DEDICATION

With love and appreciation we dedicate this book to Pam, Stephen, and Barbara

PREFACE

Needed: A Larger View of Marketing

As a discipline, the study of marketing has in recent years been risking an interesting limitation on its boundaries of thought. That is, the field has found it very useful to adopt a managerial perspective for its work, one directed to enhancing the effectiveness and efficiency of managers' marketing decisions. In turn, this requires that it be focused on the activities of the firm, its managers, and household consumers. We much agree with the value of this approach.

However, we do not believe that this is enough for those who wish to think about the huge institution that constitutes marketing in our world. We believe that it is also important that we attend to and deepen our understanding of how marketing impacts society itself on a variety of fronts. This is the role for the area of work entitled "Marketing in Society." Here we view marketing from a broader and more aggregate perspective, as an intrinsic part of our larger social and economic system. Here we find that topics such as competition in the marketplace, economic growth and prosperity of nations, and welfare of consumers are natural to raise and investigate.

Accompanying the need for such research itself is a need for these contributions to be accessible to those persons who would either like to know about them, or would be able to use them in improving their work performance. This includes students and professors, marketing planners, government officials, those devoted to improving human welfare in not-for-profit organizations, and those in nations where economic development holds promise for improving the lives of the citizenry.

While several excellent academic journals and scholarly books do exist, these tend to focus on particular portions of issues, and are not easily available to a wide audience. Thus we set out to develop a broadly based, accessible resource that assembles useful academic contributions that have already been published in journals, coupled with invited commentaries on this field by a number of its leading scholars. This book is thus intended to be of use to a wide spectrum of readers who are interested in exploring and understanding marketing from the vantage point of society and its members. We hope that you enjoy reading it.

As just mentioned, one of the distinctive features of this volume is the expert commentary on each area by our section editors, each of whom is an expert in that area and who chose the readings that appear in that section. We wish to thank these significant contributors, along with those other experts who have written special pieces for this volume and those authors whose prior contributions appear as readings. Without their intellectual contributions this book would not be possible. We thank Francesca Van Gorp-Cooley of the American Marketing Association and Steven Momper of Thomson South-Western for their enthusiasm, support, and encouragement for this project, the American Marketing Association for providing access to so many of the contributions contained in this book, and those additional publishers who have provided access to their publications as well. Finally we would like to thank our colleagues Joel Cohen, Craig Andrews, and others for voicing the need for a resource like this, and those members of the field who have provided support and encouragement throughout the development of this effort.

GG
LB
WW

CONTENTS

Section IX: Exploring Prospects for Better Decisions: Marketing Ethics   857

CONTRIBUTORS

Section Editors

Marketing and Society: What Has Marketing Thought Contributed and
What Does the Future Hold?
> Debra L. Scammon
> Marlys J. Mason

Marketing Society: An Historical Analysis
> Joshua L. Wiener
> Patrick E. Murphy

The Consumer Interest
> Robert N. Mayer

Consumer Protection
> J. Craig Andrews

Competition
> Patrick J. Kaufmann

International Consumer Policy
> Alan Mathios

Social Marketing
> Alan R. Andreasen

Macromarketing
> Clifford J. Shultz, II

Nature and Scope of Marketing Ethics
> O.C. Ferrell

Background on the Section Editors

Alan R. Andreasen is Professor of Marketing at Georgetown University and Executive Director of the Social Marketing Institute. Dr. Andreasen is a specialist in consumer behavior, marketing to nonprofit organizations and social marketing. He is the author or editor of seventeen books and numerous monographs. His most recent books are: *Social Marketing in the 21st Century* (Sage 2006); *Marketing Social Change* (Jossey Bass, 1995);

Strategic Marketing in Nonprofit Organizations (6th ed.) with Philip Kotler (Prentice-Hall 2003); *Marketing Research That Won't Break the Bank* (Jossey-Bass 2003); and *Ethics in Social Marketing* (Georgetown University Press 2001). He has also published over 120 articles and conference papers on a variety of topics. He is a member of several academic and professional associations and serves on the Editorial Boards of the *Journal of Consumer Research*, the *Journal of Consumer Policy*, *Social Marketing Quarterly*, and the *Journal of Public Policy and Marketing*.

J. Craig Andrews is Professor and Charles H. Kellstadt Chair in Marketing, Marquette University. He received his Ph.D. in marketing from the University of South Carolina. His research interests focus primarily on advertising and public health issues. He recently served on the Behavior Change Expert Panel for the National Youth Anti-Drug Media Campaign and has been Editor of the *Journal of Public Policy & Marketing*, Consumer Research Specialist in the Division of Advertising Practices with the Federal Trade Commission in Washington, DC, and Chair of the Marketing & Society Special Interest Group of the American Marketing Association. Professor Andrews currently serves on four editorial boards. His work has appeared in the *Journal of Marketing, Journal of Consumer Research, Journal of Public Policy & Marketing, Journal of Advertising, Journal of Current Issues and Research in Advertising, Journal of International Business Studies, Journal of Retailing*, and the *American Journal of Public Health*, among others.

O.C. Ferrell is Professor of Marketing and Creative Enterprise Scholar at the University of New Mexico. Before joining the faculty at UNM, he was the first Bill Daniels Distinguished Professor of Business Ethics at the University of Wyoming, raising over $3.5 million, and responsible for a statewide business ethics initiative. He is past president of the Academic Council of the American Marketing Association and chaired the American Marketing Association Ethics Committee developing the AMA Code of Ethics and Internet Code of Ethics. Ferrell is the co-author of 17 books and more than 75 articles. His articles have been published in the *Journal of Marketing Research, Journal of Marketing, Journal of Business Research, Journal of the Academy of Marketing Sciences, Journal of Public Policy & Marketing*, and *Academy of Management Executive* as well as others. He is co-author of *Marketing: Concepts and Strategy, Business Ethics: Ethical Decision Making and Cases*, and *Business and Society*.

Patrick J. Kaufmann is Professor of Marketing and Chair of the Marketing Department of Boston University. Professor Kaufmann was a practicing attorney before receiving a Ph.D. in Marketing from Northwestern University in 1985. His research is in the areas of franchising, channels of distribution and public policy and he has published articles in a wide variety of scholarly journals including the *Journal of Consumer Research*,

Journal of Marketing, the *Journal of Law and Economics,* the *Journal of Public Policy and Marketing,* and the *Journal of Retailing.* He serves on the Editorial Boards of the *Journal of Retailing* and the *Journal of Public Policy and Marketing.* He is on the executive board of the International Society of Franchising and was chair in 1992.

Marlys J. Mason is Assistant Professor of Marketing at the William S. Spears School of Business at Oklahoma State University. Prior to her academic position, Mason attained marketing management experience in the healthcare industry. Her research interests center around health policy and information, health promotions, perceived risk, life transitions and consumer vulnerability. Mason has published in the *Journal of Consumer Research, Journal of Public Policy & Marketing, Journal of Consumer Affairs, Journal of Marketing Management, Academy of Marketing Science Review,* and many conference proceedings. She has provided research expertise to the Oklahoma Department of Health, Oklahoma Tobacco Settlement Endowment Trust, Cherokee Nation, Susan G. Komen Breast Cancer Foundation, the Utah Department of Health, University of Utah Healthcare Transplant Center, and other various governmental and non-profit entities.

Alan Mathios is Professor at Cornell University and Associate Dean for Academic Affairs in the College of Human Ecology. He is a co-editor of the *Journal of Consumer Policy* and on the editorial boards of the *Journal of Consumer Affairs* and the *Journal of Public Policy and Marketing.* He came to Cornell following employment at the Federal Trade Commission, where he served as a senior staff economist in the Division of Economic Policy Analysis. He has published extensively in the area of consumer policy, advertising and health. His research has been funded by a variety of sources including the National Cancer Institute, the Robert Wood Johnson Foundation, the National Institute of Aging, and the Merck Foundation. He has been the recipient of teaching and advising awards including the State University of New York Chancellor's Award for Excellence in Teaching and the Cornell University Kendal S. Carpenter Advising Award.

Robert N. Mayer is Professor in the Department of Family and Consumer Studies at the University of Utah. He received his PhD in sociology from the University of California-Berkeley in 1978. Dr. Mayer's research has exposed consumer problems, evaluated consumer policy interventions, and examined the U.S. and global consumer movements. His recent research has focused on consumer privacy and consumer protection on the Internet. He is the author of the book The Consumer Movement: Guardians of the Marketplace and associate editor (with Stephen Brobeck and Robert Herrmann) of the Encyclopedia of the Consumer Movement. Dr. Mayer is a board member of the National Consumers League, the Consumer Federation of America, and Consumer Reports WebWatch (a project of Consumers Union).

Patrick E. Murphy is the C.R. Smith Co-Director of the Institute for Ethical Business Worldwide and Professor of Marketing in the Mendoza College of Business at the University of Notre Dame. He served as chair of the Department of Marketing for ten years. During 1993–94 he was a Fulbright Scholar at University College Cork in Ireland. Previously, Professor Murphy was a faculty member and Marketing department chair at Marquette University. He specializes in business and marketing ethics. His work has appeared in leading journals and his most recent book (with Laczniak, N. Bowie and T. Klein) is *Ethical Marketing* (Prentice Hall, 2005). Murphy was named in 1997 as one of the top researchers in Marketing for sustained contribution to the field. He served as editor of the *Journal of Public Policy & Marketing* and serves on five editorial review boards. He won teaching awards at Notre Dame in 2005 and 2006. Currently, he is an Invited Fellow of the Ethics Resource Center (Washington, DC) and is an Academic Advisor of the Business Roundtable Institute for Corporate Ethics. Professor Murphy holds a BBA from Notre Dame, an MBA from Bradley, and a Ph.D from Houston.

Debra L. Scammon is the Emma Eccles Jones Professor of Marketing at the David Eccles School of Business, University of Utah. Debra earned her Ph.D. in marketing from University of California, Los Angeles. She joined the faculty of the David Eccles School of Business in 1975. Dr. Scammon's areas of research include: consumer behavior, public policy and marketing, and health care marketing. Professor Scammon held a position as in-house marketing and advertising research consultant to the Federal Trade Commission, Bureau of Consumer Protection in 1978–79 and has conducted research related to the FTC's Food Rule, Children's Advertising Rule, and Guides on Environmental Advertising. Her recent research has focused on nutrition and health claims in both advertising and labeling of nutritional supplements as well as on factors contributing to the obesity crisis. Dr. Scammon's current work also includes examination of policies that may increase the access to health care benefits for the currently uninsured. She has published in the *Journal of Marketing, Journal of Advertising, Journal of Consumer Research, Journal of Health Care Marketing, Journal of Public Policy & Marketing, Journal of Consumer Affairs, Journal of Business Research* and other journals dealing with consumer affairs, consumer protection, and antitrust issues. Dr. Scammon is past editor of *Journal of Public Policy & Marketing* and is active in AMA's Special Interest Group on Marketing and Society and the Association for Consumer Research.

Clifford J. Shultz II is Professor and Marley Foundation Chair at the Arizona State University, Morrison School of Management and Agribusiness; he also has served as a Fulbright Scholar (Croatia and Vietnam), an Invited Scholar at the Indochina Program of the Harvard Institute for International Development, and currently serves as Faculty Affiliate at the School of Global Studies, Program for Southeast Asian Studies, Russian and

East European Studies Consortium, and is a Fellow of the Harvard-Fulbright Vietnam Program. Professor Shultz's research interests focus on marketing, development, and societal welfare, particularly in the transitioning societies of Southeast Asia, the Balkans, and other recovering economies. He has published widely on these topics and currently manages several funded projects in these areas. Professor Shultz has lectured and provided counsel on marketing, socio-economic development, and public policy issues, at universities, businesses, NGOs, research institutions, and governmental agencies and ministries on five continents.

Joshua L. Wiener is the Carson Professor of Business and Head of the Department of Marketing at Oklahoma State University. Before coming to Oklahoma State University he was at the University of Maryland and Federal Trade Commission. His research has been published in journals such as the *Journal of Marketing, Journal of Marketing Research, and Journal of Consumer Research*. He is currently an associate editor of the *Journal of Public Policy and Marketing*. His work has encompassed the public policy, social marketing, and underlying decision making/behavioral dimensions of the marketing and society domain.

INTRODUCTION

The study of "marketing in society" is interesting and exciting. It allows one to "back away" and consider broader questions about the field of marketing and what it is doing in the world around us. From this perspective, we have the option of viewing marketing from the position of society and its members, a different look from that which views marketing from more narrow vantage points such as the firm and its managers or individual consumers. Here we can consider the "aggregate marketing system"—that large and complex structure of institutions, actors, and activities that operate to serve the "marketing" needs of a society. As we adopt this perspective, new questions and new discoveries about the field of marketing arise for our attention. The result is a richer and fuller understanding of this field of study.

As we might expect, the breadth of the societal domain allows for many possible topics and approaches. Reflecting this, six separate areas of scholarship have developed over time, and are represented in this volume:

- Public policy and marketing
- Macromarketing
- Consumer interest economics
- Social marketing
- Marketing ethics
- International consumer policy

Each of these areas has its own journal and/or annual conference in which affiliated academics and practitioners participate, but there is also recognition of a community of interest with the other areas. In research terms, the differences we see are related to levels of analysis, methods, and substantive focus. For example, as described by Wilkie and Moore (2003, p. 140, see also infra):

> . . . among the six primary groups, there are people who wish to focus on social change and help those managing these efforts (social marketing), others who wish to focus on helping corporate marketers make more ethical decisions (marketing ethics), and still others who focus on the aggregate marketing system and its impact on economic development, quality of life, or other issues (macromarketing). Another set of researchers focuses either on helping government decision makers and marketers devise more efficient and effective regulatory policies or legislation or on broader issues involving the roles for government, marketers, and the legal system (public policy and marketing). Furthermore, some people are approaching problems within different cultural and political contexts (international consumer policy), and some are approaching with different aims and methods (consumer interest economics).

The differences identified by Wilkie and Moore present both advantages and disadvantages to the field and its scholarship. On the one hand, the diversity in the topics, methods, and levels of analysis affords a larger and richer body of knowledge. On the other hand, these differences make it challenging to study the entire area at once. Thus we have endeavored to bring the field together within this volume, with separate sections for each approach (public policy receives two sections, one for consumer protection and one for competition policy). Within each of these sections you will find an original contribution written by an expert on that topic, presenting an overview of the exploration that is ongoing in that area. This is followed by a selection, chosen by the guest expert of several outstanding and worthy articles representing that particular area and its approaches and issues. Finally, current problems and debates reflecting *Policy in Progress* are included through a series of several popular press articles and other readings, also selected by the guest expert for that section. We now turn to a more detailed look at what is to come.

Sections I and II: Perspectives, Retrospectives, and Prospects

The book is organized into nine sections. The first two sections provide the reader with an understanding of the overall impact of marketing in society and an appreciation for how this has evolved over time. Both Sections I and II provide current reflections on the field and previously published readings—all written by leading scholars of Marketing in Society.

SECTION I: EXPLORING THE IMPACTS OF MARKETING IN SOCIETY: FRAMEWORKS FOR THE FIELD

Section I provides the reader with several frameworks for understanding the scholarship presented in this book. The section begins with a seminal article aptly titled "Marketing's Contributions to Society," by William L. Wilkie and Elizabeth S. Moore. In this reading, Wilkie and Moore look across time and societies toward what they call the "aggregate marketing system." Their work identifies a surprisingly large number of contributions from marketing, and shows why this field is so important to a society (also, however, it recognizes that the system is not perfect, and catalogs the range of criticisms against marketing). For a reader new to the field, this article offers an immediate introduction to a broader perspective of marketing. The section continues with two readings that organize and analyze the scholarship in the field appearing in the broader literature ("The Marketing Literature in Public Policy & Marketing: 1970–1988") and specifically within the *Journal of Public Policy & Marketing* ("Two Decades of Contribution to Marketing and Public Policy: An Analysis of Research Published in *Journal of Public Policy & Marketing*"). These articles catalogue the multitude of topics that have been explored in the literature.

Section I concludes with a thoughtful analysis of the positive effects on society of the synergy between corporate marketers, policy makers, and nonprofit and social marketers by our guest contributors Debra L. Scammon and Marlys J. Mason.

SECTION II: EXPLORING DEVELOPMENTS OVER TIME: HISTORICAL PERSPECTIVES ON MARKETING IN SOCIETY

Section II addresses the field's development over time. The first reading in this section, by William L. Wilkie and Elizabeth S. Moore (2003), "Scholarly Research in Marketing: Exploring the '4 Eras' of Thought Development," examines the course of the "4 Eras" of marketing thought, and how the societal domain has been treated over time. Section II then presents a set of short essays that appeared in a special section of the *Journal of Public Policy & Marketing* entitled: "A Retrospective on the Field of Marketing and Public Policy." These include contributions by Paul N. Bloom, Alan R. Andreasen, William L. Wilkie, Stephen A. Greyser, Michael B. Mazis, and Thomas C. Kinnear, each of whom is recognized as a leading figure in this field. Each retrospective provides insights about the field's development over a recent 25-year period. Finally, guest experts Joshua L. Weiner and Patrick E. Murphy provide an original essay that builds upon the retrospectives, brings coverage up to date, and offers their thoughts on the nature of this area.

Sections III–IX: The Primary Areas of Marketing in Society

SECTION III: EXPLORING THE CONSUMER INTEREST

Much of the marketing literature views consumers from the vantage point of the firm, as customers. In Section III, however, consumers are viewed from their own perspective, as persons within the society. Guest editor Robert N. Mayer explores the consumer interest through a selection of readings that illustrate this domain's focus on *exposing* and *explaining* consumer problems. Here we become familiar with a range of consumer problems, including the realities of how marketing deception and fraud is exacerbated for vulnerable groups of consumers. Finally, the Policy in Progress selection, which discusses the rising credit card and student loan debt among young Americans, should be of special interest to students reading this book as they contemplate their economic futures.

SECTION IV: EXPLORING THE CHALLENGES OF CONSUMER PROTECTION (GOVERNMENT REGULATION I)

Section IV begins the first of three successive sections on Government Regulation. Whereas the domain of Consumer Interest focuses on exposing and explaining consumer problems, Consumer Protection picks up with possible government solutions to protect consumers. As guest editor J. Craig Andrews tells us early in his essay, consumer protection can be thought of as the study "of policy designed to protect consumers from inaccurate or misleading information, unfairness, fraud, substantial risks and other harms that might exist in the marketplace." Indeed, Andrews' selection of readings explores the theory and practice of the Federal Trade Commission's policy on corrective advertising, a proposal for identifying misleading advertising, and an evaluation of the effectiveness of anti-smoking and anti-drug advertising. In a timely consideration of the nation's current battle with rising rates of obesity, the Policy in Progress selection here is a report from the Center for Science in the Public Interest, proposing nutrition labeling at fast food and other restaurant chains.

SECTION V: EXPLORING THE CHALLENGES OF COMPETITION POLICY (GOVERNMENT REGULATION II)

The study of Government Regulation continues with Section V on Competition Policy. In this section, guest editor Patrick Kaufmann discusses competition as rivalry among sellers, having economic and legal dimensions. Each selected reading illustrates research into topics of business, economics, and the law that have competition as a central theme. In the set of Policy in Progress readings here, we examine the current competitive struggles of small local retailers and business owners against huge conglomerates with near-monopoly power.

SECTION VI: EXPLORING THE WORLD OF INTERNATIONAL CONSUMER POLICY (GOVERNMENT REGULATION III)

Regulations aimed at protecting consumers and safeguarding competitive markets, as described in the previous two sections, become increasingly complex when one takes into account the globalization of the world. In Section VI, guest editor Alan Mathios' essay explores the world of international consumer policy, an area of scholarship focused on policies designed to protect both domestic consumers and domestic industries, and on how international organizations can manage adhering to domestic regulations while participating in an increasingly global environment. Through the Mathios essay and the collection of readings here, we examine the benefits and challenges of international trade agreements (e.g., GATT) and governing bodies (e.g., the World Trade Organization). In the Policy in Progress readings here, we consider the current "hot topic" debates on biotechnology and the labeling of genetically modified foods.

SECTION VII: EXPLORATIONS IN IMPROVING SOCIETY VIA SOCIAL MARKETING INITIATIVES

In Section VII, we shift from a government regulatory focus to a non-governmental approach to benefiting society. Termed "Social Marketing," here the emphasis is on employing the familiar tools of marketing management, but for the primary purpose of social welfare rather than profits. In this section, guest editor Alan R. Andreasen, founder of the Social Marketing Institute in Washington D.C., shares with us his views of the past successes, challenges going forward, and the key topics facing social marketers today. The selected readings further define this field, and then examine a case study in which the World Health Organization employs a mass-media communication campaign to improve vaccination coverage in the Philippines. In our Policy in Progress materials, Andreasen asks us to consider three problematic societal trends: the rising rates of childhood obesity, the government-supported increase in cigarette smoking in China, and the increase in binge drinking on college campuses.

SECTION VIII: EXPLORING MACROMARKETING: TAKING A BROADENED VIEW OF OUR WORLD

In Section VIII, we return to the "larger" view of marketing as an aggregate system. Macromarketing is the study of marketing as a social process; the study of the reciprocal consequences of marketing on society and society on marketing. Our guest editor for this section, Clifford J. Shultz II, presents the sub-disciplines that reflect macromarketing today, such as the study of distributive justice and the current interest in studies on quality of life. Shultz's provocative Policy in Progress readings provide a macromarketing perspective on the allegations of Nike's unfair and unsafe labor practices in Vietnam, and the daunting marketing system challenges in Iraq, all while drawing attention to the potential repercussions to the rest of society.

SECTION IX: EXPLORING PROSPECTS FOR BETTER DECISIONS: MARKETING ETHICS

Section IX represents the belief that all personal and organizational marketing practices must be conducted with integrity and fairness to all stakeholders. Guest editor O.C. Ferrell's essay explains key issues in marketing ethics today and also provides a framework for understanding ethical decision making. The selected readings offer a normative and descriptive understanding of the dimensions of ethical decision making, as well as evidence of the organizational benefits of corporate ethical values. The Policy in Progress selections then raise specific ethically related controversies of today, including Wal-Mart's conduct in relation to society and other non-consumer stakeholders, the counterfeit products in an increasingly global marketplace, and questions of the social responsibility of food manufacturers in marketing their products.

★　★　★　★　★　★

Taken together, then, this volume contains a wide-ranging, high-quality look at important issues in our world of marketing today. We wish you a wonderful voyage as you navigate through its pages!

EXPLORING THE IMPACTS OF MARKETING IN SOCIETY: FRAMEWORKS FOR THE FIELD

Marketing's Contributions to Society

William L. Wilkie and Elizabeth S. Moore

At this unique point in time, it is appropriate to step back and deliberate on the scope of the marketing field and the contributions it offers to society. The authors adopt several perspectives to do this, looking across time, across societies, and into the operations and structure of the aggregate marketing system itself, which emerges as a huge and complex human institution. A large number of contributions to society are illustrated, ranging from aggregate inputs to the nation's economic health to individual benefits felt by some consumers. However, the system is not perfect; a range of criticisms and system problems also is summarized. The article closes with a look at lessons learned and future challenges in the century ahead.

Our Goals for this Paper

We are honored to have this opportunity to address the topic: "What does marketing contribute to society?" We originally chose to study the field of marketing because we found it to be among the most stimulating, complex, and intellectually challenging of academic areas in a university setting. In curious contrast to its general reputation as a "soft" area, we have found that this field welcomes insights from many disciplines, including economics, psychology, history, mathematics, sociology, law, political science, communications, anthropology, and the creative arts. Its scholarship combines elements of objectivity and subjectivity, demands both quantitative and qualitative insights, requires persistence yet rewards creative leaps, and allows freedom of imagination and nuance yet grounds its efforts in real actions with measured consequences. Furthermore, marketing can be studied from several intriguing perspectives.

In the spirit of this special "Millennium Issue" of the *Journal of Marketing,* we view this article as an effort to clarify, illustrate, and celebrate, but not without a critical eye, some

William L. Wilkie is the Nathe Professor of Marketing, and Elizabeth S. Moore is Assistant Professor of Marketing, University of Notre Dame. The main portion of this article was completed while the second author was on the faculty of the University of Illinois, and the authors gratefully acknowledge both Notre Dame and Illinois for their support of this work. In addition, the project has benefited from useful comments, criticisms, and suggestions from many scholars. The authors especially thank their incredibly supportive colleagues in the Marketing Department at Notre Dame, as well as David Aaker, Alan Andreasen, Craig Andrews, Neil Beckwith, Jack Calfee, Joel Cohen, Peter Dickson, John Farley, Richard Heuther, James Hunt, Shelby Hunt, Donna Kamm, Harold Kassarjian, Gene Laczniak, Lynn Lee, Donald Lehmann, Susan Lloyd, John Malone, E. Scott Maynes, Robert Nason, Thomas Reynolds, Robert Schindler, Richard Tedlow, Hans Thorelli, and three anonymous Special Issue reviewers for their inputs. Finally, the authors salute David Montgomery, George Day, and Robert Lusch for creating this opportunity for developmental articles aimed at addressing important issues for the field; this project never would have been undertaken without such a structure.

Wilkie, William L. and Elizabeth S. Moore (1999), "Marketing's Contributions to Society," *Journal of Marketing,* 63, 198-218.

of the special aspects of the marketing field and its relationship to society. We did not wish to be naïve about this and so, in developing this article, have undertaken several allied efforts with regard to the history of marketing thought, shifting criticisms of marketing, and current emphases in this area, details of which are available elsewhere (Moore and Wilkie 2000; Wilkie and Moore 1997, 2000). It is clear that the marketing system today is providing more and different benefits than in times gone by. Formal marketing thought has advanced much since its inception as the new academic area of "market distribution," shortly after 1900 (Bartels 1988).[1]

As the field nears its 100th birthday, its focus is squarely on firms, markets, and household consumers. Relatively few persons, even in the mainstream of the field, have recently been able to examine marketing's contributions to society. However, this subject is worthy of consideration by the broad college of thinkers in the field. It is worthy of exposure to thoughtful practitioners, to students in MBA and undergraduate programs, and to emerging scholars in doctoral programs (likely why the Marketing Science Institute named it a key topic for this Special Issue). Thus, our purpose here is to provide a different look at marketing, one that engages thoughtful deliberation on the larger system and its contributions. Taken together, the issues in this domain help us better determine both the nature of marketing and the remarkable potentials of the field.

One Hundred Years of Marketing

Three early insights we gained in this project were that marketing's contributions (1) accumulate over time, (2) diffuse through a society, and (3) occur within the context of everyday life. This can make them hard to discern at any given point in time. We begin, therefore, with an informal look over a very long period.

> *A View Across Time: Marketing's Impact on Daily Life in the United States, or, "It's a Wonderful Life."* Here we join Mary Bailey as she reads a diary her mother recently had given her as a family heirloom. It had been written by Mary's great-grandmother Anne at the turn of the century, 100 years ago. As she settles under her lamp on a cold winter's evening in Bedford Falls, Mary is imagining her ancestor's times and how very much life has changed.
>
> *(Daily activities)* As she reads, Mary is surprised to discover how Anne spent her days.[2] Largely dependent on walking or horses, families centered on the home and local community. Daily life meant physical labor. Equipped with only a scrub board, the typical housewife spent 7 hours a week doing laundry and carried 9000 gallons of water into the house each year, which she then had to boil before using (only 25% of homes had running water). Cooking, baking, and food preservation required substantial time, some 42 hours per week!

---

[1] In this project, we were fortunate to be able to find and consider a treasure trove of books and articles from marketing thinkers, theorists from other disciplines, and critical observers from within and outside marketing. We acknowledge our deep debt to people who have addressed these issues before us and have allowed us to build on their thoughts here.

[2] Comparative numbers are from a variety of sources, especially Lebergott (1993) and *U.S. News and World Report* (1995★).

Products that now routinely are bought, such as clothing, often were produced in the home. Central heating would not arrive until the 1920s; Anne's family heated only the kitchen for the winter, using fuel hauled in daily by family members. Only 3% of households had electrical lighting, so most families relied on coal, kerosene, or oil to light their homes. As she reads on under her bright lamp, Mary wonders how bright the lighting had been for the author whose words she was reading.

(Health and safety improvements) Mary is reading deeply as Anne described relief that her baby Aaron had survived; infant mortality was common in Bedford Falls at the time (about one in every ten births). In checking the family tree, Mary finds that Anne herself had died at a relatively young age (life expectancy in 1900 was only 47 years of age). In contrast, life expectancy today is nearly 80 years of age, and Mary has not had to worry seriously about infant mortality (now significantly less than 1%) or death from infectious disease. Thinking more about this, Mary realizes that her family's health, safety, and ability to enjoy life have been assisted by the fruits of advances in diagnostic equipment, pharmaceuticals to combat disease, pain relievers, bacteria-safe foods, safety-tested products, and so forth.

(Impacts of technology and growth of the marketing system) The academic field of "marketing" began about the time Anne was writing her diary. During the ensuing century, we have experienced many changes in daily life in the United States. The aggregate marketing system, in conjunction with the other aggregate systems with which it interacts (e.g., technology, finance, production) has delivered most of these changes to society. For example, the availability of home electricity was followed by the creation of many new appliances— clothes washers and dryers, vacuum cleaners, air conditioners, dishwashers, music systems, television, and so forth—that bring efficiency and enjoyment to homes today. Home refrigeration and supermarkets mean fewer trips to the store; together with use of appliances, this has allowed the average time spent on food preparation to fall from 42 hours to less than 10 hours per week! With economic growth (gross national product is 400 times greater than a century ago), higher incomes, and technological innovations have come new possibilities and opportunities. A vast array of goods and services is now available. Moreover, real prices for many goods (e.g., television, autos) have fallen to the point that they are accessible to almost every member of U.S. society today.

Mary Bailey closes her diary and begins to think about other changes as well. She and her family are informed readily about national and global events and easily can drive or fly from Bedford Falls to points of interest anywhere in the world. Her family's daily life is far, far removed from that of her ancestor's. As she ponders this, she realizes that the world for her children will be different from hers today, in as yet unknown ways, as the aggregate marketing system continues to deliver change to their society in the future. . . .

The Importance of Perspective

Viewing a topic from a single perspective highlights certain characteristics but can hide other aspects that also may be important. For example, a person looks different from the front than from the back and different again if viewed from the side. To understand a topic well, it is helpful to walk around it mentally, adopting different perspectives on it.

For example, four perceptual barriers in this topic involve *time, system limits, culture,* and *personal experience.* The Mary Bailey illustration addresses the issue of slow diffusion of marketing's contributions over time by contrasting two extremes. When viewed in this way, contributions the aggregate marketing system has delivered to society are apparent; it is clear that Americans today are living very differently, and mostly in better ways, than did their ancestors a century ago. With respect to system limits, not only is the marketing system vast (as we shall demonstrate shortly), but its operations converge and coordinate with the operations of other aggregate systems within a society's larger economic system. (In a Venn diagram, we might conceive of aggregate systems in marketing, finance, technology, production, and so forth as partially overlapping large circles that reflect areas in which activities are in common and those in which activities lie only in that field.)

With respect to culture, marketing is a social institution that is highly adaptive to its cultural and political context. Thus, we can move easily around the world to locate societies with very different marketing systems. In some global locations, we would find rudimentary marketing systems offering none of the conveniences Mary Bailey is enjoying; people there may be living as Anne did a century ago. Elsewhere, as in parts of Brazil, we would find people just discovering installment credit and using it to obtain the first home conveniences they have ever enjoyed. In parts of China, we would find incredible levels of investment—one of every five construction cranes in the world is reportedly at work just in Shanghai—to bring modern elevators, air conditioners, and other conveniences to the citizenry. Thus, coverage of aggregate marketing systems *is* culture-bound. We must take care to distinguish which lessons are generalizable and which are not. With regard to personal experience, many marketing contributions are "behind the scenes," unseen by those not directly involved. It is thus important that we remain mentally open to discovery of new possibilities about marketing and its relationship to society. We have come away from this project with a new and richer view of our field and hope that readers will as well.

The article consists of four major sections. The first section is an overview of marketing as an aggregate system, starting with an "up close" illustration of its operations. Our second section profiles the range of benefits marketing offers to society. The third section adds balance in summarizing criticisms and controversial aspects of this field, and our fourth section draws conclusions and implications for the future.

The Aggregate Marketing System

Studies have shown that the less familiar a person is with the marketing field, the more likely he or she is to equate marketing with advertising or selling. As a person learns more, the view broadens and he or she begins to appreciate the richness of the field of marketing (Kasper 1993★). We now turn to the aggregate marketing system. Although originally a central theme in marketing thought, we have not found much of this idea in recent years, in favor of an emphasis on managerial decisions. We begin with an illustration of one small part of the system to determine what it does. If marketing thinkers are to appreciate the range of contributions our field makes, it is good to remind ourselves about the scope and details of the work that it undertakes.

THE SYSTEM AT WORK

Our illustration begins with a U.S. household at breakfast. Here, the outputs of a small number of marketing channels are brought together for the purpose of consumption.

"Breakfast at Tiffany's." [Note: The idea for this illustration is based on Vaile, Grether, and Cox's (1952) classic textbook on marketing, though our description is different and updated. We join Tiffany Jones and her family in New York as Tiffany reaches for her breakfast pastry and blows softly across her cup of coffee. . . .]

(A cup of coffee) Although a commonplace enough event, a breakfast represents an interesting confluence of forces from the aggregate marketing system. Let us first consider Tiffany's coffee and how it got to this morning's meal. Tiffany has chosen a leading brand that delivers a consistent color, scent, and taste that is favored by its many customers. How exactly does this brand's marketing system achieve this? The coffee Tiffany has prepared is a combination of beans grown in different countries, then brought to the United States, and blended into a specified mixture to deliver this brand's unique qualities. Because of different growing seasons and bean characteristics, the source nations for the coffee change as the year progresses; coffee is grown in some 50 nations around the world.

As shown in Figure 1, Panel A, we assume that some beans in this cup came from a Colombian hillside, handpicked (to ensure ripeness) in the grower's field. The process was highly structured: From basket, to tractor, to truck, the beans were transported to the coffee grower's depulping mill, where the inner beans were separated from their cherries. Still wet and protected by a parchmentlike cellulose shell, the beans were spread on a sun-filled patio to dry for several days. They then were milled (removing the parchment sheath to produce a green bean) and graded against set national coffee standards. Samples of the beans were sent to buyers and the government coffee board to check the grading process. The beans then were put into 60 kilo (132 pound) burlap or polyester bags bearing the grower's name and quality level and warehoused at the grower's facility. Brokers and large buyers were contacted by the grower to arrange for sale and delivery. In the case of Tiffany's brand, this process continued a long-term business relationship with this grower, based on trust in the quality of the beans, his capability to deliver needed quantities at agreed on times, and his willingness to stand behind agreements. This seller has similar views about buyers and will only deal with certain buyers. Thus, the actual agreement on these beans was sealed with a handshake.

★Authors were limited in the number of references used in text, therefore, those references marked with an ★ are available at www.ama.org/pubs/jm and at www.msi.org.

Continuing with Panel A, the beans were loaded on trucks and driven from the mountains to the port city (ocean humidity levels could damage the beans had they been warehoused there). They were loaded directly into 20-ton "piggyback" containers designed to transport seamlessly among ships, trains, and trucks. After four or five days at sea, the beans arrived at the port of New Orleans, were tested again for quality, and given over to a warehouse service. This service handled custom's clearance, then unloaded the bags into trucks driven to the coffee firm's "silo" facility. Here, loads of different beans were stored, then blended together into 20-ton hopper trucks, and sent to the firm's New Orleans roasting plant (alternatively, they might have been sent to the firm's Midwest or Southwest roasting plants in 80-ton hopper cars). The final coffee was prepared carefully, tested for quality, and packaged into the familiar red cans or bricks. As indicated in Panel A, from this point, the route depends on the purchaser. It may be shipped in large volume to one of the firm's seven regional distribution centers, thence to be sold to wholesalers, and then to retail outlets, or, in the case of very large national accounts, trucked directly from the plant in 40,000-pound loads. Because Tiffany bought her coffee from the neighborhood IGA supermarket, it had taken the longer route. Even so, the vacuum-packed containers had kept it quite fresh and lent pleasure to her cup this morning. Thus, we demonstrate how one marketing system has operated to provide a branded cup of coffee to a U.S. family on a typical morning.

(A breakfast pastry) Although coffee provides useful insights, it is yet a relatively simple product. We can move to a further level of complexity with another item in Tiffany's meal: a new breakfast pastry produced by a major food marketer to compete in the fast-growing "premium" breakfast segment. Its marketing system is shown in Panel B of Figure 1 (for ease of communication, we have shown only portions of this system to complement points of the coffee channel; neither system is portrayed to its true complexity). Note at the left of Panel B that the preproduction marketing system is much more involved than the linear system for coffee, as there are 15 ingredients in each unit of this pastry. Although not shown in the panel, each ingredient has its own system, similar to coffee's, for collection and transport to its processors. The pastry brand is similar to the coffee brand in requiring a high level of uniformity in the brand units sold to consumers. Thus, we find exacting product specifications for each ingredient at the left side of Panel B.

The next set of activities focuses on product management decisions. Excited by consumer research showing unmet demand for bakery-quality pastry that can be stored at home and concerned by the success of competitors' new entries, this firm began a major new product development project. Experts in food science and nutritional technologies were challenged to translate this benefit concept into an actual food product. A long process ensued, as many attributes—size, icing, taste, consistency, flavoring, shelf-life, preparation, packaging, reasonable costs for pricing, production feasibility, and so forth—needed to be brought to acceptable levels. The process included consumer research on reactions to prototypes, in-home use tests, and BehaviorScan controlled store tests of pricing and promotions (including studies of purchase substitution patterns). The firm's board of directors had to decide whether to launch the product. Key factors included internal rate of return over a six-year period, capital needs (new plant versus conversion), options for copacking or outsourcing production, and effects on the firm's current product line. Because this would be a "bakery-quality"

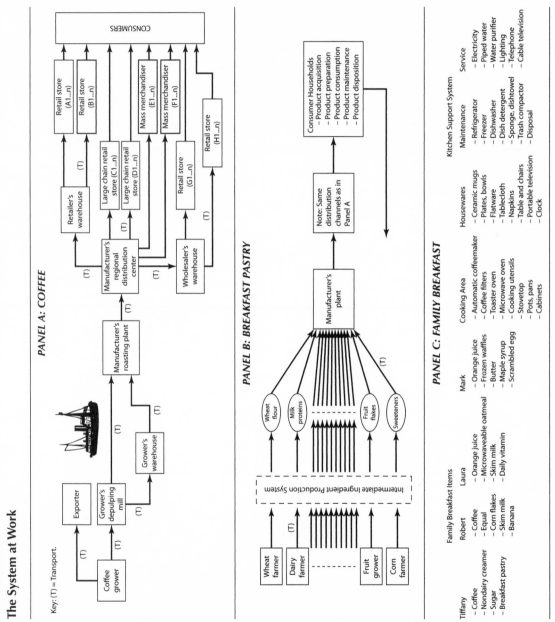

FIGURE 1

The System at Work

PANEL A: COFFEE

Key: (T) = Transport.

PANEL B: BREAKFAST PASTRY

PANEL C: FAMILY BREAKFAST

(Continued)

PANEL D: SELECTED MARKETING SYSTEM ACTIVITIES (present in the coffee and breakfast pastry examples)

Sales and Delivery

The Classic Functions of Distribution
- Transportation (2)
- Storage (2)
- Financing (2)
- Risk-bearing (2)
- Assembly (1)
- Selling (1)
- Standardization (2)
- Market information (1)

n.b., Detailed levels of activities exist: (e.g., transport activities)
- Truck to depulping mill (2)
- Beans to drying area (2)
- Ship to New Orleans (2)
- Hopper truck to roasting plant (3)
- Truck to retail store (2)
- (additional steps in text) (2)

Purchasing and Use

Organizations:
- Sourcing raw material supply (2)
- Quality specifications (2)
- Purchase of capital equipment (3)
- Outsourcing: Specialist/expert services (2)
- Purchase for resale (1)
- Assortment building (2)
- Bulk breaking (2)
- Order processing (2)
- Negotiation: Terms of sale (1)
- Transfer of ownership (2)

Consumers:
- Product acquisition (2)
- Product preparation (3)
- Product consumption (3)
- Product maintenance/repair (2)
- Product disposition (2)

Knowledge Development/Intelligence

Organizations:
- Market analysis (1)
- Market demand assessment (1)
- Analysis of competitive strategies (1)
- Market segmentation (1)
- Market forecasts (1)
- Performance monitoring (1)
- Program evaluation (1)

Consumers:
- Consumer education (2)
- Information search (2)
- Word of mouth (3)
- Store visits (2)
- Postpurchase analysis (3)

Marketing Plans and Programs/Government Actions

Organizations:
- Financial projections (2)
- Board of directors approval (2)
- Product design (2)
- Product line decisions (1)
- Budget setting (2)
- Distribution planning (1)
- Brand name selection (1)
- Packaging (1)
- Market testing (1)
- Positioning strategy (1)
- Pricing decisions (2)
- National advertising (2)
- Direct marketing (3)
- Consumer promotion (2)
- Trade promotion (3)
- Communication to sales force (1)
- Point-of-purchase materials (2)
- Publicity (1)
- Warranty terms (2)
- Customer service (2)
- Retailer assortment (1)
- Merchandising (1)
- Retail advertising (1)
- Inventory management (2)

Government Agencies:
- Standard setting (2)
- Export/import controls (2)
- Trademark protection (2)
- Financing arrangements (2)
- Nutritional labeling (2)
- Inspections (1)
- Regulatory rules and guidelines (3)

Centers of Little or No Marketing Involvement

Organizations:
- Internal management of work force (n)
- Management of plant and equipment (n)
- Financial management, accounting, and control (n)
- Basic research (n)

Government:
- All noncommerce/nonconsumer sectors (n)

Consumers:
- All non-consumer aspects of daily life (n)

Numerical Key:

(1) = Largely or entirely controlled by marketing managers.
(2) = Largely controlled by others, but influenced by or coordinated with marketing managers.
(3) = Little or no influence by marketing managers.
(n) = Activity does not involve marketing.

PANEL E: DEPICTING THE ENTIRE AGGREGATE MARKETING SYSTEM

Brand coffee system (Panel A) → **All system activities given for the cup of coffee**, beginning with harvest of beans on left, ending with consumer use and disposition on right. (note: not all activities controlled by marketers; see key)

(Multiplicative increase) → **Add all coffee systems.**

Brand pastry system (Panel B) → **All system activities given for pastry**, beginning with creation, storage, and transport of 15 pastry ingredients and ending with consumer use and disposition.

(Large geometric increase) → **Add all breakfast systems, on-premise restaurants, and home kitchen systems.**

(Large geometric increase) → **Add all other food and beverage systems.**

(Huge geometric increase) → **Add all product systems and all service systems.**

(Huge geometric increase) → **Add all not-for-profit marketing activities.**

(Huge geometric increase) → **Add all government and all consumer marketing system activities.**

(Similar sets of activities, participants, and forms of value creation)
"
"
"
"
"
"

item, the board was concerned about the system at the left of Panel B—that the ingredients be regularly available, cost-controlled, and geared to precise recipe quality. The board gave the green light, and the entire marketing mix was finalized and implemented. The distribution system (right side of Panel B) was similar to that for coffee, as was the consumer's purchase and use system (which, we note, concludes with a disposition service purchase for trash removal). In terms of the system's dynamics, each consumer purchase feeds back into stocking and production plans; through feedback derived from both internal accounting and formal market research projects, this firm will monitor and adapt its management of this offering. Over time, therefore, consumers' actual use satisfactions and repurchases will determine its success or failure.

(Further considerations) Although the illustration is getting long, we are only a little way toward capturing the true scope of the aggregate marketing system. However, we now dispense with details and simply point to key issues. We have covered only two breakfast items; as shown in Panel C, the four family members have different preferences that the aggregate marketing system is able to accommodate easily. Also, the breakfast depends on more than food, and an entire kitchen support system is available to assist this consumption episode. In terms of our broader topic, it is important to recognize that all aspects of Panel C have been brought to the Jones household through the aggregate marketing system, some many years ago (e.g., the plumbing and the furniture) and others more recently (e.g., the new dishwasher bought last week and the coffee, pastry, and fresh fruit bought yesterday). Also, each element listed in Panel C has its own complex marketing system that brought it to this point. Global sourcing was involved in some systems—the coffeemaker from Germany, artwork from the Far East, microwave from Korea, and so forth. In every case, a complete system was planned, created, and run to deliver these products to households such as Tiffany's and, in most cases, had to compete and win out over others' systems to gain Tiffany's purchase. If we were to analyze each system, many pages would be used; the total number of system interactions needed to create this meal is truly impressive. When we further recognize that the aggregate marketing system routinely provides breakfast for 100 million U.S. households every morning and that breakfast is only a trivial element of its total activity, we are ready to appreciate its immensity and significance.

THE SCOPE AND SIZE OF THE SYSTEM

The foregoing illustration is a useful basis for summarizing system scope. Panel D of Figure 1 provides a partial listing of system activities that enabled this breakfast to occur. Several points emerge:

- There are a surprisingly large number of entries; the aggregate marketing system undertakes a wide range of activities to provide for a simple breakfast meal.
- There are participants other than marketers in the aggregate marketing system. Organizational customers and ultimate consumers are key players (buying is crucial

at every stage), and governments provide services intended to facilitate system operations (shown at the right in Panel D, these cross all stages).

- As indicated by the keyed entries in Panel D, marketing managers control (1) only some of the activities of the aggregate marketing system. Other necessary activities are carried out by persons who do not consider themselves marketers. In most of these cases within organizations, marketing managers serve as influences (2) on these actions, whereas in some cases (3), necessary system activities may be carried out with little or no direct influence from marketers (note that this is particularly apparent in the consumer realm). This property of the system calls for a perspective on marketing that reaches beyond a sole focus on a manager's controllable decisions. (Note that numbers assigned to each activity are generalized. Readers may wish to consider whether they would agree.)

- The three classes of participants all engage in activities apart from the aggregate marketing system. The system is very broad but not entirely dense. Some parts of virtually every organization work on tasks only indirectly related to the marketing activities listed and carry these out independently (shown as "n" in the bottom right of Panel D). We would not define these as marketing system activities, nor would we include activities of government agencies or consumers that are directed entirely toward other sectors of society and life. Thus, our visual conception of the aggregate marketing system would resemble a cross-section of fine swiss cheese or steel mesh, similar to Panels A and B, with many linkages between organizations as we move across to the consumer sector but with holes inside each organization to represent parts where the work arguably is outside the marketing system.

- Finally, Panel D significantly understates system activity. Most listings have many detailed steps (e.g., advertising, promotion, merchandising, transportation, as in the leftmost column).

Panel E of Figure 1 next depicts an approach to assessing the scope of the U.S. aggregate marketing system. Horizontally, note that it extends from extraction of raw materials/crops at the left through many levels of value creation to end consumption and disposition in far-off locales at the right. (Again, the preceding Venn diagram analogy should clarify our conception that some of these activities are regarded properly as also belonging to other intersecting aggregate systems.) Vertically, we first add all competing coffee and pastry systems, then add all other food systems, then add all other goods and services. In concept, this process will include all organizations that engage in marketing system activities of the types shown in Panel D, all levels of government activities that affect this system, and all forms of consumer participation by all societal members. Our next illustration provides estimates of the magnitudes involved.

"From Here to Eternity." The aggregate marketing system is huge and growing rapidly.[3] As we move past the year 2000, in the United States alone, there are some 275 million final consumers arrayed in 100 million households, all on the consumption side of the system. They spend $5 trillion each year, or two-thirds of the nation's gross domestic product (GDP). To place this spending in perspective, if we were to try to count it at the rate of $1 per second, it would take more than 150,000 years, or much longer than the history of civilization. Although the aggregate marketing system in the United States may not stretch quite to "eternity," it certainly does stretch a very long way.

Furthermore, we should recall that yearly data are compiled merely for convenience and easily can understate true impacts. For example, as in Tiffany's kitchen, households accumulate many consumer durables that continue to provide benefits to them for years. As opposed to annual sales then, consider that some 200 million motor vehicles currently are registered for road use in the United States. All of these have been provided through the marketing system (and many are used to carry out its functions on a daily basis). In terms of the work of marketing, a significant portion of Americans are employed entirely or in part assisting the system to perform its functions. Although exact figures are elusive because of categorization problems, it appears that more than 30 million Americans work directly within the aggregate marketing system, with salespersons accounting for the largest portion. There are almost 20 million businesses acting as buyers, 3 million of which are retailers that resell to consumers, and another one-half million wholesaling firms (because of multiple steps in the wholesale channel, total sales of wholesalers are greater than those of retailers). Advertising spending is huge and growing, now some $200 billion per year. Other areas of recent growth include services (now more than half of all consumer spending) and direct marketing, which has doubled in recent years.

Even though these numbers are huge, we still have understated the true scope of the aggregate marketing system in U.S. society. Professional practices (attorneys, accountants, architects) were not included in these counts but must engage in accepted forms of marketing to build and maintain their clientele. Many persons in not-for-profit organizations, also not included in our formal numbers, employ marketing actions both in garnering resources and carrying out their missions. Government workers at local, state, and federal levels regularly negotiate contracts, buy goods and services, and monitor marketing performance. Furthermore, because marketing is an intrinsic function in those 20 million business firms previously noted, a portion of the responsibilities of many positions, from chief executive officer to quality inspectors to shipping and fulfillment clerks, is involved with carrying out the firm's marketing activities. Finally, the U.S. aggregate marketing system in no way stands alone in the world. By not including other nations' numbers, we have understated by many times the actual impacts of marketing around the globe. (As an aside, this analysis also helps us appreciate the enormity of the challenges faced by command systems, which cannot hope to replicate the millions of allocation decisions being made within a market system each day.)

---

[3]For a classic effort to assess magnitudes of the U.S. distribution system alone, see Cox, Goodman, and Fichandler (1965). The figures reported in the illustration are from the *Statistical Abstract of the United States* (1996★), tables 12, 66, 685, 691, 1003, 1252, 1253, 1255, 1272, 1274, 1278, 1279, and 1280. Calculated comparisons are by the authors. The advertising spending estimate is from *Advertising Age* (1997★).

FIGURE 2

Propositions on the Aggregate Marketing System

The Aggregate Marketing System:

1. *Incorporates many activities,* including the classic distribution functions, marketers' plans and programs, and actions by consumers and government;
2. *Is composed of planned and continuous flows* among participants, including flows of goods and materials, service deliveries, dollar payments, and flows of information and influence;
3. *Is extensive, in several respects,*
   a. Extending all the way from the collection of raw materials through multiple intermediate processes to use and disposition at each individual household,
   b. Combining materials/goods from around the globe into market offerings,
   c. With multiple sets of marketers, acting as competitors, performing activities in parallel, and
   d. In its geometric exchange activity, with multiple producers selling to multiple purchasers and multiple buyers purchasing from multiple sellers;
4. *Is sophisticated structurally,* relying on a massive physical and communications infrastructure that regularly and routinely creates and delivers goods and services across the society;
5. *Is a key basis for resource allocation in a market economy,* because consumer responses to market offerings determine which goods and services are created in the future;
6. *Is governed by forces for efficiency,* most notably self-interest, competition, and characteristics of market demand;
7. *Is constrained by social forces,* including laws, government regulations, cultural norms, and ethical codes of business and consumer conduct;
8. *Relies on coordinated processes,* with producers and resellers seeking interdependent purchases to fit pre-specified standards with the later expectation of purchase by consumers;
9. *Operates through human interactions, experience and trust* as participants develop and maintain marketplace relationships as a basis for conducting their system activities; and
10. *Is an open system, geared toward growth and innovation,* as participants seek to solve problems and pursue opportunities, investing with faith in the future operations of the market.

CHARACTERISTICS OF THE AGGREGATE MARKETING SYSTEM

Figure 2 completes our background on the system with a summary of key properties. Propositions 1, 3, and 4 have been discussed at length, but the others deserve brief comment. Proposition 2 provides a system perspective that we long have perceived as powerful: the concept of continuous flows in various modalities, including physical, persuasive, informational, and monetary. Flows occur in both directions (e.g., money flows backward in the system in payment for goods; information and influence flow forward from advertising and sales efforts but also backward with marketing research). Some are simultaneous, but many are not; for example, the investment flow forward (in plant, labor, production, and promotion in advance of sales) represents levels of risk-taking and confidence in marketing activity.[4] Meanwhile, Proposition 5 reflects that, in a

---

[4]We are unsure whence the concept of marketing flows originated but have found it in Vaile, Grether, and Cox's (1952), McInnes's (1964*), and Kotler's (1976*) work. This analysis also highlights marketing's contributions at the firm level by demonstrating marketing to be the function that reaches out from a firm to the outside world (marketplace) with flows of products, information, and promotion activity and further shows marketing as using its learning about that world (through an inward flow of research) to influence decisions within the firm. Finally, marketing generates an inward flow of dollars to sustain the firm's continued existence, which earns it the title of "lifeblood of the business."

market-based system, consumers' response to marketers' offerings drive supply allocations and prices. Depending on a society's decisions on public versus private ownership, the aggregate marketing system plays a greater or lesser role in allocating national resources.[5] The United States has given substantial freedoms to its aggregate marketing system. Apart from certain restrictions, a person may choose to produce almost any good or service he or she desires, in any form and name; offer it for sale at places, prices, and terms of his or her choosing; and advertise it or not, using virtually any appeal believed to be effective. Although restrictions exist in each of these areas, they are primarily to protect the rights of competing marketers or consumers.

Proposition 6 reflects that the aggregate marketing system does more than physically deliver goods and services; it also works to bring a *dynamism* to society that encourages continual growth and progress (Vaile, Grether, and Cox 1952). Marketers know that observed demand is not really fixed and that consumers can be highly responsive to different marketing programs. Thus, competition is the main driving force, leading marketers to search for areas of comparative advantage that will lead to greater financial success.[6] New competitors are attracted to areas of opportunity; over time, prices can be adjusted downward through competition and/or production efficiencies. New buyers join in buying the favored offerings, and some markets grow while others wither away. Not all marketing system programs are successful; the effort to support dynamism can lead to excesses, failures, and sometimes unforeseen consequences.

Proposition 7 reflects this underlying tension by reflecting the need for controls. A market system needs a legal infrastructure for property rights, performance of contracts, freedom of choice, and so forth. The role of government as society's representative is thus central, though this can be contravened if politicians allow cynical, self-seeking interests to circumvent either competition or desirable restraints. Thus, the issue of government achieving a proper balance to serve a society's goals best becomes a key issue for aggregate marketing systems.[7]

Propositions 8 and 9, meanwhile, refer back to the bonding forces that constitute the heart of the marketing effort. The existing infrastructure requires coordination in space, time, and fit, because offerings require intermarriage of components within a context of high efficiency. We have been impressed by the serious attention given to process quality control within this system. Furthermore, we have been reminded that, at its roots, this is a human institution in which both experience and trust play major roles, a point that

---

[5]As societal boundaries become more permeable, especially through immigration and trade, the linkages of production, employment of human resources, and end consumption become more complex.

[6]This has been the subject of significant recent theoretical developments within marketing that challenge the tradition of equilibrium economic theory (e.g., Dickson 1992, 1996★, 1999★; Hunt and Morgan 1995, 1996★).

[7]Unfortunately, extensive discussion of government's role is beyond the purview of this article. Readers may wish to access the excellent volume by Stern and Eovaldi (1984) for discussions pointed to marketing.

also has emerged recently in relationship marketing thought. Even economists have recognized the role of trust within the system. As Kenneth Arrow (1972), Nobel Laureate in Economics, explained, "virtually every commercial transaction has within itself an element of trust . . . much of the economic backwardness in the world can be explained by the lack of mutual confidence." In asking why all societies do not become equally wealthy and successful, recent work by Hunt (1997★) and others (e.g., Etzioni 1988★) points to differences in societal institutions that promote trust and personal moral codes as a key differentiator.

Finally, Proposition 10 notes that this "open system" stresses achievement, growth, and progress. These are the elements of the U.S. aggregate marketing system that have brought huge, positive changes to the daily lives of its society's members, as was indicated in our first illustration, "It's a Wonderful Life."[8]

We now turn to the system's contributions. Our discussion here is presented in three sections: (1) benefits to economic well-being, (2) benefits to buyers, and (3) several broader perspectives on benefits.[9] Although most entries will not be new to marketing thinkers, we are hopeful that in combination they will prove useful in stimulating further thought about the field and its value to society.

Marketing's Contributions to Economic Well-Being

CONTRIBUTIONS TO THE LARGER ECONOMIC SYSTEM

Whatever the political choices, an aggregate marketing system is integral to a society's economic system. In Figure 3, Part A, we list ten areas in which marketing contributes in the United States. It offers employment and incomes for the millions of persons engaged in this field, enabling them to be productive and earn money needed for consumption. As noted, consumers' exercise of freedom of choice means that the preferences of society's members largely are reflected in the system's goods and services, which should mean that aggregate satisfaction is enhanced in this sector of life. As Adam Smith pointed out in his classic *Wealth of Nations* (1776★, p. 385), "Consumption is the sole end and purpose of all production." In this regard, the aggregate marketing system is involved directly in delivering the standard of living enjoyed by society's members. Furthermore, private investments for the marketing system have been important in assisting national infrastructure development in such areas as distribution facilities, transportation, communication, medical care, and the financial sector. Related to this, monies gathered by

---

[8]Any aggregate system will bring serious issues as well. For example, probing questions can be posed about destruction of natural resources, social inequality in life chances, the nature of growth in affluence, and others. We discuss these in our section on controversies and criticisms.

[9]Although the aggregate system includes marketers, customers, and public policymakers, given the purpose of this article, we concentrate on contributions emanating from the marketing sector of the system.

FIGURE 3

Marketing's Contributions to Economic Well-Being

A. Ten Contributions to the Larger Economic System

—*Employment and personal incomes*
—*Freedom of choice in consumption*
—*Delivery of a standard of living*
—*Assistance in infrastructure development (e.g., transportation, communications, financial sector)*
—*Tax payments for public purposes*
—*Mass-market efficiencies*
—*Diffusion of innovations*
—*Enhanced balance of trade accounts*
—*International development*
—*Integral to economic growth and prosperity*

B. Insights on Marketing and Economic Development

—*Marketing employment/gross domestic product relationship*
—*Roles depend on stage of development:*
  • Traditional subsistence: assure prices
  • Transitional: infrastructure
  • Market-oriented: financing, credit
—*Roles depend on government policies*
—*Roles depend on consumers and culture*
—*Marketing expertise and systems are key*
—*Marketing's development functions:*

  • Organization of networks   • Spatial connectivity
  • Speculation in time   • Capital accumulation
  • Equalization   • Entrepreneurial entry

---

governments (sales and excise taxes) actually are gathered by operations of the marketing system. Together with income taxes paid by firms and individuals engaged in marketing, these represent substantial sources of the tax payments to fund public programs.

With respect to consumption, the system's mass-market efficiencies have led to lower costs, lower prices, and increased total consumption for citizens. The system's dynamic character also fosters diffusion of innovations, bringing new benefits to consumption. Internationally, the aggregate marketing system is a crucial contributor to the nation's balance of trade and, in seeking new areas of opportunity, is a force for international development. Overall, then, in many significant and positive ways, the aggregate marketing system has played an integral role in the economic growth and prosperity of the United States.

Although obvious in the abstract, marketing's contributions to economic well-being actually have not been recognized by many businesspersons or, indeed, by many economists. This is probably because they are not factors in the classic macroeconomic equations (Kinnear 1994). Here, aggregate supply depends on the stock of capital, labor, raw materials, and technology; Kinnear asserts that marketing's importance would be more clear if efficiencies and skills in wholesaling, retailing, and logistics were included in this equation. Similarly, aggregate demand is a function of expenditures for consumption, investment, government, and net foreign trade. However, marketing does affect aggregate demand; if economists' equations were to identify effects of marketing programs (on autonomous consumption and marginal propensity to consume, on prospects for success of an investment in a new product, and on the volume of exports and imports), the value of marketing efforts in the economic system would be more starkly obvious. Furthermore, this would stimulate interest in calibrating the magnitudes of these contributions.

MARKETING AND ECONOMIC DEVELOPMENT

The societal benefits that flow from the aggregate marketing system are nowhere more apparent than in the area of economic development. Peter Drucker, the noted business thinker, raised this issue years ago in a stirring speech at a Parlin Award dinner, reprinted by the *Journal of Marketing* as "Marketing and Economic Development" (Drucker 1958★). His view of marketing as an entrepreneurial "multiplier" and organizer of resources casts a quite different light on our field. Subsequent work has done much to explore and refine this view. The points in Figure 3, Part B, illustrate several key insights about marketing's roles and contributions.[10]

First, the role for marketing in economic development is real. Nations with higher proportions of their populations in marketing also have higher GDPs. Development of the marketing system is necessary for this to occur (e.g., Preston 1967★; Wood and Vitell 1986). However, the specific roles for the marketing system differ by stage of economic development. In a subsistence economy, production is barely sufficient for self needs and is not separated in time or distance from consumption. The immediate priority is incentives to increase production, with price assurance being most significant. In economies just becoming urbanized, the priorities are to develop distribution infrastructure (i.e., transport, storage, and selling networks). In market-oriented systems, all marketing functions are important, with investment financing and consumer credit as primary tools for market growth (U.S. Department of Agriculture 1972★).

Second, as noted in Figure 3, Part B, a host government's policies help determine opportunities for marketing's contributions to the society (e.g., Thorelli 1996). However, governments typically pursue five possibly contradictory goals—growth, fuller employment, income distribution, price control (inflation), and balance of payments—and may do so with too few tools to handle the task (Slater 1978). Treatment of the

---

[10]Much of the discussion to follow is based on overviews provided by Batra (1997), Moyer (1965), Nason and White (1981), Thorelli (1996), and Wood and Vitell (1986).

aggregate marketing system is thus part of a complex political context. As a social institution, the marketing system must be embedded in the society's culture, and this can be problematic in some societies because aspects of the culture are not welcoming of some features of the U.S. marketing system (e.g., Ger 1997⋆). Where a U.S.-style system is desired, moreover, certain consumer behaviors (e.g., handling of finances, planned saving and choice processes, defenses to persuasion) must be learned for the system to work well. With regard to linkages among efficiency, consumer behavior, and culture in developing marketing systems, Slater identifies literacy, achievement desires, cooperativism, fatalism, mass media, and innovativeness as key dimensions (cf. Nason and White 1981). Marketing experts working in the "transitional economies" (i.e., those moving from centralized planning to market-based systems) of Eastern Europe, the former Soviet Union, and China note that entrepreneurial risk-taking, marketing management expertise, and the use of strong business planning and control systems are crucial in determining success (e.g., Batra 1997). These experts differ as to ease of transfer of such knowledge, but the large number of international students educated in business schools in recent years does provide cause for optimism.

Third, Figure 3, Part B's "Marketing's Development Functions" reflect marketing's roles in more basic settings (modified from Moyer 1965). Marketing encourages increased production by conceiving, organizing, and operating networks for communication and exchange. Speculation across time is needed to bring future production and consumption using entrepreneurial risk of capital and effort. Equalization of supply and demand occurs across distance (transport), time (storage), and quantity (price), whereas spacial connectivity joins diverse locales in a larger marketplace to offer efficiencies of scale and lower prices to consumers. Over time, these can grow into a center for capital accumulation (investment) and serve as a springboard for marketing entrepreneurs' entry as industrialists. For example, some years after its nationhood, nearly half the leading industrialists of Pakistan were found to have come from the marketing sector (Papenek 1962⋆). Here they had learned, in Adam Smith's words, "the habits . . . of order, economy, and attention" that characterize success in market distribution (Smith 1776⋆, p. 385).

Contributions to Buyers from Specific Marketing Activities

We now focus on marketers' actions that benefit buyers. Because there are millions of competing firms in the aggregate marketing system, at any time a huge number of these benefits are being offered in parallel. Across time, these benefits accumulate through billions of purchase occasions to become truly formidable. Our framework in Figure 4 will be familiar to marketing thinkers, but persons outside the field likely will be surprised at the scope of contributions offered. We begin with the economic concept of utility.

FIGURE 4

Contributions to Buyers from Specific Marketing Activities

Traditional Views	Managerial Sectors	System Outcomes

A. Five Types of Utility:
– Elemental
  (marketing not a
  contributor)
– Form
  (marketing a partial
  contributor)
– Place
  (marketing a major
  contributor)
– Time
  (marketing a major
  contributor)
– Possession
  (marketing a major
  contributor)
 	
**B. Eight Classic Functions of
Market Distribution:**
– Transportation
– Storage
– Financing
– Risk-bearing
– Assembly
– Selling
– Standardization
– Market information
	C. _Marketing Mix Elements:_
	
	Product and Service Offerings
	– Two-way exchange
	– Benefits from each use occasion
	– Benefit bundles (multiattribute)
	– Frequent new offerings
	– Continued improvements
	– Considerable product variation
	– Stress on quality control
	– Guarantees and redress
	
	Branding/Trademarks
	– Identification of specific offerings
	– Efficiency in future search
	– Consumer confidence/meaning
	– Possible symbolic benefits
	
	Market Distribution
	– Most marketing functions (at left)
	– Eases access to products/services
	– Reduces information search costs
	– Enables interbrand comparisons
	– Lowers prices through competition
	– Increases quantity of information
	– Facilitates the transaction process
	– Offers credit opportunities
	– Postpurchase support structure
	  • delivery and set-up
	  • liberal return policies
	  • maintenance and repair
	– Provides entry for new competitors
		Salespersons and Representatives
		– Consultation on problem solutions
		– Crystallization of needs
		– Education about alternatives
		– Introduction of new offerings
		– Customization of offerings
		– Facilitation of transactions
		– Access to technical support
		– Customer satisfaction
		– Feedback from field
		
		Advertising and Promotion
		– Provides information
		  • product knowledge/use
		  • new products and services
		  • prices and specials
		– Decision-making enhancements
		  • shopping patronage
		  • lowers search costs
		– Enlarges market demand
		  • reduces distribution costs
		  • lowers prices
		  • entry of new competitors
		  • acceptance of innovations
		– Subsidizes media and events
		  • news and editorial
		  • entertainment and sports
		– Provides entertainment
			**D. _Summary: The Marketing System's
			Resultant Benefits:_**
			
			_I. Promotes the production of desired
			products and services_
			II. Delivers products and services
			III. Provides for market learning
			IV. Stimulates market demand
			V. Offers wide scope for choice
			VI. Close/customized fits with needs
			VII. Facilitates purchases (acquisitions)
			VIII. Saves time/promotes efficiency
			IX. Provides for postpurchase support
			X. Brings new entries to market
			XI. Fosters innovations/improvements
			XII. Enables larger total consumption
			_XIII. Seeks customer satisfaction for
			repeat purchase relationships_
			_XIV. Provides a pleasant "approach"
			environment for buyer behavior_

MARKETING'S BUNDLE OF UTILITIES

Economists traditionally employ utility to represent value. As a prominent economist observed nearly 80 years ago, "marketing and advertising are interested primarily in the creation of value" (Moriarty 1923★). Identification of marketing's special utilities, shown in Figure 4, Part A, proved helpful to economists who argued that distributive services added value beyond that of production.[11] Of the five utilities listed, note that only elemental utility, which refers to cultivation or extraction of crops and raw materials, is arguably beyond marketing's purview. The second, form utility, comes primarily from operations, but marketing activities contribute here by (1) physically supplying essential inputs to the production process and (2) providing insights from the marketplace (e.g., market research) that help decide specific attributes for goods and services. Place utility is clearly in marketing's province, representing the value added by providing goods where buyers need them. Marketing adds time utility through preplanning, inventory, and promotion activities to ensure customers can obtain goods when needed. Finally, possession utility is offered through marketing transactions and enables customers to use goods for desired purposes.

THE EIGHT CLASSIC FUNCTIONS OF MARKET DISTRIBUTION

Our appreciation of marketing's contributions is enhanced by thought on the "functional approach" to marketing, which arose early in the twentieth century in reaction to mainstream economists' lack of attention to the value of distribution. It became a basic approach for the study of marketing for more than five decades, describing marketers' activities and reasons for them. With the rise of the managerial approach, however, this descriptive view of marketing has all but disappeared (Hunt and Goolsby 1988).

Among many frameworks, the eight functions listed in Figure 4, Part B, are widely accepted (Maynard, Weidler, and Beckman 1927). With the then-emphasis on agriculture and manufacturing, functional frameworks stressed physical supply services, beginning with transportation. Closely allied, storage helps nullify timing discrepancies in supply and demand, smooths production schedules to lower costs, and enables mixing of ingredients or stock (as in our coffee bean example). Innovations in these areas (consider refrigeration and freezing) have brought major improvements to society during the past century. The next of marketing's classic functions, financing, receives little attention by marketing scholars today but is still a key topic in economic development settings. A firm must finance the time gap between start of the productive process (when machines, material, labor, marketing, and so forth must be paid for) and later receipt of

---

[11]The recent emphasis on supply chain management incorporates a systems approach to the provision of these utilities aimed at enhancing efficiencies. Although this may alter marketing's identification within a firm, these clearly remain as activities within the aggregate marketing system.

money from sales. Such investment financing may be undertaken directly by marketers or, when stakes are high, by financial institutions. Within the overall system, financing has fostered entry by many small businesses, and consumer credit has enabled purchases of millions of homes, autos, and so forth. It thus has been a key factor in society's prosperity. Assumption of risk reflects transactions and arises out of uncertainty. In marketing channels, for example, risk comes with ownership of goods for which future demand may be less than expected (e.g., negative price changes, demand shortfalls, improved designs, deterioration in quality, credit problems with repayments). Risk is substantial throughout the aggregate marketing system, a fact apparent to those who forecast demand.

Assembly refers to the broader buying process, seeking out sources of supply and deciding on goods and services to be purchased. Buying is pervasive across the aggregate marketing system and leads to successive changes in ownership that end in final consumer purchases. On the other side of a purchase is another's sale. Although much maligned, selling harnesses the forces of competition to improve the value of offerings and brings about the exchanges that enable the system to operate. Standard-setting often is unseen and quite underestimated. Once set by a society, standards serve as buying guides in a vast range of business and consumer categories. In essence, they provide assurance for critical "credence" attributes such as safety, strength, or other elements of an offering that may be difficult to determine through inspection, and they aid in price and value comparisons as well. Marketers are important users of standards in our society and also participate in their creation. (In contrast to general perceptions, the vast majority of standardization is a voluntary activity in the United States, as opposed to standards being imposed by government.) Finally, the gathering and use of market information is quite familiar. Inputs can come from sources—experts, government, customers, the sales force, library—beyond formal market research projects. As a key activity in marketing, this function increasingly stimulates improvements in the benefits we now discuss.

BENEFITS FROM PRODUCT AND SERVICE OFFERINGS

A marketing exchange relies on both transacting parties' expectations to be better off. Because sellers benefit from payments for purchases, it is not surprising to find marketers' focus on purchase processes. However, it is important to recall that benefits received by customers accrue from use or consumption. As indicated in Figure 4, Part C, this has an interesting implication: Each single-use occasion creates an opportunity for another benefit delivery from the system. Furthermore, because products and services are "benefit bundles," users are deriving multiple benefits (e.g., Green, Wind, and Jain 1972★). For example, toothpaste attributes, such as decay prevention, whitening, tartar control, and good taste, can be combined to create multiple sources of value in a single-use occasion. Extensive product variation further enables closer fits with users' preferences. In the U.S. system, frequent new offerings and improvements to current offerings also are pursued. Furthermore, we should recognize that much of the care taken by marketers in design, creation, and delivery of offerings remains unseen and, thus, is underappreciated by the general public. This care aids a brand's competitive success by providing an intended, identical service or use experience expected by loyal customers. Finally, the marketing system generally stands behind its offerings, with buyers often protected by guarantees or warranties.

To verify our impression of this system stress on quality, we checked ratings in some 200 product and service classes. Ratings were given in 1996 and 1997 in *Consumer Reports,* published by Consumers Union, an independent testing organization that accepts no advertising or other funds from the marketing community. Our tabulation of scores showed that, of 3028 ratings, only 51 items (1.7%) were rated as "poor" in quality. Including "fair" as a passing grade, 98% of marketers' offerings received satisfactory ratings; 88% received ratings of "good," "very good," or "excellent."[12] Clearly the system is delivering quality offerings to its public.

BENEFITS OF BRANDING/TRADEMARKS

Unique identification is not only significant to marketers (Aaker 1991), but also benefits buyers in four ways.[13] As shown in Figure 4, Part C, unique source names assist (1) in organizing future behaviors, because if problems are encountered, the source can be recontacted, but if satisfied, favorable attitudes can direct future decisions; (2) efficiency in locating favored sellers (though it appears innocuous, summed across products, time, and competing demands, this efficiency actually is quite significant in total); (3) rapid, confident choices in self-service settings (the average time for a single choice in a U.S. supermarket aisle is only a few seconds); and (4) in deriving symbolic benefits from purchase, ownership, or use. Symbolic benefits can be public (driving a high-status car) or private (enjoying a finely crafted product). Although at times a target for criticism, symbolic benefits' mechanisms are varied and subtle, involving sustaining personal identity as well as communicating about the self (e.g., Belk 1988,★ 1989★; Cohen 1989★; Levy 1959★).

BENEFITS FROM MARKET DISTRIBUTION

As noted in the first entry of this section in Figure 4, Part C, the key benefits in this area are captured in our discussion of marketing's eight classic functions. Because it is performed largely out of the sight of nonparticipants, however, the performance of distribution easily can be underappreciated. It is useful to recall that the marketing system

---

[12]Every quality test rating that used the five-point "excellent-poor" scale given by the organization was considered. Ratings by members were not included, nor were relative scales in which distributions were forced.

[13]Branding is being used in a broad sense, because price and value are relevant issues as well. Health insurance firms, for example, are pushing for "debranding" (generic drugs) to obtain lower prices.

performs these functions repetitively and routinely, millions of times daily, each time offering benefits to receivers. Beyond this, wholesale and retail activities offer additional benefits, as noted in the remaining listings of Figure 4, Part C. The first five of these are well recognized and need no amplification. The final four entries, however, deserve separate discussion.

One powerful aspect of the U.S. marketing system is facilitating the transaction process, which saves consumers time and effort and maximizes purchase opportunities. Consider, for example, the benefits of extended store hours, convenient locations, free parking, stocked shelves, posted prices, displays, fast and smooth checkout, advertising price specials, salespersons' pleasant and efficient completion of transactions, and so forth. (Consumers from some other cultures express surprise and delight on this discovery of the U.S. retailing system.) Furthermore, processes for extending consumer credit enable some expensive purchases to occur that otherwise would have been delayed, and bank credit cards have eased transaction processes for buyers and sellers alike. That stores pay significant fees, approximately 3%, for bank card charges is a good indicator of how much the system desires to facilitate purchase transactions. When a durable-good purchase is made, moreover, consumers enter a use phase that can last for many years. During this time, the marketing system offers a postpurchase support structure with benefits such as delivery, installation, repair services, and liberal return policies. Our final entry is quite different but has done much to improve the lives of everyone in U.S. society, in that channels of distribution serve as the entry point (gatekeeper) for new products and services. Receptivity by wholesalers and retailers to offerings that provide better value or new benefits has made this dynamic work for societal gain. Similarly, government actions to reduce barriers to entry serve to enable innovations and price competition to work to the benefit of a society's consumers and competitors.

BENEFITS FROM SALESPERSONS AND REPRESENTATIVES

Sales representatives facilitate flows within the aggregate marketing system. Although advertising receives more public attention, marketers frequently rate personal selling as more important for business success. In one study, executives rated selling five times more important than advertising for industrial goods and almost twice as important for consumer durable goods; for consumer nondurables, the two were rated approximately equally important (Udell 1972★). An estimated 20 million sales representatives are at work daily in the system, 9 million in business-to-business selling, and 11 million others dealing directly with consumers. Roles vary widely, as does level of performance. In Figure 4, Part C, we list some contributions offered in business-to-business sales, in which the salesperson is a professional representative who deals with generally well-informed buyers and with current users who may need to have problems resolved. To start, salespersons may be called on to consult on large programs (e.g., plant construction, advertising campaigns), often as part of account teams that include specialists. During this process, a representative may help crystallize client needs, educate about alternatives, introduce new entries, and customize the offering when feasible. He or she then works to facilitate the entire transaction, payment, and product delivery or project completion. During this process, which could extend for years, the sales representative provides access to technical support and offers personal service to ensure customer satisfaction and a continuing relationship. Our final entry, feedback from the field, reflects the reports back to the firm about opportunities to enhance its offerings.

BENEFITS FROM ADVERTISING AND PROMOTION

Each year, an incredible amount of money is spent on advertising and sales promotion: Advertising is a major industry in its own right, accounting for approximately 3% of U.S. GDP. Due to its high visibility, advertising is likely the most criticized facet of the aggregate marketing system, though it provides important benefits. In their classic study *Advertising in America,* Bauer and Greyser (1968; also see Pollay and Mittal 1993) asked consumers about this institution. Their findings fit four of the five entries in Figure 4, Part C. Appreciation for the information advertising provides on products and prices was expressed by a majority of consumers.[14] Few consumers noted our second benefit; clearly, however, advertising can enhance consumer decisions through lower search costs. (Product proliferation, however, raises search costs.) The consumers mentioned enlarging market demand and noted special appreciation for advertising's contribution to lowering prices. Less obvious are three related benefits in this category: reducing distribution costs, aiding entry by new competitors, and fostering acceptance of new innovations by a society. The consumer sample also recognized the final entries in Part C, applauding advertising's role in subsidizing media and expressing pleasure with advertising's creative offerings.

SUMMARY: MARKETING'S KEY BENEFITS TO BUYERS

Because our detailed listings risk "losing sight of the forest for the trees," in Figure 4, Part D, we abstract what we believe are 14 of the key benefits consumers derive from marketing activities. There is marketing's role in driving the production of offerings most desired in the marketplace. In many organizations, marketers act as internal advocates who represent the customer in decisions on what to produce, then other elements of the aggregate marketing system advance the creation of those offerings by carrying out their functions (e.g., assembly, transport) at all intermediate stages, leading to final production. The marketing system then manages the delivery of products

---

[14]Several leading marketing thinkers believe that firms would benefit from increased attention to providing consumer information/education programs that would assist consumers to make better decisions, as opposed to simple emphasis on persuasion/entertainment in advertising.

and services to consumers. It also expends funds to provide for market learning using sales representatives, advertising, brochures, specialized brokers, and so forth. The persuasive aspect of these vehicles serves to stimulate market demand, which creates sales and can lead to lowered costs and prices. Through competition, the system offers a wide array of choices, which enables consumers to judge how best to satisfy their needs to obtain desired quality. In this regard, it is interesting to realize that every available good and service is being purchased by some fellow consumers. The system's variety enables some marketers to offer close or even customized fits with a user's needs. The system also is designed to facilitate purchases, easing acquisitions of benefits for buyers. Various elements of time-saving are offered in both products and purchasing, which increase societal members' efficiency and leave time for more total activity. Also, the marketing system offers a postpurchase support structure to enable continuing benefits over time.

The marketing system continually brings new entries for customers to consider and actively works on behalf of product innovations and improvements, some of which will enhance a society's quality of life over the long run. Furthermore, it enables buyers to engage in larger total consumption than they would otherwise be able, through credit, price specials, discount versions of goods, and/or bundled attributes. Most sellers seek long-term repeat purchases from patrons, so customer satisfaction is a real goal of the system. Finally, the marketing system often offers pleasant environments within which consumers can act, a distinct benefit in itself (as those experienced with some monopolists or government agencies can attest).

Two Broader Views of Benefits

CONTRIBUTIONS FROM IMPROVEMENTS IN MARKETING SYSTEM ACTIVITIES

In our analyses to this point, it has become clear that the system's current level of performance is based on its emphasis on a continual search for improvement. Thus, our interest is in not only kinds of benefits, but also increased levels of benefits emanating daily from individual firms and people, as indicated in the following:

"Back to the Future." The constant press for improvements characterizes the world of the aggregate marketing system. Many efforts do not work out, some yield minor advances, and a few lead to norms of the future. In Figure 5, Part A, we display a few illustrative cases of recent breakthroughs. For example, trucking firms now combine onboard computers and satellite tracking systems for real-time monitoring of their cargo. One firm uses this system to coordinate routes and communicate with all 10,000 trucks in its fleet, thereby adapting instantly to weather or traffic delays. The result is better delivery service with lower costs for the firm. Similarly, containerization has added efficiency in shipping and handling; our coffee beans, for example, shifted easily from ocean to ground transport and were less

---

FIGURE 5

Some Broader Views of Benefits

A. Contributions from Improvements in Marketing System Activities

Transportation
  – e.g., real-time monitoring
Materials handling
  – e.g., containerization
Distribution
  – e.g., order processing systems
Assembly
  – e.g., global sourcing
Retailing
  – e.g., checkout scanners

Product design
  – e.g., match or better
Promotion programs
  – e.g., loyalty clubs
Product management
  – e.g., brand equity
Market segmentation
  – e.g., mass customization
Database marketing
  – e.g., personalized offerings

Marketing research
  – e.g., expert systems
Packaging innovations
  – e.g., environmental impacts
Pricing programs
  – e.g., value/bonus packs
Services marketing
  – e.g., consumer satisfaction

B. Contributions to Quality of Life

I. Illustrative Social/Psychological Benefits to Marketing Participants (Opportunities for):

– Achievement	– Creativity	– Beauty
– Success	– Humor	– Morality
– Growth	– Invention	– Interpersonal relationships
– Action	– Influence	– Understanding
– Discovery	– Service	– Trust

II. Illustrative Social/Psychological Benefits Created by Consumers Engaged Within the System:

– Accomplishment	– Bonding	– Socializing
– Beauty	– Belonging	– Learning
– Safety	– Excitement	– Authority
– Health	– Prestige	– Control
– Nurturance	– Pleasure	– Status
– Joy	– Self-enhancement	– Play
– Gift-giving	– Escape	– Leisure

III. Emerging Areas of Study:

  – Quality of life (QOL)
  – Social marketing

---

susceptible to damage, spoilage, and theft. As distribution channels have embraced relationship marketing, order processing systems have saved time and costs. For example, two firms may use electronic data interchange, in which inventories (e.g., a drugstore's entire stock in a line) automatically are replenished as sales movement data are transmitted to the wholesaler; people are limited to oversight of the system. Also, improvements in communications, transport, and technology have enabled marketers to move increasingly worldwide to obtain materials at much lower costs. Although global sourcing has generated legitimate criticisms, it also has provided consumers with quality goods at lower prices and added to the aggregate marketing systems of other societies as well. In retailing, checkout scanners brought a revolution. Computerized pricing enabled stores to lower labor costs, better manage inventory, and promote more effectively through information on what works best with each store's customers. For food manufacturers, this technology speeds adjustments to developments in the marketplace, which enables increased responsiveness to consumers.

In product development, "match or better" means a search for value parity on most key attributes, and advantage on the others. For example, in the early 1980s, Ford Motor Company had lost $3 billion when it created "Team Taurus," a group of marketers, designers, engineers, and plant personnel charged with developing a new car to rescue the firm. The team relied on consumer research, choosing 700 features for the new car from this source. In addition, the team bought models of popular competing cars, then tore them apart to analyze their best features (over 400 were "borrowed" in this process). The net result of Team Taurus's efforts? One of the most popular cars ever produced and a turnaround for Ford, whose market share rose from 16% to 29% (Wilkie 1994). The general lesson? Marketers know that demand is highly responsive to advantages consumers perceive a product to have (or lack) and can be quite responsive to price as well (e.g., Day and Wansink 1994*). At this point, we need not detail the remaining items in Figure 5, Part A, because marketing readers easily can appreciate the potentials of each. As previously noted, pressure for improvements in the system are relentless, and the positive benefits of this force should be appreciated.

CONTRIBUTIONS TO QUALITY OF LIFE

In this final section on contributions, we shift away from the economic calculus that reports on the system as if it were a relentless machine spewing out streams of utiles. Instead we examine briefly the aggregate marketing system as a human institution composed of people living their lives on a variety of fronts. Our effort here is illustrative, intended to raise this topic as worthy of further attention by marketing scholars. We first examine benefits in the work of marketing, in which aggregate effects could be very large.

Social/Psychological Benefits to Marketing Participants

In the first set of entries in Figure 5, Part B, we have listed several social and psychological benefits we believe are offered to persons who work in marketing. Drawing on the system's stress on competition, achievement is highly rewarded in this field. This is one reason for steep increases in incomes in early years of a marketer's career, in contrast to accounting or engineering, in which salaries begin at higher levels but increase much more slowly. Because of the marketing system's openness to change, opportunities abound for feelings of personal growth and individual autonomy. Whether pursuing clearer understanding of the consumer marketplace, creating a new advertising campaign, managing a retail store, closing an important sale, or planning a new product launch, marketing offers challenges to creativity and ingenuity, as well as opportunities to influence others. Marketers in many areas can offer service to others, and those in the arts can foster aesthetic values within society. Many marketing positions require teamwork to achieve a common goal, which can provide valued group affiliations. It is common for sellers to develop friendly relationships with their clients as a consequence of ongoing exchange activities. In our breakfast illustration, for example, the large transaction between the coffee buyer and major grower was sealed with a handshake. To marketing scholars, many of whom who have come to the field from other disciplines, these attributes are well understood. Furthermore, with globalization of markets, these opportunities are expanding.

Social/Psychological Benefits Created by Consumers

Since the study of consumer behavior entered marketing's mainstream during the 1950s and 1960s, consumers' goals and motivations have been studied extensively. Most research has been instrumental (e.g., what can we learn about consumers so that we can sell more effectively to them?), but some reveals interest in deeper human issues. Examples include two older books by well-known marketing consultants, Daniel Yankelovich (1981), who revealed concerns about society's direction at the time, and Arnold Mitchell (1983), who designed the VALS (values and lifestyles) system using Maslow's humanistic need theory.

More recently, the interpretivist orientation (e.g., Sherry 1991) has honed our appreciation of goods' meanings in consumers' lives. A carefully cultivated lawn and flower garden can give a homeowner a sense of accomplishment, or a parent may derive special satisfaction from selecting food, clothing, or furniture for a safe, healthy home. Gift-giving can involve significant emotional and symbolic dimensions. Movies, sporting events, or theatrical productions can lead to feelings of belonging, prestige, escape, or excitement. Consumer activities enable learning, socializing, and self-enhancement (listening to music, playing tennis); benefits are emotional, subjective, and experiential (Holbrook and Hirschman 1982★). Spending money can bring feelings of achievement, status, control, and even play. Shopping is an enjoyable activity for many. Although intangible and difficult to express, our treatment of the marketing system's contributions to consumers would be incomplete without discussion of these sometimes meaningful consequences.

Two Emerging Areas of Study on Marketing's Broader Contributions

During the 1960s and 1970s, literature on marketing and society raised questions about (1) how well society itself was faring and (2) how it might be improved. These questions spawned two different subareas: research on "quality of life" (QOL) and "social marketing." Marketers interested in QOL faced three special issues: (1) marketing is only one of many forces that combine to yield overall lifestyles, (2) daunting conceptualization and measurement issues on exactly what QOL is, and (3) difficulty in communicating across fields. Economists defined issues to fit their terms and research forms, as did psychologists, sociologists, ecologists, and political scientists (Sirgy, Samli, and Meadow 1982). The International Society for Quality of Life Studies now carries on this work. Recent work on the American Consumer Satisfaction Index shows promise in reflecting market-based performance of the system at various levels of aggregation (Fornell et al. 1996), as does work on the Index of Consumer Sentiment Toward Marketing (Etzel and Gaski 1999).

Social marketing differs from traditional marketing by aiming to benefit the target audience directly (e.g., AIDS awareness or childhood immunization) or society as a whole (e.g., recycling programs, blood donations) rather than the firm sponsoring the program (Andreasen 1994★). It has, however, faced academic difficulties on two fronts: (1) it has tended to be an "action" field in which primary emphasis is on successful intervention and (2) value judgments are made on desirable behavioral changes, so the area is also "activist" in this sense. There is potential to add to knowledge in this sphere, and an expanding set of researchers has been moving into the area (e.g., Andreasen 1991; Goldberg 1995★). Meanwhile, useful field work has been progressing for some time, applying marketing tools in health and safety, education, charitable giving, politics, the arts, and the environment.

In light of the topic for this article, these two fields of study are significant in pointing out that the aggregate marketing system is composed of more participants than just business marketers. Private marketing *is* the mainstay of the system in the United States, but government, the entire consumer sector, and many individuals in the not-for-profit sector are also participants. The system's issues extend to societal concerns and, in turn, are affected by them as well.

Criticisms and Problems of the Aggregate Marketing System

Our focus in this article has been on accomplishments, but balance calls on us to acknowledge also that the aggregate marketing system long has been controversial in some respects. In Figure 6, we summarize many of the most prominent criticisms, controversies, and problems that have been raised. Space limitations preclude an extended analysis, but it is available elsewhere (Moore and Wilkie 2000). We begin with critiques of system values. These usually are made by persons speaking from vantage points outside the system and raising philosophical points about its nature. These criticisms tend to say little directly about the practice of marketing but instead focus on broader issues such as the "consumer culture" and the economic system that sustains it. Political theory is the root of some of these critiques, but not all. These are not simplistic arguments, and we do not wish to do them an injustice in such a brief summary. Readers will find writings by Galbraith (1958) of interest, as well as the Pollay (1986★, 1987★) versus Holbrook (1987★) advertising debate and the recent collection by Goodwin, Ackerman, and Kiron (1997).

Classic social and economic debates are next in Figure 6. These have a long history, though they have evolved over time. For example, the distribution cost debate of the early 1900s had farmers questioning why they received only a low percentage of the consumer's food dollar; today, buyers (and farmers) ask why cereal brands are

FIGURE 6

Criticisms and Problems of the Aggregate Marketing System

Broad Social and Economic Concerns	Views of the Consumer Movement	Continuing Challenges for Marketing Practice	Problem Episodes Through Deliberate Behaviors
Critiques of System Values Promotes materialism – Stresses conformity – Social competitiveness, envy – Exacerbates pain of poverty Negatively affects cultural values – Creates insidious cycle of work and spend – Discourages participation in noneconomic activities (e.g., arts, community, leisure) – Undermines families, alters socialization Is fundamentally persuasive/manipulative in character – Creates artificial wants and needs – Invokes imbalance between marketer and consumer Cultural imperialism – Cultural impacts – Natural resource depletion – global warming Proposes limitless, unsustainable aggregate consumption levels Capitalist system promotes inequality in benefit distribution (fairness versus allocative efficiency) Emphasis on private consumption leads to deterioration in quality of public goods Pervasive commercialism System is inherently self-serving, directed toward no broader social purpose **"Classic" Social and Economic Debates** – Does distribution cost too much? – Is there too much advertising? Is it wasteful? – Advertising: information or market power? – Advertising: good taste and morality? – Subliminal advertising? – Is price related to quality? – Is deliberate product obsolescence good?	**The Consumer Bill of Rights** – The right of safety – The right to be informed – The right to choose – The right to be heard **Consumerism's Three Major eras: Key Issues** I. Turn of the century – Food and drug safety – Regulation of competition II. 1920s and 1930s – Objective information – Consumer representation III. 1960s and 1970s – Product safety – Advertising's social impact – Avenues for redress **Economic Imperfections: The Asymmetric Power of Marketing** – Difficult product quality assessment – Incomplete or biased information – Too few sellers in some local markets – Uncaring civil servants – Too little time for considered decisions – Underrepresentation of consumer interest – Ineffective regulatory agencies – Consumers' deficiencies **Some Continuing Controversies** – Dangerous products (e.g.., cigarettes) – Vulnerable groups (e.g., children, elderly) – Emerging problems with marketplace encroachment – Intrusiveness of advertising – Concerns regarding invasion of privacy – Restrictions on database usage – Selling as marketing research – Exploitation by price discrimination	**Limits to Information and Persuasion** Advertising content – Limits to persuasion – Themes, executions, and copy – Intrusiveness: environmental clutter – Ad approval processes Sales, pricing, and after-sales practices – Limits to persuasion – Control of sales abuses – warranties and guarantees – Retailer and distributor pricing practices Information disclosure – Limits to disclosure – Effective warning labels – Use of disclaimers **The Broader Environment** Environmental concerns – Natural resource depletion – Threats to ecology – Reusabilty and disposition Product safety – Hazardous products – Regulatory approval processes – Product failure and liability Anticompetitive practices – Effects of quotas/trade barriers – Antitrust issues **Responsible Corporate Citizenship** Consumer dissatisfaction – Rumors and negative word of mouth – Complaint handling – Problem resolution systems Corporate actions – Incorporating ethical concerns – Role of consumer affairs departments – Criteria for evaluating business performance – Industry self-regulation – Community involvement	**Marketing Sector** – Deceptive advertising – High-pressure sales techniques – Misrepresentations of sales intent – Inferior products and services – Bait and switch – Price fairness: high-low pricing – Price fixing – Predatory pricing – Franchise abuses – International: Bribery – Gray-market goods – Counterfeit goods – Internet fraud **Consumer Sector** – Uninformed decisions – Consumer fraud (e.g., shoplifting, credit abuse) – Bankruptcy – Product liability: Frivolous lawsuits – Compulsive consumption **Government Sector** – Errors of omission – Errors of commission

priced so high relative to ingredient costs. Also, much attention has been directed to advertising, as reflected in four of the eight debates. These debates likely persist because (1) strong proponents on each side will not concede; (2) generalizations are, at times, based on episodes; (3) decisive empirical evidence has not been available because of severe measurement difficulties; and (4) the underlying issues actually are complex.

The second column reflects the views of the consumer movement. These tend not to be antagonistic to the aggregate marketing system itself (recall the high ratings *Consumer Reports* gives system offerings) but are aimed at having the system serve consumers' interests rather than only those of marketers. Thus, President John F. Kennedy's 1962 proclamation of the "Consumer Bill of Rights" was regarded as crucial in placing the power of government squarely on the side of consumers in the four basic ways listed (that is, it affirmed that U.S. society would pass laws, restricting marketers if necessary, to ensure consumers received their rights). During the past century, there have been three eras (Mayer 1989) of high public receptivity to consumer movement issues. Consumer issues have shifted over time as early concerns largely have been attained (e.g., food processing safety). A root belief sustaining the consumer movement, however, is that major economic imperfections persist within the system, especially reflecting pricing and value received per dollar. These are listed in the next entries of this section (Maynes 1997). Some debates continue in part because consumers themselves disagree. Again, our treatment here cannot do justice to the arguments' sophistication, but excellent readings are available, including Aaker and Day (1982), Maynes and colleagues (1988), Mayer (1989), and Brobeck (1997).

The third column of Figure 6 highlights difficult issues that arise naturally in marketing and must be addressed.[15] Handling by some marketers may spark legitimate criticisms, whereas others may merit commendation for efforts to be responsible. Also, problems may arise in balancing goals of different stakeholders. Illustrative issues are organized in three topics. First, limits for persuasive influence arise in both advertising and selling; a firm must focus on both policy and daily control levels to address these. Second, specific problems arise from certain products or from markets that pose societal externalities if only short-term sales and profits are pursued. We expect increasing conflict here if societies' controls of marketer actions are challenged by further globalization. Third, consistently responsible actions by all members of an organization are needed. Efforts here include design of systems to assist customers with problems and formalization of the presence of influential "voices" for all stakeholders, including employees,

---

[15]The essential point here—that social issues shape aspects of marketing practice—is based on Day's (1994) framework, which we have modified to reflect our purposes in this section.

consumers, and the broader society. The right-hand column of Figure 6 then shifts to deliberate problem behavior, as in our final illustration.

"Ruthless People." On rare occasions, a participant in the aggregate marketing system chooses to act in ways that injure others. This occurs in all system sectors, as indicated in the following reports (Wilkie 1994).

(Marketing slippage) "Creating a consumer want" has a cynical meaning among a certain stratum of marketers who first alter a consumer's product, then point out the problem to gain a sale. Gas stations on interstate highways, for example, have been caught plunging ice picks into tires and placing chemicals into batteries to cause adverse reactions. "Termite inspectors" have been caught placing the bugs in houses, then informing frightened residents of an imminent home collapse unless repaired immediately. Some traveling "tree surgeons" thrive by pointing out imagined diseases in large trees over a house, then removing the trees at high prices. A classic case of this fear selling, however, was used by the Holland Furnace Company, which employed 5000 persons in its 500 U.S. offices. Its sellers were to introduce themselves as "safety inspectors," go down to the furnace and dismantle it, and then condemn it as "so hazardous that I must refuse to put it back together. I can't let myself be an accessory to murder!" Senator Warren Magnuson (Washington) called the selling "merciless." One elderly woman was sold nine new Holland furnaces in six years, which cost more than $18,000 at the time.

(Consumer slippage) We have pointed out that one hallmark of the marketing system is emphasis on providing satisfaction after sale, including liberal return policies. Some consumers abuse this service, as this quote shows: "Mark is a soccer player who needs new shoes frequently. He has developed a system to get them from a local store that takes back defective shoes. Once or twice a year, Mark removes the sole, slices off a cleat, or places a rip in the tongue, each in a way that is hard to detect. He then brings the shoes to the store to exchange . . . at last count he'd received eight new pairs this way. Mark is sure to go to a different clerk on each visit, and . . . probably won't get caught."

(Government sector) Government abuses are harder to identify because of the few legal cases and difficulty in observation. Errors of omission (failure to act when warranted) may be more common than errors of commission because of the incentive structure of a bureaucratic system. For example, New York City's health department discovered that a dispute between two laboratory managers had led to delays of up to one year in reading cancer test results for women using city clinics. Of 3000 delayed Pap smear readings, 500 abnormalities called for immediate follow-up, 93 more appeared malignant, and 11 were clearly malignant. On discovery, the commissioner denounced his department for "betrayal of the public trust" as he demoted four people (evidently, none could be fired).

Several points remain. This is a complex area involving the law; it may not be clear that an act was deliberate or that a certain party was responsible. Also, criticisms usually are aimed at marketers, but all system participants have responsibilities, including public policymakers and consumers, and negative acts occur in each sector regularly. In addition, some acts deserve to be criticized by all participants. The U.S. system is designed for dealings to be open, honest, and well-informed. Deceptive and irresponsible behaviors injure honest competitors or consumers. Thus, it is disingenuous to simply defend actions of fellow marketers or consumers because system roles are shared. It is not clear why anyone would want disreputable persons' actions to define either the standards or image for the system overall.

Conclusions and Implications

Our goal has been to stop at this unique point in time, consider the larger picture of the marketing field, then fairly portray its structure, activities, and benefits to society. The system is huge and dynamic. Its imperfections stand as challenges for improvement, and it is appropriate for participants to work to rectify them. Beyond this, the aggregate marketing system offers much that is impressive.

IN SUMMARY

This article began by comparing daily life today with that at the turn of the last century. It is evident that the aggregate marketing system has brought many improvements to society. An illustration of a breakfast then showed the confluence of marketing systems, which highlighted the physical side of marketing and the wide range of system activities. Together, these explain why the aggregate marketing system is so ubiquitous within U.S. society: It employs approximately one in five adults and includes several million firms, several hundred million consumers, and many others who deal with marketing in their work in government, the professions, services, and not-for-profit sector. In the next section of the article, we summarized a three-set series of contributions the aggregate marketing system offers to society. We examined benefits to the overall economy, as well as for economic development, in the first set. The second set compiled an impressive array of direct benefits to buyers, and the third noted continual enhancements in system performance and an array of noneconomic contributions to the quality of life of a society and its members. We followed this with a summary of criticisms of the system. As previously noted, the aggregate marketing system emerged from this overall analysis as a worthy testament to those who have shaped it over time.

INTERESTING INSIGHTS FROM THE PROJECT

Some Substantive Lessons Learned

This project has been illuminating, and five "lessons learned" stand out for us (depending on background and interests, other readers might have drawn different insights).

- *The size, power, and practiced performance of the aggregate marketing system has emerged in this project.* Several points accompany this realization: (1) There is a real need to appreciate conceptually the magnitudes involved in this system; (2) many "hidden aspects of marketing" may be being excluded from thinking about the field; and

(3) those marketing elements the public experiences directly, such as advertising and retail selling, are likely receiving disproportionate weight in its view of the field.

- *Not all lessons are entirely positive; future developments likely will place marketers at the center of further controversies.* "Society," as referenced in the article's title, may be losing cohesion, and global marketers can be described as assisting this process (though this might not be intentional). Consider challenges to ethical systems (e.g., bribery), religious beliefs and customs (e.g., interest rates), or government protections for home industries and workers (trade barriers) and growing needs for adaptations in national antitrust policies (Federal Trade Commission [FTC] 1996). Meanwhile, not only does the Internet seamlessly cross societal boundaries, but the incredible efficiency of its reach offers huge potentials for marketing fraud. In one recent FTC (1997) case, an Internet pyramid scam promised investors $60,000 per year for an initial investment of $250: 15,000 consumers had bought in before it was stopped. Overall, concerns are increasing about marketer intrusions in privacy of records, security of financial resources, and selling to children.

- *This article has concentrated on benefits and system potentials. However, at this special point in time, it is reasonable for every marketing person to ask whether the current aggregate marketing system actually represents "the best of all worlds."* Our emphasis here is not critical but philosophical. The system is very powerful, and marketers are at work to help it achieve its ends. That society has granted marketers substantial freedoms, and that these serve to allocate much of the nation's resources, is a key statement about a societal purpose of the aggregate marketing system. To what extent do marketing managers view themselves as having reponsibility for improving the public interest or acting as stewards of a society's resources? What implications do these views have for the field as presently constituted?[16]

- *The central role for innovation in improving a society's quality of life became more evident to us.* The contributions from innovations and improvements are striking. Conceptually, this underscores the value of dynamism in an aggregate marketing system, as well as the key role of competition in providing the system's impetus. In turn, the societal importance of a government's policies to foster and protect both innovation and competition—antitrust, patents, trademarks, and so forth—become clearly apparent, but global differences may impede future progress. We also find the system's twin reliance on competition as a driver and trust as a bonding agent to be impactful yet somehow paradoxical. Finally, it is clear that achievement of success in discovering, developing, and managing new products is a central issue for the field, which calls for closer ties with other areas, such as more joint programs for science and marketing.

---

[16]We thank an anonymous reviewer for suggesting this issue be raised for the field's consideration.

- *Tremendous potentials exist for marketing contributions to economic development, which can literally "change the world" for citizens of developing nations.* Each aggregate marketing system is specific to its own society and time. Although a society's choices will constrain options, development also proceeds in identifiable stages. Thus, there is a potential to transfer knowledge, products, and methods found useful in prior stages of advanced systems. Aggregate marketing systems are in flux daily across the globe. Will the "transitional" nations trying to move from command to free-market systems be successful? Strong linkages between marketing, public policy, and aggregate marketing system performance are starkly clear in these cases.

Implications for Marketing Scholarship

Overall, we are optimistic: This project has convinced us that adopting the perspective of the aggregate marketing system helps a person "see" the field of marketing in its true expanse and complexity. However, this perspective largely has disappeared from the marketing mainstream in recent years (Wilkie 1997; Wilkie and Moore 2000). Four insights address dimensions of this issue:

- *Prospects for contributions from many scholarly traditions are bright if differing perspectives are pursued.* One wonderful aspect of the academic life is its freedom to speculate. Beyond specific topics in marketing and society research, it is helpful to recognize how employing different perspectives on the aggregate marketing system could enable a much broader set of contributions to marketing thought. To wit, the goals for this journal issue directed our focus toward "marketing," "contributions," and "society," and we examined the world from this vantage point. A slightly different mandate, however, might have led us to, say, "the aggregate consumption system." In this case, consumer behavior, consumer economics, and public policy would have joined marketing on center stage, though the larger phenomenon would not differ much. Thus, this project has highlighted more generally for us the potentials of higher "levels of analysis" aggregated beyond a single firm, market, or household. Although not a new insight in itself, its potential to be meshed with differing perspectives opens many opportunities for useful investigations.
- *Of particular note, the "value of marketing" offers special potential as an organizing framework for new contributions to marketing thought.* Following on the preceding point, much current research in marketing is actually quite useful for understanding the aggregate marketing system if we invoke only a slightly different frame of reference. "Value of marketing" will work well. A multiuniversity project with this title was begun by Yoram Wind at the Wharton School in the early 1990s and led to some of the insights cited in this article. Support for Wind's project is warranted, as is a general recognition of this framework's potential. For example, assessing the value of marketing

activities is congenial to much current research in marketing management (e.g., new product development), marketing science (e.g., long-term value of promotion versus advertising), and consumer research (e.g., consumer information). Furthermore, value can be assessed at a firm level, across firms, or for society. Thus, efforts at developing theory and calibrations of the value of various marketing actions will contribute to a better understanding of the aggregate marketing system.

- *The existing infrastructure for thought on "marketing and society" offers inviting opportunities.* Many interesting research issues exist, and interested scholars should know that the present infrastructure eases entry to this area. Nearly 300 academics have joined the American Marketing Association's recently formed "Marketing and Society" special interest group, and allied professional groups exist in such areas as macromarketing, marketing and public policy, marketing ethics, the consumer interest, marketing history, and the aforementioned areas of QOL and social marketing, each of which offers periodic meetings. Many publishing outlets exist, including the *Journal of Macromarketing, Journal of Public Policy & Marketing, Journal of Consumer Policy,* and *Journal of Consumer Affairs,* which are among those that specialize in publishing research in this area. Mainstream journals long have welcomed manuscripts as well.

- *As a final note, it is troubling to realize that knowledge does not necessarily accumulate in a field; knowledge can disappear over time if it is not actively transmitted* (e.g., Wilkie 1981★). One responsibility of academia is to place a field of study into proper perspective. We believe the aggregate marketing system should come to occupy a central position in research in the marketing field. However, this issue will not receive due consideration unless current scholars are willing to consider that important knowledge is being lost from the active body of marketing thought. As research specialization has proceeded, with good reason, this risk has increased. Knowledge outside a person's specialty first may be viewed as noninstrumental, then as nonessential, then as nonimportant, then finally as nonexistent. Our concern is not for today's scholars, who may opt to make an informed choice, but for later generations of scholars who may not gain enough background to realize that a choice is available to them. To examine this risk, a survey of Doctoral Consortium participants was run as part of this project (Wilkie and Moore 1997). In brief, these concerns appear justified. Although two-thirds of current doctoral candidates report having a personal interest in learning about marketing and society, less than one in ten has taken even one course in the area at any level, and self-rated expertise is low. Doctoral programs sorely need to reconsider this issue, as might MBA and undergraduate programs.

INTO THE FUTURE

Having begun this article by looking back over a long time, we now know not to look forward very far. As just one example, new information technologies clearly will change our world in the future, though exact impacts are unknown. Some firms will gain new efficiencies, others will develop new offerings, and all will need to adapt to new competitive realities. Richard Tedlow (1998), Harvard historian of business, offers the view that the future of the Internet depends on its treatment within the aggregate marketing system:

> the word on everyone's lips is "Internet." A century ago [it] was "radio." When radio came along, everyone knew that a device of profound significance was now available . . . but for all its magic, how was radio to be commercialized? . . . It took decades to find the answer for radio. How long will it take for the Internet?

And what happens if the Internet changes consumers' buying behaviors in basic ways? Whereas "location, location, location" was long the retailing mantra for success, the Internet means that geographic location can be removed as a factor (sellers can be anywhere in the world), time can be shortened and shifted through computer access, new forms of information (with advice from neutral experts) can be consulted, and lower prices might be negotiable. How will today's fixed marketing system—malls, retailers, wholesalers, manufacturers, suppliers, shippers, advertising agencies, and salespersons—adapt, and to what extent will it be necessary? It is interesting to realize that some readers of this article will be responsible for the successful adaptations that will change the marketing systems of the future.

In closing, we reiterate that we feel privileged to have had this opportunity to step back, explore, and recognize the achievements of the aggregate marketing system. Through this process, we have gained a better understanding of the nature of the field, the challenges that it faces, and the contributions it makes to societal welfare.

References

Aaker, David A. (1991), *Managing Brand Equity*. New York: The Free Press.

___ and George S. Day (1982), *Consumerism: Search for the Public Interest,* 4th ed. New York: The Free Press.

Andreasen, Alan R. (1991), "Consumer Behavior Research and Social Policy," in *Handbook of Consumer Behavior,* Thomas S. Robertson and Harold H. Kassarjian, eds. Englewood Cliffs, NJ: Prentice Hall, 459–506.

Arrow, Kenneth (1972), "Gifts and Exchanges," *Philosophy and Public Affairs,* 343–61.

Bartels, Robert (1988), *The History of Marketing Thought,* 3d ed. Columbus, OH: Publishing Horizons.

Batra, Rajeev (1997), "Executive Insights: Marketing Issues and Challenges in Transitional Economies," *Journal of International Marketing,* 5 (4), 95–114.

Bauer, Raymond A. and Stephen A. Greyser (1968), *Advertising in America: The Consumer View.* Boston, MA: Research Division, Harvard Business School.

Brobeck, Stephen, ed. (1997), *Encyclopedia of the Consumer Movement.* Santa Barbara, CA: ABC-Clio.

Cox, Reavis, Charles S. Goodman, and Thomas C. Fichandler (1965), *Distribution in a High-Level Economy.* Englewood Cliffs, NJ: Prentice Hall.

Day, George S. (1994), "Social Issues Shaping Marketing Practice," presentation at the American Marketing Association Summer Educators' Conference, San Francisco, CA (August).

Dickson, Peter R. (1992). "Toward a General Theory of Competitive Rationality," *Journal of Marketing,* 56 (January), 69–83.

Etzel, Michael J. and John F. Gaski (1999), "A Report on Consumer Sentiment Toward Marketing," working paper, Graduate School of Business, University of Notre Dame.

Federal Trade Commission (1996), *Anticipating the 21st Century: Competition Policy in the New High-Tech, Global Marketplace.* Washington, DC: U.S. Government Printing Office.

___ (1997), *Anticipating the 21st Century* Washington, DC: U.S. Government Printing Office.

Fornell, Claes, Michael D. Johnson, Eugene W. Anderson, Jaesburg Cha, and Barbara Everitt (1996), "The American Customer Satisfaction Index: Nature, Purpose, and Findings," *Journal of Marketing,* 60 (October), 7–18.

Galbraith, John K. (1958), *The Affluent Society.* Boston, MA: Houghton Mifflin.

Goodwin, Neva R., Frank Ackerman, and David Kiron (1997), *The Consumer Society.* Washington, DC: Island Press.

Hunt, Shelby D. and Jerry Goolsby (1988), "The Rise and Fall of the Functional Approach to Marketing: A Paradigm Displacement Perspective," in *Historical Perspectives in Marketing–Essays in Honor of Stanley C. Hollander,* Terence Nevett and Ronald A. Fullerton, eds. Lexington, MA: D.C. Heath, 35–51.

___ and Robert M. Morgan (1995), "The Comparative-Advantage Theory of Competition," *Journal of Marketing,* 59 (April), 1–15.

Kinnear, Thomas C. (1994), "Marketing and Macroeconomic Welfare," presentation at the Value of Marketing Conference, Stanford University (August).

Lebergott, Stanley (1993), *Pursuing Happiness.* Princeton, NJ: Princeton University Press.

Mayer, Robert N. (1989), *The Consumer Movement: Guardians of the Marketplace.* Boston, MA: Twayne.

Maynard, Harold, W.C. Weidler, and Theodore Beckman (1927), *Principles of Marketing.* New York: The Ronald Press Co.

Maynes, E. Scott (1997), "Consumer Problems in Market Economies," in *Encyclopedia of the Consumer Movement,* Stephen Brobeck, ed. Santa Barbara, CA: ABC-Clio, 158–64.

___ et al., eds. (1988), *The Frontier of Research in the Consumer Interest.* Columbia, MO: American Council on Consumer Interests.

Mitchell, Arnold (1983), *The Nine American Lifestyles.* New York: Macmillan.

Moore, Elizabeth S. and William L. Wilkie (2000), "Criticisms, Controversies and Problems in the Aggregate Marketing System," working paper, Graduate School of Business, University of Notre Dame.

Moyer, Reed (1965), "Marketing in Economic Development," working paper, Graduate School of Business, Michigan State University.

Nason, Robert W. and Phillip D. White (1981), "The Visions of Charles C. Slater: Social Consequences of Marketing," *Journal of Macromarketing,* 1 (Fall), 4–18.

Pollay, Richard W. and Banwari Mittal (1993), "Here's the Beef: Factors, Determinants, and Segments in Consumer Criticism of Advertising," *Journal of Marketing,* 57 (July), 99–114.

Sherry, John F., Jr. (1991), "Postmodern Alternatives: The Interpretive Turn in Consumer Research," in *Handbook of Consumer Behavior,* Thomas S. Robertson and Harold H. Kassarjian, eds. Englewood Cliffs, NJ: Prentice Hall, 548–91.

Sirgy, M. Joseph, A.C. Samli, and H. Lee Meadow (1982), "The Interface Between Quality of Life and Marketing: A Theoretical Framework," *Journal of Marketing & Public Policy,* 1 (1), 69–84.

Slater, Charles C. (1978), "Toward an Operational Theory of Market Processes," in *Macro-Marketing: Distributive Processes from a Societal Perspective, An Elaboration of Issues,* Phillip White and Charles Slater, eds. Boulder, CO: University of Colorado Press, 115–29.

Stern, Louis W. and Thomas Eovaldi (1984), *Legal Aspects of Marketing Strategy.* Englewood Cliffs, NJ: Prentice Hall.

Tedlow, Richard (1998), personal correspondence, (April 7).

Thorelli, Hans B. (1996), "Marketing, Open Markets and Political Democracy: The Experience of the PACRIM Countries," *Advances in International Marketing,* 7, 33–46.

Vaile, Roland S., E.T. Grether, and Reavis Cox (1952), *Marketing in the American Economy.* New York: The Ronald Press Co.

Wilkie, William L. (1994), *Consumer Behavior,* 3d ed. New York: John Wiley & Sons.

___ (1997), "Developing Research on Public Policy and Marketing," *Journal of Public Policy & Marketing,* 16 (Spring), 132–36.

___ and Elizabeth S. Moore (1997), "Consortium Survey on Marketing and Society Issues: Summary and Results," *Journal of Macromarketing,* 17 (2), 89–95.

___ and ___ (2000), "Marketing and Society: The Four Eras of Marketing Thought," working paper, Graduate School of Business, University of Notre Dame.

Wood, Van P. and Scott Vitell (1986), "Marketing and Economic Development: Review, Synthesis and Evaluation," *Journal of Macromarketing,* 6 (1), 28–48.

Yankelovich, Daniel (1981), *New Rules: Searching for Fulfillment in a World Turned Upside Down.* New York: Random House.

The Marketing Literature in Public Policy: 1970–1988

Gregory T. Gundlach and William L. Wilkie

Nearly two decades have passed since management practices at the Federal Trade Commission (FTC) were severely criticized in separate studies by Ralph Nader and the American Bar Association.[1] These and other criticisms made during a time of increasing consumerism provided the impetus for revitalization and strengthening of the government's role in consumer protection activities during the early 1970s.

Paralleling the strengthening of regulatory activities at the FTC and other governmental agencies during this period was an increase in marketing research on consumer protection issues. Academic researchers and others, through analytical and empirical contributions, began to play a more instrumental role in the regulatory process. Consumer research emerged as a useful mechanism for detecting the incidence and severity of present or potential market failures.

By the early 1980s, however, increasing complaints by businesses affected by enforcement actions, decreasing sentiment towards the effectiveness of regulation, growing foreign competition, and the emergence of a severe recession prompted a reconsideration of the government's role in consumer protection. Congress, acting in response to these occurrences, enacted measures to reduce the effective regulatory power of governmental agencies involved in consumer protection.[2] These measures greatly reduced the regulatory development, enforcement powers, and activities of the FTC and other governmental agencies in favor of a more conservative policy protocol.

During the 1980s, consumer research contributions in the area of public policy and marketing also declined. In contrast to the rigorous governmental research programs of the 1970s, this period emphasized impact evaluation studies directed at the assessment of governmental programs, rules, cases, and enforcement activities. Academic consumer research, while continuing, was de-emphasized in the policy process.

At present, consumer research activity at the FTC has been greatly curtailed. External activity by marketing academics also appears to be declining. On the horizon, continued uncertainty as to the appropriate role of government in consumer protection suggests

GUNDLACH, GREGORY T. and WILLIAM L. WILKIE (1990) "The Marketing Literature in Public Policy: 1970–1988," Marketing and Advertising Regulation—Federal Trade Commission in the 1990's, Patrick E. Murphy and William L. Wilkie (eds.), Notre Dame, IN: Notre Dame Press, 329–344.

a questionable future for the FTC and its use of consumer research. Recently, the American Bar Association (ABA) released its study of the role of the FTC. Initial findings indicate a rather lackluster performance over the last eight years. The ABA report suggests the agency redirect its efforts to provide clearer regulatory direction for industry. Disturbingly, however, the report made no mention of a role for marketing and consumer research in FTC decision making.

Given the current political climate and the almost two decades that have passed since policy issues received research prominence in the marketing literature, it should be useful to review the academic marketing literature on public policy. In an effort to provide such a perspective, this paper reports on the contributions of marketing to public policy from 1970 to 1988. As part of a larger project, 673 published marketing contributions to public policy were classified within a framework of key public policy and marketing topics. In this paper we summarize the initial results and implications of this classification process.

Public Policy and Marketing

Policy may be defined as the general principles by which a government is guided in its management of public affairs. Public policy encompasses actions by government in its management of public affairs concerning and affecting the welfare of the general populace (Black 1979). These actions presumably include any and all governmental initiatives. Such activities encompass federal, state, and local efforts in the development and enforcement of regulations and statutes, chosen governmental courses of action, and, as well, the deliberate absence of governmental activity or interference.

Many definitions of marketing are offered in the literature (cf., Kotler 1988; McCarthy and Perreault 1984). Generally these definitions suggest that marketing includes the performance of functions that seek to satisfy human wants by facilitating exchange relationships.

Together, the intersection of these two topical areas provides the domain of public policy and marketing. A comprehensive review of marketing's contribution to public policy research requires an examination of published contributions that appear within this domain. As indicated in Figure 1, this encompassing arena includes policy issues that arise in the context of consumer protection, antitrust, and other governmental activities that interface with marketing. In addition, the deliberate absence of governmental action in the form of self-regulation, such as found within some areas of advertising, must also be included.

A Framework for Public Policy and Marketing

Within the general area of public policy and marketing lie many specific topics of interest. In order to classify the work in this area, a comprehensive framework of these topics is needed. Our development of this framework began with the organizational structure

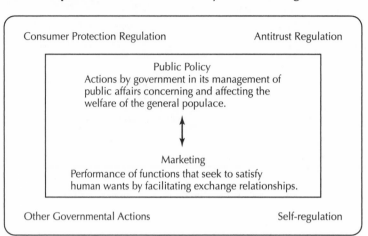

FIGURE 1

The Conceptual Domain of Public Policy and Marketing

employed by Stern and Eovaldi (1986) in their text on the legal aspects of marketing. This structure, centered around the elements of the marketing mix, was then extended into the framework for this study.

As shown in Table 1, the extended framework contains three basic subject headings with seventy-four specific topical areas. These areas provide the basis for subject classification in the review. The three basic subject headings are listed below.

> *Consumerism and Consumer Protection Topics:* This heading contains topics related to the more macrodimensions of public policy and marketing. Ten broad subject areas are identified and deal with an array of topics extending from consumerism to general consumer protection issues.
>
> *Marketing Management Topics:* Under this heading, specific subject areas which address the various elements of the marketing mix are identified. In total, fifty-three issues are listed under the classification of product, price, place, and promotion.
>
> *General Topics:* A general heading is also specified in the framework and includes international issues, policy implications of marketing research, participants in the policy process, more general antitrust topics, other governmental actions, and self-regulation issues.

Literature Analysis

A modification of the snowball sampling technique in survey research was employed for the gathering of published marketing contributions from 1970 to 1988. The technique requires an initial set of respondents to be identified and then used as a basis for identifying other respondents (Goodman 1961). Initially, journals, major conference proceedings, and

TABLE 1

Framework for Public Policy and Marketing

Consumerism and Consumer Protection Topics

- Consumerism
- Socially Conscious Consumers
- Legal Aspects
- Marketing and Society
- Marketer Behavior

- Management of Consumer Protection
- Consumer Information
- Consumer Education
- Consumer Complaining
- General Consumer Protection

Marketing Management Topics

Product Issues
- Protection of Trade Secrets
- Patents
- Copyright
- Trademarks
- Certification Marks
- Warranty
- Product Liability
- Safety
- Package and Labeling
- Nutrition Information Labeling
- Services
- General Product Issues

Place Issues
- Exclusive Dealing
- Tying Contracts
- Territorial and Customer Restrictions
- Resale Price Maintenance
- Reciprocity
- Refusals to Deal
- Functional Discounts
- Vertical Integration
- Gray Markets
- Mergers
- General Place Issues

Price Issues
- Price Fixing
- Exchanging Price Information
- Parallel Pricing
- Discriminatory Pricing
- Credit Practices
- Robinson-Patman Act
- Unit Pricing
- Reference Price
- General Price Issues

Promotion Issues
- Deceptive Advertising
- Unfairness in Advertising
- Advertising To Children
- Advertising Substantiation
- Affirmative Disclosure
- Corrective Advertising
- Multiple Product Orders
- Comparative Advertising
- Endorsements
- Price Promotions
- Warranty Promotions
- Credit Promotions
- Sweepstakes and Contests
- Personal Selling Practices
- Mail Order Selling
- Referral Sales
- Brokerage
- Promotional Allowances
- Promotion of Professional Services
- General Promotion Issues

General Topics

International
- Protectionism
- Corrupt Practices
- General International Issues

Research
- Market Research

Other Governmental Actions
- General Governmental Regulation

Public Policy Participants
- U.S. Supreme Court
- Administrative Agencies
- State and Local Government

General Antitrust
- Antitrust Regulation

Self-regulation
- Self-regulation Issues

FIGURE 2

Research Design and Publication Sources

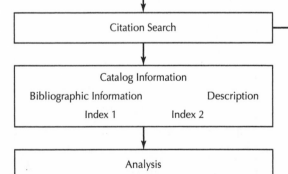

Publication Sources

Journals

- *Journal of Public Policy and Marketing*
- *Journal of Marketing*
- *Journal of Macromarketing*
- *Journal of Advertising*
- *Journal of Advertising Research*
- *Journal of Consumer Research*
- *Journal of Retailing*
- *Journal of Academy of Marketing Science*
- *Harvard Business Review*
- *Business Horizons*
- *Journal of Consumer Affairs*
- *Journal of Business Research*
- *California Management Review*
- *Journal of Consumer Policy*
- *Journal of Consumer Marketing*

Proceedings

- American Marketing Association
- Advances in Consumer Research

Books/Monographs

- Marketing Science Institute
- General

Citation Search

Catalog Information

Bibliographic Information   Description

Index 1   Index 2

Analysis

monographs containing marketing studies and articles dealing with public policy issues were identified. Figure 2 illustrates the research design and contains a full listing of the sources employed.

Subject indexes and the table of contents within each publication were reviewed for articles that by judgment of both authors addressed topical areas contained in the framework.[3] Additional studies or articles that were cited in these contributions were then examined regardless of their source. In total, 673 articles, studies, and books were included in the review.

FRAMEWORK CLASSIFICATION

Within the framework, each contribution was classified employing a major and secondary level classification. This allowed for each contribution to be classified potentially under two subject areas. For example, an article that dealt mainly with deceptive advertising may also have addressed corrective advertising. Under the major and secondary classification approach, the article would be classified under its major heading—deceptive advertising—and also under corrective advertising as a secondary heading.

Relevant bibliographic and descriptive information for each contribution was cataloged employing a database management system. This approach allowed for organization of the contributions and efficient access to each published contribution.

Publication Frequency Trends: 1970–1988

Figure 3 contains a frequency count of the number of published contributions found each year for the period 1970 to 1988. As can be seen across the yearly frequency counts, marketing contributions to public policy generally increased during the period 1970 to 1980. This trend may be reflective of the revitalized initiative of the Federal Trade Commission during the same period that was highlighted earlier.

In contrast to the period 1970 to 1980, after 1980 a gradual decline in published contributions is evident. Coincidentally, this trend parallels the diminished enforcement activity of the Federal Trade Commission during the same period under the Reagan administration.

The decline in activity during the post-1980 period appears more acute when, as illustrated in Figure 4, the contributions that were published in the *Journal of Public Policy & Marketing* are separated. Identifying only those articles and studies appearing within the nonspecialized marketing outlet sources, the frequency of marketing's contribution to public policy appears to have diminished steadily since the mid-1970s.

Trends across the major journals in marketing—*Journal of Marketing Research, Journal of Marketing*, and *Journal of Consumer Research*—are shown in Figure 5. As illustrated, the frequency counts reveal a similar gradual decline of policy contributions across the major journals from the mid-1970s to 1988.

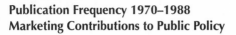

Publication Frequency 1970–1988
Marketing Contributions to Public Policy

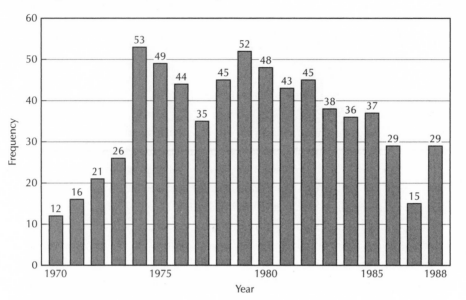

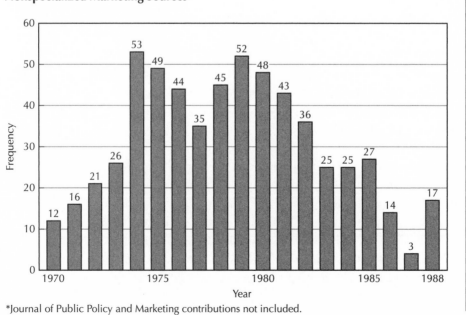

*Journal of Public Policy and Marketing contributions not included.

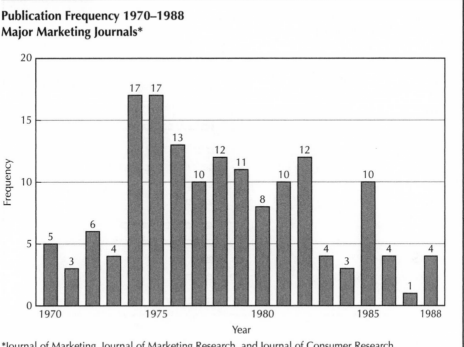

FIGURE 5

Publication Frequency 1970–1988
Major Marketing Journals*

*Journal of Marketing, Journal of Marketing Research, and Journal of Consumer Research.

Topical Classification

Tables 2a–2d contain frequency counts and median year activity for each topical area within the framework. First and second index level frequency counts, their combined total and median year of activity are listed. Bar charts are also included in order to illustrate the first and second index level frequencies. Within the bar charts, second index level frequency counts are shown as additions to each first index level frequency count. For example, under the topic *consumerism,* thirty-three published contributions were found and indexed under the first level. Two additional contributions were also located and judged to address consumerism issues as a subtopic. These contributions were classified under the second index level. In total, thirty-five published contributions were located for the topic—consumerism issues. For consumerism, the median year of published activity was found to be 1975.

CONSUMERISM AND CONSUMER PROTECTION TOPICS

In Table 2a, review of the frequency counts of published contributions for each topic under the subject heading—consumerism and consumer protection—indicates the topics: consumerism (33 first index/2 second index), legal (8/22), management of consumer

TABLE 2a

Publication Frequency and Median Year by Topic
Consumerism and Consumer Protection Topics

Framework Topic	Frequency: First Index	Frequency: Second Index	Frequency: Total	Median Year Activity
- Consumerism	33	2	35	(1975)
- Socially Conscious Consumers	6		6	
- Legal Aspects	8	22	30	
- Marketing And Society	11	1	12	(1977)
- Marketer Behavior	9		9	
- Management Of Consumer Protection	24	6	30	(1982)
- Consumer Information	42	6	48	(1977)
- Consumer Education	4		4	
- Consumer Complaining	12		12	(1978)
- General Consumer Protection	14	1	15	(1979)

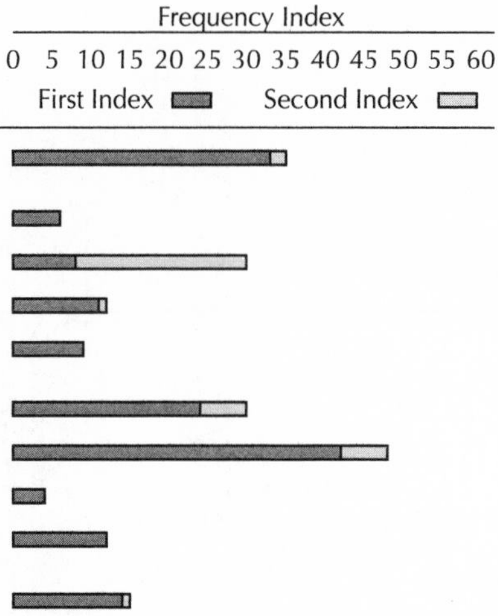
Frequency Index
0 5 10 15 20 25 30 35 40 45 50 55 60
First Index
Second Index

protection (24/6), and consumer information (42/6) topics received greater emphasis in the literature than other framework subjects under the heading.

Interestingly, across these categories the median year for contributions addressing management of consumer protection topics was 1982. In contrast, for the other categories, the median fell earlier, during the mid-to-late 1970s. This difference may have resulted from the increasing emphasis by policy makers as to the proper role of consumer protection regulation during the 1980s under the Reagan administration.

MARKETING MANAGEMENT ISSUES

As indicated within Tables 2b and 2c, of the marketing mix elements, topics dealing with promotion appear to be represented more often in the review followed by product, price, and place or market channel issues. The apparent emphasis on promotion issues is the result, in part, of the numerous contributions that addressed deceptive and corrective advertising and advertising to children. Surprisingly, in relative comparison, very few contributions were found which addressed market channel issues. One possible explanation may have been the observed emphasis on issues that had a direct impact on the consumer rather than issues which concerned business to business issues. Many of the market channel topics concern this latter category.

TABLE 2b

Publication Frequency and Median Year by Topic
Marketing Management Topics

Framework Topic	Frequency			Median Year Activity	Frequency Index 0 5 10 15 20 25 30 35 40 45 50 55 60 First Index ▰ Second Index ▱
	First Index	Second Index	Total		
Product					
- Trade Secrets					
- Patents		1	1		▯
- Copyright	1		1		▮
- Trademarks	7	2	9		▰▰▱
- Certification Marks	3		3		▰
- Warranty	19	1	20	(1980)	▰▰▰▰▰▰▰▱
- Product Liability	19		19	(1982)	▰▰▰▰▰▰▰
- Safety	10	7	17	(1978)	▰▰▰▱▱▱
- Package And Labeling	18	7	25	(1979)	▰▰▰▰▰▱▱▱
- Nutrition Information	25		25	(1980)	▰▰▰▰▰▰▰▰
- Services	6	3	9		▰▰▱▱
- General Product Issues	5	2	7		▰▰▱
Price					
- Price Fixing	2		2		▰
- Exchanging Price Info					
- Parallel Pricing					
- Predatory Pricing					
- Discriminatory Pricing	9		9		▰▰▰
- Credit Practices	14		14	(1976)	▰▰▰▰▰
- Robinson-patman Act	6		6		▰▰
- Unit Pricing	7	1	8		▰▰▱
- Reference Price	5		5		▰▰
- General Price Issues	5	1	6		▰▰▱

In addition to the divergence of emphasis in published contributions across the major topical headings representing the marketing mix elements, within each heading are several topics that received only minimal attention or none at all. These topics represent potential areas for future research. The following sections highlight the major contributions within each major topical heading and note those topics receiving minimal attention.

Product Issues   For articles addressing product issues (see Table 2b), the topics of nutrition information labeling (25/0), package and labeling (18/7), product liability (19/0),

TABLE 2c

Publication Frequency and Median Year by Topic
Marketing Management Topics

Framework Topic	Frequency			Median Year Activity	Frequency Index 0 5 10 15 20 25 30 35 40 45 50 55 60
	First Index	Second Index	Total		First Index ▬ Second Index ▭
Place					
- Exclusive Dealing					
- Tying Contracts	2		2		▪
- Territorial / Customer Restrictions	8		8		▭
- Resale Price Maint.	4		4		▪
- Reciprocity	3		3		▪
- Refusals To Deal	1		1		▪
- Functional Discounts					
- Vertical Integration					
- Gray Markets	4		4		▪
- Mergers	1		1		▪
- General Place Issues	6	13	19		▬▭
Promotion					
- Deceptive Advertising	41	15	56	(1978)	▬▬▬▬▭
- Unfairness In Adv.	2		2		▪
- Advertising To Children	24	1	25	(1978)	▬▬▬
- Adv. Substantiation	5	1	6		▬▪
- Affirmative Disclosure	7	5	12		▬▭
- Corrective Advertising	26	4	30	(1980)	▬▬▬▭
- Multiple Product Orders					
- Comparative Adv.	10	1	11	(1975)	▬▬▪
- Endorsements					
- Price Promotions		1	1		▪
- Warranty Promotions					
- Credit Promotions					
- Sweepstakes / Contests					
- Personal Selling	4	1	5		▬▪
- Mail Order Selling					
- Referral Sales					
- Brokerage					
- Promotional Allowances					
- Promotion Of Professional Services	14		14	(1980)	▬▬
- General Promotion	23	21	44	(1980)	▬▬▬▭

warranty (19/1), and safety (10/7) appear prominently in the literature. Median years of publication for these topics fell in the late 1970s and early 1980s.

As can be seen in the table, several topics contain only a few contributions or none at all. Topics in which fewer than ten publications were found for the first level index include: protection of trade secrets (0/0), patents (0/1), copyright (1/0), trademarks (7/2), certification marks (3/0), package and labeling (8/17), services (6/3), and general product issues (5/2).

Price Issues   For contributions to price-related issues (see Table 2b), credit practices (14/0) appear with the greatest frequency. The median year of publication activity for credit practices, the only median calculated, was in 1976.

Several topics, as with the product topics, are represented only minimally in the data base, with several topics containing no contributions. Topics containing fewer than ten published contributions for the first level index include: price fixing (2/0), exchanging price information (0/0), parallel pricing (0/0), predatory pricing (0/0), discriminatory pricing (9/0), Robinson-Patman Act (6/0), unit pricing (7/1), reference price (5/0), and general price issues (5/1).

Place Issues   For articles concerning place or market channel issues (see Table 2c), very few contributions were identified. Of the topics within the framework, the nongeneral topic appearing with the greatest frequency was territorial and customer restrictions (8/0). Topics containing very few contributions include: exclusive dealing (0/0), tying contracts (2/6), resale price maintenance (4/0), reciprocity (3/0), refusals to deal (1/0), functional discounts (0/0), vertical integration (0/0), mergers (1/0), and gray markets (4/0). The general place category contained a variety of contributions (6/13).

Promotional Issues   Of the contributions to promotional issues (see Table 2c), deceptive advertising (41/15), corrective advertising (26/4), advertising to children (24/1), general promotional category (23/21), and promotion of professional services (14/0) appear to have received the majority of attention. The median year of published activity for these categories generally fell in the mid-to-late 1970s or 1980.

Within the review, several topics contained only a few contributions with some topics containing none at all. Topics containing fewer than ten contributions for the first level index heading include: unfairness in advertising (2/0), advertising substantiation (5/1), affirmative disclosure (7/5), multiple product orders (0/0), endorsements (0/0), price promotions (0/1), warranty promotions (0/0), credit promotions (0/0), sweepstakes and contests (0/0), personal selling practices (4/1), mail order selling (0/0), referral sales (0/0), brokerage (0/0), and promotional allowances (0/0).

TABLE 2d

Publication Frequency and Median Year by Topic
General Topics

Framework Topic	Frequency			Median Year Activity	Frequency Index 0 5 10 15 20 25 30 35 40 45 50 55 60 First Index ▬ Second Index ▭
	First Index	Second Index	Total		
International					
- Protectionism	1		1		▪
- Corrupt Practices		5	5		▭
- General International	33	1	34	(1981)	▬▬▬▬▬▬▬▪
Research					
- Market Research	18	12	30	(1979)	▬▬▬▬▭▭
Public Policy Participants					
- U.S. Supreme Court	4		4		▬▪
- Administ. Agencies	57	1	58	(1979)	▬▬▬▬▬▬▬▬▬▬▪
- State And Local Gov't	8	1	9		▬▬▪
General Antitrust					
- General Antitrust Issues	18	4	22	(1978)	▬▬▬▬▭
Other Gov t Actions					
- General Governmental Regulation	13		13	(1982)	▬▬▬
Self-regulation					
- Self-regulation Issues	12	8	20	(1983)	▬▬▭▭

GENERAL TOPICS

Of the general topical categories contained in Table 2d, contributions that deal with administrative agency participants (57/1) in the public policy process contain the highest frequency of contributions. General international issues (33/2) and contributions that address market research (18/12), general antitrust (18/4), general governmental regulation (13/0), and self-regulation issues (12/8) also contain numerous contributions. The median year of activity for these categories ranged from 1978 to 1983.

These topics receiving fewer than ten published contributions as identified within the first level index included: protectionism (1/0) and corrupt practices (0/5) under the international issues heading; and U.S. Supreme Court (4/0) and state and local government (8/1) topics under public policy participants.

Implications and Conclusions

This initial analysis of almost twenty years of work in marketing and public policy reveals that a considerable body of work has been done, covering a broad array of topics. At the same time, many topics have as yet received little or no attention from our field. Further, examination of the timing of the research suggests a declining frequency of marketing contributions to public policy since the late 1970s. Notwithstanding contributions appearing within the *Journal of Public Policy & Marketing,* published articles appearing in the major marketing journals have almost steadily declined since the mid-1970s. Such a decline likely suggests diminished interest among academicians towards public policy and marketing topics. This apparent decline, coupled with decreasing interest towards consumer research within the FTC, suggests an uncertain future for public policy and marketing-related research.

In the future, revitalization of public policy and marketing topics may require greater internal initiative within the marketing discipline. Previous reliance on FTC-centered research may have to be shifted in favor of more independently driven research. In this capacity, the *Journal of Public Policy & Marketing* may provide an invaluable outlet for contributions by marketers.

Viewing broadly those topics that have been addressed, many appear to have focused on policy issues originating from consumer-to-organization interaction. These contributions address, largely, consumer protection related issues. Very few marketing contributions were found that addressed business-to-business or antitrust related policy topics (generally, previous research that has addressed this topic has been centered within the economics literature). At present, however, a tradition of social science research on interorganizational relations and competition is developing in marketing, and should provide a foundation for future contributions to antitrust policy issues.

Notes

[1] E. Cox, R. Fellmeth, and J. Schulz, *The Nader Report on the Federal Trade Commission VII* (1969). See also, *Report on the American Bar Association Commission to Study the Federal Trade Commission* (September 15, 1969).

[2] For a full discussion of these steps see: William J. Baer (1986), "Where to From Here: Reflection of the Recent Saga of the Federal Trade Commission," *Oklahoma Law Review* 39, 51.

[3] A modified Delphi process was employed for disagreements as to both the determination of inclusion of a contribution in the review and its proper classification. The Delphi process is a method of generating and refining group judgment and is based on the premise that several participant inputs are better than a single judgment (Jolson and Rossow 1971). The general approach is to collect individual judgments, summarize individual discrepancies, and return them to the judges for reassessment until a consensus is reached.

References

Baer, William J. (1986). "Where to From Here: Reflection of the Recent Saga of the Federal Trade Commission," *Oklahoma Law Review* 39, 51.

Black, Henry C. (1979). *Black's Law Dictionary*. St. Paul, MN: West Publishing Co.

Cox, E., R. Fellmeth, and J. Schulz (1969). *The Nader Report on the Federal Trade Commission VII.*

Goodman, Leo A. (1961). "Snowball Sampling." *Annals of Mathematical Statistics* 2, 148–170.

Jolson, Marvin A., and Gerald L. Rossow (1971). "The Delphi Process in Marketing Decision Making." *Journal of Marketing Research* (November), 443–448.

Kotler, Phillip (1988). *Marketing Management.* 6th ed. Englewood Cliffs, NJ: Prentice Hall.

McCarthy, Jerome E., and William D. Perreault, Jr. (1990). *Basic Marketing.* 10th ed. Homewood, Ill.: Richard D. Irwin.

Report on the American Bar Association Commission to Study the Federal Trade Commission (September 15, 1969).

Stern, Louis W., and Thomas L. Eovaldi (1986). *Legal Aspects of Marketing Strategy: Antitrust and Consumer Protection Issues.* Englewood Cliffs, NJ: Prentice-Hall, Inc.

Two Decades of Contributions to Marketing and Public Policy: An Analysis of Research Published in Journal of Public Policy & Marketing

David E. Sprott and Anthony D. Miyazaki

The authors examine the first 20 years of Journal of Public Policy & Marketing *(JPP&M) to understand the nature, influences, and impact of marketing and public policy research published in the journal. After discussing the history of* JPP&M, *the authors report three related sets of analyses based on all articles published since the journal's inception. Specifically, a content analysis examines the scope and depth of research topics over time. Next, publication analyses assess how various authors and institutions have influenced the field through publishing in the journal. Finally, a citation analysis shows the impact of* JPP&M *articles on research published in journals of related fields.*

With the publication of the Fall 2001 issue, *Journal of Public Policy & Marketing* (*JPP&M*) celebrated the completion of 20 years of service to the field of marketing and public policy. In these two decades, there have been considerable advancements in the field, as well as substantial growth in the reach and impact of *JPP&M*. To gain a better understanding of *JPP&M*'s influence on the discipline, as well as the roles that authors and their organizations have played, we examine all work published in what has been the key source of marketing and public policy research for the past 20 years.

Our analysis consists of three parts. First, we categorize the content of all articles published in *JPP&M* since its inception in an effort to understand the journal's historical impact. Similar to content analyses in related areas (e.g., Malhotra 1996), we track general changes in content over time and provide suggestions as to how such changes may have emerged. Second, we analyze the research contributions of authors and their institutions to identify major providers of *JPP&M* content (see, e.g., Borokhovich et al. 1995; Eaton et al. 1999; Fields and Swayne 1988; Inkpen and Beamish 1994; Malhotra 1996). The result is a tool helpful not only to understand the development of research in the field but also to benchmark publishing productivity—a primary tenure and promotion

DAVID E. SPROTT is Assistant Professor of Marketing, College of Business and Economics, Washington State University, Pullman. ANTHONY D. MIYAZAKI is Assistant Professor of Marketing, School of Business Administration, University of Miami. The authors, who contributed equally to this project, thank Sebastian Fernandez for his invaluable assistance with data collection and processing. Special thanks go to the former editors of *JPP&M*—Tom Kinnear, Pat Murphy, Michael Mazis, and Debbie Scammon—for their insights into the development of the journal and to Craig Andrews and the four anonymous *JPP&M* reviewers for their constructive commentary on previous versions of this manuscript.

Sprott, David E. and Anthony Miyazaki (2002), "Two Decades of Contributions to Marketing and Public Policy: An Analysis of Research Published in Journal of Public Policy & Marketing," *Journal of Public Policy & Marketing* 21 (1), 105–125.

criterion for many academic researchers and a significant gauge of research quality for some practitioners (Floyd, Schroeder, and Finn 1994; Schroeder, Langrehr, and Floyd 1995). Third, to assess the impact of the journal, we analyze *JPP&M*'s citations in various academic journals. Following these analyses, we discuss implications of the findings for *JPP&M* and its contributors in light of various editorial goals.

The Development of *JPP&M*

During its first 20 years, *JPP&M* published 455 articles, filling more than 5245 pages.[1] The number of articles published in each issue remained fairly constant from the first to the second decade of publication (at 14.7 articles per issue), but annual output grew from a mean of 16.2 to 29.3 articles (see Table 1). Although partially attributable to growth of the field, these increases also can be attributed to the journal's changing structure, broadening scope, and increasing reputation as a research publication outlet.

The Changing Structure of *JPP&M*

Journal of Public Policy & Marketing emerged 20 years ago during an era when researchers and society were intensely interested in issues surrounding marketing and public policy. Among the various influences on the development of *JPP&M* since that time have been the five editors of the journal (in chronological order): Thomas C. Kinnear, Patrick E. Murphy, Michael B. Mazis, Debra L. Scammon, and J. Craig Andrews. Figure 1 shows a time line of the journal and important occurrences in the history of *JPP&M* under the leadership of these editors.

Tom Kinnear founded *JPP&M* in 1982 as an annual publication of the University of Michigan School of Business Administration.[2] Originally titled *Journal of Marketing & Public Policy* (only for Volume 1), the name was changed to *Journal of Public Policy & Marketing* after the American Marketing Association expressed concerns that the journal's name might be confused with its own *Journal of Marketing* (Kinnear 2001). During its initial five years, *JPP&M* went on to publish a wide variety of articles; as Kinnear (1986, p. 1) notes, the journal had "grown and prospered during the five years to one that is considered a top flight outlet for research in the area of public policy within marketing."

During the next five years, under the primary editorship of Patrick E. Murphy, *JPP&M* experienced several structural changes. The first was the introduction of special

---

[1]All articles published during the first 20 years of *JPP&M* are examined in this research (book reviews and editorials are excluded). Articles written by three special issue editors are also included in the analyses because one (Hill 1995) was not an editorial-type article and the other two (Grewal and Compeau 1999; Milne 2000) contained mainly noneditorial content.

[2]The concept of *JPP&M* was test-marketed by Kinnear a few years prior to the journal's introduction with the 1979 reader, titled *Public Policy Issues in Marketing,* coedited with Cindy Frey and Bonnie Reece (Frey, Kinnear, and Reece 1979; Kinnear 2001).

TABLE 1

The Structure of *JPP&M* and Article Counts

Volume	Issue	Year	Editor	Traditional	Special Issue	Conference[b]	Policy Watch	Legal Developments	Total
				\<colspan: Type of *JPP&M* Article[a]\>					
1	—	1982	Kinnear	14	—	—	—	—	14
2	—	1983	Kinnear	13	—	—	—	—	13
3	—	1984	Kinnear	14	—	—	—	—	14
4	—	1985	Kinnear	14	—	—	—	—	14
5	—	1986	Kinnear	16	—	—	—	—	16
6	—	1987	Kinnear/Murphy	13	—	—	—	—	13
7	—	1988	Murphy	6	10	—	—	—	16
8	—	1989	Murphy	10	9	—	—	—	19
9	—	1990	Murphy	15	—	—	—	—	15
10	1	1991	Murphy	—	—	16	—	—	16
10	2		Murphy	3	9	—	—	—	12
11	1	1992	Murphy	11	—	—	—	—	11
11	2		Mazis	—	—	14	—	—	14
12	1	1993	Mazis	8	4	—	2	—	14
12	2		Mazis	11	—	—	2	—	14
13	1	1994	Mazis	8	3	5	2	1	16
13	2		Mazis	5	—	3	1	3	15
14	1	1995	Mazis	—	10	—	2	3	16
14	2		Mazis	8	6	1	3	2	16
15	1	1996	Scammon	—	11	—	1	3	17
15	2		Scammon	7	1	—	3	3	13
16	1	1997	Scammon	—	9	6	3	3	21
16	2		Scammon	7	—	4	2	2	15
17	1	1998	Scammon	—	8	—	4	3	15
17	2		Scammon	9	—	2	5	2	18
18	1	1999	Andrews	3	7	—	3	—	13
18	2		Andrews	9	—	—	3	1	13
19	1	2000	Andrews	3	7	—	3	1	14
19	2		Andrews	10	—	—	1	1	12
20	1	2001	Andrews	3	7	—	3	1	14
20	2		Andrews	9	—	—	1	2	12
Percent (counts) in first ten years				72.8% (118)	17.3% (28)	9.9% (16)	—	—	100% (162)
Percent (counts) in second ten years				37.9% (111)	24.9% (73)	11.9% (35)	14.7% (43)	10.6% (31)	100% (293)
Percent (counts) in 20 years				50.3% (229)	22.2% (101)	11.2% (51)	9.5% (43)	6.8% (31)	100% (455)

[a]Five types of articles have been published in *JPP&M*—those edited by the main editors, special issue editors, conference editors, and the Policy Watch and Legal Developments section editors.

[b]According to the article acknowledgments published in the journal, *JPP&M* articles from the annual conference have been edited by the following people: Mazis, Paul Bloom, Debra Ringold, Pam Scholder Ellen, Patrick Kaufmann, Hill, Ray Taylor, Easwar Iyer, and George Milne.

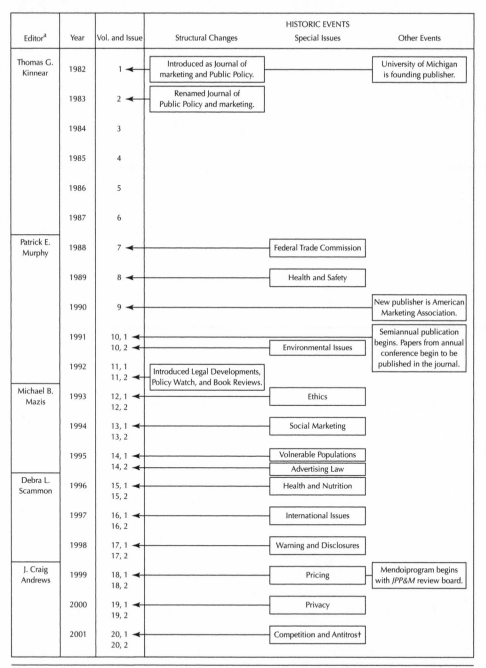

FIGURE 1

Time Line for *JPP&M*

Editor[a]	Year	Vol. and Issue	Structural Changes	Special Issues	Other Events
				HISTORIC EVENTS	
Thomas G. Kinnear	1982	1	Introduced as Journal of marketing and Public Policy.		University of Michigan is founding publisher.
	1983	2	Renamed Journal of Public Policy and marketing.		
	1984	3			
	1985	4			
	1986	5			
	1987	6			
Patrick E. Murphy	1988	7		Federal Trade Commission	
	1989	8		Health and Safety	
	1990	9			New publisher is American Marketing Association.
	1991	10, 1			Semiannual publication begins. Papers from annual conference begin to be published in the journal.
		10, 2		Environmental Issues	
	1992	11, 1			
		11, 2	Introduced Legal Developments, Policy Watch, and Book Reviews.		
Michael B. Mazis	1993	12, 1		Ethics	
		12, 2			
	1994	13, 1		Social Marketing	
		13, 2			
	1995	14, 1		Volnerable Populations	
		14, 2		Advertising Law	
Debra L. Scammon	1996	15, 1		Health and Nutrition	
		15, 2			
	1997	16, 1		International Issues	
		16, 2			
	1998	17, 1		Warning and Disclosures	
		17, 2			
J. Craig Andrews	1999	18, 1		Pricing	Mendoiprogram begins with *JPP&M* review board.
		18, 2			
	2000	19, 1		Privacy	
		19, 2			
	2001	20, 1		Competition and Antitrost	
		20, 2			

[a]Dates of editorships are based on when the editors name appeared on the journal's masthead. The end of an editor's official term does not necessarily indicate the end of an editor's impact on the journal's content. For example, some articles edited by Debra Scammon were published under the editorship of Craig Andrews, and Andrews's term as editor will extend to 2002 (Volume 21, Issue 1), with a special issue on Social Marketing, for which Andrews selected the issue editor (Andrews 2001a; Scammon 2001).

issues to the journal.[3] As Murphy (2001) notes, the underlying motivation for this change was (in part) to encourage researchers outside of marketing to submit articles and, more generally, to increase manuscript flow. Several years into Murphy's editorship, former editor Tom Kinnear negotiated a publishing agreement with the American Marketing Association, which began in 1990 and resulted in a semiannual publishing schedule in 1991 (Murphy 2001). At that same time, papers from the annual Marketing and Public Policy Conference began to be published in the journal, starting with Volume 10, Issue 1 (edited by Michael B. Mazis).

At the beginning of the second decade, editor Michael Mazis introduced new sections called Policy Watch (edited by Robert N. Mayer and Debra Scammon) and Legal Developments (edited by Ross D. Petty) to expose readers to a variety of contemporary and sometimes controversial public policy issues (Mazis 2001). These sections (appearing in *JPP&M* for the first time in Volume 12) allowed for, respectively, the debate of important policy issues by key players and the discussion of new legal cases and regulation. Mazis also instituted the Book Review section (directed under various editors Joshua Lyle Wiener, Gregory T. Gundlach, and Robert Mayer). Although the next editor, Debra Scammon, continued to support the three sections implemented by Mazis, she refined the content and style of these sections (Scammon 2001). The Policy Watch section (edited by Ronald Paul Hill) evolved into a point/counterpoint type of presentation involving practitioners and policymakers, with external commentary from an academic. The Legal Developments section (edited by Ross Petty, then Greg Gundlach) began a more rigorous review procedure similar to articles appearing in the main section of the journal. The fifth *JPP&M* editor, Craig Andrews, also maintained the same structure (Ron Hill and Greg Gundlach continued to serve, respectively, as the Policy Watch and Legal Developments editors).

THE BROADENING SCOPE OF *JPP&M*

Twenty years ago, *JPP&M* was started to provide researchers with an outlet for policy-oriented marketing research. As noted by Kinnear (2001), "it was a time of great excitement for those of us interested in public policy issues in marketing. . . . Unfortunately, there was a limited amount of space available in the standard marketing journals as public policy research competed with many other substantive topics." As such, the journal initially solicited articles that focused on the "evaluation of current or proposed public

---

[3]During the past 20 years, 13 special issues have been published in the journal. The topics (with volume, issue, and editors) include the FTC (Vol. 7, Kinnear and Murphy), health and safety (Vol. 8, Murphy), environmental issues (Vol. 10, No. 2, Murphy), ethics (Vol. 12, No. 1, Gene Laczniak), social marketing (Vol. 13, No. 1, Alan Andreasen), vulnerable populations (Vol. 14, No. 1, Hill), advertising law and regulation (Vol. 14, No. 2, Jef Richards), health and nutrition (Vol. 15, No. 1, Scammon), international issues (Vol. 16, No. 1, Gary Bamossy, Russell Belk, and Janeen Arnold Costa), warnings and disclosures (Vol. 17, No. 1, Andrews), pricing (Vol. 18, No. 1, Dhruv Grewal and Larry Compeau), privacy and ethical issues in database/interactive marketing (Vol. 19, No. 1, George Milne), and competition policy and antitrust law (Vol. 20, No. 1, Gundlach).

policy programs; antitrust and monopoly issues; special markets such as children, the elderly, or the disadvantaged; government regulation and deregulation of marketing practices and various industries; consumer information and education programs; and marketing and the legal system" (Kinnear 1982, p. 1). Although the journal sought articles in various areas dealing with "public policy effects on marketing practice" and "the application of marketing and marketing research practices to public policy issues," it specifically was "not seeking articles on social marketing or marketing in not-for-profit organizations" (Kinnear 1982). This was done in an attempt to establish a "critical mass" of articles on public policy and to avoid being overwhelmed by articles dealing with social marketing—a fairly popular topic at the time (Kinnear 2001).

Over time, the various editors have steadily broadened the scope of the journal in several ways. For example, though Patrick Murphy adhered to Tom Kinnear's initial criteria, Murphy (2001) began what he later described as an "unconscious" shift to a more broadened view of public policy by soliciting articles on topics that had not received substantial treatment in the literature. Mazis (2001) continued this effort by appointing special issue editors on a more regular basis and by branching into areas that included social and ethical issues but did not necessarily directly involve laws or regulations. To ensure that the more broadened topics received rigorous reviews, Scammon (2001) expanded the breadth of expertise of the Editorial Review Board. She also encouraged a widened set of methodological approaches such as qualitative data collection, historical research, and meta-analyses. Finally, Craig Andrews broadened the author base to more readily include students and young faculty by instituting a mentor program wherein *JPP&M*'s Editorial Review Board members volunteered their expertise to young scholars for developing their research programs. The broadening scope of *JPP&M* has continued to the present time, as illustrated by incoming editor Joel B. Cohen's (2001, p. 8) statement that the mission of the journal includes the goal of "publishing thoughtful articles on how marketing practice shapes and is shaped by societally important factors." Note, however, that *JPP&M* contributors have always been encouraged to consider the public policy implications of their research (Andrews 2001b).

THE ACADEMIC REPUTATION OF *JPP&M*

Several factors suggest that over the past 20 years, *JPP&M* has developed into the premier policy-oriented marketing journal. First, journal subscriptions (AMA 2001a) have increased from nearly 350 for the 1992–93 fiscal year to 549 for the 2000–2001 fiscal year (after peaking at 640 during 1995–96). Second, and more indicative of reputation, a recent survey of marketing academics at doctorate-granting institutions ranked *JPP&M* twelfth (of 93 publications) in terms of importance, ahead of other policy- and consumer-oriented marketing journals such as *Journal of Consumer Affairs, Journal of Business Ethics,* and *Journal of Consumer Psychology* (Hult, Neese, and Bashaw 1997). Finally, an examination of *Social Sciences Citation Index* (*SSCI*) data indicates that *JPP&M* ranks fifth in current research impact from 1986 to 2000 (behind *Journal of Marketing, Journal of Consumer Research, Journal of Marketing Research,* and *Journal of Advertising*) among marketing journals in which policy-oriented research may be published. For the most recent time frame (1992 to 2000), *JPP&M* ranks fourth. Details of this analysis are provided in Table 2. Although the impact scores need to be interpreted with some caution (Zinkhan and Leigh 1999), *JPP&M* has consistently ranked among the top marketing journals during the past 10 years of its existence, with the highest impact occurring in 1993.

Content Analysis

To assess *JPP&M*'s contribution to public policy, it is important to understand the nature of work published in the journal. To this end, a content analysis was conducted with respect to (1) the perspective and (2) the topic of the published research. The research perspective analysis captures who was studied (i.e., consumers, marketers, or policymakers), and the research topic analysis focuses on what is studied (e.g., antitrust, commercial speech, privacy, social marketing). The perspective and topic analyses are independent in that any research topic can be studied from the three different research perspectives. For example, the recent Microsoft case (an antitrust research issue) could be studied from the perspective of the consumer (e.g., How do consumers respond when court rulings are announced?), the policymaker (e.g., What is the role of various courts when developing an antitrust case?), or the marketer (e.g., How has Microsoft responded at a strategic level to the litigation?).

RESEARCH PERSPECTIVE

Marketing and public policy can be studied from three perspectives, that of the consumer, the marketer, or the policy-maker. Accordingly, all *JPP&M* articles were coded as to whether the research focused on (1) consumers (such as how consumers react to nutrition information), (2) marketers (such as how marketers operate under various types of governmental regulation), or (3) policymakers (such as how government agencies formulate policy). Two coders (the primary investigators) read the abstract and first page of all articles published in *JPP&M* ($n = 455$) and independently coded each with respect to who was studied (each article received only one code). When the abstract and first page were not sufficient to determine the research perspective, the entire article was examined. Disagreements between the coders (resolved by discussion) were minimal, as is indicated by a high intercoder reliability, I_r, of .96 (Perreault and Leigh 1989; Rust and Cooil 1994).

The results indicate that 42.6% (194 articles) of the published research focused on consumers, 32.5% (148 articles) focused on policymakers, and the remaining 24.8% (113 articles) focused on marketers. The focus has changed slightly between the first and

The Impact of Marketing Journals[a]

Journal[b]	Annual SSCI Impact Factor[c, d]															Average Impact		
	1986	1987	1988	1989	1990	1991	1992	1993	1994	1995	1996	1997	1998	1999	2000	1986–1991	1992–2000	1986–2000
1. Journal of Marketing	.98	1.54	1.04	1.36	1.73	1.74	3.15	2.00	2.37	2.43	3.25	2.78	2.93	2.55	2.04	1.40	2.61	2.28
2. Journal of Consumer Research	2.23	2.17	1.88	2.00	3.11	2.29	2.43	2.10	2.28	1.37	1.62	1.38	1.83	2.48	2.46	2.28	1.99	2.26
3. Journal of Marketing Research	1.28	1.63	1.36	1.43	1.60	1.37	1.28	1.48	1.89	1.72	1.35	1.28	1.60	2.58	1.68	1.44	1.65	1.68
4. Journal of Advertising	.62	.39	.39	.35	.67	1.00	.79	.55	.82	.52	.58	.48	.56	.71	.63	.57	.63	.65
5. JPP&M	.11	.50	.17	.48	.17	.18	.63	1.13	.65	.90	.53	.81	.62	.46	.66	.27	.71	.57
6. Journal of Retailing	.51	.47	.39	.32	.45	.12	.36	.70	.44	.49	.71	.44	.84	.68	.50	.49	.52	.54
7. Journal of Advertising Research	.43	.63	.62	.48	.41	.39	.31	.40	.50	.32	.52	.66	.78	.64	.60	.38	.58	.54
8. Journal of Business Research	.26	.18	.17	.19	.24	.14	.30	.27	.38	.32	.40	.41	.25	.30	.41	.20	.34	.30
9. Journal of Consumer Affairs	.41	.48	.13	.30	.20	.08	.23	.15	.17	.27	.15	.06	.21	.52	.34	.26	.23	.26

[a]Marketing journals included here are those likely to publish public policy–related research using data available from SSCI.
[b]Journals are rank-ordered by average impact factor from 1986 through 2000.
[c]The impact factor is an indicator of a journal's current influence on knowledge development (for a more detailed review of the measure, see Zinkhan and Leigh 1999) and Journal Citation Reports from SSCI. Data are from Zinkhan and Leigh (1999) and Journal Citation Reports from SSCI.
[d]Data are unavailable from SSCI for JPP&M prior to 1986.

second decades of the journal such that the proportion of articles centered on consumers decreased (from 47.5% to 39.9%) and those focused on marketers increased (from 21.0% to 27.0%).[4] Articles focusing on policymakers remained nearly the same between the two time periods (31.5% and 33.1%, respectively). Additional analysis using five-year time periods showed that these changes occurred primarily during the first five years of publication and that all three perspectives have been relatively equally represented for the past 15 years.

Research Topic

We performed the research topic analysis (i.e., examining what is studied in the research) using a category structure developed specifically for this research.[5] The categorization consists of four major areas: (1) protection of consumers, (2) protection of competition and marketers, (3) policy and policymaking, and (4) societal issues. The first two areas are based on traditional views—espoused by organizations such as the Federal Trade Commission (FTC; 2001) and by various academics in the field (e.g., Andrews 2001c; Cohen 1995; Gundlach 2001)—holding that public policy in the marketing arena should primarily protect the well-being of consumers and marketplace competition (FTC 2001). We based the inclusion of policy and policymaking on the observation that much research published in *JPP&M* considers policy and the process by which it is developed. Examples of this research exist across the life of the journal, ranging from studies of federal agencies to commentary on court decisions that are likely to affect the field.

Although *JPP&M* publishes much research that focuses directly on issues of public policy and encourages authors to consider policy implications of all topics, there is a substantial portion of published research that is not directly related to public policy (e.g., research investigating business ethics and social marketing). As former editor Mazis (1997, p. 140) stated, "the view of the field has broadened to include issues not only involving government policy but also affecting society at large." Indeed, the current *JPP&M* mission statement (American Marketing Association 2001b) suggests that not all research published in the journal must be directly related to public policy: "*JPP&M* endeavors to comprehend the effects on marketing of public policy issues, as well as discuss marketing issues that may result in changes to public policy. Public concerns, such as ecology, health, and privacy, are also covered from the marketing perspective." To reflect research contributions from such areas, a fourth major area, representing societal issues, was included in the category structure.

---

[4]In that these figures represent a census, no statistical analyses are presented.

[5]A potential preexisting scheme existed within the *JPP&M* subject indices. In particular, seven indices review articles published in Volumes 1–6, 1–10, and 11–15 and annual reviews for Volumes 16, 17, 18, and 19 (also see Laverie and Murphy 1993). These indices are not employed here because they do not have a collective hierarchical structure that allows aggregation across subcategories. Indeed, these subject indices are based on various approaches to categorization, including research domain, marketing-mix element, agency jurisdiction, product type, targeted group, and policy issue.

Using the four major topic areas as a supporting structure, we developed the detailed aspects of the categories in a two-stage process. In the first stage, we used subject indices from *JPP&M* (i.e., multivolume reviews for Volumes 1–6, 1–10, and 11–15 and annual reviews for Volumes 16, 17, 18, and 19) along with three edited texts from the field (Bloom 1991; Bloom and Gundlach 2001; Hill 1996) to develop a list of 84 potential categories. After examining all categories with respect to the four major areas detailed previously, we dropped from further consideration any category that did not reflect at least one of the areas. We added categories as appropriate to complete the initial category structure.

In the second stage, we refined the initial category structure using an iterative process that included the coding and recoding of large sets of randomly selected articles. As is shown in the Appendix, the final category structure is fairly elaborate. Subsumed under the four major areas are 23 main categories (e.g., antitrust, information provision) and 60 subcategories (e.g., exporting, Nutrition Labeling and Education Act).

Using this category structure, we independently coded each article at the subcategory level (unless no subcategories existed for a particular main category). Each article received one or two research topic codes (see Malhotra 1996), which represented the primary research topics in the article. The process progressed in a nonsequential manner (with respect to journal volume) to reduce possible order effects. Intercoder reliability for the overall topic analysis was high, with an I_r for all 455 articles of .93. The results of the research topic analysis are presented in Table 3 at the main category level and explained in the following sections.

Protection of Consumers

The majority of research examining issues of consumer protection surrounds information provision to consumers. Research in this category, however, has waned over time, with over a 30% reduction in the percentage of articles from the first to the second ten-year time period (from 29.0% of all articles in the first ten years to 19.5% in the second ten years). This change may be due, in part, to a shift away from the use of informational remedies by the FTC and the Food and Drug Administration (FDA) during this later time period. Indeed, a closer examination of the subcategories for information provision indicates that much of this change is due to declines in research focusing on remedies for misleading/missing information (from 6.8% to 1.4% of all articles), presentation and format of information (from 5.6% to 2.4%), and information about consumer hazards (from 8.0% to 5.8%). All other main categories for consumer protection increased across these time periods, and the percentage of articles focusing on privacy nearly doubled from 2.5% to 4.8%.

Protection of Marketers

The protection of competition and marketers encompasses the fewest research topics. Although various topics have been addressed regarding protection of competition, the

TABLE 3

Research Topics of *JPP&M* Articles

Research Topics	1982–2001	First Ten Years	Second Ten Years
Protection of Consumers			
Information provision	22.9 (104)	29.0 (47)	19.5 (57)
Product performance and safety	16.3 (74)	13.6 (22)	17.7 (52)
Deceptive and unfair practices	6.2 (28)	5.6 (9)	6.5 (19)
Privacy	4.0 (18)	2.5 (4)	4.8 (14)
Protection of Marketers			
Antitrust	6.8 (31)	3.7 (6)	8.5 (25)
Liability	5.1 (23)	8.6 (14)	3.1 (9)
Commercial speech	4.6 (21)	4.3 (7)	4.8 (14)
Self-regulation	2.9 (13)	3.1 (5)	2.7 (8)
Intellectual property	2.9 (13)	1.2 (2)	3.8 (11)
Contracts and agreements	2.2 (10)	1.9 (3)	2.4 (7)
Policy and Policymaking			
U.S. executive branch	9.7 (44)	11.1 (18)	8.9 (26)
Input to the policymaking process	7.9 (36)	9.9 (16)	6.8 (20)
U.S. legislative branch	6.6 (30)	4.9 (8)	7.5 (22)
U.S. judicial branch	5.9 (27)	4.3 (7)	6.8 (20)
Multinational policymakers	2.0 (9)	.0 (0)	3.1 (9)
Non-U.S. policymakers	1.1 (5)	1.2 (2)	1.0 (3)
Societal Issues			
Corporate social responsibility	10.8 (49)	6.8 (11)	13.0 (38)
Societal issues	10.3 (47)	6.2 (10)	12.6 (37)
Environmental protection	7.9 (36)	14.2 (23)	4.4 (13)
Politics and public opinion	4.4 (20)	6.2 (10)	3.4 (10)
Quality of life	4.0 (18)	4.3 (7)	3.8 (11)
Social marketing	3.3 (15)	3.7 (6)	3.1 (9)
International issues	2.6 (12)	3.7 (6)	2.0 (6)

Notes: Cell entries include the percentage of total articles receiving a particular topic code for a given time period. The number in parentheses indicates the number of articles receiving a specific code. For example, 6.81% (31/455) of all articles include research topics related to antitrust. The percentages sum to more than 100% because each article can receive up to 2 codes. A total of 683 codes was assigned to the 455 articles.

most predominant category during the past 20 years is antitrust, which experienced 130% growth in the percentage of articles from the first ten years (3.7%) to the second (8.5%). Conversely, articles focusing on liability experienced a notable decrease in percentage (from 8.6% to 3.1%).

Policy and Policymaking

Policy and policymaking was the third most prevalent research topic. Most of these articles were distributed relatively evenly among the three primary branches of the U.S. federal government. Relatively few articles were devoted to policymaking outside the United States. The other main category of note in this section pertains to input to the policymaking process, reflecting research that develops new research methods for use by policymakers, comments on the policy formation process, or presents other academic research directed at the development of public policy (such as commentary offered by various experts on the future of the field; Kinnear 1997; Mazis 1997).

Societal Issues

The majority of research topics related to societal issues dealt with corporate social responsibility (e.g., corporate ethics, advertising's effects on society), various types of societal issues (ranging from addiction to violence), and environmental protection. In terms of changes over the two ten-year time periods, notable increases occurred for research on corporate social responsibility (from 6.8% to 13.0%) and societal issues (from 6.2% to 12.6%), whereas research on environmental protection decreased (from 14.2% to 4.4%).

Influences on Research Topics

As demonstrated by the preceding analyses, the prevalence of research topics addressed in *JPP&M* has ebbed and flowed over the past 20 years, and such changes likely are due to one or more of the following factors: (1) the structure of the journal, (2) the interests of researchers who publish in the journal, and (3) changes in the external environment. Each of these factors is discussed subsequently.

The structure of *JPP&M* (i.e., specific sections such as Policy Watch, special issues, and so forth) is a likely influence on the topics published in the journal. Indeed, an examination of research topics across the five types of articles published in *JPP&M* (as edited by the main editors, the special issue editors, the conference editors, and the Policy Watch and Legal Developments section editors) shows that topics vary by the section in which the article appeared (see Table 4). For example, Legal Developments published a higher percentage of articles on policy and policymaking (15.2% of the total articles in this category) and marketer protection (16.2%) than on consumer protection (4.0%) and societal issues (.5%). In addition, special issues had a strong influence on the prevalence of certain topics published in the journal. For example, a substantial portion of research on privacy and antitrust (two areas that increased in proportion from the first to the second ten years) has appeared in special issues.

Another influence on research topics published in *JPP&M* is researcher interest. As Wilkie (1997) notes, a single researcher (or small group of researchers) can have a substantial impact on the field, potentially changing the nature and/or magnitude of published research topics. For example, of the articles coded as antitrust for the second ten years of the journal, Greg Gundlach has been an author on fully 20% of them. Had his efforts been directed elsewhere during this time period, the high growth rate of research in this area would have been considerably smaller (assuming that no other researchers took his place and published a similar number of articles).

Research Topics and the Structure of *JPP&M* Articles

Research Topic	Percentage by Type of Article				
	Traditional	Special Issues	Conference	Policy Watch	Legal Developments
Protection of Consumers (224)	**52.2**	**25.0**	**12.1**	**6.7**	**4.0**
Information provision (104)	57.7	24.0	7.7	7.7	2.9
Product performance and safety (74)	52.7	23.0	10.8	9.5	4.1
Deceptive and unfair practices (28)	46.4	21.4	28.6	.0	3.6
Privacy (18)	27.8	44.4	16.7	.0	11.1
Protection of Marketers (111)	**51.4**	**14.4**	**8.1**	**9.9**	**16.2**
Antitrust (31)	29.0	35.5	19.4	.0	16.1
Liability (23)	78.3	.0	.0	13.0	8.7
Commercial speech (21)	52.4	4.8	.0	23.8	19.0
Self-regulation (13)	46.2	23.1	7.7	23.1	.0
Intellectual property (13)	46.2	7.7	.0	.0	46.2
Contracts and agreements (10)	70.0	.0	20.0	.0	10.0
Policy and Policymaking (151)	**41.7**	**17.9**	**13.2**	**11.9**	**15.2**
U.S. executive branch (44)	22.7	29.5	22.7	13.6	11.4
Input to the policymaking process (36)	63.9	5.6	22.2	5.6	2.8
U.S. legislative branch (30)	46.7	10.0	3.3	23.3	16.7
U.S. judicial branch (27)	48.1	7.4	3.7	11.1	29.6
Multinational policymakers (9)	11.1	44.4	.0	.0	44.4
Non-U.S. policymakers (5)	40.0	60.0	.0	.0	.0
Societal Issues (197)	**49.2**	**30.5**	**6.1**	**13.7**	**.5**
Corporate social responsibility (49)	42.9	30.6	4.1	22.4	.0
Societal issues (47)	44.7	31.9	6.4	14.9	2.1
Environmental protection (36)	61.1	27.8	8.3	2.8	.0
Politics and public opinion (20)	60.0	20.0	5.0	15.0	.0
Quality of life (18)	50.0	27.8	.0	22.2	.0
Social marketing (15)	33.3	40.0	20.0	6.7	.0
International issues (12)	58.3	41.7	.0	.0	.0

Notes: Cell entries include the percentage of articles (by type of article) coded as the focal research topic. The percentages sum to 100% across a row. For example, of the articles coded as "information provision," 57.7% (60/104) appeared as traditional articles. A total of 683 codes was assigned to the 455 articles.

Finally, as has been observed by noted experts in the area, *JPP&M*'s research topics are influenced by various changes in the external environment (e.g., Bloom 1997; Kinnear 1997). For example, increases in research on the legislative branch (from 4.9% to 7.5%) may be due in part to new legislation (such as the Nutrition Labeling and Education Act) that directly affects the marketing field. Similarly, decreases in environmental protection research (from 14.2% to 4.4%) can be attributed partially to the high number of articles during the first ten years of *JPP&M* that responded to both the energy crisis of the late 1970s and the more general interest in the environment during that time.

Publication Analysis

Because *JPP&M* relies for the most part on submitted articles, its content greatly reflects the research interests of its authors and their supporting institutions. As such, we conducted analyses of individual and institutional contributors to the journal. The analyses include all 455 articles published during the first 20 years of the journal.

The Nature of *JPP&M* Authorship

The publication analysis begins with a brief examination of general article authorship, an issue of importance for many academic researchers with respect to tenure and promotion within their institutions (Floyd, Schroeder, and Finn 1994; Schroeder, Langrehr, and Floyd 1995; Urban, Wayland, and McDermott 1992). During its first 20 years, *JPP&M* published 455 articles by 602 different authors from 272 institutions. Of those 455 articles, 177 (39%) are sole-authored, 152 (33%) have two authors, 99 (22%) have three authors, and 27 (6%) have four or more authors. As noted in Table 5, the mean number of authors per article has gradually increased over the past ten years because of a higher percentage of articles being coauthored by four or more people, a trend also experienced by other marketing-related journals (Fields and Swayne 1988; Schroeder, Langrehr, and Floyd 1995).

Contributors to the journal are affiliated with academic, corporate, government, or nonprofit organizations. Given the focus of the journal, it is not surprising that researchers from academe constitute the vast majority (89.6%) of authors. As shown in Table 5, there has been little change in the percentage of contributions by academics over time and only slight fluctuations in contributions by other groups. A more detailed examination of academic authors, however, reveals some changes in the academic ranks of authors over time. For example, a midperiod dip in contributions by full professors occurred concurrently with a peak for assistant professors. In addition, the percentage of students publishing in the journal has slowly risen over time.

As indicated by *JPP&M*'s editorial philosophy, the journal "serves as a bridge between academic researchers interested in developing new insights and practitioners concerned with solving current problems" (e.g., Andrews 1999, p. 1). One indication of how well this bridge is being developed is the nature of nonacademic authorship in *JPP&M*. A total of 75 articles (16.5% of all articles appearing in *JPP&M*) has been published with either a nonacademic sole author (32 articles) or at least one nonacademic coauthor (43 articles). Of the joint articles, 8 had only practitioner coauthors, whereas 35 were coauthored by at least one academic and one practitioner. The latter group included academics working with corporate ($n = 18$), government ($n = 11$), and nonprofit ($n = 6$) partners. The sole-authored articles included authors from nonprofit ($n = 16$), government ($n = 8$), and corporate ($n = 8$) organizations. In a follow-up analysis, we examined whether

TABLE 5

JPP&M Authors per Article, Author Affiliation, and Author Academic Rank

Volume	Number of Authors per Article					Academic Rank					Author Affiliation			
	Mean	1	2	3	4+	Full Professor	Associate Professor	Assistant Professor	Student	Other Academic	Academic	Corporate	Nonprofit	Government
1	1.9	5	6	3	0	8	9	7	0	0	24	1	0	1
2	2.1	5	3	4	1	9	9	4	1	0	23	0	0	4
3	1.6	8	3	3	0	7	6	9	0	0	22	0	0	1
4	1.8	6	7	0	1	5	6	5	1	2	19	3	0	3
5	2.3	4	4	8	0	18	8	4	1	2	33	3	0	0
6	1.6	7	4	2	0	7	7	5	1	0	20	1	0	0
7	1.8	6	8	2	0	11	1	10	2	0	24	1	2	1
8	1.7	8	9	2	0	13	9	7	0	2	31	2	0	0
9	2.1	5	4	6	0	9	5	12	2	3	31	0	2	0
10	1.9	10	11	6	1	10	12	13	6	3	44	2	2	6
11	2.1	8	9	6	2	13	16	15	1	0	45	1	2	4
12	2.0	11	11	3	3	16	13	10	7	5	51	1	4	1
13	1.6	16	11	4	0	11	9	18	2	5	45	2	1	2
14	2.0	11	11	9	1	14	24	15	5	3	61	1	1	1
15	2.1	11	8	8	3	14	22	12	3	5	56	1	2	4
16	1.8	20	8	6	2	27	12	13	6	1	59	2	2	1
17	2.3	12	7	9	5	22	19	13	7	5	66	4	4	3
18	2.1	9	8	6	3	18	12	10	4	2	46	0	2	7
19	2.0	8	13	3	2	16	13	10	4	4	47	2	1	2
20	2.4	7	7	9	3	17	16	18	5	2	58	2	1	1
1–5[a]	1.93	39%	32%	25%	3%	34.3%	27.7%	21.2%	2.2%	2.9%	88.3%	5.1%	.0%	6.6%
6–10	1.82	40	40	20	1	29.9	20.4	28.1	6.6	4.8	89.8	3.6	2.4	4.2
11–15	1.96	39	34	21	6	23.8	29.4	24.5	6.3	6.3	90.3	2.1	3.5	4.1
16–20	2.11	38	29	22	10	32.3	23.2	20.6	8.4	4.5	89.0	3.2	3.2	4.5
Totals	1.98	39	33	22	6	29.5	25.3	23.4	6.5	4.9	89.6	3.2	2.7	4.7

[a]For 5-year and 20-year totals, the percentage of articles in the particular category (column) for that time period (row) is shown.

the nature of contributing authors varied across the five types of *JPP&M* articles. The results indicate a significant relationship between author type and the structure of *JPP&M* ($\chi^2 = 45.35, p < .001$). Specifically, few of the traditional (10.9%, $n = 25$), Legal Development (6.5%, $n = 2$), and special issue (11.9%, $n = 12$) articles had at least one nonacademic author. In contrast, a significantly higher percentage of articles in the Policy Watch section (46.5%, $n = 20$) or from a conference (31.4%, $n = 16$) had at least one nonacademic author.

CONTRIBUTIONS OF SPECIFIC AUTHORS AND INSTITUTIONS

To understand which researchers and organizations have most affected the marketing and public policy field through *JPP&M*, we examined specific contributions to the journal. Although such analyses are common, there is disagreement whether contributions (i.e., authorship counts for individual authors or institutions) should be presented in raw form or after being adjusted for the number of authors appearing on each article (Fields and Swayne 1988; see also Borokhovich et al. 1995; Clark 1985; Malhotra 1996). A raw score is calculated by summing the articles on which an individual author (or institution) appears during the reporting period, regardless of coauthorship. An adjusted score, however, gives more weight to articles with fewer authors by dividing each article by the number of authors before summing across articles. Some academic institutions use this adjusted method to determine publication productivity for tenure and promotion purposes because some scholars maintain that single-authored articles have more value than multiple-authored articles. In that (1) there is merit in both approaches, (2) prior research often reports results using both approaches (e.g., Borokhovich et al. 1995; Malhotra 1996), and (3) the two sets of results reveal some notable differences in the ordering of contributors, we present both raw and adjusted data.

Author Contributions

Contributions of individual authors to the journal are presented as raw and adjusted data, respectively, in Table 6, Panels A and B. Authors are included if their total articles exceed arbitrary cutoff points for each time period. It is clear from Table 6 that the type of analysis (raw versus adjusted counts) and the time period (first versus second ten-year period) greatly influence the ordering of the lists.

For the entire 20-year period, a total of 602 authors contributed to *JPP&M*. The raw scores ranged from 1 to 13 articles per author; 37 authors (6%) published four or more articles, 24 (4%) published three, 74 (12%) published two, and the remaining 467 (78%) published one article. For the adjusted scores, which ranged from .14 to 8.67, 37 authors (6%) had scores of 2.00 or higher, 35 (almost 6%) had between 1.00 and 2.00, and the remaining 530 (slightly more than 88%) had a score of 1.00 or lower.

TABLE 6

Publication Analysis

A: Raw Scores for *JPP&M* Authors

1982–2001		First Ten Years		Second Ten Years	
Morgan, Fred W.	13	Morgan, Fred	7	Hill, Ronald Paul	11
Hill, Ronald Paul	11	Mazis, Michael B.	5	Burton, Scot	8
Bloom, Paul N.	8	Wilkie, William	5	Gundlach, Gregory T.	7
Burton, Scot	8	Bloom, Paul N.	4	Petty, Ross D.	7
Gundlach, Gregory T.	8	Armstrong, Gary M.	3	Milne, George R.	6
Mazis, Michael B.	8	Calfee, John E.	3	Morgan, Fred W.	6
Petty, Ross D.	8	Gelb, Betsy D.	3	Compeau, Larry D.	5
Ringold, Debra Jones	8	Kinnear, Thomas C.	3	Grewal, Dhruv	5
Scammon, Debra L.	8	McCrohan, Kevin F.	3	Ringold, Debra Jones	5
Sheffet, Mary J.	7	Ringold, Debra Jones	3	Scammon, Debra L.	5
Calfee, John E.	6	Scammon, Debra L.	3	Bloom, Paul N.	4
Milne, George R.	6	Sheffet, Mary J.	3	Levy, Alan S.	4
Wilkie, William L.	6	Staelin, Richard	3	Mathios, Alan D.	4
Compeau, Larry D.	5	Bernhardt, Kenneth L.	2	Miyazaki, Anthony D.	4
Grewal, Dhruv	5	Brucks, Merrie	2	Netemeyer, Richard G.	4
Kopp, Steven W.	5	Caywood, Clarke L.	2	Preston, Ivan L.	4
Levy, Alan S.	5	Ellen, Pam Scholder	2	Sheffet, Mary J.	4
Mathios, Alan D.	5	Gleason, Sandra E.	2	Taylor, Charles R.	4
Morris, Louis A.	5	Hirschman, Elizabeth C.	2	Andreasen, Alan R.	3
Murphy, Patrick E.	5	Jones, Mary Gardiner	2	Andrews, J. Craig	3
Netemeyer, Richard G.	5	Kangun, Norman	2	Biswas, Abhijit	3
Preston, Ivan L.	5	Kopp, Steven W.	2	Boedecker, Karl A.	3
Richards, Jef L.	5	Maronick, Thomas J.	2	Calfee, John E.	3
Taylor, Charles R.	5	Mills, Michael K.	2	Carlson, Les	3
Andreasen, Alan R.	4	Morris, Louis A.	2	Franke, George R.	3
Andrews, J. Craig	4	Mowen, John C.	2	Hastak, Manoj	3
Boedecker, Karl A.	4	Muehling, Darrel D.	2	Jacoby, Jacob	3
Carlson, Les	4	Murphy, Patrick E.	2	Kopp, Steven W.	3
Franke, George	4	Reece, Bonnie B.	2	Laczniak, Gene R.	3
Hirschman, Elizabeth C.	4	Reid, Leonard N.	2	Manning, Kenneth D.	3
Kinnear, Thomas C.	4	Richards, Jef L.	2	Mazis, Michael B.	3
Laczniak, Gene R.	4	Rotfeld, Herbert J.	2	Morris, Louis A.	3
Miyazaki, Anthony D.	4	Samli, A. Coskun	2	Murphy, Patrick E.	3
Muehling, Darrel D.	4	Schucker, Raymond E.	2	Ozanne, Julie L.	3
Pappalardo, Janis K.	4	Stiff, Ronald M.	2	Pappalardo, Janis K.	3
Rotfeld, Herbert J.	4	Tyebjee, Tyzoon	2	Richards, Jef L.	3
Wiener, Joshua Lyle	4	Ursic, Michael	2	Rose, Randall L.	3
		Wiener, Joshua Lyle	2	Sprott, David E.	3
				Stewart, David W.	3

(Continued)

TABLE 6

Continued

B: Adjusted Scores for *JPP&M* Authors

1982–2001		First Ten Years		Second Ten Years	
Morgan, Fred W.	8.67	Morgan, Fred W.	5.50	Petty, Ross D.	6.00
Petty, Ross D.	7.00	Wilkie, William L.	5.00	Hill, Ronald Paul	5.92
Gundlach, Gregory T.	6.00	Bloom, Paul N.	2.33	Gundlach, Gregory T.	5.00
Wilkie, William L.	6.00	Hirschman, Elizabeth C.	2.00	Milne, George R.	4.33
Hill, Ronald Paul	5.92	Jones, Mary Gardiner	2.00	Preston, Ivan L.	3.50
Bloom, Paul N.	4.67	Richards, Jef L.	2.00	Morgan, Fred W.	3.17
Richards, Jef L.	4.50	Armstrong, Gary M.	1.83	Andreasen, Alan R.	3.00
Sheffet, Mary J.	4.50	Mazis, Michael B.	1.83	Laczniak, Gene R.	3.00
Milne, George R.	4.33	McCrohan, Kevin F.	1.83	Sheffet, Mary J.	3.00
Mazis, Michael B.	4.17	Calfee, John F.	1.50	Pappalardo, Janis K.	2.50
Andreasen, Alan R.	4.00	Mills, Michael K.	1.50	Richards, Jef L.	2.50
Preston, Ivan L.	4.00	Reece, Bonnie B.	1.50	Ringold, Debra Jones	2.50
Jones Ringold, Debra	3.75	Rotfeld, Herbert J.	1.50	Burton, Scot	2.39
Calfee, John E.	3.50	Sheffet, Mary J.	1.50	Bloom, Paul N.	2.33
Laczniak, Gene R.	3.50	Tyebjee, Tyzoon	1.50	Mathios, Alan D.	2.33
Scammon, Debra L.	3.50	Ursic, Michael	1.50	Mazis, Michael B.	2.33
Murphy, Patrick E.	3.33	Gelb, Betsy D.	1.33	Taylor, Charles R.	2.33
Cohen, Joel B.	3.00	Mowen, John C.	1.33	Compeau, Larry D.	2.17
Pappalardo, Janis K.	3.00	Murphy, Patrick E.	1.33	Grewal, Dhruv	2.17
Rotfeld, Herbert J.	3.00	Scammon, Debra L.	1.33	Scammon, Debra L.	2.17
Silverglade, Bruce A.	3.00	Wiener, Joshua Lyle	1.33	Balto, David A.	2.00
Hirschman, Elizabeth C.	2.83	Ringold, Debra Jones	1.25	Calfee, John E.	2.00
Mathios, Alan D.	2.83	Kinnear, Thomas C.	1.17	Cohen, Joel B.	2.00
Taylor, Charles R.	2.83	Staelin, Richard	1.17	Murphy, Patrick E.	2.00
Wiener, Joshua Lyle	2.83	All others ≤ 1.00		Roth, Martin S.	2.00
Kopp, Steven W.	2.50			Silverglade, Bruce A.	2.00
Burton, Scot	2.39			Stewart, David W.	2.00
Franke, George R.	2.33			Franke, George R.	1.83
Compeau, Larry D.	2.17			Cook, Don Lloyd	1.50
Grewal, Dhruv	2.17			Hoy, Mariea Grubbs	1.50
Kinnear, Thomas C.	2.17			Jacoby, Jacob	1.50
Balto, David A.	2.00			Kopp, Steven W.	1.50
Beales, J. Howard III	2.00			Mason, Marlys J.	1.50
Gardiner Jones, Mary	2.00			Miyazaki, Anthony D.	1.50
Gould, Stephen J.	2.00			Rotfeld, Herbert J.	1.50
Roth, Martin S.	2.00			Simonson, Alexander	1.50
Stewart, David W.	2.00			Wiener, Joshua Lyle	1.50
Armstrong, Gary M.	1.83			Boedecker, Karl A.	1.33
Boedecker, Karl A.	1.83			Grier, Sonya A.	1.33
Grubbs Hoy, Mariea	1.83			Levy, Alan S.	1.33
McCrohan, Kevin F.	1.83			Smith Gooding, Sandra	1.33
Mowen, John C.	1.83			Ozanne, Julie L.	1.17
Morris, Louis A.	1.58			Netemeyer, Richard G.	1.14
Levy, Alan S.	1.53			All others ≤ 1.00	
All others ≤ 1.50					

Notes: Total = 602 authors.

Institutional Contributions

Panels A and B of Table 7 present, respectively, the raw and adjusted data for institutional contributions to *JPP&M*. Institutions are included if total articles for the 20-year period exceed the arbitrary cutoff points. Similar to the author publication analysis, separate lists are presented within Table 7 for the first and second ten-year periods.

For the 20-year period, 272 institutions are represented. During this time period, institutional contributions ranged from 1 to 21; 42 (15%) institutions published six or more articles, 8 (3%) published five, 14 (5%) published four, 28 (10%) published three, 42 (15%) published two, and the remaining 138 (51%) published one article. Although some institutions (e.g., the FTC, American University) made relatively consistent contributions over the two ten-year periods, others experienced marked differences over time. For example, several institutions that were absent during the first ten years received relatively high rankings during the second ten years (e.g., Arkansas, Villanova, Miami, Portland, Georgetown). The opposite effect occurred as well, though not as often (e.g., Baltimore). Although several factors can effect such changes, one likely cause is the movement of prolific faculty members across institutions. Also of note is that nonacademic institutions such as the FTC and the FDA have provided consistent and substantial contributions to the journal.

Citation Impact Analysis

We examined all citations of *JPP&M* articles to provide an understanding of the journal's impact on the progression of marketing and public policy thought. The citation analysis is based on the 427 articles published during the first 19 years of *JPP&M* (i.e., Volumes 1–19), in that we collected data during the twentieth year of the journal. We gathered citation information using the online version of the *SSCI* and a separate examination of each article's citations.

OVERALL JOURNAL IMPACT

At the time of analysis, the 427 articles published in Volumes 1–19 of *JPP&M* had been cited a total of 1967 times by 223 journals. The majority of these journals (120, 53.8%) cited *JPP&M* only once, and a smaller portion (81, 36.3%) cited *JPP&M* between two and nine times. Only 22 journals (9.9%) cited *JPP&M* ten or more times; the citation counts for these journals are presented in Table 8 for each of the volumes and issues of *JPP&M*. Although these 22 journals constitute only 9.9% of all journals citing *JPP&M*, they represent 78.4% (1546) of the total citations.

The analysis provides several noteworthy observations. First, and not surprisingly, the most frequent citer of *JPP&M* is *JPP&M;* citations within the journal account for 42.4% (834 of 1967) of all citations. Second, aside from citations in *JPP&M*, 20 journals oriented toward marketing and consumer behavior (some of which are highlighted in Table 8) account for almost half of the non-*JPP&M* citations (47.2%, 535 of 1133) and

TABLE 7		

Publication Analysis

A: Raw Scores for *JPP&M* Institutional Contributors

1982–2001		First Ten Years		Second Ten Years	
Michigan State Univ.	21	Michigan State Univ.	15	Univ. of Arkansas	21
Univ. of Arkansas	21	Univ. of North Carolina	10	Louisiana State Univ.	15
Univ. of Utah	21	American Univ.	8	Univ. of Utah	15
FDA	20	Wayne State Univ.	8	Colorado State Univ.	13
Louisiana State Univ.	19	Arizona State Univ.	7	FDA	13
Wayne State Univ.	19	FDA	7	Univ. of Miami	12
American Univ.	18	FTC	7	Notre Dame	12
FTC	17	Univ. of Florida	7	Univ. of Massachusetts	11
Arizona State Univ.	16	George Mason Univ.	6	Univ. of Portland	11
Univ. of North Carolina	16	Georgia State Univ.	6	Villanova Univ.	11
Notre Dame	15	Univ. of Michigan	6	Wayne State Univ.	11
Colorado State Univ.	14	Oklahoma State Univ.	6	Univ. of Wisconsin	11
Clemson Univ.	13	Univ. of Utah	6	American Univ.	10
Univ. of Florida	13	Univ. of Baltimore	5	Clemson Univ.	10
Univ. of Massachusetts	13	Univ. of Houston	5	FTC	10
Univ. of Wisconsin	13	Marquette Univ.	5	Arizona State Univ.	9
Marquette Univ.	12	Univ. of Texas (Austin)	5	Babson College	9
Univ. of Miami	12	Virginia Tech	5	Georgetown Univ.	8
Babson College	11	Washington State Univ.	5	Loyola College	7
Georgia State Univ.	11	Florida State Univ.	4	Marquette Univ.	7
Oklahoma State Univ.	11	Louisiana State Univ.	4	Univ. of South Carolina	7
Univ. of Portland	11	Univ. of Southern California	4	Cornell Univ.	6
Univ. of Texas (Austin)	11	Auburn Univ.	3	Univ. of Florida	6
Villanova Univ.	11	Clemson Univ.	3	George Washington Univ.	6
Washington State Univ.	11	Florida International Univ.	3	Michigan State Univ.	6
Virginia Tech	10	Univ. of Georgia	3	Univ. of North Carolina	6
George Mason Univ.	9	Indiana Univ.	3	Rutgers Univ.	6
Univ. of South Carolina	9	Univ. of Maryland	3	Univ. of Texas (Austin)	6
George Washington Univ.	8	Memphis State Univ.	3	Washington State Univ.	6
Georgetown Univ.	8	Univ. of Minnesota	3	Clarkson Univ.	5
Loyola College	8	Notre Dame	3	Univ. of Colorado (Denver)	5
Univ. of Michigan	8	Pennsylvania State Univ.	3	Georgia State Univ.	5
Rutgers Univ.	8	Santa Clara Univ.	3	Univ. of Kentucky	5
Univ. of Southern California	8	Simon Fraser Univ.	3	Univ. of Nebraska	5
Auburn Univ.	7	All others 2 or fewer		Oklahoma State Univ.	5
Pennsylvania State Univ.	7			Virginia Tech	5
Univ. of Nebraska	7			Willamette Univ.	5
Univ. of Colorado (Denver)	6			All others 4 or fewer	
Cornell Univ.	6				
Florida International Univ.	6				
Univ. of Georgia	6				
Univ. of Houston	6				
All others 5 or fewer					

TABLE 7

Continued

B: Adjusted Scores for *JPP&M* Institutional Contributors

1982–2001		First Ten Years		Second Ten Years	
FTC	12.00	Michigan State Univ.	8.17	Babson College	8.50
Michigan St. Univ.	12.00	Univ. of Florida	6.50	Notre Dame	8.50
Notre Dame	10.83	Wayne State Univ.	6.00	Univ. of Wisconsin	8.00
Babson College	10.50	Univ. of North Carolina	5.33	Villanova Univ.	7.58
Univ. of Florida	10.50	FTC	4.50	FTC	7.50
Univ. of Utah	9.00	Oklahoma State Univ.	3.33	Univ. of Massachusetts	7.00
Univ. of Wisconsin	9.00	George Mason Univ.	3.00	Georgetown Univ.	6.67
Wayne State Univ.	8.50	Univ. of Texas (Austin)	3.00	Univ. of Utah	6.50
Univ. of North Carolina	8.33	American Univ.	2.83	Univ. of Arkansas	5.89
Univ. of Massachusetts	7.67	Arizona State Univ.	2.67	Univ. of Miami	5.00
Villanova Univ.	7.58	Marquette Univ.	2.67	Univ. of Portland	4.83
American Univ.	7.00	Univ. of Utah	2.50	George Washington Univ.	4.50
Marquette Univ.	7.00	Univ. of Houston	2.33	Marquette Univ.	4.33
Georgetown Univ.	6.67	Univ. of Michigan	2.33	American Univ.	4.17
Oklahoma State Univ.	6.33	Notre Dame	2.33	FDA	4.08
Arizona State Univ.	6.25	Simon Fraser Univ.	2.33	Univ. of Florida	4.00
Univ. of Texas (Austin)	6.25	Univ. of Southern California	2.33	Michigan State Univ.	3.83
George Washington Univ.	6.00	Virginia Tech.	2.17	Clemson Univ.	3.67
Univ. of Arkansas	5.89	Univ. of Baltimore	2.08	Louisiana State Univ.	3.65
FDA	5.68	Babson College	2.00	Arizona State Univ.	3.58
Louisiana State Univ.	5.48	Baruch College	2.00	Colorado State Univ.	3.33
Rutgers Univ.	5.17	CIRI[a]	2.00	Univ. of Texas (Austin)	3.25
Univ. of Miami	5.00	Georgia State Univ.	2.00	Rutgers Univ.	3.17
Univ. of Portland	4.83	Indiana Univ.	2.00	CSPI[b]	3.00
Univ. of So. California	4.83	NYU	2.00	Cornell Univ.	3.00
Clemson Univ.	4.67	Pennsylvania State Univ.	2.00	Univ. of Illinois	3.00
Virginia Tech.	4.67	Rutgers Univ.	2.00	Univ. of North Carolina	3.00
George Mason Univ.	4.50	Santa Clara Univ.	2.00	Oklahoma State Univ.	3.00
Colorado State Univ.	4.33	Southern Illinois Univ.	2.00	U. of Colorado (Denver).	2.83
Univ. of Illinois	4.33	Louisiana State Univ.	1.83	Loyola College	2.75
Georgia State Univ.	4.17	Florida State Univ.	1.67	Univ. of Kentucky	2.67
CSPI[a]	4.00	Washington State Univ.	1.67	Auburn Univ.	2.50
Auburn Univ.	3.83	FDA	1.60	Boston College	2.50
Univ. of Michigan	3.83	George Washington Univ.	1.50	U. of Southern California	2.50
Loyola College	3.75	Memphis State Univ.	1.50	Stanford Univ.	2.50
Pennsylvania State Univ.	3.67	Wilfrid Laurier Univ.	1.50	Univ. of Tennessee	2.50
Washington State Univ.	3.67	All others below 1.50		Virginia Tech.	2.50
NYU	3.50			Wayne State Univ.	2.50
U. of Colorado (Denver)	3.33			Willamette Univ.	2.50
Univ. of Nebraska	3.25			Univ. of South Carolina	2.42
Univ. of South Carolina	3.08			Univ. of Nebraska	2.25
Cornell Univ.	3.00			Univ. of Alabama	2.17
Baruch College	2.67			Clarkson Univ.	2.17
Univ. of Houston	2.67			Georgia State Univ.	2.17
Univ. of Kentucky	2.67			All others ≤ 2.00	
All others ≤ 2.50					

[a]Consumer Interest Research Institute.
[b]Center for Science in the Public Interest.
Notes: Total = 272 institutions.

TABLE 8

JPP&M Citation Counts Across Journals

Volume and Issue	JPP&M	J. Advertising	Adv. Consum. Res.	J. Marketing	J. Consum. Aff.	Annu. Rev. Psychol.	J. Bus. Res.	J. Consum. Res.	Psychol. Market	Am. Bus. Law J.	J. Advertising Res.	J. Bus. Ethics	Am. Behav. Sci.	J. Acad. Marketing Sci.	J. Marketing Res.	Environ. and Behav.	J. Retailing	Am. J. Public Health	Antitrust Law J.	J. Econ. Psychol.	J. Appl. Soc. Psychol.	J. Study Alcohol	Total Citations	Total Less JPP&M	Total Citations Adjusted for Time	Total Less JPP&M Adjusted for Time
1	12	2	3	2	1	0	0	2	0	0	0	0	0	0	0	0	0	0	0	0	0	0	27	15	.10	.06
2	36	2	2	1	3	0	2	3	0	2	1	0	0	0	1	0	0	0	0	0	0	0	68	32	.29	.14
3	37	4	6	3	7	2	3	8	0	0	6	2	0	3	4	2	2	3	0	0	0	0	84	47	.35	.20
4	39	9	12	2	2	1	1	4	0	0	6	2	0	1	1	1	2	0	0	1	0	2	126	87	.56	.39
5	40	4	7	2	10	6	4	4	0	2	0	0	1	0	0	0	0	0	0	0	0	0	122	82	.51	.34
6	30	9	1	1	1	3	0	0	0	2	2	2	1	0	1	0	0	0	0	1	0	0	61	31	.34	.17
7	34	9	3	3	2	0	2	0	0	0	2	2	1	0	0	0	0	0	1	1	1	0	67	33	.32	.16
8	64	8	3	5	5	0	2	5	0	0	1	1	0	0	0	1	1	1	1	1	2	0	119	55	.52	.24
9	42	2	1	3	3	0	3	3	0	3	2	0	2	0	2	0	0	0	1	1	0	1	84	42	.51	.25
10, 1	99	2	5	11	9	0	2	2	4	4	4	0	3	2	4	0	0	1	3	1	2	2	215	116	1.34	.73
10, 2	30	10	15	3	6	0	10	7	7	4	0	5	5	0	0	10	0	0	0	0	5	0	131	101	1.15	.89
11, 1	15	9	2	6	1	2	0	2	2	1	2	0	2	0	1	0	4	1	0	1	0	0	68	53	.69	.54
11, 2	22	3	4	0	0	0	2	0	0	2	1	0	1	0	0	1	0	0	1	0	2	0	51	29	.43	.24
12, 1	40	2	1	2	8	0	5	5	5	0	0	11	10	0	0	1	0	3	0	0	1	5	151	111	1.57	1.16
12, 2	42	1	3	3	4	2	0	0	1	2	2	1	2	2	2	2	0	0	0	1	1	0	85	43	.81	.41
13, 1	38	2	7	7	2	7	0	0	0	1	1	1	3	3	1	0	0	0	0	0	0	0	88	50	.79	.45
13, 2	21	2	1	4	1	3	0	1	0	1	1	0	1	2	0	1	1	0	1	1	0	0	44	23	.45	.24
14, 1	36	5	3	2	2	6	3	0	1	1	3	1	0	0	1	1	0	0	6	0	0	0	78	42	.81	.44
14, 2	14	4	1	6	1	7	1	0	1	1	0	1	0	0	0	1	1	0	0	3	0	0	49	35	.56	.40
15, 1	47	2	4	4	1	0	1	0	0	1	3	0	1	9	1	0	1	0	0	1	0	0	87	40	1.02	.47
15, 2	15	0	0	0	0	0	0	0	0	0	0	0	0	0	0	0	0	0	0	0	0	0	21	6	.36	.10
16, 1	15	3	3	2	0	0	0	0	0	1	0	1	0	0	0	0	0	0	0	0	0	0	28	13	.33	.15
16, 2	16	3	0	0	0	0	0	0	0	0	0	0	0	0	0	0	0	0	0	0	0	0	26	10	.50	.19
17, 1	9	0	0	0	1	0	0	0	0	1	1	0	0	0	0	0	0	1	0	0	0	0	22	13	.49	.29
17, 2	11	2	0	1	1	0	0	0	0	0	0	0	0	2	0	0	1	1	1	0	1	1	24	13	.53	.29
18, 1	13	2	0	2	2	0	0	0	0	0	0	0	0	0	0	0	0	0	0	0	0	0	21	8	.81	.31
18, 2	2	0	0	0	0	0	0	0	0	0	0	0	0	0	0	0	0	0	0	0	0	0	4	2	.21	.10
19, 1	13	0	0	0	0	0	0	0	0	0	0	0	0	0	0	0	0	0	0	0	0	0	14	1	1.00	.07
19, 2	2	0	0	0	0	0	0	0	0	0	0	0	0	0	0	0	0	0	0	0	0	0	2	0	.33	.00
Total	834	98	84	74	66	49	40	34	31	27	25	25	24	23	22	16	14	13	13	12	11	11	1967	1133	—	—

a substantial portion of the overall citations (27.2%, 535 of 1967). The journal was also cited by 54 health-related journals (147 citations), 17 psychology journals (102 citations), 19 law-oriented journals (86 citations), 13 environment-related journals (35 citations), and 99 other journals (228 citations). Third, 8 of the top 20 journals citing *JPP&M* are not related directly to marketing and consumer behavior. Three of these journals (*Journal of Business Ethics, American Behavioral Scientist,* and *Environment and Behavior*) typically have cited articles that appeared in *JPP&M* special issues with themes related to the content of these journals.

Finally, there is considerable variation across *JPP&M* issues in terms of citation counts. This is not surprising because (1) earlier issues have had more opportunity (i.e., more time) to be cited and (2) some issues have more articles than others (the range is from 11 to 21 articles per issue). Therefore, to control for these factors, we adjusted the citation counts for the number of years an issue has been in print (in half-year increments) and for the number of articles published in a particular issue. (Note that the use of this procedure allows potential short-term anomalies to bias recent journal issues more strongly than older issues.) The results, reported in Table 8 and illustrated in Figure 2, show that certain issues lead others in terms of average citation counts. Although the success of these issues may be influenced by their overall content (e.g., a special issue on a particular topic), further analyses (reported subsequently) show that certain key articles have a significant impact on the issue-level citation counts.

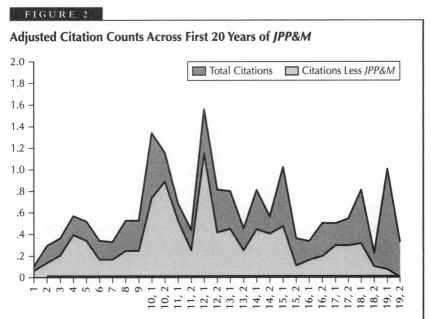

FIGURE 2

Adjusted Citation Counts Across First 20 Years of *JPP&M*

Notes: The citation counts are adjusted for the number of articles per issue and the time the issue was published.

INDIVIDUAL ARTICLE IMPACT

The 427 articles examined in the citation analysis were cited an average of 4.61 times (median = 2). Total citation counts ranged from 0 to 58 citations per article. Information for the top-cited articles—those with 20 or more total citations—is presented in Table 9. In terms of the articles published in Volumes 1–19 of *JPP&M*, these 16 articles represent 3.7% of the articles and 22.6% (444) of the citations.

Four observations are notable. First, the majority of the top-cited articles based on raw citations remain "top-cited" even after we adjust for time. Second, the high citation counts of certain issues (e.g., Vol. 10, Nos. 1 and 2) appear to be driven by several key articles. Third, 7 of the 16 top-cited articles are the first articles in their respective issues (indeed, for 12 of the 30 journal issues examined in the citation analysis, the first article was the most highly cited article of that issue). Fourth, there is a near-exclusive focus on consumers in these top-cited articles, and the majority examine some form of information provision.

Discussion

We explored the contributions of *JPP&M* to the arena of public policy and marketing using publication, citation, and content analyses. In the following sections, we discuss the findings and how they relate to the future development of the journal.

AUTHORS AND INSTITUTIONS

The publication analyses show that a wide variety of individual authors and institutions have contributed scholarly work to *JPP&M*. We discuss three notable findings regarding these contributors: First, the combined contribution from for-profit, nonprofit, and governmental organizations has remained at a relatively constant level (approximately 10%), which suggests that this particular connection with the "outside world" is stable, albeit relatively small. Although *JPP&M* is a respected academic journal, the practitioner element is important, considering the journal's many readers and contributors from government, nonprofits, and corporations. Indeed, if *JPP&M* maintains or increases the participation rates of practitioners, it presumably could benefit from improved actual and perceived relevance of published research, as well as an increased likelihood that research will be considered for use in the field (see Andrews 2001c).

Various strategies might be employed to maintain or increase authorship by practitioners. One approach is to aim calls for papers directly toward contributors from outside of academia. For example, the journal's first special issue (on the FTC in Volume 7) included several FTC commissioners who were recruited by then-editor Murphy to contribute articles (Murphy 2001). Another approach is to develop new sections and/or maintain current sections of the journal that appeal to practitioners. For example, the

TABLE 9

Most Frequently Cited *JPP&M* Articles

Author	Title	Volume, Issue	Article Position	Citations			
				Total	Non-JPP&M	Adjusted Total	Adjusted Non-JPP&M
1. Bettman, Payne, and Staelin	Cognitive Considerations in Designing Effective Labels for Presenting Risk Information	5	1	58	43	3.87	2.87
2. Levy et al.	The Impact of a Nutrition Information Program on Food Purchases	4	1	46	37	2.88	2.31
3. Granzin and Olsen	Characterizing Participants in Activities Protecting the Environment	10, 2	1	34	27	3.58	2.84
4. Brucks, Mitchell, and Staelin	The Effect of Nutriitonal Information Disclosure in Advertising: An Information Processing Approach	3	1	33	21	1.94	1.24
5. Mazis, Morris, and Swasy	An Evaluation of the Alcohol Warning Label: Initial Survey Results	10, 1	15	29	17	2.90	1.70
6. Ellen, Wiener, and Cobb-Walgren	The Role of Perceived Consumer Effectiveness in Motivating Environmentally Conscious Behaviors	10, 2	6	28	22	2.95	2.32
7. Scammon, Mayer, and Smith	Alcohol Warnings: How Do You Know When You Have Had One Too Many?	10, 1	14	24	14	2.40	1.40
8. Schwepker and Cornwell	An Examination of Ecologically Concerned Consumers and Their Intention to Purchase Ecologically Packaged Products	10, 2	5	24	18	2.53	1.89
9. Hilton	An Overview of Recent Findings on Alcoholic Beverage Warning Labels	12, 1	1	23	16	2.88	2.00
10. Stewart and Martin	Intended and Unintended Consequences of Warning Messages: A Review and Synthesis of Empirical Research	13, 1	1	22	12	2.95	1.71
11. Andrews, Netemeyer, and Durvasula	Believability and Attitudes Toward Alcohol Warning Label Information: The Role of Persuasive Communications Theory	9	1	21	11	1.91	1.00
12. Ippolito and Mathios	Health Claims in Food Marketing: Evidence on Knowledge and Behavior in the Cereal Market	10, 1	2	21	7	2.10	.70
13. Goodwin	Privacy: Recognition of a Consumer Right	10, 1	10	21	7	2.10	.70
14. Calfee and Pappalardo	Public Policy Issues in Health Claims for Food	10, 1	3	20	9	2.00	.90
15. Andrews and Franke	The Determinants of Cigarette Consumption: A Meta-analysis	10, 1	6	20	15	2.00	1.50
16. Hankin et al.	The Impact of the Alcohol Warning Label on Drinking During Pregnancy	12, 1	2	20	17	2.50	2.13

results reported herein indicate that nonacademic authors are more likely to publish articles in the Policy Watch section or through the annual conferences. Further research exploring publication motivations could be used to design additional strategies to encourage more practitioner participation. Other strategies, such as inviting articles by nonacademics or developing journal-sponsored joint-research efforts (e.g., between the FTC and new assistant professors), may also prove fruitful.

The distribution of authorship is a second issue worthy of discussion. The bulk of contributors to *JPP&M*—78% (467) of the individual authors and 51% (138) of the institutions—have published only a single article in the journal. This does not suggest that authors and institutions with a single published article in *JPP&M* have not made significant contributions. On the contrary, an examination of the 16 most-cited articles appearing in Table 9 reveals that 19 of the 43 authors on those articles appear only once in the journal (though 17 of these 19 authors published with more prolific coauthors). Indeed, the only two sole-authored articles on that list (Goodwin 1991; Hilton 1993) were contributed by authors with only one publication in *JPP&M*. These examples appear to be anomalies, thereby leaving a large number of these one-time authors with a limited influence on the journal. Using a marketing metaphor, these customers have sampled the product (i.e., publication in the journal) but have not made a repeat purchase.

There are several likely reasons a researcher would contribute only one article to *JPP&M*. For example, given the multidisciplinary nature of the journal, authors in other areas (such as sociology, anthropology, economics, and public health) may direct the majority of their scholarly efforts toward publishing in journals that are more specific to their fields. One-time authors also may find the effort-to-reward ratio too high, considering the relatively stringent review process (acceptance rates for regular submissions are under 20% for each of the past four years) and the reluctance of some institutions to rank *JPP&M* alongside journals of similarly low acceptance rates. Indeed, some of the one-time authors may be attempting to republish in the journal but have yet to overcome the acceptance rate figures. Finally, one-time authors, whether or not they are from academe, may not have the publication of academic research as a primary focus of their career efforts.

Further research could examine why authors with one *JPP&M* publication have not published additional research in the journal. Such research could examine individual publication records to determine where other policy-related research is being published. This would provide several important deliverables including a list of reasons researchers do not publish more in *JPP&M,* a list of likely "competitors" for policy-related marketing research, and directions for developing appropriate strategies to influence researchers' submission of more manuscripts to the journal.

A third issue is the steady decline in the participation of assistant professors over the past 15 years of the journal (see Table 5), as well as minimal changes in student participation.

This potential threat to the future of *JPP&M* has not gone unnoticed by leaders in the discipline (e.g., Andrews 1999; Mazis 1997). Recent research suggests that many new scholars in the field are interested in marketing topics related to public policy and society, yet they may not be familiar with the various outlets that publish this type of research (Wilkie and Moore-Shay 1997).

Introducing newer researchers to the journal and maintaining their interest would require a multifaceted approach. Wilkie and Moore-Shay (1997) suggest that increased awareness of research outlets may be helpful, as well as increased coverage of policy and society topics in marketing doctoral programs. Any promotion of the journal to young scholars would need to address a variety of issues, such as the nature of its published research, the perception of the journal's quality in the discipline, upcoming special issues, and review procedures. Similar approaches aimed at academic leaders (e.g., department chairpersons, college deans, doctoral program coordinators) may also prove beneficial and could focus on journal acceptance rates, *SSCI* impact data, and various rankings to illustrate the level of prestige the journal has obtained. In addition, established scholars in the field can continue to encourage and support those newer to the field in their efforts to conduct marketing and public policy research (Andrews 1999; Mazis 1997). The continued development of the recently established mentor program (Andrews 1999) and improved attendance of young scholars at annual conferences and consortia will be helpful in achieving this goal.

THE IMPACT OF *JPP&M*

The overall impact of *JPP&M* in the field was assessed in the current research through two approaches. First, analysis of *SSCI* impact factor data indicated that the journal ranks relatively high in the field since 1992. Note, however, that the current impact of *JPP&M* peaked in 1993 and has not reached such levels since that time. Further research needs to determine the factors that affect the impact of *JPP&M* on the field in order to develop possible strategies for increasing impact. One avenue for such research is to conduct an expanded analysis of *SSCI* data, employing measures other than the current impact factor scores used here (see Zinkhan and Leigh 1999).

Second, an examination of citations showed that nearly 58% of citations of *JPP&M* articles were by non-*JPP&M* articles. This is comparable to Cote, Leong, and Cote's (1991) analysis finding that approximately 60% of citations of *Journal of Consumer Research* were attributed to external sources. From the perspective that a higher percentage of external citations is better (Cote, Leong, and Cote 1991; Hamelman and Mazze 1973), *JPP&M* appears to be doing well. By calculating the proportion of external citations to total citations for each journal issue, we can develop a more detailed understanding of external citations. Although no clear pattern exists for these proportions over time, note that the proportion of external citations is positively related to the overall number of citations for a particular issue ($r = .52, p < .05$).[6] In that a goal of the journal may be to increase overall citations, a potential strategy would be to develop content that is likely to be cited by external sources. Such a goal would need to be balanced with the desire to have contributors accurately represent the nature of prior research as published in the journal—a goal necessitating greater referencing of *JPP&M* articles.

One obvious approach to increasing citation counts is to increase the distribution of the journal. The steady decline in *JPP&M*'s circulation, by approximately 14% over the past five years, is due to declining individual subscriptions (corporate subscriptions have increased slightly). It seems reasonable that if individual subscribers are less informed about the content of the journal (because they no longer subscribe), then citations (and the journal's impact) will decrease. Before developing strategies to combat declines in circulation, further research needs to address why decreases in circulation have occurred. For example, the declines may be due to wider availability of the journal from Web-based resources or perhaps the increased costs associated with traditional subscriptions.

The Breadth and Depth of Research Content

As demonstrated in the content analysis, the nature of what is published in *JPP&M* is broad and touches many areas that are directly and indirectly related to public policy and marketing. Nevertheless, a substantial portion of this research is restricted to relatively few topics. For example, the large majority of knowledge regarding policy and policymaking is based on the U.S. federal government, whereas research on state, local, and international policymaking is relatively isolated. Such a situation is indicative of the balance that should be struck in the journal between sufficient breadth of research topics and sufficient depth at least of what might be determined the "most important" topics.

To illustrate the issue of research breadth and depth for a particular topic area, we analyzed *JPP&M* articles that examine potentially harmful products. Using a process mirroring the content analysis, we developed a simple categorization for potentially harmful products and coded each of the 455 articles with respect to that structure.[7] The breadth of research in this area is represented by 14 categories of potentially harmful products, whereas research depth is illustrated by cigarettes (22 articles) and alcohol (28 articles) jointly accounting for 53.8% of such research in *JPP&M*. The dilemma here

---

[6]Because recent issues with small numbers of citations may bias the result, we conducted the same analysis using only journal issues with at least 20 citations. The result was similar ($r = .43$, $p < .05$).

[7]The 14 categories (number of articles in parentheses) are alcohol (28); chemicals, cleaners, and so forth (2); drugs—illegal (4); drugs—over-the-counter (4); drugs—prescription (10); equipment and appliances (1); food products and additives (5); gambling, lotteries, and sweepstakes (5); medical procedures (1); nutritional and/or dietary supplements (5); sex and pornography (3); tobacco products (22); violent entertainment (e.g., video games) (2); and weapons (1).

is whether future efforts should focus on expanding research breadth or deepening research depth. That is, should researchers be encouraged to investigate potentially harmful products that have not been addressed previously in the journal (e.g., building materials such as asbestos and lead, cosmetic surgery, weight loss products and programs) or to dig deeper into topics that have been only marginally addressed in *JPP&M* (e.g., gambling and lotteries, over-the-counter drugs, weapons)?

One way to address this dilemma is the strategic use of special issues—an obvious prior influence on both breadth and depth of research topics. Indeed, the achievement of Cohen's (2001, p. 8) goal "to broaden the Journal's scope to incorporate penetrating analyses of economic efficiency, competition and industry performance and consumer welfare" will no doubt be aided by the topics solicited in the first special issue under his editorship—an issue focusing on the consumer welfare and economic performance implications of marketing's information technology revolution. Our results indicate that, historically, increased coverage of topics such as antitrust, multinational policymakers, and privacy has been influenced significantly by the special issues that focus on those topics. It is not evident, however, that special issues will result in a stream of manuscripts on a particular topic over time. In addition, because of *JPP&M*'s semiannual publication schedule, special issues on a particular topic are unlikely to be repeated with the frequency needed to ensure steady attention to such topics without increasing the total number of special issues. Unfortunately, increasing the number of issues published per year is a strategy with its own set of drawbacks.

Conclusion

The present research should prove useful for various groups connected with marketing and public policy, including researchers with interests in the field as well as future *JPP&M* editorial teams. For example, scholars may benefit by considering the content analysis when developing their own programs of research in the area, because this analysis provides a deeper understanding of the breadth and depth of research published in the field's leading journal. In addition, current and future editorial teams may consider the results and implications of the publication, citation, and content analyses when designing efforts to enhance the nature, quality, and scope of the journal.

During the past 20 years, *JPP&M* has come to represent a wide base of authors and institutions, has been cited by a wide variety of academic journals, and has offered a varied and unique repertoire of research topics. Although certain individual authors and institutions lead in the quantity of articles published and citations garnered, it is the set of contributions as a whole that has advanced the field and has moved *JPP&M* to its position as the primary outlet for marketing and public policy research.

Appendix A

Alphabetic Listing of Research Topic Structure

Policy and Policymaking

1. Executive Branch
   - Bureau of Alcohol, Tobacco, and Firearms
   - FDA
   - FTC
   - Internal Revenue Service
   - Securities and Exchange Commission
2. Input to General Policymaking Process
   - Academic research
   - Policy formation processes
   - Research methods
3. Judicial Branch
4. Legislative Branch
   - Americans with Disabilities Act
   - Communications Decency Act
   - Dietary Supplement Health Act
   - Fair Credit Reporting Act
   - Foreign Corrupt Practices Act
   - Lanham Act
   - Magnuson—Moss Warranty Act
   - Nutrition Labeling and Education Act
   - Robinson—Patman Act
   - Sherman Antitrust Act
   - Taxation
   - Technology Innovation Act
   - Telephone Consumer Protection Act
5. Multinational Policymakers
6. Non-U.S. Policymakers

Protection of Consumers

1. Deceptive and Unfair Practices
   - Deceptive advertising
   - Other deceptive and unfair practices
   - Unfair advertising
2. Information Provision
   - General information provision
   - Information regarding hazards
   - Presentation and format of information
   - Puffery
   - Remedies for misleading information
3. Privacy
4. Product Performance and Safety
   - Potentially harmful products

- Product misuse, use, and abuse
- Product recalls
- Product warranties

Protection of Marketers

1. Antitrust
2. Commercial Speech
3. Contracts and Agreements
4. Intellectual Property Rights
5. Protection (or Lack of) from Liability
6. Self-Regulation

Societal Issues

1. Corporate Social Responsibility
   - Advertising's effects on society
   - Corporate ethics
   - Exploitative marketing practices
   - Marketing's effects on society
   - Societal marketing
2. Environmental Protection
   - Environmentally responsible behaviors
   - Pollution and waste management
   - Recycling
   - Resource conservation
3. International Issues
   - Countertrade
   - Economic development (United Nations)
   - Exporting
   - Immigration
4. Politics and Public Opinion
   - Elections
   - Lobbying
   - Marketers' perceptions of policy
   - Political activism
   - Public's perceptions of policy
5. Quality of Life
6. Social Marketing
7. Societal Issues
   - Addiction
   - Consumer debt
   - Crime
   - Disease
   - Education
   - Health care
   - Nutrition
   - Poverty
   - Violence

References

American Marketing Association (2001a), e-mail communication, (August 7).

___ (2001b), "Editorial Guidelines," (accessed May 10), [available at http://www.ama.org/pubs/jppm/info/info2.asp].

Andrews, J. Craig (1999), "Editor's Statement," *Journal of Public Policy & Marketing,* 18 (1), 1–2.

___ (2001a), personal e-mail communication, (August 23).

___ (2001b), personal written communication, (November 8).

___ (2001c), "The Use of Marketing Knowledge in Formulating and Enforcing Consumer Protection Policy," in *Handbook of Marketing and Society,* Paul N. Bloom and Gregory T. Gundlach, eds. Thousand Oaks, CA: Sage Publications, 1–33.

___, Richard G. Netemeyer, and Srinivas Durvasula (1990), "Believability and Attitudes Toward Alcohol Warning Label Information: The Role of Persuasive Communications Theory," *Journal of Public Policy & Marketing,* 9, 1–15.

Andrews, Rick and George R. Franke (1991), "The Determinants of Cigarette Consumption: A Meta-Analysis," *Journal of Public Policy & Marketing,* 10 (1), 81–100.

Bettman, James R., John W. Payne, and Richard Staelin (1986), "Cognitive Consideration in Designing Effective Labels for Presenting Risk Information," *Journal of Public Policy & Marketing,* 5, 1–28.

Bloom, Paul N., ed. (1991), *Advances in Marketing and Public Policy: A Research Annual,* Vol. 2. Greenwich, CT: JAI Press.

___ (1997), "Field of Marketing and Public Policy: Introduction and Overview," *Journal of Public Policy & Marketing,* 16 (1), 126–28.

___ and Gregory T. Gundlach, eds. (2001), *Handbook of Marketing and Society.* Thousand Oaks, CA: Sage Publications.

Borokhovich, Kenneth A., Robert J. Bricker, Kelly R. Brunarski, and Betty J. Simkins (1995), "Finance Research Productivity and Influence," *Journal of Finance,* 50 (5), 1691–717.

Brucks, Merrie, Andrew A. Mitchell, and Richard Staelin (1984), "The Effect of Nutritional Information Disclosure in Advertising: An Information Processing Approach," *Journal of Public Policy & Marketing,* 3, 1–25.

Calfee, John E. and Janis K. Pappalardo (1991), "Public Policy Issues in Health Claims for Food," *Journal of Public Policy & Marketing,* 10 (1), 33–53.

Clark, Gary L. (1985), "Productivity Ratings of Institutions Based on Publications in Eight Marketing Journals: 1983–1984," *Journal of Marketing Education,* 7 (Fall), 12–23.

Cohen, Dorothy (1995), *Legal Issues in Marketing Decision Making.* Cincinnati OH: South-Western.

Cohen, Joel B. (2001), "Consumer Behavior, Marketing and Public Policy: My Goals for *JPP&M,*" *ACR News,* (March/April), 8–9.

Cote, Joseph A., Siew Meng Leong, and Jane Cote (1991), "Assessing the Influence of *Journal of Consumer Research*: A Citation Analysis," *Journal of Consumer Research,* 18 (December), 402–10.

Eaton, John P., James C. Ward, Ajith Kumar, and Peter H. Reingen (1999), "Structural Analysis of Co-author Relationships and Author Productivity in Selected Outlets for Consumer Behavior Research," *Journal of Consumer Psychology,* 8 (1), 39–59.

Ellen, Pam Scholder, Joshua Lyle Wiener, and Cathy Cobb-Walgren (1991), "The Role of Perceived Consumer Effectiveness in Motivating Environmentally Conscious Behaviors," *Journal of Public Policy & Marketing,* 10 (2), 102–17.

Federal Trade Commission (2001), "Vision, Mission and Goals," (accessed May 12), [available at http://www.ftc.gov/ftc/mission.htm].

Fields, D. Michael and Linda E. Swayne (1988), "Publication in Major Marketing Journals: 1960–1986," *Journal of Marketing Education,* 10 (Fall), 36–48.

Floyd, Steven W., Dean M. Schroeder, and Dale M. Finn (1994), "'Only If I'm First Author': Conflict over Credit in Management Scholarship," *Academy of Management Journal,* 37 (3), 734–47.

Frey, Cynthia J., Thomas C. Kinnear, and Bonnie B. Reece (1979), *Public Policy Issues in Marketing.* Ann Arbor, MI: University of Michigan.

Goodwin, Cathy (1991), "Privacy: Recognition of a Consumer Right," *Journal of Public Policy & Marketing,* 10 (1), 149–66.

Granzin, Kent L. and Janeen E. Olsen (1991), "Characterizing Participants in Activities Protecting the Environment," *Journal of Public Policy & Marketing,* 10 (2), 1–27.

Grewal, Dhruv and Larry D. Compeau (1999), "Pricing and Public Policy: A Research Agenda and an Overview of the Special Issue," *Journal of Public Policy & Marketing,* 18(Spring), 3–11.

Gundlach, Gregory T. (2001), "Marketing and Modern Antitrust Thought," in *Handbook of Marketing and Society,* Paul N. Bloom and Gregory T. Gundlach, eds. Thousand Oaks, CA: Sage Publications, 34–50.

Hamelman, Paul W. and Edward M. Mazze (1973), "Cross-Referencing Between AMA Journals and Other Publications," *Journal of Marketing Research,* 10 (May), 215–18.

Hankin, Janet R., Ira J. Firestone, James J. Sloan, Joel W. Ager, Allen C. Goodman, Robert J. Sokol, and Susan S. Martier (1993), "The Impact of the Alcohol Warning Label on Drinking During Pregnancy," *Journal of Public Policy & Marketing,* 12 (1), 10–18.

Hill, Ronald Paul (1995), "Researching Sensitive Topics in Marketing: The Special Case of Vulnerable Populations," *Journal of Public Policy & Marketing,* 14 (Spring), 143–48.

___, ed. (1996), *Marketing and Consumer Research in the Public Interest.* Thousand Oaks, CA: Sage Publications.

Hilton, Michael E. (1993), "An Overview of Recent Findings of Alcoholic Beverage Warning Labels," *Journal of Public Policy & Marketing,* 12 (1), 1–9.

Hult, G. Tomas M., William T. Neese, and R. Edward Bashaw (1997), "Faculty Perceptions of Marketing Journals," *Journal of Marketing Education,* 19 (Spring), 37–52.

Inkpen, Andrew and Paul Beamish (1994), "An Analysis of Twenty-Five Years of Research in the *Journal of International Business Studies*," *Journal of International Business Studies,* 25 (4), 703–14.

Ippolito, Pauline M. and Alan D. Mathios (1991), "Health Claims in Food Marketing: Evidence on Knowledge and Behavior in the Cereal Market," *Journal of Public Policy & Marketing,* 10 (1), 15–32.

Kinnear, Thomas C. (1982), "Editor's Statement," *Journal of Marketing & Public Policy,* 1, 1.

___ (1986), "Editor's Statement," *Journal of Public Policy & Marketing,* 5, 1.

___ (1997), "An Historic Perspective on the Quantity and Quality of Marketing and Public Policy Research," *Journal of Public Policy & Marketing,* 16 (1), 144–46.

___ (2001), personal e-mail communication, (September 11).

Laverie, Debra A. and Patrick E. Murphy (1993), "The Marketing and Public Policy Literature: A Look at the Past Ten Years," *Journal of Public Policy & Marketing,* 12 (Fall), 258–67.

Levy, Alan S., Odonna Mathews, Marilyn Stephenson, Janet E. Tenney, and Raymond E. Schucker (1985), "The Impact of a Nutrition Information Program on Food Purchases," *Journal of Public Policy & Marketing,* 4, 1–13.

Malhotra, Naresh K. (1996), "The Impact of the Academy of Marketing Science on Marketing Scholarship: An Analysis of the Research Published in *JAMS*," *Journal of the Academy of Marketing Science,* 24 (4), 291–98.

Mazis, Michael B. (1997), "Marketing and Public Policy: Prospects for the Future," *Journal of Public Policy & Marketing,* 16 (Spring), 139–43.

___ (2001), personal e-mail communication, (August 23).

___, Louis A. Morris, and John L. Swasy (1991), "An Evaluation of the Alcohol Warning Label: Initial Survey Results," *Journal of Public Policy & Marketing,* 10 (1), 229–41.

Milne, George R. (2000), "Privacy and Ethical Issues in Database/Interactive Marketing and Public Policy: A Research Framework and Overview of the Special Issue," *Journal of Public Policy & Marketing,* 19 (Spring), 1–7.

Murphy, Patrick E. (2001), personal e-mail communication, (September 4).

Perreault, William D. and Laurence E. Leigh (1989), "Reliability of Nominal Data Based on Qualitative Judgments," *Journal of Marketing Research,* 26 (May), 135–48.

Rust, Roland T. and Bruce Cooil (1994), "Reliability Measures for Qualitative Data: Theory and Implications," *Journal of Marketing Research,* 31 (February), 1–14.

Scammon, Debra L. (2001), personal e-mail communication, (August 23).

___, Robert N. Mayer, and Ken R. Smith (1991), "Alcohol Warnings: How Do You Know When You Have Had One Too Many?" *Journal of Public Policy & Marketing,* 10 (1), 214–28.

Schroeder, Dean M., Frederick W. Langrehr, and Steven M. Floyd (1995), "Marketing Journal Coauthorship: Is It a Hit or a Miss with Coauthors?" *Journal of Marketing Education,* 15 (Summer), 45–58.

Schwepker, Charles H. and T. Bettina Cornwell (1991), "An Examination of Ecologically Concerned Consumers and Their Intention to Purchase Ecologically Packaged Products," *Journal of Public Policy & Marketing,* 10 (2), 77–101.

Stewart, David W. and Ingrid M. Martin (1994), "Intended and Unintended Consequences of Warning Messages: A Review and Synthesis of Empirical Research," *Journal of Public Policy & Marketing,* 13 (1), 1–19.

Urban, David J., Jane P. Wayland, and Dennis R. McDermott (1992), "An Empirical Investigation of Research Standards for Marketing Faculty at AACSB-Accredited Business Schools," *Journal of Marketing Education,* 14 (Summer), 53–67.

Wilkie, William L. (1997), "Developing Research on Public Policy and Marketing," *Journal of Public Policy & Marketing,* 16 (1), 132–36.

___ and Elizabeth S. Moore-Shay (1997), "Consortium Survey on Marketing and Society Issues: Summary and Results," *Journal of Macromarketing,* 17 (2), 89–95.

Zinkhan, George M. and Thomas W. Leigh (1999), "Assessing the Quality Ranking of the *Journal of Advertising,* 1986–1997," *Journal of Advertising,* 28 (2), 51–70.

Marketing and Society: What Has Marketing Thought Contributed and What Does the Future Hold?

Debra L. Scammon and Marlys J. Mason

Introduction

As the field of marketing has evolved it has become clear that marketing knowledge and tools can contribute to society in a number of ways. These contributions come not just by informing decisions made in the corporate setting, but also by guiding the activities of nonprofit and social marketers as well as by influencing the formulation of public policy. To capture the full scope of the influence of marketing knowledge, one must assess its direct and short-term impacts on marketing decisions by all types of organizations, as well as its indirect and longer-term impacts on the economy as a whole and societal and consumer well-being.

In their book, *Handbook of Marketing & Society* (2001), Bloom and Gundlach provide a succinct model depicting the variety of potential impacts of marketing knowledge and decisions throughout the economy (see Figure 1). They suggest that not only does marketing knowledge affect decisions of corporate marketers, policy makers, and nonprofit and social marketers, but there are also reciprocal effects among these three domains based upon decisions that each makes. Further, the Bloom and Gundlach model depicts decisions in each of the domains impacting competition within markets, economic growth and development, and consumer welfare. We use the Bloom and Gundlach model as a basis for discussing how the flow of marketing knowledge works its way through to these societal impacts. Throughout our discussion we highlight interrelationships within the marketplace in order to provide the reader with a broader understanding of the ways in which marketing thought has impacted market dynamics. Not all of the linkages in the Bloom and Gundlach model have attracted equal attention by researchers and these gaps in knowledge offer opportunities for future research. Recent contributions to marketing knowledge also present opportunities for taking a fresh look at public policy and social

DEBRA L. SCAMMON is the Emma Eccles Jones Professor of Marketing in the David Eccles School of Business at the University of Utah and MARLYS J. MASON is an Assistant Professor of Marketing in the William S. Spears School of Business at the Oklahoma State University.

Scammon, Debra L. and Marlys J. Mason (2006), "Marketing and Society: What Has Marketing Thought Contributed and What Does the Future Hold?"

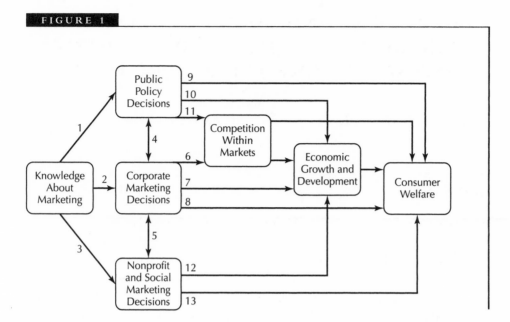

marketing activities to ensure that consumer welfare is considered at the level of both the individual consumer and society.

The formulation and implementation of public policies governing marketer actions often are stimulated by observation of breakdowns in the functioning of the marketplace. Because competition within markets is influenced by corporate marketing decisions, public policy decisions, and the reciprocal relationship between the two (as depicted in the Bloom and Gundlach model, linkages 6 and 11), we look at the flow of marketing knowledge to businesses and to public policy together. To demonstrate the successes of and potential for application of marketing knowledge by nonprofit entities and in the context of social marketing, we discuss both why and how marketing is used in this domain and the impacts upon economic development (linkage 12) and consumer welfare (linkage 13). We contend, however, that although each domain depicted in the Bloom and Gundlach model can impact consumer welfare, the greatest positive impacts are likely to be achieved through the synergy of actions in all three domains. The potential for such synergy highlights the important interrelationships of decisions in the three areas of corporate marketing, public policy, and social and nonprofit marketing. We conclude with some observations about future opportunities for refining and applying marketing knowledge.

Exploring the System

THE CONSUMER BILL OF RIGHTS

As depicted in the Bloom and Gundlach model, consumer welfare is an ultimate result from operation of the marketplace. An early expression of concern for the interests of consumers was highlighted in a historic speech to Congress in 1962 by President Kennedy in which he set out what has become known as the Consumer Bill of Rights (Lampman 1988). At their essence, the four essential consumer rights outlined in this Bill provide guidance to both policy makers and corporate marketers. According to the Bill, all consumers should enjoy: the Right to *Safety,* the Right to be *Informed,* the Right to *Choose,* and the Right to be *Heard.*

The Right to be Informed and the Right to Choose are essential to the smooth functioning of a free marketplace. The assumption is that competition within markets will be enhanced when consumers have access to relevant information that is not fraudulent or misleading, thereby enabling them to make better choices (Bloom 1989; Nelson 1970). Consumers will be more likely to meet their needs if an array of competitive offerings is available at fair prices. Importantly, consumers' choices will give clear direction to producers as to the product offerings that best meet consumers' needs and wants. The belief that information and choice are essential components of a competitive market and contribute to consumer welfare underscored many of the actions taken by the Federal Trade Commission (FTC) during the 1970s. A Task Force formed by the FTC at the end of the 1970s developed a briefing book, *"Consumer Information Remedies: Policy Review Session"* (FTC 1979) that laid out a framework for considering the impacts information could have in the marketplace and the consequences that could occur when accurate and relevant information was not available to support consumer decision making. Several members of that task force collaborated on an article published in the *Journal of Marketing* in 1981 (Mazis, Staelin, Beales and Salop) that summarized the theoretical foundation for reliance on information to enhance the competitiveness of the marketplace. Their article identified principles for the use of information to help align the interests of buyers and sellers. For example, they suggest that the information environment can be improved by reducing advertising regulation, mandating information disclosure and standards, and banning deceptive claims. They argue that if information flow is improved, then competition is improved and consumers in general will benefit. The influence of members of the original FTC Task Force on the field of marketing and public policy cannot be overemphasized. Recently, for example, Howard Beales served as the Director of the Bureau of Consumer Protection at the FTC from 2001 to 2004.

During the last two decades a number of consumer protection regulations have been enacted to enhance the information available to consumers. For example, the Nutrition Labeling and Education Act (NLEA) of 1990 requires food manufacturers to include information about the nutritional content of their products on food labels. With passage of this Act, it was also hoped that, in anticipation of consumer response to such information, the labeling requirement would also encourage sellers to begin offering a broader selection of items, some of which would have superior nutrition content. Later evaluation research by a marketing academic (Moorman 1998) demonstrated that in fact sellers did change their product lines following the passage of this rule. Moorman's findings provide evidence that more nutritious products entered the market following the passage of the NLEA. If one considers consumer welfare for consumers in general, it appears that the NLEA had the desired effects.

However, focusing upon the positive effects of enhanced information flow for consumers at large can be misleading because it overlooks the potential negative effects for individual consumers. Moorman's findings (1996, 1998) suggest that not all consumers benefited equally from competitive reactions to the NLEA. While information-seeking consumers acquired more nutritional information and influenced firms to provide better quality products, the healthier product offerings shifted away from price promotions putting them out of reach of poorer consumers. Further, not all consumers had the motivation or incentive to compare product offerings. Moorman's findings suggest that valuable insights into the ways that public policy interventions are likely to play out in the marketplace can come from recognizing that there are important differences among consumers and that the actions of members of one segment of consumers stimulated by an intervention can have both positive and negative impacts on other segments (Moorman and Price 1989).

Beyond information and choice, the Consumer Bill of Rights also emphasizes the right of consumers to be protected from products hazardous to their health. As with information and choice, the presumption of a Right to Safety has guided both corporate marketing decisions and public policy. Marketers frequently test prototypes of new products to determine how they might be used by consumers. If products are found to be unsafe, marketers may redesign them before introducing them to the market and may develop warning labels or use instructions to help consumers avoid harm. In some industries, such as the pharmaceutical industry, product safety is overseen by specific state and federal agencies. The Food and Drug Administration (FDA) monitors both product safety and efficacy, requiring that before being offered on the market, prescription drugs must meet strict standards of evidence of both safety and efficacy. The Consumer Product Safety Commission also sets standards for the composition and design of consumer products that help ensure products will not harm users. A variety of warnings, use instructions, and disclosures of contra-indications for use of products are also required to help ensure that consumers' safety is secure. In addition to pre-market activities to promote safety, there are also programs designed to identify safety problems that occur in the market. These programs curtail risks through voluntary or mandatory product recalls and require affirmative communications to consumers known to have purchased unsafe products. Important protections for consumers harmed by unsafe products are found in product liability laws that allow injured consumers to receive damages from the manufacturer and/or seller of defective products. The definition of what is defective includes products with manufacturing defects (items do not meet the manufacturer's own design specifications or design standards common in the industry), products that do not have adequate warnings or use instructions (products that do not provide information about possible risks for improper use of the product, including how to avoid the dangers and what to do if the danger is encountered), and products that have design defects (products for which a safer design is feasible but which the manufacturer has not adopted). Generally speaking, product liability is "strict," meaning that if the product is found to be defective, the manufacturer is liable regardless of fault. Manufacturers also have liability for the sale of products that fail to comply with stated warranties (Stern and Eovaldi 1984).

The final right included in the Consumer Bill of Rights is that consumers will have assurance that their interests will be heard and considered in shaping public policies (Lampman 1988). The Right to be Heard was conceived as a means of ensuring that consumers' interests had "a seat at the table" in discussions of how the marketplace was or should be functioning. A significant outcome of the articulation of this Right was President Kennedy's establishment of the Consumer Advisory Council in 1962 and later identification of a Special Assistant to the President for Consumer Affairs. The existence of these advocates for the interests of consumers influenced several actions including amendments to the Food and Drug Act, truth-in lending laws, and fair packaging and labeling rules (Lampman 1988). As another way of ensuring that consumers' voices are included in policy planning, several federal agencies have implemented hearing and comment procedures that are followed when new regulations are being proposed. Comments are frequently solicited while new regulations are being formulated, and hearings provide the opportunity for comments by consumers, businesses, and other involved spokespersons. (The call for comments on proposed regulations is frequently published in the Federal Register as are summaries and analyses of the testimony provided). This process of public participation has in several cases led to an exponential growth in the research-based literature on particular topics. For example, the FTC's proposed trade regulation rule on Children's Advertising spawned a large volume of new research on the impacts of advertising on children (National Science Foundation 1978).

These four principles outlined in the Consumer Bill of Rights paved the way for advancing consumer welfare and remain a guiding force that continues to shape both marketing and public policy actions (Andreasen 1991). Current policies and regulations are intended to enhance consumer decision making, stimulate competitive activity, and protect public health and welfare without placing undue burdens upon businesses. At the same time, many businesses are taking affirmative actions to help consumers effectively navigate the marketplace and obtain products and services that meet their needs. Thus, a meshing of the interests of consumers and businesses can be stimulated through both public and corporate policies.

MARKETING AND COMPETITION POLICY

Linkage 4 in the Bloom and Gundlach model (refer to Figure 1) makes the point that corporate marketing decisions and public policy decisions have a reciprocal impact on each other. The underlying system belief is that the smooth functioning of the marketplace depends upon competitors interacting effectively. Thus, it is also important in this area to examine how marketers' actions actually impact competition (Linkage 6 in the Bloom and Gundlach model; refer to Figure 1). For competition to flourish, competitors should not engage in unfair or anticompetitive practices. The entire field of antitrust economics has grown up around the concern that concentration of economic power in the hands of too few competitors (at the extreme, a single monopolist) could ultimately diminish consumer welfare. Here public policy decisions have also helped shape the level of competition (Linkage 11 in the Bloom and Gundlach model; Figure 1). Rules against monopolistic practices such as predatory pricing, exclusive dealing, collusion, bundling and a variety of other marketing tactics have been enacted because such practices potentially have negative impacts on other competitors, decreasing competition and ultimately harming consumers. Much of the research on these topics appears in the law and economics literature. Within marketing, Sprott and Miyazaki (2002) note that about 1/4 of the articles published over the 20-year history of the *Journal of Public Policy & Marketing* deal with protection of marketers, with an increasing trend in recent years. Some highly visible investigations and legal proceedings of suspect marketing practices have occurred during this time, including issues such as bundling (a specific Internet browser packaged as part of a branded computer), anticompetitive slotting allowances (large retailer insisting upon manufacturers paying a fee to have preferential display space), discriminatory promotional pricing practices (advertise a sale price as a discount from a fictitious prior price) and exclusive dealing arrangements (a retailer agreeing to stock a manufacturer's product only if the manufacturer agrees not to sell to a competitive retailer). With an increased interest in relationship marketing, new issues have arisen regarding how power is wielded within the channel of distribution. For example, as "big box" retailers, such as Wal-Mart, gain a more dominant place in the market for many consumer products, they may be able to use their power to make new forms of demands upon their suppliers, with new consequences for competing suppliers as well as possibly for consumers.

MARKETING AND ECONOMIC DEVELOPMENT

Both as a goal itself (Linkages 7 and 10 in Figure 1) and as a means to enhance consumer welfare, economic growth and development is highlighted in the Bloom and Gundlach model as an area on which corporate marketing and public policy decisions have a direct impact and an area on which they exert an indirect impact through competition. As

Klein and Nason (2001) point out, there is a bi-directional relationship between marketing and development. At the same time that marketing is influenced by and adapting to its environment, the outcomes from the application of marketing knowledge are impacting economic, social, political, and ecological systems. Applied to economic development, marketing makes many contributions, including improved outcomes in domestic and export markets, increased employment, standard of living, and social conditions embedded in "Quality of Life" including access to and quality of health care, education, cultural opportunities, and civic freedoms. Marketing knowledge will also impact methods of distribution, channel structure, products, pricing methods, and other features of the marketing system that is evolving within a developing economy. Notably, in recent times many countries have moved toward capitalist systems, and the expansion of these economies has been strongly shaped by modern marketing thought.

SOCIAL AND NONPROFIT MARKETING

The application of marketing knowledge to social issues and problems and in nonprofit settings (Linkage 3, Figure 1) also can lead to the enhancement of economic growth and development (Linkage 12, Figure 1) and of consumer welfare (Linkage 13, Figure 1). In the late 1960s and early 1970s marketing literature first began to consider ways in which marketing knowledge could be expanded to other settings, especially in support of nonprofit organizations. For example, Kotler and Zaltman (1971, p. 5) observed that marketers ". . . have advised churches on how to increase membership, charities on how to raise money, and art museums and symphonies on how to attract more patrons. . . ." Early advice from marketing experts emphasized more than just communications. Kotler and Zaltman (1971), for example, suggested that the design, implementation, and control of programs was best accomplished by considering the full range of marketing mix components that might be employed in reaching an organization's goals—product planning, pricing, communication, distribution, and marketing research.

In the years since, marketing knowledge has helped many nonprofit organizations to achieve their goals within constrained budgets. Cultural and educational organizations have learned to appeal to diverse target audiences through programming and targeted promotional messages. Healthcare organizations have employed concepts of effective distribution to locate new clinics and an understanding of portfolio packaging to determine which services to offer at these locations (for example, diagnostic and pharmacy services). Arts organizations have used consumer research to help design their program offerings and build consumer loyalty and patronage through the effective use of price incentives such as season ticket subscriptions and family ticket packages.

In the late 1970s and early 1980s the field began in earnest to consider whether and how marketing tools and techniques might also be applied to social causes. By then few marketers disputed the relevance of marketing to the management of nonprofit organizations but the application of marketing to the furtherance of social causes raised some controversies (Fox and Kotler 1980). Some felt that putting marketing to such uses was manipulative; others felt it was wasteful to spend money on marketing rather than the cause at hand; still others felt it would increase the "noise" in society and thus was distasteful. Despite these criticisms, the potential for societal benefits as a result of the application of a marketing perspective has been recognized by several leaders in our field.

For consumers, it is interesting to consider that marketplace exchange can also facilitate the achievement of more meaningful lives and greater social good. For example, Russell Belk (1986), in his Presidential Address to the Association for Consumer Research noted that consumer researchers needed to "recognize the full complexity of the relationship between consumption and the rest of life." A few years later, Alan Andreasen (1993) used his Presidential Address to advocate that marketing knowledge be used to help address some of the world's critical health problems such as infant mortality, juvenile delinquency, and drug abuse. Recently, in his ACR Presidential Address, David Mick reiterated the need to impact consumer welfare and quality of life and called for more transformative consumer research ". . . that strive(s) to respect, uphold, and improve life . . ." (2006, p. 2).

Recent discussions about healthcare reform have emphasized the importance of including public health initiatives, not just programs to improve access to and quality of individual medical care, in strategies to improve consumer health and societal welfare. Initiatives aimed at curtailing obesity in order to help reduce health care needs for lifestyle-related diseases and enhanced availability and use of vaccines to prevent the spread of illnesses are two such possibilities that could enhance overall quality of life. Marketing knowledge could have an important role to play in helping ensure that campaigns supporting such public health initiatives are effective.

Social issues and public health initiatives present particularly challenging problems since they frequently involve personal and immediate costs in order to achieve social and long-term desired benefits. By individuals taking preventive measures today, the future health and financial well being of citizens generally will be enhanced. Thus, with immunization campaigns, for example, individuals must be encouraged to get vaccinated today in order that both they and consumers in general will have a higher quality of life in the long run. Rothschild (1999) suggests that because of the self-interested nature of consumers, such a campaign is more likely to be effective if it recognizes differences among consumers and uses different approaches to encourage the desired behavior among different segments. He specifically suggests using different combinations of education, laws and regulations, and marketing depending upon the segment. For example, for consumers who are motivated to immunize their children and have the ability and the opportunity to do so, education efforts to increase awareness and remind of the importance of immunizations may be all that is needed to increase compliance. For persons who may be motivated to immunize their children, but lack the financial ability, marketing efforts to provide low-cost or free immunization programs would be worthwhile. Individuals who are not motivated to immunize their children because of resistance based on personal beliefs may only respond if laws are enacted that ensure compliance (for example, children not being admitted to public school without proof of immunization). Similarly, anti-smoking campaigns must encourage individual behavior change in order to create positive impacts. Those impacted include those who quit, those around them who will no longer have to deal with secondhand smoke, and ultimately members of society at large who won't have to bear the costs of premature death and debilitating health. Campaigns such as these have benefited from marketing thought both in terms of message design and target marketing. As more social causes embrace the concepts of marketing, it will be important to understand the motivation of individual consumers to engage in preventive measures and pro-social behaviors. Because such behaviors often require personal sacrifice and because the messages used to encourage such sacrifices can have very subtle interpretations by and impacts on consumers, it is important to assess in advance and monitor the impact of such campaigns on diverse segments of consumers.

Although there are many examples of the effective use of marketing knowledge to improve actions of both nonprofit and social marketers, the impacts of marketing in these settings have typically been assessed by looking at short-term results in dealing with individual issues. If one steps back from the immediate problems facing a specific organization, and looks at the larger system, even more possibilities exist for positive results from the application of marketing knowledge. When assessing the impact of marketing in the context of nonprofit organizations and social causes, consumer welfare should be assessed not just according to the material acquisitions achieved through the market, but in terms of such measures as satisfaction, consumer sentiment, and quality of life at both the individual consumer level and at the macro level of our consumer society. This perspective is reflected in a model by Ruby and Nikhilesh Dholakia (2001) that suggests that aspects of the macro environment, such as education, health, increased income, and population control can be impacted through specific targeted programs that can be enhanced with the application of marketing knowledge. In this process it is also important to recognize the constraints and opportunities presented by contextual forces such as technology, politics, and level of development of the infrastructure. They emphasize the interrelationships of base states (such as level of health in the general population) with program components (such as employment targets to increase population income) and the context within which they will be managed (such as the availability of technology). If all of these are carefully aligned, the result can be enhanced economic development and ultimate consumer welfare.

In this section we have traced the impacts of marketing thought throughout the marketplace and society at large by providing a systematic look at relationships among the primary players in the market system, how they each use marketing, and how these uses impact and are impacted by entities in the other domains. We turn now to some challenges for the future in refining and advancing the positive impacts marketing thought can have for consumers and for society at large.

Challenges for the Future

Marketing knowledge impacts the aggregate market, and ultimately consumer welfare, through both direct and indirect (mediated) effects. The interdependency of consumers and businesses emphasizes the need to carefully consider the intended and unintended consequences that may result from incentives designed to stimulate business and consumer behavior. To accurately anticipate these consequences, it is important to take a closer look at the individual characteristics of market participants. Rather than focus on consumers in general, it is important to consider the circumstances of individual consumers, and to use marketing knowledge and a broad arsenal of exchange concepts to shape pubic policies and social efforts that will enhance consumer welfare at both the individual and societal level.

INDIVIDUAL CONSUMER WELFARE

Ensuring that information is readily available for consumers to use in making sound decisions has been a priority concern of businesses, policy makers, and social and non-profit marketers. It has been assumed that more information is better both for consumers and for the efficient functioning of markets. As we have been focusing on the amount of information available in the market, the qualitative nature of the information environment has been changing as well with the appearance of new types of information, the advent of new media (the Internet, telemarketing), and the entry of new sources (consumer advocates, educators, chat room hosts). Thus, an important question for the future is whether information may also have unintended effects, increasing the "noise" in exchange, and distracting or even deceiving consumers.

Requirements for labeling on dietary supplements provides an interesting example of a new type of information (Dietary Supplement Health and Education Act 1994). In order to protect consumers from ineffective and/or potentially harmful dietary supplements, the information remedy adopted was that supplement advertisers be required to disclose the fact that the Food and Drug Administration (FDA) has not evaluated the product or its performance claims. Now, if one considers that consumers have become accustomed to the FDA testing and approving prescription drugs and their claims prior to marketing, then it is not surprising that some consumers may also expect that those same protections will be in place for dietary supplements (Mason and Scammon 2000). If so, some consumers—particularly those with a chronic illness for which they have found no other treatment—might ignore the new, unfamiliar disclaimer and not take important precautions in deciding whether to use dietary supplements.

With the proliferation of new media and sources of information, the reliability of some of the information available and consumers' ability to discern accurate and helpful information also become issues deserving attention. For example, the Internet has become a primary source of information for consumers. Health information is one of the types of information sought on the Internet and consumers often go there before (or even in lieu of) talking to a physician about a health concern. Although some self-regulation of the health information available on the Internet is beginning (Miaoulis and Bodkin 2005) consumers still may not have a clear idea of the source of information they encounter. The American Medical Association's "Guidelines for Medical and Health Information Sites on the Internet" (Winker et al. 2000) suggest that websites should clearly name the source or authors of editorial content, identify funding or sponsorship of any specific content, and distinguish advertising from editorial content. However, these guidelines apply only to AMA websites and other health sites are not policed for compliance. The reliability of information on the Internet remains an issue particularly because at least some consumers may not consider the credibility and trustworthiness (even if they make note of the source) of information they obtain.

A second issue deserving careful consideration is the assumption that consumers approach decision making with active information search and careful consideration of all alternatives. There is increasing evidence that emotions, experiences, and social influences motivate consumer behavior at least as much as deliberate and rational decision making. Recent research suggests biased reasoning, hopes and desires, and subjective knowledge can affect information search and processing (MacInnis and de Mello 2005; Mason and Scammon in progress; Moorman et al. 2004). Consumers may be driven by a longing for favorable outcomes, such as improved health or increased financial security, and seek goods, services, and sources that they believe will help them achieve those aspirations. Consumers may constrain their search for information to sources they anticipate will provide desired content; they may also "believe" information they want to hear while disregarding information contrary to the message they wish to hear. Consumers' experiences are likely to be influenced by their hopes and desires, especially when product and service performance is difficult (or impossible) for consumers to assess (for example, health and financial services). Consumers also use consumption of such products and services to help them cope emotionally with future uncertainties and fears. In such cases, there is the potential for consumer harm both with regard to their immediate experience and with regard to their intentions for future use of the product.

The concept of "experiential consumption" is also interesting to consider. Some consumers see their behaviors in the marketplace as a means of self-expression and even at times of resisting social or political forces with which they do not agree. For example, adolescents may make the decision to smoke (despite knowing the health risks associated with tobacco) as a way to demonstrate their independence and to denounce the direction from an authoritative source (like the Federal Government) that they should not smoke. Athletes, envisioning exceptional performance in their sport, may decide to take dietary supplements to boost their physical strength and/or stamina, despite knowing that the supplements may carry some health risks, both short and long term. It is also possible that some consumers may engage in risky behaviors precisely because they are risky. To risk seekers, information that suggests a particular behavior is potentially dangerous may make that behavior appear particularly attractive.

In addition to recognizing the differences among consumers and the likelihood of different reactions to changes in the information environment, it is important also to consider the possibility that some consumers may be particularly vulnerable in marketplace exchanges. Vulnerability is not merely a result of a personal characteristic (young, elderly, disabled), but can be exacerbated by situational factors (physical mobility barriers, grief, illness), complicated by society's response to personal circumstances (poverty, ethnicity), and importantly, accentuated by the simultaneous interaction of a number of these factors. Additional work to help understand the factors that contribute to consumer vulnerability, the consequences of being vulnerable, and the avenues for minimizing or eliminating vulnerability is needed. Policy solutions and/or marketplace interventions are not likely to be effective on their own; thus, it is important to understand how consumer resilience can be strengthened and the role, if any, that marketing knowledge can have in fostering self-sufficiency. Further, it is important to consider whether and how public and social policies may themselves contribute to consumers' vulnerability.

SOCIETAL WELL-BEING

Beyond the immediate impact of marketing thought on the well-being of individual consumers and the functioning of the marketplace, it is important to step back and examine the role of marketing thought on societal well-being more broadly. As discussed earlier, many public policies and social issue campaigns are designed to impact societal welfare through the actions of individual consumers and businesses. Issues such as public health, environmental quality, and economic stability, for example, are impacted by the decisions of individual consumers and businesses.

Through the implementation and evaluation of campaigns designed to influence individual consumer behaviors so that broader social goals may be reached, we have learned that messages can be interpreted in subtly different ways. For example, there appears to be a relationship between one's willingness to take personal action and perceptions of the likelihood of similar actions by others (Wiener and Doescher 1994). When individuals perceive that others are unlikely to engage in a behavior (for example, recycling) they may also elect not to adopt that pro-social behavior. In other contexts, individuals may disassociate themselves from the role/peer models or messages in social marketing campaigns causing them to tune out and ignore the message.

There is some evidence that social marketing campaigns may even boomerang, causing consumers to hold stronger positive attitudes and intentions toward the socially undesirable behavior. For example, a stop-smoking campaign that presents information on the incidence of lung cancer among smokers could result in some consumers seeing the likelihood of contracting the disease as lower than originally expected, thus reducing their perception of risks associated with smoking (Pechmann and Slater 2005). To increase the likelihood that public policies and social marketing campaigns will have their intended positive impact on the quality of life of consumers, it is important that the differences among consumers and markets be carefully considered. All of the nuances of marketing knowledge should be explored as they apply to the crafting of successful social marketing campaigns.

The quality of life experienced by consumers across multiple domains (health, education, employment) accumulates into a state of overall societal welfare. As discussed earlier, marketing thought has been applied in many domains. Because these domains are often integrally related, a systems perspective on the relationships between and among the players in the marketplace may help to identify even more ways in which marketing thought can impact quality of life in specific domains and ultimately societal welfare. Here too, it is important to pay particular attention to the possibility of unintended consequences from policy interventions as interventions designed to enhance health (for example) could have negative impacts on employment. Consideration of impacts on many quality of life domains should be heeded. More attention needs to be devoted to understanding the transferability of knowledge, such that successes and best practices in one domain can be used to enhance the activities in another. Importantly, more research is needed to understand the synergy of actions by marketers, policy makers, and social and nonprofit marketers in stimulating positive social and individual outcomes.

There is no doubt that marketing thought has found its way into the marketplace through its use by various players. As businesses, policy makers, and social and nonprofit marketers have implemented marketing approaches, they have influenced each other and have had impacts on consumers and society. The relationships among the players and the dynamics of their actions are far more complex than can be captured in even a comprehensive model. Thus, though we have learned much about the impact of information and incentives in marketplace exchanges, there is more to learn. Observations in one context can provide insights in a different setting. Careful attention to the nuisances of individuals, entities, and their relationships can offer new insights. The richness of the interrelations among the various actors in the marketplace provides opportunities for extending and fine-tuning marketing approaches to better fit particular settings and objectives. There are many interesting roles yet to be discovered for marketing knowledge in our world.

References

Andreasen, Alan R. (1991) "Consumer Research and Social Policy," *Handbook of Consumer Behavior,* Thomas Robertson and Harold Kassarjian, Editors. Englewood Cliffs, NJ: Prentice Hall, pp. 459–506.

Andreasen, Alan R. (1993), "The Future of the Association for Consumer Research: Backward to the Past," *European Advances in Consumer Research,* Vol. 1, 1–4.

Belk, Russell W. (1986), "ACR address: Happy Thought," *Advances in Consumer Research,* Melanie Wallendorf and Paul Anderson, Editors. Vol. XIV, 1–6.

Bloom, Paul N. (1989), "A Decision Model for Prioritizing and Addressing Consumer Information Problems," *Journal of Public Policy & Marketing,* 8, 161–80.

Bloom, Paul N. and Gregory T. Gundlach (2001), "Introduction," *Handbook of Marketing and Society.* Thousand Oaks, CA: Sage Publications, pp. xiii–xxii.

Dholakia, Ruby Roy and Nikhilesh Dholakia (2001), "Social Marketing and Development," *Handbook of Marketing and Society,* Paul N. Bloom and Gregory T. Gundlach, Editors. Thousand Oaks, CA: Sage Publications, pp. 486–505.

Dietary Supplement Health and Education Act (1994), Public Law No. 103–417, 108 Stat. 4325.

Federal Trade Commission, "Consumer Information Remedies: Policy Review Session," June 1, 1979. Washington, D.C.

Fox, Karen F. A. and Philip Kotler (1980), "The Marketing of Social Causes: The First 10 Years," *Journal of Marketing,* 44 (Fall), 24–33.

Gundlach, Gregory T. and William L. Wilkie (1990), "The Marketing Literature in Public Policy: 1970–1988," *Marketing and Advertising Regulation: The Federal Trade Commission in the 1990s,* Patrick E. Murphy and William L. Wilkie, Editors. Notre Dame, IN: University of Notre Dame Press, pp. 329–344.

Klein, Thomas A. and Robert W. Nason (2001), "Marketing and Development: Macromarketing Perspectives," *Handbook of Marketing and Society,* Paul N. Bloom and Gregory T. Gundlach, Editors. Thousand Oaks, CA: Sage Publications, pp. 486–505.

Kotler, Philip and Gerald Zaltman (1971), "Social Marketing: An Approach to Planned Social Change," *Journal of Marketing,* 35 (July), 3–12.

Lampman, Robert J. (1988), "JFK's Four Consumer Rights: A Retrospective View," *The Frontier of Research in The Consumer Interest,* edited by E. Scott Maynes and ACCI Research Committee. American Council on Consumer Interests, pp. 19–33.

MacInnis, Deborah and Gustavo E. de Mello (2005), "The Concept of Hope and its Relevance to Product Evaluation and Choice," *Journal of Marketing,* 69 (January), 1–14.

Mason, Marlys J. and Debra L. Scammon (2000), "Health Claims and Disclaimers: Extended Boundaries and Research Opportunities in Consumer Interpretation," *Journal of Public Policy & Marketing,* 19 (Spring), 144–150.

Mason, Marlys J. and Debra L. Scammon (in progress), "Coping and Hoping: The Role of Products and Product Environments in Facing Health Challenges," working paper.

Mazis, Michael B., Richard Staelin, Howard Beales, and Steven Salop (1981), "A Framework for Evaluating Consumer Information Regulation," *Journal of Marketing,* 45 (Winter), 11–21.

Miaoulis, George and Charles Bodkin (2005), "An Exploratory Study of Consumer Perceptions of e-Health Ethics Issues," *Proceedings of the Association for Health Care Research,* edited by Michael Weigold.

Mick, David Glen (2006), "Meaning and Mattering Through Transformative Consumer Research," *Advances in Consumer Research,* Cornelia Pechmann and Linda L. Price, Editors. Vol. XXXIII, 1–4.

Moorman, Christine (1998), "Market-Level Effects of Information: Competitive Responses and Consumer Dynamics," *Journal of Marketing Research,* 35 (February), 82–98.

Moorman, Christine (1996), "A Quasi Experiment to Assess the Consumer and Informational Determinants of Nutrition Information Processing Activities: The Case of the Nutrition Labeling and Education Act," *Journal of Public Policy & Marketing,* 15 (Spring), 28–44.

Moorman, Christine, Kristin Diehl, David Brinberg and Blair Kidwell (2004), "Subjective Knowledge, Search Locations, and Consumer Choice," *Journal of Consumer Research,* 31 (December), 673–680.

Moorman, Christine and Linda L. Price (1989), "Consumer Policy Remedies and Consumer Segment Interactions," *Journal of Public Policy & Marketing,* 8, 181–203.

National Science Foundation (1978). *Research on the Effects of Television Advertising on Children: A Review of the Literature and Recommendations for Future Research.* Washington, D.C.

Nelson, Phillip (1970), "Information and Consumer Behavior," *Journal of Political Economy,* 78 (2), 311–329.

Pechmann, Cornelia and Michael D. Slater (2005), "Social Marketing Messages That May Motivate Irresponsible Consumption Behavior," *Inside Consumption: Frontiers of Research on Consumer Motives, Goals, and Desires.* D. Mick and S. Raineshwar, Editors. London, UK: Routledge, forthcoming.

Rothschild, Michael L. (1999), "Carrots, Sticks, and Promises: A Conceptual Framework for the Management of Public Health and Social Issue Behaviors," *Journal of Marketing,* 63 (October), 24–37.

Sprott, David E. and Anthony D. Miyazaki (2002), "Two Decades of Contributions to Marketing and Public Policy: An Analysis of Research Published in Journal of Public Policy & Marketing," *Journal of Public Policy & Marketing,* 21 (Spring), 105–125.

Stern, Louis W. and Thomas L. Eovaldi (1984). *Legal Aspects of Marketing Strategy: Antitrust and Consumer Protection Issues.* Englewood Cliffs, NJ: Prentice-Hall, pp. 89–94.

Wiener, Joshua Lyle and Tabitha A. Doescher (1994), "Cooperation and Expectations of Cooperation," *Journal of Public Policy & Marketing,* 13 (Fall), 259–270.

Winker, Margaret A., Annette Fllanagin, Bonnie Chi-Lum, John White, Karen Andrews, Robert L. Kennett, Catherine D. DeAngelis, and Robert A. Musacchio (2000). *Guidelines for Medical and Health Information Sites on the Internet.* (http://www.ama-assn.org/ama/pub/category/1905.html).

EXPLORING DEVELOPMENTS OVER TIME: HISTORICAL PERSPECTIVES ON MARKETING IN SOCIETY

SCHOLARLY RESEARCH IN MARKETING: EXPLORING THE "4 ERAS" OF THOUGHT DEVELOPMENT

William L. Wilkie and Elizabeth S. Moore

Today's body of marketing thought is expanding geometrically, pushing frontiers in numerous domains—quantitatively, behaviorally, strategically—with much enhanced technology and on an increasingly globalized basis. As this pushes forward on many fronts, however, it is also worthwhile to ask what is in danger of being left behind. What is the benefit, if any, of discerning the roots of this field? On the basis of an extended look across the last century of marketing thought, this article paints a wide-ranging portrait of (1) the general course that has been taken by the body of marketing thought over its "4 Eras" and (2) how the treatment of societal dimensions of marketing has fared during each period. On the basis of these findings, the authors pose several key issues for further consideration by interested thinkers concerned with the progress of marketing scholarship.

[Note to readers: This article is the second report from an extended, multiyear project in which we have been attempting to explore the nature and scope of our academic field of marketing. The initial article, "Marketing's Contributions to Society," appeared in the millennium Special Issue of the Journal of Marketing *(1999). We originally conceived of the historical analysis presented here as serving as a useful background for that article, but it quickly spiraled far beyond the bounds of a mere section there. We therefore set it aside until that article was completed and then returned to this topic with alacrity. Several years later, we are pleased with the education we have received throughout this process. However, this very education has also caused us to become increasingly puzzled by certain aspects of our modern academic condition in the marketing field. For example, it is clear that our field has been benefiting from increasing research specializations. However, this powerful force has apparently not been accompanied by public discourse within the community of scholars as to whether we are headed toward a point wherein a central coherence for the field of marketing is being lost. Although we do not discuss it much directly in this article, we view this as an important latent dimension for*

WILLIAM L. WILKIE is the Aloysius and Eleanor Nathe Professor of Marketing, and ELIZABETH S. MOORE is Associate Professor of Marketing, University of Notre Dame. The authors thank the following people for their provision of significant background insights and information: Stephen Greyser, Thomas Klein, Daniel LeClair, Angela Lyzinski, Robert Nason, and Ross Rizley. The authors also express their appreciation for the significant editorial improvements suggested by the three anonymous *JPP&M* reviewers.

Wilkie, William L. and Elizabeth S. Moore, (2003), "Scholarly Research in Marketing: Exploring the '4 Eras' of Thought Development," *Journal of Public Policy & Marketing*, Vol. 22 (2), 116–146.

future consideration on a broad scale. More pointedly for this article, there is little question that some higher levels of marketing analysis, such as those reflecting larger views of the aggregate marketing system, have been recently disappearing from the priority perspectives of most modern marketing researchers. Thus, the primary goal for this article is to address a broad range of thoughtful people in the field with a piece that will engage interest and stimulate further thought about the scope of the field and its undertakings. It is not written with the didactic intent of advising readers what should be done, but it is meant to stimulate contemplation and discussion about the more valuable options for progressing. Thank you for your attention to it.]

The academic field of marketing formally began shortly after the turn of the last century and is now about 100 years old. Both the real world of marketing and the real world of society have undergone massive changes during this time. A rich body of marketing literature has been developed. However, all scholars should recognize that an examination only of today's research cannot come close to capturing the total expanse of thought in the marketing domain. This point is especially clear when it is recognized that the focus of today's academic field of marketing is squarely on firms and household consumers and that few people, even in the mainstream of marketing thinking, have deeply considered marketing from a broadened, more aggregate perspective. However, across the span of the last century, many interesting insights on the field of marketing have been developed. Beyond this, many interesting insights into marketing's broader relationships with society have also been developed. This article explores the advances that have occurred across this time.

Rather than a steady, cumulative advance of a unified body of marketing thought, the past century has experienced periodic shifts in dominance of prevailing modes of thinking. Table 1 outlines what we consider the "4 Eras of Marketing Thought" since the field's formal beginnings.[1] As we will discuss, distinct issues and approaches affected mainstream marketing thinking during these times and very much affected interest in and treatment of marketing's relationship to its society.

Table 1's first row, "Pre-Marketing," is included to acknowledge that considerable thought about marketing-related phenomena was available prior to the formal beginnings of this field of study. From the time of the ancient Greeks through the time of the great economists of the 1700s and 1800s (including Smith, Malthus, Jevons, Ricardo, Mill, and Marshall), the concepts of markets, marginal analysis, value, production, humans as social and economic entities, competition, and the role of governments had already been raised and extensively debated (e.g., Dixon 2002; Shaw 1995). As of the turn of the twentieth century, therefore, the area that would become "marketing" was firmly ensconced within the field of economics.

---

[1]Table 1's four time periods, era names, and descriptions represent our conclusions based on the study of many primary books and articles published over the years. Of special note, however, is that in the early stages of the project, we obtained considerable guidance from Robert Bartels's (1988) *The History of Marketing Thought*.

TABLE 1

The "4 Eras" of Marketing Thought

Era	Distinctive Characteristics
"Pre-Marketing" (Before 1900)	• No distinguishing field of study; issues are embedded within the field of economics.
I. "Founding the Field" (1900–1920)	• Development of first courses with "marketing" in title. • Emphasis on defining purview of marketing's activities as economic institution. • Focus on marketing as distribution.
II. "Formalizing the Field" (1920–1950)	• Development of generally accepted foundations or "principles of marketing." • Establishment of knowledge development infrastructure for the field: professional association (AMA), conferences, journals (*Journal of Retailing* and *Journal of Marketing*).
III. "A Paradigm Shift—Marketing, Management, and the Sciences" (1950–1980)	• Growth boom in U.S. mass market and marketing body of thought. • Two perspectives emerge to dominate the marketing mainstream: (1) the managerial viewpoint and (2) the behavioral and quantitative sciences as keys to future knowledge development. • Knowledge infrastructure undergoes major expansion and evolution.
IV. "The Shift Intensifies—A Fragmentation of the Mainstream" (1980–present)	• New challenges arise in business world: short-term financial focus, downsizing, globalization, and reengineering. • Dominant perspectives are questioned in philosophy of science debates. • Publish-or-perish pressure intensifies on academics. • Knowledge infrastructure expands and diversifies into specialized interest areas.

Meanwhile, business was changing the day-to-day life of society by investing in basic industries that fueled the growth of the United States. Key issues were presenting themselves through the sheer energy and size of productivity gains brought by the Industrial Revolution (e.g., the 20 years from 1880 to 1900 alone brought the invention of electricity, aluminum, the steam engine, automobile, telephone, phonograph, rechargeable battery, tractor, cellulose film, and various types of electric motors; Desmond 1986). During this time, societal issues were of considerable importance, as economists had long viewed the development of public policy as a central focus of their endeavor. For example, some "robber barons" found that they could amass even greater profits by using questionable business methods. These included illegally gaining control of land and raw materials, ridding themselves of competitors (by creating giant trusts or employing predatory practices), using low wages and dangerous work conditions to lower production costs, and choosing in other ways to place their avarice ahead of others' interests. The larger question of laissez-faire versus government oversight of business was increasingly raised as a social and economic issue, leading to landmark legislation that provided foundations for a government regulatory system for business, such as the Sherman Antitrust Act in 1890. *However, it is important to note that the thinkers of this booming time of market growth clearly viewed government as a balance of competing interests, that is, as both a facilitator and a restrainer of business* (e.g., Dickson and Wells 2001). Thus, in addition to restrictive legislation, considerable efforts were devoted to the ways governments could properly *assist* businesses to invest and to grow (as through railroad lands, trading treaties, mineral and water rights, patent protections, and so forth).

The remainder of this article deals with the formal body of thought from the time the academic field of marketing began. As our exploration deepened, it became increasingly clear that marketing thought has been simultaneously responsive to the exigencies of its times, yet also highly volitional in terms of the topics and approaches chosen for development. Thus, for each era in this article, we will discuss how knowledge development reflected (1) the impact of external societal events and (2) the orientations and preferences of that era's prevailing marketing thought leaders. We address the "4 Eras" in chronological order. Within each, we first explain why it is significantly distinguishable with respect to marketing thought in general, and then we specifically review how broader societal issues were treated during that time.

Era I: "Founding the Field of Marketing" (1900–1920)

GENERAL CHARACTERISTICS OF THE PERIOD

As indicated in Table 1, the first era of formal marketing thought began shortly after the turn of the twentieth century, when more structured academic attention started to be given to a specific portion of the business system that was evolving and assuming ever greater prominence in the marketplace: the area of market distribution. In general, economists had not been handling this topic, as the thrust of traditional economic theory had focused on *production* (and thus land, labor, and capital) as the creator of economic value and had placed little emphasis on services of the sort provided through distribution. This view was somewhat understandable when markets were entirely localized. By the turn of the century in the United States, however, immigration, migration to urban centers, production and technology gains, and improvements in transport and storage were combining to change the state of the marketplace dramatically, and the growth and evolution of distribution systems were developing apace. Thus, there was a genuine need for some economists to step forward to embrace and then to explain those elements of this new world that were not incorporated into the body of thought of the time.

The marketing field began to take on its own distinct identity when professors at a number of universities across the country independently began to develop new courses to examine various aspects of the marketing system, including "distributive and regulative industries" (University of Michigan), "the marketing of products" (University of Pennsylvania), "methods of marketing farm products" (University of Wisconsin), and "mercantile institutions" (New York University) (Bartels 1951b, 1988). Substantively, these courses reflected the realities of their time and place (e.g., agriculture was extremely important in those times, and significant attention was paid to distribution of farm products, so it is no happenstance that Big Ten universities have long been leading contributors to marketing scholarship).

As the period progressed, especially during the second half of Era I (from 1910 to 1920), articles in economics journals and freestanding books helped the fledgling field of marketing begin to create distinct conceptual approaches to knowledge development (Bussiere 2000; Savitt 1990). Three of these approaches later came to be known as the *commodity approach* (focusing on all marketing actions involved in a particular product category), the *institutional approach* (focusing on describing the operations of a specialized type of marketing agency, such as a wholesaler or a broker), and the *functional approach* (focusing on the purposes served by various marketing activities).

ERA I's ATTENTION TO MARKETING AND SOCIETY ISSUES

Before turning to details, it may be helpful to briefly indicate that "marketing and society" is broadly conceived here in terms of an Aggregate Marketing System: a huge, powerful, yet intricate complex operating to serve the needs of its host society (Wilkie and Moore 1999). The Aggregate Marketing System is recognized as different in each society, as an adaptive human and technological institution reflecting the idiosyncrasies of the people and their culture, geography, economic opportunities and constraints, and sociopolitical decisions. The three primary sets of actors within the system are (1) consumers, (2) marketers, and (3) government entities, whose public policy decisions are meant to facilitate the maximal operations of the system for the benefit of the host society.[2] How has the academic field of marketing dealt with this larger system? As we noted, our coverage in this article spans roughly a century of knowledge development, placing an appropriate context on how broader issues involving marketing have been viewed during various times.

During Era I, the societal domain was an implicit issue in the body of marketing thought. As we noted previously, focus was strongly on the distribution sector, with stress

---

[2]As we will discuss at the end of this article, different combinations of system actors and levels of aggregation afford numerous research areas under the umbrella of marketing and society. For example, focus on consumers might lead to consumer interest research, whereas focus on consumer/government might lead to consumer protection research. Attention to marketer/government could lead to antitrust research, and marketer/marketer could lead to research dealing with judicial challenges; moving to not-for-profit venues could lead to social marketing, whereas a focus on individual or firm behavior could involve marketing ethics; and so forth. Our focus at this point is primarily on *perspective* rather than specific topics: We employ the marketing and society rubric to suggest any of these areas.

directed at explicating the economic rationales for the development of these enhanced and more complex systems evolving in the society of the time. In a real sense, reflecting scholars' disciplinary training in economics, a strong emphasis was on understanding markets and their operation. In contrast to today's focus on managerial decision making, these approaches were more abstract and clearly encompassed societal concerns, as Shaw (1912, pp. 708, 706, and 737, respectively) demonstrates in the following:

> (1) "The accepted system of distribution was built up on the satisfying of staple needs . . . this sort of activity has . . . contributed to the progress of civilization"; (2) "Society can no more afford an ill-adjusted system of distribution than it can inefficient and wasteful methods of production"; and (3) "The middleman is a social necessity."

The stress on economic efficiency stimulated exploration of the roles being played by marketers and the government. For example, the passage of the Clayton Act and creation of the Federal Trade Commission, both in 1914, reflected serious societal concern with pricing and other competitive behaviors within the growing capitalist economy (e.g., Murphy and Wilkie 1990). In addition, contributing to the development of theory in this domain, the concept of marketers as specialists was advanced to explain efficient performance of necessary tasks within the distribution system (e.g., Weld 1915, 1916).

As befits the unstructured beginnings of a field of study, different writers employed different frameworks to address this area (Hollander, Keep, and Dickinson 1999). Shaw (1912), for example, included both personal selling and advertising as topics within distribution, Weld (1915) continued to include marketing under the production function, and Butler (1914) concentrated attention on advertising and selling as distinct activities in themselves. Cherington (1920), writing at the end of this period, added an important basis for future thought by asking whether marketing performance (and thus societal welfare) might be enhanced by focusing on the underlying functions that marketing activities serve.

Overall, it is instructive to note that the thought leaders of Era I were quite willing to use economic efficiency criteria to express negative as well as positive judgments about marketing, advertising, and selling performance and potentials. The focus was very much on business: Government appeared not to be a central concern in this literature. In contrast to today, these writers did not much address government's role as a regulator, but they did maintain an appreciation for its functioning as a facilitator of marketing through such activities as setting grades and standards (see, e.g., Weld 1916). Era I's literature was also willing to raise and address larger questions, such as the following:

- Are there too many middlemen? Does distribution cost too much?
- Does advertising raise or lower prices?
- What control, if any, should be exerted over new combinations in distribution?
- Of the total costs paid by consumers, which elements are desirable? Indispensable?
- What about "nonessential" services such as credit availability; should these be eliminated?

In the absence of elaborate theory, data, or structure, the authors then attempted to provide nonempirical but relatively objective answers about these social issues that reflected their evolving marketing system.

Era II: "Formalizing the Field" (1920–1950)

GENERAL CHARACTERISTICS OF THE PERIOD

At the start of Era II, in 1920, marketing was an ill-formed, nascent field. By 1950, at the end Era II, it was a flourishing, vibrant academic field. Some of the major characteristics of this important time in marketing are chronicled in Table 2. The rapid development of the field during this period actually accompanied (and reflected) several profound societal changes (indicated in the left-hand column of Table 2). In only 30 short years, the United States moved through boom and prosperity in the 1920s, to the Great Depression of the 1930s, to the cataclysmic World War II, and to the postwar period of the 1940s. In many respects, this was a remarkable time in U.S. history.

A key characteristic of the marketing system is that it is embedded within the day-to-day life of the society (e.g., Wilkie and Moore 1999). As the world shifted and evolved in Era II, so did the marketing system. Mass production capabilities required more complex and varied distribution systems and a more sophisticated understanding of tools to influence mass consumer demand. Technological developments led to the introduction of a vast array of new products. For example, as electricity was brought into U.S. homes (53% of homes by 1925 from only 8% in 1908), innovations such as the electric iron, washing machine, refrigerator, and vacuum cleaner eased the lives of the average consumer (Cross 2000; Lebergott 1993). Consumers' choices also expanded exponentially with the introduction of newly convenient packaged goods, delivered in new retail formats such as the supermarket (circa 1930). These developments brought new challenges to consumers who were inexperienced in this more complex and technologically sophisticated marketplace (Mayer 1989). The resurgence of the "Consumer Movement" in the 1920s and 1930s was centered in part on frustrations with prices; the quality of some products; a shortage of product information (and resultant consumer confusion); and increasing use of emotion, image, and even fear appeals in advertising (Allen 1952; Cross 2000). All of these difficulties were exacerbated by the Great Depression, then wrenched into a different domestic reality by World War II (for interesting reports on consumer contexts, see Cohen 2003; Hill, Hirschman, and Bauman 1997; Witkowski 1998), and finally launched into the dawn of an uncertain new world as the postwar period ensued.

The middle column of Table 2 reflects that the vast opportunities and difficult challenges of the time called for the academic field of marketing to become a formalized area of study. Two significant developments in this regard were (1) the creation of a formal infrastructure for the development of marketing knowledge and (2) the integration of

TABLE 2

Era II: Formalizing the Field, 1920–1950

General Features of the Period (in the United States)	Academic Thought in Marketing	Treatment of Societal Domain in Marketing (Roughly Across Time)
Across Era II: Enormous Growth but Social and Economic Upheaval	**Academic Organization (Growth in Formation of Colleges of Business and Departments of Marketing)**	**Continued General Emphasis on the Economic Efficiency of Marketing**
• Early era: mass production expands (*e.g., from 1922 to 1929 there is 34% growth in output in agriculture, manufacturing, and construction*).	1924: Formation of National Association of Teachers of Marketing and Advertising.	• Costs of distribution • Economics of advertising • Pricing policies
• Sharp income rise in the Roaring Twenties.	1930: American Marketing Society (focus on practitioners) forms.	**Laws on Pricing Practices a Major Focus**
• Burst of innovative technologies appear (*e.g., some based on electricity*).	1937: Two groups merge to form the AMA, which provides bases for sharing marketing thought.	• Impacts of Robinson-Patman Act • Fair Trade and Unfair Practices Act • Analysis of specific state laws • Taxation (especially chain stores)
• Major products diffuse in society and reach average consumers (*e.g., the number of autos registered rises from less than 2.5 million in 1915 to more than 26.5 million by 1930*).	**Academic Journals and Proceedings**	**Special Attention to Agricultural Marketing**
	1925: *Journal of Retailing* begins at New York University.	• Grade labeling, pricing issues, regulation of supply, cooperative marketing
• New media landscape changes news and entertainment (*e.g., commercial radio broadcasts begin in 1920*).	1936: • *Journal of Marketing* debut: *JM* becomes center for advancing marketing thought.	**Exploring Government's Role in the System** • As a protector of certain sectors
• Expansion of new retail forms (*e.g., first supermarkets appear in 1930*).	• Early *JM* contributors are quite diverse (39% academics, 46% business, and 15% government).	• Marketing appraisals of New Deal legislation • Regulatory agencies (especially FTC and FDA)
• Great Depression begins in 1929, economy slows sharply, and incomes and wealth decline across society.	• *JM* serves as forum for communication: encourages commentaries on prior articles ("Notes and Comments" begins in Volume 5).	• Key areas: competition, pricing, false advertising
• Consumer movement reappears in 1920s; gains strength in 1930s.	• Considerable coordination of AMA conferences and *JM* (proceedings published in *JM*: 41% of *JM* articles had been originally presented at AMA conferences).	**Questioning of Particular Marketing Activities** • Advertising appeals (e.g., fear, style, image) • Aggressive salesmanship
• Key books on consumer problems appear and serve as catalysts for protest (*e.g., 100,000 Guinea Pigs*).		**Representation of the Consumer Interest**
• Consumers' Union forms in 1936.	**Substantive Content and Orientation**	• Key areas of concern: product quality, standardization, and lack of objective information
• Tremendous growth in size, power, and complexity of federal government under New Deal and then during World War II.	For first half of Era II (until *JM*), marketing textbooks serve as the primary repositories of academic marketing knowledge (e.g., successful textbooks run through numerous editions, preserving main lines of thought).	• Impacts of the consumer movement • Roles for government and business in system
• Key business/consumer laws passed (*e.g., Robinson-Patman Act; Food, Drug, and Cosmetic Act; Wheeler-Lea Amendment*).	• Primary orientation of textbooks of Era II is descriptive of marketing operations and grounded in economic theory.	**Marketing's Role in a National Emergency** • Industrial mobilization and production • Supply rationing to retailers and consumers
• Onset of World War II alters economic priorities (*e.g., leads to diversion of production, price controls, and rationing of some products from 1941 to 1945*).	• Notable aims of textbooks of Era II are the development and integration of generally accepted marketing principles.	• Marketing of national policies (propaganda) • Analysis of wartime impacts on markets

	• Three approaches dominate Era II:
	  –Functional
	  –Commodity
	  –Institutional
		Emergence of Foreign Nation Focus

• Postwar return of soldiers unleashes a new world for marketing (*e.g., pent-up consumer demand fuels new mass market, baby boom begins*).	• At end of Era II, there is an emerging interest toward theorizing: systems and scientific approach.	**Postwar Planning** • Marketing's role in national economic planning, community betterment, and business • Industrial and regional planning • Price controls in postwar economy • Retail arrangements • Allocation of surplus goods
		Analysis of Economic Indicators • Size and scope of postwar markets • Marketing and employment • Consumer savings (and dis-savings)

113

substantive content into a coherent and generally agreed-on view of the field, reflecting "Principles of Marketing."

The Development of Marketing's Infrastructure

The availability of an academic infrastructure (i.e., formal organizations, scheduled conferences, and chronicles of knowledge developments such as newsletters and journals) is virtually a necessary condition for a vibrant body of thought in a field. Until the early 1920s, the American Economic Association's conference had served as a setting for a small number of marketing people to meet for discussion, and the association's journal had served to convey the small number of formal articles in the fledgling field (Bussiere 2000). Then, in 1925, *Journal of Retailing* was launched at New York University. It was published on a quarterly basis and contained primarily short articles (one to five pages) aimed at understanding the management of retail functions and processes (e.g., Mensch's 1925 article "The Merchandise Division: Why It Exists, and Its Job," Straus's 1926 article "Some Observations on Merchandise Control"). Thus, for the retail sector of the field, a valuable communications vehicle had become available.

Meanwhile, in 1924, the National Association of Teachers of Marketing and Advertising was formed, and in 1930 the American Marketing Society, which represented the interests of practitioners, came into being. This society began *American Marketing Journal* in 1934, which was changed in 1935 to *National Marketing Review*. In 1936 and 1937, the teaching and practitioner associations merged to form the American Marketing Association (AMA), and the new group's publication was renamed *Journal of Marketing* (*JM*), which continues today with the explicit mission of communicating across the broad range of marketing activities (Bartels 1988; Kerin 1996).

The value of the AMA's infrastructure became quickly apparent as marketing thinkers began to convey their thoughts and opinions more readily and as others read, considered, learned, and responded. In the first decade alone, *JM* published some 500 articles (Kerin 1996). In some significant ways, however, the early journal was very different from that of today. First, a much wider range of contributors was evident in these early years: Marketing academics were in the minority (contributing approximately 40% of the articles in Volumes 1–10) and were joined by business practitioners (45%) and government officials (15%) to advance thought about marketing (Appelbaum 1947). Second, these articles were brief (about five pages), nine of ten were single authored, and commentaries and debates were a common feature (a section titled "Notes and Communications" was added in Volume 5 to provide this forum). Finally, proceedings of AMA conferences were also published in early issues of *JM*, though this ceased in the 1940s in support of war-related resource conservation efforts. Thus, conference sessions afforded opportunities for discussion that could then be disseminated to a much larger audience through the journal.

Establishing a Foundation for the Field

Early textbooks served an especially important role in laying down the foundation for the academic field of marketing (e.g., Clark 1922; Converse 1924; Ivey 1922; Maynard, Weidler, and Beckman 1927; Phillips 1938). During Era II, the mainstream textbooks in effect represented much of the mainstream body of academic thought, because marketing journals did not yet exist in numbers. In addition, their reach and influence could extend over many years, as the major texts were published in multiple editions, providing a continuity of perspective across the era.[3] It was also during this time that business schools were beginning to develop on a widespread basis, and these types of textbooks represented a significant impetus to a more standardized curriculum development across the nation. Thus, marketing textbooks also facilitated the evolution of this field away from its earlier roots in economics and agriculture and into a more formal treatment of the business system in general.

The primary emphasis in the Era II textbooks was on the development and integration of generally accepted marketing principles. In addition, the essential presentation was descriptive of prevailing marketing operations. The approaches of these texts were generally similar, which enabled dissemination of a core content about marketing to the college of thinkers in this field. A reasonable understanding of typical content is available in Table 3, which illustrates chapter contents of Clark's 1922 text. Notice how reflections of the commodity, institutional, and functional approaches are each present in this listing: Some degree of integration across approaches was a common feature in these early works. Over time, the functional approach especially gained wide acceptance among marketing thinkers. It was valued as a means of defining and rationalizing the field of marketing and its numerous activities and for its usefulness in analyzing marketing problems (Fullbrook 1940). Many functions were identified, falling under three general categories: (1) physically supplying the market, (2) creating opportunities for exchange, and (3) auxiliary or facilitating functions.[4] Grounded in economic theory, functional analysis also extended interest in the efficiency with which the functions were being performed.

As Era II was ending, academic books and journal articles began to seriously address a new topic: What could the role of theory and science be for this field? Leading figures such as Paul Converse (author of the 1945 article "The Development of the Science of Marketing"), Wroe Alderson and Reavis Cox (authors of the 1948 article "Towards a Theory of Marketing" and editors of the 1950 work *Theory in Marketing*), and, dated slightly beyond our boundary, Robert Bartels (author of the 1951 article "Can Marketing Be

---

[3]For our analysis, we consulted 20 different textbooks from Era II, some mainstream and some not, according to Bartels's (1988) work. This analysis revealed the continuity in thought presented through multiple editions. For example, the original Maynard, Beckman, and Weidler (1927) text was in its fifth edition as Era II came to a close (with some changes in authorship over the years), and a sixth edition was soon to follow.

[4]Although the functional approach achieved wide currency among marketing thinkers in Era II, lists of functions varied across authors. For further discussion, see Hunt and Goolsby (1988).

TABLE 3

Illustrative Era II Textbook: Substantive Content

Chapter	Contents
I.	Introduction
II.	The Marketing Functions
III.	Marketing Farm Products
IV.	The Wholesaling of Farm Products
V.	Middleman of the Agricultural Wholesale Market
VI.	Marketing Raw Materials
VII.	Marketing Manufactured Products
VIII.	Wholesale Middleman of the Manufacturer's Market: The Jobber
IX.	Wholesale Middleman of the Manufacturer's Market (continued)
X.	Direct Marketing of Manufactured Products
XI.	Retail Distribution
XII.	Large Scale Retailing
XIII.	Distributive Cooperation
XIV.	The Elimination of Middlemen
XV.	Physical Distribution
XVI.	Market Finance
XVII.	Market Risk
XVIII.	Market News
XIX.	Standardization
XX.	Competition and Prices
XXI.	Market Price
XXII.	Price Maintenance & Unfair Competition
XXIII.	The Relation of the State to Marketing
XXIV.	The Elements of Marketing Efficiency
XXV.	The Cost of Marketing
XXVI.	Final Criticism

Notes: From Clark (1922). Text chapters that are particularly relevant to the commodity approach are 3–10; the institutional approach, 4, 5, 8–14; and the functional approach, 2, 11, 15–19.

a Science?") began to explore new parameters for the body of thought. This development presaged a major shift in the future.

Era II's Attention to Marketing and Society

As illustrated in the third column of Table 2, marketing and society topics were quite prominent between 1920 and 1950. In contrast to today, marketing was frequently examined as a social instrument, as is evident in Breyer's (1934, p. 192) work:

> [M]arketing is not primarily a means for garnering profits for individuals. It is, in the larger, more vital sense, an economic instrument used to accomplish indispensable social ends.... A marketing system designed solely for its social effectiveness would move goods with a minimum of time and effort to deficit points. In doing so, it would also provide a fair compensation, and no more, for the efforts of those engaged in the activity. At the same time it would provide the incentive needed to stimulate constant improvements in its methods. These are the prime requisites of social effectiveness.

This orientation was evident in both textbooks and *JM*. As we would expect, however, the coverage of specific topics differed between these two sources.

Textbooks' Treatment of Marketing and Society

For this section, we consulted a wide range of Era II textbooks. Substantial variability in explicit attention to marketing and society was evident, from as few as 2 chapters, or 10%, in Converse's (1924) work to as many as 13 chapters, representing almost 50% of text content in Breyer's (1934) text.

Societal Issues of General Interest   Three of the most common issues presented in most textbooks of Era II are pricing practices, costs of distribution, and value of advertising. In particular, resale price maintenance (fair trade legislation) was much debated: Should a manufacturer have the right to determine the minimum price at which a branded or trade-marked item can be resold by a wholesaler or retailer? Controversy over price maintenance was intense early on in Era II, stimulated by the price-cutting policies brought about by the rise of large, powerful retail chains. The movement to exert control at the federal level gained support during the Great Depression, which began in 1929, and achieved (at least short-term) success in 1937 with the passage of the Miller-Tydings Act.[5] The pro arguments reflected desires to protect small businesses and advanced arguments that price cutting (1) can reduce a brand's value in the eyes of consumers; (2) can interfere with proper distribution (if, over time, retailers are unwilling to carry certain price-cut brands); and (3) can pressure manufacturers to reduce product quality, much to the detriment of the consumer. The con arguments reflected beliefs that price maintenance legislation would (1) effectively eliminate price competition, resulting in higher prices, fewer options, and reduced consumer welfare, and (2) discriminate against some classes of resellers (e.g., chain stores, mail order houses) and impair competition. Later, with passage of the Robinson-Patman Act in 1936, textbooks began to discuss the merits of prohibiting price discrimination (the legality of price discounts based on quantity or class of trade). Thus, students of marketing were learning about the larger issues of the day, here the impacts of pricing practices on competition, market efficiency, and public welfare.

Significant attention during Era II was also given to widespread marketing criticisms. Advertising and channel members were particularly singled out: Two long-standing controversial topics involved the "economic value of advertising" (e.g., Moriarity 1923; Phillips 1938; Vaughan 1928) and the question, Does distribution cost too much? (e.g., Converse 1924; Maynard, Weidler, and Beckman 1927). This question was stimulated by the importance of the agricultural sector and the recognition that farmers were receiving only a low proportion of the final prices paid by consumers for their food products. The geographic location of many marketing thought leaders in Midwestern

---

[5]With the passage of the Consumer Goods Pricing Act in 1975, the Miller-Tydings Act and related federal legislation (i.e., McGuire Act of 1952) were effectively repealed (Stern and Eovaldi 1984).

universities was no accident: Distribution system cost and performance for the agricultural sector was a real and controversial issue, as were the prices charged to consumers for the food processed by this system (in contrast to a prevailing view in our field today, manufacturers at this time were not the focus of the system but were instead considered part of the distribution system that processed the food supplied by the farm sectors).

Additional Issues of Interest in Textbooks of the Time   Beyond these three foundational issues, coverage varied as a function of each author's interests and background. For example, Era II brought a tremendous growth in the size, complexity, and authority of the federal government, and it was common to find discussion of the government's role in the marketing system in textbooks (e.g., Clark 1922; Duddy and Revzan 1947; Phillips 1938; Vaughan 1928). Substantively, although the authors might be critical of potential encroachments on marketer freedoms, recognition of the government's role as a protector of certain sectors (e.g., farmers, small retailers) was also apparent. Appraisals of marketing's performance in relation to specific legislative issues were also provided, as in Breyer's (1934) examination of marketing's social effectiveness in light of New Deal legislation enacted during the depths of the Great Depression years. Some textbook authors would also question specific marketing practices, such as the increasing use of fear and other image appeals in advertising. Misrepresentations of various forms (e.g., product origin, content, workmanship), aggressive salesmanship, and actions that might impede competition were also raised for critical appraisal (e.g., Duddy and Revzan 1947; Maynard, Weidler, and Beckman 1927; Vaughan 1928; White 1927). Needs for greater consumer protections within the marketing system were also acknowledged in some texts (e.g., Alexander et al. 1940; Phillips 1938). Particular concerns centered on cases of questionable product quality, insufficient standards, and a shortage of objective product information to aid consumer decision making.

JM's Treatment of Marketing and Society

Although *Journal of Retailing* had been serving its constituency since 1925, from its start in 1936, *JM* played a crucial role in marketing's emergence as an academic field. This was also true for the area of marketing and society. The larger events of the times (the economic depression of the 1930s and World War II in the early 1940s) sparked special interest in exigencies of the marketing and society relationship, and the early years of *JM* were replete with articles on these issues. Although *JM* was only available for about half of this era (1936–1950), 146 articles and commentaries related to marketing and society appeared during this time.[6] Many of these examined marketing issues in the light of unfolding world events; thus, attention to particular topics shifted across time.

---

[6]This total is based on listings in *JM*'s cumulative index for Volumes 1–15 under the subject headings "Government Issues," "Social Marketing," and "Social, Political, and Economic Issues." However, we should note that this is a conservative number because these listings tended not to include the many articles devoted to the role of marketing in a national emergency, specifics on the war effort, or postwar planning and analysis.

At the journal's start, in the late 1930s, the proper role of the government's trying to protect both competition and competitors was among the most frequently discussed topics. As was noted about textbooks, within the context of the economic pressures of the Great Depression, chain stores had exploded into rapid growth, offering consumers sharply reduced prices from those that could be charged by existing independent small retailers. In the first several years of the journal, by the end of 1939, some 30 articles and commentaries had appeared in *JM* on pricing issues. These especially addressed the wisdom and drawbacks of the two key governmental responses mentioned previously: fair trade laws and the Robinson-Patman Act (e.g., Engle 1936; Grether 1937). The journal appeared to welcome commentary on controversial issues, and occasional criticisms of prevailing practices appeared (e.g., Montgomery 1937). Other areas of significant interest in *JM* during this time included agricultural grade labeling, price stabilization policies, taxation, and developments in government's antitrust regulation (e.g., Bain 1941; Buehler 1937; Holt 1936; McHenry 1937).

Because the Great Depression was a time of social and political upheaval among consumers, numerous articles discussed issues in this realm, including efforts to create consumer cooperatives, and controversies about advertising and pricing practices (e.g., Cassady 1939; Drury 1937). Attention was also given to understanding the rapidly expanding consumer movement (e.g., Bader and Wernette 1938). Ready contributors to discussions of this period were government officials (e.g., from the Agricultural Adjustment Administration, Bureau of Foreign and Domestic Commerce, National Resources Planning Board), business and trade association representatives (e.g., from Dun & Bradstreet, American Association of Advertising Agencies, American Retail Federation), and marketing academics.

As war progressed in Europe and tensions mounted domestically, *JM* articles about the role of marketing in a national emergency, industrial preparedness, and shifting foreign trade practices began to appear (e.g., Hobart 1940; Rutherford 1940; Thomas 1940). At the same time, ongoing assessments of marketing's efficiency, pricing policies, economic impacts of advertising, and legislative developments such as the Food, Drug, and Cosmetic Act of 1938 continued (e.g., Borden 1942; Copeland 1942; Engle 1941; Tousley 1940). The specific problems of World War II increasingly moved onto the marketing thought stage; topics included wartime rationing of goods, government price controls, consumers' shifts and adaptations, and the role of marketing in the defense program (e.g., Derber 1943; Grether 1943; Taylor 1943; Watson 1944). Discussion of forms of marketing-system industry and government cooperation was much in evidence, and academics and other interest-group members (e.g., Republic Steel Company, War Production Board, Office of Price Administration) made these contributions to the journal. *It was at this point that the proportion of JM attention to marketing and society peaked for the entire period we have studied.* With the country galvanized by the war effort, according to our calculations, 55% of *JM*'s content was devoted to societal issues.

As prospects for the war's end increased, articles began to explore prospects for the coming postwar period. Although in retrospect the postwar prosperity is known, fears of an economic downturn at the close of the wartime economy were much in evidence as well (a byproduct of the depression period, which had not been clearly resolved at the start of the war). Contributors to the journal thus focused significant attention on postwar planning and analysis. *Underpinning these efforts was an explicit recognition that the efficiency and performance of the marketing system played a critical role in ensuring economic prosperity.* Issues such as the long-term impacts of price controls, impact studies in key industries, and the forecasting of demand for postwar markets came to the fore (e.g., Alderson 1943; Grether 1944; Nance 1944; Wittausch 1944).

After 1945, in the postwar period itself, new coverage was dedicated to topics such as the growth of the mass market, employment, consumer savings, and industrial development (e.g., Grether 1948; Hahn 1946; Vance 1947). In addition, given the need to better comprehend the burgeoning consumer market, a surge of articles on developments in marketing research began to appear at the end of Era II and continued into the early stages of Era III (this surge was estimated as representing almost 50% of *JM*'s content by the early 1950s; Grether 1976). There was also a return to some older issues such as resale price maintenance, agricultural grade labeling, and false advertising (e.g., Brown 1947a, b; Grether 1947; Payne 1947). The journal continued to support in-depth scholarly analyses of significant marketing and society topics, as in the series of articles by Ralph Cassady (1946a, b; 1947a, b) on the marketing, economic, and legal aspects of price discrimination. Overall, however, the level of attention to marketing and society topics began to decline during the postwar period as thought leaders turned their attention to the set of concerns that would characterize the new Era III.

Before closing this section, we should indicate that *Journal of Retailing* also carried several marketing and society articles during this time (e.g., Howard's 1933 "The Whole Truth in Retail Advertising," Nystrom's 1948 "The Minimum Wage in Retailing," Severa's 1943 "Retail Credit in Wartime"). *Journal of Retailing* also published a notable special issue, "War Problems," in April 1942 that covered analyses of retail buying policies, customer service and advertising under war conditions, wartime rationing, and retailers' contributions to national defense. Finally, articles devoted to retail planning in the postwar period also emerged at the end of Era II.

CLOSING OBSERVATIONS ON ERA II

As we look back over the field in this second era, it is clear that marketing academics had a very different orientation to the study of marketing than we do today. Their approach was much more descriptive of marketing operations and less oriented toward solving managerial problems. Significant attention was paid to external developments and the exigencies of the time (see Hollander, Keep, and Dickinson 1999). Evident in the textbooks and *JM* is a willingness to ask important economic, social, and political questions about marketing's impacts in society. Appraisals of the performance of the marketing system are embedded in the many discussions about the costs of distribution, value of advertising, and pricing policies that appeared. Finally, in an important sense, it appears that marketing thinkers viewed their scholarly and professional roles more broadly than we do today, as Alderson (1937, pp. 189–90) demonstrates in the following:

> "It is the responsibility of the marketing profession, therefore, to provide a marketing view of competition in order to guide efforts at regulation and to revitalize certain aspects of the science of economics.... For surely no one is better qualified to play a leading part in the consideration of measures designed for the regulation of competition."

Era III: "A Paradigm Shift in the Marketing Mainstream— Marketing, Management, and the Sciences" (1950–1980)

THE BOOM ARRIVES

Era III was very much built on the arrival of mass marketing dominance and a period of booming growth in the U.S. marketing system. The infrastructure and body of marketing thought likewise expanded geometrically during the 30 years from 1950 to 1980. Table 4 provides some interesting indicators of the growth in the field and its academic infrastructure. For example, the AMA's membership rose from just less than 4000 members in 1950 to nearly 17,000 members in 1980. The annual production of doctorates in business (with marketing receiving its share) rose from about 130 per year at the beginning of Era III to more than 750 per year at its close. Both phenomena were fueled by the enormous growth experienced in university business education programs, as represented by awards of nearly 2 million business bachelor's degrees and almost a half million MBA degrees during Era III.

TABLE 4

Indicators of Growth in Field During Era III

	At Beginning of Era III	At Close of Era III	Percentage of Base Year	Cumulative Degrees in Era III[a]
AMA professional membership	3797	16,770	442%	—
Annual doctoral degrees awarded in business	129[b]	753	584	10,820
Annual bachelor's degrees awarded in business	42,813	184,867	432	1,932,854
Annual master's degrees awarded in business	3280	54,484	1661	476,212

[a]Refers to academic degrees awarded in 1955–1956, the first year data are reported.
[b]Government data report begins in 1955–1956, so five years of Era III are not represented.
Notes: Information from U.S. Department of Education (2001) and the AMA. The AMA membership is as of December 23, 1949, as reported in *JM* (14 [April], 781).

Figure 1 depicts the associated growth patterns across the period. Notice that professional AMA membership and bachelor's degree-level business education both grew strongly and steadily (fueled by the vanguard of baby boomers beginning to graduate from college in 1967) and were four to six times larger at the end of Era III than they had been at its start. Even more striking, however, was the growth in graduate business education during Era III; MBA degrees soared from some 3000 per year to more than 50,000 per year (a 1,561% increase) and helped fuel the demand for university professors to teach these courses. Doctorates, though still low on an absolute basis, also soared during this time. Between 1960 and 1965, for example, the number of business doctorates awarded per year actually tripled and then increased to seven times the 1960 rate only ten years later. Thus, on all bases, the field of marketing grew rapidly during Era III.

The Field Evolves in New Directions

Although precursors existed prior to this time and the momentum carried on afterward, the period after 1950 marked a watershed in the history of marketing thought. A new mainstream was formed during this time, a mainstream that was *(1) steeped in science as the basis for marketing thought development and (2) devoted to viewing the field from the perspective of marketing managers in order to help them undertake successful marketing programs.* In some senses, the turn to a managerial perspective was not entirely a radical shift in that marketing thinkers had always been interested in the activities undertaken by marketers. What *was* different about this perspective, however, was its overt interest in helping the individual manager make better decisions in Era III. In earlier times, the efforts of marketing thinkers were somehow more idiosyncratic: Some leading academics seemed to be standing apart more clearly to observe and describe the operations of marketing. From this perspective, they could offer expert, empathetic, and yet objective and sometimes critical evaluations of actions being taken by marketers. As Myers, Massy, and Greyser (1980, p. 96) summarize: "The study of marketing as an interesting subject to think about and reflect on gave way to a much more action-oriented view of the training of potential marketing managers."

The Turn to a Managerial Perspective

Several key factors were influential in bringing about the shift in marketing thought to viewing the field from the vantage point of the manager. This perspective certainly brought professional and vocational appeal to university courses, in the sense that it directly prepared students for jobs they would undertake after graduation. Beyond this, the field had been experiencing an increasing impatience on the part of some thinkers, such as Wroe Alderson at the Wharton School, with what they saw as a too-heavy reliance on the description of marketing institutions and activities rather than efforts to develop theory in the field.

FIGURE 1

Growth Patterns During Era III

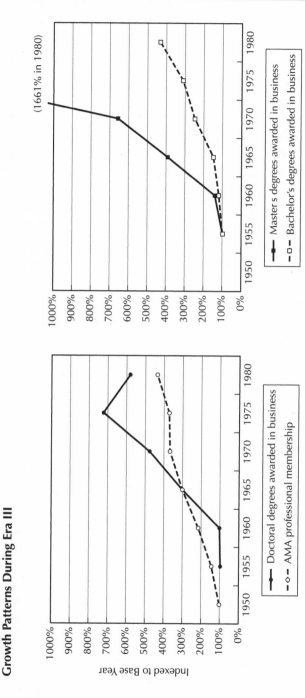

Notes: U.S. Department of Education (2001); degrees indexed relative to 1955.

External factors were also very significant at this time. The world of marketing was now dealing with an exploding mass market. This was driven by pent-up demand from the war years' restrictions on supplies of consumer goods, as well as an explosive growth in population. The baby boom had begun in 1946, bringing a cohort of an additional 4 million babies per year, which began to strain institutional and market capacities as it unfolded across time, until a total of 76 million new consumers had arrived 19 years later. In addition, marketers faced new opportunities through significant infrastructure developments for distribution (e.g., the new interstate highway system), new regions experiencing substantial growth, a shift to suburban living (altering the nature of locations in the retailing sector), and the development of a new communicator, television, and a national audience toward which to advertise each evening during "prime time."[7] Overall, the scope of the real world of marketing in the United States was becoming much larger and much more national in character. This changing world offered huge new opportunities but at the same time demanded significant adaptations, trials, and risks by companies and their marketing managers.

The strength of the shift to the managerial perspective in marketing during the early portion of Era III is strikingly evident in the burst of significant new concepts that were introduced during this time. It is startling to realize just how many of these, now almost a half century old, are still prominent in the field today: the marketing concept (John McKitterick 1957); market segmentation as a managerial strategy (Wendell Smith 1956); the marketing mix (Neil Borden 1964); the 4 P's (E. Jerome McCarthy 1960); brand image (Burleigh Gardner and Sidney Levy 1955); marketing management as analysis, planning, and control (Philip Kotler 1967); the hierarchy of effects (Robert Lavidge and Gary Steiner 1961); marketing myopia (Theodore Levitt 1960); and the wheel of retailing (Stanley Hollander 1960; Malcolm McNair 1958).

The shift toward the managerial perspective of marketing was also much enhanced by several key textbooks that appeared during the early portion of Era III. Jones and Shaw (2002) identify three textbooks in particular: Wroe Alderson's (1957) *Marketing Behavior and Executive Action,* John Howard's (1957) *Marketing Management: Analysis and Planning,* and E. Jerome McCarthy's (1960) *Basic Marketing: A Managerial Approach,* in addition to Eugene Kelley and William Lazer's readings book, *Managerial Marketing: Perspectives and Viewpoints* (1958). Alderson's work reflected efforts to develop a comprehensive theory of marketing based on concepts from the physical and social sciences, but with the intent that theory should view marketing as management behavior in an institutional and environmental context. In their historical overview of marketing thought,

---

[7]We thank an anonymous reviewer for pointing out that the explosive growth in media across the century likely led to increasing attention to societal issues involving advertising and promotion, first with increasing print modes (e.g., catalogs, newspapers, magazines, direct mail, flyers); then joined by sound (e.g., radio, telephone) and sight and sound (movies); followed by in-home sight and sound (television); and finally, today's evolution of the Internet and its concurrent concerns about personal privacy.

Lichtenthal and Beik (1984, p. 147) depict Howard's impact as follows: "In effect, John Howard's text hallmarks the arrival of the marketing management era." For McCarthy, meanwhile, they report (pp. 148–49): "Eugene J. McCarthy, in his classic text.... explains the manager's job ... [using] an essentially new unique concept, the four P's." Although perspective shifted toward management, the substance of marketing thought in these books did retain much of the key foundational elements from Eras I and II, particularly the insights contained in the functionalist approach (Myers, Massy, and Greyser 1980).

Somewhat later, in 1967, Philip Kotler virtually cemented the turn to the managerial mainstream with the publication of his classic textbook, aimed at more-advanced students in the burgeoning graduate programs of the time, with the famed Analysis, Planning, and Control framework (Kotler 1967).[8] In addition to influencing MBA students, the Kotler text influenced many young academics and developing researchers in the doctoral programs of the time and thus helped direct the research that was to come by explicitly incorporating the quantitative and behavioral sciences as part of the new thrust in marketing thought.

THE EMERGENCE OF THE QUANTITATIVE AND BEHAVIORAL SCIENCES

Management science and behavioral science emerged into the marketing mainstream at roughly the same time. Their progress into the field was assisted by the offering of some mutual support by academics in each area: Although well separated in terms of projects, specialists in the two approaches agreed with each other's beliefs in the scientific method, in underlying disciplines (science and social sciences), and in the body of marketing thought needing to be improved through new forms of knowledge and reliance on advanced empirical research methods. The sciences arrived in stages, slowly during the 1950s (*Management Science* was started in 1954), increasingly during the 1960s, and, as doctoral programs completed their adjustments, in a dominant manner through the 1970s. By the end of Era III, there was no question that the future of the mainstream of marketing thought would be governed by people who had these forms of training and these basic perspectives about the field.

The Nationally Planned Infusion of Management Science into Marketing

Although linked by science, many differences existed between management scientists and behavioral scientists in substance, orientation, and routes into the marketing field. The tale behind the rise of management science is particularly interesting. It was significantly enhanced in the United States by two external factors: (1) a national effort to infuse mathematics and statistics into business schools and (2) the development of the computer as a research tool.

---

[8]The framework is expanded to "Analysis, Planning, Implementation, and Control" in the sixth edition (Kotler 1988).

In the early 1950s, the Ford Foundation began a multiyear initiative to infuse scientific theory, methods, and analysis into the U.S. business system, in which few managers were at all technically trained. The focus of the effort was on changing the research agendas, doctoral educations, and teaching approaches of the faculty members at work in U.S. business schools. The early portion of the effort, beginning in 1953, involved a rollout of program change experiments at five selected schools in turn: Carnegie, Harvard, Columbia, Chicago, and Stanford (Schlossman, Sedlack, and Wechsler 1987). As experience accumulated at the five experimental sites, emphasis began to shift late in the decade to trickle down dissemination efforts aimed at other universities. The Ford Foundation efforts included a series of "new-developments" seminars held during the summers at the five schools (more than 1500 faculty members from some 300 schools attended) and an impactful commissioned study, the "Gordon–Howell Report" (Gordon and Howell 1959; see also Schmotter 1984), which provided powerful arguments for changes in business education. This report, together with another the same year, pointed out that business professors were teaching business in a largely descriptive fashion that represented the past, not the future, and that they were doing so in part because they had simply never been trained to do anything else.

To foster fundamental long-term changes, the Ford Foundation also sponsored a special year-long program in 1959 (The Harvard/Massachusetts Institute of Technology Institute of Basic Mathematics), in which a select group of promising young business faculty members was tutored deeply for a year by the mathematics faculty. This cadre, according to the plan, would return to their schools and begin to infuse the new knowledge into the curriculum and, more generally, into their field's body of thought by undertaking new forms of research.

The success of this effort was felt strongly and almost immediately as the program's marketing participants (including Frank Bass, Robert Buzzell, Philip Kotler, William Lazer, E. Jerome McCarthy, Edgar Pessemier, Donald Shawver, and Abraham Schuchman) returned to their universities and went to work.[9] In addition to their important personal contributions to research, members of this group contributed to the diffusion of the new perspective by writing highly influential textbooks, convening seminal conferences on research theory and methods, and training the next generations of thought leaders in this new approach to knowledge development. Their presence in the field was also helpful to new arrivals whose training had been in mathematics, statistics, or engineering, in terms of being able to discern and communicate useful problems to attack through the management science approach.

---

[9]As an aside of interest, the first author of this article was an undergraduate undecided between a liberal arts and mathematics major when he was recruited by the recently returned E. Jerome McCarthy into a new minor, management science, that Professor McCarthy was instituting in Notre Dame's College of Business Administration. Some 20 students from various fields entered the new program, and 7 went on to doctoral work in business fields.

A second external factor crucial to the success of management science was *the rapid development of computer technology* in both industry and academia, especially during the 1960s. This new tool enabled researchers to undertake sophisticated efforts to model complex marketing problems, as with optimization models of marketing processes in such areas as physical distribution, sales force allocation, and advertising budgeting. In addition, new forms of multivariate statistical analyses could now be applied to large banks of information on the mass marketplace.

The Advance of Consumer Research

In contrast to the planned introduction of marketing science, the emergence of consumer behavior within marketing appears to have been a natural response by the field to the pressing needs for insights about the mass consumer marketplace, insights for use in new product planning, advertising, retailing, and other marketing decision areas. For example, a comparison of textbooks at the beginning of Era III to its close shows sharp contrasts in the level of analysis, sophistication, and actual content in the treatment of consumer behavior: "[Previous emphases on] sociodemographic profiles, income levels, and geographic spread . . . [changed dramatically, and by 1977 drew] much more heavily from behavioral science concepts applied to marketing" (Myers, Massy, and Greyser 1980, p. 92). The growth in computers was also a positive factor, as it allowed for large-scale consumer surveys and the dissemination of new empirical research findings, their causes, and their implications.

No program similar to the Harvard mathematics training was available, however, so marketing professors who had been untrained in the underlying disciplines of psychology and sociology had to attempt to learn on their own or to hire new faculty from these fields. Upon arrival, however, those faculty members from other disciplines generally had little familiarity or experience with marketing itself, and many retained an interest in contributing to the literature in their base discipline as well as to that in marketing. Acceptance into the mainstream of marketing thought was somewhat slower for the consumer behavior area in general, and there is still some question among some of these people as to the extent their scholarly efforts are or should be directed toward assisting marketing managers (as opposed to, for example, contributing basic insights into the body of knowledge about human behavior).

GROWTH IN THE ACADEMIC INFRASTRUCTURE DURING ERA III

As we documented in Table 4 and Figure 1, Era III experienced a sharp increase in the rate of doctoral degree production in business. Given our focus on the body of marketing knowledge, moreover, the *accumulation* of these degrees is the most relevant statistic to represent growth in the group most likely to be making thought contributions. By this cumulative measure, the growth is truly striking: A total of nearly 11,000 new business doctorates

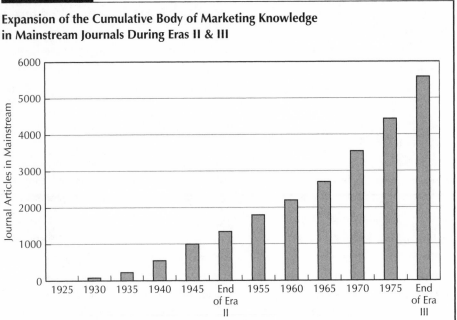

**Expansion of the Cumulative Body of Marketing Knowledge
in Mainstream Journals During Eras II & III**

Notes: This graph includes all articles in the following publications: *Journal of Retailing* (from 1925), *JM* (1936), *JAR* (1960), *JMR* (1964), and *JCR* (1974).

launched into action between 1955 and 1980. The data are not divided into fields within business, but if only 10% of degrees were in marketing, this would still represent 1100 new potential thought contributors to the field. Not surprisingly, this steady addition of many new marketing academics led to a dramatic increase in the sheer magnitude of new thought pieces relevant to marketing. Figure 2 depicts the impact of this infusion into the prevailing body of marketing thought by graphing the development of the cumulative body of new journal articles in a selection of mainstream publications of the field. Several points are notable. The body of thought reflected at the close of Era II was not insignificant: More than 1400 journal articles appeared in *JM* and *Journal of Retailing* by that time. This pace continued through the 1950s, when new journals began to appear, reflecting applications of the sciences to marketing. At this point, the slope of contributions steepened, first during the 1960s and again during the 1970s. By the end of Era III, the cumulative body of marketing thought was four times larger than it was at its start, reaching nearly 6000 articles.[10]

A Marketing Think Tank Emerges

As we noted previously, the impact of the sciences had become increasingly strong as Era III progressed. Beyond the sheer numbers, therefore, the nature of marketing's

---

[10]This discussion is essentially illustrative and undercounts the actual increase, because other significant marketing publications had also started during the latter part of Era III.

knowledge infrastructure needed to significantly expand to accommodate these new forces. Special conferences and workshops began to be held on behavioral and quantitative frontier topics, and the regular conferences incorporated sessions on them as well. New publications also emerged to accommodate this work. Another important infrastructure development also occurred during this time when a new think tank, the Marketing Science Institute (MSI), was formed in 1961. The MSI was the result of collaboration among Thomas McCabe, the president of Scott Paper Company; 29 sponsoring firms that underwrote expenses; and such leading marketing thinkers as John Howard, Albert Wesley Frey, and Wroe Alderson. According to McCabe (qtd. in Bloom 1987, p. 8), MSI's plan was to conduct research and educational activities designed to "(1) contribute to the emergence of a definitive science of Marketing and (2) stimulate increased application of scientific techniques to . . . current marketing problems." The MSI began in Philadelphia (with Wendell Smith as its first president) and in 1968 moved its offices to Cambridge, Mass., to begin a lengthy relationship with the marketing area of Harvard Business School, first under Robert Buzzell and then under Stephen Greyser. The MSI was an interesting and bold effort: Over the ensuing years, the research it stimulated and supported became a major factor in advancing thought in the marketing field (Kerin 1996; see also Bloom 1987).

Building the Research Infrastructure for Marketing Science[11]

The Ford Foundation's program during the 1950s began to bear fruit almost immediately in the 1960s. *Mathematical Models and Methods in Marketing,* a book written by the Harvard mathematics program participants (Bass et al. 1961), was soon followed by such other key books as *Quantitative Techniques in Marketing Analysis* (Frank, Kuehn, and Massy 1962), *Mathematical Models and Marketing Management* (Buzzell 1964), the comprehensive *Marketing Decision Making: A Model Building Approach* (Kotler 1971), and still others soon to follow (for a listing, see Montgomery 2001). These books provided an important foundation for the doctoral students and emerging scholars who would soon play leadership roles in advancing this new field. In addition, MSI was quite supportive of initiatives. One such impactful undertaking was the Profit Impact of Marketing Strategies (PIMS) Project, in which a number of major marketers contributed confidential information about business units' marketing strategies and operating results: This database was then explored with the latest statistical methods to learn more about the risks and rewards of various marketing alternatives (e.g., Bloom 1987).

During this time, articles on marketing topics were appearing with increasing frequency in the broader journal *Management Science.* In the mid-1960s, the "marketing college" in the Institute of Management Science (TIMS) was formed, thus providing an organizational

---

[11]This section is based on an informative history special section in the Fall 2001 issue of *Marketing Science* (pp. iii–iv, 331–81).

infrastructure for the emerging marketing science area (Montgomery 2001). From its beginnings, the goal of the college was to foster professional exchange among industry practitioners, marketing academics, and management scientists from other disciplines. The marketing college flourished during this period; its membership doubled to more than 300 members between 1966 and 1972 (Little 2001). Intellectual ferment was evident in the marketing science sessions and symposia in these early years: Sessions at TIMS meetings, AMA Summer Educators' Conferences, and workshops sponsored by universities provided important venues for sharing research (Montgomery 2001; Wittink 2001). When the specialized annual Marketing Science Conference began in 1979, the marketing college ceased participating in the annual AMA meetings, which were perceived as having become "too large and too diverse to accommodate the need for . . . serious discussion and interaction among marketing modelers" (Bass 2001, p. 360).

Additional infrastructure developments involved the academic journals. In 1969, the editorial structure of *Management Science* was altered, and marketing was given its own department; in 1971, an entire special issue, edited by David Montgomery, was devoted to marketing articles (Steckel and Brody 2001). Through the 1970s, *Journal of Marketing Research* (*JMR*) provided a key high-quality outlet for scientific articles, and output in the marketing science sphere blossomed. Storm clouds loomed, however, as the end of Era III neared. Increasingly, some marketing scientists perceived that *JMR* was not sufficiently welcoming of analytic models and that a new option was needed. Thus, just as the field was to enter Era IV, *Marketing Science,* with more of an engineering and operations research orientation than *JMR*, was ready to begin under the editorship of Donald Morrison (Montgomery 2001; Morrison 2001).

Building the Research Infrastructure for Consumer Behavior

Given that it was not the target of any organized foundation efforts, research in the consumer behavior domain began more slowly during the early portion of Era III. Some important advances did occur in the 1950s, however, on such topics as consumer purchasing, attitudes, sociodemographics, advertising research, and the controversial area of motivation research. A notable book during the early portion of the period was Lincoln Clark's (1955) edited volume *The Life Cycle and Consumer Behavior,* which featured articles by such leading researchers as David Riesman, Howard Roseborough, Burleigh Gardner, George Katona, Robert Ferber, William Whyte, and Joseph Newman. Notably, many of these research leaders reflected training in such social sciences as sociology, economics, and psychology, not marketing. Then, during the 1960s, consumer behavior's impetus was enormously enhanced by the appearance of textbooks such as Gerald Zaltman's (1965) *Marketing: Contributions from the Behavioral Sciences*; Engel, Kollat, and Blackwell's (1968) *Consumer Behavior;* the research-packed framework in John Howard and Jagdish Sheth's (1969) *The Theory of Buyer Behavior;* and Harold Kassarjian and Thomas Robertson's (1968) influential research readings book, *Perspectives in Consumer Behavior.*

As the focal point of this domain, the consumer, was positioned on the other side of transactions from the marketer, it was natural that not all research in this area would fit comfortably within the increasingly dominant managerial approach to marketing. Thus, a number of consumer researchers carried out work with some (deliberate) distance from marketing's mainstream organization: the AMA. This desire for independence led to the formation of a new group, the Association for Consumer Research (ACR), in 1970. The field grew quickly: In its first ten years, ACR expanded to more than 1000 members in some 20 nations. Numerous young academics and graduate students flocked to this new area of opportunity, and it became a major force in academic marketing. For example, by actual count, at the 1977 AMA Doctoral Consortium some two-thirds of the doctoral dissertations were being conducted on consumer behavior topics. This movement was much assisted by the appearance in 1974 of *Journal of Consumer Research* (*JCR*), with Ronald Frank as its first editor. In addition, the annual ACR conference had been healthy from the start. Thus, within only a few short years, the essential infrastructure for a field of study (an association with newsletter, journal, conference, and proceedings) had been created by the consumer behavior pioneers.[12]

NEW TOPICS IN MARKETING KNOWLEDGE DEVELOPMENT

To conclude this discussion, imagine observing the body of thought in Era III as it unfolds. The field is growing, shifting, and grappling with the new challenges of how to market successfully in a booming yet competitive mass marketplace. Articles in *JM* are becoming longer and more empirical. Many new names are appearing on the roster of thought contributors, and a higher proportion of these are from academia. The clearest shift of all is the increasing dominance of marketing research. The first major research journal focuses on advertising specifically and is driven by the practitioner community (*Journal of Advertising Research* [*JAR*] in 1960). At this time, businesses are grappling with a huge new medium (television), huge national market-growth opportunities, and highly volitional decisions about how and how much to advertise. Exploration of many new research options to better understand both consumer markets and advertising effectiveness is underway by influential research departments in advertising agencies, and *JAR* clearly serves a knowledge need.

Shortly thereafter, in 1964, *JMR* begins, offering a broader forum for frontier advances, discoveries, and debates on both marketing research methodologies and empirical research studies. In addition, there is a steady rise in the proportion of consumer behavior articles appearing in *JM* and *JMR* into the 1970s, when *JCR* appears in 1974 (as an interdisciplinary, not specifically marketing, journal). Thus, by the end of Era III, three new major research outlets, *JAR*, *JMR*, and *JCR* (as well as other significant new publications), had joined *JM* and *Journal of Retailing* as vehicles for developing marketing thought.

---

[12]An interesting set of retrospective reports on the development of ACR and *JCR* is available in Kardes and Sujan's (1995) work. See Cohen (1995); Engel (1995); Kassarjian (1995); Kernan (1995a, b); and Wells (1995).

What new content would we observe appearing during this time? Fortunately, a useful overview is readily available for almost the precise period covered in Era III. Table 5 is adapted from Myers, Massy, and Greyser's (1980) book on marketing knowledge development (this work represents the Commission on the Effectiveness of Research and Development for Marketing Management, a group of 18 prominent marketing thinkers [8 academics and 10 practitioners] sponsored as a joint activity of the AMA and MSI). Several brief points regarding Table 5 are worthy of note. First, as noted previously and expanded on in Column 1, a burst of important new managerial frameworks were being developed. *More broadly, Era III itself was a time of great change in which growth and innovation were much welcomed. In retrospect, the speed with which thought leaders adopted and worked with new ideas is a significant feature of the period.* Second, although the listing is only illustrative, it is impressive in its sheer magnitude: The domain of marketing thought was expanding considerably during this time. To be sure, not all the concepts, theories, or methods listed in Columns 2–4 were original to marketing thinkers: Unabashed borrowing and trial was characteristic and, at times, was followed by further applications and refinements. Third, the emerging power of the behavioral and quantitative sciences is quite evident, as is the way they merge within a larger "marketing research" sphere. Notice that the academic training required to contribute to many of the topics listed here has changed dramatically from Era II. This supports the observation that the people leading the mainstream research thrusts of late Era III either were new to the field or had retrained themselves in the Ford Foundation program or elsewhere. Notice also that the heterogeneity presented in Table 5 is very high. This is quite significant for the future of knowledge development in that it calls for increasing specialization by individual researchers working to push back the frontiers of knowledge. This is the characteristic that drove the development of our next period of marketing thought, Era IV.

ERA III'S ATTENTION TO MARKETING AND SOCIETY

The First Half: Moving to the Sidelines

With all these explosive developments and undercurrents at work during Era III, what was happening with respect to marketing and society? Two major points are relevant to this question: (1) In general, Era III's major thrusts (an infusion of both a scientific perspective and a managerial view of marketing) are largely indifferent to the study of marketing and society, but (2) Era III itself actually saw substantial attention paid to these issues. This was due in part to certain pressing concerns of the period (which placed both government and business in defensive postures at times) and to the efforts of certain marketing thinkers who carried on societal perspectives from Era II.

Emphasis on societal issues early in Era III, during the 1950s, generally maintained the orientation of previous years. For example, in 1952, Vaile, Grether, and Cox's notable *Marketing in the American Economy* appeared. Its thesis centered on marketing as an intrinsic

TABLE 5

Some Examples of Knowledge Developments in Marketing, 1952–1977

Managerial Frameworks and Approaches	Discipline-Based Theories	Research Methods, Models, and Measurement	

Managerial Frameworks and Approaches

- Marketing concept
- Marketing mix, 4 P's
- Product life cycle
- DAGMAR
- Development of marketing cases
- Stage approaches to strategy development
- New product development process
- Physical distribution management
- Marketing information systems
- Product positioning and perceptual mapping
- Segmentation strategies
- New marketing organization concepts (e.g., brand management)
- Territory design and sales force compensation
- Marketing audit
- Demand-state strategies
- Creative approaches and styles
- New search and screening approaches
- Refinements in test-marketing approaches

Discipline-Based Theories

- Market segmentation
- General and middle-range theories of consumer behavior
- Image and attitude theory
- Theories of motivation, personality, social class, life style, and culture
- Expectancy-value theory
- Theories of advertising processes and effects
- Information-processing theory
- Attitude-change theories (consistency and complexity theories)
- Attribution theory
- Perceptual processes
- Advertising repetition
- Distribution theory
- Refutation and distraction hypotheses
- Theories of diffusion, new product adoption, and personal influence
- Prospect theory

Research Methods, Models, and Measurement

Data Analysis: Broad and Specific

- Causal models
- Weighted belief models and determinant attributes
- Bayesian analysis
- Sensitivity analysis and validity tests
- Response functions
- Marginal analysis and linear programming
- Multidimensional scaling and attitude measurement
- Forecasting
- Econometrics
- Time-series analysis
- Trade-off analysis and conjoint analysis
- Analysis of variance
- Multivariate dependence methods: multiple regression, multiple discriminant analysis, and canonical correlation
- Multivariate interdependence methods: cluster and factor analysis and latent structure analysis

Data Gathering: Adoption and Refinement

- Advances in survey research
- Focus groups, depth interviewing
- Experimental and panel designs
- Motivation research and projective techniques
- Hypothesis formulation, inference, significance tests
- Psychographics and Activities, Interests, and Opinions studies
- Unobtrusive measures, response latency, nonverbal behavior
- Physiological techniques: (e.g., eye camera, GSR, CONPAAD)
- Probability sampling

Marketing Models

- Advertising (e.g., Mediac, Brandaid, Adbudg)
- Sales management (e.g., Dealer, Callplan)
- New product (e.g., Demon, Sprinte, Steam)
- Product planning: Perceptor, Accessor
- Bid pricing models
- Stochastic brand choice
- Market-share models

Marketing Cases and Simulations

- Simulation and marketing games
- Computer-assisted marketing cases

Notes: Adapted from Myers, Massy, and Greyser's (1980) work.

part of the U.S. economic system. Assessing marketing's performance of its social and economic tasks was an important issue for the authors. The specific element that characterized this approach was its view of marketing as a key operating system within the society, thus reflecting analysis at a higher level of aggregation than the newer emphases on the horizon of marketing thought.

Overall, however, the proportion of marketing and society articles in *JM* declined during the 1950s, reflecting the field's strong turn to new managerial and theoretical topics. This decline does not appear to reflect a change in the basic position about societal issues but rather a strong shift in research priorities, reflecting the challenges of the times in marketing. A number of articles did appear, however, and in 1951 the journal began the "Legal and Judicial Developments" section in each issue. The articles that appeared during this decade tended to focus on traditional questions in government policies toward business competition: major antitrust cases, administered price controls, and the Robinson-Patman Act. The early 1960s experienced a continuation of the shift toward the managerial perspective, now even in the work pertaining to government. Such articles dealt with how to market to the government, the effect of government actions on marketing programs, and legal advice for marketers (e.g., "How to Protect Your Trademark"), in addition to traditional antitrust issues.

The Second Half: Excitement and Exploration

Then, in the second half of the 1960s, a powerful new interest, marketing and society, began to emerge. As in earlier eras, this shift reflected the tenor of the times. Social unrest was spreading across society. Issues such as civil rights and the role of the government and the "military–industrial complex" in waging a controversial war in Vietnam rose to the forefront of everyday life. Assassinations of national leaders and role models led to further urban unrest. Thoughtful people associated with business increasingly began to examine issues and options, and some academics began to pursue new courses of investigation to try to ultimately improve the equity and operation of their society. One such area of emphasis in marketing thought reflected "social responsibility of business" issues. During this period, the AMA formed a public policy division and established committees to address such topics as inner-city marketing and minority enterprise. Furthermore, *JM* published the special issue "Marketing's Changing Social/Environmental Role" (July 1971), which featured articles on such topics as planned social change; population problems; recycling solid wastes; food prices and vulnerable groups; self-regulation; and ecology, air pollution, and marketing strategy.

Another area of emphasis was on consumers. Increasingly, marketing academics were spurred to examine the possibilities of putting their theories and methods to use in the service of poor and vulnerable consumers; for better health (e.g., cigarettes, alcohol, drug use); or for better, "wiser," or more efficient consumer purchases. This movement was greatly enhanced in the political arena in 1962, when President John F. Kennedy announced the Consumer Bill of Rights (for a first-person account, see Lampman 1988). This important declaration established that within the framework of U.S. society, consumers have the rights to expect product safety, to be fully informed, to have freedom of choice, and to have a voice in the rules for the marketplace. Thus, marketers were presented with some formal constraints well beyond any residual notions that caveat emptor ("Let the buyer beware") might still rule the U.S. marketplace. The related academic infrastructure also expanded during this time, as the American Council on Consumer Interests began publication of its *Journal of Consumer Affairs* (*JCA*) in 1967: Over the years, numerous marketing academics have published articles reflecting concern for consumer rights in this volume.

The marketing and society stream of work continued to accelerate sharply throughout the 1970s until the end of Era III. Some 20 readings books on the topic appeared between 1966 and 1974 (Bartels 1988, p. 220). These collections brought a rich panoply of perspectives, experiences, and viewpoints about marketers, consumers, responsibilities, rights, and system performance. Authors of the articles in the readers included such high-profile nonmarketing figures as Ralph Nader, John Kenneth Galbraith, Senator Warren Magnuson, FTC Commissioner Mary Gardiner Jones, John D. Rockefeller III, and the president of Pepsi-Cola, Donald Kendall. Numerous distinguished marketing academics were also well represented. Some continue to be prominent today, though not necessarily in this area. For example, one leading readings book was edited by David Aaker and George Day (1982), who would later achieve acclaim for advancing thought on brands and strategic imperatives.

The appearance of several distinct subareas fueled the acceleration of societal research in the 1970s. Some marketing thinkers focused on extending historical emphasis on issues related to performance of the marketing system, a focus that would come to be known as *macromarketing*. Others in the mainstream of marketing became embroiled in a controversy regarding the proper boundaries for the marketing field: Is marketing fundamentally a business topic, driven by the profit motive, or is it something broader, a technology or body of knowledge that can (should) be applied to social problems wherever they are found (Kotler and Levy 1969a, b; Luck 1969)? Many in the field approved of "broadening the concept of marketing," which allowed the emergence of a new and significant emphasis beyond the marketing of products and services, to such topics as the marketing of places, ideas, and personages and to consideration of such concepts as "demarketing," "network marketing," and megamarketing. This step also set the stage for development of *social marketing,* an area that would focus on the work of not-for-profit groups and government agencies concerned with effective intervention into social problem areas, such as the marketing of health, education, or alleviation of poverty.

A third division occurred when a number of academics, who typically had the new consumer behavior training, turned to study the area of *public policy*. This movement was greatly assisted by a new program sponsored by the Association to Advance Collegiate

Schools of Business (AACSB) and the Sears-Roebuck Foundation to place approximately 20 business faculty members annually in government agencies for yearlong periods of consulting work and study. Similar to the effects of the Ford Foundation's mathematics program, this program led to significant diffusion of new research perspectives during the decade. A major focus of activity was the Federal Trade Commission (FTC), the chief regulator of the U.S. marketing system.

Beginning in 1971, marketing academics moved into the FTC as in-house consultants on leaves of about one year. During the next ten years, some 30 marketing faculty worked in this capacity and contributed significantly to the development of research in the public policy sphere (for a summary of this program, see Murphy 1990). The FTC issues in consumer protection became a major focus in the marketing journals and conferences of the 1970s. Government officials spoke at research conferences, MSI coordinated a number of public policy research projects, and marketing doctoral dissertations began to address the important questions in this sphere directly. Given the right issue, academics, government officials, and marketing practitioners would converge to address controversial topics. For example, a large audience of attorneys and marketers traveled from New York and Washington to Miami to attend a single-morning session, Advertising to Children, at the ACR conference in 1978 (for a session report, see Mazis 1979). These efforts also reflected the increasing influence of marketing academics in the FTC's actions. Their contributions included research and conceptual inputs into case selection, preparation and analyses of case evidence and testimony, consultation on remedy development, program evaluation of case impacts, and background investigations into the development of trade regulation rules. Marketing academics played key roles in the influential "Consumer Information Task Force Report" for the FTC. By the end of the decade, the FTC was spending $1 million per year on marketing research, under the guidance of the marketing academic Kenneth Bernhardt.

Overview of Second-Half Activity: A Plethora of Riches

Overall, *JM*'s roster of articles during this decade well reflects the shift that had occurred, especially during the second half of Era III. In addition to social marketing topics, articles reflected the powerful impact of consumer behavior on the marketing field, with attention especially to developments at the FTC and other regulatory agencies on a range of consumerism issues, including deceptive advertising, consumer information, consumer complaints, warranties, credit practices, product safety, franchising law, and management of consumer protection activities. An excellent set of short articles describing this period is available in the Spring 1997 issue of *Journal of Public Policy & Marketing* (*JPP&M*; Andreasen 1997; Bloom 1997; Greyser 1997a; Kinnear 1997; Mazis 1997; Wilkie 1997).

As we noted previously, the range of marketing and society research both broadened and deepened during this time. We address the specifics of the range of topics in a following section; here, however, we close our discussion of Era III with Figure 3, a graphic

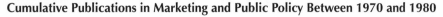

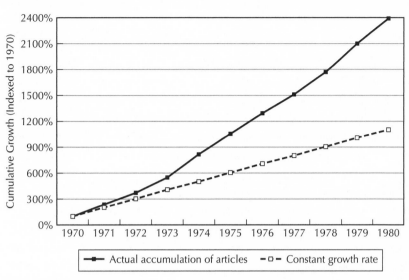

Cumulative Publications in Marketing and Public Policy Between 1970 and 1980

Source: Gundlach and Wilkie (1990).

depiction of the burst of public policy research that occurred during the 1970s. Figure 3 is based on the results of an extensive project aimed at cataloging all the marketing and public policy research published in major journals and conference proceedings during recent times.[13]

Two features of particular interest in Figure 3 are that (1) the absolute level of activity in this area (550 articles) is much larger than in any previous decades and (2) activity escalated over the period, as shown by the slope of the actual growth compared with a constant rate of publication. With respect to amount, this period produced many more publications than had appeared during the second half of Era II, a period previously described as highly involved with marketing and society issues. The primary reason for this difference is the vastly increased thought infrastructure and number of marketing contributors: The compilations in Figure 3 now represent many more outlets (12 journals alone) than the only 2 during Era II. *Thus, we may conclude that the proportional representation of marketing and society articles was lower during the end of Era III, but the absolute number of marketing and society contributions was much higher, and it was again a major topic of interest to the marketing field.* Thus, marketing and society was a vibrant, flourishing field in marketing as Era III drew to a close.

---

[13]Unpublished data courtesy of the authors (for a previous report of findings, see Gundlach and Wilkie 1990, p. 335). Note that the data presented in Figure 3 reflect only marketing and public policy topics that involve some mix of consumerism, government, and self-regulatory issues. This study represents a considerable sampling of the major research venues in marketing, including the 12 most prominent journals published during all or part of this period (*JM, JMR, JCR, Journal of Advertising, JAR, Journal of the Academy of Marketing Science, Business Horizons, Journal of Business Research, California Management Review, JCA, Harvard Business Review,* and *Journal of Retailing*), the proceedings of the conferences of the AMA (Educators') and ACR, and the publications of MSI.

Era IV: "The Shift Intensifies—A Fragmentation of the Mainstream" (1980–Present)

THE OVERALL CHARACTER OF ERA IV

Era IV, which extends from 1980 to the present, is characterized by a much changed face of the field, brought about by adaptations and reactions to the powerful shifts that had captured marketing during Era III. In a sense, it appears that the pressures that had been building on the mainstream of marketing thought finally reached a stress level that demanded relief through the infrastructure, much as an over-full dam might burst so that the pent-up waters can find their new courses and destinations. The new directions-taken during Era IV have had far-reaching consequences for both the marketing mainstream and the field's treatment of marketing and society.

Thus, in Era IV, the managerial perspective, or the belief that the major purpose for academic work is to enhance the effectiveness of managers' marketing decisions, continues to maintain a preeminent position in the field. So, too, does reliance on the scientific approach to knowledge development: Virtually all researchers today have been trained in and bring to their work some mix of behavioral and management science perspectives. In important other respects, though, the field is very different today than it was in 1980. How did this come to be?

THE PRESSURES BUILD

Since 1980, there have been significant upheavals in the worlds of both marketing practice and academia, and Era IV reflects these upheavals within the body of marketing thought. For example, it was during this period that the command economies of many communist nations faltered, then fell, and then began to be replaced with new experiments in market-based systems. Increasing globalization ensued, partially as a result of marketers from Western nations seeking new lands of opportunity and partially from people of those lands seeking to learn more and to apply business methods for successful enterprise. Then, as the Internet opened communication across international boundaries, interest in marketing concepts exploded geometrically. On the domestic front, leveraged buyouts and related financial strategies altered the domestic business landscape of the 1980s and 1990s, placing the attainment of short-term profit (and its impact on a firm's stock price) in a new, premier position. This and associated forces had important negative impacts on marketing's role within corporations, causing that role to shrink, shift, and synthesize with previously distinct functional domains (see, e.g., Day 1996; Greyser 1997b; Reibstein 2001; Webster 2002).

In addition, several controversies within the marketing thought community helped create the conditions for Era IV. One such controversy involved control of the mainstream journal for the field and the extent to which it should reflect theory and science rather than practical application. (During much of the 1970s, *JM* had encountered increasing difficulty in trading off the needs of marketing practice against an emerging consensus toward scientific perspectives of scholarship in the field. Both sides generally agreed on maintaining a managerial focus, but they disagreed sharply as to how to approach thought development.) *Just at the dawn of Era IV, a new editorial policy for* JM *was adopted: It would publish only scholarly articles* and would also strive to serve as a "bridge between the scholarly and practical . . . for the thoughtful marketing practitioner and academician" (Kerin 1996, p. 6). Although likely formulated as a compromise, this policy change actually cemented the shift that had been occurring slowly over many years: the takeover of marketing's body of thought by the academic community, together with the virtual disappearance of practitioner representation in the leading journals. To illustrate, as we reported previously, practitioners authored fully 42% of *JM* articles in the journal's first 16 years, during Era II (Appelbaum 1952), but according to Kerin (1996), this proportion has dropped to less than 1% during Era IV. Furthermore, *JM*'s editorial board membership has also shifted sharply, from 60% practitioners in the early 1960s (Era III) to less than 5% in Era IV.

A quite distinct area of controversy also arose at the beginning of Era IV that was contained almost entirely within the consumer behavior sector of the academic community. It arose in reaction to the dominance and strictures of the prevailing positivist scientific approach to research and resulted in heated debates over development of knowledge (e.g., Anderson 1983; Hunt 1983, 1990, 1992; Peter 1992; Peter and Olsen 1983; Zinkhan and Hirschheim 1992). These debates also brought to the surface a second significant reaction that had been held by many consumer behavior academics; this against what was viewed as an imposition of a managerial viewpoint for consumer research. Here, it was pointed out that consumption could (and should, according to proponents) be studied as a social phenomenon unto itself. In addition, consumers' interests clearly were not always perfectly allied with sellers' interests.

The independent status of ACR and *JCR* were instrumental in advancing these academic positions on knowledge development during the remainder of Era IV. Post-positivism has flourished during most of Era IV, joining positivist research to populate this journal and this conference. Furthermore, consumer research has progressed with some attention to a managerial rationale for its efforts, but with a major proportion of its endeavors having no such purpose whatsoever (e.g., Belk 1986; Holbrook 1987; Wilkie 1981). Following the insight of our colleague John Gaski, to get an idea of how strong this position has been within the consumer research community, our count of the nearly 900 articles published by *JCR* in its first 20 years showed that the word "marketing" appeared only three times in an article's title. Furthermore, representation from practitioners and government personnel has also dwindled across Era IV, in keeping with the broader marketing body of thought.

On related fronts, scientific advances had brought more complex concepts and methodologies into the marketing field. Growth in business school enrollment continued, particularly in MBA programs and on a global scale, and led to strong demands for new marketing faculty members. Furthermore, an increasing number of universities adopted "publish-or-perish" career paths for their new faculty, which added pressures for increasingly sophisticated research training in doctoral programs. Thus, three powerful forces were bearing on the academic infrastructure to create Era IV: (1) a growing globalization of business education and application, bringing new thinkers from around the world into the marketing field; (2) a substantial need for more opportunities for research contributions to be communicated to interested peers; and (3) a substantial and increasing need to allow for sophisticated perspectives and language as the frontiers of marketing thought were being explored.

Business Education Goes Global: Bringing New Academics into Marketing

As we noted previously, a major trend during Era IV has been a dramatic globalization of business concepts, as entire blocs of nations have moved toward market-based systems and away from centralized command and control. For example, the Russian Association of Business Education now numbers more than 50 schools, all formed within the past 15 years, and the Central and Eastern European Management Association now has more then 100 member schools, up from only 13 in 1989.[14] In China, the Ministry of Education has accredited more than 60 new MBA programs in the past ten years, and the MBA degree is now the largest single field of study for graduate program applications in China. Growth is not limited to the transitional nations, however. There are now more than 100 business schools offering MBA degrees in the United Kingdom; some 120 MBA schools in Austria, Germany, and Switzerland; and the European Union is pursuing plans to offer a single system for MBA degrees: This would be based on the U.S.–U.K. model and would facilitate economic competitiveness and employment mobility across national boundaries.

Within the United States, Era IV has maintained the momentum from Era III's increasing emphasis on higher education in business, particularly at the MBA level. Recalling Table 4, some 55,000 U.S. MBA degrees were awarded in 1980, at the close of Era III. After 20 years of Era IV, that number has more than doubled, to some 115,000 MBA degrees awarded in 2000. This has contributed to a continuing increase in academic positions available in business schools and a concomitant increase (assuming a publish-or-perish reward system in many universities) in marketing academics who wish to contribute to the body of thought.

The most important impact of globalization on marketing academia has not come from MBA programs but from the dramatic increase in international scholars contributing

---

[14]The educational program statistics in this section are courtesy of the AACSB (2003).

TABLE 6

Indicia of Era IV's Globalization Impact on the Body of Marketing Thought

		Authorships			Editorial Board Memberships		
		Early (1986–1987)	Recent (2001–2002)	Significance	Early (1986–1987)	Recent (2001–2002)	Significance
JPP&M	International	10%	21%	*	14%	11%	N.S.
	Domestic	90	79		86	89	
JCR	International	22	39	*	14	23	N.S.
	Domestic	78	61		86	77	
JM	International	22	53	**	22	33	*
	Domestic	78	47		78	67	
JMR	International	34	63	**	13	43	**
	Domestic	66	37		87	57	
Marketing Science	International	37	75	**	40	60	*
	Domestic	63	25		60	40	

$*p \leq .05; **p \leq .0005.$
Notes: N.S. = not significant.

new theories, concepts, and findings. Earlier in Era IV, a major source was the increasing number of people born outside the United States who attended U.S. doctoral programs and developed the ethos to contribute to marketing knowledge. Many of these academics remained in the United States as faculty members and productive researchers, and others moved to other nations as business faculty positions became increasingly numerous and attractive there.

Has there been a major impact of internationalization on the marketing body of thought during Era IV? Table 6 reports the findings of a modest investigation we undertook to explore the degree to which the globalization impact has been evidenced during this time in five of the most prominent journals of the marketing field.[15] As indicated by the column heads, we compared both the authorship of articles and the membership on the editorial boards for the two-year period 1986 and 1987 with the two-year period 2001 and 2002 for the following publications: *JPP&M, JCR, JM, JMR,* and *Marketing Science.* This enabled us to examine both direct contributions to the body of literature (journal articles) and gatekeeping and influence roles for academic field norms. It was our expectation that the article measure would show a substantial internationalization impact, but given lag times in research career development, we were interested to learn how strongly this had yet appeared for editorial boards.

[15]To assess the impact of internationalization, we identified individuals who were affiliated with U.S. universities, firms, or agencies and who we knew were or believed were born in the United States as "domestic U.S." We assigned the code "international" to anyone (including those who had been born in the United States) affiliated with non-U.S. institutions or who we either knew or strongly believed were born in another nation. If we could not confidently infer a given person's code, we excluded them from the analysis (this occurred in less than 5% of the cases). Thus, the totals we obtained are properly only estimates. Given the clear magnitude of the differences, however, we are confident that the patterns shown are real.

In brief, Table 6's results on both measures are extremely powerful. It is apparent that Era IV has brought about a huge change in the composition of the body of marketing thinkers. Scanning down the left-hand side of the articles section, we see that early in the era (1986–1987), the clear majority of contributors to marketing thought (in these journals) were U.S. natives and were at work in U.S. institutions. On the right-hand side, it is evident that each of these journals was operated by a majority of domestic U.S. academics. Internationally related scholars were much in evidence in both publication and editorial board activity, but they were in the minority across the outlets.

Today, however, the overall picture has changed substantially. As shown in Table 6, internationally related scholars have posted statistically significant gains on nearly every comparison. *Overall, with the exception of JPP&M, we were surprised to discover that for the four most prestigious U.S. marketing journals, internationally related scholars now constitute a majority of total article contributors* (the actual difference is small [55% international versus 45% domestic], but the trend is very strong as internationally related authors have come from very far back to now take the lead). Substantial global gains in editorial board memberships have also occurred, but likely reflecting the aforementioned lag effect, domestic U.S. academics still constitute a clear majority of board membership overall and for all journals except *Marketing Science*.

To better appreciate these overall findings, we should also note that changes in the bases for both measurements (not shown here) are relevant. For example, a noticeable gain (67%) in the size of editorial boards has occurred, from an average of about 50 in 1986 and 1987 to an average of more than 80 recently. Thus, the international gains shown in Table 6 are somewhat understated (e.g., the number of internationally related *JCR* editorial board members has more than doubled during this period, but because the overall board membership increased so much [from less than 60 to more than 90], the proportional representation did not reach statistical significance). The picture with respect to authorship opportunities is quite different but interesting nonetheless. Apart from *JPP&M* (whose number of articles per year roughly doubled across this period because of the move from one to two issues per year), *the publication opportunities in the four most prestigious U.S. marketing journals have basically not changed during this time: The number of contributions per year is about the same today as it was in 1986 and 1987.*

Finally, examination of the individual journals also reveals some interesting findings. In brief, working from the extremes, *Marketing Science* has reflected a strong internationally related presence both in authorship and in leadership since its inception at the start of the 1980s, and *JPP&M* has continued to post high domestic U.S. numbers since its inception at about the same time (more on this in a subsequent section). The second-lowest impacts of internationalization are reflected by *JCR*, but even so, the trend is strong, and the proportion of publications from this source doubled during the 15-year period. In general, *JMR*'s patterns are similar to those of *Marketing Science*, with a solid

TABLE 7

Marketing Journals Introduced During the 1980s

Date	Publication Outlet
1980	*Journal of Personal Selling & Sales Management*
1981	*Journal of Macromarketing*
1982	*Journal of Public Policy & Marketing*
1982	*Marketing Science*
1983	*Journal of Consumer Marketing*
1984	*Psychology and Marketing*
1984	*Journal of Product Innovation and Management*
1984	*International Journal of Research in Marketing*
1987	*Journal of Interactive Marketing*
1989	*Marketing Letters*

majority of internationally related scholars contributing and a tripling of international representation on its editorial board. Although our study did not extend to this issue, our observations of the strong quantitative/analytical backgrounds brought by many internationally related scholars support these results. Finally, we found *JM*'s profile to be of special interest, because this was the publication we have followed so carefully in tracking the mainstream of the marketing field during Eras II and III. In our view, the power of globalization is thus particularly well represented in the *JM* rows of Table 6, reflecting the umbrella vehicle for publication of current, mainstream marketing thought. For *JM*, internationally related scholars are now the majority of authors, with a slower rate of change on this largest of editorial boards (here slower change may reflect both the previously noted time lag and perhaps a different set of reviewing needs, given the broad expanse of topics and approaches for *JM* coverage).

An Outpouring of New Publication Outlets, 1980–1984

The confluence of forces near the end of Era III erupted in a startling burst of new and specialized journals at the very start of Era IV. As shown in Table 7, for just a brief period beginning in 1980, the introduction rate of significant new marketing journals began to rise sharply. *In the five short years from 1980 to 1984, the number of research-based marketing journal outlets more than doubled (from 7 to 15).*[16] The slowly evolving infrastructure over the previous 45 years had clearly changed its pace and direction, at least at the margin, and has continued to do so, though at a lesser rate.

A perusal of the entries in Table 7 reveals that these new outlets were directly aimed at narrower constituencies within the marketing field: The era of research specialization

---

[16]Of course, there are many types of publication outlets, so definition may be an issue for this calculation. To be clear, the seven existing marketing-related journals we used in this assumption were *JM, JMR, JCR, JAR, Journal of Retailing, Journal of the Academy of Marketing Science,* and *JCA.* Generalized publications such as *Harvard Business Review* and *Management Science* were not included here.

had now arrived in full force.[17] Numerous industry-specific trade publications were also introduced during this era, as were several magazine-style journals intended for practitioners and launched by the AMA.

The content and roles played by academic conferences also shifted during Era IV. The large general conferences continued to add simultaneous sessions, and an increasing proportion of these were "special topics" submitted by a small group of people interested in a particular issue. These have been joined by an increasing number of single-topic workshops, symposia, and "research camps" at which specialists gather to pursue advanced developments. As the era moved on, in the 1990s the AMA was forced to adapt to this trend by creating its new special-interest-group (SIG) format in which each academic member can join as many as three groups that hold targeted workshops and otherwise work to support their special facet of marketing thought. As the SIGs gained momentum, they also increased their weight in determining sessions for the AMA's annual academic conferences, thus building in further specialization over time.

Research Specialization and the Fragmentation of the Marketing Mainstream

It is clear that the evolution to research specialties has been deliberate, but it is not clear that a fragmentation of the marketing field was also desired. However, it does appear that this has been a result. *Notice that it is difficult today for a person who wishes to monitor the developments in marketing to stay current with the sheer volume of articles being published.* For example, a recent publication analysis by Baumgartner and Pieters (2003) explores citation patterns for some 49 marketing-related journals as of 1997 and indicates that this number has doubled since 1982 (during Era IV).

With respect to fragmentation, Baumgartner and Pieters (2003) find that citation patterns indicate at least five natural subareas of marketing thought, which they label as follows:

1. Core marketing (8 journals, *JMR* is most influential),
2. Consumer behavior (9 journals, *JCR* is most influential),
3. Managerial marketing (9 journals, *Harvard Business Review* is most influential),
4. Marketing applications (21 journals, *JM* is most influential), and
5. Marketing education (2 journals, *Journal of Marketing Education* is most influential).

They also point out that the spans of citation influence for *JM* and *JMR* are particularly broad, as they are rated among the top five journals for each of the five subareas. Thus, these results indicate that there are simultaneous pressures both toward and away from cohesion for the academic marketing field.

---

[17]Some older journals also were specialized, as in advertising and consumer behavior and affairs, so the phenomenon was not new. However, the new journals during this period clearly extended research specialization into many new domains. Some reflected marketing decision areas, including in the international realm, and others were geared to applications of behavioral sciences. *Marketing Science* was born in 1982 of a perceived need for a quality outlet to welcome marketing model development (Morrison 2001), and *Marketing Letters* provided an opportunity for short articles with creative insights and findings. Finally, two new journals reflected societal interests.

However, on several other fronts it appears that fewer academics are interested in making the effort to pursue the entire mainstream of marketing thought: Instead, specialization has come to play the primary role in our professional lives. It is the case that increasingly specialized languages, theories, and methods have evolved. Although this should serve to enhance the rigor of thought, it also makes it increasingly difficult for people not engaged in that research to discern what is developing there. Thus, over time, the specialty areas have become more silo-like in their activities.

Is this a positive or a negative? It appears to be a reasonable view to be pleased with the general stream of developments during Era IV, viewing fragmentation of the mainstream as an indication of the natural progression into a mature discipline. Conversely, it could be the case that this evolution has brought about a situation in which (1) communication across the field is breaking down; (2) doctoral education is failing to present sufficient history, scope, and perspective upon which future scholars can build the body of thought about marketing as a field; and (3) cumulative responsiveness to important external challenges is lagging as a result. Whichever is the overall conclusion, it is clear that at present it is difficult to summarize the state of the marketing mainstream in the early years of the new century. The shifts just described have had strong impacts on the field's viewpoints about itself and have directly affected the treatment of marketing's relationship to its society.

ERA IV's ATTENTION TO MARKETING AND SOCIETY

A Puzzling Paradox

Era IV has experienced a paradoxical evolution of interest and coverage of marketing and society. *First, this era has brought the most significant decline in mainstream interest in this topic during the entire history (nearly a century) of marketing thought.* It is fair to say that most marketing thinkers' attention has been directed elsewhere and that many have given virtually no research thought to this question during the entire Era IV. This does not appear to be due to any overt opposition to study of the issues here but rather reflects other priorities. For example, a quick look at the published lists of "MSI Research Priorities" over the past 30 years provides interesting illumination of the changes being registered at the field's think tank, MSI:

- End of Era III: From 1975 to 1980, "Marketing and the Public Interest" and/or "Government Regulation and Marketing Practice" are listed each year as a research priority.
- Start of Era IV: From 1982 to 1985, "The Marketing Environment" is listed as a priority topic.
- Early Era IV: From 1986 to 1990, there is no listing for this area among the priorities.
- Mid–Era IV: From 1990 to 1994, marketing and society topics reappear as a priority.

- Recent Era IV: Since 1994, structures of the listing change fairly often. However, a chart summarizing the top seven MSI research priorities for the next five periods (1994–2004) shows no mention of marketing and society issues in any of the 35 listings (Lehmann 2002). This is not to suggest that these topics are not of interest to MSI, but the lack of a sense of urgency is clear (e.g., public issues were ranked at 14, 15, and 15 in the late 1990s, and "Marketing and Society" is currently listed as a third-tier priority for 2002–2004). Although not high on the list of priorities, however, MSI has been a consistent financial supporter of initiatives in this area, such as the annual Marketing and Public Policy Conference.

Beyond MSI per se, an academic's choice of specific research problems also raises another key consideration: the effects of choosing a "level of analysis" appropriate to a given issue. To illustrate, for most marketing strategists and most marketing scientists, adopting the managerial perspective means focusing on the firm: Analyses of the Aggregate Marketing System (Wilkie and Moore 1999) are actually dysfunctional for solving firm-level problems.[18] Meanwhile, for many consumer researchers, emphasis has been on individual consumers or household decisions: Again, a systemwide examination of either marketing or consumers would be a dysfunctional choice given the research goals.

The paradox arrives with a second recognition that within its own smaller sphere, the area of marketing and society has actually been flourishing, especially during the second half of Era IV. This has been primarily due to an active subset of marketing thinkers who (1) have built a welcoming infrastructure to encourage thought development and (2) have continued personally to pursue research on these issues with enthusiasm and energy. Overall, then, this paradoxical state of affairs reflects the fragmentation that is more generally evident in the marketing field during Era IV. Thus, there are a number of other interest areas with similar research situations at present.

A Specialized Infrastructure Develops

As we noted previously, one of the true prerequisites of a vibrant research area is the presence of an academic infrastructure that (1) assists thinkers in learning about important

---

[18]A brief analysis of two leading textbooks indicates a differential treatment of marketing and society topics in Era IV, depending on the degree of managerial emphasis toward marketing. We explored the undergraduate-level *Principles of Marketing* by Kotler and Armstrong (2004) and Kotler's (2003) graduate-level text, *Marketing Management.* The undergraduate book contains 20 chapters, with the final chapter titled "Marketing and Society: Social Responsibility and Marketing Ethics." In addition, there are brief discussions of societal issues in chapters on pricing strategies, direct marketing, the marketing environment, and marketing in the digital age. Overall, then, this area is represented and discussed, though not as a major focus. In contrast, the graduate-level text directly reflects the managerial orientation throughout, as indicated by its title, and marketing and society topics are clearly much less in evidence, even in comparison with that above. Of the 22 chapters here, none is devoted to marketing and society. Very limited discussions appear on certain topics at several points in the book, which advances the need for a "societal marketing concept" (pp. 126–27) and addresses ethical issues, briefly, on several separate occasions. Given the managerial perspective, however, topics are primarily addressed in terms of a manager's scope of attention, motivations, interests, and span of control. Marketing and society topics are clearly not a priority set of concerns for students whose views are being shaped by this important book. (The authors thank an anonymous reviewer for suggesting both the MSI priorities analysis and this examination of modern marketing textbooks.)

developments, (2) provides vehicles for publication of quality research, and (3) generally facilitates communication and interchange among researchers who have common interests. Typically, this consists of one or more associations that offer conferences, a newsletter or Web site, and a journal. It was during Era IV that the marketing and society research area created a strong infrastructure for itself.

First came the journals. *Journal of Macromarketing* (*JMM*) began in 1981, followed shortly and independently by *JPP&M* in 1982. The founding editor of *JMM*, George Fisk (1981, p. 3), described the goal of this journal as follows: "to provide a forum in which people can debate and clarify the role of marketing and society. . . . [W]e hope to identify social issues in which improvements in knowledge can lead to improvements in the way resources are managed in private and public organizations to serve society's interest." Subsequent *JMM* editors included Stanley Shapiro, Robert Nason (whose stewardship of the journal extended for 11 years), Luis Dominguez, Sanford Grossbart, and Clifford Schultz. During his editorship, Nason (1992, p. 1) clarified that macromarketing was viewed to be both positive and normative; "positive in its dispassionate identification and measurement of macromarketing phenomena, and normative in its search for a fundamental philosophy of societal improvement." Over time, *JMM* has published articles covering a wide expanse of topics and perspectives. Recently, the structure has been altered to codify several distinct special sections to welcome particular topics, now including (1) marketing history, (2) quality-of-life studies, (3) marketing and development, (4) competition and markets, (5) global policy and environment, (6) marketing ethics, and (7) reviews and communications.

Meanwhile, according to its founding editor, Thomas Kinnear (1982, p. 2), *JPP&M* was begun to "provide a forum for dialogue on issues in marketing and public policy." Empirical studies were particularly encouraged, and many appeared in the ensuing years. Subsequent *JPP&M* editors included Patrick Murphy, Michael Mazis, Debra Scammon, J. Craig Andrews, and currently Joel Cohen. In 1990, the publication moved from the University of Michigan to the AMA. An excellent overview of the history of *JPP&M* has recently been compiled by Sprott and Miyazaki (2002), who report that some 455 articles were published in the first 20 years of the journal, written by 602 authors from 272 different institutions. Interested readers are urged to consult this article, which covers the history of *JPP&M*, a content analysis of its articles, its authors and institutions, and citation impacts (we return to *JPP&M* later in this section in describing topical frameworks for marketing and society research).

The development of marketing and society research was also spurred by conferences during Era IV. The macromarketing group had been holding an annual conference for several years preceding the advent of *JMM*, and others interested in additional aspects of marketing and society were attending their own special meetings and gathering in sessions at the mainstream marketing and consumer research conferences. In 1989, an invitation-only symposium was held on the Notre Dame campus in recognition of the FTC's seventy-fifth anniversary (Murphy and Wilkie 1990). This provided an impetus for regular meetings that grew into the annual Marketing and Public Policy Conference. Several years later, the Marketing and Society SIG was formed within the AMA and grew quickly. Thus, a strong infrastructure for knowledge development had been created and continues to serve today.

A Wide Range of Research Topics and Issues

What topics characterize marketing and society research through Era IV and up to today? This is a difficult question to answer briefly, given the vast domain of potential issues. However, several distinct frameworks highlight the diverse research dimensions of this field (that we need to review four such frameworks reflects how significant multiple perspectives are to this field of thought).

First, a simpler framework has proved useful for research in the consumer interest: the Consumer Bill of Rights. This was enunciated in 1962, when President John F. Kennedy sent the U.S. Congress his now famous declaration that asserted consumers' place within U.S. society. The four propositions are the following:

1. Right to Safety: Consumers have the right to be protected against products and services that are hazardous to health and life.
2. Right to Be Informed: Consumers have the right to be protected against fraudulent, deceitful, or misleading advertising or other practices and to be given the facts they need to make an informed choice.
3. Right to Choose: Consumers have the right to be assured, whenever possible, access to a variety of products and services at competitive prices. In industries where competition is not workable, government regulation is substituted to ensure quality and service at fair prices.
4. Right to Be Heard: Consumers have the right to be assured that consumer interests will receive full and sympathetic consideration in the formulation of government policy and fair and expeditious treatment in its administrative tribunals.

This framework provides a basis by which the "marketing/consumer environment" can be examined in society (Wilkie 1994). *The general goal is that such a marketplace be both "fair" and "efficient" for marketers, competitors, and consumers alike.* The Consumer Bill of Rights has been used as a research-organizing framework in both a major research compendium authored by consumer advocates (Maynes 1988) and in an excellent overview prepared for consumer researchers (Andreasen 1991).

Moving from a sole focus on consumer rights, a second framework of interest has recently been developed by Sprott and Miyazaki (2002) to classify the 455 articles that appeared in the first 20 years of *JPP&M*. Although restricted to just this journal, it is a much broader and more complex schema: Its hierarchical structure is based on 4 primary categories, 23 main categories under these, and 60 further subcategories under these. The four primary categories are as follows:

1. Protection of consumers,
2. Protection of marketers,
3. Policy and policymaking, and
4. Societal issues.

Note that the first three categories reflect the three institutional players in the market system—consumers, marketers, and government—and the fourth category reflects broader research issues. It is also notable that each of these four major categories received significant attention in *JPP&M* during Era IV: Protection of marketers was the smallest, but it still accounted for some 111 articles, and protection of consumers was the largest, with approximately twice this number of articles. Furthermore, the existence of some 83 subsidiary categories indicates the breadth within these headings.

A third significant framework was developed for the recent *Handbook of Marketing and Society*, edited by Paul Bloom and Gregory Gundlach (2001). Their framework is designed to encourage future work by pointing to possible areas for knowledge development. Several notable elements of the framework are its emphasis on marketing knowledge as a positive force for improved decisions and the enhancement of consumer welfare as the system's goal. Analysis of the framework helps in recognizing the means–end nature of much activity in this research field, as is evident in considering its primary organizing sectors and their chapter contents:

- *"How Knowledge About Marketing Improves Public Policy Decisions"*: This area of research assesses how marketing knowledge can improve and has improved public policy regulatory decisions on consumer protection (especially at the FTC and the Food and Drug Administration [FDA]), on antitrust policies (at the FTC and the U.S. Department of Justice), and with regard to deceptive advertising and selling techniques (at the FTC and the court system).
- *"Impacts of Corporate Marketing Decisions on Competition"*: This area focuses on mainstream marketing management research topics, but here explores their implications for potential legality and effects on competition as well as consumer decisions. Examples of topics include advertising's effects on price and competition, socioeconomic consequences of franchising distribution, and positive and negative aspects of pricing strategies.
- *"Impacts of Public Policy Decisions"*: These topics focus on the impacts of public policy decisions on both competition and consumers. Some topics here reflect attention to technical aspects of product and service offerings, such as how public policymakers and marketers can best regulate product safety and emerging issues and challenges

in the arena of consumer privacy. Other topics rely heavily on consumer research expertise, such as consumer response to warnings, the effectiveness of nutritional labels on foods, the effectiveness of environmental product claims, and the effects of deceptive advertising regulation.

- *"Social Marketing Initiatives"*: This area reflects marketing tools that increasingly are adopted by not-for-profit (whether governmental or private) agencies involved with education, health, poverty, religion, crime prevention, and myriad other social programs. Formally, social marketing differs from traditional marketing in aiming to benefit the target audience directly (e.g., AIDS awareness, childhood immunization) or society as a whole (e.g., recycling programs, blood donations) rather than the firm sponsoring the program (Andreasen 1994).

- *"Understudied Topics"*: Although not designated by this term in the *Handbook,* the remaining links in Bloom and Gundlach's framework have had little research undertaken within the marketing academic community, though interesting issues are present. Examples here include corporate response to alterations in the legal environment (e.g., how grocery manufacturers changed their marketing mixes in response to the nutritional labeling law, how companies react to antitrust enforcement) and to issues with public relations or reputational overtones (e.g., corporate responses to boycotts). Chapters are also devoted to intellectual property laws (trademarks, patents), economic development, and marketing's long-term impacts on consumer welfare.

Finally, we turn to a detailed portrayal of research topics by considering a fourth framework. It was developed by William Wilkie and Gregory Gundlach as part of a database project to capture all public policy–related articles published in marketing between 1970 and 1990 (e.g., Gundlach and Wilkie 1990). Through an iterative process, research articles were examined and then assigned to primary, secondary, and tertiary framework categories, with the creation of new categories and reassignments when necessary. Table 8 depicts an adapted version of this framework. Note that it contains more than 100 categories. *Every category has been the topic of some research by marketing academics.* Furthermore, the number of gradations within headings is a reasonable reflection of areas of greater or lesser stress.

Notice that the literature reflects a strong emphasis on marketing-mix issues in general. Promotion issues receive the most attention, but marketing authors have actually pursued each of the 4 P's to a considerable extent. It is also apparent that consumer protection has been heavily stressed, reflecting both the prominence of consumer research among many marketing academics and the fact that the FTC, the FDA, and the courts have called on marketing academics to provide expertise in operating some programs in this area. In contrast, antitrust attorneys and economists have only very recently begun to discern that marketing academia might be a source of useful expertise (see the special section on this topic in the Fall 2002 issue of *JPP&M*). Here, however, our primary concern is to

TABLE 8

The Wilkie and Gundlach Framework of Topics in Marketing and Public Policy Research

General Topics	Marketing Management Topics		Consumer Protection Topics

General Topics

International Issues
- Marketing and economic development
- Protectionism
- Corrupt practices
- General international

Public Policy Participants
- U.S. Supreme Court
- Administrative agencies
- State and local government

General Antitrust
- Antitrust regulation

Other Governmental Regulation
- Commercial speech
- General governmental regulation

Self-Regulation
- Advertising self-regulation
- Local business bureaus

Information Technology Issues
- Internet marketing
- Consumer welfare impacts of the "digital divide"
- Impacts on marketing productivity
- Consumer privacy

Market Research Issues
- Using marketing research
- Market research problems

Marketing Management Topics

Product Issues
- Protection of trade secrets
- Patents
- Copyright
- Trademarks
- Certification marks
- Warranty
- Product liability
- Safety
- Package and labeling
- Nutrition information
- Services
- Product standards
- General product

Place Issues
- Exclusive dealing
- Tying contracts
- Territorial and customer restrictions
- Resale price maintenance
- Reciprocity
- Refusals to deal
- Functional discounts
- Vertical integration
- Gray markets
- Mergers
- Franchising
- Slotting allowances
- General place

Pricing Issues
- Price fixing
- Exchanging price information
- Parallel pricing
- Predatory pricing
- Discriminatory pricing
- Credit practices
- Robinson-Patman Act
- Unit pricing
- Reference price
- Item price removal
- General price

Promotion Issues
- Deceptive advertising
- Unfairness in advertising
- Advertising to children
- Advertising substantiation
- Affirmative disclosure
- Corrective advertising
- Multiple product remedy
- Comparative advertising
- Endorsements
- Price promotions
- Warranty promotions
- Credit promotions
- Sweepstakes and contests
- Personal selling practices
- Mail order selling
- Referral selling
- Brokerage allowances
- Promotional allowances
- Promotion of professional services
- Cigarette advertising
- Political advertising
- Sex roles in advertising
- General promotion

Consumer Protection Topics

Consumerism and Consumer Protection Issues
- Consumerism
- Socially conscious consumers
- Quality of life
- Legal aspects
- Comparative marketing
- Marketing of governmental programs
- Competition
- General macro issues
- Marketer behavior
- Management of consumer protection
- Consumer information
- Consumer education
- Consumer complaining
- Vulnerable segments
- Ethnic targeting
- Consumer practices
- Environmental issues
- Energy conservation
- Minority-owned businesses
- Consumer affairs
- Ethics
- Consumer Satisfaction/ dissatisfaction
- Consumer information search
- Medical programs
- Objective price/quality
- Social marketing
- General consumer protection

communicate the wide array of research issues that has been studied. After reading through Table 8, one can easily note how distinct and advanced are its many topics, and why they would be of significance to marketers and to society in general.

Given all of the foregoing information, it seems reasonable to ask, Is this academic area large or small? Relative to its wide scope of topics and issues, the field can appear to be underpopulated and underdeveloped. However, we should recognize that at present the body of thought in this area is not small. In fact, there are well over 1000 articles in the area of marketing and public policy alone, according to an update of the Gundlach and Wilkie (1990) study (for study base, see Note 15). Thus, there is a need for perspective on the present, an issue to which we now turn.

Quo Vadis? Quo Vadimus?

Where are we going? Where should we want to go? The academic field of marketing holds vast scope, great complexity, and great promise, but the answers to these questions are surely not obvious. To assist in addressing them, in this article, we have undertaken an extended look at the development of modern thought in marketing, with special attention to broader issues for the field. In this concluding section, we present several summary conclusions, pointing to further issues and implications in need of careful consideration by thinkers in the college of marketing.

CONCLUSION 1: MARKETING'S TREATMENT OF SOCIETAL ISSUES HAS CHANGED OVER TIME

Table 9 presents a summary of our findings of the treatment of marketing's relationship to society across the 4 Eras of marketing thought. Not included in Table 9, but most relevant to it, is that a dramatic evolution of the real world of the U.S. Aggregate Marketing System underpins everything there. In magnitude, sophistication, substance, and performance, the reality of "marketing" is vastly different today than it was a century ago, as is the "society" within which it operates.

Our exploration convincingly revealed, moreover, that there is much more than sheer growth that is at issue. *Indeed, the fundamental relationship between marketing and society, as conceived by the thought leaders of the marketing field, has changed as well.* This is largely due to the conception of marketing itself having changed, giving rise to the "4 Eras," already discussed in detail. An important finding here is the extent to which the tenor of the times is reflected within the body of marketing thought. This point also applies to the right-hand column of Table 9, which addresses the treatment of marketing's relationship to society in each era. The manner in which the current world is reflected in our field's thinking about society, however, has shifted somewhat here as well. In contrast to early treatments of marketing as an economic distribution system for goods and

TABLE 9

Treatment of Marketing and Society Issues over the "4 Eras" of Marketing Thought

Era	Key Characteristics of Marketing's Treatment of Societal Issues
"Pre-Marketing" (Before 1900)	• Public policy toward economic pursuits of central interest; laissez-faire versus government constraints.
I. "Founding the Field" (1900–1920)	• Focus on value of marketing's distributive activities to consumers and society. • Stress on economic benefits: specialization by marketing agents was perceived as contributing to economic growth and efficiency.
II. "Formalizing the Field" (1920–1950)	• Continued emphasis on economic efficiency of marketing functions: A major question is, Does distribution cost too much? • New emphases in mid-era reflected tenor of the times: pricing laws and practices a major issue per 1930s economic depression. World War II focus moved to issues such as price controls, supply rationing policies, and so on. • Peak of interest during World War II; estimated 55% of *JM* articles on societal issues. • Postwar period: new focus on marketing and economic prosperity.
III. "A Paradigm Shift—Marketing, Management, and the Sciences" (1950–1980)	• Throughout era, there is continued interest in government constraints on business. • Decreasing attention to assessing system efficiency. • In 1960s, increased attention to managerial implications of government actions and to marketing to the government. • Kennedy's Consumer Bill of Rights presages onset of consumerism. • Second half of era features widespread interest in societal issues. Dramatic increase in attention to broadening the concept of marketing, social debates, and regulatory agency actions in consumer protection.
IV. "The Shift Intensifies—A Fragmentation of the Mainstream" (1980–present)	• Formal development of specialized research infrastructure for marketing and society area: *JPP&M* and *JMM* first published, annual Marketing and Public Policy Conference begins, and AMA SIG is formed. • Sharp decline in area during the 1980s and then steady increase in 1990s; wide range of academic topics and issues studied (captured in frameworks). • Six subgroups solidify with diverse substantive interests, levels of analysis, and research methods: public policy, marketing ethics, macromarketing, consumer economics, social marketing, and international consumer policy. • Potential for marginalization escalates. • Present-day paradox: Mainstream interest in marketing and society issues has declined across the era, yet area of marketing and society flourishes within itself.

services, there now is much more attention given to strategies and practices involved in effectively managing marketing-related programs, whether these be in social marketing settings, government regulatory settings, self-regulatory settings, or a gamut of responsible business practices in the private sector. As was demonstrated in the discussion of Era IV, the body of knowledge that has accumulated is impressively broad, interesting, and useful. It is, at the same time, necessarily incomplete, given the vast array of important societal issues that might be studied in depth.

CONCLUSION 2: THE "MARKETING AND SOCIETY" AREA TODAY IS ITSELF FRAGMENTED

There is also another significant characteristic to consider about the area after more than 20 years of Era IV. To wit, rather than a single unified presence, there are at least *six subgroups* hard at work on research dealing with marketing and society issues, some with their own journals and conferences. These groups are outlined and briefly described in Figure 4. When reading through it, note that though topics are related, true prospects for future integration are actually hindered by significant differences in levels of analysis, methods, and substantive focus. For example, among the six primary groups, there are people who wish to focus on social change and help those managing these efforts (*social marketing*), others who wish to focus on helping corporate marketers make more ethical decisions (*marketing ethics*), and still others who focus on the aggregate marketing system and its impacts on economic development, quality of life, or other issues (*macromarketing*). Another set of researchers focuses either on helping government decision makers and marketers devise more efficient and effective regulatory policies or legislation or on broader issues involving the roles for government, marketers, and the legal system (*public policy and marketing*). Furthermore, some people are approaching problems within different cultural and political contexts (*international consumer policy*), and some are approaching with different aims and methods (*consumer interest economists*).

It is the case that during the 1990s, efforts were undertaken to integrate these groups into a larger area of focus, and more than 200 marketing academics joined the Marketing and Society SIG of the AMA. However, true integration did not really occur for at least half of the groups listed, and each of the previously specialized conferences and journals continues to operate today. Although not a cohesive entity, however, the fact that these various vehicles exist presents a significant set of outlets for scholars seeking to publish their work. Furthermore, for publication purposes, these specialized journals have been receptive to a variety of topics and approaches, and the mainstream marketing journals, especially *JM*, have also been generally willing to publish work on marketing and society. So our discussion of Era IV ends with a visit to the paradox noted previously: The marketing and society area has been treated with "benign neglect" by the new academic mainstream of research in marketing, but this mainstream has itself been fragmented and

---

FIGURE 4

Six Subgroups in Marketing and Society

Public Policy and Marketing. This informal group has its own annual conference and the specialized *JPP&M*, published by the AMA. Its focus has been largely on the legal system and government's regulatory and legislative policies with regard to marketing, and it enjoys strong ties to MSI and to professionals at the FTC and FDA. It welcomes government, industry, and legal practitioners as well as academics from any discipline, but the dominant constituency is from marketing academia.

Macromarketing. This informal group has several annual conferences and the specialized *JMM*, published by Sage Publications. Its orientation represents the closest ties to an overall marketing system view as represented in Eras I and II. It also has formed alliances with smaller groups focused on economic development, quality-of-life studies, and marketing history.

Consumer Economics. The American Council on Consumer Interests is an organization that comprises primarily consumer economists who study marketing issues from the perspective of advancing the consumer interest. This group also holds its own annual conference and publishes the *JCA*, which has broadened its content to include additional areas such as consumer law and communications. In addition, many consumer-oriented marketing academics have published in this journal.

Social Marketing. This has been a loosely affiliated group of researchers who are interested in assisting not-for-profits and government agencies in designing effective interventions. It does not publish a journal, but it does have ties to the more practice-oriented *Social Marketing Quarterly* and the annual conference "Innovations in Social Marketing." Opportunities for volunteer projects are also available through the Social Marketing Institute, which has its headquarters in Washington, D.C.

Marketing Ethics. The Society for Business Ethics draws its membership from various business disciplines, but it does not publish its own journal. *Business Ethics Quarterly* is the major outlet in this area, and it does have a special editor for marketing. Within marketing, this is more a community than a formal group. It has been quite active in creating special sessions at the major marketing conferences. Given difficult issues in crossing cultures, the International Society of Business, Economics, and Ethics is also worthy of note.

International Consumer Policy. Distance and cultures still present barriers. These people are at work in other nations, with only sporadic interactions with the U.S. groups. They publish two journals on different aspects of this topic: *Journal of Consumer Policy* (now, however, edited at Cornell University) and *Journal of Economic Psychology*.

is less powerful. Within its own ambit, moreover, marketing and society research is also fragmented, yet in some respects it offers both fertile questions and accessible publication opportunities.

CONCLUSION 3: MARKETING AND SOCIETY BELONGS AS AN INTRINSIC PART OF MAINSTREAM MARKETING THOUGHT

As we have succinctly stated elsewhere (Wilkie and Moore 1999, p. 217), we believe the following: *"One responsibility of academia is to place a field of study into proper perspective. We believe the Aggregate Marketing System should come to occupy a central position in research in the marketing field."* It is clear that this was once the case, but it is not the case today, at least in terms of coverage in doctoral programs, research journals, and research conferences of both the quantitative and behavioral science researchers of the field. In contrast, two recent undertakings intended to advance scholarship in the field of marketing have reflected positively on this point. First, *JM*'s 1999 fifth Special Issue (known to researchers as the "Millenium Issue") was envisioned to "help the marketing discipline look to the future" (Lusch 1999, p. 1). Titled "Fundamental Issues and Directions for Marketing," its organizers focused on four key questions:

1. How do customers and consumers really behave?
2. How do markets function and evolve?
3. How do firms relate to their markets? and
4. What are the contributions of marketing to organizational performance and social welfare?

The target audience for this issue was deliberately identified by *JM* Editor Robert Lusch (1999, p. 1) as "marketing academics in general, not just specialists in some narrower subfield of marketing." Thus, this issue was directly intended to maintain a mainstream of thought for the future of the field. Moreover, MSI provided funding and support for this endeavor, in collaboration with the AMA. The editors of this special issue, George Day and David Montgomery (1999), further assessed the current state of the academic marketing field and the challenges confronting it. For our purposes here, however, it is most important to note that marketing and society was clearly included here as an integral component of the mainstream of the field.

Furthermore, this position has been maintained in another recent high-level mainstream research undertaking, *Handbook of Marketing* (Weitz and Wensley 2002). Its target audience is research-oriented academics, and it is especially designed for use in doctoral programs to provide a firm foundation across the expanse of the marketing field. Again, marketing and society is clearly identified as an integral component of the body of thought; indeed, Chapter 1's title is "Marketing's Relationship to Society." Let us not miss the point, however, that these two efforts merit special notice precisely because they are not common today, and each was constructed in part to assist directly in resisting the tidal wave of research fragmentation.

CONCLUSION 4: FRAGMENTATION OF MARKETING THOUGHT IS A POWERFUL, PERHAPS IRRESISTIBLE FORCE—HOWEVER, IT DESERVES CAREFUL CONSIDERATION AND POSSIBLE ACTION BY THE COMMUNITY OF SCHOLARS IN OUR FIELD

This we found to be an extremely complex issue. Fragmentation is in part an outgrowth of research specialization, which affords depth and sophistication, and has delivered significant advances in methodologies and concepts to the field. In this sense, it is a very positive phenomenon. However, fragmentation has been spurred in part by the spread of the publish-or-perish system, leading to a dramatic increase in journal and conference outlets into which work can be placed. For individual authors wishing to place their work, this may provide a true sense of advance and improvement, and it does contribute to the advance of a specialty area. However, for the field as a whole, other topics not selected for attention will be failing to advance at the same time.

Exacerbating this fundamental issue is the fact that there are now so many current publications (at least 49, according to Baumgartner and Pieters's [2003] recent analysis) that it is virtually impossible to keep up with the material across the field. In addition, the research-oriented doctoral student or faculty member may well encounter significant pressures to produce and publish research in a quite constrained time period. Again, there is a latent conflict, but here it involves allocation of time to be spent in learning and contemplating knowledge developed by others versus creating and producing new knowledge. A common solution is to specialize deeply in the precise sphere in which an academic is attempting to create the contribution: This affords both learning and contemplation on the selected material and can contribute to significant advances for the field. However, time and energy are not limitless: The modern research academic who would choose to devote significant time to reading literature unrelated to a specialty topic could appear to be behaving in an almost dysfunctional manner.

What about the presence of the marketing and society area in a fragmented field of marketing? Given its often-close ties to the substantive domain, it is significant that the modern infrastructure for knowledge development has been virtually taken over by academics steeped in the view that the theoretical and methodological domains naturally should take precedence over the substantive domain. There are excellent arguments for prizing excellence in both theory and method, but it should also be recognized that a too simplistic acceptance of this view can have negative consequences as well. In this regard, a good lesson of this project for us was that marketing thought has a large volitional component to it: Absent institutional strictures, marketing thinkers can choose to think about those issues that they believe are most important, interesting, or pressing and can ignore others at the same time.

This project's analysis of Era IV suggests that the ideal of a broadly balanced conceptualization of marketing on the part of individual scholars has been disappearing during Era IV, and at least portions of the substantive domain have been the losers in this process. In consumer behavior research, for example, ACR has represented quality and integrity since its founding. However, it appears that many members today may not realize that the founding mission of ACR was to bring academic researchers, marketing practitioners, and government representatives together in a collegial quest to pursue consumer research issues. Today, however, the membership of ACR appears to have only 3 members (of some 1700) from the government sector. Similarly, *JM*'s recent editorial board listed more than 100 members, of whom only 2 were from marketing practice and none from government agencies (as we noted previously, the *JM* editorial board of the early 1960s had 60% practitioners). Thus, the academic presence in the field not only has grown substantially but also has moved to insulate itself to a great extent. Whether this is good or bad is, of course, debatable, but it could well have implications for the receptivity of reviewers to marketing and society contributions representing problems of the substantive domain.

CONCLUSION 5: A MAJOR COST OF FRAGMENTATION IS THAT KNOWLEDGE IS BEING LOST FROM OUR FIELD—THIS CALLS FOR DIRECTED CONSIDERATION OF MODIFICATIONS TO DOCTORAL EDUCATION IN MARKETING

Pursuing the issue of fragmentation a bit further, this project actually underscores a point of concern that we have had for some time: *It is troubling to realize that knowledge does not necessarily accumulate in a field; knowledge can disappear over time if it is not actually transmitted* (Wilkie 1981). In crossing the span of the 4 Eras, it is evident that some insights, perspectives, and findings did not get passed on but were replaced by other, more recent discoveries. In addition, as Andreasen (1997) points out in speaking of marketing and society research, some important social problems were "left behind" (insufficient progress was achieved) as researchers turned their attention to new frontiers.

This project provided an opportunity to observe more closely the process of change in marketing thought activities across time. Two key factors have already been noted: the significance of external developments in the larger world and the volitional choices of individual thinkers as to topics of primary importance for their work (consider the substantial impact of postpositivism within consumer behavior research). A further factor is that different thought leaders come to the forefront as the field advances over time. Thus, there is a time overlap as the eras shift, with a continuity of previous approaches during an influx of the predominant new dimensions. For example, the thought leaders of Era II generally did not lead the change into Era III; instead, in the main they continued to build on and extend their previous paths of inquiry while the new wave of contributors was beginning to bring the new quantitative and behavioral research approaches that would come to characterize the research of the next decades.

This third insight prompts us to examine more closely whence the academic marketing thought leaders of the future come and how their scholarly training and predispositions are being shaped. How are they being trained to answer the question of the role, if any, for marketing and society? This issue will not receive due consideration unless current scholars are willing to consider that important knowledge has been and continues to be lost from the active body of marketing thought. *As research specialization has increased, this risk has increased: Knowledge outside of a person's specialty may first be viewed as noninstrumental, then as nonessential, then as nonimportant, and finally as nonexistent in terms of meriting attention.* Our concern is not for the aware scholar who may opt to make an informed choice, but for later generations of scholars (today's and the future's doctoral students) who may not gain enough background to realize that a choice is available to them.

To examine this risk, a survey of AMA–Sheth Doctoral Consortium participants was run as an earlier part of this project (Wilkie and Moore 1997). The results strongly suggest that these concerns are justified. Although two-thirds of the doctoral candidates reported having a personal interest in learning about marketing and society, less than one in ten has taken even one course in the subject (ever, and most were in or near their last year of formal education). Furthermore, they were honest in reporting their self-ratings of expertise to be low; regular readership of the journals most pertinent to marketing and society was very low, as was their prior participation in the conferences for this area. Finally, many of these respondents honestly answered that they do not regard this area as professionally relevant for them, at least at this stage of their careers. Doctoral programs sorely need to reconsider this issue. Fortunately, the recent appearance of *Handbook of Marketing* should offer an entry point for many more doctoral students than has been the case during Era IV. Of course, it will still be necessary that the current scholars leading these seminars assign and cover this topic.

CONCLUSION 6: A CALL TO ACTION IS APPROPRIATE FOR THE FIELD OF ACADEMIC MARKETING—IT IS TIME FOR AN ACADEMIC MARKETING SUMMIT TO EXPLORE VIABLE MEANS TO ENHANCE SCHOLARSHIP IN OUR FIELD

This project served as a cogent reminder of the promise, potential, and sheer wonder of the cumulative body of marketing thought. The previous conclusions are sufficient to demonstrate a need for wisdom in exploring means to create a better context for scholarship in the future. Worthy topics that we would suggest for consideration include the following: (1) the character of business schools' vocational objectives for university faculty members; (2) the publish-or-perish system's incentives and time constraints; (3) the character of the modern journal publication system; (4) the nature and objectives of research-oriented doctoral programs, especially the extent to which failure to provide sufficient background in intrinsic domains of marketing thought may lead to problems for the future of the field; and (5) the implications, problems, and opportunities presented by the twin forces of globalization and the Internet.

Such a summit is feasible. Similar efforts have been undertaken before in our field with interesting and impressive results. These include the "Commission on the Effectiveness of Research and Development for Marketing Management," a group of 18 prominent marketing thinkers (8 academics and 10 practitioners) sponsored by the AMA and MSI in the late 1970s (Myers, Massy, and Greyser 1980) and the AMA's "Task Force on the Development of Marketing Thought," headed by Kent Monroe in the late 1980s (AMA Task Force 1988). It seems clear to us that another effort is needed now.

A CLOSING COMMENT ON THE FUTURE

We feel privileged to have been able to undertake this most interesting venture through the literature of our field. We have learned much and have been impressed with the spirit and enthusiasm for discovery that has characterized our field across the years. There is no question that the body of thought has been impressively advanced, and in exciting ways. This will surely continue in the future, especially in light of emerging globalization challenges and opportunities, the spread of the Internet phenomenon, other new technological innovations, and a changing set of consumers and citizens. At the same time, we cannot escape the impression that in our field's advance much has also been left behind, as emphasis has been continually at advancing the frontiers. As we suspect readers of *JPP&M* will agree, the questions, insights, principles, and discoveries that constitute marketing and society should not be left out of the minds of future marketing thought leaders. It is up to us to get them there and then up to future scholars to retain and build on this base.

References

AACSB (2003), *International Doctoral Faculty Commission Draft Report.* St. Louis: AACSB.

Aaker, David A. and George S. Day (1982), *Consumerism: Search for the Public Interest,* 4th ed. New York: The Free Press.

Alderson, Wroe (1937), "A Marketing View of Competition," *Journal of Marketing,* 1 (January), 189–90.

____ (1943), "The Marketing Viewpoint in National Economic Planning," *Journal of Marketing,* 7 (April), 326–32.

____ (1957), *Marketing Behavior and Executive Action.* Home-wood, IL: Richard D. Irwin.

____ and Reavis Cox (1948), "Toward a Theory of Marketing," *Journal of Marketing,* 13 (October), 137–52.

Alexander, R.S., F.M. Surface, R.F. Elder, and Wroe Alderson (1940), *Marketing.* New York: Ginn & Company.

Allen, Frederick Lewis (1952), *The Big Change.* New York: Harper & Brothers.

AMA Task Force (1988), "Developing, Disseminating, and Utilizing Marketing Knowledge," *Journal of Marketing,* 52 (October), 1–25.

Anderson, Paul F. (1983), "Marketing, Scientific Progress, and Scientific Method," *Journal of Marketing,* 47 (Fall), 18–31.

Andreasen, Alan R. (1991), "Consumer Behavior Research and Social Policy," in *Handbook of Consumer Behavior,* Thomas S. Robertson and Harold H. Kassarjian, eds. Englewood Cliffs, NJ: Prentice Hall, 459–506.

____ (1994), "Social Marketing: Its Definition and Domain," *Journal of Public Policy & Marketing,* 13 (Spring), 108–114.

____ (1997), "From Ghetto Marketing to Social Marketing: Bringing Social Relevance to Mainstream Marketing," *Journal of Public Policy & Marketing,* 16 (Spring), 129–31.

Appelbaum, William (1947), "The *Journal of Marketing:* The First Ten Years," *Journal of Marketing,* 11 (April), 355–63.

____ (1952), "The *Journal of Marketing:* Postwar," *Journal of Marketing,* 16 (January), 294–300.

Bader, Louis and J.P. Wernette (1938), "Consumer Movements and Business," *Journal of Marketing,* 3 (July), 3–15.

Bain, Joe S. (1941), "The Sherman Act and the Bottlenecks of Business," *Journal of Marketing,* 5 (January), 254–58.

Bartels, Robert (1951a), "Can Marketing Be a Science?" *Journal of Marketing,* 15 (January), 319–28.

____ (1951b), "Influences on the Development of Marketing Thought, 1900–1923," *Journal of Marketing,* 16 (July), 1–17.

____ (1988), *The History of Marketing Thought,* 3d ed. Columbus, OH: Publishing Horizons.

Bass, Frank M. (2001), "Some History of the TIMS/INFORMS College on Marketing as Related to the Development of Marketing Science," *Marketing Science,* 20 (Fall), 360–63.

____, Robert D. Buzzell, M.R. Greene, William Lazer, Edgar A. Pessimier, Donald Shawver, Abraham Schuchman, and G.W. Wilson (1961), *Mathematical Models and Methods in Marketing.* Homewood, IL: Richard D. Irwin.

Baumgartner, Hans and Rik Pieters (2003), "The Structural Influence of Marketing Journals: A Citation Analysis of the Discipline and Its Subareas over Time," *Journal of Marketing,* 67 (April), 123–39.

Belk, Russell W. (1986), "What Should ACR Want to Be When It Grows Up?" in *Advances in Consumer Research,* Vol. 13, Richard J. Lutz, ed. Provo, UT: Association for Consumer Research, 423–24.

Bloom, Paul N. (1987), *Knowledge Development in Marketing.* Lexington, MA: D.C. Heath & Company.

____ (1997), "Field of Marketing and Public Policy: Introduction and Overview," *Journal of Public Policy & Marketing,* 16 (Spring), 126–28.

____ and Gregory T. Gundlach (2001), "Introduction," in *Handbook of Marketing and Society,* Paul N. Bloom and Gregory T. Gundlach, eds. Thousand Oaks, CA: Sage Publications, xiii–xxii.

Borden, Neil H. (1942), "Findings of the Harvard Study on the Economic Effects of Advertising," *Journal of Marketing,* 6 (April), 89–99.

____ (1964), "The Concept of the Marketing Mix," *Journal of Advertising Research,* (June), 2–7.

Breyer, Ralph F. (1934), *The Marketing Institution.* New York: McGraw-Hill.

Brown, William F. (1947a), "The Federal Trade Commission and False Advertising I," *Journal of Marketing,* 12 (July), 38–45.

____ (1947b), "The Federal Trade Commission and False Advertising II," *Journal of Marketing,* 12 (October), 193–201.

Buehler, Alfred G. (1937), "Chain Store Taxes," *Journal of Marketing,* 1 (January), 177–88.

Bussiere, Dave (2000), "Evidence of a Marketing Periodic Literature within the American Economic Association: 1895–1936," *Journal of Macromarketing,* 20 (2), 137–43.

Butler, Ralph W. (1914), *Marketing Methods and Salesmanship.* New York: Alexander Hamilton Institute.

Buzzell, Robert D. (1964), *Mathematical Models and Marketing Management.* Boston: Harvard Graduate School of Business.

Cassady, Ralph, Jr. (1939), "The Consumer and the Maintenance of Resale Prices," *Journal of Marketing,* 3 (January), 257–61.

____ (1946a), "Some Economic Aspects of Price Discrimination Under Non-Perfect Market Conditions," *Journal of Marketing,* 11 (July), 7–20.

____ (1946b), "Techniques and Purposes of Price Discrimination," *Journal of Marketing,* 11 (October), 135–50.

____ (1947a), "Legal Aspects of Price Discrimination: Federal Law," *Journal of Marketing,* 11 (January), 258–72.

____ (1947b), "Legal Aspects of Price Discrimination: State Law," *Journal of Marketing,* 11 (April), 377–89.

Cherington, Paul T. (1920), *The Elements of Marketing.* New York: Macmillan.

Clark, Fred E. (1922), *Principles of Marketing.* New York: Macmillan.

Clark, Lincoln H., ed. (1955), *The Life Cycle and Consumer Behavior.* New York: New York University Press.

Cohen, Joel B. (1995), "Abbott and Costello Meet Frankenstein: An ACR Retrospective," in *Advances in Consumer Research,* Vol. 22, Frank R. Kardes and Mita Sujan, eds. Provo, UT: Association for Consumer Research, 545–47.

Cohen, Lizabeth (2003), *A Consumers' Republic: The Politics of Mass Consumption in Postwar America.* New York: Alfred A. Knopf.

Converse, Paul D. (1924), *Marketing Methods and Policies,* 2d ed. New York: Macmillan.

___ (1945), "The Development of the Science of Marketing: An Exploratory Survey," *Journal of Marketing,* 10 (July), 14–23.

Copeland, Morris A. (1942), "A Social Appraisal of Differential Pricing," *Journal of Marketing,* 6 (April), 177–84.

Cox, Reavis and Wroe Alderson, eds. (1950), *Theory in Marketing.* Homewood, IL: Richard D. Irwin.

Cross, Gary (2000), *An All-Consuming Century: Why Commercialism Won in Modern America.* New York: Columbia University Press.

Day, George S. (1996), "Using the Past as a Guide to the Future: Reflections on the History of the *Journal of Marketing,*" *Journal of Marketing,* 60 (January), 14–16.

___ and David B. Montgomery (1999), "Charting New Directions for Marketing," *Journal of Marketing,* 63 (Special Issue), 3–13.

Derber, Milton (1943), "Gasoline Rationing Policy and Practice in Canada and the United States," *Journal of Marketing,* 8 (October), 137–44.

Desmond, Kevin (1986), *A Timetable of Inventions and Discoveries.* New York: M. Evans & Company.

Dickson, Peter R. and Philippa K. Wells (2001), "The Dubious Origins of the Sherman Antitrust Act: The Mouse That Roared," *Journal of Public Policy & Marketing,* 20 (Spring), 3–14.

Dixon, Donald F. (2002), "Emerging Macromarketing Concepts from Socrates to Alfred Marshall," *Journal of Business Research,* 55 (September), 87–95.

Drury, James Child (1937), "Consumers' Cooperation," *Journal of Marketing,* 4 (April), 385–89.

Duddy, Edward A. and David A. Revzan (1947), *Marketing: An Institutional Approach.* New York: McGraw-Hill.

Engel, James F. (1995), "ACR's 25th Anniversary: How It All Began," in *Advances in Consumer Research,* Vol. 22, Frank R. Kardes and Mita Sujan, eds. Provo, UT: Association for Consumer Research, 548–49.

___, David T. Kollat, and Roger D. Blackwell (1968), *Consumer Behavior.* New York: Holt, Rinehart & Winston.

Engle, N.H. (1936), "Implications of the Robinson-Patman Act for Marketing," *Journal of Marketing,* 1 (October), 75–81.

___ (1941), "Measurement of Economic and Marketing Efficiency," *Journal of Marketing,* 5 (April), 335–49.

Fisk, George (1981), "An Invitation to Participate in Affairs of the *Journal of Macromarketing,*" *Journal of Macromarketing,* 1 (Spring), 3–6.

Frank, Ronald E., Alfred A. Kuehn, and William F. Massy (1962), *Quantitative Techniques in Marketing Analysis.* Homewood, IL: Richard D. Irwin.

Fullbrook, Earl S. (1940), "The Functional Concept in Marketing," *Journal of Marketing,* 4 (January), 229–37.

Gardner, Burleigh B. and Sidney J. Levy (1955), "The Product and the Brand," *Harvard Business Review,* (March–April), 33–39.

Gordon, Robert and James Howell (1959), *Higher Education in Business.* New York: Columbia University Press.

Grether, E.T. (1937), "Fair Trade Legislation Restricting Price Cutting," *Journal of Marketing,* 1 (April), 334–54.

___ (1943), "Price Control and Rationing Under the Office of Price Administration: A Brief Selective Appraisal," *Journal of Marketing,* 7 (April), 300–318.

___ (1944), "Long Run Postwar Aspects of Price Control," *Journal of Marketing,* 8 (January), 296–301.

___ (1947), "The Federal Trade Commission Versus Resale Price Maintenance," *Journal of Marketing,* 12 (July), 1–13.

___ (1948), "The Postwar Market and Industrialization in California," *Journal of Marketing,* 12 (January), 311–16.

___ (1976), "The First Forty Years," *Journal of Marketing,* 40 (July), 63–69.

Greyser, Stephen A. (1997a), "Consumer Research and the Public Policy Process: Then and Now," *Journal of Public Policy & Marketing,* 16 (Spring), 137–38.

___ (1997b), "Janus and Marketing: The Past, Present, and Prospective Future of Marketing," in *Reflection on the Futures of Marketing Practice and Education,* Donald R. Lehmann and Katherine E. Jocz, eds. Cambridge, MA: Marketing Science Institute, 3–14.

Gundlach, Gregory T. and William L. Wilkie (1990), "The Marketing Literature in Public Policy: 1970–1988," in *Marketing and Advertising Regulation: The Federal Trade Commission in the 1990s,* Patrick E. Murphy and William L. Wilkie, eds. Notre Dame, IN: University of Notre Dame Press, 329–44.

Hahn, L. Albert (1946), "The Effects of Saving on Employment and Consumption," *Journal of Marketing,* 11 (July), 35–43.

Hill, Ronald Paul, Elizabeth C. Hirschman, and John F. Bauman (1997), "Consumer Survival During the Great Depression: Reports from the Field," *Journal of Macromarketing,* 17 (Spring), 107–127.

Hobart, Donald M. (1940), "Probable Effects of a National Emergency on Marketing Functions and Policies," *Journal of Marketing,* 4 (April), 59–65.

Holbrook, Morris B. (1987), "What Is Consumer Research?" *Journal of Consumer Research,* 14 (June), 128–32.

Hollander, Stanley (1960), "The Wheel of Retailing," *Journal of Marketing,* 25 (July), 37–42.

___, William W. Keep, and Roger Dickinson (1999), "Marketing Public Policy and the Evolving Role of Marketing Academics: A Historical Perspective," *Journal of Public Policy & Marketing,* 18 (Fall), 265–69.

Holt, Budd A. (1936), "Economic Provisions of Marketing Agreements for General Crops," *Journal of Marketing,* 1 (October), 115–26.

Howard, John A. (1957), *Marketing Management: Analysis and Planning.* Homewood, IL: Richard D. Irwin.

___ and Jagdish N. Sheth (1969), *The Theory of Buyer Behavior.* New York: John Wiley & Sons.

Howard, William H. (1933), "The Whole Truth in Retail Advertising," *Journal of Retailing,* 9 (October), 79–82.

Hunt, Shelby D. (1983), "General Theories and the Fundamental Explananda of Marketing," *Journal of Marketing,* 47 (Fall), 9–17.

___ (1990), "Truth in Marketing Theory and Research," *Journal of Marketing,* 54 (July), 1–15.

___ (1992), "For Reason and Realism in Marketing," *Journal of Marketing,* 56 (April), 89–102.

___ and Jerry Goolsby (1988), "The Rise and Fall of the Functional Approach to Marketing: A Paradigm Displacement Perspective," in *Historical Perspectives in Marketing: Essays in Honor of Stanley C. Hollander,* Terence Nevett and Ronald A. Fullerton, eds. Lexington, MA: D.C. Heath & Company.

Ivey, Paul Wesley (1922), *Principles of Marketing,* reprint. New York: Ronald Press Co.

Jones, D.G. Brian and Eric H. Shaw (2002), "A History of Marketing Thought," in *Handbook of Marketing,* Barton A. Weitz and Robin Wensley, eds. Thousand Oaks, CA: Sage Publications, 39–65.

Kardes, Frank R. and Mita Sujan, eds. (1995), *Advances in Consumer Research,* Vol. 22. Provo, UT: Association for Consumer Research.

Kassarjian, Harold H. (1995), "Some Recollections from a Quarter Century Ago," in *Advances in Consumer Research,* Vol. 22, Frank R. Kardes and Mita Sujan, eds. Provo, UT: Association for Consumer Research, 550–52.

____ and Thomas S. Robertson (1968), *Perspectives in Consumer Behavior.* Glenview, IL: Scott Foresman.

Kelley, Eugene J. and William Lazer, eds. (1958), *Managerial Marketing: Perspectives and Viewpoints.* Homewood, IL: Richard D. Irwin.

Kerin, Roger A. (1996), "In Pursuit of an Ideal: The Editorial and Literary History of the *Journal of Marketing,*" *Journal of Marketing,* 60 (January), 1–13.

Kernan, Jerome B. (1995a), "Declaring a Discipline: Reflections on ACR's Silver Anniversary," in *Advances in Consumer Research,* Vol. 22, Frank R. Kardes and Mita Sujan, eds. Provo, UT: Association for Consumer Research, 553–60.

____ (1995b), "Framing a Rainbow, Focusing the Light: *JCR's* First Twenty Years," in *Advances in Consumer Research,* Vol. 22, Frank R. Kardes and Mita Sujan, eds. Provo, UT: Association for Consumer Research, 488–96.

Kinnear, Thomas C. (1982), "Editor's Statement," *Journal of Marketing & Public Policy,* 1, 1–2.

____ (1997), "An Historic Perspective on the Quantity and Quality of Marketing and Public Policy Research," *Journal of Public Policy & Marketing,* 16 (Spring), 144–46.

Kotler, Philip (1967), *Marketing Management: Analysis, Planning, and Control.* Englewood Cliffs, NJ: Prentice Hall.

____ (1971), *Marketing Decision Making: A Model Building Approach.* New York: Holt, Rinehart and Winston.

____ (1988), *Marketing Management: Analysis, Planning, Implementation, and Control,* 6th ed. Englewood Cliffs, NJ: Prentice Hall.

____ (2003), *Marketing Management,* 11th ed. Upper Saddle River, NJ: Prentice Hall.

____ and Gary Armstrong (2004), *Principles of Marketing,* 10th ed. Upper Saddle River, NJ: Prentice Hall.

____ and Sidney J. Levy (1969a), "Broadening the Concept of Marketing," *Journal of Marketing,* 33 (January), 10–15.

____ and ____ (1969b), "A New Form of Marketing Myopia: Rejoinder to Professor Luck," *Journal of Marketing,* 33 (July), 55–57.

Lampman, Robert J. (1988), "JFK's Four Consumer Rights: A Retrospective View," in *The Frontier of Research in the Consumer Interest,* E. Scott Maynes, ed. Columbia, MO: American Council on Consumer Interests, 19–33.

Lavidge, Robert J. and Gary A. Steiner (1961), "A Model for Predictive Measurements of Advertising Effectiveness," *Journal of Marketing,* 25 (October), 59–62.

Lebergott, Stanley (1993), *Pursuing Happiness: American Consumers in the Twentieth Century.* Princeton, NJ: Princeton University Press.

Lehmann, Donald R. (2002), "Marketing ROI Tops 2002–04 Research Agenda," in *Marketing Science Institute Review.* Cambridge, MA: Marketing Science Institute, 1, 4–5.

Levitt, Theodore (1960), "Marketing Myopia," *Harvard Business Review,* (July-August), 45–56.

Lichtenthal, J. David and Leland L. Beik (1984), "A History of the Definition of Marketing," in *Research in Marketing,* Vol. 7, Jagdish N. Sheth, ed. Greenwich, CT: JAI Press, 133–63.

Little, John D.C. (2001), "The History of the Marketing College Is a Work in Progress," *Marketing Science,* 20 (Fall), 364–72.

Luck, David J. (1969), "Broadening the Concept of Marketing: Too Far," *Journal of Marketing,* 33 (July), 53–55.

Lusch, Robert F. (1999), "From the Editor," *Journal of Marketing,* 63 (Special Issue), 1–2.

Mayer, Robert N. (1989), *The Consumer Movement: Guardians of the Marketplace.* Boston: Twayne.

Maynard, Harold H., Walter C. Weidler, and Theodore N. Beckman (1927), *Principles of Marketing.* New York: Ronald Press Co.

Maynes, E. Scott, ed. (1988), *The Frontier of Research in the Consumer Interest.* Columbia, MO: American Council on Consumer Interests.

Mazis, Michael B. (1979), "Overview of 'Can and Should the FTC Restrict Advertising to Children' Workshop," in *Advances in Consumer Research,* Vol. 6, William L. Wilkie, ed. Ann Arbor, MI: Association for Consumer Research, 3–6.

___ (1997), "Marketing and Public Policy: Prospects for the Future," *Journal of Public Policy & Marketing,* 16 (Spring), 139–43.

McCarthy, E. Jerome (1960), *Basic Marketing: A Managerial Approach.* Homewood, IL: Richard D. Irwin.

McHenry, Lorenzo Alva (1937), "Price Stabilization Attempts in the Grocery Trade in California," *Journal of Marketing,* 2 (October), 121–28.

McKitterick, John B. (1957), "What Is the Marketing Management Concept?" in *The Frontiers of Marketing Thought and Action,* Frank M. Bass, ed. Chicago: American Marketing Association, 71–82.

McNair, Malcolm P. (1958), "Significant Trends and Developments in the Postwar Period," in *Competitive Distribution Is a Free, High-Level Economy and Its Implications for the University,* A.B. Smith, ed. Pittsburgh: University of Pittsburgh Press, 1–25.

Mench, John (1925), "The Merchandise Division: Why It Exists, and Its Job," *Journal of Retailing,* 1 (July), 3–5.

Montgomery, David B. (2001), "Management Science in Marketing: Prehistory, Origin, and Early Years of the INFORMS Marketing College," *Marketing Science,* 20 (Fall), 337–48.

Montgomery, D.E. (1937), "The Consumer Looks at Competition," *Journal of Marketing,* 1 (January), 218–22.

Moriarity, W.D. (1923), *The Economics of Marketing and Advertising.* New York: Harper & Brothers.

Morrison, Donald G. (2001), "Founding Marketing Science," *Marketing Science,* 20 (Fall), 357–59.

Murphy, Patrick E. (1990), "Past FTC Participation by Marketing Academics," in *Marketing and Advertising Regulation: The Federal Trade Commission in the 1990s,* Patrick E. Murphy and William L. Wilkie, eds. Notre Dame, IN: University of Notre Dame Press, 205–215.

___ and William L. Wilkie, eds. (1990), *Marketing and Advertising Regulation: The Federal Trade Commission in the 1990s.* Notre Dame, IN: University of Notre Dame Press.

Myers, John G., William F. Massy, and Stephen A. Greyser (1980), *Marketing Research and Knowledge Development.* Englewood Cliffs, NJ: Prentice Hall.

Nance, J.J. (1944), "War and Postwar Adjustments in Marketing Appliances," *Journal of Marketing,* 8 (January), 307–309.

Nason, Robert W. (1992), "From the Editor: The Driving Forces of Macromarketing," *Journal of Macromarketing,* 12 (Spring), 1–3.

Nystrom, Paul N. (1948), "The Minimum Wage in Retailing," *Journal of Retailing,* 24 (February), 1–5.

Payne, Happer (1947), "Standardized Description, A Form of Specification Labeling," *Journal of Marketing,* 12 (October), 234–41.

Peter, J. Paul (1992), "Realism or Relativism for Marketing Theory and Research: A Comment on Hunt's 'Scientific Realism'," *Journal of Marketing,* 56 (April), 72–79.

___ and Jerry C. Olson (1983), "Is Science Marketing?" *Journal of Marketing,* 47 (Fall), 111–25.

Phillips, Charles F. (1938), *Marketing.* New York: Houghton Mifflin.

Reibstein, David (2001), "Marketing's Present and Future," *Marketing Science Institute Review,* (Spring–Summer), 1ff.

Rutherford, H.K. (1940), "Industrial Preparedness," *Journal of Marketing,* 4 (April), 47–50.

Savitt, Ronald (1990), "Pre-Aldersonian Antecedents to Macro-marketing: Insights from the Textual Literature," *Journal of the Academy of Marketing Science,* 18 (4), 293–301.

Schlossman, S., M. Sedlack, and H. Wechsler (1987), "The 'New Look'; The Ford Foundation and the Revolution in Business Education," *Selections,* (Winter), 8–28.

Schmotter, James (1984), "An Interview with Professor James Howell," *Selections,* (Spring), 9–13.

Severa, R.M. (1943), "Retail Credit in Wartime," *Journal of Retailing,* 19 (April), 35–40.

Shaw, Arch W. (1912), "Some Problems in Market Distribution," *The Quarterly Journal of Economics,* 26 (4), 703–765.

Shaw, Eric H. (1995), "The First Dialogue on Macromarketing," *Journal of Macromarketing,* 15 (Spring), 7–20.

Smith, Wendell (1956), "Product Differentiation and Marketing Segmentation as Alternative Marketing Strategies," *Journal of Marketing,* 20 (July), 3–8.

Sprott, David E. and Anthony D. Miyazaki (2002), "Two Decades of Contributions to Marketing and Public Policy: An Analysis of Research Published in *Journal of Public Policy & Marketing,*" *Journal of Public Policy & Marketing,* 21 (Spring), 105–125.

Steckel, Joel H. and Ed Brody (2001), "Special Section 2001: A Marketing Odyssey," *Marketing Science,* 20 (Fall), 331–36.

Stern, Louis W. and Thomas L. Eovaldi (1984), *Legal Aspects of Marketing Strategy: Antitrust and Consumer Protection Issues.* Englewood Cliffs, NJ: Prentice Hall.

Straus, Percy S. (1926), "Some Observations on Merchandise Control," *Journal of Retailing,* 2 (April), 3–5.

Taylor, Malcolm D. (1943), "Allocation of Scarce Consumers' Goods to Retailers," *Journal of Marketing,* 8 (October), 123–32.

Thomas, Eugene P. (1940), "Shifting Scenes in Foreign Trade," *Journal of Marketing,* 4 (April), 51–58.

Tousley, Rayburn D. (1940), "The Federal Food, Drug, and Cosmetic Act of 1938," *Journal of Marketing,* 5 (January), 259–69.

U.S. Department of Education (2001), "Completion Survey," National Center for Education Statistics, Integrated Postsecondary Education Data System, [available at http://www.nces. ed.gov].

Vaile, Roland S., E.T. Grether, and Reavis Cox (1952), *Marketing in the American Economy.* New York: Ronald Press Co.

Vance, Lawrence L. (1947), "The Interpretation of Consumer Dis-Saving," *Journal of Marketing,* 11 (January), 243–49.

Vaughan, Floyd L. (1928), *Marketing and Advertising.* Princeton, NJ: Princeton University Press.

Watson, Alfred N. (1944), "Wartime Incomes and Consumer Markets," *Journal of Marketing,* 8 (January), 231–37.

Webster, Frederick E., Jr. (2002), "The Role of Marketing and the Firm," in *Handbook of Marketing,* Barton A. Weitz and Robin Wensley, eds. Thousand Oaks, CA: Sage Publications, 66–82.

Weitz, Barton A. and Robin Wensley, eds. (2002), *Handbook of Marketing*. Thousand Oaks, CA: Sage Publications.

Weld, Louis D.H. (1915), *Studies in the Marketing of Farm Products*. Minneapolis: Bulletin of the University of Minnesota.

___ (1916), *The Marketing of Farm Products*. New York: Macmillan.

Wells, William D. (1995), "What Do We Want to Be When We Grow Up?" in *Advances in Consumer Research*, Vol. 22, Frank R. Kardes and Mita Sujan, eds. Provo, UT: Association for Consumer Research, 561–63.

White, Percival (1927), *Scientific Marketing Management*. New York: Harper & Brothers.

Wilkie, William L. (1981), "Presidential Address: 1980," in *Advances in Consumer Research*, Vol. 8, Kent Monroe, ed. Ann Arbor, MI: Association for Consumer Research, 1–6.

___ (1994), *Consumer Behavior*, 3d ed. New York: John Wiley & Sons.

___ (1997), "Developing Research on Public Policy and Marketing," *Journal of Public Policy & Marketing*, 16 (Spring), 132–36.

___ (2002), "On Books and Scholarship: Reflections of a Marketing Academic," *Journal of Marketing*, 66 (July), 141–52.

___ and Elizabeth S. Moore (1997), "Consortium Survey on Marketing and Society Issues: Summary and Results," *Journal of Macromarketing*, 17 (2), 89–95.

___ and ___ (1999), "Marketing's Contributions to Society," *Journal of Marketing*, 63 (Special Issue), 198–218.

Witkowski, Terrence H. (1998), "The American Consumer Home Front During World War II," in *Advances in Consumer Research*, Vol. 25, Joseph W. Alba and J. Wesley Hutchinson, eds. Provo, UT: Association for Consumer Research, 568–73.

Wittausch, William (1944), "Postwar Competition for Mass-Produced Low-Cost Housing," *Journal of Marketing*, 8 (April), 375–81.

Wittink, Dick R. (2001), "Market Measurement and Analysis: The First 'Marketing Science Conference,'" *Marketing Science*, 20 (Fall), 349–56.

Zaltman, Gerald (1965), *Marketing: Contributions from the Behavioral Sciences*. New York: Harcourt, Brace & World.

Zinkhan, George M. and Rudy Hirschheim (1992), "Truth in Marketing Theory and Research: An Alternative Perspective," *Journal of Marketing*, 56 (April), 80–88.

FIELD OF MARKETING AND PUBLIC POLICY: INTRODUCTION AND OVERVIEW

Paul N. Bloom

The following five essays are expanded versions of comments made during a session of the 1996 Marketing and Public Policy Conference. The session was titled "Marketing and Public Policy: A Retrospective" and was the brainchild of Ron Hill, co-chair of the conference. Ron asked me to organize and moderate the session. We both believed that it was an appropriate time in the history of our subfield to have such an event; the conference marked the 25th anniversary of when marketing professors were first employed as visiting scholars by the Federal Trade Commission.

The five authors all have been significant contributors to the marketing and public policy subfield. They are clearly leaders of the subfield, both as researchers and research managers (i.e., editors, conference chairs, and Marketing Science Institute executive director). However, their selection for the session and this journal contribution should not be viewed as an attempt to downplay or minimize the substantial contributions of many other leaders in the subfield. Indeed, the only reason there are five authors here is because the session could have only that many.

The questions that the speakers were asked to address during the session are as follows:

1. What do you consider to be some of the major research contributions of the subfield? How have the contributions varied in different time periods?
2. What forces have caused research activity (and quality) to increase or decrease significantly in the past? Are any of those forces present today?
3. What have been the subfield's most difficult research problems? What have we learned about how not to solve these problems?
4. How has knowledge dissemination progressed in the subfield? Has the *Journal of Public Policy & Marketing* made a significant difference?
5. What role has research funding played in the knowledge creation process? Has money made a difference?

PAUL N. BLOOM is Professor of Marketing and Chair of the Faculty of Marketing, Kenan-Flagler Business School, University of North Carolina. He chaired the 1992 Marketing and Public Policy Conference and the Marketing Science Institute's research competition on "Using Marketing to Serve Society." He previously had been a visiting scholar at the Marketing Science Institute. He has been an expert witness in several antitrust and consumer protection cases.

Bloom, Paul N. (1997), "Field of Marketing and Public Policy: Introduction and Overview," *Journal of Public Policy & Marketing*, 16 (1) 126–28.

The speakers addressed some of these questions directly, but more often they addressed them indirectly, while posing and answering other questions.

The session generated considerable discussion and numerous favorable comments. As a result, Debra Scammon, editor of *JPP&M,* suggested that a collection of invited essays by the speakers would be a valuable addition to the journal. These essays are presented here. But before presenting them, I will try to offer a few answers to the questions originally posed for the session. My thoughts are based only in part on what the five speakers said and should not be viewed as a summary of their essays. My own biases and views, formed by working 25 years in the subfield, certainly come through.

Major Research Contributions

The marketing and public policy subfield has, in my opinion, made significant research contributions to (1) the broader academic field of marketing, (2) the creation of public policy, and (3) the practice of marketing. The broader academic field of marketing has benefited from the many studies that simultaneously have addressed both public policy questions and important, broader, theoretical issues. For example, we have learned much about how consumers process information from studies that have been done on public policy initiatives such as unit pricing (Russo 1977), warning labels (Stewart and Martin 1994), nutritional labels (Moorman 1996), and corrective advertising (Bernhardt, Kinnear, and Mazis 1986). Similarly, we have learned much about what creates consumer satisfaction and dissatisfaction from research that originally was focused on measuring consumer dissatisfaction for the purpose of setting public policy priorities (Andreasen and Best 1977).

Public policy in the United States has been influenced in many ways by research from our subfield. Our work has had substantial impact on the way government information programs have been implemented, including programs that have introduced warning labels, nutritional labels, and affirmative disclosures. We also have had an important impact on how advertising is regulated. We have helped policymakers see that advertising is not as all-powerful and dangerous in its effects on the general public and on certain populations (e.g., children) as some of its critics would have people believe (Greyser 1972). In addition, we have helped to establish procedures and approaches for dealing with deceptive advertising (Wilkie, McNeill, and Mazis 1984). Other areas in which we have had an impact on policymakers have been in enforcement of the antitrust, trademark, environmental protection, and product safety laws. Our work is being cited regularly in the court documents and regulatory proceedings of these areas.

Practitioners of many types have been affected by our research. Business marketers have learned much about what is legal and ethical to do in the marketplace from reading our articles and texts. And nonprofit and social marketers are drawing on our research regularly to guide them in marketing preventive health, charitable giving, and other socially beneficial behaviors (Andreasen 1995).

Our research contributions have not, in my opinion, come along in a steady stream. Although certain people have focused most of their research energies throughout their careers to marketing and public policy questions, others have contributed more sporadically to the subfield. The most active periods seem to have been the mid–1970s and the 1990s, with the 1980s representing a period of lesser activity.

Forces Influencing Research

The level of research activity seems to be driven by at least four factors: (1) the political climate, (2) the research funding climate, (3) the research publication climate, and (4) the teaching climate. These factors are interconnected with one another. At the risk of oversimplifying the situation, I argue that researchers seem to be more interested in studying public policy issues during eras of activism in Washington with respect to consumer protection and antitrust. Perhaps they are attracted by the possibilities of having an impact on policymakers, or perhaps by the greater opportunities to have their research funded, published, and taught about during those eras. It seems as though activity in Washington leads funding agencies such as the Marketing Science Institute (MSI)—whose research priorities are set by its member companies—to be more interested in supporting public policy research projects. Washington activity and MSI support also seem to affect journal editors and reviewers, making them more receptive to public policy articles. Finally, Washington activity leads students to be interested in taking courses that deal with public policy issues, and this in turn can create more teaching jobs for people who do research in this area (and consequently have more interest in doing the research).

Unfortunately, the late 1990s could be an era of reduced Washington activity with respect to consumer protection and antitrust. Reflecting this, the most recent 1996–97 MSI research priorities put "marketing and social issues" as its lowest funding priority of 15 areas. It remains to be seen whether other developments—such as the institutionalization of the marketing and public policy research area, which has occurred through the establishment of a Marketing and Society interest group within the American Marketing Association (AMA)—can counter the effects of what is happening in Washington, keeping research activity at a high level.

Difficult Research Problems

Our subfield involves extremely difficult research problems. We seek an understanding of how certain corporate or government actions affect consumers, intermediaries, and competitors, paying particular attention to how much these actions help or harm these parties. Consequently, we must focus more on behavioral effects than on effects on knowledge and attitudes. To provide guidance to public policymakers or the courts, we have an obligation to have strong support for conclusions that indicate that a particular action caused a particular helpful or harmful outcome. This requires the use of tight experimental and quasi-experimental methods with valid and reliable measures.

Some of the questions we have yet to address satisfactorily include the following:

1. How are vulnerable populations affected by certain advertising and marketing practices? For example, how does cigarette and beer advertising affect the consumption habits of children? Or how does the advertising of prescription drugs affect people with health problems?
2. How are smaller competitors affected by the aggressive use of certain marketing practices by larger competitors? Have smaller competitors been driven out of business by aggressive advertising, pricing, shelf space control efforts, or supplier alliances?
3. How effective have certain regulatory initiatives been in protecting consumers and encouraging competition? Are information remedies such as "Truth in Lending" disclosures, nutritional labeling, or alcohol warning labels having their intended effects on consumer behavior? Have consumers benefited from the government actions that were intended to bring more aggressive competition to the telecommunications, airlines, and computer industries?
4. How can individual persons be persuaded through the use of social advertising or other social marketing tools to engage in preventive health behaviors such as eating nutritious foods, exercising regularly, getting regular health screenings, and avoiding smoking and excessive drinking?

We have learned that answers to questions such as these will not come from simple surveys, correlational studies, or small laboratory experiments. We must engage in long-term, programmatic research that involves paying careful attention to internal and external validity. We also have learned that biased and advocacy-oriented research has no place in this subfield. Most of us have recognized that keeping our independence and objectivity is essential if our work is to be credible and taken seriously.

Knowledge Dissemination

As suggested previously, our research seems to be getting widely disseminated, with citations in important court cases and regulatory proceedings becoming a frequent occurrence. Clearly, the increasing availability of electronic search techniques has helped policymakers and attorneys find our work. However, studies must be published before they can be spotted in a search. Fortunately, *JPP&M* has become an excellent publication outlet, providing space for socially oriented marketing studies at a time when other marketing journals have become less likely to publish this kind of work—in part, because they have been inundated with an increase of submissions of all types as more universities require their faculties to "publish or perish."

JPP&M has benefited from the emergence in the 1990s of the annual Marketing and Public Policy Conference, because the best papers presented at this conference are accepted into the journal. The conference itself has become an important dissemination vehicle, as attendance by academics, marketing practitioners, and public policymakers has grown steadily. In addition, dissemination of our work has been improved by the development of the Marketing and Society special interest group within the AMA. This group has held several successful workshops and sessions associated with AMA conferences.

Research Funding

I believe that research funding is an important driving force in the knowledge creation process. Significant work on deceptive advertising, children's advertising, labeling, and other topics resulted from funding provided in the 1970s by such places as the National Science Foundation, the Federal Trade Commission, MSI, and the Canadian government. All but the last source tended to dry up during the 1980s, and a reduction in research activity resulted. A smattering of new funding support in the 1990s from such places as the Federal Trade Commission, MSI, the Centers for Disease Control, and the National Institutes of Health has helped to fuel some of the research resurgence discussed previously. But if places like MSI again start to put research on marketing and social issues as a low priority—which was done in its most recent priority-setting process—then the subfield could suffer.

The kind of high-quality, objective, long-term, programmatic research that must be done on marketing and public policy issues does not come cheaply. I think an important overriding goal for all of us working in this subfield should be to establish a funding agency that will regularly support our research. This agency cannot have a particular political orientation, nor can it have a pro-business or pro-consumer activist bias. It must be dedicated to seeking honest and objective answers to how marketing can become a more positive force in creating a better society.

References

Andreasen, Alan R. (1995), *Marketing Social Change,* San Francisco: Jossey-Bass Publishers.

___ and Arthur Best (1977), "Consumers Complain—Does Business Respond?" *Harvard Business Review,* 55 (July/August), 93–101.

Bernhardt, Kenneth L., Thomas C. Kinnear, and Michael B. Mazis (1986), "A Field Study of Corrective Advertising Effectiveness," *Journal of Public Policy & Marketing,* 5, 146–62.

Greyser, Stephen A. (1972), "Advertising: Attacks and Counters," *Harvard Business Review,* 50 (March/April), 20–30.

Moorman, Christine (1996), "A Quasi-Experiment to Assess the Consumer and Informational Determinants of Nutrition Information Processing Activities: The Case of the Nutritional Labeling and Education Act," *Journal of Public Policy & Marketing,* 15 (Spring), 28–44.

Russo, J. Edward (1977), "The Value of Unit Price Information," *Journal of Marketing Research,* 14 (May), 192–201.

Stewart, David W. and Ingrid M. Martin (1994), "Intended and Unintended Consequences of Warning Messages: A Review and Synthesis of Empirical Research," *Journal of Public Policy & Marketing,* 13 (Spring), 1–19.

Wilkie, William L., Dennis L. McNeill, and Michael B. Mazis (1984), "Marketing's 'Scarlet Letter': The Theory and Practice of Corrective Advertising," *Journal of Marketing,* 48 (Spring), 11–31.

From Ghetto Marketing to Social Marketing: Bringing Social Relevance to Mainstream Marketing

Alan R. Andreasen

A retrospective look at the arc of my career involvement in public policy issues reveals two major concerns. First, I have a central concern for the problems of a group I once labeled "disadvantaged consumers" (Andreasen 1975), but that has expanded beyond ghetto markets to encompass customers in need around the world. Second, I consistently have sought to bring concern for social issues into the mainstream of marketing thought and research. My involvement in these concerns has gone through three stages that reflect an ebb and flow of academic and popular interest. Today's involvement in these issues reflects a maturation of the discipline as well as a continuing neglect of some of the important challenges that marked the earliest days of interest.

The Early "Vietnam" Days

My own involvement in trying to find solutions to the problems of the disadvantaged mirror broader trends in the marketing discipline. I began my career with the traditional focus on commercial marketing, with particular attention given to the newly emerging specialty that came to be called *consumer behavior*. I began my teaching career at the State University of New York at Buffalo in the 1960s. SUNY-Buffalo had just been transformed from the localite University of Buffalo into what Norman Mailer one day called (to the dismay of many Buffalonians) the "Berkeley of the East." In the late 1960s and early 1970s, the Buffalo campus, along with many others in the United States, seethed with Vietnam era protest against the government, against Dow Chemical, and against the Reserve Officers' Training Corps. In this atmosphere, heady new educational paradigms were considered seriously and new conceptualizations of the proper interface between the Ivory Tower and the broader society were debated regularly.

ALAN R. ANDREASEN is Associate Dean for Faculty and Professor of Marketing, School of Business, Georgetown University. He is past president of the Association for Consumer Research and has been active as a scholar, expert witness, and consultant in the area of social marketing with special emphasis on problems of the economically disadvantaged.

Andreasen, Alan R. (1997), "From Ghetto Marketing to Social Marketing: Bringing Social Relevance to Mainstream Marketing," *Journal of Public Policy & Marketing,* 16 (1) 129–31.

But in the business school where I was housed formally, these upheavals were largely ignored. My colleagues were very mainstream and establishment and looked on with barely disguised horror at the ideas and antics of their hippie colleagues and students in other departments. Secretly, I felt more affinity for what these "hippies" were concerned with than I felt for the bottom line focuses of my nominal academic brethren. My chance to break free came with the urban riots of the late 1960s. During the fall of 1969, Buffalo's ghetto underwent a series of violent social and physical explosions, much of it directed against the retail establishment.

Finally, I could apply my bleeding heart liberal sensibilities and nascent scholarly skills to a real problem facing a real American underclass. I was ecstatic: finally I could hold up my head among the sociologists and political scientists with whom I had formed an affinity. And, as it turned out, I had stumbled into a career focus that, over the years, would yield some fairly useful contributions to both the basic science of the marketing profession and the resolution of important social problems.

During these early days, I pursued two broad research interests. First, I looked carefully at the ghetto marketplace itself, with a particular focus on the businesspeople who worked there. I carried out a major study of business in Buffalo's inner city (Andreasen 1971) and engaged in several interventions that were intended to help improve the skills of minority entrepreneurs who, at the time, held minuscule shares of what limited wealth there was in this urban marketplace.[1] Second, I focused on an issue that was featured in many press reports at the time and in a seminal study by a sociologist, namely that "the poor pay more" (Caplovitz 1967). Working alone and with colleagues at the University of Rochester and sharing ideas with others including Fred Sturdivant, then of Ohio State, I tried to figure out whether these allegations were true, what their causes were, and what might be done to remedy the situation.

The latter work resulted in several articles and the book *The Disadvantaged Consumer*, in which I argue that the sources of the problems of the disadvantaged are threefold. First, they have personal characteristics that cause them to receive less value in the marketplace than do others for their consumer dollars. This includes their poverty, race, and education, which tend to restrict their shopping scope and their access to low-cost goods and services. The second source of difficulty is the marketplace in which they shopped. As my research had made clear, urban ghettos in which the poor shopped were populated everywhere with small, undercapitalized stores with ill-trained businesspeople who charged high prices and held tiny inventories. Large, low-cost enterprises (supermarkets, discounters) rarely were to be found and, especially after the riots, tended to flee to the

---

[1]Ironically, it turned out that my skills were ill-suited to this task. I had been trained to provide advice to General Motors and General Electric, not Bert's Barber Shop or the Southside Deli. Indeed, at the time, I noted the paradox that those who wanted to help in the ghetto (the scholars from the elite universities) were probably the least well equipped by training and breeding, whereas those who were best equipped (scholars at the two-year community colleges and trade schools) were largely uninterested in these problems.

more lucrative suburbs. The third source of difficulty is the rapacious merchants with whom the underclass came in contact who did not hesitate to prey upon consumers' marginal social status and market fears to charge high prices and employ unconscionable contractual terms to confiscate their salaries and, in many cases, their possessions.

As I looked for solutions in this area, it was inevitable that I would become interested in the work of third-party interveners, which included the Federal Trade Commission (FTC). There I found other like-minded marketing scholars, such as Bill Wilkie, making initial forays into providing intellectual rigor in the form of a noneconomist's perspective on the work of commissioners and their staff.

The Middle "Anti-Regulation" Years

Two things happened in the mid–1970s that changed the focus of work on the disadvantaged. First, the culture changed. The Vietnam war was over. A series of Republican presidents took over the White House. The interests of America shifted to middle-class "family values" and a sympathy with corporate interests. Funding for agencies like the FTC was cut back.

Second, the initial spate of interest and research among academicians died out, and the scholars went elsewhere. In a 1978 article, "The Ghetto Marketing Life Cycle" (Andreasen 1978), I argued that among other things this exodus was caused by two factors: (1) The topic area had been subjected to a lot of quick-and-dirty early research that seemed to provide answers to initial burning questions (e.g., do supermarkets charge more in the inner city?) and (2) Perhaps because of this, it never attracted first-rate marketing scholars. By 1975, work on the problems of disadvantaged consumers virtually disappeared.

That left those of us hooked on the more general challenge of finding ways to use our academic skills to benefit the broader society casting about for new avenues of research and activism. For me, salvation came in the form of that well-known public scold, Ralph Nader.

In the mid–1970s, it was clear that government solutions to consumer problems were not going to be either popular or funded. It was an era in which the private market was supposed to hold the key to most of society's problems. Responding to this shift, others and I came to focus on the extent to which consumers could—and did—police the marketplace themselves. This, in fact, was one of Nader's major contributions. He saw himself as the voice of the consumer amplified a hundredfold to challenge the nefarious practices of evil marketers in the auto, drug, and retail industries.

In the mid–1970s, Nader had become respectable. After years of being a lonely voice challenging corporate America, he was now relatively well funded. He had established a Center for the Study of Responsive Law and hired (at shockingly low wages) a coterie of zealous attorneys to help him make the marketplace correct itself. I entered the picture when Nader decided that he needed a research base to give a strategic focus to his interventionist impulses. Before the mid–1970s Nader, and to a large extent the FTC, pursued consumer problem areas that caught their attention, whether through personal experience (or in the case of the FTC, the experience of some Congressperson) or the popular press. Nader thought that a more rational, systematic approach to prioritizing would be to conduct a survey calibrating just where problems lay and what consumers were actually doing about them—if anything.

A junior associate of his, Arthur Best, was put in charge of this project and, in the course of looking for a field organization to carry out the study, found me and the Survey Research Center at the University of Illinois, where I then was teaching. The study we produced was one of the first to count just how often consumers perceived problems in 34 product and service categories, how often they spoke up about them, and how often, when they spoke up, they were satisfied with management's responses (Andreasen and Best 1977). This information was helpful to Nader. But, more important for academics, the work, along with that of Ralph Day, Keith Hunt, and many others, led to the founding of an entirely new research area that came to be called "consumer satisfaction/dissatisfaction and complaining behavior," or CS/D research.

Three features of this new stream of research were important and led to its longevity. First, it dealt with fundamental consumer behavior processes that were of basic interest to the new field of consumer behavior. Second, perhaps because of this, it attracted some very good scholars. Along with the work of Hunt and Day, it has seen powerful *fundamental* work by such people as John Swan, Rich Oliver, Marsha Richins, and others (Andreasen 1991). Third, it turned out to be a topic that, though we did not recognize it at the time, would have a profound effect on private sector marketing behavior.

The last point is filled with irony. I can remember making presentations about the "Nader Study" to business groups in the late 1970s. On these occasions, I kept saying that CS/D data were amazing sources of consumer feedback that provided early warning of problems in the marketplace that companies might not see reflected in market share data for months or years. I urged them at least to look systematically at their own complaint data and—a radical thought—even go out and solicit complaint information. This, at the time, was seen as truly foolish: Why would businesses want to urge people to complain? First, it would just get consumers all riled up. Second, complaints were costly to resolve, and that hurt the bottom line. And, finally, complaints meant that somebody was not doing their job and heads would roll. Better not raise the lid on such a can of worms.

It took almost ten years before corporate America saw the light. And today, consumer satisfaction research is a major industry, and no self-respecting major marketer is without access to such data nor, if the numbers are favorable, unwilling to tout such results (e.g., J.D. Power ratings) in expensive advertisements.

The Present "Social Marketing" Era

During the middle years of my involvement in the interface between marketing scholarship and societal problems, I became aware of the substantial amount of solid research
on consumer problems of the disadvantaged and on CS/D in general being conducted
outside the United States. In 1977–78, Jean Manning and I undertook a partially successful attempt to replicate the Nader Study in six European countries. This experience
made clear both the value of looking to perspectives outside a scholar's own intellectual
bailiwick and the fact that the problems consumers face elsewhere, especially in the less
developed countries, are very much different from those in America.

The latter recognition dovetailed well with both the internationalization of the fields
of marketing and consumer research and the growth of social marketing. I have
recounted elsewhere my odyssey into and through the latter richly rewarding topic area
(Andreasen 1993a). A large proportion of my work in social marketing involves whole
cultures and large populations that are disadvantaged. The difference here is that their
disadvantage is not in their consumption behavior but in other dimensions of their life,
especially their health.

Although early articles on the topic are found in 1969 and 1970, the topic is still in
its formative stages as an academic area—though practitioners have been doing social
marketing for 20 years or more. I am optimistic that its fate will be very different from
that of ghetto marketing in the 1970s. There are top-flight scholars working in the area,
including Marvin Goldberg, Christine Moorman, Dana Alden, Craig Lefebrve, and
Marty Fishbein. The field is becoming institutionalized, with centers springing up in
Florida, Ottawa, and Glasgow. A conference series has been initiated, and several major
publications are emerging (e.g., Andreasen 1995).

At the same time, the specific topic of disadvantaged consumers still sparks interest
in the 1990s with a focus on what are called "vulnerable consumers." A recent issue of
this journal was devoted to several articles on this topic, and Linda Alwitt and Tom
Donley have just published a monograph on the low-income consumer (Alwitt and
Donley 1996). What is particularly pleasing about this work is that it does not just
revisit the old issues, and it uses several imaginative new methodologies. Ron Hill's
ethnographic research on the problems of the homeless is one excellent example of this
kind of thrust.

Conclusion

Two points must be made about this brief history. First, scholars should recognize the
extent to which attention to particular research topics is affected by both the general
social climate and the interests of the scholarly community. It is clear that the extent and

focus of intellectual enterprise is affected strongly by both demand and supply factors. Those who wish to ensure the longevity of particular research topics must pay special attention to both forces if their subject area is to remain viable.

Second, just as stewards of an intellectual discipline should not neglect the past, neither should substantive scholars. There are a great many questions raised in the earliest days of interest in the problems disadvantaged consumers face that remain unresolved (cf. Andreasen 1993b). We still do not know the effect of erratic—not just low—incomes on the consumption problems of the poor. We do not know why the poor and the elderly report higher purchase satisfaction than do other consumers despite our expectations that the opposite should be true. And, though we have some of the necessary data, we do not have models that would help interventionists choose among problem areas for action.

An exciting thing about working on the problems of the disadvantaged and in social marketing is that a researcher is using his or her own skills to help make the society a better place, not just through making corporations more beneficial to stockholders and employees. But, perhaps equally satisfying is that working in this area presents fundamental intellectual and research problems that can tax the best scholarly minds. I have argued in many places that research in these areas is a great way to advance basic science in our major disciplines. A careful review of the sweep of history in these domains makes this transparent.

References

Alwitt, Linda F. and Thomas D. Donley (1996), *The Low-Income Consumer.* Thousand Oaks, CA: Sage Publications.

Andreasen, Alan R. (1971), *Inner City Business: A Case Study of Buffalo, New York.* New York: Praeger Publishers Inc.

___ (1975), *The Disadvantaged Consumer.* New York: The Free Press.

___ (1978), "The Ghetto Marketing Life Cycle: A Case of Underachievement," *Journal of Marketing Research,* 15 (February), 20–28.

___ (1991), "Consumer Behavior Research and Social Policy," in *Handbook of Consumer Behavior,* Thomas S. Robertson and Harold H. Kassarjian, eds. Englewood Cliffs, NJ: Prentice Hall, Inc., 459–506.

___ (1993a), "Revisiting the Disadvantaged: Old Lessons and New Problems." *Journal of Public Policy & Marketing,* 12 (Fall), 270–75.

___ (1993b), "Presidential Address: A Social Marketing Research Agenda for Consumer Behavior Researchers," in *Advances in Consumer Research,* Vol. 20, Michael Rothschild and Leigh McAlister, eds. Provo, UT: Association for Consumer Research, 1–5.

___ (1995), *Marketing Social Change.* San Francisco, Jossey-Bass.

___ and Arthur Best (1977), "Consumers Complain—Does Business Respond?" *Harvard Business Review,* 55 (July/August), 93–101.

Caplovitz, David (1967), *The Poor Pay More.* New York: The Free Press.

Developing Research on Public Policy and Marketing

William L. Wilkie

A quarter of a century is a long time, and the past 25 years have offered us ample opportunity to recognize lessons that can be helpful to our future. In reflecting on how our field has developed, I have culled nine particular lessons, which are listed in Table 1, that I believe might be useful in better understanding both where we have been and where we might go in the future. In the brief space available I offer short commentaries on each.

Societal Forces and the Field's Development

All experienced academics realize that research is actually much more than what they read on the pages of journal articles. Instead, the process of research development—particularly in substantive domains such as public policy—involves a variety of exposures that cumulate to influence problem selection and research approaches. Therefore, it is not surprising to observe that the larger social context has played an important role in shaping our development over the past quarter-century.

The social context of the late 1960s and early 1970s was very different from today. Professor Andreasen's piece describes this nicely, so I will not delve much further here. Suffice it to say that at that time there was a much broader interest in issues of business and society. Students and faculty members discussed and debated issues of social responsibility, the value of work as a human enterprise, consumer rights, and so forth. Many of us in business schools came down on the conservative side of these issues, but in contrast to today, we certainly agreed that they *were* issues.

Within this setting, there was an active interest in marketing and society, inquiring into questions of our marketing system's activities and their impacts—both positive and negative—on the social system and its members. My impression is that this was a broader field than is ours today, with academic roots in both economics and institutional

WILLIAM L. WILKIE is the Nathe Professor of Marketing, University of Notre Dame. He was co-chair of the forerunner to the current Marketing and Public Policy Conference, which was held in 1989. He is a past-president of the Association for Consumer Research, was visiting scholar at the Marketing Science Institute, and was the first in-house academic consultant within the Bureau of Consumer Protection at the Federal Trade Commission in 1972.

Wilkie, William L. (1997), "Developing Research on Public Policy and Marketing," *Journal of Public Policy & Marketing,* 16 (1) 132–36.

TABLE 1

Nine Insights on Public Policy and Marketing

  I. Societal Forces and the Field's Development
 II. Research Ebbs and Flows
III. On Depending on the Government
 IV. Impacts from Personal Initiatives
  V. Research Impediments (1): Marketing Academia
 VI. Research Impediments (2): Public Policy Issues
VII. An Infrastructure Emerges
VIII. Marginalization Threatens
 IX. New Challenges and New Vistas

---

marketing (especially physical distribution) and with developing interest into value-laden issues such as fair pricing laws, the treatment of marginalized groups, the social and economic value of advertising, and so forth. The areas we today divide into macromarketing and social marketing were both at work then, though there was furious academic debate on whether broadening the concept of marketing (beyond the for-profit sector) was appropriate for our field. In comparison to today, what was not so evident at that time were advanced statistical and experimental methods, much of the current theory in consumer behavior (such as information processing), and academic focus on consumer protection activities by the government.

Overall, though, it seems to me that the most pertinent difference does involve the breadth of interest across both the marketing field and business academia in general. Today we face a sad situation in which most young academics are receiving no exposure or training in issues of either business and society or public policy. It is a serious concern that the topics of marketing and society have largely disappeared from the mind-set of mainstream marketing academia (I return to this issue subsequently).

Research Ebbs and Flows

It is also important to observe that research activity in this area has been anything but smooth and cumulative. It has instead reflected fits and starts, with various researchers moving in and out of the literature. At Notre Dame, my colleague Greg Gundlach and I have been working on a project to track the literature in the field since 1970 (for an early report on this research, see Gundlach and Wilkie 1990). Given publication time lags, our study supports the casual impressions many of us had: from a relatively low level in the early 1970s, the remainder of the decade saw a steady climb in activity, peaking in 1980. At this point the field of marketing began to see a drop in research interest in public policy through the decade of the 1980s, leveling off toward the end, then beginning to climb during the 1990s. Overall, then, an inverted U-curve nicely describes total activity from 1970 to the late 1980s, with a slow but steady increase in activity during the 1990s. With respect to specific topics, our study shows even larger shifts, with some "hot" topics virtually disappearing from the scene.

At this point three conclusions on research activity seem appropriate: First, total interest and participation is growing, and the future looks bright; second, there is still a need for more commitment, more consistency, and more cumulative research traditions; third, the danger of a decline in interest still lurks: It isn't clear that another "1980s decade" does not lie in our future.

On Depending on the Government

It is startling to realize how dependent our field's development has been on interest and support from key government agencies. Twenty-five years ago, a key impetus came from the Federal Trade Commission's (FTC's) decision to explore the boundaries of its mandate in the area of consumer protection and its ensuing interest in the expertise offered by our field. Many of us became involved, traveling to Washington, advising government and businesses, and undertaking studies. When FTC interests turned to rule-making in the late 1970s, our efforts moved to incorporate these issues as well.

Then the FTC began to lose its standing (and budget) in Congress, and the deregulatory forces came into power under President Reagan. In the early 1980s, free-market economists entered the FTC in numbers and apparently saw no need for inputs from our field. Thus, hobbled by both budget cuts and lack of current policymakers' interest, research in our area began its long ebb. Recently, under more moderate leadership at the FTC, interest in our field's contributions has been rekindled.

I've learned several lessons during this time. First, the forces that determine government's support for our research are largely independent of (and unresponsive to) our field of endeavor. Therefore, reliance on the government as a sustaining force for us is a dangerous strategy. Second, business seems not to be the answer either: Apart from several long-standing and laudable self-regulatory efforts, interest in the business community in public policy matters seems to be derivative in nature: it is largely absent when the pressure is off and sparks up again when the government becomes interested in a regulatory problem. Third, academics need to confront the issue of their proper purpose, level, and scope of activity. Research in our field should be more than consulting for public policymakers: A substantial proportion of our efforts should be directed toward developing generalizable theories, frameworks, and methodologies for understanding issues related to marketing, society, and regulatory activity.

Impacts from Personal Initiatives

Another surprising insight gained from a look at our recent history is just how significant the impact of a personal initiative can be. Thus our field has its own short roster of heroes and heroines who deserve to be recognized for the impacts they have had. For example, Mary Gardiner Jones began this modern era by pressing for a marketing academic on her staff while serving as an FTC commissioner. Her initiatives set off a decade-long process. She first contacted George Day (then an assistant professor at Stanford), who suggested a doctoral student of his, Murray Silverman. Upon arriving in Washington, Murray discovered that his position on a commissioner's staff meant that he could not interact with bureau personnel on pending matters. Therefore, there was a need for at least one other person from our field to work on these issues. Murray contacted me, and I arrived in mid-1972, as the first consultant within the Bureau of Consumer Protection (BCP; interestingly, the BCP Director then was Robert Pitofsky, now FTC chairman). Shortly thereafter, David Gardner (University of Illinois) arrived as a consultant in the Office of Policy Planning and Evaluation (OPPE), and the three of us began our efforts to employ and instill consumer research at the FTC. As our short-term assignments neared an end, Gardner and I arranged for top researchers to replace us (Harold Kassarjian in BCP, Neil Beckwith in OPPE). They in turn arranged for their successors, and so forth, until a total of some 30 marketing academics had served in these capacities during the 1970s (Jones 1990; Murphy 1990). Many important contributions in our literature, including dissertations, have emerged from these visits.

One problem with naming names is that you might miss some people. Therefore I'll restrict my mentions simply to those in this panel, each of whose personal initiatives have been important in developing this field. In addition to his research in this area, Stephen Greyser, in his capacity as Executive Director of the Marketing Science Institute (MSI), has initiated discussions among researchers, marketers, and public policymakers, leading to research support from such diverse sources as the American Association of Advertising Agencies and the National Science Foundation. MSI's published research and its many mini-conferences did much to foster progress and better understanding.

In addition to his work on disadvantaged consumers, Alan Andreasen initiated a national survey on consumer problems that engendered wide interest in research on consumer satisfaction, and by reporting it in the *Harvard Business Review* he reached key business leaders as well. Also, Andreasen's long commitment to high-quality research and the cause of not-for-profit groups has been a quiet inspiration to many of us in our field.

Turning to Tom Kinnear, newer members of our field might not recognize the enormous gratitude we owe him for having begun, again on his personal initiative, the *Journal of Public Policy & Marketing* at a time (the early 1980s) when there seemed to be little demand for this publication. Moreover, as an able university administrator, Kinnear managed to subsidize this publication under the auspices of the University of Michigan until it was healthy enough to be taken over by the American Marketing Association (AMA). Under its subsequent editors, Patrick Murphy, Michael Mazis, and Debra Scammon, this journal has emerged as the centerpiece of our area.

Michael Mazis, meanwhile, has contributed significant initiatives over an extended period. Among them is the work he stimulated as a policy planner at the FTC, including the influential Consumer Information Task Force in 1979, his research contributions, and *Journal of Public Policy & Marketing* editorship. Mazis also initiated the AMA's Marketing and Society special interest group and organized one of the early conferences in our current series.

Our chairman Paul Bloom has been a consistent stimulator of the field's development, through his activities with MSI, his chairing an early conference in our series, his work with doctoral students, and his creation of a number of sessions such as this one, which are all instrumental to further development of the field.

I do not really wish to persist with names, but I do believe that a note of special thanks also is due to Commissioner Andrew Strenio, who has joined our group in recent years and who worked hard to facilitate its rebirth at the FTC in the 1990s. Also, other FTC commissioners and key staffers have helped to revive research there and have contributed to our conferences and literature.

My lesson here is simple: Getting involved does make a difference. We simply would not have the field we do today if some special people had not stepped forward at the right times.

Research Impediments (1): Marketing Academia

Another observation that is somewhat surprising to me is how few of us, over time, have remained consistently in the public policy zone of research. Instead, almost all of us (myself included) have moved in and out of the area, maintaining some considerable portion of our research activity in consumer behavior, advertising, channels of distribution, or some other area of marketing itself. A surprising number of marketing's best researchers have been contributors to public policy, but only in a sporadic (often one-time) fashion. (A quiz question for newer members: What two leading academics in marketing strategy produced the leading readings book on marketing and society some 25 years ago? You will find the answer in my reference list marked with an asterisk.)

Such part-time efforts are understandable given our primary home in marketing academia. However, I must ask whether this is a positive situation with respect to the field's development. There are several factors to consider in this regard: (1) our strong reliance on the essentially unreliable support and interest from government; (2) the lack of exposure and training to public policy issues in marketing doctoral education; (3) the fact that no school has specialized in marketing and public policy work at the doctoral level, in the manner that Florida has specialized in consumer behavior, Purdue and MIT in marketing science, and so forth (such specialization has had noted impacts in advancing those fields); and (4) the likelihood that recent *Business Week* emphasis on vocational master of business administration (MBA) training will place more pressures to move academics at top MBA schools further away from this area.

Conversely, on many occasions during these 25 years I have detected a latent interest in, and respect for, the issues of our field on the part of many marketing academics. Furthermore, though it is hard to recognize while we are young, I recently have been pleasantly surprised by an increasing realization that academic careers are actually quite long, if a person simply chooses to stay active. Therefore, research on a significant number of topics is actually quite feasible over an extended period of time, and public policy topics certainly can benefit from this opportunity. This panel is a fine example of this very point!

Research Impediments (2): Public Policy Issues

In addition to sociological and institutional analyses, it is important that we recognize that there are also some essentially academic difficulties to be faced in research in this area. For me, this challenge has been nicely captured by the research validity framework proposed by Brinberg and McGrath (1985; for marketing research examples, see also Brinberg and Hirschman 1986). My simplified view of this framework is that there are three domains inherent in any research study: the theoretical, the substantive, and the methodological. If we picture a triangle with each domain at an intersection, the researcher must begin a study at only one of these points—that domain reflecting his or her top-priority question to be answered by the study. The researcher then must develop the study by choosing to move along one of the legs, toward a second domain reflecting a further study aspect of particular significance (e.g., that it be realistic, that it be theoretically clean, that it be rigorously carried out). Then, only after reaching appropriate reconciliations on these two domains can the researcher move across the triangle to the third domain. At this point, prospects for a strong representation of this third domain are bleak, as its essential demands will have been sacrificed in order to achieve the demands of the first and second domains.

Having experienced this very problem in some of my own work and having observed it in the course of reading and reviewing many other studies in our area, by now I am convinced that this is an excellent representation of the difficulties we face. The primary difficulty is that theories seem to be inherently confounded in the complex real world of public policy issues. If we start with the substantive domain, then we will likely not find a clean mapping onto a single theory. Conversely, if we start with a single theory, we are likely to oversimplify the realities of the policy problem.

Two lessons emerge from this analysis. First, if we are to be relevant and significant for public policy, the substantive domain *must* be represented strongly in much of our research. This brings with it a risk that either theory or methodology will be weaker in these studies. This, however, is unacceptable for our academic field. Therefore, it seems that the only alternative for us is programmatic research such that, over time, each domain can be explored appropriately in our work. The downside is that this could require more time (and research support) than many marketing academics wish to invest.

An Infrastructure Emerges

Against the limiting prognoses of the last several points, this one is extremely positive. It has been heartening to watch how our academic field has begun to build a solid basis for itself. The rotating research positions at the FTC, together with the staunch support of MSI, the Association for Consumer Research (ACR), and the AMA, were key factors in supporting our work during the 1970s. As one indicator of our success, by the late 1970s FTC's own budget for consumer research, under the control of Ken Bernhardt, was some $1 million. However, this supporting structure largely crumbled when the FTC began its budgetary and organizational retreat from support of our area in the 1980s.

At this point, Professor Kinnear's development of the *Journal of Public Policy & Marketing* served to offer a continuing outlet for such research (and in this sense can be seen possibly to have saved our field). As the journal got stronger, interest in the area continued. At Notre Dame, Pat Murphy and I decided to convene a special symposium to commemorate the 75th anniversary of the FTC. This 1989 event, which brought together the academic researchers who had served at the FTC and some key past and present FTC officials, was a smashing success. Its contents are captured in a book (Murphy and Wilkie 1990) that is intended as a resource for those wishing to work in this field. The spirited interaction at that symposium led to participants agreeing that this is something we should do on a more frequent basis and, thanks to the initiatives of others, led eventually to the establishment of our annual conference held each May (current plans call for the 1999 Marketing and Public Policy Conference to be held at Notre Dame for a tenth anniversary celebration).

Finally, our field's infrastructure has been strengthened further by the recent development of the Marketing and Society special interest group within the AMA, providing us with a formal organizational structure around which to build. Under its able early leaders, the special interest group is strong and active, sponsoring special workshops at AMA conferences, sponsoring our annual conference, and publishing a newsletter to foster communication and new activity.

Taken altogether, we have now seen our field develop its own journal, its own conference, and its own association, all working to offer a venue and support for academics to interact, learn, and publish research on topics in our field. In this respect, we have certainly come a long way!

Marginalization Threatens

On the downside of our field's development is a rising concern that the gap between us and mainstream marketing could be increasing. We have noted already some of the symptoms. Probably the most disturbing is that most doctoral students today are receiving little or no education on our topics. I do not know whether this is being accompanied by a negative word of mouth about these topics. (Fortunately, however, I believe that we have avoided being captured by any particular political philosophy: conservatives, liberals, and moderates are all welcomed in our sessions and journal.)

Although removal from the mainstream might not affect us personally, I believe it is serious because our topics and points of view are important for the field of marketing academia to consider. As I indicate previously, there have been numerous occasions in which I have noted a latent interest in and respect for our issues among a broad range of marketing academics. I do not believe that the marginalization threat stems from deliberate efforts, but simply from the need to allocate time and attention to matters of perceived priorities. As the emphasis on MBA and executive training becomes incredibly strong at leading research schools, moreover, we can expect for these difficulties to increase.

My suggestion, therefore, is that we make serious and strong efforts to maintain marketing and public policy issues and perspectives in the mainstream of marketing academia. This means that we would strive to produce some work for *Journal of Marketing, Journal of Marketing Research, Journal of Consumer Research,* and *Marketing Science* as well as other mainstream publications. We would support Professor Jerry Wind's "Value of Marketing" program at Wharton, and we would increase our participation in MSI's research programs. It means that we would propose special sessions at AMA, ACR, Marketing Science, and other major conferences. Finally, it means that we would make efforts to reach out to doctoral students at this critical time of their educational development.

New Challenges and New Vistas

One striking aspect of our field is how important deliberate action has been in its development. In this spirit I offer some questions that I have about where we might head from here. How large a field should we be, and what level of cohesion should we seek? What sort of relationship should we have with consumer groups such as Consumer Federation of America or Consumers Union? What sort of relationship should we have with academic groups, such as the American Council on Consumer Interests, the Society for Consumer Psychology, macromarketers, and social marketers? What role, if any, should we seek to serve for public policymakers, marketing managers, or industry associations? To what extent should our research be "problem-driven"; to what extent normative? Given that we now can take on any of a number of shapes, it is good to ask seriously what we wish to become.

Turning to research substance, in case the previous points have not raised enough issues for further consideration, we should be pleased to see that the changes in the world are bringing larger and more complex issues before us for further research. Among these topics are the impacts of *globalization* on marketers, consumers, employees, investors, citizens, and regulators. Also, the development of *database marketing* offers challenges yet to be explicated and analyzed fully. Furthermore, the *technological implications* of the World Wide Web are potentially immense and deserve attention. Finally, future *antitrust policies* well could benefit were insights from our field to be offered in depth. The FTC held an interesting set of hearings on some of these issues in Fall 1995. (Transcripts are available on the FTC's Home Page [FTC 1996].)

A Concluding Comment

Although I have ended with challenges and questions for the future, these do not fully reflect my current thoughts about our field or its accomplishments. It was an exciting journey the first time through, and it has been a pleasure to revisit it again. I hope that it is clear that I have much appreciated the chance to have participated in this area at all: It is inherently an interesting and important sphere of activity, rewarding both personally and professionally. I am pleased to have been able to play a part in our journey to this point, and I look forward to participating in our continued progress in the future.

References

*Aaker, David A. and George S. Day, eds. (1971), *Consumerism: Search for the Consumer Interest.* New York: The Free Press.

Brinberg, David and Elizabeth C. Hirschman (1986), "Multiple Orientations for the Conduct of Marketing Research: An Analysis of the Academic/Practitioner Distinction," *Journal of Marketing,* 50 (October), 161–73.

___ and Joseph E. McGrath (1985), *Validity and the Research Process.* Beverly Hills, CA: Sage Publications, Inc.

Federal Trade Commission (1996), *Anticipating the 21st Century: Consumer Protection Policy in the New High-Tech, Global Marketplace,* Volume II. Washington, DC: Federal Trade Commission.

Gundlach, Gregory T. and William L. Wilkie (1990), "The Marketing Literature in Public Policy: 1970–1988," in *Marketing and Advertising Regulation: The Federal Trade Commission in the 1990s,* Patrick E. Murphy and William L. Wilkie, eds. Notre Dame, IN: University of Notre Dame Press, 329–44.

Jones, Mary Gardiner (1990), "Marketing Academics at the FTC: Reflections and Recommendations," in *Marketing and Advertising Regulation: The Federal Trade Commission in the 1990s,* Patrick E. Murphy and William L. Wilkie, eds. Notre Dame, IN: University of Notre Dame Press, 216–20.

Murphy, Patrick E. (1990), "Past FTC Participation by Marketing Academics," in *Marketing and Advertising Regulation: The Federal Trade* Commission *in the 1990s,* Patrick E. Murphy and William L. Wilkie, eds. Notre Dame, IN: University of Notre Dame Press, 205–15.

___ and William L. Wilkie, eds. (1990), *Marketing and Advertising Regulation: The Federal Trade Commission in the 1990s.* Notre Dame, IN: University of Notre Dame Press.

Consumer Research and the Public Policy Process—Then and Now

Stephen A. Greyser

My consideration of marketing and public policy over the past quarter-century focuses principally on consumer research and its incorporation into the public policy process by business, academics, and public policymakers. An overview of "then" and "now" leads me to seven principal observations.

From Expert Opinion to Data-Based Judgment

There has been a major shift from expert opinion to data-based judgment as the basis for assessing what messages and ideas consumers take away from advertisements. "Then" the reliance was on logic and inference often derived from consumer psychology. "Now" it is on empirical data tempered by analysis and judgment.

In "My Day in Court" (Smith et al. 1973), six professionals (psychologists, professors, and lawyers) discussed their experiences in the use of psychologists as expert witnesses in Federal Trade Commission (FTC) proceedings. Former FTC Bureau of Consumer Protection official Nancy Buc succinctly described the earlier model (p. 20):

> The Commission staff would troop in ... consumers who were not part of a selected sample.... These consumers talked about what they thought the ad said. The result of these sessions was usually an opinion.

The then-growing use of consumer psychologists as expert witnesses brought psychological concepts into the courtroom. Commercial researcher Valentine Appel described the application of a halo effect in the Wonder Bread case as "the first time that a fundamental psychological law has figured so importantly in a legal decision" (p. 13). Quickly, the operational ground-rules evolved to the use of empirical data rather than relying on expert opinion alone. As Professor Raymond A. Bauer put it, "the effects of communications should not be guessed at by experts" (p. 18).

STEPHEN A. GREYSER is the Richard P. Chapman Professor, Harvard Business School, where he specializes in marketing and communications. For over 30 years, he has contributed to the marketing and public policy field. He has been longtime Editorial Board Chairman of *Harvard Business Review* and is former executive director of the Marketing Science Institute. He has testified before the Federal Trade Commission on hearings on advertising and is a public member of the National Advertising Review Board.

Greyser, Stephen A. (1997), "Consumer Research and the Public Policy Process," *Journal of Public Policy & Marketing,* 16 (1) 137–38.

Increasingly, psychologists refused to testify as to what the public would infer, when the issue was amenable to empirical data—even though the latter still would be debatable as to interpretation. This rapidly became the standard and, as I show subsequently, has led to guidelines for gathering and using data on consumer attitudes and beliefs.

Shift in Industry Behavior

In the early 1970s, as consumerism waxed, industry's position on numerous marketing regulatory initiatives was almost always a "knee-jerk no." Although industry has not fully embraced new regulation over the years, the field of advertising has developed a highly distinctive self-regulation system.

By way of background, the 1960s had been a decade of substantial criticism of truth in advertising content, especially around alleged deceptive claims. The FTC's extensive public exploration of "modern advertising practices" in 1971 brought much of this criticism to the fore. The advertising community responded by establishing a self-regulation system sponsored by the American Advertising Federation, American Association of Advertising Agencies, Association of National Advertisers, and the Council of Better Business Bureaus. Its objectives are to sustain high standards of truth and accuracy in national advertising and promote responsible advertising to children.

The system initiates inquiries, determines the issues, collects and evaluates data, and adjudicates agreements. Advertisers must submit substantiation for their claims for staff resolution. Appeals can be made to a panel of the National Advertising Review Board (NARB), which is composed of representatives of national advertisers, advertising agencies, and the public sector.

As a several-times public member of NARB, I can attest to the system's seriousness of purpose, care in gathering and assessing data, and devotion to fairness in the process. Through the hundreds of cases undertaken by both the National Advertising Division (NAD) and the Children's Advertising Review Unit, numerous advertising campaigns have been withdrawn. Furthermore, the existence of the process and its operation have led companies and agencies to prevent questionable campaigns from being mounted.

Meaningful Structural Improvements

The 1970s saw some meaningful structural improvements in making advertising more truthful. Prior substantiation of advertising claims became the law for all advertisers, though many had done this as sensible business practice. The FTC instituted corrective advertising to redress the adverse effects of proven past deceptive advertising. And with FTC encouragement, more advertisers undertook direct brand versus brand comparisons in their advertising.

Overall, through legal, regulatory, and advertising industry initiatives, a clearer under-standing emerged of what actually constituted "deceptive advertising" and unsupported claims. What seemed to many to be a mountain to climb 20 years ago now seems rather routine.

Research Welcomed

One key foundation of all the change has been the broad welcoming of consumer research, including the application of consumer research by the FTC itself. A group of academic "visitors" to the FTC played a vital role. (Others in this session will describe that aspect in more detail.)

By "broad," I mean the courts, business, network acceptance departments, and academe. From the last has streamed research studies, conferences, articles, and a dedicated journal. Funding entities, such as the Marketing Science Institute (MSI) over the years and at times the National Science Foundation and the Advertising Educational Foundation, have helped facilitate insights into consumer information processing and other areas that under-pin researchers' improved understanding of how consumers approach marketing and advertising programs.

Along the way, there have been some milestone studies. William Wilkie's early con-sumer information-processing research, Keith Hunt's series of conferences on consumer satisfaction/dissatisfaction, Jack Jacoby's volume on miscomprehension of advertising (and other) communications, and Scott Ward's pioneering research on children and tele-vision advertising are but a few. (Others here will no doubt cite additional significant studies and publications.)

Warranting note is the FTC's Joan Bernstein's call for consumer research at the 1995 Association for Consumer Research annual conference. She emphasized "how impor-tant accurate information about consumer behavior is to our mission." Her paper, both in purpose and in detailed structure, shows how far consumer research has come in the public policy process.

Progress on Guidelines for Public Policy Research

With widespread use of consumer research in the public policy arena, it was inevitable that the need for guidelines would arise. How similar/different should such guidelines be for research to be used in public policy settings compared with typical commercial applications?

MSI has been a longtime champion of more systematic approaches to such guide-lines. Some 20 years ago, it sponsored joint business-government-academic-activist conferences on the subject. In 1994, it was the aegis for a comprehensive workshop led by Paul Bloom addressing design and implementation of research for public policy on the effects of marketing communications.

Training to Prevent Problems

One aforementioned felicitous consequence of the enhanced role of consumer research are workshops for business on how to try to avoid regulatory (and self-regulatory) problems.

The National Advertising Division of the Council of Better Business Bureaus, as part of advertising's self-regulation efforts, has sponsored a series of six workshops. Five deal with substantiation and performance testing:

- Substantiating a taste claim;
- Substantiating food health claims in advertising;
- Advances in claim substantiation;
- Product performance tests: design, interpretation, and claims; and
- Uniform industry performance standards.

The sixth treats consumer perception communications surveys, covering five topics:

- Design and sampling issues,
- Survey questions and structure,
- Data analysis: tabulation and reporting results,
- Case studies of consumer perception cases, and
- Hypothetical disputed survey at NAD.

Again, this activity reflects the distance traveled by the field. Now there is an entire set of potential problems for consumers—like a giant iceberg—that will never appear in public because they will have been addressed by companies at a prior stage.

Pitfalls

My chronicle basically has been one of progress. However, pitfalls remain. Let me cite a few:

- A persistent problem for academics in this field is the traditional matter of extrapolability from on-campus or university community respondents to relevant consumers. In the public policy setting, this is particularly dangerous, compared with samples of relevant consumers.
- Many people in this area, especially professors, play multifaceted roles—researchers, consultants, advocates. Consequently, it is essential that they declare (and make it clear) what role they are in when they are in it.

- Advocacy research—in which the conclusions have been reached before always-supporting research is undertaken—is another flaw in the research landscape. Advocacy is free speech; advocacy research weakens all researchers.
- Ad hoc research on "live" cases (i.e., ones in process) must be approached carefully. The absence of a clean prior state makes interpretation difficult, if feasible at all.
- Finally, long periods of "remission" in research and research support hurt the field. The 1980s are illustrative of a period when business and government tended not to support consumer research on public policy; business was less "under the gun" than before, and government had changed its priorities. This particularly affected programs of research.

A closing question: In light of clear advances in the professional application of consumer research in public policy, are consumers better off today in terms of protection? Advertising well could be less deceptive, but what about labels? What about the thicket of health and nutritional product claims? What about the clarity of services and costs for some financial services for poor people or of others for well-off people? Let me leave this subject for another session, another discussion, another paper.

Reference

Smith, Joseph, Herbert Abelson, Valentine Appel, Raymond A. Bauer, Nancy Buc, and Bruce Montgomery (1973), "My Day in Court," *Journal of Advertising Research,* 13 (December), 9–22.

MARKETING AND PUBLIC POLICY: PROSPECTS FOR THE FUTURE

Michael B. Mazis

Over the past several years, there has been a growing interest in marketing and public policy issues. After a promising beginning in the 1960s and 1970s, the field slumped in the 1980s. However, the 1990s has been a decade of renewal and growth. Some important events have served as a catalyst to the field's regeneration.

First, the annual Marketing and Public Policy Conference has brought together academic researchers, industry representatives, and government officials to discuss current studies and emerging policy issues. This conference has provided an opportunity for interaction and has imbued participants with a sense of optimism about the field's development. The genesis of this conference was a 1989 symposium that focused on the Federal Trade Commission (FTC) and advertising regulation and was attended by 50 invited participants. This meeting was organized by Patrick Murphy and William Wilkie and was held at the University of Notre Dame (Murphy and Wilkie 1990). This successful gathering led to a one-day conference in August 1990 prior to the American Marketing Association (AMA) Educators' Conference. The substantial attendance at this conference (100) participants) led organizers to believe that an annual conference could be successful. The Marketing and Public Policy Conference has been held each spring starting in 1992, and attendance has grown to nearly 150 attendees. The conference has had two or three simultaneous tracks of papers presented over two days.

Second, the *Journal of Public Policy & Marketing* (*JPP&M*) has grown in stature over its 15-year history. Initiated by Tom Kinnear and sponsored by the University of Michigan for its first ten years, *JPP&M* published an annual issue of approximately 13 manuscripts per year. Since its purchase by the AMA in 1991, *JPP&M* now publishes approximately 25 manuscripts per year in two issues. The editorial board has been expanded, manuscript submissions have grown steadily, and the quality of articles and the reputation of authors have been impressive.

MICHAEL B. MAZIS is Professor of Marketing, American University. He was editor of *Journal of Public Policy & Marketing* from January 1992 to July 1995. He was chair of the second Marketing and Public Policy conference. He worked in the Division of National Advertising and in the Office of Policy Planning at the Federal Trade Commission between 1976 and 1979.

Mazis, Michael B. (1997), "Marketing and Public Policy: Prospects for the Future," *Journal of Public Policy & Marketing*, 16 (1) 139–43.

Third, the Marketing and Society special interest group (SIG) of the AMA has boosted the field's visibility. The SIG was developed to serve as a "home" for the annual Marketing and Public Policy Conference, develop mini-conferences, organize special sessions at AMA educators' conferences, and publish a newsletter as a means of ensuring ongoing communication with members.

Another sign that the field is flourishing is the number of special issues of marketing journals devoted to marketing and public policy topics. Special issues of the *Journal of Business Research* (legal, regulatory, and ethical issues), *Journal of Advertising* ("green" advertising), and *Psychology and Marketing* (consumer warnings) have been published recently or are about to be published. Also, Paul Bloom organized a successful Marketing Science Institute competition to fund research on public policy issues. Finally, there are flourishing social marketing and macro-marketing groups that hold annual conferences.

However, the purpose of this article is not to exalt the field's resurgence, as there are still significant barriers to further growth. My goal is to review the threats facing the field and explore the opportunities for continued expansion.

Threats to Further Growth

There are several significant threats to the growth of the field. The field could become fragmented as social marketing, macromarketing, and marketing ethics groups form their own interest groups and develop their own conferences. To the extent that bridges are built among these groups, the entire field will prosper. The current practice of holding back-to-back Social Marketing and Marketing and Public Policy conferences, which enable participants to attend both conferences at a reduced rate, should be encouraged. The initial goal of the Marketing and Society SIG was to offer a "big tent" for diverse groups to participate. It is hoped that this goal will be realized in the future.

Another problem is that few business schools offer Marketing and Public Policy, Marketing and Society, Social Marketing, or similar classes. Although there have been some recent textbooks (Cohen 1995; Smith and Quelch 1993) and cases, these efforts must be expanded. Conferences should include sessions on teaching of marketing and public policy classes, and syllabi and materials should be shared freely. The Marketing and Society SIG newsletter should be used as a vehicle for sharing materials. Significant efforts must be undertaken to institutionalize marketing and public policy as an important component of the marketing and business school curricula.

Finally, as documented by Wilkie (1997), marketing and public policy issues must play a more prominent role in doctoral programs and must be covered in articles that appear in highly rated academic journals. This is a problem that is not easily remedied. However, a concerted effort should be made to involve important marketing scholars in marketing and public policy conferences—for example, serving as discussants or delivering invited papers that apply their work to public policy, social marketing, marketing ethics, or other social issues. Involving key scholars in marketing and public policy issues is part of the broader issue of encouraging a cultural change in departments of marketing. Although departments of economics and psychology have a strong tradition of conducting research that serves society, such a practice has not emerged in business schools. Despite Harvard Business School's significant commitment to incorporating ethics into its master of business administration (MBA) program, the significant movement toward executive training and more applied MBA curricula make it difficult to change cultural values. However, continuing efforts should be made to involve opinion leaders in public policy meetings and research.

What Is Marketing and Public Policy?

Throughout this article, I use several terms to describe the field—marketing and public policy, marketing and society, macromarketing, and social marketing. Overall, the field comprises two components. First, it involves studying marketing actions or the use of marketing techniques that affect society. These activities might include a business that distributes allegedly deceptive advertisements, a government agency that promotes AIDS-preventative behaviors, or a nonprofit organization that is concerned with ethical issues involved in the sale of potentially hazardous products in Third-World countries. Second, it involves government policy or other societal change that has marketing dimensions. This might include examining a government agency's proposal to institute a change in product labeling regulations, studying consumers' attitudes toward environmental issues on recycling behavior, or examining images of minority groups as portrayed in television advertising.

Traditionally, the field has focused substantial attention on two domains: legal and regulatory. Therefore, the field's best-known work involves examining laws and court decisions in areas such as antitrust, products liability, and advertising deception and in studying the activities of U.S. regulatory agencies, such as the FTC, Food and Drug Administration, and Consumer Product Safety Commission.

However, the field has expanded its horizons in recent years. Increasingly, two other areas—ethics and social issues—now fall under the marketing and public policy umbrella. Therefore, the view of the field has been broadened to include issues not only involving government policy but also affecting society at large.

As editor of *JPP&M* I sought to reflect this change by initiating special calls for papers on marketing ethics, social marketing, and vulnerable populations, which were edited by leading scholars: Gene Laczniak, Alan Andreasen, and Ron Hill, respectively. One purpose of these sections was to signal scholars that *JPP&M* and the marketing and public policy field is receptive to these areas of study. Also, though the field has focused largely on domestic regulations and laws that affect U.S. marketing activities, there have been recent efforts to focus more attention on international matters (this *JPP&M* special issue is an example). Such progressive approaches should be continued in the future.

This leaves the question, Should the field continued to be referred to as "marketing and public policy"? The term *public policy* implies that some government action or program is involved. Although government activity is an important segment of the field, other nongovernmental issues affecting society are becoming equally important. Therefore, the label "marketing and society," which is used to describe the recently developed SIG, comes closest to portraying the range of issues currently being studied. However, the major journal in the field, *JPP&M,* and the major conference both have "public policy" in their titles. Therefore, though the expression "marketing and public policy" does not reflect the great variety of research projects that are being conducted in the field, it is well known to the community of marketing scholars. It is appropriate, therefore, to continue using a name that has acquired a significant amount of brand equity.

Research Methods in Marketing and Public Policy

Traditionally, marketing and public policy research has employed three research methods: experimental research, consumer surveys, and legal/policy analysis. Some of the field's most influential articles report on (Jacoby, Chestnut, and Silberman 1977; Russo 1977; Russo et al. 1986) or are based on (Bettman 1975) experimental research. Important new contributions to the literature (Keller and Block 1996; Pechmann and Ratneswar 1994) are also based on laboratory research. Not surprisingly, consumer surveys also are widely used in marketing and public policy research (cf. Burton, Netemeyer, and Lichtenstein 1995; Laczniak, Muehling, and Carlson 1995). In addition, legal and policy analyses by scholars such as Calfee, Gundlach, Ippolito, Morgan, Petty, Preston, Richards, Scammon, and Sheffet appear frequently in *JPP&M* and other leading marketing journals.

There is a need, however, to use a wide variety or research methods to study marketing and public policy issues. Over the past few years, there has been a significant expansion in the types of methodologies used by scholars; such a trend should be continued. For example, Scammon, Li, and Williams (1995) use focus groups to explore physicians' perceptions about the supply of providers for the medically underserved. Depth interviews are used by Drumwright (1994) to determine how and why socially responsible buying comes about in organizations and by Hill (1994) to examine the perceptions of bill collectors and debtors about loan repayment. Peñaloza (1995) uses ethnography in a recent study of immigrant consumers' behavior, and interpretative methodologies are used to explore images of African-Americans in television advertisements (Bristor, Lee, and Hunt 1995) and to examine cinematic portrayals of drug and alcohol addiction (Hirschman and McGriff 1995). These qualitative and post-positive methodologies have been used widely in consumer behavior research over the past decade and have begun to be used for examining public policy issues. To continue this trend, key scholars should be encouraged to be active in the marketing and public policy field. For example, efforts should be undertaken to develop special sessions and symposia involving qualitative and post-positive methodologies at the Marketing and Public Policy Conference.

In addition, other methodologies must be employed more frequently. With the wide availability of government and industry data, there is significant potential for using secondary data analysis to study marketing and public policy issues. Notable examples of such research include the use of public opinion data on consumer beliefs about advertising (Calfee and Ringold 1994), the use of supermarket scanner data to explore relationships between socioeconomic variables and food choices (Mathios 1996), and the use of government survey data on smoking behavior to explore relationships between cigarette advertising expenditures and cigarette brand shares among youths and adults (Pollay et al. 1995). Also, though content analysis has been used occasionally (Diener 1993; King et al. 1991; Taylor and Lee 1994), it has the potential to be used more often. Finally, though meta-analysis is an extremely powerful technique, there is only one reported use of this methodology in marketing and public policy research (Andrews and Franke 1991). The field would benefit significantly from additional meta-analysis studies.

Theory-Based or Problem-Oriented Research?

Marketing and public policy research is frequently generated by interest in a particular problem. One reason that marketing and public policy researchers find the field rewarding is that their studies can "make a difference" in helping to understand important issues related to the homeless, the environment, product safety, or consumer privacy. Marketing and public policy researchers frequently feel passionate about their research, which often leads to emotional discussions or disagreements at conferences. However, the reasons that attract many scholars to study public policy issues serve to limit the growth of the field.

Studies that focus exclusively on a particular issue such as cigarette smoking, seat belt use, or AIDS prevention can be difficult to apply to other related behaviors. However, if studies have a firm theoretical foundation, the results obtained can be generalized more easily. Theoretically based studies also have greater potential to be published in leading journals, such as the *Journal of Consumer Research, Journal of Marketing,* and *Journal of Marketing Research.* Articles that appear in highly rated journals are likely to be read and cited widely, and such articles provide important signals to doctoral students, who are making decisions about career directions.

Significant public policy research should be *both* applied to significant social issues and designed to test theory. As Petty and Cacioppo (1996, pp. 6–7) state in a recent article,

Basic theory-driven research should remain an essential part of our overall research enterprise and we should foster its integration and use in applied research. . . . For various reasons, behavioral scientists have tended to focus either on basic or applied research. . . . Because of this antagonism can arise as to which approach is more valuable. This is nonsense, because applied research is fostered by basic research and vice versa.

Influential research not only addresses consequential issues and rests on a firm theoretical foundation, but also is part of a cumulative research program. Far too often, marketing and public policy studies are "one-shot" investigations that lack necessary follow-up. Notable examples of significant cumulative research programs are Bearden and Rose's work on adolescents' attitudes toward drugs and alcohol, Gorn and Goldberg's research on children's consumer behavior, Gundlach's analyses of exchange relationships, and Hill's studies on homelessness and poverty. These are research programs that should be emulated by emerging marketing and public policy scholars; these authors are strongly committed to their research programs and have made substantial contributions to the discipline.

Areas for Further Research

There are many fruitful areas for marketing and public policy research. However, there are some topics that would benefit from research and advance the discipline significantly. I list ten important areas for marketing and public policy research here:

- *Warning Messages:* Although there has been a significant amount of research on warning label effects (cf. Stewart and Martin 1994), much additional research is needed. How can meta-analysis be used to determine the relative impact of warning label characteristics on consumer recall, knowledge, attitudes, and behavior? Are "boomerang" effects likely to exist from warning messages? Under what circumstances? What is the impact on consumers of frequent repetition of warning messages? How do individual difference factors influence response to warnings? What is the potential effectiveness of new technologies in conveying warning messages?
- *Risk Perception:* How do consumers process information about the risks associated with engaging in unhealthful activities and the benefits associated with engaging in preventative health behaviors? What trade-offs do consumers make among safety, nutrition, and environmental protection along with durability, cost, convenience, and other attributes in making product or service decisions?
- *Children:* How do children and adolescents learn about the consumption of potentially harmful products, such as alcohol and cigarettes? What role does marketing play in initiation decisions? Does advertising for alcoholic beverages and cigarettes targeted to young adults have a significant effect on children and adolescents?

- *Disadvantaged Consumers:* How can the concept "targeting" be defined conceptually and empirically? What is the ethical "boundary line" between conducting target marketing to serve a target market's special needs and conducting targeting to "exploit" a segment's vulnerabilities? What are the responses of disadvantaged groups and minorities to having products and advertising targeted to their groups? What is the potential impact of the availability of new technologies and communications on disadvantaged consumers' decision making?

- *Media Influence:* What is the influence of different media (e.g., news stories, advertising) in shaping consumer knowledge about health and safety, the environment, and other social issues? What is the influence of brand-specific and institutional advertising in affecting beliefs about the healthfulness, safety, and environmental risks associated with specific product classes?

- *Privacy:* What are the dimensions of consumers' views about privacy? What trade-offs are consumers willing to make to gain additional privacy? What conceptual frameworks can be developed to understand attitudes about privacy better? What are the optimal organizational structures to ensure privacy and facilitate organizational efficiency? What is the appropriate balance between private firms' desire for information transmission on the information superhighway and the public's desire for privacy?

- *International:* What is the impact of laws (e.g., North American Free Trade Agreement, European Community legislation) and regulations on international competitiveness? What is the impact of regulations and laws on new product development? How do marketing ethics vary across cultures? What is the appropriate balance between a developing country's desire to protect its industries and a developed county's desire to reduce protectionist trade barriers?

- *Advertising Deception:* To what extent do consumers generalize from comparative claims ("Brand X margarine is lower in fat than Brand Y margarine") to absolute claims ("Brand X margarine is a low-fat product")? To what extent do consumers generalize from specific exemplars ("Betty Smith lost 60 pounds on Brand X diet") to specific product beliefs ("Most consumers will lose 60 pounds on Brand X diet")? How can the materiality of an advertising claim be measured reliably? What are the necessary steps to prevent deception on the Internet while addressing freedom of speech concerns?

- *Corporate Decision Making:* What organizational frameworks are most effective for discouraging inappropriate or illegal activity (e.g., price fixing, bribery, export of hazardous products) and for encouraging pro-social activity (e.g., environmental consciousness, fair employment practices)? What are the most appropriate ethical frameworks for guiding long-term relationships among suppliers or alliances among firms? What are the most effective processes for improving managers' ethical and socially responsible behaviors? What is the impact of corporate social responsibility on consumer and supplier perceptions and decision making?

- *Social Marketing:* What are the characteristics of successful campaigns to demarket potentially harmful products such as cigarettes, alcohol, and illegal drugs? How can interpersonal factors be used to develop successful social marketing campaigns? What are the ethical and cultural concerns in developing social marketing campaigns, and how can these concerns be handled?

Conclusions

My purpose has been to report on the field's current status and its future prospects. Marketing and public policy is enjoying a significant resurgence. The current growth is due to several factors: the development of the annual Marketing and Public Policy Conference, the enhanced reputation of *JPP&M,* and the establishment of the Marketing and Society SIG. However, the key factor in this revival has been the time and commitment of a small body of dedicated persons who have devoted considerable effort to planning conferences, developing special sessions, serving as editorial board members or section editors, and working to improve the quality of research in the field. People who deserve a special thanks include Craig Andrews, Paul Bloom, Pam Ellen, Greg Gundlach, Ron Hill, Pat Kaufmann, Tom Kinnear, Rob Mayer, Pat Murphy, Ross Petty, Debra Ringold, Debra Scammon, Mary Jane Sheffet, and Josh Wiener.

There are fundamental impediments to the field's continued progress. The field could become fragmented into subdisciplines, such as legal/policy, macromarketing, ethics, and social marketing. Each of these groups probably lack adequate mass to be self-sustaining. Therefore, efforts should be undertaken to encourage groups with somewhat diverse interests to coalesce to the extent possible. Also, continuing efforts are needed to involve key marketing scholars in conferences as a means of enhancing the field's reputation and increasing awareness of marketing and public policy issues among doctoral students. Moreover, marketing and public policy scholars must guard against focusing too much effort on applied issues and "hot" topics. Publication in leading journals is primarily restricted to theory-based research; for the field to prosper, marketing and public policy research must appear regularly in journals such as the *Journal of Consumer Research, Journal of Marketing,* and *Journal of Marketing Research.* In addition, marketing and public policy scholars must not be too limited in the methodologies used; a wide variety of research methods are needed to address complex social issues. Finally, the most important ingredient to further growth is the continued involvement of "old" and established scholars and the development of "young" and evolving talent in the field. Therefore, established scholars must continue to mentor doctoral students and assistant professors and provide opportunities for participation in conferences and other events.

References

Andrews, Rick and George R. Franke (1991), "The Determinants of Cigarette Consumption: A Meta-Analysis," *Journal of Public Policy & Marketing,* 10 (Spring), 81–100.

Bettman, James R. (1975), "Issues in Designing Consumer Information Environments," *Journal of Consumer Research,* 2 (December), 169–77.

Bristor, Julia M., Renee Gravois Lee, and Michelle R. Hunt (1995), "Race and Ideology: African-American Images in Television Advertising," *Journal of Public Policy & Marketing,* 14 (Spring), 48–59.

Burton, Scot, Richard G. Netemeyer, and Donald R. Lichtenstein (1995), "Gender-Differences for Appearance-Related Attitudes and Behaviors," *Journal of Public Policy & Marketing,* 14 (Spring), 60–75.

Calfee, John E. and Debra Jones Ringold (1994), "The 70% Majority: Enduring Consumer Beliefs About Advertising," *Journal of Public Policy & Marketing,* 13 (Fall), 228–38.

Cohen, Dorothy (1995), *Legal Issues in Marketing Decision Making.* Cincinnati, OH: South-Western College Publishing.

Diener, Betty J. (1993), "The Frequency and Context of Alcohol and Tobacco Cues in Daytime Soap Opera Programs: Fall 1986 and Fall 1991," *Journal of Public Policy & Marketing,* 12 (Fall), 252–57.

Drumwright, Minette E. (1994), "Socially Responsible Organizational Buying: Environmental Concern as a Noneconomic Buying Criterion," *Journal of Marketing,* 58 (July), 1–19.

Hill, Ronald Paul (1994), "Bill Collectors and Consumers: A Troublesome Exchange Relationship," *Journal of Public Policy & Marketing,* 13 (Spring), 20–35.

Hirschman, Elizabeth C. and Joyce A. McGriff (1995), "Recovering Addicts' Responses to Cinematic Portrayal of Drug and Alcohol Addiction," *Journal of Public Policy & Marketing,* 14 (Spring), 95–107.

Jacoby, Jacob, Robert Chestnut, and W. Silberman (1977), "Consumer Use and Comprehension of Nutrition Information," *Journal of Consumer Research,* 4 (September), 119–28.

Keller, Punam Anand and Lauren Goldberg Block (1996), "Increasing the Persuasiveness of Fear Appeals: The Effect of Arousal and Elaboration," *Journal of Consumer Research,* 22 (March), 448–60.

King, Karen Whitehall, Leonard N. Reid, Young Sook Moon, and Debra Jones Ringold (1991), "Changes in the Visual Imagery of Print Cigarette Ads, 1954–1986," *Journal of Public Policy & Marketing,* 10 (Spring), 63–80.

Laczniak, Russell N., Darrel D. Muehling, and Les Carlson (1995), "Mothers' Attitudes Toward 900-Number Advertising Directed at Children," *Journal of Public Policy & Marketing,* 14 (Spring), 108–16.

Mathios, Alan D. (1996), "Socioeconomic Factors, Nutrition, and Food Choices: An Analysis of the Salad Dressing Market," *Journal of Public Policy & Marketing,* 15 (Spring), 45–54.

Murphy, Patrick E. and William L. Wilkie (1990), *Marketing and Advertising Regulation: The Federal Trade Commission in the 1990s.* Notre Dame, IN: University of Notre Dame.

Pechmanri, Cornelia and S. Ratneshwar (1994), "The Effects of Antismoking and Cigarette Advertising on Young Adolescents' Perceptions of Peers Who Smoke," *Journal of Consumer Research,* 21 (September), 236–51.

Peñaloza, Lisa (1995), "Immigrant Consumers: Marketing and Public Policy Considerations in a Global Economy," *Journal of Public Policy & Marketing,* 14 (Spring), 83–94.

Petty, Richard E. and John T. Cacioppo (1996), "Addressing Disturbing and Disturbed Consumer Behavior: Is It Necessary to Change the Way We Conduct Behavioral Science," *Journal of Marketing Research,* 33 (February), 1–8.

Pollay, Richard W., S. Siddarth, Michael Siegel, Anne Haddix, Robert K, Merritt, Gary A. Giovino, and Michael P. Eriksen (1996), "The Last Straw? Cigarette Advertising and Realized Market Shares Among Youths and Adults, 1979–1993," *Journal of Marketing,* 60 (April), 1–16.

Russo, J. Edward (1977), "The Value of Unit Price Information," *Journal of Marketing Research,* 14 (May), 192–201.

___, Richard Staelin, Catherine A. Nolan, Gary Russell, and Barbara Metcalf (1986), "Nutrition Information in the Supermarket," *Journal of Consumer Research,* 13 (June), 48–70.

Scammon, Debra L., Lawrence B. Li, and Scott D. Williams (1995), "Increasing the Supply of Providers for the Medically Underserved: Marketing and Public Policy Issues," *Journal of Public Policy & Marketing,* 14 (Spring), 35–47.

Smith, N. Craig and John A. Quelch (1993), *Ethics in Marketing.* Homewood, IL: Richard D. Irwin, Inc.

Stewart, David W. and Ingrid M. Martin (1994), "Intended and Unintended Consequences of Warning Messages: A Review and Synthesis of Empirical Research," *Journal of Public Policy & Marketing,* 13 (Spring), 1–19.

Taylor, Charles R. and Ju Yung-Lee (1994), "Not in *Vogue:* Portrayals of Asian Americans in Magazine Advertising," *Journal of Public Policy & Marketing,* 13 (Fall), 239–45.

Wilkie, William L. (1997), "Developing Research on Marketing and Public Policy," *Journal of Public Policy & Marketing,* 16 (Spring), 132–36.

AN HISTORIC PERSPECTIVE ON THE QUANTITY AND QUALITY OF MARKETING AND PUBLIC POLICY RESEARCH

Thomas C. Kinnear

There are many interesting issues that could be addressed in a retrospective on the subfield of marketing and public policy (M&PP). Many of these are addressed in the commentaries of the authors of other sections of this retrospective. Therefore, I limit myself to a few specific issues as follows: (1) What forces have caused research activity and its quality to vary significantly? (2) What have been the most difficult research problems? and (3) How should researchers *not* proceed to solve these problems? The comments that follow reflect my personal judgments about these issues on the basis of my experiences in writing, editing, and consulting in the subfield.

Forces Causing Variation in Research Activity

The first reason for the variation in the level of research activity in the M&PP subfield is the variation in the degree of activism in the marketing regulatory environment. High activism provides sources of both funding and research issues, and low activism lowers the salience of the issues to researchers and dries up funding sources. This funding comes from both the relevant federal and state agencies and the businesses affected by the activism. In addition, individual academic researchers move their interest and attempts to get funding grants to active areas.

The key federal agencies driving this variation have been the Federal Trade Commission (FTC) and the Food and Drug Administration (FDA). At the state government level, the level of aggressiveness of the individual attorneys general and their association, the National Association of Attorneys General (NAAG), have been influential in this ebb and flow.

As an example of this dynamic, consider the significant efforts in M&PP that arose out of the heightened activism at the FTC during the late 1970s and early 1980s. At that time,

THOMAS C. KINNEAR is Vice President for Development and D. Maynard Phelps Professor of Marketing, School of Business Administration, University of Michigan. He was the first editor of *Journal of Public Policy & Marketing* and has been an active scholar and expert witness in issues related to advertising deception.

Kinnear, Thomas C. (1997), "An Historic Perspective on the Quantity and Quality of Marketing and Public Policy Research," *Journal of Public Policy & Marketing*, 16 (1) 144–46.

the FTC's Impact Evaluation Office, which was headed by Ken Bernhardt, funded more than $1 million a year in research in M&PP. Examples include Bill Wilkie's (1983, 1987) work on affirmative disclosure and Mike Mazis's work on pricing in deregulated markets.[1] In the 1980s, the great dimunition of this funding due to reduced FTC activism and changing priorities resulted in an associated fall in related M&PP research. As the FDA's interest in food nutritional labeling increased, so did the level of related research productivity. The work of Levy and colleagues (1985) on labeling, which was sponsored by the FDA, is an example.[2] At the state level, the efforts of the NAAG in the area of cigarette advertising and associated impacts have driven interest and funding in this area. The work of Richard Pollay (1989) and Richard Mizerski[3] are but a few of many examples.

The second reason for the variation in the level of research activity in the M&PP subfield is the variation in the degree of prestige in the discipline assigned to researchers in the subfield. There has been a little bit of "now you're hot, now you're not" dynamic to this. For example, environmental issues in marketing have had two hot periods: the first in the early 1970s and the second in the early 1990s. At these times, more well-known researchers were attracted to this part of M&PP, and prize journal space was made available to these researchers and their work. At other times, interest in this subject declined, and little prestige was assigned to those who continued to labor in the area.

In addition, some of the more theoretical members of the marketing discipline never have assigned any prestige to researchers in this area. "You were never hot" seems to be their attitude. The driving force behind this attitude is the belief that an area of research that has a very practical public policy outcome in mind lacks the "purity of real science." At one time, members of regulatory agencies were a significant part of the Association for Consumer Research (ACR). Over the years, the strong theory over practice view within ACR drove these regulators out of ACR. They were considered a low-prestige group, as were most of the researchers who chose to work with them.

The third reason for the variation in the level of research activity in the M&PP subfield is the content and direction within marketing doctoral programs. In recent years the number of doctoral programs offering courses in M&PP as part of their core curriculum has declined substantially. Virtually none of the most recognized doctoral programs now offer such training. Without this training in current programs, there has developed a shortage of trained faculty to offer appropriate courses.

The fourth reason for the variation in the level of research activity in the M&PP subfield is the realities of the job market for doctoral students. Almost no schools now

---

[1] This work occured when Michael Mazis was working at the FTC and had a major impact on policy.

[2] See the Spring 1996 issue of *Journal of Public Policy & Marketing* for a special section on nutritional issues. Some of this research reflected the activist FDA of Dessler on this issue. The Spring 1993 issue of *Journal of Public Policy & Marketing* has a special section on alcohol warnings.

[3] Richard Mizerski has made many presentations about "Joe Camel" symbolism and other icons at various Marketing and Public Policy conferences.

actively seek a prospective faculty member who positions him- or herself as a M&PP person. The same also can be said for the promotion policies of most schools. An academic's prospects for promotion are much diminished by positioning him- or herself as a M&PP person. Researchers must do M&PP research on top of having established themselves as solid scholars in a more theoretical discipline. These attitudes clearly limit the flow of M&PP scholarship.

The fifth reason for the variation in the level of research activity in the M&PP subfield relates to the subjective probability that researchers assign to gaining access to the "A" level mainstream journals for M&PP topics. This perceived probability of access varies with changes in journal editors' attitudes about M&PP topic relevance. These editors must deal with significant space limitations and make judgments about the appropriate mix of article topics from the whole array of marketing. Prospective authors often edit themselves not to research a particular topic on the basis of their perception that a particular editor likely will not provide space for that topic in the relevant journal. The creation of the *Journal of Public Policy & Marketing* was one attempt to provide a consistent outlet for M&PP topics. It is hoped that this has helped reduce the variance in the amount of M&PP research.

Most Difficult Research Problems in M&PP

It could be argued that all M&PP research problems are inherently difficult. This research must address complex issues at the interface of the practice of marketing and the public policy environment. This requires a blend of solid theory, relevant empirical information, appropriate research control, and an understanding of the practical consequences of policy actions. However, within this context there are some research problems that could be called the "most difficult."

The first such difficult research problem involves regulatory impact evaluation studies. When a public policy law that affects marketing or a new FTC rule is proposed or enacted, how are its potential or actual impacts to be evaluated? Research can provide useful results in these contexts, but only if it can stand the tests of both internal and external validity. This usually means that great care must be taken in implementing the research, and that the budget for the research will be substantial.

The second difficult research problem involves measuring the secondary and long-term impacts of public policy developments. For example, in the early 1970s the FTC proposed an affirmative disclosure remedy for Hawaiian Punch fruit drink. The published evaluation of this work by Jim Taylor, Oded Gur-Arie, and myself took more than eight years of field work (Kinnear, Taylor, and Gur-Arie 1983). Results observed in the first few years were quite different than the more long-term results of the study. Just how many one-time, short-term studies have deceived us?

The third difficult research problem involves topics that are emotionally laden. The environment, food nutrition, and cigarette advertising research are three such examples. I personally have been challenged on principle on environmental issues by groups that do not accept the concept of "market failure." The book *Tainted Truth* (Crossen 1994) documents the sad saga of poor research with an emotional point of view in the food nutrition area. Finally, the "shouting matches" at M&PP conferences about cigarette research has made a scientific discourse on the subject most difficult. In all these areas, there are too many interest groups, with too little regard for "scientific truth," that pollute the nonjournal literature with questionable research.

The fourth difficult research problem involves the measurement of true behavior impacts. All too often the field has been content to measure attitude or stated intention as good measures of behavior. The M&PP arena is full of consumers and firms with good intentions. This often does not translate to real behavior. The environmental research area is a good example of this dynamic. Attitude studies from the 1970s consistently overstate true environmentally friendly behavior, as have more recently reported studies from the 1990s.[4]

To make the most meaningful contributions to the M&PP discourse, research studies must effectively deal with these complex problems. Too much research takes the easy way out and takes a path down which researchers should not proceed. In the next section, I note some of the pitfalls on this easy path.

How *Not* to Proceed to Solve Research Problems

The first way not to proceed is to do impact evaluation research on the cheap. Fundamentally, excellence in this type of research requires studies of such complexity and realism that a large budget is required. The right number of waves of a study, the breadth of a sample, the number of controls used, the sophistication of analysis, and so on, all require substantial money.

The second way not to proceed relates to the use of student subjects in research. Frankly, there are almost no real M&PP issues for which a student subject pool matches the population of relevance. M&PP issues of the aged, the poor, or young children require associated samples.

The third way not to proceed is to avoid longitudinal studies and never seek secondary effects, and the fourth is too let biases hold forth and affect research programs. Finally, assume that attitude is behavior in M&PP research. The costs and complexities of getting to real long-term behavior likely exceed the research budget. So what if the field is potentially misled?

---

[4]As an example of a recent attitudinal study that did not reach true behavioral measures, see Berger and Corbin (1992). This is a well-implemented study in its dealings with attitudes, but it does not measure actual behavior.

References

Berger, Ida E. and Ruth M. Corbin (1992), "Perceived Consumer Effectiveness and Faith in Others as Moderators of Environmentally Responsible Behaviors," *Journal of Public Policy & Marketing,* 11 (2), 79–89.

Crossen, Cynthia (1994). *Tainted Truth: The Manipulation of Fact in America.* New York: Simon & Schuster.

Kinnear, Thomas C., James R. Taylor, and Oded Gur-Arie (1983), "Affirmative Disclosure: Long-Term Monitoring of Residual Results," *Journal of Public Policy & Marketing,* 2, 38–45.

Levy, Alan, Odanna Mathews, Marilyn Stephenson, Janet E. Tenney, and Raymond E. Schucker (1985), "The Impact of a Nutritional Information Program on Food Purchasing," *Journal of Public Policy & Marketing,* 4, 1–13.

Pollay, Richard W. (1989), "The Informational Content of Cigarette Advertising: 1926–1986," *Journal of Public Policy & Marketing,* 8, 1–23.

Wilkie, William L. (1983), "Affirmative Disclosure at the FTC: Theoretical Framework and Typology of Case Selection," *Journal of Public Policy & Marketing,* 2, 3–15.

___ (1987), "Affirmative Disclosure at the FTC: Communication Decisions," *Journal of Public Policy & Marketing,* 6, 33–42.

Marketing and Society: An Historical Analysis

Joshua Wiener and Patrick E. Murphy

Introduction

The history of marketing and society is a rich one. As Wilkie and Moore (1999) have noted, formal marketing knowledge has contributed to society for over one hundred years. Marketing's societal impact in terms of advertising, sales practices, power in the channel, product safety and a host of other issues are experienced on a daily basis. Hence, the examination of marketing's role in society needs constant re-examination. One purpose of this chapter is to undertake such an analysis.

Our paper is divided into several parts. Initially, we discuss three interwoven threads that we see in this field—its intellectual history; the evolution of the field and its relationship to marketing at large; and the history of consequences in marketing and society. Finally, we propose future directions for this field.

Interwoven Threads

We see three interwoven threads in the formal study of marketing and society. The first is an intellectual history of how domain-relevant knowledge advanced and retreated. Second, an infrastructure history pertains to how the domain evolved from an informal group of scholars into a robust sub-field with conferences, and highly regarded specialty journals. Third, there are the consequential and personal histories of how the ideas and people from the marketing and public policy domain have influenced the actions of policy makers in private firms, government agencies, and nongovernmental organizations as well as the domain itself. Finally, we share an overwhelming belief that the reason for understanding the domain's history is to provide direction for the domain's future. The reader will note that most of our sections cumulate in lessons to be learned. This belief reflects the historical role played and the one currently being carried out by those who study marketing and society. Each trend adds to the field's knowledge, infrastructure, and influence over policy makers. In other words, history is being written by those who both made it, and continue to make it.

WIENER, JOSHUA and PATRICK E. MURPHY (2006), "An Historical Analysis."

Joshua L. Wiener is the Tom and Edna Mae Carson Professor of Business Administration and Director of the Center for Social and Services Marketing at the Oklahoma State University and **Patrick E. Murphy** is the C. R. Smith Co-Director, Institute for Ethical Business Worldwide and Professor of Marketing in the Mendoza College of Business at the University of Notre Dame.

It is likely that the history of many academic domains could be decomposed into multiple threads. What may be less likely is that the contributors to the domain so passionately care about each of the threads. In particular, a close reading of the selections in this volume reveals how often one seeks to balance the goals of advancing intellectual thought, improving the stature of the sub-field within the broader marketing domain, and providing information that both defines substantive problems and suggests meaningful solutions.

Intellectual History

There are (at least) three ways to view a field's intellectual history: by issues addressed, intellectual ideas advanced, and empirical findings amassed. In this section we focus on the issues addressed and trace the evolution of marketing and society's domain over time. Our goal is not to provide a history (this is provided by the Wilkie and Moore "4 Eras" reading in this section), but to highlight the underlying forces which drive society and marketing's domain.

THE EARLY YEARS (1900–1950)

In the early years of marketing scholarship was driven by a need and desire to understand marketing phenomena. The world was rapidly changing and the extant business discipline (economics) was proving too narrow in scope. Marketing scholars defined their research problems in terms such as distribution, middlemen, and advertising, i.e., regarding issues and agents that were emerging as key elements of the modern American economy (Wilkie and Moore 2003). In a broad sense, little conflict existed between research that advanced knowledge and research that addressed consequential issues.

Many of these substantive issues were either by definition or easily framed in marketing and society terms. When major changes take place in the way an economy works, questions of how these changes might impact competitors, consumer well-being or social welfare are a natural occurrence. Because marketing was only beginning to emerge from the shadow of economics, asking broad questions about the impact of significant changes of the socio-economic system at large was equally commonplace. During early 1900s two questions of great intellectual and political weight were: which economic system (capitalism or socialism) would work best for its participants, and under what conditions would capitalism produce the best (most efficient) outcome? In other words, broad higher-order levels of analysis were very much an accepted part of the research tradition.

When significant changes take place, winners and losers are likely to emerge, and inevitably many are concerned because change is ever-present. If the changes are viewed as potentially harmful to groups within the economy, social movements arise and pressures for government intervention become intense. When the political process succumbs to these pressures (rightly or wrongly), legislation is passed and rules written. In other words, a period of economic and social upheaval is tailor made for a domain that takes a special interest in assessing how marketing practices might harm (help) classes of people; and how government policies impact marketing practices.

In sum, during the early years of the marketing field, research conducted from a marketing and society perspective fit well within the overall marketing paradigm. It focused on important issues; used multiple perspectives to understand the impact of marketing phenomena on different members of society; employed several levels of analysis including broad views that took social well being as the "dependent" variable. Many of the critical issues facing marketing gave rise to or led to federal or state regulations. The growth in consumer protection legislation in the 1930s, a more activist FTC and more sympathetic courts represented some outcomes of this era (Zuckerman 1990).

MODERN TIMES (1950–PRESENT)

As time passed, the study of macro-issues, which so concerned early scholars, faded. Attention increasingly focused on how a firm could be most profitable operating within the economic system, and not on the system itself. Questions of policy and law were increasingly framed in the narrowest of terms, i.e., how specific laws might impact marketing practice, and questions of societal welfare were, for the most part, viewed as beyond the scope of marketing.

During the late 1950s and early 1960s the world began to change again. Popular books questioned the benefits of the affluent society (Carson 1962; Galbraith 1958; Packard 1957). The proliferation of television advertising raised anew questions about the impact of advertising on free-choice. Social movements both brought attention to segments such as minorities that had not benefited from post WWII growth, and the negative societal consequences of industrial/technological development. Scientific evidence mounted that many health problems sprang from choices individuals made. One specific example was the Surgeon General's Report in the early sixties on the dangerous effects of cigarette smoking. As has been the case in earlier times, proposing new public policies was one response to societal movements and concerns.

One initial wave of research springing from the ills of the affluent society largely focused on issues of choice and information.ʹ (Only in an affluent, consumer-driven society are these issues of concern. In other words, during the depression and war the key concern was simply to make consumer products available. Of course, a plethora of choices is not alone a significant problem.) The problem arises when, in the eyes of thought-leaders, consumers are making poor choices. It is clearly a marketing issue when these poor choices are blamed on marketing activities. Two reasons might explain why marketing was criticized. The first is that during the 1960s societal attitudes towards business turned negative, and towards government turned positive. President Kennedy in

1962 articulated his famous "Consumer's Bill of Rights" which clearly included the presumption that it was the government's duty to ensure these rights. The second is that the growth of television (the "information technology" revolution of the time) made advertising ubiquitous and intrusive. We will return to this wave of research when we speak of how marketing and society research influences the world.

The 1960s was also a time when the middle class increasingly began to focus on issues that transcended meeting their material needs. It was the decade of the civil rights movement, growing environmentalism, concern about the poor, etc. How marketing scholarship responded to these societal changes is best understood by examining the July 1971 special "Society and Marketing" issue of the *Journal of Marketing*. Specific topics addressed included: fund raising, health services, population control, recycling, black vs. white food costs, the social responsibility of business, and air pollution. However, it is important to note how the editor framed most of this work. He began by casting societal issues in terms of how the managers of private firms must respond to the pressures and opportunities engendered by social changes. In other words, he does not waver from the post-WWII view that marketing's primary role is to serve the needs of private enterprise.

In the ensuing years, societal concerns and the substantive issues addressed by marketing and society scholars changed. Some research just tracked the news media. An extreme example is energy research. For example, during its first ten years the *Journal of Public Policy & Marketing* published numerous papers about energy issues (in particular conservation) and then the topic almost disappeared as a distinct line of inquiry. For example, between 1978 and 1984 twenty-seven energy related papers were published in *JPP&M*, four were published between 1984 and 1989, and none since Sprott and Miyazaki (2002). A similar pattern is found in the *Journal of Consumer Research (JCR)* with articles focusing on children and adolescent consumers: 20 between 1974 and 1984; 15 in the next decade, 4 in the last half of the decade, and just two since 2000. In contrast, since 2002 the *Journal of Public Policy & Marketing* has published six papers concerned with direct to consumer advertising of drugs, six investigating diet/nutrition issues and two other health related papers. During its history the *JCR* has published only three papers which they index as health/nutrition; they all have appeared since 2002.

Prior to WWII much of the research had been driven by fundamental changes in the American economy. This driver of scholarship has returned today, particularly from the rise of information technology (which is changing how consumers search for and use information) and consolidation and integration at the retail level. With respect to retailing structure change, for many years one of the primary functions of the Federal Trade Commission was to enforce the Robinson Patman Act protecting small businesses, especially the "ma and pa" grocers (Zuckerman 1990). In recent years, however, not only has the number of consumer categories dominated by stores expanded, but the "box" stores have learned to extend their power up the supply channel. For example, Wal-Mart pressures its suppliers to continue to reduce costs year after year. As a consequence, numerous studies conducted over the past few years have focused on both broad anti-trust issues and on the issues, such as slotting allowances, which arise as a consequence of buyer power. These anti-trust issues were highlighted by a special section in the *JPP&M* in the Fall 2002 issue.

LESSONS

History provides a few clear lessons. The first is that marketing and public policy research is a venue where scholars can study the issues that interest them as citizens. The caveat is that the issues must be studied in marketing terms. The second is the marketing consequences of the ongoing information technology revolution will continue to play an increasingly important role in shaping research priorities. It will likely do so because it changes several activities: how consumers search and process/use information; how companies compete for consumers and manage channel relationships; and the salience of "ongoing" issues such as privacy and property rights. These changes create turmoil which requires both a need to understand how the changes are impacting the public good and pressures for regulations that will address the problems that change creates.

The Evolution of the Field and Its Relationship to Marketing at Large

KEY DEVELOPMENTS

Prior to the 1960s marketing and society scholarship was simply a dimension of first economics and later marketing thought. At some point in the late 1960s or early 1970s, the domain achieved self-awareness. It matters not what sign-posts one wants to use (the initial publication of the *Journal of Consumer Affairs* in 1967; the July 1971 special issue of the *Journal of Marketing,* first edition of Aaker and Day's (1971) *Consumerism: Search for the Consumer Interest*). By the early 1980s the domain had evolved into a robust academic sub-field with its own journal, conferences, and associations. However, as the field developed on its own, increasing concerns were raised about the field's place within the broader marketing discipline.

In 1982 Thomas Kinnear founded the *Journal of Public Policy & Marketing.* The journal began with the goal of publishing papers which "focused on the application of marketing and marketing practices to public policy issues" and discouraged papers concerned with social marketing or nonprofits. Over time the scope of the journal has broadened to include public policy, social marketing, nonprofit marketing, ethics, etc. Currently, the *Journal of Public Policy & Marketing* is consistently ranked as one of marketing's best field journals; the more specialized journals are well regarded as well.

A key element of the domain's infrastructure is the annual Marketing and Public Policy Conference. The conference had its genesis at an invited symposium in honor of the 75th Anniversary of the FTC held at Notre Dame in 1989 (Murphy and Wilkie 1990) which led to a one-day conference preceding the 1990 AMA Summer Marketing Educators' Conference. The idea for an ongoing conference began over lunch at the Federal Trade Commission cafeteria in April 1991. A small number of academics had been invited to speak to the Commission by then Commissioner Andrew Strenio. The following year, 1992, the Marketing and Public Policy Conference became an annual event. The conference has evolved to a large (150+) gathering with a strong focus on bringing new scholars into the field. A recent addition to the conferences is a multi-day workshop where leading academic scholars (who volunteer their time and pay their own way) teach and work with Ph.D. students, who come from around the world.

An alternative way to view the field's development is to consider the extent to which marketing and society issues have become subsumed by the marketing field at large. For example, Paul Bloom's reading in this section (1997) noted that public policy scholars have made significant contributions to the development of information processing research, and consumer satisfaction research. Furthermore, much of the initial interest in understanding children as consumers stemmed from a policy concerns over advertising directed at children, e.g., Robertson and Rossiter (1974); information economics (e.g, signaling and the search/experience/credence typology) are theories developed to address public policy concerns regarding how consumers respond to marketing communications (see Ford, Smith, and Swasy 1990; Wiener 1985). A more general example would be that the recently growing corporate reputation literature has its roots in the work of scholars whose primary concern was the corporate social responsibility. At a very broad level, it could be argued that one of the initial intellectual drivers of post-positivist scholarship was an effort to understand the holistic relationship between a consumer and the marketplace economy. In other words, the post-positivist stream of work could be considered an intellectual heir to the earliest intellectual impulses in the field which became marketing and society.

FRAMING KNOWLEDGE DEVELOPMENT

A second, almost hidden, stream of marketing and society research is revealed if one considers the context in which research is conducted. Historically, the importance of context is discussed cogently in Alan Andreasen's (originally published in 1997) reading in this section, "From Ghetto Marketing to Social Marketing: Bringing Social Relevance to Mainstream Marketing." In recent years there has been a significant amount of work focusing on the impact of emotions, and affect on how individuals process information in general and risk information in particular. Generally, these studies use health contexts and explain their motivation in terms of health communications (Pechmann et al. 2003). In a similar vein, research framed in terms of group influence typically use and frame their findings in terms of situations where the product of social influence is a behavior that policy makers would like to curb. Our point is that there is a vast amount of marketing and society research that is framed in terms of pure consumer research.

The broader views suggest that significant intellectual progress has and is being made by scholars, who work within the marketing and society domain. At times, the degree of progress is obscured by how the work is framed. As noted above, some research with public policy relevance is presented as consumer behavior or managerial work. It is equally true that often marketing and society scholars frame their projects in narrow terms. For example, social marketing research is presented in terms of issues, such as smoking, drinking, conservation, drug use, children, product safety, etc. This presentation suggests a series of episodic studies responding to daily events. The progress towards enhancing knowledge is revealed when one sees these works in terms of contributing to extensive on-going theory driven research streams such as the effect of emotions on the processing of information, fear appeals, enlisting cooperative behavior, social influence theory, the processing and meaning of risk, and so on.

The point we are making with our illustrative (not exhaustive) discussion is that because marketing and society scholars often begin with "questions concerning the world about them," instead of an extant literature stream, new lines of inquiry (theory and method) are often broached. For example, social marketing practice serves as an inspiration for seemingly pure consumer behavior research, because it reveals boundary conditions and the failures which arise when the latest state of the art theory is applied. The evolution of fear appeal research was stimulated by the frequent observation that in some cases not only did such appeals fail, but they were counter-productive. Over time this has led to the development of increasingly sophisticated models incorporating individual and situational moderating variables that could explain when and why fear appeals would be effective.

Lessons

The most important lesson that can be drawn here is that the marketing and society domain is visibly vibrant and sometimes secretly integrated. The vibrancy as evidenced by the success of *JPP&M* and the Marketing and Public Policy Conference can be seen by anyone. What is less apparent, but perhaps more important, is the field's hidden strength. Because it pushes theoretical boundaries, and addresses emerging issues which create economic turmoil, research investigating marketing and society issues are often on the cutting edge but is not labeled marketing and society.

History of Consequences

One central element of marketing and society research is that it strives to influence how policy makers behave. The work is most often framed in terms of how the findings could and should have an impact on a decision maker—in a state or federal agency, non-governmental organization, legislative body, corporate board room, or even a court house. The intended influence path may range from revealing a problem or opportunity, to altering the conceptual framework used to understand the issue, to suggesting a specific set of tactical tools, and to evaluating the consequences of a particular policy or marketing effort. Regardless, the commonality is that scholars produce knowledge to be applied and not knowledge for the sake of knowledge. For good or ill, scholars often approach the problem of identifying concerns to study by asking what societal issues are in need of greater understanding, rather than what gaps exist within an extant stream of academic work. This is not to suggest that gap-filling and prior work extension research does not take place. However, the gaps and extensions addressed are studied because the filling or extending will lead to better policy decisions. In light of this orientation, one measure of the field is the degree to which it may influence practice.

Marketing and society scholars have had their greatest impact on two broad sets of decision makers. These are (1) social marketers, and (2) federal officials, who set and enforce regulations intended to protect consumers.

One of the most significant ways by which marketing and society scholars have impacted policy makers is through the creation and development of the social marketing domain. Since the development of this domain constitutes a section of this book, we will simply point out a few important highlights. Prior to the advent of social marketing, there were educational programs and fear appeals. As in the case of many policy approaches, the first reflected a super-rational view of human behavior and the second a lay person's intuition regarding how people might be influenced. Over time, social marketing research constructed frameworks and theories for understanding how people would respond to social marketing communications. Research in social marketing identified the barriers to and motivators for acting in a manner that would further a social marketing objective. As noted above, marketing scholars play a central role in terms of both translating findings from pure consumer behavior into the underpinnings of social marketing campaigns, and identifying key issues to be investigated by consumer behavior scholars. (For a summary of this research, see the social marketing section in this book).

The second area of marketing and society influence pertains to the role of the public policy maker. Over the past thirty years, three major changes have occurred in how federal and state agencies seek to protect consumers. The changes are inter-related and track the evolution of thought in the marketing and society domain.

The first change deals with how policy makers conceptualize the consequences of marketing communications, be they advertisements or warnings. The meaning of a message can be understood from either the sender or the receiver's perspective. To embrace the receiver's perspective, one must determine how s/he will process information. Bettman (1979) identified three critical differences between how most policy makers understand consumer information processing and the view held by marketing scholars. These being: (1) possessing the ability to process vast amounts of information vs. bounded rationality; (2) being similar in how they processed a common message vs. being quite different; and (3) always benefiting from more information vs. often suffering from information overload. The implication of these differences is that what is sent is often not what is received.

The trend towards viewing messages from an information processing perspective began with scholarly research and personal salesmanship. It is not that marketers with an interest in public policy issues discovered and applied the new research stream of information processing. Much of the early motivation for information processing research stemmed from scholars, who were concerned about why consumers made choices that were contrary to the choices a purely normative (economic) model would have predicted. From a strictly commercial marketing perspective, this distinction is interesting, but not vital, since whether or not a consumer makes a normatively correct decision has no bearing on the bottom line. From a marketing and society perspective, though, it is key, since the well being of consumers and efficient functioning of the market place are important goals. Hence, much of the early information processing research was motivated by public policy concerns such as nutritional labeling (see chapter ten of Bettman 1979 for a discussion).

Unfortunately, a multitude of academic studies that have important policy or managerial implications simply gather dust. A characteristic of the marketing and society domain is that leading scholars do more than publish "truth"—they market "truth." In addition to his long list of academic publications, William Wilkie actively worked within the Federal Trade Commission to change their understanding of academic research. His efforts led to several government reports which would help guide policy makers. Of particular importance was a report prepared for the National Science Foundation (Wilkie 1975) which set out three goals: (1) to provide public policy makers with an understanding of consumer information processing (CIP) research so that this knowledge would guide policy decisions; (2) to provide consumer researchers with an understanding of the problem settings and special needs faced by policy makers; and (3) to foster the development of a cohesive stream of CIP research.

Another influence of Wilkie and the early pioneers at the Commission is that they influenced a long line of marketing academics, who would spend a year or two at the FTC pushing it towards adopting a view of consumers in accord with the latest research.

These individuals numbered over thirty from the early 1970s to the year 2000 including four past editors of the *JPP&M*—Craig Andrews, Mike Mazis, Pat Murphy and Debbie Scammon—as well as Ken Bernhardt, Gary Ford, Greg Gundlach, Tom Maronick, and Josh Wiener (Murphy 1990).

The degree of acceptance by regulatory agencies of an information processing view of humans has been uneven. The greatest shift has taken place at the FTC, at least partially attributed to the influence of marketing scholars over the years. For example, the FTC statement on deception embodies the receiver's perspective and pays special note to vulnerable segments and the distinction between literal truth and received truth (Cohen 1995). Other agencies have been slower to adapt this perspective. For example, despite the great advances which have taken place in terms of our understanding of what makes warnings more, or less, effective (Stewart and Martin 1994), the FDA disclosure requirements when prescription drugs are advertised are proof that the sender perspective still rules in some domains.

A second, and related, shift has been the increasing acceptance of extrinsic empirical evidence. To understand this change, it is useful to consider an observation made thirty years ago by David Aaker (1974).

> What evidence is employed to support or refute the interpretation of an advertisement upon which a charge of deception is based? The answer is that, to a surprising extent, the hard evidence does not influence decisions. Either it is not introduced at all, or if introduced . . . it is simply not very persuasive.

The courts, at that time, would yield to the FTC's judgment unsupported by evidence because the commission possessed special expertise and responsibility. As Stephen Greyser (1997) observes in his reading in this section, extrinsic empirical evidence is now accepted. This rise in part reflects the personal efforts of the marketing scholars who worked at the FTC during the 1970s and 80s. However, it is also indicative of the overall development of consumer behavior in general, theory advancement, and measures of how consumers respond to marketing stimuli. At first, approaches focused on measuring the extent to which consumers believed false claims. Over time, these efforts became more refined so that the degree to which consumers were misled by a false claim could be understood relative to a benchmark, such as prior beliefs. Ongoing research today investigates the conditions which may influence the beliefs a consumer may draw from any of a host of stimuli that may be present in a communication. The critical point is that as study after study investigating and measuring consumer responses to marketing stimuli were published in the *JPP&M* and elsewhere, the approach assumed the mantle of science. Thirty years ago surveys and copy tests could be dismissed as techniques used by the advertising industry. Even in the educated mind they would be confounded with all the other tools of influence associated with the *Hidden Persuaders* (Packard 1957) or motivation research (Dichter 1964). Although every study can be disputed on internal and external validity grounds, extrinsic empirical work that follows accepted methodologies is today accepted as science.

The third change involves what policy makers think about consumer protection policies. Three intertwined principles have emerged: (1) a strong preference for information remedies; (2) a belief that market based solutions are best; and (3) the application of benefit-cost analysis to any potential policy action. As Mazis et al. (1981) point out, this approach emerged from the integration of work drawn from consumer behavior, economics, and law. Marketing scholars working both inside and outside the Federal Trade Commission played a critical role in this integration.

The centrality of marketing scholars in this shift should be recognized. At an abstract level, the three principles are dictated by rudimentary micro-economics. Although micro-economics provides the intellectual basis for the principles, it does not produce the policy rationale for application of the principles. It fails on two counts. The first is that the information and rationality assumptions underlying classical micro-economics simply lack face validity. No scholar or practitioner would argue that consumer markets are typified by perfect information. The situational deterministic basis for the assumption that people would act as if they are informed Benthamite calculating machines also falls apart when the a policy maker must address a situation because individuals often make choices that are seemingly inconsistent with those a rational or informed consumer should make. The second failure is that the intellectual argument that the market would be best if people were informed does little good if a framework is lacking for providing individuals with information. In other words, to convincingly advocate information remedies, one must be able to devise concrete information remedies (Wilkie 1994).

Although marketing scholars have made a strong contribution to the movement towards information/market based remedies; one broad line of research serves as a caution. Marketers naturally think in terms of consumer segments, not representative consumers. From its beginning, marketing and society scholars have had a special concern about vulnerable segments (Andreasen 1997). A major product of research investigating how consumers process information is the knowledge that there will be significant individual differences. The consequence is that marketing scholars force policy makers to, at the least, acknowledge the inherent tension between actions which may benefit the typical consumer but neither help, and possibly even harm, the most vulnerable.

LESSONS

The history of how marketing and society scholars are changing consumer protection policy reveals the power of marketing and society research. The research which influenced the Federal Trade Commission ran the gamut from "lab" information processing studies replete with internal validity to qualitative work, experiments and surveys which investigated processing and communication issues in far richer (and less pure) contexts, to the development of conceptual frameworks. The key point is that all forms of scholarship were critical—it was their cumulative weight which influenced policy makers. Currently, marketing scholars are assisting other federal agencies, such as FDA, to rework their consumer protection policies. It is not enough for marketing and society scholars to point to pure theory, context irrelevant (but internally valid studies), or sophisticated mathematical models nor to point to the results of qualitative studies or empirical work that is seemingly ad-hoc or theory free. To change policy is not easy—policy makers must believe that recommendations are both based on solid "pure science" and relevant to the settings where they will be applied.

Future Directions

Since this paper has focused on the historical context of the marketing and society field and we do not pretend to have any greater insights than our peers, we are reluctant to provide any definitive future directions. Nevertheless, we will offer a few.

First, as indicated by Mazis (1997) in his reading in this section, the journal and conference in the marketing and society area both carry the "public policy" moniker. Although those close to the field know that marketing and society is more inclusive than exclusive, we do worry that some in the general field view this area as being primarily legal or policy oriented. We do not advocate that the name of either should be changed, but that efforts should be made by leaders and serious scholars in marketing and society to allow for broad input. We know that the subfields of marketing and society such as marketing ethics (Murphy et al. 2005), macromarketing, and social marketing will continue to be studied by serious scholars. Therefore, these areas should continue to be welcomed as part of the community of scholars in marketing and society.

Second, a point made by Wilkie several times (1997, 2002; and Moore 2003) about the marginalization of this field by the broader marketing academic field should be of concern to all who work in this area. The aforementioned lack of doctoral education, the de-emphasis of marketing and society topics by the top journals and the disparate subfields that make up this general area all combine to undermine the future of marketing and society scholarship. For this specialty to continue to contribute both in scholarly and policy directions means that it must be perceived as a legitimate area of marketing like strategy, consumer behavior and modeling.

We are optimistic, however, that marketing and society will grow in breadth and stature in the coming decade. The domain of marketing responds to changes in American economy. Hence, the more fundamental the changes the greater the importance of marketing and society. The information technology revolution is changing the nature of inter-firm competition, how firms communicate with consumers, firm-consumer relationships, and the consumer search and choice process. In all these cases, the turmoil creates the types of potential regulatory and equity issues which make up the marketing and society core. Intertwined with the information revolution is the evolution towards consumer autonomy. Increasingly, individuals are taking (or being handed) control over health and well-being decisions that were formerly the province of expert gatekeepers. Since issues such as physical health, and retirement income, remain matters of public concern, this evolution will foster significant marketing and society research opportunities. The forces of information flow and consumer autonomy also serve to highlight the role and importance of market segments. The segments may be traditional vulnerable (e.g., poor) or defined by psychographics (e.g., gay). Regardless, their importance is too great to be ignored, and once again this is a classic marketing and society issue.

Of course, achieving stature requires more than simply addressing important issues. Academic stature requires work that is of highest quality, innovative, and capable of being generalized to other domains. We believe that public policy research possesses these qualities. To provide useful information to policy makers, scholars must explicitly address very difficult substantive and methodological issues. We see this constraint not as a barrier to doing research but as a motivator for conducting the highest quality research.

In conclusion, the field of marketing and society has evolved over the years. From the early days of the 20th century when the emphasis was on major economic and structural issues to the contemporary emphasis on theory testing and "issue specific" research, this sub-discipline had undergone significant changes. We highlight three interwoven threads that hold together the area and draw important lessons from each. As mentioned above, we are optimistic about the scope and impact of this field in the future. By conducting studies that will be of value to a policy maker, scholars are forced to address critical issues that are as vital to marketing as a whole as they are to marketing and society. Thus, we see marketing and society researchers making important contributions in the future.

References

Aaker, David and George Day eds. (1971), *Consumerism: Search for the Consumer Interest,* New York NY: The Free Press.

___ (1974), "Deceptive Advertising," in *Consumerism: Search for the Consumer Interest,* Aaker, David and George Day eds., 2nd edition, New York NY: The Free Press.

Andreasen, Alan R. (1997), "From Ghetto Marketing to Social Marketing: Bringing Social Relevance to Mainstream Marketing," *Journal of Public Policy & Marketing,* Vol. 16 (1) (Spring), 129–131.

Bloom, Paul N. (1997), "Field of Marketing and Public Policy: Introduction and Overview," *Journal of Public Policy & Marketing,* Vol. 16 (1), (Spring), 126–128.

Bettman, James R. (1979), *An Information Processing Theory of Consumer Choice,* Reading, MA: Addison Wesley.

Carson, Rachel (1962), *Silent Spring,* New York: Houghton Mifflin.

Cohen, Dorothy (1995), *Legal Issues in Marketing Decision Making,* Cincinnati, OH: South-Western College Publishing.

Dichter, Ernest (1964), *Handbook of Consumer Motivation,* New York: McGraw-Hill.

Ford, Gary, Darlene Smith, and John Swasy (1990), "Consumer Skepticism of Advertising Claims: Testing Hypotheses from Economics of Information," *Journal of Consumer Research,* Vol. 14 (December) 363–371.

Greyser, Stephen A. (1997) "Consumer Research and Public Policy Process—Then and Now," *Journal of Public Policy and Marketing,* Vol. 16 (1), (Spring), 137–138.

Galbraith, John Kenneth (1958), *The Affluent Society,* (New York: Houghton Mifflin).

Kinnear, Thomas C (1997), "An Historic Perspective on the Quantity and Quality of Marketing and Public Policy Research," *Journal of Public Policy & Marketing,* Vol. 16 (1) (Spring), 144–146.

Mazis, Michael B. (1997), "Marketing and Public Policy," *Journal of Public Policy & Marketing,* Vol. 16 (1) (Spring), 139–143.

Mazis, Michael B., Richard Staelin, Howard Beales and Steven Salop (1981), "A Framework for Evaluating Consumer Information Regulation," *Journal of Marketing,* 44 (Winter), 11–21.

Murphy, Patrick E. (1990), "Past FTC Participation by Marketing Academics," in *Marketing and Advertising Regulation: The Federal Trade Commission in the 1990s,* P. E. Murphy and W. L. Wilkie, eds., Notre Dame, IN: University of Notre Dame Press, 205–215.

___, Gene R. Laczniak, Norman E. Bowie and Thomas A. Klein (2005), *Ethical Marketing,* Upper Saddle River, NJ: Pearson Prentice Hall.

Packard, Vance (1957), *The Hidden Persuaders,* New York, NY: D. Mckay Co.

Pechmann, Connie, Guangzhi Zhao, Marvin Goldberg, and Ellen Reibling (2003), "What to Convey in Antismoking Advertisements for Adolescents: The Use of Protection Motivation Theory to Identify Effective Message Themes," *Journal of Marketing,* Vol 67, (April), 1–18.

Robertson, Thomas and John Rossiter (1974), "Children and Commercial Persuasion: An Attribution Theory Analysis," *Journal of Consumer Research,* Vol. 1 (June), 13–20.

Sprott, David, and Anthony Miyazaki (2002), "Two Decades of Contributions to Marketing and Public Policy: An Analysis of Research Published in *Journal of Public Policy and Marketing,*" *Journal of Public Policy and Marketing,* Vol. 21 (1) 105–125.

Stewart, David, and Ingrid Martin (1994), "Intended and Unintended Consequences of Warning Messages: A Review and Synthesis of Empirical Research," *Journal of Public Policy & Marketing,* Vol. 13 (1) 1–19.

Wiener, Joshua (1985), "Are Warranties Accurate Signals of Product Reliability," *Journal of Consumer Research,* Vol. 12 (September), 245–250.

Wilkie, William L. (1975) "How Consumers use Product Information: An Asssessment of Research in Relation to Public Policy Needs," National Science Foundation Research Application Directorate (RANN) Division of Advanced Productivity Research and Technology, Washington DC: U.S. Government Printing Office.

___ (1994), *Consumer Behavior,* 3rd edition, New York, NY: John Wiley, Chapter 21.

___ (1997), "Developing Research on Public Policy," *Journal of Public Policy & Marketing,* Vol. 16 (1) (Spring), 132–136.

___ (2002), "On Books and Scholarship: Reflections of a Marketing Academic," *Journal of Marketing,* Vol. 66 (July), 141–152.

___ and Elizabeth S. Moore (1997), "Consortium Survey on Marketing and Society Issues: Summary and Results," *Journal of Macromarketing,* 17(2), 89–95.

___ and ___ (1999) "Marketing's Contribution to Society," *Journal of Marketing,* Vol. 63, Special Issue, 198–218.

___ and ___ (2003), "Scholarly Research in Marketing: Exploring the '4 Eras' of Thought Development," *Journal of Public Policy & Marketing,* Vol. 22 (2), 116–146.

Zuckerman, Mary Ellen (1990) "The Federal Trade Commission in Historical Perspective: The First Fifty Years," in *Marketing and Advertising Regulation: The Federal Trade Commission in the 1990s,* P. E. Murphy and W. L. Wilkie, eds., Notre Dame, IN: University of Notre Dame Press, 169–202.

EXPLORING THE CONSUMER INTEREST

The Consumer Interest

Robert N. Mayer

Introduction

The interests of consumers or the *consumer interest* is an important area of marketing in society. Capturing the concerns of consumers in relation to marketing and society, the phrase *consumer interest* provides a helpful starting point for understanding and advancing the consumer interest.

Definition

Because the word "consumer" seems almost synonymous with "citizen" and "member of the general public," the phrase "the consumer interest" has a uniquely positive valence. This simple three-word phrase is, however, notoriously difficult to define (Mayer and Brobeck 1997). Is there a single consumer interest, or are there multiple and even competing consumer interests? Is the consumer interest something objective that can be determined by an impartial observer, or does each individual consumer define his or her consumer interest, even if it includes engaging in dangerous activities such as consuming cigarettes or illegal drugs?

Rather than resolve the conceptual difficulties entailed by "the consumer interest," consumer researchers have focused instead on factors that detract from it (consumer problems) and efforts to promote it (consumer policy). This chapter concentrates on the efforts of consumer researchers to understand consumer problems, while other chapters in this volume, especially those on consumer protection and international consumer policy, focus more on solutions to consumer problems. Both are essential parts of advancing the consumer interest.

The Domain of Consumer Interest

Research on consumer problems has a venerable history that stretches back more than a hundred years in the United States. The earliest research focused on issues of health and safety, but over time, problems pertaining to information, choice, redress, and privacy have

---

MAYER, ROBERT N., Consumer Interest

Robert N. Mayer is a Professor of Family and Consumer Studies at the University of Utah.

been added to the mix. Whether conducted by activists, academics, or government officials, research on consumer problems usually has two goals: to *expose* and *explain* these problems. These goals, in turn, lead to resolving or at least ameliorating consumer problems.

Exposing consumer problems is unavoidably a political act. Consumer activists conduct research on consumer problems to advance their causes. Academic and government researchers may regard themselves as more objective and dispassionate than activists, but their choice to study a particular consumer problem is, at a minimum, an implicit assertion of that problem's importance. For example, a study that quantifies the costs to consumers of identity theft or Internet fraud is essentially a plea for businesses and government policy makers to reduce this problem. Publication of research reinforces this implied importance by bringing a subject to the attention of a broader audience.

While exposing consumer problems is a crucial first step in the research process, it quickly gives way to *explaining* consumer problems, which also has its political dimensions. By exposing the roots or causes of a problem, research assigns responsibility and sometimes blame to certain actors and institutions. For example, the first studies of identity theft were content to bring public attention to a problem that was growing rapidly; later studies tried to explain whether identity theft was caused primarily by acquaintances of the victim or faceless criminals (Phan 2005; Synovate 2003). Similarly, rising personal bankruptcy rates throughout the 1990s led to research by Elizabeth Warren and several others who argued forcefully that most bankruptcies are precipitated by uncontrollable events like illness, job loss, and divorce rather than indolence and immorality (Himmelstein et al. 2005; Sullivan et al. 2000).

PERSPECTIVES AND HISTORICAL DEVELOPMENT

Research on consumer problems is as old as the consumer movement itself (Mayer 1989). During the last decade of the 19th century, consumer leagues were formed by activists to expose problems, specifically, the need for safer food and drugs (and better working conditions). Muckrakers like Upton Sinclair and scientists such as Dr. Harvey Washington Wiley and Ellen Swallow Richards also worked to uncover consumer problems.

Upton Sinclair's novel, *The Jungle,* exposed unsavory and unhealthy practices in the meatpacking industry and generated public support for government oversight of it. Dr. Wiley engaged in a primitive form of "consumer research." He convened a group of healthy young men from his employees at the U.S. Department of Agriculture to sample suspect food additives and waited to observe any ill-health effects on his "poison squad." His research led to new protections for consumers. Home economist Ellen Richards, the first woman to earn a doctorate from M.I.T., applied her knowledge of chemistry to expose contaminants in public water supplies. In addition to problems of health and safety, activists, scientists, and government officials at the turn of the 20th century exposed the anti-competitive practices of monopolies and "trusts" in industries such as oil, railroads, and tobacco. The explanation that underlay all these exposé activities was simple: big businesses, when left unchecked by the forces of competition, exploited the public as well as smaller businesses.

After a hiatus during World War I, efforts to uncover consumer problems resumed during the 1920s and 30s. The roles of activist and scientist often blended in efforts to galvanize the consumer public (for example, Kallet and Schlink's 1933 book, *100,000,000 Guinea Pigs*) or educate it about the relative merits of competing products (for example, publication of *Consumers' Research* and *Consumer Reports* magazines). As in earlier decades, consumer problems were given a relatively simple explanation: consumer ignorance in the face of increasingly complex products. Economist Stuart Chase and engineer Frederick Schlink (1927) described consumers in their book *Your Money's Worth* as "Alices in a Wonderland of conflicting claims, bright claims, fancy packages, soaring words, and almost impenetrable ignorance."

Despite important precursors, research on consumer problems did not become common and institutionalized until the 1960s. The exposé tradition begun by the muckrakers at the turn of the 20th century was continued by Vance Packard (*Hidden Persuaders* 1957), Rachel Carson (*Silent Spring* 1962), David Caplovitz (*The Poor Pay More* 1963), Ralph Nader (*Unsafe at any Speed* 1965), and U.S. Senator Warren Magnuson (*The Dark Side of the Marketplace* 1968). The Nader Reports of the early 1970s, written by "Nader's Raiders," had a more anti-corporate tone than previous research and called explicitly for government action to correct consumer and environmental problems.

At roughly the same time Nader and his associates were showing that consumer research could be ideological and action-oriented, other researchers were bringing legitimacy and theoretical depth to the study of consumer problems. The launching of the *Journal of Consumer Affairs* in 1967 by the American Council on Consumer Interests was a key event as it provided an academic venue for research on consumer problems. Developments in the "economics of information" also provided impetus for research on consumer problems (Ippolito 1988), as did the growth of many university-level programs in consumer economics and consumer studies (Bryant 1997). In addition, scholars in the field of marketing became more interested in consumer problems. Beginning in the early 1970s, the U.S. Federal Trade Commission actively enlisted the help of marketing scholars, inviting them to spend semesters or years at the Commission to provide guidance on cases and rule-making. These scholars helped the agency think about the nature and effects of deceptive advertising as well as craft remedies to consumer information problems.

One would imagine that, over time, research on the consumer interest would shift from exposing and explaining problems to shaping and evaluating policy interventions. Indeed, this has been the case. Nevertheless, research that exposes and explains consumer problems remains vibrant because "old" problems transmogrify (for example, food safety in an age of bioengineering) and "new" problems emerge (for example, threats to consumer privacy from new technologies such as radio frequency identification tags and genetic tests).

KEY TOPICS

Research to Expose Consumer Problems

The most basic form of contemporary research on the consumer interest consists of studies that bring consumer problems to light. These studies often are preliminary and lack solid quantitative data, disclosing, as they do, problems that some parties would like to keep hidden (for example, a defective product or a deceptive sales technique). Building on "classics" already mentioned by authors such as Upton Sinclair, Stuart Chase and Frederick Schlink, and David Caplovitz, more recent efforts to expose consumer problems are exemplified by the spate of "nation" books—*Fast Food Nation* (Schlosser 2001), *Credit Card Nation* (Manning 2000), and *Database Nation* (Garfinkel 2000).

Attention-grabbing, muckraking-style books have been complemented by more systematic data collection efforts by academics and government officials, sometimes with the financial help of enlightened businesss. One example is the annual survey of consumer complaints compiled jointly by the National Association of Consumer Agency Administrators (NACAA) and the Consumer Federation of America (CFA). NACAA, as the name suggests, is a professional association whose members are mostly consumer protection officials working in state and local agencies. These officials are often the first entities to which consumers bring their serious problems. Since 1992, NACAA and CFA have surveyed these agencies annually and compiled their complaint data. The 2005 report, covering the 2003–4 period, revealed that home improvements and repairs topped the complaint list. Auto sales and auto repairs held down the second and third spots, respectively, followed by credit (including credit repair services), and telecommunications/cable/satellite companies (NACAA/CFA 2005).

The National Fraud Information Center is a second source of data on consumer problems. The Center is a creation of the National Consumers League, which brought together a variety of for-profit, nonprofit, and governmental groups in 1989 to fund a telephone hotline to handle consumer complaints about possible fraud, especially involving telemarketing. The Center has evolved to cover other types of fraud, including Internet fraud. Based on the phone calls it receives, the Center compiles—and shares with law enforcement agencies—data on consumer problems and the amounts of money involved. Statistics are kept separately for telemarketing and Internet fraud. In 2005, for example, the largest number of complaints about telemarketing fraud concerned prizes and sweepstakes, with this combined category accounting for average financial losses of over $3000 (National Fraud Information Center 2006a). Online auctions accounted for 90% of complaints about Internet fraud in 2005, with an average financial loss of about $1155 (National Fraud Information Center 2006b).

The data on consumer problems compiled by NACAA/CFA and the National Fraud Information Center have a tip-of-the-iceberg quality inasmuch as they represent problems whose severity is sufficient to motivate a person to complain to an unfamiliar organization. Problems may also exist that cause "death by a thousand cuts" yet go largely unreported. The American Consumer Satisfaction Index is intended to be a measure of these everyday household experiences. Guided by Professor Claes Fornell of the University of Michigan, the Index has since 1994 generated brand-specific satisfaction measures for durable goods like personal computers, consumer electronics, household appliances, and automobiles and also services such as Internet Web sites, airlines, restaurants, gas stations, and even government agencies. The Index measures satisfaction itself as well as its presumed determinants (perceived quality, perceived value, and consumer expectations) and consequences (complaints and customer loyalty). An aggregate, 38-industry measure of consumer satisfaction is also created and used as a macroeconomic indicator (American Consumer Satisfaction Index 2004).

The Federal Trade Commission is an additional source of research on the prevalence of consumer problems. In the last few years, the FTC has sponsored major national consumer surveys on identity theft (Synovate 2003) and consumer fraud (Anderson 2004). The resulting press coverage has yielded eye-popping headlines like "ID Theft Costs Consumers $53 Billion" and "More Than One-In-10 Americans Fell Victim to Fraud." Research that exposes consumer problems is not confined to surveys of consumers. An alternative approach is to apply content analysis to the marketing communications of firms, such as weight-loss advertisements (Cleland et al. 2002), dietary supplement claims (Morris and Avorn 2003), and Internet spam (Federal Trade Commission 2003).

Research on the Causes of Consumer Problems

Beyond documenting the existence and frequency of consumer problems, research can explore the causes of these problems. Explanations, in turn, point the way to solutions to consumer problems. There are four especially important explanations in the literature on the consumer interest. The first two—asymmetric information and market power—refer to ways in which consumer sovereignty and efficiency are undermined by deviations from the competitive market in which consumers make well-informed choices based on their preferences. The second two explanations address problems of equity rather than efficiency—vulnerable consumers and barriers to mobilizing consumers.

Asymmetric Information Can Hurt Consumers

Whereas consumer problems were originally attributed to either business greed or consumer ignorance, explanations of consumer problems became more sophisticated beginning in the early 1960s. First, economists identified "information asymmetries" as a chief cause of consumer problems. Second, both liberal activists and conservative economists

drew attention to the role of government in creating and perpetuating business dominance over consumers.

George Stigler's classic 1961 article, "The Economics of Information," is generally
recognized as having kick-started work on the role of information in markets. Stigler
pointed out that, because information is costly for consumers to acquire, some degree
of price dispersion among sellers is inevitable, even in competitive markets. True, this
dispersion rewards consumers who acquire information to compare alternatives, but
only up to the point where the marginal benefits of search equal its marginal costs.
Whereas Stigler focused on reasons consumers might pay more for goods than would
be expected, George Akerlof's 1970 classic article, "The Market for 'Lemons': Quality
Uncertainty and the Market Mechanism," explained why markets might not deliver
products of high quality. If acquiring information about an item's quality is costly, sellers
have little incentive to provide a level of quality above the market average. Indeed, they
have an incentive to provide lower levels of quality to the extent that consumers have
difficulty judging quality. Philip Nelson (1970) and Darby and Karni (1973) strengthened Akerlof's conclusion by pointing out that quality information may be more than
costly; it may be impossible for a consumer to learn prior to purchase.

Several researchers lent empirical support to the theoretical insights of what became
known as "the economics of information" (Ippolito 1988). In summary, when consumers
are deficient in information about prices or product quality attributes, their ignorance
contributes to "market imperfections"; that is, the possible or even likely misallocation
of their resources.

Market Power Can Hurt Consumers

There is a second, and perhaps more ominous, source of market imperfections—market
power. Market power is the ability of firms to dictate rather than participate in the determination of prices and quality levels. The extreme case of market power is a monopoly,
but unregulated monopolies are rare. More common are oligopolies (industries dominated by a few large firms that do their best to discourage new competitors and avoid
price competition with their fellow oligopolists) or government-regulated monopolies
(such as local telephone companies and energy utilities).

Whereas oligopoly and its putatively negative consequences have typically been
blamed on oligopolists themselves, economists beginning in the 1960s and 1970s exposed the role of government in creating monopoly power. They took government regulatory agencies to task for creating unnecessary barriers to competition in industries
such as the airlines, trucking, energy, and banking. The most prominent of these scholars
was Alfred Kahn, but George Stigler (1971) and Richard Posner (1974) were early proponents of this position, and Murray Weidenbaum (1977) did much to publicize the
costs of regulation for the consumer and taxpayer. Some consumer activists, notably

Mark Green (1973), joined the chorus of critics. Whereas economists tended to be suspicious of all forms of regulation, consumer activists had to carefully distinguish the economic regulation they opposed (control of prices, profits, and number of competitors) from the social regulation (control of health, safety, and employment practices) they supported. Over the past several decades, marketing scholars have made substantial contributions toward understanding the impact of competition—and its abridgement—on competitors and, to a less extent, on consumers (Sprott and Miyazaki 2002). These contributions are viewed in the competition section of this volume. Research conducted by consumer advocates has tended to focus more narrowly on consumers. This research has illustrated the negative impacts on consumers when mergers and deregulation occur in the absence of adequate competitive pressures (Cooper 2002). Recently, there has been cross-fertilization between marketing scholars and consumer activists. This partnership is best exemplified by the collaboration between Albert Foer, head of the American Antitrust Institute, and Gregory Gundlach, one of the editors of this volume (Desrochers, Gundlach, and Foer 2003).

Most recently, consumer activists have criticized government-sanctioned monopolies over intellectual property through patents, trademarks, and copyrights. While recognizing the need to grant intellectual property rights as a means of encouraging innovations, consumer advocates have been lobbying for relatively permissive intellectual property rules governing, for instance, peer-to-peer file sharing and links to material found on Web sites. At the same time, more dispassionate consumer researchers have begun to document the impacts of strict vs. lenient intellectual property regimes (Committee on Economic Development 2004; Lessig 2001).

Vulnerable Consumers Can Be Harmed

While framing consumer problems as matters of market imperfections gave consumer advocates a degree of respectability within the halls of academia and in legislative chambers, many advocates and even some academics preferred to see consumer problems as matters of injustice rather than inefficiency. Two problems have received particular attention as matters that lay outside the framework of market imperfections: vulnerable consumers and the unequal political power of consumers relative to businesses.

Recall that sociologist David Caplovitz had already drawn attention to the problem of low-income, and racial minority consumers in his 1963 book, *The Poor Pay More*. The 1968 Kerner Commission, a federal body appointed to explore the roots of race riots that rocked urban centers during the mid-1960s, considered the perceived exploitation of black consumers by white merchants to be one cause of the rioting. Alan Andreasen added the perspective of a marketing scholar in his 1975 book, *The Disadvantaged Consumer,* and helped to legitimize this topic of research among business academics. Like Caplovitz, Andreasen recognized that the problems of vulnerable consumers are a function of a harsh and discriminatory environment coupled with their own lack of education and information.

During the 1990s, research on the unequal treatment of low-income and minority consumers had a renaissance among consumer-oriented academics, consumer activists, and their governmental allies. Researchers discovered the existence of "fringe banking" (Caskey 1994) and the "alternative financial sector" (Swagler, Burton, and Lewis 1995). Studies showed that low-income and minority consumers had been largely abandoned by mainstream financial institutions. As a result, these consumers were left in the hands of check cashers, payday lenders, pawn shops, rent-to-own stores, subprime mortgage lenders, all of whom charged high and, according to consumer advocates, outrageous fees and interest rates. Research by activists and academics has deepened understanding of the problems experienced by consumers in the alternative financial sector as well as the dilemmas faced by financial providers (Barr 2004; Ernst, Farris, and Young 2004; Hogarth et al. 2004; Squires 2004; Sawyer and Temkin 2004). Once the notion of consumer vulnerability based on income and race was established, it was a relatively small step to discuss additional groups of consumers who were ill-served by the marketplace. These groups included young children, the elderly, the physically challenged, women, and the recently bereaved. Again, a solid body of research has been produced by consumer activists, government agencies, and scholars in a variety of fields, including marketing (Alwitt 1996; Hill 2001). Whereas the problems of children as consumers received a great deal of attention during the 1970s, the "graying" of the consumer market has heightened awareness of the problems of elderly consumers. The AARP has probably been most active in sponsoring and disseminating research in this area (Gaberlavage 2004), and researchers from a variety of disciplines have made contributions (Lee and Geistfeld 1999).

Recently, the vulnerabilities of two additional groups of consumers have drawn the attention of researchers interested in documenting consumer problems: college students who can accumulate crushing levels of debt (Draut and Silva 2004; Hystad and Heavner 2004; King and Bannon 2002; Lyons 2004) and immigrants who often pay exorbitant fees to send remittances to family members overseas (De La Garza and Lowell 2002). And, as further evidence of continuing interest in vulnerable consumers, a special issue of the *Journal of Macromarketing* was devoted to this topic in 2005.

Consumers Are Politically Weaker Than Businesses

A second strand of equity-inspired research on consumer problems focuses less on the economic marketplace than on the political arena. Here, the central problem for consumers is, and has been, political mobilization. Although the U.S. consumer movement is the envy of the world in terms of its organizational breadth and its independence from government or business funding, a pressing research question is how it can lobby successfully against far more formidable business organizations. Little of the research on this question has been conducted by consumer activists; they don't have the time to wonder at their own existence. Academics, on the other hand, find it intriguing that consumer activists continue to overcome several structural impediments to sustaining a consumer movement.

The general problem of mobilizing extremely large groups to pursue their common interests was powerfully stated by Mancur Olson, Jr. in his 1965 book, *The Logic of Collective Action*. Although Olson did not focus on consumers *per se*, his analysis leads to the question: How can rational consumers be expected to voluntarily bear the financial, time, and other costs of a social movement whose benefits go to all consumers? When a consumer movement successfully lobbies for a new auto safety standard, a new food label, or more vigorous competition among telephone companies, all consumers benefit regardless of whether they helped in the lobbying effort. As a result, most consumers try to free ride on the backs of their peers; but if too many people are free riders, nothing is accomplished.

Political scientist Mark Nadel (1971) applied Olson's analysis explicitly to the problem of mobilizing consumers to act on behalf of themselves. Nadel identified three characteristics of the consumer interest that make its representation difficult. First, the consumer interest is diffuse, that is, it is widely shared. There is no subset of consumers that stands to benefit disproportionately from consumer protection measures and hence no subset willing to "carry the ball" for the remainder of consumers. Second, the consumer interest lacks intensity relative to interests associated with other social roles. People may care about prices and quality, but they *really* care about their jobs and racial identity. If consumer interests compete for time, energy, and funds with these more intense interests, the consumer interest will lose out. Finally, the consumer interest is plagued by the gap between objective and subjective needs. By this Nadel means that the issues that seem most important to consumer leaders, scientists, and other consumer professionals may not be the same as those that excite members of the general public. Hence, consumer professionals may have difficulty pursuing the consumer issues that they deem most important.

Resource mobilization theory (McCarthy and Zald 1977) in sociology provided an answer to the dilemmas posed by Olson for public interest movements such as the consumer movement. The core of its answer is that modern-day social movement leaders do not need to mobilize the masses. Rather, these leaders raise funds by selling publications, receiving foundation support and government grants, winning lawsuits, and exploiting other sources of support beyond soliciting dues and time from members. In the process, these leaders have been able to build a profession in which long-term careers within social movement organizations are possible.

Marketing scholars Paul Bloom and Stephen Greyser (1981) applied resource mobilization to the consumer movement. Bloom and Greyser were attracted to the obvious business allusions in resource mobilization theory: social movement leaders as *entrepreneurs,* organizations as *competitors* in a social movement *industry,* organizational goals as *products,* adherence to organizations as *demand,* and *advertising* and celebrity *endorsements* as means of appealing to potential constituents. In their *Harvard Business Review* article, Bloom and Greyser took these allusions literally and divided the U.S. consumer movement into competing *brands,* including "nationals" (reformist organizations that engage in a variety of lobbying and education activities), "corporates" (politically cautious organizations that advise and work with corporations), and "anti-industrialists" (radicals who are highly distrustful of businesses, government, and technology). In addition to the answer provided by resource mobilization theory, other social science scholars have explained consumer movement successes and failures in terms of alliances and interest group politics (Mayer 1988, 1989; Vogel 1989). Recently, researchers have asked whether a new problem exists in mobilizing consumers in an age of globalization and anti-corporate protests: the subjugation of consumer issues to those of the environmental and labor movements (Buttel and Gould 2004).

In sum, research on consumer problems highlights four basic causes: information asymmetries, market power, vulnerabilities of certain consumer subgroups, and barriers to mobilizing consumers. Whereas the research foundation for these four explanations was laid mainly during the 1970s, each explanation has been refined and applied to new consumer problems.

Delving Deeper into Consumer Interest: Selected Readings

A CLASSIC ARTICLE ON INFORMATION ASYMMETRY

Many consumer economists view asymmetric information as *the* root of consumer problems. The high cost to consumers of acquiring information allows markets to deviate from the situation in which you "get what you pay for." Among the researchers who have tried to document the extent to which prices and quality may be only weakly correlated in particular markets, Cornell University economist Scott Maynes has been the most devoted. Studying everything from cameras to condoms, Maynes identified the "perfect information frontier" at which price and quality are most closely related, and he demonstrated how far most markets are from this ideal. Not surprisingly, Maynes has been an indefatigable supporter of product testing magazines, like *Consumer Reports,* as a way to reduce information costs for consumers. In his 1977 article, "The Local Consumer Information System: An Institution-To-Be?" (reprinted in this volume), Maynes and his co-authors expose the low correlation between price and quality in local markets for most goods and then argue for a local version of *Consumer Reports* to rectify the problem. The idea of a local consumer information system did not take off at the time Maynes published his article, but some of his suggestions—notably the use of large-scale consumer surveys to rate retailers and other service providers—have been adopted at the national level by *Consumer Reports* magazine and at the local level by *Consumers' Checkbook* magazine.

Documenting an Intractable Consumer Problem

The FTC is, arguably, the most important federal agency in the area of consumer protection. In attempting to reduce physical and financial harm to consumers, the Commission not only relies on studies conducted by other entities; it also conducts studies itself. In recent years, the Commission has conducted research to understand the dimensions and causes of such problems as identity theft, Internet spam, fraud (on and offline), violent entertainment directed at children, abuses in the rent-to-own industry, and exaggerated claims for weight loss products. In the latter case, Commission researchers collected 300 advertisements disseminated through television, radio, magazines, newspapers, direct mail, email, and Internet. The Executive Summary of the report (reprinted in this volume) concludes that "the use of false or misleading claims in weight-loss advertising is rampant." The report summary gives some flavor of the way that testimonials, guarantees of results, and before/after pictorial comparisons entice consumers to buy products of questionable value. If you believe that you can "lose 44 pounds in 30 days . . . without diet or exercise," you probably should read the entire report. Studies like this one help the Commission fine tune its enforcement activities as well as stimulate trade associations, individual firms, the media, and consumers themselves to step up their efforts against deception.

Vulnerable Consumers

At various points in time, different subgroups of consumers have been deemed especially "vulnerable": low-income and minority consumers in the 1960s, women and young children in the 1970s, low-income urban consumers in the 1990s, and immigrants sending money home to their families in other countries in recent years. Across the decades, researchers have been drawn to the consumer problems of an additional consumer subgroup—elderly consumers. With the aging of the U.S. population in general and the Baby Boom generation in particular, interest in this topic is unlikely to wane. Telemarketing fraud is an especially vexing problem for elderly consumers, not only because the financial stakes are often high, but also because elderly consumers spend more time at home where they receive, and sometimes appreciate the interaction afforded by, telemarketing calls.

Jinkook Lee and Loren Geistfeld, in their article "Elderly Consumers' Receptiveness to Telemarketing Fraud," try to unravel—theoretically and empirically—the various social, cognitive, and biophysical factors that make older consumers more receptive to telemarketing fraud than younger people. Using a large data set commissioned by the advocacy organization AARP, Lee and Geistfeld studied receptiveness to fraud (for example, willingness to listen to telephone solicitors and frequency of sending money to unknown sellers), not victimization itself. Like many studies, the results provided only partial support for the researchers' hypotheses, indicating the depth of the challenge of understanding how and why oldsters (and others) end up losing billions of dollars annually to fraudsters (Anderson, 2004; United States Senate, 1983).

Policy in Progress: Illustrative Action Issue

Many of the readers of this volume are students who owe thousands of dollars in student loans and other forms of credit. You are not alone. In a 2002 report titled "The Burden of Borrowing," (King and Bannon 2002), researchers representing the State PIRGS' Higher Education Project found that the amount of borrowing by students rose dramatically during the 1990s to the point where by the end of the decade, a third of college seniors graduated with more than $20,000 in debt and more than a third of all students and more than half of Hispanic and African-American students graduate with "unmanageable" levels of debt.

Indebtedness hardly disappears after students graduate from college; it just shifts from student loans to credit card debt. According to a new study by Draut and Silva (2004), average credit card debt among indebted young adults (25–34 years old) increased by 55 percent between 1992 and 2001, to $4,088 (measured in 2001 dollars). Young people between the ages of 18 and 24 experienced an even sharper rise in credit card debt during the 1992–2001 period—104 percent—to an average of $2,985 (2001 dollars).

The report containing these findings makes a number of policy recommendations, including expanding grants for higher education and providing greater health care coverage. Some campuses have tried to reduce marketing of credit cards on campus. In early 2005, a bill was discussed in the New Jersey Legislature that would have made it illegal for a credit card to be issued to an individual under 21 years of age who is claimed as a dependent by a parent or legal guardian (Rozenfeld 2005). Proposals such as this one reveal a broader philosophical debate about consumer problems: to what extent should consumers be blamed for irresponsible and undisciplined behavior, and to what extent should sellers be blamed for aggressive, manipulative, and sometimes even deceptive practices?

Conclusion

In a sense, researchers who dedicate themselves to exposing and explaining consumer problems want to put themselves out of work. They intend that their research is the first step in a process that will lead other researchers to propose policy solutions and then evaluate the effectiveness of policy interventions. The world is too dynamic for that, though. As quickly as consumer problems are solved, or at least reduced in intensity, new ones arise due to a variety of technological, demographic, economic, and political factors.

Sometimes the cause of a new consumer problem is technological, as in consumer concerns over genetically engineered food and radio frequency identification tags. Other times the cause is demographic. For example, the increasing number of elderly drivers is sure to result in an increase in deaths and injuries for drivers and pedestrians alike. Research will be needed to disentangle the visual, physical, and cognitive contributors to accidents among elderly drivers. Research will be needed as well to evaluate the success of any programs developed on the basis of this knowledge.

As has been true in the past, new consumer problems arise in response to changing economic conditions. When conditions deteriorate during recessionary periods, consumers enter unfamiliar and relatively unregulated portions of the marketplace. Instead of new car dealerships, consumers shop at used car lots and private sellers. Instead of traditional banks and credit unions, consumers patronize check cashing outlets, payday lenders, pawn shops, and unqualified or unscrupulous financial counselors. Upturns in economic conditions can also create new consumer problems, as higher wages and more working hours allow consumers to afford new products while squeezing the time available for careful shopping.

Finally, the causes of new consumer problems can be political in nature. The current political climate emphasizes personal financial responsibility. At a practical level, this translates into new domains of consumer decision making, especially with respect to investments. For instance, pension coverage is shifting from defined benefit plans to defined contribution plans, in which consumers must decide how their retirement funds will be invested. Similarly, some workers are being encouraged to set up and manage Medical Savings Accounts to augment their health insurance coverage. As a final example, when the political climate favors privatization and deregulation of industries, consumers end up having new choices, whether they want them or not. In the past, deregulation of financial, transportation, and telecommunication services has meant new and sometimes complex choices for consumers. The future may bring further privatization and deregulation with respect to education, health care, and water delivery services. Even when privatization and deregulation are beneficial to consumers as a whole, consumer problems typically arise for subgroups of consumers, such as low-income people, the elderly, or rural residents.

Technological, demographic, economic, and political factors are currently combining to highlight two types of consumer problems: privacy and environmental sustainability. With respect to privacy, new technologies such as spyware, miniature cameras, and biometric devices are making some consumers nervous about their privacy. Problems related to spam, phishing, and identity theft are already all too real and well documented

(Synovate 2003). Unfortunately, efforts to protect consumer privacy are costly and may even be unpopular in a political environment poisoned by terrorism. Hence, researchers will need to not only expose and explain privacy-related problems; they will have to study how to balance privacy against other desired goals.

A second problem that will likely stimulate a new round of consumer research is the environmental degradation that results from consumption. This topic has had its ups and downs among marketing researchers and social scientists more generally. Surges in interest occurred after the energy crises of the 1970s and 1980s and again during the 1990s, when recycling and solid waste reduction became important issues (Mayer et al. 2001). Despite all the research that has been conducted on environmental issues, a fundamental problem remains: How can marketers close the gap between the interest in green products that consumers claim to have and their actual willingness to make buying decisions based on environmental criteria? As the world's population continues to grow and as economic progress raises standards of living around the world, competition for the Earth's natural resources will inevitably increase. Hence, a continuing challenge for marketing research is helping societies reconcile their consumption with their environmental impacts.

In short, new consumer problems are the partner of new consumer opportunities. As a result, the study of consumer problems and their causes will remain a growth industry for the foreseeable future.

Questions for Discussion

1. No one expects the world to be perfect, and we learn to live with many problems that, in theory, could be corrected. What are the societal mechanisms that transform a problem into an issue that the activists, researchers, and ultimately public policy makers can no longer ignore?

2. What consumer problems have you experienced personally? Perhaps you purchased a used car that turned out to need far more repairs than you anticipated, or perhaps you were treated rudely by a waiter, bank teller, or representative of a cell phone company. Whatever problem you choose to analyze, whom do you consider most responsible for it: you as a consumer, a retailer, a manufacturer, some other entity in the business community, or even a government body?

3. A narrow view of marketing scholarship holds that its role is to assist firms in successfully selling goods and services to consumers. Why then do so many marketing scholars examine consumer problems and their causes? Is it just that consumer problems create profit opportunities for the alert marketer? For inspiration in answering these questions, read William L. Wilkie's article, "Marketing's Contributions to Society" in the October 1999 issue of the *Journal of Marketing.*

4. The reading by E. Scott Maynes points to a consumer utopia in which consumers are well informed and can count on a very close connection between price and quality. Has the Internet, with its ability to disseminate customized information quickly and inexpensively, made Maynes' vision more practical, or will time and money pressures always keep consumers from being well informed enough to discipline the marketplace?

5. It is easy to poke fun at bogus advertisements for weight-loss products and treatments, but the reading based on the FTC's study raises a larger and tougher question: How does the government protect consumers from bad information without discouraging firms from providing consumers with good information? In the case of nutritional claims for food products, the FTC has argued for a more lenient approach while the Food and Drug Administration has chosen a stricter course. Do you prefer a marketplace with less information, including less accurate and helpful information, or one with more information, including more false and misleading information?

6. The reading by Lee and Geistfeld highlights the fact that consumer problems are often the result of deficiencies on the part of both the buyer and seller. For every fraud, there is a gullible consumer in addition to an unscrupulous perpetrator. Hence, any reduction in fraud will have to result from actions on both sides of the equation. Education is the best way to help consumers help themselves, yet consumer education is rarely required in schools. It becomes even more difficult to educate adults once they have finished their schooling. What, if anything, do you think should be done to increase the amount and improve the quality of consumer education for people of all ages?

References

Allwit, Linda F. and Thomas D. Donley. *The Low-Income Consumer.* Thousand Oaks, CA: Sage Publications, 1996.

American Consumer Satisfaction Index, "Latest Increase in ACSI Bodes Well for the Economy," Press Release, June 4, 2004. http://www.asq.org/media-room/news/2004/06/20040603acsi.html

Anderson, Keith B. 2004. *Consumer Fraud in the United States: An FTC Survey.* Washington, D.C.: FTC, Bureaus of Economics and Consumer Protection, August.

Barr, Michael S., "Banking the Poor: Policies to Bring Low-Income Americans into the Financial Mainstream," *Brookings Institution Research Brief,* September 2004.

Bloom, Paul N. and Stephen A. Greyser. "The Maturing of Consumerism," Harvard Business Review 59 (November/December, 1978), 130–9.

Bryant, W. Keith. "Consumer Economics/Studies," in *Encyclopedia of the Consumer Movement.* Stephen Brobeck (ed.) Santa Barbara, CA: ABC-CLIO, 1997, pp. 133–8.

Buttel, Frederick H. and Kenneth A. Gould. "Global Social Movement(s) at the Crossroads: Observations on the Trajectory of the Anti-Corporate Globalization Movement," *Journal of World-Systems Research,* 10, 1 (Winter 2004): 36–67.

Caskey, John P. *Fringe Banking.* New York: Russell Sage Foundation, 1994.

Chase, Stuart and F.J. Schlink. *Your Money's Worth.* New York: The MacMillan Company, 1927, p. 2.

Cleland, Richard L., Walter C. Gross, Laura D. Koss, Matthew Daynard, and Karen M. Muoio. 2002. *Weight-Loss Advertising: An Analysis of Current Trends.* Washington, D.C.: Federal Trade Commission, September.

Committee on Economic Development. *Promoting Innovation and Economic Growth: The Special Problem of Digital Intellectual Property.* Washington, D.C. (March 2004).

Cooper, Mark. 2002. *The Failure of "Intermodal" Competition in Cable Markets.* Washington, D.C.: Consumer Federation of America, April.

De la Garza, Rodolfo O. and Briant Lindsay Lowell, eds. *Sending Money Home: Hispanic Remittances and Community Development.* Lanham, MD: Rowman & Littlefied, 2002.

Desrochers, Debra M. Gregory T. Gundlach, and Albert A. Foer. "Analysis of Antitrust Challenges to Category Captain Arrangements," *Journal of Public Policy & Marketing,* 22, 2 (Fall 2003): 201–22.

Draut, Tamara and Javier Silva. *Generation Broke: The Growth of Debt Among Young Americans.* New York: Demos, 2004.

Ernst, Keith, John Farris, and Uriah Young. *Quantifying the Economic Loss of Predatory Payday Lending.* Durham, NC: Center for Responsible Lending, 2004.

Federal Trade Commission, Division of Marketing Practices. 2003. *False Claims in Spam.* Washington, D.C.: Federal Trade Commission, April 30.

Gaberlavage, George. *Beyond 50,04: A Report to the Nation on Consumers in the Marketplace.* Washington, DC: AARP, 2004.

Garfinkel, Simson. *Database Nation.* Sebastopol, CA: O'Reilly & Associates, 2000.

Green, Mark J. "Uncle Sam, the Monopoly Man," in *The Monopoly Makers: Ralph Nader's Study Group Report on Regulation and Competition,* Mark J. Green, ed. New York: Grossman Publishers, 1973.

Hill, Ronald Paul. *Surviving in a Material World.* Notre Dame, IN: Notre Dame University Press, 2001.

Himmelstein, David U., Elizabeth Warren, Deborah Thorne, and Steffie Woolhandler. 2005. "Illness and Injury as Contributors to Bankruptcy," *Health Affairs,* Web Exclusive, February 2.

Hogarth, Jeanne M., Chris E. Angulov, and Jinkook Lee. 2004. "Why Don't Households Have a Checking Account?" *Journal of Consumer Affairs* 38 (Summer): 1–34.

Hystad, Cheryl and Brad Heavner. *Credit Card Marketing on Maryland College Campuses.* Baltimore, MD: Maryland Consumer Rights Coalition. (February 2004).

Ippolito, Pauline M. "The Economics of Information in Consumer Markets: What Do We Know? What Do We Need to Know?" in *The Frontier of Research in the Consumer Interest.* E. Scott Maynes (ed.) Columbia, MO: American Council on Consumer Interests, 1988, pp. 235–64.

King, Tracey and Ellynne Bannon. *The Burden of Borrowing: The Rising Rates of Student Loan Debt.* Washington, D.C.: State PIRGs' Higher Education Project (March 2002).

Lee, Jinkook and Loren V. Geistfeld. "Elderly Consumers' Receptiveness to Telemarketing Fraud," *Journal of Public Policy & Marketing,* 18, 2 (Fall 1999): 208–218.

Lessig, Lawrence. *The Future of Ideas: The Fate of the Commons in a Connected World.* New York: Random House, 2001.

Lyons, Angela C. 2004. "A Profile of Financially At-Risk College Students," *Journal of Consumer Affairs,* 38 (Summer): 56–80.

Manning, Robert D. *Credit Card Nation.* New York: Basic Books, 2000.

Mayer, R.N. *The Consumer Movement: Guardians of the Marketplace.* Boston: Twayne/G.K.Hall & Company, 1989.

Mayer, R.N. "When Businesses Oppose Businesses in Support of Consumerist Goals," *Journal of Consumer Policy* 11 (December 1988): 375–94.

Mayer, Robert N. and Stephen Brobeck. "Consumer Interest," in *Encyclopedia of the Consumer Movement.* Stephen Brobeck (ed.) Santa Barbara, CA: ABC-CLIO, 1997, pp. 153–5.

Mayer, Robert N., Linda A. Lewis, and Debra L. Scammon. "The Effectiveness of Environmental Marketing Claims: The Roles of Consumers, Competitors, and Policy Makers," in *Handbook of Marketing and Society.* Paul N. Bloom and Gregory T. Gundlach, (eds.) Thousand Oaks, CA: Sage Publications, 2001, pp. 399–420.

Maynes, E. Scott, James N. Morgan, Weston Vivian, and Greg J. Duncan. "The Local Consumer Information System: An Institution-To-Be?" *Journal of Consumer Affairs,* 11, 1 (Summer 1977): 17–33.

McCarthy, John D. and Mayer N. Zald. "Resource Mobilization and Social Movements: A Partial Theory." *American Journal of Sociology* 82 (1977), 1212–39.

Morris, Charles A. and Jerry Avorn. 2003. "Internet Marketing of Herbal Products," *Journal of the American Medical Association,* Vo. 290, No. 11, September 17, pp. 1505–9.

Nadel, Mark V. *The Politics of Consumer Protection.* Indianapolis, IN: Bobbs-Merrill, 1971.

National Association of Consumer Agency Administrators/Consumer Federation of America. *Thirteen Annual NACAA/CFA Consumer Complaint Survey.* Washington, D.C., February 10, 2005.

National Fraud Information Center. *2005 Telemarketing Fraud Report.* Washington, DC: National Consumers League, 2006a. http://www.fraud.org/toolbox/2005_Telemarketing_Fraud_Report.pdf

National Fraud Information Center. *2005 Internet Fraud Statistics.* Washington, DC: National Consumers League, 2006b. http://www.fraud.org/2005_Internet_Fraud_Report.pdf

Phan, Don. 2005. *2005 Identity Theft Survey Report.* Pleasonton, CA: Javelin Strategy and Research.

Posner, Richard A. "Theories of Economic Regulation." *Bell Journal of Economics and Management Science* 5 (Autumn 1974): 355–58.

Rozenfeld, Monica. 2005. "State May Require Credit-Card Consent," *The Daily Targum,* February 16.

Sawyer, Noah and Kenneth Temkin. *Analysis of Alternative Financial Service Providers,* Washington, D.C.: Fannie Mae Foundation, 2004.

Schlosser, Eric. *Fast Food Nation.* New York: Houghton Mifflin, 2001.

Sprott, David E. and Anthony D. Miyazaki. "Two Decades of Contributions to Marketing and Public Policy: An Analysis of Research Published in Journal of Public Policy & Marketing," *Journal of Public Policy & Marketing,* 21, 1 (Spring 2002): 105–25.

Squires, Gregory D., ed. *Why the Poor Pay More: How to Stop Predatory Lending.* Westport, CN: Greenwood Publishing, 2004.

Stigler, George J. "The Theory of Economic Regulation. *Bell Journal of Economics and Management Science* 2 (Spring 1971), 3–21.

Sullivan, Teresa, Elizabeth Warren, and Jay Lawrence Westbrook. *The Fragile Middle Class.* New Haven, CT: Yale University Press, 2000.

Swagler, Roger, John Burton, and Joan Koonce Lewis. "The Operations, Appeals, and Costs of the Alternative Financial Sector: Implications for Financial Counselors." *Financial Counseling and Planning,* 6 (1995), 93–98.

Synovate. 2003. *Identity Theft Survey.* Washington, D.C.: Federal Trade Commission, September.

U.S. Senate, Special Committee on Aging. 1983. Consumer Frauds and Elderly Persons: A Growing Problem.

Vogel, David. *Fluctuating Fortunes: The Political Power of Business in America.* New York: Basic Books, 1989.

Weidenbaum, Murray L. *Business, Government, and the Public.* Englewood Cliffs, NJ: Prentice Hall, 1977.

Readings

1. "Classic" on information asymmetry:

    Maynes, E. Scott, James N. Morgan, Weston Vivian, and Greg J. Duncan. "The Local Consumer Information System: An Institution-To-Be?" *Journal of Consumer Affairs,* 11, 1 (Summer 1977): 17–33.

2. Exposing a consumer problem:

    Cleland, Richard L., Walter C. Gross, Laura D. Koss, Matthew Daynard, and Karen M. Muoio. 2002. *Weight-Loss Advertising: An Analysis of Current Trends.* Washington, D.C.: Federal Trade Commission, September. **EXECUTIVE SUMMARY ONLY (pp. vii–x).**

3. Vulnerable groups

    Lee, Jinkook and Loren V. Geistfeld. "Elderly Consumers' Receptiveness to Telemarketing Fraud," *Journal of Public Policy & Marketing* 18, 2 (Fall 1999): 208–218.

4. Hot Topic: A CFA Report

    "Generation Broke": Debt Among College Students (pp. 1–14 only)
    http://www.demos-usa.org/pubs/Generation_Broke.pdf

THE LOCAL CONSUMER INFORMATION SYSTEM: AN INSTITUTION-TO-BE?

E. Scott Maynes, James N. Morgan, Weston Vivian and Greg J. Duncan

This paper makes the case for the creation, testing and perfection of a new economic institution—a local consumer information system. The heart of the system would be a data bank to which the consumer could address questions and receive answers repeatedly regarding the local market. The purpose of the system would be to deliver relevant consumer information more efficiently. For the individual consumer this new institution would help identify his best buy variety of a product, quickly and at low cost. It would also tell him, again quickly and at low cost, from what local retailers and at what local prices this best buy variety might be purchased. This new institution would serve all consumers in a given community by lowering many prices, quality constant. By reproducing itself in different locales, as the product testing organizations have, it might be expected to multiply and serve consumers in many communities. The paper discusses the types of information to be provided, methods of information collection and dissemination, means of insuring accuracy and fairness and how it might be financed.

Together affluence, urbanization and the technical complexity of products have formed an unholy trinity that condemns consumers to increasingly ill-informed purchase decisions and to less informationally perfect consumer markets *unless* the delivery of consumer information is made more effective.

The supporting argument is straightforward. First, affluence has exacerbated the consumer's information problem by enlarging the average number of purchases that each family can make as well as expanding the set of products, brands, models and retailers from which choices are to be made. At the same time affluence has increased the value of the individual's time and hence reduced the extent of his shopping or search activities. Second, urbanization—itself the consequence of vastly improved agricultural productivity and the automobile—has also added to the set of products, brands, models and

E. Scott Maynes is Professor and Chairman, Department of Consumer Economics and Public Policy, College of Human Ecology, Cornell University; James N. Morgan is Professor of Economics and Program Director, Survey Research Center, University of Michigan; Weston Vivian is Director, Program in Engineering for Public Systems, Graduate School, University of Michigan; Greg J. Duncan is Study Director, Survey Research Center and Assistant Professor of Economics, University of Michigan.

The proposal presented here has been submitted to the National Science Foundation for possible funding.

The authors are indebted to W. Keith Bryant for helpful comments.

Maynes, E. Scott, James N. Morgan, Weston Vivian, and Greg J. Duncan, "The Local Consumer Information System: An Institution-To-Be?" *Journal of Consumer Affairs*, 11, 1 (Summer), 1977, pp. 17–33.

retailers to which a consumer has access. Third, the technical complexity and multi-component nature of products has made it difficult for consumers to assess both quality and price accurately. Finally, the consumer is still the prisoner of the same 168-hour week in which to undertake these more numerous and more difficult choices that his affluence, urbanization and technical progress now make possible.[1]

The local consumer information system proposed here is designed to reduce the consumer's information problem by delivering relevant local consumer information more efficiently. Specifically the system and the research proposal designed to create and test it have four objectives: (1) to provide individual payoffs to the system's users; (2) to improve the working of the particular local market in which it operates; (3) to reproduce itself and to thus improve the functioning of markets other than the one in which it was spawned; and (4) to document the informational perfection or imperfection of local markets over many types of products and areas of varying population densities.

The Background of This Idea

The notion of a local consumer information system is hardly new. In the form of a voluntary association of friends–acquaintances who pool local consumer information it has been tried in a number of places but never successfully. All faltered as the dominant enthusiasts finally ran out of energy and enthusiasm.

This proposal would substitute a professional, commercial, non-profit organization for these voluntary exchange arrangements. At present one local consumer organization exists—the Washington Center for the Study of Services [2]. In content it somewhat resembles the system proposed here, but it differs with respect to information dissemination, eschewing repeated contacts with its members and instead publishing essentially a local *Consumer Reports*. As of January 1976 the Washington center had 15,000 members.

We now turn to discussion of the proposed local consumer information system.

Types of Information Provided

The system would provide four types of information as follows:

1. *Local Price Information.* What is the range of prices in the local market? Where is the cheapest place locally to buy products characterized by relatively little quality variation, such as term life insurance?
2. *Local Accessibility to Products Quality-Rated by Consumers Union.* What does the local price–quality map look like? What models are least expensive, quality constant? What retailers sell these models? For a given model, what range of prices is available?

---

[1] These ideas are further developed in [3, 5, 6].

3. *Experience Rating of Vendor Services.* Where should I take my disabled television set (or car, high-fidelity system or other consumer durable) to have it repaired cheaply and effectively?

4. *Consumer Ratings of Retailers.* What have been consumers' reactions to particular local retailers—their advertising, salespersons, promptness, post-purchase service, refund practices and correction of grievances?

Local Price and Access: Some Instructive Examples

A more realistic view of what a local consumer information system might do for the consumer and of the problem of organizing and delivering information in such a system comes from four examples—life insurance, Kodachrome color film, single-lens reflex cameras and 10-speed bicyles.

Before discussing the examples, some background information is necessary. The local market for the examples is Ann Arbor, Michigan with a population of 150,000. In 1974 professional shoppers identified all retail establishments selling a given product and obtained price estimates from each, asking the retailer for the "lowest price he would quote knowing that the information would be widely distributed."

The first two products, term life insurance and Kodachrome 126 film, are roughly of uniform quality.[2]

NONPARTICIPATING 5-YEAR RENEWABLE TERM LIFE INSURANCE

The relevant facts on term life insurance, presumably stored in the system, are as follows:

1. Prices ranged from $1680 to $3100 for a 25-year-old male in good health.
2. Prices for these 62 policies formed a normal distribution.

Consider the needs and reactions of a typical consumer. If he is rational he will first ask about the price *range*. If he is typical he will be astonished to discover that the highest price is almost twice as high as the lowest price (for many audiences the median guess of the *highest* price was $2,000 when told that the *lowest* price was $1,680).

His next question is likely to be the identity of one or more of the lowest-priced companies. In response the system would supply the name and address of the local agent or the telephone number and mailing address of the nearest out-of-town agent or office.

Some consumers will come to the system with another question: How does the price charged by my company—the Faithful—compare?

---

[2]Essentially term life insurance embodies a single characteristic: protection. Die, and the payment of the policy's face value provides income replacement or protection for your beneficiary.

Kodachrome color film is probably unchanged from one retailer to another. However the characteristics of retailers such as convenience, decor, friendliness, etc. do vary and should reasonably affect the consumer's purchase decision. The text discusses how.

A skeptical consumer may ask the system, where does this information come from? To this query the system would answer: the prices come from *Consumer Reports,* January 1974, pp. 35–66 while information on the identity of the nearest agent or office comes from the insurance companies themselves.[3]

The price dispersion of life insurance prices coupled with the 3 1/2 percent of income that is devoted to the product mean large payoffs to the system's users.

KODACHROME 126 COLOR FILM

The relevant facts:

1. Prices range from $1.45 to $2.50 per roll.
2. The prices offered by the 35 retail outlets in Ann Arbor formed a normal distribution.

Consider again the needs and reactions of a typical consumer. Again his first question will be the *range* of prices. He will note that the maximum gain is $1.05 per roll. The second obvious question is, which retailers are low?

Would he use the information? The answer to this question depends upon the consumer's usual marginal net gain calculation. Should he buy 10 rolls at one time, the gross gain is greater *ceteris paribus.* However his marginal cost includes both time costs and any per-service fee. Immediate delivery of the information via telephone or cable TV coupled with a zero or small per-service fee would make usage more likely.

Should the system include price information or small-ticket products? The answer can only be given empirically, depending upon observed consumer demand and the cost of collecting and delivering the information.

SINGLE-LENS REFLEX CAMERAS

The product is single-lens reflex cameras and the data are depicted in Figure 1. Each letter represents a *variety* of camera, for example an Olympus OM-1, and each point represents a price quoted by one of eleven retail establishments. The numerical quality scores are those published in *Consumer Reports.*[4] Regarding their accuracy, *Consumer Reports* stated (p. 798), "Differences of less than about 10 points ... were judged not very significant."

It should be noted that these quality scores pertain to varieties of cameras and hence do not reflect characteristics of retailers such as convenience and courtesy. Furthermore they take account of only those characteristics of single-lens cameras for which satisfactory tests of performance could be devised. Thus they ignore such subjective properties as the maker's reputation. Finally they reflect the weights and the interpretation of

---

[3]Information on means of contacting the company was obtained either from the yellow pages or from parent companies. The list of companies—and these companies account for 70 percent of life insurance sold—and the price data come from *Consumer Reports,* January 1974, pp. 35–66.

[4]Consumers Union's quality scores correspond closely to the concept of quality proposed by Maynes. See [4] for a technical exposition and [6, Ch. 4] for a less technical exposition.

FIGURE 1

Prices and Quality in the Local Ann Arbor Market, Single-Lens Reflex Cameras

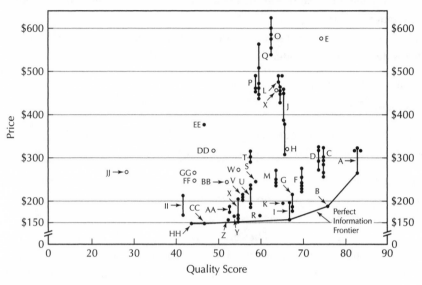

Source: Quality scores from *Consumer Reports,* November 1974. Prices collected by Blanche R. Maynes, November 18–26, 1974. The symbol ∘ denotes the list prices of specimens which could not be purchased in Ann Arbor. Other points represent actual prices.

performance tests of a committee, Consumers Union's engineers, whose assessment may differ from the users.

The perfect information frontier in Figure 1 is defined as the positively sloped line segments connecting those points, representing price and quality, for which a given quality may be purchased for the lowest price.

With these definitions and limitations in mind we are ready to consider the needs and reactions of different types of consumers. All will ask about (1) the *range* of prices above the perfect information frontier, and (2) the *range* of prices *for each variety.* The answers given by the system will reveal large payoffs for each answer.

Some consumers will accept Consumers Union's quality scores as sufficient, imperfect and incomplete though they may be.[5] These consumers will obviously want to know the identity of the on-frontier variety/retailer combinations. Recognizing that above-frontier retailers may possess advantages such as easy-return policies, convenient locations, and so forth, they may be willing to pay above-frontier prices to these retailers. So for particular varieties they will want to know the names and addresses of some above-frontier retailers.

[5] According to a 1970 survey 48 to 81 percent of the subscribers to *Consumer Reports* reported purchasing in various product classes models that were top-rated by *Consumer Reports* [1].

Other consumers, desiring more information or more skeptical, will ask for detailed discussions of the factors behind the quality scores. The system will provide them with the citation of the *Consumer Reports* article. Or, the system could store some of this information for immediate retrieval.

Finally those who made their choice of variety after consulting the basic article or from other sources may ask for prices charged by all retailers selling their preferred variety of camera.

Should the system present the perfect information frontier diagram itself? Or how could the information in Figure 1 be stored and delivered for efficient information processing by the consumer? These are questions that will have to be considered in the design of the system.

MEN'S 10-SPEED BICYCLES

The other end of the price-quality spectrum is illustrated by men's 10-speed racing bicycles [*Consumer Reports,* January 1974, pp. 18–28]. In this case there is a high, curvi-linear correlation between price and quality with very few above-frontier prices. Here the consumer advantage in knowing the relationship between price and quality is very great, and the payoff to information regarding particular varieties and retailers is much less since in this case price is roughly an indicator of quality.

Ratings of Vendor Services: An Example

Suppose a consumer asked the system: Where in Ann Arbor is the best place to have my car repaired? A first approximation answer might be based on Table 1 which presents overall satisfaction ratings by customers of 10 automobile repair firms. The system could also provide similar data on customer ratings of promptness, quality of work and reason-ableness of price.

These data were obtained from a pilot study using telephone interviews of 408 adults representing a probability sample of Ann Arbor telephone subscribers. The response rate was 86 percent. The character and quality of the results correspond closely with those obtained by a mail survey of home improvements customers conducted in St. Paul, Minnesota in 1970 and with ratings of automobile repair firms obtained by mail by the Washington Center for the Study of Services [1].

Are these results useful to a typical consumer? We first note that Table 1 discloses considerable differences in ratings between top-rated firm A and bottom-rated firm J. Similar large differences in ratings were obtained in the two studies just mentioned. It is clear that with larger samples many statistically significant differences would be obtained. Although no formal efforts were made to validate the ratings assigned by respondents, they did seem broadly consistent with the details of repair episodes that

TABLE 1

Ratings of Automobile Repair Firms, Ann Arbor, Michigan, April, 1974

Firm	Number of Consumers Expressing Satisfaction[1]					Mean Rating[2]
	Very Satisfied	**Somewhat Satisfied**	**Pro-Con**	**Somewhat Dissatisfied**	**Very Dissatisfied**	
A	5	4				4.6
B	4	2	1	1		4.1
C	2	4	1	1		3.9
D	5	4			2	3.9
E	3	8		3		3.8
F	4	7		2	4	3.6
G	8	7	1	3	4	3.4
H	4		1	1	2	3.4
I	2	5	1	1	1	3.6
J		5		1	4	2.6

[1]The questions asked were: "Considering everything, how satisfied were you? If "satisfied": Were you very satisfied, or just satisfied? If pro-con: Would you say on balance you were satisfied or not? If "dissatisfied": Were you very dissatisfied or somewhat dissatisfied?" The tabulations were confined, for illustrative purposes, to firms rated by 8 or more respondents. In an operating system much larger samples would be required.
[2]Mean ratings were obtained by assigning values to each response category as follows: Very satisfied (5), Somewhat Satisfied (4), Pro-Con (3), Somewhat Dissatisfied (2), Very Dissatisfied (1).

were reported in answers to various questions. Qualitatively, interviewers reported no particular problems with the questionnaire.

Some may question the decision to seek consumer ratings rather than more sophisticated assessments of the quality of local services. There are several reasons for utilizing consumer ratings. In the first place they are easily understood and economically collected. Second, there exists considerable evidence that for many products a sufficient sharing of standards exists so that the mean reported satisfaction ratings of a sample will prove useful to other consumers. As examples, consider the use of controlled taste tests performed on wines, meat pies, beer and other products by Consumers Union. Or consider further the widespread acceptance of critics' or consumer panels' ratings of movies, recordings, hotels and restaurants. Finally evidence from the Ann Arbor pilot study reveals that the respondents who supplied vendor ratings both found them meaningful and stood ready to purchase and use them.

Data Collection and Promotion

The sample sizes required for statistically reliable vendor ratings depend upon the relative frequency of usage of various service and repair facilities. The pilot study revealed the following repair frequencies: automobiles (2.4 episodes per household per year);

television (19.5% reported one or more contacts); washing machine (8.5% reported one or more); other appliances (22% reported one or more).

Digested, these results led to a decision to collect vendor ratings from quarterly surveys with samples of about 10,000 each. This sample size was expected to yield vendor ratings by 25 or more respondents for most of the 130 automobile repair firms and the 35 television service firms in Ann Arbor. Applying conventional standards, this minimal sample size would be sufficient to detect statistically significant differences among vendors.

At the same time it was thought that samples of 10,000 would enable the system to provide experience ratings of vendors for about 25 products per year. The rate at which vendor information becomes obsolete will be a subject of investigation early in the larger project. The results of such an investigation will in turn influence the frequency and size of the periodic surveys over the longer run.

The decision as to whether rating surveys would utilize mail or telephone interviews for data collection was left open. Clearly, both are feasible. The final choice will depend upon further investigations of relative costs.

For promotion purposes the need for large-scale data collection becomes a virtue. Almost automatically, the interview in which experience ratings of vendors are sought conveys the nature and character of the information bank to a potential user in a most persuasive way. Consequently most of those responding to the survey expressed a willingness to purchase the experience ratings to which they were contributing.

A virtue of local price and local access information is its low cost. A second pilot study probed the problems and costs of obtaining these data. The products involved were those cited earlier plus regular gasoline, portable sewing machines and straight life insurance. For each product three types of information were obtained: (1) a list of the varieties of each product on sale in Ann Arbor; (2) a list of all the local retailers selling each variety; and (3) the price charged by each retailer for each variety.

What became clear was that only one person-year was required to obtain local access information for all the products tested by Consumers Union in a year (about 75) as well as to obtain local price information for perhaps 25 more products of uniform quality.

Add 100 local access/local price products to 25 products for which vendor ratings have been obtained and you obtain a stock of information on 125 products. This raises the question as to the useful life of local access and ratings information.

The results of the pilot study support the belief that local access and local price information are relatively long-lived. For both cameras and 10-speed bicycles the level and shape of the perfect information frontier changed but little over a six-month period. Nor were there many changes in the identity of on-frontier varieties or on-frontier retailers. It is noteworthy that many of the models of bicycles for which test reports were published in January 1974 were still available in May 1975. Obviously the obsolescence rate for such information is product-specific. But these preliminary results were encouraging.

We have no evidence of the life of vendor ratings. A crucial consideration here is the effect of feedback from the system. Will a highly favorable rating in the system "spoil" Vendor A and at the same time invalidate his rating? The effect of feedback on ratings as well as on local access, local prices and the perfect information frontier is a subject for early research once the system is established.

A virtue of a large stock of products (125 products) is that the system becomes self-promoting. With only 10 products in the system for example consumers would have to be reminded rather frequently to use the system. As the numbers of products increases, the need to be reminded by advertising and other promotion declines.

Methods of Information Dissemination

The methods of data *collection* involved in a local consumer information system are relatively familiar. Not so the methods of information *dissemination*. In exploring this unknown territory, a first step is to state our objectives. They are:

1. To make the information available *where the consumer wants it*—at the point of purchase or perhaps in his home.
2. To give the consumer information as *speedily* as possible.
3. To *convey the information in a portable form* so that he can consider and reconsider it.
4. To give the consumer *as much information as he wants*—neither too much nor too little.
5. To *deliver* the information at *low cost*.
6. Possibly, to make the information mode *perishable*. Why make the mode perishable? There are two reasons: (1) to prevent its resale (thereby reducing the system's revenues) and (2) to avoid purchase errors arising from the use of obsolete information.

Table 2 lists the most likely means of dissemination and some of their properties. Though one would be rash to assert at this point what means a new system really would employ, it seems plausible that experimentation would start with some thoroughly conventional means such as mail or telephone and then proceed by stages to tests of the more exotic forms of information delivery.

Accuracy, Fairness and Legal Jeopardy

Consider for a moment the Ann Arbor retailer who sells Specimen O in Figure 1 for $635, a price almost four times as high as that charged by a competitor for a different camera which Consumers Union judges to be of about the same quality. Now contemplate his reaction to the local consumer information system which proposes to publicize this difference in prices. The point of this? The fear of reprisals by locally powerful retailers reinforces the natural inclinations to establish a local information system that is

TABLE 2

Means for Dissemination

Inquiry Received by	Report Delivered by	Time Delay	Shareability	Scan Field	Approximate Cost per 1000 Words
Telephone digital	Cable TV-Neighborhood public[1]	few seconds	many can watch	100 words	10¢
Telephone digital	CATV-Neighborhood semi-public	few seconds	only information service subscribers can watch	100 words	10¢
Telephone digital (also CATV digital)	CATV Private[1]	few seconds	only inquirer	100 words	10¢
Telephone digital	Telephone voice computer-actuated	few seconds	only inquirer	20 words	50¢
Telephone voice	Telephone voice conversation	few seconds	only inquirer	20 words	40¢
Telephone digital	Mail	one day	print copy	1,000 words to 10,000 words	20¢
Vending device[2]	Vending device[2] no copy	few seconds	only inquirer	100 words to 1,000 words	20¢
Vending device[1]	Vending device released copy[2]	few seconds	print copy	1,000 words to 10,000 words	20¢

[1]Requires device in each home.
[2]Shopping centers only.

both accurate and fair. To this end, we propose a number of procedural steps to insure fairness and to protect the system from legal jeopardy.

An overriding requirement would be that methods of data collection and dissemination conform to accepted scientific standards. For ratings of vendor services this would imply the use of probability sampling, the publication of ratings for a particular vendor only after the attainment of minimally acceptable sample sizes, the identification and explanation of statistically significant differences, the communication of the conditions under which the data were collected, sample checks to insure the authenticity of question answers, as well as the accuracy of data processing. The data on quality ratings would usually be those of Consumers Union. Hence they embody methods which have passed the test of criticism and public scrutiny over a considerable period. Data on prices would be checked on a sample basis to insure that they are authentic and they have been processed accurately.

A second major ingredient would be the establishment of suitable review and grievance procedures for retailers. One preventive procedure in the case of vendor ratings would be to show each vendor his rating *prior* to publication and to provide him with an opportunity to state his side of the case. Possibly comments by retailers might be inserted into the data bank. There would also be a community-developed procedure for resolving any disputes with respect to ratings between retailers and the system.

Retailers would be told beforehand that the prices they quote will be widely distributed. They will be asked further the extent to which the prices they quote pertain only to a limited stock of sale items. By the same token explanations of the conditions under which prices were obtained will be provided to users who will also be advised of the possibility of bargaining to obtain lower prices.

These precautionary steps represent just a sample of those that might be adopted. One of the objectives of this first testing of the consumer information system concept will be to develop a set of procedures that will make it easier for subsequent local systems to get started without making any false steps in this sensitive area.

The Question of Financing

A fundamental issue in the establishment of a local consumer information system is whether the system should be financed primarily from user fees or from a public subsidy. This issue is particularly intractable because its proper answer depends upon the ultimate effect of the system on local markets. One possibility is that the system makes local markets informationally perfect by pushing all prices down to the perfect information frontier. Such results would not rob the system of its reason for experience. The reasons are that first, the lever of open information may have to be applied repeatedly to keep prices in the vicinity of the frontier, and secondly, such results for a system with limited capacity would enable the system to turn its attention to other products. To the extent that the system drives prices of many products to the perfect information frontier persistently, all consumers will be the beneficiaries. Thus the system would be a public good and deserve a public subsidy.

Alternately it is possible that the system will enable its users to make advantageous purchases and improve their economic welfare by obtaining better quality at lower prices without however pushing most prices to the frontier. Should this be the case, then user fees of some sort would represent the most appropriate form of financing. Unfortunately, the effects of the system on local markets will not be known until considerable experience has been accumulated.

Should it be necessary to finance the system from user fees, some findings from the 1974 Ann Arbor pretest are encouraging. Ann Arbor consumers were asked whether they would be willing to pay to "get the latest up-to-date information ranking different repair businessess." The responses to the question were emphatically and encouragingly positive (Table 3).

At best answers to hypothetical questions such as this are suggestive. But it is probable that these responses are biased on the down side since most people tend to underestimate the extent to which prices are dispersed above the perfect information frontier. If so, they probably underestimate one of the major payoffs from such a system. One should note that these questions were asked with respect to information about vendor services and not about local prices or local access information.

A large volume of promotion or advertising will be necessary to recruit users to the system. But the problem of advertising is different for a local consumer information

---

TABLE 3

Consumers' Willingness to Finance the Information System

| | Percent of Consumers Expressing Willingness to Pay[1] | |
Hypothetical Service Fee	Unqualified yes	Unqualified no
25¢	81%	11
50¢	72	19
75¢	73	13

[1]Respondents consisted of a probability sample of adults residing in Ann Arbor, Michigan in April, 1974. The question asked was: "It would cost money to collect information from a large number of people to get the latest up-to-date information ranking different repair businesses. Do you think people would be willing to pay a charge of say 25¢ (50¢, 75¢) for this information?" In a previous question, 90 percent of respondents had answered yes to the question: "Do you think that people will be interested in the average ratings other people give about particular businesses in Ann Arbor?"

system than it is for an ordinary business. This is true because the operation of the local consumer information system will require the conduct of periodic surveys involving 10,000 or so respondents out of a total market size of approximately 150,000 people or 50,000 families. Hence the data collection itself is in part an exercise in informing the population about the existence of the system, the nature of the information it collects and the possibility of becoming a user of the system.

The size of the data bank maintained is likely to affect the volume of advertising required. With 110 products in the local accessibility file, 25 products in the vendor rating file, and with some additional products (of uniform quality) in the local price file it is possible that the system may be entirely self-sustaining from a promotional viewpoint, requiring no outside advertising.

Local Access Information and Consumers Union

For the system to include access information on *Consumer Reports* ratings, negotiations must be undertaken with Consumers Union. A number of issues must be resolved. One pertains to the question of how much the information published in *Consumer Reports* should be reproduced in the local consumer information system. An important question to be answered would be the effect, if any, of the system on the volume of local subscriptions to *Consumer Reports*. Should studies show that the system has a positive effect on the number of subscriptions, obviously it will be easier to negotiate continued cooperation from Consumers Union.

In the past Consumers Union has been cautious about permitting other organizations to distribute or use its data. This attitude is readily understood. Consumers Union's greatest asset is its reputation, and it is only natural that it should feel that the protection of its reputation is most easily achieved by having all uses of its data under its control. Necessarily, participation in a local consumer information system would require it to relinquish close control over the use of its data. So an important problem is to specify the steps the system would have to take in order to protect the reputation of Consumers Union.

Still another important question would pertain to what subsidy, if any, the system should pay to Consumers Union. Or, indeed, whether Consumers Union should pay a subsidy to the system. Obviously the direction of any subsidy depends upon the direction of any net benefits between the system and Consumers Union.

The Matter of Governance

We view the creation of a local consumer information system, at least in its initial stages, as the testing of an immensely attractive idea. For this reason we propose to vest the governance of the local consumer information system initially in a board consisting predominantly of research oriented academics. As the research stage is succeeded by a consolidation state—assuming the project to be successful—control would then be shifted to the members, and the system would be organized as an independent cooperative. It is worth noting that the establishment of a cooperative would conform to historical precedence. With but few exceptions, brand-specific price and quality information has been collected and distributed by cooperative or nonprofit organizations.[6]

The Need for a Minimum Scale and a Fair Test of the Concept

All of those involved in the development of the concept of the local consumer information system have been tremendously taken by the idea. All these people are concerned that, when it is finally tested, the test be a fair one. This clearly requires a large scale. Many facets of this proposal are subject to large economies of scale—the collection of all four types of information, the development and use of alternative methods of dissemination, promotion and the volume of information contained in the information library of the system. Statistical considerations also support the need for a large scale: statistically significant differences in ratings of vendors can be obtained only with large samples.

Thus a caveat is directed toward potential adopters: experiment with this idea only if relatively large financial and personnel resources are in sight.

Summary

This paper has sought to give an overview of a yet-to-be economic institution, the local consumer information system. In place and successful, this institution would improve the informational functioning of local consumer markets, enabling consumers to achieve better quality and lower prices in their purchases.

Selected References

1. Benson and Benson, "Survey of Present and Former Subscribers to Consumer Reports." Mount Vernon, New York, unpublished report, 1970.
2. *Checkbook,* Summer 1976, Vol. 1. No. 2, periodical published quarterly by the Washington Center for the Study of Services, 1910 K Street, NW, Suite 201.
3. Linder, Staffan B., *The Harried Leisure Class,* New York, Columbia University Press, 1970.

---

[6] Travel guides and ratings of municipal bonds come to mind as notable exceptions.

4. Maynes, E. Scott, "The Concept and Measurement of Product Quality," in Nestor E. Terlecki, editor, *Household Production and Consumption, Studies in Income and Wealth,* Volume Forty, New York, National Bureau of Economic Research, 1976, pp. 529–560.

5. ___, "Consumerism: Origin and Research Implications," in Eleanor B. Sheldon, editor. *Family Economic Behavior, Problem and Prospects,* Philadelphia, Lippincott, 1973.

6. ___, *Decision-Making for Consumers, An Introduction to Consumer Economics,* New York, Macmillan, 1976.

7. Wilkie, William L., *How Consumers Use Product Information, An Assessment of Research in Relation to Public Policy Needs,* stock number 038-000-00237-6, Washington, Government Printing Office, 1975.

Weight-Loss Advertising:
An Analysis of Current Trends

Richard L. Cleland
Walter C. Gross
Laura D. Koss
Matthew Daynard
Karen M. Muoio

(Principal Authors)

A Report of the Staff of the Federal Trade Commission

September 2002

Cleland, Richard L., Walter C. Gross, Laura D. Koss, Matthew Daynard, and Karen M. Muoio (2002), *Weight-Loss Advertising: An Analysis of Current Trends*. Washington, D.C.: Federal Trade Commission, September EXECUTIVE SUMMARY ONLY (pp. vii–x).

EXECUTIVE SUMMARY

This report attempts to take a comprehensive look at weight loss advertising. The need to do so is compelling. In the last decade, the number of FTC law enforcement cases involving weight loss products or services equaled those filed in the previous seven decades. Consumers spend billions of dollars a year on weight loss products and services, money wasted if spent on worthless remedies. This report highlights the scope of the problem facing consumers as they consider the thousands of purported remedies on the market, as well as the serious challenge facing law enforcement agencies attempting to prevent deceptive advertising.

According to the U.S. Surgeon General, overweight and obesity have reached epidemic proportions, afflicting 6 out of every 10 Americans. Overweight and obesity constitute the second leading cause of preventable death, after smoking, resulting in an estimated 300,000 deaths per year. The costs, direct and indirect, associated with overweight and obesity are estimated to exceed $100 billion a year.

At the same time, survey data suggest that millions of Americans are trying to lose weight. The marketplace has responded with a proliferating array of products and services, many promising miraculous, quick-fix remedies. Tens of millions of consumers have turned to over-the-counter remedies, spending billions of dollars on products and services that purport to promote weight loss. In the end, these quick-fixes do nothing to address the nation's or the individual's weight problem, and, if anything, may contribute to an already serious health crisis.

Once the province of supermarket tabloids and the back sections of certain magazines, over-the-top weight loss advertisements promising quick, easy weight loss are now pervasive in almost all media forms. At least that is the impression. But are the obviously deceptive advertisements really as widespread as they might appear watching late night television or leafing through magazines at the local newsstand? To answer this and other questions, we collected and analyzed a nonrandom sample of 300 advertisements, mostly disseminated during the first half of 2001, from broadcast and cable television, infomercials, radio, magazines, newspapers, supermarket tabloids, direct mail, commercial e-mail (spam), and Internet websites. In addition, to evaluate how weight-loss advertising has changed over the past decade, we collected ads disseminated in 1992 in eight national magazines to compare with ads appearing in 2001 in the same publications.

We conclude that false or misleading claims are common in weight-loss advertising, and, based on our comparison of 1992 magazine ads with magazines ads for 2001, the number of products and the amount of advertising, much of it deceptive, appears to have increased dramatically over the last decade.

Of particular concern in ads in 2001 are grossly exaggerated or clearly unsubstantiated performance claims. Although we did not evaluate the substantiation for specific products and advertising claims as part of this report, many of the claims we reviewed are so contrary to existing scientific evidence, or so clearly unsupported by the available evidence, that there is little doubt that they are false or deceptive. In addition to the obviously false claims, many other advertisements contain claims that appear likely to be misleading or unsubstantiated.

Falling into the too-good-to-be-true category are claims that: the user can lose a pound a day or more over extended periods of time; that substantial weight loss (without surgery) can be achieved without diet or exercise; and that users can lose weight regardless of how much they eat. Also falling into this category are claims that a diet pill can cause weight loss in selective parts of the body or block absorption of all fat in the diet. These types of claims are simply inconsistent with existing scientific knowledge.

This report catalogues the most common marketing techniques used in 300 weight loss advertisements. Nearly all of the ads reviewed used at least one and sometimes several of the following techniques, many of which should raise red flags about the veracity of the claims.

Consumer Testimonials; Before/After Photos. The headline proclaimed: "I lost 46 lbs in 30 days." Another blared, "How I lost 54 pounds without dieting or medication in less than 6 weeks!" The use of consumer testimonials is pervasive in weight-loss advertising. One hundred and ninety-five (65%) of the advertisements in the sample used consumer testimonials and 42% contained before-and-after pictures. These testimonials and photos rarely portrayed realistic weight loss. The average for the largest amount of weight loss reported in each of the 195 advertisements was 71 pounds. Fifty-seven ads reported weight loss exceeding 70 pounds, and 38 ads reported weight loss exceeding 100 pounds. The advertised weight loss ranges are, in all likelihood, simply not achievable for the products being promoted. Thirty-six ads used 71 different testimonials claiming weight loss of nearly a pound a day for time periods of 13 days or more.

Rapid Weight-Loss Claims. Rapid weight-loss claims were made in 57% of the advertisements in the sample. In some cases, the falsity of such claims is obvious, as in the ad that claimed that users could lose up to 8 to 10 pounds *per* week while using the advertised product.

No Diet or Exercise Required. Despite the well-accepted prescription of diet and exercise for successful weight management, 42% of all of the ads reviewed promote an array of quick-fix pills, patches, potions, and programs for effortless weight loss and 64% of those ads also promised fast results. The ads claim that results can be achieved without reducing caloric intake or increasing physical activity. Some even go so far as to tell consumers "you can eat as much as you want and still lose weight."

Long-Term/Permanent Weight-Loss Claims. "Take it off and keep it off" (long-term/permanent weight loss) claims were used in 41% of the ads in the sample. In fact, the publicly available scientific research contains very little that would substantiate long-term or permanent weight-loss claims for most of today's popular diet products. Accordingly, long-term or permanent weight-loss claims are inherently suspect.

Clinically Proven/Doctor Approved Claims. Clinically proven and doctor approved claims are also fairly common in weight-loss advertisements, the former occurring in 40% and the latter in 25% of the ads in the sample. Some of the specific claims are virtually meaningless. For example, a representation such as, "Clinical studies show people lost 300% more weight even without dieting," may cause consumers to conclude mistakenly that the clinically proven benefits are substantial, whereas, in fact, the difference between use of the product and dieting alone could be quite small (1.5 lbs. vs. .5 lbs.). These claims do little to inform consumers and most ads fail to provide consumers with sufficient information to allow them to verify the advertisers' representations. Moreover, the Federal Trade Commission, in past law enforcement actions, has evaluated the available scientific evidence for many of the *ingredients* expressly advertised as clinically proven, and challenged the weight-loss efficacy claims for these ingredients.

Natural/Safe Weight-Loss Claims. Safety claims are also prevalent in weight-loss advertising. Nearly half of all the ads in the sample (42%) contained specific claims that the advertised products or services are safe and 71% of those ads also claimed that the products were "all natural."

Safety claims can be difficult to evaluate, especially when so many ads fail to disclose the active ingredients in the product. On the other hand, some advertisements disclose ingredients, *e.g.*, ephedra alkaloids, that make unqualified safety claims misleading. Nevertheless, marketers in almost half (48%) of the ads that identified ephedra as a product ingredient made safety claims. Only 30% of the ads that identified ephedra as an ingredient included a specific health warning about its potential adverse effects.

Historical Comparison. To develop a perspective on how weight-loss advertising has changed over time, this report also compares advertisements appearing in a sample of magazines published in 2001 with ads in the same magazines in 1992. Compared to 1992, readers in 2001 saw more diet ads, more often, and for more products. Specifically,

- The frequency of weight-loss advertisements in these magazines more than doubled, and
- The number of separate and distinct advertisements tripled.

Moreover, the type of weight-loss products and services advertised dramatically shifted from "meal replacements" (57%), in 1992 to dietary supplements (66%), in 2001. Meal replacement products typically facilitate the reduction of caloric intake by replacing high-calorie foods with lower-calorie substitutes, whereas dietary supplements are commonly marketed (55%) with claims that reducing caloric intake or increasing physical activity is unnecessary.

The considerable changes in the methods used to promote weight-loss products are the most revealing indication of the downward spiral to deception in weight-loss advertising. The 2001 advertisements were much more likely than the 1992 ads to use dramatic consumer testimonials and before-and-after photos, promise permanent weight loss, guarantee weight-loss success, claim that weight loss can be achieved without diet or exercise, claim that results can be achieved quickly, claim that the product is all natural, and make express or implied claims that the product is safe. Finally, although both the 1992 and 2001 examples include unobjectionable representations, as well as almost certainly false claims, the 2001 advertisements appear much more likely to make specific performance promises that are misleading.

Conclusion. The use of false or misleading claims in weight-loss advertising is rampant. Nearly 40% of the ads in our sample made at least one representation that almost certainly is false and 55% of the ads made at least one representation that is very likely to be false or, at the very least, lacks adequate substantiation. The proliferation of such ads has proceeded in the face of, and in spite of, an unprecedented level of FTC enforcement activity, including the filing of more than 80 cases during the last decade. The need for critical evaluation seems readily apparent. Government agencies with oversight over weight-loss advertising must continually reassess the effectiveness of enforcement and consumer and business education strategies. Trade associations and self-regulatory groups must do a better job of educating their members about standards for truthful advertising and enforcing those standards. The media must be encouraged to adopt meaningful clearance standards that weed out facially deceptive or misleading weight-loss claims. The past efforts of the FTC and the others to encourage the adoption of media screening standards have been largely unsuccessful. Nevertheless, as this report demonstrates, the adoption and enforcement of standards would reduce the amount of blatantly deceptive advertising disseminated to consumers and efforts to encourage the adoption of such standards should continue. Finally, individual consumers must become more knowledgeable about the importance of achieving and maintaining healthy weight, more informed about how to shop for weight-loss products and services, and more skeptical of ads promising quick-fixes.

Elderly Consumers' Receptiveness to Telemarketing Fraud

Jinkook Lee and Loren V. Geistfeld

The authors use data from the 1996 and 1997 EXCEL Omnibus Survey commissioned by the American Association of Retired Persons to investigate the receptiveness of consumers 50 years of age or older to telemarketing fraud. The authors investigate elderly consumers' receptiveness to telemarketing fraud, as reflected by a consumer's psychological orientation (willingness to listen to sales pitch and attitude toward callers) and actual engagement in risky behavior (responding to unknown callers) using setwise regression. They conclude with policy implications.

Marketing and telecommunications advances give everyone, even con artists, the power to boost the sophistication and reach of a sales pitch (Pitofsky 1997; Starek 1996). Telemarketing fraud is one of the most pervasive deceptions identified by the Federal Trade Commission (FTC) (1998a, b; Thompson 1999). Although most telephone sales pitches are made on behalf of legitimate organizations, many sales calls are fraudulent. Consumers lose more than $40 billion a year to telemarketing fraud (Thompson 1999).

The Federal Bureau of Investigation estimates there are 14,000 fraudulent telemarketing firms operating in the United States, with 80% of these directing their activities at older people (American Association of Retired Persons [hereafter, AARP] 1996; Boosalis 1998; Harris 1995). When the FTC brought fraud charges against telemarketing companies that solicited charitable contributions in return for a prize, 85% of the victims were 65 years of age or older (Pitofsky 1997). Furthermore, 56% of the names on "mooch lists" (what fraudulent telemarketers call their lists of most likely victims) were 50 years of age or older (AARP 1999).

Although the seriousness of fraudulent telemarketing practices directed toward older consumers has been recognized widely, research efforts examining older consumers'

Jinkook Lee is an associate professor, Department of Consumer and Industry Services Management, University of Tennessee, Knoxville. Loren V. Geistfeld is a professor, Department of Consumer and Textile Sciences, the Ohio State University. The authors thank Richard Widdows and Monroe Friedman for their insightful comments on the previous version and two editors and four JPP&M reviewers for their constructive reviews and guidance. Gratitude also is extended to Jane Takeuchi, Bridget Small, Lee Norrgard, and the American Association of Retired Persons for generously providing the data sets, funding, and enthusiasm.

Lee, Jinkook and Loren V. Geistfeld, "Elderly Consumers' Receptiveness to Telemarketing Fraud," Journal of Public Policy & Marketing, 18, 2 (Fall) 1999, pp. 208–218.

receptiveness to telemarketing fraud are limited. Many explanations of consumer receptiveness have been offered (Brill 1992; Butler 1968; Friedman 1992; Gentry et al. 1995; Lord and Kim 1995; McGhee 1983; Peñaloza 1995); however, few of these have been subjected to empirical analysis (Lee and Soberon-Ferrer 1997). Building on Lee and Soberon-Ferrer's (1997) study of consumer vulnerability, we further investigate older consumers' receptiveness to telemarketing fraud. Whereas Lee and Soberon-Ferrer's study broadly examined consumer vulnerability in the marketplace, this study focuses on elderly consumers' vulnerability to telemarketing fraud. Also, in this study, consumer vulnerability is investigated in more depth because we examine multiple facets of the construct instead of treat it as a single measure.

Related Literature and Hypotheses

The uniqueness of fraud as opposed to other types of crime makes it particularly difficult to document and study (Friedman 1992; Lee and Soberon-Ferrer 1997; McGhee 1983). Consumer fraud victims must be persuaded rather than forced to give up their money. In these circumstances, it is possible that an individual consumer may be unaware of his or her victimization or too embarrassed to report the crime for fear of appearing foolish and gullible. Therefore, instead of relying on self-reported vulnerability, indirect methods are used to infer susceptibility to consumer fraud (Friedman 1992; Lee and Soberon-Ferrer 1997; Moschis 1992).

RECEPTIVENESS TO TELEMARKETING

Receptiveness to telemarketing reflects consumers' predisposition to respond to legitimate and fraudulent telemarketers. Consumers' willingness to listen to telemarketers is one manifestation of receptiveness. There are consumers who are interested in direct marketing offers and enjoy being solicited (Lee and McGowan 1998). These consumers are interested in a particular product or service offered by a telemarketer or use direct marketing offers as a matter of convenience, a means to gather information, or even a way to satisfy a need to socialize. Because of their willingness to listen to telemarketers, these consumers are more likely to respond to fraudulent telemarketing calls.

McGhee (1983) and Lord and Kim (1995) suggest that consumers' attitudes toward sellers are related to receptiveness to marketing activities. Consumers with positive attitudes toward telemarketers are more likely to be receptive because they are predisposed positively toward all telemarketers, even those engaged in fraudulent practices.

FACTORS ASSOCIATED WITH CONSUMER RECEPTIVENESS

Exposure to market fraud creates an opportunity for a consumer to be victimized (Butler 1968; Friedman 1992; Phillips and Sternthal 1977). In the case of telemarketing fraud, a consumer's exposure is determined by the number of telemarketing solicitations received (Golodner 1991). Greater exposure to telemarketing solicitations increases the likelihood that a consumer will be exposed to a fraudulent telemarketer. When a consumer is identified as an easy prey or placed on a mooch list, increasing numbers of fraudulent telemarketers try to call and exploit the consumer.

Several theoretical explanations can be used to identify consumers who are susceptible to telemarketing fraud. Social integration and activity theories suggest that consumers' openness to sellers may result from social isolation. Social isolation makes people feel less connected to friends and other support systems and makes them more likely to respond to sellers who pay attention to them (Butler 1968; Friedman 1992; Kang and Ridgway 1996; Phillips and Sternthal 1977). Nahemow (1980, p. 81) explains the relationship between social isolation and the ability to persuade, as follows:

> Individuals who, by virtue of their social isolation, are not in a position to argue their opinions for the benefits of others ultimately become unsure of their own point of view and are, therefore, highly vulnerable to persuasive communication.

Several scholars have acknowledged that marketers play an important, active role in providing social relationships (Blau 1973; Bradach and Eccles 1989; Granovetter 1985; Kang and Ridgway 1996). Most market transactions contain social interaction elements (Granovetter 1985), and more important, marketers usually try to be nice to their customers (Bradach and Eccles 1989; Granovetter 1985). Furthermore, as relationship marketing has become an increasingly common marketing strategy, the social content of market interactions has increased (Kang and Ridgway 1996). Social exchange theory suggests that, in responding to marketers' friendliness, consumers feel obligated to return the friendly overture (Blau 1973; Kang and Ridgway 1996). This provides the unscrupulous marketer an opportunity to harm consumers financially or emotionally.

There are specific components of social integration that are particularly important to the existence of competent consumer functioning (McGhee 1983). A consumer becomes familiar with unfair business practices, appropriate complaining behavior, and sources of information through relationships with other people and organizations (Lee and Soberon-Ferrer 1997; McGhee 1983; Warland, Herrman, and Willits 1975). Socially isolated consumers tend to be less aware of normative beliefs related to fair treatment in the marketplace, as well as of unfair business practices.

Whereas social integration theory identifies social isolation as a lifelong state, activity theory considers social isolation a result of lost roles, which have caused a significant disruption in a person's relationship to society. Retirement, loss of spouse, and children leaving home (empty nest) reduce the opportunities for social interaction (Butler 1968; Kuypers and Bengston 1973; Moon 1990). This suggests that consumers who are retired and/or living alone are more likely to be socially isolated.

As consumers get older, they are likely to experience loss of companionship, which suggests a positive relationship between age and social isolation (Moschis 1992). In addition, a decline in the ability to hear and other physical limitations are likely to affect the elderly's social interaction. The elderly may be able to compensate for loss of companionship by devoting more time to socializing in continuing or new relationships. If increased time allows for successful substitution of lost social interactions, a person's psychological well-being is maintained (Moschis 1992; Smith and Moschis 1985). Social integration researchers also have found that ethnic minorities and the poor tend to be less socially integrated (House, Landis, and Umberson 1988; House, Umberson, and Landis 1988).

Cognitive ability is also likely to influence consumer receptiveness to market fraud (Lee and Soberon-Ferrer 1997; Lord and Kim 1995; McGhee 1983). Consumers with limited cognitive ability may find it difficult to process information (Lee and Soberon-Ferrer 1997; Lord and Kim 1995; McGhee 1983). To avoid telemarketing fraud, consumers must have the ability to gather critical information by asking relevant questions, understand the given information, and evaluate the opportunities. Consumers with limited cognitive ability are more likely to fail in one or more of these information-processing tasks.

Moschis (1992) explains the relationship between cognitive ability and receptiveness to persuasion using the level of processing framework, which describes memory performance as a function of the depth and elaboration of cognitive processing. Elaboration refers to the richness or extensiveness of processing at any level and may include activities such as rehearsal of information and counterarguments. Deeper and more elaborate processing requires more effort and processing resources to achieve.

Previous researchers have found that education and age are correlated highly with cognitive ability. Education provides the reading and decision-making skills needed to cope with marketplace complexities (McGhee 1983), and higher educational level is found to be associated with greater awareness of fraudulent business practices (Butler 1968; McGhee 1983).

Aging is found to be associated with reduced cognitive ability, because those skills used to evaluate market offerings, such as memory retrieval and information-processing speed, deteriorate with age (John and Cole 1986; Moschis 1994). Biophysical studies find that aging is accompanied by a slower reaction time for the brain and nervous system; short-range memory loss; and diminished visual, hearing, and other sensory acuity (Smith and Moschis 1985). In particular, speed of response and perceptual integrative ability (such as the ability to understand new concepts and make deductive inferences in concept learning) show a much greater decline with age than do verbal ability and ability to store information. The elderly tend to overlook relevant information about the problem at hand (Moschis 1992). According to Salthouse (1991), aging affects the central nervous system by reducing the resources needed to perform encoding and retrieval of information, and processing resources decline with advancing age. These phenomena influence older consumers' ability to use deep processing, which involves the use of counterarguments. Smith, Moschis, and Moore (1987) find empirical evidence that deficiencies in information-processing ability influence the elderly's susceptibility to advertising puffery.

Finally, socially and economically underprivileged consumers are more vulnerable to consumer fraud than dominant consumers are (Marx [1887] 1970; McCarney 1990). It has been argued that social and economic relationships generate underprivileged groups of consumers (Marx [1887] 1970; McCarney 1990). Power is derived from a social exchange imbalance (Dowd 1975). A consumer's market power (the ability of a consumer to negotiate the best possible deal in the marketplace) is associated directly with his or her social power, but a consumer's compliance is related inversely to social power (Lee and Soberon-Ferrer 1997; Martin 1971). The asymmetry of social power creates inequitable exchange relationships that place underprivileged groups in an inferior position during negotiation, which makes them easily coerced by a dominant group (Brill 1992). Underprivileged consumers are more susceptible to consumer fraud than privileged consumers because of the asymmetry of power relationships between the groups.

Less privileged groups include women, nonwhites, and the poor, whereas dominant groups include men, whites, and the rich (Bristor, Lee, and Hunt 1995; Hirschman 1993; Peñaloza 1995). As both Marxists and feminists have asserted, patriarchy is a dominant ideology that frequently discriminates against women (Hirschman 1993). Furthermore, women are expected by society to behave less assertively than men are, which predisposes women to fraud and unfair business practices.

Non-Hispanic whites are the dominant group in the United States and have the greatest social power (Bristor, Lee, and Hunt 1995). Loro (1996) reports that Hispanics have a more positive attitude toward direct marketing than non-Hispanic whites do. This favorable attitude is attributed to unpleasant in-store shopping experiences.

Income is a resource that influences a consumer's social status, which thereby determines social power. The theory of perceived adequacy of resources suggests that a person who perceives resources as inadequate might be inclined to try to improve his or her financial situation by responding to telemarketers (Walters 1990). This would make that person more receptive to misleading and deceptive practices that are believed to be financially beneficial. In contrast, other researchers have suggested that favorable financial circumstances attract consumer swindlers (Friedman 1992; Harris 1995).

Hypotheses

The following hypotheses were developed on the basis of the discussion of consumer receptiveness and factors affecting receptiveness.

Consumers' exposure to fraudulent telemarketers is associated with receptiveness to telemarketing fraud.

H_1: Increased exposure to telemarketing solicitation increases receptiveness to telemarketing fraud.

Social integration and activity theories suggest that social isolation is related positively to consumer's receptiveness to telemarketing fraud. Working status, household size, and age are indicators of consumers' social isolation.

H_{2a}: Retired consumers are more receptive to telemarketing fraud than are those who are in the workforce.

H_{2b}: Single consumers are more receptive to telemarketing fraud than are those who live with someone.

H_{2c}: Age is related positively to consumer's receptiveness to telemarketing fraud.

Cognitive ability is related negatively to consumers' receptiveness to telemarketing fraud. Education reflects consumers' cognitive ability.

H_3: Less educated consumers are more receptive to telemarketing fraud than are more educated consumers.

Socioeconomic power and consumers' receptiveness to telemarketing fraud are associated negatively with each other. Race/ethnicity, income, and gender reflect a consumer's socioeconomic power.

H_{4a}: Racial and ethnic minorities are more receptive to telemarketing fraud than are non-Hispanic whites.

H_{4b}: Income is related negatively to consumer's receptiveness to telemarketing fraud.

H_{4c}: Female consumers are more receptive to telemarketing fraud than are male consumers.

Methods

DATA

We used data from the 1996 and 1997 EXCEL Omnibus Survey commissioned by the AARP to investigate elderly consumers' vulnerability to telemarketing fraud. The data set was based on responses to telephone interviews of a random sample of persons 50 years of age or older. The data were collected between February 14 and February 25, 1996 and 1997. The ICR Survey Research Group conducted the survey. Questions were asked regarding the number of calls subjects received from telemarketers, how they responded to the calls, how they handled telemarketing solicitations, and their awareness of organizations fighting telemarketing fraud. Demographic data also were collected.

The study sample consisted of respondents who had received a telemarketing solic-itation (n = 661 in 1996, and n = 675 in 1997). Distributions of demographic vari-ables appear in Table 1. No statistically significant difference between the two years was found for the demographic characteristics. More than 75% of the respondents had at least a high school education, and more than 40% reported an income in excess of $30,000 per year. Nearly 54% of the respondents were women. More than 30% of the respondents were 70 years of age or older, and nearly 70% were married or living with a partner. Approximately 90% were non-Hispanic white, and approximately 40% were employed at least part-time.

VARIABLES

Consumer receptiveness to telemarketing fraud was measured using three proxy vari-ables. The first two were noted in the literature review: consumers' willingness to listen to telemarketing solicitation and negative attitude toward callers (Lee and Soberon-Ferrer 1997; Lord and Kim 1995; McGhee 1983). These measures reflect a consumer's psychological orientation toward telemarketers. A third measure was used in the empirical analysis: frequency of sending money to unknown sellers. This measure re-flects actual behavior by consumers and was included because consumer victimization occurs only when consumers act on the offers of fraudulent sellers. In the case of tele-marketing, consumers are victimized when they actually give a credit card number or send a check in response to the offers of fraudulent telemarketers.

Willingness to listen to telemarketing solicitations is measured on a four-level ordinal scale, ranging from "very likely to listen" (4) to "not at all likely to listen" (1). The following question was asked to determine the respondents' willingness to lis-ten: "In general, if someone calls you over the phone and tries to sell you something or get you to enter a sweepstakes, make an investment, or asks for a donation, how likely are you to listen?"

Negative attitude toward telephone callers is based on the response to the following question: "Thinking about the callers who contact you to sell you something or tell you you've won a prize, which of the following comes closest to describing your impression of who these callers are?" The forced choice responses were as follows:

1. They are probably just people doing their jobs for a legitimate business;
2. They are probably honest people who are unaware that they are working for a shady business;
3. They are probably con artists trying to take advantage of you; and
4. They are probably hardened criminals running an organized illegal operation.

Frequency of sending money to unknown sellers is the number of times during the pre-ceding year a consumer responded to telephone offers from unfamiliar organizations by

TABLE 1

Demographic Characteristics

Demographic Characteristics		1996 Sample (n = 661)	1997 Sample (n = 675)
Education	Less than high school	22.3%	24.1%
	High school or technical/trade	32.6%	33.0%
	Some college	17.7%	18.1%
	Bachelor's degree	17.3%	16.0%
	Graduate degree	9.4%	8.1%
	Refused to answer	.7%	.9%
		100 %	100 %
Income	Less than $10,000	9.8%	8.2%
	$10,000–$14,999	10.2%	6.9%
	$15,000–$29,999	18.5%	22.1%
	$30,000–$49,999	17.0%	18.6%
	$50,000–$74,999	13.2%	10.4%
	More than $75,000	11.2%	7.7%
	Refused to answer	20.1%	26.1%
		100 %	100 %
Gender	Male	46.4%	46.5%
	Female	53.6%	53.5%
		100 %	100 %
Age	50–59	35.8%	36.8%
	60–69	33.4%	29.5%
	70–79	24.5%	25.5%
	80 or older	6.2%	8.3%
		100 %	100 %
Marital status	Married/living with partner	69.3%	69.7%
	Separated/divorced	10.0%	9.7%
	Widowed	18.4%	19.1%
	Never been married	1.5%	.9%
	Refused to answer	.6%	.7%
		100 %	100 %
Household size	1	19.7%	18.9%
	2	55.3%	50.4%
	3	12.7%	17.7%
	4 or more	12.3%	13.0%
		100 %	100 %
Race	White	87.3%	88.2%
	Black	6.2%	5.7%
	Hispanic	4.5%	2.3%
	Other	2.0%	3.8%
		100 %	100 %
Employment status	Full-time employed	31.0%	27.7%
	Part-time employed	9.0%	9.5%
	Retired	50.4%	51.0%
	Unemployed	9.6%	11.8%
		100 %	100 %

Notes: The sample is not representative of the entire population because no one younger than 50 years of age was included in the survey; however, it is representative of the population 50 years of age and older.

sending money or giving a credit card number to purchase something, enter a contest, make an investment, or donate to a charity. This is a continuous variable ranging from 0 to 30.

As noted in the literature review section, the number of telephone solicitations received was an independent variable. This variable is the number of calls received in a typical week from an unknown organization asking the respondent to buy something, enter a sweepstakes or contest, make an investment, or make a donation to a charity. It is a continuous variable ranging from 0 to 25.

The other independent variables were working status, household size, age, race/ethnicity, income, education, and gender. These variables were measured as follows:

- Working status was three binary variables (yes = 1, no = 0): retired, unemployed, and employed (base category);
- Household size was a binary variable (single person household = 1, living with someone else = 0);
- Age was a continuous variable;
- Race/ethnicity was a binary variable (non-Hispanic white = 0, nonwhite or Hispanic = 1);
- Income was a continuous variable, ranging from 1 to 9: (1) less than $10,000, (2) $10,000 to less than $15,000, (3) $15,000 to less than $20,000, (4) $20,000 to less than $25,000, (5) $25,000 to less than $30,000, (6) $30,000 to less than $40,000, (7) $40,000 to less than $50,000, (8) $50,000 to less than $75,000, and (9) $75,000 or more;
- Level of education consisted of four binary variables (yes = 1, no = 0): less than high school education, high school graduate (base category), some college education, and bachelor's degree or more; and
- Gender was a binary variable (male = 0, female = 1).

ANALYSIS

We examined descriptive statistics for variables that reflected consumer receptiveness to telemarketing fraud: consumers' willingness to listen to unknown callers, negative attitudes toward callers, and frequency of responding to unfamiliar telemarketers' offers by sending money or giving a credit card number. We then used multivariate analyses to assess the association between the independent and dependent variables. We performed a separate setwise regression analysis for each proxy measure of consumer vulnerability.

Setwise regression analysis is a modification of multiple regression analysis. Whereas multiple regression uses single variables as independent variables, setwise regression uses sets of single variables as independent variables (Cohen and Cohen 1983). In this study, we use the following independent variables: exposure to telemarketing, a set of variables associated with social isolation (working status, household size, and age), cognitive ability as reflected in education, and a set of variables associated with socioeconomic power (race/ethnicity, income, and gender). We also use simultaneous procedures, which assess variance for a given set with the remaining sets partialled. We report F-statistics as a test of statistical significance for the variance due to a partialled set, as well as the parameter estimates for each independent variable of the full model.

Finally, we conduct a multivariate analysis of the number of phone calls received using the same independent variables. This analysis enables us to identify the variables associated with a consumer's exposure to telemarketing.[1]

Findings

DESCRIPTIVE STATISTICS

Four percent of the respondents indicated they were very likely to listen to a solicitation, and 68% said that they were not at all likely to listen (Table 2). Approximately 30% of the respondents had a positive attitude toward telemarketing solicitors, whereas 38% perceived solicitors as con artists or criminals. Fourteen percent of the respondents who received a telephone call from an unfamiliar organization sent money or gave a credit card number to purchase something, enter a contest, make an investment, or donate to a charity at least once within the preceding year.

SETWISE REGRESSION ANALYSES

The results of the setwise regression analyses appear in Tables 3 and 4. The squared multiple partial correlation, partial R^2, indicates the unique variance explained by a set of variables as a proportion of the variance not estimable by other sets of variables (Cohen and Cohen 1983). The general F-test statistics are reported to examine the significance of an increment. Both partial R^2 and F-statistics appear in Table 3.

The set of variables reflecting socioeconomic power—race/ethnicity, income, and gender—was found to influence negative attitude toward callers at .01 significance level. This set of variables uniquely explains approximately 3% of the variance. F-tests indicate that the other sets of variables were not associated significantly with negative attitude toward callers.

Willingness to listen was influenced significantly by a set of variables related to social isolation—working status, household size, and age. Other variable sets did not affect willingness to listen significantly. The partial R^2 of the social isolation variable set was .02.

The socioeconomic power variable set was associated significantly with number of times money was sent to unfamiliar telemarketers. The partial R^2 of the socioeconomic power variable set was .02. Other sets of variables were found to be insignificant.

---

[1]In addition, we examined a possibility of yearly difference between 1996 and 1997 by including a year dummy variable in full model. The results of the analyses of the full model including a year dummy variable yielded that there was no yearly difference.

TABLE 2

Descriptive Statistics of Consumer Receptiveness to Telemarketing

Variables	Responses	1996	1997
Number of calls received	Less than once a week	16.7%	20.6%
	1	22.9%	18.5%
	2	15.4%	15.3%
	3	15.2%	11.8%
	4–5	11.7%	11.6%
	6–10	7.3%	9.4%
	11–25	3.6%	3.5%
	Don't know/Refused to answer	7.3%	9.5%
		100 %	100 %
Willingness to listen	1. Not at all likely	67.4%	65.8%
	2. Not very likely	18.6%	21.5%
	3. Somewhat likely	8.2%	9.1%
	4. Very likely	3.6%	3.2%
	Don't know/Refused to answer	2.2%	.4%
		100 %	100 %
Attitude toward callers	1. People doing their jobs for a legitimate business.	30.3%	32.5%
	2. Honest people who are unaware that they are working for a shady business.	22.3%	17.1%
	3. Con artists trying to take advantage of you.	34.5%	31.5%
	4. Hardened criminals running an organized illegal operation.	1.6%	3.8%
	Don't know/Refused to answer	11.3%	15.1%
		100 %	100 %
Number of times responded to unknown telemarketers	0	83.5%	87.3%
	1	4.3%	3.6%
	2–3	4.2%	4.2%
	4–9	3.7%	3.0%
	10–30	1.5%	.9%
	Don't know/Refused to answer	2.8%	1.1%
		100 %	100 %

Whether demographic characteristics were associated with number of calls received was also investigated with setwise regression analysis. F-tests indicate that the sets of independent variables were not associated significantly with this variable.

HYPOTHESES TESTING

Results of the setwise regression analyses indicate that elderly consumers' receptiveness to telemarketing fraud, as reflected by negative attitude toward caller and number of times money was sent in response to calls, is influenced by the socioeconomic power variable set. Receptiveness, as reflected by consumers' willingness to listen, is affected by

TABLE 3

Results of Setwise Regression Analyses: Partial R^2 and F-statistics

Set of Variables	Attitude Toward Caller		Willingness to Listen		Number of Times Money Sent		Number of Calls Received	
	Partial R^2	F-statistic	Partial R^2	F-statistic	Partial R^2	F-statistic	Partial R^2	F-statistic
Number of calls received	.0003	.05	.0028	.43	.0006	.08	NA	NA

Social isolation
  Working status
  Household size
  Age
	.1095	1.85	.0208	3.24*	.0019	.37	.0076	1.58

Education	.0005	.08	.0067	1.03	.0021	.35	.0052	.92

Socioeconomic power
  Race/ethnicity
  Income
  Gender
	.0297	4.47*	.0041	.63	.0160	2.69*	.0037	.65

*$p < .01$.

the social isolation variable set. To test specific hypotheses developed previously, we examine the parameter estimates of the full regression model (Table 4).

Based on the findings reported in Tables 3 and 4, consumers' receptiveness to telemarketing fraud is not affected by exposure to telemarketing solicitation. This suggests that the number of telephone solicitations received does not influence willingness to listen, negative attitude toward callers, or response to the offers by sending money. Therefore, H_1 is not supported.

With regard to working status, retirement has no significant effect on consumer receptiveness to telemarketing fraud. Retired consumers were hypothesized to be more receptive to telemarketing fraud, but retired respondents do not show any significant difference in terms of their willingness to listen, negative attitude toward callers, or the number of times they sent money to unfamiliar telemarketers than those who currently are employed. Therefore, H_{2a} is not supported.

Living alone does not affect negative attitude toward callers, willingness to listen, or number of times money was sent by the elderly respondent. Therefore, H_{2b} is not supported.

Older consumers were hypothesized to be more receptive to telemarketing fraud (H_{2c}). The results of regression analyses reveal that older consumers are more likely to listen to a telemarketer's sales pitch. As social integration and activity theories suggest, elderly consumers might be more socially isolated and therefore seek social interactions from marketers. However, age is not found to influence the frequency of responses to

TABLE 4

Results of Setwise Regression Analyses: Parameter Estimates

Set of Variables	Attitude Toward Caller	Willingness to Listen	Number of Times Money Sent	Number of Calls Received
Number of calls received	.0138	−.0096	−.0029	NA
Working Status (working as base)				
Retired	−.1647	.0303	.0295	.0017
Unemployed	−.4235*	.2816	−.1086	.0504
Single household (living with someone else as base)	.2256	−.2176	.1966	−.4760
Age	−.0107	.0308***	−.0063	−.0231
Education (high school graduates as base)				
Less than high school	−.0138	.0141	−.2434	−.074
Some college	.0138	.2557	−.1678	.5730*
Bachelor's degree or more	.0927	.3685*	−.2159	.5193*
Nonwhites (Caucasian whites as base)	−.5964**	−.2089	.7983***	−.3368
Income	.0346	−.0376	−.0159	.0689
Female (male as base)	.5212***	.0253	−.0180	−.0180
R^2	.0422***	.0355***	.0206*	.0268***

*$p < .05$.
**$p < .01$.
***$p < .001$.

unknown telemarketers or negative attitude toward callers.[2] Therefore, H_{2c} is supported partially.

Less educated consumers were hypothesized to be more receptive to telemarketing fraud (H_3). Both the setwise analysis and the parameter estimates from the full regression model indicate that education is not associated significantly with negative attitude toward callers or number of times money was sent. With regard to consumers' willingness to listen, consumers with a bachelor's degree or higher education were more likely to listen to telephone solicitations than high school graduates, which is opposite the hypothesized direction. Therefore, H_3 is not supported.

Under the socioeconomic power paradigm, racial and ethnic minorities were hypothesized to be more receptive to telemarketing fraud (H_{4a}). Racial and ethnic minorities are found to have a more positive attitude toward callers. This is consistent with

---

[2] To confirm the effect of age, we conducted further analyses in which we treated age as a binary variable (young-old, 50–69 = 0, and old-old, 70+ = 1). With the age dummy variable, we found no age impact on the number of times money was sent to unfamiliar telemarketers, but a marginally significant ($p = .10$) age impact on negative attitude toward callers. Young-old consumers tended to have a more negative attitude toward callers than old-old consumers did.

Loro's (1996) finding that Hispanics have a more positive attitude toward direct marketing than non-Hispanic whites do. Racial and ethnic minorities also are found to send money to unfamiliar telemarketers more often than non-Hispanic whites, but race/ethnicity is not found to affect willingness to listen. Therefore, H_{4a} is partially supported.

H_{4b}, that less affluent consumers are more receptive to telemarketing fraud, is not supported. Income is not found to be associated with any of the proxy measures of consumer receptiveness.

The last hypothesis, H_{4c}, states that women are expected to be more receptive to telemarketing fraud than men. However, it was found that women are more likely to have a negative attitude toward callers than men are. Gender is found not to influence willingness to listen or number of times money was sent to unknown telemarketers. Although H_{4c} is not supported, it was important to note that men have a more positive attitude toward callers than women. A summary of the hypotheses tests appears in Table 5.

Discussion, Conclusions, and Limitations

What concerns exist with respect to those elderly consumers who tend be more responsive to telemarketing solicitations (older, racial/ethnic minorities, and male consumers)? Answers to this question may be found by examining the nature of telemarketing fraud and how these more responsive elderly consumers relate to the nature of telemarketing fraud.

According to the U.S. Department of Justice (1998), telemarketing fraud operations use deception and misrepresentation for three purposes: "(1) To make it appear that the good, service, or charitable cause their telemarketers offer to the public is worth the money that they are asking the consumer to send. (2) To obtain immediate payment before the victim can inspect the item of value they expect to receive. (3) To create an aura of legitimacy about their operations, by trying to resemble legitimate telemarketing operations, legitimate businesses, or legitimate government agencies that refers generally to any scheme to defraud."

How might elderly consumers react in this environment? As discussed in the literature review, if elderly consumers seek social interaction from the fraudulent telemarketers, they likely will be oblivious to what is happening to them with respect to the fraudulent offer because they are responding to the immediate need for social interaction with the caller. Results from the setwise analysis that social isolation influences willingness to listen to telemarketers support this explanation. An effective way to protect the elderly from falling into telemarketing scams may be to provide information related to fraudulent telemarketing practices through personal interaction. This type of personal interaction could satisfy the need for social interaction while providing information to make the elderly more wary of fraudulent telemarketers.

TABLE 5

A Summary of Hypotheses Testing and Policy Implications

Hypotheses	Findings	Implications
H_1: Increased exposure to telemarketing solicitation increases receptiveness to telemarketing fraud.	Not supported	Number of times calls received does not affect receptiveness to telemarketing.
H_{2a}: Retired consumers are more receptive to telemarketing fraud than are those who are in the workforce.	Not supported	Neither retirement nor living alone is related to consumer receptiveness to telemarketing. Further research is needed to capture psychological nature of social isolation.
H_{2b}: Single consumers are more receptive to telemarketing fraud than are those who are living with someone.	Not supported	
H_{2c}: Age is positively related to consumers' receptiveness to telemarketing fraud.	Partially supported: significantly influences willingness to listen	Consumer education programs for elderly should involve personal interaction rather than the media and/or printed materials.
H_3: Less educated consumers are more receptive to telemarketing fraud than are more educated consumers.	Not supported	Education appears not to affect consumer receptiveness to telemarketing.
H_{4a}: Racial and ethnic minorities are more receptive to telemarketing fraud than are non-Hispanic whites.	Partially supported: significantly influences attitude toward caller and number of times money sent	Consumer education programs should address fraudulent telemarketing as an organized criminal activity.
H_{4b}: Income is related negatively to consumers' receptiveness to telemarketing fraud.	Not supported	Income does not influence consumer receptiveness to telemarketing.
H_{4c}: Female consumers are more receptive to telemarketing fraud than are male consumers.	Not supported	Although not the expected finding, it is important to note that men have a more positive attitude toward callers than women do.

The Protection Against Scams on Seniors Act is currently under debate in the 106th U.S. House of Representatives (1999). Recognizing the pervasiveness of telemarketing fraud targeting the elderly, this bill was introduced to protect the public, especially seniors, against telemarketing fraud and fraud over the Internet. It authorizes an educational campaign to improve senior citizens' ability to protect themselves against telemarketing fraud. Section 104 of H.R. 612 proposes that information be disseminated in the following ways: public service announcements, a printed manual or pamphlet, an Internet Web site, and telephone outreach to persons whose names appear on mooch lists.

Of the various approaches to information dissemination, the telephone outreach is the most important because is it is directed at the elderly who willingly listen to telephone calls. As we discussed previously, this approach is an effective way to reach receptive elderly because it is based on interpersonal interaction.

According to the FTC (1998, p. 3),

> people who engage in telemarketing fraud treat it as a profession. In order to perpetrate their scheme, they recruit and train others to that same criminal profession. Once these new telemarketers have been "trained," they set up their own telemarketing establishments, and begin the cycle again. When a boiler room is shut down by state or federal authorities, the telemarketers working at that room do not leave the industry, they merely find another establishment at which to practice their trade.

Recognizing the criminal nature of fraudulent telemarketing industry, the 105th Congress enacted the Telemarketing Fraud Prevention Act (1998) on June 23, 1998. This Act amends the federal criminal code by increasing penalties for fraudulent schemes committed by illegitimate, criminal telemarketers.

This suggests a different picture of telemarketing fraud than most consumers appear to have. One-third of the respondents in this study viewed telemarketers as con artists or "flimflam men" who likely work individually. Less than 4% of the respondents perceived telemarketers as criminals running an organized illegal operation. This suggests that the FTC's description of the fraudulent telemarketers (FTC 1998 a, b, c) is much different than the average consumer's perception. Considering that one-tenth of telemarketing firms are fraudulent (United States–Canada Working Group 1997), this is a concern, particularly for racial/ethnic minorities and men, who tend to have positive attitudes toward telemarketers. These groups tend to perceive telemarketers as people doing their jobs for a legitimate business. This suggests a need to educate consumers about the criminal nature of the fraudulent telemarketing industry. In addition, compounding the more positive attitude of racial/ethnic minorities is the finding that they are more likely to send money in response to telemarketing solicitations.

The discussion and conclusions should be viewed within the limitations of this study. First, the three proxy measures of consumer receptiveness to telemarketing fraud—attitude toward callers, willingness to listen, and number of times money was sent to unfamiliar organizations—were not pretested or validated. Although they appear to have face validity, validation of these measures of consumer receptiveness to telemarketing fraud should be a priority for further research. In addition, using self-reported measures of attitude and behavior is potentially problematic.

Second, direct measures of competing but not necessarily alternative theoretical arguments, such as social isolation, cognitive ability, and socioeconomic power, are needed. Data limitations did not permit direct measures in this study; therefore, setwise regression was used to examine the impact of a set of variables related to these constructs.

This approach is limited by the extent to which the single variables in a set actually reflect the associated constructs. In addition, some of the demographic variables relate to more than one theoretical construct. For example, age is related not only to social isolation, but also to cognitive ability. Considering the significant age impact, we cannot conclude that cognitive ability is not associated with consumer vulnerability. What we empirically find is that education is not associated with consumer receptiveness to telemarketing. Therefore, future research efforts need to investigate factors that affect receptiveness to telemarketing fraud using direct measures of constructs.

References

American Association of Retired Persons (AARP) (1996), "AARP Calls for New Approach in Fight Against Telemarketing Fraud," News Release, (August 6).

____ (1999), "Facts About Fraudulent Telemarketing," (accessed April 27), [available at http://www.aarp.org/fraud/1fraud.htm].

Blau, Zena Smith (1973), *Old Age in Changing Society.* New York: New Viewpoints.

Boosalis, Helen (1998), "Testimony of Helen Boosalis, AARP Board of Directors, Before the Commerce, Justice, State and Judiciary Subcommittee of the Senate Appropriations Committee," (accessed April 27), [available at http://www.aarp.org/wwstand/testimony/1998/boosalis.html].

Bradach, Jeffrey L. and Robert G. Eccles (1989), "Price, Authority, and Trust: From Ideal Types to Plural Forms," *Annual Review of Sociology,* 15, 97–118.

Brill, Jonathan E. (1992), "Interpersonal Interaction Styles of Adult Retail Shoppers: A Social and Aging Perspective," doctoral dissertation, Temple University.

Bristor, Julia M., R. Gravois Lee, and Michelle R. Hunt (1995), "Race and Ideology: African-American Images in Television Advertising," *Journal of Public Policy & Marketing,* 14 (Spring), 48–59.

Butler, R.N. (1968), "Why Are Older Consumers So Susceptible," *Geriatrics,* 23 (12), 83–88.

Cohen, Jacob and Patricia Cohen (1983), *Applied Multiple Regression/Correlation Analysis for the Behavioral Sciences,* 2d ed. Hillsdale, NJ: Lawrence Erlbaum Associates.

Dowd, James J. (1975), "Aging as Exchange: A Preface to Theory," *Journal of Gerontology,* 30 (5), 584–94.

Federal Trade Commission (1998a), "1995–1996 Report, Staff Summary of Federal Trade Commission Activities Affecting Older Americans," (accessed April 27), [available at http://www.ftc.gov/os/1998/9803/aging98.rpt.html].

____ (1998b), "Fraudulent Marketing Schemes. Before the Subcommittee on Commerce, Justice, State and the Judiciary of the Senate Appropriations Committee," (accessed April 27), [available at http://www.ftc.gov/os/1998/9802/greggtes.fin.html].

____ (1998c), "Comments of the Federal Trade Commission Regarding Proposed Amendments to the U.S. Sentencing Guidelines," (accessed April 27), [available at http://www.ftc.gov/be/v980003.html].

Friedman, Monroe (1992), "Confidence Swindles of Older Consumers," *Journal of Consumer Affairs,* 26 (1), 20–46.

Gentry, James W., Patricia F. Kennedy, Katherine Paul, and Ronald Paul Hill (1995), "The Vulnerability of Those Grieving the Death of a Loved One: Implications for Public Policy," *Journal of Public Policy & Marketing,* 13 (Fall), 128–42.

Golodner, L.G. (1991), "Telemarketing: Enhancing Consumer Choice of the Market Place: Enhancing Opportunities for Fraud," in *Enhancing Consumer Choice: Proceedings of the Second*

International Conference on Research in the Consumer Interest, R.N. Mayer, ed. Columbia, MO: American Council on Consumer Interests, 315–24.

Granovetter, Mark (1985), "Economic Action and Social Structure: The Problem of Embeddedness," *American Journal of Sociology,* 91 (3), 481–510.

Harris, Marlys J. (1995), "Elder Fraud," *Money,* 24 (11), 144–54.

Hirschman, Elizabeth C. (1993), "Ideology in Consumer Research, 1980 and 1990: A Marxist and Feminist Critique," *Journal of Consumer Research,* 19 (1), 537–55.

House, James S., Karl R. Landis, and Debra Umberson (1988), "Social Relationships and Health," *Science,* 241 (July), 540–45.

___, Debra Umberson, and Karl R. Landis (1988), "Structure and Processes of Social Support," *Annual Review of Sociology,* 14, 293–318.

John, Deborah Roedder and Catherine A. Cole (1986), "Age Differences in Information Processing: Understanding Deficits in Young and Elderly Consumers," *Journal of Consumer Research,* 13 (3), 297–315.

Kang, Yong-Soon and Nancy M. Ridgway (1996), "The Importance of Consumer Market Interactions as a Form of Social Support for Elderly Consumers," *Journal of Public Policy & Marketing,* 15 (Spring), 108–17.

Kuypers, J.A. and V.L. Bengston (1973), "Social Behavior and Competence: A Model of Normal Aging," *Human Development,* 16 (3), 181–201.

Lee, Jinkook and Karen M. McGowan (1998), "Direct Marketing Solicitations: Do They Generate Sales or Consumer Annoyance?" *Journal of Marketing Management,* 8 (1), 63–71.

___ and Horacio Soberon-Ferrer (1997), "Consumer Vulnerability to Fraud: Influencing Factors," *Journal of Consumer Affairs,* 31 (1), 70–89.

Lord, Kenneth R. and Chung K. Kim (1995), "Inoculating Consumers Against Deception: The Influence of Framing and Executional Style," *Journal of Consumer Policy,* 18 (1), 1–23.

Loro, L. (1996), "Direct Mail Thriving Through Better Executions, Lists," *Advertising Age,* 67 (12), 32.

Martin, Rodrick (1971), "The Concept of Power: A Critical Defense," *British Journal of Sociology,* 22 (3), 240–57.

Marx, Karl ([1887] 1970), *Capital: A Critique of Political Economy.* London: Lawrence & Wishart.

McCarney, Joseph (1990), "Analytical Marxism: A New Paradigm," in *Socialism, Feminism and Philosophy: A Radical Philosophy Reader,* Sean Sayers and Peter Osborne, eds. London: Routledge, 169–78.

McGhee, Jerrie L. (1983), "Vulnerability of Elderly Consumers," *International Journal of Aging and Human Development,* 17 (3), 223–46.

Moon, Marilyn (1990), "Consumer Issues and the Elderly," *Journal of Consumer Affairs,* 24 (2), 235–44.

Moschis, George P. (1992), *Marketing to Older Consumers: A Handbook of Information for Strategy Development,* Westport, CT: Quorum Books.

___ (1994), "Consumer Behavior in Later Life: Multidisciplinary Contributions and Implications for Research," *Journal of the Academy of Marketing Science,* 22 (3), 195–204.

Nahemow, Lucile (1980), "Isolation and Attitudinal Dependency," in *Aging, Isolation and Resocialization,* Keith Bennett, ed. New York: Van Nostrand Reinhold.

Peñaloza, Lisa (1995), "Immigrant Consumers: Marketing and Public Policy Considerations in the Global Economy," *Journal of Public Policy & Marketing,* 14 (Spring), 83–94.

Phillips, L. and B. Sternthal (1977), "Age Differences in Information Processing: A Perspective on the Aged Consumer," *Journal of Marketing Research,* 14 (November), 444–57.

Pitofsky, Robert (1997), *Fighting Consumer Fraud: The Challenge and the Campaign,* (accessed October 22), [available at http://www.ftc.gov/reorts/Fraud/].

Salthouse, Timothy A. (1991), *Theoretical Perspectives on Cognitive Aging.* Hillsdale, NJ: Lawrence Erlbaum Associates.

Smith, Ruth B. and George P. Moschis (1985), "A Socialization Perspective on Selected Consumer Characteristics of the Elderly," *Journal of Consumer Affairs,* 19 (1), 74–95.

____, ____, and Roy L. Moore (1987), "Social Effects of Advertising and Personal Communication on the Elderly Consumer," in *Advances in Marketing and Public Policy,* Vol. 1, Paul Bloom, ed. Greenwich, CT: JAI Press, 65–92.

Starek, Roscoe B., III (1996), "Consumer Protection in the Information Society: A View from the United States," in *The European Consumer Forum on the Consumer and the Information Society,* Dublin Castle, (September 4).

Telemarketing Fraud Prevention Act (1998), Public Law No. 105–184, H.R. 1847.

Thompson, Mozelle W. (1999), "Presentation Before the International Conference on Consumer Policy Sponsored by the Japanese Economic Planning Agency," (accessed April 19), [available at http://www.ftc.gov/speeches/thompson/japan22.htm].

United States–Canada Working Group (1997), "Report of the United States–Canada Working Group to President Bill Clinton and Prime Minister Jean Chretien," (accessed July 14), [available at http://www.usdoj.gov/criminal/fraud/uscwgrtf.htm].

United States Department of Justice (1998), "What Is Telemarketing Fraud?" (accessed January 7), [available at http://www.usdoj.gov/criminal/fraud/telemarketing/whatis.htm].

U.S. House (1999), Protection Against Scams on Seniors Act, 106th Cong., 1st sess., H.R. 612 1H.

Walters, T.A. (1990), "The Elderly Consumer: Social Integration, Perceived Adequacy of Resources, and Complaint Behavior," doctoral dissertation, Florida State University.

Warland, R.H., R.O. Herrman, and J. Willits (1975), "Dissatisfied Consumers: Who Gets Upset and Who Takes Action," *Journal of Consumer Affairs,* 9, 148–63.

Generation Broke: The Growth of Debt Among Young Americans

Tamara Draut and Javier Silva

Over the 1990s, credit card debt among young Americans rose dramatically—leaving many young adults over-extended and vulnerable to financial collapse. This briefing paper documents the rise in credit card and student loan debt between 1992 and 2001 and examines the factors contributing to young adults' increased reliance on credit cards. Rising costs combined with slow real wage growth and skyrocketing college debt have eroded the economic security of today's young adults. Generation Broke is the second in a series of Borrowing to Make Ends Meet Briefing Papers documenting trends in debt among subgroups of the population.

Key Findings

YOUNG ADULTS (25–34 YEARS OLD)

- Average credit card debt among indebted young adults increased by 55 percent between 1992 and 2001, to $4,088 (2001 dollars).
- The average credit card indebted young adult household now spends nearly 24 percent of its income on debt payments, four percentage points more, on average, than young adults did in 1992.
- Among young adult households with incomes below $50,000 (2/3 of young households), nearly one in five with credit card debt is in debt hardship—spending over 40 percent of their income servicing debt, including mortgages and student loans.
- Young Americans now have the second highest rate of bankruptcy, just after those aged 35 to 44. The rate among 25–34 year olds increased between 1991 and 2001, indicating that Gen Xers were more likely to file bankruptcy as young adults than were young Boomers at the same age.[1]

THE YOUNGEST ADULTS (18–24 YEARS OLD)

- The youngest adults saw a sharper rise in credit card debt—104 percent—to an average of $2,985 (2001 dollars).

Draut, Tamara and Javier Silva (2004), "Generation Broke: The Growth of Debt Among College Students," Demos, (pp. 1–14 only)
http://www.demos-usa.org/pubs/Generation_Broke.pdf
Borrowing to Make Ends Meet Briefing Paper #2, October 2004.

- The average credit card indebted household in this age group spends nearly 30 percent of its income on debt payments, double the percentage spent on average in 1992.
- Among the youngest adult households with incomes below $50,000 (2/3 of younger households), nearly one in seven with credit card debt is in debt hardship.

Introduction

The average credit card debt of Americans aged 25 to 34 years old increased by 55 percent between 1992 and 2001, to a self-reported household average of $4,088. Estimates of card debt based on aggregate data put the dollar amount as much as three times higher.[2] This age group's bankruptcy rate grew by 19 percent over the same period—so that by 2001 nearly 12 out of every 1,000 young adults were filing for bankruptcy.[3] Young adults now have the second highest rate of bankruptcy, just after those aged 35 to 44. Their rate of bankruptcy is higher than it was for young Boomers who were 25–34 years old in 1991.

Why are today's young adults going into debt and going broke? During the boom of the 1990s, the popular media showered attention on the rising fortunes of Generation X, who appeared to be riding the tech boom to great heights. However, in 2001 adults aged 25 to 34 were showing signs that the path to adulthood had become more financially perilous than it was for the previous generation of late Baby Boomers in 1992. The major adult costs that begin to mount between the ages of 25 and 34—housing, child care, and health care—have all increased dramatically over the past decade. And the rising unemployment, slow real wage growth, and skyrocketing tuition and resulting student loan debts have combined to erode the economic security of today's young adults. Additionally, just at this time the newly-deregulated credit industry began aggressively marketing to young people on college campuses. Deregulation also brought higher rates and fees, making it increasingly difficult for young Americans to get out of debt.

Compared to the population as a whole, young adults are more likely to be in debt.

Methodology. The credit card data analyzed in this brief are drawn from the Survey of Consumer Finances (SCF), a triennial Federal Reserve survey of the assets and liabilities of American families. The survey years 1992 and 2001 (the most recent data available) were chosen to allow analysis of change in debt trends during the 1990s. The survey years were also selected to allow comparison between the Baby Boomers in 1992 and Generation X in 2001. In 1992, those aged 25 to 34 were mostly late Baby Boomers, while in 2001, those aged 25 to 34 were mostly Generation Xers (See Table 1). **All debt amounts are inflation-adjusted, in 2001 dollars.**

TABLE 1

Defining Baby Boomers and Generation X in the 1992 and 2001 Data

	1992	2001
	Aged 25–34 **(born 1958–1967)**	**Aged 25–34** **(born 1967–1976)**
Baby Boomers (born 1946–1964)	*X*	
Generation X (born 1965–1976)		*X*

Demos' Findings on Credit Card Debt Among Younger Americans, 1992–2001

Prevalence of Credit Cards and Indebtedness. Nearly 7 out of 10 young Americans aged 25 to 34 have one or more credit cards, a level basically unchanged since 1992. Compared to the population as a whole, however, young adult cardholders are much more likely to be in debt: 71 percent of young adult cardholders revolve their balances, compared to 55 percent of all cardholders.

Higher Balances. Credit card debt among young adults has increased significantly since 1992, outpacing the rise among the population as a whole. (Table 2) The average credit card debt among indebted 25 to 34 year olds increased by 55 percent, to $4,088.

Debt by Income Level. All but the lowest-income young households experienced dramatic increases in credit card debt over the decade. Middle-income young adults experienced the fastest growth of any income group. Credit card debt rose 37 percent among moderate-income young adults earning between $10,000 and $24,999. (Figure 1A) Middle-income young adults—those with incomes between $25,000 and $49,999—experienced a 65 percent increase in credit card debt. Upper middle-income young adults with incomes between $50,000 and $74,999 experienced a 55 percent increase in debt. (Figure 1B)

TABLE 2

Average Credit Card Debt Among Young Households with Credit Card Debt (2001 Dollars)

	1992	2001	% change 1992–2001
All households	$2,991	$4,126	38%
Aged 25–34	$2,640	$4,088	55%

Source: Dēmos' Calculations from the 1992 and 2001 Survey of Consumer Finances.

FIGURE 1A

Average Credit Card Debt Among Low- and Moderate-Income Adults Aged 25 to 34 (in 2001 dollars)

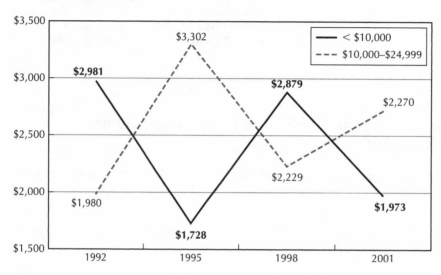

FIGURE 1B

Average Credit Card Debt Among Middle- and Upper-Middle-Income Adults Aged 25 to 34

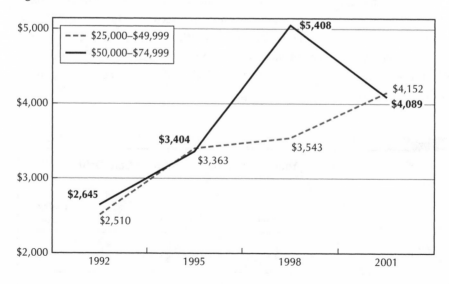

Debt Service-to-Income Ratio. The true financial impact of debt is best understood by examining the percentage of income young adults must devote to debt payments, which is typically called the debt service-to-income ratio. Debt service-to-income ratios have been steadily rising for young Americans since 1992, when the average ratio for indebted young adults was 19. By 2001, the average debt service-to-income ratio for 25 to 34 year olds had risen to 24 percent— meaning that the average indebted young American spends nearly a quarter of every dollar earned servicing debt. However, the debt service-to-income ratio severely

> *The average indebted young adult spends nearly 25 cents of every dollar of income on debt payments.*

underestimates the financial burdens facing young Americans in several ways. First, the ratio only measures outstanding mortgage and consumer debt, such as credit cards and auto loans—excluding what is often a young household's largest expense: rent. Second, since the figure doesn't include auto lease payments, the cost of a car may not be reflected in the ratio. Finally, the ratio significantly underestimates credit card debt burden because it can only measure the minimum payment burden—which is typically 2 1/2 percent of the total outstanding balance. That means that a credit card debt of $10,000 is counted as $250 in debt service. But the key to paying off credit card debt is making more than the minimum payment. If a young American were to only pay the minimum on a $10,000 balance with a 15% APR, it would take them more than 39 years and cost them over $16,000 in interest charges.

Debt Hardship. A family spending more than 40 percent of their income on debt payments, including mortgages and student loan debt, is traditionally considered in a state of *debt hardship.* Overall, 13 percent of indebted young Americans experience debt hardship—nearly double the percentage in 1992. Lowest income households are the most likely to be in debt hardship, but middle-income young adults are also experiencing

TABLE 3

Percent of Credit Card Indebted Young Americans Aged 25 to 34 in Debt Hardship (Debt Payment to Income Ratio > 40%)

Income Group (25–34)	1992	2001
Overall	7.9%	13.3%
Income Group		
Under $10,000	37.1%	57.6%
$10,000–$24,999	8.4	22.3
$25,000–$49,999	6.7	13.4
$50,000–$74,999	7.8	5.2

Source: Dēmos' Calculations from the 1992 and 2001 Survey of Consumer Finances.

higher levels of debt hardship. About 13 percent of indebted young adults with incomes between $10,000 and $75,000 are in debt hardship. (See Table 3). Young adults are having a harder time making payments, too. Nearly 1 out of 5 of reported being late or missing payments within the last year on any loan, up from 1 out of every 6 in 1992.

What Is Driving Debt?

Several factors may be driving the rise in credit card debt among young adults. In many ways, young families are just like other households—often their paychecks are just enough to cover the rent, groceries and car payment, so that any additional or unexpected expense is financed through credit. But there are unique economic circumstances that may contribute to young adults' greater reliance on credit cards to make ends meet. Young adults are often still servicing student loan debt, have higher unemployment rates and earn lower, entry-level wages. Likewise, today's young adults have come of financial age during an era of banking deregulation that has dramatically increased the availability and cost of credit.

Earnings of young adults have not kept up with inflation or the costs of basic necessities.

Slow Real Wage Growth. The earnings of 25 to 34 year olds have not kept up with inflation or the costs of basic necessities including housing, healthcare and student loan repayment obligations. Between 1992 and 2001, the median annual earnings of all male workers grew by 5 percent in real terms (See Table 4). Female workers made greater gains in their annual earnings, which rose by 6.7 percent in real terms. Both male and female workers with bachelor's degrees made greater gains than their non-degree holding counterparts. However, given the higher amounts of debt borrowed by those attending

| TABLE 4 |

Median Annual Earnings of All Wage and Salary Workers Age 25 to 34 (in 2002 dollars)

	Males			Females		
	All Males	Some College	Bachelor's Degree or Higher	All Females	Some College	Bachelor's Degree or Higher
1992	$34,051	$34,024	$45,756	$27,834	$27,134	$36,177
2001	35,778	35,598	48,782	29,723	26,769	38,331
2002	35,487	35,552	48,955	30,093	26,828	40,021

Source: National Center for Education Statistics, based on data from US Department of Commerce, Bureau of the Census. March Current Population Surveys, 1972–2003.

college in the 1990s, much of the annual earnings advantage by young college workers is diminished by debt service.

In 2001, the average starting salary for college grads was about $36,000, with wide variations among different fields.[4] Salaries in marketing started at $34,000; advertising jobs started at $28,000, and education majors got on average $39,000 out of the gate. It would be valuable to break down the budget for a typical college grad in 2001 (See Figure 2).

The sample budget below is for an average college graduate earning about $36,000. The budget makes conservative estimates and does not include expenses for entertainment, clothing, furniture or even household cleaning supplies or toiletries. At the end of the month, our average college grad has just $34 unaccounted for by monthly bills. That money must cover any additional expenses, such as car repairs, new work clothes or even a movie.

FIGURE 2

Sample Budget for Recent College Graduate

$2,058 Monthly Take Home Pay
($36,000 a year, average starting salary of college grads in 2001, minus taxes and a monthly health care contribution of $42[5])

Absolute Expenses

$182 Student Loan Monthly Payment
(average monthly student loan payment reported by undergraduate borrowers)

$797 Rent and Utilities
(median monthly rent for single, college educated adults in 2000)

$456 Food and Groceries
(average monthly amount spent on food by 25–34 year olds, 2001)

$464 Transportation
(average monthly amount for car, auto repairs, insurance and gas)

$125 Credit Card Minimum Payment
(average credit card debt of 25–34 year olds; $4,008 balance at 16% APR)

= $1,933 Total Monthly Expenses

Money Left Over for Everything Else

$34 For child care, entertainment, clothing, furniture, Internet access, etc.

Starting Salary: Alexis M. Herman. "Invasion of the College Grads." MonsterTrak, Young Money Interactive. Accessed online at www.young-money.com/careers/monstertrak/job_hunt/053.

Health Care Costs: The average monthly worker contribution for single coverage was $42 in 2003. *Employer Health Benefits Survey 2003,* Kaiser Family Foundation.

Student Loan Payment: Sandy Baum and Marie O'Malley. "College on Credit: How Borrowers Perceive their Education Debt. Results of the 2002 National Student Loan Survey." Nellie Mae Corporation, Feb. 6, 2003.

Rent: US Census Bureau, Median Gross Rents, Census 2000. The $797 is the average of the top 5 metropolitan cities median monthly rents for college-educated, single young adults (San Francisco, Los Angeles, Atlanta, Washington, DC and New York City.

Food: Consumer Expenditure Survey 2002, Average Annual Expenditures on Food for 25–34 year olds is $5,471.

Transportation: Consumer Expenditure Survey 2002, Average annual expenditures for transportation by singles, aged 25 to 34. $5,567 yearly; $464 monthly.

Under- and Un-Employment. Today's young adults are entering a labor market radically different from that of their parents. Many young adults are part of the new contingent labor force, working in temporary jobs that pay less than full-time permanent positions and don't offer health or pension benefits. In 1999, one out of four contingent workers★ was between the ages of 25 and 34, a higher percentage than any other age group.[6] College graduates make up the largest percentage of contingent workers, with nearly 38 percent holding bachelor's degrees or higher. Young adults under 24 tend to prefer their contingent arrangement to a full-time job, usually because they're balancing work and school. But the large majority of contingent workers over age 25 would prefer a full-time job.[7]

Not only are young adults frequently *under*-employed, they are also more likely to be unemployed, because young workers have less job tenure. The recent recession has been particularly bad for younger workers, as their unemployment rate rose faster than that of older workers. Almost one in ten young workers were unemployed in mid-2003.[8] Young adults of color face particularly dim prospects in the job market. In 2003, the unemployment rate was 17.9 percent for young African Americans; 9.6 percent for young Latinos and 7.6 percent for young whites.[9] Even during the boom year of 2000, young African Americans unemployment rate was more than double that of young whites.

Workers with college degrees—who are typically more secure in jobs than those without—have been hit hard since the 2001 recession. In March 2004, the number of unemployed college graduates reached 1.17 million, higher than the number of unemployed high school dropouts. While statistics indicate that college education pays-off over the long term, over the short-term many young college grads are finding it difficult to secure jobs.

Student Loan Debt. This generation is also the first to shoulder the costs of their college primarily through interest-bearing loans rather than grants. Most of the 25 to 34 year olds in the 2001 sample went to college in the 1990s—when college costs increased by

> *This generation is the first to shoulder the costs of college primarily through loans rather than grants.*

an average of 38 percent, borrowing became more common among students, and the amount borrowed grew rapidly.[10] For example, in the 1992–1993 school year, 42 percent of students borrowed money for college. By the end of the decade, almost two-thirds of students had borrowed.[11] A survey of college borrowers conducted by Nellie Mae found that the average college senior graduated with $18,900 in student loans in 2002—taking a big $182 monthly bite out of their paychecks each month.[12] That's more than double the just over $9,000 average loan amount carried by young adults in the previous generation in 1992.[13] For young adults who pursued graduate degrees, the student loan burdens are even higher: the average

---

★The findings presented here are based on the Bureau of Labor Statistics definition of contingent worker: individuals who hold jobs that are temporary and not expected to continue.

combined student loan debt for grad school students is $45,900.[14] Young adults who went to grad school pay an average of $388 per month for student loans, amounting to nearly 13.5 percent of their income.

The average undergraduate student loan debt represents about 9 percent of young adults' income today.[15] The commonly accepted rule, used by credit counselors and lenders, is that total monthly debt payments should not exceed 36 percent of gross income. The debt included would be the rent or mortgage, credit cards, student loans, car leases and any other revolving type of loan. With student loan debt taking up 9 percent of young adults' income on average, that leaves just 27 percent of their paychecks to allocate to rent or a car loan without risking financial hardship—not to mention a damaged credit rating. With one out of every five young adults reporting that they have been late on or missed a loan payment in the past year, it is clear that servicing debt has become increasingly risky, and at a time when credit scores are growing more relevant for employment, housing, and even cell phones.

Aggressive Marketing to College Students. While many younger Americans are going into debt to make ends meet, aggressive marketing tactics by the credit card industry have helped fuel the use of credit cards. Across college and university campuses at the beginning of each semester, credit card companies engage in "tabling" offering free t-shirts, mugs, pizza, and other incentives for students to fill out credit card applications. These tactics work exceedingly well—a recent study found that 96 percent of college seniors had a credit card. With little or no financial literacy training, many students fall victim to the aggressive marketing tactics offered by credit card companies.

Ninety-six percent of college seniors have credit cards.

Rising Housing and Transportation Costs. During the last decade, both home prices and rents have grown faster than inflation. In 2001, 3.2 million households earning between $17,500 and $50,000—which includes the median earnings of today's 25 to 34 year olds—spent more than half their incomes on housing.[16] Compared to the late Boomers in 1992, Generation Xers were spending considerably more on average for rent and transportation, according to Consumer Expenditure Survey data.[17] On average, Gen X renters spent $6,815 annually on rent, about 10 percent more than Boomers of the same age spent in 1992. Young adult households are also spending more on getting around: $8,423 on average for transportation in 2002 compared to $6,820 in 1992 (inflation adjusted dollars).

The Cost of Being Uninsured. Young adults are much more likely to be uninsured than older workers, putting many young adults at both physical and financial risk. Contrary to popular perception, young adults are not uninsured because they decline coverage from their employer. Only 3 percent of uninsured young workers were offered but declined insurance coverage.[18]

Young adults are more likely to work in jobs that don't offer health care benefits. Nearly half of full-time workers aged 19 to 29 lack job-based health benefits, compared to less than one-third percent of all workers under 65.[19] As a result, young adults are more likely to be uninsured than the population as a whole: approximately 1 in 3 young adults lacks health insurance compared to 1 in 6 Americans overall.[20] Not having health insurance exerts a physical and financial cost on young adults. About half of young adults aged 19 to 29 without health insurance reported having problems paying medical bills.[21]

Child Care Costs. The ages of 25 to 34 are the prime years when young adults begin to start families. Today, the average woman will have her first child around the age of 25.[22] But unlike three decades ago, today's young families are more likely to have two parents working full-time. Today, mothers with infants are more likely to be working full-time than part-time—adding the expense of child care to the family budget.[23] According to the U.S. Census Bureau, 59 percent of mothers with a child under age 1, and 64 percent of mothers with a child under age 6, are in the workforce. Nationwide, about half of all working families with children under age 13 pay for child care, spending an average of $303 per month, or 9 percent of their earnings.[24] With full-day care ranging from $4,000 to $10,000 a year per child, the cost of child care is a major strain on young families' already tight budgets.

The Youngest Adults: Indebted from the Start

Today's 18 to 24 year olds are experiencing the pinnacle of two trends fueling the rise in debt: dramatic increases in the cost of college and aggressive marketing of credit cards on college campuses. In this section, we take a closer look at the debt among the youngest adults, those aged 18 to 24.

Credit card debt among 18 to 24 year olds rose sharply over the decade, by 104 percent, to an average of $2,985 in 2001 (See Table 5). Although the Survey of Consumer Finances does not survey current students, it is clear that the youngest adults' increased debt loads are to some extent a result of rising credit card debt among college students. On-campus credit card marketing exploded during the 1990s, as creditors sought

TABLE 5

Average Credit Card Debt Among Young Households with Credit Card Debt (2001 dollars)

	1992	2001	% change 1992–2001
Aged 18–24	$1,461	$2,985	104%

Source: Dēmos' Calculations from the 1992 and 2001 Survey of Consumer Finances.

to saturate the youth market for the first time.[25] The co-branded college cards and student-conscious advertising and rewards programs were successful: in 2001, fully 83 percent of all undergraduates had at least one credit card. By their senior year, 96 percent of all students have credit cards, carrying an average of six cards. Balances among college students have risen sharply over the last decade. Between 1990 and 1995, one survey found credit debt had shot up 134 percent, from $900 to $2,100.[26] In 2001, college seniors graduated with an average of $3,262 in credit card debt.[27]

ACCORDING TO DEMOS' FINDINGS

- The youngest adults saw a sharp rise in credit card debt—104 percent—to an average of $2,985.
- The youngest adults are the age group most likely to be indebted: nearly three out of four carry balances on their cards.
- The average credit card indebted household in this age group spends nearly 30 percent of its income on debt payments, double the percentage spent on average in 1992.

> *Nearly one out of five 18 to 24 year olds reported being late or missing payments within the last year on a loan.*

- Among the youngest adult households with incomes below $50,000 (2/3 of younger households), nearly one in seven with credit card debt is in debt hardship.
- Nearly one out of five households in this age group reported being late or missing payments within the last year on a loan, a 27 percent increase since 1992.

Policy Recommendations

Young adults are servicing higher amounts of debt than they were at the start of the 1990s. The trends fueling the growth in debt among this age group include slow or stagnant wage growth, rising tuition costs and declining grant aid, as well as growing costs of transportation, child care and housing. For younger Americans struggling to make ends meet, the promise of a better future than the previous generation seems uncertain, if not unlikely. The following policy recommendations are aimed at providing more economic stability for today's young adults—those who should be entering the most productive years of their lives but are now constrained by mounting debts and slow economic growth.

ADDRESSING ECONOMIC INSECURITY

The following policy changes would help ensure younger Americans the opportunity to get ahead and build strong, financially secure futures for themselves and their families.

Enacting just one of these reforms would help reduce the need for younger Americans to borrow to make ends meet—both before and after they complete their education.

Expand Health Insurance Coverage. The growing number of younger Americans without health insurance is cause for concern about the state of the nation's health insurance system. Young adults have a very high stake in the nation addressing the problem of uninsurance among all age groups in the nation. Any policy change that moves the United States toward some system of universal coverage would benefit young adults as well. In the meantime, there are several discrete policy changes that could specifically address the drop-off in insurance coverage that happens after young adults turn 19. The first would be to require private insurers and employers to provide dependent coverage through age 23. And for the 2.7 million uninsured young adults living in poverty, Congress could require that eligibility for Medicaid and CHIP coverage be extended to age 23.[28] Finally, states could require all colleges to provide health insurance to both full-time and part-time students—which would help cover the 2 million students who currently are uninsured.

Expand Grants for Higher Education. The cost of post-secondary education has risen steadily over the last decade, rising faster than inflation and family income. The rise in student loan debt over the 1990s can be attributed to rising tuition costs and changes in federal financial aid. Over the last 20 years, federal financial aid has steadily shifted away from grant-based aid to a predominantly loan-based system. In 1980, grants comprised 52 percent of federal aid while loans totaled 45 percent of aid. By 2000, grant aid made up only 41 percent of federal aid and loans had increased to 58 percent. As a result, borrowing has become the most common way for students to finance their education. Today, students with bachelor's degrees graduate on average with over $18,000 in loans and graduate students accumulate a combined debt of $45,900.[29] And more than 1 in 4 students report using credit cards to help finance their education.[30] Many students leave college in debt, but without a degree—one-third of students who left school without completing a degree had borrowed between $10,000 and $20,000.[31] The student loan burden is taking a toll on young adults: almost 1 in 5 significantly changed their career plans because of student loans; nearly 40 percent delayed buying a home and just over 20 percent reported their debt burden caused them to postpone having children.[32] Finally, many qualified students fail to enroll or complete degrees because they can't afford the costs of college.[33]

Our nation must return to grant-based federal financial aid for college.

Our nation must dramatically rethink its federal aid policies. Demos has proposed a new "Contract for College" that would reorient federal aid to a grant-based system and better align aid with the real cost of college. The Contract also would provide early and up-front knowledge to high school students about the amount of aid available. Students

The Contract for College

Based on the Average Annual Cost of Attendance at 4-year Public Colleges (Approx. $12,000)

Household Income below $25,000			*Household Income $75,000–$99,000*	
Grant to cover 75% of costs	$9,000		Grant to cover 40% of costs	$4,800
Work-study	1,500		Work-study	1,500
Subsidized loan	1,500		Subsidized loan	2,350
			Unsubsidized loan	2,350
Household Income $25,000–49,999				
Grant to cover 65% of costs	$7,800		*Household Income above $100,000*	
Work-study	1,500		Unsubsidized loan	$10,000
Subsidized loan	2,700			
Household Income $50,000–$74,999				
Grant to cover 55% of costs	$6,600			
Work-study	1,500			
Subsidized loan	3,900			

would be guaranteed a combination of grants and loans, with grants making up the bulk of aid to students from low- and moderate-income households. Table 3 below offers an example of how the Contract for College would vary for different income levels (the real plan would include more gradual phase-outs for each subsequent income level). For more details on the "Contract for College," see Demos policy brief on higher education, *Leveling the Playing Field* at www.demos-usa.org/opportunity.

Help Young Adults Build Savings by Extending Deferment of Student Loans.

As young people leave college to start their newly independent lives, the presence of high student loan debt as well as college credit card debt leaves very little slack in the household budget. To help young adults gain their financial footing after college, extended deferment periods on student loans should be considered. Currently, students are required to begin paying back federal loans six months after graduation. Allowing students to defer payment for 12 or 18 months would provide more time for new graduates to stabilize their financial situations, as well as divert what would have been student loan payments into savings or high-interest credit card debt reduction. The organization 18to35.org proposes a policy to require students who choose extended deferments to contribute to a tax-deferred savings account. (see www.18to35.org for more details.)

Increase the Minimum Wage.

In the United States today, a quarter of all workers make $8 or less an hour. In 2003, 10.5 percent of workers aged 25 to 34 earned at or below $8 per hour. The minimum wage, instituted in 1938, has failed to keep pace with inflation and doesn't protect against poverty. It has lost 24 percent of its purchasing power since 1979. The minimum wage should be increased gradually to $8.40 an hour by 2010—a level that would help increase the wages of young adults who currently earn between

The minimum wage should be increased gradually to $8.40 an hour by 2010.

$5.15 and $8 an hour. The new minimum wage should also be indexed to inflation, so that it retains its purchasing power.

ADDRESSING INDUSTRY PRACTICES

While the long-term goals of increased economic security and opportunity for young adults will help future generations avoid the pitfalls of debt, certain policy changes at the federal level could help today's young adults pay down their debt at reasonable rates, over reasonable amounts of time.

Enact a Borrower's Security Act. Today there are no legal bounds to the amount of fees and interest credit card companies can charge borrowers. In addition, credit card companies, unlike other lenders, are allowed to change the terms on the card at any time, for any reason. As a result, cardholders routinely borrow money under one set of conditions and end up paying it back under a different set of conditions. Legal limits on interest rates and fees have traditionally been established by the states. But because card companies can export interest rates from the state in which they're based, consumers are left unprotected from excessive rates, fees and capricious changes in account terms. Congress needs to pass new legislation that provides borrowers with the security of knowing the upper limit on the interest rates and fees they can be charged and that the terms of their original agreement can not altered at any time, for any reason. The Borrower's Security Act would ideally prohibit a range of existing exploitative and unfair practices:

- Require card companies to provide a late-payment grace period of at least 5 days before fees or interest rate hikes can be assessed; limit penalty rates to an amount no higher than 50 percent of the original rate (e.g., if the original APR is 9 percent, the penalty rate cannot be above 13.5 percent).
- Require disclosure of the full costs of only paying the minimum payments, including the number of years and total dollars it will take to pay off the debt. Raise the minimum payment requirement to 5 percent of the total balance for new cardholders to curtail excessive debt loads and interest payments.
- Require credit cards issued to individuals under 21 to have a co-signer, unless they can prove they have independent means of support.
- Prohibit card companies from raising a cardholder's interest rate based on payments to other creditors.
- Limit any rate increase to future activity on the card only.

Maintain Existing Bankruptcy Laws For Individuals In Severe Economic Distress. Over half a million adults under the age of 34 filed for bankruptcy in 2001.[34] Congress has considered legislation that would make it more difficult for individuals to recover from financial collapse. The growing presence of younger Americans in the bankruptcy courts should warn policymakers of the importance of safeguarding this difficult last resort for consumers.

Conclusion

Rising student loan and credit card debt remains a growing concern for the future economic success of today's young adults. To cope with entry-level wages that haven't kept up with rising costs, young adults are turning to credit cards to meet their monthly expenses. Addressing this problem will necessarily entail a multi-pronged approach that includes policies aimed at bolstering incomes, reducing costs, and expanding access to financial literacy and asset-building programs. As this generation struggles to begin their lives with high levels of debt, there are consequences for both these individuals and for our national economy. The ability for young adults to build wealth and accumulate assets is greatly undermined by debt burdens that stymie their economic advancement now and well into their adult lives.

PERSONAL STORY

Randy Carter, Communications Professional, Age 28

Randy Carter got his first credit card from a mail solicitation at age 18. He didn't have to prove any source of income for the $800 credit line, just that he was a student at the University of Wisconsin in Madison. A combination of student loans and a part-time job at a hardware store weren't enough to meet the cost of going to school full-time, so the new Citibank credit card helped make up the difference. After six months of small, steady charges for things like books and meals, Citibank more than doubled Randy's limit to $2,000. Randy then took a new job more in line with his career ambitions that required him to drive around the state. Unfortunately, the nonprofit employer didn't reimburse gasoline expenses, so he filled up his tank regularly on the card. "It was clear to the bank that I'd use just about as much credit as they gave me, and that I would make the minimum payments," he realizes now. So Citibank doubled his limit again, to $4,000. More offers poured in the mail, and by his senior year, Randy had four cards and was $7,500 in debt. The minimum payments grew to be more than he could handle, so he began using the cash advance checks MBNA sent him to pay Citibank, and vice-versa. These checks carried immediate interest charges in the high twenty percent range, and the result was rapidly rising balances, even when he slowed his purchases. When Randy's older brother learned how deep in debt he was, he took out a low-interest personal loan and paid off most of his debt. "I sent the cards back to be cut up, except for the Citibank card, with a couple thousand dollars on it, because I wanted to take some responsibility for some of my debt," Randy explains.

"I'M 28 YEARS OLD, AND I'M WORSE THAN BROKE."

His first job out of school was with a public television station that could only pay him $9 an hour for 20 hours of work a week, although he put in more than 50 hours a week. "I was committed to the job, and was hoping to translate my effort into a full-time job, which happened, finally, after two years of making under $15,000 a year." Credit continued to fill the gap between his salary and his living expenses, which were low by most standards. His rent in the college town was only $300, but his student loan payments were over $400. He eventually had to put his college loans in forbearance. When Randy finally got his full-time position, the salary was $27,000—lower than expected and with no raise in sight due to a Wisconsin state budget salary freeze.

In September of 2001, Randy decided he needed to take control of his career and his finances and follow a job lead in New York. Taking stock of $18,000 in credit card debt, he paid a $778 establishment fee for a debt settlement company to take $389 a month with the promise of using the savings to settle his debts in three years. Randy's new job at a New York dot-com documentary company paid him $650 a week with no benefits, but he was able to live on his brother's couch rent-free. But the city's economy was in a tailspin, and he was laid off four months later. Randy cashed out his retirement savings, taking a substantial tax penalty to access only a few thousand dollars. He needed the money and couldn't get un-employment benefits for nearly two months because he'd worked in two different states. "I started to have to pay rent, which was a bargain in New York at $500, but with the $389 debt payment, I was left with less than $100 a month to live on. I applied for over 300 jobs and got nothing." When his unemployment ran out, he cobbled together a work week of odd jobs— babysitting, filing, light construc-tion—until finally a temp agency took him on. "By this time, I was severely de-pressed, I had gone to college and worked hard and had so little to show for it."

After almost a year, he finally got a full-time job in his field, and is now doing better. "It still doesn't pay a fair or sustainable wage for New York, but it is stable and has advanced my career." Randy's bad credit has made getting an apartment of his own nearly impossible. "I've been told to pay the full year's rent up front. If I could do that, would I be so deep in debt?" He's also been told that he would have been better off filing for bankruptcy. "I always thought it would be better for me to pay, to honor my debts even when I was unemployed and under-employed. But I've spent over $14,000 in the past 3 years, servicing my debt instead of going to the doctor. I'm 28 years old, and I'm worse than broke."

Notes

[1] Teresa A. Sullivan, Deborah Thorne and Elizabeth Warren. "Young, Old, and In Between: Who Files for Bankruptcy?." *Norton Bankruptcy Law Advisor,* Issue No. 9A, September 2001.

[2] The absolute figures (for example, the average household reported $4,126 in credit card debt) are based on data that consumers reported about themselves in the Survey of Consumer Finance. Aggregate data on outstanding revolving credit reported by the Federal Reserve estimates the average credit card debt per household at about $12,000—nearly three times more than the self-reported amount. See also Robert Manning, "*Credit Card Nation,*" pp. 319.

[3] Teresa A. Sullivan, Deborah Thorne and Elizabeth Warren. "Young, Old, and In Between: Who Files for Bankruptcy?." *Norton Bankruptcy Law Advisor,* Issue No. 9A, September 2001.

[4] Alexis M. Herman. "Invasion of the College Grads." MonsterTrak, Young Money Interactive. Accessed online at www.youngmoney.com/careers/monstertrak/job_hunt/053.

[5] The average monthly worker contribution for single coverage was $42 in 2003. *Employer Health Benefits Survey 2003,* Kaiser Family Foundation.

[6] Steven Hipple. "Contingent Work in the late 1990s." *Monthly Labor Review.* March 2001.

[7] Steven Hipple. "Contingent Work in the late 1990s." *Monthly Labor Review.* March 2001.

[8] Heather Boushey and John Schmitt. "Hard Times in the New Millenium." Center for Economic and Policy Research. November 2003.

[9] Heather Boushey and John Schmitt. "Hard Times in the New Millenium." Center for Economic and Policy Research. November 2003.

[10] After adjusting for inflation, tuition and fees at both public and private four-year colleges arose 38 percent between 1992–1993 and 2002–2003. College Board, "Trends in College Pricing." 2002.

[11] Tracey King and Ellynne Bannon. "The Burden of Borrowing: A Report on the Rising Rates of Student Loan Debt." State PIRGs Higher Education Project. March 2002.

[12] Sandy Baum and Marie O'Malley. "College on Credit: How Borrowers Perceive their Education Debt. Results of the 2002 National Student Loan Survey." Nellie Mae Corporation, February 6, 2003.

[13] Tracey King and Ellynne Bannon. "The Burden of Borrowing: A Report on the Rising Rates of Student Loan Debt." State PIRGs Higher Education Project. March 2002.

[14] Sandy Baum and Marie O'Malley. "College on Credit: How Borrowers Perceive their Education Debt. Results of the 2002 National Student Loan Survey." Nellie Mae Corporation, February 6, 2003.

[15] Sandy Baum and Marie O'Malley. "College on Credit: How Borrowers Perceive their Education Debt. Results of the 2002 National Student Loan Survey." Nellie Mae Corporation, February 6, 2003.

[16] "The State of the Nation's Housing." Fact Sheet. Harvard University Joint Center for Housing Studies. June 17, 2003.

[17] Consumer Expenditure Survey Tables for age 25–34, years 1991–1992 and 2000–2001, adjusted for inflation for 2002 dollars.

[18] Kevin Quinn, Cathy Schoen, Louisa Buatti. "On Their Own: Young Adults Living Without Health Insurance." The Commonwealth Fund. May 2000.

[19] Kevin Quinn, Cathy Schoen, Louisa Buatti. "On Their Own: Young Adults Living Without Health Insurance." The Commonwealth Fund. May 2000.

[20] 18to35.org. Health Care Factsheet. Downloaded online July 28, 2004 at www.18to35.org/policy/fact-health.html.

[21] Sara R. Collins, Cathy Schoen, et al. "Rite of Passage? Why Young Adults Become Uninsured and How New Policies Can Help." The Commonwealth Fund. May 2004.

[22] National Vital Statistics Report. "Mean Age of Mother, 1970–2000." December 11, 2002.

[23] "Fertility of American Women." Current Population Reports, US Census Bureau. October 2003.

[24] Adelman, S., Giannarelli, L., and Schmidt, S. (Feb. 2003) *Getting Help with Child Care Expenses.* Washington, DC: The Urban Institute.

[25] For a good discussion of campus marketing, see Robert R. Manning, *Credit Card Nation,* (Basic Books, New York) 2000.

[26] Robert R. Manning, *Credit Card Nation,* (Basic Books, New York) 2000, p. 169 citing a study conducted by marketing research firm Claritas, Inc.

[27] Nellie Mae Corporation. "Undergraduate Students and Credit Cards: An Analysis of Usage Rates and Trends." April 2002.

[28] Sara R. Collins, Cathy Schoen, et al. "Rite of Passage? Why Young Adults Become Uninsured and How New Policies Can Help." The Commonwealth Fund. May 2004.

[29] Sandy Baum and Marie O'Malley. "College on Credit: How Borrowers Perceive their Education Debt. Results of the 2002 National Student Loan Survey." Nellie Mae Corporation, February 6, 2003.

[30] Sandy Baum and Marie O'Malley. "College on Credit: How Borrowers Perceive their Education Debt. Results of the 2002 National Student Loan Survey." Nellie Mae Corporation, February 6, 2003.

[31] Ibid.

[32] Ibid.

[33] *Empty Promises: The Myth of College Access in America.* Report of the Advisory Committee on Student Financial Assistance, June 2002. In 2001-2002 alone, it's estimated that 410,000 college-qualified students did not enroll in a 4-year institution and 168,000 more did not enroll in any college at all.

[34] Teresa A. Sullivan, Deborah Thorne and Elizabeth Warren. "Young, Old, and In Between: Who Files for Bankruptcy?." *Norton Bankruptcy Law Advisor,* Issue No. 9A, September.

Exploring the Challenges of Consumer Protection (Government Regulation I)

Consumer Protection

J. Craig Andrews

Introduction

An important and essential area of regulation and law relating to marketing in society involves consumer protection. Protecting consumers against potential harms found in the marketplace enables our economy to operate more effectively and efficiently and directly benefits consumer and societal welfare. This chapter first defines consumer protection and details its substantive domain. It then summarizes its historical development and several key topic areas, offering selected readings and insights, and concluding with important questions for discussion.

Definition

Given the extensive and diverse nature of research on consumer protection issues, providing a single definition for "consumer protection" is no easy task. Nonetheless, based on a review of the literature, the field of consumer protection can be thought of as the study of policy designed to protect consumers from inaccurate or misleading information, unfairness, fraud, substantial risks, and other harms that might exist in the marketplace. This treatment focuses on the study and research of *policy* in protecting consumers rather than the examination of the consumer interest per se that represents a separate chapter in this volume. Such policy may focus on regulatory efforts, but can also involve self-regulation (e.g., National Advertising Division of the Council of Better Business Bureaus), judicial decisions (e.g., Lanham Act cases), and legislative (e.g., Congressional) actions. It also is distinct from the study of competition (e.g., anti-trust actions; mergers/acquisitions) as reviewed in this volume, although anti-competitive actions in the marketplace (e.g., price fixing/discrimination; channel exclusion) may also have an effect on consumers (Cohen, 1995). In addition, even though consumers may be "protected" through the implementation of social marketing campaigns (e.g., anti-drug advertising) or the application of marketing ethics programs/standards, these will represent separate chapters in this volume.

From a regulatory perspective, the term "consumer protection" has long been an important part of efforts at U.S. federal agencies, such as the Federal Trade Commission

ANDREWS, J. CRAIG, Consumer Protection.

J. Craig Andrews is the Charles H. Kellstadt Chair in Marketing in the College of Business Administration at Marquette University.

(FTC; www.ftc.gov) and Food and Drug Administration (FDA; www.fda.gov). Since the Wheeler-Lea Amendment to the FTC Act in 1938, consumer protection has been officially incorporated into the Commission's mandate with "affording protection to the purchasing public" (FTC, 1939, p. 163). Currently, the FTC's Bureau of Consumer Protection serves to protect consumers from unfair, deceptive, or fraudulent practices. It also enforces a variety of consumer protection laws enacted by Congress, as well as industry-wide trade regulation rules issued by the Commission. The U.S. FDA is a scientific, regulatory, and public health agency that oversees products and services accounting for 25 cents of every dollar spent by consumers (Swann, 1998). Its consumer protection jurisdiction encompasses most food products (other than meat and poultry), human drugs, therapeutic agents of biological origin, medical devices, radiation-emitting products for consumer and medical use, and cosmetics. Consumer protection activities also have been an important part of state and local governments in the form of "mini-FTC acts" at the state level, zoning, weights and measures, licensing of sellers, and other regulatory and policy initiatives.

The Domain of Consumer Protection

Substantive Domain

Research in the consumer protection domain dates back to the early 20th century (cf. Hollander, Keep, and Dickinson, 1999; Wilkie and Moore, 2003) and can be categorized along the following three general areas (Andrews, 1999; Scammon, 1997):

1. *Application/Use of Marketing Knowledge for Consumer Protection Policy/Regulation.* This research tradition examines how marketing knowledge and skills can benefit public policy and the evaluation of regulatory efforts. For example, marketing researchers have made a significant impact on consumer protection policy in the application of advertising copy testing principles in FTC, NAD, and Lanham Act cases (Maronick, 1991). Other researchers in the marketing field have applied their expertise using meta-analyses (Franke, 2001), longitudinal studies, or numerous other analytic techniques for important consumer protection topics, such as children's advertising (Martin, 1997), warnings and disclosures (Argo and Main, 2004; Cox et al., 1997), and nutrition labeling (Ippolito and Mathios, 1991; Pappalardo and Ringold, 2000).
2. *The Influence of Consumer Protection Policy/Regulation on Marketing.* This category examines consumer protection policy's impact on marketing practice. For instance, research has examined the impact of the Americans with Disabilities Act on company and consumer responses (Baker, Stephens, and Hill, 2001) and the impact of the Nutrition Labeling Education Act on consumers, firms, advertising, and stock prices (cf. Balasubramanian and Cole, 2002; Ghani and Childs, 1999).

3. *The Study of Consumer Protection Policy/Regulation Per Se.* Beginning with early research on the Federal Food, Drug, and Cosmetic Act of 1938 (Tousley, 1941), and the Wheeler-Lea Amendment and false advertising cases (Brown, 1947a; 1947b), there have been numerous articles that have studied consumer protection policy or regulation per se. Many are consumer, economic, and legal analyses of legislation, such as the Alcohol Labeling and Education Act, Fair Credit Reporting Act, and the Nutrition Labeling and Education Act.

The substantive domain of the study of consumer protection also involves an examination of the *process* by which marketing knowledge is transferred in the formulation of consumer protection policy. As noted in Andrews (2001, Figure 1.1, p. 8), marketing knowledge and information provided by marketing consultants/academics is valued and at times serves as direct input into consumer protection agency decisions via staff and agency directors. At other times, such knowledge is integrated with that of other disciplines (such as advertising, economics, law, medicine, nutrition, psychology), legal precedent, and prior agency policy and rules to impact changes in policy. Quite often, there is a "change agent" (such as Congress or a consumer group) that serves at a catalyst for change in agency policy. In turn, such change also provides input for further consumer protection policy research and contributions to marketing knowledge. In sum, research on consumer protection issues and policies can serve to bridge important knowledge gaps between marketing academics/consultants and agency staff/practitioners.

Perspectives and Historical Development

Early Days of Consumer Protection

Although the United States embraced an open market view in its early days of existence, the term "consumer protection" dates back to 18th- and 19th-century efforts by states to regulate rates and services (such as prices, railroads), foods and drugs, and provide minimum safety standards for products and services (cf. Hollander, Keep, and Dickinson, 1999). These activities were rooted in European restrictions on mercantilism, as American colonial communities set rules and regulations for the marketplace. For example, as early as 1785, Massachusetts passed the first state-sponsored food and drug law. At the national level, the Vaccine Act of 1813, though short-lived, was the first federal law dealing with consumer protection and therapeutic substances (Swann, 1998). At the federal level, a Division of Chemistry was then established in 1862 as part of the Department of Agriculture and eventually began investigating the adulteration and misbranding of agricultural commodities. By the early 1900s, there was pressure for a more comprehensive law regulating foods and drugs, motivated by journalists uncovering marketplace hazards and Upton Sinclair's (1906) vivid description of problems in the meat-packing industry. In response, the 1906 Food and Drugs Act "prohibited the interstate transport of unlawful food and drugs under penalty of seizure of the questionable products and/or prosecution of the responsible parties" (Swann, 1998). The focus of the Act was on identifying misbranding of product labels rather than pre-market approval. The law addressed harmful chemical additives to foods and misbranding of patent medicines, although Supreme Court review ruled that false therapeutic claims were not covered by the legislation. Thus, in 1938, Congress passed the Food, Drug, and Cosmetics Act mandating pre-market approval of all new drugs and prohibiting all false therapeutic claims for drugs (e.g., Elixir Sulfanilamide contained a toxic analogue of antifreeze solvent and led to 100 deaths in 1937).

The Federal Trade Commission

In the case of the FTC, 1938 was also an important date with the passage of the Wheeler-Lea Amendment that gave the Commission a specific mandate to protect consumers from deceptive and unfair practices. Although the framers of the FTC Act had not envisioned consumer protection as part of the Commission's original mission, it nonetheless emerged as a key component of FTC enforcement and increased in prominence following World War II (Zuckerman, 1990; Winerman, 2004). However, as Brown (1947a, p. 38) notes, the Commission's success often depended "not only upon its own interpretation of the law, but also upon its ability to obtain court approval of its decisions." This difficulty is seen in the early days of the Commission (prior to Wheeler-Lea) in trying to take action against false advertising by having to show indirect injury to *competitors* (*FTC v. Sears* 1919; *FTC v. Winsted Hoisery* 1922). The court, however, had a more narrow interpretation of later cases (e.g., *FTC v. Raladam* 1931 for false anti-obesity claims) and felt direct injury to competitors was needed. This, in turn, led to the passage of the Wheeler-Lea Amendment in 1938. In her review of the first 50 years of the FTC, Zuckerman (1990) concludes that the Commission has continually dealt with difficult consumer protection policy issues, including (1) whether to employ an adversarial or negotiational approach with regulation (e.g., trade rules), (2) the expansion and contraction of FTC powers due to Congressional and judicial oversight, (3) the conflicts inherent in being pro-consumer and also protecting small business, and (4) funding and staffing concerns.

Academic Research on Consumer Protection Issues

As noted by Hollander et al. (1999), much of the early academic work on marketing and public policy dealt with the study of agricultural policy (Duddy, 1936; Agricultural Adjustment Administration), truth-in-advertising (Brown, 1947a;b), price legislation (Bader, 1944) or fair trade and chain store practices (Grether, 1947; 1948). For example, the effects of resale price maintenance and price discrimination on consumers were important topics of interest in the early 20th century. Other important areas of concern included consumer grade labeling, trademarks, credit practices, installment selling, and other consumer protection issues (cf. Bader and Hotchkiss, 1941; Cox, 1948; Hollander et al. 1999; Rewoldt, 1947). The early marketing academic interest in consumer protection issues has been characterized as somewhat situational and dependent upon prevailing interest groups and the political environment of the time (cf. Hollander et al., 1999). Many of these research efforts had focused primarily on aspects of the regulations per se (e.g., category #3 in the last section).

Later, given consumer concerns about the quality and equality of the marketplace in the 1960s, statements from a 1969 American Bar Association report and consumer advocates (e.g., Ralph Nader) that were critical of the FTC, and encouragement from key executive branch and federal agency staff for stronger consumer protection (cf. Jones, 1990), research on consumer protection issues enjoyed renewed importance in the field of marketing. Trade regulation rules against industry-wide deceptive and unfair practices were started in 1962, and the formalization of the Bureau of Consumer Protection occurred in 1970. Special attention was paid by the Commission to vulnerable consumers, such as children, the poor, and elderly. Also, the first "Public Policy & Marketing" Conference was held in 1972 and ". . . was not intended to be a vehicle for reporting the scant research findings that exist[ed] in this area, but rather to serve as a stimulus to thinking and research" on the topic (Allvine, 1973, p. ix). As such, the focus of the conference was on the need, extent, and character of regulation in the marketplace and the edited volume from the conference contained many important research frameworks, analyses, suggestions, and calls to action. (The Marketing and Public Policy Conference continued in 1989 [Wilkie and Murphy, 1990] and remains an annual event today.)

Later in the 1970s, the Commission had two major initiatives: (1) important input from marketing academics on televised advertising to children (FTC, 1978) and (2) consumer information remedies (FTC, 1979). In their review of 20 years of research in the *Journal of Public Policy & Marketing* that appears elsewhere in this volume, Sprott and Miyazaki (2002) list "protection of consumers" as the leading topical area, and include subdivisions of information provision, product performance and safety, deceptive and unfair practices, and privacy. In general, and as noted by Andrews (2001), marketing and public policy research enjoyed a resurgence in the 1990s with important research contributions, texts on legal decision making in marketing (Cohen, 1995), and edited volumes on consumer issues in public policy (cf. Bloom and Gundlach, 2001; Hill, 1996; Macklin and Carlson, 1999). Finally, the series of retrospective articles that appear elsewhere in this volume provide a historical viewpoint of consumer protection and other marketing and public policy topics and represents an important contribution to our field (Andreasen, 1997; Bloom, 1997; Greyser, 1997; Kinnear, 1997; Mazis, 1997; Wilkie, 1997).

Research Conclusions

Several conclusions have been made in the review of early research on consumer protection issues and interactions with consumer protection agencies and remain pertinent today. First, as noted by Greyser (1973), Wilkie and Gardner (1974) and Bernhardt and Stiff (1981), there can be substantial information and communication gaps between marketing researchers and those involved in public policy decisions. For example, constraints such as limited time to prepare cases, little training in the legal and economics professions in behavioral sciences, and balancing the internal validity and external validity of studies can contribute to these information and knowledge gaps. From a broader academic perspective, the field of consumer protection (as part of marketing and public policy) represents an active, but smaller subset of researchers that examine marketing and society issues (e.g., macromarketing, social marketing, marketing ethics, consumer economics, international consumer policy). As such, it has been argued that these subfields might have a stronger impact on the field of marketing if they would be better integrated with one another and studied consistently within doctoral marketing curricula (Wilkie and Moore, 2003). Certainly, however, many of these sub-areas of consumer protection research have had a profound impact on the marketing field and other disciplines and will now be examined.

KEY TOPICS OF INTEREST

The purpose of this section is to present a series of five leading topics of research in the consumer protection field: information remedies for deception and unfairness; warnings and disclosures; tobacco advertising, regulation, and anti-tobacco campaigns; children's advertising; and nutrition labeling and advertising claims. This section provides several examples of research in each topical area rather than an exhaustive set of studies. Also, a more comprehensive treatment of consumer protection research topics can be found in Andrews (2001).

Information Remedies for Deception and Unfairness

In FTC cases, as well as under the Lanham Act in which companies can sue one another in federal court, extrinsic evidence can provide important insight into potentially deceptive or unfair ad claims. Quite often, this evidence is presented in the form of advertising copy tests conducted by experts from the marketing profession. Researchers have offered generally accepted principles for such copy tests, addressing issues such as the universe, sample selected, method of questioning, experience, designs and controls, data collection, and analysis (cf. Andrews and Maronick, 1995; Maronick, 1991; Morgan, 1990; Preston, 1987; Stewart, 1995). Copy test guidelines recently have been applied to public health and social marketing campaigns as well (cf. Foley and Pechmann, 2004). Other contributions in this area have examined important changes in FTC deception policy (Ford and Calfee, 1986), as well experimental effects of misleading advertising and remedies to reduce such misleadingness (cf. Andrews, Netemeyer, and Burton, 1998; Burke et al., 1988; Johar 1995; Olson and Dover, 1978; Pechmann, 1996; Russo, Metcalf, and Stephens, 1981). Quite often, the effectiveness of such remedies may depend on consumer motivation, ability/ knowledge, or opportunity to process such information. For example, the effects of nutrition ad disclosures have been found to be dependent on nutrition knowledge levels in the case of foods perceived to be "good for you" (cf. Andrews, Burton, and Netemeyer, 2000). Finally, the marketing discipline has made important contributions in the study of remedy application, such as affirmative and triggered disclosures (Wilkie, 1985), warnings (cf. Stewart, Folkes, and Martin, 2001), and corrective advertising (Wilkie, McNeil, and Mazis, 1984; Mazis, 2001).

Warnings and Disclosures

Information disclosures can be potentially helpful in reducing misleading impressions from ad and package claims, messages, and other cues in the marketplace. A beginning point for research in this area can be found in a series of studies offered by Wilkie (1985) providing a thorough classification of FTC cases involving affirmative disclosures. However, this area poses many challenges for both advertisers and regulators. For example, Hoy and Stankey's (1993) extensive content analysis of adherence of televised ad disclosures to the FTC's "clear and conspicuous standard" (CCS) indicated that approximately 25 percent of prime time television ads in 1990 contained disclosures and none adhered to all of the CCS guidelines. A comparison of the 1990 data with 2002 in Hoy and Andrews (2004) found that approximately 67 percent of televised ads now contained disclosures, yet adherence had declined or remained unchanged for most of the CCS guidelines.

Experimental studies of print ad disclosures show that they can play an important role to consumers in highlighting related ad copy (Foxman, Muehling, and Moore, 1988). Experimental manipulation of disclosure statements in advertising has shown that evaluative disclosures can have a greater impact than relative or absolute disclosures (Andrews, Netemeyer, and Burton, 1998), yet this can depend on the type of product advertised and moderating effects such as consumer knowledge (Andrews, Burton, and Netemeyer, 2000).

"Warnings" constitutes a special class of disclosures for the purpose of alerting consumers to special risks from a product or service. A recent meta-analysis of warning label effectiveness (Argo and Main, 2004) indicates that consumer attention to warning labels is affected by vividness, location, and familiarity, but not by the type of product. However, product type did affect perceptions of risk and familiarity, and costs were found to affect behavioral compliance. (See also Cox et al., 1997 for an earlier meta-analysis.) Also, readers should examine Stewart, Folkes, and Martin's (2001) thorough examination of consumer information processing effects of warnings. More targeted reviews can be found in Andrews and Netemeyer's (1996) examination of alcohol warning labels (with addiction and policy issues) and Bettman, Payne, and Stayman's (1986) suggestions for warning labels based on consumer information processing theory. Finally, readers are encouraged to see the Spring 2004 special issue of *JPP&M* on how consumers view, evaluate, and manage risk and the associated public policy implications of such an analysis (cf. Johnson, 2004).

Tobacco Advertising, Regulation, and Anti-Tobacco Campaigns

Several consumer protection studies have examined the challenges that researchers face in evaluating the effectiveness of tobacco advertising regulation and attempts to examine cause-and-effect relationships (e.g., Does advertising contribute to smoking behavior, and if so, how and how much?) (cf., Calfee, 1986; Cohen, 1990). A direct application to the "Joe Camel" (RJR) case at the FTC can be found in the analysis of court documents (Cohen, 2000) and overall data and causal issues (Calfee, 2000) associated with the campaign. As a result of increased litigation, and proposed FDA regulations against the tobacco industry, the states initiated and succeeded in obtaining a master settlement agreement with the industry in the amount of $246 billion over 25 years (NAAG, 1998; Tobacco Free Kids, 2004). This settlement helps fund many state anti-tobacco media campaigns; however critics have noted that some states have diverted some of these funds to other uses, and have failed to use funds wisely in the fight against tobacco initiation and use by children and adolescents (Tobacco Free Kids, 2004). Subsequent experimental research in this area has helped to determine which of many anti-tobacco advertising themes served to significantly increase nonsmoking intentions of adolescents (Pechmann et al., 2003; Pechmann and Ratneshwar, 1994). Other recent work has shown the success of state anti-tobacco advertising aimed at adolescents, especially for those facing social influence (smoking peers/family) and prior trial experience (Andrews et al., 2004). In the case of adult smokers, quitting consideration is shown to be positively affected by the interaction between the number of children at home and anti-tobacco advertising beliefs about deceptive industry practices (Netemeyer, Andrews, and Burton, 2005). Other consumer research has shown the positive impact of processing interventions in anti-smoking appeals (Keller and Block, 1996), as well as young adult perceptions of addiction and risks associated with smoking (Rindfleisch and Crockett, 1999). Also, recent findings indicate that the addition of graphic visual package warnings (such as those used in Canada) to current U.S. verbal package warnings increases smokers' intentions of quitting compared with the verbal warning statements alone (Kees et al., 2006). Insight into the overall impact of tobacco advertising can be found in studies employing meta-analytic and market share estimation methods (Andrews and Franke, 1991; Pollay et al., 1996).

Children's Advertising

In the late 1970s to early 1980s, extensive hearings were held by the FTC to examine young children's understanding of televised advertising and whether such advertising was unfair (FTC, 1978). This generated substantial research interest on the part of marketing academics, including the identification of different processing capabilities of children (limited, cued, and strategic) based on storage and retrieval differences that varied by age (Roedder, 1981). Other research examples include an experimental examination of snack commercials and public service announcements (Goldberg, Gorn, and Gibson, 1978), whether young children understood the selling intent of commercials (Macklin, 1985), the formulation and use of cognitive defense strategies to promotion (Brucks, Armstrong, and Goldberg, 1988), and children's adaptive decision making (Gregan-Paxton and Roedder John, 1997). Meta-analyses of research on children's understanding of the intent of commercials (Martin, 1997) and updated findings and perspectives on children's advertising (Macklin and Carlson, 1999) have helped advance the field, as have extensive reviews of consumer socialization of children (John, 1999). Recent topics of addressing childhood obesity and the Children's Online Privacy Protection Act are beginning to generate additional research efforts. For example, the first systematic study of online food marketing to children details significant online exposure via "advergaming," viral marketing, and ad claims targeted to children (Moore, 2006). Suggestions on programmatic research and conceptual/methodological issues regarding children's advertising research can be found in work by Freistad and Wright (2005).

Nutrition Labeling and Advertising Claims

The implementation of the Nutrition Labeling and Education Act (NLEA) (1990) via the FDA food regulations and the FTC operating policy statement on food advertising generated substantial interest in the 1990s from consumer researchers. Examples of studies in this area include examining the effectiveness of alternative label formats (Levy, Fein, and Schucker, 1996), consumer processing of nutrient and health claims on packages (Ford et al., 1996), and consumer acquisition and comprehension of nutrition information (Moorman, 1996). Other examples of research in this area include the experimental variation of nutrition label format information (Burton, Biswas, and Netemeyer, 1994), examination of age effects (Burton and Andrews, 1996), experimental and field studies of nutrient, health claim, and disclosure information (Andrews, Burton, and Netemeyer, 2000; Andrews, Netemeyer, and Burton, 1998; Ippolito and Mathios, 1991; Roe, Levy, and Derby, 1999), content analysis and tracking reviews (Pappalardo and Ringold, 2000), and interactions between claims and labeling (Keller et al., 1997; Kozup, Creyer, and Burton, 2003; Mitra et al., 1999; Szykman, Bloom, and Levy, 1997). A common theme of many of the studies above is that consumer characteristics (such as motivation, nutrition knowledge, age, opportunity) can drive the processing and effectiveness of nutrition labeling and claim information. For example, a pre-post NLEA analysis of search activity for nutrition information indicated that highly motivated and less knowledgeable consumers benefited more from the changes (Balasubramanian and Cole, 2002; see also Derby and Levy, 2001 on tracking awareness). The recent national focus on the alarming increase in cases of obesity will no doubt generate much further research interest in this area.

Emerging Areas

One additional area that has been emerging of late is that of *consumer privacy* associated with the notice, consent, access, and security of personal information, especially in an online environment (cf. Milne, 2001; Culnan, 2000). Recent policy issues associated with the national do-not-call list, peer-to-peer file sharing, and e-mail spam are likely to generate research interest. Also, as noted in a special section of the Fall 2002 issue of *JPPM*, work is emerging on the role of the regulatory policy in *direct-to-consumer prescription drug advertising*. In addition, attention is beginning to develop on *covert marketing activities* (e.g., product placement, buzz marketing, viral marketing), as indicated by a planned Spring 2008 special issue of *JPP&M*. Finally, it is suggested that readers see Andrews (2001) for broader theoretical contributions and applications to consumer protection research. Interested readers also are directed to other categorizations of consumer protection topics that differ from those presented here (cf. Sprott and Miyazaki, 2002; Wilkie and Moore, 2003).

Delving Deeper into Consumer Protection: Selected Readings

Seminal/Classic Article

A major criterion in the selection of the seminal or classic article in this chapter is that the article should take a broader perspective in motivating the consumer protection field to strengthen their overall impact or contribution to the discipline. The article selected, Wilkie and Gardner's "The Role of Marketing Research in Public Policy Decision Making" (*Journal of Marketing* 1974), does a wonderful job in this respect by offering clear suggestions to researchers and public policy staff to help close the research understanding gap between the two disciplines. Erroneous assumptions about consumer processing are discussed, as well as suggestions for researchers to better understand policy needs and efforts in order to make their research more relevant to agency staff.

Chapters on Consumer Protection

A common theme among the four example articles selected is that they address important consumer information processing issues associated with consumer protection, as well as examining some of the major consumer protection topics previously discussed. These articles also stand out among the most popular readings rated by graduate students enrolled in marketing and public policy coursework. The selections provide clearly articulated objectives and implications, as well as empirical evidence for their arguments.

The first selected article is Russo, Metcalf, and Stephens' "Identifying Misleading Advertising" (*Journal of Consumer Research* 1981). This article provides an excellent comparison to the FTC's process in advertising deception. Three approaches to measuring deceptive advertising (fraud, falsity, and misleadingness) are first discussed and evidence from specific ads is then presented. The challenge of limited consumer knowledge and the FTC's role in developing true corrected versions of the ads are important issues to discuss in class as well. Overall, this is one of the best articles to generate discussion on the nature of deceptive advertising as well as helping to truly understand measurement issues associated with consumer processing of such ads. The second article is Wilkie, McNeil, and Mazis' "Marketing's 'Scarlet Letter': The Theory and Practice of Corrective Advertising," (*Journal of Marketing* 1984). This classic article provides one of the best and most complete analyses of corrective advertising, including an in-depth examination of the FTC program and early cases, its supporting theory, and clear recommendations for changing FTC policy in this area.

Pechmann, Zhao, Goldberg, and Reibling's "What to Convey in Antismoking Advertisements for Adolescents: The Use of Protection Motivation Theory to Identify Effective Message Themes" (*Journal of Marketing* 2003) is the third selection. This article is extremely important to efforts by many state governments in the development of anti-smoking campaigns as a result of the Master Settlement with the industry (NAAG 1998). Findings indicate that three ("Endangers Others," "Smokers' Negative Life Circumstances," and "Refusal Skills Role Model") of seven message themes increased adolescents' nonsmoking intentions versus a control. Other important dependent measures (health risk perceptions, self-efficacy) are also examined across the message themes. Finally, the fourth article selected is Block, Morwitz, Putsis, and Sen's "Assessing the Impact of Antidrug Advertising on Adolescent Drug Consumption: Results From a Behavioral Economic Model" (*American Journal of Public Health* 2002). This study provides an important analysis of the effectiveness of the first four years of national anti-drug advertising from the Partnership for a Drug-Free America (PDFA) through their Partnership Attitude Tracking Survey (PATS). The study features a careful methodology including a multi-wave analysis controlling for prior drug use and demographic variables. Findings indicate that recall of anti-drug advertising was associated with a lower probability of illegal drug use, not with a decision of how much of a drug to use.

Policy in Progress: Illustrative Action Issue

Finally, for the "hot topic" reading, there is perhaps no other public policy topic more pressing than the alarming increase in those who are overweight and obese in the United States. Currently, 65 percent of all Americans are overweight (BMI > 25) and 30 percent are obese (BMI > 30), and the trend is worsening (CDC, 2004). Fifteen percent of all children aged 6–19 are overweight, double the rate 20 years ago (CDC, 2004). Research has linked being overweight and obese to a multitude of medical problems. As almost half of the food dollar is spent on foods consumed away from home, and because such foods have much higher caloric content, the Center for Science in the Public Interest (CSPI, 2003) has encouraged state and local legislatures to require a more complete disclosure of nutritional content on restaurant menus. This initiative has emerged in the form of the MEAL (Menu Education and Labeling) Act that has been proposed and discussed in Congress. Thus, the "hot topic" paper for this chapter is CSPI's (2003), "Anyone's

Guess: The Need for Nutrition Labeling at Fast Food and Other Chain Restaurants." This policy piece provides a clear discussion of the impact of restaurant foods on American diets and offers several recommendations for menu labeling and examples of model menus. Such policy items can provide important input for subsequent research on the topic (Kozup et al., 2003), and in turn, offer consumer groups better extrinsic evidence. For other social marketing ideas for bringing about behavioral change in reversing the overweight and obesity trend, readers are encouraged to see the Policy in Progress section in Alan Andreasen's chapter in this volume.

Conclusions

INSIGHTS IN EXAMINING RESEARCH ON CONSUMER PROTECTION TOPICS

In studying research on consumer protection issues, there are several issues that might be considered in the evaluation process. First, a thorough examination of the multiple views and perspectives on an issue is critical, as interested parties such as attorneys, economists, consumer activists, and industry representatives are likely to have differing viewpoints and backgrounds. As noted by Mazis (1980, pp. 5–8), consumer protection can sometimes be viewed myopically by each discipline, with behavioral scientists focusing on maximizing information processing benefits, economists focusing on cost minimization to the market and sellers, attorneys seeking to minimize violations of law or policy, and consumer activists attempting to maximize information flow. (As noted in Scammon [1977], information overload clearly can be a problem with this latter perspective.) Interaction with all parties on an issue from workshops, conferences, trade reports, etc. can help form a more balanced, informed, and objective view of the problem.

A second consideration is to try to apply the right balance between *internal and external validity* in the relevant research. Achieving both insight as to causal effects (internal validity) and the generalization/relevance of effects to the policy situation (external validity) is an important but often difficult undertaking (Cook and Campbell, 1979). That is, a theoretical piece without relevance to policy or, conversely, research without a firm grounding in theory or the policy problem can be viewed as being incomplete. A third consideration is to search for *methodology that is rigorous and relevant* to the policy issue. Is the design rigorous enough to infer causality if such claims are made? Does the approach follow generally-accepted principles for the research methodology? Is there adequate pretesting of the design, manipulated variables (if any), and stimuli? To enhance external validity, are realistic stimuli, procedures, and measures used? Is the sample representative of the population studied for the policy issue?

A final consideration is to try to think through *possible implications and contributions of the research to public policy* even before any research is conducted. That is, *why* is this research important to the policy debate or issue at hand? What are possible implications of the research to current and future public policy? The idea is to try to lead rather than lag policy issues in research contributions (Wilkie and Gardner, 1974). A review of agency workshops and points of contention by consumer activist groups (such as the Center for Science in the Public Interest; Public Citizen) can help in this regard.

STATE OF FIELD AND FUTURE DIRECTIONS

The consumer protection field and its research tradition are enjoying a renewed interest that began in the early 1990s and has continued to date, although challenges for the field certainly exist as noted previously. In terms of research productivity, consumer protection topics have appeared recently in a wide variety of top outlets, such as *Journal of Marketing, American Journal of Public Health, Journal of Public Policy & Marketing, Journal of Advertising, Journal of Consumer Affairs,* among others. The annual Marketing & Public Policy Conference and Marketing & Society special interest group of the AMA provide important forums for the continued discussion of consumer protection research. No doubt, emerging topics such as childhood obesity (Moore, 2006), violent entertainment, and children (Grier, 2001), graphic tobacco warnings (Kees et al., 2006), and new threats to privacy (Milne, 2001) are among many issues that will continued to be studied in the near future. For example, will changes to nutrition facts panels, menu disclosures, and caloric claims in helping to combat obesity ultimately depend on the consumer's nutrition knowledge/motivation on calories/obesity? Can peer-to-peer file sharing risks (data security, unwanted exposure, spyware/adware, copyright infringement) be effectively communicated to consumers via online disclosures? Also, there exists a wide variety of federal agencies with consumer protection missions that currently are understudied (see www.consumer.gov to learn more about these agencies and recent consumer protection information).

Questions for Discussion

In general, it is hoped that the following discussion questions will prompt readers to extend their thinking on knowledge generation, integration, and applications to consumer protection topics. The following represents a sample of many possible questions that have been used successfully in marketing and public policy coursework. They cover many of the key interest areas on consumer protection topics previously discussed in this chapter.

1. *Nutrition and obesity.* Can regulatory initiatives from the FDA and FTC help contribute to the war on obesity? Specifically, will proposed changes to the Nutrition Facts Panels highlighting calories and making serving sizes more realistic (e.g., 20 ounce bottle of soda) help in this battle? Should the FTC be more proactive in regulating false caloric/low carb claims in advertising? Can disclosures in advertising be effective in reducing misperceptions or do consumers' nutrition knowledge, motivation, and other factors

need to be taken into account? (See research in the Nutrition Labeling and Advertising Claims section in this chapter.)

2. *Prescription drug marketing.* Do you agree with a strict regulation of prescription drugs on the United States even though Canadian imports from the very same manufacturing facilities can be sent to U.S. seniors for 40 percent of the cost? What do you think about recent direct-to-consumer prescription drug advertising? Should celebrities be used in such ads? Are there any other distractions in the ads reducing the processing of key warning information? How effective are disclosures about possible drug side effects in such ads? Do the recent amounts spent on such advertising contribute to higher prescription drug pricing?

3. *Tobacco regulation.* Is the $246 billion settlement of the states with the tobacco industry working? Should states be forced to use the settlement money on anti-tobacco initiatives as it was intended or should they be allowed to decide the best use for the money? (See http://tobaccofreekids.org/reports/settlements) What role does cigarette advertising play in influencing kids to smoke (Calfee, 2000; Cohen, 2000)? Could new graphic visuals and warnings on cigarette packages used in Canada, Australia, and the EU work here in the United States (Kees et al., 2006)? Also, discuss the influence of cigarette advertising on sales and the influence of cigarette advertising throughout stages of information processing. What are the methodological problems in assessing the effect of tobacco advertising (Cohen, 1990)?

4. *Advertising copy testing in litigation or for public health campaigns.* What methodological issues should be considered in the design of an advertising copy test for litigation involving deceptive or unfair advertising? For major public health campaigns? What problems might be experienced in the process? Discuss the tradeoffs inherent in the choice of different study designs, sampling procedures, measures, and control groups (see Andrews and Maronick, 1995; Foley and Pechmann, 2004; Maronick, 1991).

5. *Corrective advertising.* In theory, corrective advertising represents a potentially valuable remedy for regulating deceptive advertising. In practice, however, corrective advertising must perform a very delicate balancing act by being strong enough without being too strong. Explain the nature of this dilemma (Mazis, 2001; Wilkie et al., 1984).

6. *Warnings and disclosures.* Under what specific circumstances are product warnings and disclosures effective? Describe contributions from theory and research on fear appeals, information processing, and persuasion as they apply to the implementation of product warnings and disclosures (see previous section on "Warnings and Disclosures" in this chapter). Also, provide arguments for and against the use of warnings for cigarettes, cigars, over-the-counter drugs, children's cribs, power tools, household cleaning products, electrical equipment, and alcoholic beverages (see www.cpsc.gov for recent examples). Do the same for specific medical informed-consent information (such as for immunizations).

As a final note, insight from Wilkie and Gardner (1974) is especially appropriate as we conclude this chapter on consumer protection. As they suggest (p. 38), "Marketers should recognize that public policy will continue to be created, with or without their research." As it was when the field of consumer protection first emerged, it is incumbent on us to help guide efforts in consumer protection and public policy in general. It is hoped that this chapter will help provide students and researchers with the first step in making this effort a reality.

References

Allvine, Fred C. 1973. "Preface," in *Public Policy and Marketing Practices*. Fred C. Allvine (ed.) Chicago, IL: American Marketing Association, ix.

Andreasen, Alan R. 1997. "From Ghetto Marketing to Social Marketing: Bringing Social Relevance to Mainstream Marketing," *Journal of Public Policy & Marketing*, 16 (Spring): 129–131.

Andrews, J. Craig. 1999. "Editor's Statement," *Journal of Public Policy & Marketing*, 18 (Spring): 1–2.

____. 2001. "The Use of Marketing Knowledge in the Formulating and Enforcing Consumer Protection Policy," in *Handbook of Marketing and Society*. Paul N. Bloom and Gregory T. Gundlach, (eds.) Thousand Oaks, CA: Sage Publications, 1–33.

____, Scot Burton, and Richard G. Netemeyer. 2000. "Are Some Comparative Nutrition Claims Misleading? The Role of Nutrition Knowledge, Ad Claim Type, and Disclosure Conditions," *Journal of Advertising*, 29 (Fall): 29–42.

____ and Thomas J. Maronick. 1995. "Advertising Research Issues from *FTC versus Stouffer Foods Corporation*," *Journal of Public Policy & Marketing*, 14 (Fall): 301–309.

____ and Richard G. Netemeyer. 1996. "Alcohol Warning Label Effects: Socialization, Addiction, and Public Policy Issues," in *Marketing and Consumer Research in the Public Interest*, Ronald Paul Hill, (ed.) Thousand Oaks, CA: Sage, 153–175.

____, ____, and Scot Burton. 1998. "Consumer Generalization of Nutrient Content Claims in Advertising," *Journal of Marketing*, 62 (October): 62–75.

____, ____, ____, D. Paul Moberg, and Ann Christiansen. 2004. "Understanding Adolescent Intentions to Smoke: An Examination of Relationships Among Social Influence, Prior Trial Behavior, and Anti-tobacco Campaign Advertising," *Journal of Marketing*, 68 (July): 110–123.

Andrews, Rick and George R. Franke. 1991. "The Determinants of Cigarette Consumption: A Meta-Analysis," *Journal of Public Policy & Marketing*, 10 (Spring): 81–100.

Argo, Jennifer J. and Kelley J. Main. 2004. "Meta-Analyses of the Effectiveness of Warning Labels," *Journal of Public Policy & Marketing*, 23 (Fall): 193–208.

Bader, Louis. 1944. "Recent Price Legislation and Economic Theory," *Journal of Marketing*, 3 (2): 166–172.

____ and George B. Hotchkiss. 1941. "Attitudes of Teachers of Marketing Toward Consumer Grade Labeling," *Journal of Marketing*, 6 (3): 274–279.

Baker, Stacy Menzel, Debra Lynn Stephens, and Ronald Paul Hill. 2001. "Marketplace Experiences of Consumers with Visual Impairments: Beyond the Americans with Disabilities Act," *Journal of Public Policy & Marketing*, 20 (Fall): 215–224.

Balasubramanian, Siva K. and Catherine Cole. 2002. "Consumers' Search and Use of Nutrition Information: The Challenge and Promise of the Nutrition Labeling Education Act," *Journal of Marketing*, 66 (July): 112–127.

Bernhardt, Kenneth L. and Ronald Stiff. 1981. "Public Policy Update: Perspective in the Federal Trade Commission," in *Advances in Consumer Research,* 8. Kent B. Monroe, (ed.) Ann Arbor, MI: Association for Consumer Research, 452–454.

Bettman, James R., John W. Payne, and Richard Staelin. 1986. "Cognitive Considerations in Designing Effective Labels for Presenting Risk Information," *Journal of Public Policy & Marketing,* 5, 1–28.

Block, Lauren G., Vicki G. Morwitz, William P. Putsis, and Subrata K. Sen. 2002. "Assessing the Impact of Antidrug Advertising on Adolescent Drug Consumption: Results From a Behavioral Economic Model," *American Journal of Public Health,* 92 (8): 1346–1351.

Bloom, Paul N. 1997. "Field of Marketing and Public Policy: Introduction and Overview," *Journal of Public Policy & Marketing,* 16 (Spring): 126–128.

___ and Gregory T. Gundlach. 2001. *Handbook of Marketing and Society.* Thousand Oaks, CA: Sage Publications.

Brown, William F. 1947a. "The Federal Tarde Commission and False Advertising: I," *Journal of Marketing,* 12 (July): 38–46.

___. 1947b. "The Federal Trade Commission and False Advertising: II," *Journal of Marketing,* 12 (October): 193–201.

Brucks, Merrie, Gary T. Armstrong, and Marvin E. Goldberg. 1988. "Children's Use of Cognitive Defenses against Television Advertising: A Cognitive Defense Approach," *Journal of Consumer Research,* 14 (4): 471–482.

Burke, Raymond R., Wayne S. DeSarbo, Richard L. Oliver, and Thomas S. Robertson. 1988. "Deception by Implication: An Experimental Investigation," *Journal of Consumer Research,* 14 (March): 483–494.

Burton, Scot and J. Craig Andrews. 1996. "An Examination of Age, Product Nutrition, and Nutrition Label Effects on Consumer Perceptions and Product Evaluations," *The Journal of Consumer Affairs,* 30 (Summer): 68–89.

___, Abe Biswas, and Richard G. Netemeyer. 1994. "Effects of Alternative Nutrition Label Formats and Nutrition Reference Information on Consumer Perceptions, Comprehension, and Product Evaluations," *Journal of Public Policy & Marketing,* 13 (Spring): 36–47.

Calfee, John E. 1986. "The Ghost of Cigarette Advertising Past," *Regulation,* November–December, 35–45.

___. 2000. "The Historical Significance of Joe Camel," *Journal of Public Policy & Marketing,* 19 (Fall): 168–182.

Center for Science in the Public Interest (CSPI). 2003. "Anyone's Guess: The Need for Nutrition Labeling at Fast-Food and Other Chain Restaurants," Washington, DC: CSPI, 1–22+ [http://www.cspinet.org/restaurantreport.pdf].

Centers for Disease Control and Prevention (CDC). 2004. "Overweight and Obesity," U.S. Department of Health and Human Services, September [http://www.cdc.gov/nccdphp/dnpa/obesity/index.htm].

Cohen, Dorothy. 1995. *Legal Issues in Marketing Decision Making.* Cincinnati, OH: South-Western Publishing.

Cohen, Joel B. 1990. "Charting a Public Policy Agenda for Cigarettes," in *Marketing and Advertising Regulation: The Federal Trade Commission in the 1990s.* Patrick E. Murphy and William L. Wilkie, (eds.) Notre Dame, IN: University of Notre Dame Press, 234–254.

___. 2000. "Playing to Win: Marketing and Public Policy at Odds over Joe Camel," *Journal of Public Policy & Marketing,* 19 (Fall): 155–167.

Cook, Thomas D. and Donald T. Campbell. 1979. *Quasi-Experimentation: Design and Analysis Issues for Field Settings.* Boston, MA: Houghton Mifflin.

Cox, Eli P. III, Michael S. Wogalter, Sara L. Stokes, and Elizabeth J. Tipton Murff. 1997. "Do Product Warnings Increase Safe Behavior? A Meta-Analysis," *Journal of Public Policy & Marketing,* 16 (Fall): 195–204.

Cox, Reavis. 1948. *The Economics of Installment Buying,* New York, NY: The Ronald Press Company.

Culnan, Mary J. 2000. "Protecting Privacy Online: Is Self-Regulation Working?" *Journal of Public Policy & Marketing,* 19 (Spring): 20–26.

Derby, Brenda M. and Alan S. Levy. 2001. "Do Food Labels Work? Gauging the Effectiveness of Food Labels Pre- and Post-NLEA," in *Handbook of Marketing and Society.* Paul N. Bloom and Gregory T. Gundlach, (eds.) Thousand Oaks, CA: Sage Publications, 372–398.

Duddy, Edward A. 1936. "Comments on 'The Consumer and the Agricultural Adjustment Administration'," *Journal of Marketing,* 1 (1): 9–12.

Federal Trade Commission (1919) v. Sears, Roebuck & Company, 258 F. 307 (7th Circuit).

___ (1922) v. Winsted Hoisery Company, 258 U.S. 483.

___ (1931) v. Raladam Company, 283 U.S. 643.

___ (1939), *Annual Report of the Federal Trade Commission:* Washington, DC: FTC.

___ (1978), *Staff Report on Televised Advertising to Children,* Washington, DC: FTC, February, 1–346+.

___ (1979), *Consumer Information Remedies: Policy Review Session,* Washington, DC: FTC, June 1, 1–320+.

Foley, Diane and Cornelia Pechmann. 2004. "The National Youth Anti-Drug Media Campaign Copy Test System," *Social Marketing Quarterly,* 10 (Summer): 34–42.

Ford, Gary T. and John E. Calfee 1986. "Recent Developments in FTC Policy on Deception," *Journal of Marketing,* 50 (July): 82–103.

___, Manoj Hastak, Anusree Mitra, and Debra J. Ringold. 1996. "Can Consumers Interpret Nutrition Information in the Presence of a Health Claim? A Laboratory Investigation," *Journal of Public Policy & Marketing,* 15 (Spring): 16–27.

Foxman, Ellen, Darrel D. Muehling, and Patrick A. Moore. 1988. "Disclaimer Footnotes in Ads: Discrepancies between Purpose and Performance," *Journal of Public Policy & Marketing,* 7, 127–137.

Franke, George. 2001. "Applications of Meta-Analysis for Marketing and Public Policy: A Review," *Journal of Public Policy & Marketing,* 20 (Fall): 186–200.

Freistad, Marian and Peter Wright. 2005. "The Next Generation: Research for Twenty-First Century Public Policy on Children and Advertising," *Journal of Public Policy & Marketing,* 23 (Fall): 183–185.

Ghani, WaQar I. and Nancy M. Childs. 1999. "Wealth Effects of the Passage of the Nutrition Labeling and Education Act of 1990 for Large U.S. Multinational Food Corporations," *Journal of Public Policy & Marketing,* 18 (Fall): 147–158.

Goldberg, Marvin E., Gerald J. Gorn, and Wendy Gibson. 1978. "TV Messages for Snack and Breakfast Foods: Do They Influence Children's Preferences?" *Journal of Consumer Research,* 5 (September): 73–81.

Gregan-Paxton, Jennifer and Deborah Roedder John. 1997. "The Emergence of Adaptive Decision Making in Children," *Journal of Consumer Research,* 24 (June): 43–56.

Grether, E.T. 1947. "The Federal Trade Commission Versus Retail Price Maintenance," *Journal of Marketing,* 12 (July): 1–13.

___. 1948. "In Defense of 'Fair Trade': A Rejoinder," *Journal of Marketing,* 13 (July): 85–88.

Greyser, Stephen A. 1973. "Public Policy and the Marketing Practitioner: Toward Bridging the Gap," in *Public Policy and Marketing Practices*. Fred C. Allvine, (ed.) Chicago, IL: American Marketing Association, 219–232.

___. 1997. "Consumer Research and the Public Policy Process: Then and Now," *Journal of Public Policy and Marketing*, 16 (Spring): 137–138.

Grier, Sonya A. 2001. "The Federal Trade Commission's Report on the Marketing of Violent Entertainment to Youth: Developing Policy-Tuned Research," *Journal of Public Policy & Marketing*, 20 (Spring): 123–132.

Hill, Ronald Paul. 1996. *Marketing and Consumer Research in the Public Interest*, Thousand Oaks, CA: Sage Publications.

Hollander, Stanley C., William W. Keep, and Roger Dickinson. 1999. "Marketing Public Policy and the Evolving Role of Marketing Academics: A Historical Perspective," *Journal of Public Policy & Marketing*, 18 (Spring): 265–269.

Hoy, Mariea Grubbs and J. Craig Andrews. 2004. "Adherence of Prime-Time Televised Advertising Disclosures to the "Clear and Conspicuous" Standard: 1990 Versus 2002," *Journal of Public Policy & Marketing*, 23 (Fall): 170–182.

___ and Michael J. Stankey. 1993. "Structural Characteristics of Televised Advertising Disclosures: A Comparison with the FTC Clear and Conspicuous Standard," *Journal of Advertising*, 22 (2): 47–58.

Ippolito, Pauline M. and Alan D. Mathios. 1991. "Health Claims in Food Marketing: Evidence on Knowledge and Behavior in the Cereal Market," *Journal of Public Policy & Marketing*, 10 (1): 15–32.

Johar, Gita Venkataramani. 1995. "Consumer Involvement and Deception from Implied Advertising Claims," *Journal of Marketing Research*, 32 (August): 267–279.

John, Deborah Roedder. 1999. "Consumer Socialization of Children: A Retrospective Look at Twenty-Five Years of Research," *Journal of Consumer Research*, 26 (December): 183–213.

Johnson, Eric. 2004. "Rediscovering Risk," *Journal of Public Policy & Marketing*, 23 (Spring): 2–6.

Jones, Mary Gardiner. 1990. "Marketing Academics at the FTC: Reflections and Recommendations," in *Marketing and Advertising Regulation: The Federal Trade Commission in the 1990s*. Patrick E. Murphy and William L. Wilkie, (eds.) Notre Dame, IN: University of Notre Dame Press, 216–220.

Kees, Jeremy, Scot Burton, J. Craig Andrews, and John Kozup. 2006. "Tests of Graphic Visuals and Cigarette Package Warning Combinations: Implications for the Framework Convention on Tobacco Control," *Journal of Public Policy & Marketing*, 25 (Fall): forthcoming.

Keller, Punam Anand and Lauren Goldberg Block. 1996. "Increasing the Persuasiveness of Fear Appeals: The Effect of Arousal and Elaboration," *Journal of Consumer Research*, 22 (March): 448–459.

Keller, Scott B., Mike Landry, Jeanne Olson, Anne M. Velliquette, Scot Burton, and J. Craig Andrews. 1997. "The Effects of Nutrition Package Claims, Nutrition Facts Panels, and Motivation to Process Nutrition Information on Consumer Product Evaluations," *Journal of Public Policy & Marketing*, 16 (Fall): 256–269.

Kinnear, Thomas C. 1997. "An Historic Perspective on the Quantity and Quality of Marketing and Public Policy Research," *Journal of Public Policy & Marketing*, 16 (Spring): 144–146.

Kozup, John C., Elizabeth H. Creyer, and Scot Burton. 2003. "Making Healthful Food Choices: The Influence of Health Claims and Nutrition Information on Consumer Evaluations of Packaged Food Products and Restaurant Menu Items," *Journal of Marketing*, 67 (April): 19–34.

Levy, Alan S., Sara B. Fein, and Raymond E. Schucker. 1996. "Performance Characteristics of Seven Nutrition Label Formats," *Journal of Public Policy & Marketing,* 15 (1): 1–15.

Macklin, M. Carole. 1985. "Do Young Children Understand the Selling Intent of Commercials?" *Journal of Consumer Affairs,* 19 (2): 293–304.

___ and Les Carlson. 1999 *Advertising to Children: Concepts and Controversies.* Thousand Oaks, CA: Sage Publications.

Maronick, Thomas J. 1991. "Copy Tests in FTC Deception Cases: Guidelines for Researchers," *Journal of Advertising Research,* 31 (December): 9–17.

Martin, Mary C. 1997. "Children's Understanding of the Intent of Advertising: A Meta-Analysis," *Journal of Public Policy & Marketing,* 16 (Fall): 205–216.

Mazis, Michael B. 1980. "An Overview of Product Labeling and Health Risks," in *Banbury Report 6: Product Labeling and Health Risks.* Louis A. Morris, Michael B. Mazis, and Ivan Barofsky, (eds.) Cold Spring Harbor, NY: Cold Spring Harbor Laboratory, 3–11.

___. 1997. "Marketing and Public Policy: Prospects for the Future," *Journal of Public Policy & Marketing,* 16 (Spring): 139–143.

___. 2001. "*FTC v. Novartis*: The Return of Corrective Advertising?" *Journal of Public Policy & Marketing,* 20 (Spring): 114–122.

Milne, George R. 2001. "The Effectiveness of Self-Regulated Privacy Protection: A Review and Framework for Future Research," in *Handbook of Marketing and Society.* Paul N. Bloom and Gregory T. Gundlach, (eds.) Thousand Oaks, CA: Sage Publications, 462–485.

Mitra, Anusree, Manoj Hastak, Gary T. Ford, and Debra Jones Ringold. 1999. "Can the Educationally Disadvantaged Interpret the FDA-Mandated Nutrition Facts Panel in the Presence of an Implied Health Claim?" *Journal of Public Policy & Marketing,* 18 (Spring): 106–117.

Moore, Elizabeth S. 2006. *It's Child's Play: Advergaming and the Online Marketing of Food to Children.* Menlo Park, CA: Kaiser Family Foundation, July: 1–57.

Moorman, Christine. 1996. "A Quasi-Experiment to Assess the Consumer and Informational Determinants of Nutrition Information Processing Activities: The Case of the Nutrition Labeling and Education Act," *Journal of Public Policy & Marketing,* 15 (Spring): 28–44.

Morgan, Fred W. 1990. "Judicial Standards for Survey Research: An Update and Guidelines," *Journal of Marketing,* 54 (January): 59–70.

National Association of Attorneys General (1998), *Master Settlement Agreement,* November 23, 1–118+ [http://www.naag.org/upload/1032468605_cigmsa.pdf].

Netemeyer, Richard G., J. Craig Andrews, and Scot Burton. 2005. "The Effects of Anti-Smoking Advertising-Based Beliefs on Adult Smokers' Consideration of Quitting," *American Journal of Public Health,* 95 (June): 1062–1066.

Nutrition Labeling and Education Act (1990), Public Law 101-535, 21 USC 301 (November 8).

Olson, Jerry C. and Philip A. Dover. 1978. "Cognitive Effects of Deceptive Advertising," *Journal of Marketing Research,* 15 (February): 29–38.

Pappalardo, Janis Kohanski, and Debra Jones Ringold. 2000. "Regulating Commercial Speech in a Dynamic Environment: Forty Years of Margarine and Oil Advertising Before the NLEA," *Journal of Public Policy & Marketing,* 19 (Spring): 74–92.

Pechmann, Cornelia. 1996. "Do Consumers Overgeneralize One-Sided Comparative Price Claims, and Are More Stringent Regulations Needed?" *Journal of Marketing Research,* 33 (May): 150–162.

___ and S. Ratneshwar. 1994. "The Effects of Antismoking and Cigarette Advertising on Adolescents' Perceptions of Peers Who Smoke," *Journal of Consumer Research,* 21 (September): 236–251.

___, Guangzhi Zhao, Marvin E. Goldberg, and Ellen Thomas Reibling. 2003. "What to Convey in Antismoking Advertisements for Adolescents: The Use of Protection Motivation Theory to Identify Effective Message Themes," *Journal of Marketing,* 67 (April): 1–18.

Pollay, Richard W., S. Siddarth, Michael Siegel, Anne Haddix, Robert Merritt, Gary A. Giovino, and Michael Ericksen. 1996. "The Last Straw? Cigarette Advertising and Realized Market Shares among Youths and Adults: 1979–1993," *Journal of Marketing,* 60 (April): 1–16.

Preston, Ivan L. 1987. "Extrinsic Evidence in Federal Trade Commission Deceptiveness Cases," *Columbia Business Law Review,* 633–694.

Rewoldt, Stewart H. 1947. "The Assignment of Trade-Marks," *Journal of Marketing,* 12 (4), 483–487.

Rindfleisch, Aric and David Crockett. 1999. "Cigarette Smoking and Perceived Risk: A Multidimensional Investigation," *Journal of Public Policy & Marketing,* 18 (Fall): 159–171.

Roe, Brian, Alan S. Levy, and Brenda M. Derby. 1999. "The Impact of Health Claims on Consumer Search and Product Evaluation Outcomes: Results from FDA Experimental Data," *Journal of Public Policy & Marketing,* 18 (Spring): 89–105.

Roedder, Deborah L. 1981 "Age Differences in Children's Responses to Television Advertising: An Information-Processing Approach," *Journal of Consumer Research,* 8 (September): 144–153.

Russo, J. Edward, Barbara L. Metcalf, and Debra Stephens. 1981. "Identifying Misleading Advertising," *Journal of Consumer Research,* 8 (September): 119–131.

Scammon, Debra L. 1977. "'Information Load' and Consumers," *Journal of Consumer Research,* 4 (December): 148–155.

___. 1997. "Journal of Public Policy & Marketing," "Meet the Editors" session presentation at the 1997 Summer American Marketing Association Educators' Conference, Chicago, IL: August.

Sinclair, Upton Beall. 1906. *The Jungle,* New York, NY: Doubleday and Page.

Stewart, David W. 1995. "Deception, Materiality, and Survey Research: Some Lessons From Kraft," *Journal of Public Policy & Marketing,* 14 (Spring): 15–28.

___, Valerie S. Folkes, and Ingrid Martin. 2001. "Consumer Response to Warnings and Other Types of Product Hazard Information: Future Public Policy and Research Directions," in *Handbook of Marketing and Society.* Paul N. Bloom and Gregory T. Gundlach, (eds.) Thousand Oaks, CA: Sage Publications, 335–371.

Sprott, David E. and Anthony D. Miyazaki. 2002. "Two Decades of Contributions to Marketing and Public Policy: An Analysis of Research Published in *Journal of Public Policy & Marketing,* 21 (Spring): 105–125.

Swann, John P. 1998. "History of the FDA," Rockville, MD: U.S. Food and Drug Administration [http://www.fda.gov/oc/history/historyoffda/default.htm].

Szykman, Lisa R., Paul N. Bloom, and Alan S. Levy. 1997. "A Proposed Model of the Use of Package Claims and Nutrition Labels," *Journal of Public Policy & Marketing,* 16 (Fall): 228–241.

Tobacco Free Kids. 2004. "A Broken Promise to Our Children: The 1998 State Tobacco Settlement Six Years Later," December 2, Washington, DC: Campaign for Tobacco Free Kids, 1–141 [http://www.tobaccofreekids.org/reports/settlements/2005/fullreport.pdf].

Tousley, Rayburn D. 1941. "The Federal Food, Drug, and Cosmetic Act of 1938," *Journal of Marketing,* 5 (January): 259–269.

Wilkie, William L. 1985. "Affirmative Disclosure at the FTC: Objectives for the Remedy and Outcome of Past Orders," *Journal of Public Policy & Marketing,* 4: 91–111.

___. 1997. "Developing Research on Public Policy and Marketing," 16 (Spring): 132–137.

___ and David M. Gardner. 1974. "The Role of Marketing Research in Public Policy Decision Making," *Journal of Marketing*, 38 (January): 38–47.

___, Dennis B. McNeil, and Michael B. Mazis. 1984. "Marketing's 'Scarlet Letter': The Theory and Practice of Corrective Advertising," *Journal of Marketing*, 48 (Spring): 11–31.

___ and Elizabeth S. Moore. 2003. "Scholarly Research in Marketing: Exploring the "4 Eras" of Thought Development," *Journal of Public Policy & Marketing*, 22 (Fall): 116–146.

___ and Patrick E. Murphy. 1990. *Marketing and Advertising Regulation: The Federal Trade Commission in the 1990s,* Notre Dame, IN: University of Notre Dame Press.

Winerman, Marc. 2004. "A Brief History of the Federal Trade Commission," 90th Anniversary Program, Washington, DC: FTC, 6–9. [http://www.ftc.gov/ftc/history/90thAnniv_Program.pdf].

Zuckerman, Mary Ellen. 1990. "The Federal Trade Commission in Historical Perspective: The First Fifty Years," in *Marketing and Advertising Regulation: The Federal Trade Commission in the 1990s.* Patrick E. Murphy and William L. Wilkie, (eds.) Notre Dame, IN: University of Notre Dame Press.

THE ROLE OF MARKETING RESEARCH IN PUBLIC POLICY DECISION MAKING

William L. Wilkie and David M. Gardner

How Can Marketing Research Aid the Public Policy Maker?

Government agencies are making increasingly active attempts to assure and maintain a "fair competitive environment" for consumers. One important characteristic of these public policy activities has been an underutilization of the skills and insights of researchers in marketing and consumer behavior. This article explores reasons for this underrepresentation and proposes means by which marketing research can contribute to future policy decisions.

Although many points made here can apply across government agencies, attention will focus upon the Federal Trade Commission (FTC), where the authors recently completed extensive in-house consulting assignments for the purpose of effecting increased utilization of marketing research by the organization. This experience resulted in several significant conclusions:

1. Public policy makers have a sincere interest in contributions from marketing and consumer behavior research.[1]
2. This interest is well founded; effective research could significantly improve many public policy decisions.
3. There is currently, however, a substantial gap between information needs and the nature of available research inputs.
4. Marketers are thus faced with the alternatives of either increased participation in enlightened policy making or continued reaction in the political arena. The research gap can be closed if the marketer is willing to understand and adapt to the exigencies of policy decisions. Marketers should recognize that public policy will continue to be created, with or without their research.

WILLIAM L. WILKIE is a visiting lecturer at Harvard University and a visiting research associate at the Marketing Science Institute while on leave from the Krannert Graduate School of Industrial Administration, Purdue University, Lafayette, Indiana. DAVID M. GARDNER is associate professor of business administration in the College of Commerce and Business Administration, University of Illinois, Urbana-Champaign.

Wilkie, William L. and David M. Gardner (1974), "The Role of Marketing Research in Public Policy Decision Making," *Journal of Marketing*, 38 (January), 38–47.

[1]Comments by FTC Commissioner Mary Gardiner Jones are especially relevant; see Mary Gardiner Jones, "The FTC's Need for Social Science Research," in *Proceedings of the 2nd Annual Conference, Association for Consumer Research*, David Gardner, ed. (College Park, Md., 1971), pp. 1–9.

The above points are amplified in the sections which follow. First, a brief discussion of the background and decision processes of the FTC outlines information needs of the organization and highlights a crucial distinction in problem perspective between marketers and consumerists. Next, a detailed analysis of the research gap indicates necessary shifts in research emphasis that should be made by marketers if their research is to be useful to policy makers. The third section of the paper offers suggested areas of inquiry for future research.

A Brief Perspective on the FTC

The Federal Trade Commission is broadly charged with the responsibility for providing a fair competitive environment for the nation's economic system. Its mandate, apart from administering several specific acts, is surprisingly vague. Section 5 of the Federal Trade Commission Act originally declared "unfair methods of competition in commerce" to be unlawful and was later amended to include "unfair or deceptive acts or practices" in this category. These statements historically have been interpreted as assigning responsibility and authority in areas of industry structure (competition) and trade practices (consumer protection).

Critics have often questioned commission activities in both competition and consumer protection. Much of the FTC's recent activity can be attributed to charges leveled in 1969 studies by "Nader's Raiders"[2] and an American Bar Association committee commissioned by President Nixon.[3] The primary responses by the FTC under Chairmen Weinberger, Kirkpatrick, and Engman have been to make major internal changes in organization and staffing and to increase efforts to seek effective impacts externally.[4]

A brief overview of the FTC's decision process is useful in assessing the rationale for these shifts. As outlined in Figure 1, there are essentially three decision stages for the organization. Stage 1 requires the determination of program priorities and, within programs, selection of specific cases for further involvement. Stage 2 represents decision sequences in staff investigations, commission complaint procedures, consent negotiations, and formal adjudicatory procedures. Stage 3, remedy generation and compliance monitoring, determines the actual impact of commission activities.

Public criticisms by Nader and the ABA concerned FTC performance at each stage. Charges included too little activity and that what activity there was centered on trivial problems (Stage 1); excessive time delays (e.g., four or more years) in Stage 2; and weak, ineffective remedies in Stage 3. The FTC has since attempted to improve performance within each decision sector. A new Office of Policy Planning and Evaluation was created

---

[2]E. Cox, R. Fellmeth, and J. Schultz, *The Nader Report on the Federal Trade Commission* (New York: Richard W. Baron, 1969).
[3]*Report of the American Bar Association Commission to Study the Federal Trade Commission,* committee print, September 15, 1969.
[4]A summary of important changes is presented in R. E. Freer, "The Federal Trade Commission—A Study in Survival," *The Business Lawyer,* Vol. 26 (July 1971), pp. 1505–1526.

FIGURE 1

FTC Decision Stages

1	2	3
Area or Case Selection	Investigation, Complaint Issuance, Fact-Finding	Remedy and Compliance

to report directly to the commissioners on program planning and resource allocation. A management information system is being developed to streamline Stage 2, and power to seek preliminary injunctions has been requested. The search for more effective remedies at Stage 3, of course, has been the most obvious of all changes at the FTC.

There are four areas of new remedies of particular interest to marketers:

1. Advertising substantiation
2. Corrective advertising (affirmative disclosure by single firms)
3. Product information (affirmative disclosures by all firms within an industry)
4. Consumer education

The much publicized advertising substantiation program was developed to provide public documentation of the basis for competitive copy claims. Corrective advertising reflects the dual concerns of rectifying "ill-gotten" competitive advantages and correcting the "residual effects" consumers may have received from deceptive advertising campaigns. Product information programs are aimed at providing consumers with information to help improve purchasing decisions, while consumer education is concerned with developing consumers' abilities to deal effectively with complex purchasing problems.

While these programs are open to, and have been receiving, legitimate criticisms on legal and economic grounds, the intent here is neither to advocate nor disparage their value. The *concepts* are significant in that they reveal a shift by the FTC from *re*action to *pro*action. Rather than rely solely on rectifying isolated and recognizable abuses, the agency has begun an attempt to change the consumer environment so as to reduce the probability of abuses.

Two rationales can be advanced to account for this shift in FTC activity. The first follows from the above-mentioned charges of inefficiencies in internal procedures and external effects; the new remedies are clearly aimed at increasing impact per FTC resource dollar. The second is less obvious but more important in that it symbolizes a significantly different perspective of the consumer environment than that implicitly held by most marketers and researchers. Consumer advocates place primary emphasis on perceived shortcomings of the extant consumer environment as compared to a more desirable environment characterized by full information, quality and price competition, and rational purchasing. The current environment is attributed solely to marketers having exercised "marketing freedoms" in their own best interests. The marketing researcher should recognize the existence and implications of this viewpoint whether or not he chooses to accept it, for it appears to underlie much of the disagreement as to appropriate roles and tactics for governmental policy.

In summary, present research needs of the FTC can be identified with respect to its three decision points: program priorities, fact-finding, and development of equitable and effective remedies. A number of worthwhile suggestions for the incorporation of consumer research were advanced by Dorothy Cohen four years ago in the JOURNAL OF MARKETING.[5] Despite the obvious insights that marketing research can offer the commission, little influence has yet been evidenced at the FTC. This situation can be traced to a basic gap in understanding between policy makers and consumer researchers.

The Current Gap

That a gap in understanding exists is obvious. Specification of the nature of the gap will aid both marketers and public policy makers to better understand the elements that they are trying to influence. The least understood element in the implicit models of competition used by the FTC staff seems to be consumer behavior. The following misconceptions are widespread in the agency among those who have not studied the behavioral sciences.

ECONOMIC MAN ASSUMPTION

The study of consumer behavior has repeatedly shown that the economic man assumption in its purest form is not valid. Nonetheless, this assumption has certain intrinsic attractions to the policy maker who is trying to reduce a complex situation into a manageable one. In addition, there is little likelihood that there will be any educational experience in the background of the public policy maker to make him aware of the fallacies of an assumption that rests heavily on the further assumption of "all other things being equal." Consequently, it is common to find at least the following three ideas underlying much of the thinking of the FTC.

First, it seems that price, brand, store, advertising, and quality are often considered to be completely independent of each other and other factors. The idea that a person would be willing to pay more for a certain brand, even though the almost identical product is available at less cost, is thought by many to signal some flaw in the system and represent anticompetitive behavior on the part of some business firm. Likewise, advertising expenditures often are viewed with suspicion and in isolation.

---

[5]Dorothy Cohen, "The Federal Trade Commission and the Regulation of Advertising in the Consumer Interest," JOURNAL OF MARKETING, Vol. 33 (January 1969), pp. 40–44.

Second, frequently it is assumed that the consumer has unlimited shopping time to make numerous comparisons and unlimited time to acquire the necessary information to achieve the lowest economic cost. This belief, unfortunately, ignores *total* economic cost.

Third, psychological needs of consumers are often ignored or, if included, are said to be the result of marketing and advertising practices. Incorporated here is the failure to recognize the relatively large amount of disposable income in the hands of consumers after "basic" needs have been satisfied.

DEFINITION OF RATIONALITY

While the economist can use the theoretical results of pure or perfect competition to measure actual competitive organizations and strategies, no similar model of consumer behavior is widely accepted. In the absence of such a model, various normative models are applied. Unfortunately, these are often inductive models based mainly on personal experience and observation. They are not, therefore, representative and do not generalize beyond rather narrow limits.

PROXY VARIABLES

Through experience, word-of-mouth information, and expectations, consumers learn to use certain aspects of the purchase situation as cues or proxy variables to provide them with information about products. The policy maker often acts as if information transmitted by price, brand name, and store is not related to the product itself. This can easily lead to the assumption that the consumer needs more information and would use it if available. Conversely, it may be maintained by some policy makers that in some situations one of the variables is so important that no other variable matters. Complaints which focus on a brand name, a price strategy, or a store name and purposely or otherwise ignore other variables represent this view.

CONSUMER INFORMATION PROCESSING

The most serious misconception or assumption is the belief that the consumer is highly impressionable and that by saying the right words he will blindly obey what he is told by an advertisement or other source of product information. This is the belief that leads people to attribute great powers to advertising. It denies the concept of consumer information processing and, especially, selective perception. Three conclusions follow from this view of consumer information processing.

First, *more information is better*. The more information consumers have, the better decisions they can make. Little recognition is given to the actual needs of consumers, the environment in which the information is used, and accumulation of relevant information through product usage and word-of-mouth. Considerable consternation results when information provided to consumers is ignored. Likewise, the policy maker often does not understand the failure of education campaigns which try to provide customers with information to help them be better decision makers.

Closely related is the *lack of concern with the quality or content of the message*. The study of consumer information processing indicates a variety of factors necessary to insure that the consumer receives the same meaning from the communication as the communicator desires. However, there is an inherent belief that if you say something in plain English, it will be clearly understood in the intended manner by all.

The third idea is that *information is processed in a uniform manner by all consumers*. This idea ignores differential processing of information according to experience, anticipated use for the product, and the importance of the product. A related assumption is that most products are relatively important to customers.

Howard and Sheth suggest that decision making can be divided into three stages during which purchase criteria are crystallized and the range of alternatives is narrowed.[6] It is clear that the type of information desired and useful to the consumer varies from stage to stage. It also appears that information has a greater capacity to influence consumers who are in the earlier stages of search. These sorts of insights should be incorporated into policy decisions aimed at consumer utilization of information.

CORRECTIVE ADVERTISING

To illustrate the problems that these misconceptions can cause, the relatively recent FTC program of corrective advertising is reviewed below. These comments in no way should be construed as value judgments, but only as observations. By presenting these observations, the authors hope to clarify the need for the incorporation of research into decision processes.

The primary goal of corrective advertising is to eradicate the "residual effects" of deceptive advertisements. An effective program of corrective advertising would seem to benefit consumers as well as honest competitors and provide a strong deterrent to deceptive advertising in general. It should be noted, however, that a number of difficult decisions are required of the FTC in order to create an effective program.[7]

First, it must be determined whether or not the advertisement at issue is deceptive. If deceptive, a second decision must be made as to the need for corrective advertising. This involves a determination of the extent and magnitude of the residual effects of the deception. If residual effects are held to exist, it is necessary to specify the best program by which to "correct" them. Such diverse concepts as media selection and scheduling, time period for

---

[6]John A. Howard and Jagdish N. Sheth, *The Theory of Buyer Behavior* (New York: John Wiley & Sons, 1969).
[7]A detailed discussion of these issues is given in W. L. Wilkie, "Research on Counter and Corrective Advertising" (Paper delivered to the American Marketing Association Conference on Advertising and the Public Interest, Washington, D.C., May 9–11, 1973).

correction, budget, and copy elements are included in this decision. Early corrective advertising orders have typically required that 25% of the brand's advertising budget be expended in normal media schedules for one year, with the corrective copy subject to FTC approval.

A failure to consider research perspectives and evidence raises several significant issues for the commission. While it may be reasonable to assert that advertising can have residual effects in general, how are these effects to be assessed in any particular case? This problem would seem to require both a precise definition of "residual effect" and an effort to obtain evidence on whether or not such effects are present in the minds of consumers.

Assuming that residual effects are present, how can they be eradicated? An important constraint in this regard is that FTC remedies cannot be punitive in intent. This suggests that considerable *precision* is required in the FTC's specifications for the corrective advertising order. Guidelines for corrective copy are surely required; research has shown that strong corrective copy can lead to negative brand attitudes, decreased intentions to purchase the brand, and unfavorable corporate and brand images.[8] These negative predispositions could be viewed as punitive and should be avoided through copy specifications focused on less affective dimensions of consumer information.

Delivery of the corrective message also requires precision. Consider the strong assumptions implicit in requiring that 25% of an advertising budget be devoted to corrective copy for a one-year period. It is much more logical to assume that each case will require its own budget formula and its own time frame if eradication is to be achieved without punitive effects upon the respondent firm.

In light of these problems, an alternative approach to the FTC's corrective advertising program has been advanced.[9] This approach requires, first, that the nature of "residual effects" be carefully defined in terms of consumer behavior. Second, evidence as to the existence and magnitude of the residual effect must be used to decide whether or not corrective advertising is needed in a given case. Finally, the FTC should withdraw from its new role as the public's advertising agency; it is simply not clear that legal training and expertise provide a basis for developing copy, budgeting, media, and timing decisions aimed at precision without punishment. Instead, the FTC's order would simply require that the previously defined and measured residual effects be reduced to a minimal baseline level. Respondents would retain flexibility in the manner by which this is accomplished. Failure to accomplish the eradication or to meet secondary measures of "good faith compliance" would constitute violation of the order and subject the respondent to the heavy penalties of violation.

The basis for such an approach lies in consumer research rather than intuition or introspection. Resistance to such a change is one characteristic of the current gap between consumer research and public policy.

---

[8]Same reference as footnote 7, p. 11.
[9]Same reference as footnote 7, p. 11.

INFORMATION PROCESSING CONSTRAINTS

Most policy makers received their formal academic training prior to the emphasis on the behavioral sciences. In addition, especially within the FTC, most policy makers are lawyers by training. With a few notable exceptions, there is little if any training in the behavioral sciences offered by present day law schools. Since policy makers are not familiar with the potential contributions of the behavioral sciences, they appear to be reluctant to incorporate the findings of behavioral science and incapable of understanding inferential research as it bears on their problem.

Even if the lawyer understands the scientific method and inferential research, he generally avoids the use of research findings if the design or conclusions can be attacked in any manner. Since all inferential research can be attacked, it is generally not used because any attack on evidence is apt to leave a negative halo effect that may carry over to other points of the case.

Lastly, the pressure is on the lawyer or policy maker to find a solution NOW! The difficulties of incorporating formal planning within a political environment contribute to a timing problem. Very seldom does the policy maker have the time to conduct an extensive research investigation. It is not uncommon for an attorney to have less than two months to gather his complete legal brief for a case to be heard before an administrative law judge. Yet carefully designed research projects typically take much longer and even then the lack of replication would open questions of reliability and validity.

But the gap is two-sided. While the lawyer may find it difficult to use information because of his training and inclinations, there is a serious problem with the type of information available to him.

Policy makers are decision makers. Generally, they are not interested in theory—they want practical, unambiguous information. In addition, they want "specific and absolute" proof. But what information is available to the policy maker? The immediate reply is: quite a bit. A closer look at this situation is warranted. The inspection is best handled by breaking existing research evidence into two categories: (1) consumer belief and attitude research, and (2) consumer decision-making research.

CONSUMER BELIEF AND ATTITUDE RESEARCH

The first category includes all research directed at demonstrating how consumer beliefs and attitudes are formed, organized, and used to give meaning to products and services. Much of what is known about this category comes from research carried on by social psychologists. While a great deal has been learned about motivation, personality, learning, socialization, and group interaction, careful assessment should be made as to whether what has been "learned" is readily usable by the policy maker.

The objectives of social psychology should not automatically be equated with the objectives of the study of consumer behavior. Since social psychology is primarily concerned with the social behavior of man in society, few of its findings or tools had as their genesis the need or desire to know about the consumer. While many of the findings from social psychology are indeed transferable to the study of consumer behavior, they have often been accepted with an uncritical attitude.

With the exception of those who specifically call themselves consumer psychologists, most social psychologists who study consumer behavior do not do so as an area of primary interest, but because such study might allow them to investigate a general phenomenon. It should also be noted that, for the most part, social psychologists are not concerned with external validity. Consequently, two difficulties arise when one tries to apply to public policy knowledge borrowed from the findings of social psychology about consumers. The first is that psychology is generally concerned with exploring a small aspect of behavior in a rigorous manner. The objective is often to increase knowledge simply for its own sake. The second difficulty is that certain problems which are basic to the understanding of consumer behavior have not been given adequate attention by social psychologists. The result of this gap in an understanding of consumer information is that one can only talk in generalities about the formation of consumer information. This level of knowledge is not sufficient for the implementation of public policy. Therefore, much of what the marketer claims to know about attitude and belief formation with regard to products and purchase situations is not readily applicable to the needs of the policy maker.

CONSUMER DECISION-MAKING RESEARCH

The research evidence available to the policy maker on consumer decision making is more in line with his needs. Even so, this considerable amount of information about the consumer's use of unit pricing information, open dating, interest rate disclosure and the availability of consumer product rating publications has hardly scratched the surface. The gaps in this area of research are not to be blamed on social psychology; rather, they represent the results of a piecemeal attack, often based on questionable or nonexistent theoretical foundations.

The major deficiency is that many studies attempt only to describe consumer behavior rather than explain it. For example, many studies on brand loyalty, unit pricing, price/quality and advertising/sales relationships present quite simplistic explanations for the behavior described. Marketers have perceptual maps of many products and have seen canonical correlation and discriminant analysis applied to many problems. But why are these developments not directly useful to the policy maker?

The reasons are complex, of course, but the major components are: an implicit marketing management orientation, a strong interest in techniques, and a lack of research programming.

An implicit marketing management orientation is not to deny the high quality of research useful to marketing managers. As just two examples, the body of research dealing with market segmentation and that dealing with market share analysis make fine contributions to the body of knowledge needed to be a successful marketing manager. However, these two areas, as well as most research in marketing, deal only indirectly with how consumers process information. This research is focused on controllable decisions of marketing management, while little attention has been given to controllable decisions of public policy makers. The latter orientation might begin, for example, by carefully considering the scope and character of a desirable consumer environment.

There is a very understandable interest in developing techniques associated with consumer behavior. The unidimensional techniques used for many years simply are not appropriate for the complex, multidimensional world of the consumer. Likewise, the development of techniques is often a very rewarding experience personally. But the application of these techniques to the study of consumer behavior lags many years behind their development. Marketers must ask themselves serious questions about the value of devoting increasingly greater resources to development and refinement of new techniques as opposed to encouraging the use of existing techniques to develop information about consumers for the policy maker.

Within the field of consumer behavior, no research traditions apart from short-lived interest areas have emerged. The net result is that *no research programming exists*. Three major models have been proposed: Nicosia in 1966;[10] Engel, Kollat, and Blackwell in 1968;[11] and Howard and Sheth in 1969.[12] Although interesting and sometimes controversial attacks have been directed at components of these models, no comprehensive program is yet in sight. Academic researchers are often too ready to blame the lack of funding for this deficiency. The interest in small "do-able" pieces of research because of the need to "publish or perish," coupled with the absence of any organized groups of researchers, may go further toward explaining the absence of a coordinated, comprehensive approach.

If research on consumer behavior is to have an impact on public policy, it must be useful and available to the policy maker. Therefore, it is imperative that marketing researchers examine their strong interest in research techniques, reconsider their biases, and start pooling their talents and research efforts in comprehensive programs.

The Negative Halo Effect of Business-Sponsored Research

A final basic constraint is that research conducted or sponsored by business firms and organizations of business firms is often subject to suspicion by policy makers. Since policy makers typically are not sophisticated in research design and analysis, they are apt to rely on the assumption that the only reason a business firm would sponsor research would be

---

[10]Francesco M. Nicosia, *Consumer Decision Processes* (Englewood Cliffs, N.J.: Prentice-Hall, 1966).

[11]James F. Engel, David T. Kollat, and Roger D. Blackwell, *Consumer Behavior* (New York: Holt, Rinehart & Winston, 1968).

[12]Same reference as footnote 6, p. 10.

to support the firm's position. Unfortunately, there is some validity to this general assumption of the policy maker. Therefore, any research directed at the policy maker must be conducted in such a manner as to allow him to completely remove these suspicions.

Implications for Future Research

A significant increase in the use and effectiveness of research in public policy is likely to occur when researchers begin to anticipate future information needs and make insights available when they are needed. A primary objective for interested researchers should thus be to *lead rather than lag* public policy issues.

Future decision needs of the FTC and marketers concerned with public policy and consumer protection offer challenging topics for research. As noted earlier in this article, recent activities of the FTC indicate a willingness both to challenge the quality of the existing consumer environment and to effect changes in it. It seems highly appropriate that businessmen and researchers add their insights to this decision process. The authors' impressions of the most prominent topics are listed in Table 1 and discussed below.

PROGRAM PRIORITIES

The most important and complex decisions made by the FTC involve choices concerning areas of activity. While philosophical disagreements will occur as to the appropriate scope of governmental regulation, it is hoped that most marketers will choose to participate

---

TABLE 1

Topics for Future Research

A. Program Priorities
1. Consumer environment descriptions
2. Models for resource allocation
3. Social cost-benefit measurements
4. Structural versus trade practice remedy

B. Stimulus Research
1. Advertising effects
2. Personal selling and promotion
3. Pricing
4. Product quality
5. Guarantee and warranty

C. Response Research
1. Product information
2. Consumer education

D. Product and Segment Research
1. Special markets
2. Specific products and services

in this process rather than ignore it entirely. Four decision areas in particular require research on priorities: description of consumer environments, resource allocation models, social cost/benefit measures, and remedy approaches.

Consumer environment descriptions refer to measures of the state of the consumer world, both present and future. While considerable information on aggregate consumer behavior currently exists, interpretation is difficult without bases for comparison. Such bases might include aggregate models of an "optimal" consumer environment or individual data on problems and satisfactions with existing conditions. Either form of information could be used to measure "deviations" indicative of program needs.

Models for resource allocation should include explicit considerations of nonregulatory remedies such as industry self-regulation or consumer education. While internal costs might be accurately predicted for these models, major work is clearly needed to obtain external program costs and social benefits. Improved methods of measuring or analyzing nonquantifiable costs and benefits are also required for these models. *Social cost/benefit measures*, in addition to acting as model inputs, could also serve as performance indicators for the FTC and the macro-marketing system.

Structural versus trade practice remedy issues concern the alternative means by which consumer benefits can be gained, ranging from forced divestitures in concentrated industries; through limitations on, or prohibitions of, certain marketing activities; to case approaches of single problems. Marketer and consumer behavior are key elements in predicting the effects of these alternatives; yet they are often subject to simplistic assumptions in such analyses.

STIMULUS RESEARCH

Much of the recent activity of the FTC has been directed at stimuli created and disseminated by brand-competitive marketers. Concern with the nature of such stimuli as they foster or impede brand comparisons is evident. Interest in stimulus research and experience was exemplified by the FTC advertising hearings held in 1971. One major benefit which resulted from marketer testimony at these hearings has been an increasing recognition by the FTC of stimulus complexity and appreciation of the need for advanced forms of stimulus research. It should also be noted, however, that some slight reorientation is required for stimulus research to fit public policy decisions. The essence of this orientation reflects needs for aggregate or macro-analysis, research standards or protocols, and generalizable constructs around which useful FTC programs can be developed. Many of the issues listed below can be viewed in this regard.

Advertising effects have received the greatest attention recently and thus present many significant research topics. Can advertising deception be behaviorally defined and measured? Should advertising be more informative? Are brand comparison advertisements likely to improve consumers' choices? What are the role and effects of emotional copy themes? Are testimonials particularly susceptible to deception? Is advertising substantiation a desirable program? Does advertising really have little or no lagged effect? Is repetition actually more important than advertising copy? Does advertising lead to increased or decreased prices; does this effect depend upon industry conditions and analysis mode? Is industry self-regulation a viable alternative to further government involvement? Is there a need for corrective advertising and can it be expected to meet its nonpunitive objectives? Note the simplistic phrasing of these questions; given that answers will differ as a function of conditions, the present need is for careful identification of such conditions by researchers.

Personal selling and other promotional forms are subject to many of the above questions but have as yet received little focused research attention. Although there are likely to be increased difficulties in investigation and evidence, plus compliance monitoring by the FTC, the sheer size and nature of these activities indicate major effects on social welfare. Remedies are likely to require considerable research due to probable choices between seller requirements or consumer education. Research and analysis may be most efficiently accomplished when conducted on a product- or service-specific basis, with particular attention paid to high-ticket, infrequent purchases utilizing product as well as brand demand stimulation. Topic areas might include door-to-door sales, games and sweepstakes, cents-off coupons, "free" trips, or arrangements between suppliers and salesmen.

Pricing and product quality, in addition to relating to issues discussed above, present important topics for further research. Findings by Morris and Bronson, for example, show low correlations between list prices and quality ratings presented in *Consumer Reports*.[13] Is it desirable that high correlations exist? What are the implications of consumer research on imputed price-quality relationships? Does price competition actually exist in many industries? With respect to quality, is it possible to assess accurately psychic value in addition to functional performance? Should more attention to quality improvements be given at the expense of promotional stress? Are consumers presently concerned with these issues and, if so, in which industries?

Guarantee and warranty issues also involve questions of promotion, performance, and consumer expectations. Are there certain products or services which do not deliver expected performance due to weak or nonexistent service arrangements? Are standards or guidelines for guarantee desirable or is this a promotable product differentiation variable? Do consumers presently use guarantees as brand differentiators? Is this area susceptible to complex payoff analysis by marketers?

---

[13]R. T. Morris and C. S. Bronson, "The Chaos of Competition Indicated by Consumer Reports," JOURNAL OF MARKETING, Vol. 33 (July 1969), pp. 26–34.

Response Research

The explicit distinction between stimulus and response research points to the differences which arise when attempting to research potential rather than past or present stimuli. The distinction follows from the aforementioned orientation of public agencies to effect new environments for the consumer. This in essence places these agencies in the role of *stimulus generators* and requires that they recognize the responsibilities and difficulties of this role. Problems exist in developing criteria for stimulus generation, implementing and evaluating communication vehicles, and determining audience segments and topic areas. There are, in addition, critical decisions as to appropriate public agency participation in programs which could potentially be handled by the private sector. The value of consumer research is becoming increasingly evident as simplistic models of the "rational" consumer or "helpless" consumer continue to prove unrealistic.

Product information provides particularly interesting examples of consumer research needs. It is commonly agreed that few, if any, consumers use comparative product information to reach optimal purchase decisions. It is also agreed that such information is not readily available in many product categories and that, in some of these (e.g., high-ticket, infrequently purchased goods which are difficult to evaluate) decision costs can be high. It is not clear, however, whether such information can be effectively gathered and communicated.

Difficult problems in developing standards for measurement can be anticipated in at least some product categories. The major difficulties lie, however, in deciding how much and what kinds of information should be made available and the means by which such information should be communicated.

Much of the required input must come from researchers, and at present it is not clear that either this information or the methods for obtaining it are available. For example, two basic criteria for public information programs might be (1) *effectiveness* and (2) *neutrality* with respect to directing choice. Experience and expertise in marketing, however, have been developed in providing effective *nonneutral*, persuasive communications. Are there adaptable evaluation methods for neutral information? Is behavior change an appropriate objective? Are consumer self-reports of usage or satisfaction sufficient, or is information-processing research the key to this question?

Within information processing, is it true that consumers typically operate in few dimensions—that relatively low cognitive capacity limits the quantity of information that can be communicated? If so, what are the implications for neutral disclosure of full information on complex products? How can potential segment differences be anticipated and provided for? In what form should information be provided, by whom, and with which vehicles?

Consumer education offers many of the same researchable topics but is distinct in that criteria and methods may differ substantially. The focus is less likely to be on particular brand information, with more attention paid to hints for the decision process. Neutrality is a less significant criterion but no less a problem for public agencies. Evaluation appears especially difficult in that both criteria and the "market" are less well defined. Marketing research methods can potentially offer great benefits to this activity, but only by moving into new territories.

PRODUCT AND SEGMENT RESEARCH

Issues in this area reflect public policy concern with special topics, and can provide data and focus for pursuit of research in the areas discussed above: program priorities, stimulus research, and response research.

Special markets reflect attention on those segments of the population who appear least able to deal effectively with certain aspects of the consumer environment. Children, the poor, those with little education, and the elderly are some of these markets. Children's television, ghetto prices and fraud, vocational school deceptions, home repairs, and retirement residencies are examples of topics which have been attacked. Possible remedial actions range from criminal charges to consumer education. Investigation, remedy, and compliance are complex, but involved program research is needed.

Specific products and services are often stressed due to either high social costs or conditions of consumer inability to adequately evaluate alternatives and anticipate effects. Health and safety provide a number of possible topics, including nutrition, fire hazards, OTC drugs, and medical care. Purchasing power issues include consumer credit practices, insurance, encyclopedias, and self-improvement products.

Conclusion

Public policy regarding consumer behavior is going to be made, with or without research evidence. If marketers feel that public policy regarding consumer behavior could benefit from research evidence, it behooves them to recognize the weakness of present research and to conduct studies that are more relevant to public policy decision making.

Unfortunately, researchers operate at severe disadvantages in providing information that will be used by public policy makers. For the purposes of this discussion, no distinction is made between legislative, regulatory, and judicial policy makers and policy making. However, one thing must be clearly understood: policy makers are decision makers. They are not interested in theory; they want practical, useful information.

The most severe disadvantage researchers must overcome is that most public policy makers have neither training nor experience in the use of research evidence. Public policy makers with legal training and backgrounds may not include working knowledge of the scientific method among their skills. Legal practice often avoids the use of research findings if the design or conclusions can be attacked in some manner. Instead, reliance is placed on the use of qualitative statements by "experts." Meehl suggests that "legislators and judges have relied upon the 'fireside inductions' (common sense, anecdotal, introspective, and culturally transmitted beliefs about human behavior) in making and enforcing law as a mode of social control."[14]

The second disadvantage researchers face is that many public policy makers desire "specific and absolute" proof. They are not comfortable with the use of probability statements and, furthermore, they want the evidence to be directly relevant to the specific topic, not some "similar" topic.

Not all policy makers, fortunately, are reluctant to use research evidence. Two encouraging trends are evident. First, many law schools are now giving their students some exposure to research as a component of the legal process. The research tradition of "sociology of law" is receiving increasing attention in these schools. Second, there is an increasing tendency among firms to introduce research as evidence in proceedings instigated by government agencies. This practice will force more people to become aware of the value of research evidence and how it can be used.

What should be the posture of researchers interested in doing research on consumer behavior relevant to public policy making?

1. Recognize the inadequacies of research based on untested assumptions, conducted on non-representative samples, and oriented too specifically toward marketing management.

2. Tailor the study to the needs of the policy maker. This requires that the research also have a forward orientation. Therefore, *it is absolutely imperative* that the researcher be in constant touch with policy makers to learn what their problems are and what types of research are most appropriate. As those researchers who have done otherwise will testify, an impeccable piece of research has little or no value unless the policy maker sees its value and it fits into his perceived set of needs.

3. Since research is somewhat foreign to many policy makers, it behooves the researcher to do more than just present his study and the results. The concept of research must be sold along with the findings.

4. Researchers might usefully segment their market for research. There are public agencies such as the National Science Foundation whose mission is to promote basic research. Most government agencies, however, deal in policy decisions and require research applied to their policy environment. Policy makers are not using existing consumer research because it does not answer their questions.

---

[14]Paul E. Meehl, "Law and the Fireside Inductions: Some Reflections of a Clinical Psychologist," *Journal of Social Issues*, Vol. 27, No. 4, 1971, pp. 65–100.

Will the FTC use marketing research in he future? An educated guess is a definite yes. Open systems theory would predict a positive response and a few limited, but hesitant, steps have been taken by the FTC.[15] The question yet to be answered, however, is the willingness and readiness of market researchers to be adaptive.

---

[15]David M. Gardner, "Dynamic Homeostasis: Behavioral Research and the FTC" (Paper presented at the 4th Annual Conference of the Association for Consumer Research, Boston, November 9–11, 1973).

The authors wish to acknowledge the assistance of Professor Murray Silverman of San Francisco State University in conceptualizing the potential contributions of marketing research to public policy decisions.

IDENTIFYING MISLEADING ADVERTISING

J. Edward Russo, Barbara L. Metcalf and Debra Stephens

A procedure for identifying misleading advertising is presented, based solely on measured consumer beliefs. An advertisement is misleading if an exposed group holds more false beliefs than a comparison group. When ten allegedly misleading advertisements were tested, two were identified as incrementally misleading, and four others were shown to be exploitively misleading.

Determining whether an ad is misleading continues to prove difficult and controversial. Naturally, advertisers and consumer advocates rarely agree on whether a particular ad is misleading. More disappointing, however, is the failure of researchers to agree on a broadly applicable definition of misleadingness or a procedure for identifying it (Gardner 1975; Jacoby and Small 1975; Preston 1976). The problem is further complicated by the conflict between the behavioral paradigm of researchers and the jurisprudential view of regulatory organizations.

In this paper, we propose and test a procedure for identifying misleading advertising. Contrary to custom, the procedural problem is confronted first, and a definition of misleadingness follows. The procedure is empirically based, as it relies on the measurement of consumer beliefs.

PRESUMPTIONS

We make certain presumptions when we speak of misleading advertising. First and most important is the discrepancy between the claims of an ad and the facts of actual product performance.[1] If such a discrepancy does not exist, no one can be misled. The second presumption is that consumers cannot by themselves correct all claim-fact discrepancies. Individual consumers cannot correct some claims because verification is technically impossible or prohibitively expensive. For example, how can the ordinary consumer determine whether Volvos are built better than Fords? Manufacturers themselves are

---

J. EDWARD RUSSO is Associate Professor and BARBARA L. METCALF is a former Research Project Manager, both at the Graduate School of Business, University of Chicago, Chicago, IL 60637. DEBRA STEPHENS is a doctoral candidate in the Department of Behavioral Sciences, University of Chicago. This article has benefited from the comments of Julie A. Edell, Hillel J. Einhorn, Michael B. Mazis, Andrew A. Mitchell, John Paul Russo, and especially from those of Ivan L. Preston. The senior author acknowledges Jacob Jacoby for introducing him to the problem, and Jeffery Godlis and Michael Hyman for collaboration on an early pilot study. This research was supported in part by Grant DAR 76-81806 from the National Science Foundation.

Russo, J. Edward, Barbara L. Metcalf, and Debra Stephens (1981), "Identifying Misleading Advertising," *Journal of Consumer Research*, 8 (September), 119–131.

[1]A major assertion of this paper is that the focus of misleading advertising should shift from "an advertisement's claims" to "consumer beliefs." This change is discussed shortly. Until then, we continue to use the traditional term, claims.

generally unable or unwilling to provide consumers with substantiation for such claims (Corey and Patti 1979). The final presumption is that not all claim-fact discrepancies can be corrected by natural market mechanisms (Eighmey 1978). In some cases the market is self-correcting, as when a false claim is corrected by a competitor's advertising. And, of course, economic self-interest dictates the correction of any false impressions of one's own products that reduce sales. In spite of some self-correction, however, there are many instances where natural market mechanisms are inadequate. Clearly, claim-fact discrepancies do exist at market equilibrium, and misleading advertising does increase sales.

These presumptions impose two requirements on any solution to the problem of misleading advertising. There must be some extramarket, institutionalized system for detecting misleading advertising. Such a regulatory system may be public, private, or mixed (as we currently have in the United States). Second, whatever combination of public or private institutions regulates advertising, there should be some equitable, standard procedure to determine whether an ad is misleading. The focus of this paper is on such a procedure.

Three Approaches to Unjust Advertising

One may best understand our procedure in the context of three alternative views of unjust advertising: fraud, falsity, and misleadingness.[2] These views parallel the three components of an advertising communication: the advertiser, the message itself, and the resultant consumer beliefs about the advertised product.

FRAUD

Fraud focuses on the advertiser and assumes a deliberate *intent* to create false beliefs about the product. We believe that fraud is neither a valid nor practical approach. It is invalid because the advertiser's intent may be irrelevant to the harm done to consumers. It is impractical because the requirement of proof of intent makes it difficult to take action against the ad, and thereby stop the harm it is doing to consumers.

For both reasons, fraud plays a declining role in current regulatory practice. The Federal Trade Commission has not been required to prove intent for over 30 years.[3] Similarly, the main industry regulator, the National Advertising Division (NAD) of the Better Business Bureau, does not need to prove fraud in order to find that an ad should be withdrawn

---

[2]There is some confusion among the jurisprudential, scientific, and ordinary meanings of the terminology of misleading advertising. We use *unjust advertising* as a superordinate label, and *fraudulent, false,* and *misleading* as distinct subordinates. Not used are the two terms Congress wrote into the FTC's mandate declaring "unfair or deceptive" advertising to be unlawful. *Unfair* has a special legal meaning (Cohen 1974), and *deception's* ordinary meaning, which connotes the intent to mislead, differs too widely from its legal meaning, misleadingness, whether intended or not. The terms *misrepresentation* and *misperception/miscomprehension* are avoided because they suggest the locus of blame, the advertiser and the consumer, respectively.

[3]For brief histories of the FTC's regulation of advertising, see Jentz (1968), Chapter 9 of Preston (1975), or the broader review of Aaker (1974).

(Ashmen, Hasenjaeger, Hunt, Katz, Miracle, Preston, and Schultz 1979, p. 57). Unfortunately, current statutes still require proof of fraud in some situations, such as the U.S. Postal Service's regulation of advertising through the mails.

Falsity

Falsity in advertising refers to the existence of a *claim-fact discrepancy.* Examples include price and availability claims, as when a vendor advertises a product at a reduced price. "Literal truthfulness" requires both that the item be sold at the advertised price and also that a reasonable number of such items be available for sale.

In order to demonstrate falsity in advertising, one must verify the existence of a discrepancy. For prices, this is a simple task, accomplished with numerical certainty. For availability, however, it becomes more complicated. What is the minimum number of advertised items a vendor must have available for purchase? To answer such questions, numerical certainty must give way to subjective judgment. The most common approach is the use of expert testimony; but, of course, experts do not always agree. Especially if the issue is important, experts can usually be found to support each opposing viewpoint.

Standardization of Meaning
The usefulness of the falsity approach is greatly enhanced if a regulatory institution has the power to standardize the meaning of critical words. How else can one resolve the falsity of a claim like "nutritious"? There is some nutritional value in even the worst junk food, and experts do not agree on what constitutes a "nutritious" food. Standardization of meaning removes the ambiguity and potential misleadingness of such terms.

Standardization has become a widely used regulatory strategy. Many trade associations regulate the use of product descriptions, and governmental agencies standardize product labels. For example, the Department of Agriculture sets standards for grades of fruits, and even determines whether a product name, like peanut butter, can be used at all. As "unconscionable lies" have disappeared from advertising, the role of standardization of meaning has become increasingly important in demonstrating the falsity of an advertised claim.[4]

Insufficiency of Falsity
In spite of the efficacy of a demonstration of falsity, it is neither sufficient nor necessary to prove that an ad is misleading. What matters is what consumers believe. A false claim does not harm consumers unless it is believed, and a true claim can cause great harm if it generates a false belief.

Some false claims are clearly harmless. Fanciful cartoon characters, though literally false, can enhance the belief of a valid claim. Similarly, true claims can create false, harmful beliefs. Consider the following (hypothetical) audio commercial: "Aren't you tired of the

---

[4]In spite of its general acceptance, some believe that this approach is bound to fail. They argue that advertisers are too clever and will always circumvent simple prohibitions on terminology.

sniffles and runny noses all winter? Tired of always feeling less than your best? Get through a whole winter without colds. Take Eradicold pills as directed" (Harris 1977; Harris and Monaco 1978). The ad's claim that Eradicold pills will prevent winter colds is not linguistically asserted, yet it is clearly implied. Preston (1975, p. 7) describes a television ad for toy racing cars that the FTC found to be deceptive. Through clever close-up photography, the impression was created that the cars were traveling faster than they actually could.

In short, we believe that falsity is the wrong criterion. What is claimed and what is believed can be quite different, and it is what is believed that harms consumers.

MISLEADINGNESS

The third view, misleadingness, focuses exclusively on consumer beliefs. A demonstration of misleadingness requires the observation of false consumer beliefs in conjunction with exposure to the ad. Whereas falsity refers to a claim-fact discrepancy, misleadingness refers to a belief-fact discrepancy. During the last two decades, the FTC altered its approach to unjust advertising, so that the focus gradually shifted from the message itself to the resulting beliefs of consumers. In keeping with this change in focus, the percentage of FTC advertising cases using behavioral evidence has increased from four percent prior to 1954 to 54 percent in the early 1970s (Brandt and Preston 1977). A thorough legal analysis of the various definitions of unjust advertising, including the need to rely on consumers' beliefs or "expectations," is presented by Beales, Craswell, and Salop (1981).

Rationale of the Procedure

The proposed procedure for identifying misleading advertising requires the assessment of consumer beliefs about a false claim. This means that consumer beliefs must be measured and then classified as correct or incorrect. The incorrect beliefs must be further partitioned into those that can harm consumers to the benefit of advertisers, and those that cannot harm consumers. Thus, the category of incorrect beliefs is divided into *misleadingly false* and *correctably false*. This coding scheme is most easily explained with an example.

MISLEADINGLY FALSE VERSUS CORRECTABLY FALSE BELIEFS

Consider a banana ad that claims "there's only 85 calories [in a banana]." This claim is false because an average banana contains 101 calories. There are *two* types of incorrect beliefs: an average banana contains fewer than 100 calories (100 is considered correct as a rounded encoding of 101), or it contains more than 101 calories. Although both inaccuracies are potentially harmful to the consumer, only the former serves the advertiser's goal of selling more of the product (except for those very few consumers seeking more calories). Any belief that calories exceed 101 can be presumed to be correctable by natural market mechanisms. That is, the advertiser has the incentive of increased sales to correct the impression that there are more than 101 calories in a banana. We call such beliefs *correctably false*. However, if consumers believe that calories number below 100, the advertiser benefits at the expense of the consumer. These *misleadingly false* beliefs are the ones that require extramarketplace regulation. Therefore, the proposed procedure for detecting misleading advertising focuses only on these beliefs. As the proposed procedure is best introduced through example, we describe the experiment that was performed.

Experimental Evidence

SUMMARY

Ten magazine ads were selected for testing. All had a verifiable claim-fact discrepancy, and were independently correctable. The latter phrase means that the ad can be altered to remove all of the misleadingness and none of the legitimate persuasiveness. The original and corrected versions, combined with a no-ad (control) treatment formed the three treatment conditions of the experiment.

One hundred consumers were recruited from city and suburban social organizations. They were instructed to read and evaluate the entire advertising message. They then answered questions designed to assess belief in the misleading claim and in an important legitimate claim. Responses to these questions form the evidence on which misleadingness is to be identified.

Two potentially confounding effects were evaluated and found to be absent. Beliefs were unaffected by the ads' construction, which was below professional quality. Different interest levels in purchasing a product did not affect the likelihood of a misleading belief.

CONSUMER SUBJECTS

One hundred members of PTA, church and women's organizations were recruited as experimental subjects. All organizations were from Chicago area suburbs or city neighborhoods with middle rankings (median 110 out of 200) on the recent reports of socioeconomic status of Chicago area communities. Citing her husband's job in advertising, one person declined to participate, leaving a sample of 99. Subjects earned a flat rate of $4.00 for their participation, as well as a 10-cent bonus for correctly answering each of ten selected questions. Payment was credited to the subjects' organizations; no payments were made directly to individuals.

Based on self-reported sociodemographic data, the average participant was female, age 39, with slightly more than two years of college completed, and an annual household income of $25,000. (The 1978 estimated average Chicago household income *after* taxes was $21,679.) Consumers who are above average in income and education were probably overrepresented in our sample. Thus, the reported results may not generalize across the entire United States population. However, as subjects were partitioned into four groups as demographically balanced as possible, within the time schedule and location constraints of field testing, any atypicality was evenly balanced across treatment groups.

At the end of the experimental session, participants were asked whether they had trouble reading any of the 12 ads. As the ads contained large amounts of text, it is not surprising that 51 percent reported some trouble with at least one. The 17 subjects who reported some difficulty with four or more ads were dropped from the study. This left a total of 82 subjects distributed in groups of 19, 17, 26, and 20. We tested for differences in subject characteristics across these four groups, and found none. An analysis of variance revealed no significant ($p < 0.05$) differences for any of the measured sociodemographic characteristics: income, education, age, occupation, and number of younger (under six years) and older (six to 17 years) children living at home.

TASK

Participating consumers were shown a series of ads. Their task was to read and comprehend the entire advertising message, and to evaluate the product. To assure that the entire message was perceived and understood, subjects were asked a simple factual question immediately after seeing each ad, and were paid a ten-cent bonus for each correct answer. To simulate realistic viewing, subjects were also asked if the ad made it more or less likely that they would purchase the product or, if the product was one for which they had no use, recommend purchase to a friend. After all ads had been shown, a second group of questions was presented. One question was designed to assess misleadingness and the other to measure the effectiveness of some legitimate claim. In general, the subject's task was to process each ad completely in preparation for factual, evaluative, and substantive questions.

ADVERTISEMENTS TESTED

Ten ads were chosen to satisfy several criteria. First, there had to be a verifiable claim-fact discrepancy. Because we had no special testing facilities to verify product claims, we had to rely on publicly available criteria or our own judgment. The public criteria were decisions of the NAD and a proposed FTC Trade Regulation Rule on the use of nutritional claims in food advertising (Federal Trade Commission 1974).

The second selection criterion was correctability. An ad is correctable if the misleading claim can be removed without reducing its legitimate power to persuade. For example, the banana ad that falsely claims 85 calories for what people presume to be a banana of medium size can be corrected by substituting the true caloric value, 101 calories, for the false one. This does not change the central legitimate claim that a banana and a glass of milk is a superior "60-second breakfast."

The introduction of corrected versions of each tested ad restricted us to print sources. We did not have the facilities to duplicate and modify broadcast ads. Thus, the ten ads selected for testing were taken from popular magazines, including 1975–1978 issues of *Better Homes and Gardens, Good Housekeeping, Newsweek,* and *Redbook.*

The ads were also chosen to represent a wide variety of products. They included the following product categories: acne treatments (Mudd), automobiles (Chevrolet Nova), bananas (Dole), breakfast cereals (Cheerios and Kellogg's), breakfast drinks (Tang), cigarettes (Carlton), margarine (Diet Imperial and Fleischmann's), and snack foods (Granola Bars). Summaries of five of these ten ads are presented in Exhibit 1.

Preparation and Display

We prepared corrected versions of the ads by removing the misleading part of the message and substituting a revised portion. Some revisions were typed, so the appearance of the ad

---

EXHIBIT 1

Misleadingly False, Legitimate, and Corrected Claims for Selected Advertisements

Advertised Product and Type of Claim	Content of Claim
Dole Bananas	
Misleadingly false	"and there's [sic] only about 85 calories (in a banana)." This number is true only for small bananas. A typical medium-sized banana contains 101 calories.
Legitimate	The central theme of the ad is that a banana and a glass of milk are relatively healthful as a very fast breakfast. The headline reads "the 60-second breakfast from Dole."
Corrected	The corrected ad substituted 101 for 85 in the calorie claim.
Chevy Nova Automobile	
Misleadingly false	The bottom of the ad prominently displays a picture of a Chevrolet Nova with a price. The car is shown with white striped tires, wheel covers, and body side molding. The price shown, $3,823, is not the price of the car shown. The actual price is $3,948, a value that can be obtained only by adding three additional prices (white striped tires $44; wheel covers $39; body side molding $42). These latter values are given in the text of the ad.
Legitimate	The ad's theme is that a Chevy Nova is inexpensive, yet rugged enough to be a police car.
Corrected	The boldly printed price at the bottom of the ad is changed from $3,823 to $3,948. Thus, the price shown becomes that of the car shown.
Nature Valley Granola Bars	
Misleadingly false	"Nature Valley Granola bars [are] crunchy, wholesome, delicious." According to a proposed Trade Regulation Rule of the FTC the word "wholesome" may connote "nutritious" and cannot be used unless the product satisfies a minimum standard of nutrition (defined in terms of the percent U.S. RDA of the eight nutrients listed on the food label). Granola bars fall far short of the minimum standard.
Legitimate	The theme of the ad is that Granola bars are a "100 percent natural" snack. They contain "no additives [and] no preservatives." The headline is "Go Natural."
Corrected	The word "wholesome" was removed, eliminating the nutrition claim. This was judged to be an advertiser's likely response. The only alternative permitted by the FTC's proposed rule is the inclusion of a very unflattering table of percent of U.S. RDA.

(Continued)

EXHIBIT 1

Continued

Advertised Product and Type of Claim	Content of Claim
Carlton Cigarettes	
Misleadingly false	The ad includes a list of alternative "low tar" brands and their mg. of tar per cigarette. This list is shown in the left panel of Exhibit 2. The alternative brands listed are not those lowest in tar. The misleading implied claim is that no other "low tar" brands are nearly as low as Carlton; specifically, that even if one smokes the second lowest brand, one must inhale five times the tar of Carlton.
Legitimate	The ad truthfully claims that Carlton has less than all other brands. This claim is stated in the headline, "Carlton is lowest."
Corrected	The misleading panel is changed to contain the six brands lowest in mg. of tar, in order and without omissions, as shown on the right of Exhibit 2.
Diet Imperial Margarine	
Misleadingly false	The ad states no restriction on the use of Diet Imperial, implying that it can be substituted for regular margarine in any situation. This implied claim is true when margarine is used as a spread, a use pictured in the ad; but it is not true when margarine is used in cooking. As Diet Imperial achieves its caloric reduction by diluting regular margarine with water, there is 50 percent less oil per tablespoon.
Legitimate	The central claim is that Diet Imperial has 50 instead of 100 calories per tablespoon. The headline reads, "Try delicious, new Diet Imperial. Still only half the calories of butter or margarine."
Corrected	A disclaimer is added, "Do not use in baking."

Note: A complete description of all ten ads can be found in Russo, Metcalf, and Stephens (1979).

clearly showed that it had been altered. So that this "cut-and-paste" appearance did not differentially affect the corrected versions, cosmetic alterations were also made on the original versions. Thus, both sets of ads appeared equally altered.

To test whether this cosmetic alteration affected consumers' comprehension of an ad's message, four untouched original versions were shown. These untouched originals were exact copies of the ads that appeared in the magazine. Note that there was no difference in content (pictures and text) between the untouched and altered versions. The latter merely substituted identical typewritten segments for what had been typeset in the untouched originals.[5] For both versions of each ad, we computed the proportion of consumers holding misleadingly incorrect beliefs. These proportions showed no significant differences ($p < 0.05$), either in aggregate or for the four ads tested individually.

After all ads had been prepared, they were photographed and printed as 2-inch × 2-inch slides. Subjects viewed these slides at a convenient viewing distance.

---

[5]The four ads for which both untouched and cosmetically altered original versions were prepared are Carlton cigarettes, Diet Imperial margarine, Fleischmann's margarine, and Tang breakfast drink.

EXPERIMENTAL DESIGN

The experimental design contained three homogeneous and one mixed-treatment condition. Each of these conditions contained one version of all ten experimental ads.

The first treatment condition contained the ten (cosmetically altered) original ads. The second contained the corrected ads. The third group contained no ads, which is to say that the same questions were asked of subjects, but without exposure to any version of the ad. A fourth treatment was mixed. It included the four untouched originals and variations of the six other ads.[6]

The four subject groups should not be confused with the four treatment groups. To counterbalance any subject differences, each subject group saw two or three ads from each treatment condition in an approximation of a Latin square design. That is, each subject group saw seven or eight of the ten ads once, but not in the same treatment condition. For example, a subject in the first group saw the original Tang ad, the corrected Chevy Nova ad, no version (the control treatment) of the Fleischmann's ad, and the unaltered Carlton ad. The results depend only on the differences across treatment conditions, not subject groups. It should be remembered that within the same treatment condition different ads were seen by different subjects. This will explain the differences in sample sizes within the same treatment condition.

PROCEDURE

Consumer subjects participated in small groups (range of group size, four to 11) in a subject's home. After two practice ads and samples of the questions, subjects saw seven or eight of the ten experimental ads. (Recall that two or three ads occurred in the no-ad treatment.) In addition, two or three distractor ads were shown. The (cosmetically modified) distractors were included to reduce any suspicion that the ads were selected to be misleading. The exposure time for each ad ranged from 30 to 90 seconds, as determined by laboratory and field pretests. After viewing each ad, the subjects answered the factual question and rated the likelihood of purchase. After all ten ads had been seen, they completed a questionnaire that included the questions about misleading and legitimate beliefs, a seven-point rating scale of interest in the product category, reading difficulty, and various sociodemographic characteristics.[7]

---

[6]These variations are not relevant to the results reported here. They are described in Russo et al. (1979).

[7]We tested for a possible relation between each consumer's level of product interest and the likelihood of a misleading belief. In order to maximize any effect of interest level, only extreme responses were included. The low-interest group qualified by a response of 1 or 2 on the seven-point scale; inclusion in the high-interest group required a 6 or 7. A total of 233 low-interest and 184 high-interest responses were available. The proportions misled were essentially identical, 0.67 for low-interest and 0.68 for high-interest subjects.

To test each advertisement individually, we increased the smaller sample size. Those responding 3 were added to the low-interest group; those responding 5 were added to the high-interest group. No difference was significant ($p < 0.05$), except for the Cheerios advertisement. We could find no reason for this exception, and concluded that it was probably a false alarm. (Whenever ten tests at $\alpha = 0.05$ are performed, at least one such false alarm will occur 40 percent of the time.)

Procedures for Detection of Misleadingness

The experiment just described provides the following evidence on which to base a judgment that an ad is misleading: false beliefs held by consumers who did and did not see an ad, and also by consumers who saw a corrected version of the same ad. Based on this evidence, how can a misleading ad be identified?

CRITERION 1: CONSUMER BELIEF OF A FALSE CLAIM

Is it sufficient to demonstrate that a claim is false and that people believe the claim? This is a claim-fact discrepancy coupled with direct evidence that people believe the claim. Many researchers would answer yes to this question, with one qualification.[8] They would require that the percentage of misled consumers exceed some minimum (*n* percent) needed to declare an ad misleading (Gellhorn 1969; Jacoby and Small 1975). As has been argued elsewhere, the problem of finding the best value, or even several values, of *n* percent is insoluble (Russo 1976). For each ad the observed percentage of misled consumers must be judged against its own standard, not against some universally applicable cutoff.

As an example of the belief in a false claim, consider the ad for a Granola Bar (Exhibit 1). This product is claimed to be "wholesome" in the sense of nutritious. Consumers who saw the original ad were asked their belief about the nutrition in a Granola Bar. The average percent U.S. RDA (Recommended Daily Allowance) for the eight "leader" nutrients was believed to be 32 percent. The true value is two percent. Eighty-two percent of consumers believed the average U.S. RDA exceeded five percent. These data indicate extensive belief of a false claim; 82 percent must surely exceed anyone's *n* percent cutoff. Nonetheless, the question remains whether this evidence of a false belief is sufficient to demonstrate that the Granola Bar ad is misleading. Phrased differently, does this evidence show that the false belief was caused by reading the ad?

Our answer is no. Consumer belief of a false claim is necessary to demonstrate misleadingness, but it is not sufficient. The problem is simple: this evidence does not exclude the possibility that consumers would hold the same false belief even if they had not seen the ad.

The design of our experiment permits a test of this alternative hypothesis. In the control treatment consumer subjects answered the same question about nutritional content without having viewed the ad. The control group's mean was 28 percent of the U.S. RDA, a value not reliably different from 32 percent. The proportion of people providing misleadingly false answers also showed no significant difference, 87 percent for no-ad versus 82 percent for the original ad. Thus, though a claim-fact discrepancy exists and a large percentage of consumers believe the claim, the evidence does not show that the ad is responsible.

---

[8]Some researchers would not qualify an affirmative answer at all. Gardner and Barbour (1980) measured price errors after exposure to four tire advertisements. Because the mean error is large, 26 percent, and "a sizable portion of the sample" held the erroneous belief, they conclude that the advertisements are misleading.

The trouble with identifying misleadingness solely from false beliefs is that it uses an absolute criterion, *n* percent of consumers holding a misleadingly false belief. No matter how high this cutoff, the level of false belief could exceed it (and trigger the condemnation of the ad as misleading), even though the false beliefs were derived entirely from preexisting misconceptions.

CRITERION 2: INCREASED BELIEF IN A FALSE CLAIM AFTER EXPOSURE TO AN ADVERTISEMENT

A second approach rectifies the main flaw of the first one by requiring a causal demonstration of misleadingness. *An ad is identified as misleading whenever exposure to that ad increases the false belief held by consumers.* That is, the proportion of consumers holding a misleadingly false belief is greater for the group that views the ad than for the control group that does not view the ad. We call this incremental misleadingness. It is probably the clearest, least controversial form of misleadingness. The rationale for identifying incremental misleadingness is based on a standard before-after comparison in which the before group provides the criterion against which the level of false belief is compared. A comparison similar to this has been proposed by Armstrong, Gurol, and Russ (1978), although Jacoby, Hoyer, and Sheluga (1980) found this approach to be impractical.

To see how this procedure works, consider the Dole banana ad described in Exhibit 1. It claims 85 calories per banana, while the truth is 101. A misleadingly incorrect answer is anything less than 100 calories. (Recall that both 100 and 101 calories are considered correct because consumers are likely to encode 101 as "a hundred.") The proportion of misleadingly incorrect beliefs is 0.92 for the original group and 0.44 for the control group. This difference is both large and statistically significant ($p < 0.05$). We conclude that viewing the ad caused an increase in the level of false belief, and we find it incrementally misleading.

The causal assertion of misleadingness can be strengthened by examining those answers that are "exactly misleading," in this case the 85 calories stated in the ad. If the ad is changing consumers' beliefs about caloric content, then more consumers in the original treatment than in the no-ad (control) treatment should answer exactly 85 calories. The proportions are 0.50 (13 of 26) for the original group and 0.03 (1 of 36) for the control group, again a significant difference.

This criterion for misleadingness was applied to all ten ads. That is, we tested for a higher level of misleadingly false beliefs in the original treatment than in the no-ad (control) treatment. Table 1 reports the two proportions and the results of a chi-square test for their equality.[9] Significant misleadingness was found in only two cases, the Dole banana and Chevy Nova ads.

---

[9]Unfortunately, the chi-square test is two-tailed, whereas our hypothesis is one-tailed. However, all nonsignificant *p* values exceeded 0.10. In one case (the Kellogg advertisement), all sample size requirements for a chi-square test were not met, and a Fisher's Exact test was used ($p = 0.07$).

TABLE 1

Proportion of Misleadingly Incorrect Answers after Viewing Original Ad

Product	Advertisement Seen	
	Original	None (Control)
Carlton	.92 (25)[a]	.94 (18)
Cheerios	.68 (19)	.60 (20)
Chevy Nova	.65[b] (20)	.00 (17)
Diet Imperial	1.00 (20)	.85 (26)
Dole	.92[b] (26)	.44 (36)
Fleischmann's	.94 (17)	.88 (26)
Granola Bar	.82 (17)	.87 (15)
Kellogg's	.88 (17)	.60 (20)
Mudd	.82 (17)	.61 (46)
Tang	.40 (20)	.39 (18)
Mean	.80	.62

[a]Numbers in parentheses are sample sizes.
[b]$p < 0.05$.

What about the other eight supposedly misleading ads? Are they really not misleading at all, or only not incrementally misleading? There is at least one other form of misleadingness that Criterion 2 overlooks, exploitive misleadingness. The criterion of increased false belief after exposure to an ad is *sufficient* evidence of misleadingness, but it is not *necessary*. Specifically, it fails to detect non-incremental forms of misleadingness.

EXPLOITIVE MISLEADINGNESS

All advertisers feel that changing people's beliefs is a very difficult task. It takes many exposures, usually to different ads, for a campaign to *change* beliefs. It is much easier to link a product to existing beliefs. Granola Bars are believed to be nutritious because Granola cereal has that image. Trying to raise the existing belief about nutritional content would be costly and unnecessary. Better to free-ride on this existing belief, reinforcing and utilizing it to sell the product. We call this *exploitive misleadingness*. The advertiser does not mislead by increasing false beliefs, but by exploiting those that already exist.

If this type of misleading advertising exists, how can it be detected? Obviously, the previous procedure will fail. By the very nature of exploitive misleadingness there is no increase in the level of false belief. At least two approaches are possible. The first is to show an increase in something other than the misleadingly false belief. The confidence in the belief and the importance of the belief to an overall product evaluation are secondary beliefs that may be increased by exposure to the ad. For example, Armstrong, Gurol, and Russ (1978) found that a Listerine mouthwash ad increased only the importance of a false belief. This approach retains from Criterion 2 the concept of an increase as a *causal* demonstration of the effect of the ad. However, it changes the focal observation from primary to secondary beliefs. The development of this approach is an important goal of future research.

Alternatively, one can continue to focus directly on the misleadingly false belief and search for a more sensitive comparison than the no-ad (control) treatment. The second approach, a more sensitive comparison, forms the basis of Criterion 3.

CRITERION 3: LESS MISLEADINGLY FALSE BELIEFS FOR CORRECTED THAN FOR ORIGINAL ADVERTISEMENTS

We believe that a properly corrected ad provides the desired comparison. For each of the ten original ads a corrected version was designed to remove the original claim-fact discrepancy, and to affect no other aspects of the ads. For example, in the Granola Bar ad the word "wholesome" was eliminated. In the Carlton ad, the table of mg. of tar for selected brands was replaced by one containing the lowest brands, as shown in Exhibit 2.

If a significantly lower level of misleadingly false belief is produced by the corrected ad, we conclude that the product attribute involved in the false claim is perceived by consumers and exploited by the advertiser. For example, 92 percent of consumers exposed to the original Carlton ad believed that the brand second lowest in tar contained more than 1 mg. By comparison, only 40 percent of consumers who saw the corrected version held this false belief. The corresponding mean estimate of mg. of tar dropped from 4.5 to 1.9.

Using a corrected version to provide the standard of comparison comforms to a common scientific principle. A comparison condition should alter only the variable of interest and hold constant everything else. Because the corrected ad changes only the misleading component, it is better able than the no-ad condition to sense whether consumers

---

EXHIBIT 2

Panels of Tar Ratings for Competing Brands in the Carlton Cigarette Advertisement

Original*			Corrected		
Winston Lights		12	Tempo		7
Vantage		11	Pall Mall		6
Salem Lights		11	True		5
Kent Golden Lights		8	Iceberg		3
Merit		8	Lucky		3
True		5	Now		1
Carlton Soft Pack		1	Carlton Soft Pack		1
Carlton Menthol	less than	1	Carlton Menthol	less than	1
Carlton Box	less than	1	Carlton Box	less than	1

*These panels occupied about 10 percent of the area of each advertisement.

TABLE 2

Proportion of Misleadingly Incorrect Answers after Viewing Corrected Ad

Product	Corrected Advertisement	Reduction Compared to Original Advertisement
Carlton	.40 (19)[a]	.52[b]
Cheerios	.69 (26)	−.01
Chevy Nova	.16 (19)	.49[b]
Diet Imperial	.24 (17)	.76[b]
Dole	.20 (20)	.72[b]
Fleischmann's	.95 (19)	−.01
Granola Bar	.56 (16)	.26[b]
Kellogg's	.92 (26)	−.04
Mudd	.74 (19)	.08
Tang	.12 (17)	.28[b]
Mean	.50	.30

[a]Numbers in parentheses are sample sizes.
[b]$p < 0.05$.

are perceiving, and being exploited by, this misleading component.[10] The use of a corrected ad as the standard of comparison was proposed by Jacoby and Small (1975).

This third criterion was applied to all ten ads. The reduction in the proportion of misleadingly false beliefs between the original and the corrected treatments is shown in Table 2, along with the results of a chi-square test for equality of two proportions. Based on this test, six of the ten ads are found to be misleading: Carlton, Chevy Nova, Diet Imperial, Dole, Granola Bar, and Tang.

What about the remaining four supposedly misleading ads? Does this mean that they are actually not misleading? Possibly, but there is at least one other explanation for the failure to find original-corrected differences in the proportion of false beliefs. Maybe the corrections were ineffective, either because they were not persuasive, or because consumers ignored them. For the two ads with nutritional claims, Cheerios and Kellogg's, evidence indicated that the correction was ineffective.[11] In general, however, it is not possible to discriminate between a poor correction and the absence of exploitive misleadingness.

---

[10]Cohen (1977) and Wright (1977) have each proposed a similar procedure for identifying misleadingness. Both proposals compare consumer beliefs after exposure to original and corrected ads. These proposals differed from ours mainly in the rationale for designing the corrected versions. The authors of these proposals work from an information provision strategy in which the corrected ad is limited to factual, truthful claims. In the context of the Food and Drug Administration's regulation of drug advertising, Wright's (1977) corrected ad is "an unadorned text that describes non-blacklisted conditions the product can alleviate, in the direct terms the FDA sanctions" (p. 14). Similarly, Cohen (1977, p. 15) favors "a true 'bare bones' version, closer in substance and mode of presentation to what is on the label." Both proposals differ from our strategy of making the corrected and original ads as similar as possible in all respects, except the misleading claim. The approach of Cohen and Wright seems to be motivated by a belief that many misleading claims are manifest throughout an ad, including its pictorial and verbal content. Cohen (1977, p. 15) states that the "use of a 'bare bones' base-line would, in my opinion, quite properly make the advertiser responsible for the entire ad." We are more optimistic that misleadingness can be removed without turning the ad into a label.

[11]The details of this analysis can be found in Russo et al. (1979).

WHAT IS A PROPER CORRECTION?

Not every corrected ad can legitimately serve as a comparison to the original. For example, in the extreme it is possible to correct an ad by gutting it, that is by destroying its ability to communicate any product claims, misleading or otherwise. Such an alteration is obviously improper.

Two aspects of the correction are critical: independence, or whether reducing the misleading claim interferes with the persuasiveness of legitimate claims, and informativeness, or how much the correction depends on providing correcting information.

Independent Correction

The correction should reduce the misleading belief without affecting legitimate persuasiveness. This has not always been easy to achieve. At least two studies tested the FTC correction of Listerine ads and found attenuation of belief in claims other than the target of correction (Dyer and Kuehl 1978; Mazis and Adkinson 1976).[12]

Recall that the ten ads were selected partly on the basis of a clear separation between the misleading claim and an important legitimate claim. If the corrections were independent, consumer belief in these legitimate claims should be just as high for the corrected ads as for the original ones. The critical proportions are shown in Table 3.

The mean proportions show no difference between the corrected and original treatment groups. Tests of individual ads also reveal no significant differences. To make clear that both versions were genuinely persuasive, the proportion of correct responses for the no-ad treatment is also shown in Table 3. The corrected and original treatments exhibit a much higher belief level than does the no-ad group: 0.73 versus 0.44 on the average. We conclude that the corrections were independent in that they did not reduce the considerable legitimate persuasiveness of the original ads.

Informativeness

There are two corrective strategies: provide nonmisleading information, or cease mentioning the misleading attribute. Because the misleading table of alternative brands in the Carlton ad was replaced, as shown in Exhibit 2, the correction was informative. If the misleading table had been removed without being replaced, the correction would have been uninformative. The Granola Bar ad was uninformatively corrected by dropping the nutritional claim, "wholesome." In contrast, it could have been informatively corrected by adding a table of percent of U.S. RDA (Russo et al. 1979).

---

[12]Note that we tested only one legitimate claim for each ad. To show that one claim is not infirmed is not to show that all were not. However, we did try to select a major thematic claim whenever possible, and it is fair to say that the present results could not be more supportive of the assertion that legitimate persuasiveness was preserved.

TABLE 3

Proportion of Correct Answers to Questions Assessing Legitimate Persuasiveness

Product	Version of the Advertisement		
	Corrected	Original	No Advertisement
Carlton	.95 (20)[a]	.92 (26)	.28 (18)
Cheerios	.88 (26)	.95 (19)	.65 (20)
Chevy Nova	.79 (19)	.90 (20)	.35 (17)
Diet Imperial	.88 (17)	.90 (20)	.46 (26)
Dole	.90 (20)	.92 (26)	.89 (36)
Fleischmann's	.16 (19)	.06 (17)	.27 (26)
Granola Bar	.65 (20)	.69 (16)	.18 (17)
Kellogg's	.42 (26)	.53 (17)	.15 (20)
Mudd	1.00 (19)	1.00 (17)	.80 (46)
Tang	.65 (17)	.45 (20)	.39 (18)
Mean	.73	.73	.44

[a]Numbers in parentheses are sample sizes.

An uninformative correction is not always possible. If the misleading belief is not explicitly activated by some component of the original ad, there is nothing to remove. The only way to correct such an ad is to add information. The Diet Imperial margarine advertisement provides such an example (Exhibit 1). To correct the false belief that Diet Imperial can be used in cooking (which it cannot because it is 50 percent water), an informative disclaimer had to be added.

Both the informative and uninformative corrections provide valuable evidence about the level of exploitive misleadingness. The uninformative does less correcting, and will almost certainly be the choice of advertisers. It also provides the more conservative test. We expect a smaller original-corrected difference in misleading belief when the correction is uninformative. Not saying anything ought not to reduce a false belief as much as telling people the truth.

Forced Education

Advertisers may claim that by comparing an ad to its corrected version they are being held to an unreasonable standard. They are being required to educate the public. Not only might such a requirement violate their freedom of speech, but it would be impossible for an ad to provide enough factual information to correct every existing false belief.

This argument is groundless. A regulatory organization is often justified in requiring that the advertiser explicitly provide information in order to decrease some existing false belief (Beales et al. 1981). A warning on the use of a drug is a common example. The disclaimer that Diet Imperial margarine should not be used in cooking is another example. The question of whether to reduce misleadingness by requiring additional information in an ad really involves the severity of harm. This, in turn, is a question of utility and action selection. Although it is essential in any regulatory context, we would like to keep it separate as long as possible from the more scientific question of the existence of misleadingness. We return to this topic later.

SUMMARY OF RECOMMENDED PROCEDURE

The prerequisite to our recommended procedure for identifying misleading advertising is empirical evidence of consumer belief. Specifically, we require the proportions of a representative group of potential purchasers that hold a misleadingly false belief after exposure to: the original ad, one or more corrected versions, and no ad at all.

Given this evidence, the identification of incremental misleadingness is straightforward. If the level of misleading belief is (statistically significantly) higher for the original group than for the no-ad (control) group, then the ad is found to be incrementally misleading. Exposure to the ad increases the level of false belief.

Exploitive misleadingness occurs when the ad does not increase, but free-rides on, an existing level of misleading belief. If the level of misleading belief is (statistically significantly) higher for the original ad than for the corrected version, the ad is found to be exploitively misleading. The selection of a corrected version is critical. The most conservative correction is both independent and uninformative. This provides the most conservative test.

Theoretical Issues

THE *n* PERCENT PROBLEM

The inadequacy of Criterion 1 is essentially a statement about the insolubility of the *n* percent problem. The difficulty with establishing a single standard of *n* percent (or even a sliding standard) is that this task confounds two concepts, the existence of misleadingness and its importance. Criterion 2, for identifying incremental misleadingness, succeeds precisely because it separates existence from importance. It accomplishes this in the same way that classical statistical hypothesis testing separates statistical significance from practical importance. When statistical techniques show that there is significantly more misleading belief in the original group than in the no-ad (control) group, all we have demonstrated is that misleadingness exists. There is no judgment about the importance of that misleadingness, in terms of the seriousness of the potential harm to consumers.[13]

---

[13]A remaining problem is determining the appropriate sample size of the test of misleadingness. A close analysis will reveal that the issue of sample size reintroduces the judgment of seriousness of harm, but in a less damaging way. Ideally, the appropriate sample size is partially determined by the utilities of the two statistical errors (Hamburg 1970). The more harmful a given level of misleadingness, the more important is its detection and the larger should be the sample size. The appropriate sample size is a decision that should be jointly made by researchers and policy makers. Although it is an untidy remnant of the *n* percent problem, it should affect only a few marginal determinations of misleadingness. These cases will occur when relatively few people are misled, but the potential damage is great, such as a misleading drug ad to physicians.

The judgment of seriousness depends on the nature of the advertised claim. In our procedure it remains, as it must remain, the prerogative of the regulator. It is worth noting that as n percent increases, both the existence and seriousness of misleadingness increase. This partly explains why these separate issues have been confused in the past.

Remedial Action and Utility

If an ad is misleading, what remedial action, if any, should be taken? The problem of action selection is, of course, one of judging the severity of harm to consumers. In principle, the existence and severity of misleadingness are separate issues. In practice this distinction cannot always be achieved.

Consider an (hypothetical) ad for Efficax, a new powerful nonprescription pain reliever. Efficax has only one qualification, it relieves all but one common pain, say, angina of effort. (This is the temporary pain caused by too little blood to a working muscle.) As consumers' past experiences are only with drugs that relieve all common pain, it is likely that an initial advertising campaign will find a linkage between the legitimate belief of the relief of most pain and the misleading belief of angina relief. The more effectively an ad persuades consumers of Efficax's power, the more it is apt to increase the level of false belief, even with a clear disclaimer that angina is excluded. Such an effective ad might, according to Criterion 2, be identified as incrementally misleading. However, the net benefit to society could still be positive, because the benefit of the legitimate belief might outweigh the damage of the misleadingly false belief.

This example illustrates a situation that affects the applicability of Criterion 3 for detecting exploitive misleadingness. The legitimate and misleading beliefs may be interdependent. The promoting of Efficax as powerful increases both the legitimate and misleading claims. These beliefs are similar and naturally linked.

For the ten ads that we corrected and tested, legitimate persuasiveness was undiminished. In each case the legitimate and misleading beliefs were independent. In general, however, we cannot expect independence among beliefs. And once the legitimate and misleading claims are linked, correction comes only at the expense of legitimate persuasiveness. Because some correction can always be attained (if necessary, by turning the ad into an informative label), the use of the corrected ad as a comparison loses its validity. Thus, we stop short of applying Criterion 3 to the case of a link between the misleading and legitimate beliefs.

This is not to say that regulators cannot honestly find an ad misleading in the face of such a linkage. But to do so they must consider severity of damage, or disutility. For example, if a correction lowered the legitimate belief by one percent and the misleading belief by 40 percent, the regulating agency might well find the ad misleading or, more properly, *unnecessarily* misleading. Note that this judgment implicitly involves the relative utilities of a one percent decrease in the legitimate belief versus a 40 percent decrease in the misleading beliefs. Normally one would opt for the 40 percent and sacrifice the one percent, but not always. The decision must depend on the specific utilities (Beales et al. 1981).

Although we restrict our procedure to the independent case, we suggest that one topic of future research is the formal extension of the procedure to *action selection*. Such an extension would incorporate utility judgments, possibly the marginal utilities of the various decreases in the legitimate and misleading belief levels caused by different corrections.

A DEFINITION OF MISLEADINGNESS

The conventional strategy for measuring misleadingness starts with a definition of misleading advertising and develops a measurement procedure by operationalizing that definition (Jacoby and Small 1975; Olson and Dover 1978). We have reversed that process, first constructing a procedure and now defining misleadingness:

> An advertisement is misleading if it creates, increases, or exploits a false belief about expected product performance.

The key words in this definition are "belief" and "false." We focus on what consumers believe as a result of reading an ad, regardless of what the ad claims or what the advertiser intended it to claim. We also require that resulting beliefs not be false, i.e., that the expectation of product benefits be justified. This definition is compatible with several other "behavioral" definitions of misleadingness, especially those of Gardner (1976) and Olson and Dover (1978).

OTHER MEASURES OF MISLEADINGNESS: PERCENT MISLED VERSUS AMOUNT MISLED

The only evidence used by the proposed procedure is the percentage of misled consumers. A measure of the amount of misleadingness would provide more information from the same number of consumer subjects. For example, the size of the misleadingness in the Carlton ad could be measured by how far above 1 mg. each consumer believed the second lowest brand to be. That is, instead of scoring responses of 2 and 10 mg. as identically incorrect, the greater error reflected by the 10 mg. belief could be preserved by measuring the size of these two errors as 1 and 9 mg., respectively.

Although numerical measures of misleadingness would increase the efficiency of the test procedure, they have their disadvantages. The proportion of misled consumers is more intuitively understandable than a corresponding numerical measure. Also, across ads the proportion remains comparable, whereas different numerical measures would be required, such as mg. of tar for one, percent of U.S. RDA for another, and so forth. Nonetheless, the use of numerical measures should not be excluded, but rather explored. Their advantages may be essential in some situations.

Application of the Procedure

PUFFERY

The proposed procedure applies to all advertising claims, including puffs. These are transparent exaggerations, often in the form of superlatives ("the finest beer you can buy") or hyperbole ("pain relief so effective you'll think you're 20 again"). The law considers the falsity of such claims so transparent as to render them harmless. Consumers are assumed to see through the exaggeration, and to place no credence in puffed claims (Preston 1975; Rotfeld 1979). Essentially, the law embodies two extreme assumptions about the beliefs of consumers: fact-based claims are credible to all, while puffs are credible to none.[14]

The procedure proposed here makes no distinction between puffs and other claims. More generally, the increasing use of behavioral evidence should reduce, and eventually eliminate, the distinction between puffed and fact-based claims (Oliver 1979).

This is not to say that the problem of puffery in advertising is now solved, because the elusiveness of puffed advertising reappears in a different form. Recall that besides demonstrating belief in the claim, our procedure requires that the claim be verifiably false. To identify a puffed claim as misleading, one must be able to demonstrate that the corresponding belief is false. How do we decide whether Giordano's really makes "the best pizza in Chicago," or that some hair transplant "will restore your sense of manhood"? Depending on the regulatory criteria for verifying such falsity, this demonstration can be more or less difficult. Nonetheless, by abandoning the presumption that no one ever believes puffery, and substituting a test for misleadingness based on measured consumer beliefs, we can begin to deal with the real impact of puffed claims on consumers' beliefs and purchases.

LIMITATIONS

Verifiability

The proposed procedure requires that the allegedly misleading claim/belief be verifiably true or false. This becomes problematical when the beliefs are evaluative and subjective rather than factual. Is a cigarette ad's implicit claim that the smoker will appear more sophisticated obviously false? A simple yes or no answer is not possible. Although many people would agree that the primary outcome of cigarette smoking is the risk of lung cancer, many teenage girls see cigarettes as genuinely conferring a sophisticated status.[15]

---

[14]Unfortunately, this dichotomy has been necessary. Regulatory judgment of fact-based claims, like those tested in our experiment, is difficult enough. The additional burden of puffed claims would have strained the existing jurisprudential system past endurance.

[15]A psychologically deep issue underlies this phenomenon. Expectations can influence reality, especially social reality. Your chance of appearing to others as sophisticated (or sexy or friendly) increases if you *believe* that you are sophisticated (or sexy or friendly). The communication by ads of such "social psychological representations" has been examined by Shimp (1979).

A task of future research is the development of methods for verifying claims that are essentially evaluative/subjective. One hopeful factor is that a misleading claim, such as enhanced sophistication, may engender many subclaims. Misleadingness can be demonstrated with any one of these. Thus, if misleadingness is genuinely present, the problem of verifiability may be overcome by finding *any* verifiable subclaim.

Creating the Correction

For some ads a correction may be possible in theory only. Consider a TV ad for a health-related, but not medical, product such as a breakfast cereal without chemical additives. The advertiser might misleadingly imply a medical claim by dressing the spokesperson in a white lab coat or setting the testimonial in a hospital. Correction of such an ad is straightforward, exchange the lab coat and hospital setting for typical non-medical counterparts. But, what if the spokesperson is an actor who is closely identified with his role as a physician in a movie or TV series? It may not be possible to find a "corrected" actor, one with no false medical image, but with equal appeal and legitimate credibility.

Devising a proper corrected ad requires cleverness and effort. Like its reflection, the control group in experimental science, the corrected ad may pose practical difficulties, but at least the goal is clear.

NATURALISTIC MEASUREMENT

For a valid assessment of consumer belief, the ad must first be presented as naturalistically as possible. This might mean embedding a print ad in editorial material and a broadcast ad in regular programming (Collins and Jacobson 1978). It might also require multiple exposures ("Multiple Exposure Test Needed to Evaluate Commercials" 1979) or testing on split-sample cable TV to obtain matched groups of viewers (Mizerski, Allison, and Calvert 1980). In general, the goal is to create a natural exposure context, often with so-called "low involvement" by the consumer (Mitchell 1979; Mitchell, Russo, and Gardner 1981). Advertisers have developed many techniques for naturalistic presentation and, within cost constraints, we recommend their use.

Even with naturalistic presentation, however, one must still measure beliefs nonreactively. A nonreactive measurement technique is one that does *not* change the behavior it is trying to measure (Webb, Campbell, Schwartz, and Sechrest 1966). Suppose that we want to know how advertising affects the beliefs of potential purchasers of state lottery tickets about their chances of winning. They are exposed to a persuasive ad that emphasizes the wonderful ways of spending one million dollars. If we now ask, "What do you think your chances are of winning the million-dollar grand prize?" most would correctly respond that their chances are small. But this response probably reflects the effect of the question, not what it was supposed to measure, the effect of the message.

Answering the question activates a rational consideration of the probability of winning that would not otherwise occur. Such questions would never be asked under normal conditions of exposure to an ad. If we were then to measure purchase intention, we would almost certainly find it lower than that of an exposed group not asked the misleading question.

The problem of reactivity to the measurement procedure is worse for questions about misleadingness. Because such beliefs are false, deliberation about them is more apt to reverse them. Simple solutions to the problem of nonreactive measurement do not exist. Each case requires a different creative approach to posing a question subtly enough that people respond without reacting.

USE BY ADVERTISERS

If a standardized procedure for identifying misleadingness were established, advertisers could pretest to avoid regulatory action. If they knew the evidence that the NAD or FTC would use to judge misleadingness, they could collect that evidence prior to public exposure of the ad. There would be no need to second guess regulators' judgments.

Besides helping to avoid costly regulatory action, a pretest may reveal that the misleading claim is not essential to selling the product. One of the striking findings of our experiment is that the main thrust of the ads was not attenuated by removal of the misleading claim. Consumers still believed that Carlton is lowest in tar or that a Chevy Nova is good enough to be a police car. Our procedure enables advertisers to evaluate the contribution of any specific claim (not only a possibly misleading claim) to a major thematic belief about the product.

USE BY REGULATORS

Standardized procedures reduce both the cost and the uncertainty of regulatory action. Beyond these advantages, the use of our procedure over time poses some interesting possibilities. The cumulative body of empirical evidence would constitute a partial census of misleading advertising. Types of claims that are particularly troublesome could be exposed. One could also map the various values of n percent of consumers who hold false beliefs. It would be interesting to know for which product category advertising is the most misleading, and for which the level of false belief is highest.

This type of census can be used to help establish long-range priorities for the regulatory agency, such as those that exist in the field of consumer satisfaction/dissatisfaction (Hunt 1977). A census of dissatisfaction across product categories reveals where dissatisfaction is highest and remedial action most needed.[16]

---

[16]The highest dissatisfaction is uniformly found for automobile repairs; see, for example, Andreasen and Best 1977.

References

Aaker, David A. (1974), "Deceptive Advertising," in *Consumerism: Search for the Consumer Interest,* eds., David A. Aaker and George S. Day, New York: The Free Press.

Andreasen, Alan R., and Best, Arthur (1977), "Consumers Complain—Does Business Respond?" *Harvard Business Review,* 55, 93–101.

Armstrong, Gary M., Gurol, Metin N., and Russ, Frederick A. (1978), "Detecting and Correcting Deceptive Advertising," *Journal of Consumer Research,* 6, 237–46.

Ashmen, Roy, Hasenjaeger, John, Hunt, H. Keith, Katz, Benjamin J., Miracle, Gordon E., Preston, Ivan L., and Schultz, Don E. (1979), *Advertising and Government Regulation,* Cambridge, MA: Marketing Science Institute.

Beales, Howard, Craswell, Richard, and Salop, Steven (1981), "The Efficient Provision of Consumer Information," working paper, Federal Trade Commission.

Brandt, Michael T., and Preston, Ivan L. (1977), "The Federal Trade Commission's Use of Evidence to Determine Deception," *Journal of Marketing,* 41, 54–62.

Cohen, Dorothy (1974), "The Concept of Unfairness as It Relates to Advertising Legislation," *Journal of Marketing,* 38, 8–13.

Cohen, Joel B. (1977), "Prepared Statement and Comment in re: Proposed Trade Regulation Rule Concerning Advertising Claims for Over-the-Counter Drugs," (unpublished results).

Collins, Sy, and Jacobson, Sol (1978), "A Pretest of Intrusiveness of Radio Commercials," *Journal of Advertising Research,* 18, 37–43.

Corey, Kenneth A., and Patti, Charles H. (1979), "Advertisers' Responses to Requests for Substantiation of Product Claims: Differences by Product Category, Type of Claim and Advertising Medium," *The Journal of Consumer Affairs,* 13, 224–35.

Dyer, Robert F., and Keuhl, Philip G. (1978), "A Longitudinal Study of Corrective Advertising," *Journal of Marketing Research,* 15, 39–48.

Eighmey, John (1978), "Consumer Research and the Policy Planning of Advertising Regulation," in *The Effect of Information on Consumer and Market Behavior,* ed. Andrew A. Mitchell, Chicago: American Marketing Association.

Federal Trade Commission (1974), "Food Advertising: Proposed Trade Regulation Rule," *Federal Register,* 39, 39842–51.

Gardner, David M. (1975), "Deception in Advertising: A Conceptual Approach," *Journal of Marketing,* 39, 40–6.

___ (1976), "Deception in Advertising: A Receiver Oriented Approach to Understanding," *Journal of Advertising,* 5, 5–11, 19.

___, and Barbour, Frederic L. (1980), "Deceptive Advertising: A Practical Approach to Measurement," faculty working paper No. 724, Department of Business Administration, University of Illinois at Urbana-Champaign.

Gellhorn, Ernest (1969), "Proof of Consumer Deception Before the FTC," *Kansas Law Review,* 17, 559–72.

Hamburg, Morris (1970), *Statistical Analysis for Decision Making,* New York: Harcourt, Brace and World.

Harris, Richard J. (1977), "Comprehension of Pragmatic Implications in Advertising," *Journal of Applied Psychology,* 62, 603–8.

___, and Monaco, G. (1978), "Psychology of Pragmatic Implication: Information Processing Between the Lines," *Journal of Experimental Psychology: General,* 107, 1–22.

Hunt, H. Keith (ed.) (1977), *Conceptualization and Measurement of Consumer Satisfaction/Dissatisfaction,* Cambridge, MA: Marketing Science Institute.

Jacoby, Jacob, Hoyer, Wayne D., and Sheluga, David A. (1980), *Consumer Miscomprehension of Televised Communications,* New York: American Association of Advertising Agencies.

___, and Small, Constance (1975), "The FDA Approach to Defining Misleading Advertising," *Journal of Marketing,* 39, 65–8.

Jentz, Gaylord A. (1968), "Federal Regulation of Advertising," *American Business Law Journal,* 6, 409–27.

Mazis, Michael B., and Adkinson, Janice E. (1976), "An Experimental Evaluation of a Proposed Corrective Advertising Remedy," *Journal of Marketing Research,* 13, 178–83.

Mitchell, Andrew A. (1979), "Involvement: A Potentially Important Mediator of Consumer Behavior," in *Advances in Consumer Research, Vol. 6,* ed. William L. Wilkie, Ann Arbor, MI: Association for Consumer Research.

___, Russo, J. Edward, and Gardner, Meryl P. (1981), "Strategy-induced Low Involvement Processing of Advertising Messages," technical report, Carnegie-Mellon University, July.

Mizerski, Richard W., Allison, Neil K., and Calvert, Stephen (1980), "A Controlled Field Study of Corrective Advertising Using Multiple Exposures and a Commercial Medium," *Journal of Marketing Research,* 17, 341–8.

"Multiple Exposure Test Needed to Evaluate Commercials," (1979), *Marketing News,* September 21, 13–14.

Oliver, Richard L. (1979), "An Interpretation of the Attitudinal and Behavioral Effects of Puffery," *Journal of Consumer Affairs,* 13, 8–27.

Olson, Jerry C., and Dover, Philip A. (1978), "Cognitive Effects of Deceptive Advertising," *Journal of Marketing Research,* 15, 29–38.

Preston, Ivan L. (1975), *The Great American Blow-up: Puffing in Advertising and Selling,* Madison, WI: The University of Wisconsin Press.

___ (1976), "The FTC's Handling of Puffery and Other Selling Claims Made By Implication," *Journal of Business Research,* 5, 155–81.

Rotfeld, Herbert J. (1979), "Conceptualizing Research on Deceptive Advertising Issues: The Example of Puffery," working paper 79–11, Boston College.

Russo, J. Edward (1976), "When Do Advertisements Mislead the Consumer: An Answer From Experimental Psychology," in *Advances in Consumer Research, Vol. 3,* ed. Beverlee B. Anderson, Ann Arbor, MI: Association for Consumer Research.

___, Metcalf, Barbara L., and Stephens, Debra (1979), "Toward An Empirical Technology for Identifying Misleading Advertising," working paper, Center for Decision Research, University of Chicago.

Sawyer, Alan, and Semenik, Richard J. (1978), "Carryover Effects of Corrective Advertising," in *Advances in Consumer Research, Vol. 5,* ed. H. Keith Hunt, Ann Arbor, MI: Association for Consumer Research.

Shimp, Terence A. (1979), "Social Psychological (Mis)representations in Advertising," *Journal of Consumer Affairs,* 13, 28–40.

Webb, Eugene J., Campbell, Donald T., Schwartz, Richard D., and Sechrest, Lee (1966), *Unobtrusive Measures: Nonreactive Research in the Social Sciences,* Chicago: Rand McNally.

Wright, Peter (1977), Testimony to the Federal Trade Commission on the Proposed Trade Regulation Rule Concerning Advertising Claims for Over-the-Counter Drugs, Washington, D.C.

Marketing's "Scarlet Letter": The Theory and Practice of Corrective Advertising

William L. Wilkie, Dennis L. McNeill, and Michael B. Mazis

Corrective advertising is one of the most controversial regulatory proposals made in recent years. This article provides an in-depth look at this FTC program, analyzes the theory behind FTC's management of this power, and reviews research findings. It then proposes a significant change in the program to make it more equitable and efficient than in the past.

Introduction

THE REGULATORY SETTING

The period since 1968 has been a turbulent time in marketing regulation. Activism and deregulation have each held center stage during this time. New concepts of marketing regulation have been advanced, among them the FTC's program for corrective advertising.

The impetus for more active regulation of marketers came from a diverse set of institutions and represented a strong set of forces. First, a book by "Nader's Raiders" harshly criticized the FTC's low profile during the 1960s (Cox, Fellmeth, and Shultz 1969). At this point the FTC was issuing less than 70 complaints a year against deceptive promotional practices in the entire nation. Cast against the massive promotional activity of the American economy, it was obvious that the chance of detection and prosecution was extremely slim (Pitofsky 1977). A special American Bar Association report (1969) followed, with findings similar to those of Nader's group. The ABA report had been requested by the President of the United States. It concluded that drastic changes within the agency were needed. If such changes were not made, moreover, the ABA report called for disbanding the entire FTC and assigning its tasks to other agencies. President Nixon and the Congress decided to support the changes; new appointments were made, and the agency's budget was increased.

WILLIAM L. WILKIE is Graduate Research Professor, University of Florida; DENNIS L. McNEILL is Associate Professor of Marketing, University of Denver; and MICHAEL B. MAZIS is Professor of Marketing, American University. The authors have served as in-house consultants to the FTC and have worked on the corrective advertising program at various stages of its development. Support from the Public Policy Research Center, University of Florida, is gratefully acknowledged. The authors also wish to thank Ivan Preston, Richard Lutz, Terence Shimp, Priscilla LaBarbera, Wayne Hoyer, and two JM reviewers for their insights and suggestions to this work.

Wilkie, William L., Dennis B. McNeil, and Michael B. Mazis (1984), "Marketing's 'Scarlet Letter': The Theory and Practice of Corrective Advertising," Journal of Marketing, 48 (Spring), 11–31.

During the ensuing decade the FTC emphasized new powers and programs. Advertising was a major target: new proposals were advanced on such topics as advertising substantiation (Cohen 1980), comparative advertising (Wilkie and Farris 1975), affirmative disclosure (Wilkie 1981, 1982), advertising to children (Mazis 1979, Ratner et al. 1978), and advertising code barriers (e.g., eyeglasses, drugs, the professions). The net effect during the 1970s was to create a much more powerful regulatory agency, supported by a 500% budget rise over the decade. However, the increase in power and activity sparked a strong backlash from the business community. To date, the 1980s have been marked by restrictions on FTC powers in several regulatory areas.[1]

THE CONCEPT OF CORRECTIVE ADVERTISING

Corrective advertising—in which a firm that had misled consumers would have to rectify its deception in its future ads—was a key FTC proposal of the early 1970s. Proponents saw it as a benefit for both consumers and competitors, as well as a means to deny the wrong-doer any further gains from deceptive residuals in consumers' minds. Also, the threat of this stronger remedy might help deter deceptive advertising generally (Pitofsky 1977).

Opponents of corrective advertising argued that the remedy was beyond the FTC's powers. In addition to being illegal, it represented an unwelcome intrusion of government bureaucrats into the market system. Here, corrective advertising was viewed as a punishment proposal—a "Scarlet Letter"—requiring a public confession of having sinned (Brozen 1972).

After years of acrimony and argument, the courts have sanctioned the FTC's use of corrective advertising in key advertising cases. It is thus important for the marketing community to appreciate the nuances of this remedy, and to recognize some critical issues of marketing regulation that corrective advertising brings to the surface.

AN OVERVIEW

This article presents a comprehensive analysis covering a variety of perspectives on corrective advertising. There are five sections:

- The *historical* background of corrective advertising is first described, including its origins and cases.
- The key *legal* questions are analyzed in the second section. These will place important constraints on any future actions.
- The third section examines *managerial* issues for this program. Here we will contend that the process has been deficient in the past and needs to be overhauled.

---

[1]Legislative actions in the early 1980s required, for example, Congressional oversight hearings every six months, as well as other restrictive measures. The overall impacts were to reduce the number and strength of FTC "rulemaking" actions aimed at entire industries. Individual cases will thus become relatively more significant, which could increase the importance of the corrective advertising remedy in the future. At this time, however, President Reagan's administration is stressing less restrictive regulation of business and has not pursued corrective advertising orders. This likely reflects in part a judgment that the remedy is not clearly cost effective. Much of this article is germane to improving effectiveness.

- The fourth section reviews the *research* available on the actual impacts of corrective advertising.
- The final section provides conclusions on the first decade of corrective advertising, together with *suggestions* for improving the FTC's management of this power.

A Historical Perspective

THE SOUP CASE

The seeds for corrective advertising were planted in late 1969 by a small group of law students from George Washington University. The FTC had brought a case against Campbell Soup (1970) advertisements in which clear marbles had been placed in the bottom of soup bowls, forcing the vegetable soup ingredients to the surface where they were photographed. The FTC had proposed a cease and desist order that would ban the firm from this practice, on the grounds that it held a potential to deceive viewers as to the actual quantity of vegetables in the soup. The students, using the acronym "SOUP" (Students Opposed to Unfair Practices), petitioned to intervene in the case. SOUP argued that a "corrective" message was needed to inform consumers of the deception; otherwise, they would never become aware they had been deceived.

The Commission denied intervention, but stated that the concept of corrective advertising was of interest and could be considered in more serious case circumstances. Less than six months later, the Commission began to include corrective advertising in some of its proposed complaints (Thain 1972–73). Table 1 lists some of the large advertisers against whom these early complaints were issued.

COMPANIES' QUESTIONS: FIGHT OR CONSENT?

In each case the company faced an option of fighting the complaint in formal litigation or negotiating a consent agreement. Consent negotiations usually allow the company to avoid

TABLE 1

Early Corrective Advertising Complaints against National Advertisers

Firm (Product)	Firm (Product)
Standard Oil of California (F-310 gasoline)	Coca-Cola (Hi-C fruit drink)
Firestone Tire and Rubber (Firestone Safety Champion Tires)	Chemway (Dr. West's Germ Fighter Toothbrush)
Ocean Spray Cranberry (Ocean Spray Cranberry Juice Cocktail)	ITT Continental Baking (Profile Bread, Wonder Bread, and Hostess Snack Cakes)
American Home Products (Easy-Off Window Clearner, Easy-On Speed Starch, Aero Wax Floor Wax, and Black Flag Ant and Roach Killer)	Amstar (Domino and Spreckels sugar)
	Sun Oil (Sunoco gasoline)
	Sugar Information, Inc. (refined sugar)
Warner-Lambert (Listerine Mouthwash)	Bristol-Myers (Bufferin and Excedrin)
Sterling Drug (Lysol Disinfectant)	American Home Products (Anacin and Arthritis Pain Formula)
Sterling Drug (Bayer Aspirin, Cope, Vanquish, and Midol)	

admitting deception, but at the cost of agreeing to comply with an official FTC order. The terms of the order are open to negotiation and are likely to be softened in return for the firm's agreement. Formal litigation, in contrast, is more risky. If the firm wins, the complaint is dismissed, but if it loses, all order specifications are set by FTC. Also, win or lose, the firm must bear the dollar and time costs of litigation, as well as face more publicity about the case.

The first corrective ad case to reach conclusion was the negotiated Profile Bread order. In it, ITT–Continental (1971) agreed to devote 25% of the next year's Profile Bread ad expenditures to disclose that the brand, contrary to past advertising, was not effective for weight reduction. The FTC-approved corrective message which ensued from the consent negotiations began to appear in September 1971. Table 2 displays the text of this correction, together with the texts of three other early negotiated orders. In all four cases, note that the corrective message is relatively weak.

TABLE 2

Texts of Four Early Corrective Ads

Profile Bread

"Hi, (celebrity's name) for Profile Bread. Like all mothers, I'm concerned about nutrition and balanced meals. So, I'd like to clear up any misunderstanding you may have about Profile Bread from its advertising or even its name.

"Does Profile have fewer calories than any other breads? No. Profile has about the same per ounce as other breads. To be exact, Profile has seven fewer calories per slice. That's because Profile is sliced thinner. But eating Profile will not cause you to lose weight. A reduction of seven calories is insignificant. It's total calories and balanced nutrition that count. And Profile can help you achieve a balanced meal because it provides protein and B vitamins as well as other nutrients.

"How does my family feel about Profile? Well, my husband likes Profile toast, the children love Profile sandwiches, and I prefer Profile to any other bread. So you see, at our house, delicious taste makes Profile a family affair."

(To be run in 25% of brand's advertising, for one year.)

Amstar

"Do you recall some of our past messages saying that Domino Sugar gives you strength, energy, and stamina? Actually, Domino is not a special or unique source of strength, energy, and stamina. No sugar is, because what you need is a balanced diet and plenty of rest and exercise."

(To be run in one of every four ads for one year.)

Ocean Spray

"If you've wondered what some of our earlier advertising meant when we said Ocean Spray Cranberry Juice Cocktail has more food energy than orange juice or tomato juice, let us make it clear: we didn't mean vitamins and minerals. Food energy means calories. Nothing more.

"Food energy is important at breakfast since many of us may not get enough calories, or food energy, to get off to a good start. Ocean Spray Cranberry Juice Cocktail helps because it contains more food energy than most other breakfast drinks.

"And Ocean Spray Cranberry Juice Cocktail gives you and your family Vitamin C plus a great wake-up taste. It's . . . the other breakfast drink." (To be run in one of every four ads for one year.)

Sugar Information, Inc.

"Do you recall the messages we brought you in the past about sugar? How something with sugar in it before meals could help you curb your appetite? We hope you didn't get the idea that our little diet tip was any magic formula for losing weight. Because there are no tricks or short-cuts; the whole diet subject is very complicated. Research hasn't established that consuming sugar before meals will contribute to weight reduction or even keep you from gaining weight."

(To be run for one insertion in each of seven magazines.)

TABLE 3

History of Corrective Advertising Cases

Company	Product	Claim	Order Type	Disclosure Features
Amstar Corp. (1973)	Domino sugar	sugar benefits	consent	25% of ad costs
Beauty-Rama Carpet Center (1973)	retailer	prices	consent	firm used "bait & switch"
Boise Tire Co. (1973)	Uniroyal tires	tire ratings	consent	one ad
ITT Continental Baking (1971)	Profile bread	caloric content	consent	25% of one year's ads
Lens Craft Research (1974)	contact lenses	medical claims	consent	four weeks
Matsushita Electric of Hawaii (1971)	Panasonic TV sets	hazard ratings	consent	one ad
National Carpet (1973)	retailer	prices	consent	firm used "bait & switch"
Ocean Spray Cranberries (1972)	cranberry drink	food energy claim	consent	one of every four ads
Payless Drug Co. (1973)	motorcycle helmets	safety	consent	equal number to original ads
Rhode Island Carpets (1974)	retailer	prices	consent	firm used "bait & switch"
RJR Foods Inc. (1973)	Hawaiian punch	juice content	consent	every ad until effects are shown
Shangri La Industries (1972)	swimming pools	availability and terms	consent	25% of one year's ads
STP Corp. (1976)	oil additive	effectiveness	consent	one ad, 14 media
Sugar Information (1974)	sugar	sugar benefits	consent	one ad, seven media
Warner-Lambert (1975)	Listerine	effectiveness claim	litigated	correction in $10 million of ads
Wasems Inc. (1974)	Wasems vitamins	vitamin benefits	consent	one ad, seven insertions
Yamaha International (1974)	Yamaha motorcycle	motorcycle safety	consent	corrective letter

The marketers who resisted corrective advertising in the early cases generally fared well. Chemway and American Home Products negotiated the deletion of corrective provisions in their consent orders. In litigated cases against Firestone (1972), Standard Oil, Coca-Cola (Hi-C) (1972), I.T.T. (Wonder Bread) (1973), and Sun Oil (1974), the Commission ultimately decided not to include corrective advertising provisions. In total, therefore, most of the early complaints against major marketers did *not* result in corrective advertising.

The FTC also brought a number of actions against smaller marketers, with some resulting in corrective orders. Table 3 provides a history of all FTC corrective ad orders.[2] Note that the smaller case orders were often for short-term retractions.

---

[2]See Scammon and Semenik (1982) for an interesting discussion of further aspects of the early program, plus more detailed coverage of corrective advertising requirements in each order.

CONCLUSION FROM THE EARLY CASES: A PAPER TIGER?

Most of the early corrective ad complaints did not yield corrective ad orders. Most of the orders which were issued, moreover, did not seem to contain strong disclosure requirements. In retrospect, the anxiety experienced in the marketing/advertising community at the time may seem overly strong in light of the actual orders. Corrective advertising at that point may have been a paper tiger which did little to affect either consumers or companies in the marketplace.[3]

Careful observers may recall, however, that the early orders were not the only cause for concern within the business community. Beyond any single case, corrective advertising represented an additional set of regulatory powers of government over business. Once in place, the spectre of expansion and/or abuse of such powers would always be a threat. For this reason, *litigation* was an important issue, for litigation would provide the route by which government power would be tested and legal issues clarified.

The FTC's Legal Authority for Corrective Advertising

A VAGUE MANDATE

The FTC was established in 1914 as the government's chief economic regulatory agency. Its goal is broad: to provide a "fair competitive and consumer environment" for our nation's economic system (Wilkie and Gardner 1974). Its written mandate is brief and vague.

One effect of a vague mandate is uncertainty as to an agency's legal authority to undertake new programs. Traditionally, the route to clarify FTC's authority is for it to bring and litigate a test case, then have its order appealed to the federal courts. In resolving the appeal, the courts must decide whether the new program exceeds FTC's power.

In the case of corrective advertising, the FTC's litigated 1975 order against Warner-Lambert (*Listerine* 1975) was appealed by the firm. The U.S. Court of Appeals upheld this order in a 1977 decision. In 1978 the U.S. Supreme Court declined to hear a further appeal (562 F. 2d 749 (D.C. Cir. 1977), *cert. denied,* 98 S. Ct. 1575 (1978)). These actions established the FTC's basic authority to order corrective advertising. There are, however, five key legal issues relating to this power. These create basic constraints on the FTC's corrective ad decisions.

THE FIVE UNDERLYING LEGAL CRITERIA

Table 4 summarizes the five legal standards that govern FTC's authority to employ corrective advertising. A brief consideration of the list indicates that it is both complex and

---

[3]Unfortunately, no formal evaluations of the effects of these orders were undertaken, and actual effects are unknown (Wilkie 1982). In the Profile Bread case, a confused picture emerged in the trade press. Early reports indicated brand sales were up, while later reports (and sworn testimony in the Wonder Bread case) indicated that Profile's sales fell substantially during the campaign. The firm, however, changed its marketing mix at the time, and indicated that publicity about the case was likely to have been responsible for the fall in sales (*Advertising Age* 1972, *Broadcasting* 1972, Wilkie 1973).

TABLE 4

The Five Legal Criteria for Corrective Advertising

Issue	Requirement for the Order
1. Orientation	The remedy must be prospective rather than retrospective in nature.
2. Goal	The remedy must be nonpunitive in nature.
3. Substance	The remedy must bear a reasonable relation to the violation in question.
4. Scope	The remedy must not infringe on the First Amendment rights of the firm.
5. Form	The remedy should be in the least burdensome form necessary to achieve an effective order.

interrelated.[4] While detailed legal discussions are beyond the scope of this article, the following paragraphs briefly describe the essentials of each criterion. For each criterion, a summary of the Circuit Court's *Listerine* decision is also provided, as these interpretations will guide future decisions in this area.[5]

1. *The "Prospective Remedy" Requirement.* The literal wording of the FTC Act empowers the agency to order firms to "cease and desist" from unfair or deceptive practices. Thus, FTC orders must serve to stop current violations and prevent future violations. Corrective advertising, however, seems to be a retrospective remedy. It seeks to have the consumer audience return to a consideration of *past* deceptions in order to rectify them. On the other hand, it can be argued that corrective advertising is *prospective* in that it seeks to have consumers not continue to rely upon false beliefs in their future purchasing: accordingly, corrective ads would be necessary to prevent future deceptions.

The key legal question at present is whether an FTC remedy can have both prospective and retrospective qualities, or whether corrective ads must be geared only to prevent prospective deceptions. Those opposed to corrective advertising stress a strict reading of the Act's language. Those in favor of the remedy as well as official FTC opinions (e.g., *Curtis Publishing Co.* 1971) argue, to the contrary, that in reality, almost all orders involve elements of both past and future—that this distinction is no barrier to corrective advertising.

Listerine and "Prospective Remedy" Summary.
The Circuit Court's *Listerine* opinion appears to narrow the interpretation of prospective remedy. The reasoning is subtle but significant. Essentially, the court chose not to accept the typical view of corrective advertising as aimed at removing deceptive residual effects which would likely influence future purchases. Instead, the court suggested that the key impact of residual effects is that they would likely make future Listerine ads deceptive. This

---

[4]See especially "Corrective Advertising" 1971, Cornfield 1977, "First Amendment" 1978.
[5]The court did not refer to these criteria specifically. This summary represents the authors' interpretations of each dimension. Interested readers should also consult interpretations provided in "Warner-Lambert" 1978, "First Amendment" 1978, "Recent Development" 1978.

would presumably be the case even if the ads were literally true, and even if the ads were entirely directed to a different promotional theme. In this legal sense, therefore, corrective advertising would be needed to prevent future deceptions. It would thus be solely prospective in nature.

This interpretation introduces additional complexities for future cases. For example, it appears that the FTC now has an additional burden of proof: not only must it prove (1) that past ads tended to deceive, and (2) that residual effects continue to exist, but it must also now demonstrate (3) that even truthful ads in the future are likely to have deceptive effects. On the other side, advertisers now face the task of demonstrating that future ads would not be made deceptive.

With respect to residual effects, this ruling could lead to a situation in which consumers might continue to purchase a brand on deceptive grounds (based on mistaken beliefs they hold about a brand) because the advertiser was able to demonstrate that certain new ads would not evoke the false associations, thereby avoiding corrective advertising. This type of loophole makes it likely that the prospective/retrospective issue will be tested in the future. The *Listerine* opinion, however, appears to have created a narrow basis at present.

2. *Nonpunitive Remedies*. The nonpunitive rule stems from the FTC's basic responsibility to stop unlawful practices and prevent their recurrence. It is clearly inappropriate, therefore, for the FTC to issue an order aimed at punishing an offender for past actions (unless he/she has violated a prior order).

An advertiser might argue, for example, that a requirement to make disclosures that result in losses of image or sales constitutes punishment (Cornfield 1977). However, this is likely to depend on the nature of the order itself. If sales or image losses were the effects of informed consumer behavior and were not designed as necessary outcomes of the order, the order would not have been punitive in intent (the fact that sales were lost, moreover, might be seen as good evidence that a corrective order was needed). If, on the other hand, the order had been designed to yield sales decreases, the firm would seem to have a strong case on the nonpunitive criterion.

Listerine and Nonpunitive Remedies Summary.
This issue was not treated in depth in the Circuit Court's opinion in *Listerine*. Instead, the court inserted the following footnote:

> "We express no view on the question whether an order intended to humiliate the wrongdoer would be so punitive as to be outside the Commission's proper authority."

Clearly, however, the court did not view corrective ads to be necessarily punitive in nature. As such, it now appears that the nonpunitive criterion is not a threat to corrective advertising, although it may still impact on the exact form of the order.

3. *The "Reasonable Relation" Rule*. The reasonable relation criterion is an elusive yet fundamental requirement for all FTC orders. In many cases, especially those involving disreputable marketing tactics, the violator is in fact likely to engage again in these types

of practices. If the Commission writes a very narrow and specific order, it runs the risk of the violator simply altering some details of the scheme so as to escape the bounds of the order. The FTC is thus prone to write broader orders, whenever possible, to foreclose such related violations that otherwise might occur. Legally, however, broader orders may tend to suppress lawful activity and may therefore be "unreasonable."

In essence, then, this criterion reflects the need for an FTC order to be appropriate, given the nature and facts of the case. It should go no further than necessary to effectively remedy the wrong.

> *Listerine and "Reasonable Remedies" Summary.*
> Here the Circuit Court's opinion stressed an examination of the case facts regarding: (1) the existence of residual effects in the consumer marketplace, and (2) the detailed FTC plan for removing these effects (the FTC plan is discussed in the next section of this article). In general, the court deferred to an FTC expertise in fashioning the remedy and appeared to view the plan as generally appropriate.

4. *First Amendment Rights.* The fourth criterion is that an FTC order should not infringe upon the advertiser's First Amendment rights of freedom of speech (FTC 1979). Advertisers have the right to express ideas, as well as the right to remain silent. It is clear that the constitutional protection afforded commercial speech does not extend to deceptive speech, however ("First Amendment" 1978). This removes most impediments to a corrective advertising remedy, assuming the other criteria are met.

There are, however, two potential issues lurking in this area. First, it is not clear that a corrective advertising order can legally suppress the free expression of other ideas by the advertiser. It may be, then, that an advertiser could attempt to undercut the effectiveness of the correction by disseminating other material counter to the corrective message's claims.

Also, the First Amendment right to remain silent may become a critical issue. For example, when American Home Products was ordered by an FTC administrative law judge (Hyun 1978) to engage in corrective advertising for Anacin's tension claims, the company replied that it might instead decide not to advertise at all. The Commission decided, on appeal, not to require corrective ads, however, so this issue went untested at that time.

> *Listerine and the First Amendment Summary.*
> The court opinion was clear as to the fact that deceptive commercial speech does not enjoy freedom from regulation. The opinion also dealt with the question of whether an advertiser might be precluded from the right to freely advertise truthfully, if ordered to include a required statement in ads. In dealing with this troublesome question, the court was able to rely on its "prospective remedy" rationale as follows: Since future Listerine ads would be deceptive without the required disclosure (according to the court), Warner-Lambert's constitutional right to advertise truthfully would not be threatened by the required disclosure.

With respect to an advertiser's right *not* to speak (i.e., not to advertise at all), the court was silent. It is likely, therefore, that this issue will be tested in a future case.

Overall, given that the First Amendment's relationship to commercial speech has recently been undergoing substantial analysis in the judicial sector, it would not be surprising to see further developments in the future.

5. *Least Burdensome Remedy.* The final standard reflects that the remedy should be in the least burdensome form to the marketer, consistent with effectively handling the problem. This means that the FTC's orders should minimize implementation costs, disruption of normal business, and other side effects.

While this criterion is not entirely settled, courts have used it to modify several recent FTC orders in other cases. In *Beneficial Finance Corporation* (1976), for example, the FTC's order had banned the phrase *Instant Tax Refund* from future advertising. The Commission concluded: "No brief language is equal to the task of explaining the Instant Tax Refund slogan, for the phrase is inherently contradictory to the truth of Beneficial's offer."

The Court of Appeals, however, stressed the least burdensome criterion, and instead offered the FTC the following disclosure as an example of what the firm might do to clarify the phrase: "Beneficial's everyday loan service can provide to regularly qualified borrowers an Instant Tax Refund Anticipation Loan whether or not the borrower uses our tax service." Having decided that an affirmative disclosure requirement, such as this statement, would be less burdensome than a ban of the phrase, the court remanded the case to the FTC for a new order.

Other courts, on appeal, have likewise demonstrated increased judicial concern with the burden of FTC remedies, and this will continue to be an issue for corrective advertising in the future.

Listerine and Least Burdensome Remedy.

The court decision displayed concern that the FTC had gone beyond the minimum required disclosure consistent with achieving an effective remedy. The FTC had ordered Listerine to disclose: "Contrary to prior advertising, Listerine will not help prevent colds or sore throats or lessen their severity." The court, calling the first phrase a "confessional preamble," determined that it was not necessary to include it in order to attract attention to the disclosure. The court then removed the phrase "contrary to prior advertising" from the corrective advertising order. With this modification, the court found the order to constitute a reasonable burden in relation to the violation found, and required Listerine to undertake corrective advertising.

CONCLUSIONS: THE LEGAL SETTING

In addition to the specific issues discussed, two key points emerge from our analysis of the legal setting for corrective advertising. One is that the area is quite complex and still under development. Particular case facts and arguments will impact on future court decisions and interpretations. The FTC and marketers will need to adapt to these considerations.

The second point is that the legal setting has some important deficiencies to consider. A careful reading of the legal treatment of corrective advertising provides convincing evidence of a *need for managerial and research understanding of marketing and consumer behavior*. Topics such as advertising strategy, consumer attitudes and decisions, and persuasive communication theory are all critical issues. The FTC and the courts are forced to deal with these issues, even though their attorneys and decision makers are likely to lack requisite training or experience in the area. The next section takes up this issue, concentrating on the FTC's management of the corrective advertising program.

FTC's Management of Corrective Advertising

THE CASE PROCESS

Concentrated attention on public debates and legal procedures has helped to obscure the fact that the FTC has been engaged in managing a new program. Even inside the agency, this recognition is often overcome by pressures of day-to-day concerns and focus on individual cases. In addition, different levels of the organization participate at different times in a case's progress; this adds to the difficulty of developing a coherent and streamlined program.

Figure 1 outlines the seven major stages of a case and the location of key decision points. Each stage takes considerable time. A "normal" span for a case may be three to

FIGURE 1

The FTC Case Decision Process[a]

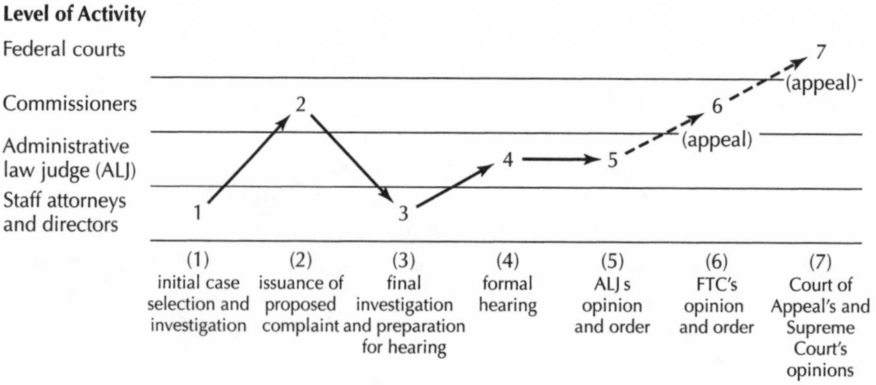

Level of Activity

Federal courts

Commissioners

Administrative law judge (ALJ)

Staff attorneys and directors

(1)	(2)	(3)	(4)	(5)	(6)	(7)
initial case selection and investigation	issuance of proposed complaint	final investigation and preparation for hearing	formal hearing	ALJ's opinion and order	FTC's opinion and order	Court of Appeal's and Supreme Court's opinions

Involvement by Levels	Stage	Decision	Brief or Argument
Federal courts	stage 7 only	stage 7	
Commissioners	stages 2 and 6 only	stages 2 and 6	stage 7[b]
Administrative law judge	stages 4 and 5 only	stage 5	
Staff attorneys and directors	stages 1, 2, 3, 4, 6	stages 1 and 3	stages 2, 4, 5, 6, 7

Type of Involvement

[a]This chart represents a fully adjudicated case. Consent orders can be issued at any point, thus terminating the process.
[b]The FTC is formally represented in the federal courts by its General Counsel's office.

four years, with major cases taking even longer (*Listerine* stretched over eight years). During this time span, moreover, many persons are involved in making case related decisions.

The Commissioners' Dual Role. Of special interest is the position of the Commission itself. FTC commissioners *cannot* participate in a case during most of its progress because of a dual role built into their positions. The five Commissioners must serve as *both top executives and impartial judges* at the FTC. As top managers, they must determine general policy and provide agency direction. As impartial judges, however, they must take care not to prejudge any individual case or rule proceeding.

This places severe pressure on the internal management system of the FTC. For example, the Commission must vote to issue a proposed complaint (stage 2 in Figure 1), but this is done as an administrative step and does not constitute a judgment on the actual outcome of that case.

Following this decision, the Commissioners and their assistants may not participate in any aspect of that case until it is ready for a final decision. At that time, they must rely upon the formal record, briefs, and opinion of the administrative law judge (ALJ) to reach their verdict.

Functions of the Staff. The net effect of this structure places most of the responsibility for program management on the shoulders of the "staff," consisting of Bureau directors and case attorneys. These persons identify potential cases, conduct initial investigations, engage in consent negotiations, develop proposed complaints and orders (all denoted as stage 1 in the Figure), and argue to the commissioners in favor of a case's initial complaint (stage 2). In stage 3 the staff develops further evidence, finetunes its case strategy, contacts expert witnesses, develops testimony, and takes depositions of opposing witnesses. Stage 4 involves the formal hearing: here the staff personnel carry out their strategy for developing a total record, and conduct direct and cross-examination of witnesses. In stage 5 they prepare written briefs and propose legal findings and an exact suggested order for the ALJ to issue against the marketer.

The ALJ then determines findings of fact, writes an opinion, and proposes an order; the order may be identical to one proposed by either side, or it may be a new form entirely. If, as is typical, the ALJ's opinion is appealed by either or both parties to the Commission, the staff prepares further briefs and engages in oral argument before the Commission (stage 6). If the resulting Commission order is then appealed to the court system by the firm (stage 7), the staff participates in developing the FTC's positions for arguments before the Court of Appeals and the U.S. Supreme Court.

Unfortunately, several characteristics of the FTC's staff role can hinder program development. There has been rapid turnover of FTC legal personnel, with many persons staying only two or three years before moving to private practice. Attorneys assigned to a given case may change several times during its progress. The recent changes in administrations and political philosophies, moreover, have also led to heavy turnover in the higher levels of the bureaus, where the overall programs are managed.

Case Pressures. Finally, the major pressures in a case are to "win" a verdict. In order to raise the probability of winning, most attorneys try to provide an arsenal of legal theories, facts, opinions, and arguments. Since this happens on both sides, rarely is a case neatly focused. Therefore, it is likely that a corrective ad case will *not* be brought and argued on a single, well-defined program basis, but instead will contain a range of reasoning.

Also, as Wilkie and Gardner (1974) have pointed out, the historic legal stress is on a "guilty-not guilty" verdict rather than the details of an order. We should recognize that the primary training of involved persons, particularly the staff attorneys, lies almost entirely with fact-finding and adversarial processes, not with questions of remedy development.

THE CORRECTIVE AD DECISION PROCESS

The creation of a corrective advertising order involves a series of judgments to be made. Figure 2 outlines the key decision stages. The process is geared toward three basic questions:

• Is a corrective ad order needed?
• If so, what exactly should the order require?
• (at a later time) Is the order achieving its objectives?

Need for a Corrective Order. As shown in Figure 2, the first phase of a corrective ad case requires three distinct decisions.

Decision 1 determines whether or not an advertisement has the "tendency and capacity" to deceive the consumer. This stage usually involves some showing of facts to provide the basis (or "factual predicate") for judging that an ad is misleading or deceptive. Marketing academics have recently begun to develop definitions and measurement methods to assist in this decision (see, e.g., Aaker 1974; Armstrong and Russ 1975; Gardner 1975; Jacoby and Small 1975; Preston 1976; and Russo, Metcalf, and Stephens 1981). Historically, however, the final interpretation of "tendency and capacity to deceive" has rested with the endowed expertise of the Commission. Preston (1982) provides an interesting discussion of the issues in this topic.

If the ad is judged deceptive, *Decision 2* involves whether to issue a traditional cease and desist order, or whether another form of remedy is needed to handle deceptive effects that will continue into the future. Several types of lingering deceptive effects are possible. For example, some deceptive practices lead to large one-time purchases by consumers, such as land purchases or contracts for vocational school education. In these areas, the FTC has sought restitution orders (decision 3 in Figure 2) under which offending firms had to refund money to consumers who were misled.

Returning to decision 2, at times future deceptive effects can involve consumers' knowledge gained from advertising. One problem the FTC often encounters is that some

---

FIGURE 2

Corrective and Decision Stages

A. Determining the Basis for the Order:

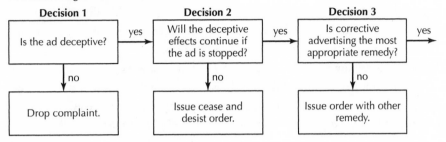

| Decision 1 | Decision 2 | Decision 3 |

| Is the ad deceptive? | →yes | Will the deceptive effects continue if the ad is stopped? | →yes | Is corrective advertising the most appropriate remedy? | →yes |

| ↓no | ↓no | ↓no |

| Drop complaint. | Issue cease and desist order. | Issue order with other remedy. |

B. Developing the Corrective Ad Order:

Decision 4

Determine exact requirements for the order.[a]

C. Monitoring Effectiveness of the Order:

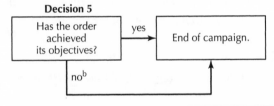

Decision 5

Has the order achieved its objectives? →yes→ End of campaign.

no[b]

---

[a]Decision 4 is a series of decisions, which include determination of exact objectives for the correction, content of the statement, wording of the statement, placement of the statement in the ad, duration of the campaign, media mix and schedule, and budget for the campaign.

[b]Failure to achieve objectives could possibly lead to a revision of the order, though this would present other problems concerning "due process" rights of the advertiser, and is not likely under the current corrective advertising programs.

---

deceptive ads do not disclose certain material information to consumers. Rather than having an entirely mistaken belief about the products, consumers in these cases are instead ignorant of an important fact about the offering. In these instances, affirmative disclosure orders can be employed, under which the advertiser must provide such information in future ads. During a recent eight-year period, the FTC issued over 200 orders of this type (Wilkie 1981, 1982).

Corrective advertising is a type of affirmative disclosure. Here the residual effects at issue are mistaken opinions spread by the ad campaign and held by consumers. In order to determine whether such effects exist in the market, substantial evidence is likely to be developed and evaluated within the adversarial process. This evidence can range from background facts on the campaign (e.g., length, budget, etc.), to copy test results, to surveys of consumers. (Also, as noted earlier, the *Listerine* decision may require a showing that future truthful ads will be rendered deceptive through residual effects at the consumer level. This would seem to call for experimental forms of evidence as well.)

Decision 3 then represents the choice of a stronger remedy such as a restitution order, affirmative disclosure, or corrective advertising, given the facts just developed. In extreme cases of health or safety danger, an injunctive remedy—stopping the sale of a dangerous product—may be sought by Commission staff. At the other extreme, the case facts may appear sufficiently innocuous to issue a cease and desist order.[6]

If the case facts call for a corrective ad order, *Decision 4* requires that a precise and entire order be developed. Although Figure 2 shows this as a single decision stage, there is no yes–no policy decision possible at this point; a number of arbitrary decisions must be made. *A detailed corrective advertising campaign must be developed, whether or not the attorneys involved know exactly how to dispel residual effects.*

Some illustrative decisions are outlined in the figure. These include: the determination of precise objectives for the corrective campaign, exact content of the statement, wording of the statement, placement in an ad, length of time for the campaign to be run, the campaign's budget, its media mix and scheduling, and so forth. Also, these decisions must factor in the severe constraints of the five legal criteria.

Decision 5, the evaluation, must also be planned at the time of the other decisions in order to obtain accurate "before" (baseline) measures. The evaluation's basic question involves the order's achieving its objective: Is the corrective campaign removing the lingering effects of the deception?

Only recently has the FTC built this monitoring stage into its decision process (results of two of the first evaluations are discussed in a later section). At present, there is a strange paradox associated with this stage. As noted in the figure, the monitoring stage has *no impact* on the process. Even if the evaluation said, "No, the corrective campaign is not working . . .," the campaign would continue exactly as per the order's requirements. Then, when the order's time limit is reached—even if the objectives have not been met—the campaign would end.

In summary, the overall corrective ad decision process is a complicated phenomenon, even in the abstract. In reality, it is even more complex; the *Listerine* case provides an excellent illustration of this point.

EXAMPLE: THE LISTERINE DECISIONS

This case arose as one of the 1971 set of FTC complaints seeking corrective advertising. Warner-Lambert had advertised for over 50 years that gargling with Listerine

---

[6]A much more active posture toward corrective advertising was formally advocated to the FTC in a 1976 petition from the Institute for Public Interest Representation (INSPIRE). This group proposed that, rather than rely on data on residual effects, corrective advertising be automatically required in all cases of deceptive ad campaigns involving health, safety, or nutrition, if the campaign had been run for a certain time period (six months or one year) (INSPIRE 1976). The FTC questioned the nature of this approach and did not proceed with the rulemaking process requested by the petitioners.

mouthwash helped prevent colds and sore throats by killing the germs that caused these illnesses. Given the long history of extensive advertising, the dominant market share (at one point over 60%), and the importance of cold prevention to consumers, FTC staff proposed corrective advertising as a necessary remedy.

Consent negotiations broke down, and the case went into litigation. Hearings were held for four months. Over 4,000 pages of testimony from 46 witnesses was offered. Almost all testimony concentrated on decision stages 1 and 2 of Figure 2. Within stage 1, the wording of the ads showed the claims had been made. A judgment of deception thus hinged on medical evidence as to the truth of the claims. Following testimony by expert witnesses, it was determined that the claims were not true; the ads were therefore judged deceptive.

Attention then turned to decisions 2 and 3—whether deceptive "residual effects" existed from these ads, and whether corrective advertising was warranted. Research evidence here involved three aspects of residual effects from Listerine advertising. These were advertising recall (consumers' memory after exposure), "ad registration" (consumers' perceptions of ad themes), and "product image" (consumers' beliefs about mouthwash brands). Company market research reports were subpoenaed and entered as evidence by the FTC attorneys, who argued that the data showed massive advertising impacts. Further, expert witnesses (Professors Frank Bass and Peter Rossi) asserted that the effects were likely to persist unless corrective advertising was used. Given the adversarial setting, Warner-Lambert was placed in the position of arguing that its ads had only minimal impacts and that these would not persist over time. The later judges, commenting on this line of argument, indicated doubt that advertisers would be willing to spend large sums of money in the expectation of such small returns.

Notably, *no testimony was introduced into the hearing on the question of how to remedy residual effects* (decision 4 in Figure 2). The drafting of the corrective ad order thus moved each decision maker into uncharted territory.

The nature of problems encountered can be appreciated if we trace the progression of the Listerine corrective ad order through the various levels of that case (see Table 5). First, the FTC staff attorneys proposed their desired order ("A" in the Table) in their brief to the ALJ. It provided a fairly long statement to be placed in every advertisement for a five-year period. A provision to shorten this period was included, in the event that a showing of the eradication of residual effects was to be made by the company. No dollar budget was given in this proposal.

Columns B, C, and D indicate the changes made by the ensuing decision makers. Administrative Law Judge Berman's order (shown in column B) shortened the statement slightly, removing the mention of FTC findings of deception. He retained most of the suggested specifications but shortened the campaign's duration to two years, while removing the company's option to provide evidence to lift the order.

TABLE 5

Listerine Order Provisions

Elements	A Proposal by FTC Staff in Hearing	B ALJ Berman's Order	C Commission's Order	D Court of Appeal's Order (final)
Required statement:	"The Federal Trade Commission has found, contrary to the prior advertising of the Warner-Lambert Company, the makers of Listerine, that Listerine will not prevent colds or sore throats, Listerine will not cure colds or sore throats, and Listerine will not be beneficial in the treatment of cold symptoms or sore throats."	"Contrary to prior advertising of Listerine, Listerine will not prevent or cure colds or sore throats, and Listerine will not be beneficial in the treatment of cold symptoms or sore throats."	"Contrary to prior advertising, Listerine will not help prevent colds or sore throats or lessen their severity."	"Listerine will not help prevent colds or sore throats or lessen their severity."
Specifications:				
print	Separated from text; type size at least as large as text, such that can be readily noticed.	(same as A)	(same as A)	(same as A)
broadcast	Presented in both audio and visual portions; no other sound in audio portion; in language principally employed in the ad.	(same as A)	(same as A)	(same as A)
both	Nothing in ad and should be inconsistent with or detract from the required disclosure.	(deleted)	(deleted)	(deleted)
Campaign duration:	Five years (plus provision to end earlier upon showing that residual effect had been dissipated).	two years	variable, likely one year	(same as C)
Required budget:	Variable (to be included in every Listerine ad during the period).	(same as A)	average annual expenditure 1962–72 (about $10 million)	(same as C)

The five FTC Commissioners, upon appeal of the ALJ's opinion and order, shortened the statement further (column C in Table 5) and maintained the specifications. However, they chose to change the type of budget decision. Noting that the variable budget allowed Listerine to escape the disclosure if it opted not to advertise the brand at all, the Commissioners required that the statement be disseminated. Rather than a time limit for the campaign, they set a budget of one year's average advertising expenditures, which amounted to about $10 million.[7]

When Warner-Lambert appealed the FTC's order to the courts, the final step in campaign development occurred. The Circuit Court of Appeals decided that all of the FTC's order decisions were reasonable, with one exception. The court felt that the introductory preamble, "Contrary to prior advertising . . .," was not necessary to ensure an effective campaign. This phrase was deleted from the final order which Listerine had to carry out.

A final twist occurred when Listerine placed the required disclosure into effect by creating advertising's first "corrective, comparative commercial." Mouthwash marketers had discovered that an onion theme was a useful symbol for evidence of product power. Listerine's corrective commercial featured two couples, with each husband finding himself having "onion breath." Each used mouthwash, one trying Scope and the other Listerine. After sniffing her husband's breath, one wife stated that she hadn't known that "clinical tests prove Listerine fights onion breath better than Scope." The other replied, "We always knew." The corrective disclosure had been placed midway in the 30-second spot as follows: "While [Listerine will not help prevent colds or sore throats or lessen their severity], breath tests prove Listerine fights onion breath better than Scope" (Giges 1978).

In terms of decision 5 in Figure 2, the FTC did plan and conduct a formal evaluation of the effectiveness of Listerine's corrective campaign. These recently available results are summarized next.

Research Evidence on Corrective Advertising's Impact

TYPES OF RESEARCH

This section is divided into two parts. First, we briefly examine findings from consumer laboratory experiments on corrective advertising. Second, we discuss recent field evaluations of consumer reactions to actual corrective ads, using three case histories. Each type of research offers special strengths and limitations, and each provides interesting insights.

CONSUMER EXPERIMENTS ON CORRECTIVE ADVERTISING

Table 6 summarizes this body of research. Studies were done in laboratory settings, with students as subjects, exposed to one or a few messages designed by the researchers. The

---

[7]This represented an average over a number of years and was thus understated to the extent that inflation, media costs, and market growth had increased recent expenditure levels.

TABLE 6

Summary of the Experimental Studies on Corrective Advertising Research

Researchers and Year of Experiment	Hunt (1973)	Dyer & Kuehl (1974)	Kassarjian et al. (1975)	Mazis & Adkinson (1976)	Sawyer & Semenik (1978)	Dyer & Kuehl (1978)	Armstrong et al. (1979)	Mizerski et al. (1980)
I. Background								
Place	lab	lab	lab	lab	lab	lab	lab	field
Advertised product	Chevron gasoline	soft drinks, suntan lotion	motorcycle helmet	Listerine	Listerine	Listerine	Listerine	Listerine
Medium	print	print/radio	print	radio	TV	print	TV	radio
Respondents	students	adults	students	students	adults	adults	adults	students
Number of exposures	one	one	one	one	one	one	one	four
Measurement over time	no	no	no	no	yes	yes	yes	yes
II. Results[a]								
Source effect	yes	yes	—	ns	—	ns	ns	—
Message content effect	yes	yes	ns	—	ns	—	—	—
Time effect	—	—	—	—	ns	yes	ns	—
Attitudes	yes	yes	yes	yes	—	—	—	ns
Target beliefs	—	—	—	yes	ns	yes	yes	yes
Nontarget beliefs	—	—	—	yes	ns	yes	—	ns
Evaluations[b]	—	—	—	yes	ns	—	ns	ns
Company image	yes	yes	ns	—	—	—	—	ns
Recall	—	yes	—	yes	—	—	—	—

[a]Results are summarized as follows: yes = a statistically significant effect was observed on this variable.
ns = no significant effect was observed on this variable.
— = not tested in the study.

[b]Refers to the a_i component of the Fishbein model of attitudes: it is a measure of a consumer's evaluation of specific product characteristics.

goals of this work, however, were to initially gauge the reactions consumers might have to corrective messages, and to study specific effects of different corrective conditions. Research control was thus needed.

Summary of the Early Studies. The earliest empirical studies were by Hunt (1973), Dyer and Kuehl (1974), and Kassarjian, Carlson, and Rosin (1975). In their contemporaneous Ph.D. dissertations, Dyer and Hunt varied corrective ads to examine consumers' sensitivity to different types of corrective messages. Both studies used student subjects. Dyer developed print and radio ads for soft drink and suntan lotion brands. Hunt used actual print ads from an FTC case against Chevron F-310 gasoline. Dyer varied the "strength" of corrective ad copy, the source of the message (FTC or company), and number of exposures. Hunt studied degrees of corrective explicitness and use of countering arguments (inoculations) by the advertiser.

Although methodologies differed, results were consistent. Both studies indicated that strongly worded corrective ads could have negative impacts on consumer brand perceptions. Hunt, for example, used three types of copy. His "normal" condition, a typical company ad, led to favorable brand ratings from consumers. His "general attack" corrective message reduced brand liking, yet still led to a slightly favorable attitude. His "explicit attack," however, resulted in negative brand attitudes (25% of the ad copy space used a statement that the FTC had found prior ads to be deceptive, specifying each deceptive selling point).

Dyer found strong corrective ads, in the form of FTC news releases, decreased intentions to purchase the brand. He also reported lower attribute ratings when corrections were repeated.

Kassarjian, Carlson, and Rosin tested a series of layout and message variations on perceptions of a motorcycle safety helmet that had been the subject of an FTC case. Results showed exposure to a correction lowered the favorableness in brand perceptions created by the misleading ad. Variations in corrective copy, however, did not produce differential results.

Conclusions from the Early Studies. The three early studies provided important findings. They showed corrective advertising to have a potential to shift consumers' brand perceptions. Such changes could extend to overall company image and might injure sales and share of market. The fact that a correction was being made seemed more important to consumers than minor variations in the messages themselves. Finally, this early research provoked the interest of other academic researchers in pursuing these issues.

Changes for the Later Experimental Studies. The later studies reflected three key changes in research approach. First, Wilkie's (1973, 1974, 1975) conceptual analyses of corrective advertising had pointed out the dangers of focus on attitudes and intentions and had proposed that consumers' brand beliefs should instead be the key dependent variable. The later studies adopted this view.

Second, the later research shifted its emphasis away from managerial issues (e.g., who should be named as the source of the correction or how strong the copy should be). This shift was stimulated in part by the weak results of these variables in the earlier studies, and in part by the appearance, in 1975, of the FTC's Listerine order, which was the topic in five of the key later studies.

A third major change reflected an increased emphasis on experimental design and conditions under which consumer impacts were being studied. Variables such as viewing or listening context, message repetition, and repeated measurement became important factors in these studies.

Summary of the Later Studies. In the first of these, Mazis and Adkinson (1976) exposed students to messages inserted in a television program. The broader context was intended to lessen subjects' concentration on the ads alone. Messages were developed from actual Listerine ads. Results showed corrective ads changed beliefs on Listerine's ability to prevent colds and sore throats. However, beliefs about Listerine's germ-killing capacity, not a target of the correction, were also affected, indicating a potential for possible punitive effects from corrective ads.

Later studies maintained the emphasis on beliefs and more natural settings. Dyer and Kuehl (1978) used a longitudinal design with adult education subjects. The first session presented print ads for several mouthwash brands, including a deceptive Listerine ad. Baseline belief measures were taken at this time. Three weeks later, subjects were shown corrective ads and asked again for their beliefs. Results showed corrective ads to lead to significant reductions in beliefs about Listerine's prevention of colds and germ-killing power (however, some persons continued to be deceived; the researchers indicated that increased repetitions would be necessary to eradicate the deception for these persons). Repeat measures taken again three weeks later showed the corrective effects to have persisted.

The question of persistence of corrective ad effects was also raised by Sawyer and Semenik (1978). Based on social psychology, they predicted a rapid loss of the corrective effect (a "decay") during the weeks following exposure to a correction. Their study inserted test corrective ads into a videotaped TV program. The initial corrections had little impact, however, obviating a test of the decay hypothesis.

Armstrong, Gurol, and Russ (1979) employed a similar design to that of Dyer and Kuehl, except that TV ads and student subjects were used. Results of this study showed the FTC-specified Listerine correction to reduce deception levels. A second set of measures showed these corrective effects to have largely persisted over a six-week period. However, the decay predicted by Sawyer and Semenik was also evident to some extent; deception levels were higher at six weeks than they had been immediately after exposure.

A fifth academic Listerine experiment by Mizerski, Allison, and Calvert (1980) was designed to improve upon some elements of the earlier studies. This study exposed students to repeated broadcasts of Listerine corrective ads on the campus radio station.

Results showed the corrective ad to have a significant impact on the target belief (prevention of colds and sore throats), but no impact on related beliefs such as germ-killing ability.

FIELD EVALUATIONS OF THREE CORRECTIVE AD CAMPAIGNS

The consumer experiments provided interesting and potentially important insights. In order to obtain effective manipulations, however, these studies had to employ limiting research controls. There is thus a question as to their generalizability to corrective campaigns run in the low involvement, real world marketplace.

Fortunately, six studies have recently been conducted on the effects of three FTC-ordered corrective ad campaigns: RJR Foods (Hawaiian Punch) (1973), STP Corporation (STP Oil Additive) (1976), and Warner-Lambert (Listerine) (1975). Three studies were sponsored by the FTC as part of its evaluation program; the other three are smaller scale studies undertaken within academic sponsorship. Results, however, are generally consistent across the set.

The Hawaiian Punch Case.
Hawaiian Punch, made by RJR Foods at the time, has been a strong brand name for some years. In 1971 the FTC investigated possible deception in the brand's advertising, which featured the catchy jingle, "Seven Natural Fruit Juices in Hawaiian Punch," together with colorful photos of natural fruits. In reality, however, the brand is called a "fruit drink" because its main ingredients are sugar and water—it contains only 11–15% fruit juice.

After extensive consent negotiations, RJR agreed to place, on the package and in all future advertising, a disclosure (not a strict correction) of the amount of fruit juice in the drink. In November 1972, six months before the FTC order was issued, the company began a voluntary disclosure ". . . contains *not less than* 11% natural fruit juices" (emphasis added).

Research Findings: Hawaiian Punch Order Effectiveness. Kinnear, Taylor, and Gur-Arie (1984) conducted a 17-wave series of semiannual telephone surveys, asking consumers in Ann Arbor, Michigan, about Hawaiian Punch. The sample is not projectable to the U.S. population, and could be biased upward. The results are nonetheless interesting. Over the 1974–82 period, the proportion of consumers who believed that Hawaiian Punch had 20% or less fruit juice increased from 20% (1974) to 40% (1975), to 50% (1979), to 70% in 1982. Substantial changes in belief levels thus have occurred (similar disclosures had been voluntarily made by Hi-C during this period, which may have contributed to this overall change). Looking at the results another way, however, this means that, *after 10 years of disclosure, 30% of the consumer market still holds false impressions about the actual fruit juice content of Hawaiian Punch.*

The STP Case.
In the late 1970s the STP Corporation allegedly violated the terms of an earlier FTC deceptive advertising order. As a result, STP signed a consent order in February 1978, agreeing to discontinue unsubstantiated oil savings claims, and pay $700,000 in settlement, including $200,000 to place corrective public notices in 14 periodicals. The STP

FIGURE 3

Required STP Corrective Notice

FTC NOTICE

As a result of an investigation by the Federal Trade Commission into certain allegedly inaccurate past advertisements for STP's oil additive, STP Corporation has agreed to a $700,000 settlement. With regard to that settlement, STP is making the following statement:

> It is the policy of STP to support its advertising with objective information and test data. In 1974 and 1975 an independent laboratory ran tests of the company's oil additive which led to claims of reduced oil consumption. However, these tests cannot be relied on to support the oil consumption reduction claim made by STP.
>
> The FTC has taken the position that, in making the claim, the company violated the terms of a consent order. When STP learned that the test did not support the claim, it stopped advertising containing that claim. New tests have been undertaken to determine the extent to which the oil additive affects oil consumption. Agreement to this settlement does not constitute an admission by STP that the law has been violated. Rather, STP has agreed to resolve the dispute with the FTC to avoid protracted and prohibitively expensive litigation.

---

disclosure, appearing once in each periodical, is given in Figure 3. The exact text was specified in the FTC order. The FTC's objectives for this order were never disclosed, but likely included both informing consumers about the unsubstantiated claims and alerting business that strong penalties were possible for violating FTC orders.[8]

Research Findings: STP Order Effectiveness. An FTC evaluation study, reported by Bernhardt et al. (1981), involved national surveys of consumers, businesspersons, and advertising managers, taken before and after the corrective ads appeared. Claimed (aided) recall of the ad tended to be low among the total general public (6%) and business (12%) samples, but considerably higher among advertising managers (32%). Overall, only about 2% of the general public and business samples could play back any specific elements of the corrective message.

However, a comparison of the before and after measures found that intentions to purchase STP had declined, and that awareness of problems with STP ads had significantly increased, for both consumers and businesspersons. The campaign did seem to be successful in informing consumers about STP's unsubstantiated advertising and in affecting their purchase intentions. Unintended side effects, such as negative beliefs about all oil additive products or the STP firm's overall image, did not materialize.

However, because ad recall had been so low, the true cause of consumer shifts in perceptions was unclear. The authors suggest that *publicity*—through television and newspaper accounts of the settlement—likely produced most of the effects, rather than the corrective ads themselves.

The role of publicity was further examined in research by Tyebjee (1982), who interviewed MBA students after the announcement of STP's $700,000 settlement but before the actual

---

[8]As noted earlier, a potentially important *indirect* consumer effect of corrective advertising may stem from a direct effect an order might have on the decisions of other advertisers. This deterrent effect might include fewer deceptive ads, modifications in wording, and checks built into the ad development process. It might also be too strong, of course, and tend to suppress useful claims and lawful activity. Orders such as STP thus also raise the question of the proper bounds on regulatory objectives.

appearance of the corrective messages. Precampaign publicity was found to have reached 38% of this admittedly nonrepresentative sample. The author concluded: "Public policy-makers must recognize that the press release, on which media publicity is based, is an important element in the intended remedy.... A concomitant responsibility is that the press releases do not engender damaging consequences beyond the mandated scope of the regulatory action" (Tyebjee 1982). As a result, it is clear that emphasis must be given to the total information outputs, including publicity, of a corrective advertising campaign.

The Listerine Case.
Warner-Lambert's corrective campaign, described earlier, ran for 16 months, beginning in September 1978 and ending in February 1980. In total, $10.3 million was spent, almost all on TV ads. The firm's spending rate was lower than for previous campaigns, averaging about 60% of normal levels during the first year. As noted, the ads stressed breath protection, with the five-second corrective disclosure placed midway (in both audio and video) in the thirty-second spots.

Research Findings: Listerine Order Effectiveness. Three field studies, two sponsored by the FTC, provide excellent evidence on the impacts of the Listerine order. The first FTC study focused on ad communication, using Burke day after recall tests. This test monitors the first-time showing of a commercial in an area with delayed telephone interviews of a sample of consumers. Consumers' abilities to recall the commercial are measured, together with which details are recalled.

Results of the Burke tests early in the campaign did not bode well for the ultimate impact of the Listerine correction. The ad itself was well-recalled. Its chief promotional themes (breath protection and the Scope comparison) were well-communicated. A special test to assess whether the correction would hinder such promotional efforts indicated that it did not; the authors concluded that "... inclusion of the corrective message did not enhance or reduce the overall memorability of the ad" (Mazis, McNeill, and Bernhardt 1981).

The corrective disclosure itself, however, was not nearly as memorable as the promotional themes. It was the fourth most recalled message in the ad, with only about 5%, or 1 in 20, of the commercial's viewers mentioning the presence of the corrective message. When prompted for aided recall, results did not much improve. Only about one person in every five who remembered the commercial was able to identify the content of the corrective disclosure. Overall, considering the entire audience who viewed the commercial, *seven out of eight consumers could not recall the corrective message the day after having seen it.*

Two studies focused on before-after changes in consumers' beliefs about Listerine. Armstrong, Russ, and Gurol (1981) employed four waves of telephone interviews; one wave just before the corrective campaign, two more at six-month intervals during the campaign, and the fourth just after the campaign ended. Among its complex set of analyses, this study reported a reduction of only about 20% in overall deceptive beliefs about Listerine's effectiveness. The authors concluded that, while the corrective campaign had worked to some extent, its overall impact was not large.

This conclusion was reinforced by results of an FTC field study consisting of seven waves of questionnaire mailings, before and during the campaign, to the Market Facts consumer panel (Mazis 1981). Over 10,000 questionnaires were returned, a 70% response rate. The findings demonstrate a clear pattern of effects. For example:

- 22% of Listerine users associated the corrective message with the advertising campaign.
- beliefs that Listerine is effective for colds and sore throats fell about 11% (down 14% for Listerine users).
- consumers believing cold/sore throat effectiveness is extremely important in mouth-wash declined from 25% to 21% (for Listerine users, from 37% to 33%).
- a 40% drop in the amount of mouthwash used for colds and sore throats was reported.

Analysis indicated that the effects were due to the corrective advertising order and its attendant publicity, but publicity's impact alone could not be separated out.

While significant effects were observed, it is also true that *substantial problems were not rectified* through the corrective campaign. For example:

- 42% of Listerine users still believed, at the *end* of the campaign, that Listerine was still being promoted as effective for colds and sore throats.
- 57% of Listerine users continued to rate cold and sore throat effectiveness as a key attribute in their purchasing (only 15% of Scope users reported a similar goal).
- 39% of Listerine users reported continued use of mouthwash to relieve or prevent a cold/sore throat.
- as of the end of the study, 45% of the Listerine users continued to hold that the brand is "one of the best" for cold/sore throat relief or prevention. Listerine was the *only* mouthwash brand strongly associated with this attribute.

The overall pattern of results on other measures in the study provides further support for Mazis' (1981) conclusion: ". . . while the FTC remedy appears to have had an impact on consumers, the approach used falls short of fully informing consumers . . . the use of Listerine for [cold/sore throat relief and prevention] is still quite prevalent" (p. 3).

Conclusions: Consumer Research Findings

The accumulated body of research is extremely helpful in assessing this remedy's impact. Corrective ads have potential to provide consumers with useful information, which may change beliefs and modify purchase behavior. They do not appear to have a substantial impact on company image, or on that of the general product category. They do seem capable of modifying consumers' views of key product attributes and of spreading such effects to closely related product beliefs. Minor variations in messages are not likely to strongly affect consumers. Major changes, however, such as Hunt's (1973) "explicit attack" copy, can have significant effects. Future sales gains can accrue to a firm having to run corrective ads. Publicity, which is partially controlled by releases from FTC's Public Information Office and partially determined by the uncontrolled press, appears to have been an important factor in at least three cases—Profile Bread, STP, and Listerine. Publicity may play a much more significant role than had previously been recognized.

Beyond these points, the evaluation research on actual corrective orders reveals a strikingly consistent pattern of general results:

Corrective advertising has "worked," but not nearly well enough to even approach correcting the misimpression levels in the marketplace.

Analysis and a Proposal

LESSONS LEARNED

What have we learned from over a decade of corrective advertising cases and research? Table 7 advances 10 conclusions. No. 7 is perhaps the most surprising: *Consumer effectiveness of corrective advertising has not been the primary concern of the orders issued to date.* The reasons for this are relatively straightforward: Most of the cases were begun when corrective advertising was an experimental regulatory effort. Policymakers recognized that signed consent orders would establish an actual rather than proposed program. These would also serve as precedents for later cases in which corrective ads were sought by the FTC.

In each early case, details of order were prime negotiating points. In the FTC's view, a weaker provision (but one to which an advertiser would agree) might still be attractive. Not only would protracted, costly, and possibly unsuccessful litigation be avoided, but

---

TABLE 7

Summary Conclusions on Corrective Advertising

1. The FTC is empowered to order corrective advertising as a remedy against deceptive advertising campaigns.
2. There are important legal constraints as to when and in what manner the FTC can employ this remedy form.
3. Corrective advertising holds the potential to yield beneficial effects for consumers.
4. Corrective advertising appears to hold the potential to affect the sales and/or image of the advertised brand.
5. There is little evidence of a systematic FTC program for corrective advertising:
   - bursts of case activity have been followed by long periods of inactivity.
   - philosophical and personnel changes occurred throughout the 1970s and early 1980s at both the staff and Commissioner levels.
   - past orders have used a wide range of requirements for corrective advertising.
6. Consent negotiations between FTC staff members and company representatives have played a key role in the exact requirements in almost every case to date.
7. Consumer effectiveness of corrective advertising has not been the primary concern of the orders issued to date.
8. In communication terms, past corrective advertising orders against major advertisers appear to have been weak.
9. In terms of consumer impacts, the major corrective advertising orders appear *not* to have been successful in remedying consumer misimpressions across the marketplace.
10. If corrective advertising is to continue as an FTC remedy, some changes in the form of the orders will be required.

signed consent orders also meant that issues of legal constraints and advertisers' rights were under control. Finally, and not to be underestimated, there was general uncertainty on both sides about how strong the effects of these new disclosures might be. In the face of this uncertainty, conservative orders might again have seemed a reasonable course to follow.

Thus there were many important concerns at work, all within a turbulent, adversarial setting. Quite simply, the matter of ensuring consumer effectiveness was subordinated to other issues. This continued in *Listerine,* even with several levels of authority involved in the decisions and order. While the regulators and court undoubtedly desired consumer effectiveness, their serious attentions were directed at other stages of the case (e.g., evidence on deception, residual effects, and the need for correction), and at legal issues of FTC authority.

Was consumer effectiveness a primary facet of the *Listerine* order? Clearly not. No testimony on this point was included in the voluminous record of evidence. While each review level did alter details of the order's required text, budget, and campaign duration, each such change was made only on the basis of judgment, without any apparent use of research or other inputs as to which alternative might work more effectively at the consumer level.

Finally, no provision was made for revising the disclosure requirements in the event they weren't effectively informing consumers, or for stopping the disclosure early if it had already done its job. Instead, all aspects of the order were fixed, then run, then terminated. In referring to the overt lack of concern with consumer impacts, Wilkie (1982) has commented:

> An observer familiar with marketing must wonder at the sight of a judge removing a significant phrase in an ad, and a corporation embarking on a $10 million campaign, all without any apparent testing to ascertain possible effects (p. 101).

Three Knotty Problems

The low priority of actual consumer effectiveness in past cases is particularly unfortunate: in theory, consumer effectiveness *is* the fundamental rationale for corrective advertising. There are, however, formidable barriers to achieving consumer effectiveness. In particular, three characteristics of the setting, fairness, communication, and motivation, can conflict, thus presenting serious dilemmas for policymakers.

1. *The Need for Fairness to the Advertiser.* The five legal criteria (Table 4) actually represent restrictions on governmental abuse of power. Each is intended to protect marketers' rights in our society. The five criteria also, however, complicate the development of an "effective" order. The FTC's order must strive to be strong enough to eradicate deception, but must not be too strong so as to unfairly injure the advertiser. Thus there is a need for great precision.

2. *The Inherent Complexity of Consumer Communications.* Unfortunately, the demand for great precision is made on an area which does not lend itself to precision. Communicating with consumers is inherently complex; their attention must be captured, their interest in the message sustained, their beliefs altered, and the new cognitions retained.

The FTC has taken on the role of explicating exactly what must be done to achieve these purposes. Its orders have generally failed in this task. This is not surprising, however, when we consider the difficulty of these tactical decisions. For example, how long should the campaign run, in which media, and with which schedules? What budget is needed for the total effort? Should the correction be separated from other brand promotions, or can it be integrated into them? What exactly should the corrective copy say? How should it be delivered, by whom, and for how much time or space?

Marketers will recognize that these kinds of questions are no different than those asked every day for all advertising campaigns. The legal constraints, however, make these questions more pointed, since overkill must be avoided. For example, in the Listerine case, how could it have been known before the fact that precisely $10 million was needed? Perhaps the necessary sum was double or triple this amount, or perhaps it was only one-tenth of it. Also, the required statement may have been too weak or too strong. A better statement might have needed a substantially lower budget, which might then have saved a few million dollars.

3. *The Minimal Motivation of the Firm.* The third troublesome characteristic of the present situation is that once the FTC's order is issued, no one is actively working for its success at the consumer level. The advertisers' chief objectives are to maintain and enhance the brand's sales levels. While legally bound to carry out the exact dictates of the order, the advertiser is in no way obligated to do more than that.

At the practical level, almost all past orders have allowed the company to employ corrective disclosures within their normal promotional ads. Since these are designed to leave consumers with highly favorable brand images, it is not surprising that the corrections have not exactly been highlighted within the ads. They've not been used as openers, to set a somber or remorseful tone, nor have they been used to close the commercials, leaving consumers with a last important piece of information. Instead, the corrective statements have generally been sandwiched somewhere in the middle, sometimes out of context, and always with other promotional thoughts following.

This point is not intended as a criticism of advertisers; they were doing only what could be expected in this situation. Nor is it intended as a particular criticism of FTC decision makers; they had to attend carefully to the legal and political environment. Instead, our belief is simply that the legal system poses these types of barriers from the consumer perspective.

A Proposal: Take the FTC Out of the Business of Creating Advertising!

The past approach has clearly fallen short on consumer impact and is likely to continue to fail unless revised in important ways. We would therefore suggest several key revisions as part of an improved approach to corrective advertising decisions. This approach realigns the activities and responsibilities of both the FTC and the offending advertiser.

The essence of this approach, originally developed by Wilkie (1973), is to focus on *consumer effectiveness* in corrective advertising orders. This proposal has two distinct implications: (1) Instead of stressing the details of the required corrective *stimulus* before the campaign, the FTC should shift its stress to actual consumer *responses* during the campaign; and (2) instead of using their experience and expertise to *minimize* consumer impact from the disclosure, advertisers should be given incentives to seek effective corrective communication. The goal of the approach is to be more equitable, more efficient, and more effective than the traditional system.

The Improved System

Figure 4 outlines the essentials. Stage I parallels the traditional approach; deception and its residual misimpressions are assessed here. At stage II, however, the approaches diverge

---

FIGURE 4

Essentials of the "Effectiveness Standard" System Proposal

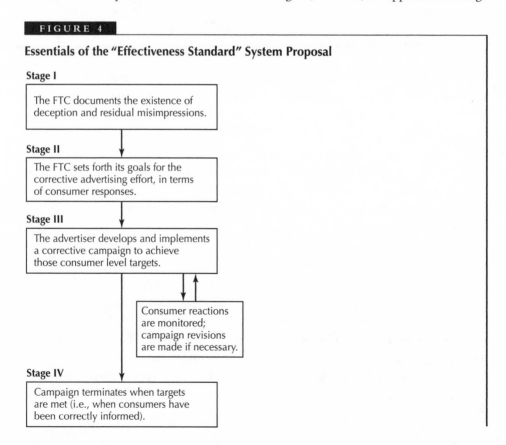

Stage I

The FTC documents the existence of deception and residual misimpressions.

Stage II

The FTC sets forth its goals for the corrective advertising effort, in terms of consumer responses.

Stage III

The advertiser develops and implements a corrective campaign to achieve those consumer level targets.

Consumer reactions are monitored; campaign revisions are made if necessary.

Stage IV

Campaign terminates when targets are met (i.e., when consumers have been correctly informed).

sharply. Rather than assuming the mantle of "the public's advertising agency" and asserting a degree of expertise that no advertiser possesses (that is, the ability to completely design an entire ad program which is not too strong, not too weak, but precisely right for achieving neutral informational impacts across the consumer market), *the Commission could offer the respondent company the option of remedying its own deception in its own ways.*

Thus, in stage II the FTC would need only to formalize its own corrective advertising objectives in terms of desired effects on consumers and a time frame for the effort. In general, it appears that the brand beliefs that consumers hold is the appropriate level for definition of consumer effects (see Wilkie 1973 for a more detailed analysis of this issue).[9]

Two types of consumer effect standards could be set, absolute or relative. Absolute levels might, for example, specify the exact percentages of target consumers who would need to be correctly informed about the brand's actual characteristics.[10] Relative levels, on the other hand, would involve consumer belief comparisons (termed normative belief levels by Gardner 1975) with competitive brands that had *not* been deceptively advertised. This would recognize that some consumers will make some inferences about products which are not the result of advertising.

Stage III represents the actual corrective campaign. The key difference here is that *the advertiser is free to plan and conduct any type of marketing effort to achieve the targeted results.* Advertising would not be required if other options (e.g., letters, posters, stickers, shelf displays, labels, etc.) could better accomplish the goals. Cost would not be an issue either—the advertiser would keep whatever was saved through a more efficient campaign.

Motivation for an effective corrective effort would come from the consumer target levels, and the need to achieve these levels within a specified time period of perhaps one year. If the target levels were not reached, the firm would be subject to penalties for violating an FTC order; such penalties are currently $10,000 per day per violation.

The prospect of penalties makes it likely that the firm would closely monitor the progress of the corrective campaign. The FTC would also monitor at this time, for two reasons: (1) to protect consumers and competitors from new deceptions that could accompany the corrective efforts, and (2) to protect the interests of the advertiser who is attempting to meet the consumer targets in good faith but is unable to do so.

While their interests will likely never coincide, this arrangement offers some prospect of the two parties working together, rather than at cross-purposes, to achieve consumer effectiveness. When the desired outcome is reached (stage IV), the firm would be relieved of further corrective disclosure requirements, even if this were to occur soon after the onset of the corrective advertising effort.[11]

---

[9]Hoyer, Jacoby, and Nelson (1982) suggest tactical considerations in changing beliefs under conditions of low involvement and/or holistic processing.

[10]Absolute levels face a political problem, in terms of how the press might treat them. If, for example, the FTC were to set a 75% level, this could be headlined, "Government Sanctions Deception of One-Fourth of the Population: Says 50 Million Can Be Deceived!" Also, legal precedents may be set which might not be appropriate for other cases having different consumer market settings.

[11]Given the Sawyer and Semenik decay hypothesis, however, it might be argued that a follow-up check should be taken at a later time.

A PARTIAL APPLICATION: THE HAWAIIAN PUNCH CASE

In working with FTC staff attorneys, the senior author had the opportunity of partially applying the approach in the RJR Hawaiian Punch case. The order emerged from protracted consent negotiations involving disclosure of the actual fruit juice content in the product. The order did not specify a budget for the disclosure ("contains not less than 11% natural fruit juice"), nor did it set a specific time limit. Instead, the Hawaiian Punch disclosure was required to be run continuously into the future; it could be stopped only when a consumer survey was submitted, demonstrating that consumers no longer held incorrect impressions of actual fruit juice content.

The order went on to specify the exact survey protocol—method, sampling, independence of the research house, interviewer training and control, and questionnaire. Criterion levels for consumer beliefs were set in the order: RJR could cease the disclosure when the survey revealed that a target percent of consumers are aware that Hawaiian Punch contains no more than 20% natural fruit juice. The target percent varied, depending on the likelihood of a consumer's consumption of the brand:

- disclosure ends if 67% of fruit drink purchasers are aware.
- disclosure ends if 80% of current or prospective Hawaiian Punch purchasers are aware.
- disclosure ends if 95% of consumers who have purchased Hawaiian Punch within the month preceding the survey are aware.

In retrospect, several points about the order deserve mention. First, it now seems clear that the choice of a flexible time period rather than a specific time limit (within which the knowledge had to be communicated) was an unfortunate decision. As the Kinnear, Taylor, and Gur-Arie (1984) results so graphically point out, consumer beliefs changed very slowly in this case, probably due to a weak disclosure requirement in the order. It was not until *nine years after the start of the disclosure* that the first target level (67%) was reached.

Second, Kinnear, Taylor, and Gur-Arie (1984) found essentially no differences in the belief levels of the three target segments in the order. That is, consumers who bought Hawaiian Punch within the past month are no more aware of the actual juice levels of the brand than are those who use the product class generally. As a result, the order could allow the termination of the disclosure (through the 67% target), even though research also showed that over 30% of the target market of Hawaiian Punch buyers continues to hold erroneous beliefs about the brand's juice content.

Third, however, the Hawaiian Punch order represented a tentative step toward concern with consumer effectiveness on the part of a number of FTC staffers and the Commissioners themselves. The appearance of this type of order was applauded by both business media and consumer advocates; in each case the approach was viewed as an improvement over traditional practices.

ADDITIONAL REFINEMENTS AND CONSIDERATIONS

Other issues naturally arise in moving toward a consumer effectiveness system. Chiefly among these are: good faith compliance efforts, untoward side effects, and related types of effectiveness standards.

Good Faith Compliance. The underlying issue here is that every order issued by the FTC must be constructed so that a firm is able to successfully perform its dictates if it makes "good faith" efforts to do so. With corrections, however, it is possible that some consumer beliefs could prove resistant to all reasonable efforts. In this case, if able to demonstrate such efforts, the firm should *not* be held to have violated the terms of the original order (although it may be appropriate to reopen the case to improve the order).

Untoward Side Effects. Similarly, but on the other side of the coin, the order should not allow an advertiser to create new marketplace problems while correcting old ones. Monitoring the progress of the corrective campaign should help reduce risks of either good faith or side effect problems. As most large consumer product companies already maintain periodic tracking studies, incremental costs of monitoring would be low in these cases. For some smaller marketers though, incremental costs could be relatively high. In these cases some form of cost sharing, or some restricted form of the effectiveness approach, may need to be developed.

Copytest Standards. Some forms of copytests could be used to accompany consumer effectiveness standards, to assess the messages consumers are likely to take away from the corrective disclosures under consideration by the firm. Either standard testing services or special designs could be used, with testing as either a formal part of the order or an informal step in the process. In contrast to consumer belief levels (representing postcampaign effect measures), copytest standards would reflect precampaign attempts to ensure that planned efforts will succeed. This would reduce risks for both sides by proving evidence for good faith questions as well as information on the likely effectiveness of the correction.

In *Listerine,* for example, the day after recall results (reported earlier) played no role in the decision process, despite the fact that the corrective message was shown to be performing poorly. Under a consumer effectiveness approach, however, these results would likely have led to substantial improvements made on the disclosure before it was aired. Overall, some form of precampaign monitoring could attempt to efficiently screen out ineffective corrective ads before they were run, thus reducing risks for the advertiser and raising the prospects for consumer effectiveness.

Conclusion

This article attempts to trace the major threads comprising the history, controversy, theory, and practice of corrective advertising. It is clear that corrective advertising is a complex phenomenon. It cannot be comprehended within any single perspective, whether this be a legal, economic, managerial, or consumer research viewpoint. Separate sections were thus devoted to covering the beginnings and cases of this remedy, the legal issues involved in its application, the complex managerial questions and decision system, and the findings from consumer research on impacts of this remedy in the past. After considering all of these factors, a number of conclusions were reached about the remedy, and a proposal for an improved decision system was advanced.

More broadly, though not stressed in this article, we believe that "The Case of Corrective Advertising" is representative of many topic areas within the rubric of marketing regulation. The underlying analytical framework in this article, therefore, should also be useful for persons in marketing who seek to understand other areas of marketing regulation. Over the longer run, we would hope that increased inputs from persons in marketing and consumer behavior would help to produce more effective, efficient, and equitable public policies in our field.

References

Aaker, David A. (1974), "Deceptive Advertising," in *Consumerism: Search for the Public Interest*, David A. Aaker and George S. Day, eds., New York: Free Press.

American Bar Association (1969), *Report of the American Bar Association to Study the Federal Trade Commission*, Washington, DC: The Association.

Amstar Corp. (1973), D8887 (October 2), 83 FTC 659.

Armstrong, Gary M., Metin N. Gurol, and Frederick A. Russ (1979), "Detecting and Correcting Deceptive Advertising," *Journal of Consumer Research*, 6 (December), 237–246.

___ and Frederick A. Russ (1975), "Detecting Deception in Advertising," *MSU Business Topics*, 23 (no. 2), 21–32.

___, ___, and Metin Gurol (1981), "Attitude and Belief Changes from Corrective Ads," working paper, University of North Carolina.

Beauty-Rama Carpet Center (1973), C-2398 (May 2), 82 FTC 1340.

Beneficial Finance Corp. v. FTC, 542 F2d. 611 (3d. Cir. 1976).

Bernhardt, Kenneth, Thomas C. Kinnear, Michael B. Mazis, and Bonnie Reece (1981), "Impact of Publicity on Corrective Advertising Effects," in *Advances in Consumer Research*, Kent B. Monroe, ed., 8, 414–415.

Boise Tire Co. (1973), C2425 (July 16) 83 FTC 21.

Brozen, Yale (1972), "No Scarlet Letters: Advertising Has Come under Dangerous and Unfair Attack," advertisement, *Wall Street Journal*, 179 (March 7), 16.

Campbell Soup Co. (1970), 77 FTC 664.

Cohen, Dorothy (1980), "The FTC's Advertising Substantiation Program," *Journal of Marketing*, 44 (Winter), 26–35.

Cornfield, Richard A. (1977), "A New Approach to an Old Remedy: Corrective Advertising and the FTC," *Iowa Law Review*, 61 (no. 2), 439–474.

"Corrective Advertising Orders and the FTC" (1971), *Harvard Law Review*, 85 (no. 2), 477–506.

Cox, Edward, R. Fellmeth, and J. Schultz (1969), *The Consumer and the Federal Trade Commission*, Washington, DC: American Bar Association.

Curtis Publishing Co. (1971), 78 FTC 1472, 1514.

Dyer, Robert F. and Philip G. Kuehl (1974), "The Corrective Advertising Remedy of the FTC: An Experimental Evaluation," *Journal of Marketing,* 38 (January), 48–54.

____ and ____ (1978), "A Longitudinal Study of Corrective Advertising," *Journal of Marketing Research,* 15 (February), 39–48.

Firestone Tire and Rubber Co. (1972), 8818, 81 FTC 393.

"First Amendment Limitations on FTC Corrective Advertising Orders" (1978), *Georgetown Law Review,* 66 (August), 1473–1513.

FTC (1979), "Consumer Information Remedies," FTC Bureau of Consumer Protection (June).

Gardner, David M. (1975), "Deception in Advertising: A Conceptual Approach," *Journal of Marketing,* 34 (January), 40–46.

Giges, Nancy (1978), "Listerine Slips in Disclaimer," *Advertising Age,* 49 (September 11), 2, 128.

Hoyer, Wayne D., Jacob Jacoby, and Margaret Nelson (1982), "A Model for the Development, Evaluation, and Supplementation of Remedial Advertising Statements," in *Proceedings, Southwestern Marketing Association,* D. Corrigan, F. Kraft, and R. Ross, eds., 9–12.

Hunt, H. Keith (1973), "Effects of Corrective Advertising," *Journal of Advertising Research,* 13 (October), 15–24.

Hyun, Montgomery K. (1978), "Initial Decision: FTC v. American Home Products and Clyne Maxon," FTC Dkt. 8918 (September 1).

Institute for Public Interest Representation (INSPIRE) (1976), *Petition for Rulemaking before the Federal Trade Commission,* Washington, DC: The Institute.

ITT Continental Baking Co. (1971), C2015 (August 17), 79 FTC 248.

____ (1973), 8860, 83 FTC 865.

Jacoby, Jacob and Constance Small (1975), "The FDA Approach to Defining Misleading Advertising," *Journal of Marketing,* 34 (October), 65–68.

Kassarjian, Harold H., Cynthia J. Carlson, and Paula E. Rosin (1975), "A Corrective Advertising Study," in *Advances in Consumer Research,* 2, M. J. Schlinger, ed., 631–642.

Kinnear, Thomas C., James Taylor, and Odee Gur-Arie (1984), "Affirmative Disclosure: Long-term Monitoring of Residual Effects," *Journal of Business Policy and Marketing,* 2, forthcoming.

Lens Craft Research and Development Co. (1974), D8950 (September 4), 84 FTC 355.

Matushita Electric of Hawaii Inc. (1971), CI867 (February 19), 78 FTC 353.

Mazis, Michael B. (1979), "Can and Should the FTC Restrict Advertising to Children," in *Advances in Consumer Research,* 6, William L. Wilkie, ed., 3–6.

____ (1981), "The Effects of FTC's Listerine Corrective Advertising Order," A Report to the FTC, Washington, DC: FTC.

____ and Janice Adkinson (1976), "An Experimental Evaluation of a Proposed Corrective Advertising Remedy," *Journal of Marketing Research,* 13 (May), 178–183.

____, Dennis L. McNeill, and Kenneth Bernhardt (1981), "Day after Recall of Listerine Corrective Commercials," working paper, Washington, DC: American University.

Mizerski, Richard W., Neil K. Allison, and Stephen Calvert (1980), "A Controlled Field Study of Corrective Advertising Using Multiple Exposures and a Commercial Medium," *Journal of Marketing Research,* 17 (August), 341–348.

National Carpet (1973), C-2399 (May 2), 82 FTC 1354.

Ocean Spray Cranberry (1972), D8840 (June 23), 80 FTC 975.

Payless Drug Stores (1973), C2406 (May 25), 82 FTC 1473.

Pitofsky, Robert (1977), "Beyond Nader: Consumer Protection and the Regulation of Advertising," *Harvard Law Review,* 90 (no. 4), 661–695.

Preston, Ivan L. (1976), "A Comment on 'Defining Misleading Advertising' and 'Deception in Advertising'," *Journal of Marketing,* 35 (July), 54–57.

___ (1983), "Research on Deceptive Advertising: Commentary," in *Information Processing Research in Advertising,* Hillsdale, NJ: Erlbaum, 289–305.

Ratner, Ellis et al. (1978), *FTC Staff Report on Television Advertising to Children,* Washington, DC: FTC, Bureau of Consumer Protection.

"Recent Development: First Amendment Restrictions on the FTC's Regulation of Advertising" (1978), *Vanderbilt Law Review,* 31 (no. 2), 349–373.

Rhode Island Carpets (1974), 8946, 84 FTC 555.

RJR Foods Inc. (1973), C2424 (July 13).

Russo, J. Edward, Barbara Metcalf, and Debra Stephens (1981), "Identifying Misleading Advertising," *Journal of Consumer Research,* 8 (September), 119–131.

Sawyer, Alan G. and Richard J. Semenik (1978), "Carryover Effects of Corrective Advertising," in *Advances in Consumer Research,* 5, H. Keith Hunt, ed., 343–351.

Scammon, Debra L. and Richard J. Semenik (1982), "Corrective Advertising: Evolution of the Legal Theory and Application of the Remedy," *Journal of Advertising,* 11 (no. 1), 10–20.

Shangri La Industries, Inc. (1972), C2301, 81 FTC 596.

STP Corp. (1976), C-2777, 87 FTC 56.

Sugar Information, Inc. (1974), C2308 (November 1), 81 FTC 711.

Sun Oil Co. (1974), 8889, 84 FTC 247.

Thain, Gerald (1972–73), "Advertising Regulation: The Contemporary FTC Approach," *Fordham Urban Law Journal,* 1, 349–394.

Tyebjee, Tyzoon T. (1982), "The Role of Publicity in FTC Corrective Advertising Remedies," *Journal of Marketing and Public Policy,* 1 (Winter), 111–122.

Warner-Lambert (1975), 8891, 86 FTC 1398.

"Warner-Lambert v. FTC: Corrective Advertising Gives Listerine a Taste of Its Own Medicine" (1978), *Northwestern University Law Review,* 73 (December), 957–979.

Wasems, Inc. (1974), C2524 (July 23), 84 FTC 209.

Wilkie, William L. (1973), *Consumer Research and Corrective Advertising,* Cambridge, MA: Marketing Science Institute.

___ (1974), "Research on Counter and Corrective Advertising," in *Advertising and the Public Interest,* S.V. Divita, ed., Chicago: American Marketing, 189–202.

___ (1975), *Applying Attitude Research in Public Policy,* Cambridge, MA: Marketing Science Institute.

___ (1981), *Affirmative Disclosure: A Survey and Evaluation of FTC Orders Issued from 1970–1977,* Washington, DC: Federal Trade Commission.

___ (1982), "Affirmative Disclosure: Perspectives on FTC Orders," *Journal of Marketing and Public Policy,* 1 (Winter), 95–110.

___ and Paul Farris (1975), "Comparison Advertising: Problems and Potential," *Journal of Marketing,* 39 (October), 7–15.

___ and David M. Gardner (1974), "The Role of Marketing Research in Public Policy Decisionmaking," *Journal of Marketing,* 38 (January), 38–47.

Yamaha International, Inc. (1974), C2747 (October 23), 86 FTC 973.

What to Convey in Antismoking Advertisements for Adolescents: The Use of Protection Motivation Theory to Identify Effective Message Themes

Cornelia Pechmann, Guangzhi Zhao, Marvin E. Goldberg, and Ellen Thomas Reibling

Antismoking advertising is increasingly used, but its message content is controversial. In an initial study in which adolescents coded 194 advertisements, the authors identified seven common message themes. Using protection motivation theory, the authors develop hypotheses regarding the message theme effects on cognitions and intentions and test them in an experiment involving 1667 adolescents. Three of the seven message themes increased adolescents' nonsmoking intentions compared with a control; all did so by enhancing adolescents' perceptions that smoking poses severe social disapproval risks. Other message themes increased health risk severity perceptions but were undermined by low perceived vulnerability.

There is considerable agreement that programs should be undertaken to prevent minors from smoking cigarettes (Centers for Disease Control and Prevention [CDC] 1999). The number of U.S. states that use paid antismoking advertising targeted at youths has increased from 1 in 1986 (Minnesota Department of Health 1991) to more than 21 in 2002 (Campaign for Tobacco-Free Kids 2002). Also, the American Legacy Foundation (2002) runs antismoking television advertisements nationwide. Funding primarily comes from the 1997 settlement between tobacco firms and the U.S. attorneys general (National Association of Attorneys General 2000). The sponsors of antismoking advertising use diverse message themes, and though there is widespread agreement that choice

CORNELIA PECHMANN is Associate Professor of Marketing and GUANGZHI ZHAO is a doctoral student in marketing, Graduate School of Management, University of California, Irvine. MARVIN E. GOLDBERG is Irving and Irene Bard Professor of Marketing, Smeal College of Business Administration, Pennsylvania State University. ELLEN THOMAS REIBLING is Director of the Health Education Center and a doctoral student, School of Social Ecology, University of California, Irvine. This research was funded by a grant to the first author from the California Tobacco-Related Disease Research Program. The authors sincerely thank University of California, Irvine MBA students Marion McHugh, Deborah Thompson, and George Chen for their assistance with data collection and Gerald Gorn and the anonymous *JM* reviewers for their feedback on previous drafts of this article.

Pechmann, Cornelia, Guangzhi Zhao, Marvin E. Goldberg, and Ellen Thomas Reibling (2003), "What to Convey in Antismoking Advertisements for Adolescents: The Use of Protection Motivation Theory to Identify Effective Message Themes," *Journal of Marketing*, 67 (April), 1–18.

of theme matters, there is considerable disagreement as to what choice to make. As Teinowitz (1998, p. C1) explains,

> Do you warn teens, many of whom think they are invincible, about death and disfigurement? Or do you suggest that Big Tobacco is the new evil empire . . . or that not smoking is much cooler than engaging in it? If you think the answer is obvious, you haven't seen the distinctly different approaches taken by the four states that have recently run anti-smoking ad campaigns. . . . History shows you get less smoking but how much less will depend, to a large degree, on the message used.

Evidence of the efficacy of different antismoking message themes is limited and conflicting. A report by Teenage Research Unlimited (1999) concludes that health messages are efficacious, whereas Goldman and Glantz (1998) advocate messages attacking the tobacco industry and Worden, Flynn, and Secker-Walker (1998) recommend social norm messages. Many of these conclusions are based on focus group research, which can be unreliable (Blankenship and Breen 1993), as can uncontrolled field studies. Florida has reported that its "Truth" advertisements attacking tobacco firms are effective, on the basis of surveys showing 40% and 16% declines in smoking among middle and high school students in the state, respectively (Bauer et al. 2000; see also Farrelly et al. 2002). However, Monitoring the Future (Johnston, O'Malley, and Bachman 2001) shows nearly comparable declines (30% and 14%) in the southern region of the United States as a whole, where no antismoking advertisements were running. Apparently, most of the decline was due to a macro trend, rather than to an advertisement-specific effect. Therefore, it is unclear whether anti–tobacco industry advertisements work.

The most fundamental question that must be addressed is whether using any of the common antismoking messages makes sense from a public health perspective, compared with doing nothing at all (Pechmann 2002). That is, will any of these message themes dissuade youths from smoking? To address this question, we examined 194 antismoking advertisements and created a typology of commonly used message themes. Then, we conducted an experiment to investigate the effects of each message theme on adolescents' smoking-related cognitions and intentions compared with a no-message control. We employed protection motivation theory (Rogers 1983) to help us predict why certain message themes might work or not work, because it is a highly comprehensive theory of health communication (Boer and Seydel 1996). Moreover, the antismoking advertisement sponsors sought to influence many of the cognitions that are the focus of this theory (Parpis 1997). Although our research primarily addresses social marketing, it also explores the broader issue of how youths make decisions about risky behaviors (Benthin, Slovic, and Severson 1993; Fischhoff et al. 2000). In particular, we examine the weight placed on health versus social risks (Ho 1998) and the integration of data about risk severity versus vulnerability (Weinstein 2000).

Protection Motivation Theory

Protection motivation theory (Rogers 1983) posits that people's motivations or intentions to protect themselves from harm are enhanced by four critical cognitions or perceptions, regarding the severity of the risks, vulnerability to the risks, self-efficacy at performing the advocated risk-reducing behavior, and the response efficacy of the advocated behavior. In addition, the theory posits that people's intentions to protect themselves are weakened by the perceived costs of the advocated risk-reducing behavior and the perceived benefits of the opposing risk-enhancing behavior. These cognitive processes are divided into two subprocesses: threat appraisal (severity, vulnerability, and benefits) and coping appraisal (self-efficacy, response efficacy, and costs). In general, the factors underlying each appraisal process have been studied separately, though occasionally threat or coping appraisal has been studied as a whole (Sturges and Rogers 1996; Tanner, Hunt, and Eppright 1991). According to the theory, people can be motivated to engage in desirable health behaviors not only to avoid health risks but also to avoid social or interpersonal risks (Rogers 1983). Of late, researchers have increasingly focused on messages that stress social risks (Dijkstra, De Vries, and Roijackers 1998; Mahler et al. 1997; Schoenbachler and Whittler 1996). Furthermore, protection motivation theory has recently been extended formally to include social risks (Ho 1998). Some researchers have argued that cognitive mediators are insufficient for explaining people's intentions to avoid risks and that fear should be included as an added affective mediator (Tanner, Hunt, and Eppright 1991; Witte 1992). Rogers (1983, p. 165) disagrees, however, and cites his results showing that "fear arousal does not facilitate attitude change unless this arousal directly affects . . . cognitive appraisal."

Protection motivation theory (Rogers 1975, 1983) posits that, in most cases, cognitions will affect intentions directly and additively, though at times, certain cognitions will function interactively or synergistically. The 1975 version of the theory posits two- and three-way interactions among severity, vulnerability, and efficacy. The 1983 version of the theory excludes all three-way interactions, as well as the two-way interactions of severity with vulnerability and self-efficacy with response efficacy. However, a recent meta-analysis (Floyd, Prentice-Dunn, and Rogers 2000) suggests that these two-way interactions may be important after all (see also Weinstein 2000).

Researchers have sometimes tested protection motivation theory using surveys. They have measured all the cognitive variables and intentions and examined the cognition–intentions links (e.g., Flynn, Lyman, and Prentice-Dunn 1995; Ho 1998). More commonly, though, researchers have conducted experiments in which they have manipulated a subset of the cognitive factors through social marketing messages, frequently using real messages from practitioners, as we do here (Burgess and Wurtele 1998; Castle, Skinner, and Hampson 1999; Steffen 1990; Weinstein, Sandman, and Roberts 1991). They have examined the effects of these messages on the target cognitions and intentions, often compared with a no-message control group (Mahler et al. 1997; Tanner, Hunt, and Eppright 1991; Witte 1992). This is the approach we adopt. To our knowledge, no experiment has sought to manipulate all six protection motivation theory cognitions because doing so would be too unwieldy, particularly given a standard full-factorial design. The perceived costs of the risk-reducing behavior and the perceived benefits of the risk-enhancing behavior have been studied the least (Floyd, Prentice-Dunn, and Rogers 2000; Milne, Sheeran, and Orbell 2000), perhaps because these factors weaken protection motivation intentions, and researchers have pragmatically focused on factors that strengthen intentions.

In this research, we use protection motivation theory to formulate hypotheses regarding the likely impact of seven common antismoking message themes on the cognitions that they attempt to influence, namely, health and social risk severity and self-efficacy at refusing cigarette offers and resisting tobacco marketing. In formulating these hypotheses, we review prior experiments to assess "cognitive malleability," or the ease with which severity and efficacy perceptions can be influenced. Furthermore, we assess the likelihood that if a message theme affects a cognition, it will also affect intentions. Here, we refer to meta-analysis results regarding the average effect size of each cognition on intentions (Floyd, Prentice-Dunn, and Rogers 2000; Milne, Sheeran, and Orbell 2000). In considering effects on intentions, we also examine possible two-way interactions between cognitions, because a cognitive variable could have a weak effect on intentions as a result of a moderator that reduces, nullifies, or even at times reverses its impact (Rogers 1975, 1983). We studied all of the protection motivation theory cognitions except response efficacy, which we presumed to be irrelevant in this context, because refraining from smoking is 100% effective for avoiding the risks incurred by becoming a smoker.

Hypotheses Regarding the Effects of Message Themes on Cognitions

DISEASE AND DEATH MESSAGE THEME

Disease and Death messages discuss how smokers suffer from serious diseases, such as emphysema and lung cancer, and often die prematurely. The goal of these advertisements is to convey the "harsh medical realities of the effects of smoking" (Parpis 1997, p. 35). In one stimulus advertisement used in our study, a camera follows smoke going down the throat of an adult smoker, which reveals fleshy lumps starting to grow; a voice-over states, "One damaged cell is all it takes to start lung cancer growing." Another advertisement talks about how smokers inhale poisons such as "arsenic, carbon monoxide, and formaldehyde" that "immediately affect their hearts, lungs, and brains." A third advertisement shows an adolescent male smoking, who slowly turns into a skeleton; it states, "Smoking: it's only a matter of time."

From the perspective of protection motivation theory (Rogers 1983), the intent is to increase perceptions of health risk severity. Prior studies have used similar manipulations to increase the perceived severity of unhealthy behaviors such as smoking (Maddux and Rogers 1983), unprotected sex (Block and Keller 1998), illicit drug use (Schoenbachler and Whittler 1996), and alcohol abuse (Kleinot and Rogers 1982). Manipulating health risk severity seems fairly easy to do through brief text or graphics, as in a brochure stating that unprotected sex can cause AIDS or syphilis (Block and Keller 1998) or a graphic print advertisement showing a person in a hospital who has overdosed on a drug (Schoenbachler and Whittler 1996).

We did not expect the Disease and Death messages to affect health risk vulnerability perceptions, however. These messages included none of the information that is known to enhance vulnerability perceptions, such as personal or genetic risk factors (Rippetoe and Rogers 1987; Weinstein 1983; Wurtele and Maddux 1987), probabilities of occurrence (Maddux and Rogers 1983; Mulilis and Lippa 1990), or familiar symptoms (DePalma, McCall, and English 1996). Instead, we predicted a single effect for Disease and Death messages on cognitions.

H$_1$: The Disease and Death (versus control) antismoking message theme will enhance adolescents' perceptions of the severity of the health risks of smoking.

ENDANGERS OTHERS MESSAGE THEME

Endangers Others messages stress how secondhand smoke, and smoking in general, can seriously harm smokers' family members, coworkers, and peers. The primary intent of these advertisements is "raising individuals' awareness of environmental tobacco smoke (ETS), with advertisements that portray the risks of breathing someone else's smoke" (California Department of Health Services [CA DHS] 2001, p. 84). Some advertisements also stress that when smokers die prematurely, family members suffer emotionally and financially. In one stimulus advertisement, an uncaring father's cigarette smoke envelops his frightened toddler who, in a plea for help, spells out "sudden infant death syndrome" in alphabet blocks. Another advertisement shows smoke entering rooms in a home with children and states, "Your children don't smoke and they don't want to; but when your home fills with second hand smoke, they don't have a choice; instead, every innocent breath they take eats away at them, causing asthma. . . ." In yet another advertisement, a teenager sadly explains that her mother has died of a smoking-related disease and will never attend her graduation or wedding: "All the important stuff, she won't be there."

Endangers Others advertisements are similar to Disease and Death advertisements in terms of depicting severe health risks. What is unique about Endangers Others advertisements is that they also convey that smokers may encounter strong social disapproval from nonsmokers. The advertisements suggest that many nonsmokers are disappointed in or angry at smokers for their lack of consideration of others. Some advertisements also subtly chastise smokers for hurting others. Surveys have found that Endangers Others advertising often prompts nonsmokers to voice their disapproval of smoking by asking the smokers in their midst—for example, family members or friends—not to smoke around them or even to stop smoking altogether (CA DHS 2001; Connolly and Robbins 1998).

According to protection motivation theory, Endangers Others messages seek to increase the perceived severity of the health and social disapproval risks of smoking. On the basis of prior studies, it appears to be fairly easy to manipulate social risk severity perceptions (Jones and Leary 1994; Mahler et al. 1997), just as it is with health risk severity perceptions. Schoenbachler and Whittler (1996) used a print advertisement showing young people rejecting a teenage drug user. Dijkstra, De Vries, and Roijackers (1998) sent letters to smokers stating that their family members would appreciate it if they quit. Therefore, we predict that

H2: The Endangers Others (versus control) antismoking message theme will enhance adolescents' perceptions of (a) the severity of the health risks and (b) the severity of the social disapproval risks of smoking.

COSMETICS MESSAGE THEME

Cosmetics messages stress that smokers must cope with highly unattractive and annoying side effects that are cosmetic in nature, such as smelliness. The messages attempt to convey that "smoking has many unpleasant consequences that can lead to social disapproval, such as bad breath, yellow teeth, smelling bad" (Minnesota Department of Health 1991, p. 52). In one stimulus advertisement, a teen compares a smoker's breath to a dog's breath and concludes that the latter "is slightly less putrid." In another advertisement, a teen offers strategies to enhance guys' attractiveness to girls and warns, "Nix the smoking; that yellow teeth and cigarette stench thing; it's not working." In a third advertisement, youths brush their teeth after smoking but find that their mouths are full of ashes; the advertisement warns, "You can brush, you can gargle, but you can't get rid of cigarette mouth."

From the perspective of protection motivation theory, Cosmetics messages attempt to enhance perceptions that smoking poses severe social disapproval risks because of its unattractive side effects. However, it is possible that adolescents might not be too concerned about such problems, which cosmetic products such as breath sprays and gums can easily remedy. In most prior studies that enhanced perceptions of social risk severity, the messages stressed appearance-related risks that cosmetics products could not remedy, such as curvature of the spine from osteoporosis (Klohn and Rogers 1991) or wrinkles from excessive sun exposure (Jones and Leary 1994). The Endangers Others messages seem to convey more serious social concerns as well, by stressing that many nonsmokers believe that smoking is inconsiderate and violates their right to breathe clean air. However, given adolescents' hypersensitivity to being evaluated by others (Graham, Marks, and Hansen 1991), we predict that even Cosmetics messages will be effective.

H₃: The Cosmetics (versus control) antismoking message theme will enhance adolescents' perceptions of the severity of the social disapproval risks of smoking.

Smokers' Negative Life Circumstances Message Theme

Most adolescents want to appear mature, independent, savvy, attractive, and cool, and many think that smoking will help them realize these goals (CA DHS 1990, p. xi; see also Miller 1998). Smokers' Negative Life Circumstances messages suggest that smoking "is a barrier to achieving [these] goals" (Miller 1998, p. 2743). Specifically, the advertisements use graphic, gross, and antisocial images to convey that smoking is a hindrance, rather than a pathway, to achieving higher-order aspirational goals (Parpis 1997; Pechmann and Shih 1999). Smokers are depicted as disheveled "losers" in a variety of unattractive life circumstances, who have quite obviously taken the wrong path in life.

In one stimulus advertisement, an attractive young male demonstrates to a disheveled and befuddled smoker that smoking is as ill-conceived as sticking one's head in a toilet; "Smoke away," the advertisement jeers at the end. Another advertisement pokes fun at a sophomore who unwisely "started smoking in junior high," showing him as a scrawny old man with a whiney voice and a cigarette poking out of his mouth. One more advertisement shows a young female smoker who tries to beautify herself for a date; instead, she turns into an ugly witch sitting in a bathtub, giggling inanely. The graphic, negative imagery in Smokers' Negative Life Circumstances advertising is designed to suggest that smokers are viewed as losers and will experience severe social disapproval from peers. Translating this idea into protection motivation theory terms, we predict that

H₄: The Smokers' Negative Life Circumstances (versus control) antismoking message theme will enhance adolescents' perceptions of the severity of the social disapproval risks of smoking.

Refusal Skills Role Model Message Theme

Refusal Skills Role Model messages explain why many attractive role models view smoking as unappealing and demonstrate refusals of cigarette offers (Worden et al. 1988). In one advertisement, a girl confides to a friend, "I don't want to go out with him; he was smoking and he thought it was cool"; instead, she is impressed with another boy who says "no thanks" when offered a cigarette. A different advertisement shows kids being stalked by a cigarette, and one strong, brave boy knocks the cigarette out with boxing gloves. In yet another advertisement, a famous football player symbolically kicks a cigarette away like a football, stating, "No way was I going to lose to some tiny little cigarette."

Turning to protection motivation theory, one goal of the advertising is to increase perceptions that smoking poses social disapproval risks. The attractive role models clearly indicate that they disapprove of smoking and smokers. These role models could make quite an impression because, as was mentioned previously, social risk perceptions generally appear to be malleable (Dijkstra, De Vries, and Roijackers 1998; Jones and Leary 1994;

Mahler et al. 1997; Schoenbachler and Whittler 1996). Refusal Skills Role Model advertising also attempts to enhance adolescents' perceptions of self-efficacy at refusing cigarette offers (Worden et al. 1988). The advertising shows role models successfully refusing cigarettes, which may teach skills and raise viewers' expectations that they too are capable of refusing (Bandura 1997).

However, self-efficacy perceptions have proved to be quite rigid and often cannot be changed unless intense interventions are used that permit practice and mastery of focal skills (Bandura 1997). Rohrbach and colleagues (1987) increased adolescents' feelings of self-efficacy at refusing alcohol offers with a three-hour intervention involving demonstrations and practice that progressed from simple rehearsals to extended role plays. Bryan, Aiken, and West (1996) boosted female subjects' self-efficacy regarding condom use with a multifaceted intervention including a video of condom purchases, role-playing of asking a partner to wear a condom, and demonstrations of how to put a condom on a partner. Refusal Skills Role Model advertising relies on passive observation, so we were uncertain whether it would influence self-efficacy perceptions. However, we expected the advertising to influence social risk perceptions.

> H_5: The Refusal Skills Role Model (versus control) antismoking message theme (a) will enhance adolescents' perceptions of the severity of the social disapproval risks of smoking and (b) may enhance their perceptions of self-efficacy at refusing cigarette offers.

MARKETING TACTICS MESSAGE THEME

Marketing Tactics messages stress that tobacco firms use powerful marketing tactics such as image advertising and target marketing and that children, women, and minorities are prime targets. The advertising sponsors believe that "the strategy makes [children] stop and consider that smoking may not be an act of their own free will" (CA DHS 1990, p. 26). In one stimulus advertisement, cigarettes rain down on a schoolyard while a tobacco executive explains, "We have to sell cigarettes to your kids; we need half a million new smokers a year just to stay in business, so we advertise near schools, at candy counters. . . . We have to." Another advertisement features a former tobacco lobbyist who says, "Maybe they'll get to your little brother or sister, or maybe they'll get to the kid down the block, but one thing is perfectly clear to me: the tobacco companies are after children." One more advertisement shows a cigarette billboard claiming that women want "rich flavor." The billboard peels away to reveal the company's true motive: "Women are making us rich."

Marketing Tactics messages attempt to increase adolescents' knowledge about cigarette marketing tactics, including the perpetrators, target audiences, effects, and ethics. This multidimensional knowledge base has been labeled "persuasion knowledge" (Friestad and Wright 1994). Ideally, such knowledge should enhance youths' perceptions of control over tobacco marketers' persuasion attempts (Campbell and Kirmani 2000). As Friestad and Wright (1994) explain, when a person understands that an agent's action is a persuasion attempt, a "change of meaning" occurs, wherein the person can exert control over the persuasion attempt.

In protection motivation theory terms, Marketing Tactics advertising seeks to boost adolescents' knowledge regarding tobacco marketing tactics and, ultimately, their self-efficacy at resisting such tactics. The advertising may increase knowledge, as many media literacy programs have been shown to do (Banspach, Lefebvre, and Carleton 1989; Brucks, Armstrong, and Goldberg 1988). However, it is less clear whether the advertising will enhance skills and self-efficacy, because it relies on passive observation (Bandura 1997). Media literacy programs that have improved skills typically have enabled students to practice and master those skills (Dorr, Graves, and Phelps 1980; Feshbach, Feshbach, and Cohen 1982). Consider, for example, Peterson and Lewis's (1988, p. 167) successful program:

> The individual learning module for that day was defined . . . and modeled by the experimenter who gave several examples. . . . Then, an advertisement that included the item relevant to that learning module was shown. . . . The rest of the session was spent with the children viewing advertisements and identifying items relevant to the present learning module, and helping the children make up their own examples.

Because watching advertising is fundamentally different from this type of program, we predict that

> H_6: The Marketing Tactics (versus control) antismoking message theme may enhance adolescents' perceptions of self-efficacy at resisting tobacco marketing.

SELLING DISEASE AND DEATH MESSAGE THEME

Selling Disease and Death messages claim that tobacco firms use manipulation and deception to pressure consumers into purchasing a product that causes serious diseases and even death. The advertising seeks to persuade adolescents to resist tobacco marketers' tactics. As one advertising sponsor explains, youths "are quick to excuse the tobacco executives as simply doing their jobs," and so it is important to "expose the tobacco industry as different from other industries" (Miller 1998, pp. 2743–44). One advertisement features a former cigarette model who pleads with viewers in a grossly distorted voice due to throat cancer. She says, "I was a model in cigarette ads, and I convinced many young people to smoke; I hope I can convince you not to." A second advertisement shows the brother of a Marlboro Man who has died from lung cancer; he explains, "The tobacco industry used my brother . . . to create an image that smoking makes you independent; don't believe it; lying there with all those tubes in you, how independent can you really be?" A third advertisement shows a woman who has lost her trachea because of smoking; she smokes from a hole in her throat and states, "They say nicotine isn't addictive; how can they say that?" These advertisements stress smoking's severe health effects. They also seek to enhance persuasion knowledge, so youths will be less influenced by tobacco marketing and feel a greater sense of control over it, which should translate into en-hanced self-efficacy. On the basis of our previous assumption that severity perceptions are more malleable than self-efficacy perceptions, we posit that

> H_7:   The Selling Disease and Death (versus control) antismoking message theme (a) will en-hance adolescents' perceptions of the severity of the health risks of smoking and (b) may enhance their perceptions of self-efficacy at resisting tobacco marketing.

SUBSTANTIVE VARIATION MESSAGE CONDITION

In our experiment, each subject saw just one of the previously discussed message themes, which was represented by eight stimulus advertisements. We also tested a heterogeneous, or Substantive Variation, condition (Schumann, Petty, and Clemons 1990), in which subjects saw all themes, one advertisement per theme. The Disease and Death, Selling Disease and Death, and Endangers Others advertisements dealt with health risk severity. The Endangers Others, Cosmetics, Smokers' Negative Life Circumstances, and Refusal Skills Role Model advertisements dealt with social risk severity. The Marketing Tactics and Selling Disease and Death advertisements addressed self-efficacy at resisting tobacco marketing. The Refusal Skills Role Model advertisement addressed self-efficacy at refusing cigarette offers.

In the Substantive Variation condition, just one or at most two advertisements con-veyed each message theme, so that the total number of stimulus advertisements could be held constant, at eight advertisements, across message conditions. Ideally, the one or two advertisements on each theme would influence the focal cognitions almost as effectively as the set of eight similar advertisements in each other message condition. Prior protec-tion motivation studies have included substantively varied or heterogeneous message con-ditions and have found them to be highly effective at influencing cognitions (Sturges and Rogers 1996). For example, Maddux and Rogers (1983) find that essays that discuss health risk severity and vulnerability and self- and response efficacy enhance all four types of cognitions. On the basis of this rationale, we predict that

> H_8:   The Substantive Variation (versus control) antismoking message condition (a) will en-hance adolescents' perceptions of the severity of the health and social disapproval risks of smoking and (b) may enhance their perceptions of self-efficacy at resisting tobacco marketing and refusing cigarette offers.

Hypotheses Regarding Effects of Cognitions on Intentions

Next, we turn to the issue of whether antismoking message themes that induce changes in adolescents' risk severity or self-efficacy cognitions will produce corresponding changes in their intentions. Meta-analyses indicate that all of the protection motivation theory cogni-tions significantly affect youths' and adults' intentions and behaviors (Floyd, Prentice-Dunn, and Rogers 2000; Milne, Sheeran, and Orbell 2000). However, self-efficacy perceptions seem to have at least twice as much influence as risk severity perceptions. Milne, Sheeran, and Orbell (2000) report mean effect sizes of .10 for severity and .33 for self-efficacy. Floyd, Prentice-Dunn, and Rogers's (2000) estimates are .39 for severity and .88 for self-efficacy. Therefore, although we posited previously that severity perceptions are more malleable and more likely to be affected by antismoking advertising, self-efficacy perceptions seem to be more important in terms of influencing intentions.

It should be noted, though, that these meta-analysis results are based primarily on messages that stress health risks. The effect sizes for social disapproval risks are unknown. Recent studies suggest that young people may be more influenced by social risks than health risks (Ho 1998; Jones and Leary 1994; Schoenbachler and Whittler 1996). With regard to smoking, youths' perceptions of social norms have been found to be among the strongest predictors of their smoking intentions (Chassin et al. 1984; Collins et al. 1987; Conrad, Flay, and Hill 1991). For parsimony, though, we base our formal hypothesis on protection motivation theory (Rogers 1975, 1983), which makes no predictions regarding the relative impact of different cognitions on intentions, thus implying roughly equivalent effects for each cognition.

H_9: Adolescents' intentions not to smoke will be a positive function of perceived (a) health risk severity and vulnerability, (b) social disapproval risk severity and vulnerability, (c) self-efficacy at refusing peers' cigarette offers, and (d) self-efficacy at resisting tobacco marketing; these intentions will be a negative function of perceived (e) benefits of smoking and (f) costs of not smoking. Therefore, if anti-smoking advertising influences risk severity or self-efficacy perceptions (H_1–H_8), it should influence intentions too.

Meta-analyses have examined only two potential interactive effects (Floyd, Prentice-Dunn, and Rogers 2000). The joint effect of self-efficacy and response efficacy was found to have a .41 effect size, but as discussed previously, response efficacy does not seem to be relevant in the context of smoking prevention. (Not smoking is clearly an effective response for avoiding the risks of being a smoker.) Of greater interest here is that the joint effect of health risk severity and vulnerability had an effect size of .54. What is most notable is that when these variables were manipulated separately, their effect sizes were .39 and .41, respectively. The variables' combined effect might be expected to be .80 (.39 + .41), yet it was only .54, which suggests a negative synergistic effect. For example, the combined manipulation might have increased severity perceptions a great deal and vulnerability perceptions much less so. This result could be problematic, because increases in severity given low vulnerability could have null or even counterproductive effects on intentions (Mulilis and Lippa 1990).

Considerable research shows that stressing the severe health risks a behavior poses can enhance its allure by making it more thrilling or positively arousing, if perceived vulnerability is low (Benthin, Slovic, and Severson 1993; Klein 1993; Wood et al. 1995). This phenomenon has been referred to as a "forbidden fruit" reaction (Pechmann and Shih 1999).

For example, the most extreme roller coaster ride often has the greatest appeal because riders can experience an intense thrill and feel brave and macho with no apparent risk to themselves. Adolescents in particular seem to be attracted to forbidden fruit, because many believe they are invulnerable to physical harm (Arnett 2000; Cohen et al. 1995; Pechmann and Shih 1999; Urberg and Robbins 1984). However, youths do not feel immune to social disapproval risks; on the contrary, most youths are hypersensitive to how peers evaluate them (Graham, Marks, and Hansen 1991; McNeal and Hansen 1999). Therefore, any forbidden fruit reaction should be restricted to health risk severity messages and should not be evoked by social risk severity messages.

H_{10}: If an antismoking (versus control) message theme enhances adolescents' perceptions of health risk severity but perceived health risk vulnerability is low, nonsmoking intentions could be weakened.

Advertisement Coding Study

SUBJECTS AND PROCEDURE

We obtained 194 antismoking television advertisements that had aired between 1986 and 1997. Most came from Arizona, California, Canada, Massachusetts, Minnesota, or the University of Vermont, but some came from the American Cancer Society, Australia, Michigan, New Hampshire, or the U.S. CDC. We used real television advertisements because we wanted to generalize our results to such advertisements. To the best of our knowledge, only the Vermont advertisements had been pretested for message content (Worden et al. 1988). Therefore, it seemed important to conduct a preliminary study to identify advertisements that contained the focal message themes. The study involved 1129 seventh and tenth graders, representing middle school and high school, respectively.

The 194 antismoking advertisements were copied onto 24 videotapes, so that each videotape contained eight or nine randomly selected advertisements. Groups of seventh and tenth graders watched each videotape. After each advertisement was viewed twice, the videotape was paused and subjects answered a series of "yes"/"no" questions regarding its message content (see Table 1). Perceived ad effectiveness was also measured with the question, "Overall, I think this ad is effective for kids my age" (1 = "strongly disagree," 5 = "strongly agree"; Biener 2000). The other procedures were similar to those used in the main experiment.

RESULTS

The criterion for determining if an advertisement contained a message theme was 80% or higher agreement among the roughly 45 subjects who viewed that advertisement. A total of 129 advertisements fell into one of the seven thematic message categories shown in

TABLE 1

Antismoking Message Themes Tested in the Main Experiment

Message Theme Labels	Message Content	Adolescents' Agreement That Advertisements Contained Content: % (Standard Deviation)	Adolescents' Perceptions of Ad Effectiveness: Mean (Standard Deviation)
Disease and Death	Smokers suffer from health effects such as cancer, lung disease, and premature death.	92 (6.4)	3.63 (.064)
Endangers Others	Smokers endanger the health and well-being of their families and others, primarily because of secondhand smoke.	91 (6.3)	3.63 (.064)
Cosmetics	Smokers must cope with unattractive side effects, such as bad breath and smelly clothes, hair, and ashtrays.	91 (7.8)	3.42 (.065)
Smokers' Negative Life Circumstances	Smokers have adopted a grotesque, loser lifestyle and have therefore chosen the wrong life path.	91 (5.3)	3.64 (.061)
Refusal Skills Role Model	Attractive role models do not smoke because they view it as highly unappealing, and they refuse others' cigarette offers.	89 (4.5)	3.51 (.066)
Marketing Tactics	Tobacco firms use powerful tactics, such as target marketing and image advertising, to reach youths and others.	91 (5.2)	3.22* (.068)
Selling Disease and Death	Tobacco firms use manipulation and deception to sell a product that causes serious diseases and even death.	90 (4.3)	3.62 (.065)
Substantive Variation	Included advertisements from each condition to test the efficacy of a heterogeneous message approach.	92 (4.4)	3.65 (.065)

*Indicates that the designated antismoking message theme differed from the others ($p < .05$).
Notes: These results are from the advertisement coding study, when eight advertisements representing each message theme were selected at random for the main experiment.

Table 1.[1] The largest category was Selling Disease and Death, with 27 advertisements; the smallest was Marketing Tactics, with 9 advertisements. We randomly selected 8 advertisements from each message category (56 advertisements total) to be used in the main experiment. For the selected advertisements, the intersubject agreement on message content averaged 91%. We also created a Substantive Variation condition, with 2 Selling Disease and Death advertisements and 1 advertisement from each other condition (8 advertisements total). The advertisements were chosen at random so that any differences in sponsor, year, quality, or style would be randomly distributed across conditions. Each condition contained advertisements from approximately four sponsors and spanned roughly nine years of advertising. The advertisement selection procedure seems to have controlled for any major quality differences, in that subjects perceived the advertisements in each condition to be similar in terms of their effectiveness ($p > .30$), except the Marketing Tactics advertisements, which were rated as slightly weaker than the others ($p < .05$). For the selected advertisements, the average effectiveness rating was 3.5, slightly above the midpoint of 3.0.

Main Experiment

SUBJECTS AND DESIGN

Subjects were 1667 students (46% male), consisting of 788 seventh graders (47%) and 879 tenth graders. Subjects were recruited from four middle schools and four high schools; each school contributed roughly 200 students. Schools were paid $1,000 honorariums. Student assent and parental consent were obtained, and participation rates exceeded 90%. The schools were publicly funded and ethnically diverse and were located in middle- to lower-middle-class neighborhoods. Of the subjects, 44% were Hispanic, 35% were White, and 21% were some other ethnicity. Only 4% of the subjects were regular smokers.

The design was a between-subjects factorial with one factor, antismoking message theme, and nine manipulated levels (eight treatment, one control). We randomly assigned approximately 185 subjects to each condition. Each treatment condition consisted of eight advertisements selected randomly from among the set identified in the advertisement coding study. Using eight advertisements enabled us to assess thematic message effects rather than individual ad effects and minimized the influence of extraneous executional factors, in that each message theme was represented by several ad executions. The control

---

[1] Our initial categorization scheme included two additional message themes: smoking's effect on athletic performance and youths' involvement in antismoking political activities. The athletics category yielded too few advertisements (n = 7) to be included. The activism category was slightly larger (n = 10), but it appeared that the primary goal was to encourage adamantly antismoking youths to become antismoking activists, not to deter the average youth from smoking, so we did not study this message theme. Twenty-two advertisements fell into miscellaneous combination categories, such as Selling Disease and Death plus Endangers Others, none of which were prevalent enough to study. Twenty-six advertisements did not seem to contain any clear-cut message, in that fewer than 80% of subjects responded "yes" to any of the message content questions, so these advertisements were excluded from further analyses as well.

condition consisted of eight randomly selected advertisements from the Ad Council on the health and social risks of drunk driving. We copied the advertisements onto videotapes in random order. To ensure a strong manipulation, we showed each advertisement twice in succession, and there was no filler material.

Data Collection Procedures

At each school, two classrooms were equipped with rented televisions and videocassette recorders. Subjects were released from class to participate in the study and were randomly assigned to one of these classrooms. The videotape to be shown in each classroom was determined in advance through a random-number algorithm. Data collection at each school was completed in one day to minimize subject contamination. Each data collection session lasted 50 minutes. Subjects were told they would view a videotape of advertisements and then complete an anonymous survey. Subjects viewed the videotapes in groups of 25–40, and no talking was permitted. Immediately after watching the entire videotape of advertisements, subjects completed a written survey with the dependent measures. Subjects placed their completed surveys in sealed envelopes and were instructed not to discuss the study with others. Subjects in the control condition reported no problems completing a survey about smoking, perhaps because the anti–drunk driving advertisements appropriately primed them by addressing a drug-related issue.

Measures

Behavioral intentions. We derived the dependent measures from prior protection motivation studies on smoking (Maddux and Rogers 1983; Sturges and Rogers 1996) as well as surveys of adolescent tobacco and alcohol use (Bauman 1997; Grube 1997; Rose 1997). Five-point (1–5) scales were used unless otherwise stated. We assessed behavioral intentions with a previously validated three-item scale (Pierce et al. 1996): "In the future, you might smoke one puff or more of a cigarette," "You might try out cigarette smoking for a while," and "If one of your best friends were to offer you a cigarette, you would smoke it" ("definitely yes" to "definitely no").

Health risk perceptions. We assessed perceived severity of and vulnerability to the health risks of smoking using nine items pertaining to dying early; contracting diseases; becoming addicted; breathing poisons; premature aging; causing others to die, get diseases, or breathe poisons; and harming babies. The health severity question asked subjects to mark each outcome they viewed as very serious. The health vulnerability question asked subjects the likelihood that they would personally experience each outcome if they smoked regularly ("sure it would not happen" to "sure it would happen").

Social risk perceptions. To assess the perceived severity of social disapproval risks, we used five semantic differentials: "How acceptable is smoking cigarettes to your close friends?"

"How do you think your close friends feel, or would feel, about you smoking?" "How attractive would you look to others if you smoked?" "How attractive would you look to dates, or potential dates, if you smoked?" and "How well would you fit in with kids your age if you smoked?" To assess the perceived vulnerability to social disapproval risks, we asked subjects how important it was for them to look attractive to others, look attractive to dates, fit in with kids their age, and fit in at parties ("not important" to "very important").

Efficacy, cost, and benefit perceptions. We assessed perceived self-efficacy at refusing cigarette offers with three items: "If others pressure you to smoke, you can say no, walk away, or change the subject" ("sure you cannot" to "sure you can"). We measured self-efficacy at resisting tobacco marketing with two items (same scale): "You can resist being fooled by cigarette advertisements and by cigarette promotions." For completeness, we also assessed perceptions of the costs of not smoking on a two-item "disagree"/"agree" scale ("being made fun of," "being looked down upon") and the benefits of smoking on a similar four-item scale ("feel less stressed," "feel in a good mood," "concentrate better," "look confident").

ANALYSIS OF VARIANCE RESULTS ON HOW MESSAGE THEMES AFFECTED COGNITIONS

Analysis plan and control variables. We used fixed effects analyses of variance to assess whether the antismoking (versus control) message themes affected cognitions. If there was a significant message theme effect, we conducted follow-up t-tests in which each antismoking message mean was compared with the control mean. Because we used the control mean multiple times, we used Dunn–Sidak critical t-statistics to avoid an inflated Type I error rate. Initially, sex, ethnicity, and perceived ad effectiveness were included as covariates but were dropped because they had no effect on the results. The sex and ethnicity covariates were nonsignificant, indicating that randomly assigning subjects to message conditions had ensured that the conditions were closely matched on these variables. Perceived ad effectiveness was a significant covariate, indicating that the message conditions were slightly imbalanced on this factor. Here, the Refusal Skills Role Model message theme was perceived as somewhat less effective than the other message themes $(p < .05)$.[2] However, when we conducted the pairwise comparisons of means, we obtained the same pattern of results regardless of whether we used covariate adjusted or unadjusted means; for parsimony, we report unadjusted means.

A final control variable, grade in school, was included as a blocking factor because of concerns about possible ceiling effects among seventh graders. We included seventh graders

---

[2] Refusal Skills Role Model advertisements were rated lowest on perceived ad effectiveness in the main experiment, and Marketing Tactics advertisements were rated lowest in the advertisement coding study (Table 1). We suspect that the difference may arise because advertisements were rated in sets of eight in the main experiment and individually in the advertisement coding study. Apparently, for Refusal Skills Role Model advertisements, the whole was perceived to be less than the sum of the parts. For Marketing Tactics advertisements, the whole was perceived to be greater than the sum of the parts.

in the research because most smoking prevention campaigns target middle school as well as high school students (e.g., Worden et al. 1988). It is believed that the opportunity to fore-warn and inoculate youths against smoking is present in middle school, before significant numbers of them have even tried a cigarette (CDC 1994; Glynn 1989). However, because the prevalence of current (i.e., past month) smoking among seventh graders is only about 4% (U.S. Department of Health and Human Services 1999), we were concerned that our seventh graders might report strong antismoking intentions or cognitions, leaving little room for improvement after exposure to antismoking advertisements. By including seventh graders, we left our options open. If it was possible to detect ad effects among this group, we would be able to do so and determine which message themes work best for them. If effects among seventh graders were masked because of ceiling effects, we could use grade as a block to detect effects among tenth graders. Among tenth graders, the prevalence of current smoking is much higher, approximately 26% (U.S. Department of Health and Human Services 1999), so ceiling effects were much less likely.

Results. Table 2 shows the omnibus F-statistics and cell means; t-tests follow. Among all subjects, four message themes enhanced health risk severity perceptions: Disease and Death ($t = 2.79$, $p < .05$), Endangers Others ($t = 3.33$, $p < .01$), Selling Disease and Death ($t = 4.11$, $p < .01$), and Substantive Variation ($t = 3.40$, $p < .01$). Three message themes enhanced the perceived severity of the social disapproval risks of smoking: Endangers Others ($t = 2.71$, $p < .06$), Smokers' Negative Life Circumstances ($t = 2.82$, $p < .05$), and Refusal Skills Role Model ($t = 2.73$, $p < .05$). Intentions not to smoke were bolstered by the same three message themes: Endangers Others ($t = 3.96$, $p < .01$), Smokers' Negative Life Circumstances ($t = 3.51$, $p < .01$), and Refusal Skills Role Model ($t = 2.81$, $p < .05$). However, the effects on social risk severity perceptions and intentions were confined to tenth graders, so the preceding t-tests pertain to this group. Seventh graders' social risk perceptions and intentions were unaffected. (For social risk severity: message effect $F(8, 1649) = 1.34$, $p = .22$; message by grade $F(8, 1649) = 2.33$, $p < .05$. For intentions: message effect $F(8, 1643) = 2.23$, $p < .05$, but among seventh graders, there were no effects for antismoking versus control messages; message by grade $F(8, 1643) = 3.08$, $p < .01$.)

None of the message themes affected self-efficacy at refusing cigarette offers, self-efficacy at resisting tobacco marketing, health risk vulnerability, the benefits of smoking, or the costs of not smoking ($p > .10$), but null results were expected in the last three cases because the message themes did not address these topics. Finally, the Marketing Tactics message theme unexpectedly bolstered tenth graders' perceived vulnerability to social disapproval risks ($t = 3.37$, $p < .01$). This theme apparently implied that if marketers make such a concerted effort to influence societal opinions, those opinions must be important. To reiterate, the Disease and Death, Selling Disease and Death, Marketing Tactics, Cosmetics, and Substantive Variation message themes did not significantly affect

TABLE 2

Effects of Antismoking Message Themes on Adolescents: Mean Postexposure Responses

Dependent Measure	Message Effect: F (d.f.)	Antismoking Message Theme								
		Disease and Death	Endangers Others	Cosmetics	Smokers' Negative Life Circumstances	Refusal Skills Role Model	Marketing Tactics	Selling Disease and Death	Substantive Variation (All Messages)	Messages Unrelated to Smoking (Control)
Severity of health risks	3.84*** (8, 1649)	7.68**	7.91***	7.46	7.10	7.54	7.14	8.15***	7.90***	6.68
Vulnerability to health risks	1.16 (8, 1631)	4.43	4.42	4.40	4.55	4.35	4.32	4.39	4.42	4.34
Severity of social disapproval risks	2.10** (8, 870)	3.98	4.09*	3.98	4.09***	4.10**	3.89	3.96	3.82	3.77
Vulnerability to social disapproval risks	2.90*** (8, 870)	2.30	1.96	2.02	2.48	2.17	2.76***	2.29	2.22	2.10
Self-efficacy at refusing cigarette offers	.39 (8, 1639)	4.25	4.25	4.32	4.35	4.33	4.29	4.31	4.27	4.23
Self-efficacy at resisting tobacco marketing	1.68 (8, 1640)	4.16	4.25	4.35	4.04	4.38	4.12	4.31	4.29	4.22
Benefits of smoking	1.20 (8, 1632)	2.06	1.83	1.88	2.01	1.82	1.97	1.98	1.99	2.04
Costs of not smoking	1.23 (8, 1589)	2.37	2.36	2.28	2.22	2.48	2.50	2.32	2.39	2.50
Intentions not to smoke	3.56*** (8, 866)	3.95	4.22***	3.87	4.13***	4.03**	3.68	3.88	3.64	3.53

Notes: Higher numbers indicate higher scores on the indicated variables. All scales are 1–5 except severity of health risks (0–9). F-statistics and means for social disapproval risks and intentions not to smoke are based on the tenth grade sample, because message theme effects were confined to these subjects. Asterisks indicate either an omnibus message theme effect or an anti-smoking message theme (versus control group) effect: *$p < .06$, **$p < .05$, ***$p < .01$.

intentions. None of the antismoking (versus control) message themes had any effects beyond those reported previously ($p > .10$).[3,4]

LISREL RESULTS ON HOW COGNITIONS AFFECTED INTENTIONS

Analysis plan. We predicted that the eight measured protection motivation theory cognitions should directly, and possibly also interactively, influence intentions. To test these interrelationships, we pooled the data from all experimental conditions.[5] We then used LISREL analyses, because all focal variables were measured and LISREL models errors in measurement and estimates path coefficients with less bias than analysis of variance or regression (Jöreskog and Sörbom 1993). We used 24 indicators to measure our nine latent constructs (eight cognitions plus intentions), with 2 to 4 indicators per construct. If a construct was measured by several items, the items were randomly divided into 2 or 3 indicator variables to enhance parsimony and facilitate model estimation (Jöreskog and Sörbom 1996a). We restricted all indicators to load onto their respective latent constructs. We allowed the eight latent cognitive variables to covary freely. We assumed error terms to be independent. Because the data were ordinal and skewed, we used weighted least square estimation (Jöreskog and Sörbom 1996a). We used PRELIS 2 to generate input matrices and LISREL 8 to estimate the models (Jöreskog and Sörbom 1996a, b).

To test for two-way interactions among cognitions, we applied multiple-group structural equation modeling (Bollen 1989; Jöreskog and Sörbom 1993). For each variable that theoretically could be involved in an interaction (severity, vulnerability, and efficacy; Rogers 1975), we divided subjects into two levels on the basis of whether they scored above the variable's mean. Then, for each theorized two-way interaction, we estimated two models of effects on intentions. In the constrained model, we restricted the effect of the first variable in the two-way interaction to be equal across both levels of the second variable. In the unconstrained model, we allowed the effect of this first variable to vary freely. If the unconstrained (versus constrained) model produced a significant χ^2 reduction ($p < .05$), we concluded that there was an interaction effect.[6]

Measurement properties. We first examined the psychometric properties of our measurement model by conducting a confirmatory factor analysis using LISREL 8, and the

---

[3]Additional analyses revealed that message, past smoking behavior, and grade interactively influenced intentions (F(8, 1581) = 2.72, $p < .01$). The Endangers Others, Smokers' Negative Life Circumstances, and Refusal Skills Role Model (versus control) message themes boosted intentions not to smoke among tenth graders who had tried smoking (t = 2.79, 3.40, and 2.74; $p < .05$). The absence of effects among tenth graders who had never smoked seems to be attributable to ceiling effects on intentions (mean = 4.52, maximum = 5); likewise for seventh graders who had never smoked (mean = 4.42). Too few seventh graders had tried smoking to permit meaningful tests of our hypotheses.

[4]We also assessed subjects' knowledge of the sources, tactics, effects, and ethics of pro-tobacco messages, which are the key dimensions of persuasion knowledge (Friestad and Wright 1994). The Marketing Tactics, Selling Disease and Death, and Substantive Variation (versus control) message themes enhanced subjects' persuasion knowledge ($p < .05$), but this knowledge failed to bolster subjects' feelings of self-efficacy at being able to resist tobacco marketing.

[5]The data were also analyzed separately within each message condition, but the pattern of findings was unchanged. In other words, the antismoking message theme affected the mean levels of cognitions and intentions, but not the relationships between cognitions and intentions. These findings are consistent with protection motivation theory, which assumes that the cognition–intention relationships are relatively stable and predictable.

[6]In these model pairs, cost effects were constrained to be equal, as were benefit effects, because neither variable has been theorized to be involved in any interaction. The remaining four cognitive variables were allowed to vary freely.

results were favorable. The reliability estimates for the indicators ranged from .87 to .99. Furthermore, the indicators had large and significant ($p < .001$) factor loadings on their respective latent constructs, and the variance extracted by each latent construct was greater than the recommended level of .50 (Fornell and Larcker 1981). The discriminant validity results were also favorable. Using a series of nested confirmatory factor analysis models, we found that whenever the correlation between two latent constructs was restricted to one rather than being allowed to vary, the fit of the model worsened, as indicated by a significant increase in χ^2. In addition, the variance extracted by each latent construct was substantially larger than its shared variance with other latent constructs (Fornell and Larcker 1981). For details, see Table 3.

Main effects. The main effects structural model predicting a direct relationship between each cognition and intentions fits the data well. The model χ^2 is 539.79 (216 degrees of freedom [d.f.], $p < .01$). The χ^2 divided by the degrees of freedom (2.50), root mean square error of approximation (.031), goodness-of-fit index (.998), adjusted goodness-of-fit index (.997), normed fit index (.997), nonnormed fit index (.998), and comparative fit index (.998) all indicate an adequate fit of the model. The following cognitions, listed from most to least influential, enhanced intentions not to smoke: severity of social disapproval risks, self-efficacy at refusing cigarette offers, vulnerability to social disapproval risks, and vulnerability to health risks (which is qualified by an interaction; see the subsequent discussion). Also, the perceived benefits of smoking lowered nonsmoking intentions. Severity of health risks, self-efficacy at resisting tobacco marketing, and costs of not smoking were not associated with intentions. For coefficients and t-values, see Table 4.

Interaction effects. We examined all theoretically possible two-way interactions among severity, vulnerability, and efficacy (Rogers 1975). There were ten such interactions (see Table 5). All theorized three-way interactions were also tested, but no meaningful patterns emerged, so these analyses are not discussed further. Two two-way interactions were significant (see Figure 1). Health risk severity and health risk vulnerability interactively influenced intentions. Among subjects who were at or below the mean on health risk vulnerability (n = 511), higher perceived health risk severity was associated with weaker nonsmoking intentions. Among subjects who were above the mean (n = 1069, a larger group due to a skewed distribution), health risk severity perceptions and intentions were unassociated. It appears that these subjects felt only moderately vulnerable because, had they felt highly vulnerable, there would have been a positive association between severity and intentions (Block and Keller 1998; Kleinot and Rogers 1982).[7] Health risk vulnerability and self-efficacy at refusing cigarette offers also functioned synergistically. Higher perceived health risk vulnerability was associated with stronger nonsmoking intentions among

---

[7] We split the sample into three vulnerability groups in an attempt to find high-vulnerability subjects. However, the pattern of results was unchanged, which indicates that few subjects felt highly vulnerable to smoking's health risks.

TABLE 3

LISREL Model Latent Constructs: Summary Information

Dependent Measures	1	2	3	4	5	6	7	8	9	Variance Extracted	Factor Loadings
1. Intentions not to smoke	**.94**	.01	.06	.34	.00	.10	.02	.22	.01	.85	.907, .928, .925
2. Severity of health risks	.09	**.99**	.03	.02	.01	.01	.03	.02	.00	.96	.960, .998, .980
3. Vulnerability to health risks	.25	.16	**.96**	.07	.01	.08	.04	.06	.04	.89	.964, .924, .935
4. Severity of social disapproval risks	.58	.13	.27	**.89**	.00	.09	.03	.45	.01	.79	.915, .867
5. Vulnerability to social disapproval risks	.01	-.09	-.08	-.02	**.96**	.00	.04	.00	.00	.85	.940, .964, .858, .916
6. Self-efficacy at refusing cigarette offers	.32	.10	.29	.30	-.06	**.87**	.14	.07	.01	.70	.856, .908, .739
7. Self-efficacy at resisting tobacco marketing	.14	.17	.20	.16	-.19	.38	**.95**	.03	.00	.91	.931, .980
8. Benefits of smoking	-.47	-.15	-.25	-.67	.06	-.27	-.17	**.93**	.01	.87	.904, .959
9. Costs of not smoking	-.10	-.05	-.21	-.09	.05	-.08	-.03	.08	**.93**	.87	.881, .983

Notes: For columns 1–9, the numbers below the diagonal are correlations, the numbers above the diagonal are shared variances, and the boldface numbers on the diagonal are construct reliabilities. Factor loadings are standardized; all $p < .001$. Factor loading for the specific scale items can be obtained from the first author.

TABLE 4

LISREL Results for Main Effects Model

Variables Posited to Affect Intentions Not to Smoke, Based on Protection Motivation Theory (Expected Signs)	Standardized Coefficient	t-Value
Severity of health risks (+)	−.028	−1.13
Vulnerability to health risks (+)	.062	2.23*
Severity of social disapproval risks (+)	.502	11.42**
Vulnerability to social disapproval risks (+)	.079	3.29**
Self-efficacy at refusing cigarette offers (+)	.213	6.09**
Self-efficacy at resisting tobacco marketing (+)	.007	.21
Benefits of smoking (−)	−.093	−2.04*
Costs of not smoking (−)	−.019	−.83

*$p < .05$.
**$p < .01$.

TABLE 5

LISREL Results for Interaction Effects Models

Possible Interaction Effects Posited by Protection Motivation Theory	χ^2	d.f.	χ^2 Difference	d.f.
Health risk severity × health risk vulnerability				
Unconstrained (interaction) model	689.58	337		
Constrained model	699.51	338	9.93**	1
Health risk severity × self-efficacy at refusing offers				
Unconstrained (interaction) model	689.29	337		
Constrained model	689.62	338	.33	1
Health risk vulnerability × self-efficacy at refusing offers				
Unconstrained (interaction) model	689.29	337		
Constrained model	694.70	338	5.41*	1
Health risk severity × self-efficacy at resisting marketing				
Unconstrained (interaction) model	800.07	379		
Constrained model	800.33	380	.26	1
Health risk vulnerability × self-efficacy at resisting marketing				
Unconstrained (interaction) model	800.07	379		
Constrained model	800.39	380	.32	1
Social risk severity × social risk vulnerability				
Unconstrained (interaction) model	475.71	298		
Constrained model	478.80	299	3.09	1
Social risk severity × self-efficacy at refusing offers				
Unconstrained (interaction) model	689.29	337		
Constrained model	691.82	338	2.53	1
Social risk vulnerability × self-efficacy at refusing offers				
Unconstrained (interaction) model	689.29	337		
Constrained model	689.51	338	.22	1
Social risk severity × self-efficacy at resisting marketing				
Unconstrained (interaction) model	800.07	379		
Constrained model	800.16	380	.09	1
Social risk vulnerability × self-efficacy at resisting marketing				
Unconstrained (interaction) model	800.07	379		
Constrained model	800.08	380	.01	1

*$p < .05$.
**$p < .01$.
Notes: A smaller χ^2 indicates a better fit between the observed and estimated covariation matrices.

Illustrations of Interactions Detected in LISREL

A: Health Risk Severity × Health Risk Vulnerability

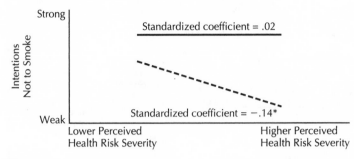

Key:

───── Subjects who were above the mean on health risk vulnerability.
- - - Subjects who were at or below the mean on health risk vulnerability.

B: Health Risk Vulnerability × Self-Efficacy at Refusing Offers

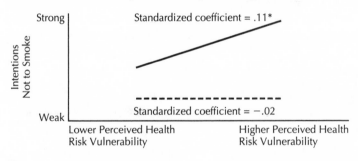

Key:

───── Subjects who were above the mean on self-efficacy at refusing cigarette offers.
- - - Subjects who were at or below the mean on self-efficacy at refusing cigarette offers.

*$p < .01$.

subjects who were above the mean on self efficacy at refusing offers (n = 1097), whereas health risk vulnerability and intentions were unassociated among subjects who were at or below the mean (n = 483).

Final Discussion

SUMMARY OF MAIN RESULTS

Of the seven antismoking message themes we tested, only three (Endangers Others, Refusal Skills Role Model, and Smokers' Negative Life Circumstances) bolstered adolescents'

FIGURE 2

Summary of Key Findings

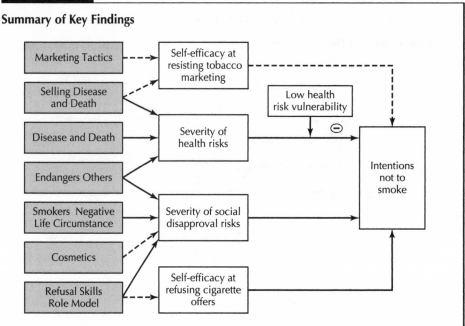

Notes: Solid lines show significant effects; dotted lines show hypothesized but nonsignificant effects. All relationships are positive, except the negative effect of perceived severity of health risks on intentions given low perceived health risk vulnerability. For parsimony, the Substantive Variation message condition is not included in this figure. It was hypothesized to enhance all of the cognitive variables and intentions not to smoke, but it only enhanced the perceived severity of health risks.

intentions not to smoke, and all did so by conveying that smoking cigarettes poses severe social disapproval risks (see Figure 2). Cosmetics messages sought to influence social risk severity perceptions but failed, apparently because the problems stressed (e.g., bad breath) could be minimized by using cosmetic products. Refusal Skills Role Model messages had a secondary aim: to boost adolescents' perceived self-efficacy at refusing cigarette offers. However, such perceptions seemed to be relatively unmalleable, as they were unaltered by ad exposure, though they were predictive of behavioral intentions. To boost self-efficacy perceptions, it may be necessary to implement media literacy programs that enable practice and mastery of focal skills.

Two message themes (Disease and Death and Selling Disease and Death) increased health, rather than social, risk severity perceptions. However, it seems that few adolescents felt vulnerable to the health risks, which undercut the efficacy of health severity messages. Among youths who felt immune to health risks, higher perceived health risk severity was associated with stronger intentions to smoke. In other words, in the context of low perceived vulnerability, stressing health risks could increase smoking's symbolic value as a risk-seeking, rebellious, and thus attractive behavior. Two message themes (Marketing Tactics and Selling Disease and Death) discussed tobacco marketing tactics. However, these message themes failed to influence adolescents' perceived self-efficacy at resisting tobacco marketing tactics, and in any event, such perceptions were not predictive of behavioral intentions. Finally, we tested a heterogeneous, or Substantive Variation, message condition, with essentially one advertisement per message theme. This message condition boosted health risk severity perceptions, but not social risk severity or self-efficacy perceptions, and had no effect on intentions. We speculate as to why in the next section.

Substantive Contributions and Implications

On the basis of our findings, when policy officials and advertising agencies design antismoking campaigns for adolescents, they should seriously consider using norm-based appeals—specifically, appeals that convey that smoking poses severe social disapproval risks (see also Pechmann and Shih 1999). This strategy would be consistent with considerable prior research that suggests a strong link between adolescents' perceptions of smoking norms and their intentions and behaviors (Chassin et al. 1984; Collins et al. 1987; Conrad, Flay, and Hill 1991; Pechmann and Knight 2002; Pechmann and Ratneshwar 1994). Our latest research indicates that norm-based appeals are declining in prevalence, which would appear to be an undesirable trend. Although many of the recent Philip Morris antismoking advertisements seem to contain social norm messages, they do not appear to be effective (Farrelly et al. 2002), perhaps because their messages are mixed. In our view, many of the Philip Morris advertisements seem to imply that both nonsmoking and smoking are socially acceptable behaviors, which does not constitute a clear antismoking message. Furthermore, the Philip Morris advertisements tend to show nonsmokers who are clean-cut and stereotypically "good" and might imply that adolescents should smoke if they want to demonstrate that they are not "goody two shoes" (Amos et al. 1998).

When youths are targeted, stressing the severity of long-term health risks does not appear to be an effective strategy; indeed, doing so could enhance smoking's forbidden fruit allure. However, our recent findings indicate that advertisements that stress health risk vulnerability, not severity, seem to work. Therefore, if policy officials want to use health-based appeals, we recommend that the appeals convey that adolescents are highly vulnerable to smoking's health risks. The advertisements might, for example, tell true-life stories of younger victims, stress how quickly these victims became addicted to smoking, and show how much they have suffered (Biener 2000; Teenage Research Unlimited 1999). When health risk vulnerability advertisements are developed, it may be useful to keep in mind the vulnerability $\times$ efficacy interaction that we observed. This interaction suggests that advertisements about health risk vulnerability bolster nonsmoking intentions among youths who feel capable of refusing cigarette offers, but not among youths who feel incapable of refusing (Rogers 1975, 1983). On the basis of this finding, it may be beneficial to supplement vulnerability-focused advertisements with school programs that teach refusal skills (CDC 1994; Glynn 1989).

Our findings to date suggest that tobacco marketing (anti-industry) advertisements may not be especially effective with adolescents, though such advertisements are popular, in part because of the apparent success of the Florida Truth campaign (Bauer et al. 2000; Farrelly et al. 2002). The advertisements we studied did not alter adolescents' behavioral intentions. It is possible that advertisements of this type may work if they elicit stronger reactance or rebellion against tobacco firms. According to reactance theory (Brehm 1972), it should be possible to intensify reactance by, for example, showing tobacco firms using heavy-handed tactics to persuade youths to smoke or stressing the number and importance of the threatened freedoms (Clee and Wicklund 1980). Alternatively, what may be needed are advertisements that address youths' primary misconception about why they smoke. Most youths naively believe they smoke not because of tobacco marketing but because their friends look cool doing it (Pechmann and Knight 2002). According to Pechmann and Knight's (2002) research, youths perceive that smokers "look cool" in large part because the attractive, cool models in cigarette advertisements prime or make salient positive smoker stereotypes and bias social perceptions (see also Romer and Jamieson 2001). Therefore, tobacco marketing advertisements may be needed that educate youth about this priming phenomenon. We recommend further research on these issues.

In the current research, the Substantive Variation (heterogeneous) message condition did not perform as well as expected, having no impact on intentions. However, this may be due to the way we set up the Substantive Variation condition. We used only one advertisement (at most two) to convey each theme, so the total number of advertisements was eight, the same as in the other message conditions. Furthermore, we selected the advertisements in the Substantive Variation condition at random from those used in the other conditions. We did this to equate the message conditions as much as possible and thus minimize confounds. As it turns out, though, the advertisements that were used to convey social risk severity in the Substantive Variation condition may have been too few in number or too weak to do much good. Because the advertisements did not affect this critical social cognition, the Substantive Variation condition as a whole had no impact on intentions. On the basis of these findings, we do not recommend that sponsors of antismoking advertising campaigns use all seven of the message themes studied here concurrently, particularly if they are on a limited budget. However, they may want to use the three most effective themes identified here (Endangers Others, Refusal Skills Role Model, and Smokers' Negative Life Circumstances) if they have an adequate budget. Substantively varied advertising campaigns have been shown to forestall tedium and wearout, particularly when the advertising topic is highly relevant to viewers (Schumann, Petty, and Clemons 1990), as the antismoking issue may well be.

Because it is a challenge to create good advertising, quantitative copy testing should be conducted to ensure that any advertisement that is included in a campaign actually bolsters antismoking beliefs and intentions (Pechmann and Reibling 2000). Furthermore, we recommend copy testing advertisements among ninth or tenth graders, not among middle school students. Our findings indicate that middle school youths' survey responses may be so strongly antismoking that no ad effects can be discerned because of ceiling effects. Finally, we do not recommend that advertisements be evaluated on the basis of viewers' ratings of perceived ad effectiveness (Biener 2000; Teenage Research Unlimited 1999). In our research, all sets of advertisements were virtually equivalent on perceived ad effectiveness, yet they were found to differ in their effects on both beliefs and intentions.

THEORETICAL CONTRIBUTIONS

This research supports recent efforts by Ho (1998) to extend protection motivation theory formally to include social risks. We find that social risk severity and vulnerability are distinguishable from their health risk counterparts and that social risk severity perceptions are especially predictive of adolescents' behavioral intentions. Our results further indicate that Rogers's (1983) decision to drop the health risk severity $\times$ vulnerability interaction from protection motivation theory and to focus on threat $\times$ coping appraisal interactions may have been ill advised; his original formulation seems preferable.

We also contribute to the literature on decision making and risk, in which severity $\times$ vulnerability interactions have been theorized but rarely observed in health contexts (Weinstein 1993, 2000). Weinstein (2000) argues that important interactions between health risk severity and vulnerability have not been documented because prior studies have examined mid-level variable values, and interactive effects occur at more extreme levels. Here, we document an interaction that has rarely been observed. Given low perceived vulnerability, higher perceived health risk severity was associated with increased intentions to engage in a risky behavior. Given moderate vulnerability, severity and intentions were unassociated. If found to be prevalent, this interaction would appear to have important implications. Most theories posit that health risk severity messages will discourage risky behaviors (Rogers 1975, 1983; Weinstein 1993), yet they could have the opposite effect among people who view themselves as invincible.

RESEARCH LIMITATIONS

We studied antismoking advertising's impact on intentions, not behavior, because a field experiment of seven message themes would have been too costly. Also, to differentiate our study from prior work on multifaceted tobacco control efforts, we focused strictly on advertising. It is conceivable that advertising that is ineffective on its own becomes effective when combined with other efforts. We used a forced-exposure copy test method; therefore, if a certain message theme was more attention getting than others, this effect would have been masked. We did not embed the advertisements in television programming, because a cluttered copy test environment "adds complexity and is possibly confounding" (Aaker, Batra, and Myers 1992, p. 425). Because subjects were told that the study was about advertisements, they could conceivably have sought to provide socially desirable, proad-vertisement responses (Aaker, Batra, and Myers 1992). If this bias was operative, though, all of the message themes should have been effective, and many were found to be ineffec-tive. Nevertheless, it would be beneficial to conduct a follow-up study that uses a more naturalistic exposure environment.

There was a weak correspondence between message theme and execution. To examine this issue post hoc, three trained research assistants coded the stimulus advertisements on several executional variables, including spokesperson age, emotional tone and intensity, and sensation value (Schoenbachler and Whittler 1996). The findings indicate that these vari-ables alone cannot explain the results. For example, compared with other message themes, the Refusal Skills Role Model and Cosmetics message themes used somewhat more youthful spokespeople, yet only the former bolstered nonsmoking intentions. Also, both the Selling Disease and Death and Endangers Others message themes scored relatively highly on emotional intensity, but only the latter influenced intentions. However, researchers may want to address the possible moderating effects of these and other executional variables. The funding that is available for antismoking advertising is unprecedented, and sound market-ing research should play a major role in helping ensure that the money is wisely spent.

References

Aaker, David A., Rajeev Batra, and John G. Myers (1992), *Advertising Management*. Englewood Cliffs, NJ: Prentice Hall.

American Legacy Foundation (2002), (accessed January 13, 2003), [available at http://www.americanlegacy.org/].

Amos, Amanda, Candice Currie, David Gray, and Rob Elton (1998), "Perceptions of Fashion Images from Youth Magazines: Does a Cigarette Make a Difference?" *Health Education Research*, 13 (December), 491–501.

Arnett, Jeffrey J. (2000), "Optimistic Bias in Adolescent and Adult Smokers and Nonsmokers," *Addictive Behaviors*, 25 (July/August), 625–32.

Bandura, Albert (1997), *Self-Efficacy: The Exercise of Control*. New York: W.H. Freeman.

Banspach, Stephen W., R. Craig Lefebvre, and Richard A. Carleton (1989), "Increasing Awareness of the Pressures Related to Smoking: An Analysis of Two Models of Anti-smoking Curriculum in the Classroom," *Health Education Research*, 4 (March), 69–78.

Bauer, Ursula E., Tammie M. Johnson, Richard S. Hopkins, and Robert G. Brooks (2000), "Changes in Youth Cigarette Use and Intentions Following Implementation of a Tobacco Control Program: Findings from the Florida Youth Tobacco Survey, 1998–2000," *Journal of the American Medical Association*, 284 (August), 723–34.

Bauman, Karl E. (1997), Written correspondence regarding "A Study of Cigarette Smoking Behavior Among Youth: Adolescent Questionnaire," School of Public Health, Department of Maternal and Child Health, University of North Carolina, Chapel Hill (Fall).

Benthin, Alida, Paul Slovic, and Herbert Severson (1993), "A Psychometric Study of Adolescent Risk Perception," *Journal of Adolescence*, 16 (June), 153–68.

Biener, Lois (2000), "Adult and Youth Response to the Massachusetts Anti-tobacco Television Campaign," *Journal of Public Health Management and Practice,* 6 (May), 40–44.

Blankenship, Albert B. and George E. Breen (1993), *State-of-the-Art Marketing Research.* Lincolnwood, IL: NTC Business Books.

Block, Lauren G. and Punam A. Keller (1998), "Beyond Protection Motivation: an Integrative Theory of Health Appeals," *Journal of Applied Social Psychology,* 28 (September), 1548–608.

Boer, Henk and Erwin R. Seydel (1996), "Protection Motivation Theory," in *Predicting Health Behaviour,* Mark Conner and Paul Norman, eds. Buckingham, UK: Open University Press, 95–120.

Bollen, Kenneth A. (1989), *Structural Equations with Latent Variables.* New York: John Wiley & Sons.

Brehm, Jack W. (1972), *Responses to Loss of Freedom: A Theory of Psychological Reactance.* Morristown, NJ: General Learning Press.

Brucks, Merrie, Gary M. Armstrong, and Marvin E. Goldberg (1988), "Children's Use of Cognitive Defenses Against Television Advertising: A Cognitive Response Approach," *Journal of Consumer Research,* 14 (March), 471–82.

Bryan, Angela D., Leona S. Aiken, and Stephen G. West (1996), "Increasing Condom Use: Evaluation of a Theory-Based Intervention to Prevent Sexually Transmitted Diseases in Young Women," *Health Psychology,* 15 (September), 371–82.

Burgess, Erika Swift and Sandy K. Wurtele (1998), "Enhancing Parent–Child Communication About Sexual Abuse: A Pilot Study," *Child Abuse and Neglect,* 22 (November), 1167–75.

California Department of Health Services (1990), *Toward a Tobacco Free California.* Sacramento, CA: Department of Health Services.

____ (2001), *Independent Evaluation of the California Tobacco Control Prevention and Education Program.* Sacramento, CA: Department of Health Services.

Campaign for Tobacco Free-Kids (2002), "Show Us the Money: An Update on the States' Allocation of the Tobacco Settlement Dollars," (accessed January 13, 2003), [available at http://www. tobaccofreekids.org/].

Campbell, Margaret C. and Amna Kirmani (2000), "Consumers' Use of Persuasion Knowledge: The Effects of Accessibility and Cognitive Capacity on Perceptions of an Influence Agent," *Journal of Consumer Research,* 27 (June), 69–83.

Castle, Catherine M., T. Chas Skinner, and Sarah E. Hampson (1999), "Young Women and Suntanning: An Evaluation of a Health Education Leaflet," *Psychology and Health,* 14 (May), 517–27.

Centers for Disease Control and Prevention (1994), "Guidelines for School Health Programs to Prevent Tobacco Use and Addiction," *Morbidity and Mortality Weekly Report,* 43 (RR-2), 1–15.

____ (1999), *Best Practices for Comprehensive Tobacco Control Programs.* Atlanta, GA: Office on Smoking and Health.

Chassin, Laurie, Clark C. Presson, Steven J. Sherman, Eric Corty, and Richard W. Olshavsky (1984), "Predicting the Onset of Cigarette Smoking in Adolescents: A Longitudinal Study," *Journal of Applied Social Psychology,* 14 (May/June), 224–43.

Clee, Mona A. and Robert A. Wicklund (1980), "Consumer Behavior and Psychological Reactance," *Journal of Consumer Research,* 6 (March), 389–405.

Cohen, Lawrence D., Susan Macfarlane, Claudia Yanez, and Walter K. Imai (1995), "Risk-Perception: Differences Between Adolescents and Adults," *Health Psychology,* 14 (May), 217–22.

Collins, Linda M., Steve Sussman, Jill Meste, Clyde W. Dent, C. Anderson Johnson, William B. Hansen, and Brian R. Flay (1987), "Psychosocial Predictors of Adolescent Cigarette Smoking: A Sixteen-Month, Three-Wave Longitudinal Study," *Journal of Applied Social Psychology,* 17 (June), 554–73.

Connolly, Gregory and Harriett Robbins (1998), "Designing and Effective Statewide Tobacco Control Program—Massachusetts," *Cancer,* 83 (December), 2722–27.

Conrad, Karen M., Brian R. Flay, and David Hill (1991), "Why Children Start Smoking Cigarettes: Predictors of Onset," *British Journal of Addiction,* 87 (December), 1711–24.

DePalma, Mary Turner, Michael McCall, and Gary English (1996), "Increasing Perceptions of Disease Vulnerability Through Imagery," *College Health,* 44 (March), 227–34.

Dijkstra, Arie, Hein De Vries, and Jolanda Roijackers (1998), "Computerized Tailored Feedback to Change Cognitive Determinants of Smoking: A Dutch Field Experiment," *Health Education Research,* 13 (June), 197–206.

Dorr, Aimee, Sherryl Browne Graves, and Erin Phelps (1980), "Television Literacy for Young Children," *Journal of Communication,* 30 (3), 71–83.

Farrelly, Matthew C., Cheryl G. Healton, Kevin C. Davis, Peter Messeri, James C. Hersey, and M. Lyndon Haviland (2002), "Getting to the Truth: Evaluating National Tobacco Counter-marketing Campaigns," *American Journal of Public Health,* 92 (June), 901–907.

Feshbach, Seymour, Norma D. Feshbach, and Sarale E. Cohen (1982), "Enhancing Children's Discrimination in Response to Television Advertising: The Effects of Psychoeducational Training in Two Elementary School-Age Groups," *Developmental Review,* 2 (December), 385–403.

Fischhoff, Baruch, Andrew M. Parker, Wandi De Bruin, Julie Downs, Claire Palmgreen, Robyn Dawes, and Charles F. Manski (2000), "Teen Expectations for Significant Life Events," *Public Opinion Quarterly,* 64 (Summer), 189–205.

Floyd, Donna L., Steven Prentice-Dunn, and Ronald W. Rogers (2000), "A Meta-Analysis of Research on Protection Motivation Theory," *Journal of Applied Social Psychology,* 30 (February), 407–29.

Flynn, Mary F., Robert D. Lyman, and Steven Prentice-Dunn (1995), "Protection Motivation Theory and Adherence to Medical Treatment Regimes for Muscular Dystrophy," *Journal of Social and Clinical Psychology,* 14 (Spring), 61–75.

Fornell, Claes and David F. Larcker (1981), "Evaluating Structural Equation Models with Unobserved Variables and Measurement Error," *Journal of Marketing Research,* 18 (February), 39–50.

Friestad, Marian and Peter Wright (1994), "The Persuasion Knowledge Model: How People Cope with Persuasion Attempts," *Journal of Consumer Research,* 21 (June), 1–31.

Glynn, Thomas J. (1989), "Essential Elements of School-Based Smoking Prevention Programs," *Journal of School Health,* 59 (May), 181–88.

Goldman, Lisa and Stanton A. Glantz (1998), "Evaluation of Anti-smoking Advertising Campaigns," *Journal of the American Medical Association,* 279 (March), 772–77.

Graham, John W., Gary Marks, and William B. Hansen (1991), "Social Influence Processes Affecting Adolescent Substance Use," *Journal of Applied Psychology,* 76 (April), 291–98.

Grube, Joel (1997), Written correspondence regarding "Parents and Children: a Survey, SCR R 1206, Forms C1 and C2," Prevention Research Center, Berkeley, CA (Fall).

Ho, Robert (1998), "The Intention to Give Up Smoking: Disease Versus Social Dimensions," *Journal of Social Psychology,* 138 (June), 368–80.

Johnston, Lloyd D., P.M. O'Malley, and Jerald G. Bachman (2001), "Cigarette Smoking Among American Teens Declines Sharply in 2001," University of Michigan News and Information Services, (accessed January 13, 2003), [available at http://www.monitoringthefuture.org/].

Jones, Jody L. and Mark R. Leary (1994), "Effects of Appearance-Based Admonitions Against Sun Exposure on Tanning Intentions in Young Adults," *Health Psychology,* 13 (January), 86–90.

Jöreskog, Karl and Dag Sörbom (1993), *LISREL 8: Structural Equation Modeling with SIMPLIS Command Language*. Chicago: Scientific Software International.

___ and ___ (1996a), *LISREL 8: User's Reference Guide*. Lincolnwood, IL: Scientific Software International.

___ and ___ (1996b), *PRELIS 2: User's Reference Guide*. Lincolnwood, IL: Scientific Software International.

Klein, Richard (1993), *Cigarettes Are Sublime*. Durham, NC: Duke University Press.

Kleinot, Michael C. and Ronald W. Rogers (1982), "Identifying Effective Components of Alcohol Misuse Prevention Programs," *Journal of Studies on Alcohol,* 43 (July), 802–11.

Klohn, Lisa S. and Ronald W. Rogers (1991), "Dimensions of the Severity of a Health Threat: The Persuasive Effects of Visibility, Time of Onset, and Rate of Onset on Young Women's Intentions to Prevent Osteoporosis," *Health Psychology,* 10 (5), 323–29.

Maddux, James E. and Ronald W. Rogers (1983), "Protection Motivation and Self-Efficacy: A Revised Theory of Fear Appeals and Attitude Change," *Journal of Experimental Social Psychology,* 19 (September), 469–79.

Mahler, Heike I.M., Betsy Fitzpatrick, Patricia Parker, and Angela Lapin (1997), "The Relative Effects of a Health-Based Versus an Appearance-Based Intervention Designed to Increase Sunscreen Use," *American Journal of Health Promotion,* 11 (July/August), 426–29.

McNeal, Ralph B. and William B. Hansen (1999), "Developmental Patterns Associated with the Onset of Drug Use: Changes in Postulated Mediators During Adolescence," *Journal of Drug Issues,* 29 (Spring), 381–400.

Miller, Anne (1998), "Designing an Effective Counter Advertising Campaign—Massachusetts," *Cancer,* 83 (December), 2742–45.

Milne, Sarah, Paschal Sheeran, and Shejna Orbell (2000), "Prediction and Intervention in Health-Related Behavior: A Meta-Analytic Review of Protection Motivation Theory," *Journal of Applied Social Psychology,* 30 (January), 106–43.

Minnesota Department of Health (1991), *Minnesota Tobacco-Use Prevention Initiative 1989–1990: A Report to the 1991 Legislature*. Minneapolis, MN: Department of Health.

Mulilis, John-Paul and Richard Lippa (1990), "Behavioral Changes in Earthquake Preparedness Due to Negative Threat Appeals: A Test of Protection Motivation Theory," *Journal of Applied Social Psychology,* 20 (May), 619–38.

National Association of Attorneys General (2000), "Master Settlement Agreement," (accessed January 13, 2003), [available at http://www.naag.org/tobac/].

Parpis, Eleftheria (1997), "Up in Smoke: Kicking Butt," *AdWeek* (Eastern Edition), 38 (41), 33–38.

Pechmann, Cornelia (2002), "Changing Adolescent Smoking Prevalence: Impact of Advertising Interventions," in *Changing Adolescent Smoking Prevalence: Where It Is and Why,* David Burns, ed. Silver Spring, MD: National Cancer Institute, 171–81.

___ and Susan J. Knight (2002), "An Experimental Investigation of the Joint Effects of Advertising and Peers on Adolescents' Beliefs and Intentions About Cigarette Consumption," *Journal of Consumer Research,* 29 (June), 5–19.

___ and Srinivasan Ratneshwar (1994), "The Effects of Anti-smoking and Cigarette Advertising on Young Adolescents' Perceptions of Peers Who Smoke," *Journal of Consumer Research,* 21 (September), 236–51.

___ and Ellen Thomas Reibling (2000), "Planning an Effective Anti-smoking Mass Media Campaign Targeting Adolescents," *Journal of Public Health Management and Practice,* 6 (May), 80–94.

___ and Chuan-Fong Shih (1999), "Smoking in Movies and Antismoking Advertisements Before Movies: Effects on Youth," *Journal of Marketing,* 63 (July), 1–13.

Peterson, Lizette and Katherine E. Lewis (1988), "Preventive Intervention to Improve Children's Discrimination of the Persuasive Tactics in Televised Advertising," *Journal of Pediatric Psychology,* 13 (June), 163–70.

Pierce, John P., Won S. Choi, Elizabeth Gilpin, Arthur J. Farkas, and Robert K. Merritt (1996), "Validation of Susceptibility as a Predictor of Which Adolescents Take Up Smoking in the United States," *Health Psychology,* 15 (September), 355–61.

Rippetoe, Patricia A. and Ronald W. Rogers (1987), "Effects of Components of Protection-Motivation Theory on Adaptive and Maladaptive Coping with a Health Threat," *Journal of Personality and Social Psychology,* 52 (March), 596–604.

Rogers, Ronald W. (1975), "A Protection Motivation Theory of Fear Appeals and Attitude Change," *Journal of Psychology,* 91 (September), 93–114.

___ (1983), "Cognitive and Physiological Process in Fear Appeals and Attitude Change: A Revised Theory of Protection Motivation," in *Social Psychophysiology: A Source Book,* John Cacioppo and Richard Petty, eds. New York: Guilford Press, 153–76.

Rohrbach, Louise, John W. Graham, William B. Hansen, Brian R. Flay, and C. Anderson Johnson (1987), "Evaluation of Resistance Skills Training Using Multitrait–Multimethod Role-Play Skills Assessment," *Health Education Research,* 2 (December), 401–407.

Romer, Daniel and Patrick Jamieson (2001), "Advertising, Smoker Imagery, and the Diffusion of Smoking Behavior," in *Smoking Risk, Perception, and Policy,* Paul Slovic, ed. Thousand Oaks, CA: Sage Publications, 127–55.

Rose, Richard J. (1997), Written correspondence regarding the "I.U. Smoking Questionnaire," Department of Psychology, Indiana University, Bloomington, IN (Fall).

Schoenbachler, Denise D. and Tommy E. Whittler (1996), "Adolescent Processing of Social and Physical Threat Communications," *Journal of Advertising,* 25 (Winter), 37–54.

Schumann, David W., Richard E. Petty, and D. Scott Clemons (1990), "Predicting the Effectiveness of Different Strategies of Advertising Variation: A Test of the Repetition–Variation Hypotheses," *Journal of Consumer Research,* 17 (September), 192–202.

Steffen, Valerie J. (1990), "Men's Motivation to Perform the Testicle Self-Exam: Effects of Prior Knowledge and an Educational Brochure," *Journal of Applied Social Psychology,* 20 (May), 681–702.

Sturges, James W. and Ronald W. Rogers (1996), "Preventive Health Psychology from a Developmental Perspective: An Extension of Protection Motivation Theory," *Health Psychology,* 15 (May), 158–66.

Tanner, John F., Jr., James B. Hunt, and David R. Eppright (1991), "The Protection Motivation Model: A Normative Model of Fear Appeals," *Journal of Marketing,* 55 (July), 36–45.

Teenage Research Unlimited (1999), "Counter-tobacco Advertising Exploratory Summary Report January–March 1999," (accessed January 13, 2003), [available at http://tobaccofreekids.org/reports/smokescreen/study.shtml/].

Teinowitz, Ira (1998), "After the Tobacco Settlement: Take the Money and Run (Ads)," *Washington Post,* (December 6), C1.

Urberg, Kathryn A. and Rochelle Robbins (1984), "Perceived Vulnerability in Adolescents to the Health Consequences of Cigarette Smoking," *Preventive Medicine,* 13 (3), 367–76.

U.S. Department of Health and Human Services (1999), "Summary of Findings from the 1999 National Household Survey on Drug Abuse," (accessed January 13, 2003), [available at http://www.icpsr.umich.edu/SAMHDA/].

Weinstein, Neil D. (1983), "Reducing Unrealistic Optimism About Illness Susceptibility," *Health Psychology,* 2 (Winter), 11–20.

___ (1993), "Testing Four Competing Theories of Health-Protective Behavior," *Health Psychology,* 12 (July), 324–33.

___ (2000), "Perceived Probability, Perceived Severity, and Health-Protective Behavior," *Health Psychology,* 19 (January), 65–74.

___, Peter M. Sandman, and Nancy E. Roberts (1991), "Perceived Susceptibility and Self-Protective Behavior: A Field Experiment to Encourage Home Radon Testing," *Health Psychology,* 10 (1), 25–33.

Witte, Kim (1992), "The Role of Threat and Efficacy in AIDS Prevention," *International Quarterly of Community Health Education,* 12 (3), 225–49.

Wood, Peter B., John K. Cochran, Betty Pfefferbaum, and Bruce J. Arneklev (1995), "Sensation-Seeking and Delinquent Substance Use: An Extension of Learning Theory," *The Journal of Drug Issues,* 25 (Winter), 173–93.

Worden, John K., Brian S. Flynn, Berta M. Geller, Milton Chen, Lawrence G. Shelton, Roger H. Secker-Walker, Douglas S. Solomon, Laura Solomon, Sidney Souchey, and Michael C. Costanza (1988), "Development of Smoking Prevention Mass Media Program Using Diagnostic and Formative Research," *Social Science and Medicine,* 17 (2), 531–58.

___, ___, and Roger H. Secker-Walker (1998), "Antismoking Advertising Campaigns for Youth," *Journal of the American Medical Association,* 280 (July), 323.

Wurtele, Sandy K. and James E. Maddux (1987), "Relative Contributions of Protection Motivation Theory Components in Predicting Exercise Intentions and Behavior," *Health Psychology,* 6 (5), 453–66.

Assessing the Impact of Antidrug Advertising on Adolescent Drug Consumption: Results from a Behavioral Economic Model

Lauren G. Block, Vicki G. Morwitz, William P. Putsis Jr, and Subrata K. Sen

Objectives. This study examined whether adolescents' recall of antidrug advertising is associated with a decreased probability of using illicit drugs and, given drug use, a reduced volume of use.

Methods. A behavioral economic model of influences on drug consumption was developed with survey data from a nationally representative sample of adolescents to determine the incremental impact of antidrug advertising.

Results. The findings provided evidence that recall of antidrug advertising was associated with a lower probability of marijuana a and cocaine/crack use. Recall of such advertising was not associated with the decision of how much marijuana or cocaine/crack to use. Results suggest that individuals predisposed to try marijuana are also predisposed to try cocaine/crack.

Conclusions. The present results provide support for the effectiveness of antidrug advertising programs.

In the present study, we evaluated the effectiveness of the national antidrug advertisements of the Partnership for a Drug-Free America (PDFA). Over the years, PDFA has received more than $3 billion in donated media from a variety of sources, including the major television networks, 11 cable networks. 11 radio networks, more than 1000 newspapers, and more than 100 magazines and medical journals (M. Townsend, chief marketing officer, Partnership for a Drug-Free America; written correspondence; May 1998). PDFA's donated media make it the largest advertiser of a "single product" in the United States after McDonald's.[1]

LAUREN G. BLOCK is with the Department of Marketing, Baruch College, New York City. VICKI G. MORWITZ is with the Department of Marketing, New York University, New York City. WILLIAM P. PUTSIS JR is with the Department of Marketing, London Business School, London, England. SUBRATA K. SEN is with the Department of Marketing, Yale University, New Haven, Conn.

Requests for reprints should be sent to William P. Putsis Jr, London Business School, Regent's Park, London NW1 4SA, United Kingdom (e-mail: bputsis@london.edu).

Block, Lauren G., Vicki G. Morwitz, William P. Putsis, Jr. and Subrata K. Sen, (2002), "Assessing the Impact of Anti-Drug Advertising on Adolescent Drug Consumption: Results from a Behavioral Economic Model." *American Journal of Public Health,* Vol. 92, 1346–1351.

We analyzed data from the first 4 years of the Partnership Attitude Tracking Survey (PATS), an annual survey conducted by PDFA to independently test whether the commencement of the advertising campaign was associated with a change in adolescents' drug use. The first "wave" of PATS was initiated during February and March 1987, 3 months before the first antidrug messages were aired. Additional waves, which took place during February and March of each year thereafter, measured respondents' recall of PDFA advertisements. These waves formed a "natural experiment" in that respondents during the first wave were not exposed to PDFA advertising, whereas respondents in subsequent waves were subjected to PDFA advertising.

A preliminary examination of the PATS data reveals that the percentages of respondents who reported marijuana or cocaine/crack use in the previous 12 months decreased significantly over the years 1987 to 1990. Other sources of data corroborate this pattern (e.g., survey data from the University of Michigan's Institute of Social Research, National Household Survey on Drug Abuse).[2,3] Although this overall pattern is consistent with the hypothesis that antidrug advertising reduces drug consumption, such a simple analysis does not accommodate other potential explanations for changes in drug consumption over time. To adjust for these other factors, we used a detailed behavioral economic model that investigated the relationship between adolescents' recall of antidrug advertising and their probability of using marijuana, cocaine, or crack, as well as their volume of use given that they were already using these drugs.

Methods

DATA SOURCES

Data were obtained through multiple-site central location sampling, usually conducted at shopping malls (see Black et al.[4] for a detailed report on the PATS methodology). Respondents at selected sites approximated a national probability sample. Sites were selected along 2 dimensions: (1) regional and (2) urban, suburban, and rural distribution of the population. At each site, sex and race quotas were established. The sample sizes of adolescents aged 13–17 years (numbers of locations from which adolescents were sampled are shown in parentheses) during 1987 through 1990 were 797 (96), 1031 (89), 870 (85), and 1497 (99), respectively.

Self-administered questionnaires were completed by respondents in a private facility and returned anonymously in a blank envelope. This data collection method should have resulted in an increased willingness among participants to reveal illicit or undesirable behaviors compared with other methods.[5] Although evidence indicates that drug use self-reports are highly reliable and valid,[6,7] we also conducted a detailed analysis of the impact of potential reporting biases on the results.

THEORY AND KEY CONSTRUCTS

We began with an individual-level behavioral economic model of drug use, focusing on the impact of advertising. This well-established economic framework provided the rigorous link between the underlying theory and the statistical model needed to estimate individual behaviors.[8–10] We then relied on health behavior theory to select the specific variables used within this empirical specification. The measures used in the analysis represented the predominant benefits and costs of drug use identified in major health behavior theories.[11–13] Because factor analyses indicated that all of the multi-item measures described below loaded on 1 factor, items were averaged.

Measures of drug consumption. We analyzed marijuana use separately from cocaine/crack use because reasons for use differ for specific drugs.[14] We combined cocaine and crack into a single category because 92% of respondents reported using both with equal frequency. Respondents indicated how often in the past 12 months they had used each drug by selecting 1 of 7 alternatives: (1) no use, (2) once, (3) 2 to 3 times, (4) 4 to 9 times, (5) 10 to 19 times, (6) 20 to 39 times, or (7) 40 or more times. We used these responses to determine both the percentages of respondents who reported using each drug in the previous 12 months (0 = no use, 1 = any use in the past 12 months) and the volumes of use among those reporting use. In the case of users of both drugs, we divided their volume of use at the median and considered those below the median to be light users (coded as 0; representing 1 to 9 times) and those above the median to be heavy users (coded as 1; representing 10 to 40 or more times).

Perceived susceptibility. The more adolescents perceive themselves to be susceptible to the negative consequences of drug abuse, the less likely they are to use drugs.[15] Perceived susceptibility was measured by asking respondents to rate 3 items (on 4-point scales) indicating the degree to which people risk harming themselves by using drugs (physically or in other ways); low scores corresponded to no risk. Scale α values were .86 (marijuana susceptibility) and .94 (cocaine/crack susceptibility).

Perceived severity. The more adolescents perceive the consequences of drug abuse to be severe, the less likely they are to use drugs.[13] Respondents rated 4 items (on 4-point scales) indicating the degree to which they would fear the consequences of being caught with drugs; low scores corresponded to no fear. The perceived severity scale α value was .88.

Attitudes toward drugs. The more favorable teenagers' attitudes toward drugs, the higher their likelihood of using drugs.[15–17] Respondents indicated their level of agreement with 14 items (on 5-point scales) describing benefits of drug use; high scores represented unfavorable attitudes toward drugs. The α value for the attitude scale was .89.

Attitudes toward drug users. As evidenced by national[14] and regional[17] surveys, adolescents with positive attitudes toward drug users are more likely to use drugs. Attitude toward drug users was measured by having respondents indicate whether each of 27 personality characteristics would describe a marijuana, cocaine, or crack user; high scores represented unfavorable attitudes toward drug users. The α values were .80 for the marijuana scale and .82 for the cocaine/crack scale.

Peer pressure. Drug use is influenced by social norms and peer pressures.[18,19] Peer pressure was assessed with 2 items rated on 5-point scales: number of friends who use each drug occasionally at parties or social events and how many close friends get "stoned" or "high" on each drug once a week or more (low scores corresponded to no close friends).

Drug availability. The supply or availability of drugs is also a significant factor in drug use. Respondents rated how difficult it would be for them to obtain each drug on a single-item 5-point scale (low scores corresponded to extreme difficulty).

Addictive properties of drugs. Past drug usage accounts for a significant degree of variability in subsequent drug consumption.[16,20,21] Previous addiction (1 = yes, 0 = no) was measured via asking respondents whether they had ever thought they were hooked on marijuana, cocaine, or crack.

Antidrug advertising. Recall was measured by asking respondents to read a short description of each advertisement and to indicate how often they had seen the advertisement. Ratings were made on a 3-point scale (low scores corresponded to not at all). All 6 advertisements were aired nationally, and there were no known differences in frequency or reach for the intended teenage audience. The α value for the recall scale was .81.

Demographic covariates. Three covariates in our model controlled for individual heterogeneity. Respondents indicated their sex (0 = female, 1 = male), their race (1 = White, 0 = other), and whether they lived in an urban or rural area (1 = city or suburb of a city, 2 = town/village or rural area).

STATISTICAL ANALYSES

We present an abbreviated description of the statistical methodology here. A comprehensive explanation of the models and analyses is available separately.[22]

Stage 1: The decision to use marijuana or cocaine/crack. The probabilities of a respondent's reporting use of marijuana and cocaine/crack over the previous 12 months were expressed in a standard "probit" formulation[23] as a function of both the attributes of the individual (e.g., demographic characteristics) and his or her perceptions of drug use itself (e.g., perceived severity). We considered 3 versions of this formulation, each involving a slightly different assumption about the relationship between the cocaine/crack and marijuana use decisions.

First, we estimated the marijuana and cocaine/crack equations independently, assuming that the decision to try the 2 drugs is independent. However, empirical research suggests that the process may be sequential; that is, one first tries marijuana and then cocaine/crack.[17,24] Second, the common-syndrome theory[25] suggests that individuals have a "predisposition" to use drugs that manifests itself first in marijuana use. Third, certain factors associated with the experience of using marijuana could lead people to use harder drugs, such as cocaine/crack; this has been referred to as a "gateway" or "stepping stone" theory.[26,27] These 3 alternatives resulted in different statistical specifications, allowing us to test the hypotheses with the available data.

Stage 2: The volume decision. In addition to the "use" choice, we investigated the decision regarding how much to use (the "volume" decision), given that an individual has reported using marijuana or cocaine/crack. Although the decision regarding how much to use is a continuous one, data limitations (data were reported categorically, and there were too few observations in key cells)[22] forced us to categorize individuals as "light" or "heavy" users.

The result is a classic sequential-choice decision: an individual uses the drug and then, on the basis of his or her experience and additional information (e.g., antidrug advertising), decides whether or not to use the drug again.[22,23] Accordingly, for each drug, we initially estimated stage 1 probability equations and then estimated the probability of a given individual's being a light or heavy user conditional on previous use. Thus, including only those who had previously used drugs, we estimated each second stage equation using a dichotomous dependent variable that took on a value of 1 if the respondent was a "heavy" user and 0 if he or she was a "light" user.

Stage 3: Evaluation of advertising effectiveness. The first "wave" of PATS (conducted before the initiation of antidrug advertising) provided us with the data necessary to assess the determinants of drug use in the absence of PDFA advertising (the "control" in our natural experiment). We were then able to assess the significance of recall of PDFA advertising in terms of use and volume decisions via a series of "treatment" groups consisting of each of the subsequent waves exposed to advertising.

We began by estimating the 3 sets of probability-of-use equations ("independent," "gateway," and "predisposition") using the wave 1 data for marijuana and cocaine/crack. Then, on the basis of the best fitting of these equations, we estimated the second stage regressions for the probability of being a light vs heavy user, also using the wave 1 data. This provided us with a detailed analysis of the factors influencing the decision to use and the volume of use for each drug before the commencement of PDFA advertising.

One way of assessing the impact of PDFA advertising would be to repeat the stage 1 and stage 2 probability equations for waves 2, 3, and 4, including the additional variable capturing respondent recall of advertising. The problem with this approach is that advertising recall may be related to an individual's previous drug use behavior. For example, a heavy drug user may tune out antidrug advertising. Accordingly, in measuring the impact of PDFA advertising in waves 2, 3, and 4, we had to control for the endogeneity of advertising recall by adjusting for probability of use at the individual level. Fortunately, we had a ready-made estimate of an individual's probability of use from the wave 1 control group probability equations.

Specifically, using the estimated coefficients from the wave 1 control group, we predicted the probability of use for each individual in wave 2 (the first wave exposed to PDFA advertising). This provided us with estimates of the probability of use of marijuana (Ψ_{MJ}^2) and cocaine/crack (Ψ_{CC}^2) in wave 2 in the absence of PDFA advertising (because the parameter estimates were generated by control-group relationships).

The probability of using drugs in wave 2 was expressed as a function of 2 variables: probability of use in the absence of PDFA advertising and recall of PDFA advertising. The coefficient for the advertising-recall variable provided a test of the impact of PDFA advertising on the 2 probability-of-use equations for respondents in wave 2.

This process was repeated for marijuana and cocaine/crack use in waves 3 and 4. The same methodology was then employed for the set of users based on the stage 2 analysis of volume of marijuana and cocaine/crack use among existing users.

Because the 3-stage methodology involved the use of the results from the wave 1 "control" group data as the basis for the subsequent analysis, many of the statistical problems associated with self-reported survey data were alleviated. For example, consider "social desirability bias," the tendency of individuals to provide responses that they think are socially desirable. A detailed analysis of this potential reporting bias suggested[22] that it served only to strengthen the results by (1) lowering the estimated marginal impact of antidrug advertising on drug use and (2) inflating coefficient standard errors,[28] thereby increasing the likelihood of concluding that advertising had no effect. Thus, our results represent a conservative estimate of the impact of antidrug advertising.

Results

STAGE 1 ("USE") AND STAGE 2 ("VOLUME") PROBITS: WAVE 1 DATA

Using nested tests, we concluded that the "predisposition" formulation fit significantly better than the "independent" process. Consequently, we used this formulation throughout. In addition, in the "gateway" formulation, the binary variable representing previous marijuana usage in the cocaine-use probit was statistically nonsignificant, leading us to reject the hypothesis that marijuana use increases the probability of cocaine/crack use. Although individuals who have used marijuana in the past are indeed more likely to use cocaine/crack, the reason is that, statistically, individuals who are predisposed to try marijuana are also predisposed to try cocaine/crack.

Table 1 presents the wave 1 results of the stage 1 equations for marijuana and cocaine/crack use. All of the variables were of the predicted sign, and the overall fit was excellent.

We next estimated the stage 2 volume-of-use equations (Table 2). The fit and parameter estimates for volume of marijuana use were quite good, but the overall equation for volume of cocaine/crack use was barely significant, at $\alpha = 0.10$. In regard to the marijuana volume

TABLE 1

Wave 1 Probits on Probabilities of Marijuana and Cocaine/Crack Use

	Coefficient	SE	z (β/SE)	P (Z > z)
Marijuana Use[a]				
Constant	0.4343	—	—	—
Attitude toward drugs	−0.5719	0.1093	−5.233	0.000
Perceived severity	−0.2854	0.0870	−3.280	0.001
Attitude toward users	−0.2043	0.5808	−0.352	0.363
Peer pressure	0.6479	0.0801	8.086	0.000
Perceived susceptibility	−0.3085	0.0954	−3.232	0.001
Previous addiction	0.8349	0.3423	2.439	0.007
Availability	0.0901	0.0542	1.664	0.048
Urban residence	0.0860	0.1587	0.542	0.588
Male	0.1675	0.1438	1.165	0.244
Race	0.4100	0.2116	1.938	0.053
Cocaine/Crack Use[b]				
Constant	5.0748	—	—	—
Attitude toward drugs	−0.5279	0.1480	−3.567	0.000
Perceived severity	−0.4407	0.1309	−3.366	0.001
Attitude toward users	0.0731	0.6707	0.109	0.457
Peer pressure	0.6592	0.1134	5.814	0.000
Perceived susceptibility	−0.3891	0.1437	−2.709	0.004
Previous addiction	2.2655	0.5876	3.856	0.000
Availability	0.0991	0.0869	1.151	0.125
Urban residence	0.2870	0.2535	1.132	0.258
Male	0.3205	0.2371	1.352	0.177
Race	0.0198	0.3397	0.058	0.954
Decision independence	0.8549	0.1854	4.612	0.000

[a]No. of observations = 642, log-likelihood = −402.87, χ^2 = 383.54 (P = .0000).
[b]No. of observations = 630, log-likelihood = −202.60, χ^2 = 232.85 (P = .0000).

equation, White and male respondents were more likely to be heavy (vs light) users. (Note that a positive and significant "decision independence" value implies that the decision to use marijuana and the decision to use cocaine/crack are not independent; that is, the use probability influences the volume decision.[22])

STAGE 3 PROBITS AND THE IMPACT OF ANTIDRUG ADVERTISING: ANALYSIS OF WAVES 2, 3, AND 4

This analysis, conducted with the wave 1 "control" group, provided the basis for analyzing the significance of recall of PDFA advertising in waves 2, 3, and 4. The results are presented in Table 3.

The findings demonstrate that recall of antidrug advertising was associated with a decreased probability of marijuana use. The advertising coefficients in the marijuana use equation (see top section of Table 3) were all statistically significant and of the "correct" sign.

TABLE 2

Wave 1 Second-Stage Probits for Light vs Heavy Marijuana and Cocaine/Crack Use

	Coefficient	SE	z (β/SE)	P (Z > z)
Marijuana Volume[a] (0 = light user, 1 = heavy user)				
Constant	−2.0510	—	—	—
Attitude toward drugs	−0.6927	0.3065	−2.260	0.012
Perceived severity	−0.4294	0.1729	−2.483	0.007
Attitude toward users	−1.0230	0.7443	−1.374	0.085
Peer pressure	0.8800	0.2744	3.206	0.001
Perceived susceptibility	−0.4023	0.2005	−2.007	0.023
Previous addiction	1.5386	0.5398	2.850	0.002
Availability	0.0763	0.1012	0.753	0.226
Urban residence	0.2008	0.2505	0.801	0.423
Male	0.5896	0.2430	2.426	0.015
Race	0.9078	0.4038	2.248	0.025
Decision independence	1.3481	0.7885	1.710	0.087
Cocaine/Crack Volume[b] (0 = light user, 1 = heavy user)				
Constant	0.7405	—	—	—
Attitude toward drugs	−0.0259	0.2373	−0.109	0.457
Perceived severity	−0.1925	0.2532	−0.760	0.224
Attitude toward users	0.3341	0.8981	0.372	0.355
Peer pressure	0.3167	0.1856	1.706	0.044
Perceived susceptibility	−0.4509	0.2567	−1.757	0.040
Previous addiction	−0.9231	0.5627	−1.641	0.051
Availability	0.0641	0.1556	0.412	0.341
Urban residence	0.4104	0.4477	0.917	0.359
Male	0.4210	0.4206	−1.001	0.317
Race	0.0561	0.5535	−0.101	0.920

[a]Stage 2 dependent. No. of observations = 206, log-likelihood = −137.61, χ^2 = 234.34 (P = .0000).
[b]Stage 2 independent. No. of observations = 64, log-likelihood = −43.86, χ^2 = 234.34 (P = .0861).

In the case of cocaine/crack use, the advertising variables were also significant in waves 2 through 4. The estimated advertising coefficients in the bottom section of Table 3, however, were all statistically nonsignificant with the exception of the wave 4 marijuana volume-of-use equation. This suggests that recall of PDFA's antidrug advertising had little or no impact on the volume of use among existing users.

Finally, to ensure that the negative advertising coefficients imply that recall of advertising leads to lower marijuana and cocaine/crack use and are not due to omitted-variable bias (e.g., omission of variables such as exposure to other antidrug programs), we examined the correlation between the advertising-recall variable and the estimated equation error. This correlation was found to be statistically nonsignificant (according to a significance level of $P < .0001$) for each equation, suggesting that omitted-variable bias was not a significant problem.

TABLE 3

"Stage 3" Advertising Impact Coefficients, Use Decision, and Light/Heavy Use Decision: Waves 2, 3, and 4

Equation and Variable	Wave 2	Wave 3	Wave 4
Use Decision			
Marijuana			
Recall of advertising	−0.183	−0.305	−0.303
	(P = .043)	(P = .005)	(P = .001)
ψ_{MJ}	3.429	2.973	3.581
	(z = 19.03)	(z = 15.731)	(z = 20.94)
Log-likelihood	−574.02	−410.19	−659.97
df	864	672	1184
χ^2 (P)	538.62 (.0000)	344.31 (.0000)	707.00 (.0000)
Cocaine/crack			
Recall of advertising	−0.205	−0.162	−0.421
	(P = .05)	(P = .05)	(P = .000)
ψ_{CC}	3.490	2.665	3.600
	(z = 12.59)	(z = 10.13)	(z = 14.60)
Log-likelihood	−333.90	−216.27	−320.75
df	880	700	1211
χ^2 (P)	210.71 (.0000)	123.51 (.0000)	308.48 (.0000)
Light/Heavy Use Decision			
Marijuana			
Recall of advertising	−0.087	−0.086	−0.406
	(P = .273)	(P = .330)	(P = .003)
ψ_{MJ}	2.166	1.847	2.263
	(z = 5.73)	(z = 6.81)	(z = 8.00)
Log-likelihood	−214.40	−129.89	−193.90
df	315	191	276
χ^2 (P)	48.65 (.0000)	52.19 (.0000)	91.95 (.0000)
Cocaine/crack			
Recall of advertising	−0.048	−0.076	−0.289
	(P = .389)	(P = .400)	(P = .127)
ψ_{CC}	2.946	2.531	3.004
	(z = 2.45)	(z = 2.00)	(z = 2.97)
Log-likelihood	−60.58	−37.36	−57.71
df	101	73	83
χ^2 (P)	9.46 (.0088)	4.41 (.1101)	14.05 (.0009)

Marginal Impact of Advertising

We also estimated the marginal impact of the advertising–recall variable[23] to determine the change in the probability of use associated with a 1-unit change in advertising recall. We estimated the cumulative impact on use probability given a particular wave's level of advertising awareness by subtracting the average predicted probability of use in the absence of PDFA advertising from the average predicted probability given the level of recall generated by PDFA advertising in that wave.

Marginal effects of PDFA advertising on the probability of drug use were estimated to be 6.8%, 9.2%, and 6.5% for marijuana and 3.3%, 2.8%, and 2.5% for cocaine/crack across waves 2, 3, and 4, respectively. In wave 2, for example, a 1-unit change in advertising recall (measured on a 3-point scale) would have resulted in 6.8% and 3.3% reductions in the probability of using marijuana and cocaine/crack, respectively. Cumulative effects of PDFA advertisements were estimated to be 9.6%, 11.98%, and 9.25% for marijuana and 4.7%, 3.6%, and 3.6% for cocaine/crack, respectively, across the 3 waves. These measures suggest that, after 3 years of PDFA advertising, approximately 9.25% fewer adolescents were using marijuana.

Discussion

Our results are consistent with the hypothesis that antidrug advertising reduces the probability of marijuana and cocaine/crack use among adolescents. However, our results also suggest that recall of antidrug advertising is not associated with adolescents' decisions regarding how much marijuana or cocaine/crack to use among those already using each drug.

This study was not without limitations. Although the sample was constructed to be representative of American adolescents, central-location sampling was used. Sudman[29] has shown that when central-location sampling is used carefully, it will provide close estimates of the total population. It is also possible that respondents were exposed to other antidrug intervention programs in addition to their exposure to antidrug advertising. However, past research has demonstrated that these alternative programs have been largely ineffective.[30]

Despite these potential limitations, our findings have important public policy implications. Our model, based on survey data from 1987 to 1990, indicates that increases in amounts of antidrug advertising are associated with decreases in teenage drug use. During this time period, media financial support for antidrug advertising increased, from a low of $115 million in 1987 to a high of $365 million in 1991.[31,32] Given our results, this increase appears to have been a worthwhile investment.

CONTRIBUTORS

All of the authors contributed equally to article preparation and data analysis.

ACKNOWLEDGMENTS

We thank Gordon Black and Edgar Adams for providing the data and Scott Armstrong, Ravi Dhar, George Foltin, Eric Greenleaf, Edward Kaplan, Elisa Montaguti, Bob Shoemaker, and 3 anonymous reviewers for their helpful comments on earlier versions of the article. We also thank Elisa Montaguti for computational assistance.

HUMAN PARTICIPANT PROTECTION

No protocol approval was needed for this study.

References

1. Levine J. Don't fry your brain. *Forbes.* February 4, 1991:116–117.

2. *What Americas Users Spend on Illegal Drugs, 1988–1993.* Cambridge, Mass: Abt Associates Inc; 1995.

3. *Leading Drug Indicators.* Washington, DC: Office of National Drug Control Policy; 1990.

4. Black GS, Zastowny TR, Green PJ, Adams EH, Lawton KB. The consistency of estimates obtained through central-location sampling: analysis of the Partnership for a Drug-Free America Attitude Tracking Study. *Am J Drug Alcohol Abuse.* 1994;20:199–222.

5. Aquilino WS. Interview mode effects in surveys of drug and alcohol use. *Public Opin Q.* 1994;58:210–240.

6. Sickles R, Taubman P. Who uses illegal drugs? *Am Econ Rev.* 1991;81:248–251.

7. O'Malley PM, Bachman JG, Johnston LD. Reliability and consistency in self-reports of drug use. *Int J Addict.* 1983;18:805–824.

8. Hanemann WM. Discrete/continuous models of consumer demand. *Econometrica.* 1984;52: 541–562.

9. Putsis WP Jr, Srinivasan N. Buying or just browsing? The duration of purchase deliberation. *J Marketing Res.* August 1994:393–402.

10. Bickel WK, Vuchinich RE. *Reframing Health Behavior With Behavioral Economics.* Mahwah, NJ: Lawrence Erlbaum Associates; 2000.

11. Maiman LA, Becker MH. The Health Belief Model: origins and correlates in psychological theory. In: Becker Marshall H, ed. *The Health Belief Model and Personal Health Behavior.* Thorofare, NJ: Charles B Slack Inc; 1974:9–26.

12. Leventhal H. Findings and theory in the study of fear communication. In: Berkowitz L, ed. *Advances in Experimental Social Psychology,* vol. 5. New York, NY: Academic Press Inc; 1970: 119–186.

13. Rogers RW. Cognitive and physiological processes in fear appeals and attitude change: a revised theory of protection motivation. In: Cacioppo JT, Petty RE, eds. *Social Psychophysiology.* New York, NY: Guilford Press; 1983:153–176.

14. Johnston LD. O'Malley PM. Why do the nation's students use drugs and alcohol? Self-reported reasons from nine national surveys. *J Drug Issues.* 1986;16:29–66.

15. Bachman JG, Johnston LD, O'Malley P. Explaining recent increases in students' marijuana use: impacts of perceived risks and disapproval, 1976 through 1996. *Am J Public Health.* 1998;88: 887–892.

16. Brook JS, Balka EB, Whiteman M. The risks for late adolescence of early adolescent marijuana use. *Am J Public Health.* 1999;89:1549–1554.

17. Kosterman R, Hawkins JD, Guo J, Catalano RF, Abbott RD. The dynamics of alcohol and marijuana initiation: patterns and predictors of first use in adolescence. *Am J Public Health.* 2000;90:360–366.

18. Rosenstock IM. Historical origins of the Health Belief Model. In: Becker Marshall H, ed. *The Health Belief Model and Personal Health Behavior.* Thorofare. NJ: Charles B Slack Inc; 1974:1–8.

19. Rose RL, Bearden WO, Teel JE. An attributional analysis of resistance to group pressure regarding illicit drug and alcohol consumption. *J Consumer Res.* 1992;19:1–13.

20. Bentler PM, Speckart G. Models of attitude–behavior relations. *Psychol Rev.* 1979;86:452–464.

21. Becker GS, Grossman M, Murphy KM. An empirical analysis of cigarette addiction. *Am Econ Rev.* 1994;84:396–418.

22. Block L, Morwitz V, Putsis P, Sen S. *Does Anti-Drug Advertising Work?* New Haven, Conn: Yale University; 1999. Working paper.

23. Maddala GS. *Limited-Dependent and Qualitative Variables in Econometrics.* Cambridge, England: Cambridge University Press; 1983.

24. *Cigarettes, Alcohol, Marijuana: Gateways to Illicit Drug Use.* New York, NY: Center for Addiction and Substance Abuse, Columbia University; 1994.

25. Donovan J, Jessor R. Structure of problem behavior in adolescence and young adulthood. *J Consult Clin Psychol.* 1985;53:890–904.

26. Kandel DB, Yamaguchi K, Chen K. Stages of progression in drug involvement from adolescence to adulthood: further evidence for the gateway theory. *J Stud Alcohol.* 1992;53:447–457.

27. Goode E. Cigarette smoking and drug use on a college campus. *Int J Addict.* 1972;7:133–140.

28. Madger LS, Hughes JP. Logistic regression when the outcome is measured with uncertainty. *Am J Epidemiol.* 1997;146:195–203.

29. Sudman S. Improving the quality of shopping center sampling. *J Marketing Res.* 1980;17:423–431.

30. Ennett ST, Rosenbaum DP, Flewelling RL. Biehler GS, Ringwalt CL, Bailey SL. Long-term evaluation of drug abuse resistance education. *Addict Behav.* 1994;19:113–125.

31. Marwick C. Administration attacks increasing use of marijuana. *JAMA.* 1995;274:598–599.

32. Crain R. Ad biz needs to reinvigorate once-strong anti-drug message. *Advertising Age.* September 2, 1996:17.

Anyone's Guess:
The Need for Nutrition Labeling at Fast-Food and Other Chain Restaurants

Center for Science in the Public Interest

For more information or model legislation, please contact:

Dr. Margo G. Wootan

Center for Science in the Public Interest

1875 Connecticut Avenue, NW, Suite 300

Washington, DC 20009

phone: 202-777-8352

fax: 202-265-4954

email: nutritionpolicy@cspinet.org

November 2003

Anyone's Guess is available online (free of charge) at www.cspinet.org/restaurantreport
or by mailing a check for $7 ($10 in Canada) to CSPI at the above address.

Summary: Nutrition Labeling at Fast-Food and Other Chain Restaurants

- Obesity is one of the greatest public health challenges of our time.
  - Obesity rates in adults doubled over the last twenty years. Currently, two-thirds of American adults (65%) are overweight or obese. Obesity rates have doubled in children and tripled in teens over the past two decades.
  - Obesity costs American families, businesses, and governments about $117 billion each year in health-care and related costs.
  - The negative health consequences of obesity already are evident. Between 1990 and 2001, diabetes rates rose by 60%. Type 2 diabetes can no longer be called "adult onset" because of rising rates in children.
- Only 12% of Americans eat a healthy diet according to the U.S. Department of Agriculture's (USDA) Healthy Eating Index. Between 1978 and 1995, the average person's calorie intake increased by 167 calories, from 1,876 to 2,043 calories.
- The 1990 Nutrition Labeling and Education Act (NLEA) requires food manufacturers to provide nutrition information on nearly all packaged foods. However, NLEA explicitly exempts restaurants. At most restaurants, people can only guess the nutritional content of the food.
  - Yet, Americans are increasingly relying on restaurants to feed themselves and their families. In 1970, Americans spent just 26% of their food dollars on restaurant meals and other foods prepared outside their homes. Today, we spend almost half (46%) our food dollars on away-from-home foods. The average American consumes about one-third of his or her calories from foods from restaurants and other food-service establishments.

  > "Despite nutritional gains at home, Americans will find it difficult to improve their diets because they purchase so many meals outside the home," U.S. Department of Agriculture (Lin et al., 1999).

- Increases in Americans' caloric intake over the past two decades are due in part to increases in the frequency of eating out. Studies have found a positive association between eating out and higher caloric intakes and higher body weights. Children eat almost twice as many calories when they eat a meal at a restaurant (770 calories) as at home (420 calories).
- The nutritional quality of restaurant foods and meals varies widely, and a range of options is usually available. However, without nutrition information, it can be difficult to compare options and make informed decisions. Americans rank nutrition second only to taste in determining their food purchases. Studies show that estimating the calorie and fat content of restaurant foods is difficult.

- Foods that people eat from restaurants and other food-service establishments are generally higher in nutrients for which over-consumption is a problem (like fat and saturated fat) and lower in nutrients that people need to eat more of (like calcium and fiber) as compared to home-prepared foods.

The U.S. Surgeon General's "Call to Action" to reduce obesity recommended: "increase availability of nutrition information for foods eaten and prepared away from home" (2001).

- It is not uncommon for a restaurant entree to provide half of a day's calories, saturated and trans fat, or sodium. Include an appetizer, drink and dessert, and it is easy to consume a whole day's calories, saturated and trans fat, and sodium in a single meal.

- Portion sizes at restaurants are often large, pricing can make larger serving sizes more appealing, and studies show that people tend to eat greater quantities of food when they are served more.

- The current system of voluntary labeling at restaurants is inadequate given the large role that restaurant foods play in Americans' diets. Approximately two-thirds of the largest chain restaurants do not provide any nutrition information about their foods to their customers.

Recommendation: Congress and/or state or local legislatures should require food-service chains with ten or more units to list on their menus the calorie, saturated and trans fat (combined), and sodium contents of standard menu items. Restaurants that use menu boards, where space is limited, should be required to provide at least calorie information on their menu boards. While listing other nutrition information could help consumers make healthier choices, calorie, saturated and trans fat, and sodium information is most needed, given that cardiovascular diseases are the leading causes of death and obesity rates are rising rapidly. Such information, clearly displayed at the point of decision, would allow consumers to make informed choices at restaurants and is an important strategy for reducing obesity and protecting the nation's health.

The Importance of Food Choices to Health

Unhealthy diets and physical inactivity are leading causes of premature death, disabilities, and high health-care costs in the United States. According to the U.S. Department of Health and Human Services (DHHS), poor diets, along with physical inactivity, cause about 310,000 to 580,000 premature deaths each year (Table 1; McGinnis & Foege, 1993). That is five times the number of people killed by guns, AIDS, and drug use combined.

Unhealthy eating is a major cause of obesity, heart disease, cancer, stroke, diabetes, high blood cholesterol, high blood pressure, osteoporosis, tooth decay and other health problems. Poor diet can result in disabilities and loss of independence from stroke, heart

TABLE 1	
Leading Contributors to Premature Death (Deaths per Year)	
Diet and Physical Inactivity	310,000–580,000
Tobacco	260,000–470,000
Alcohol	70,000–110,000
Microbial Agents	90,000
Toxic Agents	60,000–110,000
Firearms	35,000
Sexual Behavior	30,000
Motor Vehicles	25,000

disease or osteoporosis-related hip fracture, or blindness and limb amputations due to diabetes.

Obesity is one of the greatest health challenges of our time. Rates are increasing rapidly in both adults and children. Obesity rates in adults doubled over the last twenty years (Flegal et al., 2002). **Currently, two-thirds of American adults (65%) are overweight or obese.** Obesity rates have doubled in children and tripled in teens over the past two decades (Ogden et al., 2002). Obesity costs American families, businesses, and governments about $117 billion in health-care and related costs each year (US DHHS, 2001).

Obesity costs American families, businesses and governments about $117 billion in health-care and related costs each year (U.S. Department of Health and Human Services, 2001).

The negative health consequences of obesity already are evident. Between 1990 and 2001, diabetes rates rose by 60% (Mokdad et al., 2003). Type 2 diabetes can no longer be called "adult onset" because of rising rates in children. In one study, the incidence of type 2 diabetes in adolescents increased ten-fold between 1982 and 1994 (Pinhas-Hamiel et al., 1996). Employers pay an average of $4,410 more per year for employee beneficiaries who have diabetes than for beneficiaries who do not have diabetes (Ramsey et al., 2002), and the federal government spends $14.5 billion a year on diabetes through Medicare and Medicaid (NIH, 2000).

Americans' Eating Habits

According to the U.S. Department of Agriculture (USDA), though "Americans' eating patterns, as measured by the Healthy Eating Index, have slightly but significantly improved since 1989 . . . the diets of most Americans still need improvement" (Bowman et al., 1998). Only 12% of Americans eat a healthy diet (i.e., a diet consistent with federal nutrition recommendations) (Bowman et al., 1998). Less than 1/3 of Americans meet dietary recommendations for grains (22%), fruits (17%) and vegetables (31%) (Bowman et al., 1998), and our diets are too high in saturated fat, added sugars, sodium, and calories. Only 2% of children eat a healthy diet (Munoz et al., 1997). Children's diets generally are too high in fat, saturated fat, and sodium and too low in fiber (Lin et al., 1996).

Between 1978 and 1995, average calorie intake increased by 167 calories per day, from 1,876 to 2,043 calories according to national nutrition surveys (Lin et al., 1999). Note, however, that self-reported intake data underestimates calorie consumption. Food supply data, which overestimate calorie intake but provide reliable time-trend data, also show that Americans are eating more calories. From 1970 to 1983, the number of available calories was relatively stable at about 3,200 to 3,300 calories per person per day (Putnam & Allshouse, 1999). Then, it started to increase. **In 1994, there were 3,800 calories available for each person per day, which is 1,800 calories more than a sedentary adult needs.**

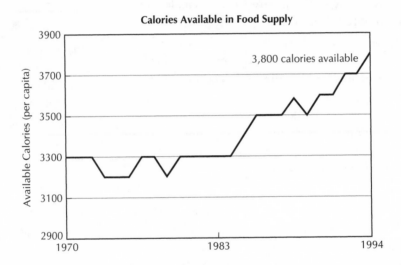

Calories Available in Food Supply

Eating Out Trends

Restaurant foods are an increasingly important part of Americans' diets. In 1970, Americans spent just 26% of their food dollars on restaurant meals and other meals prepared outside their homes (Lin et al., 1999). Today, we spend almost half (46%) our food dollars at restaurants (NRA, 2002). Almost half (44%) of adults patronize a restaurant on any given day (Ad Age, 2001).

On average, Americans (age 8 and older) eat 218 restaurant meals per year (NRA, 2002). Although people with higher incomes eat out more often than those with lower incomes, people with household incomes below $15,000 per year eat out 3.2 meals per week (compared to 4.9 restaurant meals per week for people with household incomes over $75,000 per year) (Ebbin, 2000).

Reasons why Americans are eating out more frequently include higher incomes, more affordable and convenient fast-food outlets, increased marketing by restaurants, more women working outside the home, and more two-earner households (Lin et al., 1999).

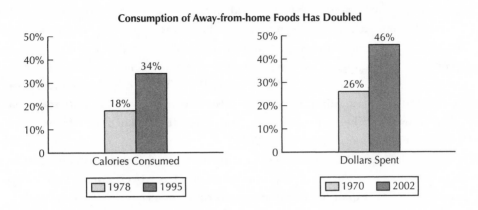

Consumption of Away-from-home Foods Has Doubled

Impact of Restaurant Foods on Americans' Diets

In the past, when eating out was an occasional treat, few had to worry about the nutritional quality of restaurant foods. Today, however, restaurant foods make up a sizeable proportion of the American diet. Over the last two decades, meals and snacks from restaurants and other food-service establishments have increased by almost 70%, from 16% of meals and snacks in 1978 to 27% in 1995 (Lin et al., 1999). **According to USDA, away-from-home food provided 34% of total calories in 1995, compared to 18% of calories in 1978** (Lin et al., 1999).

Increases in Americans' caloric intake over the past two decades may be due in part to increases in eating out (Lin et al., 1999). **Children eat almost twice as many calories when they eat at a restaurant (770 calories) compared to at home (420 calories)** (Zoumas-Morse et al., 2001). One study found that women who eat out more often (more than 5 times a week) consume 288 more calories each day than women who eat out less often (Clemens et al., 1999). (Despite eating more calories, the women did not consume more of beneficial nutrients such as calcium or fiber.) Fast-food meals also are linked to eating more calories, more saturated fat, fewer fruits and vegetables, and less milk (French et al., 2001; Jeffery & French, 1998; McNutt et al., 1997).

Children eat almost twice as many calories when they eat at a restaurant (770 calories) compared to at home (420 calories) (Zoumas-Morse et al., 2001).

Although away-from-home foods make up 27% of meals and snacks, as noted above, they provide 34% of calories. This suggests that when people eat out, they either eat larger quantities of food, higher-calorie foods, or both than when eating at home (Lin et al., 1999). Several, though not all (French et al., 2001), studies have found a **positive association between eating out and body weight or body fatness** (Binkley et al., 2000; Jeffery & French, 1998; Ma et al., 2003; McCrory et al., 2000; McCrory et al., 1999).

Foods that people eat from restaurants and other food-service establishments are generally higher in nutrients for which over-consumption is a problem (like fat and saturated fat) and lower in nutrients that people need to eat more of (like calcium and fiber) as compared to home-prepared foods (Lin et al., 1999; Clemens et al., 1999; Jeffery & French, 1998; Ma et al., 2003; McCrory et al., 1999). The **foods that children eat from fast-food and other restaurants also are higher in fat and saturated fat and lower in fiber, iron, calcium, and cholesterol than foods from home** (Lin et al., 1996; Zoumas-Morse et al., 2001).

Although many Americans have made nutritional improvements to their diets over the past 20 years, the improvements have been smaller for away-from-home foods than for home-prepared foods (Lin et al., 1999). For example in 1978, the total fat content of foods was the same for home-prepared and away-from-home foods (41% of calories). In 1995, the fat content of home-prepared foods dropped to 31.5% of calories compared to 37.6% of calories for foods eaten from restaurants and other food-service establishments (Lin et al., 1999). In 1995, Americans' average saturated-fat intake from home foods was 10.9% of calories, compared with 12.5% of calories from restaurants and 13.8% of calories from fast-food establishments (Lin et al., 1999).

Over the last two decades, calcium intake from foods prepared at home increased (from 402 mg to 425 mg per 1,000 calories). In contrast, the calcium density from away-from-home foods decreased (from 368 mg to 343 mg per 1,000 calories) (Lin et al., 1999). Home-prepared foods also provide more fiber (8.1 g/1,000 cal) than fast foods (5.6 g/1,000 cal) and other restaurant foods (6.2 g/1,000 cal) (Lin et al., 1999).

Nutritional Quality of Restaurant Foods

Restaurant foods are often 1) high in calories, saturated and trans fat, and sodium, 2) served in large portions, and 3) priced in a way that makes larger serving sizes more appealing. In addition, "away-from-home foods are typically ready-to-eat and consumed 'as is,' and the consumer has less control over or knowledge of their nutritional content" (Lin et al., 1999).

"Foods prepared at home are generally much more healthful than away-from-home foods," USDA (Lin et al., 1999).

Nutritional quality of popular restaurant foods. According to studies conducted by the Center for Science in the Public Interest (CSPI) and nutrition information obtained from restaurants (Jacobson &

Hurley, 2002), it is not uncommon for restaurant meals to provide half a day's to a whole day's worth of calories (1,100 to 2,350 calories) (Table 2).

Restaurant appetizers can use up half a day's calories before people even get to their meal. Buffalo wings with blue cheese dressing (1,010 calories) and stuffed potato skins with sour cream (1,260 calories) each provide about a half a day's calories. No one would mistake cheese fries with ranch dressing for a health food, but few

---

TABLE 2

Restaurant Foods Can Be High in Calories, Saturated and Trans Fat and Sodium*

	Calories	Saturated and Trans Fat (g)	Sodium (mg)
Appetizers			
Buffalo Wings (12 wings, 13 oz.)	700	16	1,750
with Blue Cheese Dressing	1,010	22	2,460
Stuffed Potato Skins (8 skins, 12 oz.)	1,120	40	1,270
with Sour Cream (5 Tb.)	1,260	48	1,300
Cheese Fries (4 cups, 27 oz.)	2,380	79	4,020
with Ranch Dressing (8 Tb.)	3,010	91	4,890
Drinks			
McDonald's Coca-Cola, Super Size (42 oz.)	410	0	40
7-Eleven Double Gulp, Coca-Cola (64 oz.)	600	0	60
Dunkin' Donuts Coolatta, Made with Cream, Large (32 oz.)	820	22[†]	144
McDonald's Shake, Large (32 oz.)	1,010	19[†]	530
Entrees/Meals			
French Toast (3 slices) with Syrup ($^{1}/_{4}$ cup) and Margarine	910	13	1,030
Schlotzsky's Chicken Breast Sandwich, Light & Flavorful (Large, 29 oz.)	1,010	4[†]	4,520
House Lo Mein (4$^{1}/_{2}$ cups)	1,060	7[†]	3,460
Spaghetti with Meatballs (3$^{1}/_{2}$ cups)	1,160	10[†]	2,210
Dinner House Mushroom Cheeseburger	900	28	1,070
with Onion Rings (11 rings)	1,800	52	2,130
Grand Slam-type Platter (2 Scrambled Eggs, 2 Pancakes with Syrup and Margarine, 2 Sausage Links and 2 Strips of Bacon)	1,010	19	1,770
Fried Seafood Combo Platter (with 4 Tb. Tartar Sauce, Fries, Coleslaw and 2 Biscuits with Butter [2 Pats])	2,170	39	4,390
Burger King Double Whopper with Cheese Value Meal, King Size (with King Fries and King Coca-Cola Classic)	2,180	48	2,600
Dessert			
Cinnabon Classic (7$^{1}/_{2}$ oz.)	670	14	800
Fudge Brownie Sundae (10 oz.)	1,130	30	400
Cheesecake Factory Carrot Cake (1 slice)	1,560	23[†]	520

Note: Recommended daily limits for a 2,000 calorie diet are 20 grams of saturated fat and 2,400 mg of sodium.
*Jacobson & Hurley, 2002.
[†]Includes only saturated fat.

would guess that a typical serving uses up more than a whole day's worth of calories (3,010 calories).

Drinks can pack the calories of a meal. A large shake from McDonald's has 1,010 calories. A large Dunkin' Donuts Coolatta made with cream has 820 calories.

Restaurant entrees such as a large Schlotzsky's Light and Flavorful chicken breast sandwich (1,010 calories), spaghetti with meatballs (1,160 calories), and French toast with syrup and margarine (910 calories) each provide about a thousand calories, before adding side dishes. The calorie contents of whole meals are higher. A fried seafood platter has 2,170 calories. A king size Burger King Double Whopper with Cheese Value Meal provides 2,180 calories.

Though people know that dessert is a splurge, many do not realize how many calories it can add. A Cinnabon Classic has 670 calories, and just one slice of the Cheesecake Factory's Carrot Cake has 1,560 calories.

The nutritional quality of restaurant foods and meals varies widely and a range of options is usually available (Table 3). However, without nutrition information, it can be difficult to compare options and make informed decisions. For example, Szechuan Shrimp and Kung Pao Chicken may look equally attractive at a Chinese restaurant until their calories and saturated fat are revealed: 930 versus 1,620 calories and 2 versus 13 grams of saturated fat. Without nutrition information, many may not realize that a tuna salad sandwich from a typical deli has 50% more calories and twice as much saturated fat as a roast beef sandwich with mustard. While most people probably know that the vegetable of the day is a healthier choice than an order of French fries, many may not realize that the fries contain ten times as many calories. Ordering a venti Caffe Mocha with whole milk instead of a grande Caffe Latte with skim milk at Starbucks will more than triple the calories in your drink and add three-quarters of a day's worth of saturated fat.

Portion sizes. The large portion sizes served at restaurants greatly affect the nutritional quality of the foods and their impact on Americans' diets and waistlines. **It is common for restaurants to serve two to three times more than what is considered a standard serving size** (see Table 4). A Double Gulp from 7-Eleven contains six servings, meaning it provides six times as many calories as would a standard serving size of soft drink. A porterhouse steak from a typical steak house restaurant weighs more than a pound. According to USDA serving sizes, that is enough meat to serve a family of six. A typical pastry from a sit-down restaurant is often twice as big as the Food and Drug Administration's (FDA) standard serving size. Larger portions also mean higher saturated fat and sodium numbers.

Portion sizes have grown over time. In the 1950s, a "family size" bottle of Coke was 26 ounces, while now a single-serve bottle is 20 ounces. McDonald's original burger, fries, and 12-ounce Coke provided 590 calories. Today, a Super Size Value Meal that

TABLE 3			

Nutritional Quality of Restaurant Foods Vary Widely*

Menu Item	Calories	Saturated + Trans Fat (g)	Sodium (mg)
Entrees/Meals			
Szechuan Shrimp (3^1/$_2$ cups)	930	2[†]	2,460
Kung Pao Chicken (4^1/$_2$ cups)	1,620	13[†]	2,610
Grilled Chicken (6 oz.) with Baked Potato with Sour Cream (1 Tb.) and Vegetable (1 cup)	640	5	820
Chicken Fingers (5 pieces, 9 oz.) with French Fries (2 cups) and Coleslaw (1 cup)	1,640	30	2,640
Roast Beef with Mustard Sandwich (9 oz.)	460	4	990
Tuna Salad Sandwich (11 oz.)	720	8	1,320
Overstuffed Tuna Salad with Mayo Sandwich (13 oz.)	980	11	1,310
Burger King Sandwiches			
Hamburger	310	6	580
Chicken Whopper			
without Mayonnaise	420	3	1,250
with Mayonnaise	580	6	1,370
Whopper	760	15	1,000
Whopper with Cheese	850	32	1,430
Double Whopper with Cheese	1,150	33	1,530
Dinner House Side Dishes			
Vegetable of the Day	60	1	150
Baked Potato with Sour Cream (1 Tb.)	310	2	30
French Fries (2 cups)	590	12	460
Loaded Baked Potato (bacon, butter, cheese, etc.)	620	19	570
Onion Rings (11)	900	23	1,050
Starbucks			
Caffe Latte with Skim Milk, Grande (16 oz.)	160	1[†]	220
Caffe Latte with Whole Milk, Grande (16 oz.)	270	9[†]	210
Caffe Mocha with Whole Milk, Whipped Cream, Grande (16 oz.)	420	13[†]	190
Caffe Mocha with Whole Milk, Whipped Cream, Venti (20 oz.)	530	16[†]	250

Note: Recommended daily limits for a 2,000 calorie diet are 20 grams of saturated fat and 2,400 mg of sodium.
*Jacobson & Hurley, 2002.
[†]Includes only saturated fat.

includes a Quarter Pounder with Cheese, Super Size Fries, and a Super Size Coke delivers 1,550 calories. A typical bagel used to weigh 2 to 3 ounces, compared to 4 to 7 ounces today (Young & Nestle, 1995).

Although portion sizes started to increase in the 1970s, they grew sharply in the 1980s and have continued to increase since then (Young & Nestle, 2002). This trend has occurred in parallel with increases in overall calorie intake, available

TABLE 4		
Portion Sizes at Restaurants		
Menu Item	**Serving Size**	**Calories**
Soda Pop (Cola)		
FDA Official Serving	1 cup (8 oz.)	100
12 oz. Can	1½ cups (12 oz.)	150
20 oz. Bottle	2½ cups (20 oz.)	250
Burger King, King Size w/ Ice	4 cups of Soda (42 oz. cup)	430
7-Eleven Double Gulp w/ Ice	6 cups of Soda (64 oz. cup)	600
Steaks		
USDA Official Serving (Sirloin)	3 oz.	220
Dinner House Serving (Sirloin)	7 oz.	410
Steak House Serving (Porterhouse)	20 oz.	1,100
Muffins		
FDA Official Serving	2 oz.	160
Restaurant Serving	4 oz.	430

calories in the food supply, and the prevalence of overweight and obesity (Young & Nestle, 2002).

Large portions are a problem not only because they provide more calories, but also because **studies show that when adults and children are served more food, they eat more food** (Booth et al., 1981; Orlet Fisher, et al., 2003; Rolls et al., 2000; Wansink, 1996; Young & Nestle, 2002).

In addition, a national survey found that when people eat out, 67% report that they eat all of their entree either all or most of the time (AICR, 2001). Most restaurant owners believe that people generally do not share restaurant entrees. Rather, entrees are purchased for consumption by individuals (Young & Nestle, 1995). Thus, the large portion sizes at fast-food and other restaurants likely contribute to overeating.

Portions and price. Food pricing can move people toward larger portions. For food manufacturers and restaurants, the actual monetary costs of larger portions are small because the cost of the food itself is small (on average about 20% of retail costs) compared to marketing, labor, overhead, distribution, and other costs (Nestle, 2002). Thus, even the relatively small amounts of extra money consumers spend when upgrading to larger portions mean larger corporate profits. In addition, consumers perceive larger portions as better monetary values.

A national study found that a medium-sized movie-theater popcorn costs just 71 cents more than the small. People may not realize that it also "costs" them 500 more calories

TABLE 5				

Portions and Price*

Menu Item	Serving Size	Calories	Saturated + Trans Fat (g)	Average Price ($)
Wendy's				
Classic Double with Cheese	11 oz.	760	19[†]	3.32
Classic Double with Cheese Old Fashioned Combo Meal 2 (with Biggie Fries and Medium Cola)		1,360	26[†]	4.89
McDonald's French Fries				
Small	2$\frac{1}{2}$ oz.	210	3	1.03
Medium	5 oz.	450	8	1.50
Large	6 oz.	540	9	1.67
Super Size	7 oz.	610	10	1.90
Movie Theater Popcorn without "Butter"				
Small	7 cups	400	19	3.13
Medium	16 cups	900	43	3.84
7-Eleven, Coca-Cola Classic				
Gulp	16 oz.	150	0	0.89
Double Gulp	64 oz.	600	0	1.26
Cinnabon				
Minibon	3 oz.	300	5	2.01
Cinnabon Classic	7$\frac{1}{2}$ oz.	670	14	2.49

Note: Recommended daily limits for a 2,000 calorie diet are 20 grams of saturated fat and 2,400 mg of sodium.
*NANA, 2002.
[†]Includes only saturated fat.

and 24 extra grams of saturated and trans fat (Table 5; NANA, 2002). A Cinnabon Classic costs 24% more than a Minibon, but it contains 123% more calories. Purchasing a Double Gulp instead of a Gulp at 7-Eleven costs 37 cents more, but adds 450 more calories. **Restaurant customers often get many more calories and more saturated fat and sodium for a small difference in price. Providing nutrition information on menus and menu boards would reveal the nutritional cost of choosing larger portions at restaurants.**

Without nutrition information, it is difficult to estimate the caloric content of restaurant foods. Numerous studies show that people have a difficult time estimating portion sizes, especially large portions (Young & Nestle, 1995). In addition, a study published by the University of Mississippi found that people underestimate the calorie content of meals purchased at restaurants (Johnson et al., 1990).

Dietitians' Estimates of the Calorie Content of Popular Restaurant Foods*

Food Item	Actual Calorie Content	Average Calorie Estimate	% Difference
Whole Milk (1 cup)	150	155	3% over
Lasagna (2 cups)	960	695	**28% under**
Grilled Chicken Caesar Salad with Dressing (4 cups)	660	440	**33% under**
Porterhouse Steak Dinner[†]	1,860	1,240	**33% under**
Hamburger (10 oz.) and Onion Rings (11 rings)	1,550	865	**44% under**
Tuna Salad Sandwich (11 oz.)	720	375	**48% under**

*Backstrand et al., 1997.
[†]The dinner included a porterhouse steak (20 oz.) with a Caesar salad (2 cups), vegetable of the day (1 cup) and a baked potato with butter (1 Tb.).

The USDA concluded that "differences in information may also impede healthful eating, in that the nutritional quality of away-from-home foods may be less apparent to consumers than for food at home," USDA (Lin et al., 1999).

A study conducted by the Center for Science in the Public Interest and New York University found that even well-trained nutrition professionals could not accurately estimate the calorie content of typical restaurant meals (Table 6; Backstrand et al., 1997). Although the dietitians were able to accurately estimate the caloric content of a cup of whole milk (the control in the study), they consistently underestimated the calories in restaurant foods and meals. Their estimates were off by large amounts—by 200 to 600 calories. For example, when shown a typical dinner-house hamburger and onion rings, the dietitians on average estimated that it had 865 calories, when it actually contained 1,550 calories. Since not even experts in the field of nutrition are able to accurately estimate the caloric content of restaurant foods, consumers are unlikely to do better.

Nutrition Information at Restaurants

Nutrition labeling in supermarkets. The Nutrition Labeling and Education Act (NLEA), which was signed into law by President George H.W. Bush in 1990, requires comprehensive, consistent food labeling on almost all packaged foods sold at supermarkets, convenience stores, and other retail stores. Three-quarters of adults report using food labels (US DHHS, 2001b), and using food labels is associated with eating more-healthful diets (Kim et al., 2000; Kreuter et al., 1997; Neuhouser et al., 1999). About half (48%) of people report that the nutrition information on food labels has caused them to change their minds about buying a food product—a 50% increase over the number in a survey conducted before the new food labeling law was implemented (Levy & Derby, 1996).

Strengthening food labeling is likely to yield significant health and economic benefits. The FDA estimated that requiring trans fat to be listed on packaged-food labels would save 2,100 to 5,600 lives a year and $3 billion to $8 billion a year (FDA, 1999). USDA estimated the economic benefits of extending nutrition labeling to fresh meat and poultry to be $62 million to $125 million per year (Crutchfield et al., 2001).

About half (48%) of people report that the nutrition information on food labels has caused them to change their minds about buying a food product (Levy & Derby, 1996).

Nutrition information at restaurants. The NLEA explicitly exempts restaurants. Under current law, the only requirement is that when restaurants make a health or nutrient-content claim for a food or meal, nutrition information relevant to that claim must be available (FDA, 2001). For example, if a menu board claims that a sandwich is low fat, the restaurant is required to have available—somewhere in the store—information about the fat content of that sandwich. Unlike for processed foods, for which nutrition information is determined by laboratory analyses of the food, nutrition information to substantiate restaurant claims may be determined from nutrient databases, cookbooks, or "other reasonable bases." The provision of that nutrition information can take various forms.

Some restaurants, particularly fast-food chains, provide brochures or posters with nutrition information regarding their menu items. Several fast-food chains provided in-store nutrition information only after pressure from state attorneys general and consumer groups. **In 1986, state attorneys general from several states, including Texas, New York, and California, negotiated an agreement with McDonald's, Burger King, Jack in the Box, KFC, and Wendy's to provide nutrition and ingredient information in their restaurants.**

There are a number of limitations with the current voluntary system for providing nutrition information in chain restaurants. First, most chain restaurants do not provide nutrition information. McDonald's and Burger King are the exceptions rather than the norm. **A survey of the largest chain restaurants found that two-thirds (65%) do not provide customers with any nutrition information** (including on menus, menu boards, pamphlets, table tents, or posters) (Almanza et al., 1997). Second, the nutrition information is not always accessible. Even when restaurants have developed nutrition pamphlets, they can be hard to find in individual outlets. Brochures may not be in an obvious location, and employees may not know where to find them. Third, **the nutrition information provided can be difficult to use.** Large, complicated tables listing everything from protein and cholesterol to iron and vitamin A can be hard to use because they present an overwhelming amount of nutrition information in small print for each food item. Also, not many harried diners want to lose their place in line to decipher a poster. In addition, it is unlikely that many more restaurants will provide nutrition information under a voluntary system. Two-thirds of the largest chain restaurants believe that they do not have a responsibility to provide nutrition labeling (Almanza et al., 1997).

A number of restaurant chains offer nutrition information on their websites (see Appendix A for examples). While nutrition information on the web is of value, it is not convenient or accessible to the customer at the point of decision making in the restaurant. Also, the information may be displayed in a hard-to-read format. If restaurants can provide nutrition information on websites and through printed materials, they should be able to place some of that information on their menus and menu boards. (Note: those restaurants that already have nutrition information electronically available would not incur additional cost to analyze their menu items if calorie labeling were required on menus and menu boards).

Some restaurants provide menu items that are labeled as "light fare," "healthy heart," or other "healthy" designation. Although some of those programs have been shown to increase the sales of the healthy-designated items (Albright et al., 1990; Anderson & Haas, 1990), there are a number of limitations with this approach. First, there usually are a limited number of "healthy fare" items on the menu, and nutrition information regarding those items is not always provided on the menu or menu board. In addition, providing nutrition information for only the "healthy" foods or meals does not allow patrons to compare the "healthy" items to other menu options and determine what tradeoffs they may be making by forgoing a dish off the regular menu. For example, providing calorie labeling for all menu items would reveal that at a Mexican restaurant you could save 570 calories by choosing the low-fat chicken enchiladas platter (690 calories) instead of a regular chicken enchiladas platter (1,260 calories).

In summary, most restaurants do not provide any nutrition information about their foods. While several major fast-food chains provide complete information about their products, that information is often presented in a hard-to-read, hard-to-use format.

In a study in a cafeteria setting, signs indicating the calorie content of available foods significantly decreased the number of calories that people purchased (Milich et al., 1976). An unpublished evaluation of a menu labeling program at four northwest table-service restaurants also found that calorie labeling on menus led to entree selections that were lower in calories (Heart Institute of Spokane, 2002).

Product reformulation: a key benefit of nutrition labeling. A key benefit of mandatory nutrition labeling on packaged foods has been the reformulation of existing products and the introduction of new nutritionally improved products (Silverglade, 1995).

Between 1991 (before implementation of the Nutrition Labeling and Education Act) and 1995 (after implementation), the number of available fat-modified cheese products tripled and the market share for fat-modified cookies increased from zero percent of the market to 15% (Levy & Derby, 1996). In a similar fashion, nutrition labeling on menus and menu boards may spur nutritional improvements in restaurant foods.

Recommendations

In their "Call to Action" to reduce obesity, the U.S. Surgeon General and the U.S. Department of Health and Human Services recommended: "increase availability of nutrition information for foods eaten and prepared away from home" (US DHHS, 2001). In 1999, a report from the U.S. Department of Agriculture and Food and Drug Administration recommended that "Americans could adopt nutrition policy, educational programs, and promotion strategies to improve both the nutritional quality of food away from home and consumers' food choices when eating out" (Lin et al., 1999).

Given 1) the rising rates of obesity, 2) the increasing role of restaurant foods in Americans' diets, 3) the negative impact of eating out on the nutritional quality of our diets, 4) the large portion sizes and high calorie, saturated and trans fat, and sodium contents of restaurant foods, and 5) the lack of nutrition information available in most restaurants, **Congress and/or state or local legislatures should require food-service chains with ten or more units to list the calorie, saturated and trans fat (combined), and sodium contents of standard menu items on their menus. Restaurants that use menu boards, where space is limited, should be required to provide at least calorie information next to each item on their menu boards.** Maine, New Hampshire, New York, Pennsylvania and the District of Columbia legislatures (at the time this report went to press) were considering legislation to require calorie and other nutrition labeling on menus and menu boards at chain restaurants. A similar federal bill has been introduced.

Sample Restaurant Menu Board

Ice Cream & Sorbet	Calories	Price
Sorbet, 1 scoop	120	2.95
Law Fat Ice Cream, 1 scoop	170	2.95
Vanilla Ice Cream, 1 scoop	270	2.95
Vanilla Ice Cream, 2 scoops	540	4.95
Vanilla Ice Cream, 2 scoops	810	5.25
Bailey's Irish Cream Shake	960	5.45
Banana Split	1,100	6.35
Dulce Split Dazzler	1,180	6.35
Mint Chip Dazzler	1,270	6.35

While listing other nutrition information could help consumers make healthier choices, calorie, saturated and trans fat, and sodium information is most needed, given that cardiovascular diseases are the leading causes of death and obesity rates are rising rapidly. Such information, clearly displayed at the point of decision, would help consumers to make more informed choices at restaurants and is an important strategy for reducing obesity and protecting the nation's health.

> *The nutrition information should be placed directly on menus and menu boards to provide information in an easy-to-use, consistent manner where customers are making food choices.*

It is essential that the nutrition information be placed directly on menus and menu boards to provide the information in an easy-to-use, consistent manner where customers are making food choices.[1]

Restaurant chains could voluntarily provide additional nutrition information (such as carbohydrates, fiber, calcium, etc.) on menus or through brochures, posters, labels on food item packaging, tray liners, web sites, or other means.

Chains with ten or more units typically have standardized menus and are large enough to have management capable of implementing new regulations. Locally-owned, neighborhood (mom and pop) restaurants should be exempt from the law.

Public interest in nutrition and nutrition information is high. In national surveys, 85% of Americans say that nutrition is personally important to them (ADA, 2000). Sixty percent of Americans report that the healthfulness of the food is an important factor in choosing a restaurant (AICR, 2001). **Two-thirds of Americans support requiring restaurants to provide nutrition information, including calories, on menus** (Global Strategy Group, 2003; Harvard, 2003). Though people are provided good nutrition information in supermarkets, they usually can only guess what they are getting in restaurants. In addition, studies show that people eat more calories and saturated fat when they eat out than when they eat at home. Providing calorie and other key nutrition information at restaurants, and thus helping people to make healthier choices when eating out, is an important and necessary strategy for reducing obesity and protecting the nation's health.

References

Advertising Age. "Ad Age Almanac: Eating Out." *Advertising Age* December 31, 2001, p. 22.

Albright CL, Flora JA, Fortmann SP. "Restaurant Menu Labeling: Impact of Nutrition Information on Entree Sales and Patron Attitudes." *Health Education Quarterly* 1990, vol. 17, pp. 157–167.

Almanza BA, Nelson D, Chai S. "Obstacles to Nutrition Labeling in Restaurants." *Journal of the American Dietetic Association* 1997, vol. 97, pp. 157–161.

---

[1] Standard menu items should be analyzed by collecting a representative sample from several units of the chain and subjecting them to nutrient analysis in a laboratory. Many commercial laboratories can provide nutritional analyses. Costs vary between labs and range from about $55–$95 for calorie analysis per meal, food or beverage. Analysis of calories, saturated plus trans fat, and sodium averages about $220 per menu item.

American Dietetic Association (ADA). "Nutrition and You: Trends 2000." *Journal of the American Dietetic Association* 2000, vol. 100, pp. 626–627.

American Institute for Cancer Research (AICR). "As Restaurant Portions Grow, Vast Majority of Americans Still Belong to 'Clean Plate Club,' New Survey Finds." Washington, DC: AICR News Release, January 15, 2001.

Anderson J, Haas MH. "Impact of a Nutrition Education Program on Food Sales in Restaurants." *Journal of Nutrition Education* 1990, vol. 22, pp. 232–238.

Backstrand J, Wootan MG, Young LR, Hurley J. *Fat Chance.* Washington, DC: Center for Science in the Public Interest, 1997.

Binkley JK, Eales J, Jekanowski M. "The Relation Between Dietary Change and Rising US Obesity." *International Journal of Obesity* 2000, vol. 24, pp. 1032–1039.

Booth DA, Fuller J, Lewis V. "Human Control of Body Weight: Cognitive or Physiological? Some Energy Related Perceptions and Misperceptions." In: Cioffi LA, James WPT, Van Itallie TB, eds. *The Body Weight Regulatory System: Normal and Disturbed Mechanisms.* New York, NY: Raven Press, 1981, pp. 305–314.

Bowman S, Lino M, Gerrior S, Basiotis P. *The Healthy Eating Index: 1994–96.* Washington, DC: U.S. Department of Agriculture, Center for Nutrition Policy and Promotion, 1998.

Clemens LHE, Slawson DL, Klesges RC. "The Effect of Eating Out on Quality of Diet in Premenopausal Women." *Journal of the American Dietetic Association* 1999, vol. 99, pp. 442–444.

Crutchfield S, Kuchler F, Variyam JN. "The Economic Benefits of Nutrition Labeling: A Case Study for Fresh Meat and Poultry Products." *Journal of Consumer Policy* 2001, vol. 24, 185–207.

Ebbin R. "Americans' Dining-Out Habits." *Restaurants USA*, November 2000. Accessed at <http://www.restaurant.org/rusa/magArticle.cfm?ArticleID=138> on April 12, 2002.

Flegal KM, Carroll MD, Ogden CL, Johnson CL. "Prevalence and Trends in Obesity Among US Adults, 1999–2000." *Journal of the American Medical Association* 2002, vol. 288, pp. 1723–1727.

Food and Drug Administration (FDA), U.S. Department of Health and Human Services. "Nutrition Labeling of Restaurant Foods." 21 C.F.R., sec. 101.10, 2001, p. 47.

Food and Drug Administration (FDA), U.S. Department of Health and Human Services. *Federal Register* 1999, vol. 64, pp. 62772–62774.

French SA, Story M, Jeffery RW. "Environmental Influences on Eating and Physical Activity." *Annual Review of Public Health* 2001, vol. 22, pp. 309–335.

French SA, Story M, Neumark-Sztainer D, Fulkerson JA, Hannan P. "Fast Food Restaurant Use among Adolescents: Associations with Nutrient Intake, Food Choices and Behavioral and Psychosocial Variables." *International Journal of Obesity* 2001, vol. 25, pp. 1823–1833.

Global Strategy Group. Nationally representative poll commissioned by the Center for Science in the Public Interest. Washington, D.C.; September 4–8, 2003.

Harvard Forums on Health. "Obesity as a Public Health Issue: A Look at Solutions." National poll by Lake Snell Perry & Associates, June 2003.

Heart Institute of Spokane. "Menu2 Pilot Results." Accessed at <http://www.this.org./comm_edu/mn2rest.html> on December 22, 2002.

Jacobson MF, Hurley JG. *Restaurant Confidential.* New York, NY: Workman Publishing, 2002.

Jeffery RW, French SA. "Epidemic Obesity in the United States: Are Fast Food and Television Viewing Contributing?" *American Journal of Public Health* 1998, vol. 88, pp. 277–280.

Johnson WG, Corrigan SA, Schlundt DG, Dubbert PM. "Dietary Restraint and Eating Behavior in the Natural Environment." *Addictive Behaviors* 1990, vol. 15, pp. 285–290.

Kim SY, Nayga RM, Capps O. "The Effect of Food Label Use on Nutrient Intakes: An Endogenous Switching Regression Analysis." *Journal of Agricultural and Resource Economics* 2000, vol. 25, pp. 215–231.

Kreuter MW, Brennan LK, Scharff DP, Lukwago SN. "Do Nutrition Label Readers Eat Healthier Diets? Behavioral Correlates of Adults' Use of Food Labels." *American Journal of Preventive Medicine* 1997, vol. 13, pp. 277–283.

Levy AS, Derby BM. *The Impact of the NLEA on Consumers: Recent Findings from FDA's Food Label and Nutrition Tracking System.* Washington, DC: Center for Food Safety and Applied Nutrition, Food and Drug Administration, 1996.

Lin B, Guthrie J, Frazao E. *Away-From-Home Foods Increasingly Important to Quality of American Diet.* Washington, DC: U.S. Department of Agriculture, Economic Research Service, 1999. Agriculture Information Bulletin No. 749.

Lin B, Guthrie J, Frazao E. "Nutrient Contribution of Food Away From Home." *America's Eating Habits: Changes and Consequences.* Washington, DC: U.S. Department of Agriculture, Economic Research Service, 1999b. Agriculture Information Bulletin No. 750, pp. 213–242.

Lin BH, Guthrie J, Blaylock JR. *The Diets of America's Children: Influence of Dining Out, Household Characteristics, and Nutrition Knowledge.* Washington, DC: U.S. Department of Agriculture, Economic Research Service, 1996. Agricultural Economic Report No. 746.

Ma Y, Bertone ER, Stanek III EJ, Reed GW, Hebert JR, Cohen NL, Merriam PA, Ockene IS. "Association between Eating Patterns and Obesity in a Free-living US Adult Population." *American Journal of Epidemiology* 2003, vol. 158, pp. 85–92.

McCrory MA, Fuss PJ, Saltzman E, Roberts SB. "Dietary Determinants of Energy Intake and Weight Regulation in Healthy Adults." *Journal of Nutrition* 2000, vol. 130 (Supplement), pp. 276S–279S.

McCrory MA, Fuss PJ, Hays NP, Vinken AG, Greenberg AS, Roberts SB. "Overeating in America: Associations between Restaurant Food Consumption and Body Fatness in Healthy Adult Men and Women Ages 19 to 80." *Obesity Research* 1999, vol. 7, pp. 564–571.

McGinnis JM, Foege WH. "Actual Causes of Death in the United States." *Journal of the American Medical Association* 1993, vol. 270, pp. 2207–2212.

McNutt SW, Hu Y, Schreiber GB, Crawford PB, Obarzanek E, Mellin L. "A Longitudinal Study of the Dietary Practices of Black and White Girls 9 and 10 Years Old at Enrollment: The NHLBI Growth and Health Study." *Journal of Adolescent Health* 1997, vol. 20, pp. 27–37.

Milich R, Anderson J, Mills M. "Effects of Visual Presentation of Caloric Values on Food Buying by Normal and Obese Persons." *Perceptual and Motor Skills* 1976, vol. 42, pp. 155–162.

Mokdad AH, Ford ES, Bowman BA, Dietz WH, Vinicor F, Bales VS, Marks J. "Prevalence of Obesity, Diabetes, and Obesity-Related Health Risk Factors, 2001." *Journal of the American Medical Association* 2003, vol. 289, pp. 76–79.

Munoz K, Krebs-Smith S, Ballard-Barbash R, Cleveland L. "Food Intakes of U.S. Children and Adolescents Compared with Recommendations." *Pediatrics* 1997, vol. 100, pp. 323–329.

National Alliance for Nutrition and Activity (NANA). *From Wallet to Waistline: The Hidden Costs of Super Sizing.* Washington, DC: NANA, June 2002.

National Institutes of Health (NIH), Office of the Director, U.S. Department of Health and Human Services. *Disease-Specific Estimates of Direct and Indirect Costs of Illness and NIH Support.* Bethesda, MD: NIH, 2000.

National Restaurant Association (NRA). "Industry at a Glance." Accessed at <http://www.restaurant.org/research/ind_glance.cfm> on April 12, 2002.

Nestle M. *Food Politics.* Berkeley, CA: University of California Press, 2002.

Neuhouser ML, Kristal AR, Patterson RE. "Use of Food Nutrition Labels Is Associated with Lower Fat Intake." *Journal of the American Dietetic Association* 1999, vol. 99, pp. 45–50, 53.

Ogden CL, Flegal KM, Carroll MD, Johnson CL. "Prevalence and Trends in Overweight Among US Children and Adolescents, 1999–2000." *Journal of the American Medical Association* 2002, vol. 288, pp. 1728–1732.

Orlet Fisher J, Rolls BJ, Birch LL. "Children's Bite Size and Intake of an Entree are Greater with Large Portions than with Age-Appropriate or Self-Selected Portions." *American Journal of Clinical Nutrition* 2003, vol. 77, pp. 1164–1170.

Pinhas-Hamiel O, Dolan L, Daniels S, et al. "Increased Incidence of Non-Insulin-Dependent Diabetes Mellitus among Adolescents." *The Journal of Pediatrics* 1996, vol. 128, pp. 608–615.

Putnam JJ, Allshouse JE. *Food Consumption, Prices, and Expenditures.* Washington, DC: U.S. Department of Agriculture, Economic Research Service, 1999. Statistical Bulletin No. 965.

Ramsey S, Summers K, Leong S, et al. "Productivity and Medical Costs of Diabetes in a Large Employer Population." *Diabetes Care* 2002, vol. 25, pp. 23–29.

Rolls BJ, Engell D, Birch LL. "Serving Portion Size Influences 5-Year-Old But Not 3-Year-Old Children's Food Intake." *Journal of the American Dietetic Association* 2000, vol. 100, pp. 232–234.

Silverglade BA. "Food Labeling: Rules You Can Live By." *Legal Times,* July 17, 1995, pp. 21–24.

U.S. Department of Health and Human Services (US DHHS). *The Surgeon General's Call to Action to Prevent and Decrease Overweight and Obesity.* Rockville, MD: U.S. Department of Health and Human Services, Public Health Service, Office of the Surgeon General, 2001.

U.S. Department of Health and Human Services (US DHHS), Centers for Disease Control and Prevention, National Center for Health Statistics. *Healthy People 2000 Final Review.* Hyattsville, MD: U.S. Department of Health and Human Services, Centers for Disease Control and Prevention, National Center for Health Statistics, 2001b. DHHS Publication No. 01-0256.

Wansink B. "Can Package Size Accelerate Usage Volume?" *Journal of Marketing* 1996, vol. 60, pp. 1–14.

Young LR, Nestle M. "The Contribution of Expanding Portion Sizes to the US Obesity Epidemic." *American Journal of Public Health* 2002, vol. 92, pp. 246–249.

Young LR, Nestle M. "Portion Sizes in Dietary Assessment: Issues and Policy Implications." *Nutrition Reviews* 1995, vol. 53, pp. 149–158.

Zoumas-Morse C, Rock CL, Sobo EJ, Neuhouser ML. "Children's Patterns of Macronutrient Intake and Associations with Restaurant and Home Eating." *Journal of the American Dietetic Association* 2001, vol. 101, pp. 923–925.

Appendix A

Examples of Restaurants that Provide Nutrition Information on the Internet

Arby's: http://www.arbys.com/arb06.html

Baja Fresh: http://www.bajafresh.com/jump.jsp?itemID=68&itemType=CATEGORY
&iMainCat=4&iSubCat=10&i3Cat=68

Baskin-Robbins: http://www.baskinrobbins.com/about/nutritional.shtml

Blimpie Subs and Salads: http://www.blimpie.com/framesets/sfs_nutrition.htm

Boston Market: http://www.boston-market.com/food/index.jsp?page=nutrition

Burger King: http://www.burgerking.com/Food/index.aspx

Carl's Jr.: http://www.carlsjr.com/home

Chick-fil-A: http://www.chick-fil-a.com/content/nutri/nutriInnerFrame.htm

Chuck E. Cheese's: http://www.chuckecheese.com/cec2002/restaurants/nutritional.html

Church's Chicken: http://www.churchs.com/home.asp

Domino's Pizza: http://www.dominos.com/C1256B420054FF48/vwContentByKey/
W256QR93351DENNEN#

Dunkin' Donuts: http://www.dunkindonuts.com/nutrition/

El Pollo Loco: http://www.crazychicken.com/consumer/con_index.html

Fazoli's: http://www.fazolis.com/nutrition.asp

Godfather's Pizza: http://www.godfathers.com/nutrition.html

Haagen-Dazs Ice Cream Café: http://www.haagen-dazs.com/

Hardee's: http://www.hardeesrestaurants.com/nutrition/

KFC: http://www.kfc.com/kitchen/nutrition.htm

Krispy Kreme Doughnuts: http://www.krispykreme.com/varieties.html

Krystal: http://www.krystalco.com/food/nutrition/home.asp

Little Caesars: http://littlecaesars.com/menu/nutrition.asp?category=menu

Long John Silver's: http://www.ljsilvers.com/nutrition/default.htm

McDonald's: http://www.mcdonalds.com/countries/usa/food/index.html

Pizza Hut: http://www.pizzahut.com/menu/nutritioninfo.asp

Round Table Pizza: http://www.roundtablepizza.com/RTP/LO/default.asp

Schlotzsky's Deli: http://www.schlotzskys.com/nutrition.html

Subway: http://subway.com/applications/NutritionInfo/index.aspx

Taco Bell: http://www.tacobell.com/

TCBY: http://www.tcby.com/TCBY_Sorbet_and_%20Yogurt_Nutrition_Chart.pdf

Wendy's: http://www.wendys.com/food/index.jsp?country=US&lang=EN

Whataburger: http://www.whataburger.com/menulist.cfm

White Castle: http://www.whitecastle.com/_pages/nutrition.as

SANDWICHES

HAMBURGER	280 Cal	.89
CHEESEBURGER	330 Cal	.99
FILET-O-FISH®	470 Cal	1.99
CRISPY CHICKEN	550 Cal	2.79
QUARTER POUNDER®	430 Cal	2.29
BIG N' TASTY®	540 Cal	2.29
BIG MAC®	590 Cal	2.39
CHICKEN McGRILL®	450 Cal	2.89
DOUBLE QUARTER POUNDER®	760 Cal	2.99

Model Menu Boards: Fast Food

SANDWICHES

BIG BURGER	590 cal	2.39
BIG N' TASTY	540 cal	2.29
QUARTER POUNDER with CHEESE	530 cal	2.29
QUARTER POUNDER	430 cal	2.29
DOUBLE QUARTER POUNDER	760 cal	2.99
CHEESEBURGER	330 cal	0.99
HAMBURGER	280 cal	0.89
CHICKEN NUGGETS (6PC)	290 cal	2.29
CHICKEN NUGGETS (9PC)	430 cal	2.89
CRISPY CHICKEN	550 cal	2.79
CHICKEN GRILL	450 cal	2.89
FILET OF FISH	470 cal	1.99

SALADS

CHICKEN CAESAR[†]   230 cal   2.59   CHEF[†]   280 cal   2.89   GARDEN[†]   230 cal   1.99

KIDS' MEAL   ## BIG KIDS' MEAL

Comes with sm. french fry, child-size drink and toy. For kids under 12. Comes with sm. french fry and child-size drink.

HAMBURGER	600 cal	1.99	DOUBLE HAMBURGER	700 cal	2.80
CHEESEBURGER	650 cal	2.49	DOUBLE CHEESEBURGER	800 cal	3.30
4 CHICKEN NUGGETS	510 cal	2.89	6 CHICKEN NUGGETS	610 cal	3.30

FRENCH FRIES

SMALL   210 cal 1.03   MEDIUM   450 cal 1.50   LARGE   540 cal 1.67   SUPER SIZE   610 cal 1.90

BEVERAGES

	Small		Medium		Large		Super Size	
SODA	150 cal	0.99	220 cal	1.29	330 cal	1.49	430 cal	1.69
SHAKE*	360 cal	1.59	510 cal	1.89	770 cal	2.29	1,010 cal	2.49
ORANGE JUICE	210 cal	1.29	280 cal	1.49	430 cal	1.69	560 cal	2.59
COFFEE**	5 cal	0.89	10 cal	0.99	15 cal	1.09		
1% MILK	100 cal	0.99						

(Continued)

DESSERTS

FRUIT 'N YOGURT PARFAIT	380 cal	1.99	CONE	150 cal	0.99
without Granola	280 cal	1.99			
FLURRY*	610 cal	2.16	BAKED PIE	260 cal	0.99
SUNDAE*	330 cal	1.29	COOKIES*	250 cal	0.99

Daily Values are based on a 2,000 calorie diet.

†Calories include reduced calorie dressing. Please see nutrition brochure for other dressing information.
*Calories depend on flavor/variety. Average for line. Please see nutrition brochure for more details.
**Calories without cream or sugar. Please see nutrition brochure for details.

Model Menu Board: Mall Restaurant

Grilled Sandwiches

served w/lettuce, tomato, and mayo

GREAT STEAK	660 cal	**$4.49**
w/Onions & Provolone		
SUPER STEAK	660 cal	**$4.69**
w/Onions, Peppers, Mushrooms & Provolone		
HAM EXPLOSION	710 cal	**$4.69**
w/Onions, Peppers, Mushrooms & Swiss		
HAM DELIGHT	710 cal	**$4.49**
w/Pineapple & Swiss		
CHICKEN PHILLY	640 cal	**$4.69**
w/Onions & Swiss		
CHICKEN TERIYAKI	580 cal	**$4.69**
w/Onions, Swiss & Teriyaki		
TURKEY PHILLY	690 cal	**$4.49**
w/Onions & Swiss		
VEGGIE DELIGHT	570 cal	**$4.19**
Fresh Grilled Veggies w/Provolone & Swiss		
COMBO IT! Add Small Fry & Drink	+610 cal	**$6.39**

Baked Potatoes

GREAT POTATO	600 cal	**$4.49**
w/Steak or Turkey, Onions & Cheese		
BROCCOLI & CHEESE	340 cal	**$3.29**

Fresh Cut Fries

Cooked in 100% Cholesterol Free Peanut Oil

SM.	460 cal	**$1.49**	REG.	540 cal	**$1.99**	LRG.	920 cal **$2.79**

♦ *Daily Values are based on a 2,000 calorie diet.* ♦

Model Menu: Dinner House Restaurant

Starters & Snacks

SPICY BUFFALO WINGS
   Tossed in our hot or mild Buffalo sauce. Served with blue
   cheese dressing and celery sticks.
   1,010 cal, 22 g sat fat, 2,460 mg sodium   **$6.99**
FRIED MOZZARELLA STICKS
   Mozzarella cheese lightly breaded and deep fried.
   Served with marinara sauce.
   830 cal, 28 g sat fat, 1,890 mg sodium   **$5.99**
BLOOMING ONION
   A whole onion, cut like a flower, battered and golden fried.
   Served with zesty dipping sauce.
   2,130 cal, 57 g sat fat, 3,840 mg sodium   **$6.99**
STUFFED POTATO SKINS
   Large potato shells fried golden brown, filled with
   Jack and Cheddar cheese, crisp smoked bacon,
   green onions, parsley and sour cream.
   1,260 cal, 48 g sat fat, 1,300 mg sodium   **$6.69**
CHEESE FRIES
   French fries smothered in cheese, sprinkled with bacon
   and served with ranch dressing.
   3,010 cal, 91 g sat fat, 4,890 mg sodium   **$6.99**

Salads

CHICKEN CAESAR SALAD
   Grilled chicken over Romaine lettuce. Served with croutons,
   Parmesan cheese, and our special Caesar dressing.
   660 cal, 11 g sat fat, 1,490 mg sodium   **$6.99**
ORIENTAL CHICKEN SALAD
   A quarter pound of skinless chicken breast over a mound of Romaine
   lettuce, snow peas, water chestnuts, red cabbage, carrots and other
   fixings. Topped with our homemade Oriental dressing.
   750 cal, 12 g sat fat, 1,140 mg sodium   **$6.99**

◆ The Daily Values for a 2,000 calorie diet are 20 g of saturated
fat and 2,400 mg of sodium. ◆
Saturated fat numbers include trans fat.

Lunch/Dinner Entrees

SIRLOIN STEAK
   Seven ounces USDA choice steak, grilled to your satisfaction.
   Served with French fries and seasonal vegetables.
   1,060 cal, 23 g sat fat, 1,000 mg sodium   **$12.99**
BBQ BABY BACK RIBS
   A one pound platter of slow roasted ribs, basted in our special
   barbeque sauce and served with French fries and cole slaw.
   1,530 cal, 36 g sat fat, 1,610 mg sodium   **$10.59**

(Continued)

CHICKEN FINGERS
   Lightly breaded chicken tenders served with French fries,
   cole slaw and dipping sauce.
   1,640 cal, 30 g sat fat, 2,640 mg sodium   **$7.99**
STEAK FAJITAS
   Sliced steak over sauteed onions and bell peppers. Served with
   soft tortillas, guacamole, sour cream, salsa and cheese.
   1,190 cal, 28 g sat fat, 2,810 mg sodium   **$11.69**
GRILLED CHICKEN
   We grill a tender boneless marinated chicken breast and serve with
   vegetables and a baked potato with a dollop of sour cream on the side.
   640 cal, 5 g sat fat, 820 mg sodium   **$9.79**

Burgers

Our burgers are 100% USDA ground beef. Each is grilled to medium-well unless otherwise requested and served on a toasted roll with French fries and fixings. (Nutrition information includes sides.)
BACON & CHEESE GRILLED CHICKEN SANDWICH
   Grilled chicken, crisp bacon, tomato, onion, mayo,
   lettuce and cheese on a toasted bun.
   1,230 cal, 24 g sat fat, 2,110 mg sodium   **$7.99**
HAMBURGER
   Tender USDA ground beef, grilled to your liking.
   1,240 cal, 29 g sat fat, 1,270 mg sodium   **$7.99**
MUSHROOM CHEESEBURGER
   Sauteed mushrooms over our All-American Burger with
   melted Jack cheese.
   1,490 cal, 40 g sat fat, 1,540 mg sodium   **$7.50**

Sides

VEGETABLE OF THE DAY
   60 cal, 1 g sat fat, 150 mg sodium   **$1.99**
BAKED POTATO W/SOUR CREAM
   310 cal, 2 g sat fat, 30 mg sodium   **$2.99**
LOADED BAKED POTATO
   620 cal, 19 g sat fat, 570 mg sodium   **$4.99**
FRENCH FRIES
   590 cal, 12 g sat fat, 460 mg sodium   **$1.99**
ONION RINGS
   900 cal, 23 g sat fat, 1,050 mg sodium   **$1.99**

    ♦ The Daily Values for a 2,000 calorie diet are 20 g of saturated fat and 2,400 mg of sodium. ♦
                   Saturated fat numbers include trans fat.

Model Menu: Pizza Restaurant

Specialty Pizzas*

Medium $12.29	**Large $15.29**

Lover's Line
Get more of the toppings you love. Our Lover's Line pizzas pack on more of your favorite toppings!

Supreme Pizzas
Our most famous selections, top of the line in every way.

Pepperoni Lover's
Loaded with more cheese and more pepperoni.
    900 cal **19** g sat fat **2,070** mg sodium

Supreme
Our signature blend of pepperoni, beef and pork toppings, green peppers, ham, red onions and mushrooms.
    870 cal **16** g sat fat **1,820** mg sodium

Meat Lover's
A combination of pepperoni, Italian sausage, bacon, beef and pork toppings.
    980 cal **19** g sat fat **2,290** mg sodium

Super Supreme ($1.00 more)
A nine-topping feast of pepperoni, ham, Italian sausage, beef, pork, green peppers, red onions, fresh mushrooms and black olives.
    930 cal **16** g sat fat **2,120** mg sodium

Veggie Lover's
Fresh mushrooms, red onions, green peppers, tomatoes and black olives.
    730 cal **11** g sat fat **1,390** mg sodium

Chicken Supreme
Tender chunks of grilled chicken breast with green peppers, red onions and mushrooms.
    730 cal **11** g sat fat **1,580** mg sodium .

*Nutrition information is for three slices with pan style crust. See nutrition brochure for other crust types.

BREADSTICKS
Crispy on the outside, soft & chewy on the inside. Served with tangy marinara sauce.

Single order of 5 sticks	**800** cal	**5** g sat fat	**1,700** mg sodium	**$1.99**
Family order of 10 sticks	**320** cal	**2** g sat fat	**680** mg sodium	**$3.99**
(Nutrition information for 2 stick serving)				

PERSONAL PAN PIZZA
All the tempting flavor of our pan pizza packed into an individual serving.

CHEESE	**630** cal	**12** g sat fat	**1,370** mg sodium	**$2.99**
1 TOPPING**	**660** cal	**11** g sat fat	**1,550** mg sodium	**$2.99**

**Nutrient values vary with crust type and topping. See nutrition brochure for more details.

    ♦ The Daily Values for a 2,000 calorie diet are 20 g of saturated fat and 2,400 mg of sodium. ♦

Model Menu: Breakfast Restaurant

Legendary Breakfasts

CRACK OF DAWN
Two eggs,* any style, two hotcakes with syrup and
margarine, two sausage links and two strips of bacon.
1,010 cal **19** g sat fat **1,770** mg sodium $5.39

FARMER'S HEARTY BREAKFAST
Two eggs,* two fluffy pancakes with syrup and margarine,
two sausage links, two strips of crisp bacon and hash browns.
Sure to satisfy your hearty appetite!
1,230 cal **22** g sat fat **1,970** mg sodium $6.69

EARLY RISER
A bowl of hot cereal, served with 2% milk, orange juice,
seasonal fresh fruit and toast.
600 cal **3** g sat fat **660** mg sodium $6.39

COUNTRY BISCUIT
A biscuit split and topped with eggs over-easy and our
country gravy. Served with two sausage links and two strips of bacon
1,110 cal **27** g sat fat **2,580** mg sodium $5.49

Pancakes n' Such

THICK-SLICED FRENCH TOAST
Three slices of our own bread dipped in our egg and
milk mixture, then grilled to perfection. Served with syrup
and margarine and your choice of breakfast meat.**
1,130 cal **20** g sat fat **1,740** mg sodium $5.29

MOMMA'S PANCAKE BREAKFAST
A classic. Four of our traditional pancakes served up
with syrup, margarine and your choice of breakfast meat.**
1,160 cal **19** g sat fat **2,680** mg sodium $5.49

BELGIAN WAFFLE
Topped with strawberries and whipped cream. Served with
your choice of breakfast meat.**
1,020 cal **22** g sat fat **1,740** mg sodium $6.39

Eggs, Etc.

LIGHTEN UP
Two scrambled Egg Beaters, served with hash browns
and toast to get you off to a good start.
480 cal **6** g sat fat **670** mg sodium $3.69

TWO EGG COMBO
Two eggs,* any style, served with hashed browns and toast.
650 cal **8** g sat fat **660** mg sodium $3.69

HAM AND CHEESE OMELETTE
A combo of diced, smoked ham with sharp cheese.
Served with hash browns and toast with margarine.
990 cal **26** g sat fat **1,790** mg sodium $6.49

(Continued)

Sides			
breakfast ham	**100** cal	**1** g sat fat	**910** mg sodium	$2.89
hash browns	**220** cal	**3** g sat fat	**200** mg sodium	$1.69
toast (2 slices) with margarine	**260** cal	**4** g sat fat	**390** mg sodium	$1.35
thick-sliced bacon (4)	**130** cal	**4** g sat fat	**530** mg sodium	$2.29
sausage links (4)	**340** cal	**13** g sat fat	**670** mg sodium	$2.29
pancakes (3) with syrup and	**770** cal	**9** g sat fat	**1,490** mg sodium	$2.49
cold cereal with 2% milk	**210** cal	**2** g sat fat	**380** mg sodium	$1.89
oatmeal with 2% milk	**210** cal	**2** g sat fat	**380** mg sodium	$1.89

*Nutrition information listed for scrambled eggs. Please see nutrition brochure for other types of eggs.
**Nutrient values vary depending on meat selection. Please see nutrition brochure for more details.

♦ The Daily Values for a 2,000 calorie diet are 20 g of saturated fat and 2,400 mg of sodium. ♦
Saturated fat numbers include trans fat.

Model Menu Board: Coffee Shop

	Coffee Drinks					
	Small		**Medium**		**Large**	
COFFEE OF THE DAY[†]	10 cal	1.40	10 cal	1.60	10 cal	1.70
DECAF COFFEE OF THE DAY[†]	10 cal	1.40	10 cal	1.60	10 cal	1.70
CAPPUCCINO*	110 cal	2.55	140 cal	3.10	180 cal	3.40
CAFFE LATTE*	160 cal	2.55	210 cal	3.10	270 cal	3.40
CAFFE MOCHA*[§]	250 cal	2.75	330 cal	3.30	410 cal	3.55
WHITE CHOCOLATE MOCHA*[§]	330 cal	3.20	440 cal	3.75	550 cal	4.00
COLD BEVERAGES						
ICED CAFFE LATTE*	100 cal	2.55	130 cal	3.10	160 cal	3.50
ICED CARAMEL LATTE*	160 cal	2.80	220 cal	3.40	270 cal	3.80
ICED CAFFE MOCHA*[†]	150 cal	2.75	190 cal	3.30	240 cal	3.55
ICED CAFFE AMERICANO[†]	10 cal	1.75	10 cal	2.05	10 cal	2.40
COFFEE ALTERNATIVES						
TAZO CHAI*	200 cal	2.70	260 cal	3.10	330 cal	3.35
STEAMED CIDER	170 cal	1.75	230 cal	2.00	290 cal	2.25
HOT CHOCOLATE*[†]	270 cal	2.20	350 cal	2.45	440 cal	2.70

*Calorie content depends on type of milk used. See nutrition brochure for more information.
[†] without milk   [§] with whipped cream   [†]without whipped cream

2 TB skim milk = 10 cal   2 TB 2% milk = 15 cal   2 TB whole milk = 20 cal   2 TB half and half = 40 cal
whipped cream = 100 cal

♦ Daily Values are based on a 2,000 calorie diet. ♦

Actual Menu Brochure: Baja Fresh

Enchiladas Verano   **$5.95**

Charbroiled chicken, grilled peppers, chilis, onions topped with Salsa Verde & shaved cheese, served w/rice & beans and Pico de Gallo.

    580 Calories   9g Fat   38g Protein   21g Fiber*

Bare Burrito™   **$5.65**
(Served in a Bowl, No Tortilla)

Charbroiled chicken, grilled peppers, chilis & onions, rice, beans, Pico de Gallo and Salsa Verde.

    650 Calories   7g Fat   45g Protein   22g Fiber*

Vegetarian Bare Burrito™   **$4.95**
(Served in a Bowl, No Tortilla)

Grilled peppers, chilis & onions, rice, beans, lettuce, jack cheese, Pico de Gallo and "Salsa Baja™".

    560 Calories   8g Fat   20g Protein   22g Fiber*

Grilled Veggie Tacos   **$3.80**

Two soft tacos on corn tortillas, shaved cheese, guacamole, beans, grilled peppers, chilis & onions, lettuce, Pico de Gallo and Salsa Verde.

    420 Calories   10g Fat   16g Protein   14g Fiber*

"Side-by-Side"   **$4.90**

Our side salad with fat-free Salsa Verde, paired with a generous side order of Charbroiled chicken.

    320 Calories   6g Fat   52g Protein   6g Fiber*

Shrimp Ensalada   **$7.40**

Charbroiled "Wild" Gulf Shrimp, romaine lettuce, Pico de Gallo salsa, Salsa Verde, topped with tomato slices and shaved cheese.

    180 Calories   4g Fat   22g Protein   6g Fiber*

*As all our food is hand-crafted, all nutritional information is approximate.
To view all our nutritional information, please visit us at www.bajafresh.com

EXPLORING THE CHALLENGES OF COMPETITION POLICY (GOVERNMENT REGULATION II)

COMPETITION

Patrick Kaufmann

Introduction

Competition and competition policy are essential aspects of our free market and relate directly to marketing in society. Competition is important as it reflects the form of exchange found in free markets. Competition policy in the form of laws and regulations is also important as it protects and insures competition.

Definition

Although most would agree that competition is the engine of our economic system, like the fabled elephant, its essence depends to a great extent on one's vantage point. Economists view competition as a useful abstraction with which to compare economic institutions and policies, lawyers as a benchmark for judging the legality of various practices, and businesses as a threat to their insecure market share (Berhard, 1967 in Stern and Grabner, 1970). In its most basic sense, competition is the rivalry that exists among multiple parties on one side of a dyad to establish an exchange with the other side of the dyad. Thus, we have firms competing for the patronage of customers, candidates competing for the support of voters, and employees competing for a job. In this sense competition is a process in a zero sum game. When the focal exchange occurs, someone has won and someone has lost. In this chapter we concentrate on competition in the business or economic sense of rivalry among sellers for the patronage of buyers.

Although business competition refers generally to this process of rivalry among sellers, as suggested above, economists, lawyers and businesses think very differently about the concept and use it in different ways. In this chapter, we introduce four papers that provide examples of those perspectives. The chosen articles are not articulations or summaries of the alternative viewpoints, but rather represent research into topics of specific interest in economics, business, and the law that have competition as a central theme or an underlying assumption. To set the stage for the papers, therefore, we discuss some of the widely divergent aspects of competition that become relevant to these streams of research.

Patrick J. Kaufmann is Professor of Marketing and Chair of the Marketing Department in the School of Management at Boston University.

The Domain of Competition

PERSPECTIVES AND HISTORICAL DEVELOPMENT

The Economists' View of Competition

Competition in Classical and Neo-Classical Economics

Since Adam Smith's writings at the same time as the American Revolution (1776), competition has been the centerpiece of free market economic analysis. Through his empirical observations and interpretation of natural law, Smith concluded that competition had two distinct aspects, *conduct* and *structure*. According to Smith, the conduct of competition entailed the independent striving of independent actors for patronage in the market. He saw the structural aspects of competition to include the long-term movement of resources to industries with high returns, assuming the absence of entry barriers. These structural aspects of competition became more central as economics became more mathematical and the formal models of classical and neoclassical economics were developed (Scherer, 1980 at 10). Critical to this analysis was the idea that any interference with the price-signaled free flow of resources away from low return industries into high return industries was to society's detriment. The initial basis for the classical political economists' preference for freely competing markets, however, was not the derived mathematical models (which came later) but Smith's observations and intuitive reasoning that competition had a positive and dynamic effect on the incentives of the individual actors. It was the subsequent effort to rigorously prove that this free flowing competition produced a mathematically optimal allocation of resources that ultimately led economists to the severely restrictive models of pure competition (Atiyah, 1979 at 300).

> *Two economists were walking down the street and see a $10 bill lying on the sidewalk. One says, "Why don't you pick that up?" and the other answers, "If it were a real $10 bill, someone would have already picked it up." (Unknown)*

Evolution of the Model of Competition

It is tempting to set up the highly stylized neoclassical model of pure competition as a straw man noting that its assumptions of perfect information and homogeneous products and tastes are far removed from observed reality. However, the fact is that economists have made great strides in making their models more realistic. Perhaps the most seismic change was the introduction of the concept of *monopolistic competition* (Chamberlain, 1962). Chamberlain's analysis incorporated the fact that products are not really all the same and do not compete directly with one another, and that each has some level of *market power* derived from that differentiation. This market power allows the manufacturer to increase price over what would be the normal competitive price taken by a manufacturer in an atomistic market. The diversification giving rise to this market power could come from product differences, service differences, location, and so on but the important point is that firms are not powerless price takers but could be strategic decision makers competing in a much more complex marketplace than that captured in the original models of pure competition (Scherer, 1980 at 24). The strategic interaction, or rivalry, among these firms as they jockey for position, therefore, replaced the reactive cost-cutting and price-taking behavior of purely competitive firms as the assumed conduct of business (Weitz, 1985).

This is not the end of the story, however. Because the increased prices precipitated by the differentiated products are assumed to attract new entrants to the market, in the long run prices would again be forced back down toward the differentiated manufacturer's average costs. So although much more realistic than the pure competition model, the model of monopolistic competition produces much of the same message: that industry structure is critical to economists' view of competition and at the heart of this analysis is the question of whether or when we might expect there to be enduring entry barriers, or as they are sometimes called *market imperfections*.

Industrial Organization Economics

The focus on the structure of industries and its impact on competition are at the heart of modern industrial organization economics. Industry structure is important because it leads to predictable conduct which in turn leads to predictable performance (Scherer, 198). Industrial organization economics, and its offshoots of agency theory and transaction cost analysis, departs from the simple rigor of microeconomic theory to incorporate more realistic but messier concepts such as asymmetric information. It includes empirical models that examine the evolution of industry structures that result from strategic behavior on the part of individual firms. From the perspective of industrial organization economics, therefore, competition among firms is not a simplifying assumption but a highly complex and dynamic activity. Moreover, because industrial organization economists are typically deeply committed to the public policy goal of enhancing industry performance through competition, one of the critical points of debate is the stability of entry barriers.

Some industrial organization economists take a strong neo-classical approach to entry barriers believing them to be typically transitory as long as they are not exogenously imposed by government and that entry by additional competitors will act to reestablish competitive markets and force prices down. Other economists see the potential for more enduring entry barriers resulting from the strategic behavior of firms. They see strategy dominating structure and the purposeful behavior of firms eroding the efficiency of the marketplace. This debate has significant implications for the legal analysis of competition and will be discussed below. Whatever one's perspective, it seems clear that a key empirical question relevant to competitive entry is whether firms seeing a market with high profit potential are prone to enter with products similar to those producing the high profits or are likely to choose strategies that further fracture the market with even more differentiated offerings. Does industry structure determine strategy or does strategy determine industry structure? In other words, what is the business view of competition?

The Business View of Competition

Competition as a Game

Although economists might see competition as a great leveling device whereby resources are allocated to their most efficient use, businessmen and women generally see competition as a game to be won or lost and competitors as threats to their winning. Firms win in the market game by achieving a lasting advantage over other players (Porter, 1985). However under the economists' traditional view of competition if the market is working and there are either a sufficient number of competitors

> *"To a blackbird, a mole may be a competitor, but it is not nearly so important a competitor as another blackbird."* (Richard Dawkins *The Selfish Gene at 72*)

or entry is relatively unimpeded, all such advantages are short-lived. Firms quickly lose their cost advantages as direct competitors copy their efficient allocation of inputs. Thus, firms that provide essentially the same product or service as their competitors are relegated to a game whose outcome will be determined in the short run by who figures out the most efficient allocation of resources first, and in the long run, by the fact that everyone will either adopt the survival technology and come out about the same—or be gone. As trade among countries with significant labor (or other resource) cost differences has increased, the inability of some competitors to match radically lower production costs has exacerbated the problem. In a truly competitive market, strategy gives way to predestination. This is not the kind of game that most managers like to play.

Dynamic Differentiation and Competitive Advantage

Businesses operating in relatively high-wage economies, therefore, not only seek out the most efficient production function possible to them for their particular offering but even more aggressively seek *differentiation strategies* designed to make their products unique among their competitors and to maintain that position for as long as possible. The primary goal in this form of competition is not to become better at doing what their competitors are doing but to do something that separates the firm from the rest of the pack. One benefit of this approach is that whereas a strategy of cost leadership is typically available to one firm in an industry, multiple firms can adopt differentiation strategies (Porter, 1985). Furthermore, if the firm's unique offering is particularly well suited to the needs of some segment of a presumably heterogeneous consumer base, the firm will be able to exploit this fit to gain additional resources from the market. Finding innovative ways to gain and retain *comparative advantage,* therefore, has become the foundation of modern business.

The key to this approach is constant dynamic change and adjustment, staying one step ahead of competition in identifying market opportunities and being fast on your feet. Larger, often more cost-efficient, companies are quick to spot opportunities to copy profitable product offerings (see the reading by Engardio and Keenan on "The Copycat Economy"). These "me too" products reflect corporate strategies focused on a reactive form of competition. In some product markets, the ability to rapidly change product design occasioned by advances in manufacturing has shortened product life cycles to the point where by the time a "me-too" competitor enters the market, the firm has already moved on to derive high returns from new features, an even newer model or a new product entirely. The real danger is in believing that your firm's products are somehow immune from this cloned competition and relaxing into complacency.

Certainly, the firm must also always seek to drive its costs down, but in the dynamic innovation approach to competition, cost reduction is sometimes more a byproduct of gradually expanding the differentiation strategy to attract those consumers for whom the initial value proposition is unattractive than it is a strategy in itself. As prices drop to enlarge the market, pressure is put on costs. This primary focus on product and demand rather than cost and price seems to be the preferred response of firms defending against new product entries as well as those on the offensive. Kuester et al. (1999) found that firms facing new product entries are more likely to respond with product improvements, repositioning or new products of their own than to defend by reducing price. It appears that whether rivals are on the offense or defense differentiation is the preferred course. It is no wonder that firms operating in a world of dynamic differentiation often find the economists' models of long run static equilibrium somewhat irrelevant.

Differentiation strategies do not necessarily target only small market segments and sometimes can lead to longer-term low-cost positions. The largest retailer in the world, Wal-Mart initially targeted only small town America. The uniqueness of its positioning was derived from bringing a very broad assortment of general merchandise to areas of the country where the existing retail establishments provided little choice to consumers. However, Wal-Mart aggressively extended the breadth of its concept and the variety of its locations. Eventually, the size of its target market (which they call the "Big Middle"), together with the firm's constant attention to supply chain design delivered significant cost advantages. The important point is that, whether the target is broad or narrow, an aggressive differentiation strategy supported by clear branding provides a way to circumvent direct price competition. Furthermore, although the reduction in direct price competition causes some concerns from a public policy standpoint, it is clear that buyers benefit from the increased choice derived from constant innovation and reward the companies that provide it (Baker, 1997). Segmentation, dynamic differentiation, brand positioning, and niche marketing are synonymous with modern business practice and reflect the view of business that in competition you win the race not only by running faster but by finding a better route to the finish line.

Marketing Scholarship on Competition

Marketing helps businesses find a better route and so marketing scholars have long been, and continue to be, intimately involved in research involving issues of competition. Weitz (1985) identified five questions concerning competition that are relevant to marketing scholars: 1) Who is the firm/brand's competitor? 2) How intense is the competition in the market? 3) How does competition affect market evolution and structure? 4) How do competitive actions affect marketing decisions?, and 5) How do firms achieve and maintain a competitive advantage? Marketing studies of competitive interaction, first mover effects and the sources of entry barriers help firms in their efforts to win the game by developing defensible strategies, but also inform policy makers of the potential for market imperfections. Thus, we have also included in this volume an award winning article by Hunt and Morgan (1995) in which they incorporate insights from the marketing concept and marketing orientation to create a new theory of competition based on "comparative" advantage.

In winning the competitive game, understanding how products and brands substitute for one another is also a critical success factor. Here the contributions of marketing scholars on topics like brand switching, variety seeking, and choice behavior help firms understand the underlying forces in their competitive environment (Weitz, 1985). Far from assuming an atomistic market with perfect information, marketing scholars have focused on the complexity of the purchase decision. A classic example of that type of examination is found in our reading on customers' consideration sets by Roberts and Lattin (1991) included below. It should be remembered, however, that when marketers study the consumer purchase decisions it is "the way(s) that fishermen study fish rather than as marine biologists study them" (Tucker, 1974). Business studies consumers because firms want to "catch more fish" and win the game. In contrast, protecting the quality of the choice process has been the focus of the law for centuries, so we turn now to the legal view of competition.

The Legal View of Competition

Early Common Law of Contract

Lawyers and regulators see competition as a method for judging acts and practices as they relate to the well-being of society. What we think of now as business law and regulation has its roots in contract law, the law of

"I don't meet competition, I crush it." (Charles Revson of Revlon, Inc., *Time* 16 June 1958).

property and what I will call the law of the marketplace. Initially, the law of contract focused entirely on the conduct of commerce and the practices of unscrupulous sellers and not on the structure of the markets. Early common law of contract, therefore, dealt with ensuring that in their dealings with buyers, sellers would deliver what they had promised. Thus, the rule that a binding contract was created when the promise was made for consideration (which could be another promise) became part of the common law. When more than one seller competed for the patronage of a buyer, these legal principles relating to contracts supported the creation of efficient competitive markets where buyers could make choices among the alternatives based on fact and reasonable expectations of outcomes. The modern extensions of these contracting principles are found in the specific rules pertaining to deceptive advertising, product liability, warranty, and so on that are dealt with elsewhere in this book, but the overall impact of a predictable law of contract was to smooth the playing field for competing rivals. Contract was not the only area of early common law that related to the issue of competition, however; property law also had a direct relationship to the creation of competitive markets.

Property Law and Monopoly Power

It is hard now in our modern economy to imagine a time when property law was essentially a law of monopolies. Nevertheless, when all property rights ultimately came from the sovereign or from devices like adverse possession and long-term continuous use, they carried with them an assumption of continued protection from other claims. For example, if an individual were granted the right to build a mill on a stream, he could be assured of gaining the expected returns for that investment only if the flow of the stream would be protected from other interests. Thus, when mill owners were granted rights to interrupt the flow of streams to which other mill owners had been given rights, the common law courts had to decide whether to foster competition or maintain absolute rights of priority which essentially granted a monopoly to one mill. Initial decisions in the United States favored economic development through efficiency and supported the prior rights of one mill to foreclose all others if that would allow it to operate more efficiently. Subsequently however, the courts moved to adopt a rule that allowed multiple reasonable claims on the flow of streams so that the public would benefit from the competition that would ensue. Thus, through the 18th and early 19th centuries, competition gradually replaced planned and allocated monopoly rights in early American property law as the preferred path to economic development (Horwitz, 1977).

The Law of the Marketplace

The early common law of the marketplace had a strong pro-competition stance and several of these early legal concepts represent some of the first forms of what would become antitrust law. Foremost among these rules were the laws against regrating, forestalling and engrossing. These were all offenses against the free working of the early markets and all dealt with the creation of some form of *intermediation*. Intermediation, i.e., the purchase of commodities not for one's own use but for further sale, was considered detrimental to the working of the market because it was believed to increase prices. Specifically, regrating involved buying commodities and selling them in the same market, forestalling dealt with the interruption of the flow of goods to a market so as to wait for prices to rise, and engrossing with the purchase of large amounts of a product to corner the market of some type of supply (Atiyah, 1979 at 129). The focus of these and other laws of the marketplace, therefore, was to foster a fair exchange of goods between seller and end user. They implicitly, if not explicitly, recognized the fact that any distortion of that free flow of commerce would be detrimental to the overall public good and equated intermediaries with that distortion. It would have been hard for early courts to imagine the market-friendly behavior of modern channel members, but they laid the groundwork for concerns about the kinds of exclusionary vertical restraints that are still at issue today.

The Foundation of Antitrust Law

In the 1600s monopolies arose from government grants that resembled modern day patents. As early as 1602, the common law courts were registering their distaste for government established monopolies and finding reasons to declare them void (Atiyah, 1979 at 118). In 1623 the Statute on Monopolies affirmed the government's power to grant patent rights but at the same time curbed the market power of the guilds and provided for the private right of action by persons harmed by unauthorized monopolies (Baker, 2004). By the 18th century the common law reflected the free market thinking of the liberal political economists and was strongly supportive of competitive markets. Nevertheless, by the late 1800s in the United States, huge trusts such as John D. Rockefeller's Standard Oil Trust placed the control of many if not all of the firms in a particular industry in the hands of one person or small group. These trusts dominated the railroads, oil, sugar, coal, steel, and textile industries. Firms joined the trusts or were run out of business (Shaw and Wolfe, 1991 at 350). Because the common law was perceived as ineffective in fighting these abuses, in 1890 Congress passed the Sherman Act, the first of the American antitrust laws. With the Sherman Act's passage, it became clear that public policy in the United States was firmly against monopolization of any kind.

It is a subject of debate whether the initial antitrust legislation actually reflected a policy concern for the small firms who were forced out of business by the powerful trusts or for the consumers who would not receive the benefits of competition. Passage of the oft derided Robinson Patman Act (also know as the anti-chain store act) in 1936 seemed to be consistent with the "competitor protection" argument. The question was ostensibly put to rest in 1962 in the Brown Shoe Case (*Brown Shoe Co. v. U.S.*, 370 U.S. 294) when the Supreme Courts interpreted Sherman as protecting competition not competitors

(Stern and Eovaldi, 1984), and yet some would argue that cases like that recently brought against Microsoft signal the Justice Department's growing dissatisfaction with that single-minded test (Sowell, 1995; Henderson, 1998).

U.S. Antitrust Policy

In protecting competition, it is important to note that the policy expressed in Sherman was not against the existence of monopolies but rather a policy against the act of actively creating a "contract, combination or conspiracy in restraint of trade" or against a firm that "monopolizes or attempts to monopolize" an industry. This seems a fine point but it remains a crucial part of the law as it relates to competition. The fact that a firm happens to have monopoly power either through historical accident or through the ineffectiveness of its competitors does not amount to a violation. However, if a firm with monopoly power actively seeks to maintain or increase that power, it will run afoul of the Sherman Act. The Sherman Act equally prohibits the active formation of any formal or informal cartel among firms that leads to a state of monopoly power. This prohibition covers typically covert activities such as horizontal price fixing agreements, but it also is the provision that bestows the power to review the potential anticompetitive effects of proposed mergers. Although the Sherman Act (as it was interpreted by the court) was a powerful tool in combating the trusts, it was found to be incomplete and was followed by the Clayton Act in 1914 and the Federal Trade Commission Act also enacted in 1914 and significantly extended in the 1938 amendment, both of which enhanced the government's range of review over potentially anticompetitive activities, as well as creating in the Federal Trade Commission an alternative to Justice Department enforcement.

As mentioned above, the antitrust laws focus on prohibited acts. In other words, the statutes primarily look at the conduct-performance link and not at structure. Nevertheless, the structure of industries in terms of the numbers and concentration of competitors is important in the sense that prohibited conduct is more likely to occur. Thus, exclusionary behavior that might be tolerated in fragmented industries is prohibited when a firm with market power engages in such behavior. An example of this is the fact that in order to find an illegal tie between the sale of one product and the sale of another requires the suspect firm to have market power in the tying product market.

There have been instances, however, when what appears to be mere market structure was claimed to have anticompetitive effects. In 1972 the FTC brought suit against the dry cereal producers alleging a theory of shared monopoly (*In the matter of Kellogg Co. et al,* Doc. No. 8934 January 24, 1972). Essentially, the FTC believed that, although no collusion was alleged, the oligopoly that existed in the cereal market led to anticompetitive pricing as well as to advertising policies that were designed to prevent entry by new competitors. Ultimately, that suit was dismissed and conduct was retained as the foundation of antitrust policy (Stern and Eovaldi, 1984 at 492).

In reviewing alleged anticompetitive behavior the courts have become much more astute at examining the relevant managerial and economic arguments. In some instances, they have become convinced of valid (i.e., pro-competitive) marketing reasons for various kinds of vertical restraints that had been previously considered illegal *per se* (e.g., *Continental TV, Inc. et al. v. GTE-Sylvania Inc.,* 433 U.S. 36, 1977). They have recognized the complexity of product market definitions when products lock in customers though technology (e.g., *Eastman Kodak Company v. Image Technical Service,* 504 U.S. 451, 1992). Essentially, the courts have taken a strong public policy in favor of competition that had its birth in the medieval marketplace and have incorporated into that policy modern day marketing and economic reasoning.

Current Issues in Antitrust

The current debate in antitrust policy relates back to issues discussed in the section on economics. In the 1980s, antitrust law underwent a significant shift as neo-classical economic reasoning became the clear starting point for all competitive analysis. Called the Chicago school of antitrust economics because of its close ties to the thinking of Milton Friedman and his successors at the University of Chicago, its proponents in the Justice Department and on the courts adopted the general position that in the absence of government intervention, most markets are inherently efficient and entry barriers relatively low. Thus, a rational firm would be unlikely to incur costs related to creating a monopoly because if entry is easy, it would never be able to recoup those costs by raising prices to a supra-competitive level. For example, if a firm uses predatory pricing designed to drive competitors out of business in order to achieve a monopoly position, it must ultimately raise prices to make that behavior worthwhile. If the threat of easy entry by new competitors prevents that, it makes no sense for the firm to engage in predatory pricing in the first place. And so the argument goes that if we observe very aggressive pricing by presumably rational firms, it must be for procompetitive and not anticompetitive reasons. In fact, this is the subject of one of the articles in this section's collection of readings (Guiltinan and Gundlach, 1996).

The Chicago school's reliance on simplified neo-classical models appeared to some economists as unnecessarily abstract in light of advances in economic theory. Thus, economists in the Post-Chicago school of thought focused on concepts such as information asymmetry, non-transferable assets and network externalities in their analysis of firm behavior and competitive markets (Gundlach, 2001). They also took a more dynamic view of consumer welfare. In addition to the allocative and productive efficiency goals of the Chicago school, Post Chicago economists sought "gains to consumer welfare extending from improvements to existing market conditions as precipitated through innovation" (Gundlach, 2001 at 41). Overall, the Post-Chicago school focused on the sources of market imperfections and was highly suspicious of strategic behavior of firms designed to distort competitive markets.

Although the role of economic theory in antitrust law had been growing for many years, the legacy of both the Chicago and Post-Chicago schools has been to deeply and permanently imbed sophisticated economic analysis into the interpretation of the Sherman, Clayton, Robison-Patman and FTC Acts. Although different on many important dimensions, both "schools" have had significant impact in continuing to move antitrust law further away from a reflection of social policy toward a reflection of economic policy. Although some would argue that too much economic reasoning and not enough marketing reasoning has been employed in that endeavor (Gundlach, 2001), it is clear that economics, business and the law each continue to offer unique, important and interrelated perspectives in the creation of competition policy.

Delving Deeper into Competition: Selected Readings

The following articles present examples of how the different perspectives, economics, business (i.e., marketing) and the law, intertwine to form a complex interpretation of the concept of competition.

COMPETITION AS A STRATEGIC PROCESS

In the first article, *The Comparative Advantage Theory of Competition,* Shelby Hunt and Robert Morgan add a marketing scholar's perspective to the various theories of competition. They develop a theory that uses insights from marketing research to improve on the explanatory power of existing approaches. They trace the source of competitive advantage to resource-based comparative advantages to show how individual firms can achieve superior financial performance while at the same time providing society the benefits of enhanced quality, efficiency and innovation. In 1995 this article won the prestigious *Harold H. Maynard Award* given each year to the *Journal of Marketing* article that has made the most significant contribution to marketing theory and thought.

CONSUMER CHOICE AND COMPETITIVE SETS

At the heart of all competition, whether from an economic, business or legal perspective, is the concept of consumer choice. Competitors are those products or services from which one is chosen by the consumer. It is clear, however, that consumers do not (and can not) consider all of the potential choices that may be available to them. Imagine a person in a book store. Can we really consider all of the books as competing for that consumer's business? And yet, so much of the legal and economic analysis seems to treat markets as containing all available suppliers of similar products or services. In *Development and Testing of a Model of Consideration Set Composition,* John Roberts and James Lattin bring marketing insight to bear on these issues as they examine the purchase decision itself to see where the boundaries of competition really are. They provide evidence in support of a two-stage choice process that begins with the creation of a consideration set. These findings have significant implications for how we think about competitors and their rivalry for consumer patronage and the policy issues that arise from that rivalry. For example, should we treat competition for inclusion in a consideration set the same as we treat competition among its members? In 1996, Roberts and Lattin's article received the *William F. O'Dell Award* for the most significant long-term contribution to marketing theory, methodology and/or practice made by an article appearing in the *Journal of Marketing Research* in the previous five years.

BRINGING MARKETING ANALYSIS TO ANTITRUST LAW

In the third article, *Aggressive and Predatory Pricing: A Framework for Analysis,* Joseph Guiltinan and Gregory Gundlach pull together law, economics and marketing reasoning in arguing that the lack of marketing input to antitrust law leads to misinterpretation of firm activity and to potential public policy mistakes. They focus here on issues relating to predatory pricing, but clearly their point applies to many other areas of antitrust. This article demonstrates the importance of understanding marketing strategies and tactics in evaluating firm behavior and their impact on competition and provides a critical bridge between competitive theory and the analysis of actual business practice.

Policy in Progress: Illustrative Action Issues

In this section we include two articles from the popular press that reflect some of the current issues in competition and competitive policy. In the first article *The Copycat Economy,* Pete Engardio and Faith Keenan present a view of an economy consistent with some of the ideas expressed by neo-classical economics where differentiation is fleeting and competitors copy ideas as fast as the innovators can come up with them, prices plunge and consumers (if not producers) thrive. In the second article, *Dominant Firms Attract Antitrust Probes and Investors,* Greg Ip discusses the long term success of brands like Microsoft and Coca-Cola and the near monopoly power that dominant blue-chip companies seem to enjoy. Recognizing this power, shareholders bid up the stock while policy makers and regulators worry, and sometimes act.

Conclusion

Economics, business and the law offer three very different perspectives on competition. All three, however, rightly share a focus on the consumer. With its historical origins in political economy the economic analysis of competition takes the actions of rational human actors as its building blocks. Consumers making rational consumption choices interact with sellers making rational resource allocation choices. The shift from observation of these phenomena to optimization analysis leads to the economists' concern for competitive structures that support efficient choices by both consumers and producers.

The law, on the other hand, is charged with the task of ordering societal activities such as competition to protect individual and group interests. Like economics, the law is interested in both sides of the exchange dyad. Thus, the law protects competing sellers by requiring buyers to honor their promises to pay for the goods and services that they have enjoyed. But the law has been even more active in protecting the consumer side of the exchange. Recognizing that informed choice among alternatives in a market setting protects the interests of consumers, the law has sought to insure the quality of that choice through a broad range of statutes and common law doctrines in support of effective competition. Sometimes these two interests coincide as when the law protects small competitors from the aggressive activities of their overzealous larger rivals. But this protection is typically explained as necessary to ultimately maintain choice for the consumer. Although originally based on rather vague concepts of justice, in determining what kinds of seller activities interfere with consumer choice the law has increasingly looked to economics to inform those decisions.

Business goals bear a complex relationship to the goals of the law relating to competition. It is clear that seeking profit for their investors, firms would prefer to operate in a profit-maximizing environment free from competition of any kind. In an economy subject to laws protecting competition and consumer choice, however, firms instead use the methods of marketing in their attempt to achieve positions of comparative advantage over their rivals. The complexity of the relationship between the policy of protecting consumer choice and the firm's marketing activities is exacerbated by the fact that assumptions of how consumers choose among alternatives are far too simplistic. The fact that ostensible substitutes are not necessarily considered by consumers in one single choice process but are rather subjected to a hierarchical decision process has significant implications for the legal and economic analysis of competition.

As marketing and consumer behavior researchers delve deeper into the consumer choice process, the simplifying assumptions associated with traditional views of competition become more and more tenuous. The challenge of scholars interested in understanding competition and devising policy recommendations to enhance the interests of consumers is to incorporate these insights in a systematic and comprehensive way. Until the complexity of consumer behavior research is linked to the concept of competition in a sufficiently rigorous fashion, the abstract models of competition will continue to dominate the policy debate.

Questions

1. What are the downsides to a "Copycat Economy"? Are the lower prices inherent in the "Copycat Economy" worth it?
2. The law protects competitors from some kinds of behavior of their rivals, for example deceptive advertising or product disparagement. How much rivalry is too much? If there are no substantial entry barriers keeping other entrants out, should aggressive pricing that successfully drives a competitor from the market be permitted?
3. Economists who believe in the structure-strategy-performance paradigm are frequently concerned about industry concentration. If consumers form a consideration set from the set of brands of which they are aware as an intermediate step in the final choice decision, at what level do brands compete? At what level is concentration important? If very few brands in a particular category are ever really considered by consumers is that cause for concern?
4. Are businesses that attempt to undermine direct price comparison by differentiating their product or service offerings from those of their rivals hurting consumers?
5. How will/should globalization impact the views of competition by economics, the law and business?
6. What other insights from marketing would make the antitrust analysis of competition more realistic?

References

Atiyah, P.S. 1979. *The Rise and Fall of Freedom of Contract,* Oxford: Clarendon Press.

Baker, Donald I. 2004. "Revisiting History—What Have We Learned About Private Antitrust Enforcement That We Would Recommend To Others?" *Loyola Consumer Law Review,* 16, 379–408.

Baker, Jonathan B. 1997. "Product Differentiation through Space and Time: Some Antitrust Policy Issues," *The Antitrust Bulletin,* 42 (1): 177–196.

Bernard, Richard C. 1967. "Competition in Law and Economics," *Antitrust Bulletin,* 12 (Winter): 1099–1163.

Chamberlin, Edward. 1962. *The Theory of Monopolistic Competition: A Re-orientation of the Theory of Value, 8th Ed.* Harvard University Press: Cambridge.

Dawkins, Richard. 1976. *The Selfish Gene.* Oxford University Press: Oxford.

Engardio, Pete and Faith Keenan. 2002. "The Copycat Economy," *Business Week,* August 19, 2002, 94–95.

Guiltinan, Joseph P. and Gregory T. Gundlach. 1996. "Aggressive and Predatory Pricing: A Framework for Analysis," *Journal of Marketing,* 60 (July): 87–102.

Gundlach, Gregory T. 2001. "Marketing and Modern Antitrust Thought," *in Handbook of Marketing and Society,* Paul N. Bloom and Gregory T. Gundlach (eds.) Sage: Thousand Oaks, CA, 34–50.

Henderson, David R. 1998. "The Case Against Antitrust," *Fortune,* 137 (8): 40–41.

Horwitz, Morton J. 1977. *The Transformation of American Law 1780–1860.* Cambridge: Harvard University Press.

Hunt, Shelby D. and Robert M. Morgan. 1995. "The Comparative Advantage Theory of Competition," *Journal of Marketing,* 59 (April): 1–15.

Ip, Greg. 1998. "Dominant Firms Attract Antitrust Probes and Investors," *Wall Street Journal,* (May 12, 1998): C1.

Kuester, Sabine, Christian Homburg and Thomas S. Robertson. 1999. "Retaliatory Behavior to New Product Entry," *Journal of Marketing,* 63 (October): 90–106.

Porter, Michael. 1985. *Competitive Advantage,* New York: The Free Press.

Revson, Charles. 1958. *Time Magazine,* (June 16, 1958).

Roberts, John H. and James M. Lattin. 1991. "Development and Testing of a Model of Consideration Set Composition," *Journal of Marketing Research,* 28 (November): 429–440.

Scherer, F.M. 1980. *Industrial Market Structure and Economic Performance,* Chicago: Rand McNally College Publishing Company.

Shaw, Bill and Art Wolfe. 1991. *The Structure of the Legal Environment, 2nd Ed.,* Boston: PWS-Kent Publishing Co.

Stern, Louis W. and John R. Grabner, Jr. 1970. *Competition in the Marketplace.* Scott, Glenview, IL: Foresman and Company.

Stern, Louis W. and Thomas L. Eovaldi. 1984. *Legal Aspects of Marketing Strategy.* Englewoods Cliffs, NJ: Prentice-Hall, Inc.

Sowell, Thomas. 1995. "Sinister Theory," *Forbes,* 156 (5): 50.

Tucker, W.T. 1974. "Future Directions of Marketing Theory," *Journal of Marketing,* 38 (April): 30–35.

Weitz, Barton A. 1985. "Introduction to Special Issue on Competition," *Journal of Marketing,* 22 (August): 229–236.

THE COMPARATIVE ADVANTAGE THEORY
OF COMPETITION

Shelby D. Hunt and Robert M. Morgan

A new theory of competition is evolving in the strategy literature. The authors explicate the foundations of this new theory, the "comparative advantage theory of competition," and contrast them with the neoclassical theory of perfect competition. They argue that the new theory of competition explains key macro and micro phenomena better than neoclassical perfect competition theory. Finally, they further explicate the theory of comparative advantage by evaluating a market orientation as a potential resource for comparative advantage.

Three recent streams of research portend major changes in marketing theory and practice: works addressing strategic issues in marketing theory and research (Aaker 1988; Bharadwaj, Varadarajan, and Fahy 1993; Day and Wensley 1988; McKee, Varadarajan, and Pride 1989), those advocating a market orientation for superior firm performance (Day 1984; Day and Nedungadi 1994; Kohli and Jaworski 1990; Narver and Slater 1990; Shapiro 1988; Webster 1994), and those emphasizing the desirability of relationship marketing in strategic network competition (Berry and Parasuraman 1991; Dwyer, Schurr, and Oh 1987; Morgan and Hunt 1994; Parvatiyar, Sheth, and Whittington 1992; Thorelli 1986; Webster 1992). However, not all marketers are sanguine about the prospects for these three streams. Day (1992, p. 324, 328) points out that "within academic circles, the contribution of marketing to the development, testing, and dissemination of strategy theories and concepts has been marginalized over the past decade," and he observes that "the marketing concept is nowhere to be found in . . . discussion[s] of competing principles of management presumed to be causally related to the effectiveness of organizations." Moreover, he concludes that "the prognosis for marketing . . . is not encouraging" in the ongoing "strategy dialogue" regarding networks and alliances.

The emperor has no clothes.
—Hans Christian Andersen

SHELBY D. HUNT is J.B. Hoskins and P.W. Horn Professor of Marketing, Marketing Area, College of Business Administration, Texas Tech University. ROBERT M. MORGAN is an Assistant Professor of Marketing, Department of Management and Marketing, College of Commerce and Business Administration, University of Alabama. The authors thank Chris Cox, Nicholls State University; Kim Boal, Steve Edison, Anil Menon, Robert Phillips, John R. Sparks, James B. Wilcox, and Robert E. Wilkes, Texas Tech University; and the anonymous *JM* reviewers for their helpful comments on drafts of this article.

Hunt, Shelby D. and Robert M. Morgan (1995), "The Comparative Advantage Theory of Competition," *Journal of Marketing*, 59 (April), 1–15.

489

Our central thesis is that the strategy dialogue Day refers to is evolving toward a new theory of competition—one that has significant advantages over neoclassical theory. Our article contributes to the development of this new theory and examines its implications for marketing. Specifically, we draw on (1) the evolving resource-based theory of the firm from the strategy literature (Barney 1991; Conner 1991), (2) the works on competitive advantage from marketing and industrial organization economics (Bharadwaj, Varadarajan, and Fahy 1993; Day and Wensley 1988; Day and Nedungadi 1994; Porter 1980, 1985, 1990), (3) the theory of competitive rationality from Austrian economics (Dickson 1992), and (4) the theory of differential advantage from marketing and economics (Alderson 1957, 1965; Clark 1961) to develop the foundations for a theory of competition that we label the "comparative advantage theory of competition."[1] We argue that this theory explains key macro and micro phenomena better than does neoclassical theory.

By "neoclassical theory" we mean the theory of perfect competition, and "neoclassicist," then, is anyone whose work derives from, is consistent with, or assumes the foundational premises of perfect competition. Because economics texts present perfect competition as the ideal form of competition, it is the basis for most public policy (at least in North America). Furthermore, perfect competition is the only theory of competition that college students ever see. Although perfect competition theory casts marketing activities as "creators of market imperfections," because marketing texts themselves present no rival theory, our own students see only perfect competition theory. Indeed, even marketing's academic literature often adopts the neoclassical view. Consider such phrases as "assume a competitive market," "abnormal profits," and "economic rents." These expressions—not uncommon in marketing—are terms of art in neoclassical theory and mean, respectively, "assume perfect competition," "profits different from that of a firm in an industry characterized by perfect competition," and "profits in excess of the minimum necessary to keep a firm in business in long-run competitive equilibrium." Because perfect competition is ideal, when marketing scholars refer to a marketing activity as "rent seeking," they imply that the activity is economically undesirable from a public policy perspective. We should be mindful that when one adopts a term of art from neoclassical theory, one also adopts implicitly the theory that gives the term its meaning. Therefore, we argue that marketing academics and practitioners should avoid certain neoclassical terms.

The dominant status of perfect competition notwithstanding, there have been numerous critiques of neoclassical theory, ranging from Austrian to evolutionary schools of economics. (Even the works of many industrial organizational economists can be viewed as resulting from a dissatisfaction with neoclassical theory.) Although we acknowledge and

---

[1]Given the prominent role of the resource-based theory of the firm in our own theory, an alternative, equally appropriate label would be the "resource-advantage theory of competition."

appreciate these critiques, we do not overview them. We develop the foundations for a rival to perfect competition theory—we do not just critique it. One reason that perfect competition theory has retained its dominant status despite its many deficiencies is the absence of a well-articulated rival that has superior explanatory power. We maintain that the strategy literature is evolving toward just such a rival and our objective here is to articulate its foundational premises.

First, we identify the key phenomena that any satisfactory theory of competition should be capable of explaining, and then we examine how perfect competition attempts to explain these key phenomena. Next, we develop the foundations for our theory and discuss its explanatory power. Finally, we evaluate a market orientation within the context of the comparative advantage theory of competition.

Competition and Explanation

Theories contribute to scientific understanding by explaining and predicting phenomena (Hunt 1991). Although a theory of competition might be required to explain numerous phenomena, the single most important macroeconomic phenomenon of the twentieth century has undoubtedly been the collapse of planned or "command" economies, which were premised on cooperation among state-owned firms under the direction of a central planning board, and the concomitant triumph of market-based economies, which are premised on competition among self-directed, privately owned firms. Perhaps the greatest "natural experiment" in recorded history is now complete and the results are in: Economies premised on competing firms are far superior to economies premised on cooperating firms in terms of total wealth creation, innovativeness, and overall quality of goods and services. Both the quantitative lack of goods and services (i.e., low gross domestic product) and the qualitative fact that the goods that were produced were so shoddy plagued Eastern bloc economics. Therefore, why economies premised on competition are far superior to command economies in terms of the quantity, quality, and innovativeness of goods and services produced is a macro-level question that should be answered by any satisfactory theory of competition.

The micro phenomenon of the radical heterogeneity of firms is strikingly evident throughout the world's market-based economies. Across and within countries, and across and within industries, firms differ radically as to size, scope, methods of operations, and financial performance:

1. Some firms are so large that their sales exceed the GDP of many countries, whereas others sell flowers on a single street corner;
2. Some produce hundreds of products and others sell only one;
3. Some are vertically integrated "hierarchies" (Williamson 1975) and others specialize in one activity;

4. Some are profitable and others are unprofitable; and
5. Some consistently maintain relatively high profits and others "fall back into the pack."

A theory of competition, we argue, should satisfactorily explain the micro phenomenon of firm diversity. Specifically, why do market-based economies have such an extraordinarily diverse, ever-changing assortment of firms? We now examine the theory of perfect competition and explore how it attempts to explain both the macro and micro phenomena.

The Neoclassical Explanation

Table 1 displays the foundational premises of the neoclassical theory of perfect competition.[2] As to consumer behavior, neoclassical theory assumes that demand is homogeneous for every industry's product. That is, though consumers are allowed to prefer different quantities of each industry's product (heterogeneity across generic products), their tastes and preferences are assumed to be identical with respect to desired product features and characteristics (homogeneous within industries). Consumers also are assumed to have perfect information, which is costless to them, about the availability, characteristics, benefits, and prices of all products. Consumer motivation, one dimension of human motivation, is self-interest or utility maximization.[3]

The firm's objective is profit maximization or, in more sophisticated versions, wealth maximization, that is, the maximization of the net present value of future profits. Acting under conditions of perfect and costless information, neoclassical theory focuses on the firm producing a single product using the resources of capital, labor, and sometimes land. These "factors of production" are assumed to be homogeneous and perfectly mobile; that is, each unit of labor or capital equipment is assumed to be identical with other units and can "flow" from firm to firm without restrictions. The role of management is to respond to changes in the environment by determining the quantity of product to produce and implementing a production function that is identical across all firms in each industry.

Competition in neoclassical theory, then, is each firm in an industry (1) in the short run adjusting its quantity of product produced in reaction to changes in the market price of its product and the prices (costs) of its resources and other inputs and (2) in the long run adjusting the scale of its plant. Therefore, the firm's environment strictly determines its conduct. In particular, all firms in an industry will inexorably produce at the output rate at which marginal cost equals marginal revenue (the product's market price). In the

---

[2]These foundational premises are implied by the standard treatment of the axioms of perfect competition found in economics texts (e.g., Gould and Lazear 1989).

[3]Etzioni (1988) discusses the three conceptualizations of utility and utility maximization in neoclassical economics: (1) a pleasure utility (ethical egoism in moral philosophy terms), (2) a tautology, and (3) an empty mathematical abstraction. He notes that only pleasure utility, or "P-utility," maximization is a substantive thesis that could potentially be empirically tested. Furthermore, in empirical works and public policy recommendations, P-utility is assumed. (See also Hunt and Vasquez-Parraga 1993, p. 79–80.)

TABLE 1

Foundations of the Neoclassical and Comparative Advantage Theories of Competition

	Neoclassical Theory	**Comparative Advantage Theory**
1. Demand	Homogeneous within industries	Heterogeneous within industries
2. Consumer information	Perfect and costless	Imperfect and costly
3. Human motivation	Self-interest maximization	Constrained self-interest
4. Firm's objective	Profit maximization	Superior financial performance
5. Firm's information	Perfect and costless	Imperfect and costly
6. Resources	Capital, labor, and land	Financial, physical, legal, human, organizational, informational, and relational
7. Resource characteristics	Homogeneous, perfectly mobile	Heterogeneous, imperfectly mobile
8. Role of management	Determine quantity and implement production function	Recognize, understand, create, select, implement, and modify strategies
9. Role of environment	Totally determines conduct and performance	Influences conduct and performance
10. Competition	Quantity adjustment	Comparative advantage

short run, in which such resources as plant and equipment are relatively fixed, each firm will incur profits or losses depending on whether price is greater than or less than the average total cost of producing the profit-maximizing quantity. However, in long-run equilibrium in a perfectly competitive market, all resources are variable and each firm produces the quantity at which market price equals long-run marginal cost, which itself equals the minimum long-run average cost. The position of long-run equilibrium is a "no-profit" situation—firms have neither a pure profit (or "rent") nor a pure loss, only an accounting profit equal to the rate of return obtainable in other perfectly competitive industries. Therefore, the firm's environment strictly determines its performance (i.e., its profits).

The welfare economics literature investigates the conditions prevailing at the position of long-run general equilibrium. If all industries in an economy are perfectly competitive and no further adjustments in quantity produced are made by any firm in any industry, then at this general equilibrium position every firm has the optimum sized plant and operates it at the point of minimum cost. Furthermore, every resource or "factor" employed is allocated to its most productive use and receives the value of its marginal product. Moreover, the distribution of products produced is (Pareto) optimal at general equilibrium because the price of each product (reflecting what consumers are *willing* to pay for an additional unit) and its marginal cost (the extra resource cost society *must* pay for an additional unit) will be exactly equal. Therefore, the adjective "perfect" is taken literally in neoclassical theory: perfect competition is perfect.

EXPLAINING ABUNDANCE

Neoclassicists readily admit that such abundant economies as that of the United States are not characterized by perfect competition. However, they claim that the U.S. economy is close enough to perfect competition to benefit from its efficiency-producing characteristics (Shepherd 1982; Stigler 1949). Therefore, neoclassical theory could potentially explain abundance by focusing on the efficiency of perfect competition.[4] Whereas command economies misallocate resources because of the lack of "signals" from the marketplace as to where planners should deploy resources, prices and profits in market-based economies serve as signals and motivators for efficient resource allocation. For example, because firms in a command economy are not profit maximizers, their survival does not depend on finding the most efficient scale of operation. As a second example, the absence of marketplace-determined prices would mean that such resources as aluminum and steel would likely not be allocated to their greatest value-producing uses. Consequently, overall efficiency suffers and output is lowered.

As for explaining the superior innovativeness of market-based economies, though neoclassical economists no doubt have beliefs, their views are not derived from perfect competition theory. Indeed, long-run equilibrium, a cornerstone of neoclassical theory, is precisely the situation that would prevail after all innovation has ceased. That is, firms have maximally adjusted their product output, plant sizes, and consumption of various resources. These adjustments are the only kinds of innovativeness permitted by perfect competition theory; all other forms of innovation are exogenous variables in perfect competition. Indeed, under perfect competition, introducing an innovative feature to an industry's product can be considered a marketplace "imperfection" that would disturb the equilibrium and move the system away from an ideal state. In this vein, for example, neoclassical studies have considered the innovative features in yearly automobile model changes to have no benefits for consumers, only injurious "product differentiation" costs (Fisher, Griliches, and Kaysen 1962).

Similarly, perfect competition cannot explain why market-based economies have higher quality products than do command economies. The assumptions of homogeneous consumer demand and identical within-industry production functions mean that (1) all consumers must desire precisely the same quality level within each product class and (2) firm-specific competencies are disallowed. Therefore, there is no reason to believe that Eastern bloc firms in each industry could not (and would not) have implemented in

---

[4]We add the qualifier "potentially" because in fact the standard view of neoclassicists up until the collapse of the Eastern bloc was that neoclassical theory provided no grounds for preferring market-based over planned economies (Knight 1936; Lavoie 1985). For example, the neoclassicist Lekachman (1985, p. 396–97) concludes that socialist economists have "proved that a Central Planning Board could impose rules upon socialist managers which allocated resources and set prices as efficiently as a capitalist society of the purest stripe, and *much more efficiently* than the capitalist communities of experience" (italics added). Similarly, Balassa (1974, p. 17) concludes that "economic arguments are not sufficient to make a choice between economic systems." See Lavoie (1985) for a review of this issue.

an equally competent manner the same standard production functions to produce the same quality products as did their Western market-based counterparts. Unless consumers in Eastern bloc economies *desired* lower quality products (an assumption refuted by the premium prices commanded by Western goods in such economies) or the resource endowment (e.g., labor) was intrinsically inferior in command economies (also a tenuous assumption), perfect competition cannot explain the historical shoddiness of Eastern bloc products.

We should note also the implications of perfect competition for quality improvement. No firm in perfect competition would or could incur the extra expense of producing a product with a quality level higher than the standard product because the homogeneous demand assumption implies that it could not charge a higher price. Moreover, if a firm did produce a higher quality product and received a higher price for it, then this again could be interpreted as a market imperfection that moves the market away from the ideal state of equilibrium.

Theories of monopolistic and oligopolistic competition could potentially have served as the starting point for overcoming the explanatory deficiencies of perfect competition theory because they—as neoclassicists put it—"relax" some of its foundational premises. In actuality, however, extant versions of these theories are not presented in neoclassical theory as having any beneficial consequences for society. Rather, they are discussed as undesirable departures from the preferred form of competition (note the pejorative tone to the labels "monopolistic" and "oligopolistic").

Consider, for example, Chamberlin's theory of monopolistic competition. He (1933/ 1962, p. 214) realized that the "explicit recognition that product is differentiated . . . makes it clear that pure competition may no longer be regarded as in any sense 'ideal' for purposes of welfare economics." However, as a neoclassicist, he was methodologically wedded to finding equilibrium solutions to his theory. His equilibrium analyses conclude that product differentiation (e.g., some firms producing higher quality products or products with innovative features) always results in (1) product prices higher than perfect competition's (p. 67) and (2) output rates that are not at the lowest point on firms' long-run average cost curves (p. 77). Therefore, the theoretical import of Chamberlin's work for neoclassicists is not the deficiencies of perfect competition (i.e., his conclusion that pure competition is not "in any sense ideal"), but just how *imperfect* monopolistic competition is. Furthermore, when neoclassical works attempt to explore empirically the effects of deviations from perfect competition, they focus on estimating the "social costs" resulting from misallocations of resources (e.g., Cowling and Mueller 1978; Harberger 1954; Siegfried and Tieman 1974).[5] Tellingly for our purposes, no potential social benefits are estimated in such studies, such as those that might be related to innovativeness or quality.

---

[5]These social cost estimates commonly range from .1% to 13% of GDP.

Indeed, why should they? How could departures from perfection possibly have beneficial consequences?

Explaining Firm Diversity

Explaining the diverse assortment of firms in market-based economies poses even more problems for neoclassical theory. Perfect competition implies numerous small firms in every industry, with each producing a single product in the quantity dictated by its most efficient plant size. But many industries in market economies are characterized by a few firms of very large size that produce numerous products. Because perfect competition is perfect, such large corporations must necessarily be inefficient and represent "market failures" brought about through collusive behaviors or the existence (or erection) of "barriers to entry." Similarly, a firm with profits higher than the industry average is prima facie evidence of market imperfections and the existence of "market power." Thus, perfect competition provides the foundations for suspecting that such large and profitable firms as IBM in the 1960s, 1970s, and 1980s resulted from impermissible imperfections (Taylor 1982). Likewise, the continuing financial success of Microsoft in the 1990s is, again, an imperfection that should be eliminated as a matter of public policy (*Business Week* 1991, 1994a, b).

Two schools of economists have attempted to explain the diversity of firms without resorting to such hypotheses as "collusion" or "barriers to entry." First, Chicago-school economists modify the assumption of identical, industry-wide production functions by acknowledging firm-specific competency differences (Demsetz 1975; Stigler 1951, 1964). For them, because "individuals are not all alike, . . . the teams that make up business firms are not alike, and the effectiveness of firms differs" (McGee 1975, p. 101). Therefore, large firms may exist because of differences in production efficiency rather than collusion. "Bigness" for the Chicago school is not necessarily "badness." Nonetheless, Chicago economists still adhere to the neoclassical belief that superior earnings based on efficiency differences will be competed away by imitators in the long run and equilibrium restored. Therefore, sustained superior performance remains suspect (Demsetz 1973; Stigler 1966). Furthermore, Chicago economists address only efficiency differentials, not the possibility that superior earnings would result from either more innovative or higher quality products, that is, effectiveness differentials (Conner 1991).

Transaction cost economics also criticizes the neoclassical view. Coase (1937) pointed out over half a century ago that firms can avoid both search and contract-negotiation costs by producing some of their own production inputs. Therefore, he maintained, each firm expands its operations until the marginal cost of producing an input in house equals the market price of that input. Indeed, his extension of perfect competition explains not only the existence of large firms on the basis of minimizing the costs associated with market exchange, but the existence of small firms as well. That is, individuals band together under the direction of an entrepreneur to purchase inputs and jointly produce an output because, compared with each individual acting alone, "certain marketing costs are saved" (Coase 1937/1952, p. 338).

Extending Coase's ideas, Williamson (1981, p. 1537) believes that "the modern corporation is mainly to be understood as the product of a series of organizational innovations that have had the purpose and effect of economizing on transaction costs," where such costs include all the "negotiation, monitoring, and enforcement costs necessary to assure that contracted goods and services between and within firms are forthcoming" (Alston and Gillespie 1989, p. 193). Williamson's work (1975, 1981, 1983, 1985, 1989) identifies circumstances in which a firm's avoidance of marketplace transaction costs are critical. If all human behavior is unrestrained self-interest maximization and all firms maximize profits, then all firms will seek profits through opportunism, that is, "self-interest seeking with guile" (1975, p. 6). Indeed, he maintains, without the assumption of opportunism, "the study of economic organization is pointless" (1981, p. 1545).[6] Because opportunism is the "deceit-oriented violation of implicit or explicit promises about one's appropriate or required role behavior" (John 1984, p. 279), it will occur whenever producing a product requires a "transaction-specific asset," that is, an asset whose value depends significantly on its being employed in conjunction with another specific asset. According to transaction cost economics, therefore, large, vertically integrated firms exist because of the fear of marketplace opportunism (Conner 1991).

A Summary Evaluation

How well does neoclassical theory explain either the abundance of or the diversity in market economies? As we have seen, though neoclassical theory can potentially contribute to explaining the greater wealth-producing potential of market-based economies on efficiency grounds, it cannot explain their greater innovativeness or their goods and services' superior quality. As to the diversity of firms in market economies, this diversity is directly contrary to perfect competition theory.

With respect to the Chicago school approach, though it allows some human agency in the production function, its retention of other neoclassical assumptions limits the school's explanatory power. The situation with respect to transaction cost economics is more complex. Williamson (1981) identifies as foundational the behavioral assumptions of opportunism and bounded rationality (managers are intendedly rational, but only limitedly so). He also accepts the neoclassical maximizing tradition: "Neoclassical economics maintains a maximizing orientation. This is unobjectionable, if all the relevant

---

[6] Although Williamson acknowledges that not all economic agents behave opportunistically, he argues for assuming universal opportunism because it is "ubiquitous" (1981, p. 1550) and opportunistic "types cannot be distinguished ex ante from sincere types" (1975, p. 27) or, at the very least, "it is very costly to distinguish opportunistic from nonopportunistic types ex ante" (1981, p. 1545; italics added).

costs [i.e., the transaction costs] are included" (1985, p. 45). However, if all firms in an industry engage in opportunism, then the maximizing tradition would imply that all firms in an industry would ultimately wind up at precisely the same size, scope, and profitability—the one that minimizes total costs, including each firm's identical costs of opportunism. Therefore, transaction cost economics can contribute to explaining firm diversity only by diverging from such neoclassical assumptions as homogenous demand.[7] What is needed to explain firm diversity is a new theory of competition, one that reexamines all the foundations of perfect competition. To this task we now turn.

The Comparative Advantage Theory of Competition

In Table 1, we display the foundational premises of the proposed theory.[8] Both the content and epistemology of each premise differ from its perfect competition counterpart. Specifically, because we adopt the epistemology of scientific realism (Hunt 1991), each premise is offered as a proposition that can and should be subjected to empirical testing. Thus, unlike the epistemology of perfect competition, if any foundational premise is found to be false, then it should be replaced with a premise that better describes the real world of competition in market-based economies.

First, rejecting the neoclassical assumption of the gray sameness of human consumption preferences within generic product classes, we view industry demand as significantly heterogeneous and dynamic (Alderson 1957; Dickson 1992). That is, consumers' tastes and preferences within a generic product class, for example, footwear, not only differ greatly as to desired product features and characteristics, but they are always changing. Second, consumers have imperfect information concerning products that might match their tastes and preferences, and obtaining such information is often costly in terms of both time and money. Note that heterogeneity implies that few, if any, *industry markets* exist; there are only market segments within industries. For example, there is no "market for shoes," or even separate markets for women's and men's shoes. Even though all consumers require footwear and one can readily identify a group of firms that manufacture shoes, the group of firms that constitutes the shoe industry does not collectively

---

[7]Williamson's (1981, p. 1551) profit maximizing equation appears, among other things, to deny the neoclassical assumption of homogeneity of demand. Nonetheless, Williamson (1975, p. xi) views transaction cost theory as a "complement" to rather than being "in essential conflict with received microtheory."

[8]The use of the label "comparative advantage" is drawn in part from its use in international trade. There, classical Ricardian analysis provides that international trade is beneficial for all if each country specializes in those products for which its "factors" of production (which are heterogeneous and immobile across countries) make it, compared with other countries, more efficient. It need not have an absolute efficiency advantage in producing any product over all countries; it need only be relatively more efficient in producing some products than others. Similarly, our analysis assumes significant resource heterogeneity and immobility across firms in an industry. A firm, therefore, gains comparative advantage over other firms by making the best use of its heterogeneous resources. Note, however, that the resources assumed here are much more sophisticated than the traditional land, labor, and capital of international trade economics. Furthermore, such resources are not considered to be "natural" endowments (cf. Jones and Kenen 1984). Rather, some of the most important resources are those intangible ones that collectively constitute competencies of the firm.

face a single, downward sloping demand curve—such an industry demand curve would imply homogenous tastes and preferences. Indeed, to the extent that demand curves exist at all, they exist at a level of (dis)aggregation that is too fine to be an industry. For example, even if there were a men's walking shoe *market,* one certainly would not speak of the men's walking shoe *industry.*

Third, in their roles as both consumers of products and managers of firms, humans are motivated by constrained self-interest seeking. This premise draws on Etzioni's (1988) argument that people have two irreducible sources of valuation: pleasure (or, in Etzioni's notation, "P-utility") and morality. Because people do pursue pleasure and avoid pain, P-utility explains much behavior. However, both consumers and managers are constrained in their self-interest seeking by considerations of what is right, proper, ethical, moral, or appropriate. In ethical theory terms, deontological considerations constrain teleological considerations (Hunt and Vasquez-Parraga 1993). This premise implies that opportunism is not assumed to prevail in all circumstances. We reject transaction cost theory's "guilt by axiom" (Donaldson 1990, p. 373). The extent to which people behave opportunistically in various contexts is a research question to be explored and explained—not presumed.

Fourth and fifth, the firm's primary objective is superior financial performance, which, consistent with Austrian economics (Jacobson 1992), it pursues under conditions of imperfect (and often costly to obtain) information about customers and competitors. Our view parallels Porter (1991, p. 96), who identifies firm success as "superior and sustainable performance . . . relative to the world's best rivals." There are, no doubt, other objectives—such as contributing to social causes or, as Porter (1991, p. 96) puts it, individuals "enjoying slack"—but we maintain that such secondary objectives are enabled by the accomplishment of superior financial performance. "Superior" implies that firms seek a level of financial performance that exceeds that of its referents, often its closest competitors. Why "superior" instead of maximum financial performance? Because firms do not maximize profits both because of the well-documented fact that they lack the information to do so (i.e., they operate under bounded rationality [Simon 1979]), and because morality considerations at times constrain them (or some of them) from doing so. In short, superior financial performance is constrained by managers' views of morality. For example, many managers resist cheating or opportunistically exploiting their customers and suppliers not only because of the P-utility fear of "getting caught," but also because they believe such cheating and exploitation to be deontologically wrong.

Financial performance is indicated by such measures as profits and return on investment, with the relative importance of specific financial indicators assumed to vary somewhat from firm to firm, industry to industry, and country to country. For example, in Germany and Switzerland, where banks and other major shareholders rarely trade their shares, long-term capital appreciation is valued more highly than it is in the United States (Porter 1990). Rewards flow to firms (and then to their owners, managers, and employees) that produce superior financial results. Rewards include not only stock dividends, capital appreciation, salaries, wages, and bonuses, but also promotions, expanded career opportunities, prestige, and feelings of accomplishment.

Note that we do not characterize the firm's objective as "abnormal" profits or "rents" that result from market "imperfections," as does neoclassical theory. We urge all marketers to eschew such neoclassical expressions. Although one can compute such things as the average profits of a group of rivals for comparison purposes, the notion of "normal profits," that is, the average firm's profits in a purely competitive industry in long-run equilibrium, is an empirically meaningless, arguably pernicious abstraction. Long-run equilibrium is neither something that exists nor something that groups of rivals are "tending toward" nor something that, if achieved, would be desirable (let alone perfect). Rather, markets are *never* in equilibrium (Dickson 1992; Jacobson 1992) and activities that produce turmoil in markets have positive benefits because they are the engine of economic growth: "Capitalism, then, is by nature a form or method of economic change and not only never is but never can be stationary" (Schumpeter 1950, p. 82).

Sixth, resources are the tangible and intangible entities available to the firm that enable it to produce efficiently and/or effectively a market offering that has value for some market segment or segments (cf. Barney 1991; Wernerfelt 1984).[9] For example, a firm's core competencies (Prahalad and Hamel 1990) are intangible, higher order resources that enable it to perform—better perhaps than its competitors—the activities in Porter's (1985) "value chain."[10] Drawing on Barney (1991), Day and Wensley (1988), and Hofer and Schendel (1978), we propose that the multitude of potential resources can be most usefully categorized as financial (e.g., cash reserves, access to financial markets), physical (e.g., plant, equipment), legal (e.g., trademarks, licenses), human (e.g., the skills and knowledge of individual employees), organizational (e.g., competencies, controls, policies, culture), informational (e.g., knowledge resulting from consumer and competitor intelligence), and relational (e.g., relationships with suppliers and customers).

Seventh, resources are both significantly heterogeneous across firms and imperfectly mobile. Resource heterogeneity means that every firm has an assortment of resources that is at least in some ways unique. Immobility implies that firm resources, to varying degrees, are not commonly, easily, or readily bought and sold in the marketplace (the neoclassical "factor" markets). Because of resource immobility, resource heterogeneity can persist through time despite attempts by firms to acquire the same resources of particularly successful competitors (Collis 1991; Dierickx and Cool 1989; Peteraf 1993).

---

[9]As used here, "value" refers to the sum total of all benefits that consumers perceive they will receive if they accept the market offering. It does not imply a ratio of benefits received to price paid, as in the trade's use of "value pricing."

[10]Porter (1991, p. 108), however, is critical of extant versions of resource-based theory: "At worst, the resource-based view is circular." For him, discussions of core competencies are "inward looking and most troubling" and "stress on resources must complement, not substitute for, stress on marketplace positions." For him, selecting the right industry and generic strategy within an industry is key because industry is the "most significant predictor of firm performance" (Montgomery and Porter 1991, p. xiv).

FIGURE 1

Competitive Position Matrix[a]

Relative Resource-Produced Value

	Lower	Parity	Superior
Lower	1 **?**	2 Competitive Advantage	3 Competitive Advantage
Parity	4 Competitive Disadvantage	5 Parity Position	6 Competitive Advantage
Higher	7 Competitive Disadvantage	8 Competitive Disadvantage	9 **?**

Relative Resource Costs

[a]*Read:* The marketplace position of competitive advantage identified as cell 3 results from the firm, relative to its competitors, being able to produce an offering for some market segment or segments that is (1) perceived to be of superior value and is (2) produced at lower costs.

When a firm has a resource (or, more often, a specific assortment of resources) that is rare among competitors, it has the potential for producing a comparative advantage for that firm (Barney 1991). A comparative advantage in resources exists when a firm's resource assortment (e.g., its competencies) enables it to produce a market offering that, relative to extant offerings by competitors, (1) is perceived by some market segments to have superior value and/or (2) can be produced at lower costs. As Conner (1991, p. 132) notes, "distinctiveness in the product offering or low costs are tied directly to the distinctiveness in the inputs—resources—used to produce the product, much as the quality and cost of boeuf bourguignonne depend on the particular ingredients used and the way in which they are mixed." A comparative advantage in resources, then, can translate into a position of competitive advantage in the marketplace and superior financial performance—but not necessarily.

Figure 1 shows nine possible competitive positions for the various combinations of a firm's relative (to competitors) resource-produced value for some segments and relative resource costs for producing such value.[11] Ideally, of course, a firm would prefer the

---

[11]Note that we use "relative resource-produced value" and not "relative differentiation advantage." We do so because (1) to be simply different from one's competitors does not yield a position of competitive advantages, (2) differentiation is an outcome of producing superior value (not the same thing as producing superior value), (3) as marketers we should (of all groups) be using terms that focus on customers, and (4) the word "differentiation" has the connotation—pernicious, in our judgment—from its use in neoclassical economics that the purpose of offering superior value to one's customers is to "escape the rigors" of perfect competition.

competitive position of cell 3, where its comparative advantage in resources produces superior value at lower cost. The Japanese automobile companies, for example, had this position throughout the 1970s and into the 1980s in the United States because their more efficient and effective manufacturing processes produced higher quality products at lower costs. Positions identified as cells 2 and 6 also bring competitive advantage and superior financial returns, whereas cell 5, the parity position, produces average returns. But firms occupying positions 1 and 9, though having a comparative advantage in either value or costs, may or may not have superior returns.

In position 1 the advantage of lower relative resource costs is associated with (or results from) a sacrifice in relative value for consumers. Consequently, the offerings of firms in such a position will generally have lower prices than those, say, in cell 2. Depending on the extent to which the price reductions are less than, equal to, or greater than their relative advantage in resource costs, cell 1 firms are at positions of competitive advantage, parity, or competitive disadvantage, respectively. For example, though American car companies in the 1970s and 1980s occupied position 7, in the 1990s they have a relative cost advantage over imported Japanese makes (Lavin 1994). Nonetheless, because many consumers still perceive American cars to be of somewhat lower quality, they occupy position 1 and competitive advantage is not assured. Position 9, on the other hand, is equally indeterminate and describes the German car companies in the 1990s. Although the resources of the German auto manufacturers continue to produce products of superior perceived value, they do so at much higher resource costs (Keller 1993). Unlike the 1970s and 1980s, when the German car companies occupied position 6, competitive advantage is now no longer assured.

Cell 5, the parity position, is the marketplace situation addressed in part by perfect competition theory. If no firm can produce superior value for some particular market segments and no firm has a cost advantage (which implies that all innovation has stopped), then an equilibrating model of competition might apply. We should note, however, that this, the degenerative case, is unlikely to persist in many markets through time.

Eighth, the role of management in the firm is to recognize and understand current strategies, create new strategies, select preferred strategies, implement or manage those selected, and modify them through time.[12] Strategies that yield a position of competitive advantage and superior financial performance will do so because they rely on those resources in which the firm has a comparative advantage over its rivals. Sometimes it is a single resource, such as a trademark; more often it is a combination of interconnected resources, that is, a resource assortment. Sustained, superior financial performance occurs only when a firm's comparative advantage in resources continues to yield a position of competitive advantage despite the actions of competitors.

---

[12]The rationale for including the recognition and understanding of strategies is that sometimes a firm's strategies emerge or are implicit (Mintzberg 1987). In such cases, it is important for firms to recognize and understand their emergent or implicit strategies.

Because all firms seek superior financial performance, competitors of a firm having a comparative advantage will attempt to neutralize their rival's advantage by obtaining the same value-producing resource. If the resource is mobile, that is, readily available for sale in the marketplace, then it will be acquired by competitors, and the comparative advantage is neutralized quickly and effectively. If it is immobile, then competitors innovate. According to Barney (1991), the innovating behavior can be either imitating the resource or finding a substitute resource that is strategically equivalent. A third alternative, which we propose is more important than either imitation or substitution, is major innovation, that is, finding a new resource that produces value that is superior to—not strategically equivalent to—the advantaged competitor. Why more important? Because, whereas neutralizing a competitor's advantage through imitation or substitution produces only parity returns (cell 5 in Figure 1), identifying and obtaining a new resource can result in a position of competitive advantage and superior returns (cells 2, 3, or 6).

Ninth, whereas neoclassical theory—including traditional industrial organization economics views (Bain 1956)—assumes that the firm's environment, particularly the structure of its industry, strictly determines its conduct (or strategy) and performance (profits), our theory maintains that environmental factors only influence conduct and performance. Relative resource heterogeneity and immobility imply that strategic choices must be made and that these choices influence performance. All firms in an industry will not adopt the same strategy—nor should they. Different resource assortments suggest targeting different market segments and/or competing against different competitors.

Competition, then, consists of the constant struggle among firms for a comparative advantage in resources that will yield a marketplace position of competitive advantage and, thereby, superior financial performance. Once a firm's comparative advantage in resources enables it to achieve superior performance through a position of competitive advantage in some market segment or segments, competitors attempt to neutralize and/or leapfrog the advantaged firm through acquisition, imitation, substitution, or major innovation. The comparative advantage theory of competition is, therefore, inherently dynamic. Disequilibrium, not equilibrium, is the norm, in the sense of a normal state of affairs. It is also the norm in the sense of a preferred state of affairs, as we now show.

Explaining Abundance

Instead of the "assume we stop the world and see how everything would be allocated" procedure of neoclassical, long-run equilibrium, the comparative advantage theory of competition, displayed in Figure 2, explains the greater abundance in market-based economies on the basis that rewards, through time, flow to the efficient and the effective. First, the comparative advantage theory expands the kinds of resources (from land, labor, and capital) to include such intangible resources as organizational culture, knowledge, and competencies.

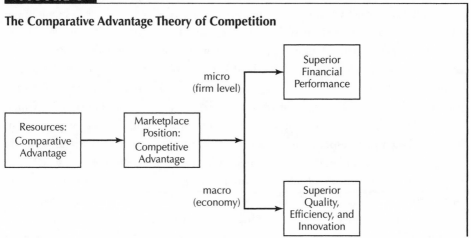

FIGURE 2

The Comparative Advantage Theory of Competition

These higher order, complex resources are most important for modern companies and their respective economies, as attested to by such modern-day successes as Japan, Singapore, and Hong Kong, which have virtually no natural resources.

Second, the theory identifies the search for a comparative advantage in resources as the powerful motivation for not only the efficient use of existing resources, but also for the creation of new ones. Thus, compared with command economies, market-based economies are more effective in creating new resources, such as distinctive organizational competencies, that can then be used efficiently. After all, determining such things as optimum plant sizes, a major part of neoclassical efficiency, is a narrow technical problem that could be solved to a high degree of precision by central planners.[13] But both central planners and individual plant managers lack the motivation for creating new resources and, hence, new efficiencies. Therefore, the comparative advantage theory explains why market-based economies continuously create resources that can produce ever more efficient production processes, which in turn produce abundance. Thus, our theory explains not only why nations that are poor in natural resources can be wealthy, but also why market-based economies keep getting more efficient and more abundant.

Comparative advantage theory straightforwardly explains why market-based economies are more innovative. Whereas in command economies there are no mechanisms for automatically rewarding innovation, rewards in market-based economies flow to firms and individuals that develop innovative processes and products. First, breakthrough innovations or "Schumpeterian shocks" (Barney 1991; Rumelt and Wensley 1981) provide

---

[13]This is one of the arguments by advocates of planned economies that was so effective in convincing neoclassicists of the superior benefits of socialism. (See references in footnote 4.)

the innovator a significant comparative advantage that can often be sustained through time. For example, Xerox's plain paper copier in the 1960s provided an advantage that endured for about a decade (Ghemawat 1986). Second, the many small innovations in processes and products that also characterize market-based economies are predicted by comparative advantage theory. These small innovations, through time, have a cumulative effect on resource advantage and, hence, on efficiency and effectiveness. Indeed, continually improving processes and products is foundational for quality assurance programs such as those advocated by Deming (Gitlow and Gitlow 1987).

As to explaining quality, rather than being exogenous or a market imperfection, superior quality is a natural outcome of a system characterized by the search for comparative advantage—rewards accrue to firms producing high-quality products. In contrast, firms in planned economies have no natural mechanisms for rewarding higher quality goods and services. Consider again the case of the Japanese car makers in the 1970s and 1980s and their adoption of Deming's views on quality. Such production competencies as just-in-time purchasing constituted a resource that produced not just lower costs but more durable, more reliable, higher quality products. Their position of competitive advantage yielded superior returns.

Explaining Firm Diversity

The comparative advantage theory of competition explains the diversity in size, scope, and profitability of firms in each industry on several grounds. First, because universal opportunism is not assumed, different firm sizes and scopes can be explained on the basis that some firms develop relationships with suppliers and/or customers that they can trust not to exploit them (Morgan and Hunt 1994), while others integrate backwards or forwards because they can find no such trustworthy partners.[14] Second, a firm may decide to conduct an activity in house, rather than contract it out, because it constitutes, or is part of an assortment of resources that constitutes, a competency. Simply put, firms do in house those activities they believe—sometimes wrongly—they have the capability of doing better. For example, whereas one auto manufacturer may perceive itself to have a distinct competency in producing engine blocks and thus be reluctant to purchase them from suppliers, another may outsource blocks because it lacks this competency resource. Third, each firm in an industry is a unique entity in time and space as a result of its history. Because of this unique history in obtaining and deploying resources, firms will differ from their competitors (Barney 1991; Dierickx and Cool 1989). For example, a firm's acquisition of a piece of property in its distant past may be now providing it a unique source of comparative advantage and influencing its size, scope, or profitability.

---

[14]Note the troubling implications for trustworthiness of the studies by Marwell and Ames (1981) showing a positive correlation between formal training in economics and prevalence of "free-riding."

Fourth, different assortments of resources may be equally efficient or effective in producing the same value for some market segments. These different assortments, therefore, lead to firms of varying size and scope, where "scope" refers to product-market diversity (Chandler 1990). Fifth, because of heterogeneous demand, servicing different market segments will likely lead to firms in the same industry with different sizes and scopes, for example, "niche" marketers. Sixth, some individual resources produce comparative advantage for only certain firms, even though their competitors service the same market segments. This is because, as discussed, it often is an assortment of interconnected resources that produce such advantages as distinct competencies. Seventh, if one or more firms servicing some market segments have a comparative advantage in resources that competitors cannot imitate, find substitutes for, or leapfrog with an entirely new resource, then these circumstances will produce diverse firms within the same industry. Eighth, the mixture of firms in an industry changes because of both changes in consumer preferences and the continuing search by all firms for a comparative advantage in resources that will yield a position of competitive advantage in the marketplace. Sometimes these efforts at innovation succeed; sometimes they do not.

Consider the substantial differences in profitability among firms. Are these differences primarily, or exclusively, attributable to differences in industry structure, as the determinism of neoclassical theory implies? Or do environmental factors just influence profitability, as maintained by our theory and the strategic choice school of researchers? Using 1975 Federal Trade Commission (FTC) line of business data, Schmalensee (1985) investigated the relative importance of firm versus industry effects on firm profitability (firm return on assets in each industry). Whereas industry effects accounted for 19.5% of the variance in firm profitability, firm effects were not significant, leading him to conclude that corporate strategy effects "simply do not exist" (p. 346).[15] Since then, several studies have questioned Schmalensee's finding that corporate strategy has no effect on firm profitability (Cubbin and Geroski 1987; Hansen and Wernerfelt 1989). For example, Rumelt (1991) extended the Schmalensee FTC study by adding data for 1974, 1976, and 1977. He found that industry effects explained only 8% of the variance in rate of return, whereas 46% of the variance was explained by business unit effects. Supporting Rumelt, Roquebert, Phillips, and Westfall (1994) found industry versus total firm (corporate plus business unit) effects to be 10% and 57%, respectively. Roquebert, Phillips, and Westfall's findings are particularly noteworthy because their sample was much larger (over 6800 corporations), had a broader base (over 940 Standard Industrial Classification four-digit categories), and included both small and large corporations. The accumulated evidence, therefore, strongly supports our

---

[15]Note that, with 80% of the variance attributed to error and only 20% attributed to industry effects, even Schmalensee's results do not imply that industry structure determines firm profitability.

theory's position that environmental factors merely influence, not totally determine, firm performance. In short, human agency matters. Strategic choices matter.

In conclusion, the comparative advantage theory of competition performs much better than neoclassical theory in explaining why market-based economies are more bountiful and innovative and have higher quality goods and services than do command economies. It also explains better why market-based economies exhibit a rich diversity of firms, even within the same industry.

Marketing and Comparative Advantage

Williamson (1981) laments the "inhospitality tradition" in economics that views with suspicion all organizational forms that depart from perfect competition. Equally lamentable is the neoclassical view that marketing is unnecessary or a presumptively nefarious market imperfection creator, or that it is to "escape" the rigors of perfect competition that firms engage in most marketing activities. As to advertising, this inhospitality tradition has resulted in the question "Is advertising anti-competitive?" being a cottage industry for neoclassicists. Much worse, it led the neoclassical historian Kuhn (1970, p. 453) to see no difference between market economies permitting advertising and command economies imposing "a common scale of values . . . by *force* and propaganda" (italics added). As to product innovations, it led neoclassicists to argue that the introduction of new breakfast cereals by cereal manufacturers is inherently anti-competitive (Cohen and Gordon 1981). As to trademarks, it led Chamberlin (1962, p. 270ff) to argue against firms having exclusive use of their brand names on the grounds that "the protection of trademarks . . . is the protection of monopoly." His "trademarks are monopolies" view led to the (unsuccessful) argument by FTC attorneys that Borden's equity in its ReaLemon trademark was anti-competitive (*Wall Street Journal* 1978).

In contrast, recall that competition in the comparative advantage theory is the constant struggle for a comparative advantage in resources that will yield a marketplace position of competitive advantage and, thereby, superior financial performance. All activities that contribute to positions of competitive advantage or the absence of which would contribute to positions of competitive disadvantage are presumptively pro-competitive— marketing activities are no exception to this rule. "Presumptively" pro-competitive does not imply that all the ways in which marketing activities are carried out are efficient, effective, or ethical or even ought to be legal. For example, it does not mean that all forms of advertising should necessarily be allowed or encouraged by society. Rather, it means that all forms of marketing activities are specifically assumed to promote competition unless (1) a form is demonstrated to be anti-competitive on the basis of evidence, where (2) such evidence does not include the fact that the activity is inconsistent with or moves away from perfect competition.

What we are arguing is analogous to the difference between a system of justice in which the defendant is presumed guilty until proved innocent versus one in which one is presumed innocent until proved guilty. Treatises on such topics as "Is advertising pro-competitive?" have historically started from the premise that "pro-competitive" meant "consistent with" or "leads in the direction of" perfect competition. Not only is perfect competition imperfect, but such a procedure—being "guilt by axiom" (Donaldson 1990)—improperly places the burden of proof on those engaging in the marketing activity.

If marketing is presumptively pro-competitive, what resources are distinctively marketing that might yield a comparative advantage? The marketing function within organizations has been, at least since the 1960s, associated with the marketing concept and the "four P's." Guided by the marketing concept, marketing has focused on decisions related to analyzing and selecting target markets, product and brand development, promotion, and channels of distribution. The activities related to each of these decision areas, it can be argued, are distinctly marketing, even though the degree of control marketing has over each decision area varies across firms and industries. Therefore, competencies with respect to these areas constitute resources when they contribute to the firm's ability to produce efficiently and/or effectively market offerings that have value. Similarly, legal rights (e.g., trademarks), physical assets (e.g., corporate-owned retail outlets), and relational assets (e.g., brand equity) can be resources. Given the recent prominence of market orientation and the controversy it has raised, we focus on it as a potential resource. In doing so, we further explicate the comparative advantage theory, show how it can be deployed, and highlight the role of resource-advantage in our theory.

The Nature of Market Orientation

The idea of market orientation traces to the marketing concept (Kohli and Jaworski 1990). Considered a marketing cornerstone since its articulation and development in the 1950s and 1960s, the marketing concept maintains that (1) all areas of the firm should be customer oriented, (2) all marketing activities should be integrated, and (3) profits, not just sales, should be the objective. As conventionally interpreted, the concept's customer-orientation component, that is, knowing one's customers and developing products to satisfy their needs, wants, and desires, has been considered paramount. Historically contrasted with the production and sales orientations, the marketing concept is considered to be a philosophy of doing business that should be a major part of a successful firm's culture (Baker, Black, and Hart 1994; Houston 1986; Wong and Saunders 1993). "In other words, the marketing concept defines a distinct organizational culture . . . that put[s] the customer in the center of the firm's thinking about strategy and operations" (Deshpandé and Webster 1989, p. 3). Indeed, "marketing should be viewed . . . as a guiding philosophy for the whole organization [because] our evidence points to improved performances among companies that adopt this wider approach" (Hooley, Lynch, and Shepherd 1990, p. 21–22). Therefore, though the marketing concept guides policies and behaviors, its cultural status makes it more permanent, more foundational, than, say, a strategy. Corporate cultures can be influenced, modified, formed, or shaped, but, unlike strategies, they are not selected.

Specifically, then, how does a market orientation relate to the marketing concept? In contrast with the marketing concept's single focus on customers, a market orientation involves a dual focus on both customers and competitors (Day and Nedungadi 1994; Jaworski and Kohli 1993; Kohli and Jaworski 1990; Narver and Slater 1990; Slater and Narver 1994; Webster 1994). Therefore, we know what a market orientation is not. It is not the same thing as, nor a different form of, nor the implementation of, the marketing concept. Rather, it would seem that a market orientation should be conceptualized as supplementary to the marketing concept. Specifically, keeping in mind the role of management in the theory of comparative advantage (see Table 1), we propose that a market orientation is (1) the systematic gathering of information on customers and competitors, both present and potential, (2) the systematic analysis of the information for the purpose of developing market knowledge, and (3) the systematic use of such knowledge to guide strategy recognition, understanding, creation, selection, implementation, and modification. We include potential customers to guard against the hazards of firms being "customer-led" (Hamel and Prahalad 1994), that is, focusing only on the articulated needs, wants, and desires of present customers. We include potential competitors to guard against the hazards of changing technology resulting in new competitors. We do not include interfunctional coordination (Narver and Slater 1990) because, though it is a factor that can contribute to implementing successfully a market orientation, such implementation factors should not appear in a concept's definition.

As to its ontological status, a market orientation should be considered a kind of organizing framework that, if adopted and implemented, could through time become culturally embedded in an organization. As such it would be intermediate between a business strategy (e.g., cost leadership) that can be selected and the preeminently cultural business philosophy identified as the marketing concept. Just as a market orientation would guide strategy selection, the marketing concept would inform the use of the components of market orientation by reminding managers to keep customers, as Webster (1994) puts it, "on a pedestal," because they always have the "final say."

Market Orientation as a Resource

Is a market orientation a resource? Marketing's strategy literature has historically categorized sources of advantage into skills and resources, in which the former are "the distinctive capabilities of personnel" and the latter are the "more tangible requirements for advantage" (Day and Wensley 1988, p. 2–3). Although its successful implementation requires skills, a market orientation is itself not a skill, nor is it more tangible than a skill. Thus, it seems not to fit this schema. Our theory views resources as the tangible and intangible entities that enable a firm to produce efficiently and/or effectively a market offering that has value for some market segment or segments. In this view, a market orientation would be an intangible entity that would be a resource if it provided information that enabled a firm to produce, for example, an offering well tailored to a market segment's specific tastes and preferences. (Note that Table 1 includes information as a basic kind of resource.)

Could a market orientation be a resource leading to comparative advantage? A market orientation stresses the importance of using information about both customers and competitors in the formulation of strategy. Therefore, the knowledge about one's competitors—their products, prices, and strategies, for example—gleaned from implementing a market orientation could potentially enable a firm to produce a market offering for some market segments more efficiently or effectively than one's competitors (Glazer 1991). We say "potentially" because a market orientation can produce a comparative advantage only if it is rare among competitors (Barney 1991). If all competitors adopt a market orientation and implement it equally well, then a comparative advantage accrues to none. Like the ante in a poker game, a market orientation would be a necessary precondition for playing the game.

Is a market orientation rare? Two studies suggest "yes." First, Jaworski and Kohli (1993, p. 64) investigate the antecedents and consequences of market orientation and conclude, "the findings of the studies suggest that the market orientation of a business is an important determinant of its performance, regardless of the market turbulence, competitive intensity or the technological turbulence of the environment in which it operates." Second, Narver and Slater (1990, p. 32) investigate the effect of a market orientation on business profitability using a sample of 140 strategic business units of a large forest-products corporation and conclude, "for both the commodity and noncommodity businesses, market orientation is an important determinant of profitability." These studies suggest that a market orientation is a resource that is rare among competitors because, if it were not, it would not be expected to lead to a position of competitive advantage (cells 2, 3, or 6 in Figure 1) and hence superior performance.

Is a market orientation a resource potentially leading to a sustainable comparative advantage and hence a position of sustainable competitive advantage and, thereby, superior long-run financial performance? The life span of a particular comparative advantage in resources—its sustainability—is determined by factors both internal and external to the firm.

INTERNAL FACTORS

A comparative advantage in resources can be dissipated, allowed to atrophy, or just plain squandered by several internal factors: (1) a failure to reinvest, (2) the presence of causal ambiguity, and (3) a failure to adapt. All resources require constant monitoring and maintenance expenditures (Dierickx and Cool 1989). For example, "a business with a reputation for superior quality could experience an erosion in quality as a source of SCA [sustainable competitive advantage] if it fails to continue investing in processes that contributed to the business's reputation for quality" (Bharadwaj, Varadarajan, and Fahy 1993). A firm may also allow a comparative advantage in resources to dissipate because the relationship between their competitive advantage in the marketplace and their comparative advantage in resources is causally ambiguous (Reed and DeFillippi 1990). In this respect, firms are like nations—both may lack an accurate understanding of their sources of wealth and both may squander such resources (Hayek 1960). Finally, a firm may fail to modify, sell, relinquish, or abandon a resource or an assortment of resources in response to a changed environment. An asset that is a resource in one environment can become a nonresource in another if it no longer contributes toward the creation of value in the firm's market offerings. Even more seriously, something that was previously a resource can become what we label a "contra-resource" and actually inhibit the creation of value in the firm's market offerings. As a case in point, consider the permanent employment issue.

Because "viewing employment as permanent creates the best incentive both for the company and its employees to invest in upgrading skills," Porter (1990, p. 594) recommends that all companies "make the commitment to maintain permanent employment to the maximum extent possible." In contrast, the view here is that permanent employment, either as a formal policy or as an informal element of a firm's culture, is not necessarily a resource in all environments. Consider IBM, an example used by Porter (1990). It is true that IBM successfully resisted involuntary layoffs for over 70 years and that this fostered worker loyalty and a low personnel turnover rate. By the 1990s, however, according to Hays (1994), the permanent employment aspect of IBM's culture appears to have been transformed into a feeling by IBM employees that they were "entitled to their jobs," which then led to employee "lethargy." Thus, the resource of permanent employment became the contra-resource of job entitlement (Hays 1994, p. A5):

> Through the mid-1980s Big Blue enjoyed 40 percent of the industry's world-wide sales and 70 percent of all profits. The no-layoffs vow backfired badly when trouble hit in the late 1980s. From 1986–1993, IBM took $28 billion in charges, half of it for voluntary buy outs and cut the payroll by 37 percent.

A policy of permanent employment may be a resource, nonresource, or contra-resource, depending on a firm's competitive position and its environment.

EXTERNAL FACTORS

A firm's comparative advantage in resources can be neutralized by the actions of consumers, government, or competitors. Changes in consumer tastes and preferences in a market segment can turn a resource into a nonresource or contra-resource. Thus, for example, a distribution system that emphasizes franchised dealers can shift from resource to nonresource if consumers decide that they desire to purchase the items in question from discount stores. In like manner, governmental actions can destroy the value-creating potential of a resource through laws and regulation. Changes in patent, trademark, franchising, and other laws can destroy a resource's comparative advantage.

Competitors' actions that can neutralize a resource's comparative advantage include attempting to purchase the same resource as an advantaged competitor, imitating the competitor's resource, searching for a strategically equivalent resource, or searching for a strategically superior resource, that is, a major innovation (Barney 1991; Dierickx and Cool 1989; Lippman and Rumelt 1982; Peteraf 1993; Reed and DeFillipi 1990; Wernerfelt 1984). The effectiveness of these actions and the time it takes for them to neutralize a specific competitor's resource advantage successfully depend on characteristics of the marketplace offering, the resources producing the offering, and the competitor's resources.

As to the marketplace offering, the key characteristic is ambiguity. Although competitors may know that consumers in the market segments strongly prefer their rival's offering, there may be great ambiguity as to precisely what attributes of the offering are making it perceived to be superior. Furthermore, there may be great ambiguity as to specifically which resources are being used to produce the highly valued attributes. These two sources of causal ambiguity (resource → offering; offering → consumer) can create great uncertainty and thus render ineffective attempts to neutralize a competitor's comparative advantage.

As to resources, the major characteristics affecting the life span of an advantage are mobility, complexity, interconnectedness, mass efficiencies, tacitness, and time compression diseconomies. The advantage brought by mobile resources, those that are commonly bought and sold in the marketplace (such as machinery), can be neutralized effectively and quickly. Intangible, higher order resources, such as an organizational competency in new product testing, cannot be neutralized as quickly. Often difficult to neutralize are complex resources, those involving combinations of many resources, and interconnected resources, those for which competitors may lack access to a critical component. Mass efficiencies spring from the fact that some resources require a "critical mass" before they can be deployed effectively. Tacit resources encompass skills that are noncodifiable and must be learned by doing and thus cannot be bought. Time compression diseconomies refers to the fact that some resources, such as a reputation for trustworthiness, by their very nature take time to acquire. All these factors make it more difficult for a competitor to acquire or imitate a competitor's advantage-producing resource, making such a resource, to varying degrees, sustainable.

In light of the preceding, is a market orientation a source of sustainable comparative advantage? Consider a hypothetical firm that is market oriented and enjoying a comparative advantage. (Its competitors, as Aaker [1988, p. 13] puts it, are "internally oriented.")

Thus, this firm chooses its target markets more wisely than its competitors and its offerings are better tailored to its customers' preferences. Could its advantage be sustained? As to internal factors, though the firm might fail to reinvest in its information-gathering activities (allowing its advantage to dissipate), adapting to changing customer requirements and competitor actions is a specific component of the firm's orientation. Furthermore, because the firm knows its customers and its competitors, this would contribute greatly to knowing itself, thus attenuating any causal ambiguity as to why it is enjoying superior financial performance.

As to external factors, knowing its customers and competitors should allow the firm to respond to changes in consumer preferences and competitor strategies in an informed, perhaps even optimal, manner. Furthermore, just as many firms give "lip service" (Aaker 1988, p. 212) to being customer oriented, competitors may not recognize a genuinely market-oriented competitor when they encounter one. Moreover, a market orientation is intangible, cannot be purchased in the marketplace, is socially complex in its structure, has components that are highly interconnected, has mass efficiencies, and is probably increasingly effective the longer it has been in place. Finally, there is probably a significant tacit dimension to implementing a market orientation effectively. Employees learn how to be market oriented not solely from reading policy manuals or textbooks but from associating with other employees that are already market oriented. Consequently, there are good grounds for believing that a truly market-oriented firm can enjoy a sustainable comparative advantage that can lead to a position of sustainable competitive advantage and superior long-run financial performance.

Conclusion

The "strategy dialogue," having already produced a new theory of the firm, is evolving toward a new theory of competition. Our purpose has been to identify the foundations of this new theory and its implications for marketing. The set of ten foundational premises in Table 1 constitute, we propose, the grounds for the comparative advantage theory of competition. Although these premises, taken individually, have been discussed by others at numerous times in many places, this article is the first to place them into a cohesive theory. Contrasting the theory's premises with those of neoclassical perfect competition facilitates understanding the structure of this new theory. A theory of competition should be required to explain not only why economies premised on competing firms are superior to economies premised on cooperating firms in terms of the quantity, quality, and innovativeness of goods and services, but also the phenomenon of firm diversity in market-based economies. Our analysis indicates that the comparative advantage theory of competition explains these key macro and micro phenomena better than its perfect competition rival.

Because competition is the constant struggle among firms for a comparative advantage in resources that will yield a marketplace position of competitive advantage and, thereby, superior financial performance, marketing activities shift from being a presumptively nefarious market imperfection creator to being, like other firm activities, presumptively pro-competitive. As a consequence, some may view (and perhaps attack) the comparative advantage theory as self-serving for marketing. In response, self-servingness is a red herring. Though our theory does indeed serve, and serve well, the interests of marketing academe and practice, the self-servingness of our theory is irrelevant. The relevant questions are, "Is the theory true? Is the real world constructed as the theory suggests, or is it not?" (Hunt 1990, p.1). That our theory explains key macro and micro phenomena gives us good reason, according to scientific realism (Hunt 1990), to believe that something exists that is like the entities and structure postulated by the theory.

Much conceptual and empirical work must be done to test, explore, and further explicate the structure and implications of the theory. Are there additional foundational premises that should be included? If so, which ones, and why? What other resources are distinctively marketing that might provide a comparative advantage? For example, is relationship marketing such a resource and, if so, under what conditions? If perfect competition should not be the norm for guiding public policy, how can and should comparative advantage theory be employed? Can and should the theory be mathematized?

Finally, marketing should harbor no illusions, let alone delusions. We can and should work on developing the comparative advantage theory, use it as a foundation for research, promote it as superior to perfect competition, and—for our students—incorporate it in our texts. We also can expunge such neoclassical locutions as "economic rents," "abnormal profits," "market imperfections," and "assuming perfect competition" from our discipline's lexicon. However, as the epigraph reminds us, what we cannot do is have an impact on neoclassical economic theory. The edifice of general equilibrium theory, with its base of perfect competition theory, is elegant, mathematically formalized, and aesthetically pleasing.[16] It is deeply embedded within a discipline that is large and influential, especially when compared with marketing. Neoclassical economics has enormous sunk costs in perfect competition. Indeed, all evidence of the theoretical, predictive, explanatory, and normative deficiencies of the set of beliefs that has perfect competition at its core has always been summarily dismissed. Perfect competition is unshakable, immutable, and impregnable. Nothing can be done.

Then again, Ptolemaic astronomy had all the preceding going for it plus the imprimatur of the Church. Hmm. . . .

---

[16]Rosenberg (1992) argues that neoclassical economics has become neither an empirical science nor an appropriate normative ideal for public policy. Rather, he maintains that neoclassical economics has become a branch of applied mathematics.

References

Aaker, David A. (1988), *Strategic Market Management*. New York: John Wiley & Sons.

Alderson, Wroe (1957), *Marketing Behavior and Executive Action*. Homewood, IL: Richard D. Irwin, Inc.

___ (1965), *Dynamic Marketing Behavior*. Homewood, IL: Richard D. Irwin, Inc.

Alston, Lee J. and William Gillespie (1989), "Resource Coordination and Transaction Costs: A Framework for Analyzing the Firm/Market Boundary," *Journal of Economic Behavior and Organization*, 11 (2), 191–212.

Bain, Joe S. (1956), *Barriers to New Competition*. Cambridge, MA: Harvard University Press.

Baker, Michael J., C.D. Black and S.J. Hart (1994), "Competitive Success in Sunrise and Sunset Industries," in *The Marketing Initiative*, J. Sunders, ed. London: Prentice Hall, 1994.

Balassa, Bela A. (1974), "Success Criteria for Economic Systems," in *Comparative Economic Systems*, Morris Bernstein, ed. Homewood, IL: Richard D. Irwin, 2–18.

Barney, Jay (1991), "Firm Resources and Sustained Competitive Advantage," *Journal of Management*, 17 (1), 99–120.

Berry, Leonard L. and A. Parasuraman (1991), *Marketing Services*. New York: The Free Press.

Bharadwaj, Sundar, P. Rajan Varadarajan, and John Fahy (1993). "Sustainable Competitive Advantage in Service Industries: A Conceptual Model and Research Propositions," *Journal of Marketing*, 57 (October), 83–99.

Business Week (1991), "Don't Persecute Microsoft for Doing Things Well" (April 29), 29.

___ (1994a), "Gunning for Microsoft" (May 9), 90.

___ (1994b), "Bill Gate's Soft Landing: A Settlement" (July 25), 40.

Chamberlin, Edward (1933/1962), *The Theory of Monopolistic Competition*. Cambridge, MA: Harvard University Press.

Chandler, Alfred D. (1990), *Scale and Scope: The Dynamics of Industrial Capitalism*. Cambridge, MA: Harvard University Press.

Clark, John Maurice (1961), *Competition as a Dynamic Process*. Washington, DC: Brookings Institution.

Coase, R. H. (1937/1952), "The Nature of the Firm," in *Readings in Price Theory*, G.J. Stigler and K.E. Boulding, eds. Chicago: Irwin, 331–51.

Cohen, Stanley T. and Richard L. Gordon (1981), "FTC Judge Tosses Cereal Industry Case," *Advertising Age* (September 14), 121.

Collis, David J. (1991), "A Resource Board Analysis of Global Competition," *Strategic Management Journal*, 12 (1), 49–68.

Conner, Kathleen (1991), "A Historical Comparison of Resource-Based Theory and Five Schools of Thought Within Industrial-Organization Economics: Do We Have a New Theory of the Firm?" *Journal of Management*, 17 (March), 121–54.

Cowling, K. and D.C. Mueller (1978), "The Social Cost of Monopoly Power," *Economic Journal*, 88 (December), 727–48.

Cubbin, J. and P. Geroski (1987), "The Convergence of Profits in the Long Run: Inter-firm and Inter-industry Comparisons," *Journal of Industrial Economics*, 35, 427–42.

Day, George (1984), *Strategic Market Planning: The Pursuit of Competitive Advantage*. Minneapolis: West Publishing Co.

___ (1992), "Marketing's Contribution to the Strategy Dialogue," *Journal of the Academy of Marketing Science*, 20 (Fall), 323–30.

___ and Prakesh Nedungadi (1994), "Managerial Representations of Competitive Advantage," *Journal of Marketing,* 58 (April), 31–44.

Day, George S. and Robin Wensley (1988), "Assessing Advantage: A Framework for Diagnosing Competitive Superiority," *Journal of Marketing,* 52 (April), 1–20.

Demsetz, H. (1973), "Industry Structure, Market Rivalry, and Public Policy," *Journal of Law and Economics,* 16, 1–9.

___ (1975), "Two Systems of Belief About Monopoly," in *Industrial Concentration: The New Learning,* H. Goldschmid, H.M. Mann, and J.F. Weston, eds. Boston: Little, Brown, 164–84.

Deshpandé, Rohit and Frederick E. Webster, Jr. (1989), "Organizational Culture and Marketing: Defining the Research Agenda," *Journal of Marketing,* 53 (January), 3–15.

Dickson, Peter Reid (1992), "Toward a General Theory of Competitive Rationality," *Journal of Marketing,* 56 (January), 69–83.

Dierickx, Ingemar and Karel Cool (1989), "Asset Stock Accumulation and Sustainability of Competitive Advantage," *Management Science,* 35 (December), 1504–11.

Donaldson, Lex (1990), "The Ethereal Hand: Organization Economics and Management Theory," *Academy of Management Journal,* 15 (3), 369–81.

Dwyer, F. Robert, Paul H. Schurr, and Sejo Oh (1987), "Developing Buyer-Seller Relationships," *Journal of Marketing,* 51 (April), 11–27.

Etzioni, Amitai (1988), *The Moral Dimension: Toward a New Economics.* New York: The Free Press.

Fisher, F., Z. Griliches, and C. Kaysen (1962), "The Cost of Automobile Model Changes Since 1949," *Journal of Political Economy,* 70 (October), 433–51.

Ghemawat, Pankaj (1986), "Sustainable Advantage," *Harvard Business Review* (September-October), 53–58.

Gitlow, Howard S. and Shelly J. Gitlow (1987), *The Deming Guide to Quality and Competitive Position.* Englewood Cliffs, NJ: Prentice Hall.

Glazer, Rashi (1991), "Marketing in an Information-Intensive Environment: Strategic Implications of Knowledge as an Asset," *Journal of Marketing,* 55 (October), 1–19.

Gould, John P. and Edward P. Lazear (1989), *Microeconomic Theory.* Homewood, IL: Richard D. Irwin, Inc.

Hamel, Gary and C. K. Prahalad (1994), *Competing for the Future.* Cambridge, MA: Harvard Business School Press.

Hansen, Gary S. and Birger Wernerfelt (1989), "Determinants of Firm Performance: The Relative Importance of Economic and Organizational Factors," *Strategic Management Journal,* 10 (September–October), 399–411.

Harberger, A. (1954), "Monopoly and Resource Allocation," *American Economic Review,* 44 (May), 77–87.

Hayek, Frederick A. (1960), *The Constitution of Liberty.* Chicago: University of Chicago Press.

Hays, Laurie (1994), "Blue Period: Gerstner is Struggling as He Tries to Change Ingrained IBM Culture," *Wall Street Journal* (May 13), 1, A5.

Hofer, C. and Dan Schendel (1978), *Strategy Formulation: Analytical Concepts.* St. Paul, MN: West Publishing Co.

Hooley, George J., J.E. Lynch and J. Shepherd (1990), "The Marketing Concept: Putting the Theory Into Practice," *European Journal of Marketing,* 24 (9), 7–23.

Houston, Franklin (1986), "The Marketing Concept: What It Is and What It Is Not," *Journal of Marketing,* 50 (April), 81–87.

Hunt, Shelby D. (1990), "Truth in Marketing Theory and Research," *Journal of Marketing,* 54 (July), 1–15.

___ (1991), *Modern Marketing Theory: Critical Issues in the Philosophy of Marketing Science.* Cincinnati: South-Western Publishing Co.

____ and Arturo Vasquez-Parraga (1993), "Organizational Consequences, Marketing Ethics, and Salesforce Supervision," *Journal of Marketing Research,* 30 (February), 78–90.

Jacobson, Robert (1992), "The 'Austrian' School of Strategy," *Academy of Management Review,* 17 (4), 782–807.

Jaworski, Bernard J. and Ajay K. Kohli (1993), "Market Orientation: Antecedents and Consequences," *Journal of Marketing,* 57 (July), 53–70.

John, George (1984), "An Empirical Investigation of Some Antecedents of Opportunism in a Marketing Channel," *Journal of Marketing Research,* 21 (August), 278–89.

Jones, Ronald W. and Peter B. Kenen (1984), *Handbook of International Economics.* Amsterdam: North-Holland.

Keller, Mary Ann (1993), *Collision: GM, Toyota, Volkswagen and the Race to Own the 21st Century.* New York: Currency Doubleday.

Knight, Frank H. (1936), "The Place of Marginal Economics in Socialist Calculation," *American Economic Review, Papers and Proceedings,* 26, 255–66.

Kohli, Ajay K. and Bernard J. Jaworski (1990), "Market Orientation: The Construct, Research Propositions, and Managerial Implications," *Journal of Marketing,* 54 (April), 1–18.

Kuhn, William E. (1970), *The Evolution of Economic Thought.* Cincinnati: South-Western Publishing Co.

Lavin, Douglas (1994), "Chrysler Is Now Lowest-Cost Producer in Auto Industry, Harbour Report Says," *Wall Street Journal* (June 23), B3.

Lavoie, Don (1985), *Rivalry and Central Planning.* Cambridge: Cambridge University Press.

Lekachman, Robert (1959), *A History of Economic Ideas.* New York: Harper.

Lippman, S.A. and R.P. Rumelt (1982), "Uncertain Imitability," *Bell Journal of Economics,* 13, 418–38.

Marwell, Gerald and Ruth E. Ames (1981), "Economists Free Ride: Does Anyone Else?" *Journal of Public Economics,* 15, 295–310.

McGee, J.S. (1975), "Efficiency and Economies of Size," in *Industrial Concentration: The New Learning,* H. Goldschmid, H.M. Mann, and J.F. Weston, eds. Boston: Little, Brown, 55–105.

McKee, Daryl O., P. Rajan Varadarajan, and William M. Pride (1989), "Strategic Adaptability and Firm Performance: A Market-Contingent Perspective," *Journal of Marketing,* 53 (July), 21–35.

Mintzberg, Henry (1987), "Crafting Strategy," *Harvard Business Review* (July–August), 66–75.

Montgomery, C.A. and Michael E. Porter (1991), *Strategy: Seeking and Securing Competitive Advantage.* Boston: Harvard Business School Publishing.

Morgan, Robert M. and Shelby D. Hunt (1994), "The Commitment-Trust Theory of Relationship Marketing," *Journal of Marketing,* 58 (July), 20–38.

Narver, John C. and Stanley F. Slater (1990), "The Effect of Market Orientation on Business Profitability," *Journal of Marketing,* 54 (October), 20–35.

Parvatiyar, Atul, Jagdish N. Sheth, and F. Brown Whittington, Jr. (1992), "Paradigm Shift in Interfirm Marketing Relationships: Emerging Research Issues," working paper, Emory University.

Peteraf, Margaret A. (1993), "The Cornerstones of Competitive Advantage: A Resource-Based View," *Strategic Management Journal,* 14(3), 179–91.

Porter, Michael E. (1980), *Competitive Advantage.* New York: The Free Press.

____ (1985), *Competitive Strategy.* New York: The Free Press.

____ (1990), *The Competitive Advantage of Nations.* New York: The Free Press.

____ (1991), "Towards a Dynamic Theory of Strategy," *Strategic Management Journal,* 12, 95–117.

Prahalad, C.K. and Gary Hamel (1990), "The Core Competence of the Corporation," *Harvard Business Review* (May–June), 79–91.

Reed, Richard and Robert J. DeFillippi (1990), "Causal Ambiguity, Barriers to Imitation, and Sustainable Competitive Advantage," *Academy of Management Review,* 15 (January), 88–117.

Roquebert, Jaime A., Robert L. Phillips and Peter A. Westfall (1994), "Markets Versus Management: What 'Drives' Profitability," working paper, Texas Tech University.

Rosenberg, Alexander (1992), *Economics: Mathematical Politics or Science of Diminishing Returns?* Chicago: University of Chicago Press.

Rumelt, Richard P. (1991), "How Much Does Industry Matter?" *Strategic Management Journal* 12, 167–85.

___ and Robin Wensley (1981), "In Search of the Market Share Effect," in *Academy of Management Proceedings,* K. Chung, ed. Hanover, PA: Sheridan Press, 2–6.

Schmalensee, Robert (1985), "Do Markets Differ Much?" *American Economic Review,* 75 (3), 341–50.

Schumpeter, Joseph A. (1950), *Capitalism, Socialism, and Democracy.* New York: Harper & Row.

Shapiro, Benson P. (1988), "What the Hell is Market Oriented," *Harvard Business Review,* 66 (November–December), 119–25.

Shepherd, William G. (1982), "Causes of Increased Competition in the U.S. Economy, 1939–1980," *Review of Economics and Statistics* (November), 613–26.

Siegfried, J. J. and T. K. Tieman (1974), "The Welfare Cost of Monopoly: An Inter-Industry Analysis," *Economic Inquiry,* 12 (June), 190–202.

Simon, Herbert A. (1979), "Rational Decision Making in Business Organizations," *American Economic Review,* 69 (September), 493–512.

Slater, Stanley F. and John C. Narver (1994), "Does Competitive Environment Moderate the Market Orientation-Performance Relationship?" *Journal of Marketing,* 58 (January), 46–55.

Stigler, George J. (1949), *Five Lectures on Economic Problems.* New York: The Macmillan Co.

___ (1951), "The Division of Labor is Limited by the Extent of the Market," *Journal of Political Economy,* 59 (3), 185–93.

___ (1964), "A Theory of Oligopoly," *Journal of Political Economy,* 72(1), 44–61.

___ (1966), *The Theory of Price.* New York: Macmillan Co.

Taylor, Robert E. (1982), "Antitrust Enforcement Will Be More Selective," *Wall Street Journal* (January 11), 6.

Thorelli, Hans (1986), "Networks: Between Markets and Hierarchies," *Strategic Management Journal,* 7, 37–51.

Wall Street Journal (1978), "Borden Ordered to Alter Pricing for ReaLemon" (November 24), 8.

Webster, Frederick E., Jr. (1992), "The Changing Role of Marketing in the Corporation," *Journal of Marketing,* 56 (October), 1–17.

___ (1994), "Executing the Marketing Concept," *Marketing Management,* 3 (1), 9–16.

Wernerfelt, B. (1984), "A Resource-based View of the Firm," *Strategic Management Journal,* 5, 171–80.

Williamson, Oliver E. (1975), *Markets and Hierarchies: Analysis and Anti-trust Implications.* New York: The Free Press.

___ (1981), "The Modern Corporation: Origins, Evolution, Attributes," *Journal of Economic Literature,* 19 (December), 1537–68.

___ (1983), "Credible Commitments: Using Hostages to Support Exchange," *American Economic Review,* 73, 519–40

___ (1985), *The Economic Institutions of Capitalism.* New York: The Free Press.

___ (1989), "Transaction Cost Economics," in *Handbook of Industrial Organization,* R. Schmalensee and R. D. Willig, eds. Amsterdam: North Holland, 136–82.

Wong, V. and J. Saunders (1993), "Business Organization and Corporate Success," *Journal of Strategic Marketing,* 1 (March), 20–40.

DEVELOPMENT AND TESTING OF A MODEL OF CONSIDERATION SET COMPOSITION

John H. Roberts and James M. Lattin

The authors develop a model of consideration set composition. The approach taken is to compare the marginal expected benefits of including an additional brand in the consideration set with its associated costs of consideration. From an expression of the utility that a brand needs to gain membership in an existing consideration set, the authors derive an expression for set composition and optimal set size. They develop a measurement method to test the model at the individual level and apply it to the ready-to-eat cereal market. The model is tested in two ways. First, the utility function is calibrated at the individual level and the model is used to predict consideration of existing brands. The calibrated model also is used to forecast individual consideration of three new product concepts. Second, the predictive ability of a two-stage model of consideration and choice is tested against a traditional one-stage choice model. The authors conclude with a discussion of management implications of the model in terms of auditing currently available brands and new product management.

In the study of consumer choice processes, most marketing texts describe a sequence of stages during which the number of brands decreases (though perhaps not monotonically) until a final choice is made (e.g., Kotler 1988, Figure 6–5). For a given consumer, the brands available on the market usually are divided into brands of which the consumer is aware and those of which he or she is not aware. This *awareness set* is divided further into brands the consumer would consider purchasing, sometimes called the *evoked set* or the *consideration set,* and those that are not considered. The purchase decision is restricted to the brands in the consideration set. See also Campbell (1969) and Howard and Sheth (1969).

Consideration is a key element of consumer behavior that is attracting increasing academic and managerial attention (see Shocker et al. 1991 for a review of contemporary research questions). In many product categories, leading brands may derive large share

JOHN H. ROBERTS is Associate Professor of Marketing, Australian Graduate School of Management, University of New South Wales. JAMES M. LATTIN is Associate Professor of Marketing and Management Science, Graduate School of Business, Stanford University.

The authors acknowledge the financial support of Pacific Dunlop and Kellogg Australia. Sue Jenkins, Deborah Gifford. Dennis Gensch, Gary Lilien, Peter McBurney, David Midgley, Pam Morrison, and Brian Ratchford provided considerable input to the article, and Chan Su Park gave valuable support in analyzing the data. The authors also appreciate the insightful comments of four anonymous *JMR* reviewers. The order of the authors' names has been chosen arbitrarily, not as a reflection of their relative contributions to the research.

Roberts, John H. and James M. Lattin (1991), "Development and Testing of a Model of Consideration Set Composition," *Journal of Marketing Research,* 28 (November), 429–440.

advantages by entering the consideration sets of more consumers than do their principal competitors. Analysis of consideration sets is important if the consideration stage is of managerial interest in its own right (e.g., for a computer manufacturer wanting to ensure that it is included in a request for proposal to tender) or if consumers' evoked set sizes are small in relation to the number of brands of which they are aware. Despite the importance of consideration, its determinants have received relatively little attention in the literature; there is a distinct lack of systematic studies to model and test the process by which brands enter the consideration set.

We develop and test a model of consideration set composition and discuss its implications. In contrast to Hauser and Wernerfelt (1990), who concentrate on the aggregate, market-level implications of consideration, we focus on individual decision making. Assuming a utility-maximizing consumer, we show how utility (represented by using a compensatory multiattribute model) and mental processing costs determine consideration. Our model provides a closed-form algebraic expression that enables us to describe the circumstances under which a brand will or will not enter the consideration set. With some simplifying assumptions about the nature of costs, we are also able to use the model to characterize the composition of the consumer's consideration set at a given point in time. Thus, we are able to forecast consideration behavior at the individual level. We also derive an expression for the optimal number of brands in the consideration set as a function of brand utilities and consideration costs.

To test the model, we develop a measurement method and apply it to the ready-to-eat cereal market. Using individual-level data, we test the model in two ways. First, we calibrate the utility function at the individual level, and use a jackknife validation to predict consideration of currently available brands. We also use the calibrated model to forecast individual consideration of three new product concepts. Second, we test the predictive ability of a two-stage model of consideration and choice versus some simple reference models.

Having modeled consideration as a function of multiattribute utility, we can determine how it will be affected by elements of the marketing mix (e.g., product features, price, and advertising aimed at changing the perceptual position). That information enables us to determine the effect of different marketing strategies on the consideration of currently available brands. We also can estimate the consideration of new products under different marketing mix scenarios. In addition to evaluating strategies aimed specifically at consideration, we can use the method as one component in a two-stage model of consideration and choice.

Literature

The study of consideration was pursued initially under the rubric of evoked set analysis, first used by Howard (1963) and Campbell (1969). However, "evoked set" has been used with several different meanings, from "brands the consumer would consider" to "brands acceptable to the customer." Wright and Barbour (1977) use the term "consideration set" to describe "brands that a consumer will consider." Because it is not clouded by the ambiguity surrounding evoked sets, we use the latter term. We define a consideration set to be "the brands that a consumer would consider buying in the near future." In studying consideration sets, one can model their dynamics as search occurs or model their composition at any point in time. Both are interesting problems. Here, we develop a model that describes the consideration set at a given point in time. Examples of cases in which the model is relevant include a company's request for tenders (which happens at a specific point in time) and a consumer's choice of frequently purchased packaged goods (when the consumer maintains a repertoire of products appropriate to various occasions).

The concept of consideration fits well with theory in consumer behavior, which suggests that for complex decisions or those involving many alternatives a consumer is likely to employ a decision process that can be represented by a phased decision rule (see Bettman 1979, p. 215). For example, the consumer might undertake a two-stage process, first filtering available alternatives and then undertaking detailed analysis of the reduced set (e.g., Wright and Barbour 1977). Bettman (1979) suggests that phased decision strategies, with an elimination phase and a choice phase, are likely to be used when the number of alternatives is large. Gensch (1987b) provides empirical support for the notion that screening rules may be invoked for as few as four alternatives.

The concept of consideration is also a logical outcome of the literature on information search in economics. That research is based on the premise that a consumer will continue to search for information as long as the expected returns from search (in terms of making a choice of higher expected utility) exceed the marginal cost of further searching (e.g., Stigler 1961). In marketing, Shugan (1980) developed a model of mental processing costs, which showed that the cost of search is proportional to the number of brands the consumer evaluates and the difficulty of making comparisons. Ratchford (1980) estimated the expected benefit of searching second, third, and fourth brands for various household appliances.

Consideration also has an important role in the field of transportation economics. Gaudry and Dagenais (1979) differentiated between consumers who considered all available brands and "captive" consumers (i.e., consumers with consideration sets of a single choice alternative). Other researchers have developed models to account for consideration sets probabilistically. For example, Swait and Ben-Akiva (1987) suggest a theory of constraints, which operate on different consumers to different degrees, to describe the probability distribution of all possible consideration sets.

In addition to their theoretical basis, consideration sets have strong empirical support. Consideration sets have been studied for consumer durable goods and packaged goods, as well as industrial products. Most of the empirical work has been largely descriptive, reporting evoked or consideration set sizes and searching for correlates of the size of an individual's evoked set in terms of attitudes to the category, innovativeness, information search, and sociodemographic characteristics (e.g., Reilly and Parkinson 1985). See Hauser and Wernerfelt (1990) for a list of average evoked set sizes from several published and unpublished studies.

Though research in other areas has offered both theoretical rationale and empirical support for consideration sets, marketing modelers have been slow to develop frameworks that specify the way in which determinants of consideration operate. The consumer behavior literature strongly favors noncompensatory models at the consideration phase (e.g., Gensch 1987b), though compensatory models also have been shown to give good fits. In studies comparing the relative fit of the two types of model, Brisoux and Laroche (1981) found a conjunctive model superior to a compensatory model, whereas Parkinson and Reilly (1979) found the converse. In both cases, the difference in fit was very low. Roberts (1989) argues that both formulations are appropriate on the basis of Narayana and Markin's (1975) classification of nonconsidered alternatives into *inept* and *inert* brands. Consumers may use a conjunctive rule to screen out unacceptable brands (inept) and a compensatory rule to screen out brands of insufficient utility (inert).

We choose to model consideration as a compensatory process, which we feel serves as a useful first approximation. Though the consumer behavior literature argues for noncompensatory screening processes on theoretical grounds, a substantial literature suggests that under a wide range of situations, compensatory models provide a reasonably accurate approximation to noncompensatory processes (see Johnson and Meyer 1984 for a review). That may well explain why compensatory models have performed so well in practice. Hence, though we argue that the cost-benefit framework we propose is a realistic description of the process consumers actually undertake, it may well be that modeling it in a compensatory way is merely a representation of a different form of decision rule.

Two developments in the modeling of consideration as a compensatory process are those of Roberts (1983, 1989) and Hauser and Wernerfelt (1990). Both assume utility-maximizing consumers who form consideration sets by a tradeoff of the expected future benefits of having more brands from which to chose against the cost of processing them. The primary difference between the two is in emphasis. Roberts concentrates at the individual level, examining the conditions under which brands enter or leave the consideration set; Hauser and Wernerfelt use their general theory to test specific hypotheses about market structure at the aggregate level. The tests include the distribution of consideration set sizes, order-of-entry effects, asymmetric advertising effects, and competitive activity. Our intended contribution is to model overall consideration set membership (not just whether a new brand will join a current set) and to determine the size of the consideration set as a function of brand utilities and consideration costs.

Model Development

In this section, we present the criterion for a brand to enter the consumer's consideration set, expressed as a tradeoff between utility and mental storage and processing costs. Assuming linear costs of consideration, we are able to use this criterion to describe consideration set composition and optimal consideration set size. Finally, taking into account the error in the consideration process, we develop a two-stage model including both consideration and choice components.

Given awareness of the brand by the consumer, we model consideration as a cost-benefit evaluation. The benefit provided by the consideration set is reflected in the expected maximum utility of a choice from the set, modeled by means of a logit choice framework. The cost is determined by the total costs associated with maintaining the consideration set (e.g., search costs, thinking costs, mental processing and storage costs, etc.), which we refer to as *consideration costs*. Because significant cognitive costs are involved as well as physical search costs, consideration costs cannot be measured by direct observation. We therefore impute them by using information on consideration set composition. By comparing the expected value of a consideration set with the costs involved in maintaining it, we are able to determine which brands should enter the set.

As has been pointed out, consideration sets have been observed for both packaged goods and durable goods. The formulation of our model can be expected to hold for both types of products. In both cases, adding more brands to the consideration set yields increasing expected utility at a decreasing rate, which at some point is more than offset by the additional costs of consideration.

CONSIDERATION

We begin with the modeling framework used by Roberts (1989) to describe the consideration of a single brand. We use that framework to develop a model of the total composition of the consideration set and to derive a closed-form expression for consideration set size. Let N denote the number of brands in the awareness set of the consumer. We model the consumer's utility for brand i, u_i, by using an additive utility function (Keeney and Raiffa 1976, p. 295). Thus,

$$u_i = \sum_k w_k y_{ki}, \tag{1}$$

where y_{ki} is the amount of attribute k possessed by brand i (measured directly) and w_k are the estimated utility function coefficients.[1] Without loss of generality, we find it useful

---

[1]Equation 1 and all those that follow hold at the individual level. We choose to omit the subscript for notational simplicity. A more complicated formulation of equation 1, in which one allows for variability in w_k (due to phenomena such as variety seeking) and in y_{ki} (due to product marketing activity, etc.), is also possible.

to index the brands in order of decreasing utility to the consumer. Thus, brand 1 provides the consumer with the highest utility and brand N provides the least.

Note that u_i represents the consumer's *beliefs* about the average utility offered by brand i. On a given choice occasion, those beliefs may not be exact because of uncertainty about product attributes (likely to be a significant factor in consumer durable goods) and various contextual factors such as variety seeking, occasional lack of availability, different users and uses within the household, and promotional activity. It is this uncertainty about which brand will provide the maximum utility on any given choice occasion that leads the consumer to consider more than one brand. We chose to model the uncertainty in utility (e.g., the variation due to contextual factors, etc.) by using a stochastic additive component (ϵ_i) that is independently and identically distributed according to the double exponential distribution.[2]

Roberts' (1989) model of consideration is based on the utility derived by the consumer from the chosen brand at the time of purchase. If we assume that the consumer chooses the brand with highest utility on a given choice occasion (i.e., the brand with the highest $u_i + \epsilon_i$) from the consideration set, the probability of choosing brand i from consideration set C, denoted p_i, is given by the following multinomial logit model (McFadden 1973).

$$p_i = \exp(u_i) \Big/ \sum_{j \in C} \exp(u_j) \tag{2}$$

Roberts (1989) also uses the logit framework to establish the total expected benefit associated with any consideration set C. Ben-Akiva and Lerman (1985) show that under the assumptions of the logit model, the expected maximum utility of a choice from C, denoted $EU(C)$, is given by

$$EU(C) = \ln \left(\sum_{j \in C} \exp(u_j) \right). \tag{3}$$

Though the logit formulation of brand choice provides an extremely tractable form of analysis, it does not come without cost. The first cost is that our model involves independence of irrelevant alternatives (IIA), so we can say nothing about brand interaction in the formation of the set. The second cost is the logit model assumption that the error term associated with utility (ϵ_i) is identically distributed across brands, which precludes looking at the extra benefits that high variance brands can offer the consumer. The latter phenomenon has been well studied in the literature on the economics of information (e.g., Weitzman 1979).

---

[2]If the mean of the stochastic error term ϵ_i were zero, we could refer to u_i as the consumer's *expected* utility for brand i. However, under the assumptions of the logit model (which implies a double-exponential distribution of ϵ_i), that would not be strictly correct. We therefore refer to u_i as utility, recognizing that it captures the component that does not vary across choice occasions because of contextual effects (etc.).

Brand i will enter the consideration set if the increase in expected utility due to choosing from the enlarged set $C \cup \{i\}$ more than offsets the associated costs of adding brand i. In other words, brand i enters if

$$(4) \qquad\qquad EU(C \cup i) - EU(C) > c_i,$$

where c_i are the incremental costs (over and above the costs already incurred in maintaining consideration set C) of maintaining the set $C \cup \{i\}$. The costs of considering a brand may have many aspects. Searching for more information will be one that is important for one-time purchases such as consumer and industrial durable goods. For packaged goods, for which experience is more easily obtained, mental maintenance (or storage) and processing costs may predominate.

Substituting the expression for $EU(C)$ from equation 3 and rearranging terms, we can express the criterion either as the maximum cost that a consumer will bear (given the utility of brand i) or the minimum utility brand i needs to enter the consideration set (given the associated costs of adding the brand):[3]

$$c_i < \ln \left[1 + \left(\exp(u_i) \Big/ \sum_{j \in C} \exp(u_j) \right) \right] \qquad (5)$$

and

$$u_i > \ln \left[\left(\sum_{j \in C} \exp(u_j) \right) \left(\exp(c_i) - 1 \right) \right]. \qquad (6)$$

From equation 6, we see that for $c_i > 0$, the threshold utility level for entrance into the consideration set is strictly positive and depends on the utilities of the brands already in the set. We see that the higher the utilities of the brands in C, the higher u_i must be to gain entrance to the set. Several other implications stemming from this model are summarized by Roberts (1989).

CONSIDERATION SET COMPOSITION

Without a less general specification of consideration costs, it is difficult to say anything about the composition of the consideration set. If we continue to allow for brand-specific costs, we are more or less limited to examining the addition of a single brand to a current consideration set. So that we can examine the composition of the consideration set, we depart from the previous approach (Roberts 1989) by assuming equal costs across all brands (i.e., $c_j = c$ for all brands j).[4]

---

[3]These criteria hold provided the existing consideration set C is not empty.

[4]Shugan (1980) suggests that evaluation costs are linear in the number of brands. Search costs will be linear unless there are economies of scale to search, in which case they will be convex. If the most easily searched brands are considered first, search costs will be concave. The implications of relaxing this assumption can be examined numerically.

It is now possible to describe the composition of the consumer's optimal consideration set. Because costs are the same across brands, the consumer can use a "greedy" algorithm to obtain an optimal solution: a consideration set consisting of the brands that provide the highest expected maximum utility.[5] The consumer begins with a null consideration set, which we denote C_0. The consumer then adds brand 1 to the set (recall that brands are indexed according to decreasing utility) to form C_1, provided $u_1 > c$. The consumer will add brand 2 to the set to form C_2 provided the increased expected benefit from choosing from the set $\{1,2\}$ is greater than the costs of adding the second brand—that is, so long as $EU(C_2) - EU(C_1) > c$ or $u_2 > u_1 + \ln(\exp(c) - 1)$ (by equation 6). The consumer will continue adding brands to the set so long as the incremental expected utility exceeds the associated costs. The optimal composition of the consideration set is given by the first n brands, where n is an integer satisfying the following two expressions:

$$u_n > EU(C_{n-1}) + \ln(\exp(c) - 1) \tag{7}$$

and

$$u_{n+1} < EU(C_n) + \ln(\exp(c) - 1), \tag{8}$$

where C_n is the set of brands from 1 to n. Because $EU(C_n)$ is increasing in n, each new brand under consideration faces a higher threshold for inclusion into the set.[6]

We can be more specific about the size of the consideration set, n, if we make some assumptions about the distribution of utility across the N brands in the awareness set. If we assume that the utility of the brands to the consumer decreases linearly[7] (i.e., $u_i = u - i\alpha$), then from equation 8 the optimal consideration set size is given by the largest integer n satisfying

$$u - n\alpha > \ln\left\{\left(\sum_j \exp(u - j\alpha)\right)(\exp(c) - 1)\right\},$$

where j indexes the brands from 1 to $n - 1$. Summing the first expression on the right side[8] and taking exponents, we obtain

$$\exp(u - n\alpha) > \exp(u)(\exp(c) - 1)\left[\frac{\exp(-\alpha) - \exp(-n\alpha)}{1 - \exp(-\alpha)}\right].$$

---

[5]Following from equation 3, if $u_i > u_j$ for brands i and j not in C and consideration costs are equal, then $EU(C \cup i) - EU(C \cup j) > 0$.

[6]A special case of this formulation, with all brands of equal utility, shows the order-of-entry effect noted by Hauser and Wernerfelt (1990).

[7]An examination of the stated utilities of the brands in consumers' awareness sets showed this to be a reasonable assumption for acceptable brands. We also examined the optimal consideration set size, assuming geometric decay in utility (using a numerical procedure); the results were qualitatively similar to those presented here.

[8]Recognizing that $\sum_j x^j = x(1 - x^{n-1})/(1 - x)$, where $x = \exp(-\alpha)$.

Rearranging terms and solving for n yields

$$n < 1 + (1/\alpha) \ln \left[\frac{\exp(c) - \exp(\alpha)}{\exp(c) - 1} \right], \alpha > 0. \tag{9}$$

For $\alpha = 0$ (the case of identically distributed brands), inequality 9 becomes $n < \exp(c)/(\exp(c) - 1)$. In any case, n must be less than or equal to N (the size of the awareness set).

Figure 1 shows how the optimal consideration set size varies as a function of α and c. We set $u = 1$ so that α and c can be interpreted as proportions. If rank-ordered utility decreases linearly by .05 (i.e., .95, .90, .85, .80, etc.) and consideration costs are equal to .05, the optimal size of the consideration set is 14. As α increases (resulting in increased brand heterogeneity in terms of utility), the optimal consideration set size decreases; when $\alpha = .20$ (with $c = .05$), n is 9. Increasing the costs of consideration affects consideration set size more severely; when $c = .20$ (with $\alpha = .05$), n is only 5.

MODEL CALIBRATION

Equation 6 suggests that a brand will be considered so long as its utility surpasses a certain threshold. If we assume equal costs of consideration across brands, that threshold is given by $u^\star = \ln[(\Sigma_{j \in C_n} \exp(u_j))(\exp(c) - 1)]$. With a perfectly specified model of utility, we should observe that $u_i > u^\star$ for all brands $i = 1, 2, 3, \ldots, n$, and that $u_k < u^\star$ for all brands $k = n + 1, n + 2, \ldots, N$. However, our multiattribute model may not be exact (i.e., there may be some specification error).[9] In that case, we might find that an individual tells us he would consider brand $i + 1$ and would not consider brand i, even though our multiattribute model suggests that $\Sigma_k w_k y_{ki} > \Sigma_k w_k y_{ki+1}$. In other words, if our multiattribute model is not a perfect specification of utility, our model will not predict consideration perfectly.

We calibrate our model by choosing the coefficients w_k so that our multiattribute utility model is as consistent as possible with the actual consideration behavior of the individual. A brand with true utility $u_i > u^\star$ will be considered only so long as the specification error associated with the multiattribute model is less than $\Sigma_k w_k y_{ki} - u^\star$, which happens with probability $F(\Sigma_k w_k y_{ki} - u^\star)$, where F is the cumulative distribution function associated with the model specification error. Similarly, brand i will not be considered when the specification error is greater than $\Sigma_k w_k y_{ki} - u^\star$, which occurs with probability $1 - F(\Sigma_k w_k y_{ki} - u^\star)$. Given information on the attributes of the available brands and the self-reported consideration, we calibrate the model by

---

[9]Note that this model specification error by the analyst is different from the stochastic component of utility given by ϵ_i.

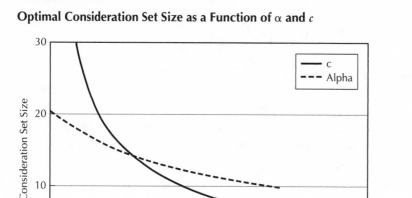

Optimal Consideration Set Size as a Function of α and c

choosing values of w_k and $u^\star$ to maximize the following log likelihood function for each consumer:

$$LL = \sum_{i \in A} \left\{ z_i \ln\left[F\left(\sum_k w_k \gamma_{ki} - u^\star\right)\right] \right.$$

$$\left. + (1 - z_i) \ln\left[1 - F\left(\sum_k w_k \gamma_{ki} - u^\star\right)\right]\right\}, \tag{10}$$

where $z_i = 1$ if the consumer considers brand i and zero otherwise, and A is the awareness set. In our estimation, we assume $F(x) = \exp(-\exp(-x))$, the cumulative double-exponential distribution. Having calibrated the model (using standard nonlinear gradient search techniques), we can use it to predict whether or not a new brand will enter the consideration set of the consumer, or the likelihood that a currently available brand will be a member of the set.

CONSIDERATION AND CHOICE

We have developed a testable model of consideration set composition. The closed-form solution enables us to examine the optimal size of the consideration set and how it varies with utility and cost. The model can be used to study consideration in its own right as an important part of the purchase process.

The proposed framework also can be used to forecast brand choice behavior. Without taking consideration into account (i.e., assuming the consumer makes his or her choice from among all N brands in the awareness set), the probability of choosing brand i is given by equation 2 with $C = A$. Taking consideration into account leads to the following expression for the probability of choosing brand i:

$$p_i = \begin{cases} \exp(u_i)\Big/\sum_{j \in C} \exp(u_j), \ i \in C, \\ 0 \ \text{otherwise}, \end{cases} \tag{11}$$

where C is the set of all brands i such that $u_i > u^*$. If consideration is an important element of the consumer decision process, we should improve our ability to fit and forecast brand choice behavior by using the two-stage model in equation 11.

Application

Overview

We calibrate and test the model with data on the Australian ready-to-eat cereal market. Kellogg Australia wanted to launch a new children's cereal in an already crowded market of more than two dozen major brands, as well as determine consideration levels for its currently available brands. The cereal market is one with large consideration sets and even larger awareness sets, making it ideal for testing the model.

We test the model in two stages. First, after an examination of consumer perceptions, we calibrate the model and use it to predict consideration of currently available brands at the individual level. We then use the calibrated model to predict consideration of three new product concepts on the basis of perceived positioning. These tests help to establish the validity of the model in describing the consideration process. Second, we test the predictive performance of the two-stage model of consideration and choice implied by our framework against some simple reference models.

Survey Design

A sample of 121 households were selected from two suburbs of Sydney. Cooperation was sought by letter and appointments were made by telephone. An incentive of $10 was offered for participation; interviews were conducted in respondents' homes. Kellogg Australia was interested in one particular segment of buyers, so participation was limited to households with at least one of three chosen brands in home and with children between the ages of 2 and 11 years. The sample was therefore reasonably homogeneous. Gensch (1985, 1987a) warns of the need to ensure homogeneity of the population before fitting choice models of this type. The level of homogeneity we need is very low: we assume homogeneous perceptions but allow individuals to vary on preference and consideration costs.

The sample consisted of 111 women and 10 men; in each case, the respondent was the primary shopper for the household. The sample was split into halves, which were administered different questionnaires. Only half of the sample (60 respondents) provided sufficient data on nonconsidered brands to allow calibration of the model; hence, the model was calibrated and validated with the consideration and choice data from respondents in that half of the sample. The data from the remaining respondents were used only in determining factor loadings and factor scores.

Respondents first were asked to evaluate brands currently on the market. Each respondent indicated his or her awareness (unaided and aided), consideration given aided and unaided awareness ("Would you consider buying this brand in the next 12 months?"), and usage patterns (brands in home and brands purchased in the past 12 months). Respondents rated their top three brands on 25 descriptive attributes. For each of the 26 major brands on the market, respondents indicated how much the family valued the brand (on a 100-point thermometer scale) and their familiarity with the brand (on a verbally anchored 5-point scale).

Respondents then were exposed to three new product concepts, each consisting of a color photograph and a description of the brand. Two of the three concepts were included to act as controls for yea-saying (one was on sale in the U.S. but not in Australia and the other was being test-marketed in a different state). The measures used for evaluation of the existing market were used also for the concepts (with the exception of awareness, which was forced): consideration, value, familiarity, and attribute perceptions. Price was included as a concept descriptor.

PERCEPTIONS

It is not possible to illustrate concisely the position of each brand on all 25 attributes; nor is it particularly parsimonious to fit a model with 25 attributes. We therefore factor analyzed the attribute ratings by all 121 respondents to determine a single underlying factor space[10] and underlying positions for each of the 26 major brands. The 121 respondents provided a total of 341 ratings (in 22 cases, subjects rated an "outside" brand). Using principal components on the mean-centered attribute ratings, we extracted four factors (based on a scree test) accounting for 53.3% of the total variance. This level of explanation is not unusual with as many as 25 attributes.[11] A varimax rotation suggested the following factor interpretations (see Table 1): healthful, artificial, interesting, and nonadult. With only

---

[10]Though we would have preferred to generate individual-level perceptual maps, the measurement task would have been onerous. The lack of such individual-level maps works against the fit of our model: we suspect the reason the model still seems to perform well is that we are sampling from a population that is relatively homogeneous in terms of its perceptions.

[11]Losing 47% of the attribute information should, if anything, make it more difficult for us to obtain good model fits.

TABLE 1

Rotated Factor Loadings (loadings greater than .40 are underlined)

	Factor 1 Healthful	Factor 2 Artificial	Factor 3 Interesting	Factor 4 Nonadult
Filling	.76	−.02	.06	.09
Natural	.63	−.39	−.17	−.07
Fiber	.66	−.37	−.14	−.30
Sweet	−.03	.70	.34	−.08
Easy	.09	.06	−.01	−.27
Low salt	−.13	.60	−.17	−.07
Satisfying	.68	−.11	.16	.25
Energy	.71	.01	.16	.04
Fun	−.05	.12	.68	.16
Kids	−.14	.00	.13	.81
Soggy	−.02	.09	−.63	.21
Economical	−.03	−.42	−.27	.38
Healthy	.67	−.51	−.11	−.11
Family	.07	−.18	.10	.70
Low calorie	−.00	.74	−.02	.02
Plain	−.25	−.04	−.67	.13
Crisp	−.21	−.05	.63	.10
Regularity	.38	−.40	.07	−.36
No sugar	−.34	.74	.17	−.10
Fruit	.38	.18	.23	−.45
Processed	−.26	.46	−.14	−.00
Quality	.50	−.50	.08	−.05
Treat	.04	.13	−.76	.01
Boring	−.26	.12	−.58	−.19
Nutritious	.67	−.48	−.07	−.17

two exceptions (the attributes easy and processed), the four factors account for at least 40% of the variation in each of the 25 attributes.

Using the factor score coefficients from the principal components analysis, we calculated the average factor scores for each of the 26 major brands (designated by γ_{ki}). The positions of the brands in the factor space have reasonable face validity, which increases our confidence in the rating procedure.

UTILITY FUNCTION AND CONSIDERATION THRESHOLD

We now calibrate the consideration model. We do not assume that each subject is equally familiar with all brands. By including our 5-point measure of familiarity in the utility function, we allow each subject to discount the utility of brands with which he or she is unfamiliar. Unlike the average factor scores, which are the same for a given brand across subjects, our measure of familiarity takes into account the fact that different households are familiar with different brands. Our measure of familiarity reflects the information uncertainty associated with the brand; the literature in modeling preference provides both theoretical and empirical support of its importance (see Roberts and Urban 1988). Thus, for each respondent, we use equation 10 to estimate six parameters: four describing the weights of the four underlying factors, one capturing the impact of familiarity, and one representing the utility threshold of consideration, $u^\star$.

Across respondents, the consideration set sizes range from a low of 4 to a high of 24, with a median of 14.[12] The average values of the utility function coefficients w_k (taken across respondents) follow.

	Name	Average	Same Sign
w_1	Healthful	.618	51/60
w_2	Artificial	−.800	48/60
w_3	Interesting	.251	37/60
w_4	Nonadult	.405	39/60
w_5	Familiarity	.599	52/60

The last column of the table suggests fairly strong homogeneity in the valuation of healthful and artificial qualities of cereals, and somewhat less agreement on interesting and nonadult. Furthermore, we can see that most respondents are likely to discount the utility of brands with which they are unfamiliar. On average, the value of the log-likelihood function across respondents is $LL = -8.88$, which represents an average U^2 value greater than .50.

If we use these fitted values to assess our ability to discriminate between considered and nonconsidered brands, we are likely to overstate the predictive ability of the model. The reason is that the observations we are "predicting" are the same ones we have used to fit the model. We therefore use a jackknife method (Crask and Perreault 1977) to assess the discriminant validity of our model. For each respondent, we use the information on all but one brand to calibrate the utility function. We then use those parameter estimates to predict whether or not the respondent will consider the holdout brand. We do this for all brands and for all respondents. The validation results follow.

	Actual	
	Consider	**Not Consider**
Predicted		
Consider	578	143
Not consider	276	563

---

[12]This average is higher than that in other studies, because we use aided rather than unaided consideration. Unaided awareness is the more appropriate measure when the search and evaluation process is such that brands must be retrieved spontaneously. Aided awareness is more appropriate for situations (such as this) in which retrieval cues are present at the time of choice. See Nedungadi (1990) for a discussion of the role of salience in consideration.

The hit rate (defined as the number of correct predictions over the total number) is $1141/1560 = 73\%$. It is considerably above the hit rate from a random discrimination rule, which is just over 50%. Thus, we have shown that the multiattribute representation of utility is able to recreate consideration set membership with reasonable accuracy. Because the model is calibrated at the individual level (effectively 26 observations per respondent), the model parameters are not estimated with a great amount of power. However, the robustness of our results is reflected in the success of the model in forecasting consideration by means of the jackknife procedure.

PREDICTING CONSIDERATION OF NEW PRODUCT CONCEPTS

As a further test of the validity of our consideration model, we use the calibrated utility functions to predict consideration of the three new product concepts. To do so, we first calculate the average factor scores for each of the three concepts using the factor score coefficients from the principal components analysis reported previously. The average scores are based on 50 ratings of concept A, 50 ratings of concept B, and 52 ratings of concept C.

	Healthful	Artificial	Interesting	Nonadult
A	.93	−.02	.72	−.01
B	−.14	.59	.70	.77
C	.58	−.70	.21	.66

In comparison with concepts A and C, concept B is perceived to be somewhat unhealthful and artificial. Analysis of variance reveals significant differences across concepts on all four factors.

Table 2 shows the discriminant results for each of the three concepts. At the individual level, across all three concepts, the hit rate for consideration as predicted by our model is $92/152 = 61\%$. It is somewhat less than the 73% reported in our cross-validation, but is still significantly better than a random discrimination rule ($t = 2.60$). Furthermore, at the aggregate product level, our model does a very good job of separating the good concepts from the bad. We predict 70% and 65% consideration for concepts A and C (vs. actual consideration of 74% and 71%, respectively), and predict only 38% consideration for concept B (vs. actual consideration of 32%).

PREDICTING CHOICE

As a final test of the validity of our proposed consideration model, we use it to predict choice behavior. This two-stage model, which we refer to as the PROPOSED model, is given in equation 11. Louviere (1989) and Swait and Ben-Akiva (1987) have shown that

TABLE 2

Discriminant Validation: Results by Concept

	ACTUAL	
	Consider	**Not Consider**
Concept A		
PREDICT		
Consider	28	7
Not consider	9	6
Hit rate: 34/50 = 68% ($t = 2.55$)		
Concept B		
PREDICT		
Consider	6	13
Not consider	10	21
Hit rate: 27/50 = 54% ($t = .57$)		
Concept C		
PREDICT		
Consider	25	9
Not consider	12	6
Hit rate: 31/52 = 60% ($t = 1.39$)		

logit model parameters based on the full choice set may be significantly different from those based on the choice set defined by consideration. Our interest here centers on whether the choice model derived from the proposed consideration framework results in improved predictions of consumer choice behavior.

We assess the predictive performance of the PROPOSED model against two reasonable benchmarks (or null models). For the first benchmark, we combine a reasonable model of consideration with a naïve model of choice. For the second benchmark, we combine a reasonable model of choice with a naïve model of consideration. Thus, each of the benchmarks is itself a two-stage model (like the proposed model). Comparing the proposed two-stage model with the first benchmark reveals the benefits from the choice stage of the model; comparison with the second benchmark reveals the benefits from the consideration stage.

The first benchmark model, which we label CONSID, uses consideration as stated by the respondent. Thus, rather than modeling consideration, we are in fact measuring it directly. In the choice stage, we assume the respondent will choose from among the brands in the consideration set with equal probability; that is,

$$p_i = \begin{cases} 1/n, i \in C, \\ 0 \text{ otherwise,} \end{cases} \qquad (12)$$

where C is the set containing the n brands considered by the respondent.

In the second benchmark model, which we label CHOICE, we assume that the respondent will consider all available brands. In the choice stage, we assume that the probability of choice is given by a logit expression; that is,

$$p_i = \exp(\beta V_i) \Big/ \sum_k \exp(\beta V_k), \tag{13}$$

where V_i denotes the mean-corrected value points for brand i (which differs across respondents, depending on their valuation of the brand). The value of the parameter β is estimated across individuals from the actual choice data by maximum likelihood.

We also compare the proposed two-stage model with another two-stage model that combines the consideration stage from CONSID with the choice stage from CHOICE. In this model, which we label C&C (for consideration and choice), we assume that respondents choose brands from their stated consideration set with probability given by the logit model; that is,

$$p_i = \begin{cases} \exp(\beta V_i) \Big/ \sum_k \exp(\beta V_k), & i \in C, \\ 0 \text{ otherwise.} \end{cases} \tag{14}$$

Note that we do not refer to the C&C model as a benchmark model. The reason is that the model embodies information on both consideration and choice, which is what we advocate. Therefore, we would expect this model to perform comparably to the proposed model. Nonetheless, a comparison enables us to assess the performance of our particular model specification (fitted on consideration data only) in relation to a reasonably strong and realistic alternative.

We use the measure of brands in home at the time of the study as our indicator of choice behavior.[13] We calculate the market share of each cereal brand by weighting respondents equally and weighting each brand in home equally (thus, if the subject has four brands of cereal at home, each brand is given a weight of .25).[14] We then try to predict those market shares.

The choice share predictions from each of the four models (as well as the actual choice shares) are reported in Table 3. The results show that the C&C model predicts choice shares better than either the CONSID or CHOICE benchmarks, providing support for a general model involving both consideration and choice. C&C has lower mean square error and mean absolute deviation and a higher correlation with the actual choice shares. We also note that the PROPOSED model (which uses fitted

---

[13]Actual purchase incidence or purchase intent might have been a more appropriate variable, but we did not collect those data. Our measure of the brands purchased in the last 12 months correlated highly with brands in home.

[14]We also calculated market shares by weighting each household according to usage (number of packages of cereal bought per month). The results were essentially the same as those described subsequently.

> ### TABLE 3

> **Predicted and Actual Choice Shares by Brand**

Brand	Name	CONSID	CHOICE	C&C	PROPOSED	Actual
1	All Bran	4.0	5.4	5.2	7.1	4.6
2	Bran Flakes	3.4	3.4	3.1	1.6	1.2
3	Cerola Muesli	3.5	4.3	3.6	4.0	2.0
4	Coco Pops	3.7	1.9	2.4	2.1	3.9
5	Crunchy Nut Flakes	2.1	2.1	1.4	.6	.1
6	Extra G	3.2	3.0	2.8	1.6	.5
7	Fibre Plus	2.7	4.1	3.0	2.8	3.8
8	Froot Loops	1.1	.8	.5	1.4	.8
9	Frosties	.8	1.1	.7	.7	.5
10	Fruit N Bran Flakes	2.8	2.6	1.7	2.0	.1
11	Good Start	3.5	3.3	3.1	.7	.9
12	Honey Smacks	1.1	1.0	.8	1.5	.3
13	Just Right	4.7	4.5	4.7	2.2	1.9
14	Kellogg's Corn Flakes	7.4	5.5	7.4	6.7	10.3
15	Kellogg's Muesli	4.2	2.8	3.0	1.3	.2
16	Nutrigrain	6.2	4.4	5.5	5.3	5.2
17	Parina Muesli	4.5	5.9	5.7	6.1	5.2
18	Ready Wheats	1.9	1.9	1.3	0.8	1.1
19	Rice Bubbles	5.9	4.6	5.6	7.9	11.5
20	Skippy Corn Flakes	3.6	3.6	3.2	1.4	.8
21	Special K	4.9	4.3	4.7	4.7	4.3
22	Sultana Bran	5.1	4.4	4.9	5.8	2.4
23	Sustain	4.2	4.0	4.0	7.2	1.3
24	Vita Brits	5.8	7.5	8.1	10.5	12.0
25	Weet Bix	7.1	9.4	11.0	11.9	18.9
26	Weeties	2.7	4.0	3.0	2.1	2.9
Between model and actual						
	Mean square error	11.59	9.92	6.97	5.72	
	Mean absolute deviation	2.38	2.34	1.93	1.66	
	Correlation	.76	.83	.89	.87	

consideration rather than directly stated consideration) does extremely well. In comparison with C&C, it has lower mean square error and mean absolute deviation but a lower correlation with the actual data. This finding suggests that our particular model specification is not a bad one. The fact that the PROPOSED model does well in relation to C&C is even more notable because our model is calibrated with only information on consideration (whereas C&C requires actual choice data to estimate the logit parameter β).

To illustrate the diagnostic value of the PROPOSED model, we also used it to predict the choice shares of the three new product concepts. Our predictions do not allow for dynamic changes to the consideration set after entry of the new brand (e.g., we have assumed that no brands actually leave the consideration set if a new product concept enters). These shares (along with those predicted by the CONSID and CHOICE reference models) follow.

Concept	CONSID	CHOICE	PROPOSED
A	4.8	3.6	6.7
B	1.8	1.4	1.9
C	3.8	4.2	11.3

These shares are interpretable as share of choice (first trial) at the awareness stage (e.g., after taste, position might change and familiarity will change).

All three models identify concept B as a product with low share potential among this particular segment of consumers. The two benchmark models predict concepts A and C will be roughly the same, but the PROPOSED model shows concept C will be much stronger in this segment. The reason is that concept C achieves a stronger position for subjects who consider it. Unfortunately, we have no purchase incidence or intention measures with which to validate the predictions.

Note that the PROPOSED model will predict a higher share than the CHOICE model when the new concept is above the threshold $u^\star$ for a sufficiently large number of consumers (i.e., if it obtains more than its fair share of consideration from the awareness set). The reason is that the CHOICE model always assumes a larger choice set (hence, larger denominator) than is in fact the case. The share predictions of the PROPOSED model will be lower than those of the CHOICE model when the perceptual position is very weak and the new concept fails to achieve consideration, as illustrated in Figure 2.

Discussion

In addition to providing a tool for determining the consideration of new products (forecasting), the model enables us to assess the ways in which product positioning can be used to improve consideration. The multiattribute utility model outlined in equation 1 can be used to calculate the change in attribute perceptions necessary to generate sufficient utility to ensure consideration by any given individual.

Though the model has been developed and tested at the individual level, clustering individuals into segments may be desirable to determine more general marketing implications. When the number of brands considered is relatively small, clustering consumers on the basis of consideration set composition prior to analysis will increase the degrees of freedom in estimation. Consumers could also be clustered on the basis of the determinants of consideration. For example, differences in utility function coefficients across attributes would allow for the targeting of strategies to ensure consideration among as broad a group

FIGURE 2

Comparison of Choice Probabilities: One-Stage and Two-Stage Choice Models

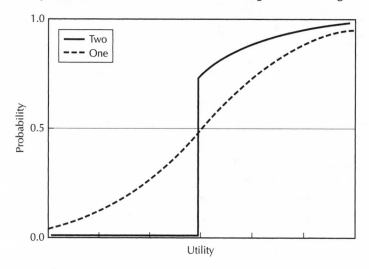

as possible. Our model suggests that effective marketing communication strategies must not only enhance choice, but also ensure consideration (e.g., generate a request to tender) across market segments.

The method could be applied in two major ways. Kellogg Australia now undertakes a quarterly survey of the ready-to-eat cereal market in which it monitors perceptions, preferences, and behavior. Measurement of consideration and the reasons for nonconsideration is an integral part of Kellogg's survey. Our method can be used also for new brand forecasting and marketing optimization. Gensch (1987b) has shown that modeling choice as a two-stage process (in which brands are first screened and then evaluated for choice) improves forecasting performance. Our model can be used as a consideration and choice simulator to predict the levels of consideration and choice for new products and how they will vary aross different formulations.

In addition to improved forecasting performance, the model has brand management implications. Figure 2 compares the brand choice forecasts for our proposed model with those of a logit model in which consumers choose from among all available brands. In the case of a market with relatively homogeneous preferences, our model suggests a very different level of marketing mix effort at $u^\star - \delta$ than at $u^\star + \delta$. That is, if the brand is just missing out on consideration (by an amount δ), putting extra marketing resources into improving the perceived utility of the brand yields a substantial reward in market share. In the more interesting case of a population with relatively heterogeneous preferences, we can compare the distributions of $(u_i - u^\star)$ under different positioning strategies.

A targeted positioning strategy would have higher $(u_i - u\star)$ for the chosen market segmen and lower $(u_i - u\star)$ elsewhere. If consideration were ignored, some of these effects might be missed or smoothed over.

Conclusion

Consideration sets have been shown to be subsets of the awareness set. In our study, we tried to show why consideration is important and how we can benefit from better understanding of its determinants. Consideration will be a more binding constraint (and thus of greater managerial relevance) when consideration sets are small in relation to the awareness set. That situation occurs when the costs of consideration are high in relation to the differences in utility across brands. As brands proliferate, that phenomenon will become increasingly prevalent (the study of awareness sets may also increase in importance).

We present one model of consideration, which is not without limitations. First, we assume that the consideration of a brand is independent of its similarity to other brands in the set. Hence, little can be said about the "shape" of the consideration set (i.e., whether or not the consideration of one brand is affected by its similarity to another brand already in the set). One way around this problem is to structure the market into relatively homogeneous groups of brands. For example, Bechtel (1990), also examining the ready-to-eat cereal market, found that the nested multinomial logit model was effective in avoiding problems with IIA. A more ambitious approach would involve using a generalized logit to model the consumer's choice of consideration set from all possible consideration sets.

A second limitation arises because we examine the composition of the consideration set at a given point in time; we therefore cannot describe the changes to the consideration set as the consumer searches for information. Additionally, we examine only the compensatory aspects of the consideration process; directly modeling the conjunctive aspects of the process is an area that warrants further attention.

Finally, though the construct of consideration is now well accepted, there is no unanimity on its operationalization. In some situations a fuzzy set approach, which allows for different degrees of consideration, may have more process validity than a discrete approach. All such issues are beyond the scope of our article, but are worthwhile areas for future research.

What we have done is build on previous work to develop a model of consideration set composition and optimal consideration set size. In designing an instrument and collecting data to test our model, we have begun to meet the need for studies of consideration at the individual level. The tests of our model address important issues in the study of consideration. First, our model helps to explain consideration set membership of currently available brands in the market. Second, when calibrated with informaton about existing products, our model can be used to predict consideration of new product concepts. Finally, our model of consideration and choice affords an improvement in predicting market-level purchase behavior.

Our model offers two managerial benefits. First, when consideration is of interest in its own right (e.g., when a brand's biggest problem is getting considered at all), our model can be used to help diagnose the problem and evaluate alternative scenarios. Second, when the overall choice process is of interest, our model of consideration and choice yields improved forecasts of aggregate choice behavior.

References

Bechtel, Gordon (1990), "Share-Ratio Estimation of the Nested Multinomial Logit Model," *Journal of Marketing Research,* 27 (May), 232–7.

Ben-Akiva, Moshe and Steven R. Lerman (1985), *Discrete Choice Analysis.* Cambridge, MA: MIT Press.

Bettman, James (1979), *An Information Processing Theory of Consumer Choice.* Chicago: Addison-Wesley Publishing Company.

Brisoux, Jacques E. and Michel Laroche (1981), "Evoked Set Formation and Composition: An Empirical Investigation Under a Routinized Response Behavior Situation." in *Advances in Consumer Research,* Vol. 8, Kent B. Monroe, ed. Washington: Association for Consumer Research, 357–61.

Campbell, Brian M. (1969). "The Existence of Evoked Set and Determinants of Its Magnitude in Brand Choice Behavior," unpublished PhD dissertation, Columbia University.

Crask, Melvin R. and William D. Perreault (1977), "Validaton of Discriminant Analysis in Marketing Research," *Journal of Marketing Research,* 14 (February), 60–8.

Gaudry, Marc and Marcel Dagenais (1979), "The Dogit Model," *Transportation Research B,* 13B, 105–11.

Gensch, Dennis H. (1985), "Empirically Testing a Disaggregate Choice Model for Segments," *Journal of Marketing Research,* 22 (November), 462–7.

___ (1987a), "Empirical Evidence Supporting the Use of Multiple Choice Models in Analyzing a Population," *Journal of Marketing Research,* 24 (May), 197–207.

___ (1987b), "A Two-Stage Disaggregate Attribute Choice Model," *Marketing Science,* 6 (Summer), 223–31.

Hauser, John R. and Birger Wernerfelt (1990), "An Evaluation Cost Model of Evoked Sets," *Journal of Consumer Research,* 16 (March), 393–408.

Howard, John A. (1963), *Consumer Behavior: Application of Theory.* New York: McGraw-Hill Book Company.

___ and Jagdish N. Sheth (1969), *The Theory of Buyer Behavior.* New York: John Wiley & Sons, Inc.

Johnson. Eric and Robert Meyer (1984), "Compensatory Choice Models of Non-Compensatory Processes: The Effect of Varying Context," *Journal of Consumer Research,* 11 (June), 528–41.

Keeney, Ralph L. and Howard Raiffa (1976), *Decision Making With Multiple Objectives: Preferences and Value Tradeoffs.* New York: John Wiley & Sons, Inc.

Kotler, Philip (1988), *Marketing Management: Analysis, Planning, Implementation and Control,* 6th ed. Englewood Cliffs, NJ: Prentice-Hall, Inc.

Louviere, Jordan (1989), "On the Consequences of Misspecifying Consumers' Choice Sets in Multinomial Logit Choice Models," working paper #89-004, Department of Marketing and Economic Analysis, University of Alberta.

McFadden, Daniel (1973) "Conditional Logit Analysis of Qualitative Choice Behavior," in *Frontiers in Econometrics,* Philip Zarembka, ed. New York: Academic Press, Inc.

Narayana, Chem L. and Rom J. Markin (1975), "Consumer Behavior and Product Performance: An Alternative Conceptualization," *Journal of Marketing,* 39 (October), 1–6.

Nedungadi, Prakash (1990), "Recall and Consumer Consideration Sets: Influencing Choice Without Altering Brand Evaluations," *Journal of Consumer Research,* 17 (3), 263–76.

Parkinson, Thomas L. and Michael Reilly (1979), "An Information Processing Approach to Evoked Set Formation," in *Advances in Consumer Research,* Vol. 6, W. L. Wilkie, ed. Miami: Association for Consumer Research, 227–31.

Ratchford, Brian T. (1980), "The Value of Information for Selected Appliances," *Journal of Marketing Research,* 17 (February), 14–25.

Reilly, Michael and Thomas L. Parkinson (1985), "Individual and Product Correlates of Evoked Set Size for Consumer Package Goods," in *Advances in Consumer Research,* Vol. 12, E. Hirschman and M. Holbrook, eds. Ann Arbor, MI: Association for Consumer Research, 492–7.

Roberts, John H. (1983), "A Multiattribute Utility Diffusion Model: Theory and Application to the Pre-Launch Forecasting of Automobiles," unpublished PhD dissertation, Sloan School of Management, MIT.

___ (1989), "A Grounded Model of Consideration Set Size and Composition," in *Advances in Consumer Research,* Vol. 16, T. Srull, ed. Provo, UT: Association for Consumer Research, 749–57.

___ and Glen L. Urban (1988), "Modeling Multiattribute Utilty, Risk, and Belief Dynamics for New Consumer Durable Brand Choice," *Management Science,* 34 (February), 167–85.

Shocker, Allan, Moshe Ben-Akiva, Bruno Boccara, and Prakash Nedungadi (1991), "Consideration Set Influences on Consumer Decision-Making and Choice: Issues, Models and Suggestions," *Marketing Letters,* forthcoming.

Shugan, Steven M. (1980), "The Cost of Thinking," *Journal of Consumer Research,* 7 (September), 99–111.

Stigler, George (1961), "The Economics of Information," *Journal of Political Economy,* 69 (3), 213–25.

Swait, Joffre and Moshe Ben-Akiva (1987), "Incorporating Random Coefficients in Discrete Models of Choice Set Generation." *Transportation Research B,* 21, 92–102.

Weitzman, Martin L. (1979), "Optimal Search for the Best Alternative," *Econometrica,* 47, 641–54.

Wright, Peter and Frederick Barbour (1977), "Phased Decision Strategies: Sequels to Initial Screening," in *Multiple Criteria Decision Making: North Holland TIMS Studies in the Management Science,* M. Starr and M. Zeleny, eds. Amsterdam: North-Holland Publishing Company, 91–109.

AGGRESSIVE AND PREDATORY PRICING: A FRAMEWORK FOR ANALYSIS

Joseph P. Guiltinan and Gregory T. Gundlach

The authors examine competitive interaction in the context of aggressive pricing strategies. Although aggressive pricing by one firm may initially provide lower prices to consumers, the behavior also can be predatory and ultimately result in undesirable welfare consequences. To date, public policy analysis of such behavior has relied on traditional economic theory, with State and Federal policies creating conflicting guidelines for managers. The authors offer a framework for understanding aggressive and predatory pricing that incorporates research from marketing and related disciplines as well as traditional and newer streams of economic analysis. Distinguishing features of the framework include a broader delineation of indicators that potentially predatory behavior might have occurred, an expanded view of the possible motivations for aggressive and predatory pricing behavior that are not admitted into current analyses, and a more comprehensive analysis of competitors' strategic responses to such pricing and the varying consequences of these responses. They further argue that the field of marketing is uniquely positioned to provide the kind of comprehensive measurement and modeling contributions needed to create policy guidelines that can be implemented in this area.

In recent years theorists in marketing, economics, and strategic planning have begun to examine competitive strategies—actions directed toward influencing the behavior of rival firms and encompassing competitive moves and countermoves between firms (cf. Porter 1980; Weitz 1985). Within marketing, much of this research has focused on measuring the type and intensity of firms' reactions to the strategic moves of rivals (cf. Chen and Miller 1994; Gatignon 1984; Gatignon, Anderson, and Helsen 1989; Hanssens 1980). Recently, marketers have begun to examine firms' reactions to competitors' signals regarding future actions (cf. Heil and Robertson 1991; Heil and Walters 1992; Moore 1992; Robertson, Eliashberg, and Rymon 1995).

Often, researchers focus on actions or signals that represent significant departures from competitive norms, for example, deep price cuts or large increases in advertising.

JOSEPH P. GUILTINAN is professor and GREGORY T. GUNDLACH is an associate professor, Department of Marketing, College of Business Administration, University of Notre Dame. The authors thank Joel Urbany and Ralph Chami for their helpful comments on earlier versions of this article. They are also grateful for the insights and suggestions of the editor and four anonymous JM reviewers.

Guiltinan, Joseph P. and Gregory T. Gundlach (1996), "Aggressive Predatory Pricing: A Framework for Analysis," Journal of Marketing, 60 (July), 87–102.

Such actions may be termed *aggressive* if they are motivated by the desire to force rivals to react by taking actions that significantly impair the rivals' performance or competitive viability. When these actions lead to a reduction in competition and undermine consumer welfare, they may be considered *predatory*. As Sullivan (1977, p. 111) observes, in contrast to the aggressive competitor,

> the predator seeks not to win the field by greater efficiency, better services, or lower prices reflective of cost savings or modest profits. The predatory firm tries to inhibit others in ways independent of the predator's own ability to perform effectively in the market. Its [conduct] is calculated to impose losses on other firms, not to garner gains for itself.

Predatory pricing is the best known form of predatory behavior. It involves lowering prices to an unreasonably low (usually below-cost) or unprofitable level in a market in a effort to weaken, eliminate, or block the entry of a rival. While capturing the attention of law and economics scholars and the concern of policy makers, predation and predatory pricing has only recently begun to be addressed by marketers. For example, Gundlach (1990) surveys the nature, regulatory framework, and alternative rules for the various forms of predation, including both price and nonprice strategies. More recently, both Sheffet (1994) and Gundlach (1995) examine key Supreme Court decisions that address predatory pricing and the emergence of alternative economic explanations based on asymmetries of information for understanding such actions. In a related work, Heil and Langvardt (1994) focus on the implications of this research for antitrust in general, including predatory pricing.

We combine the previous contributions with insights developed by researchers in marketing and related disciplines to offer a more expansive critique of the theoretical foundations of current thinking and public policy toward predatory pricing. We offer a framework for understanding predation within the context of aggressive pricing. As in the recent economic scholarship cited in studies by Gundlach (1995), Sheffet (1994), and Heil and Langvardt (1994), in our framework, we view aggressive and predatory pricing in the light of dynamic competitive strategy. However, we extend that thinking to show how the specific situational opportunities, marketing strategies, and strategic orientations of individual businesses may condition competitive responses to a given aggressive pricing scenario. In turn, we show the varying consequences of these competitive interactions for consumer welfare.

Background

The primary objective of public policy that addresses competitive interaction is distinguishing those strategies that are anticompetitive from those that simply involve aggressive competition and are procompetitive (Scherer 1976). As can be surmised, this task is extremely difficult when price is involved. As stated by the Supreme Court,

> [T]he mechanism by which a firm engages in predatory pricing—lowering prices—is the same mechanism by which a firm stimulates competition; because 'cutting prices in order to increase business often is the very essence of competition . . . [;] mistaken inferences . . . are especially costly, because they chill the very conduct the antitrust laws are designed to protect (*Brooke Group v. Brown & Williamson Tobacco Corporation* 1993, p. 4699).

The Marlboro example (see Appendix A) illustrates the complexity of understanding and distinguishing predatory pricing. As we discuss subsequently, depending on the perspective taken, Philip Morris' price cuts on its Marlboro brand cigarettes may be viewed as simply aggressive price competition or alternately as a basis for achieving anticompetitive goals through predatory pricing. The difficulty of judging the welfare implications of such actions highlights the challenge facing policymakers.

PUBLIC POLICY

Current policy assessments of predatory pricing rely on the narrow behavioral assumptions of neoclassical price theory. This body of thought envisions a model of economic behavior in which parties are assumed to be motivated exclusively by profit maximization, to possess perfect information, and to act calculatedly rational in their decisions.

Federal. According to the federal view, predatory pricing is considered "rarely tried and even more rarely successful" (*Matsushita Electric Industrial Company v. Zenith Radio Corporation* 1986, p. 589). This skepticism is due to the presumed irrationality of a firm pricing at predatory levels to maximize profits. Assuming a perfectly competitive environment, a firm engaging in such conduct would incur such severe short-term losses in its attempt at disadvantaging rivals that it would not rationally consider such a strategy. Even were the firm to engage in such conduct and successfully eliminate rivals, to be profitable, the predating firm would need to recover losses through raising prices later to supracompetitive (i.e., above normal competitive) levels. In an environment of complete information, prices at such levels would attract new competitors (hoping to obtain surplus profits), thereby reducing the firm's chances of recouping its losses. Realizing this, the firm would calculate the probability of recovering lost profits to be low and avoid such conduct.

Policy embracing this view has developed in the Courts and federal antitrust agencies.[1] In *Brooke Group Limited v. Brown & Williamson Tobacco Corporation* (1993, pp. 4702–703), the

---

[1]Both the Federal Trade Commission and the Justice Department have espoused similar policy perspectives toward predatory pricing (Rule 1988). A statement by then Federal Trade Commissioner Oliver (Antitrust & Trade Regulation Report 1987, p. 340) summarizes this view: "[T]he Supreme Court has said, correctly we think, that predatory pricing is rarely tried and rarely successful." Few cases alleging this practise have been brought by either agency in recent years.

Supreme Court established a two-pronged framework for analyzing predatory pricing claims:

> First, a plaintiff . . . must prove that the prices complained of are below an appropriate measure of its rival's costs . . . second . . . is a demonstration that the competitor has a reasonable prospect [under Section 2a of the Robinson-Patman Act], or under Section 2 of the Sherman Act, a dangerous probability, of recouping its investment in below-cost prices.

For the first element, the cost measure normally applied is average variable cost; a surrogate for marginal cost (Areeda and Turner 1975). Pricing below this level is presumed to be irrational for the profit-maximizing firm and therefore considered to infer predation. Above-cost pricing is almost always deemed procompetitive. Applying this standard to Marlboro, the above-cost price cuts of Philip Morris would not be considered predatory. For the second element, because predation requires recovery of lost profits, recoupment also is essential. It involves the determination that there is a "reasonable expectation" or "dangerous probability," given market circumstances, of recovering losses through supracompetitive prices. The absence of conditions favoring recoupment presents a situation in which it is difficult for the firm to achieve the (presumed) aims of predation. In the event that both below-cost pricing and recoupment are found, the welfare effects of such conduct are considered anticompetitive. Supracompetitive pricing is thought to lower consumer welfare through reducing *allocative efficiency*, or the efficient allocation of resources across society.

State. In contrast to federal skepticism, state courts have taken a more aggressive stance toward predatory pricing by adopting the single element of below-cost pricing as prima facie evidence of anticompetitive injury. Many states have "sales below cost" statutes or minimum markup laws (for a review of these laws, see Haynes 1988). Although the definition of *below cost* varies by state, the majority define it as average total cost, with others employing criterion similar to average total cost or average variable cost (Jordan 1995). Generally, each state requires that a price be set below cost for the purpose of injuring competition. Purpose itself, may be inferred from the below-cost price or through other means.

Juxtaposed against federal policy, the state view is characteristic of a more traditional industrial-organization perspective of antitrust—it focuses on industry concentration and as a consequence is adverse to large-scale firms. The loss of small competitors is an important consideration at the state level. State and federal standards differ primarily in that the state approach does not explicitly address recoupment, yet holds greater expectations that below-cost pricing by large firms will successfully achieve the aims of predation.

MANAGERIAL AND PUBLIC POLICY ISSUES

Pragmatically, the presence of different federal and state approaches underscores the importance of developing a more broadly accepted understanding of aggressive and predatory pricing. Separate standards increase the managerial uncertainty and costs of pricing decisions for firms through elevating their compliance burden. The noncomplementary nature of the theoretical views informing these standards further magnifies this burden. Managerial efficiency favors a unified perspective and approach for public policy assessment of predatory pricing.

At a more fundamental level, examination of the key theoretical assumptions that inform the federal and state approaches raises substantive questions as to whether these postulates appropriately reflect competitive and managerial behavior in today's complex and evolving business environment. For example,

1. Is it correct to assume that organizations are motivated exclusively by profit-maximization goals in determining price, or are other goals important in their decision making?
2. Do firms indeed possess complete information as a basis for making such decisions?
3. Are the decisions made always calculatedly rational in the traditional economic sense?
4. Finally, should the welfare of consumers be judged solely on the basis of allocative efficiency, or are other determinants important in assessing consumer welfare?

The restrictive nature of these assumptions raises theoretical concerns for using them as a basis on which to establish public policy.

In the quest for a more comprehensive and unified understanding of aggressive and predatory pricing that is unencumbered by the restrictive assumptions of neoclassical price theory, we argue that current policy could benefit from insights regarding competitive interaction and strategic decision making developed in marketing and its related fields. In the following sections, these insights are reviewed and their potential contribution examined. Applying these insights, we develop a marketing-based framework for analyzing aggressive and predatory pricing behavior. We then discuss the potential implications for application of such a framework to public policy, academic research, and marketing practice.

Insights from Marketing and Related Disciplines on Competitive Pricing Behavior

For analyzing predatory pricing, the federal model, as informed by traditional economic thinking, essentially seeks to determine whether

1. A firm is pricing below some measure of cost (e.g., sacrificing current profits);
2. The basis of such a price strategy is predicated on the rational calculation that losses incurred may be later recouped through increased prices (e.g., does it make economic sense that foregone profits may be recovered through later price increases?);
3. Competitors would likely respond by exiting the market, reducing output, or deciding not to enter (e.g., will the pricing strategy injure relevant competitors?); and

4. Given such an outcome, if consumers will be injured through later price increases on the part of the predator (e.g., will there be injury to consumer welfare?).

These determinations are made against the backdrop of stringent assumptions, including competitors possessing complete information, being motivated exclusively by profit maximization, operating within market conditions that generally mitigate market power, and being completely rational in their decision making, as well as injury to consumers occurring only through supracompetitive pricing. Put another way, the Supreme Court is pursuing a theory of predatory pricing that abides by the basic tenets of "economic reason" as constructed from the assumptions and logic that underlie neoclassical price theory (cf. Jordan 1995).

The expectation that any theory of predation should make sense or be based on economic reason is certainly a desirable attribute underlying any public policy. But, as researchers in both economics and marketing continue to examine business decision making from a dynamic, strategic perspective, the more apparent it becomes that the assumptions that underlie the current thinking may be insufficient for explaining aggressive and predatory pricing in today's competitive environments. In short, for explaining such conduct, a less restrictive understanding of competitive interaction and managerial decision making may be required. In this respect, researchers in marketing and its related disciplines are currently developing insights on how managers set pricing goals, the various ways in which price competition affects profitability and consumer choice, and how managers deal with the dynamics of the marketplace and imperfect information in arriving at price decisions. In Table 1, we summarize how these insights differ from the assumptions and thinking of the traditional economic perspective. In the following sections, we discuss the implications of such thinking for understanding predatory pricing.

Motivations Underlying Predatory Conduct

A key assumption underlying the economic perspectives of predatory pricing is that managers act to maximize profits through their price decisions. That is, their pricing decisions are driven by the singular goal to maximize profits. The traditional view is that managers would find it difficult to maximize profits in a perfectly competitive market through first incurring losses from pricing below cost and then attempting to recoup these losses later. This logic yields the view that predatory pricing rarely occurs or is rarely successful. It also underlies the recent Supreme Court standard, which now requires evidence of recoupment.

Nonprofit Maximizing Goals in Pricing. Evidence from marketing and other disciplines has historically questioned the assumption of profit maximization as the exclusive motive for managerial decision making. There is general acceptance that managers often settle for satisfactory levels of outcomes rather than optimal levels (cf. Baumol 1967; Simon 1979). Recent research indicates that managers are motivated by a variety of

| TABLE 1 |

Contrasting Perspectives Toward Predatory Pricing

Perspective	Traditional, Economics-Oriented	Emerging, Marketing-Oriented
Conditions fostering predation	• Firm behavior is a function of industry structure; structural forces set conditions for predation	• Firm behavior is strategic, industry structure is important, but additional opportunities arise from differences in product or corporate goals, segment cross-elasticities, or informational asymmetries
Motives for aggressive pricing	• Purpose of predatory pricing is to defend or maintain market power to maximize profitability	• Multiple purposes exist, especially volume-related
Evidence of potential predation	• Only below-cost prices can be predatory	• Prices need not be below cost to be predatory
Managerial information	• Managers possess "perfect" information and can calculate payoffs	• Managers possess incomplete and asymmetric information but only make "procedurally" rational evaluations of outcomes
Managers' risk attitudes	• Managers are risk-neutral or risk-averse	• Managers are risk-averse on gains; "risk-affinitive" on losses
Conjectures about competitors	• Managers predict competitors' actions from industry structure	• Managers rely on signals and history, conjecture imperfectly, and often do not understand competitors' payoffs
Recoupment assumptions	• Recoupment requires gains in market power and is unlikely	• Recoupment is frequently hard to predict, but the impact on competitive capabilities is predictable
Consumer welfare criteria	• Consumer welfare is defined as allocative efficiency and may be determined by changes in industry price or quantity of output	• Consumer welfare effects also include impact on quality, innovation, and satisfaction

other considerations in their pricing decision making. In the context of predatory pricing, Stelzer (1987, p. 5), for example, suggests that managers often may make decisions (including below-cost pricing) for reasons known only to themselves: "In short, predation [below-cost pricing] may not maximize profits. But it may nevertheless be a rational, far from unthinkable policy for business managers seeking to maximize their own career opportunities." In particular, below-cost pricing can result in dramatic changes in market share, which, if employed as a criteria for evaluating managerial performance, may motivate some business managers to engage in such pricing decisions for nonpredatory reasons.

In the context of marketing, a variety of motivations for below-cost pricing which are not oriented toward profit maximization have been identified. In particular, motivations for below-cost pricing often stem from strategic objectives that focus on volume sales. For example, Urbany and Dickson (1994) provide empirical evidence on the preference for volume-oriented pricing over profit-oriented pricing. In an experimental setting, they found that decision makers in manufacturing firms favored a price strategy that was volume-oriented and considered customers as long-term assets. The Marlboro example generally reflects this orientation. Philip Morris appears to have been willing to risk its immediate profit goals in an attempt to bolster volume-related objectives. Volume-oriented strategies emphasizing customer retention and "customer lifetime value" are increasingly pervasive among marketing managers today. The development of database marketing techniques enables managers to target deep discounts toward their most valued customers (cf. Blattberg and Deighton 1991). Because these discounts are linked to cumulative quantity purchases, they can effectively preempt competitors from that part of the firm's customer base.

Pricing that is designed to achieve long-term customer satisfaction or other volume-oriented objectives can be characterized as profit-oriented, because short-term profits may be traded for long-term gains. However, under such logic the long-term payback, or recoupment period, may be difficult to calculate precisely, and the profit nature of such gains may be difficult to identify clearly. For this to occur, managers must be able to project when "normal" prices will return so as to provide such payback returns. But in many industries, particularly in high fixed-cost markets (e.g., airlines), in which volume-oriented pricing practices are often employed, aggressive pricing can easily lead to long periods of depressed prices that frustrate such projections. Furthermore, the ability to project repeat business or other long-term gains from customers whose loyalty has been purchased by abnormally low prices is tenuous. So even if managers think aggressive, volume-oriented pricing is profit-based (i.e., likely to lead to profit-maximizing outcomes), the difficulty of identifying the recovery period and nature of returns makes such a determination extremely difficult.

Finally, economists might argue that if managers were indeed maximizing something other than profits, then more efficient firms would drive these irrational firms out of business. However, firms that attempt to maximize volume may well enjoy adequate profits to remain viable. Or, firms may be able to rely on a stable of other profitable products and divisions to remain profitable. Moreover, if competitors are truly injured by aggressive volume pricing, they may not be in a position to retaliate and drive inefficient firms from the market.

The implication of finding that managers may be driven by motives other than profit maximization for current public policy toward predatory pricing is to raise questions regarding the basic logic that underlies evidentiary requirements of legal inquiries at the state (below-cost pricing) and federal (below-cost pricing and recoupment) levels. If managers can be viewed as rationally engaging in nonprofit-maximizing strategies that result in below-cost pricing for nonpredatory reasons, any standard that relies on a finding of the same or relies on it for its basis (i.e., recoupment) must be viewed as indeterminate for identifying anticompetitive predation.

CONDITIONS INFLUENCING PREDATION

Traditional economic thought maintains that predation is only feasible if certain market conditions hold (cf. Isaac and Smith 1985; Scherer 1976). These conditions inure to the predator the requisite market power (i.e., power to control price) and therefore the ability to recoup lost profits that attend a predatory pricing episode. Some conditions provide predators with the ability to drive out competitors in a price war and thus enhance market power. To the extent that a predator's only competitors are small, fringe suppliers and that the predator has superior financial resources (i.e., "deep pockets") from which to draw, the likelihood of outlasting competitors is enhanced. Often these deep pockets are available through using profits in one business unit to subsidize another. Another set of conditions are those that keep a predator's potential losses from low prices below those of its rivals. If a predator has a lower cost structure or a lower cost of capital than a competitor, then the losses incurred at below-cost pricing are larger for the targeted rival. Similarly, a predator that enjoys a price premium normally has a larger unit profit margin and thus in a price war enjoys the advantage of lesser absolute losses per unit.

Although the assumption of a perfectly competitive market, which underlies traditional economic theory, presumes these conditions are unlikely to occur, current policy perspectives that adopt this view admit such circumstances do arise. In this context, the large retailer seems to be an excellent model of a predator capable of recouping lost profits from below-cost pricing. Such firms have size advantages that yield lower costs of goods sold and other scale economies, they have multiple stores in multiple markets to enable cross-subsidization, and much of their competition is from small (fringe) stores. Thus, even under current policy, the potential that predation may occur under certain conditions appears to be, at least, accepted.

Additional Influences. An important issue, however, is whether these traditional structural indicators of market power are sufficiently inclusive and therefore instructive for predicting conditions favorable toward predatory pricing. Recent models in economics have admitted informational asymmetry to the conditions that may facilitate predation. The presence of informational asymmetries permits a firm to induce rivals to act in such a way (e.g., exit a market, set a price, determine output) as to result in a predatory outcome (cf. Ordover and Saloner 1989).

The so-called market signaling models are predicated on the notion that rival firms' reactions to a verbal statement (e.g., an announced plan to change price) or an action (e.g., an actual price change) are based on that firm's inferences about the motives and intentions of the acting firm. Thus, one firm may interpret a rival's price cut as a signal that the rival has superior knowledge of falling demand or has a cost advantage. This perception may cause the firm to reduce output or exit the market and thus enable the predator to recoup initial losses. Note that below-cost pricing is not necessary to achieve predation in these cases. A firm need only convince the prey that the predator's cost function will allow it to set prices that will make it difficult for the prey to recover long-term average costs (cf. Milgrom and Roberts 1990).

Reputational models portray situations in which asymmetries of information exist about the payoff function of rivals. By using aggressive pricing in some markets, a firm may convince rivals that it is irrational (i.e., accepts short-term losses willingly), so they should anticipate similar behavior in future markets (see Weigelt and Camerer 1988). McCall (1987) notes that predatory reputation may enable a firm to discipline incumbent rivals to follow a particular pricing system or other tacitly agreed to policy (e.g., price fixing).

More extensive discussions of these models and their application to marketing thought are available in studies by Gundlach (1995), Heil and Langvardt (1994), and Moorthy (1985). For some industries, the extent to which firms can retain informational advantages envisioned under these models seems limited if only because of the vested interests of nonpartisan information gatherers in the financial community. In the context of the tobacco industry (see Appendix A for the Marlboro example), it seems unlikely that R. J. Reynolds (RJR) would be significantly informationally disadvantaged relative to costs or demand given the extensive Wall Street scouting of firms in this business. The announcement that Philip Morris was prepared to lose $2 billion clearly signaled a hostile intent and might be interpreted as an attempt to develop a reputation for aggressive conduct, but RJR's competitive response would be unlikely to be shaped solely by Philip Morris' action. A pervasive exception to this thinking concerns professionally managed, large-scale firms that compete with small, family-owned fringe competitors (as is the case in many retail sectors). In general, powerful incumbents are likely to be the competitors holding informational advantages when such asymmetries do exist. Thus, informational advantages appear to be correlated with the traditional market power indicators.

Additional asymmetry issues identifiable from the context of marketing are those related to goals or demand segments served by a firm. These conditions further extend the domain of circumstances favorable toward predation. With respect to goals, it is well known that family businesses often have different goals (e.g., "being the boss" or maintaining family control) that are not as profit-driven as those of their corporate competition. (Indeed, such goals are important exit barriers in some industries.) Similarly, in large corporations, business goals for the various units are often a reflection of some business portfolio model. For example, it is certainly likely that the cigarette business has a different role in the product portfolio of product-market specialist Liggett & Myers than in that of

Philip Morris. Because cigarettes may play different roles in the long-term plans of each corporation, the relative importance of volume and profit goals (both short- and long-term) and therefore the willingness to sacrifice short-term profits for volume is also likely to vary.

Viewed in terms of demand segments served, current research shows that price competition among brands of different quality levels is often asymmetric. Blattberg and Wisniewski's (1989) work, for example, suggests that in markets with both high-price-tier, high-quality brands and low-price-tier, low-quality brands, the distribution of consumer preferences may be bimodal. The evidence cited for this inference is that price "deals" on brands in the high-price tier draw sales from other high-price brands and lower-tier brands as the price gap between tiers narrows. (This pattern is observable in the Marlboro case.) However, price deals for low-tier brands do not result in substantial shifts in sales from high-tier brands. (Bemmaor and Mouchoux [1991] report similar findings.) The consequence of these findings is that private label brands are extremely dependent on the price umbrella of higher-priced national brands. Thus, differences in real or perceived quality can facilitate predation even at above-cost prices because of the asymmetric cross-elasticities between demand segments. Indeed, mere brand awareness may be sufficient to establish such asymmetric demand if incumbent brands are competing with fledgling firms (cf. Rosenbaum 1987).

Because competing firms have differing resources, market power, and managerial capabilities, it is conceivable that these differences occasionally result in informational asymmetries that could foster predation. We argue, however, that differences across firms in the goals established for a given product category or in the cross-elasticities their brands face in the marketplace are fundamentally much more important to the decision to engage in aggressive pricing behavior. For example, product line consequences of price can be important. Philip Morris' decision to slash prices on Marlboro was likely made only after considering the cross-elasticity of demand with respect to other brands in its line, such as Basic and Virginia Slims. (Reibstein and Gatignon [1984] offer a framework for assessing the impact of product line price differentials.) Precisely because predatory pricing is a strategic behavior, we must appreciate the strategic role a given product category plays in an organization's long-range plan to adequately predict pricing behavior. However, assessments of the differences in the elasticity of demand curves facing different competitors (resulting from product differentiation) and in strategically sourced product goals are not evident in traditional explanations for predatory pricing. Their incorporation in developing thought on predation seems especially relevant.

MANAGERIAL DECISION MAKING UNDER UNCERTAINTY

Traditional economic thinking regarding managerial decision-making processes is based on a narrow model of calculated, profit-maximizing behavior under conditions of complete information concerning demand, competitors, and so on. Advocates of judgment-based marketing decision models do not appear to accept this assumption. Rather, they argue that managers tap multiple sources of objective and subjective information in making decisions rather than in calibrating data sets (cf. Little and Lodish 1981). Business-people may make good decisions on the basis of poor information, because either the measurements or models required for optimal decisions are nonexistent. Although decision support systems are designed to help reduce the magnitude of this problem, judgmental inputs remain important, as even the best models are inexact when attempting to model dynamic effects (Little 1979). As Little (p. 22) states, "Managers . . . do not formulate problems in model terms because that is not the way they naturally think. They want to think about strategy not analysis."

As we noted previously, though some economists admit incomplete information into the mix to show the possibility of "rational" predation, the signaling and reputation models make strong assumptions concerning managerial conjecturing and information processing (cf. Milgrom and Roberts 1990; Moorthy 1985). For example, the signaling models to which we previously alluded presume that managers make correct conjectures about the meaning of rivals' signals. Recent behavioral research is less sanguine about these assumptions.

The Rationality of Decision Making. Several researchers from management (Amit, Domowitz, and Fershtman 1988; Porter 1980) and marketing (Dolan 1981; Moore and Urbany 1994; Moorthy 1985), for example, have begun to focus on the extent to which the process of conjecturing and decision making by individual people and managers is only *procedurally* rational. That is, rather than being perfectly rational, these processes reflect only a desire and ability to make the best possible decision under the circumstances to achieve particular goals.[2] Such research recognizes the possibility of multiple and complex goals and is concerned with how decision makers collect information, form expectations regarding outcomes, and use information in making decisions. One conclusion of this research shows that managers rarely may be assumed to engage in perfectly calculated decision making in an economic sense. In the instance of Philip Morris, with the extremely negative reaction of the stock market, it seems unlikely that the firm had a precise calculation of when the $2 billion loss for 1993 might be recouped. Perhaps Philip Morris had other goals in mind for which this aggressive price cut seemed necessary. Although the literature on decision making under uncertainty is vast and growing, a few research streams seem of special relevance to the issue of predatory pricing.

One area of importance is well summarized by Gerla (1985), who notes that the psychology of risk taking has potential applicability for understanding predatory pricing behavior. Evidence suggests that managers considering risky strategies do not estimate or weigh probabilities accurately, are risk-averse with respect to strategies for gains, and

---

[2]According to Dickson (1992, p. 69), "Imperfect procedural rationality is deliberation under conditions of limited knowledge and uncertainty. Competitive rationality is the imperfect procedural rationality of economic rivals."

are "risk-affinitive" with respect to losses. For example, when the choice is between a certain but modest loss of share to competitors from no action and the risky option of predatory pricing, managers are likely to be predisposed toward the risky option. (Such a situation seems similar to that faced by Philip Morris in the cigarette business in early 1993 with the erosion of Marlboro's share.) This tendency is reinforced by the likelihood that the small probability of success through predation will likely be overestimated.

The accuracy of managers' conjectures is also the subject of several recent inquiries. Moore and Urbany (1994), for example, discuss three factors that can lead to misjudgments of competitors' reactions to a strategic move. As they point out, managers (1) may not bother to forecast competitors' capabilities or situations, (2) may misunderstand competitors' capabilities or situations, or (3) may predict reactions incorrectly because of a failure to see things from the competitor's point of view. It also has been pointed out that a potentially dangerous judgmental bias is to expect competitors to act the same way as the decision-making firm would act (Boulding et al. 1994).

Others have made similar arguments: Zajac and Bazerman (1991), for example, note that managers have blind spots in assessing competitive reactions and may not consider competitors' payoffs. Indeed, Moorthy (1985, p. 276) argues that price wars often result because competitors are uncertain about each other's payoffs and mistakenly pursue tough reputational strategies. On the other hand, Saporito (1992) suggests that price wars may be due simply to errors firms make in forecasting the length of time it takes to drive weaker competitors from a market; when exit barriers are strong and prolonged by unexpected bankruptcy, price cutting begets more price cutting.

Errors in predicting competitive response or in the consequences of responses have also been found to occur from inadequate information processing by so-called experts. Mahajan's (1992) experiments examining the "overconfidence effect" suggest that decision makers may overestimate their ability to "diagnose" the information they initially retrieve. Those with greater domain expertise are especially likely to overinflate the value of initial information and reduce their processing efforts.

In the terminology of game theory, a sequence of competitive decisions made over time is a *repeated game*. The contribution of the previously described signaling and reputation models is their identification of possible predatory strategies extending from such sequential processes and managerial decision making. However, these models do not account for manager risk taking or for variance in the accuracy of conjectures employed for making decisions. The previous findings suggest that these models could be fruitfully extended to recognize that (1) managers' assessments of the risk of an action may be situationally determined and (2) competitive conjecturing is (understandably) mediocre or erroneous in many settings.

The implication of such an extension relates directly to the recoupment standard by challenging prior assumptions regarding managers' assessments of the prospect of recovering lost profits after a predatory episode. In short, if we accept that managers may apply differing risk propensities as well as be incapable of accurately assessing the potential of recoupment, the basis of requiring such a finding for predation is questionable.

Those who defend the recoupment standard may point out that the recoupment argument does not assume that managers are always capable of accurately assessing the chances for recoupment, only that recoupment is the motive. That managers may err does not mean there are not serious consequences (e.g., destructive price wars or reductions in quality, output, or innovation) that ultimately result in diminished vigor of competition with potentially adverse effects on consumer welfare. The recoupment standard thus fails to protect the market from myopic or "risk-affinitive" managers engaging in aggressive pricing that causes such consequences. In other words, because the Supreme Court's standard only blocks low prices as anticompetitive if it forecasts a high probability of recoupment, it would not attempt to block low prices that it deems are based on "errors" in judgment or are "irrational." In either case injury to consumer welfare may well occur.

CONSUMER WELFARE CONSEQUENCES OF PREDATION

A final issue involves extant views of predatory pricing, which relate to the notion of consumer welfare. The federal perspective on consumer welfare (conditioned by economic theory) is that healthy competition should ensure allocative efficiency and low prices. As long as aggressive pricing is procompetitive, policymakers should take no action that insulates inefficient competitors from price competition. In contrast, the state views sometimes seem to reflect an overriding concern for preserving competitors. A market-oriented view shares the economics view that consumer welfare is enhanced by healthy competition and not by preserving weak competitors for their own sakes. Yet, this view suggests that the benefits of competition not only include low prices, but also nonprice benefits such as high quality, innovation, and variety.

It is well known that consumers switch brands regularly in many categories and that some of this switching reflects a desire for variety (cf. McAlister and Pessemier 1982). Indeed, many brands and retailers survive in markets by virtue of "niching" strategies that offer unique benefits (including low prices) to narrowly targeted segments. These brands can be threatened when the price gap between the dominant, mainstream offering and such fringe competitors grows. As Scherer (1976) points out, a dominant premium-priced brand can often use periodic price cuts (at above cost) to reduce the attractiveness of an industry to new low-priced potential entrants, which results in increased demand for a premium product from those who would prefer a lesser-priced alternative.

Although some economists may argue that such is the nature of competition "on the merits," our point is that consumer welfare can be judged on dimensions beyond prices and aggregate output levels; the diversity in output and the average quality of output are nontrivial dimensions of consumer welfare. Some economists might observe, however, that if consumers really valued variety, the demand for the weaker firms' varieties should be relatively insensitive to price competition. This is a difficult point to refute if the buyers' desire for variety is just a preference for having many choices available at a given point in time. But in some markets the benefit of variety is the ability to vary brand choices over time (i.e., to have a mix of consumption experiences). Such brands tend to have low purchase frequencies relative to their rate of household penetration (Kahn, Kalwani, and Morrison 1988). Buyers may well stock up on steeply discounted alternatives in the short run, thus unintentionally causing the collapse of shallow-pocketed firms that provide variety.

That consumers lose when price competition is arbitrarily restricted to preserve inefficient competitors or those offering minor nonprice benefits is indisputable; but to ignore the relevance of nonprice benefits to consumers is to accept a view of competition that presumes homogeneity. In fact, outside of pure commodity markets, nonprice competition is often the most vibrant aspect of a market, and marketers would argue that markets containing both price and nonprice competitors best serve the welfare of consumers.[3]

Toward a Marketing-Based Framework for Analyzing Aggressive and Predatory Pricing

Applying the previous insights and building on current thinking, we here frame an approach for understanding and analyzing predatory pricing in the context of aggressive pricing behavior. Following our contention that extant thought is unnecessarily constrained in its ability to sufficiently reflect today's competitive and organizational decision making, we propose a framework that is not restricted by the narrow assumptions of traditional economic price theory. However, its foundation parallels the basic outline of extant thinking. That thinking is based on four principles:

1. Aggressive pricing involves an *economic sacrifice* to the aggressor firm.
2. The firm's pricing behavior is presumably based on managerial evaluations of the possible outcomes of the behavior so that the long-term benefits are thought to be worth the sacrifice (i.e., makes *economic sense*).
3. A consequence of aggressive pricing is *harm to one or more competitors*.
4. To be predatory, the consequence of the injury to competitors must be *injury to consumer welfare*.

---

[3]Indeed, Dixit and Stiglitz (1977) demonstrate that even in monopolistically competitive situations, economists' market solutions to the number of competitors are likely to yield too few firms to reflect demand satisfactorily. With asymmetric demand and cost considerations, they observe a bias against competitors with high costs and inelastic demands.

TABLE 2

Traditional Versus Prospective Analysis of Aggressive Pricing

Principles	Traditional Economics Perspective	Additional Dimensions in Marketing-Oriented View
Economic sacrifice	Below-cost pricing	Significant reduction in short-term profits resulting from steep price reductions lasting for more than one purchase cycle
Economic sense	Set supracompetitive prices in the future to recoup losses from below-cost prices	Set prices to • Control discounting • Stop erosion of share • Cross-sell existing customers • Shift demand to more profitable segments • Retain high-volume buyers • Force competitors to shift resources across categories
Harm to competitors	Entry likely to be deterred, exit forced, or output reduced	Competitors may be forced to retrench to core markets or reduce fixed or variable costs
Consumer welfare consequences	Impact of competitors' responses on • Demand/supply balance • Competitive price levels	Impact of competitors' responses on • Innovation • Choice • Competitive price levels • Quality of output (as reflected in customer satisfaction)

Important differences, however, distinguish our view of aggressive and predatory pricing in terms of how these principles are interpreted and applied. First, our view differs in that we offer a less restrictive interpretation of these principles. In Table 2, we summarize these key differences across the principles identified for analyzing aggressive pricing with a view toward judging predation. Under the marketing-oriented view, additional dimensions supplement the traditional perspective for each of these principles. Second, as with the traditional perspective, all four principles are fundamental to a finding of predatory pricing. In applying these principles, however, our framework incorporates a broader view of competitive responses to aggressive pricing in terms of the strategic options and enabling conditions underlying competitors' choices of response.

Interpretation of the Four Principles

Economic Sacrifice. Current policy requires prices to be below cost to consider a claim of predation. More precisely, average variable cost appears to be the preferred measure of whether sufficient economic sacrifice has been incurred. As we previously noted, though, scholars adopting a dynamic perspective of competition have shown that the aims of predation may be achieved even at above-cost prices. Such arguments, however, are not new. Various economists have argued against the use of short-term marginal cost or average variable costs as indicators that equally efficient firms are likely to be excluded because of a predatory pricing episode (cf. Posner 1976; Scherer 1976). Scherer (1976), for example, has suggested that prices above marginal costs are likely to be exclusionary in many cases. This is especially true if one competitor is advantaged in terms of retailer relations or brand image (Rosenbaum 1987). Joskow and Klevorick (1979) also note that firms cannot be expected to earn normal returns on investments if they are forced to set prices below average *total* cost. Indeed, for high fixed-cost industries, the gap between average variable cost and average total cost can be enormous; therefore, substantial sacrifices may be incurred even at prices that are well above average variable costs.

The meaningfulness of a below-cost test is even more problematic in the case of the multiproduct firm. Above-cost reductions in profitability on cash cows can represent a substantial sacrifice to the firm even beyond their direct effect on corporate earnings, because these products are expected to underwrite the firm's efforts to develop successful products in other categories. Although Philip Morris has deep pockets, its decision to pursue a strategy for one strategic business unit that management knew would cost the company $2 billion in one year is clearly an economic sacrifice.

With these limitations, we eschew the use of narrow cost tests in favor of a less restrictive interpretation of economic sacrifice. In our view, price reductions can create sufficient economic sacrifice to be of concern if the cuts result in substantial profit reductions. Although it is likely that in high variable-cost firms such profit reductions most often result from prices that are below average variable costs, prices below average total cost can cause equal or greater absolute losses in high fixed-cost firms. On the other hand, in each of these cases, aggressive pricing does not constitute economic sacrifice if short-term volume gains offset the lower margin.

Economic Sense. The current view is that economic sense reflects the narrow logic that economic sacrifices will be incurred by an aggressive firm only when a reasonable inference is held that such sacrifices may be recovered through future price increases. This perspective underlies the court's requirement that a reasonable prospect or dangerous probability of recoupment in the form of price increases be established for any claim of predation. Such a view of managerial decision making, however, does not take into consideration the strategic nature of competitive interaction and the multitude of tactical scenarios that can attend a pricing decision.

As is indicated in Table 2, we believe that aggressive and potentially predatory pricing may make economic sense for a variety of reasons, with the logic of future recoupment in the form of supracompetitive prices representing only one such reason. Indeed, competitive strategy is extremely complex and varied. Just as retailers may recover losses from price leaders through increased sales of complementary products without setting supra-competitive prices, firms may reap many kinds of benefits that may not have recoupment as an aim. For example, under some competitive conditions, profit reductions due to lower margins may be less damaging than reductions that result from eroding market share if no pricing action were taken. In such cases, aggressive pricing may simply represent a lower loss strategy. Alternatively, a firm competing across several product markets may sacrifice profits in one category to induce a rival to shift resources away from another category. Giving up profit in one market may enable the firm to achieve greater profits overall. Or, firms selling a line of substitute products at different margins may sacrifice margins on high-end products if the result is a shifting of volume out of the low-priced end of the market. Finally, aggressive pricing in markets characterized by extensive discounting may signal competitors to reduce promotions or face the risk of a price war. (Note that all of these examples are potential explanations of the Philip Morris action.)

In each example, the decision to risk economic sacrifice may make sense to an aggressive firm, yet not involve future price increases or any other form of recoupment. That said, economic sense is assumed if there is a logical competitive rationale for using aggressive pricing.

Harm to Competitors. It is well established that it is not the purpose of antitrust policy to protect individual competitors. However, unless one or more competitors are injured through aggressive pricing, there can be no injury to competition; and injury to competition is a necessary condition for injuring consumer welfare.

In the traditional theory of predation, competitive injury occurs when entry is deterred (lower prices make markets less attractive) or when existing competitors are forced to reduce output or to exit. Injury of this form yields the requisite conditions that enable a predatory firm to harm competition through raising prices above supracompetitive levels. When injured, the competition is reduced, leaving the predator with sufficient market power to control prices.

Competitive injury may occur through the traditional means of entry deterrence, reduced output, and exit, but we believe there also are other forms of competitor injury. Harm to competition need not be limited to injury that results in competitive exit or retrenchment with resultant supracompetitive prices. As we have pointed out, firms that face aggressive pricing by their rivals often defy traditional logic by remaining in markets at the lower prices even though they sustain significant profit losses. Rather than exiting or reducing their output, these firms adjust to the new, lower profit level through nonprice responses, such as reducing research and development, advertising, customer service, or variety. Marlboro certainly could benefit from forcing competitors to exit the discount segment (thereby reducing variety) and restrict advertising and new product development efforts in response to a substantial decline in industry profitability. Firms' specific reactions to an aggressive pricing episode depend on their unique organizational goals, competitive conditions, and decision-making processes. Because aggressive pricing causes major competitors to reduce nonprice competitive initiatives in order to remain viable, a market can gravitate toward commodity status. Once this occurs, the aggressor—having successfully disciplined the market through a price war (or threat of one)—may be able to exert some form of price leadership to achieve supracompetitive prices. Thus, competitive harm can include not only forced exit or output reduction, but also—from a marketing perspective—a decline in competitive mentality and nonprice initiatives. Moreover, as we discuss subsequently, traditional assessments of market conditions must be supplemented to foresee the full possibilities of such harm.

Consequences for Welfare. Extant theory relies on a narrow, efficiency-based conception of consumer welfare; in contrast, in a marketing perspective, consumer welfare is more broadly defined. From the marketing perspective, allocative efficiency requires a continuously vibrant market of independent actors. If competitive exit or output reduction occur (the traditional routes to facilitate recoupment), supracompetitive prices will emerge. But discarding key points of differentiation is much like output reduction; rivals give up their ambitions. The demise of nonprice competition can be directly detrimental (e.g., fewer flights from Denver to Phoenix; substitution for high-cost, natural ingredients in food products) because vibrant, nonprice competition is gone, or indirectly detrimental, if the loss of competition occurs because of market disciplining. In the latter case, firms that have pared costs to remain in a market are unlikely to be aggressive competitors on either price or nonprice dimensions. As marketers learn more about the nature of competitive interaction, the partial substitutability of price and nonprice strategies becomes more evident (cf. Ramaswamy, Gatignon, and Reibstein 1994). Thus, a dynamic perspective on aggressive pricing and predation must recognize the possibility of reduced consumer welfare due to the loss of nonprice benefits and the potential for price leadership and collusion that results from the loss of product differentiation in the market.

CONDITIONS INFLUENCING SUCCESSFUL PREDATION: THE ROLE OF COMPETITORS' RESPONSES

In the traditional view, the principles previously discussed are applied through the concept of market power (cf. Baldwin 1987). That is, predatory pricing is deemed possible (i.e., makes economic sense) only if the economic sacrifices incurred (i.e., from below-cost prices) can be recouped through later supracompetitive prices. Recoupment itself requires market power or the ability to set supracompetitive prices, which means that harm to competitors and consumers has (necessarily) resulted. Market power is determined through evaluation of market structure conditions. In the context of the traditional perspective, knowledge of a firm's market power therefore provides a parsimonious set of conditions for assessing the response of competitors to an aggressive and potentially predatory pricing episode. Rather than be confined to traditional assessments of market power as informed by market structure analysis, our framework relies on a broader set of conditions. Hence, for evaluating the conditions that influence the possibility of predatory pricing, we go beyond considering market structure to embrace the strategic process of competitive interaction and managerial decision making that underlie the responses of individual firms to aggressive pricing.

Some work in marketing on competitive reactions presumes that competitive reactivity (i.e., the magnitude of response to a rival's market action) is a characteristic of a market (Gatignon 1984, p. 389). Other research concludes that the likelihood and magnitude of response are shaped by the visibility and reversibility of the aggressor's action and the case with which rivals can respond (Chen and MacMillan 1992; Chen and Miller 1994). However, that individual firms in the same market facing the same competitive conditions will not all react to a competitor's action in the same way is well established by empirical research in marketing (cf. Ramaswamy, Gatignon, and Reibstein 1994). Research on responses to competitive entry indicates that incumbent firms respond by using those marketing variables that are the firm's best weapons in terms of elasticity of market response (Gatignon, Anderson, and Helson 1989). Thus, price actions may stimulate price responses from some competitors and nonprice responses from others. Similarly, some competitors may exit a market when confronted with aggressive pricing, whereas others may remain and attempt to adapt or respond. As Dickson (1992, p. 71, emphasis added) points out, "In a theory of dynamic competition . . . the focus shifts to the study of variation in the *adaptability* of individual sellers over time."

Such observations suggest that firms' responses to aggressive pricing are truly strategic behaviors, as opposed to exogenously determined reactions. Therefore, we view market structure considerations as but one element in the set of conditions influencing responses to aggressive pricing and the prospect of successful predation. For example, if price responses were viewed in the context of a typical strategic planning portfolio model, it would be recognized that firms would need to respond in the context of their competitive market structures. At the same time, a certain level of free will exists as firms decide on the appropriate goals and strategies for individual products or business units; a firm may choose share gains over profit gains and elect to withdraw, defend, or aggressively respond. In a dynamic setting, how a particular firm responds also depends on how its organizational culture, information resources, and personality (risk orientation) and skills of the decision maker shape the decision-making process (Dickson 1992).

With the questions in Appendix B, we use the insights emerging from scholars in marketing and related disciplines to provide a basis for assessing the potential competitive responses and consequences associated with aggressive pricing that tends toward predation. These insights are categorized into four sets of conditions (see Appendix B) that influence the willingness and ability of firms to respond to aggressive and potentially predatory pricing. The specific conditions reflect the relative resources, constraints, or positions of advantage (i.e., power and countervailing power) that might be available to various competitors in a market. A governing assumption is that power is not simply binary (firms have either deep or shallow pockets) but that there are shades of difference, whose gradations reflect differences in the opportunities, information, or strategic orientation that facilitate a firm's ability to adapt to a changing competitive situation (i.e., yield the firm some countervailing power).

Thus, opportunities may be available to one competitor in a market but not others, which creates variations between firms in terms of the range of available response strategies[4] (e.g., one competitor may have greater cross-subsidization opportunities, be less reliant on a market as a source of cash flow, or have a stronger commitment to a market than another competitor). These additional conditions can confer countervailing power to firms with lesser resources than an aggressive price leader, thus reducing the extent of competitive injury sustained. Examples of countervailing power include finding market niches, being able to accept substantially lower sales or profit goals, and being willing and able to take a risk that the predator is bluffing.

Recent research that addresses reactions to signals and actions appears to broadly support our viewpoint. A fundamental question addressed by much of this research is, What determines the magnitude of a firm's competitive response? (cf. Heil and Walters 1992; Robertson, Eliashberg, and Rymon 1995). Whether a response is retaliatory (high magnitude), matching, or passive (low magnitude) appears to be influenced by characteristics of the signal (e.g., the hostility and severity of consequences embedded in it), the reacting firm's strategic situation (e.g., opportunities for niching strategies, channel power, commitment to the market), and traditional industry market structure variables (Chen and MacMillan 1992; Heil and Robertson 1991). For assessing the prospect of successful predation involving price, we consider each of these factors an important element of inquiry.

ANALYZING AN AGGRESSIVE AND POTENTIALLY PREDATORY PRICING EPISODE

In the Figure, we portray the flow of analysis and key linkages among the four principles in our framework. Fundamental to this process is a view of competitive response to aggressive pricing that is based on the previously discussed expanded notion of countervailing power. If there is some economic sacrifice by an aggressive firm, rivals may respond in

---

[4]Lambkin and Day (1989) offer a parallel perspective, showing how a competitive shake-out results in failures, subpar performers, and survivors.

FIGURE

Predicting Competitive and Welfare Consequences of Aggressive Pricing

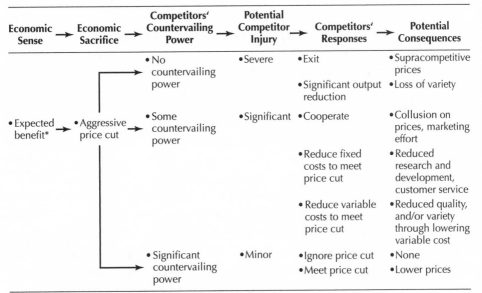

Economic Sense	Economic Sacrifice	Competitors' Coundervailing Power	Potential Competitor Injury	Competitors' Responses	Potential Consequences
		• No countervailing power	• Severe	• Exit	• Supracompetitive prices
				• Significant output reduction	• Loss of variety
• Expected benefit*	• Aggressive price cut	• Some countervailing power	• Significant	• Cooperate	• Collusion on prices, marketing effort
				• Reduce fixed costs to meet price cut	• Reduced research and development, customer service
				• Reduce variable costs to meet price cut	• Reduced quality, and/or variety through lowering variable cost
		• Significant countervailing power	• Minor	• Ignore price cut	• None
				• Meet price cut	• Lower prices

*See list of economic sense dimensions in Table 2.

various ways, depending on their perceptions and countervailing power. These responses determine the potential consequences to competitive rivalry and consumer welfare.

If the countervailing power of competitors is sufficient to either meet or ignore the aggressive pricing without incurring substantial economic harm, neither competition nor consumer welfare is at risk. Indeed, consumer welfare is enhanced if prices remain low. In the absence of countervailing power, aggressive pricing is more likely to result in significant exit or output reduction; therefore, the traditional market power indicators are likely to be sufficient for the analysis. If competitors possess enough countervailing power to remain in business, but only at the cost of economically damaging losses, we argue that both price and nonprice determinants of consumer welfare may be at risk. To salvage a minimum level of profitability in such an environment, management's choices are the following:

1. Reduce variable costs by lowering labor, material, or setup costs (by reducing product quality or variety) to offset the lower price.
2. Offset price reductions by lowering fixed costs for advertising, customer service, and research and development or by reducing selling and distribution costs by retreating to the most profitable channels or territories.

3. Cooperatively establish a "fair" price or marketing effort level either through collusion or by pursuing the "tit-for-tat" strategy that has been judged as best in prisoner dilemma–type game situations (cf. Axelrod 1980; Fader and Hauser 1988).[5]

Economic theory and marketing logic suggest that firms that unilaterally reduce marketing efforts cause their own demise. However, just as in the case of price, a broad loss in competitive effort on quality, variety, customer service, or innovation reduces pressure on the leader to continue offering these benefits, thereby further compounding the loss to consumer welfare. Whether these consequences are harmful enough to warrant a charge of predation remains a policy question that can only be answered in the context of an individual case.

Discussion

That price aggression is a highly visible action as well as one that can be swiftly matched means that a relatively high probability of retaliation can be expected (Chen and Miller 1994). So why do firms attack with price? Chen and Miller (1994, p. 97) suggest that "[p]aradoxically, it may be that the attacks that have the greatest potential payoffs are the most likely to be visible." In other words, aggressive behavior must, in some way, make economic sense. The framework we present offers an approach for understanding the economic sense of aggressive pricing and competitors' responses to aggressive and potentially predatory pricing, as well as for identifying the potential consequences for competition and consumer welfare. Although its principle foundations parallel extant thinking, important differences distinguish the application and interpretation of these principles for analyzing such conduct. As we observed, the dominant economic theory currently informing public policy argues that predation is irrational and would therefore not occur. But the stringent assumptions underlying that thinking challenge its legitimacy. Although parsimonious models of managerial decision making can be useful, rivals in markets characterized by intensive competition require complex decision-making processes to judge the sense of their actions. As Dickson (1992, p. 72) argues. "Competitive innovation-imitation depends on the accuracy of a firm's environmental analyses. Little attention has been paid to how marketing decision-makers scan the entire marketplace environment, [and] structure such analysis . . . in their innovation-imitation decision-making."

Recent scholarship focusing on competitive interactions and managers' strategic decision-making processes argues for a dynamic view of price and nonprice competition,

---

[5]The notion that cooperatively established prices may be a consequence of an aggressive pricing policy that is met with some countervailing power apparently underlies the Justice Department's investigation of Archer-Daniels-Midland (ADM). When ADM entered the market for lysine (a feed additive made from corn), prices were around $2.25 per pound. By 1991, due to ADM's pricing (and increased industry capacity), prices fell to $.65 per pound—well below the estimated ADM break-even price level of $.85 per pound. Despite the increased capacity, however, prices rebounded sharply in 1992 and reached $1.35 per pound by 1994, with ADM holding about 50% of the market (Burton, Kilmar, and Gibson 1995; Yales 1995).

in which complex goals, signals, and conjectures under imperfect information dominate. To date, little of this research has emphasized pricing strategy. Chen and MacMillan (1992) argue that researchers interested in competitive interaction have underestimated the role of price decisions because they appear to be tactical actions when in fact they are often decisions of great magnitude (as in aggressive pricing). Because price is a readily measurable competitive instrument, it is relatively easy to include in econometric estimations of reaction matrices. But, though such studies help document the nature of competitors' reactions, they do not help us understand the strategic reasons for the observed reaction patterns (Weitz 1985). Additionally, the nature of competitive responses can be varied—even across rivals in the same market. In this respect, one of our key motivations is to foster further research on competitive interaction and strategic decision making in the area of pricing and on the choice between price and nonprice dimensions of competitive strategy.

Because the framework presented here integrates various explanations underlying aggressive pricing behavior and competitive response, it offers a guide for structuring further public policy thinking regarding predation. A consequence of this framework is to open the vast middle ground between those situations in which aggressive pricing causes no competitive harm and those in which competitors are driven out of a market. As we suggest in the figure, the middle ground (i.e., where significant injury occurs) recognizes the potential impact of aggressive pricing on collusive pricing practices, nonprice competition, and nonprice dimensions of consumer welfare. Current thinking ignores these consequences.

Application of the framework and principles to public policy requires the development of indicators of economic sacrifice, nonprice competition, and welfare consequences. Doubtless there will be controversy over such measures. On the other hand, there has been considerable disagreement over the measurement of below cost, and the welfare consequence known as *supracompetitive prices* is not amenable to precise calibration. Because the field of marketing is frequently involved in measurement challenges and underscores the virtues of quality, service, variety, and innovation to consumers and strategists, it is especially well positioned to tackle the challenge of developing multidimensional indicators of consumer welfare.

As researchers in marketing begin to examine further the nature of aggressive and predatory pricing, they also may wish to consider the related practices of dumping and nonprice predation. A practice that has been related to predatory pricing involves *international dumping,* or the importation of products into the United States at prices substantially less than the actual market value or wholesale price in the principal market of the country of their production and the attendant costs of importation combined. This practice has received considerable attention by both policymakers and managers, with analogies to predatory pricing in an international context. Although similarities in conduct exist, the basis for policy development of U.S. antidumping laws has been below-market price, "fairness," and free trade, whereas predation policy's concern is for below-cost price and consumer welfare (cf. Feltham et al. 1991). With respect to nonprice predation, whereas marketing traditionally has viewed the marketing mix as composed of interchangeable variables for addressing consumer needs and competing amongst rivals, antitrust policy has distinguished predatory pricing conduct from conduct involving other marketing mix variables. However, in addition to pricing strategies, firms may employ strategies of predation that attempt to increase competitors' costs. Gundlach (1990) reviews a variety of different forms of nonprice predation that may result in anticompetitive outcomes. Research addressing the nature of both these practices and the contrasting philosophies that inform each provide fruitful inquiry for further research.

Finally, it is notable that antitrust inquiry based on strict adherence to the simplifying assumptions and deductive logic of neoclassical price theory so prevalent in the 1980s appears to be evolving toward more careful examination and factual inquiry. Considerable antitrust scholarship (see Royall 1995) and at least one Supreme Court decision (*Eastman Kodak Company v. Image Technical Service* 1992) have observed the limited usefulness of simplified economic models and tests for understanding the complex economic forces operating in today's business environments. Rather than relying on such circumscribed views, these scholars and judges favor a melding of prior antitrust thinking with the enriched explanations of less constrained thought. Our framework offers such an integration within the domain of predatory pricing.

Appendix A

The Marlboro Story: Aggressive Competition or Predatory Pricing?

In April of 1993, Philip Morris announced major price cuts on its Marlboro brand, the cigarette industry leader, admitting that the proposed plan could cost the company $2 billion in lost operating income for the year. The announcement led Wall Street to mark down Philip Morris' market value by 20% in one day. Within a few months it became apparent that the plan was not simply a short-term promotion but a price cut that would be in effect for some time.

What strategic objectives motivated these cuts? Industry analyses fell into two camps. In one, the strategic target was viewed as the growing discount segment of the market. Price-oriented competitors had been taking a steadily increasing share of the market for several years, with a substantial portion of this growth coming from Marlboro. Although Philip Morris was a player in that segment (primarily with its Basic brand), it was estimated that a pack of discount cigarettes earned only about one nickel per pack for the manufacturer—about one-tenth the margin of premium cigarettes. By narrowing the gap between premiums and discount from as much as $1 to perhaps 45¢, arguably Marlboro would draw market share back from the discount segment—both from lower margin Philip Morris brands and from competitors' brands (*Financial Times* 1993). As one Wall Street analyst put it, "The job that has to be done is . . . destroying the two price points below the full-price brands. That's the objective and what they want to do" (*Supermarket News* 1993, p. 15).

The alternative view was that Philip Morris' real target was its major competitor, RJR, manufacturer of half a dozen strong brands, including Winston, Camel, and Vantage. Heavily burdened by the debt from its famous leveraged buyout in 1989, RJR was viewed as ill-equipped for a price war involving its premium priced cash cows. RJR was said to need 9¢ per $1 of sales just for debt service. Being highly leveraged, RJR's effective tax rate was only 8%, whereas Philip Morris' 32% rate enabled it to significantly share any earnings reductions with the U.S. Treasury. Moreover, market tests conducted in Oregon the previous winter demonstrated that Marlboro share gains came equally from discount and competing premium brands. The conclusion was that Philip Morris hoped to inflict significant damage on RJR by increasing Marlboro's market share in the premium segment or forcing RJR to cut prices on its premium brands and push up prices on RJR discount brands (Chakravarthy and Feldman 1993).

As events unfolded, RJR ultimately reduced its premium prices. Discount competitors also unveiled new brands in lower (but not in superdiscount) price ranges. The narrowing price gap between premium and discount brands did result in sales growth for the Marlboro brand. Philip Morris' discount brand suffered a 10% decline, and RJR chose to exit the generic and private label segment altogether. R. J. Reynolds lagged behind Philip Morris's Marlboro in cutting prices, and its premium brands did not keep pace with Marlboro's growth. Overall, RJR's share of the total cigarette market fell from 32.5% in the first half of 1993 to 27.4% in the first half of 1994 (Teinowitz 1994). According to one analysis, the value of the Marlboro brand fell 36% in 1993 due to a 32% decline in brand-related operating profits. But the value of RJR Nabisco's Camel and Winston brands declined by 59% in the same period (Ourusoff 1994, p. 14).

Did consumers benefit (health questions aside) from the price competition unleashed by Philip Morris? Did Philip Morris benefit? Did Philip Morris have a high probability of recouping the profits lost from this price action if RJR could be eliminated or rendered less competitive? Did Philip Morris' management do a poor job of conjecturing RJR's response? Did they underestimate the cost of the price war, or overestimate the gain in market share, or was the decision made without regard to any profit goal? Did management even attempt to calculate the long-term profit impact of this action? Did Philip Morris act out of confidence by "sending a message" to its competitors that they should refrain from aggressive behavior? Or, did Philip Morris act out of fear, "rolling the dice" in the belief that inaction could only result in continued erosion of its premium cigarette business? Was Philip Morris management acting rationally?

Viewed from a legal perspective, the foregoing questions are moot. The cost of the price war finally became too high for Philip Morris, which gradually ended its deep discounting program. But had the aggressive pricing continued, what would have been the consequences? Would the prospect of significant damage to RJR, Brown & Williamson, or Liggett & Myers have provided fertile ground for predatory pricing charges? Or does any price above cost constitute competition "on the merits"?

Appendix B

Assessing Conditions Influencing the Competitive Responses and Consequences of Aggressive Pricing

1. Are there asymmetries in the abilities of firms to conduct a price war or recoup lost profits (*market power*)?
   - Superior financial resources
   - Larger market share
   - Cross-subsidization opportunities from other business units
   - Lower production or capital costs
   - Higher profit margins
2. Are there *informational asymmetries* that enable a predator to influence the exit, entry, output, or pricing decisions of competitors?
   - Prey believes predator has superior knowledge of cost or demand conditions
   - Prey believes predator has deeper pockets
   - Prey believes predator is likely to repeat history of aggressive pricing
   - Prey lacks knowledge of predator's payoffs
3. Are there differences in the *strategic product and/or market opportunities* that enable one firm to use price more aggressively than the competition to build sales?
   - Firm has a premium price and/or quality image creating asymmetric cross-elasticity (making price competition advantageous for the aggressor)
   - Firm has a wider range of complementary goods and services (facilitating recoupment)
   - No niches are available to rivals to hide from price competition
4. Are there differences in firms' *strategic orientations* that moderate the importance of profitability?
   - Differences in a product's role in the firm's portfolio (e.g., cash cow, star)
   - Differences in overall firm goals that may create exit barriers (e.g., family business)
   - Differences in the tolerance for risk

References

Amit, Raphael, Ian Domonitz, and Chaim Fershtman (1988), "Thinking One Step Ahead: The Use of Conjectures in Competitive Analysis," *Strategic Management Journal,* 9 (September/October), 431–42.

Antitrust & Trade Regulation Report (1987), "Oliver Recommends Against Changes in Resale Price Maintenance Standard," *The Bureau of National Affairs,* August 20, Issue 1329, 340.

Areeda, Philip and Donald Turner (1975), "Predatory Pricing and Related Practices Under Section 2 of the Sherman Act," *Harvard Law Review,* 88 (4), 720–32.

Axelrod, R. (1980), "More Effective Choice in the Prisoner's Dilemma," *Journal of Conflict Resolution,* 24 (3), 379–403.

Baldwin, William L. (1987), *Market Power, Competition and Antitrust Policy.* Homewood, IL: Richard D. Irwin.

Baumol, William J. (1967), *Business Behavior, Value and Growth,* revised ed. New York: Harcourt, Brace and Worth.

Bemmaor, Albert and Dominique Mouchoux (1991), "Measuring the Short-Term Effect of In-Store Promotion and Retail Advertising on Brand Sales: A Factorial Experiment," *Journal of Marketing Research,* 28 (May), 202–14.

Blattberg, Robert and John Deighton (1991), "Interactive Marketing: Exploiting the Age of Addressability," *Sloan Management Review,* 33 (Fall), 5–14.

___ and Kenneth Wisniewski (1989), "Price-Induced Patterns of Competition," *Marketing Science,* 8 (Fall), 291–309.

Boulding, William et al. (1994), "Understanding Managers' Strategic Decision-Making Processes," *Marketing Letters,* 5 (Fall), 413–26.

Brooke Group Limited v. Brown & Williamson Tobacco Corporation (1993), 113 S.Ct. 2578.

Burton, Thomas, Scott Kilman, and Richard Gibson (1995), "Investigators Suspect a Global Conspiracy in Archer-Daniels Case," *Wall Street Journal,* (July 28), A1, A5.

Chakravarthy, Subrata and Amy Feldman (1993), "Don't Underestimate the Champ," *Forbes,* (May 10), 106.

Chen, Ming-Hu and Ian MacMillan (1992), "Non-Response and Delayed Response to Competitive Moves," *Academy of Management Journal,* 35 (3), 539–70.

___ and Danny Miller (1994), "Competitive Attack, Retaliation and Performance," *Strategic Management Journal,* 15 (February), 85–102.

Dickson, Peter (1992), "Toward A General Theory of Competitive Rationality," *Journal of Marketing,* 56 (January), 69–83.

Dixit, Avinash and Joseph Stiglitz (1977), "Monopolistic Competition and Optimum Product Diversity," *American Economic Review,* 67 (June), 297–308.

Dolan, Robert (1981), "Models of Competition: A Review of Theory and Empirical Evidence," in *Review of Marketing,* Ben M. Enis and Kenneth J. Roering, eds. Chicago: American Marketing Association, 224–34.

Eastman Kodak Company v. Image Technical Service (1992), 112 S.Ct. 2072.

Fader, Peter and John Hauser (1988), "Implicit Coalitions in a Generalized Prisoner's Dilemma," *Journal of Conflict Resolution,* 32 (3), 553–82.

Feltham, Ivan, Stuart Salen, Robert Mathieson, and Ronald Wonnacott (1991), "Competition (Antitrust) and Anti-Dumping Laws in the Context of the Canada–United States Free Trade Agreement," *Canada–United States Law Journal,* 17 (1), 71–168.

Financial Times (London) (1993), "Old Loyalties Tested by Price War: Philip Morris' Efforts to Lure U.S. Smokers Back to Marlboro Country," (July 23), 21.

Gatignon, Hubert (1984), "Competition as Moderator of the Effect of Advertising on Sales," *Journal of Marketing Research,* 17 (November), 470–85.

___, Erin Anderson, and Kristiaan Helsen (1989), "Competitive Reactions to Market Entry: Explaining Interfirm Differences," *Journal of Marketing Research,* 26 (February), 44–55.

Gerla, Harry (1985), "The Psychology of Predatory Pricing: Why Predatory Pricing Pays," *Southwestern Law Journal,* 39 (3), 755–780.

Gundlach, Gregory (1990), "Predatory Practices in Competitive Interaction: Legal Limits and Antitrust Considerations," *Journal of Public Policy & Marketing,* 9 (1), 129–53.

___ (1995), "Price Predation: Legal Limits and Antitrust Considerations," *Journal of Public Policy & Marketing,* 14 (Fall), 278–89.

Hanssens, Dominique (1980), "Market Response, Competitive Behavior, and Time Series Analysis," *Journal of Marketing Research,* 17 (November), 470–485.

Haynes, William J., Jr. (1988), *State Antitrust Laws.* Washington, DC: Bureau of National Affairs.

Heil, Oliver and Arlen Langvardt (1994), "The Interface Between Competitive Market Signaling and Antitrust Law," *Journal of Marketing,* 58 (July), 81–96.

___ and Thomas Robertson (1991), "Toward a Theory of Competitive Market Signaling: A Research Agenda," *Strategic Management Journal,* 12 (September/October), 403–18.

___ and Rockney Walters (1992), "Explaining Competitive Reactions to New Product Signals: An Empirical Study," *Journal of Product Innovation Management,* 10 (January), 53–65.

Isaac, R. Mark and Vernon Smith (1985), "In Search of Predatory Pricing," *Journal of Political Economy,* 93 (2), 320–45.

Jordan, William H. (1995), "Predatory Pricing After *Brooke Group*: The Problem of State 'Sales Below Cost' Statutes," *Emory Law Journal,* 44 (1), 267–318.

Joskow, Paul and Alvin Klevorick (1979), "A Framework for Analyzing Predatory Pricing Policy," *Yale Law Journal,* 89 (March), 213–70.

Kahn, Barbara, Manohar Kalwani, and Donald Morrison (1988), "Niching Versus Change-of-Pace Brands: Using Purchase Frequencies and Penetration Rates to Infer Brand Positionings," *Journal of Marketing Research,* 25 (November), 384–90.

Lambkin, Mary and George Day (1989), "Evolutionary Processes in Competitive Markets," *Journal of Marketing,* 53 (July), 4–20.

Little, John D. C. (1979), "Decision Support Systems for Marketing Managers," *Journal of Marketing,* 43 (Summer), 9–27.

___ and Leonard Lodish (1981), "Commentary on Judgment Based Marketing Models," *Journal of Marketing,* 45 (Fall), 24–29.

Mahajan, Jayashee (1992), "The Overconfidence Effect in Marketing Management Predictions," *Journal of Marketing Research,* 29 (August), 329–42.

Matsushita Electric Industrial Company v. Zenith Radio Corporation (1986), 475 U.S. 574.

McAlister, Leigh and Edgar Pessemier (1982), "Variety Seeking Behavior: An Interdisciplinary View," *Journal of Consumer Research,* 9 (December), 311–22.

McCall, Charles W. (1987), "Predatory Pricing: An Economic and Legal Analysis," *Antitrust Bulletin,* 32 (Spring), 1–59.

Milgrom, Paul and John Roberts (1990), "New Theories of Predatory Pricing" in *Industrial Structure in the New Industrial Economics,* G. Bonanno and D. Brandolini, eds. Oxford: Clarendon Press, 112–37.

Moore, Marian (1992), "Signals and Choices in a Competitive Interaction: The Role of Moves and Messages," *Management Science,* 38 (April), 483–500.

___ and Joel Urbany (1994), "Blinders, Fuzzy Lenses, and the Wrong Shoes: Pitfalls in Competitive Conjecture," *Marketing Letters,* 5 (Fall), 247–58.

Moorthy, K. Sridhar (1985), "Using Game Theory to Model Competition," *Journal of Marketing Research,* 22 (August), 262–82.

Ordover, Janusz and Garth Saloner (1989), "Predation, Monopolization, and Antitrust" in *The Handbook of Industrial Organization,* Richard Schmalensee and Robert Willig, eds. Amsterdam: North Holland, 537–96.

Ourusoff, Alexandra (1994), "Brands: What's Hot, What's Not," *Financial World,* (August 2), 40–56.

Porter, Michael E. (1980), *Competitive Strategy: Techniques for Analyzing Industries and Competition,* New York: The Free Press.

Posner, Richard (1976), *Antitrust Law: An Economic Perspective.* Chicago: University of Chicago Press.

Ramaswamy, Venkatram, Hubert Gatignon, and David Reibstein (1994), "Competitive Marketing Behavior in Industrial Markets," *Journal of Marketing,* 58 (April), 45–55.

Reibstein, David and Hubert Gatignon (1984), "Optimal Product Line Pricing: The Influence of Elasticities and Cross-Elasticities" *Journal of Marketing Research,* 21 (August), 259–67.

Robertson, Thomas, Jehoshua Eliashberg, and Talia Rymon (1995), "New Product Announcement Signals and Incumbent Reactions," *Journal of Marketing,* 59 (July), 1–15.

Rosenbaum, David (1987), "Predatory Pricing and the Lemon Juice Industry," *Journal of Economic Issues,* 21 (1), 237–58.

Royall, M. Sean (1995), "Symposium: Post-Chicago Economics," *Antitrust Law Journal,* 63 (2), 445–54.

Rule, Charles F. (1988), "Claims of Predation in a Competitive Marketplace: When Is an Antitrust Response Appropriate?" *Antitrust Law Journal,* 57 (Summer), 421–34.

Saporito, Bill (1992), "Why the Price Wars Never End," *Fortune,* (March 23), 68–72.

Scherer, Frederic (1976), "Predatory Pricing and the Sherman Act: A Comment," *Harvard Law Review,* 89 (4), 869–90.

Sheffet, Mary Jane (1994), "The Supreme Court and Predatory Pricing." *Journal of Public Policy & Marketing,* 13 (Spring), 163–67.

Simon, Herbert A. (1979), "Rational Decision-Making In Business Organizations," *American Economic Review,* 69 (September), 493–512.

Stelzer, Irwin M. (1987), "Changing Antitrust Standards," remarks before the Workshop on Antitrust Issues in Today's Economy, The Conference Board, New York (March 5).

Sullivan, Lawrence A. (1977), *Handbook of the Law of Antitrust.* St. Paul, MN: West Publishing Company.

Supermarket News (1993), "Marlboro Price Cuts Extended Into August," (June 14), 15.

Teinowitz, I. (1994), "RJR Gets Burned in Cigarette War." *Advertising Age,* (August 29), 42.

Urbany, Joel and Peter Dickson (1994), "Evidence on the Risk Taking of Price Setters," *Journal of Economic Psychology,* 15 (1), 127–48.

Weitz, Barton A. (1985), "Introduction to Special Issue on Competition in Marketing," *Journal of Marketing Research,* 22 (August), 229–36.

Weigelt, Keith and Colin Camerer (1988), "Reputation and Corporate Strategy: A Review of Recent Theory and Applications," *Strategic Management Journal,* 9 (September/October), 443–54.

Yates, Ronald (1995), "Rival Says ADM Copied Its Process," *Chicago Tribune,* (July 28), C1–C2.

Zajac, Edward and Max Bazerman (1991), "Blind Spots in Industry and Competitive Analysis: Implications of Interfirm (Mis) Perceptions for Strategic Decisions," *Academy of Management Review,* 16 (3), 37–36.

THE COPYCAT ECONOMY

Pete Engardio and Faith Keenan

Once, a hot new idea spelled years of fat profits. But these days, rivals are moving into markets before you can say "clone"

Scenes from the corporate battlefield:

- For a decade, the refrigerator-size Symmetrix unit was the Goliath of the data-storage industry. Costing up to $3 million, it enabled its maker, EMC Corp., to reap fat profit margins. Then, in 2001, IBM and Hitachi Data Systems launched similar boxes. Prices plunged 60% last year, and are down about 35% this year.
- Kyocera Corp.'s QCP 6035 Smartphone, a combination personal digital assistant and Web-ready phone priced at $500, looked like a winner when it appeared in early 2001—until Samsung Electronics Co. launched a smaller PDA-phone with a color screen months later. The Smartphone now retails for $150.
- Last fall, Procter & Gamble Co. thought its $50 Swiffer WetJet mop, which sprays water on floors, would be the killer app of housecleaning. But then Clorox Co.'s ReadyMop forced P&G to cut its price by half in seven months.

Competition is the essence of a market economy. But rarely has it been this brutal. In numerous industries, companies are finding it increasingly hard to maintain a unique advantage long enough to make good profits on an innovation. Time was, companies could milk a novel product for years before cut-rate clones arrived. Now, new TVs, packaged foods, telecom routers, e-commerce concepts, and wireless services are barely out the door before rivals are on their tails, bludgeoning prices.

Call it the copycat economy. And it raises some critical questions: How do you make money in such an environment, especially when demand is flat? Already, the lack of pricing power partly explains why productivity gains of 3% to 4% aren't always translating into higher corporate profits. Longer term, it suggests companies may find it harder to sustain strong growth.

Many factors are at work. In pharmaceuticals, where drugmakers are hyping derivatives of old blockbusters like Claritin as their patents expire and generics swarm in, there's a paucity of technology breakthroughs. In electronics, digitization makes hardware easier to copy, since change is propelled by constant semiconductor and software advances. There has been an explosion of low-cost Asian rivals. And the rise of contract manufacturing and design has lowered the entry barrier for new players who lack factories and big labs. As a result, says CEO Michael E. Marks of contract manufacturer Flextronics Corp., keeping a product from becoming a commodity "will just get harder and harder."

Even many innovative productivity-boosting strategies of the '90s are commonplace. Nearly everyone now boasts of near-zero-defect quality, efficient supply chains, and virtual design. Often, they use the same contractors, consultants, and software. The shift of business to the Net also quickens the spread of management processes. "Everyone has the same capabilities," says Allen J. Delattre, head of Accenture Ltd.'s supply-chain consulting practice for electronics. "Even speed and quality are commodities."

For consumers and the U.S. economy, this dog-eat-dog battle is terrific. The rapid dissemination of innovation has helped spur America's productivity gains. It also means lower prices and greater choice. When color TV appeared in 1956, it took two decades before the price dropped in half. It took a decade for VCR prices to halve. In contrast, prices for DVD players, launched in 1997 for $700, halved in about two years, and now they sell for $153 on average, says market researcher NPD Techworld. Deflation has accelerated in other sectors. Since 1997, retail prices for women's apparel are down 8% on average, reports the Bureau of Labor Statistics. Television prices are down 30% in the U.S.; monthly cell-phone service, 32%.

For companies, though, benefits can be fleeting. A Mercer Management Consulting Inc. study suggests tech leaders are flaming out at a faster rate. In the 1980s, five years lapsed from the time the stocks of Digital Equipment, Wang Labs, Control Data Systems, and other highfliers went from 50% of their peak value, hit their highs, then dropped again by 50%. By then, rivals had saturated their markets or offered better technologies. In the early '90s, Cray, Sybase, and Lotus blasted off and fell in four years. In the late '90s, Lucent, Palm, Cisco Systems, Novell, and others peaked and stumbled in less than three. Their revenues followed similar curves. Mercer's Richard Wise thinks the shrinking half-life of tech leaders points to a critical issue. "A lot of companies are hitting a growth and value-creation wall," Wise says. Less tolerance for accounting tricks exacerbates the task.

Some companies are special. Dell Computer and Wal-Mart Stores are so good at execution that they always seem to be two steps ahead of the pack. Some winners control an industry standard, like Microsoft's Windows operating system. But it's getting harder for companies to establish such standards, Wise notes. Customers and rivals have ganged up to keep Nokia, America Online, Gemstar, and others from becoming the Microsofts of their industries.

There are ways to avoid the trap. For example, more companies view their hardware as platforms for pushing upgrades, spare parts, and software. That's how General Electric Co. and Sony Corp. make most of their money on aircraft engines and game players. EMC hopes software and services for banks, airlines, and others using its data-storage gear will drive future profits. Other companies constantly pump out cutting-edge products that fetch premium prices, however fleeting. To succeed in this game, companies often must get costs down to mass-production levels as soon as a new product hits the market—rather than months later. "Otherwise, you'll never make money," says Dellatre. That's one reason behind Samsung's success in new cell phones.

Another gambit is to tweak existing formulas and designs constantly. Thus, Colgate markets some 10 variations of toothpaste. Spanish clothing company Zara takes this to the extreme. It can modify a garment sold in its retail stores in two weeks, based on customer feedback from salespeople taking notes on handheld PCs.

Some companies are doing the opposite. They focus their research on fewer products, tenaciously defend patents, and back well-established brands with heavy marketing. A $500 million annual ad budget helps Gillette Co. charge $30 for its new Mach3Turbo razor and 12 replacement cartridges—while disposable razors go for $3.29 a dozen. As part of its goal to double profit margins in five years, Unilever Group has whittled its brands from 1,600 to 400. "It is increasingly difficult to develop consumer products that are truly breakthroughs," says Randy Quinn, senior vice-president for brand development. Instead, Unilever slaps its best brands on more products. Dove now appears on shower gel, deodorant, and skin cleanser.

But how long can such strategies produce growth? And as imitators try the same tactics, who is generating new demand? Or is everyone just cannibalizing each other? Eventually, companies must intensify the search for technology breakthroughs and new business models that deliver sustainable advantages. Until then, it will be hard to escape the copycat jungle.

Dominant Firms Attract Antitrust Probes and Investors

Greg Ip

Microsoft Corp., Intel Corp. and Coca-Cola Co. have been among the biggest creators of shareholder wealth during the 1990s bull market. They have also all come in for antitrust scrutiny.

These blue-chip growth companies boast enormous market shares, strong franchises and brand names and often the ability to expand profit margins in a highly competitive economy. These qualities are key to delivering consistent, above-average earnings, which is why investors attach such high values to them. But they are also the characteristics often associated with near-monopolies. As such, they are likely to attract antitrust scrutiny from regulators or competitors.

"The franchise is probably the No. 1 thing creating economies of scale," Mr. Paulsen says. "The franchises of Coke, Gillette, General Electric and so forth are very much like the barriers to entry of natural monopolies. There's a huge cost to establishing the franchise. (It) prevents other entries into their field, and allows almost perpetual ability to lower costs through more unit growth."

Microsoft Corp., Intel Corp. and Coca-Cola Co. have been among the biggest creators of shareholder wealth during the 1990s bull market. They have also all come in for antitrust scrutiny.

It may not be a coincidence.

These blue-chip growth companies boast enormous market shares, strong franchises and brand names and often the ability to expand profit margins in a highly competitive economy. These qualities are key to delivering consistent, above-average earnings, which is why investors attach such high values to them. But they are also the characteristics often associated with near-monopolies. As such, they are likely to attract antitrust scrutiny from regulators or competitors.

There is nothing illegal about a dominant market share per se. Indeed, whether these companies have actually done anything wrong is the subject of debate in Washington and in the courts. But their dominant, and in some cases near-monopolistic positions, are certainly one of the things investors love about them.

"The world is becoming increasingly dominated by monopoly power and the stock market reflects that, in the dominance of large capitalization companies, not just here but around the world," says James Paulsen, chief investment officer at Norwest Investment Management.

But unlike classic monopolists, he says today's giant companies use their size not to jack up prices but to spread their costs, hold down prices and keep competitors on the ropes.

"The franchise is probably the No. 1 thing creating economies of scale," Mr. Paulsen says. "The franchises of Coke, Gillette, General Electric and so forth are very much like the barriers to entry of natural monopolies. There's a huge cost to establishing the franchise. [It] prevents other entries into their field, and allows almost perpetual ability to lower costs through more unit growth."

The value that investors place in such franchises is obvious from stock prices. Coca-Cola trades at 49 times trailing 12-month earnings, Gillette Co. at 45 and Microsoft at 58. Standard & Poor's 500-stock index has a price/earnings ratio of 28.

Monopoly or franchise value has often been a mark of stock market leaders, from the railroads and industrial trusts at the turn of the century to International Business Machines Corp. and AT&T Corp. in the postwar period, and most of those have had their turn dealing with trust-busters' scrutiny.

What is noteworthy now is the contribution U.S. companies' dominant world market shares are making to their remarkable profit growth.

"Global brands that carry with them at least a modicum of pricing power now have a distinctly American flavor," says Douglas Cliggott, U.S. equity strategist at J.P. Morgan Securities Inc. in a report. "The active nourishment of these brand images, coupled with dramatic product innovation, particularly in the technology sector, have served as barriers to entry in a world that is awash in capital."

What investors love about these companies is the high growth and consistency of earnings such barriers to entry bring, Mr. Cliggott says. Indeed, when he scanned 63 industry groups to find out which had the highest P/E ratios and earnings growth and lowest earnings volatility in the past 10 years, he found five, four of which were obvious franchise businesses: large-cap software (notably Microsoft), household products and cosmetics, beverages (such as Coke) and restaurants (like McDonald's Corp.).

Franchise value or dominant market position can explain much of these companies' seemingly high valuations. Coke, for example, owes its 50% share of the world soft drink market not to government-granted monopoly or a costly fixed infrastructure, but to its painstakingly developed brand and distribution network.

Murray Stahl, chairman of New York money manager Horizon Asset Management, notes that Coke's shareholder equity is only $7.3 billion, or a piddling $2.96 per share.

But he calculates that since 1919, Coke has spent a staggering $78 billion, in current, inflation-adjusted dollars, on marketing, or $31 a share. If that marketing expense were treated as invested capital, the stock at yesterday's close of $77.4375 arguably trades at only 2.3 times book value, not 27 times. "Let's say we want to start a competitor to Coke. Even if someone gave me $78 billion, I think I'd need a lot more."

For anyone contemplating a challenge to Microsoft, Mr. Stahl says, "It would cost a lot more than Microsoft ever spent to develop their operating system. Then, the real barrier is, how do you convince a computer manufacturer to use a different operating system? So de facto, you have a barrier to entry. It doesn't have anything to do with money, and the only one that can really challenge it is the U.S. government."

The challenge to investors is finding other near monopolies worth buying. Beth Cotner, manager of Putnam Investment Management's large-cap Investors fund, is comfortable with high valuations on pharmaceuticals giants "because they have patents. Once you have a new drug approved, like [Warner-Lambert's] Lipitor or [Pfizer's] Viagra, you have patents in place that limit the competition for a number of years, and some of these new drugs address billion dollar-plus markets. If you can establish a dominant position and have little competition, it's going to be a very profitable endeavor." Warner-Lambert Co. trades at 60 times and Pfizer Inc. at 63 times trailing earnings.

Dominance in an industry can be fleeting. Utility stocks' underperformance reflects the new competition deregulation has permitted in their former government-granted monopolies. On the other hand, airlines, which routinely gushed red ink in bruising price wars, are pairing up in alliances: Continental Airlines with Northwest Airlines, Delta Air Lines with UAL Corp.'s United Airlines, and AMR Corp.'s American Airlines with U.S. Airways Group.

"To the extent that less direct competition means slower growth and higher margins— i.e. an oligopoly—the overall implications for airline industry profits and P/E multiples are positive," Merrill Lynch analysts say in a report. Certainly one reason SBC Communications Inc. wants to acquire Ameritech Corp. is the prospect of controlling one-third of the nation's local access phone lines, each a miniature near-monopoly into a consumer's home.

Sometimes competition chews away at what seems to be a monopoly. Intel Corp. has all the signs of a near-monopoly: an 83.5% share of the market for microprocessor chips, the ability to charge higher prices than its competitors and a well-established brand. It is also the subject of a Federal Trade Commission probe, with which it is co-operating. But William Fleckenstein, president of Seattle hedge-fund manager Fleckenstein Capital, says Intel has begun losing market share to lower-priced competitors in low-end computers. "People perceive Intel to be a monopoly. We will look back in time and people will laugh at that notion," says Mr. Fleckenstein, who has sold Intel short—that is, bet the stock price will drop.

Finally, government watchdogs and private lawsuits are always a factor for perceived monopolists. WorldCom Inc., whose merger with MCI Communications Corp. is already under review by the Justice Department and European Commission, faces a lawsuit by GTE Corp. alleging that combination would have unfair dominance over the primary long-distance networks that carry Internet data traffic globally.

Historians might note that both IBM and AT&T faced Justice Department antitrust investigations in the early 1980s, around the time their stocks began their falls from grace.

TABLE

Antitrust Problem? What Problem?

MARKET CAP. P/E
COMPANY (billions) (trailing)

Microsoft $205.1 57.8
COMMENT: Expected to soon be subject of Justice Dept. antitrust suit

Coca-Cola 191.5 48.7
COMMENT: PepsiCo lawsuit alleges Coke violates antitrust law in soda fountain sales; Coke says
   suit has no merit

Intel 135.0 24.0
COMMENT: Subject of Federal Trade Commission probe over access to chips and technical
   information

WorldCom 43.5 108.8
COMMENT: GTE Corp. sues to block WorldCom's merger with MCI Communications over share of
   Internet, long-distance traffic

Sources: News reports, Baseline, Dow Jones Markets.

EXPLORING THE WORLD OF INTERNATIONAL CONSUMER POLICY (GOVERNMENT REGULATION III)

INTERNATIONAL CONSUMER POLICY

Alan Mathios

Introduction

International consumer policy is no longer an easily ignored topic for government law-makers, policy analysts, consumer researchers, or consumer advocates. The globalization of markets along with the establishment of world bodies that focus on the implications of domestic consumer protection policy on world trade has made international consumer policy an important domain to study.

Definition of Themes Related to International Consumer Policy

International consumer policy can best be defined by considering two types of consumer protection. The first definition relates to the large set of laws and regulations that domestic governments initiate to protect consumers in the marketplace. These sets of governing structures often have common themes across countries and focus on similar types of market failures. However, in many cases, these sets of rules and regulations differ across countries thereby presenting a complex array of competing and sometimes contradictory rules when considering international exchange and trade. Governments throughout the world, for example, require different disclosures regarding nutritional aspects of food, environmental features of products, and even the methods that are utilized to assess the risk associated with products. Consequently, *international consumer policy is focused on how international organizations can best manage the common and sometimes conflicting domestic requirements in an increasingly global marketplace.* The second definition relates to the potential conflicts between domestic consumer protection actions and attempts by governments to engage in protectionism of domestic industry. *International consumer policy is focused on distinguishing consumer protection policies that are designed to protect consumers in the marketplace versus those that are enacted to create barriers to free trade.*

The Domain of International Consumer Policy

The domain of international consumer policy is broad and covers the diverse set of issues that are related to the globalization of markets and the main institutions that address international consumer policy issues. To best describe this broad domain the first

ALAN MATHIOS is a Professor at Cornell University and the Associate Dean for Academic Affairs in the College of Human Ecology at Cornell University.
Mathios, Alan: International Consumer Policy.

section examines common consumer protection themes across countries. The second section describes globalization as the key issue underlying international consumer policy. The third section provides background on the most significant institutions governing international trade. The fourth section concludes by illustrating, using biotechnology as an example, the types of conflicts that arise as institutions grapple with the conflicts between domestic consumer policy protection and free trade.

COMMON CONSUMER PROTECTION THEMES

Consumer policy has become a key focus of government and regulatory agencies thoughout the world. Cross-sectional variation in consumer policy across contries can be explained, in part, by country-specific differences in social forces, unexpected domestic tragedies, advocacy movements, government philosophical approaches to regulation, movements in public opinion, and reactions to new technologies. Despite the variations, however, there are common themes that emerge as governments develop policies to protect consumers in the marketplace. These common themes relate to accurate information about product quality, protection of potentially vulnerable consumers in contract law, consumers protection through product liability and product safety regulation, the regulation of advertising and marketing, competition/antitrust and trade practice law, and consumer redress through small claims courts. Explicit policies that emerge from these themes include mandatory labeling, minimum quality standards, licensing, simple language requirements in contracts, substantiation doctrines in adveritising law, restrictions and/or bans on certain types of advertising, punitive damages in liability cases, movements from negligence to strict liability in torts for product defects, and development of competition law. Moreover, there have been attempts by international bodies to have common practices. For example, in 1985, the General Assembly of the United Nations adopted guidelines for consumer protection laying out a set of principles for consumer protection for the world. The guidelines focus on similar themes such as health, regulation of product quality and labeling and education.

A country-by-country description of how these themes have manifested themselves in policy outcomes is beyond the scope of this chapter. However, it is instructive to browse the titles of one of the key research journals in international consumer policy. The Journal of Consumer Policy (JCP) was first published in 1977 and has continuously tracked the historical development of consumer policy from an international perspective. The editors of the journal are currently from the United States, Denmark, Germany, and the UK, and the editorial board of the journal reflects a much larger number of countries.[1] The journal also has a unique relationship with government policy makers. Over the years a number of bodies have sponsored issues of the JCP including the European

---

[1] The author currently serves as one of the editors of the journal.

TABLE 1

Consumer Policy Across Countries and Themes as Published by the Journal of Consumer Policy

Title	Theme	Country/Area
Consumer Protection in Switzerland: Strengthening Countervailing Power or Competition	Competition Law	Switzerland
The Provision of Information on Consumer Rights: British Experiences	Information	United Kingdom
Advertising Self Regulation Under Scrutiny in Austria	Advertising	Austria
The Swedish Product Safety Legislation	Product Liability	Sweden
Control of Unfair Terms in Consumer Contracts in Israeli: Law and Practice	Contract Law	Israel
Product Liability in Finland	Product Liability	Finland
Product Liability in Norway	Product Liability	Norway
Functioning and Reforms of Small Claims Tribunals in New Zealand	Small Claims	New Zealand
Small Claims: Recent Developments in Scotland	Small Claims	Scotland
Protection Against Unfair Trade Practices in Malaysia—Law, Enforcement, and Redress in a Developing Country	Competition Law	Malaysia
Reform of the Law of Product Liability in Australia	Product Liability	Australia
The Hungarian Cocktail of Competition Law and Consumer Protection: Should It Be Dissolved?	Competition Law	Hungary
Consumer Protection in Bangladesh: Law and Practice	Multiple Themes	Bangladesh
The Development of Portuguese Consumer Law with Special Regard to Conflict Resolution	Contract Law	Portugal
Consumer Sales Law in Poland: Changing the Law, Changing Attitudes	Contract Law	Poland
Consumer Law in Argentina and the MERCOSUR	Multiple Themes	Argentina
Implementation of EEC Consumer Protection Directives in Italy	Multiple Themes	Italy
Consumer Protection Act, 1986: Law and Policy in India	Multiple Themes	India
Consumer Protection in Greek Legislation	Multiple Themes	Greece

Reference information to each of these papers is included at the end of the paper.

Commission's Consumer Policy Service, the Office of Consumer Affairs of Industry Canada, the Norwegian Research Council and the National Consumer Research Center in Finland. Table 1 documents the titles of selected papers that reflect the diversity of consumer policy issues across different countries. It also provides a source for obtaining information about consumer protection policies in countries throughout the world.

The titles listed in Table 1 demonstrate some of the common themes in consumer protection through much of the world. However, one of the most important domains and certainly the most dynamic aspect of international consumer policy is its interaction with the increased interdependence of economic systems across countries. The remainder of this chapter focuses on two specific topics that relate to consumer policy developments in light of the globalization of markets. The first will deal with the history and emergence of the World Trade Organization as the key international structure for enhancing free trade and the consumer protection issues that flow from this international body. The second will deal with the emergence of biotechnology and how different social perspectives on this technology lead to domestic consumer protection policies that could give rise to international trade conflicts.

INTERNATIONAL CONSUMER POLICY AND THE GLOBALIZATION OF MARKETS

The movement towards globalization is evidenced by a number of key developments over the last decade and the dramatic growth in world trade. Merchandise exports grew on average by 6% annually and the total amount of trade in 2000 was more than 20 times the level that existed 50 years earlier.[2] Perhaps the most visible symbol of globalization is the World Trade Organization (WTO). The WTO is the successor to a longer standing set of agreements known as the General Agreement on Tarrifs and Trade (GATT). The WTO was created in 1995 by a series of trade negotiations, or rounds, held under GATT. The last of these rounds, known as the Uruguay Round resulted in the creation of the WTO. The WTO has been a highly controversial governing body. Opponents of the WTO argue that the authority of the organization to rule that country-specific consumer protection policies can constitute a barrier to trade will move governments away from implementing needed domestic consumer protection policy. Because the WTO can impose sanctions on countries who erect barriers to trade, it is argued that multinational corporate interests can preempt the effectiveness and willingness of governments to protect consumers and the environment. The thousands of protesters at the Seattle WTO meetings in 1999 reflect the depth of the controversy.

The basic premise of both GATT and subsequently the WTO is that consumers will benefit from lower prices because of the promotion of free trade. The benefits from trade are deeply rooted in basic economic principles of comparative advantage and specialization, which posits that trade with other countries provides enormous benefits to social welfare. A country has a comparative advantage over another in the production of a specific product if the cost of making this good is lower relative to the cost of other goods. So even countries with significantly higher labor costs than another country (and thus with an absolute disadvantage in the cost of production) can have comparative advantages for producing one good rather than another. Given trade agreements with other countries, social welfare is enhanced by having that country specialize in the production of the good for which it has a comparative advantage. This way it exports products that are relatively cheap to produce and imports products that are relatively expensive to produce. This leads to lower prices to consumers and allows a country to

---

[2]See www.wto.org.

consume beyond what it could if it was limited to only what can be produced domestically. Virtually every intermediate microeconomic textbook has a diagram that illustrates how consumers fare with and without free trade. For example, Mansfield and Yohe (2004) illustrate a diagram where firms can produce at any point on their domestic production possibilities frontier. Without trade they produce on this frontier and with free trade they choose a different point on the frontier (they specialize more) and through trade end up on a consumption point that is well beyond the frontier. Thus, with similar resources devoted to production, more is available for consumption thereby lowering price and increasing welfare.

As will be discussed below, however, many consumer advocates have been against the WTO and the current movement toward free trade. To understand the source of these concerns it is imperative to describe in more detail how the WTO operates and the types of issues that arise in implementation.

THE WTO AND INTERNATIONAL CONSUMER PROTECTION POLICIES

The WTO is essentially a clearing house for trade negotiations with agreements being formed and disputes being resolved. From a consumer protection perspective, consumers will gain by preventing local producer interests from erecting protectionist policies that serve the producer interest at the expense of consumer prices. As Mayer (1998) points out, however, most of the major consumer advocacy organizations were critical of the Uruguay negotiations. The concern was that the focus on free-trade might preempt and undermine consumer protection efforts by member countries. Many of the concerns were focused in particular on health regulations and regulations that are designed to protect the environment. Given the difficulty of distinguishing between legitimate consumer protection measures and those designed to protect local markets the fear was that the producer interest would rule. Mayer (1998) provides useful examples of GATT decisions that deal with this conflict.

Traditional consumer utility theory posits that consumers maximize utility subject to a budget constraint. Consumption of goods yields utility and the prices of these goods and the income of the consumer determine the constraints. The simple model does not take into account, however, that consumers may value not only the consumption of the product but also aspects of how that product was produced. Yet the quality of the production process leading to the final product, rather than the quality of the product itself is becoming the focus of international consumer protection policy. Examples include whether animals were treated humanely, whether there was environmental harm in the production of the product, whether low wages were employed in the production of the good, whether the product is consistent with sustainable consumption, and whether the product uses genetically modified inputs. As countries become increasingly interested in regulating and labeling how a product is produced there are new concerns that these regulations might conflict with the goals of the WTO. Recent rounds of WTO meetings have focused on the integration of these consumer concerns, but it has become clear that the relationship between free trade and consumer protection is becoming increasingly complex.

The WTO is based on several principles established in the original GATT agreements. These principles prohibit discrimination among the products imported by member states (Article I), and prohibit discrimination between imported and domestic goods (Article III). These two concepts establish equal treatment for like products. The question then becomes whether differences in the production process that lead to an observably similar product are like products. It becomes difficult to resolve disputes over whether countries are being protectionist by trying to prevent the import of products that do not meet criterion related to animal welfare, biotechnology and other related issues or whether these criteria legitimately allow the country to treat and market these products as fundamentally different and therefore not required to adhere to Articles I and III for like products.

Without labeling requirements, an argument can be made that consumer welfare may not be enhanced by free trade because consumers are not able to identify products with attributes that consumers are willing to pay to avoid. As a result, labeling and marketing initiatives have become one of the key regulatory methods for dealing with international consumer protection issues. Hobbs et al. (2002) provide a nice summary of these issues with respect to the European Union's attempt to adopt an animal welfare standard. The authors note that safety- or hazard-based labeling is supported by WTO policies. However, they also note that labeling based on a consumer's right to know about the production process generating the product is not clearly defined. Animal welfare standards, use of low wage workers, and genetically modified inputs all fall into a category where there is no clear direct safety or hazard issue. A review of the literature will quickly reveal how many consumer protection issues now revolve around the marketing and labeling of features of the production process. In just the last few years articles have been written about the assessments of chemicals in food (Chen, 2004), genetically modified foods in India (Gahukar, 2002), food ethics for a globalizing market (Brom, 2000), and environmental labeling of electricity delivery contracts in Sweden (Kaberger, 2003). As we will see in the next section, however, the emergence of biotechnology has been one of the key new areas where the marketing and labeling of the production process has become the focus of controversy throughout the world.

BIOTECHNOLOGY AND THE CONSUMER: AN INTERNATIONAL CONSUMER PROTECTION PERSPECTIVE

The Canadian Environmental Protection Act defines biotechnology as "The application of science and engineering in the direct use of living organisms or parts or products of living organisms in their natural or modified forms" (Knoppers and Mathios, 1999). Biotechnology is a rapidly developing sector of the economy for many countries throughout the world. The rapid development has led to heated debate about the risks and benefits of using this technology, especially in areas of agriculture and trade. The current debate about the use of genetic engineering in agricultural production reveals substantial cross-country differences in perceptions of the risks and benefits. Consequently, adoption rates vary significantly across countries. The United States, Argentina, Mexico and China have rapidly adopted genetically modified crops (Neilsen, Thierfelder and Robinson, 2003). However, in some parts of the world, including a good portion of Western Europe and Japan, there is great concern about the use of these products. Adoption rates are slower in these countries. Moreover, as a result of this higher perception of risk there has been significant legislation surrounding the mandatory labeling of these products and domestic bans on the use of some of these products. For example, many different countries, in addition to the European Union, have either adopted or have announced plans to adopt labels for genetically modified foods.

These labeling schemes include a mixture of voluntary and mandatory labeling and there is little international consensus concerning labeling standards. With labeling, those who want the choice to purchase GM-free foods will have the opportunity to purchase these foods. Researchers have focused on whether and to what degree consumers are willing to pay to avoid genetically modified foods or other biotechnology products. For example, Huffman et al. (2003), and Lusk et al. (2001) examine willingness to pay for GM-free products and find evidence that consumers are willing to pay to avoid these products. Chern (2003) examines international differences in consumer acceptance of genetically modified foods. His research compares the United States, Taiwan, Norway and Japan. He concludes that consumers in the U.S. and Taiwan are more willing to consume genetically modified foods and that consumers in general are willing to pay price premiums to avoid these foods.

Given consumers' willingness to pay a lot of attention has been focused on mandatory labeling. However, because regulatory agencies in the United States have not found GM foods to be riskier than traditional products there has been a reluctance to adopt mandatory labeling, especially given the significant costs associated with labeling. Labeling requires identity verification, which potentially involves separating production facilities and tracking distribution networks. This becomes even more difficult for processed foods with many ingredients. Moreover, some argue that the use of mandatory labeling could falsely imply that GM food products or ingredients are harmful or of lower quality than traditional products. In fact, regulatory agencies in the United States have classified many GM foods as generally recognized as safe and in many cases these products have gone through more extensive testing than traditional products. Thus, if labeling is interpreted as a warning, consumers may overreact and unnecessarily reduce their consumption of these products.

Given the willingness of consumers to pay to avoid GM foods it is not difficult to predict that the WTO will be dealing with a potential conflict between free trade and local consumer movements and regulatory attempts to restrict or label these products in the marketplace. This potential consumer protection conflict is best represented by the passage of the Cartagena Biosafety Protocol (Protocol). Recently passed and ratified in the last few years, it is one of the first multi-national agreements dealing with potential risks associated with biotechnology. A central theme of the Protocol is the formal recognition of the precautionary principle.[3] Article 10(6) of the Protocol that was adopted in January 2000 states that

> Lack of scientific certainty due to insufficient relevant scientific information and knowledge regarding the extent of the possible adverse effects of a living modified organism on the conservation and sustainable use of biological diversity in the Party of import, taking also into account risks to human health, shall not prevent that Party from taking a decision as appropriate, with regard to the import of that living modified organism intended for direct use as food or feed or for processing, in order to avoid or minimize such potential adverse effects.

In both the preamble and article 1 the protocol adopts the precautionary principle as outlined in principle 15 of the Rio Declaration on Environment and Development as the key approach for dealing with consumer and environmental protection. Principle 15 states

> In order to protect the environment, the precautionary approach shall be widely applied by States according to their capabilities. Where there are threats of serious or irreversible damage, lack of full scientific certainty shall not be used as a reason for postponing cost-effective measures to prevent environmental degradation.

The use of the precautionary principle has been quite controversial. Risks that scientific studies fail to identify no longer necessarily move lawmakers away from policy action. Instead, lack of data on long term outcomes can itself be a reason to invoke the precautionary principle leading to action on part of the policymaker. Some fear that excessive preoccupation with hypothetical novel risk will be harmful to consumers as it delays or otherwise increases the costs of new technologies. The emergence of the precautionary principle is likely to lead to fundamental issues of whether actions based on threat to consumer harm without scientific evidence of that harm will be viewed as protectionist policies or legitimate consumer protection actions by the WTO.

Delving Deeper into International Consumer Policy: Selected Readings

A starting point for gaining a better understanding of international consumer policy is to explore the three themes outlined below. For each section a suggested reading provides an overview of this area.

---

[3] A separate agreement on food safety and animal and plant health standards is the Sanitary and Phytosanitary Measures Agreement (SPS). Article 5.7 of the SPS Agreement allows temporary precautionary measures.

THE GLOBAL PERSPECTIVE ON CONSUMER PROTECTION

Countries approach consumer protection from different perspectives yet there are broad categories that provide an organizing principle for understanding international policy. The paper entitled "Consumer Protection: A Global Perspective" written by Robert Mayer provides a global overview of consumer protection policy. One contribution of this article is to classify the countries of the world into categories that go beyond the simple GNP per capita basis of the World Bank. Countries are classified into six categories based on their economic, political, and cultural characteristics and this classification is used to try to explain global variation in consumer protection policies. The analysis makes clear that the objectives of consumer protection policy differ by these categories and that the focus on product process features of products is likely to vary. Consequently, the conflicts between consumer protection policy and free trade will also result in predictable differences in how groups will respond to consumer protection policies focused on production process quality.

RISK ASSESSMENT AND INTERNATIONAL TRADE

One of the key areas where the WTO is predicted to have a large effect is on government efforts to regulate the health and safety of products and the environment more generally. The WTO, in implementing its dispute-settlement process, is increasingly relying on risk assessment to determine whether a country is implementing legitimate consumer protection policies or whether public health and environment concerns are being utilized to pass protectionist policies that favor the domestic economy. The article "The Contrast Between Risk Assessment and Rules of Evidence in the Context of International Trade Disputes: Can the U.S. Experience Inform the Process?" by Elizabeth Anderson and Catherine St. Hilaire sets the stage for understanding how risk assessment is approached by the United States and identifies key issues that face the WTO as it uses risk assessment as a major factor in its regulatory decisions. The article provides a broad overview of the history and methods of risk assessment as practiced in the United States, relates it to the precautionary principle discussed earlier and focuses on the relationship between risk assessment and the WTO.

INTERNATIONAL LABELING SCHEMES

Labeling is increasingly becoming a common international regulatory approach toward information failures in the marketplace. As discussed earlier, labeling is fundamentally linked to WTO proceedings as the agency considers whether information disclosure through labeling can constitute a barrier to trade. The rising interest in labeling leads one to question the effectiveness of labeling schemes and how different countries have used labels to address consumer information issues. An insightful overview of how labels have been used in the context of environmental protection is provided in the paper entitled

"Promoting Green Consumer Behavior with Eco-Labels." by John Thogersen. This paper examines consumer behavior with respect to environmental marketing through labeling and describes labeling initiatives throughout the world. The article examines awareness of labels, comprehension of labels, attitudes towards labels, and intention and behavior with respect to eco-labeled products.

Policy in Progress

One of the largest WTO disputes is currently underway. The article in the Wall Street Journal (2005) entitled "U.S. to Take Airbus-Aid Spat to WTO: Negotiations with EU Stall—Global Trade Body Will Get Biggest Case in Its History" describes the battle between Boeing and Airbus. This serves as a useful reminder that WTO disputes are an ongoing process and continue to lead to high profile cases that have large implications for businesses and consumers. It is clear from this overview of disputes that the tension between domestic protection and world trade is a current policy issue that will not fade from the limelight. All of the issues discussed on international consumer policy in this chapter, in fact, continue to unfold in real time. Different organizations provide extremely different perspectives on these issues. Public Citizen, an advocacy organization provides arguments against WTO policies. Its motto is "promoting democracy by challenging corporate globalization." Reading and following its critiques of WTO policy will bring into focus the deep divides between stakeholders. In contrast, documents from the WTO provide a different perspective on the issues it currently is facing. The Director provides an overview of what can be learned from the first 10 years of the WTO and how that might shape future WTO policies. Particularly insightful is to read about particular disputes. For example, the Dispute Settlement Body recently set up panels (in February 2005) to examine the United States' and Canada's disputes against the European Communities' import ban on hormone-treated beef. With the potential that import bans will spread to other GM foods, the way in which the Dispute Settlement Panel deals with this becomes increasingly important. Particularly interesting will be whether the protests against the WTO materialize at the next Ministerial Conference. An article in the International Herald Tribune (2004) discusses the ripple effects that European reluctance to adopt and use GM foods has on the politics of world trade.

As suggested in the article by Lindsey (2000), advocates of free trade are increasingly feeling under siege. Will the sixth WTO Ministerial Conference, which will be held in Hong Kong in December 2005 bring a repeat of the Seattle experience or have citizen advocacy groups begun to accept the evolving globalization of markets? These events will undoubtedly receive widespread press coverage and those interested in the most up-to-date policy debates in this area will have no difficulty obtaining news articles with various perspectives on these developments.

Conclusion

Approaches to consumer policy vary across countries but there are fundamental principles that underlie much of consumer policy throughout the world. Perhaps the most common themes relate to safety especially in the area of product safety and food safety. Consumer policy can no longer be analyzed in isolation from broader global issues. Instead one must develop a model of consumer protection policy that is integrated into an international perspective. The post World War II period witnessed the emergence of GATT, which led to the establishment of the WTO. As the influence of the WTO has grown so too has the integration of consumer policy into free trade discussions and negotiations. Distinguishing consumer policies that protect consumers in the marketplace from those that create barriers to trade is of fundamental importance to the consumer interest. Issues surrounding the regulation of marketing and labeling have become some of the primary mechanisms by which countries try to find the balance between protecting consumers and using minimal regulatory approaches so as not to incur WTO scrutiny with respect to protectionist policies. These approaches are based on the view that labeling allows consumers to make informed choices thereby creating market opportunities to purchase products that have quality aspects that meet consumer preferences.

Simultaneous with the increasing focus on free trade, consumers have also begun to focus more on the process by which final goods are produced. Rather than evaluating the product based on price and simple measures of quality, consumers are focused on the inputs of the production function. Whether animals were fed genetically modified seed, how the animals were treated, whether the producer used low wage workers have become part of the quality assessment for many consumers. This has, in turn, increased the demand for import bans and/or other regulatory mechanisms to limit the inflow of products that have features that consumers want to avoid. Given these trends, international consumer policy is likely to remain focused on labeling and other regulatory approaches that help consumers identify or avoid products that have been produced through mechanisms that consumers find objectionable. This is especially likely in the area of biotechnology where the rapid increase in the use of this technology continues. How these regulatory approaches interplay with global trade will be some of the key issues facing the WTO in the next decade.

Finally, consumer policy focused on features of the production process raises interesting and challenging questions. Even expert analysis of a product cannot identify whether the product was produced in a manner consistent with animal welfare standards or other quality features. Consequently, the verification, certification, substantiation of marketing claims becomes even more difficult to enforce. Moreover, the variation in attitudes and demand for information about the production process will create widely varying demand for not only final products but the way final products are produced. For example, countries with low per-capita GNP may have different willingness to pay for quality features relating to the production process. While this may raise tricky trade negotiations, the gains from trade are also deeply rooted in variation in preferences. All of these issues suggest that the interplay of marketing and public policy will be at the forefront of international consumer policy in the years to come.

Questions for Discussion

As the issues surrounding international consumer policy are debated the following questions are useful for framing the discussion:

Q1: Should different production processes that lead to the identical consumer good be a basis for imposing labeling regulation?

Q2: Should different production processes that lead to the identical consumer good be a basis for banning the import of goods?

Q3: If labeling becomes more commonplace for environmental features of products, how will consumers verify the accuracy of the labeling? Will third party certification be sufficient to ensure the quality of claims? Will government need to alter advertising law to ensure the truthfulness of labeling? Will consumers discount these claims as they cannot be verified even by independent experts?

Q4: Should countries be free to impose import quotas and tariffs without being sanctioned by the World Trade Organization? Is the WTO necessary for governments to avoid trade wars in which one country enacts protectionist policies in response to other countries' protectionist actions? What does game theory predict about how governments will behave with and without the WTO?

Q5: Is the precautionary principle a useful way for governments to react to risk and uncertainty? Will the precautionary principle lead to a slow down in innovation as governments prevent investment in new technologies based on unproven but potential risks? How should government trade off known risks from current technology versus the unknown risks from future technology?

References

Alexandridou, Elise (1988), "Consumer Protection in Greek Legislation," *Journal of Consumer Policy* 11 (3): 347–359.

Anderson, Elizabeth and Catherine St. Hilaire. 2004. "The Contrast Between Risk Assessment and Rules of Evidence in the Context of International Trade Disputes: Can the U.S. Experience Inform the Process?" *Risk Analysis,* 24 (2): 449–459.

Blakeney, Michael. 1986. "Advertising Self Regulation Under Scrutiny in Austria," *Journal of Consumer Policy* 9 (2): 181–190.

Burgenmeier, Beat. 1985. "Consumer Protection in Switzerland—Strengthening Countervailing Power or Competition," *Journal of Consumer Policy* 8 (1): 45–52.

Brom, Franz W.A. 2000. "Food, Consumer Concerns, and Trust: Food Ethics for a Globalizing Market," *Journal of Agricultural and Environmental Ethics* 12 (2): 127–139.

Cabecadas, Isabel M. 1994. "The Development of Portuguese Consumer Law with Special Regard to Conflict Resolution," *Journal of Consumer Policy* 17 (1): 113–122.

Chen, Junshi. 2004 "Challenges to Developing Countries After Joining WTO: Risk Assessment of Chemicals in Food," *Toxicology* 198 (1–3): 3–7.

Chern Wen. 2003. Presentation at www.cau.edu.cn/cem/baiwang/chen04.ppt

Cotterli, Simonetta, Paulo Marinello, and Carlo M. Verardi. 1994. "Implementation of EEC Consumer Protection Directives in Italy," *Journal of Consumer Policy* 17 (1): 63–82.

Cowan, W. and H. Ervine. 1986. "Small Claims—Recent Developments in Scotland." *Journal of Consumer Policy* 9 (2): 191–203.

Deutch, Sinai 1990. "Control of Unfair Terms in Consumer Contracts in Israel: Law and Practice," *Journal of Consumer Policy* 13 (2): 181–199.

Gahukar, R. 2002 "Status of Genetically Modified Food Crops in India," *Outlook on Agriculture* 31 (1): 43–49.

Harland, David. 1992. "Reform of the Law of Product Liability in Australia," *Journal of Consumer Policy* 15 (2): 191–206.

Hawes, Cynthia. 1989. "Functioning and Reforms of Small Claims Tribunals In New Zealand," *Journal of Consumer Policy* 12 (1): 71–94.

Hobbs, A., J. Hobbs, G. Isaac, and W. Kerr. 2002. "Ethics, Domestic Food Policy and Trade Law: Assessing the EU Animal Welfare Proposal to the WTO," *Food Policy* 27 (5/6): 437–454.

Huffman, Wallace, Jason F. Shogren, Matthew Rousu, and T. Abebayehu. 2003. "Consumer Willingness to Pay for Genetically Modified Food Labels in a Market With Diverse Information," *American Journal of Agriculture and Resource Economics* 28 (3): 481–502.

Kaberger, Tomas. 2003. "Environmental Labeling of Electricity Delivery Contracts in Sweden," *Energy Policy* 31 (7): 633–640.

Katalin, Cseres. 2004. "The Hungarian Cocktail of Competition Law and Consumer Protection: Should it Be Dissolved?" *The Journal of Consumer Policy* 27 (1): 43–74.

Knoppers, Bartha, and Alan D. Mathios. 1999. "Biotechnology and the Consumer: Introduction." In *Biotechnology and the Consumer*. Bartha Knoppers and Alan D. Mathios, (eds.) Kluwer Academic Publishers.

Lindsey, Brink. 2000. "Kick Me, I'm For Free Trade," *Reason* 31 (10): 52–53.

Lodrup, Peter. 1991. "Product Liability in Norway," *Journal of Consumer Policy* 14 (1): 7–14.

Lusk, J.L., M.S. Daniel, D.R. Mark, and C.L. Lusk. 2001. "Alternative Calibration and Auction Institutions for Predicting Consumer Willingness to Pay For Non-Genetically Modified Corn Chips," *Journal of Agricultural and Resource Economics* 26 (1): 40–57.

Magdalena, Sengayen. 2002. "Consumer Sales Law in Poland: Changing the Law, Changing Attitudes," *Journal of Consumer Policy* 25 (3/4): 403–437

Mansfield, Edwin and Gary Yohe. 2004 *Microeconomics: Theory/Applications* 11th edition, W.W. Norton and Company Inc.

Mayer, Robert. 1998. "Protectionism, Intellectual Property, and Consumer Protection: Was the Uraguay Round Good for Consumers?" *Journal of Consumer Policy* 21 (2): 195–215.

Mayer, Robert. 1997. "Consumer Protection: A Global Perspective" in *Regulation and Consumer Protection*. Kenneth J. Meier, E. Thomas Garman, and Lael R. Keiser (eds.) 3rd edition (Houston, TX: Dame): 417–34.

Nayak, Rajendra K. 1987. "Consumer Protection Act—1986: Law and Policy in India," *Journal of Consumer Policy* 10 (4): 417–423.

Neilson, Chantal P., Karen Thierfelder, and Sherman Robinson. 2003. "Consumer Preferences and Trade in Genetically Modified Foods," *Journal of Policy Modeling* 25 (8): 777–794.

Nordin, Gunilla H. 1989. "The Swedish Product Safety Legislation," *Journal of Consumer Policy* 12 (1): 95–104.

Perry, John. 1986. "The Provision of Information on Consumer Rights: British Experiences," *Journal of Consumer Policy* 9 (3): 345–358.

Rachagan, Sothi S. 1992. "Protection Against Unfair Trade Practices in Malaysia—Law, Enforcement and Redress in a Developing Country," *Journal of Consumer Policy* 15 (3): 255–274.

Rahman, Mizanur. 1994. "Consumer Protection in Bangladesh: Law and Practice." *Journal of Consumer Policy* 17 (3): 349–362.

Rosenthal, Elisabeth. 2004. "Europe is United: No Bioengineered Food," *International Herald Tribune*. Oct 6, 2004 p1.

Stiglitz, Gabriel A. 1994. "Consumer Law in Argentina and the MERCOSUR," *Journal of Consumer Policy* 17 (4): 459–469.

Thogersen, John. 2002 "Promoting Green Consumer Behavior With Eco-Labels." In *New Tools for Environmental Protection: Education, Information, and Voluntary Measures,*" National Academy of Sciences.

Scott Miller in Brussels, Daniel Michaels in Paris and J. Lynn Lunsford in Dallas, 2005. "U.S. to Take Airbus-Aid Spat to WTO: Negotiations with EU Stall—Global Trade Body Will Get Biggest Case in Its History," *Wall Street Journal*. May 31, 2005 A-3.

Wilhelmsson, Thomas. 1991. "Product Liability in Finland," *Journal of Consumer Policy* 14 (1): 15–27.

Consumer Protection: A Global Perspective

Robert Mayer

Introduction

The purpose of this chapter is to provide a global overview of consumer protection. There are many reasons why it is important to understand consumer protection outside the borders of one's own country. First, the marketplace is increasingly global. We therefore need to know about the consumer protection efforts of other countries if we want to be successful in that marketplace. Second, as government regulators, consumer advocates, and involved citizens, we can learn from nations that have found policies that are more effective than those in our own. Similarly, we should learn from the positive feedback represented by other nations successfully adopting our consumer protection policies. Finally, many consumer problems require global solutions. We must understand consumer protection outside our own country if we are to work constructively with our neighbors.

In describing consumer protection around the world, it would be convenient if there was a strict and simple connection between the strength and quality of a nation's consumer protection policies and its level of economic development. Reality is more complex. Even when comparing two countries at comparable levels of economic development, one finds variations in consumer protection that stem from differences in economic systems, political institutions, and cultural values. To understand the variability of consumer protection around the world, this chapter places nations into groups defined by certain economic, political, and cultural characteristics. It then searches for commonalities in the consumer protection policies in each group.

It would also be convenient if there were a single yardstick with which to measure a nation's consumer protection accomplishments. If one attempts to measure the extent to which "consumer rights" (Garman, 1996) have been secured, one notices that consumer rights are defined differently around the world. As enumerated in the United States, consumer rights presume that people have satisfied their basic needs and need help in making choices in the pursuit of higher order pursuits. In the context of less developed nations, "process" rights like choice, information, education, representation, and redress are subordinate to providing basic necessities and eliminating major threats to safety and health.

MAYER ROBERT. (1997) Consumer Protection: A Global Perspective, Kenneth J. Meier, E. Thomas Garman, and Lael R. Keiser (eds.), *Regulation and Consumer Protection, 3rd edition* (Houston, TX: Dame), pp. 417–33.

The approach of this chapter begins where the Meier Model of the regulatory process ... leaves off. The Meier Model is based on the United States; its purpose is to explain particular regulatory outcomes as a function of the interplay between regulators and interest groups in the context set by non-regulatory political elites and environmental factors. For the purpose of understanding differences among nations in their consumer protection policies, we must begin with and broaden these environmental factors. We examine environmental factors such as a nation's level of economic development, the nature of its economic system, its political institutions and traditions, and its cultural values. Then, we explore the ways in which consumer protection priorities and policies are connected to these broad environmental factors.

Classification of Nations

Although national differences in consumer protection policy cannot be attributed entirely to variations in economic development, economic development nevertheless is critically important. There are several systems of classifying nations by their level of economic development, each of which seems to offend someone. At one point in time, it was common to place nations into either the first, second, or third world. The first world consisted of affluent, market-based economies located primarily in North America and Western Europe. The second world referred to the centrally planned economies dominated by the Soviet Union and China. The third world was just about everyone else, that is, the poorer nations of the world. The first-second-third world classification has been largely abandoned in official publications. The idea of being third out of three wasn't very complimentary. Plus, the defining characteristic of second world nations, their command economies, has largely disappeared.

Some people prefer to divide nations between "developed and developing" or "more developed and less developed," but these terms also carry value judgments. They suggest that all countries should pursue the same goals of development and follow the same methods of development. Moreover, these terms imply that some nations are better than others, a suggestion that is likely to be resisted by people in the "worse" nations. A final set of terms used to categorize nations is North vs. South. These two terms seem freer of implicit value judgments, which explains their use by people in poor nations. The terms are highly imprecise, though, implying that all the world's rich nations lie in the northern hemisphere and the all the world's poor nations in the southern.

The World Bank is an institution that has grappled with these dilemmas of nomenclature and classification. The Bank now groups nations on the basis on gross national product (GNP) per capita. It places the world's economies into low-income, middle-income, and high-income groups. Middle-income economies are further divided into lower and upper in recognition of the enormous variation within this group. The Bank refers to low-income and middle-income economies as "developing," although it does not mean to imply that some economies have reached a preferred or final stage of development.

For the purposes of cross-national analysis of consumer protection, the World Bank's classification can be modified. Starting with GNP per capita, we examine three additional factors: (1) the level of government involvement in the economy, (2) the degree of political openness to the participation of consumers, and (3) the cultural emphasis on collective welfare versus individual freedom and opportunity (Triandis et al., 1990).

Using these four major concepts, the high-income economies are divided into two clusters: the Anglo-Capitalists and the Northern European Corporatists. The first group consists of countries like the United States, the United Kingdom, and Australia with an especially strong allegiance to free market principles, longstanding democratic institutions, and relatively strong and independent private consumer organizations.

Corporatism implies the interpenetration of the economic and political spheres. Whereas most of the countries of western Europe are marked by an increasing level of corporatism, the extreme cases are northern European countries like Sweden, the Netherlands, and Germany. In these nations, the line between private and public institutions (including consumer organizations) is far more blurred than in the Anglo-Capitalist countries, the economy is a mixture of private and state-owned enterprise, and political traditions emphasize collective good over individual freedom. Of particular interest in the domain of consumer protection is the way in which government brings together relevant stakeholders in an effort to work out policy solutions that are widely accepted (Kelman, 1981).

A third group, the Trade Integrationists, spans the high-income and middle-income categories. It is composed of diverse nations which, despite more recent and less intense commitments to capitalism and democracy, are intimately connected with the nations in the first two groups by virtue of trade relations. Examples of such countries are Japan, Hong Kong, Singapore, the Korean Republic, Saudi Arabia, Israel, Chile, and Mexico.

A fourth group, the Former Central Planners, consists of nations that are also becoming increasingly integrated into regional trading blocks and the global trading system, but their experience is strongly influenced by the legacies of totalitarian governments and command economies. These countries typically fall in the lower portion of the World Bank's middle-income category. Examples of countries in this group are Hungary, Poland, Russia, the Czech and Slovak Republics, and the Baltic nations of Estonia, Latvia, and Lithuania.

Two final groups will be discussed: the Earnest Strivers and the Hopeful Starters. The Earnest Strivers category is composed of countries that typically fall in the middle income category of the World Bank's classification. These countries are culturally diverse but share a non-Western past. They have made substantial strides in recent years in addressing basic issues of human capital investment: bringing the fertility rate more in

line with available resources, reducing infant mortality, increasing primary school enrollment, reducing illiteracy, and extending life expectancy. Their growing economies are
marked by strong government involvement but with an increasing reliance on market
principles and private ownership. They are exemplified by Mauritius, Indonesia, Fiji, the
Philippines, Venezuela, El Salvador, and Turkey.

Finally, there are the Hopeful Starters—low-income countries which, while still facing
enormous economic challenges, have achieved sufficient political stability to formulate
economic programs and provide the basic necessities of life for the majority of their
populations. Nevertheless, people in the Hopeful Starters may still feel that their fate is
primarily out of their hands, whether because of powerful foreign-based corporations or
unpredictable natural forces like floods and droughts. These countries include India,
Bangladesh, Burkina Faso, and Guyana, and Kenya.

Figure 1 summarizes the central characteristics of the six country categories. Before
proceeding to a more detailed discussion, a few caveats are necessary. First, the six

FIGURE 1

Summary of Country Classifications

Category	GNP Per Capita-World Bank	Government Involvement in Economy	Strength of Democratic Institutions	Cultural Values	Examples
Anglo-Capitalists	High	Low	High with Strong Private Associations	Individual Freedom and Opportunity: Private Property	US UK Canada Australia
Northern European Corporatists	High	Moderate	High with Strong Labor Unions and Parties	Group Welfare: Protection of Vulnerable	Sweden Norway Netherlands Germany
Trade Integrationists	Upper Middle	Moderate with Emphasis on Promoting Exports	Moderate with Single Party Dominance	Too Diverse for Generalization	Italy Japan Malaysia Mexico
Former Central Planners	Upper and Lower Middle	High but Decreasing with Privatization	Low but Increasing	Government Provides Basic Necessities and Public Goods	Poland Hungary Russia Latvia
Earnest Strivers	Upper and Lower Middle	Moderate and Encourages Foreign Investment	Low with Strong Influence of Military	Social Hierarchy Importance of Group and Family	Indonesia Philippines El Salvador Turkey
Hopeful Starters	Lower Middle and Low	Moderate but Decreasing with Structural Adjustment	Low with Strong Ethnic Divisions	Ethnic Identity; Traditionalism; Fatalism	India Kenya Guyana Bangladesh

categories of countries are not exhaustive. There is, sadly, a seventh category of nations which are desperately poor and/or racked by civil strife. While it is possible to describe the economies, polities, and cultures of countries like Somalia, Liberia, Burundi, and Lebanon, and Bosnia, there are virtually no consumer protection activities there at present, so they will not be discussed. Second, the six groups of countries are not mutually exclusive in any strict sense. There are countries which appear to fall in between the Hopeful Starters and the Earnest Strivers or between the Earnest Strivers and the Trader Integrationists. Third, and most important, it is always perilous to try to squeeze the vast diversity of the world's nations into a few categorizations. Some overgeneralization is inevitable. The reader is urged to keep in mind that the point of the exercise undertaken here is to emphasize homogeneities within what are inherently heterogeneous categories. In all, one must tolerate these shortcomings of the approach adopted here if one is to hope to understand how broad economic, political, and cultural features of nations are related to their consumer protection policies.

Consumer Protection Policies

Anglo-Capitalists

In the Anglo-Capitalist countries, consumer protection policies gain legitimacy to the extent that they contribute to the efficient functioning of free markets. Anti-trust policy, as pursued in the U.S. by the Federal Trade Commission and Department of Justice, is clearly designed to achieve this goal by protecting competition. Providing consumers with information helps the market mechanism as well by directing consumer dollars toward the most efficient firms. Policies to promote safety, representation, and redress can also be justified in terms of market efficiency; these policies correct "market failures" associated with externalities (costs and benefits that are unaccounted for in prices). Thus, policies designed to promote the consumer rights can be viewed as part of this market-perfecting activity.

Some consumer policies in the Anglo-Capitalist countries are justified on the grounds of compassion and fairness, without any reference to market efficiency. Examples include anti-discrimination provisions in the granting of consumer credit; protection of children from manipulative sales techniques; subsidized telephone and banking rates for low-income consumers; and prohibitions on terminating heat during the winter months for non-payment of utility bills. But these policies are in the distinct minority.

The notion that consumer protection policies improve the performance of markets both justifies and sets limits on the government's role. It is appropriate for government to enforce anti-trust laws, but determining market entry, limiting the number of firms that may compete, setting prices, and controlling profits is to be avoided. Accordingly, two of the most important trends in the Anglo-Capitalist countries during the last two decades have been industry-specific deregulation and privatization. Deregulation and/or privatization have been dramatic with respect to the airline, banking, energy, and telecommunications industries.

The regulation of advertising also exemplifies the unique emphasis on competition in the consumer protection policies of the Anglo-Capitalist countries. Banning deceptive advertisements can be seen as an attempt to help efficient firms communicate the superiority of their goods and services to consumers, so virtually all nations restrict false and misleading advertisements. What is unique to the Anglo-Capitalist countries, though, are their efforts to push the pro-competitive aspects of advertising to their limits. Thus, these countries were typically the first to encourage comparative ads in which brand-to-brand differences are highlighted, the first to permit health claims in food advertisements, and the first to allow ads for prescription drugs.

There is a history of active political participation by the citizens in Anglo-Capitalist countries. Accordingly, consumer policy is based on the assumption that consumers have the ability to mobilize to articulate and promote their collective interests. That is, special subsidies and assistance rarely need to be provided for consumer representation even though the consumer interest is dispersed, lacks cohesiveness, and does not have the intensity of worker interests (Nadel, 1971). At the extreme, consumer groups like the National Consumers League in the U.S. and the Consumers Association of Canada are expected to be financially self-supporting. In the U.K., product testing is not subsidized, but organizations dedicated to representing consumers (e.g., National Consumers Council) or advising them (e.g., local consumer advice centers) do receive government funding. When consumer representatives or "ombuds" have been established in the Anglo-Capitalist countries, they typically have been funded voluntarily by particular industries or firms, not required or funded by governments.

The expectation of active citizen participation is also reflected in the consumer redress policies in the Anglo-Capitalist countries. Barriers to legal action are relatively low in these countries. The extreme case is the United States where consumers can use a contingency fee system to encourage lawyers to take high-risk but high-return cases, where class action law suits facilitate the aggregation of many small claims, and where jury trials are available for civil cases. But countries like Canada, Australia, and the United Kingdom are moving toward the U.S. model, with all three having abandoned long-standing restrictions on advertising by legal professionals.

Finally, preserving freedom of individual choice is a strong cultural value in the consumer protection policies of the Anglo-Capitalist countries. Consider the United States and the three most serious threats to the health and safety of its consumers: motor vehicles, alcohol, and cigarettes. The United States is virtually the only western country without a national mandatory seat belt use law or national motorcycle helmet use law. Its laws against driving under the influence of alcohol are laughably weak. While it might appear that the United States has restricted individual choice through prohibitions on smoking in public places, the individual right to smoke is supported in a far more powerful way—by some of the lowest cigarette taxes among western countries.

In sum, consumer protection policies among the Anglo-Capitalist countries reflect the freedoms associated with their economic and political systems. Consumer protection is most often justified as an effort to sustain free and competitive markets. The democratic voter finds his parallel in the capitalist consumer. Both are expected to exercise informed choice and, therefore, be allowed freedom of choice as well.

Northern European Corporatists

A variety of characteristics differentiate the Northern European Corporatists from the Anglo-Capitalists. First, there is a tradition of their governments owning or conspicuously directing industries; prominent examples involve the automobile, steel, petroleum, and telephone industries. Second, while these countries are certainly democracies, the tradition of direct political participation is somewhat weaker than in the Anglo-Capitalist countries. At the most superficial level, several of these countries are still in monarchies. More important, political participation is often linked firmly to occupation groups, with more diffuse interests like the consumer interest not serving as the basis of group affiliation. Thus, labor parties play a more important role in the political system than in the Anglo-Capitalist countries. Consumer organizations are more likely to be non-partisan cooperatives (often organized by labor unions) than consumer advocacy groups.

The Northern European Corporatists are further distinguished by their cultural emphasis on collective welfare, social justice, and protection of vulnerable groups. Northern European Corporative countries like Sweden, Norway, Denmark, the Netherlands, and even Germany and France are often described as "welfare states" inasmuch as their programs providing income support, health care, housing, and child care are more generous than those of the Anglo-Capitalist countries. Income equality is higher as well. Moreover, the position of women is high by international standards, especially in the political domain. For example, over a third of national legislators in Finland, Norway, Sweden, and Denmark are women, compared to less than ten percent in the U.S. and U.K. (Kidron and Segal, 1995).

The economic, political, and cultural characteristics of the Northern European Corporatist countries have direct implications for the nature of consumer protection in these nations. Most important, there is a willingness to tolerate concentration of economic power in government-owned companies or oligopolies in industries such as telecommunications, banking, insurance, and air transportation. The flipside of this tolerance, however, is the expectation that government has a responsibility to champion the interests of consumers. This typically entails establishment of strong, centralized protection agencies and specialized consumer representatives, such as the consumer ombuds of the Nordic countries (Graver, 1986; Jeleby, 1995). Government responsibility for consumer welfare is also expressed in state funding for product testing (e.g., Stiftung Warentest in Germany), research organizations (e.g., SWOKA in the Netherlands), and consumer education.

Because competition has traditionally been less vigorous in the Northern European Corporatist countries than in the Anglo-Capitalist nations, consumer cooperatives emerged to make private sellers more responsive to consumer needs. In Sweden, for example, consumer cooperatives broke producer cartels for essential items like margarine, flour, and galoshes; pioneered self-service in grocery stores and at gas stations; introduced unit pricing and full refunds; and brought home insurance and vacation services to working class consumers who had been written off as "unprofitable" (DeLoss, 1985). More recently, the role of cooperatives has diminished as trade barriers have been reduced and competition has been interjected by foreign firms.

The close connection between consumer cooperatives and labor unions suggests an additional dimension of consumer protection policy in the Northern European Corporatist countries. While consumer protection has been embraced by both labor and non-labor political parties in these countries, the labor (or social democratic) parties provide a base for the consumer movement and a source of political clout. Before the 1970s, labor organizations often served as consumer representatives on government bodies constituted to provide consumer input.

The group-oriented values of the Northern European Corporatist countries are also expressed in efforts to provide basic consumer necessities to less fortunate consumers and to protect vulnerable consumers. These countries have attempted to protect children from the effects of television advertising. In the Nordic countries at least, one also observes aggressive efforts to protect women from sexist portrayals in advertising (Sverdrup and Stø, 1992).

Group-oriented values are also expressed in "paternalistic" policies governing safety. In the domain of auto safety, the Northern European Corporatists were among the first to enact nationals mandatory seat belt use laws, withhold the privilege of driving until age 18, and come down hard on people who drive under the influence of alcohol. In all these instances, the individual freedom of the driver is subordinated to a collective notion of the proper amount of safety. Regarding the safety risks posed by cigarettes and alcohol, there is significant variation within the Northern European Corporatists, but the Nordic countries have been leaders in imposing high taxes on these items, restricting their advertising, and requiring warnings on their packaging.

Currently, the Northern European Corporatists are adopting many of the economic policies of the Anglo-Capitalist countries. Privatization, industry deregulation, and scaling back of generous welfare state programs are prominent examples. These trends, in turn, raise the possibility that the consumer protection policies of these two categories of wealthy nations will converge as well.

TRADE INTEGRATIONISTS

There is substantial variation among Trade Integrationist nations, whether in GNP per capita (ranging from $3,000 in Mexico and Chile to $30,000 in Japan) or the extent to which major industries are owned by domestic or foreign investors. Nevertheless, their economies are all heavily reliant on exports of manufactured goods. Trade Integrationist nations such as Japan, Italy, Hong Kong, Singapore, Korea, Spain, Mexico, and Malaysia all rank among the world's top merchandise exporters (World Trade Organization, 1995). The rate of growth in their exporters is impressive as well, typically exceeding 10% per year (World Bank, 1994). The governments of the Trade Integrationist countries play a strong role in supporting exports, and these countries rely heavily on free trade agreements such as the General Agreement on Tariffs and Trade (GATT) and trade blocs like the European Union and the North American Free Trade Agreement (NAFTA).

Traditions of economic and political equality are not strong in the Trade Integrationist nations. The level of income inequality in them often exceeds that of Anglo-Capitalist and North European Corporatist countries, with Japan being a notable exception (World Bank, 1994). Similarly, democratic practices are relatively recent and often weak. Although elections take place in these nations, political power is often passed from one leader to another within a single, dominant political party. Because the cultures of the Trade Integrationist nations do not emphasize political individualism, it is also possible to place group values ahead of individual ones in the economic system as well. Their export-oriented economies often deny domestic consumption for the sake of maintaining high levels of employment. This is especially true of the Trade Integrationist nations of Southeast Asia, including Japan.

Consumer protection in the Trade Integrationist countries is best understood as part of their participation in the international trading system rather than as a response to domestic consumer demand. This is even true in those Trade Integrationist nations where GNP per capita is similar to that of many Anglo-Capitalist and North European Corporatist countries. The result is that consumer protection policies in Trade Integrationist nations closely resemble (although often with a time lag) those of the Anglo-Capitalist and Northern European Corporatist nations, despite major differences in political institutions and cultural values.

This process of homogenization in consumer protection policies is driven by several factors. In some cases, trade relations involve formal agreements under which the Trade Integrationist nations coordinate and, typically, elevate their consumer protection policies (Vogel, 1995). This would apply to nations like Spain, Portugal, Italy and Greece which are members of the European Union as well as to Mexico, a partner with the United States and Canada in the NAFTA. In other cases, trade integration influences consumer protection within an exporting nation simply because a company will use the same technology to produce goods for export as it will to make goods for domestic consumption. For example, Korean consumers may find certain automobile safety features in domestically produced vehicles because of U.S. import standards or U.S. consumer demand. At a more basic level, trade relations can raise the awareness of businesses and the expectations of consumers in a nation with a relatively less advanced system of consumer protection. The effect is an overall lifting in the level of consumer protection even over what might be expected by simply knowing the per capita GNP of a country like Israel, Korea, or Chile.

Some of the best examples of this "leveling upward" process are in Europe, where less wealthy countries like Spain, Portugal, Italy, and Greece share a market with more wealthy countries like Germany, Denmark, and France. In discussions of consumer protection issues, the more wealthy nations typically outvote the less wealthy ones and thereby impose fairly strict standards. Nations wishing less stringent standards can sometimes complain that strict standards constitute barriers to trade, but this argument is rarely sustained.

Compared to non-Western countries like Japan and Malaysia, the nations of the European Union are relatively homogeneous politically and culturally. Nevertheless, the same process of homogenization takes in non-western Trade Integrationist nations. Although these non-western nations often modify western consumer protection policies to suit their cultural traditions and values, the level of similarity in consumer protection policies that results from trade integration is still striking. For example, Japan is often portrayed as a non-litigious society, especially when contrasted with the United States. Yet, Japanese public opinion led to the implementation in 1995 of a product liability law that draws heavily upon U.S. strict liability doctrine (Fumitoshi, 1996). Similarly, the use of a seal of approval to direct consumers to environmentally superior brands was pioneered in Germany beginning in 1977; today such a seal can be found not only in the Anglo-Capitalist and Northern European Corporatists nations but also in Japan, Korea, Singapore, and India (Abt Associates, 1993).

Given the non-western political traditions of many Trade Integrationists, one finds fewer private, independent consumer advocacy groups there. Instead, government bodies are the major forces in consumer protection. In Mexico, for example, one finds the private consumer organization AMEDC (the Mexican Association of Studies for Consumer Defense) publishing a magazine and conducting consumer education via the mass media, but the organization exists due to the extraordinary efforts of just two people—Arturo and Lila Lomeli (Moffett, 1988). In contrast, the Procuraduria Federal del Consumidor is a federal entity with a large budget and offices throughout the country. The same public sector dominance in the areas of product testing, consumer education, and consumer complaint handling prevails in other Latin American countries such as Argentina and Brazil but also in Asian countries like Korea and Japan.

The Trade Integrationist nations are playing an increasingly important role in the push for consumer protection around the world. The most important international consumer organization is Consumers International (CI), formerly known as the International Organization of Consumers Unions. CI was founded in 1960 and initially reflected the priorities of Anglo-Capitalist countries, such as the U.S. and U.K., and Northern European Corporatists, such as Belgium and the Netherlands. Today, however, Trade Integrationist nations have come to play a major role in CI. Its 20-body governing council includes consumer organizations from such Trade Integrationist countries as Spain, Argentina, Brazil, Mexico, Israel, Hong Kong, and South Korea. (Add the incipient Trade Integrationists on the Council, like Slovenia and Poland, and the increasing role of the Trade Integrationists becomes even more evident.) The participation of Trade Integrationist countries in CI provides an important bridge between the interests of its members from the more and less developed nations. This bridging role is seen in the fact that CI's Regional Offices for the Asia-Pacific and Latin American regions are located in the Trade Integrationist nations of Malaysia and Chile, respectively.

FORMER CENTRAL PLANNERS

Alastair Macgeorge (1997), a U.K.-based consultant on consumer affairs, has written succinctly, "Totalitarian regimes and command economies are infertile ground for traditional consumer organizations." Totalitarian regimes have little need to satisfy people as consumers because these regimes are not accountable to people as voters. Totalitarian regimes view private consumer organizations as subversive, given their intent to express discontent and call for improvements, and therefore repress them.

Command economies were those in which central planners rather than the free market decided the quantity, quality, price, production methods, and distribution of each category of goods. Central planning was supposedly based on consumer needs, but it was planners, not consumers, who interpreted these needs. While central planners devoted themselves to obtaining vast amounts of information about production, transportation, and distribution technology, planners made little effort to obtain demand-side information from consumers (Kozminski, 1992).

The situation of consumers in command economies is difficult, especially when compared to western standards. While westerners might appreciate the attention of command economies to basic human needs for food, clothing, shelter, and health care, westerners have frequently reacted with shock to the basic scarcity of goods in command economies. Consumers are forced to wait on long lines (for nondurable goods like food and cosmetics) or lists (for automobiles and apartment units). When goods are available, one rarely has a choice about their features. If you want to dye your hair, you better want to dye it red because that's sometimes the only color available (Draculic, 1991). Finding complementary goods is often a problem, like film for cameras or gasoline for cars. And while central planners emphasize the output of goods, little attention is given to product quality or to providing spare parts when products break down. Not surprisingly, these conditions give rise to a huge black market, an exchange system of personal favors, and hoarding (Auzan, 1995).

The Former Central Planners are primarily located in Eastern Europe and Central Asia. In terms of per capita GNP, they fall either in the upper (e.g., Estonia, Hungary, Slovenia) or lower (e.g., Czech Republic, Latvia, Lithuania, Poland, Russian Federation, Slovak Republic) tiers of the World Bank's middle-income category. These countries are today in various stages of transformation toward market-based economics. Market entry, prices, and profits were once tightly controlled but are now increasingly determined by market forces. Some countries have opted for a gradual transition, while others have chosen "shock therapy" (e.g., Poland). In many cases, economic and political reform have occurred simultaneously, but market liberalization has occurred even in countries like Communist China, where democracy is still embryonic.

The first signs of a consumer movement and consumer protection policies predated the dramatic changes that have occurred in Eastern Europe and the former Soviet Union since the late 1980s. As examples, the Consumers Federation of Poland was founded in 1981, the Hungarian Consumer Council in 1982, and local consumer organizations in the Soviet Union during 1987.

Unlike the Trade Integrationist countries in which external relations provided the primary impulse for consumer protection and where governments tended to lead private consumer organizations, consumer protection in the Former Communist countries has been driven more by internal demands and has been characterized by determined, although fledgling, private organizations. In the Former Communist countries, government ministries of trade and industry and offices of quality control might be asked to take a more consumer-oriented stance, but the legacy of the planned economies is typically too great. It falls to consumer organizations to press for consumer protection measures and ensure their proper application. In a few instances (notably Russia and Ukraine), consumer groups have even been able to exercise quasi-governmental powers—to inspect shops, seize and test goods, and even initiate prosecutions (Ivanova, 1992).

Consumer protection in the Former Communist countries is not an entirely domestic matter, however. The nascent consumer organizations there have received substantial economic and technical assistance, especially from Consumers International and some of its individual members and from the European Union. In 1993, CI created a Program for Economies in Transition to assist and encourage networking among the growing number of consumer groups in Central and Eastern Europe. Funding for this program came, in part, from the European Union through its PHARE and TACIS technical assistance programs. The major product testing organizations of the U.S., U.K., Netherlands, and Germany have involved themselves in various initiatives and programs, and Germany's consumer organization AgV has played a leading part in helping to establish consumer advice centers in Poland, Hungary, Slovakia, Romania, and Estonia.

While the general goal of assistance from CI and individual consumer organizations is to build strong private and public consumer organizations, a more specific objective has been to launch product testing magazines in the Former Communist countries. These magazines can provide a vital source of income for the private consumer movement, and, in countries with large enough populations, lead to financial independence and large memberships. Another specific objective of outside assistance to the consumer organizations of the Former Central Planners has been to remind these countries of the need for consumer protection policies, especially antitrust policies, as they rush headlong toward capitalism.

Some of the Former Communist countries are strongly motivated to implement consumer protection policies. For one thing, leaders are more accountable to the electorate, and displeasing consumers can lead to their removal from power. (This cuts both ways: economic reformers have themselves been rejected when the pain of moving toward free markets has become too great.) For another, several countries (e.g., Hungary, Poland, the Czech Republic, and Slovakia) aspire to membership in the European Union, and a KEY way of demonstrating their worthiness is by raising consumer protection standards to those found in EU countries.

The picture for consumer organizations in the former planned economies is not so rosy, though. They face a deep-rooted culture of dependency on the state in which consumers are doubtful that anything can be done to improve their lot and are mistrustful of anyone purporting to be acting on their behalf. This tends to deny the independent consumer organizations of both a constituency and a source of income, and thereby weakens the democratic process as a whole (Macgeorge, 1996). Thus, despite the appearance of consumer organizations in virtually all of the former communist countries (even war-torn Bosnia), government consumer protection has been slow to develop. Poland, Hungary, and Slovenia, for instance, still lack a general consumer protection law. The state of consumer protection in the public sector, as well as the strength of consumer advocacy in the independent sector, is summarized in the *Handbook of Consumer Policy and Consumer Organisations in Central and Eastern Europe* (1996).

EARNEST STRIVERS

The Earnest Strivers are countries like Mauritius, Indonesia, Fiji, the Philippines, El Salvador, and Turkey. They fall in the lower-middle category of the World Bank's classification scheme. Per capita incomes fall in the $1000–$3000 range. These countries are making efforts to improve both the quantity and quality of life. Infant mortality and child malnutrition is decreasing, and life expectancy has generally reached 70 years or more. During those 70 years, people will have access to the basic necessities of life, they will learn to read and write (literacy rates are 75% or more), and they will likely enjoy some democratic privileges but under fairly coercive and, often, military-dominated governments.

The Earnest Striver countries are not as closely linked to the Anglo-Capitalists and Northern European Corporatists as the Trade Integrationist countries, but they are still part of a technology-driven world economic system. According to Harvard professor Theodore Levitt (1983):

> A powerful force drives the world toward a converging commonality, and that force is technology. It has proletarianized communication, transport, and travel. It has made isolated places and impoverished peoples eager for modernity's allurements. Almost everyone everywhere wants all the things they have heard about, seen, or experienced via the new technologies (p. 92).

People in the Earnest Striver countries have personally enjoyed or at least witnessed many of the consumer delights of the modern world. With their basic consumer needs generally met, their material expectations are on the rise. It is no longer good enough for them to have food; they would like it to be unadulterated and wholesome. Drugs should be safe and effective. Owning items such as radios, televisions, and refrigerators is sufficiently common that consumers now expect these items to be durable and safe. Consumers want something done about sellers who engage in deception or refuse to stand behind their products when a malfunction occurs.

In short, consumers in these countries want the consumer rights to safety, information, choice, representation, education, and redress to be institutionalized in national legislation. In addition to specific laws addressing particular problems, some of these countries have enacted more comprehensive legislation. When El Salvador's civil war ended in 1992, the peace accord signed between the government and Marxist-led insurgents required the government to draft a national consumer protection law within two months. In 1993, their Consumer Protection Act was passed, setting up a National Consumer Affairs Council to improve the effectiveness of consumer programs.

Unlike the Former Communist countries in which advocacy is typically less than a decade old, the tradition of consumer organization in the Earnest Striver countries is substantially older. The first consumer organization in the Philippines was formed in 1963; the first consumer group in Indonesia was established in 1973.

Systematic product testing is in its infancy in the Earnest Striver countries. Consumer groups find it difficult to raise the money to conduct tests and have little prospect of recouping their expenditures through selling magazines. Governments have higher priorities than running product testing labs and are even reluctant to subsidize private product testing efforts. In 1994, El Salvador's Consumer Defense Center defied this generalization by becoming Central America's first independent consumer group to engage in comparative testing, starting with a test of pasteurized milks and creams.

Consumer groups in the Earnest Striver countries are active at the international level. Representatives of consumer groups in Indonesia and Mauritius serve on CI's governing council. In addition, Indonesia has provided CI with its presidential leadership for most of the 1990s in the person of Erna Witoelar. Although CI's Regional Office for Asia and the Pacific is located in Malaysia, its priorities are primarily reflective of the less prosperous Earnest Strivers of the region. From this regional office, global networks have been spawned to combat misuse use of pesticides, pharmaceuticals, and infant milk formula.

HOPEFUL STARTERS

As basic as the consumer problems are in the Earnest Striver nations, these problems are even more pressing in the Striver nations. These are nations such as India, Bangladesh, Guyana, Burkina Faso, Kenya, and Mali. They fall in the World Bank's low-income category based on per capita GNP. While growth rates for the economies of these countries are often 2–3 percent, annual per capita income is still only about $300. Infant mortality is 2–4 times greater than in the Earnest Striver nations, and life expectancy is substantially shorter (60 years or less). Large portions of the population lack basic necessities such as clean water, food, and fuel. Where democratic regimes exist, they are fragile, often subverted by ethnic and religious tensions. Even where governments are stable and relatively benign, people feel that their destiny is subject to powerful foreign-based corporations and lending organizations, on the one hand, and unpredictable Mother Nature, on the other.

In the context of unmet human needs and a sense of political powerlessness, the danger exists that western-style consumer protection can appear to be a superfluous luxury. To avoid being irrelevant, consumer organizations in the Hopeful Starter nations have focused on extremely basic consumer problems. For instance, a consumer group in Senegal succeeded in stopping the abusive practice of demanding that new customers pay any unpaid utility bills left by previous tenants of their houses and apartments. Along the same lines, a group in Burkina Faso helped reverse a long-standing practice under which utility companies suspend service when a customer disputes a bill. Consumer groups have also attempted to raise the status of consumer protection legislation. Consumer International's regional office in Zimbabwe has published a review of existing legislation, convened workshops, drafted a "model law for Africa" based on the 1985 United Nations Guidelines for Consumer Protection, and assisted in lobbying campaigns to enact consumer protection laws.

Even with the help of the U.N. Guidelines, it can be difficult for Hopeful Starter nations to set their consumer protection priorities. On the one hand, measures that control the quality of products and the behavior of sellers seem to be the quickest and surest way of improving the welfare of consumers. On the other hand, measures to promote consumer education and consumer information are politically more palatable to business and less expensive for government to enforce. Hence, a Hopeful Starter nation must carefully craft a combination of consumer policies that is appropriate to its situation (Thorelli, 1983).

In the Hopeful Starter nations, consumer protection is difficult to separate from several other economic and social goals, including reducing poverty, encouraging economic growth and development, promoting democracy, achieving national unity and autonomy, improving the status of women, and protecting the natural environment. Thus, programs to halt erosion or provide small loans for female-owned enterprises may be called "consumer" programs.

Along with the Earnest Striver nations, the citizens of the Hopeful Starter nations are increasingly exposed to production methods and products embodying the most modern technologies and lifestyles (Barber, 1995; Ger and Belk, 1996). At the same time, the Hopeful Starter nations are struggling to address very basic consumer needs. Consumer protection initiatives in these nations often involve the intersection of modern technology and basic consumer concerns. Two examples are the campaign to encourage breastfeeding and the establishment of essential drugs lists.

In response to severe problems arising from the sale of infant milk formula in the Hopeful Starter nations, the World Alliance for Breastfeeding Action (WABA) was formed. Under the best of conditions, formula is an expensive substitute for breastfeeding. In a nation where clean water is difficult to obtain, sterilization of bottles is difficult to achieve, and the price of formula represents a large portion of a poor person's income, infant milk formula can result in malnutrition and death. In response to these problems, and some questionable marketing practices by the sellers of formula, WABA secured industry agreement to abide by a set of marketing guidelines. While compliance with the guidelines has been far from perfect, substantial improvements have been made in some countries.

The creation of an essential drugs list is a response to the high cost of imported pharmaceutical products. The idea of the list is to encourage domestic firms to produce the listed drugs at low cost by narrowing the allowable drugs that can be prescribed by publicly-owned medical institutions. Bangladesh was the pioneer in the creation of an essential drugs list, and its efforts have been emulated by other Hopeful Starter nations.

While consumers in the Hopeful Starter nations often have a strong preference for foreign-made products, they can also be subject to double standards (Kerton, 1990) by which products banned, severely restricted, or past peak usability are "dumped" into their markets. These products are typically pharmaceuticals, pesticides, packaged foods, and materials destined for recycling. Consumers in developing countries may not be aware of the risks associated with these items or, if they are, be able to use, apply, or work with the products safety. While some importing and exporting countries have put restrictions on the sale of these potentially dangerous items, this practice remains difficult to control with traditional consumer protection methods.

Conclusion

It takes a lot of chutzpah to reduce the countries of the world to six categories based on their economic, political, and cultural characteristics, and even more to suggest that this categorization can explain global variation in consumer protection policies. The alternatives, however, are even more problematic: to either assume that all nations are following a single, evolutionary path toward the "correct" consumer policies or, at the other extreme, to provide separate descriptions of the consumer protection policies of the world's more than 200 nations.

While one can argue with the exact divisions drawn here and their relationship to consumer protection, it seems undeniable that global variation in consumer protection is rooted in more than simple economics. The challenge for future research is to move from ideographic and particularistic explanations of consumer policy to more general ones in which relationships are identified that apply across different times and settings. These nomothetic explanations will likely have to take account of economic, political, demographic, social, and cultural factors in explaining differences in consumer protection policies.

At best, the six categories used here have temporary utility because the economic, political, and cultural variables that underlie the categories are constantly changing. But what is the direction of change? If the world's nations are converging in terms of their economic development, political institutions, and cultural values, then we can expect greater homogeneity in consumer protection policies. If differing political traditions and cultural values remain resistant to change or if substantial economic inequality among nations persists, differences in consumer protection policies can be expected.

For the foreseeable future at least, there will be international variation in consumer protection policies despite the homogenizing effects of mass production, multinational corporations, modern technology, and free trade agreements. If nature is any guide, this is probably for the good; diversity is the key to adaptability. We must take advantage of the opportunity to learn from the consumer protection experiences of countries other than our own. Just as nations trade goods and services, hoping to take advantage of what other nations do best, nations should exchange consumer policies, learning from each others' successes and failures. Unlike trade in goods, there is no payment when one country's consumer policies are imported by another. There is, however, the satisfaction in knowing that imitation is the sincerest form of flattery.

References

Abt Associates, 1993, *Status Report on the Use of Environmental Labels Worldwide*. Washington, D.C.: U.S. Environmental Protection Agency.

Barber, Benjamin R., 1995, *Jihad vs. McWorld*. NY: Times Books.

DeLoss, Gary, 1985, "Making Change: Consumer Cooperatives in Sweden," in Ralph Nader Task Force on European Cooperatives, *Making Change: Learning from Europe's Consumer Cooperatives.* Washington, D.C.: Center for Study of Responsive Law, pp. 63–92.

Draculic, Slavenka, 1991, *How We Survived Communism and Even Laughed*. NY: W.W. Norton.

Fumitoshi, Takahasi, 1996, "Japan's Product Liability Law: Issues and Implications," *Journal of Japanese Studies*, Vol. 22, No. 1, pp. 105–28.

Garman, E. Thomas, 1996, *Consumer Economic Issues In America,* 4th edition. Houston, TX: DAME Publications, Inc.

Ger, Güliz and Russell W. Belk (1986), "I'd Like to Buy the World a Coke: Consumptionscapes of the 'Less Affluent World,'" *Journal of Consumer Policy,* V. 19, (September), pp. 271–304.

Graver, Kjersti, 1986, "A Study of the Consumer Ombudsman Institution in Norway with Some References to the Other Nordic Countries. Part I. Background and Description," *Journal of Consumer Policy.* V. 9, pp. 1–23.

Handbook of Consumer Policy and Consumer Organisations in Central and Eastern Europe, 2nd edition (1996), Report produced by the International Consumer Research Institute (Slovenia) and the International Consumer Policy Bureau (Scotland).

Ivanova, Natasha, 1992, "Rising to the Challenge," *World Consumer,* No. 202, July, pp. 1–5.

Jeleby, Hans, ed., 1995, *Facts and Views on Nordic Consumer Policy: An Anthology*. Copenhagen, Denmark: Nordic Council of Ministers.

Kerton, Robert R., 1990, *Double Standards: Consumer and Worker Protection in an Unequal World*. Ottawa, Canada: North-South Institute.

Kelman, Steven, 1981, *Regulating America, Regulating Sweden*. Cambridge, MA: MIT Press.

Kidron, Michael and Ronald Segal, 1995, *The State of the World Atlas*. London: Penguin.

Kozminski, Andrzej K., 1992, "Consumers in Transition From the Centrally Planned Economy to the Market Economy," *Journal of Consumer Policy,* V. 14, pp. 351–369.

Levitt, Theodore, 1983, "The Globalization of Markets," *Harvard Business Review,* Vol 83 (May–June), pp. 92–102.

Macgeorge, Alastair (1997), "Consumer Movements in Central and Eastern Europe" in Steve Brobeck, Robert N. Mayer, and Robert O. Herrmann, eds., *Encyclopedia of the Consumer Movement*. Garland Publishing, in press.

Macgeorge, Alastair (1996), personal communication.

Moffett, Matt, 1988, "Mexican Consumers Have a Stout Friend in Arturo Lomeli," *Wall Street Journal,* January 18, p. 1+.

Nadel, Mark V., 1971, *The Politics of Consumer Protection*. Indianapolis: Bobbs-Merrill Company, Inc.

Sverdrup, Sidsel G. and Eivind Stø, 1992, "Regulation of Sex Discrimination in Advertising: An Empirical Inquiry into the Norwegian Case," *Journal of Consumer Policy,* V. 14, pp. 371–91.

Thorelli, Hans B., 1983, "Consumer Policy in Developing Countries," in Karen P. Goebel (ed.), *Proceedings of the 29th ACCI Annual Conference*. Columbia, MO: American Council on Consumer Interests, pp. 147–53.

Triandis, Harry C., Christopher McCusker, and C. Harry Hui, 1990, "Multimethod Probes of Individualism and Collectivism," *Journal of Personality and Social Psychology*, V. 59, No. 5, pp. 1006–1020.

Vogel, David, 1995, *Trading Up: Consumer and Environmental Regulation in a Global Economy*. Cambridge, MA: Harvard University Press.

World Bank, 1994, *World Development Report—1994*. Oxford University Press, 1994.

World Trade Organization, 1995, *International Trade: Trends and Statistics*.

THE CONTRAST BETWEEN RISK ASSESSMENT AND RULES OF EVIDENCE IN THE CONTEXT OF INTERNATIONAL TRADE DISPUTES: CAN THE U.S. EXPERIENCE INFORM THE PROCESS?

Elizabeth L. Anderson[1][*] and Catherine St. Hilaire[1]

Risk assessment provides a formalized process to evaluate human, animal, and ecological responses associated with exposure to environmental agents. The purpose of risk assessment is to answer two related questions.

- How likely is an (adverse) event to occur?
- If it does, how severe will the impact be?

In the United States, the science of risk assessment has evolved out of the necessity to make public health decisions in the face of scientific uncertainty. Its basic propositions have been established over the past three decades and its applications have impacted virtually every aspect of public health and environmental protection in many countries, including the United States. More recently, the World Trade Organization's (WTO) dispute-settlement process has provided additional incentive for the reliance on risk assessments internationally through the requirement that member countries be able to provide scientific justification, based on a risk assessment, for public health and environmental regulatory measures that are challenged. The purpose of this article is to review the history of risk assessment in the United States, emphasizing the development of both its scientific and policy aspects, as one example of the development of institutional capacity for risk assessment. This article discusses the importance of the social, political, and economic contexts of risk assessment and risk management in shaping the approaches taken while highlighting the reality that the analytic or risk assessment part of the decision-making process, in the absence of scientific data, can be completed only by inserting inferences, or policy judgments, which may differ among countries. This article recognizes these differences, and the consequent difference between risk

Anderson, Elizabeth L. and Catherine St. Hilaire (2004), "The Contrast Between Risk Assessment and Rules of Evidence in the Context of International Trade Disputes: Can the U.S. Experience Inform the Process?" *Risk Analysis,* Vol. 24 (2) 449–59.

[1] Sciences International, Inc., 1800 Diagonal Road, Suite 500, Alexandria, VA 22314, USA.

[*]Address correspondence to Elizabeth L. Anderson, Sciences International, Inc., 1800 Diagonal Road, Suite 500, Alexandria, VA 22314, USA; elanderson@sciences.com.

assessment that incorporates public health protective assumptions and the rules of evidence that seek to answer questions of causality, and discusses implications for the WTO dispute-settlement process. It further explores the value of country-specific risk assessment guidelines to facilitate consistency within a country along with the appropriateness and feasibility of international risk assessment guidelines.

KEY WORDS: Risk assessment; public health policy; international trade litigation

Introduction

The World Trade Organization (WTO) Agreement on Sanitary and Phytosanitary (SPS) Measures negotiated in the Uruguay Round came into effect on January 1, 1995. It requires that countries either adopt harmonized international standards or, if they choose to maintain stricter regulations, standards based on risk assessment, scientific principles, and scientific evidence[2] (Howse, 2000; GATT, 1947; Sanitary and Phytosanitary Measures, 1994, Article 3.3). The North American Free Trade Agreement (NAFTA) also contains a section on SPS measures (Chapter 7) that requires SPS regulations to have a scientific basis and result from a risk assessment (Atik, 1996–1997).

The WTO provides a mechanism to resolve disputes over the appropriateness of national standards that are more restrictive than other national or international standards. To date, 301 disputes have been brought to the WTO (http://www.wto.org). Several of these disputes have focused on the scientific basis for SPS standards, e.g., EC—Hormones, Australia—Salmon, and Japan—Varietals, and have been highlighted in companion articles. . . .

In this article, we review the history of risk assessment procedures relied upon within the United States to protect human health (one aspect of the SPS agreement). This is not a comprehensive review; rather, it focuses on key issues that were addressed as the risk assessment process evolved that are relevant to the WTO dispute-settlement process. These issues include the following:

1. definitions of risk assessment/management,
2. relationship/interface of risk assessment/management,
3. method to determine weight and sufficiency of evidence,
4. qualitative versus quantitative risk assessment,
5. uncertainty in scientific knowledge, including absence of data,
6. science and policy in the risk assessment process,

---

[2]Article 20 of the General Agreement on Tariffs and Trade (GATT 1947) allows governments to act on trade in order to protect human, animal, or plant life or health, provided they do not discriminate or use this as disguised protectionism. In addition, there are two specific WTO agreements dealing with food safety and animal and plant health and safety—the SPS Measures agreement—and with product standards—the Technical Barriers to Trade Agreement (TBT).

7. role of precaution/precautionary principle versus evidence of causality,

8. exposure assessment, and

9. risk assessment guidelines.

The History of Risk Assessment

Despite the attention given to it during the last several decades, risk assessment is not new or novel. Koch (1984) provided an early risk assessment process in the form of "Koch's Postulates," which are intended to define the scientific evidence required to demonstrate causation as it relates to infectious disease.

1. An organism can be isolated from a host suffering from the disease.

2. The organism can be cultured in the laboratory.

3. The organism causes the same disease when introduced into another host.

4. The organism can be reisolated from that host.

One century later Bradford-Hill (1965) published a set of criteria to be applied while attempting to establish causality between an environmental exposure to a (noninfectious) agent and a particular disease in humans.

1. Is there a temporal relationship?

2. How strong is the association between exposure and disease?

3. Is there a dose-response relationship?

4. Have the results been replicated?

5. Is the association biologically plausible?

6. Have alternative explanations been considered?

7. What is the effect of ceasing exposure?

8. Does the association exhibit specificity?

9. Are the findings consistent with other relevant knowledge?

The preceding examples are qualitative determinations of the likelihood, or strength of the evidence, that agent A causes disease B. This type of analysis, including the use of results from experimental laboratory studies, was relied upon by U.S. regulatory agencies, e.g., the Occupational Safety and Health Agency (OSHA), the Food and Drug Administration (FDA), and the Environmental Protection Agency (EPA), until the 1970s when it became apparent within FDA and EPA that a zero-risk policy was not achievable. These agencies recognized that considerations beyond qualitative evidence including potency differences and exposure information are essential for sound public health policies.

In the case of FDA, the 1958 Food Additives Amendment to the Food, Drugs, and Cosmetics Act prohibited the use of food additives found to be carcinogenic. In 1962, Congress amended the law to permit the use of a carcinogenic animal drug if the agency determined that no residue of the drug would be detected in edible animal tissues. In the early 1970s, because of the difficulty of enforcing a law based on detection limits that were constantly lowered through analytic advances, FDA proposed sensitivity of method guidelines that defined "not detected" through the use of quantitative risk assessment methods. Although the guidelines were never adopted, the principles have been applied on numerous occasions to food contaminants, trace contaminants of food additives and food packaging material, and veterinary drug residues (FDA, 1987, 1995, 2002), including the use of the proposed definition of "significant risk"—a 10^{-6} lifetime risk of cancer.

At about the same time, in the early to mid 1970s, when faced with the necessity of regulating hundreds of potentially carcinogenic agents under a rapid cascade of regulatory authorities that covered toxicants in all environmental media and a wide variety of use patterns, EPA scientists and policy makers realized that its zero-risk policy for carcinogens, based solely on the qualitative determination that a substance had carcinogenic potential in exposed humans or animals, was unobtainable. The Agency moved instead to the concept of an "acceptable level" of risk. This approach required the Agency to be able to correlate exposure levels to risk levels through a quantitative risk assessment process. In 1976, the EPA Administrator, Russell Train, announced a new policy that emphasized a two-part process for making policy decisions regarding carcinogens as follows:

1. the first step was to determine whether an agent was a carcinogenic hazard (qualitative and quantitative aspects) and
2. the second step was to determine what level of regulation was necessary to protect public health, taking into consideration social and economic factors as prescribed by statutory language.

(This two-step process later surfaced as the distinction between risk assessment and risk management.) Further, the risk assessment process for environmental agents was described for the first time as including both a qualitative analysis (How likely is the agent to be a human carcinogen?) and a quantitative analysis (Assuming the agent is a carcinogen, what is the extent of the impact of a proposed regulatory policy?). The concept of assessing qualitative and quantitative risks for hundreds of agents in the environment and using this information to support acceptance of some level of residual risk was novel at that time.

The methods to be followed by the Agency were collected into a set of guidelines that were published in the *Federal Register* in 1976 (EPA, 1976). These guidelines put in motion the analytic or risk assessment process for hundreds of agents that incorporated all the scientific evidence, which was evaluated in a "weight-of-evidence" approach that gave the greatest weight to epidemiologic data and data from animal studies conducted in multiple strains/species. Epidemiologic and animal studies that had been replicated and showed dose-response associations were given greater weight in reaching the overall conclusion. The guidelines also included the appropriate inferences, or policy-based assumptions, which were intentionally chosen to be biased toward public health protection, to be used when scientific information was incomplete. For example, the use of a linear, nonthreshold dose-response curve was to be used to place an upper bound on risks at environmental exposure levels where no data existed. These guidelines also called for the establishment of a senior health committee, the Carcinogen Assessment Group, which would report directly to EPA's Administrator. These approaches were further emphasized by publication of an article co-authored by EPA Administrator Train in the *Journal of the National Cancer Institute* (Albert *et al.,* 1977).

Largely because policy-based judgments were essential to the risk assessment process, efforts to bring continuity to the risk assessment process across the four major regulatory agencies, EPA, FDA, OSHA, and the Consumer Product Safety Commission (CPSC), were attempted by the Inter-Agency Regulatory Liaison Group (IRLG), which reported out interagency guidelines for performing risk assessment (IRLG, 1979). As expected, EPA and FDA were largely in agreement about the use of quantitative risk assessment but OSHA was opposed to the use of dose-response information in regulatory decision making. Consequently, the document reported guidance on the use of quantitative methods if an agency chose to use them.

The movement by regulatory agencies from qualitative to quantitative expressions of risk was not made without substantial controversy—on both sides of the issue. For example, the risk assessment process was debated as to the appropriateness of certain inference assumptions. The risk management process was challenged by the environmental and other public interest groups who opposed the idea that there could be an "acceptable" level of risk, while the regulated community believed very strongly that the regulatory levels corresponding to acceptable risk levels were many times lower than necessary to protect public health. This controversy ultimately led to a congressional mandate that the National Academy of Sciences (NAS) conduct a study of the risk assessment process used by federal regulatory agencies.

Risk Assessment in the Federal Government: Managing the Process

The report "Risk Assessment in the Federal Government: Managing the Process" (NAS, 1983) provided much needed clarity and legitimacy to the risk assessment process that had evolved over time in U.S. regulatory agencies (Anderson, 2003). This report was prepared in response to a congressional directive to assess the merits of separating the risk assessment process from the regulatory policy-setting process. Congress was responding to concern within the regulated community that the analytic process in risk assessment was being inappropriately influenced by the desire to regulate within some agencies, such as the EPA. The NAS Committee conducting the study, however, found that the basic problem in risk assessment was not its organizational location but "the sparseness and uncertainty of the scientific knowledge of the health hazards addressed . . ."

The Committee went on to identify and address critical aspects of risk assessment, including the following:

1. definitions,
2. science and policy in risk assessment,
3. risk assessment/risk management interface, and
4. development of guidelines.

DEFINITIONS

The NAS Committee defined risk assessment as "the characterization of the potential adverse effects of human exposure to environmental hazards." Prior to the establishment of this definition, much of the debate surrounding risk assessment was unnecessarily complicated by inconsistency in the use of the term. For example, the Committee intended the definition to include *qualitative* risk assessments, in contrast to others who used the term narrowly to refer only to *quantitative* risk assessments.

SCIENCE AND POLICY IN RISK ASSESSMENT

A key observation of the Committee was that "[w]hen scientific uncertainty is encountered in the risk assessment process, inferential bridges are needed to allow the process to continue . . . The judgments made by the scientist/risk assessor . . . often entail a choice among several scientifically plausible options . . . [and] . . . policy considerations inevitably affect, and perhaps determine, some of the choices . . ." That is, gaps in knowledge are bridged through a set of inferences that consist of default assumptions based on "risk assessment policy." This recognition of the necessity and appropriateness of relying on default assumptions when gaps in scientific knowledge were encountered in an assessment was a crucial step forward in fostering transparency in risk assessment procedures and in legitimizing the process relied upon by regulatory agencies. Thus, the NRC Committee differentiated between *risk assessment science* and *risk assessment policy,* the latter term referring to the use of default assumptions. Risk assessment policy was distinct from the types of policy considerations required when the risk management/regulatory decision was made (e.g., economic concerns, technical feasibility).

INTERFACE OF RISK ASSESSMENT/RISK MANAGEMENT

The Committee recommended that agencies maintain a clear conceptual distinction between assessment of risks and the consideration of risk management alternatives: "The goal of risk assessment is to describe as accurately as possible the possible health consequences of exposure to hazardous substances using the best available science supplemented as necessary by assumptions that are consistent with the science. The ultimate goal of risk management on the other hand is to evaluate trade-offs between health consequences and other effects of specific regulatory actions." That is, the Committee emphasized that an agency's desire to regulate, or not to regulate, a specific substance must not influence the conduct of the risk assessment. In fact, it recommended that agencies develop mechanisms to minimize even the *perception* that this could occur. In this way the integrity of the science is more likely to be maintained.

RISK ASSESSMENT GUIDELINES

The NAS Committee concluded that the best way to ensure integrity and consistency in the risk assessment process was to develop guidelines for the performance of risk assessments. *Guidelines* were defined as the principles followed by risk assessors in interpreting and reaching judgments based on scientific data. Ideally, such guidelines would be consistent across all public health agencies in the United States, but at the very least they were expected to be consistent within a given agency.

Following the publication of the NRC (1983) report, EPA (EPA, 1986a) published updated cancer risk assessment guidelines and guidelines for developmental, mutagenicity, chemical mixtures, estimating exposure, reproductive toxicity, and neurotoxicity (EPA, 1986b, 1986c, 1986d, 1986e, 1996b, 1998). (Several of these have since been updated (EPA, 1991, 1996a, 1996b, 1999, 2003).) In another federal-government-wide effort to harmonize risk assessment approaches for assessment of carcinogens, the Office of Science and Technology Policy (OSTP) convened an interagency committee to develop a statement of the scientific basis for risk assessment. This committee published its findings in the *Federal Register* in 1985 (OSTP, 1985).

NAS 1994 released a second report that provided further guidance on methods to improve the process of risk assessment and risk management decision making. Again, in response to the NAS recommendations, the EPA issued revised draft cancer guidelines. However, in contrast to the relative ease of finalizing the 1976 and 1986 guidelines, these new cancer risk assessment guidelines have been in draft since 1996 (EPA, 1996a, 1999) and have only recently been again released in draft (EPA, 2003).

The Scientific Basis for Risk Assessment

Because the science underlying risk assessment is not fixed, a key aspect of continued application of this tool is the ability to accommodate the advances in our understanding of toxicity caused by environmental agents. In the following discussion, current approaches, including several recent developments in risk assessment methods, are highlighted. The risk assessment paradigm (consisting of four separate steps—hazard identification, dose-response assessment, exposure assessment, and risk characterization—developed in the

NAS (1983) report (and adopted by U.S. regulatory agencies) is used to describe the scientific underpinnings of the risk assessment process (Figure 1).

HAZARD IDENTIFICATION

This is the first step in risk assessment—determining whether exposure to an agent can cause an increase in the incidence of a health condition, e.g., cancer. This determination requires that all relevant data from epidemiology, animal studies, *in vitro* studies, and molecular structure be considered. The relevant information from these types of studies is considered in the case of carcinogens within an overall weight-of-the evidence determination. The EPA first incorporated this concept into its 1976 guidelines. The 1986 guidelines included a categorization approach, similar to that of the International Agency for Research on Cancer, for describing the weight of the evidence (or scientific

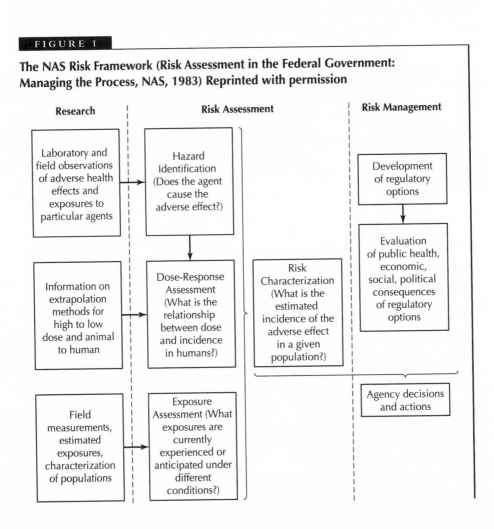

FIGURE 1

The NAS Risk Framework (Risk Assessment in the Federal Government: Managing the Process, NAS, 1983) Reprinted with permission

Research	Risk Assessment	Risk Management

Laboratory and field observations of adverse health effects and exposures to particular agents

Hazard Identification (Does the agent cause the adverse effect?)

Development of regulatory options

Information on extrapolation methods for high to low dose and animal to human

Dose-Response Assessment (What is the relationship between dose and incidence in humans?)

Risk Characterization (What is the estimated incidence of the adverse effect in a given population?)

Evaluation of public health, economic, social, political consequences of regulatory options

Field measurements, estimated exposures, characterization of populations

Exposure Assessment (What exposures are currently experienced or anticipated under different conditions?)

Agency decisions and actions

confidence) that the agent was a human carcinogen. Although the terminology relied upon by the Agency has changed somewhat in its most recent set of proposed guidelines, the evidence required in each of the categories has not. Similarly, although the terminology used by other organizations for their weight-of-evidence categories varies, the evidence required for each category is remarkably consistent (Table 1). As noted earlier, given the historical development of qualitative methods to assess evidence for causation, consistency in the approaches is expected.

DOSE-RESPONSE ASSESSMENT

Different agents have differing capacities to induce disease and a major aspect of understanding an agent's potential to cause disease is an understanding of how the exposure/dose is related to the adverse health effect. A major issue here is extrapolating from experimental conditions to those experienced by exposed populations. In epidemiology, extrapolation from the population in the study (usually occupational groups where exposure is high compared to environmental levels) is required. If animal studies are relied upon, extrapolation involves interspecies and high-to-low dose extrapolations, which introduce considerable uncertainty, especially when experimental doses are several orders of magnitude higher than doses resulting from environmental exposures (Figure 2).

The most recent EPA guidelines recommend that a benchmark dose corresponding to the lower 95th confidence limit of the dose corresponding to a 10% increased tumor incidence (LED_{10}) be identified as a point of departure for low-dose extrapolation. The default approach requires the extension of a straight line from the point of departure dose to zero dose, zero response based on an assumption of linearity. This is a significant change from the Agency's past practice of applying the linearized multistage procedure (adopted in 1979) or the linear, nonthreshold approach, which has been used since the first set of guidelines was developed in 1976. In either case, the extrapolation procedure results in a range of potential risks (Figure 3).

In cases where the mechanism of action is a threshold event, a margin of exposure analysis, in which a point of departure (e.g., the LED_{10}) is divided by uncertainty factors, is used. Uncertainty factors are used to account for database uncertainties such as the absence of a no-observed-adverse-effect level (NOAEL), insufficient experimental conditions (e.g., duration of exposure) and inter-and intraspecies extrapolations. For example, in the absence of a reliable PBPK model, extrapolation from animal doses to human equivalent doses continues to rely on scaling factors for carcinogens (e.g., $BW^{0.75}$) or the application of a 10-fold uncertainty factor (noncarcinogenic effects). The choice of uncertainty factors is determined by agency staff based on a number of factors, with one exception. In a very unusual and highly controversial move, the U.S. Congress legislated the policy choice of a 10-fold safety (uncertainty) factor to be used

TABLE 1

Weight-of-Evidence Classification Systems of Various Organizations for Chemical Carcinogens

EPA 1986	EPA 1996	EPA (2003)	IARC	NTP (2002)	EC (2003)
A Known human carcinogen (convincing epidemiologic evidence that exposure is causal)	Known/likely*	"Carcinogenic to humans" (convincing epidemiologic evidence that exposure is causal)	1 Known human (convincing epidemiologic evidence that exposure is causal)	Known human (convincing epidemiologic evidence that exposure is causal)	1 Substances known to be carcinogenic to man (sufficient evidence to establish a causal association between human exposure and cancer)
B1 Probable human carcinogen (limited human, adequate animal)		"Likely to be carcinogenic to humans" (data indicate carcinogenic potential)	2A Probably carcinogenic to humans (limited human, adequate animal)	Reasonably anticipated to be a human carcinogen (limited human evidence or adequate animal, or convincing SAR evidence)	2 Substances that should be regarded as if they are carcinogenic to man. ("sufficient evidence to provide strong presumption . . . [for] the development of cancer [in man], generally on the basis of animal studies")
B2 Probable human carcinogen (inadequate human, adequate animal)			NA	NA	NA
C Possible human carcinogen (inadequate human, limited animal)		"Suggestive evidence of carcinogenic potential" (data are suggestive of carcinogenicity—a concern for potential carcinogenic effects in humans is raised, but the data are judged not sufficient for a stronger conclusion)	2B Possibly carcinogenic in humans (inadequate human, limited animal)	NA	3 Substances that cause concern for man owing to possible carcinogenic effects but available information is not adequate for making a satisfactory assessment
D Not classifiable as to human carcinogenicity (inadequate human and animal)	Cannot be determined	Inadequate information	3 Not classifiable (inadequate human and animal)	NA	NA
E Evidence of noncarcinogenicity for humans	Not likely	"Not likely to be carcinogenic to humans"	4 Probably not carcinogenic to humans	NA	NA

*In the 1996 guidelines, "known/likely," "cannot be determined," and "not likely" replaced the six alphanumeric categories (A, B1, B2, C, D, E) in the 1986 cancer guidelines. Subdescriptors such as "highly likely" could also be used. The weight of evidence was to be presented as a narrative intended for the risk manager, which summarized the key evidence, described the agent's mode of action, characterized the conditions of hazard expression, and recommended appropriate dose-response approach(es). Significant strengths, weaknesses, and uncertainties of contributing evidence were also to be highlighted. The overall conclusion as to the likelihood of human carcinogenicity was to be given by route of exposure.

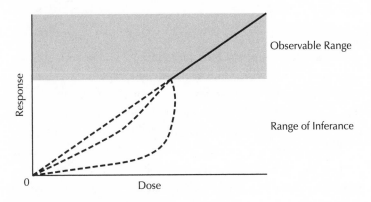

FIGURE 2

High-to-Low Dose Problem

Observable Range

Range of Inferance

Response

0   Dose

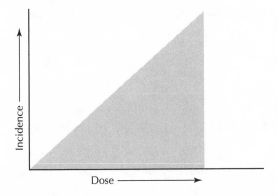

FIGURE 3

Bounding Carcinogenic Risk

Incidence

Dose

in risk assessments for pesticides to address the issue of children as a sensitive subpopulation (EPA, 1996c). The factor included in the law must be used unless it can be shown to be unnecessary.

EXPOSURE ASSESSMENT

The starting point for this process is the concentration of the agent in exposure media (e.g., air, water, food). This value may be measured or modeled and it may be expressed as a statistical definition of exposure concentration, e.g., 95% UCL or central tendency. The level of exposure received by individuals in the exposed population is characterized based on the magnitude, frequency, duration, and route(s) of exposure. In general, the exposure scenario that yields a reasonable maximum exposure (RME), which is the highest exposure that is reasonably expected to occur, is developed. The relationship between exposure and dose is determined by quantifying intake, e.g., volume of water ingested per day.

Risk Characterization

The last step in the risk assessment process is risk characterization, where both qualitative (hazard identification) and quantitative (dose-response and exposure assessment) information are presented. Combining the dose-response information with the estimates of human exposure to the agent prior to regulation provides a "baseline" estimate of current risks and establishes a basis for regulatory action. The dose-response information, combined with the Agency's determination of "acceptable risk," can then be used to determine how much of the agent can remain in the environment and still be protective of human health (e.g., drinking water levels, hazardous waste cleanup goals, permitted air releases). The EPA has developed a handbook for the risk characterization step of risk assessment (EPA, 2000a, 2000b).

A critical part of the risk characterization is a discussion of the uncertainties in the analysis and conclusions. It is this aspect of the risk assessment—dealing with uncertainty—that is the main focus of requirements that the risk assessment process be transparent so that precautionary approaches to address the uncertainties can be identified.

Discussion

Two primary issues pertinent to the WTO dispute-settlement process converge in light of the evolution of risk assessment as practiced by U.S. regulatory and public health agencies:

1. while science remains constant, inference guidelines may differ among countries, and
2. the primary use of risk assessment as a precautionary approach to preventing future disease also limits its usefulness in answering questions asked in the context of legal rules of evidence to establish causality.

If we retrace the evolution of public health risk assessment in the United States, we find that, prior to the late 1970s, regulatory agencies were independently developing approaches to risk assessment in support of regulatory decision making. A series of events led to efforts to coordinate and standardize risk assessment procedures, including a review by an independent scientific body, the NAS.

The international marketplace could be described as being at a similar juncture at this point in time. That is, risk assessments are being performed in individual countries and public attention has become focused on the scientific basis of country-specific regulatory decision making as a result of the WTO process for resolving trade disputes.

The question that the WTO must answer is whether the regulations (and the associated restrictions in trade) are legitimate. The SPS agreement has been the basis for several disputes, including one concerning the EU ban on the import of beef treated with hormones. In its ruling, the WTO Appellate Body emphasized the importance of basing public health measures on an objective assessment of risks: "In our opinion, there is a 'scientific justification' for an SPS measure, within the meaning of Article 3.3, if there is a rational relationship between the SPS measure at issue and the available scientific information."

In this article, critical issues related to risk assessment and the scientific basis for WTO decision making have been identified. A concerted effort to address them (in a process, such as that used by the NAS, which is separate and independent of specific trade disputes) is likely to benefit the process substantially. However, the specifics associated with resolution of critical issues must, of necessity, conform to the legal framework within which the WTO operates. That is, the legal context for risk assessment will influence the scientific judgments (assumptions) that must be made. This is of course true for risk assessments performed in different nations. In the case of protection of public health, conservative or precautionary measures are necessary; however, the degree of conservatism will vary among different national authorities.

For example, the EPA mission is, first and foremost, "to protect human health and to safeguard the natural environment—air, water, and land—upon which life depends" (EPA, Mission Statement, www.epa.gov). EPA is charged with anticipating potential risks to human health and the environment; thus, the policy component of a default assumption is "be protective." The question to the EPA and other agencies charged with protection of human health is not "Has this agent been scientifically proven to cause disease?" but rather, "Has it been scientifically demonstrated that this agent could, under appropriate circumstances, cause disease?"

Thus, the EPA (2003), in its most recent draft Carcinogen Risk Assessment Guidelines, provides the following explanation of the Agency's use of conservative assumptions: "Since the primary goal of EPA actions is public health protection and that, accordingly, as an Agency policy, the defaults used in the absence of scientific data to the contrary have been chosen to be health protective." The same health-protective approach is made by public health organizations outside the United States. For example, in the case of the European Union (EU), public health and environmental decision making incorporate conservatism (precaution) through the appropriate application of the "precautionary principle"[3] during the risk management phase of regulatory action (Byrne, 2000). The WTO framework is consistent with the goal of public health

---

[3] The precautionary principle addresses how to proceed when information for risk assessment is inadequate. Principle 15 of the Rio Declaration on the Environment and Development is often referred to in international discussions of the precautionary principle. It states "lack of full scientific certainty shall not be used as a reason for postponing cost-effective measures."

protection and thus the validity of using precautionary approaches has been recognized (WTO, 2003).

Different approaches to scientific uncertainty are seen in different social and economic contexts. For example, developed countries may be able to weigh cost and benefit to be more precautionary, while developing countries may choose a less precautionary approach. Conversely, countries with populations that could be at increased susceptibility to chemical toxicity due to malnutrition, endemic infections, or chronic diseases might set regulatory limits in light of these concerns.

Different legal contexts will also influence the way scientific uncertainty is addressed. For example, in the United States, litigation related to personal injury claims usually requires a determination that, in the case of environmental contaminants, past exposures have "more likely than not" caused the disease(s) of the plaintiff (or, in some jurisdictions, have been a "substantial factor" in causation). In this situation, a higher degree of scientific certainty is required, e.g., human evidence is often called for even in the presence of data from animal studies. In addition, court decisions such as *Daubert v. Merrill-Dow* (1993) have placed judges as "gate keepers" of scientific evidence through the requirement that expert testimony must be "relevant" and "reliable." In this regard, the WTO Dispute Resolution Body has a similar task of determining the scientific credibility of differing interpretations of the scientific evidence (including "minority" opinions).

An example of the impact of different legal contexts on risk assessment methods (and outcomes) is seen by comparing the weight-of-evidence criteria of public health organizations with those of a committee of the Institute of Medicine (IOM) that had been directed to evaluate the scientific evidence regarding the weight of the evidence for causation of a variety of diseases by exposures of Gulf War military personnel to a variety of substances (IOM, 2000). The IOM committee's framework, while similar on its face to those of the public health agencies[4] (Table 1), considered only *controlled epidemiologic* studies (i.e., cohort and case-control studies) in its evaluation. Other types of epidemiologic investigations (e.g., ecological) were not considered, nor were animal studies, except in those cases where the human data were sufficient to establish a positive association between an agent and a disease—in this case the animal data were used to assess the biological plausibility of the committee's finding. A review of the committee's second report (IOM, 2003) shows that the IOM committee consensus findings on certain agents do not match conclusions reached by public health agencies on these same agents. Neither is necessarily wrong—different outcomes are expected when the degree of scientific proof required differs due to the legal context (public health regulation vs. litigation related to proof of individual causation).

---

[4]The IOM categories were: "sufficient evidence of a causal relationship," "sufficient evidence of an association," "limited/suggestive evidence of an association," and "inadequate/insufficient evidence to determine whether an association exists."

Clearly, the WTO operates in its own unique legal setting and the determination of the appropriate use of scientific evidence presents a particularly interesting and challenging task for scientists (social and natural), policy makers, attorneys, and others involved in the process.

Conclusion

The historical review presented in this article provides insight into one approach in the development of institutional risk assessment capacity. It is important to recognize the context within which risk assessment evolved in the United States, beginning with the pressing need to respond to legal requirements to regulate hundreds of chemicals to protect public health. A workable, health-protective, scientifically-sound approach that would be accepted by the public was urgently needed. The risk assessment process that was developed was grounded in science and based on all available relevant data. However, where data were unavailable, the risk assessor was to rely on inference assumptions that were deliberately biased to be health protective in order to complete the risk assessment process. The highly varied contexts (social, political, economic, etc.) found among countries involved in world trade will require different approaches to the treatment of scientific gaps or uncertainties. That is, although the scientific evidence relied upon is expected to be consistent among different countries, the inferences and assumptions will not be universally applicable; i.e., different priorities and local conditions will influence the selection of assumptions used to address scientific uncertainty.

While the WTO process does not specify how risk assessment is to be performed and, hence, permits a wide diversity of approaches, it requires that a country's risk management approach for a particular product be consistent with the underlying science and with risk management of similar products, including domestic products within that country (Caswell, 2000). Thus, in addition to providing scientific justification for regulatory measures, a country must also withstand the scrutiny of other regulations in force within that country to ensure that the risk assessment procedures and regulatory actions are consistently applied. In the United States, the use of guidelines has enhanced consistency, transparency, and integrity of the risk assessment process. Development of country-specific risk assessment guidelines will also yield the same benefits and render risk management decisions less likely to be successfully challenged. It is also reasonable to assume that the development of international guidelines for risk assessment would aid in the WTO dispute-resolution process, especially if general principles can be applied to disputed regulations that are similar in nature; that is, the process would become less *ad hoc*. Of course, development of useful international guidelines with sufficient flexibility to accommodate legitimately different risk assessment approaches would be a challenging undertaking. Other international organizations, such as the Codex Alimentarius Commission (2001), have been in the process of developing risk assessment policies and principles since the early 1990s and a number of the Codex Committees have or are compiling "risk analysis procedures" used by the Committee. The EU has developed detailed guidelines for its member countries (EC, 2003). In addition, the International Programme on Chemical Safety (IPCS, 2003) has an ongoing project to harmonize approaches to the assessment of risk from exposure to chemicals. The overall goal of this project is to globally harmonize approaches to risk assessment through increased understanding, focusing on specific issues, and striving for agreement on basic principles. The short-term goal of the program is to improve acceptance of assessments that use different approaches, with convergence of methods being the long-term goal.

In conclusion, despite the complexities and challenges associated with its development and use, the science of risk assessment has been demonstrated to be a powerful, and some would argue indispensable, means to ensure that informed decisions concerning human and environmental health are made. However, the inference choices to bridge gaps in scientific knowledge must be considered in the context of country-specific policies. The implications of public health policy choices imbedded in the risk assessment must also be considered in answering evidence-based questions of causality.

References

Albert, R. E., Train, R. R., & Anderson, E. L. (1977). Rationale developed by the Environmental Protection Agency for the assessment of carcinogenic risks. *Journal of the National Cancer Institute, 58,* 1537.

Anderson, E. L. (2003). The red book in context: Science at the center. *Human and Ecological Risk Assessment, 9,* 1197–1202.

Atik, J. (1996–1997). Science and international regulatory convergence. *NW Journal of International Law and Business, 17,* 736.

Bradford-Hill, A. (1965). The environment and disease: Association or causation? *Proceedings of Royal Society of Medicine, 58,* 295.

Byrne, D. (2000). How governments can meet consumer concerns on the trade agenda. Speech to Plenary Meeting of the Transatlantic Consumer Dialogue. Washington, D.C.

Caswell J. A. (2000). Overview. In *Incorporating Science, Economics, and Sociology in Developing Sanitary and Phytosanitary Standards in International Trade.* Washington, DC: National Academy Press.

Codex Alimentarius Commission. (2001). *Risk Analysis Policies of the Codex Alimentarius Commission.* ALINORM 01/9.

Commission of the European Communities. (2001). *White Paper. Strategy for a Future Chemicals Policy.* Brussels, February 27, 2001, COM(2001) 88 final.

EC (European Commission). (2003). *Technical Guidance Document on Risk Assessment. Part 1.* Joint Research Centre. EU 20418 EN/1.

EPA (U.S. Environmental Protection Agency). *Mission Statement.* Available at http://www.epa.gov/history/org/origins/mission.htm.

EPA. (1976). Health risk and economic impact assessments of suspected carcinogens: Interim procedures and guidelines. *Federal Register, 41*(102), 21402–21405.

EPA. (1986a). Guidelines for carcinogen risk assessment. *Federal Register, 51*(185), 33992–34008.

EPA. (1986b). Guidelines for the health risk assessment of suspect developmental toxicants, *Federal Register, 51,* 34028.

EPA. (1986c). Guidelines for mutagenicity risk assessment. *Federal Register, 51,* 34006–34012.

EPA. (1986d). Guidelines for the health risk assessment of chemical mixtures. *Federal Register, 51*(185), 34014–34025.

EPA. (1986e). Guidelines for estimating exposure. *Federal Register, 51*(185), 34042–34058.

EPA. (1991). Guidelines for developmental toxicity risk assessment. *Federal Register, 56,* 63798–63826.

EPA. (1996a). Proposed guidelines for carcinogen risk assessment. *Federal Register, 61,* 17960–18011.

EPA. (1996b). Guidelines for reproductive toxicity risk assessment. *Federal Register, 61,* 56274–56322.

EPA. (1996c). *The Food Quality Protection Act of 1996.* Washington, DC, August, 1996.

EPA. (1998). *Guidelines for Neurotoxicity Risk Assessment.* 630/R-95/001F. April 30, 1998. Washington, DC: U.S. EPA, Risk Assessment Forum, p. 90.

EPA. (1999). *Draft Guidelines for Carcinogen Risk Assessment.* NCEA-F-0644, July 1999. Review draft. Available at http://www.epa.gov/ncea/raf/pdfs/cancer_gls.pdf.

EPA. (2000a). *Supplementary Guidance for Conducting Health Risk Assessment of Chemical Mixtures.* EPA/630/R-00/002, August 2000.

EPA. (2000b). *Science Policy Council Handbook: Risk Characterization.* EPA 100-B-00–002. Dec. 2000.

EPA. (2003). *Draft Final Guidelines for Carcinogen Risk Assessment.* EPA/630/P-03/001A. NCEA F0644A. February. Available at www.epa.gov/NCEA/RAF/Cancer2003.htm. Accessed in 2003.

FDA (Food and Drug Administration). (1987). *Regulation of Carcinogenic Compounds Used in Food-Producing Animals. Title 21, Parts 500.80–500.92 of the Code of Federal Regulations.*

FDA. (1995). Food additives: Threshold of regulation for substances used in food-contact articles; final rule. *Federal Register, 60*(136), 36581–36596.

FDA. (2002). Revision of the definition of the term "no residue" in the new Animal Drug Regulations. *Federal Register, 67*(246), 78172–78174.

GATT (General Agreement on Tariffs and Trade). (1947). Art X. Oct. 30.

Howse, R. (2000). Democracy, science and free trade risk regulation on trial at the World Trade Organization. *Michigan Law Review, 98,* 23–29.

IOM (Institute of Medicine). (2000). Gulf war and health. In C. E. Fulco & C. T. Liverman (Eds.), *Depleted Uranium, Pyridostigmine Bromide, Sarin, and Vaccines, Vol. 1.* Committee on Health Effects Associated with Exposures During the Gulf War, Division of Health Promotion and Disease Prevention.

IOM. (2003). Gulf war and health. *Insecticides and Solvents, Vol. 2.* Committee on Gulf War and Health: Literature Review of Pesticides and Solvents.

IARC (International Agency for Research on Cancer). (2003). *Preamble to the IARC Monographs.* Available at http://monographs.iarc.fr/monoeval/preamble.html. Accessed in 2003.

IPCS (International Programme on Chemical Safety). (2003). *IPCS Harmonization Project.* Available at http://www.who.int/ipcs/methods/harmonization/en/.

IRLG. (1979). Scientific bases for identification of potential carcinogens and estimation of risks. *Journal of the National Cancer Institute, 63,* 241–268.

Koch, R. (1984). Die Aetiologie der Tuberkulose. *Mittheilongen aus dem Kasiserlichen Gesundheitsamte, 2,* 1–88.

NAS (National Academy of Sciences). (1983). *Risk Assessment in the Federal Government: Managing the Process.* Washington, DC: National Academy Press.

NAS (National Academy of Sciences). (1994). *Science and Judgment in Risk Assessment.* Washington, DC: National Academy Press.

NTP (National Toxicology Program). (2002). *Report on Carcinogens,* 10th ed. U.S. Dep't of Health and Human Services, Public Health Service, National Toxicology Program.

OSTP (Office of Science and Technology Policy, Executive Office of the President). (1985). Chemical carcinogens: A review of the science and its associated principles. *Federal Register, 50,* 10371–10442.

Sanitary and Phytosanitary Measures. (1994). *Marrakesh Agreement Establishing the World Trade Organization. Art 7 and Annex B.* Reprinted in H.R. Doc. No. 103–316 at 69–81.

WTO. (2003). Available at http://www.wto.org/english/thewto_e/whatis_e/whatis_e.htm.

PROMOTING "GREEN" CONSUMER BEHAVIOR WITH ECO-LABELS

John Thøgersen*

Eco-labeling is one among a number of policy tools that are used in what has been termed an Integrated Product Policy (Nordic Council of Ministers, 2001). The increasing popularity of product-oriented environmental policy in Europe and elsewhere is based on the perception that the abatement of pollution from industrial and other large sources is now within reach. Hence, the relative importance of pollution from "nonpoint" sources (Miljøstyrelsen, 1996), particularly pollution (and resource use) associated with private consumption (Geyer-Allély and Eppel, 1997; Norwegian Ministry of Environment, 1994; Organization for Economic Co-operation [OECD], 1997b; Sitarz, 1994), has increased. However, not only the composition, but also the volume of consumption in the industrialized countries is increasingly acknowledged to be unsustainable. If widely accepted prognoses for the growth in global consumption are realized, a factor 4 or greater reduction in the environmental impact per produced unit is needed in the next 40 to 50 years just to keep the total environmental impact at the current level (Miljøstyrelsen, 1996).

As a means to reduce the pollution and resource use following from consumption, attempts are made to motivate consumers to switch to less environmentally harmful and resource-consuming products. One of the increasingly popular tools is to label the least harmful products in such a way that consumers can distinguish them from others (OECD, 1991,1997a; U.S. Environmental Protection Agency [EPA], 1998). The hope is that consumers' choices will give producers of (relatively) environment-friendly products a competitive advantage, allowing them to gradually push less environment-friendly products out of the market (Miljø- og Energiministeriet, 1995; OECD, 1991). In addition, it is hoped that the anticipated competitive advantage gives companies an incentive to develop new products that are more friendly to the environment (Backman et al., 1995; Miljøstyrelsen, 1996; OECD, 1991; EPA, 1998).

Other tools in the Integrated Product Policy toolbox are mandatory standards, taxes and subsidies, and voluntary agreements. These means are not necessarily alternatives to

Thøgersen, John, "Promoting green consumer behavior with eco-labels. I: New tools for environmental protection: Education, information, and voluntary measures," Thomas Dietz, Paul Stern (eds). Washington DC: National Academy Press, 2002, s. 83–104.

*The author would like to express gratitude to Doug McKenzie-Mohr and Paul Stern for helpful comments on an earlier draft of this chapter.

labeling, of course. They may be—and have been—used in combination. An important advantage of voluntary means is that they make it possible to proceed faster than is politically feasible by means of legal restrictions and taxes. Eco-labeling is unique in that it rewards proactive companies and thereby has the capacity to harness their innovative creativity to the environmental policy carriage, instead of directing it toward ways of avoiding the consequences of regulation (e.g., Tenbrunsel et al., 1997). In addition, it is hoped that eco-labeling will help increase consumer attention toward, and knowledge about, the environmental risks associated with consumption (Backman et al., 1995; Miljø- og Energiministeriet, 1999; Nordic Council of Ministers, 2001; OECD, 1991, 1997a; EPA, 1998).

Others have expressed fear that environmental claims on products may legitimize continued consumerism (e.g., Davis, 1992; Durning, 1992) and that the possible environmental gain from a shift to less harmful products may be more than offset by the continued rapid growth in the volume of consumption (e.g., Matthews et al., 2000; United Nations Environment Program, 1994). For example, many serious environmental impacts from traffic are still increasing in spite of more energy-efficient engines and catalytic converters (Mackenzie, 1997; Noorman and Uiterkamp, 1998), and the volume of waste is still growing in spite of increased recycling (Miljø- og Energiministeriet, 1999; Waller-Hunter, 2000). Whether eco-labeling contributes to consumer ignorance concerning such developments or, on the contrary, makes them more attentive to the problems associated with growing consumption is a question still not settled by research, to my knowledge.

The effectiveness of eco-labeling, in a narrow sense, is reflected in the reduction in pollution and resource use that can be attributed to the labeling. To calculate its efficiency, the costs of using this measure also should be included (Morris, 1996). However, the full picture of eco-labeling's effectiveness and efficiency includes positive and negative effects on consumer/citizens' perceptions about, attentiveness toward, and readiness to act to solve environmental problems in general. To complicate the issue further, the effectiveness of eco-labels, both in a narrow and in a wider sense, may depend on the mutual implementation of other policy measures (e.g., Gardner and Stern, 1996), notably environmental education and information about the labels.[1]

Eco-Labels and Consumer Decision Making

Consumer decision making concerning eco-labeled products involves considerations about the label as well as about the specific product itself. To reduce the analytical complexity, I consider the decision making as consisting of two interwoven, but partly independent decision—and learning—processes: one concerning a specific product and one concerning a specific label.

At least in the eyes of the consumer, a product that suddenly comes with an eco-label is an innovation, that is, a new product that differs more or less from the nonlabeled product that it may have replaced and from other nonlabeled products in the same category. The eco-label documents and communicates that the product has certain characteristics leading to outstanding eco-performance. Innovation adoption theory describes the decision to buy such a product as a learning process, consisting of a number of successive phases, where the consumer obtains, accumulates, and integrates knowledge about the product and evaluates its self-relevance (e.g., Peter et al., 1999; Rogers, 1995). Communicationwise, the process may be conceived as a hierarchy of stages (or effects) that the consumer needs to go through before making a decision to buy the new product. What these stages are, as well as their succession, depends on a number of circumstances, notably how risky the decision is perceived to be (e.g., Hoyer and MacInnis, 1997). Because the decision making process may be lengthy, and can be interrupted anywhere in the process, the evaluation of an eco-labeling scheme's success should be based not only on its eventual environmental outcomes, but also on its influence on the move from one stage in the decision process to the next (Abt Associates Inc., 1994; Nordic Council of Ministers, 2001).

An eco-label is an innovation in itself. Hence, the process through which the consumer learns about and adopts the eco-label also may be described as an innovation adoption process in which the final adoption is reflected in the purchase of products carrying the label.

The purchase of "x-labeled" (an eco-label) products is a behavioral category consisting of many independent actions, rather than just a single action (Ajzen and Fishbein, 1980). An important question, which to my knowledge remains to be answered, is whether consumers form mental categories based on eco-labels, as they have been known to do based on (some) other product characteristics (e.g., Cohen, 1982; Sujan, 1985). Because eco-labels typically are not restricted to one established product category, new mental categories based on eco-labels may cross established boundaries. The formation of such new mental categories is not likely unless consumers perceive environment friendliness as an important product attribute, both in an absolute sense and relative to other salient attributes (Gutman, 1982). Therefore, new cross-boundary eco-categories seem more likely to emerge in traditional low-involvement areas, such as groceries, than in traditional high-involvement areas, such as furniture, white goods, and electronic equipment. For example, it seems more likely that consumers will form a new cross-boundary product category for organic food products carrying a third-party eco-label, such as the Danish Ø-label, than for energy-efficient white goods carrying, say, European Union's (EU's) mandatory energy labeling's A-classification. If consumers form such categories, they may use them as the basis for category-based decision making in future choice situations when encountering labeled products of the same or different kind(s) (Cohen, 1982; Fiske and Pavelchak, 1986; Sujan, 1985). This would increase the likelihood of repeat purchase of eco-labeled products and speed up the adoption process for other new products wearing the same label. There is evidence that mental categories carry affect, which is used when evaluating entities that fit the category (Cohen, 1982; Fiske and Pavelchak, 1986). Because environmental attitudes seem to have acquired a moral basis for many people in modern society (e.g., Harland et al., 1999; Heberlein, 1972; Thøgersen, 1996b, 1999), the affect associated with eco-categories may be more charged than usual product-related attitudes (e.g., Peter et al., 1999). Strong category-based affect further increases the likelihood that eco-categories have behavioral implications (Verplanken et al., 1998).

Research on the Effectiveness of Eco-Labels

Of course, environmental labels are useful from an environmental policy perspective only if consumers use them in their decision making. However, there are still few published studies of the effectiveness of labeling schemes in this respect (OECD, 1997a). Most of the published studies focus on consumers' recognition of or knowledge about labels and/or their trust in them (Bekholm and Sejersen, 1997; Tufte and Lavik, 1997), implicitly or explicitly assuming that these are fundamental prerequisites for the use of a label in decision making. However, practically all studies are purely descriptive, leaving the question of *why* consumers know, notice, and use labels only sporadically answered. With few exceptions (e.g., Verplanken and Weenig, 1993), it is not systematically considered how the decisions that the labels are meant to influence are made and/or the implications of the decision making process for the functioning and effectiveness of labeling. For example, plenty of evidence shows that how and how much consumers attend to information in a buying situation depends on their involvement (e.g., Celsi and Olson, 1988; Herr and Fazio, 1993; Kokkinaki, 1997). In general, one cannot count on information about environmental consequences, in the form of a label or otherwise, producing high involvement in itself. The isolated consequences—environmental as well as personal—of each individual decision are simply too small in most cases (Thøgersen, 1998). If this is the case, and if other self-relevant information competes for the consumer's attention—sometimes to a degree to which the consumer experiences information overload (Jacoby, 1984)—consumers may easily fail to notice relevant labels in the buying situation.

In a recent publication, I have reasoned at length about how and why consumers attend to eco-labels (Thøgersen, 2000b). It is emphasized that "paying attention to eco-labels" is hardly a goal in itself, but rather a means to a goal: buying environment-friendly products, which is a means to a more abstract goal about protecting the environment.

Thus, it is unlikely that a consumer will pay attention to an environmental label unless he or she values protecting the environment, perceives that buying (more) environment-friendly products is an effective means to achieve this goal, and finds that the information the label conveys is useful for this purpose. In addition, the availability of eco-labeled products in the shops and the consumer's ability to recognize and understand the labels undoubtedly influence attention toward this type of label.

Empirically, I find that a large majority of the consumers in four analyzed countries pay attention to eco-labels at least sometimes. As predicted, paying attention to eco-labels is strongly influenced by the belief in considerate buying as a means to protect the environment and by the trust in the labels. The personal importance of environmental protection (proenvironmental attitude) and perceived effectiveness regarding the solving of environmental problems also influence paying attention to eco-labels, but this influence is mediated through the former two concepts (belief and trust). In three of the analyzed cases, there is also an interaction effect between proenvironmental attitude and trust, meaning that the influence of proenvironmental attitude on paying attention is higher when the consumer trusts the label (and the influence of trust higher when the consumer holds a proenvironmental attitude).

ENVIRONMENTAL OUTCOMES

Only a few studies have attempted to estimate the environmental impact of eco-labels. The most thoroughly evaluated schemes—the Swedish Society for Nature Conservation's "Good Environmental Choice" label, the Nordic Council of Ministers' Swan label, and the German Blue Angel label—are presumably also the most successful ones. For example, the Blue Angel has been credited for a reduction in emissions of sulphur dioxide, carbon monoxide, and nitrogen oxides from oil and gas heating appliances by more than 30 percent and for a reduction in the amount of solvents emitted from paints and varnishes into the environment by some 40,000 tons (United Nations Conference on Trade and Development, 1995). In Sweden, the Good Environmental Choice and the Nordic Swan labels have been credited for a considerable reduction in (1) chlorinated compounds, acids, and other pollutants from the Swedish forest industry (paper products) (Naturvårdsverket, 1997), and (2) the volume and toxicity of household chemical emissions, particularly laundry detergents, down the drains (Beckerus and Rosander HB, 1999; Scandia Consult Sverige AB, 1999; The Swedish Society for Nature Conservation, 1999). I will elaborate on the latter case.

Laundry detergents represent 70 percent of the annual consumption of household chemicals in Sweden,[2] which makes it a particularly environmentally significant product category. Since the Good Environmental Choice and the Nordic Swan labels were introduced in the late 1980s, Swedish consumers have changed their demand from less to more concentrated products and have rejected the most environmentally harmful chemicals, a development that has been largely attributed to the two labels (Backman et al., 1995). Specifically, the sales volume of household chemicals for cleaning and personal care decreased by 15 percent between 1988 and 1996. Furthermore, in 1996, 60 percent of the chemical ingredients used in soap, shampoo, detergents, and cleaners in 1988 had been removed or replaced by less harmful substances. In 1997, eco-labeled detergents had a market share of more than 90 percent in Sweden.

As already mentioned, these are undoubtedly some of the most successful eco-labeling schemes. But still, they encouragingly demonstrate that under the right circumstances, eco-labeling has the power to produce a substantial reduction in the environmental pressure from serious sources of household pollution. Important prerequisites are consumer receptiveness to information about products' environmental attributes (i.e., environmental concern and belief in responsible consumer behavior as a means to solve the problem), company willingness to adopt eco-labeling schemes, and sufficient effort in promoting the schemes to consumers. Together, these conditions decisively influence the speed by which consumers become aware of eco-labels and of new eco-labeled products and by which they pass through the subsequent stages in the decision making process.

THE ECO-LABEL HIERARCHY OF EFFECTS

Awareness

Knowing that a label exists is a prerequisite for using it in decision making. This basic type of knowledge is typically measured as (aided and/or unaided) recall in surveys (e.g., Dyer and Maronick, 1988; OECD, 1997a). The results vary widely, reflecting the presence of labels in the stores, the efforts put into promoting a label, the clarity of the label's profile, and its perceived self-relevance for consumers (Van Dam and Reuvekamp, 1995). A 1999 survey in the Nordic countries found that between 61 and 75 percent of random samples in Norway, Sweden, and Finland were able to recall the Swan label unaided when asked about which eco-labels could be found on products in their country (Palm and Jarlbro, 1999). Recurrent surveys show that awareness about the Swan label was built gradually in these countries since its introduction in the early 1990s (Backman et al., 1995). In Denmark the unaided recall in 1999 was a much lower 18 percent. Although the Swan label was introduced in the other Nordic countries in 1989, Denmark only became a full member of this labeling scheme in the beginning of 1998, which undoubtedly explains the difference. Between 1997 and 1999, aided recall of the Swan label in Denmark rose from 37 to 51 percent. During that time, the label was promoted through newspaper and magazine ads, leaflets in shops, and public relations work and the number of Swan-labeled products in the shops rose from 1,000 to 1,300 (Kampmann, 2000). In Denmark, 31 percent of the respondents mentioned the national organic food label (the Ø-label) unaided, which is substantially higher than in the other Nordic countries.[3] The unaided recall of EU's Flower label was below

2 percent in all four countries, and most other environment-related labels also achieved low unaided recall (Palm and Jarlbro, 1999).

An indicator of label awareness with particularly high face validity is the recognition of visual images of the label. A Dutch study found a wide variation in the recognition of 11 environment-related labels—from 11.5 percent recognition of the Society of Plastic Industry Symbol to 92.7 percent recognition of the chasing-arrows recycling symbol (Van Dam and Reuvekamp, 1995). The length of time a label was on the market generally correlated with an increase in recognition. Recognition also depended on the type and amount of promotion backing the label. A similar study in Denmark in 1997 investigated the recognition of five environment-related and five safety and/or health-related labels (Bekholm and Sejersen, 1997). On average, the environment-related labels were better known, but as in the Netherlands, recognition varied widely, from 18 percent recognizing EU's Flower label to 89 percent recognizing the chasing-arrows recycling symbol. This study was conducted a few months before Denmark joined the Nordic Swan labeling scheme. Hence, with few Swan-labeled products in the shops and no official promotion of the label, it is no wonder that the Swan label was recognized by only 29 percent of respondents. The promotion campaign and increased presence of Swan-labeled products boosted the recognition of the label to just over 40 percent in June 1998 and 52 percent in October 1999 (Palm and Jarlbro, 1999). Also reflecting promotion activities and presence in the shops, the Danish Ø-label ("State Controlled Organic" label for organic food products) was recognized by 43 percent of a broad sample of consumers in 1995, 5 years after its introduction (Thøgersen and Andersen, 1996), and by 79 percent in 1997 (Bekholm and Sejersen, 1997).[4]

Even consumers who know a relevant environmental label will not use it if they fail to notice it because of information overload (Jacoby, 1984) or for other reasons. For example, in 1992 it was estimated that 400 to 600 private labels, in addition to 36 labeling schemes issued by public authorities, targeted Danish consumers (Forbrugerstyrelsen, 1993). In 1996, a study found environmental claims on 63 percent of the packaged goods within 16 product categories in the major supermarkets in Oslo (Enger, 1998). A minority of 8 percent of the goods carried a third-party environmental label. The study was a partial replication of a 1994 U.S. study that found environmental claims on 65 percent of the packaged goods in 16 product categories in major supermarkets in five large population centers throughout the United States (Mayer and Gray-Lee, 1995). Only 0.3 percent of the American packages carried an environmental label issued by a third party.

Comprehension

Recognizing a label is not the same as understanding the exact, or even the approximate, meaning of it. It is well known from other areas that consumers often have a hard time understanding labels (e.g., Laric and Sarel, 1981; Parkinson, 1975). Van Dam and

Reuvekamp (1995) suggest that eco-labels suffer from a double confusion: the "generic" confusion from the limited meaning of seals and certifications and a remarkable amount of uncertainty and misunderstanding concerning environmental claims and terminology. Confirming this, one study found that only about 5 percent of a representative sample of U.S. consumers exhibited a thorough understanding of the terms "recycled" and "recyclable" (Hastak et al., 1994; see also Morris et al., 1995). Hence, campaigns that effectively target the confusion may lead to a substantial increase in the sale of labeled products, as illustrated by the "Get in the Loop, Buy Recycled" campaign in the state of Washington in 1994–1995.[5] Through a focused effort to increase awareness of products with recycled content and comprehension of the claim, the campaign produced a 58-percent increase in sales of recycled products in participating grocery stores. The campaign included prompts placed below products, which served to highlight product availability and substantiate manufacturer recycled content claims. In addition, posters, employee buttons, and door decals served as reminders for consumers.

Of course, less than a thorough understanding may be sufficient for decision making, particularly under low-risk circumstances. Van Dam and Reuvekamp (1995) classified respondents' understanding of 11 seals found on Dutch packages in three groups: adequate, underestimation, and overestimation of environmental implications. Among those recognizing a label, from 9 to 95 percent, depending on the label, had an adequate understanding of its environmental implications. Misunderstandings more often were in the direction of underestimation than overestimation. The higher the recognition of a label, the more likely it was also understood accurately (see also Bekholm and Sejersen, 1997), attention seemingly shading off into comprehension (e.g., Peter et al., 1999). As with recognition, there was a positive relationship between understanding and the length of time the label had been on the market. Understanding also depended on the type and extent of promotion, on the label's self-relevance, and on the clarity of its environmental profile. For example, two labels that particularly few understood were the German "Green Dot" and the Dutch Union of Housewives' seal. The former appears on many Dutch packages, but it has no relevance outside Germany. With regard to the latter, the environmental assessment is drowning in the long range of criteria influencing whether the Union endorses the product.

Uncertainty about what a label means often is accompanied by mistrust. A consumer only will use a label (as intended) in decision making if he or she trusts the message it conveys (Hansen and Kull, 1994). A large number of studies have found that consumers tend to be skeptical towards "green" product claims (see Peattie, 1995). One study cited by Peattie (1995) found that 71 percent of British consumers thought that companies were using green issues as an excuse to charge higher prices. However, many studies find that third-party labels and environmental information are trusted more than information provided by producers or retailers (e.g., Bekholm and Sejersen, 1997; Eden, 1994/95;

Enger and Lavik, 1995; Tufte and Lavik, 1997). Unfortunately, and perhaps because they are outnumbered so many times by private labels and other types of environmental information, consumers often are uncertain or hold outright erroneous beliefs about who issues third-party labels (e.g., Bekholm and Sejersen, 1997; Tufte and Lavik, 1997). A Norwegian study found that such mistakes reduce the trust in the Nordic Swan label (Tufte and Lavik, 1997).

Attitude

Consumers generally welcome informative product labeling (Bekholm and Sejersen, 1997; Forbrugerstyrelsen, 1993). Specifically regarding eco-labels, a previously mentioned study found that from 64 to 91 percent of representative samples in Denmark, Norway, Sweden, and Finland agreed that eco-labels are needed (Palm and Jarlbro, 1999). A positive attitude toward eco-labels depends on the consumer believing that he or she can help attain a valued goal (e.g., Forbrugerstyrelsen, 1993; Nilsson et al., 1999; Palm and Windahl, 1998). Just as unit pricing helps the consumer obtain the goal of value for money and nutrition declarations facilitate health-related goals, environmental labeling helps consumers obtain environmental goals. Hence, a positive attitude toward eco-labels is only likely if consumers desire environment-friendly products.[6]

Intention and Behavior

The intention to buy eco-labeled products is reflected most clearly in consumers' search for and attention to this kind of information. Based on survey data collected by the European Consortium for Comparative Social Surveys (COMPASS) in 1993, I analyzed the frequency of paying attention to eco-labels in Britain, Ireland, Italy, and (two samples from) Germany (Thøgersen, 2000b). A large majority of consumers in these countries seem to pay attention to eco-labels when they shop, at least sometimes. Only from 8 percent (Great Britain) to 15 percent (Ireland) never do that. Other more recent studies find a similar attentiveness to environmental information. For example, a survey in 1997 found that 61 to 71 percent of random samples of consumers in the Nordic countries claimed that they "sometimes" or "always" check out the environment friendliness of the products they buy (Lindberg, 1998).

The Swedish Consumer Agency monitored the self-reported purchase of eco-labeled products yearly between 1993 and 1997. In this period, the share of respondents claiming that they bought eco-labeled products regularly rose from 37 to 51 percent (Konsumentverket, 1993, 1995/96, 1998). These numbers are supported by market data. For example, in 1994 eco-labeled products already had captured more than 60 percent of the detergent market and more than 80 percent of the copying and printing paper market in Sweden (Backman et al., 1995).

TABLE 1

Breadth and Depth of Organic Buying Within 16 Product Categories and Length of Buying Experience, Aarhus, Denmark, 1998 (N = 232)

	<1 Year	1–3 Years	3–5 Years	>5 Years	F test
Pct. of food products organic*	2.3	2.6	2.8	3.5	13.0
Number of organic foods bought	6	8	9	11	13.8

*1 = 0%, 2 = 10%, 3 = 25%, 4 = 50%, 5 = 75%, 6 = 100%.

Repeat Purchase

There is a lack of studies of repeat purchase of eco-labeled products. It seems that most researchers implicitly assume that all decisions to purchase such products are the same, independent of the consumer's buying history. That this is hardly true is indicated by some of my own research (Thøgersen, 1998). Not unexpectedly, I found that a person's beliefs about product attributes and consequences of buying Ø-labeled products depend on the length of his or her experience with buying such products. Beliefs are changed or strengthened based on experience. I also found that experience has a direct and positive influence on the attitude toward buying organic products (after controlling for salient beliefs). Therefore, it seems that the longer a person has bought (labeled) organic products, the more positive the person's attitude is toward buying such products and the less it is based on thorough consideration of the pros and cons of doing so.

A followup study by two of my master students[7] investigated consumer purchase of 16 different food products (Andersen and Vestergaard, 1998). Based on their data set, I have made the calculations presented in Table 1.

Table 1 indicates that once consumers have started to buy Ø-labeled products, they tend to do so increasingly over time, and their propensity to choose labeled products is extended to an increasing number of product categories. Both tendencies are highly significant. In the beginning of this chapter, it was suggested that eco-labels may lead consumers to form new mental categories and that affect related to such a category can have a strong influence on their subsequent behavior. The results presented in Table 1 are consistent with this suggestion.

THE ENVIRONMENT-FRIENDLY PRODUCT HIERARCHY OF EFFECTS

Studies have found that large segments of Western European and North American consumers demand environment-friendly products in diverse areas such as packaging (Bech-Larsen, 1996; Thøgersen, 1996a), food products (Biel and Dahlstrand, 1997; Grunert and Juhl, 1995; Sparks and Shepherd, 1992; Thøgersen, 1998), paint (Buchtele and Holzmuller, 1990), and heating systems (Berger et al., 1994). Few products are acquired with the sole (or main) purpose of protecting the environment, however. Typically, consumers buy goods for the private utility they provide. Still, many consumers are willing to make an effort to diminish the negative environmental impact of their consumption, and environmental labels are welcomed as a tool for this purpose. Given that environmental attributes—as long as they do not represent any personal threat—are peripheral to what the consumer wants to achieve through their purchase, the issue usually should not be expected to be a high-involvement one. It is well documented in the cited studies that proenvironmental attitudes increase consumers' propensity to buy environment-friendly products. Less researched in this connection is Fazio's (1986; Roskos-Ewoldsen and Fazio, 1992) proposition that attitudes also influence which information about a product a consumer pays attention to, including information about the product's environmentally relevant characteristics (but see Thøgersen, 1999).

The limited space available here makes it impossible to thoroughly review the huge literature on environment-friendly consumer behavior. Thus, I concentrate on the two areas where I believe that eco-labels have the greatest potential impact: (1) increasing consumer confidence in green claims, and (2) helping consumers carry out intentions to choose environment-friendly products.

Confidence in Green Claims

Basically green purchase behavior depends on the compromise consumers have to make in the form of higher price and/or lower quality and on the confidence they have in their choice leading to desirable environmental consequences (Peattie, 1999). The toughest green products to sell are those that require a large compromise and where consumers' confidence in it making any environmental difference is low. Successful green products typically enjoy high confidence and demand no or low compromise from consumers. Thus, by increasing consumer confidence in the credibility and the significance of green claims, third-party eco-labels may greatly improve the market prospects of environment-friendly products. Calculations based on data collected for a master thesis that I supervised may serve as an illustration (Andersen, 1995).

Respondents were a broad sample of individuals[8] responsible for their household's food shopping. One sample was interviewed about their purchase of organic milk, another about organic carrots. The most important environmental benefit from organic production is that it leads to less groundwater pollution than chemically based agriculture. Hence, agreement with the statement that by buying the organic product in question the consumer contributes to groundwater protection is used as an indicator of confidence in it making an environmental difference. In Denmark, the only real compromise when buying organic food products is higher price. Thus, agreement with the statement that the organic product in question is expensive is used as an indicator

FIGURE 1

The Purchase of Organic Milk and Carrots in Groups Differing in Confidence in Environmental Consequences and Perceived Compromise, Denmark 1995

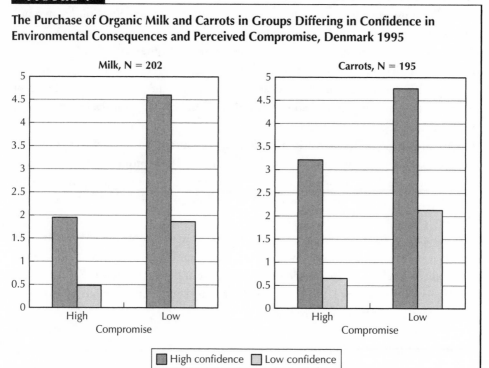

of perceived compromise. The average number of times the respondent reportedly chose organic out of the last 10 purchases of the product is shown graphically in Figure 1, using the confidence and perceived compromise indicators (split at the scale's midpoint) as grouping variables. In both cases, both grouping variables make a highly significant difference (F-test), the lowest F-value being 5.664. There are no significant interactions.

It is obvious from Figure 1 that consumers with a high confidence and who perceive the compromise as low are also most likely to buy organic products, and that the reverse combination of beliefs is much less facilitating. It is also apparent that even consumers who perceive the compromise to be high are much more likely to buy organic products if they also have a high confidence in the contribution's environmental implications. Therefore, if an eco-label increases consumer confidence in the implied green claim, the impact on the purchase of an environment-friendly product may be substantial. In fact, in the present case an eco-label had exactly this effect. In Denmark, organic food products carry the Ø-label (with the text "State Controlled Organic"). Respondents in this study were asked to point out the correct Ø-label among three alternative designs. Forty-three percent of both samples were able to do that. Those who knew the label (i.e., who picked the right one) had a significantly higher confidence in the choice making an environmental difference than those who did not ($t_{milk} = 3.467, p < .001; t_{carrots} = 3.488, p < .001$).

The Implementation of Decisions to Buy Green

Several studies have demonstrated that environment-friendly behavior often depends on specific, task-related information (e.g., Bell et al., 1996; Kearney and De Young, 1995; Pieters, 1991; Thøgersen, 2000a). Consumers need specific and reliable information in order to be able to choose the most environmentally friendly alternative when competing options are offered or to do the right thing when asked to change a behavioral routine.

Figure 2 illustrates the importance of (knowing) an environmental label, the Danish Ø-label for organic products, for transforming environment-friendly buying intentions into action. The data set is the same as that used in Figure 1, but in this case I analyze whether the respondent's ability to point out the true Ø-label among three alternative designs influences the relationship between buying intentions and buying frequency (number of organic out of the last 10 liter/kilo). Separate regression analyses were made for split samples concerning each product: those choosing the correct design (43 percent of the sample in each case) and the rest. The lines are regression lines.

FIGURE 2

The Influence of Knowing the Ø-label on the Relationship Between Buying Intention and Buying Frequency Regarding Organic Milk and Organic Carrots, Denmark, 1995

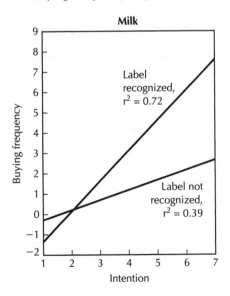 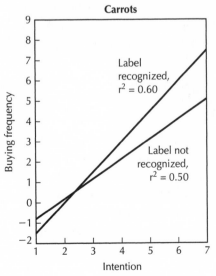

The results are in principle identical in the two cases, but the effect of knowing the Ø-label is somewhat stronger for milk than for carrots.[9] The difference may be due to some organic carrots being grown in one's own garden or bought at open markets, where there are other means to identify an organic product than the Ø-label, while organic milk can only be bought only from retail outlets.

The regression analyses illustrate that knowing the Ø-label has a substantial effect on buying frequency among those with a high buying intention, but no effect among those with a low buying intention. They also show that the relationship between buying intentions and buying frequency is stronger among consumers who are able to identify the correct Ø-label than among consumers who are not.[10] Hence, the study shows that by increasing consumers' ability to distinguish environment-friendly products, eco-labels can facilitate the implementation of environment-friendly intentions.

Summary, Conclusions, and Implications

Eco-labeling is aimed at reducing pollution and resource use associated with consumption by influencing consumer choices and, through these, companies' product policies. In the past couple of decades, eco-labeling has become a popular environment policy instrument in countries all over the world. Few schemes have been sufficiently thoroughly evaluated to be able to draw conclusions about their success. From those that have, it seems that, under the right conditions, eco-labeling can indeed lead to a substantial reduction in pollution and resource use. However, it takes time and a committed effort to build eco-labeling success. In particular, consumers have to go through an often time-consuming decision making process through which they first become aware of the label, and of labeled products, and then acquire sufficient knowledge to use it as a guide in decision making and to trust the message it conveys. A positive attitude toward eco-labels probably follows more or less automatically from knowledge and trust, but forming a positive attitude toward buying a specific eco-labeled product may take longer because time-consuming tradeoffs need to be made. Therefore, decision making about eco-labels is a gradual process and one that consumers go through at an uneven pace. Among other things, consumer receptiveness toward this kind of information and, hence, the pace depends on their environmental concern. The speed of diffusion of eco-labels also depends on the clarity of the label's profile, the intensity of its promotion, and its presence in the shops. The latter is particularly crucial for the outcome of the decision making.

There are, of course, a variety of other means that governments can use in their efforts to reduce the environmental impact of consumption. Labeling is obviously no substitute for legal restrictions and standards regulating, for example, the flow of harmful substances through the household, and taxes and subsidies—attempting to secure that nonmarket environmental impacts are reflected in the relative prices—may effectively influence consumer choices (e.g., Andersen and Sprenger, 2000; Von Weizsacker and Jesinghaus, 1992). There is no reason to believe that eco-labeling renders any of these means obsolete—on the contrary. Just keeping the environmental impact of consumption from increasing is an ambitious goal that will demand the effective use of all available means. In addition, there may be important synergies to be obtained from the coordinated implementation of several means (see, e.g., Gardner and Stern, 1996; Stern, 1999).

The fact that eco-labels compete with many other types of information in the shopping situation, including other informative labels and producers' noncertified green claims, acts as a noise wall that third-party eco-labels need to break through. Studies have shown that many consumers are uncertain about who issues third-party eco-labels and that this uncertainty reduces the trust in such labels. On the other hand, it has been shown that third-party eco-labels can increase the confidence in green claims and help distinguish environment-friendly products, thus increasing the likelihood of such products being bought. There is also evidence that experience with buying a product with an eco-label facilitates future decisions about buying this product, as well as other products wearing the same label. I suggested that the latter effect might be due to consumers forming new mental categories based on eco-labels and that such categories may carry affect. Research on the commitment approach to behavior change is informative regarding the type of affect in question (see, e.g., McKenzie-Mohr and Smith, 1999). According to this line of research, the purchase of an eco-labeled product can alter a person's self-perception to that as the type of person who buys eco-labeled products (cf., e.g., Hutton, 1982). There is plenty of evidence indicating that many people perceive a strong internal pressure to behave consistently with such a self-perception. Expressions of commitment seem to have stronger impacts on future behavior when they are voluntary (e.g., Shippee and Gregory, 1982) and public (e.g., Pallak et al., 1980), both of which typically characterize individual purchase acts.

The mentioned conclusions are based on scattered evidence and the evaluation of few schemes. There is a need for more, and more thorough and systematic, evaluations of eco-labeling schemes, particularly with a view to better identify manageable conditions for success. Special attention should be directed toward design characteristics that influence how consumers use labeling schemes in their decision making, including characteristics that facilitate and amplify the use of eco-labels as a basis for category-based decision making. Other more basic questions about eco-labeling remain unanswered, such as whether it contributes to consumer ignorance or makes them more attentive toward the problems associated with the continued rapid growth in private consumption. Hopefully this chapter will inspire future research on these topics.

Notes

[1] In Chapter 6 of original volume, Valente and Schuster, make a similar point with regard to public health communication.

[2] Dry weight.

[3] The national organic food label was mentioned by 16 percent in Sweden, 5 percent in Finland, and 1.4 percent in Norway.

[4] The two studies used different ways to measure recognition, meaning they are not strictly comparable.

[5] More information about this case can be found at http://www.toolsofchange.com/English/CaseStudies/default.asp?ID=8 and at McKenzie-Mohr's Web site, http://www.cbsm.com. I am grateful to him for bringing the case to my attention.

[6] Unless they believe other advantages are associated with environmental friendliness (Thøgersen, 1998). A recent Danish study found that "quality conscious" consumers use the Danish Ø-label as one among several cues indicating high product quality (Juhl et al., 2000).

[7] A mall-intercept survey carried out in three shopping centers in Aarhus, Denmark, in 1998.

[8] Fourteen acquaintances of the master students all over Denmark distributed questionnaires to some of their acquaintances, with the instruction to cover age groups (above 20 years) as broadly as possible. The data were collected in 1995.

[9] The interaction between buying intention and knowing the Ø-label is statistically significant ($p <$ than 0.05) in both cases. The hierarchical regression analysis used to test for the interaction effect is reported in Thøgersen and Andersen (1996).

[10] The somewhat surprising positive correlation between intention and behavior among those who are not able to identify the correct design may be because only one label design is available in the supermarket or because consumers in some cases—correct or mistakenly—use other cues to identify organic products. Of course, it also may be caused by a tendency to exaggerate organic buying that is correlated with stated buying intentions.

References

Abt Associates Inc.
  1994   *Determinants of Effectiveness for Environmental Certification and Labeling Programs.* Cambridge, MA: U.S. Environmental Protection Agency.

Ajzen, I., and M. Fishbein
  1980   *Understanding Attitudes and Predicting Social Behavior.* Englewood Cliffs, NJ: Prentice-Hall.

Andersen, A.K.
  1995   Vigtige aspekter ved forminskelsen af inkonsistensen mellem forbrugerens positive holdning til at købe økologiske landbrugsprodukter og forbrugerens reelle køb af økologiske landbrugsprodukter (Important Aspects Regarding the Inconsistency Between Consumer Attitudes and Purchase of Organic Products). Unpublished MSc dissertation. Århus, Den.: Handelshøjskolen i Århus.

Andersen, M., and L. Vestergaard
  1998   Markedet for afsætning af økologiskc fødevarer. Herunder en afdækning af hvilke faktorer der har betydning for forbrugernes køb/fravalg af de forskellige økologiske produktkategorier (The Market for Organic Food Products). Unpublished MSc dissertation. Århus, Den.: Handelshøjskolen i Århus.

Andersen, M.S., and R.U. Sprenger, eds.
  2000   *Market-Based Instruments for Environmental Management: Politics and Institutions.* Cheltenham, Eng.: Edward Elgar.

Backman, M., T. Lindkvist, and Å. Thidell
  1995   The Nordic white swan: Issues concerning some key problems in environmental labelling. In *Sustainable Consumption—Report from the International Conference on*

Sustainable Consumption, Eivind Stø, ed. Lysaker, Nor.: National Institute for Consumer Research (SIFO).

Bech-Larsen, T.
  1996   Danish consumers' attitudes to the functional and environmental characteristics of food packaging. *Journal of Consumer Policy* 19:339–363.

Beckerus and Rosander HB
  1999   *What Effect Has the Eco-Labelling of Household Detergents Had on Sewage Treatment Plants?* Stockholm, SE: Kemi & Miljö AB.

Bekholm, M., and B. Sejersen
  1997   Mærkeanvendelse og associationer. Personlig omnibus 44. Udarbejdet for Forbrugerstyrelsen (Labeling Use and Associations). Copenhagen, Den.: AIM Nielsen.

Bell, S.J., P.J. Erwin, and C.S. McLeod
  1996   Attitudes, norms and knowledge: Implications for ecologically sound purchasing behavior. In *1996 Winter Educators' Conference: Marketing Theory and Applications,* Vol. 7, E.A. Blair, and W.A. Kamakura, eds. Chicago: American Marketing Association.

Berger, I.E., B.T. Ratchford, and G.H. Haines, Jr.
  1994   Subjective product knowledge as a moderator of the relationship between attitudes and purchase intentions for a durable product. *Journal of Economic Psychology* 15:301–314.

Biel, A., and U. Dahlstrand
  1997   Habits and the establishment of ecological purchase behavior. In *IAREP XXII Conference,* Valencia, Spain: Corpas, C.B.

Buchtele, F., and H.H. Holzmuller
  1990   Die Bedeutung der Umweltverträglichkeit von Produkten für die Kaufpraëferenz (The importance of product's environmental friendliness for buying preferences). *Jahrbuch der Absatz- und Verbrauchsforschung* 36(1):86–103.

Celsi, R.L., and J.C. Olson
  1988   The role of involvement in attention and comprehension processes. *Journal of Consumer Research* 15:210–224.

Cohen, J.B.
  1982   The role of affect in categorization: Towards a reconsideration of the concept of attitude. In *Advances In Consumer Research,* Vol. 9, Andrew A. Mitchell, ed. Ann Arbor, MI: Association for Consumer Research.

Davis, J.J.
  1992   Ethics and environmental marketing. *Journal of Business Ethics* 11:81–87.

Durning, A.T.
  1992   *How Much Is Enough? The Consumer Society and the Future of the Earth.* London: Earthscan Publications Ltd.

Dyer, R.F., and T.J. Maronick
  1988   An evaluation of consumer awareness and use of energy labels in the purchase of major appliances: A longitudinal analysis. *Journal of Public Policy and Marketing* 7:83–97.

Eden, S.
  1994/   Business, trust and environmental information: Perceptions from consumers and retailers.
  1995   *Business Strategy and the Environment* 3(4):1–7.

Enger, A.
  1998   *Miljøargumentasjon i markedsføring (Environmental Arguments in Marketing).* Oslo: SIFO.

Enger, A., and R. Lavik
    1995   Eco-labeling in Norway: Consumer knowledge and attitudes. In *Sustainable Consumption—Report from the International Conference on Sustainable Consumption,* Eivind Stø, ed. Lysaker, Nor.: National Institute for Consumer Research (SIFO).

Fazio, R.H.
    1986   How do attitudes guide behavior? In *The Handbook of Motivation and Cognition: Foundations of Social Behavior,* R.M. Sorrentino and E.T. Higgins, eds. New York: Guilford Press.

Fiske, S.T., and M.A. Pavelchak
    1986   Category-based versus piecemeal-based affective responses. In *The Handbook of Motivation and Cognition: Foundations of Social Behavior,* R.M. Sorrentino and E.T. Higgins, eds. New York: Guilford Press.

Forbrugerstyrelsen
    1993   *Mærkning rettet til forbrugerne (Labeling Targeting the Consumers).* Copenhagen: Forbrugerstyrelsen.

Gardner, G.T., and P.C. Stern
    1996   *Environmental Problems and Human Behavior.* Boston, MA: Allyn and Bacon.

Geyer-Allély, E., and J. Eppel
    1997   *Consumption and Production Patterns: Making the Change.* Paris: Organization for Economic Co-operation and Development.

Grunert, S.C., and H. Jørn Juhl
    1995   Values, environmental attitudes, and buying of organic foods. *Journal of Economic Psychology* 16:39–62.

Gutman, J.
    1982   A means-end chain model based on consumer categorization processes. *Journal of Marketing* 46(Spring):60–72.

Hansen, U., and S. Kull
    1994   Öko-Label als umweltbezogenes Informationsinstrument: Begründungszusammenhänge und Interessen (Eco-labels as environmental information tool: Reasoning and interest). *Marketing* 4(4. kvartal):265–273.

Harland, P., H. Staats, and H.A.M. Wilke
    1999   Explaining pro-environmental intention and behavior by personal norms and the theory of planned behavior. *Journal of Applied Social Psychology* 29:2505–2528.

Hastak, M., R.L. Horst, and M.B. Mazis
    1994   Consumer perceptions about and comprehension of environmental terms: Evidence from survey research studies. In *Proceedings of the 1994 Marketing and Public Policy Conference,* D.J. Tingold, ed. Arlington, VA: American Marketing Association.

Heberlein, T.A.
    1972   The land ethic realized: Some social psychological explanations for changing environmental attitudes. *Journal of Social Issues* 28(4):79–87.

Herr, P.M., and R.H. Fazio
    1993   The attitude-to-behavior process: Implications for consumer behavior. In *Advertising Exposure, Memory, and Choice: Advertising and Consumer Psychology,* A.A. Mitchell et al., eds. Hillsdale, NJ: Lawrence Erlbaum Associates.

Hoyer, W.D., and D.J. MacInnis
    1997   *Consumer Behavior.* Boston: Houghton Mifflin.

Hutton, R.R.
   1982   Advertising and the Department of Energy's campaign for energy conservation. *Journal of Advertising* 11(2):27–39.

Jacoby, J.
   1984   Perspectives on information overload. *Journal of Consumer Research* 11:569–573.

Juhl, H.J., E. Høg, and C.S. Poulsen
   2000   *Forbrugernes Vurdering af Nogle Udvalgte Kvalitetsmærkninger for Hakket Oksekød–Undersøgelsens Design, Gennemførelse og Resultater (The Consumers' Evaluation of Selected Quality Labels for Minced Beef).* MAPP Working Paper. Århus, Den.: Handelshøjskolen i Århus.

Kampmann, L.
   2000   Miljø er vigtigt for danskerne (Environmental consequences are important for the Danes). *Miljømærkenyt* 1(1):3–4.

Kearney, A.R., and R. De Young
   1995   A knowledge-based intervention for promoting carpooling. *Environment and Behavior* 27(5):650–678.

Kokkinaki, F.
   1997   Involvement as a determinant of the process through which attitudes guide behaviour. In *IAREP XXII Conference.* Valencia, Spain: Corpas, C.B.

Konsumentverket
   1993   *Konsumenten og Miljön. Resultat från en undersökning av svenska konsumenters miljömedvetenhet (The Consumer and the Environment. A study of Swedish Consumers' Environmental Awareness).* Stockholm: Konsumentverket.
   1995/ *The consumer and the environment: Results of a survey into awareness of the environ-*
   1996   *ment amongst Swedish consumers.* Stockholm: Konsumentverket.
   1998   *Allmänhetens kunskaper, attityder och agerande i miljöfrågor (The Public's Knowledge, Attitudes, and Behavior in Environmental Matters).* Stockholm: Konsumentverket.

Larie, R.J., and D. Sarel
   1981   Consumer (mis)perceptions and usage of third party certification marks, 1972 and 1980: Did public policy have an impact? *Journal of Marketing* 45(Summer):135–142.

Lindberg, K.-E.
   1998   *Nordisk omnibus svanemerket. Utarbeidet for Nordisk Miljömärkning (Nordic Survey About the Swan Label).* Oslo: Markeds- og Mediainstituttet.

Mackenzie, J.J.
   1997   Driving the road to sustainable ground transportation. In *Frontiers of Sustainability,* R. Dower, D. Ditz, P. Faeth, N. Johnson, K. Kozloff, and J.J. Mackenzie, eds. Washington, DC: Island Press.

Matthews, E., C. Amann, S. Bringezu, M. Fischer-Kowalski, W. Hüttler, R. Kleijn, Y. Moriguchi, C. Ottke, E. Rodenburg, D. Rogisch, H. Schandl, H. Schütz, E. Van der Voet, and H. Weisz
   2000   *The Weight of Nations—Material Outflows from Industrial Economies.* Washington, DC: World Resource Institute.

Mayer, R.W., and J. Gray-Lee
   1995   Environmental marketing claims in the U.S.A.: Trends since issuance of the FTC guides. In *Sustainable Consumption—Report from the International Conference on Sustainable Consumption,* Eivind Stø, ed. Lysaker, Nor.: National Institute for Consumer Research (SIFO).

McKenzie-Mohr, D., and W. Smith

    1999   *Fostering Sustainable Behavior: An Introduction to Community-Based Social Marketing.*
        Gabriola Island, British Columbia, Can.: New Society Publishers.

Miljø- og Energiministeriet

    1995   *Natur- og miljøpolitisk redegørelse 1995 (Nature and Environmental Policy Report 1995).*
        Copenhagen: Miljø- og Energiministeriet.

    1999   *Natur- og miljøpolitisk redegørelse 1999 (Nature and Environmental Policy Report 1999).*
        Copenhagen: Miljø- og Energiministeriet.

Miljøstyrelsen

    1996   *En styrket produktorienteret miljøindsats. Et debatoplæg (A Strengthened Product Oriented*
        Environmental Effort: Discussion Paper). Copenhagen: Miljøstyrelsen.

Morris, J.

    1996   *Buying Green: Consumers, Product Labels and the Environment.* Los Angeles: Reason Foundation.

Morris, L.A., M. Hastak, and M.B. Mazis

    1995   Consumer comprehension of environmental advertising and labeling claims. *The Journal*
        of Consumer Affairs 29:328–350.

Naturvårdsverket

    1997   *En studie hur olika styrmedel påverkat skogsindustrin (A Study of How Various Regulation*
        Means Influence the Forest Industry). Stockholm: Naturvårdsverket.

Nilsson, O.S., N.P. Nissen, J. Thøgersen, and K. Vilby

    1999   Rapport fra "forbrugergruppen" under Erhvervsministeriets mærkningsudvalg (Report
        from the "Consumer Committee" of the Ministry of Business' Labeling Committee). In
        Mærkning. Mærkningsudvalgets redegørelse (labeling. Report from the Labeling Committee).
        Copenhagen: Forbrugerstyrelsen, Erhvervsministeriet.

Noorman, K.J., and T.S. Uiterkamp, eds.

    1998   *Green Households? Domestic Consumers, Environment and Sustainability.* London: Earthscan.

Nordic Council of Ministers

    2001   *Evaluation of the Environmental Effects of the Swan Eco-Label—Final Analysis.* Copenhagen:
        Nordic Council of Ministers.

Norwegian Ministry of Environment

    1994   *Symposium: Sustainable Consumption. 19–20 January 1994, Oslo, Norway.* Oslo: Ministry
        of Environment, Norway.

Organization for Economic Co-operation and Development

    1991   *Environmental Labeling in OECD Countries.* Paris: Organization for Economic Co-operation
        and Development.

    1997a   *Eco-Labeling: Actual Effects of Selected Programmes.* Paris: Organization for Economic
        Co-operation and Development/GD(97)105.

    1997b   *Sustainable Consumption and Production—Clarifying the Concepts.* Paris: Organization for
        Economic Co-operation and Development.

Pallak, M.S., D.A. Cook, and J.J. Sullivan

    1980   Commitment and energy conservation. In *Applied Social Psychology Annual,* Vol. 1,
        L. Bickman, ed. Beverly Hill, CA: Sage.

Palm, L., and G. Jarlbro

    1999   *Nordiska konsumenter om Svanen—livsstil, kännedom, attityd och förtroende (Nordic Consumers*
        About the Swan—Lifestyle, Awareness, Attitude, and Trust), Report 1999:592. Copenhagen:
        Nordisk Ministerråd.

Palm, L., and S. Windahl

    1998   *How Swedish Consumers Interpret and Use Environmental Information: A Study of Quantitative Environmental Product Declarations.* Stockholm: Konsumentverket.

Parkinson, T.L.

    1975   The role of seals and certifications of approval in consumer decision-making. *Journal of Consumer Affairs* 9(1):1–14.

Peattie, K.

    1995   *Environmental Marketing Management: Meeting the Green Challenge.* London: Pitman Publishing.

    1999   Rethinking marketing: Shifting to a greener paradigm. In *Greener Marketing: A Global Perspective on Greening Marketing Practice,* M. Charter and M.J. Polonsky, eds. Aizlewood's Mill, UK: Greenleaf.

Peter, J.P., J.C. Olson, and K.G. Grunert

    1999   *Consumer Behavior and Marketing Strategy.* European ed. London: McGraw Hill.

Pieters, Rik G.M.

    1991   Changing garbage disposal patterns of consumers: Motivation, ability, and performance. *Journal of Public Policy and Marketing* 10:59–76.

Rogers, E.M.

    1995   *Diffusion of Innovations.* 4th ed. New York: Free Press.

Roskos-Ewoldsen, D.R., and R.H. Fazio

    1992   On the orienting value of attitudes: Attitude accessibility as a determinant of an object's attraction of visual attention. *Journal of Personality and Social Psychology* 63:198–211.

Scandia Consult Sverige AB

    1999   *Eco-Evaluation of the 'Good Environmental Choice'—Label on Household Chemicals.* Stockholm: Scandia Consult Sverige AB.

Shippee, G.E., and W.L. Gregory

    1982   Public commitment and energy conservation. *American Journal of Community Psychology* 10:81–93.

Sitarz, D., ed.

    1994   *Agenda 21: The Earth Summit Strategy to Save Our Planet.* Boulder, CO: EarthPress.

Sparks, P., and R. Shepherd

    1992   Self-identity and the theory of planned behavior: Assessing the role of identification with green consumerism. *Social Psychology Quarterly* 55:388–399.

Stern, P.C.

    1999   Information, incentives, and proenvironmental consumer behavior. *Journal for Consumer Policy* 22:461–478.

Sujan, M.

    1985   Consumer knowledge: Effects on evaluation strategies mediating consumer judgments. *Journal of Consumer Research* 12(June):31–46.

Tenbrunsel, A.E., K.A. Wade-Benzoni, D.M. Messick, and M.H. Bazerman

    1997   The dysfunctional aspects of environmental standards. In *Environment, Ethics, and Behavior: The Psychology of Environmental Valuation and Degradation,* M.H. Bazerman, D.M. Messick, A.E. Tenbrunsel, and K.A. Wade-Benzoni, eds. San Francisco: New Lexington Press.

The Swedish Society for Nature Conservation

    1999   *Changes in Household Detergents: A Statistical Comparison Between 1988 and 1996.* Stockholm: Swedish Society for Nature Conservation.

Thøgersen, J.

1996a   *The Demand for Environmentally Friendly Packaging in Germany.* MAPP Working Paper No. 30. Aarhus, Den.: The Aarhus School of Business.

1996b   Recycling and morality. A critical review of the literature. *Environment and Behavior* 28:536–558.

1998   *Understanding Behaviours with Mixed Motives: An Application of a Modified Theory of Reasoned Action on Consumer Purchase of Organic Food Products.* Working Paper No. 98:2. Aarhus, Den.: Department of Marketing, The Aarhus School of Business.

1999   The ethical consumer. Moral norms and packaging choice. *Journal of Consumer Policy* 22:439–460.

2000a   Knowledge barriers to sustainable consumption. In *Marketing and Public Policy Conference Proceedings 2000,* P.F. Bone, K.R. France, and J. Wiener, eds. Chicago: American Marketing Association.

2000b   Psychological determinants of paying attention to eco-labels in purchase decisions: Model development and multinational validation. *Journal of Consumer Policy* 23:285–313.

Thøgersen, J., and A.K. Andersen

1996   Environmentally friendly consumer behavior: The interplay of moral attitudes, private costs, and facilitating conditions. In *Marketing and Public Policy Conference Proceedings,* Vol. 6, R.P. Hill and C.R. Taylor, eds. Chicago: American Marketing Association.

Tufte, P.A., and R. Lavik

1997   *Helse- og miljøinformasjon. Forbrukernes behov for informasjon om skadelige stoffer i produkter (Health and Environmental Information: The Consumers' Need for Information About Harmful Substances in Products).* Lysaker, Nor.: Statens Institutt for Forbruksforskning, National Institute for Consumer Research (SIFO).

United Nations Conference on Trade and Development

1995   *Trade, Environment and Development Aspects of Establishing and Operating Eco-Labeling Programmes.* Geneva: United Nations Conference on Trade and Development.

United Nations Environment Program

1994   Elements for policies for sustainable consumption. In *Symposium: Sustainable Consumption. 19–20 January 1994, Oslo, Norway.* Oslo: Ministry of Environment, Norway.

U.S. Environmental Protection Agency

1998   *Environmental Labeling Issues, Policies, and Practices Worldwide.* Washington DC: U.S. Environmental Protection Agency.

Van Dam, Y.K., and M. Reuvekamp

1995   Consumer knowledge and understanding of environmental seals in the Netherlands. In *European Advances in Consumer Research,* F. Hansen, ed. Provo, UT: Association for Consumer Research.

Verplanken, B., G. Hofstee, and H. J.W. Janssen

1998   Accessibility of affective versus cognitive components of attitude. *European Journal of Social Psychology* 28:23–35.

Verplanken, B., and M.W.H. Weenig

1993   Graphical energy labels and consumers' decisions about home appliances: A process tracing approach. *Journal of Economic Psychology* 14:739–752.

Von Weizsacker, E.U., and J. Jesinghaus

1992   *Ecological Tax Reform.* London, NJ: Zed.

Waller-Hunter, J.

2000   2020: A clearer view for the environment. *OECD Observer* 221/222:58–60.

U.S. to Take Airbus-Aid Spat to WTO; Negotiations With EU Stall; Global Trade Body Will Get Biggest Case in Its History

Scott Miller, Daniel Michaels and J. Lynn Lunsford

The U.S. will take its case against Airbus subsidies to the World Trade Organization despite months of talks with the European Union, in what would likely be the most-expensive case ever brought before the global trade body.

The U.S. Trade Representative office said it will ask the global trade enforcer today to appoint a panel to decide the fate of billions of dollars of government aid doled out on each side of the Atlantic to the two aircraft makers.

EU negotiators had hoped to stave off the move, making offers over the weekend to trim by a third the so-called launch aid that European countries give Airbus to help it develop new aircraft. The U.S., however, has long demanded that the EU completely eliminate that aid before it would consider negotiating away money Boeing Co. receives, such as local-government tax credits, or research-and-development grants for defense projects.

The dispute is coming to a head now because it is widely believed Airbus will be awarded more than a billion dollars in European launch aid for a new aircraft, the A350—a midrange plane that will compete against the Boeing 787—as early as mid-June.

"For almost a year, the United States has tried to convince the EU to negotiate an end to subsidies for large civil aircraft," said U.S. Trade Representative Rob Portman. "Unfortunately, at this point, the EU is no longer willing to hold off on launch aid, and has only proposed to reduce subsidies, not end them."

The U.S. statement said the EU still could reconsider and stop the WTO process—but only by ending launch aid. The EU has said several times it didn't want to hold separate negotiations once a WTO case was launched. Airbus is a unit of European Aeronautic Defence & Space Co., and is minority-owned by Britain's BAE Systems PLC.

A WTO case, which normally takes two years or more to resolve, threatens to further strain U.S.-EU trade relations. The effects could reach to the two powers' efforts in

---

Wall Street Journal (2005), "U.S. to Take Airbus-Aid Spat to WTO; Negotiations With EU Stall; Global Trade Body Will Get Biggest Case in Its History," Scott Miller in Brussels, Daniel Michaels in Paris and J. Lynn Lunsford in Dallas, May 31, 2005 A-3.

continuing international trade talks known as the Doha Round, in which they have often combined to advance negotiation at critical junctures. A senior U.S. trade official said that by asking the WTO to intervene, the U.S. was seeking to isolate the aircraft fight so that it wouldn't "pollute" other trade matters with the EU like Doha.

The dispute figures to be the most far-reaching in the WTO's 10-year history, potentially reordering the aircraft business, with repercussions for both companies' suppliers. The WTO's trade court, under mounting criticism from Congress, has authorized billions of dollars of sanctions on U.S. companies alone in recent years. Within the past year, for example, Congress was forced to rewrite part of the tax code to eliminate tax breaks for exporters that the trade court had found violate trade agreements.

Fueling American discontent has been Airbus's steady rise in the passenger-aircraft business, recently overtaking Boeing in market share. U.S. trade officials have argued that Airbus's launch aid has largely made it the market leader.

Europeans counter that Boeing receives billions of dollars in indirect subsidies through research and military contracts. Launch aid, they maintain, is only a more-efficient way of subsidizing aircraft makers. They point to more than $3 billion in tax incentives that the state of Washington, where Boeing formerly was based, has offered to aircraft makers as an example of state aid. Europe further argues that the Japanese government is engaging in a program akin to launch aid that benefits Boeing, by helping its own aircraft makers, which are making the wing of the new 787 "Dreamliner."

The U.S. stance on European support to Airbus, while primarily focused on the proposed A350 passenger jetliner, is also aimed at protecting Boeing's lucrative position as the sole supplier of in-flight refueling tankers to the Defense Department. Boeing last year was stripped of a $23 billion contract to supply the Pentagon with tankers after Boeing officials were implicated in a procurement scandal.

In a sign of the case's sensitivity, Mr. Portman and his EU counterpart, Peter Mandelson, published an unusual joint statement, aimed at tamping down worries about broader breakdowns in trade relations. "We remain united in our determination that this dispute shall not affect our cooperation on wider bilateral and multilateral trade issues," the statement said. "We have worked together well so far, and intend to continue to do so."

The EU declined to detail its reaction until today. "This is a disappointing move by the United States given the proposals for a negotiated solution the EU side made on Friday. The EU will make its own position known tomorrow." said Claude Veron-Reville, European Commission spokesperson for trade.

For Airbus, operating without direct subsidies would be a step into the unknown, because for its entire 35-year history, it has used government financing to cover at least some costs of developing new aircraft. Until the 1992 agreement, subsidies were unlimited and varied widely by country. The French and Spanish Airbus operations were state-owned and received significant state support, while the private British and German operations received less.

After 1992, government loans were limited to 33% of the one-time costs of developing a new jetliner. Each new Airbus plane model has used launch aid, while the development of some recent models derived from existing planes didn't use the aid.

For its 555-seat A380 superjumbo, which is now being tested for certification, Airbus received almost $4 billion in launch aid as part of its $10.7 billion up-front costs. For the proposed A350, Airbus late last year applied to the governments of France, Germany, Britain and Spain for roughly $1 billion in aid.

EUROPE IS UNITED: NO BIOENGINEERED FOOD

Elisabeth Rosenthal

GENEVA—Some are smokers. Some drink too much. Some admit they love red meat. But virtually all shoppers here at the Migros Supermarket on the bustling Rue des Paquis are united in avoiding a risk they regard as unacceptable: genetically modified food.

That is easy to do here in Switzerland, as in the rest of Europe, where food containing such ingredients must be labeled by law. Many large retailers, like Migros, have essentially stopped stocking the products, regarding them as bad for public image.

"I try not to eat any of it and always read the boxes," said Marco Feline, 32, an artist in jeans, getting onto his bike (with no helmet). "It scares me because we don't know what the long-term effects will be on people or the environment."

The majority of corn and soy in the United States is now grown from genetically modified seeds, altered to increase their resistance to pests or reduce their need for water, for example. In the past decade, Americans have happily, if unknowingly, gobbled down hundreds of millions of servings of genetically modified foods. The U.S. Food and Drug Administration says there have been no adverse effects, and there is no specific labeling.

But in Europe—where food is high culture, if not religion—farmers, consumers, chefs, and environmental groups have joined voices loudly and stubbornly to oppose bioengineered foods, effectively blocking their arrival at the farms and on the tables of the continent. And that, in turn, has created a huge ripple effect on trade and politics, from North America to Africa.

The United States, Canada, and Argentina have filed a complaint that is pending before the World Trade Organization, contending that European laws and procedures that discriminate against genetically modified products are irrational and unscientific, and so constitute an unfair trade barrier.

U.S. companies like Monsanto, which invested heavily in the technology, suffered huge losses when Europe balked. As part of a public relations effort, the U.S. State Department enlisted a Vatican academy last month as a co-sponsor of a conference in Rome, "Feeding a Hungry World: The Moral Imperative of Biotechnology."

International Herald Tribune (2004), "Europe is United: No Bioengineered Food," Elisabeth Rosenthal, Oct 6, 2004 p1.
Copyright © 2004 International Herald Tribune.

In response to such pressure, the European Union has relaxed legal restrictions on genetically modified foods.

In May, the EU approved for sale a genetically modified sweet corn, lifting a five-year moratorium on new imports. Last month the European Commission gave its seal of approval to 17 types of genetically modified corn seed for farming. But no one expects a wide-open market.

"We have no illusion that the market will change anytime soon," said Markus Payer, spokesman for Syngenta, the Swiss agribusiness company whose BT-11 corn got the approval in May. "That will only be created by consumer acceptance in Europe."

"There is currently no inclination among European consumers to buy these things," Payer went on. "But the atmosphere of rejection is not based on facts. That is a political, cultural and media-driven decision. And so we are convinced that more and more consumers will see the benefits."

Indeed, the battle lines between countries for and against genetically modified foods seem to be hardening. Several African countries, following Europe's lead, have rejected donations of genetically engineered food and seeds. In Asia, reluctance appears to be spreading. While countries like China and India are enthusiastically planting biotech crops like cotton, genetically modified food crops are having trouble winning approval.

Africa's rejection is based partly on health and local environmental concerns, but also on economic interests: Zambia and Mozambique have discovered a good market in selling unmodified grain and soy to Europe, supplanting the United States as European suppliers.

Mauro Albrizio, vice president of the European Environmental Bureau, a policy group based in Brussels, said: "In the U.S., genetically modified foods were a fait accompli; here in Europe we succeeded in preventing that."

Genetically modified foods arrived on America's dinner plates with little fanfare in the mid-1990s as large-scale farmers in the United States enthusiastically started planting the seeds, which increased production and reduced the amount of pesticide required. Convinced that bioengineered food was, "at least as safe as conventional food," the U.S. Food and Drug Administration declared that a bioengineered lemon was the same as an ordinary lemon, and did not require special labeling or regulation.

Today, nearly two-thirds of the genetically modified crops in the world are grown in the United States, mostly corn and soybeans. "In the U.S., a large part of the diet is actually bioengineered," said Lester Crawford, acting commissioner of the Food and Drug agency.

"The first thing other nations want to know is how many illnesses or adverse reactions we've seen," he added. "But we haven't actually had any problems at all with bioengineered foods."

Vast amounts of money are at stake. Believing that genetically modified foods would quickly catch on throughout the world as they had the United States, large biotech companies like Monsanto invested billions of dollars.

Since the late 1990s the European Union has required that all food containing more than tiny amounts of genetically modified materials be labeled, and that all genetically modified products be submitted for approval before sale in Europe. No products were approved during an informal moratorium from 1998 to 2003. In the past five years, many parts of Europe have enacted local bans on growing such foods.

In fact, most scientific panels have concluded that, "foods derived from the transgenic crops currently on the market are safe to eat," in the words of a recent report from the UN's Food and Agricultural Organization. But the report also cautioned that crops must be evaluated case by case.

And low risk is not no risk. The 87 member states of the UN-sponsored Cartegena Protocol on Biosafety required labeling this year of all bulk shipments of food containing genetically modified products. The United States has not signed the pact.

More important, though, is that the assessment of risk depends largely on the degree of proof that a country's consumers demand.

"In their personal lives people take lots of risk—they drive too fast and bungee-jump—but for food their acceptance of risk is very low," said Philipp Hubner of the Basel-Stadt Canton Laboratory in Switzerland, which tests products in that country for contamination with genetically modified organisms. But Hubner sees his work as detecting fraud in labeling rather than as safeguarding the public health.

"For most scientists it is not so much a safety issue, but an ethical and societal question," he said. "This is what the public here has chosen, like Muslims choosing not to eat pork."

In a survey by the European Opinion Research Group in late 2002, 88.6 percent of Europeans listed the "quality of food products" as an environmental issue with health implications.

But health fears, which can move markets, are not always consistent. In some parts of Europe, like Bordeaux, that have declared themselves free of genetically modified organisms, energy is supplied by nuclear power plants.

To sell Sugar Pops cereal to European consumers, Kellogg's imports unmodified corn from Argentina and spends extra money to make sure that the entire transportation and processing chain is free of bioengineered products, said Chris Wermann, a company spokesman. The same cereal contains genetically modified corn in the United States. Both varieties contain all the usual sugars, artificial colors and flavors.

European advocates defend their right to be finicky. "This is not ideology—it's a pragmatic stand because of potential risks to health and the environment," said Albrizio of the European Environmental Bureau, noting that there is some evidence that genetically modified crops may trigger more allergies.

In terms of agriculture, there are some very clear-cut effects, since genetically modified seeds tend to spread in the environment once they have been planted, making it hard to maintain crops that are organic and free of genetic modification. Scientists call this phenomenon "co-mixing."

To environmentalists and especially to farmers, "co-mixing" it is potentially devastating "contamination." That is why the farmers of Tuscany and 11 other regions of Italy have declared themselves free of bioengineering.

In fact, European farmers and consumers have so far created a firewall against genetically modified organisms, one that the changing laws and World Trade Organization challenges may not breach easily.

"In theory you could sell GMO products here, with labeling," Hubner said. "But I'm not aware of any products that are now being sold, because no store wants them on their shelves."

KICK ME, I'M FOR FREE TRADE

Brink Lindsey

For those of you who didn't get your fill of World Trade Organization bashing from the demonstrators in Seattle, you can look forward to more of the same this spring—this time in the other Washington. In all likelihood Congress will soon be voting on whether the United States should remain a member of the trade body.

When the United States entered the WTO back in 1995 at the close of the Uruguay Round of trade talks, a time bomb was slipped into the implementing legislation. Section 125 of the Uruguay Round Agreements Act allows any member of Congress to propose a joint resolution this year to withdraw authorization for U.S. membership in the WTO. Such a resolution would then be considered under special, expedited procedures. While there's almost no chance that the measure could really be enacted into law, it's conceivable that the House of Representatives might pass it. For that to occur would deal another serious blow to the WTO's already battered prestige.

The sad fact is that, in this country at least, the WTO has become a giant, flashing "Kick Me" sign affixed to the free trade cause. In light of that fact, it's worth remembering why creating the WTO ever made sense. It wasn't because of any mercantilist nonsense about "fair trade." As any Economics 101 textbook will tell you, we benefit from opening our own markets regardless of what other countries do. And it certainly wasn't because of any woollyheaded notion that a world economy needs a world government. That's the last thing it needs.

No, the only good reason for having a body like the WTO is to make it politically easier for our own government, and for governments abroad, to reduce restrictions on trade and investment flows. International trade agreements facilitate liberalization by adding the sugar of improved market access abroad to the political medicine of increased exposure to foreign competition at home. As a result, exporting interests eager to penetrate foreign markets are induced to lobby for the free trade cause. And once barriers have fallen, it's harder to backtrack toward renewed protectionism when doing so violates an international obligation. To cite just one recent example, Congress last year voted down import quotas on foreign steel in large part because of an unwillingness to flout the WTO's ban on such restrictions.

But if the WTO is supposed to reduce and deflect protectionist pressures, it clearly isn't working. On the contrary, it is galvanizing what would otherwise be vague and

Lindsey, Brink (2000), "Kick Me, I'm For Free Trade," *Reason* 31 (10) 52–53.

unfocused anxiety about globalization into an energetic and potent political movement. While the protesters in Seattle may not represent mainstream American public opinion, any cause that can get tens of thousands of people into the streets can't be dismissed lightly. The fact is that the WTO has boomeranged on free-traders.

The fault does not lie with the WTO. In the five years of its existence, it has served as a forum for important new agreements on information technology, telecommunications, and financial services. And its dispute settlement mechanism has performed remarkably well; it has lent a credibility to market-opening rules that never existed in the old days of the toothless GATT.

But the WTO needs help. And the supporters of trade liberalization, in politics and in business, have failed to give it. They have failed to create the domestic political conditions that are necessary if the WTO is to operate effectively. In fact, they have actively contributed to a political culture in which the WTO is a natural whipping boy. Free-traders, through a botched political strategy, have turned what should be an asset into a serious liability.

Here's the nub of the problem. The pro-trade camp in this country has tried to sell free trade generally, and the WTO in particular, on the grounds that free trade in other countries is a good idea. When other countries drop their trade barriers, American companies export more, and consequently create more export-related jobs. All true enough, but what free-traders fail to talk about—and their silence is deafening—is that free trade here at home is a good idea. It's widely believed among free-traders that talking about open U.S. markets amounts to leading with your chin, and so the less said on that subject, the better. (See "Fast-Track Impasse," February 1999.)

But by defending free trade entirely on the basis of what other countries do, supporters of open markets set themselves up for a fall. The fact is that the United States is much more open than most countries around the world—which is a strength, not a weakness. If, however, the WTO is to be justified solely on the benefits of opening markets abroad, then it always looks like we've gotten the short end of the stick. When the benefits of our own open markets are ignored, the argument that we are giving up our rights to faceless bureaucrats in Geneva begins to look plausible.

Meanwhile, by remaining silent in the face of anti-trade claims about job losses and a "race to the bottom," free-traders allow misplaced fears about globalization to spread by default. Trumpeting the prospect of increased exports by U.S. multinationals simply isn't responsive to those fears; indeed, it actually plays to suspicions that the WTO is a front for big corporations that seek to profit at the expense of ordinary Americans.

Over the past couple of decades, the U.S. economy has experienced a sharp surge in the intensity of competition. Much of this surge has had nothing to do with globalization. Deregulation, disinflation, and the revolution in information and communications technologies have all contributed. But our increasing economic ties with the rest of the world have been a significant factor. And while the increase in competition—from both domestic and foreign quarters—has been highly beneficial, it has also raised a lot of people's blood pressure. As a result, Americans are highly susceptible to demagoguery pinning the blame for all the recent tumult on foreigners—and in particular, on an obscure little bureaucracy like the WTO.

If the WTO is to facilitate trade liberalization rather than complicate it, an overhaul in political strategy is needed. In addition to their existing arguments, free-traders will have to make abundantly clear that open markets here at home serve the American national economic interest, even when other countries pursue less enlightened policies. Along those lines, they will have to argue, forthrightly and unapologetically, that a major benefit of WTO membership is the assistance it lends to reducing and holding down U.S. trade barriers against foreign competition. And then U.S. trade policy makers will actually have to walk the walk—they'll have to put American protectionist policies on the negotiating table, not defend them as though antidumping laws and textile quotas and tariffs were the crown jewels (as the Clinton administration did in Seattle).

If this about-face is made, free-traders will be in a strong position to respond to the WTO bashers. The WTO is being lambasted for its inattention to human rights, labor conditions, and environmental standards in developing countries. But once it is clear that our primary reason for joining the WTO is to open our own markets and keep them open, why on earth would we want to invent new reasons for closing them? We shouldn't rob ourselves of the benefits of openness simply because other countries are poorer or more poorly governed than ours. And as to the argument that trade sanctions are needed to help people in poor countries, how exactly do we help them by crushing their livelihoods? Burning the village in order to save it went out of fashion in Vietnam.

If free-traders don't change course, though, the WTO's usefulness will be seriously undermined—and perhaps even extinguished. Trade negotiations, rather than a pragmatic tool for speeding up liberalization, will become a quagmire of proliferating excuses for retarding and reversing it. If that happens, free-traders will have only themselves to blame.

EXPLORATIONS IN IMPROVING SOCIETY VIA SOCIAL MARKETING INITIATIVES

Social Marketing

Alan R. Andreasen

Introduction

Social marketing is an increasingly important area of marketing. Its focus is on improving the personal welfare of members of society through the application of marketing. Therefore, it necessarily differs from traditional forms of marketing in important respects.

Definition

Social marketing is the application of commercial marketing technologies to the analysis, planning, execution, and evaluation of programs designed to influence the voluntary behavior of target audiences in order to improve their personal welfare and that of the society of which they are a part (Andreasen, 1994). It is based on the assumption that all marketing is really about influencing the behavior of target audiences. In the private sector, this means sales and customer loyalty. In the social sector, it is about stopping smoking or getting your boyfriend to use a condom to prevent AIDS. The challenges in the social environment are often much more difficult and complex than in the private sector. Many of the behaviors are *really* high involvement—such as losing weight or confronting an abusive spouse (Celsi and Olsen 1988). Some socially desirable behaviors have no obvious effects, such as inoculating your child, while others involve personal costs but with benefits that mostly go to third parties, such as recycling. It is challenging to see how private sector marketing concepts and tools can be used in such different, non-economic settings.

The Domain of Social Marketing

Social Marketing as a Field of Practice and Scholarship

As will be clear in the discussion to follow, social marketing should be considered an area of practice within the broader domain of marketing practice just as retailing or internet marketing are also distinguishable practice areas. Similarly, as in these other domains, social marketing is an academic specialization. But it is an especially enticing one. As one ventures intellectually farther and farther away from the core discipline, marketing scholars need to rethink core concepts and tools and sometimes develop new frameworks that

ANDREASEN, ALAN: Social Marketing

Alan R. Andreasen is Professor of Marketing in the McDonough School of Business at Georgetown University and Executive Director of the Social Marketing Institute.

promise to apply better in these unusual contexts. I would argue that social marketing presents challenges to scholars that are dramatically different from extensions of traditional marketing to new product categories or new communication channels. Adaptation is far from easy when the transactions one seeks to influence involve no money, no tangible products and no direct services—for example, in influencing target audiences to exercise more.

While I am less than objective on the matter, these characteristics make social marketing one of the most promising new domains for marketing research and scholarship. By pushing the boundaries of our arsenal of conventional concepts and tools, we will not only provide distinctive added value to an important social domain but potentially transfer new insights back to the core discipline.

HISTORICAL DEVELOPMENT

As William Wilkie and Elizabeth Moore made clear in their recent overview of marketing and society (Wilkie and Moore, 2003), academic study and application of marketing to broader issues in society has a long history. Over that history, the term "social marketing" has had a number of meanings that, in part, reflect the broader field's evolution but have led to some confusion from time to time. The term first appeared in the seminal work emerging from what Elliott (1991) called "the Northwestern School" in the period 1969 through 1971. In 1969, Philip Kotler and Sid Levy, in a groundbreaking article in the *Journal of Marketing* (Kotler and Levy, 1969) proposed that marketing ought to move beyond its traditional focus on purely economic transactions to encompass marketing challenges faced by nonprofit organizations and government agencies. This proposal for breaking out of the conventional economic boundary of the field did not sit well with many scholars (Luck, 1974; Bartels, 1974). However, the traditional view did not prevail and the field soon saw the appearance of nonprofit textbooks and a rash of articles that made clear that scholars were quite willing to take the more expansive view.

Then, in 1971, Kotler and Gerald Zaltman introduced the term *social marketing* for the first time defining it as "the design, implementation and control of programs calculated to influence the acceptability of social ideas and involving considerations of product planning, pricing, communication, distribution and marketing research" (Kotler and Zaltman, 1971, p. 5). The concept of social marketing had already been adopted in the field—if not always labeled as such. Early applications were found in areas that were most similar to marketing applications in the economic sector, most prominently in the area of family planning in the developing world (Indian Institute of Management, 1964; Manoff, 1985; Harvey, 1999). In such instances, pioneering nonprofits were simply marketing a product line at drastically reduced prices (and later providing services) to address a significant social problem. Subsequent applications involved the marketing of social and nonprofit services in areas like the arts and education that, again, were not very different from the traditional field (Andreasen, 2001).

Confusion around the term had been common before 1971 but increased later in the 1970s as marketing scholars became more concerned with what I and others have called the "dark side" of marketing (Magnuson and Carper, 1968; Hirschman, 1991). During this period, many academics caught up in the protest movements of the period began to take a harder look at marketing's potential negative impacts on society. This included issues of deception, the plight of disadvantaged consumers, and environmental degradation. Many scholars thought of the work as studying "social marketing." Indeed, in 1973 William Lazer and Eugene Kelley put together a collection of readings that included these topics and called it *Social Marketing: Perspectives and Viewpoints* (Lazer and Kelley, 1973). The volume included such topics as consumerism, governmental regulation of marketing and issues around recycling and environmental quality.

In the period between 1971 and the late 1980s, interest in application of marketing to solving social problems grew relatively slowly. Part of the problem was marketing's suspect image in the broader society fueled by books like Packard's *Hidden Persuaders* (1957). Many nonprofits were reluctant to fully embrace marketing ideas, considering them somehow tainted and inappropriate for their mission-driven environments. Government agencies also avoided the "marketing word," choosing instead to call their efforts "public education" or "social communications" (Hill 2001).

However, by the 1990s, the environment changed dramatically—social marketing became much more acceptable. A principal driving force in this repositioning was the Centers for Disease Control and Prevention. The CDC saw the potential power of the methodology and applied it vigorously to their HIV/AIDS work. Subsequently, a number of other major governmental programs such as the Office of National Drug Control Policy began using the term and the underlying concepts and tools routinely (Denniston 2004). Foundations began to ask for social marketing components in their RFPs (Requests for Proposals). This encouraged many consultants and public relations/ advertising agencies to add social marketing to their array of skills and individuals with social marketing in their job titles began to appear.

This accelerated acceptance was abetted by the establishment of centers for social marketing in Washington, DC, Ottawa, Canada and Glasgow, Scotland (and later in Warsaw, Poland and Lethbridge, Alberta). Several textbooks and a handbook appeared and a rash of project reports and practitioner guides became widely available from specific social marketing practitioner organizations. A journal, *Social Marketing Quarterly,* emerged and a listserver started at Georgetown University to eventually link over 1,200 social marketers worldwide. And the field's supply of new talent and application was accelerated by major annual conferences organized by the University of South Florida and the Social Marketing Institute.

As practitioners and non-marketing scholars looked further at social marketing, a growing concern was the diversity of approaches. In particular, it became clear that, despite the burgeoning literature, many people (and organizations) were claiming to be doing social marketing when they were not. This development threatened the field's future growth, and it became increasingly important that the field agree on a basic set of concepts and tools that would constitute a "true" social marketing approach. To this end, the field itself engaged in vigorous debate (Blair, 1995; Bonaguro and Miaoulis, 1983; Buchanan, Reddy and Hossain, 1994; Grace, 1991; Hastings and Haywood, 1991, 1994; Lefebvre and Flora, 1988; Maben and Clark, 1995; McBrien, 1986; Syre and Wilson, 1990; Timmereck, 1987; Tones, 1994; Winett, 1995) with, for a time, no clear consensus emerging.

A consensus view of what makes social marketing potentially unique began to emerge in the late 1990s. It is now well accepted that a true social marketing approach: (a) holds behavioral influence[1] as its "bottom line"; (b) is fanatically customer-driven; and (c) emphasizes creating attractive exchanges that offer compelling benefits, minimal costs, and easy-to-implement opportunities to respond. This behavioral focus also means that there is a central role for consumer research, pretesting and program monitoring and for careful market segmentation. Creating social behavior exchanges necessarily involves the private sector's 4Ps (product, price, place and promotion) appropriately adapted to social exchange contexts. Finally, social marketers recognize that all behaviors face competition. In the social sector, this competition can take the form of inaction (e.g., continuing to smoke) or some alternative new action (e.g., vigorous biking rather than dieting).

KEY TOPICS

Theoretical underpinnings for social marketing have been drawn from both the social sciences and commercial marketing. Because of the behavioral focus, most social marketing approaches make some attempt to adapt one or more of the following frameworks: Stages of Change (Prochaska and DiClemente, 1983), Theory of Reasoned Action (Fishbein and Ajzen, 1975), Theory of Planned Behavior (Ajzen, 1991), Health Belief Model (Rosenstock, 1990), Protection Motivation Theory (Maddux and Rogers, 1983), Diffusion Theory (Rogers, 1995) and Social Cognitive Theory (Bandura, 1977). Strategy models drawn from commercial marketing include segmentation approaches (Maibach and Cotton, 1995), and formative research techniques such as focus groups, branding, and distribution planning. A great many sourcebooks, chapters, and articles are available to further spell out these elements (Kotler, Roberto and Lee, 2002; Andreasen, 1995; Donovan and Henley, 2003).

There are, of course, a number of important substantive topics that are challenging social marketers in the 21st century. Among these are:

1. How to get physicians, psychologists and other health professionals to implement evidence-based best practices;

---

[1] It should be noted that I intentionally use the term "behavioral influence" rather than "behavior change" as the focus (as I had done in earlier writing). Many social marketing campaigns are really designed to get target audiences not to act—not to drink and drive, not to smoke, or not to abuse their spouse or children.

2. How to measure the impacts of campaigns which have outcomes that are very long run, difficult to discern, and subject to influences from a many endogenous and indogenous influences;

3. How to influence media gatekeepers and others to raise specific issues to greater significance such as rampant use of prescription drugs for children, African genocide, and environmentally injurious practices;

4. How to have an impact on the global HIV/AIDS crisis or combat the spread of malaria that kills thousands of children in Africa daily ("President Bush's Emergency Plan . . . 2004)".

Delving Deeper into Social Marketing: Selected Readings

READING #1: CRAFTING A NEW DEFINITION

A major academic contribution to the rapid growth of social marketing was the appearance of my new definition of social marketing in 1994. The original definition proposed by Kotler and Zaltman in 1971 and repeated in essence in Kotler and Roberto's 1989 text book, *Social Marketing* had been the most frequently cited to this point. The essence of this definition was that social marketing was all about achieving the acceptability of social *ideas* (Kotler and Roberto, 1989). A major problem with this formulation was that practitioners and scholars in other fields reasonably interpreted it to mean that social marketing was primarily a tool for education and attitude change. Communications scholars and practitioners said, "But, that's what we do," as did those in Health Education or Health Promotion. They saw little reason to explore and understand this potentially powerful new approach.

My article "Social Marketing: Its Definition and Domain" in the *Journal of Public Policy and Marketing* (reprinted in this section) sought to break social marketing free of this intellectual dead end. The insight was to ask not, "How is social marketing different from traditional marketing?" as Bloom and Novelli creatively did in 1981 but to ask, "How is it *the same*?" It has been my argument for some time now that marketing in all its many contexts is all about *influencing behavior*. In the private sector, the behaviors in question involve getting target audiences (customers) to purchase products and services, choose Brand A over Brand B, and/or keep coming back to provider X or product Z. These behaviors are solicited by offering target audiences compelling exchanges of personally valuable benefits for reasonable costs. In these private sector contexts, the ultimate objective is to meet the needs of the firm's stockholders.

Social marketing is also about influencing behavior. Sometimes the behavior is like the private sector in that it involves products (e.g., for family planning or for the prevention of diarrhea) or services (e.g., getting an immunization shot or participating in a quit-smoking group). Sometimes these exchanges involve payment of money or some other kind of donation (e.g., volunteer labor); often they do not. But it was important to recognize that a great many social marketing programs did not involve any products or services at all! Take efforts to get an overweight person to start exercising on their own or to get a smoker to quit or to get a father to stop abusing his child. These cases involve social marketing but in each instance, no product or service is central to the approach and no money changes hands. These are instances of what I call "pure behavioral influence."

It is important, however, to understand that *all* marketing is about influencing behavior. It is simply the case that in the social sector, the behaviors often involve unusual kinds of exchanges and the goal is not to make money for stockholders but to benefit the target audience or the larger society of which they are a part.[2]

READING #2: PUTTING SOCIAL MARKETING INTO CONTEXT

The 1994 definitional breakthrough was salutary in that potential users of social marketing could see how it might be different from "communications" or "health education" and so they were open to looking further into the array of concepts and tools that social marketers have adapted from the commercial sector to address social problems. However, questions still remained of just where the boundaries of the new discipline might lie, particularly between social marketing and other traditional methods of behavioral influence such as education and the law.

Michael Rothschild's 2002 article in the *Journal of Marketing* provided this critical linchpin. Rothschild asked, "How do social behavior challenges differ and are there ways in which they differ that are both researchable and are likely to lead to choices between education, marketing, and the law?" His answer lay in earlier work by MacInnis, Moorman, and Jaworski (1991) that proposed that one could classify a target audience member at a point in time into planning segments depending on whether they were high or low on three dimensions: *Motivation* to act, *Ability* to act, and *Opportunity* to act. These MOA factors allowed Rothschild to conclude, for example, that if someone has motivation, ability and opportunity, then probably all that is needed is education (as in the case of SIDS). Alternatively, if a person has ability and opportunity but lacks motivation, then perhaps the law must be brought to bear. In most other cases, the appropriate methodology is social marketing.

The challenge for social marketers is how to coordinate social marketing approaches with education and the law to addresses challenges like teen smoking and obesity. Does one need interdisciplinary teams? Should social marketers lead such teams or is their role just one of many? How can one measure the MOA factors in practice and use them to guide strategy? Should one use social marketing approaches to influence the behavior of "educators" (including the media, teachers, mentors, etc.) or those in the law (legislators, police, prosecutors, etc.)?

---

[2]This is not to adopt the Pollyanna view that all government agencies and nonprofits doing social marketing are doing so purely for the benefit of others. These organizations want to grow and be successful. They want to win awards. They want to build their intellectual capital so that they can be more powerful change agents in future.

Readings #3: Taking Social Marketing Concepts and Tools to the Field

There has been a growing array of high quality research in the area of social marketing. Some of this research has appeared in traditional marketing journals. Other findings have been published in other social science journals, especially those in public health, as well as in the *Social Marketing Quarterly*. Among the various application areas that have been addressed include:

- Tobacco cessation (Marks, 1998; Zucker et al., 2000)
- Preventing domestic violence (Nabi, Southwell, and Hornik, 2002)
- Increasing fruit and vegetable consumption (Heimendinger et al., 1996)
- Reducing the effects of high blood pressure (National Heart, Lung and Blood Institute, 1992)
- Increasing traffic safety (Barbas and Horn, 1993)
- Illicit drug use in Australia (Jones and Rossiter, 2002)
- Smoking by low-income consumer in the UK (Macaskil, Stead, Mackintosh and Hastings, 2002)
- Immunization in Australia (Carroll and Van Veen, 2002)
- Preventing skin cancer (Peattie, Peattie and Clarke, 2001)
- Improving the diet of low-income pregnant women (Brinberg and Axelson, 2002)
- Motivating organ donations in Singapore (Lwin, Williams and Lan, 2002)

The reading included in this section by Susan Zimicki and her colleagues is a representative example of a range of evaluation studies in the field (Zimicki et al., 2002). These studies are often required by funding agencies but also are driven by researchers' eagerness to understand what works and what does not. The intervention analyzed in the article is typical of how social marketing has been used in the field. The project was carried out in 1989 and 1990 and focused on measles vaccination behavior. It was part of a 14-year project called Communication for Child Survival funded by the U.S. Agency for International Development. Principal contractor for the project was the Academy for Educational Development and the major subcontractor was Porter Novelli. (Both these organizations, one a nonprofit and one a for-profit, have been at the forefront of developments in the field.) Implementation was carried out by the Philippines Department of Health's Maternal and Child Services in collaboration with the country's Public Information and Health Education Service. Evaluations were carried out by the Center for International, Health, and Development Communications at the Annenberg School of Communications at the University of Pennsylvania.

Readers should note several key features of this research. First, because the focus was on underserved markets, very careful attention was given to the sampling component of the survey methodology. In many social marketing contexts in the developing world, nice convenient databases and sampling frames have not been available and often researchers must do much basic enumeration themselves. Second, after assessing overall campaign effectiveness (positive), the researchers dug deeply into the data to establish a plausible causal pathway from exposure to the campaign to vaccination behavior and concluded that education is a key intervening variable. Third, the researchers sought to rule out other potentially causal elements of a social marketing campaign, particularly the behavior of health workers or other elements of clinic practice.

A caveat: it is important to note that the intervention studied in the article is described as a *communication campaign*. That is, the researchers were principally focused on the influence of the communication element of the overall program. But, there were other elements to the program that make it a social marketing intervention. Many of these elements were contributed by the Philippines health service. This is clear in the campaign communications themselves. Considerable attention in the campaign was given to the importance of the Place variable in the 4Ps—or what Rothschild and MacInnis, Moorman and Jaworski would call "opportunity." As the article notes, the communications specifically focused on "logistical knowledge—[telling target audiences] the age for vaccinations and the times and places vaccinations would be available."

However, to insure that the field does not regress to earlier states of confusion, it must be remembered that a campaign that only employs one element of the 4Ps (i.e., advertising or communications) should not claim to be social marketing.

Policy in Progress

CHILDHOOD OBESITY

As noted by Craig Andrews in the section on Consumer Protection in this volume, among the most critical social problems that social marketing has lately been asked to address is overweight and obesity. This is a public health issue that has recently risen to high prominence (Huddleston and Perlowski 2003). Trend data in the U. S. make clear the dramatic increase in the presence of overweight, particularly for children. In regard to the latter, the Centers for Disease Control and Prevention reported the following percentage of children overweight in various surveys from 1963 to 2000:

Year	Age 6–11	Age 12–19
1963–70	4.2	4.6
1971–74	4.0	6.1
1976–80	6.5	5.0
1988–94	11.3	10.5
1999–2000	15.3	15.5

Sources: Centers for Disease Control and Prevention, National Center for Health Statistics, National Health and Nutrition Examination Survey, Hispanic Health and Nutrition Examination Survey (1982–84) and National Health Examination Survey (1966–70).

What is particularly noticeable here is the almost threefold increase in rates of overweight in the 20-year period from 1976–80 to 1999–2000. The Surgeon General and others now label the problem "an epidemic" and state that overweight and obesity currently represents the number two preventable cause of morbidity and mortality in the United States (similar patterns are also found in other developing and developed countries.) Overweight and obesity has shifted dramatically in the eyes of the public (Critser, 2003). There was a time where it was considered an individual problem—much as smoking was 50 years ago. But, now it is recognized that society has an obligation to address the issue directly. In the article by Peter Perl in this section, we see the challenges that a family faces in trying to cope with an obesity problem.

1. How would a social marketer tackle the problem so that families like the Duyers could achieve their weight loss objectives?
2. If one addresses childhood obesity, should the focus be on the children themselves and their parents? What about the school administrators who could change school lunch and vending programs? Should product marketers be urged—or required—to provide better labeling information and fast food chains to change their portion sizes and provide more nutrition information? Should legislators be urged to put more money into physical education programs in schools and invest in playgrounds and bike paths?

SMOKING IN CHINA

One of the great social marketing success stories in the US and Canada has been the reduction in smoking rates for all ages, ethnic groups and genders over the last twenty years. And the truth® campaign of the American Legacy Foundation continues to have major impacts on both starting and quitting behaviors.[3] But, worldwide, the story is much different. While WHO reports adult smoking rates of 23.8 percent for the United States, they find rates of 40.5 percent in Venezuela, 33.5 percent in Switzerland, 50 percent in Namibia, 35 percent in Korea and 48 percent in Bosnia Herzegovina.

As the article on the smoking problem in China makes clear, there are many forces that lead to high smoking rates in other countries and make the challenges for social marketers particularly daunting. In China, the government owns the market! And Western cigarette manufacturers are eager to enter the market because of its size. If the Chinese soon are exposed to Marlboros and Camels, one might speculate that smoking rates will rise significantly—especially if young people see smoking as a way to be "cool" in the Western sense.

1. If you were the medical student Li Dongbo, where would you focus your initial efforts? Would you focus on smokers, on retailers selling tobacco products, or on the government and its promotion strategies?

---

[3]See their website at: www.americanlegacy.org.

2. How would you organize your efforts? What allies would you seek and what roles would they play?

3. What role should education play? Should there be a mass campaign or should one segment the target audience and use limited funds on priority segments? If so, what segments would be most likely to respond—and what social marketing approaches might be most effective with them?

COLLEGE BINGE DRINKING

Students on almost every university campus know that binge drinking is a major problem. Too many students—especially those just entering college—think that bingeing is the norm and is what one must do to be "cool." Yet during their college careers, they will also learn about students who have done things while terribly drunk that they profoundly regret—cases of date rape, car crashes, missed or botched schoolwork, and falls—sometimes fatal—from apartment balconies. Still, as the binge drinking article in this section makes clear, students like Nick think that heavy alcohol consumption is important enough that it is something for which he has to train!! And Lily thinks that she has to have 21 drinks or she won't REALLY be an adult.

1. Where would you begin with someone like Nick? What should be the behavioral objective? Does it make sense to get him to (a) cut back a little; (b) make a major change in his drinking levels; or (c) find other ways to be cool?

2. Can Lily's parents play a role with her? What about Nick's parents or other relatives—what would it take to get them involved and what might they contribute?

3. What should the university's role be? Should they be educators? Police? Confidants? Should they try to get potential bingers into other party activities? Do they have an ethical responsibility *in loco parentis* to spend significant resources on the problem? If so, what is "significant"?

Conclusion

STATE OF THE FIELD: A CRITICAL CROSSROADS

Social marketing is now at a most interesting juncture in its history with the potential to make another significant leap forward. As suggested in the discussion of the obesity "hot topic," most complex social problems comprise a great many potential intervention points. Ironically, over the years, social marketing has been criticized by Lawrence Wallack and others as being solely focused "downstream" (Wallack et al., 1993). That is, social marketers appeared to be fixated on individuals who exhibited problem behaviors—those who smoked, abused their wives, did drugs or didn't recycle.

Wallack pointed out that, consistent with Rothschild, many "victims" had the motivation to change but lacked the opportunity or ability to change. For example, a child may want to exercise more but there is no playground at school (or nearby), no school Phys Ed program, and no sports teams for unskilled kids. The child may think of playing on the street but it is unsafe, even dangerous. For many children, there are no role models and no caregivers with the time or energy to play actively with the child. Wallack (and others) argued that the way to achieve *significant* social change in these cases is to work "upstream" to change the policies and practices that make the desired behaviors difficult or impossible. A downstream focus was simply a diversion from the real problem.

Social marketers have come to accept this challenge. Further, they recognize other arguments for an upstream approach. For example, sometimes changes in structures and policies will make individual behavior change *unnecessary* either because the behavioral problems are largely avoided (e.g., the cigarette industry is dramatically inhibited) or because problematic behaviors are no longer dangerous (e.g., air bags protect drivers who neglect to wear seat belts and iodized salt prevents goiter in the Philippines without citizens having to consciously change their diets). Finally, Goldberg, Sandikci, and Litvack (1997) argue that upstream changes in social norms and role models around a problem behavior can have critical influences on individuals without the latter being approached directly.

This presents a new challenge for social marketing. Social marketers need to "embrace a broader perspective that encompasses not just individual behavior change, but also the social and physical determinants of that behavior." (Hastings and Donovan, 2002, p. 4).

FUTURE DIRECTIONS

But how are social marketing concepts and tools useful—and superior—when one is trying to influence policy and upstream practice?

First, I need to modify my own definition of social marketing to replace "and" with "or" when specifying the objectives of social marketing. That is, social marketing should be defined as influencing behavior "in order to improve their personal welfare *or* that of the society of which they are a part." This slight revision makes space for upstream interventions that influence, say, a legislator's behavior where the legislator doesn't personally benefit but society does.

Upstream intervention is consistent with the view that social marketing is all about influencing individual behaviors. Upstream interventions require that individuals take action—but now we are talking about different kinds of individuals in different roles. Legislators have to pass laws and regulators must enforce them. Police have to patrol unsafe neighborhoods. Foundation executives have to fund desirable programs. Business leaders have to change workplace practices and media gatekeepers have to tell stories and present facts to move an issue higher on the social agenda (Yankelovich, 1991). The field simply needs to understand more extensively these new target audiences and consider how social marketing approaches need to be adapted for these different circumstances, if at all.

Questions for Discussion

This broadened purview of the field also presents dramatic new challenges for scholars and students. Among the important practical and theoretical questions are the following:

1. If you are trying to get someone to stop smoking, should you use a different approach than if you are trying to get someone not to start?
2. Jeffrey Sachs, head of the United Nations Millennium Challenge Project, has said that efforts by social marketers in Africa to sell insecticide-treated bed nets to prevent malaria for a small price are unconscionable. He says that the people are too poor and the nets should be given away. How would you respond to his charge?
3. How would you get obese children to start exercising and eating better if their caregivers are overweight and say "people like us are just naturally heavy?"
4. What is the role of branding in social marketing programs? The American Legacy Foundation calls its effort the *truth*® anti-smoking campaign (Zucker, Hopkins, et al., 2000) and the Office of National Drug Control Policy's promotes the "anti-drug." Are these good branding strategies and why? Where else can brands be useful in social marketing campaigns?
5. Congress mandates that three-quarters of the Office of National Drug Control Policy anti-marijuana campaign funding go to media advertising. Is this a good idea given that their principal target is teenagers? How would you allocate the budget and why? What data would you need to make your allocations?

References

Ajzen, Icek. 1991. "The Theory of Planned Behavior: Some Unresolved Issues," *Organizational Behavior and Human Decision Processes,* 50: 179–211.

Andreasen, Alan R. 1995. *Marketing Social Change.* San Francisco: Jossey-Bass, Inc.

___. 2001. "Intersector Transfer of Marketing Knowledge" in *Handbook of Marketing and Society.* Paul N. Boom and Gregory T. Gundlach (eds.) Thousand Oaks, CA: Sage Publications, Ltd., 80–104.

___. 2002. "Marketing Social Marketing in the Social Change Marketplace," *Journal of Public Policy & Marketing,* 21 (1) (Spring): 3–13.

Bandura, Albert. 1977. "Self-Efficacy: Toward a Unifying Theory of Behavior Change," *Psychological Review,* 84: 191–215.

Barbas, A. and B. Horn. 1993. "Marketing Traffic Safety," *The OECD Observer,* 181: 30–32.

Bartels, Robert. 1974. "The Identity Crisis in Marketing," *Journal of Marketing,* 38, 73–76.

Blair, J. E. 1995. "Social Marketing: Consumer-Focused Health Promotion," *AAOHN Journal,* 43 (10): 527–531.

Bloom, Paul N. and William D. Novelli. 1981. "Problems and Challenges in Social Marketing," *Journal of Marketing*, 45 (2): 79–88.

Bonaguro, J.A. and George Miaoulis. 1983. "Marketing: A Tool for Health Education," *Health Education*, 14 (1): 6–11.

Brinberg, David and Maria L. Axelson. 2002. "Improving the Dietary Status of Low Income Pregnant Women at Nutritional Risk," *Journal of Public Policy and Marketing* (Spring): 100–104.

Buchanan, D.R., S. Reddy and Z. Hossain. 1994. "Social Marketing: A Critical Appraisal," *Health Promotion International*, 9 (1): 49–57.

Carroll, Tom E. and Laurie Van Veen. 2002. "Public Health Social Marketing: The Immunize Australia Program," *Social Marketing Quarterly*, 7 (1) (Spring): 62–65.

Critser, Greg. 2003. *Fat Land: How Americans Became the Fattest People in the World*. Boston: Houghton Mifflin Company.

Denniston, Robert. 2004. "Planning, Implementing, and Managing an Unprecedented Government-Funded Prevention Communications Initiative," *Social Marketing Quarterly*, 10 (2): 6–12.

Donovan, Rob and Nadine Henley. 2003. *Social Marketing: Principles and Practice*. Melbourne: IP Communications.

Elliott, Barrie J. 1991. *A Re-examination of the Social Marketing Concept*. Sydney: Elliott & Shanahan Research.

Fishbein, Martin and Icek Ajzen. 1975. *Belief, Attitude, Intention and Behavior*. Reading, MA: Addison-Wesley.

Goldberg, Marvin E., Ozlem Sandikci and David Litvack. 1997. "Reducing the Level of Violence in Hockey," in *Social Marketing: Theoretical and Practical Perspectives*. Marvin E. Goldberg, Martin Fishbein and Susan Middlestadt, (eds.) Mahwah, NJ: Lawrence Erlbaum Associates.

Grace, V.M. 1991. "The Marketing of Empowerment and the Construction of the Health Consumer: A Critique of Health Promotion," *International Journal of Health Services*, 21 (2): 329–343.

Harvey, Philip D. 1999. *Let Every Child Be Wanted: How Social Marketing Is Revolutionizing Contraceptive Use Around the World*. Westport, CT: Auburn House.

Hastings, Gerard and A. Haywood. 1991. "Social Marketing and Communication Health Promotion," *Health Promotion International*, 6 (2): 135–145.

___ and ___. 1994. "Social Marketing: A Critical Response," *Health Promotion International*, 69 (1): 59–63.

Heimendinger, J., M.A. Van Duyn, D. Chapelsky, S. Foerster and G. Stables. 1996. "The National 5 A Day for Better Health Program: A Large Scale Nutrition Intervention," *Journal of Pubic Health Management and Practice*, 2: 27–35.

Hill, Railton. 2001. "The Marketing Concept and Health Promotion: A Survey and Analysis of Recent 'Health Promotion' Literature," *Social Marketing Quarterly*, 7 (1): 29–53.

Hirschman, Elizabeth. 1991. "Secular Mortality and the Dark Side of Consumer Behavior, Presidential Address," in *Advances in Consumer Research*, Vol. XVII. Michael R. Solomon and Rebecca Holman (eds.) Provo, UT: Association for Consumer Research.

Huddleston, Charles T. and Henry Perlowski (2003), *Employers Beware: Obese Workers Suffer Discrimination on the Job, Lawsuits Likely*. AGG Press release, November 6, http://www.agg.com/Contents/NewsArticleDetail.aspx?ID=775.

Indian Institute of Management. 1964 "Proposals for Family Planning Promotion: A Marketing Plan," *Studies in Family Planning*, 1, no. (6) (March): 7ff.

Jones, Sandra C. and John R. Rossiter. 2002. "The Applicability of Commercial Advertising Theory to Social Marketing: Two Case Studies of Current Australian Social Marketing Campaigns," *Social Marketing Quarterly,* 8 (1): 6–18.

Kotler, Philip and Sidney J. Levy. 1969. "Broadening the Concept of Marketing," *Journal of Marketing.* 33: 10–15.

Kotler, Philip and Gerald Zaltman. 1971. "Social Marketing: An Approach to Planned Social Change," *Journal of Marketing* 35: 3–12.

Kotler, Philip and Eduardo Roberto. 1989. *Social Marketing: Strategies for Changing Public Behavior.* New York: The Free Press.

Kotler, Philip, Eduardo Roberto and Nancy Lee. 2002. *Social Marketing: Strategies for Changing Public Behavior.* Thousand Oaks, CA: Sage Publications.

Lazer, William and Eugene J. Kelley (eds.) (1973). *Social Marketing: Perspectives and Viewpoints.* Homewood, IL: Richard D. Irwin.

Lefebvre, R. Craig and June A. Flora. 1988. "Social Marketing and Public Health Intervention," *Health Education Quarterly,* 15 (3): 299–315.

Luck, David J. 1974. "Social Marketing: Confusion Compounded," *Journal of Marketing,* 38: 70–72.

Lwin, May O., Jerome D. Williams and Luh Luh Lam. 2002. "Social Marketing Initiatives: National Kidney Foundation's Organ Donation Programs in Singapore," *Journal of Public Policy and Marketing* (Spring): 66–77.

Maben, J. and J.M. Clark. 1995. "Health Promotion: A Concept Analysis," *Journal of Advanced Nursing,* 22 (6): 1158–1165.

MacInnis, Deborah J., Christine Moorman and Bernard Jaworski. 1991. "Enhancing and Measuring Consumers' Motivation, Opportunity, and Ability to Process Brand Information from Ads," *Journal of Marketing* 55 (October): 32–53.

Macaskill, Susan, Martine Stead, Anne Marie Mackintosh and Gerard Hastings. 2002. "'You Cannae Just Take Cigarettes Away from Somebody and No' Gie Them Something Back': Can Social Marketing Help Solve the Problem of Low Income Smoking?" *Social Marketing Quarterly* 7 (1) (Spring): 19–34.

Maddux, J.E. and Robert W. Rogers. 1983. "Protection Motivation and Self-Efficacy: A Revised Theory of Fear Appeals and Attitude Change," *Journal of Experimental Social Psychology,* 19 (5): 469–479.

Magnuson, Warren G. and Jean Carper. 1968. *The Dark Side of the Marketplace: The Plight of the American Consumer.* Englewood Cliffs, NJ: Prentice-Hall.

Maibach, Edward and D. Cotton. 1995. "Moving People to Behavior Change: A Staged Social Cognitive Approach to Message Design," in *Designing Health Messages.* Edward Maibach and Roxanne Louiselle Parrott (eds.) Newbury Park, CA: Sage Publications, 41–64.

Manoff, Richard K. 1985. *Social Marketing.* New York: Praeger Publishers.

Marks, Amy S. 1998. "Behaviour Management of the Tobacco Addiction Cycle: What Does Social Marketing Have to Offer" in *The Economics of Tobacco Control: Towards an Optimal Policy Mix.* Iraj Abedian, Rowena van der Merwe and Nick Williams (eds.) Cape Town: The University of Cape Town Press, 210–231.

McBrien, M. 1986. "Health Promotion: Education or Marketing Strategy?" *Nursing Success Today,* 3 (5): 16–17.

Nabi, Robin L., Brian Southwell and Robert Hornik. 2002. "Predicting Intentions Versus Predicting Behaviors: Domestic Violence Prevention from a Theory of Reasoned Action Perspective," *Health Communication,* 14 (4): 429–450.

National Heart, Lung, and Blood Institute. 1992. *The Fifth Report of the Joint National Committee on Detection, Evaluation, and Treatment of High Blood Pressure.* Bethesda, MD: National Heart, Lung, and Blood Institute.

Packard, Vance. 1957. *The Hidden Persuaders.* New York: D. Mckay Co.

Peattie, Ken, Sue Peattie and Philip Clarke. 2001. "Skin Cancer Prevention: Reevaluating the Public Policy Implications," *Journal of Public Policy & Marketing,* 20 (2): 268–279.

Pechmann, C. and E.T. Reibling. 2000. "Planning an Effective Anti-Smoking Mass Media Campaign Targeting Adolescents, *Journal of Public Health Management Practice,* (May): 80–94.

Perl, Peter. 2003. "The Incredible Shrinking Duyers," *The Washington Post Magazine,* March 30, pp. 6 ff.

Prochaska, James O. and C.C. DiClemente. 1983 "Stages and Processes of Self-Change of Smoking: Toward an Integrative Model of Change," *Journal of Consulting and Clinical Psychology,* 51: 390–395.

"President Bush's Emergency Plan for AIDS Relief to Award $100 Million to Help Orphans and Vulnerable Children" (2004), Press release, U.S. Agency for International Development, October 25 at http://www.usaid.gov/press/releases/2004/pr041025.html. Retrieved June 16, 2005.

Rogers, Everett M. 1995. *Diffusion of Innovations,* 4th ed. New York: Free Press.

Rosenstock, Irwin M. 1990. "The Health Belief Model: Explaining Health Behavior Through Expectancies," in *Health Behavior and Health Education,* Karen Glanz, Francis Marcus Lewis, and Barbara K. Rimer, (eds.) San Francisco: Jossey-Bass Publishers, 39–62.

Rothschild, Michael. 1999. "Carrots, Sticks and Promises: A Conceptual Framework for the Management of Public Health and Social Issue Behaviors," *Journal of Marketing,* 63 (4): 24–37.

Syre, T.R. and R.W. Wilson. 1990. "Health Care Marketing: Role Evolution of the Community Health Educator," *Health Education,* 21 (1): 6–8.

Timmereck, T.C. 1987. "Health Education and health Promotion: A Look at the Jungle of Supportive Fields, Philosophies, and Theoretical Foundations," *Health Education,* 18 (6): 23–28.

Tones, K. 1994. "Marketing and the Mass Media: Theory and Myth," *Health Education Research,* 9 (2): 165–169.

Wallack, Lawrence, L. Dorfman, D. Jernigan, and M. Themba. 1993. *Media Advocacy and Public Health,* Newbury Park, CA: Sage Publications.

Wilkie, William L. and Elizabeth S. Moore. 2003. "Scholarly Research in Marketing: Exploring the '4 Eras' of Thought Development," *Journal of Public Policy and Marketing* 22 (2) (Fall): 116–146.

Winett, R.A. 1995. "A Framework for Health Promotion and Disease Prevention Programs," *American Psychologist,* 50 (5): 341–350.

Yankelovich, Daniel. 1991. *Coming to Public Judgment: Making Democracy Work in a Complex World.* Syracuse, NY: Syracuse University Press.

Zimicki, Susan, Robert C. Hornik, Cecelia Verzosa, José R. Fernandez, Eleanora de Guzman, Manolet Dayrit, Adora Fausto and Mary Bessie Lee. 2002. in *Public Health Communication: Evidence for Behavior Change.* Robert Hornik (ed.) Mahway, NJ: Lawrence Erlbaum Associates. 197–218.

Zucker, David, R.S. Hopkins, D. F. Sly, J. Urich, J. M. Kershaw and S. Solari. 2000. "Florida's 'Truth' Campaign: A Counter-Marketing Anti-Tobacco Media Campaign," *Journal of Public Health Management Practice,* 6 (3): 1–6.

Social Marketing: Its Definition and Domain

Alan R. Andreasen

The author argues that social marketing has been defined improperly in much of the literature. A revised definition is proposed and the domain of social marketing defined. He concludes with suggestions for implications for future growth of the discipline.

It is clear that the term *social marketing* is now a well-established part of the marketing vocabulary in universities, government agencies, private nonprofit organizations, and private for-profit firms. There are now social marketing textbooks (Kotler and Roberto 1989; Manoff 1975), readings books (Fine 1990), chapters within mainstream texts (Kotler and Andreasen 1991) and a Harvard teaching note (Rangun and Karim 1991). There have been reviews of the accomplishments of social marketing (Fox and Kotler 1980; Malafarina and Loken 1993) and calls to researchers to become more deeply involved in studies of social marketing to advance the science of marketing (Andreasen 1993). Major international and domestic behavior change programs now routinely have social marketing components (Debus 1987; Ramah 1992; Smith 1989). People with titles like Manager of Social Marketing now can be found in private consulting organizations.

Why Definitions Matter

There have been critics of the expansion of marketing beyond its traditional private sector origins from the beginning (cf. Bartels 1974; Luck 1974). However, today, a great many scholars and practitioners now see social marketing as a viable subject of research, teaching, and practice. They see the field as growing and expanding and thereby increasing the relevance of marketing education and scholarship to the problems of the broader society. It also has been argued that involvement in these new areas has had an important reciprocal effect on marketing scholarship. I note one example of the latter in my

ALAN R. ANDREASEN is Professor of Marketing, Georgetown University. The author thanks William Smith of the Academy for Educational Development for comments on an earlier draft of this article.

Alan R. Andreasen (1994), "Social Marketing: Its Definition and Domain," *Journal of Public Policy and Marketing,* Vol. 13(1), 108–114.

1992 Association for Consumer Research Presidential Address on social marketing (Andreasen 1993, p. 1):

> The rise of exchange theory, I believe, was given a major stimulus by marketing scholars trying to expand the concept of 'consumer behavior' and 'marketing' to encompass something as nontraditional as going to college, wearing seat belts, or giving blood. For example, promoting blood donations seemed to be an opportunity for 'marketing,' yet there were no products or services offered and no monetary payment made by the consumer. In fact, the consumer often *voluntarily* suffered when making the 'purchase.' Traditional unidirectional views of consumer behavior could not encompass such a strange case. We *needed* a new paradigm. The old way, like earth-centered astronomy before Copernicus, was simply not elastic enough to contain these new transactions. Thus, we slowly embraced exchange theory.

However, despite the rapid growth of interest in social marketing (or perhaps because of it), there is still considerable disagreement about what social marketing is and how it differs from similar fields like communications and behavior mobilization. This disagreement is not uncommon for a new discipline. Debates about definition and domain in other fields are quite common within university walls. Careful definition of any field is important to the advancement of scholarship and the training of future researchers. However, in the present case, the issue has an additional, important implication.

Many believe that social marketing can have a major impact on society's myriad social problems. However, this impact can be seriously compromised if the technology is applied incorrectly or to areas in which it is not appropriate. If practitioners misuse the concept, its effectiveness may be limited. If researchers and scholars assess its performance in areas for which it *should not* be responsible, social marketing may be blamed for failures for which it should not be held accountable.

It is time, therefore, to introduce precision into the dialogue by establishing a clear consensus on what social marketing is and is not and what its "legitimate" domains are and are not. These definitions and distinctions have important implications for present and future practical applications, academic discussions, and field research. The central premise of the article is that social marketing stands a significant chance of failure if existing issues of definition and domain are not adequately resolved.

The Emergence of Social Marketing[1]

Although in the 1960s, marketing scholars wrote and carried out research on topics that today would be considered social marketing (e.g., Simon 1968), the origins of the term *social marketing* can be traced to Kotler and Zaltman's classic 1971 article in the *Journal of Marketing* titled "Social Marketing: An Approach to Planned Social Change" (Kotler and Zaltman 1971). As Elliott (1991) points out, the emergence of social marketing at just

---

[1]This section draws significantly from Elliott (1991).

that moment in time was a logical outgrowth of the attempt of the Northwestern School to broaden the discipline of marketing (cf. Kotler and Levy 1969). Elliott suggests that this development reflected both significant increases in the pressures within the marketing discipline to be more socially relevant and the emergence of technologies in other disciplines that could be applied to social change. The latter was represented in the work of Rogers (1962), Weibe (1951/52), and others.

Brown (1986) concurs in this assessment, arguing that social marketing is a natural outgrowth of several developments in and out of marketing, including the following:

1. Increased needs of nonbusiness organizations for marketing services,
2. Attacks on marketing's negative impact on society,
3. The emergence of exchange theory,
4. The coalescence of social marketing oriented theory, and
5. The decline of consensus-oriented perceptions of social reality.

In the years that followed the Kotler–Zaltman (1971) article, the growth of social marketing continued to be fueled by both supply and demand pressures within the field of academic marketing. Marketing scholars found more opportunities to work with nonprofit and government organizations to apply marketing skills to social change programs. This demand already was being met partially by rival academic disciplines including "social advertising" (Davison 1959; Hyman and Sheatsley 1947; Merton, Fiske, and Curtis 1946) and public relations (e.g., Bernays 1952), but government and nonprofit practitioners sensed that marketing had a broader role to play.

It was during this period that marketing was being infiltrated by a growing number of young marketing scholars who were energized by the general social unrest and campus turmoil of the late 1960s and wanted to become more "socially relevant." My own early involvement in social marketing reflects this phenomenon (Andreasen 1993, p. 1):

> I was an academic product of the social revolution of the late sixties and early seventies and frustrated with what I was doing. My friends in Sociology and Political Science were worrying about issues like poverty, the Viet Nam war, and military recruiting on campus, and so on, while I was busy teaching my students how to market Chevrolets and Clairol Shampoo.... My 1975 encounter with (social marketing) opened my eyes to the potential for marketing to work *positively* for the good of society beyond merely (to use a classroom cliché of the time) 'delivering a better standard of living.'

Despite a growing interest in the topic by marketing scholars in the 1970s, the first major book on the subject was published in 1975 by a social marketing *practitioner,* Richard Manoff. In his pioneering volume, Manoff set forth several principles he had derived from his years of work on social change projects in the areas of food and nutrition and family planning in developing countries. Academics were slow to respond. It was six years before Manoff's contribution was followed by the first book by an academician on the topic, Seymour

Fine's *The Marketing of Ideas and Social Issues* (1981). It was eight more years before Kotler and Roberto's book *Social Marketing: Strategies for Changing Public Behavior* was published, and one more year before we saw the first readings book on *Social Marketing: Promoting the Causes of Public and Nonprofit Organizations* (Fine 1990). The latter and other books in preparation (e.g., Andreasen, forthcoming) suggest that interest in the topic is accelerating.

There is now a modest body of social marketing research produced in the 1980s and early 1990s that is beginning to find its way into the marketing and social science literature. The present section of the *Journal of Marketing and Public Policy* is one such example. In a recent review, Malafarina and Loken (1993) catalogue 76 empirical articles that already have appeared in the five leading marketing publications since 1980. Their review documents the scope of work in this area. But it also makes another important contribution by showing that early concerns expressed by Bloom and Novelli (1981) about the difficulties of doing research in this new area "were not borne out to the degree anticipated" (Malafarina and Loken 1993, p. 403). This bodes well for even greater growth of the field in future.

This makes even stronger the need for clear guideposts.

Defining Social Marketing

The very first formal definition of social marketing was that offered by Kotler and Zaltman in 1971 (p. 5):

> Social marketing is the design, implementation and control of programs calculated to influence the acceptability of social ideas and involving considerations of product planning, pricing, communication, distribution, and marketing research.

This definition proved problematic in several ways. First, the choice of the term *social marketing* was itself a source of early confusion. As Rangun and Karim (1991) note, this term tended to lead individuals to confuse social marketing with *societal* marketing. Rangun and Karim (1991, p. 3) argue that social marketing "involves: (a) changing attitudes, beliefs, and behaviors of individuals or organizations for a social benefit, and (b) the social change is the primary (rather than secondary) purpose of the campaign." In their view, societal marketing deals with regulatory issues and other efforts to protect consumers from what Hirschman terms the "dark side of the marketplace" (Hirschman 1992; cf. Magnuson and Carper 1965) and does not necessarily involve influencing target consumers in any way. Therefore, it is clearly distinguishable from social marketing.

A second problem in early discussions of social marketing was confusion over whether its practice was limited to public and nonprofit marketers. It can be argued that private sector firms engage in "social marketing," for example, when the insurance industry encourages seat belt usage or the beer industry promotes "responsible drinking." Again, Rangun and Karim (1991) would argue that such efforts should not fall within the domain of social marketing because social change is a secondary purpose of the campaign from the private sector firm's standpoint.

A third problem with this first definition is that it limits its objective to influencing "the acceptability of social ideas." Some authors, most prominently Seymour Fine, support such a restrictive definition. Fine (1991, p. xiv) defines social marketing "at its simplest [as]...the application of marketing methods to the dissemination of ideas—socially beneficial ideas like cancer research, energy conservation, and carpooling."

Most scholars and researchers, however, believe that social marketing involves much more than ideas—specifically, attitudes and behavior. This broadened review is reflected in Kotler and Roberto's (1989) social marketing text. Here, the authors equate social marketing with a social change campaign, which they define as "an organized effort conducted by one group (the change agent), which intends to persuade others (the target adopters) to accept, modify, or abandon certain ideas, attitudes, practices, and behaviors" (p. 6). They indicate that a social marketing campaign can include the "mere" provision of information on important issues or, in some cases, just change values and beliefs.

Although an improvement, Kotler and Roberto's (1989) expanded definition still leaves unanswered some other important questions about social marketing's legitimate domain. For example:

1. Is social marketing really any different from other technologies, such as "health education" or "health promotion," with which it shares many common features (cf. Glanz, Lewis, and Rimer 1990)?
2. Is any technique "fair game" to be called social marketing if it helps to achieve social marketing objectives? For example, is the imposition of a government regulation such as a ban on smoking in public buildings a legitimate social marketing strategy?
3. Is it appropriate to use attempts to include ideas and attitudes as legitimate objectives of social marketing programs?
4. Should the domain of social marketing be limited, as many government agency directors would have it, only to programs that market products, such as condoms and birth control pills or oral rehydration solutions, or services, such as immunizations and vasectomies?

A Proposed Definition

In my view, what is needed is a definition of social marketing that would (1) keep practicing social marketers focused on the outcomes they are best suited to influence, (2) keep the discipline of social marketing distinguishable from its academic "competitors," and (3) keep social marketing programs out of areas in which their likelihood of failure is high. With these objectives in mind, I propose the following definition:

> Social marketing is the adaptation of commercial marketing technologies to programs designed to influence the voluntary behavior of target audiences to improve their personal welfare and that of the society of which they are a part.

Key elements of this definition merit further elaboration.

Social Marketing Is an Adaptation of Commercial Marketing Technologies

Implicit in most definitions of social marketing is that we borrow our technology from the private sector. However, other authors appear to forget that the bottom line of all private sector marketing is *the production of sales.* To achieve their sales objectives, private sector marketers engage in a great many activities that are designed to change beliefs, attitudes, and values. But their only reason for doing this is that they expect such changes to lead to increased sales.[2] Sales are examples of consumer behavior, and it is my contention that, if we are borrowing commercial technology, we should hold social marketing to the same objectives; that is, social marketing should be designed to have as its "bottom line" *influencing behavior.*

Social Marketing Is Applied to Programs

Social advertising is synonymous with campaigns. Campaigns have a fixed termination point. Programs, by contrast, may last decades and contain several campaigns within them. Thus, the American Cancer Society has a long-run social marketing program to reduce the incidence of smoking, within which they have annual campaigns, such as each year's Great American Smokeout. An important strength of social marketing is that it takes a programmatic rather than campaign view of its mission.

Social marketing is not synonymous with organizations. Many organizations that are primarily social marketers also carry on activities that are not social marketing. Thus, in the 1970s, contraceptive social marketing programs in Colombia, Thailand, and Pakistan experimented with various sales programs that were strictly commercial but would enhance the limited revenues they were deriving from social marketing contraceptive sales (Andreasen 1988). Although supportive of the overall mission of the organization, such programs would not be considered social marketing.

Social Marketing Focuses on Behavior as its Bottom Line

The "bottom line" of social marketing is behavior change. A major shortcoming of a wide range of social marketing programs that I have observed in the field is that, though their managers consider themselves at least in part social marketers, they fail to keep their eye on the bottom line. They think that all they must do is provide information (ideas) or change beliefs. Sometimes they think this way because they were trained in other disciplines and tend to equate marketing with advertising. So they think their goal is to "get the word out" or to "change attitudes" without asking whether either of these activities is likely to lead to the desired behavior. They seem to assume that this will happen in some mystical "long run."

---

[2]As with social marketing, sometimes private sector marketers conduct campaigns that are designed to prevent change, e.g., switching to a newly introduced brand.

Ironically, in my view, a factor contributing to this confusion is the original definition of social marketing proposed by Kotler and Zaltman in 1971, a definition that is routinely (often uncritically) repeated by others (e.g., Malafarina and Loken 1993). This overly broad definition only encourages practicing social marketers to think that all they have to do is change attitudes and ideas to be successful. It keeps them from asking the question every first-rate private sector marketer asks: Does the communication of an idea or the changing of an attitude really influence behavior? This neglect of the bottom line can lead to enormous waste of inevitably scarce resources. In my judgment, it is sinful for marketing scholars to neglect their true private sector "heritage" and contribute—even indirectly—to such waste in areas that are so crucial to the welfare of society.

The sole emphasis on behavior as social marketing's bottom line also helps keep the field distinct from other disciplines. As I have noted elsewhere (Andreasen 1993, p. 2):

> Too many in social marketing confuse marketing with communication. While marketers communicate information, we are not in the *education* business. While we attempt to convince people of the rightness of certain beliefs, we are also not in the *propaganda* business. Many of the health programs I have observed or worked with around the world are, in fact, largely education and propaganda programs. . . . Education and propaganda are only *useful* to marketers if they *lead to behavior change.*

The emphasis on behavior also forces social marketers to adopt what I would argue is commercial marketing's second major contribution, its fanatical emphasis on the customer. What I believe distinguishes the best professional social marketers from a great many others I have encountered in social marketing programs is their "natural" tendency to ask constantly, "How will this (strategy, tactic) affect consumers?" This customer focus leads them to begin every social marketing program with formative research designed to understand target audiences fully before the development of expensive programs. It encourages them to test key strategies and tactics against real consumers and monitor behavior as programs unfold to make sure that they are on track.

The behavioral emphasis also ensures that marketers have the appropriate evaluation criteria for everything they do. Those without a "behavioral bottom line" are more inclined to evaluate program success in nonbehavioral terms such as number of messages distributed, beliefs changed, images improved, or lectures given. They tend to measure success by what can be measured rather than tackle the harder problem of figuring out what should be measured and then attempting to do so. It is a tendency reinforced by well-meaning consultants who forget (or never learned) that social marketing is really all about influencing behavior.

This focus on behavior has a fourth advantage. It keeps social marketing from being given responsibility for objectives in areas in which I do not believe it has any particular differential advantage—education and propaganda. Consider the challenge of persuading a woman who has little understanding of conception—let alone the prevention of conception—to undertake family planning. A moment's reflection suggests that there are several steps involved in taking a woman from the stage at which she does not understand how babies are made all the way to the point at which she is correctly and continually practicing family planning. These steps can be grouped into five broad categories: basic education, value change, attitude change, motivation to act, and training and reinforcement.

In my opinion, social marketers should not be tasked with the burden of carrying out either basic education or value change if these present massive challenges. First, such undertakings can be very long term, and marketers are best at producing "sales" in the relatively short run. Second, as argued previously, these tasks are more properly the domain of educators and propagandists. The latter know how to inform entire populations about new ideas or practices, for example, through textbooks or the school system. And they know how to bring about major value changes through speeches and pronouncements by government, religious, and civic leaders. Social marketers should be brought in to "do their thing" when these other specialists have achieved a considerable amount of success. My fear is that, if social marketers are called in to achieve behavior change objectives where massive changes in knowledge and values have not already been achieved, they will misapply their valuable skills, waste scarce resources, and show very limited success, at least in the short term. I fear that such failures will not only discourage them and their sponsors, it also will give a black eye to this fledgling discipline.

Let me be clear: I am not arguing that social marketing should never attempt to educate or change values as part of a behavior change program. Such components are essential to most of the social marketing programs with which I am familiar. I am arguing only that social marketing should not be the technology of choice if dramatically large segments of the target population are still ignorant of the behavior and/or opposed to it on the grounds that it offends central community values.

Social Marketing Programs Influence Behavior—They Do Not Always Change It

Social marketing campaigns need not involve behavior change. Definitions such as Kotler and Roberto's (1971) that speak of social marketing goals as necessitating that consumers "adopt, modify, or abandon" something ignores the fact that some social marketing programs are designed to discourage behavior. For example, campaigns to prevent children from using drugs (e.g., the "Just Say No" campaign in the United States) are clearly intended to discourage change.

Social Marketing Seeks to Influence Voluntary Behavior

In the private sector, marketers seek to influence voluntary consumer spending and choice and stop short of outright coercion. (Coercion sometimes is employed in relationships with distributors, though it is often characterized as a tactic of last resort.) Marketers can attempt to influence behavior through behavioral shaping or reinforcement strategies but, ultimately, consumers do have the choice not to buy. Thus, we should be clear that marketer's basic talents lie in influencing voluntary behavior, and these are the talents they bring to social marketing.

Experience has shown that coercion can be very effective in achieving social behavior goals, for example, inducing consumers to wear seat belts or stop smoking. It should be clear, however, that these are not parts of social marketing campaigns. In some cases, they can be substitutes for social marketing (e.g., when the latter has not been effective) or combined with social marketing efforts. Indeed, a social marketer may wish to argue that legal solutions would be more effective than social marketing to achieve particular behavioral goals and, at this point, step out of the program.[3]

Social Marketing Seeks to Benefit Target Consumers and/or the Society as a Whole, Not the Marketer

Social marketing programs benefit either individuals or society. In some programs, the primary beneficiary is the target consumer or his or her family. This would be the case in programs designed to promote breast self-examination, dieting, or the immunization of children. Other programs target the society at large as the major beneficiary, as in efforts to increase consumer recycling or induce homebuilders to plant more trees. Finally, some programs have joint beneficiaries. The latter would include efforts to get drivers to obey the 55 miles per hour speed limit, which would help save the lives of drivers and their passengers, reduce society's health care costs, free its law enforcement officers for other tasks, and reduce the country's dependence on foreign oil.

Note that the definition of social marketing omits cases in which the beneficiary is the social marketing organization. This is a major distinction between private sector and social marketing and, as Rangun and Karim (1991) argue, it prevents us from including efforts of private sector organizations to achieve social ends, as in the insurance industry's seat belt campaign. Also note that the proposed definition would not include such nonprofit marketing activities as fundraising and political campaigning, in which the major objective is to benefit the marketer.

Finally, it should be pointed out that the definition is silent about who is to define well-being. The definition of social marketing only requires that the social marketer not undertake programs to benefit him- or herself; that he or she must believe that the program will improve long run individual or societal well-being. This is a point I return to subsequently.

---

[3]I have argued that social marketing technology can be applied to getting laws passed because there one again is dealing with influencing the voluntary behavior of legislators.

Social Marketing Criteria

Implicit in the definition of social marketing outlined here are the following criteria. To be labeled social marketing, a program must

- apply commercial marketing technology.
- have as its bottom line the influencing of voluntary behavior, and
- primarily seek to benefit individuals/families or the broader society and not the marketing organization itself.

These characteristics, however, comprise necessary but not sufficient criteria for labeling a program as social marketing. A great many approaches to influencing behavior that carry other labels like health communication meet the last two criteria. So the truly distinguishing trait for social marketing is that it applies marketing technology. What, then, are the defining characteristics of such a technology? This is a topic that heretofore has not been addressed systematically (although cf. Hunt 1991). In my own efforts to use social marketing to influence voluntary behaviors, I have developed a modest set of characteristics that distinguish the very best social marketing:

1. Program managers understand the target audience's needs, wants, perceptions, and present behavior patterns before acting, in many cases through the use of specific formative research. Managers do not make assumptions about these characteristics.
2. Program managers segment target markets wherever politically feasible and devise budgets and strategies that are specifically adapted to the characteristics of each defined segment.
3. Whenever economically feasible, all major elements of program strategy and tactics are pretested with members of the target audience.
4. Program managers conceive of the decision process by which target consumers come to undertake a target behavior as comprising the following steps:
   a. Acquire the necessary knowledge to be aware of the option;
   b. Embrace the values that permit the behavior to be considered for adoption;
   c. Perceive the behavior as potentially relevant to their own circumstances, those of a member of their family or those of the broader society;
   d. Conclude that the positive consequences of the behavior exceed the negative consequences to a degree that is superior to realistic alternatives;
   e. Believe that they have the ability to carry out the action; and
   f. Believe that others who are important to them support their action.
5. The program explicitly recognizes that it faces direct or indirect competition for the target consumer's behavioral choices.
6. Strategies designed to effect behavioral change always comprise all four elements of the marketing mix (the four Ps):

a. Design of a *product* (i.e., the behavior to be promoted) that is fully responsive to the target consumers' needs and wants, in other words, that is easy and satisfying;

b. Making the *place* at which the behavior can be carried out convenient and accessible;

c. Minimizing to the extent possible the economic, social and psychological *price* of the behavior; and

d. Seeking to *promote* the behavior with messages through personal or impersonal media appropriate to the target audience's lifestyle patterns and preferences.

The need to have a full complement of marketing mix elements is very often one of the key traits on which programs fail to be true marketing programs. Too many practitioners are really doing social advertising and think it is social marketing. This misapplication of the term has caused some of our very best practitioners to despair. Recently, Bill Smith of the Academy for Educational Development (Smith 1993, p. 2, 5) said:

> I think the future of Social Marketing is in doubt. I believe that unless we do something now, it will either pass away as just another fad of the 80's, or worse yet, be institutionalized as a new bureaucratic routine of the 90's. In both cases it may die, or become fossilized, without ever having been understood. The problem with social marketing today is clear. There is often little or no marketing. . . . Social Marketing was taken over by social advertising early in its history. Whenever I mention the Four Ps (Product, Place, Price, and Promotion) these days you can see the audience glaze over, sit back and say 'where has this guy been—the Four Ps—we're way beyond the Four Ps.' We have come to believe that the Four Ps are boring, because we are only truly doing anything about the fourth P—promotion.

Smith's solution (p. 8) is to "go back to basics—to stop stressing awareness, acceptance and knowledge before we figure out what new services people need, what benefits they want, and what barriers we can make easier to overcome. Marketing is about programs, it's not about posters."

Clearly, practitioners of social marketing find that good definitions, like good theories, have very practical implications. It is important that the field come to a clear agreement about what social marketing comprises and how it differs from its rivals. A clear, accepted definition will ensure that social marketing is applied where it is appropriate and withheld where it is not. And it will ensure that those carrying out social marketing are not misapplying its basic tenets. Only under these circumstances will social marketing have a fair chance to fulfill the great potential many of us believe that it has for doing "social good."

An Ethical Concern

Social marketing is supposed to be applied to achieving social good (cf. Murphy and Bloom 1990). But social marketing is in one sense merely a technology to be employed by those who wish to achieve social good. As such, it can be used by anyone who claims (or believes) that it is being used for such an end. The determination of what is social good is entirely in the hands of the would-be social marketer. This means that, inevitably, social marketing technologies will be applied by partisans promoting their own particular visions of social welfare, which can differ significantly from those held be the general society.

Thus, social marketing could be used by the Ku Klux Klan, the German National Socialist (Nazi) Party, Mother Teresa, and both pro-life and pro-choice forces. This possibility raises a critical ethical issue: How do we ensure that this exciting new technology is used for "good" ends? Those of us who wish to promote the use of social marketing are faced with two challenges. First, we must ensure that the characteristics of good social marketing enunciated previously are adhered to—that is, that we teach and advise others in the very best social marketing practice. Second, we must make personal ethical judgments about the kinds of organizations and individuals to whom we offer our social marketing services.

Leo Szilard was instrumental to the development of atomic bomb technology. However, at the end of his career, he also spent much of his time lobbying to ensure that his legacy was put to peaceful usage. There is a lesson here for those of us who wish to be "social marketing experts." We must devote our energies to building the best technology that we can. But we also owe it to ourselves and our communities to see that it is used for what a broad consensus of society agrees is its own social good.

References

Andreasen, Alan R. (1988), "Alternative Growth Strategies for Contraceptive Social Marketing Programs." *Journal of Health Care Marketing,* 8 (June), 38–46.

___ (1993), "A Social Marketing Research Agenda for Consumer Behavior Researchers," in *Advances in Consumer Research,* Vol. 20, Michael Rothschild and Leigh McAlister, eds. Provo, UT: Association for Consumer Research, 1–5.

___ (forthcoming), *Marketing for Social Change.* San Francisco: Jossey-Bass.

Bartels, Robert (1974), "The Identity Crisis in Marketing," *Journal of Marketing,* 38 (October), 73–76.

Bernays, Eugene (1952), *Public Relations.* Norman, OK: University of Oklahoma Press.

Bloom, Paul and William D. Novelli (1981), "Problems and Challenges in Social Marketing," *Journal of Marketing,* 45 (Spring) 79–88.

Brown, B. (1986), "Social Marketing and the Construction of a New Policy Domain: An Understanding of the Convergence Which Made Social Marketing Possible," doctoral thesis, Virginia Commonwealth University (quoted in Elliott 1991).

Davison, P. (1959), "On the Effects of Communications," *Public Opinion Quarterly,* 23, 3343–60.

Debus, Mary (1987), *Lessons Learned from the Dualima Condom Test Market.* Washington, DC: SOMARC/The Futures Group.

Elliott, Barry J. (1991), A *Re-examination of the Social Marketing Concept.* Sydney: Elliott & Shanahan Research.

Fine, Seymour (1981), *The Marketing of Ideas and Social Issues.* New York: Praeger.

___, ed. (1990), *Social Marketing: Promoting the Causes of Public and Nonprofit Agencies.* Boston: Allyn & Bacon.

Fox, Karen F. A. and Philip Kotler, (1980), "The Marketing of Social Causes: The First Ten Years," *Journal of Marketing* 44, 24–33.

Glanz, Karen, Frances Marcus Lewis and Barbara K. Rimer, eds. (1990), *Health Behavior and Health Education.* San Francisco: Jossey-Bass Publishers.

Hirschman, Elizabeth (1991), "Secular Morality and the Dark Side of Consumer Behavior: Or How Semiotics Saved My Life," *Advances in Consumer Research,* 18, 1–4.

Hunt, Shelby D. (1991), *Modern Marketing Theory.* Cincinnati: South-Western Publishing Co.

Hyman, Herbert and Paul Sheatsley (1947), "Some Reasons Why Information Campaigns Fail," *Public Opinion Quarterly* 11, 412–23.

Kotler, Philip and Alan R. Andreasen (1991), *Strategic Marketing for Nonprofit Organizations,* 4th ed. Englewood Cliffs, NJ: Prentice-Hall, Inc.

___ and Sidney Levy (1969), "Broadening the Concept of Marketing," *Journal of Marketing,* 33, 10–15.

___ and Eduardo Roberto (1989), *Social Marketing: Strategies for Changing Public Behavior.* New York: The Free Press.

___ and Gerald Zaltman (1971), "Social Marketing: An Approach to Planned Social Change," *Journal of Marketing,* 35, 3–12.

Luck, David J. (1974), "Social Marketing: Confusion Compounded." *Journal of Marketing,* 38 (October), 70–72.

Magnuson, Warren G. and Jean Carper (1968), *The Dark Side of the Marketplace.* Englewood Cliffs, NJ: Prentice-Hall, Inc.

Malafarina, Katryna and Barbara Loken (1993), "Progress and Limitations of Social Marketing: A Review of Empirical Literature on the Consumption of Social Ideas," in *Advances in Consumer Research,* Vol. 20, Michael Rothschild and Leigh McAlister, eds. Provo, UT: Association for Consumer Research, 397–404.

Manoff, Richard K. (1985), *Social Marketing.* New York: Praeger Publishers.

Merton, Robert, M. Fiske, and A. Curtis (1946), *Mass Persuasion.* New York: Harper & Row.

Murphy, Philip and Paul Bloom (1990), "Ethical Issues in Social Marketing," in *Social Marketing: Promoting the Causes of Public and Nonprofit Agencies,* Seymour Fine, ed. Boston: Allyn & Bacon, 68–86.

Ramah, Michael (1992), *Social Marketing and the Prevention of AIDS.* Washington, DC: Academy for Educational Development AIDSCOM Project.

Rangun, V.K. and S. Karim (1991), *Teaching Note: Focusing the Concept of Social Marketing.* Cambridge, MA: Harvard Business School.

Rogers, Everett M. (1962), *Diffusion of Innovations.* New York: The Free Press.

Rothschild, Michael (1979), "Marketing Communications in Non Business Situations or Why It's So Hard to Sell Brotherhood Like Soap," *Journal of Marketing* 43, 11–20.

Simon, Julian (1968), "Some 'Marketing Correct' Recommendations for Family Planning Campaigns," *Demography,* 5, 504–7.

Smith, William A. (1989), *Lifestyles for Survival: The Role of Social Marketing in Mass Education.* Washington, DC: Academy for Educational Development.

___ (1993), "The Future of Social Marketing," paper presented to the Marketing Conference on Creating Successful Partnerships, Carleton University, Ottawa, Canada.

Weibe, G.D. (1951/52), "Merchandising Commodities and Citizenship in Television," *Public Opinion Quarterly,* 15 (Winter), 679–91.

Carrots, Sticks, and Promises: A Conceptual Framework for the Management of Public Health and Social Issue Behaviors

Michael L. Rothschild

The author presents a framework that considers public health and social issue behaviors and is based on self-interest, exchange, competition, free choice, and externalities. Targets that are prone, resistant, or unable to respond to the manager's goal behave on the basis of their motivation, opportunity, and ability and on a manager's use of the strategies and tactics inherent in education, marketing, and law.

Two million U.S. residents die each year; it is estimated that half of these deaths are "premature" and attributable to lifestyle and environmental factors (*UC Berkeley Wellness Letter* 1997). Advances in biomedical sciences, mass immunization, and sanitation have resulted in a decrease in the incidence of infectious diseases (Matarazzo 1984), so that the health status of the population in economically developed countries now has less to do with acute illness than with lifestyle issues such as excessive drinking, unhealthy diet, or the use of tobacco products (Walsh et al. 1993). Influencing lifestyle can do more to increase the health of the population and lower the cost of health care than can treatment of illness.

In this article, a conceptual framework is proposed for the management of public health and social issue behaviors. The article relies on education, marketing, and law as its three primary classes of strategic tools. These tools will be considered with respect to specific targets and specific public health or social issues for which the targets may or may not have any motivation, opportunity, and/or ability to cooperate but that nevertheless have been selected for management (e.g. keeping preteen girls from beginning to smoke). The tools are considered with respect to targets who are prone, resistant, or unable to comply with the manager's goals.[1] The relative appropriateness of the use of various

---

[1]*Manager* is used here as a generic term that includes, but is not limited to, various persons such as civil servants, nonprofit administrators, and/or private sector managers who attempt to direct the behavior of individuals for the good of society (as defined by the managers, the leaders, and/or the constituents of the society).

MICHAEL L. ROTHSCHILD is Professor, School of Business, University of Wisconsin, Madison. The author gratefully acknowledges the financial support of the Rennebohm Foundation, the Robert Wood Johnson Foundation, and the Comprehensive Cancer Center, School of Medicine, University of Wisconsin. The author gratefully acknowledges the intellectual contributions of Alan Andreasen, Gary Bamossy, Jan Willem Bol, Robert Drane, Jan Heide, Marvin Goldberg, Amy Marks, Daniel Wikler, the reviewers, and many, many others whose input made this article better. Ultimately, any errors in fact or logic are the author's.

Michael L. Rothschild, (1999), "Carrots, Sticks and Promises: A Conceptual Framework for the Management of Public Health and Social Issue Behaviors," *Journal of Marketing*, 63 (4), 24–37.

combinations of education, marketing, and law will be determined by these states for the purpose of assisting managers in dealing with tremendously complex societal problems.

These issues are of societal concern when they tie to freely chosen behaviors that result in social costs for which other members of the society must pay either directly or indirectly (externalities). This article also considers the macro policy trade-offs between the free choice rights of individuals and the rights of others not to have resulting externalities thrust on them. The selection of issues for which the use of education, marketing, and/or law are appropriate will be determined on the basis of this trade-off of conflicting rights.

Given the existence of these trade-offs, cooperation between parties may be necessary for the manager's goals to be met. As Ouchi (1980, p. 130) points out, "Cooperative action necessarily involves interdependence between individuals. This interdependence calls for a transaction or exchange in which each individual gives something of value . . . and receives something of value . . . in return." This article considers the potential impact of transactions when cooperation may be hindered by the competing self-interested views of the target group (whose members may be comfortable with their current behaviors) and the manager (who seeks a particular behavior).[2]

Current public health behavior management relies heavily on education and law while neglecting the underlying philosophy of marketing and exchange. A goal of this research, therefore, is to show the relevance of marketing along with education and law while recognizing that each tool set has its own strengths, weaknesses, and most appropriate application opportunities. Major tasks are to determine the circumstances in which education, marketing, and law are most appropriate, as well as to determine the societal values as to the desire to impose society's interests on individuals through the several sets of available tools.

Introducing Education, Marketing, and Law

The use of the tripartite classification of education, marketing, and law is based on previous work. Lindblom (1977) frames his macro analysis of the major politicoeconomic systems of the world into three classes of social control: persuasion, exchange, and authority. Smith (1996) has five classes of micro management tools, which he refers to as the 5Fs: facts (informational education), feelings (emotional education), facilitation (product, price, and place), freebies (promotions), and force (force of law). Hastings and Elliott (1993) use 3Es—education, environment, and enforcement—in their micro level framework. Before proceeding, several terms must be clarified.

---

[2]There also are cases in which the individual may not be comfortable with the current behavior but is unable to make changes. In these cases, the target and manager are not competing, but the manager still must choose among education, marketing, and law as tools to manage behavior.

Here, *education* refers to messages of any type that attempt to inform and/or persuade a target to behave voluntarily in a particular manner but do not provide, on their own, direct and/or immediate reward or punishment (e.g., "Quitting isn't easy—keep trying," "Just don't do it," "Eat five fruits and vegetables per day"). Education can teach and create awareness about existing benefits but cannot deliver them, even though the resultant knowledge may have value for long-run behavior in the pursuit of benefits. Education (alone) requires the target to initiate the quest for the benefit and/or solicits voluntary compliance. Compliance may be for a previously known reward (e.g., "Stop smoking and reduce the chances of heart disease"), a reward not previously received (e.g., teens are taught that "kissing a smoker is like licking an ashtray"), or for no explicitly apparent reward (e.g., "Don't forget to vote"). Education, if alone, can suggest an exchange but cannot deliver the benefit of the exchange explicitly.

Lindblom's *persuasion* is similar and comprises several forms of social control from ideological instruction and propaganda found in totalitarian systems to the free competition of ideas found in liberal democracies. Education is also similar to what Wiener and Doescher (1991) term a *behavioral solution,* that is, a solution that asks people to make voluntary sacrifices. Finally, education is similar to what Rasmuson and colleagues (1988) define as *health communications,* that is, "the development and diffusion of messages to specific audiences in order to influence their knowledge, attitudes, and beliefs in favor of healthy behavioral choice."

Although messages often are used to inform or persuade, as an aid to the marketing of a product or service in an exchange or as an aid in the enforcement of law, these supporting tactics are not included under the rubric of education here. Messages that support in these ways are important to the overall integrated behavior management process but are different from messages that stand in isolation. The former are included under marketing and law; the latter are considered education.

Marketing refers to attempts to manage behavior by offering reinforcing incentives and/or consequences in an environment that invites voluntary exchange. The environment is made favorable for appropriate behavior through the development of choices with comparative advantage (products and services), favorable cost-benefit relationships (pricing), and time and place utility enhancement (channels of distribution). Positive reinforcement is provided when a transaction is completed.

Lindblom regards *exchange* as the fundamental relationship on which market systems are built; one party gives up something to get something from another party. Kotler and Roberto (1989, p. 24) define *social marketing* as "a program planning process that promotes the voluntary behavior of target audiences by offering benefits they want, reducing barriers they are concerned about, and using persuasion to motivate their participation in program activity." Marketing offers a direct and timely exchange for a desired behavior.

Law involves the use of coercion to achieve behavior in a nonvoluntary manner (e.g., military conscription) or to threaten with punishment for noncompliance or inappropriate behavior (e.g., penalties for littering). Law also can be used to increase (by the use of price subsidies) or decrease (by the use of taxes, which effectively raise prices) the probability of transactions that might not develop as desired through free-market mechanisms; in these ways, law can be used to facilitate marketing solutions. According to Black's Law Dictionary (1990, p. 884), "law, in its generic sense, is a body of rules of action or conduct prescribed by controlling authority, and having binding legal force.... That which must be obeyed and followed by citizens subject to sanctions or legal consequences is a law."

Lindblom's *authority* is similar and exists when one individual or group implicitly or explicitly, freely or by force, recognizes the control of another individual or group. Authority consists of commands backed by specific penalties that threaten to disadvantage noncompliance. Law is also similar to what Wiener and Doescher (1991) term a *structural solution,* that is, a political act that mandates individual behavior. For Taylor and Singleton (1993), the distinction between marketing and law could be that marketing works through self-monitoring and self-sanctioning after negotiating, whereas law is used as external monitoring and sanctioning when the transaction costs of marketing are too high and the community is not strong enough to reduce these costs on its own.

Although the use of law generally is thought of as coercive and punishing, the coercion also can be positive and of assistance. The use of law can force a behavior that is desirable to the target but is not viable because of pressure to conform to a different standard. In this case, the law can provide an external motivator when an internal one cannot be accepted by the target (e.g., forcing a motorcyclist to wear a motorcycle helmet by legal means can work when no individual motorcyclist would choose this option freely). Law and marketing both can offer environmental opportunities and reinforcement for behavior, but in marketing the behavior is voluntary, whereas in law it is coerced.

In still other cases, law is used to create marketing exchanges. When the law is used to set up voluntary programs such as Head Start, such action is categorized as marketing. Law (herein) is used to manage by coercive punishing of inappropriate behavior without choice; marketing manages by offering incentives and choice.[3]

Education and marketing are similar in that both propose uncoerced, free-choice behavior. In addition, marketing offers a specific timely and explicit payback, whereas education can offer only a promise of future potential payback and is unable to reinforce

---

[3]There are cases in which there is a thin line between marketing and law or in which the law is used to create an exchange situation. As with marketing, law can be used to create offerings, manage price, facilitate distribution, or disseminate messages. Many government programs that offer freely chosen exchanges are examples of products or services being created and marketed by the passage of laws.

directly. Whereas marketing offers an explicit exchange and brings it to the target, education implies that an exchange might exist but the target must search for it. Marketing adds choices to the environment, whereas education informs and persuades within the set of choices that already exist. Law is similar to marketing in that both offer exchanges in the target's environment; marketing's offerings, though, are presented with free choice that is rewarded, whereas the force of law generally imposes sanctions for noncompliance with the proffered choice. In general, the presence of a reinforcer is incentive (marketing), whereas the withholding of a reinforcer or the onset of a punishment is coercive (backed by the force of law).

Consider the following example of how the three classes of tools might be used: A social issue with behavior management implications facing many societies involves genetic testing and the opportunity to lessen the occurrence of disabilities. If society wishes such management, while also considering the rights of its citizens, should the management be through education, marketing, or law?

- With education, the government could inform and persuade citizens with respect to the value for the individual and the society of genetic testing and, for individuals with relevant genetic markers, could provide education on the value of voluntarily choosing not to have children. Education offers free choice to citizens and accepts the externality costs that would result from socially undesirable choices.

- Through the use of marketing, the government could encourage voluntary genetic testing by setting up test sites in shopping malls and, in exchange, could offer counseling on the topic of family planning using the test results and other issues of concern to the family. For those with relevant genetic markers, voluntarily choosing not to have children might be compensated for with a priority status for adoption. Marketing offers free choice and attempts to minimize externalities by offering benefits in exchange for behaviors with fewer externalities.

- Through law, the government could require genetic testing of all citizens as they approach the age of reproduction and involuntary sterilization of those who carry genes that might lead to disabilities. Failure to comply could be punished harshly. Law restricts free choice by punishing socially undesirable choices but manages behavior to minimize externality costs.

These options are presented to show the differences among, and the opportunities and limitations of, the three major classes of tools and how an evaluation of these tools is relevant to behavior management. In reality, an issue such as genetic testing probably would be managed through a combination of the three classes of tools both over time and across different targets, and the relative weighting of the tools would be a function of individual and societal values as well as macro public policy considerations.

Before integrating education, marketing, and law in a behavior management framework, some issues of marketing and political philosophy are considered in the following section.

Issues that Influence the Potential Value of Marketing in Public Health and Social Issue Behavior Management

Because many managers are not trained formally in marketing, they often tend to neglect key issues that are important in the use of a marketing perspective. An appreciation of the self-interest of the target, the benefits of an exchange, and the constraining nature of power and competition are needed if marketing is to be used successfully as a class of behavior-management tools. These issues are considered next in comparison with their use in commercial marketing.

SELF-INTEREST

In most situations, people act primarily out of self-interest; in commercial marketing, this self-interest clearly and consistently is acknowledged and pursued. In the commercial sector, managers appeal to consumers' self-perception of short- and long-run self-interest (e.g., "buy my brand and you will be better off," "buy my brand and you will feel better about yourself"). In public health and social issues, managers often ask members of the target market to behave in ways that appear to be the opposite of that member's perception of self-interest and are often the opposite of the current manifestation of that self-interest as observed through the member's current behavior. People choose to eat junk food, not exercise, smoke and drink to excess, or engage in unsafe sex because they have evaluated their own situation and environment and made a self-interested decision to behave as they do.

Primary and selective demand. Commercial managers generally seek changes in selective demand after the primary demand decision with respect to the product class already has been made. That is, the major self-interest decision with respect to the product class has been made, and only the minor brand choice decision remains. For social managers, the desired behavior is more likely to be a change in primary demand (e.g., start behaving in a way that is new; stop behaving in a way that has been enjoyable). This difference in emphasis on primary versus selective demand makes the social manager's task more difficult.

When making a selective demand decision, consumers' ambivalence is overcome fairly easily because the differences among choices are often minor. The primary demand decisions sought with respect to public health issues generate more powerful levels of ambivalence. Most people who smoke know they should stop; many people who drink to excess "hate themselves in the morning." Many smokers make primary demand decisions several times each hour; they are determined to quit after each cigarette but then are determined to have just one more when their need for nicotine builds a few minutes later. This ambivalence with respect to the primary demand decision makes public health behavior management difficult and often calls for explicit reinforcement of the behavior that is sought by the manager.[4]

---

[4]This idea was generated from the comment of an anonymous reviewer.

Although commercial and social issues differ greatly with respect to how managers accommodate self-interest, it is important to note that the targets are behaving similarly in both domains. Individuals act in their own self-interest whether they are given the opportunity to change brands or to change health-related behavior. If the individual can discern immediate self-interest in the behavior, it is more likely to occur; if there is no perceived benefit, it is less likely to occur. If the change is minor (selective demand), it is more likely to occur; if the change is major (primary demand), it is less likely to occur.

Self-interest. Mansbridge (1990) has edited a book of readings put together to show that there are determinants of behavior other than self-interest. In the introduction to *Beyond Self-interest* (p. ix), though, she states that "Self-interest explains most of human interaction in some contexts, and it explains some role in almost every context. Institutions that allow self-interest as a primary motive, like the market and majority rule, are indispensable when vast groups of people who have no other contact with one another need to coordinate their activities or make collective decisions." This article involves what happens in the vast majority of individual decisions and when self-interest may or may not be consistent with societal goals and needs.

Whereas marketing generally plays on short-run self-interest through an exchange of reinforcers, education and law play on self-interest in quite different ways. Education often recommends and encourages behaviors by promising a self-interested future return on the behavior investment; though there is no explicit exchange, there are offers of possible returns. Some education campaigns clearly show the target why there would be self-interest in behaving appropriately (e.g., "If you use a condom, you will be less likely to contract a sexually transmitted disease"), others show a societal benefit but no direct self-interest (e.g., "If you drive more slowly, the nation will have greater fuel reserves"), and others do not show either societal or individual benefit but merely present moral platitudes (e.g., "Just say no"). Some campaigns offer immediate self-interest reinforcers (e.g., "If you immunize your baby today, it will be less susceptible to a variety of childhood diseases"), whereas others offer the possibility of future self-interested rewards (e.g., "If you drink milk today, you are less likely to contract osteoporosis when you are old"). Some of these campaigns compete directly with the behavior they are trying to change (e.g., "If you don't smoke, your mouth will taste fresher; you will be more sexually attractive and cool").

Law demands nonvoluntary behavior and offers a self-interested return by promising not to punish those who behave correctly (e.g., "If you continue to drive without drinking, we will not take away your driver's license") or cease behaving incorrectly (e.g., "If you stop drinking and driving, we will reinstate your license"). In both education and law, the self-interest of the society and its managers is pursued, but it is not always clear to the target that its self-interest is being considered.

There are several bodies of literature that support the importance of considering self-interest. These include behaviorism (beginning with Skinner 1935); evolutionary psychology (Dawkins 1976; Wright 1994); the evolution of cultures, norms, and conventions (Coleman 1990; Young 1996); neoclassical economics (Block 1994; Hausmann and McPherson 1996); behavioral decision theory (Kahneman, Slovic, and Thersky 1982); and economic sociology (Coleman 1990). Work that does not support the importance of self-interest often does so by showing exceptions to its universality (Mansbridge 1990; Sober and Wilson 1998).

THE EXCHANGE

In addition to self-interest, the fundamental nature of the exchange must be considered. In commercial marketing, the payback in the transaction is defined by an implicit or explicit contract, and its timing occurs closely behind, or simultaneous to, the initial behavior of the target. With public health and social issues, the payback is often vague, uncertain, and in the distant future.

Exchange theory. Although the exchange and transaction are at the heart of marketing philosophy (Alderson 1957; Hunt 1976; Sheth, Gardner, and Garrett 1988), much of what has been called social marketing in the past has neglected the exchange (Andreasen 1994). The functionalist school of marketing thought (Alderson 1957; Sheth, Gardner, and Garrett 1988) presents a perspective that often is missing in public health behavior management.

Marketing occurs when there is an attempt to transfer value from one entity's assortment to another's for the purpose of enhancing the assortment of the first party (Alderson 1957). Alderson puts forth the idea that there must be a common stake in the survival of both sides; both sides must perceive the opportunity for enhancing their own value but also recognize that there is risk for each involved in the transaction. According to the functionalist school, each side must assume potential costs and risks to achieve potential added value, but society places the burden of costs and risks on the individual when it uses only education or law.

Timing and payback. Houston, Gassenheimer, and Maskulka (1992) raise two issues that tie directly to the transference of marketing to social and public health issues. In most cases of commercial marketing, (1) the timing of the two parts of any transaction are temporally close and (2) the payback is agreed upon explicitly and clearly by both sides. In many noncommercial cases, these conditions do not hold, and as a result, targets are reluctant to engage in the behavior being advocated.

Explicit and temporally close payback, the offer of an immediate positive behavioral reward, and accommodation of self-interest are some of the conditions that differentiate strong and weak exchanges and may result in immediate positive reinforcement. Education, marketing, and law all offer exchanges, but those in education are weak (they generally are not temporally close and do not show explicit payback), and the exchanges in law may be temporally close and explicit but generally are based on coercion and are often negative.

In many public health behavior-management cases, there is no temporally close or tangible payback in return for the behavior. For example, many individuals have made a decision, in their own perception of self-interest, to be slothful with respect to exercise and diet. The educational messages that the social manager presents ask the individual to begin to exercise and eat more vegetables while watching less television and eating fewer high-fat foods. In return, the individual is promised some vaguely lower probability of having a heart attack that may or may not occur at some undetermined time in the future. Such a message proposes an exchange that offers neither a temporally close transaction nor an explicit payback. The individual is called on to make a choice between a behavior that definitely leads to an easy-to-see, certain, immediate, pleasant outcome and a very different behavior that may lead to a less certain but longer-run pleasant outcome.

Behavior with respect to public health and social issues comes about in much the same way as it does for commercial exchanges; individuals act out of self-interest, accepting "good" deals and rejecting "bad" ones. The difference is that the public health manager often asks for behavior that is not perceived by the individual to be of self-interest. Public health issues benefit society and often benefit the individual in the long run; the problem lies in showing the individual that immediate and sometimes continuous (undesirable) behavior must take place to achieve the long-run benefit. Although education can present long-run benefits, marketing exchanges may be needed to initiate behavior, or law may be needed to overcome the perception of a lack of benefit.

POWER AND COMPETITION

A third set of commercial–social differences involves power in the relationship and competition in the marketplace. Because of the existence of competition in most commercial marketing situations, managers know that the target has the power to choose from any of the existing vendors. This consumer power leads to an accommodation of needs.

In addition, consumer apathy, or low involvement, puts more pressure on the manager to show an immediate benefit for the target; it is this logic, at least in part, that has led to the huge increase in consumer sales promotions that lead to immediate purchase behavior for frequently purchased convenience goods. Commercial marketers long have known that the nature and outcome of an exchange will be influenced strongly by the relative power of the parties (Gaski 1984), but social behavior managers often seem to make implicit assumptions about the extent of their own power when they represent society or an agency thereof. This assumption is manifested through the choice of education or law as the preferred tools of behavior management, as managers fail to recognize that in a free-choice society, they actually have little power.

As a group, apathetic, or low-involvement, individuals in the target population have tremendous latent power to extract benefits from the society in return for desirable behavior and curtailment of externalities (Coleman 1990). Because the locus of actual power (the individual) is recognized by managers to be different from the locus of apparent power (government), the need for tools that work differently than those of law and education becomes more necessary. On the individual's side of the ledger, apathy is a strong source of power. The greater the value of the exchange for one side, the more power can be brought to bear by the other through its seeming apathy (Coleman 1990). Although apathetic individuals often do not realize the power they have and may be too disorganized to use it, managers must respond to this latent power if they are to achieve their goals. In this situation, an implicit form of negotiation takes place that consists of rejection of offers by the apathetic individuals until the manager creates an exchange that is worthy of attention.

Many social managers are equally presumptuous when they assume that they are operating in an environment devoid of competition; free choice, apathy, and inertia are powerful competitive forces that often are ignored. Social managers must recognize that there is always competition. For every choice there is an alternative: to be or not to be, to binge drink or drink in moderation, to exercise or remain a "couch potato." In a free-choice society, many laws are not followed if the target cannot discern the reward in doing so.

Dickson (1992) discusses the invisible hand of competition that constrains the self-interest of the firm and forces the firm to serve the interests of customers so that the value of behavior opportunities will be recognized. The result of recognition of power and competition in the marketplace leads to a greater balance between buyer and seller, which calls for mutual accommodation.

Issues of Public Policy Philosophy that Relate to Public Health and Social Issue Behavior Management

Managers also must consider the normative macro issues of political philosophy within which their micro level management is to be considered. These issues center on the rights and responsibilities of the individual and the society, when the individual lives in a free-choice society, and when the individual's actions may create externalities (costs) that affect other individuals without their explicit agreement (Buchanan 1971).

FREE CHOICE AND EXTERNALITIES

A classic example of this trade-off involves the right of the state to impose helmet laws on motorcycle riders versus the right of the individual to ride without a helmet. If the society allows free choice, it must be prepared to accept the externalities that come from the increased health costs that accompany accidents when riders have not worn helmets. If the society wishes to limit externalities, it must be prepared to limit free choice as well. Should the state impose helmet sanctions through law, should it try to educate and persuade its citizens to wear helmets, or should it develop an exchange that allows citizens the opportunity to go without helmets but imposes all health care costs back on the helmetless individual (or his or her insurance provider) through an exchange contract?

THE TRAGEDY OF THE COMMONS

A large subset of the cases dealing with these trade-offs of free choice and externalities involves the issue of overuse of a limited resource. Freely choosing to use a limited resource can lead to externalities as the resource is exhausted. The classic example here involves a common grazing area: Each unit of the community pursues personal self-interest by adding one more head of cattle to its own herd to increase its own fortune, but when each continues to add cattle, the common area becomes overgrazed and all suffer. Although each has acted rationally and with self-interest, the collective actions are tragic for the community.

This scenario first was presented by Lloyd (1833) as a rebuttal to Adam Smith's notion of the invisible hand that promotes the public interest through increased competition and capitalism (Smith 1776). Some behaviors that are individually uninhibited but collectively costly include behaving in an unhealthy manner (e.g., smoking, drinking excessively, having a high-fat diet), having large families, polluting, and littering. When society is asked to fund the health care needs of those with unhealthy lifestyles, these behaviors yield eternality costs for other citizens and taxpayers. How does a society manage population growth, moderation in alcohol consumption, or sensibility in diet and exercise? Hardin (1968) notes that these sorts of issues cannot be controlled in the long run by appeals to conscience (education). In the short run, some members of society may restrain their use of the commons, but in the long run, they will see that others are taking advantage of their good nature. As a result, over time more members of society will act in their own self-interests to the detriment of the greater good.

To balance this, Hardin (1968) suggests that there must be costs associated with the use of the commons such that the costs will lead to proper behavior. This can be done, for example, by increasing the tax burden for families as they continue to have children or taxing alcohol usage at a level that develops funds to pay for the health care costs associated with its abuse (law). Conversely, children from small families can be offered college scholarship subsidies that are not made available to children from larger families (marketing). Hardin's initial work has led to a vast literature and many studies involving the conditions in which his model holds.

SOCIAL DILEMMAS AND SOCIAL TRAPS

Social dilemmas (Dawes 1980; Wiener and Doescher 1991) are characterized as situations in which each individual receives a higher payoff for a socially defecting choice, but all individuals are better off if all cooperate than if all defect. For example, there is a net benefit to society when all citizens recycle, even though each citizen is inconvenienced by the activity; if no one recycles, all suffer the costs of a larger waste management problem.

Social traps (Dawes 1980) occur when a behavior that results in a short-term benefit leads to a long-term cost. There are many health issues for which individuals can find short-run benefit in not behaving in a cooperative manner (e.g., smoking, drinking, having a poor diet, not exercising), but these behaviors often lead to long-term individual costs and also impose future health care costs on the society.

In addition, individuals may perceive themselves as playing the role of the sucker when others are not behaving appropriately or when they are giving up the opportunity to be a free rider (Messick and Brewer 1983). Information asymmetry and monitoring problems often make it easy to defect and free ride. Many social issues have these characteristics; some, such as recycling, provide little direct personal benefit to the individual regardless of effort, whereas others, such as health issues, have the potential to provide personal payback over time. Society must consider these tragedies, dilemmas, and traps in the development of fair and compassionate policy, as well as of workable micro level strategies.

WHAT ARE SOME OF THE RIGHTS AND RESPONSIBILITIES OF THE STATE?

In the present context, it commonly is agreed that the (democratic) state has the right and responsibility not only to protect the rights of free choice of its citizens, but also to protect them from the externalities caused by others. The difficult judgments arise when considering the level of externalities that society should accept, the level at which it must protect others from these externalities, and the level of free choice it wishes to maintain.

WHAT ARE SOME OF THE RIGHTS AND RESPONSIBILITIES OF THE INDIVIDUAL?

The individual's rights and responsibilities (in democratic states) include the right to free choice, tempered with the responsibility to not impose externalities on others through either active creation of costs or being a free rider. In addition, individuals have the right to be free of externalities caused by others. This balance is difficult, as it is often in each individual's self-interest to allow externalities to be imposed on others, to be a free rider, and to not pay a fair share for services received. When each individual acts with self-interest (micro motivations), society overall may suffer to the point at which no individual is able to be maximally efficient (macro behaviors) (Schelling 1978).

There are many philosophies of government that consider these conflicts between the individual and the state. *Paternalism* operates from the view that the state knows what is best for the individual; it then imposes this knowledge on its constituents. Paternalism has been described as actions by society for the benefit of the individual without the consent of, or contrary to the wishes of, the individual (Brock 1983). *Libertarianism* operates from the view that the individual knows what is best and should be left alone to make choices freely. Libertarianism allows free choice and maximum liberty, but there is a resulting concern that free choice will lead to greater externalities as individuals make choices that impose costs on others.

The three classes of management tools map onto these philosophies as follows: Education clearly offers free choice when it is used to inform and/or persuade, but also can lead to greater externalities when citizens choose not to act as managers wish. If a libertarian were to allow any form of governmental intervention, it would be through informative education. Education suggests society's view of the individual's self-interest to the individual. Law is clearly coercive; even if used with the best of intentions, it would be a tool of a paternalistic government and would limit free choice to control externalities. Law imposes society's view of the individual's self-interest on the individual.

What, though, is marketing? One view is that marketing offers free-choice opportunities in a competitive environment by providing incentives that can be accepted or rejected within the environment. Another view is that marketing presents a package that is so appealing as to be coercive and, therefore, reduces choice and manipulates behavior. A third view is that marketing assesses the individual's self-interest and makes behavioral opportunities available that satisfy that self-interest; in the resulting exchange, the individual gives up a behavior that leads to the externalities and receives satisfaction of self-interested needs.

What Is Marketing, and How Does It Differ from Education and Force of Law?

The previous literature and discussion lead to the following definition of marketing:

> Marketing consists of voluntary exchange between two or more parties, in which each is trying to further its own perceived self-interest while recognizing the need to accommodate the perceived self-interest of the other to achieve its own ends.

This definition is based explicitly on the self-interest and behaviorist notions that emerge from several of the basic disciplines that have had a great impact on marketing. It is an extension of the marketing concept, which "holds that achieving organizational goals depends on determining the needs and wants of target markets and delivering the desired satisfactions more effectively and efficiently than competitors do" (Kotler and Armstrong 1994, p. G-6). Organizations succeed (i.e., fulfill their own self-interests) by assessing and meeting needs (i.e., accommodate the self-interest of the other). The definition of marketing presented here is consistent with Alderson's (1957) and Dickson's (1992) writings.

Marketers attempt to manage behavior by creating alternative choices in the target's environment that lead to voluntary self-interested exchange. Direct immediate positive reinforcement in the self-interest of the target is given when a transaction is completed or consumption occurs. Marketing is used in an attempt to assess and meet needs and to create a direct free-market exchange between the manager and the target with the greatest efficiency for each party. This separates marketing from education and law.

Education assesses and discusses needs but urges the targets to figure out how to meet their own needs. Education is used to assist targets by helping them realize their needs and be motivated to pursue them, but it cannot be used to satisfy needs because it offers no direct rewards.

Law operates in at least two ways: It is used (1) to assess needs and then force some endogenous subset of the environment to behave in a way that enables the target to meet its needs and (2) to force target behavior to meet the manager's own needs. When used in the first way, law is close to marketing in accommodating the self-interests of a target, though it does so at the expense of creating potential inefficiency for some other entity that is forced to behave to accommodate the manager and the target. (See, for example, the case of iodized salt discussed in P_2 in the section "A Conceptual Framework for Public Health and Social Issue Behavior Management.") The exchange in law is indirect and/or potentially inefficient, in that it forces either a third party to accommodate a need that was not pursued in the past or the target to behave inefficiently for the benefit of the manager.

Another way to consider differences among education, marketing, and law is in relation to the congruence of preexisting self-interests held by the target and the manager. Education will be an appropriate tool when individual self-interest is strong and consistent with societal goals but the target merely is uninformed; in such cases, no additional reinforcement is necessary. For example, in the 1970s it was discovered that aspirin taken to relieve the symptoms of chicken pox caused Reyes' Syndrome in some children. By educating parents about this finding, the incidence of the syndrome almost was eliminated. Marketing will be appropriate when the level of self-interest is insufficiently consistent with societal goals to elicit behavior. For example, the Peruvian government wishes to control births, but merely educating the population has not been sufficient to gain the desired result; the government now has begun to offer an exchange of clothing, food, and money to women who agree to voluntary sterilization. Law will be appropriate when the preexisting self-interest of the target cannot be overcome with additional rewards through exchange, when rewarding is inconsistent with societal goals, or when the rights of the target are believed to be irrelevant. For example, California now has 90% compliance to seat belt laws, whereas the overall U.S. compliance level is 70%. Some believe this higher level is due to stricter enforcement of laws that permit spot checks of drivers.

COSTS AND BENEFITS OF THE ISSUE

Rangan, Karim, and Sandberg (1996) present a 2 × 2 matrix that considers costs versus benefits and suggests another perspective for the issues at hand. It could be inferred from the matrix that the more favorable the individual cost–benefit relationship (low cost; tangible, personal benefits), the more likely that education will be sufficient. Similarly, the less favorable the individual cost–benefit relationship (high cost; intangible, societal benefits), the more likely that law will be needed. The middle cases (mixed costs and benefits) would be most likely to use marketing solutions to improve the cost–benefit relationship.

A Conceptual Framework for Public Health and Social Issue Behavior Management

In this section, education, marketing, and the force of law are considered from a micro normative managerial application perspective within the context of the prior macro public policy discussion. In considering any public health or social issue, a target may be prone, resistant, or unable to accommodate the manager's goals. The selection of tools to be used in the management of any target will be a function of where the target is perceived to be in this set.

MacInnis, Moorman, and Jaworski (1991) have presented a model of information processing of advertising in which *motivation, opportunity*, and *ability* (MOA) influence consumers' level of processing and shed light on the sort of tactics that might be useful in developing an advertising campaign. These components are modified here to have value for the management of public health and social issues. Tactics can be developed to match existing levels of MOA or enhance the probability of achieving future desired levels of MOA.

A target will be more prone to accept the manager's goals if it is easy for that target to discern the self-interest in changing or if it is easy for the manager to convey this point. Conversely, a target will be resistant or unable to accommodate the manager's goals if one or more of the set of MOA are lacking.

Figure 1 presents an overview of the relationship among (1) targets who are prone, resistant, or unable to accommodate the manager's goals; (2) the target's MOA; and (3) the use of the tools of education, marketing, and law. Figure 1 shows the eight segments of any market that result from the combinations of the presence or absence of MOA and in what conditions education, marketing, or law can be superior at achieving the manager's goals of obtaining appropriate behavior from a variety of targets.

The first three propositions consider MOA separately. Motivation is goal-directed arousal (MacInnis, Moorman, and Jaworski 1991; Park and Mittal 1985). Individuals are motivated to behave when they can discern that their self-interest will be served. As such, self-interest is a strong component of motivation.[5] For many issues, there is no inherent

---

[5]The term self-interest has been used previously in this article because it is used commonly in the literature being referenced. Motivation is the more common term of choice in the consumer behavior literature.

FIGURE 1

Applications of Education, Marketing, and Law

MOTIVATION	yes		no	
OPPORTUNITY	yes	no	yes	no
ABILITY yes	① prone to behave *education*	② unable to behave *marketing*	③ resistant to behave *law*	④ resistant to behave *marketing, law*
no	⑤ unable to behave *education, marketing*	⑥ unable to behave *education, marketing*	⑦ resistant to behave *education, marketing, law*	⑧ resistant to behave *education, marketing, law*

motivation to comply because there is no perception of the potential accommodation of self-interest. An analogous situation in profit marketing exists when brands in a product class are perceived to be similar. Advertising may have a slight impact, but a larger impact results from sales promotions (Tellis 1988). Therefore, the following is proposed:

> P_1: Motivation to act voluntarily will be increased slightly through education by discussing self-interest or increased moderately by accommodating self-interest through marketing. Law will be called on when the target cannot be motivated to act voluntarily.

Lack of opportunity includes situations in which the individual wants to act but is unable to do so because there is no environmental mechanism at hand. For example, students who binge drink on college campuses located in small towns often complain that they do so because there just is not anything else to do on the weekend. Marketing could lead to the introduction of alternative forms of recreation to compete with binge drinking. P_2 is based, in part, on the previous discussion of exchange.

Situations in which there is lack of opportunity also can be overcome by use of law. Marks (1997) presents a case in which South Africans in rural areas and townships traditionally did not have ready access to iodized salt because it was only distributed in urban areas, where demand was higher. Free-market incentives for manufacturers to market iodized as well as regular table salt to these poor segments did not exist. Regulations to iodize all salt were passed in 1995, and though consumer motivation (nonurban residents' demand) had not been addressed by policymakers, mandating opportunity led to universal usage of the healthier alternative. It follows that

> P₂: Although education will make the target aware of existing opportunities, it cannot create opportunity; opportunity can be created through marketing or indirectly through law.

Ability to act is the third element of MacInnis, Moorman, and Jaworski's (1991) model and is referred to as consumers' skills or proficiencies in interpreting brand information in an advertisement (see also Alba and Hutchinson 1987). In the present case, ability refers to individual skill or proficiency at solving problems and may include breaking a well-formed or addictive habit or countering the arguments of peers. Another relevant determinant of ability comes from Bandura's (1997) self-efficacy theory, in which those with high expectancies of personal achievement show greater abilities on a variety of tasks that relate to personal and public health issues.

P₃ is based, in part, on the preceding discussion of power and competition. A dominant competitor can impede the ability of the target to behave, either directly or through the peer group. For example, teenagers in a drug-prone environment often talk about their inability to resist the pressure put on them by their friends. It is proposed, therefore, that

> P₃: The ability to behave can be developed through education; marketing will assist in imparting ability by reinforcing a newly developed skill. The force of law may frustrate a target who is unable to act or does not have the ability to make appropriate choices.

Returning to Figure 1, a target is totally receptive to the goals of the manager and prone to behave appropriately only when MOA are all present (cell 1). In such a case, education will be sufficient to manage behavior; the target wishes to act, knows how to act, and can find the environmental mechanisms to do so. The power of competition would be minimal with respect to this target; the target only needs to be reminded to engage in the proper manner. In cases in which opportunity is missing (cell 2), marketing may be sufficient to gain behavior by introducing a product/service into the environment that enables the target to manifest its motivation and ability. Similarly, if only ability is missing (cell 5), education and/or marketing may be sufficient to teach the target how to behave and pursue its motivation through existing opportunities. When motivation exists but cannot be executed, there should be no need for the use of law. Self-interest will drive the target to the proper behavior when the hurdles associated with lack of ability and lack of opportunity are removed.

A target is resistant to the manager's goals when motivation does not exist, regardless of existing opportunities or abilities. In the extreme case in which there is opportunity and ability but no motivation (cell 3), it may be necessary to resort to the law to manage behavior. In cases in which opportunity also is missing (cell 4), marketing should be attempted before law is used. Similarly, if ability is missing (cell 7), education and marketing may be sufficient and should be used before law. Often when opportunity and ability problems are remedied, motivation follows; in these cases, it may be proper for the manager to resist the temptation to resort quickly to the use of law.

Figure 1 can be used to segment a market. Consider, for example, binge drinking on college campuses. It has been proposed (Saur 1998) that students who become binge drinkers almost always do so shortly after arriving on campus as freshmen; as they mature, many give up their bingeing habits during their junior and senior years. The manager's goals here are to minimize the number of freshmen who begin to binge drink and to maximize the number of juniors and seniors who become more moderate and responsible drinkers. In this case, there is a self-interested need to belong, explore identity, and experiment with new-found independence. Easy access to alcohol provides strong competition, and the university has little power to control behavior easily. The benefits of binge drinking tie directly and immediately to self-interested needs, and the benefits of moderation and/or abstention often are presented as vague and distant. Binge drinking has become a serious problem because secondary effects—such as damage to property, sexual harassment, drunk driving, unprotected sex, and, occasionally, death—lead to unacceptable levels of externalities. The following example involves the onset of freshmen binge drinking.

Students in cell 1 only need to be reminded not to binge drink; they will be receptive to educational messages. Cell 2 students know they should not binge and are motivated not to do so but cannot find other recreational opportunities; therefore, they binge. Offering a midnight intramural basketball league on Friday and Saturday nights provides one example of alternative opportunity. Cell 5 students also know they should not binge, are motivated not to do so, and know that midnight basketball is available; however, they do not have the ability to tell their friends that they would rather play ball than drink. They continue to drink because they do not want to be perceived as socially deviant; they need to develop the ability to stand up to their peers. This is a task to be accomplished through education and then reinforced through the good feelings that come from, for example, playing ball. Cell 6 combines the issues of cells 2 and 5. The members of cells 2, 5, and 6 are motivated to comply with the goals of the manager but need help in doing so. Marketing and/or education can provide this help and aid in reducing externalities.

In cell 3, students are quite happy with their binge drinking behavior; they see no need to change even though they are in an environment that offers choice and they have the ability to change their behavior. Marketing and education tactics may have been presented in the past, but behavior has not changed. In this case, law is necessary if it is important to manage behavior. Cells 4, 7, and 8 correspond to cells 2, 5, and 6, respectively. Education and marketing are appropriate here and should be used before relying on the law. Cell 4 students may have no motivation to stop bingeing because there are no alternative forms of recreation available to them. Cell 7 students may have no motivation to stop because they do not have the ability to deal with the resultant social situation within their peer group. Marketing and/or education interventions indirectly may create motivation and remove the need to use law.

Public health and social issue cases such as binge drinking currently may overuse education and law. The power of education is limited because it does not offer a short-run reinforcing exchange of self-interest; though this is not an issue when the target is clearly receptive to the goals of the manager, it may be that managers are relying on education in cases in which the target is lacking in opportunity and/or ability.

Another explanation (which does not seem appropriate to binge drinking) would hold that the cells in which there is no motivation are dominated by a lack of awareness, and that by using education to raise awareness, motivation would result. Such a case would exist if education had been underused.

In other cases, managers may overrely on the force of law. Although there clearly are cases in which the only way to achieve appropriate behavior is to use the law, there are also cases in which an unnecessary overuse of the law leads to resentment. College students do not seem to be drinking less as a result of relevant laws, but they are becoming more resentful of their universities and the local police for enforcing these laws. In some recent cases, this resentment has led to rioting and property damage. Marketing provides opportunity, and with the onset of opportunity, motivation may increase.

The previous discussion presents various scenarios in which only education, marketing, or law dominates. The real world is, of course, not that simple, and as a result, the manager will need to consider the proper ordering with which to bring these tools to bear on a situation. For example, in cell 5, education and marketing will be used most often to manage students who have motivation and opportunity but no ability to reject binge drinking. There are, though, cases in which law may be appropriate if education and marketing do not work. Consider the case in which pressure is so great that students need some outside force to prohibit them from behaving, so that they do not lose face with peers. Ability to behave appropriately can be enhanced when the target is forced to do the right thing. It may be more comfortable to behave and be able to blame the law than it is to behave and be ridiculed by peers.

Similarly, the segments in cells 4, 7, and 8 can be pursued with marketing and/or education strategies. If the resulting opportunity and ability does not raise motivation, the legal strategies used in cell 3 can be brought to bear; if motivation increases with the onset of opportunity, the education strategies of cell 1 can be brought to bear.

OTHER VARIABLES INFLUENCING THE SELECTION OF EDUCATION, MARKETING, AND LAW

There are many other variables that can influence managers in their selection of education, marketing, and/or law as classes of strategic tools. The following sections suggest several of these.

Current usage as an indicator of readiness to behave. Targets who are not yet engaging in an unwanted behavior may be more prone to exhibit the desired behavior; these targets are more likely to be found in cell 1 of Figure 1. Those currently engaged in the unwanted behavior will be more resistant to change; they will have less motivation to change and will be less able to do so. These targets are more likely to be in cells 7 and 8 but also might be in cells 3 and 4. For example, Hankin and colleagues (1993) show that warning labels on alcohol beverages decreased consumption during pregnancy for light drinkers but had no effect on women who drank more heavily at the time of conception. Therefore, the following is proposed:

P_4: Those who are not engaging in a socially undesirable behavior will be more receptive to continuing the desired behavior and more responsive to education, whereas those who are behaving, realizing the benefits of the previously selected reinforcing behavior, will be more resistant and more likely to need marketing or law to effect a change.

Level of competition. The more passive the competitive choice, the more likely it is that education can be a sufficient tool for eliciting the desired behavior. For example, there are few strong arguments to be made against childhood immunizations; when parents of young children are urged to get their children immunized, most parents respond appropriately (cell 1). There are, though, some parents for whom apathy can be a competitive force that subverts action. In these cases, marketing may be more appropriate (perhaps through channels tactics that would make immunizations more easily available, or through sales promotions) (cells 2 and, perhaps, 6). In other cases, parents may oppose immunization on religious or philosophic grounds; now the competition can be regarded as severe, and force of law may be needed to achieve the desired behavior. In these cases there are, for example, laws requiring immunization before children can begin school (cells 3 and, perhaps, 7). The diffusion of innovation literature (Rogers 1962) provides strategies for cases in which competition is passive or moderate. Therefore, the following is proposed:

P_5: When competition is passive, education may be sufficient; as the competition of other behavioral options, or of apathy, intensifies, a more obvious exchange will be needed, and marketing should be called on. As the power of the alternative behavior choice intensifies even more, marketing no longer will achieve the desired result, and the force of law will become appropriate.

Developing a target of critical mass. There are behaviors that can be influenced by pursuing one individual at a time (e.g., spousal abuse), whereas with other issues, behavior will not occur until all in the target agree to change at the same time. Schelling (1978) uses the example of professional hockey players who would wear helmets but cannot do so until all are forced to do so, lest their macho image be lessened. It may be more difficult to stop a single student from binge drinking and deviating from peer norms than it would be to manage the behavior of the entire group. Those who may not have the ability to resist the group's norms individually (cells 5–8), may be able to behave collectively (at least in cells 5 and 6).

A related issue deals with the free rider problem; an individual will be reluctant to behave if there is a perception that this will allow others to free ride off that behavior. Education may lead to enough people volunteering, but marketing and law can provide an exchange so that those behaving appropriately will feel rewarded; pricing that rewards prudence and penalizes flagrancy provides a marketing solution that offsets the advantages otherwise accruing to free riders. Soda and beer bottle and can deposits attempt to serve this purpose. Free riders are most likely to be found in cells 3, 4, 7, and 8.

Force of law may be needed to produce a critical mass when individuals do not have the opportunity or ability to act alone. Although citizens could be told of the virtues of fluoridating their own water or given the opportunity to buy fluoride powder to sprinkle in each glass of water, a law that forces the provision of fluoridated water to all may be a more efficient way to provide opportunity. Cells 3, 4, 7, and 8 contain individuals who are resistant to being part of the critical mass needed in these cases. Individuals in cells 1, 2, 5, and 6 are unable to effect behavior without the cooperation of those who are resistant.

Although individuals in small groups are often willing to make sacrifices to help one another, this is less likely to happen in larger, more heterogeneous communities (Schelling 1978). A consideration of social dilemmas and social traps (Dawes 1980) plays an important role here. Some efficient choices are self-sustaining through education after they are discovered, but others need the incentives of a marketing exchange or the coercion of law to be maintained.

When the target of critical mass consists of the entire community, the force of law is used to protect the majority from an aberrant minority. An extreme example occurred when Sweden changed its legal driving side from left to right. Although education could be used to manage those who would make the proper free-choice decision, the law could threaten to punish those for whom free choice was inadequate. Therefore,

P_6: When individuals can respond to the manager's goals without feeling that they are at a disadvantage relative to others in the community, marketing and education should be used. If a critical mass of support is needed, marketing or law will be required. If the entire market must behave simultaneously, law will be required.

Sharing community costs and benefits. Related to the preceding proposition is the perceived share of the community cost imposed on, and the benefit to be garnered by, the individual. The greater the perception of a payoff, the easier it will be for the individual to behave. For example, parents generally will support a bond drive to pay for a swimming pool for the local school; others in the community will support the pool if they are given an exchange that offers them the opportunity to use it outside classroom hours. Other members of the community reluctantly will pay taxes to support it when the first two groups have enough votes to force a bond issue on them. Behavior is most likely to occur when there is a payoff to the individual and those most similar to him or her (Olson 1965). Those who are most supportive of the issue are likely to be in cell 1; those most resistant are in cells 3, 4, 7, and 8; and members of 4, 7, and 8 may be managed by allowing them the opportunity and/or ability to share in the benefits. P_7 returns to a consideration of the importance of self-interest and provides more depth to the issues of motivation and self-interest presented in P_1:

> P_7: When individuals perceive that they will receive a large share of the community benefit (and/or some nonsocial benefit), education will suffice to manage behavior. When individuals perceive that they will receive a share of the community benefit, marketing will be used if it can provide additional benefit. Law will be used when individuals perceive they will receive a very small or no share of the community benefit, with no opportunity to share in any future benefits.

In addition to the preceding issues, it also is necessary to consider the sequencing of the movement of a target across the cells of Figure 1. For example, as members of cell 4 are given opportunities to behave and are made aware of them, they may move to cells 3 or 1. Those in cell 1 are now prone to behave and will respond to an educational push, but those who remain unmotivated, despite now having both opportunity and ability, will move to cell 3 and should face the threat of legal intervention.

Consider that the level of smoking in the United States decreased from approximately 40% of the population to approximately 20% in the past 25 years. The reduction was mostly in response to a tremendous education effort, which did an excellent job on the members of cells 1 and 5. As managers continued in their attempts to reduce smoking levels, it was necessary to concentrate more on the other cells with stronger legal efforts, such as forbidding smoking in public buildings and commercial establishments. The future may bring other legal and marketing efforts.

How Public Policy Issues Affect the Use of the Conceptual Framework

Democratic societies have an ongoing concern with the balance of free choice and externalities. Although the philosophy of marketing can provide a compromise position between the extremes of paternalism and libertarianism, the practice of marketing often is neglected in favor of education and law when such considerations are made. Marketing can offer a middle ground by allowing exchange through management of the environment (paternalism), as well as free choice and accommodation of self-interest (libertarianism). Trade-offs between individual and societal needs and rights create behavior management difficulties. This allocation of rights is central to the functioning of any social system as the questions of who acquires what and who gives up what are considered (Coleman 1990). The following section considers several variables that might yield insight into the relationships between the philosophies and tools discussed previously and leads to several propositions.

PROPOSITIONS RELATED TO PUBLIC POLICY

Predicted level of externalities. Selection of a tool of behavior management will depend on the externalities predicted to result from the behavior. For example, drug abuse may be believed to have unacceptable externalities because of the perceptions of related crime or lack of productivity in the workforce, so there are laws to manage its abuse. Alcohol abuse, in contrast, may be believed to have lower externalities, so policymakers have passed less severe laws and advocate education to inform and persuade relevant populations as to appropriate behavior. The predicted and tolerable level of externalities for tobacco use have changed dramatically in the past years, and as a result, policy with respect to managing tobacco usage behavior also has changed. The relationship of behavior management and externalities has a long history in political philosophy under the concept of "harm to others" (Feinberg 1984; Mill 1859). Therefore,

> P$_8$: If externalities are predicted to be low, a policy advocating education will be sufficient. Conversely, government will impose itself through the force of law when the predicted cost to society of an undesired individual behavior is high. Marketing will be used when neither extreme exists.

Whose rights dominate? In a free-choice society, individual rights dominate unless there is a compelling reason to favor the state (Feinberg 1984). For example, in many democratic countries (other than the United States), individuals are not believed to have strong rights with respect to drinking and driving; therefore, strong laws protect other motorists. In the United States, the rights of individual drinkers are of greater concern, with the result that laws are weaker and greater emphasis is placed on education. Therefore,

> P$_9$: If the issue is perceived to be one in which the rights of the greater society dominate, managers will turn to a strong legal system, but without this perception, education or marketing will be used.

Locus of power. When managers perceive that they have power, they have less need to offer an exchange. It is only when they perceive a lessening of their own relative power that they would engage in a transaction that involves compromise. P$_{10}$ is derived from the previous discussion of power:

> P$_{10}$: If managers perceive that they have power, they will use either force of law or education. If power is balanced between the society and the individual, or resides with the individual, the manager will need to offer an exchange and will call on the use of marketing.

Homogeneity and behavior management. In their work on collective action problems and transaction costs, Taylor and Singleton (1993) propose that the stronger the community, the less need there is for institutions that manage behavior (and their costs) or for outside forces to enforce and coerce behavior. This model suggests that more homogeneous communities can manage with education, but as homogeneity breaks down, more formal exchange relationships are needed, and eventually laws must be enforced to solve collective problems. As communities get larger and less homogeneous, there is less reliance on education, though solutions still can be negotiated through cooperation (marketing?). As still more individuals enter the community with different self-interests, there is ever less cooperation, and managers rely more heavily on law.

Similarly, Ouchi (1980) considers the transactions costs of clans, markets, and bureaucracies and posits that clans are efficient when goal incongruence is low and performance ambiguity is high; markets are efficient when goal incongruence is high and performance ambiguity is low. Bureaucracies are efficient when both goal incongruity and performance ambiguity are high. As Taylor and Singleton (1993) do, Ouchi concludes that members of a closely knit community are more prone to behave as per the group norms and will do so in response to education. Congruence of goals is most likely to occur when there is overlap in self-interest. Therefore,

> P_{11}: The most homogeneous communities will manage behavior primarily through the use of education, moderately homogeneous communities manage with marketing, and the least homogeneous communities will rely on law to manage behavior.

WHAT DOES MARKETING OFFER PUBLIC POLICY?

In an era of increasing political centrism and economic deregulation, marketing offers a philosophic and pragmatic middle ground. In an era of increasing individual self-interested demands, decreasing homogeneity, and diminished respect for government, marketing offers the philosophy of exchange. Marketing may offer a philosophic middle ground between paternalism and libertarianism on several dimensions. It offers free choice, while also offering behavior management through environmental changes.

Marketing offers a mechanism to find a cooperative balance between the rights of the individual and the rights of society. By operating through free choice, marketing protects the rights of the individual, because none is forced to accept the societal offering. Marketing assists society in achieving its rights by offering an incentive to the citizenry to behave in a societally appropriate manner. Ultimately, marketing offers free choice, consistent with the philosophies of both capitalism and democratic processes, as well as with the American mythic philosophy of rugged individualism.

Some Concluding Thoughts

This research has brought together several disparate themes with the goals of creating a conceptual framework for social marketing and of showing that social marketing is unique in relation both to commercial marketing and to education and the force of law. Within this framework, the manager can consider variables relevant to the selection of education, marketing, and law as sets of tools that can be brought to bear on the management of public health and social issue behaviors. The article continues with a consideration of the decline and reemergence of marketing philosophy in social marketing.

THE DECLINE OF MARKETING PHILOSOPHY IN SOCIAL MARKETING

Social marketing emerged in the late 1960s and 1970s from the work of Bagozzi (1978), Kotler and Levy (1969), Kotler and Zaltman (1971), Rothschild (1979), and Shapiro (1973), among others. In this literature, the core concept of marketing was perceived as the exchange (Bagozzi 1978; Kotler and Levy 1969) or the transaction (Kotler 1972) and was regarded as being in the self-interest of both the manager and the target (Shapiro 1973). Although this focus remains at the core of commercial marketing, many who claim to practice social marketing have drifted far afield from this philosophic base.

Many policymakers and social marketing managers now seem to regard social marketing as consisting of educational (informative and/or persuasive) messages and seem to be unaware that the core concept of marketing resides in the exchange (Andreasen 1995). It is possible that this shift in focus has occurred in large part because most social marketing managers come from a public health or mass communications background, and few have had broad training in marketing. William Smith (1993), one of the leading practitioners of social marketing, has said that "the problem with social marketing practice is clear, there is often little or no marketing."[6]

"Social marketing" has become a generic term that encompasses education and marketing but too often has been co-opted by education. Without a clear commitment to a social marketing that is rooted in the philosophy of the exchange, the field will remain focused on education and communications, but exchange and transactions are necessary and important in a framework of behavior management. Education should be used when no explicit exchange is possible or necessary or when the target is prone to behave appropriately without the development of an exchange; marketing should be used when the target is unlikely to behave as desired without receiving something (tangible or intangible) in return.

THE REEMERGENCE OF MARKETING PHILOSOPHY IN BEHAVIOR MANAGEMENT

When used properly, education, marketing, and law can help move the target from its current state to that of the manager's goal. To do so, managers must have a good understanding of and accommodate the target's MOAs and the trade-off of free choice and externalities.

The potential for success of the three sets of tools is derived from the target's assessment of the "risk premium" (Ouchi 1980) associated with an action. When this is close

---

[6]To support this point, a search of the PSYCLIT database 1991–1997 was conducted using "social marketing" as the keyword. There were 32 articles; 6 of them used marketing in the way that this article has separated marketing from education. At the 1997 Innovations in Social Marketing Conference, 6 of 18 papers discussed marketing; in 1998, 10 of 25 did so.

to zero, education will be sufficient to elicit behavior; when the risk premium is low to moderate, marketing-based exchanges can compensate for the cost of the risk; when it is too high, law often is needed because the manager is unable to compensate for the risk premium. The goals of the manager should be to reduce the perception of the risk premium (education), compensate for the risk premium (marketing), and force behavior so that no individual can take advantage of another's incurred risk premium (law).

As Weibe (1951) noted almost 50 years ago, it is difficult to sell brotherhood like soap. When marketers sell soap, they have a product that has certain benefits; when they advertise, they can refer buyers to these benefits. Too often, managers of public health behaviors, in effect, tell the target to stop being dirty or threaten to fine those who remain dirty, rather than offering the target a brand of soap and a rationale as to why the soap's benefits and rewards are superior to remaining dirty. To sell brotherhood like soap, there must be soap; however, in too many cases there is no immediately apparent soap, and as a consequence, it is difficult to show why behavior should occur.

Developing social marketing to its next level of growth and contribution calls for a wider focus on behavior management. The current focus leads managers to biases that are based on their backgrounds and the singular choice of education, marketing, or force of law as a paradigm of choice. Each paradigm has a role to play in behavior management; behavior management must be considered from the pragmatic reality created by targets and environments (What are the MOAs?), coupled with the normative perspective of policy development (How should society address a particular issue?).

In the early 1970s, it was said that the question was not whether to do social marketing but rather whether to do it well or poorly. Because all societies attempt to manage the behavior of their citizens at some level, the question now is not whether to manage public health and social issue behavior but rather how to do so appropriately.

References

Alba, Joseph W. and J. Wesley Hutchinson (1987), "Dimensions of Consumer Expertise," *Journal of Consumer Research,* 13 (March), 411–54.

Alderson, Wroe (1957), *Marketing Behavior and Executive Action: A Functionalist Approach to Marketing Theory.* Homewood, IL: Richard D. Irwin.

Andreasen, Alan R. (1994), "Social Marketing: Its Definition and Domain," *Journal of Public Policy & Marketing,* 13 (Spring), 108–14.

___ (1995), *Marketing Social Change.* San Francisco, CA: Jossey-Bass Publishers.

Bagozzi, Richard P. (1978), "Marketing as Exchange: A Theory of Transactions in the Marketplace," *American Behavioral Scientist,* 21 (March/April), 535–56.

Bandura, Albert (1997), *Self-Efficacy: The Exercise of Control.* New York: W.H. Freeman and Company.

Black's Law Dictionary (1990), 6th ed. St. Paul, MN: West Publishing Co.

Block, Fred (1994), "The Roles of the State in the Economy," in *The Handbook of Economic Sociology,* Neil J. Smelser and Richard Swedberg, eds. Princeton, NJ: Princeton University Press, 691–710.

Brock, Dan (1983), "Paternalism and Promoting the Good," in *Paternalism,* Rolf Sartorius ed. Minneapolis, MN: University of Minnesota Press, 237–60.

Buchanan, J.M. (1971), *The Bases for Collective Action.* New York: General Learning Press.

Coleman, James S. (1990), *Foundations of Social Theory.* Cambridge, MA: Harvard University Press.

Dawes, Richard (1980), "Social Dilemmas," *Annual Review of Psychology,* 31, 69–93.

Dawkins, Richard (1976), *The Selfish Gene.* Oxford: Oxford University Press.

Dickson, Peter Reid (1992), "Toward a General Theory of Competitive Rationality," *Journal of Marketing,* 56 (January), 69–83.

Feinberg, Joel (1984), *The Moral Limits of Criminal Law: Harm to Others,* Vol. 1. New York: Oxford University Press.

Gaski, John F. (1984), "The Theory of Power and Conflict in Channels of Distribution," *Journal of Marketing,* 48 (Summer), 9–29.

Hankin, Janet R., Ira J. Firestone, James J. Sloan, Joel W. Ager, Allen C. Goodman, Robert J. Sokol, and Susan S. Martier (1993), "The Impact of the Alcohol Warning Label on Drinking During Pregnancy," *Journal of Public Policy & Marketing,* 12 (1), 10–18.

Hardin, Garrett (1968), "The Tragedy of the Commons," *Science,* 162, 1243–48.

Hastings, G.B. and B. Elliott (1993), "Social Marketing Practice in Traffic Safety," in *Marketing of Traffic Safety,* Chapter 3, 35–53.

Hausman, Daniel M. and Michael S. McPherson (1996), *Economic Analysis and Moral Philosophy.* New York: Cambridge University Press.

Houston, Franklin S., Jule B. Gassenheimer, and James M. Maskulka (1992), *Marketing Exchange Transactions and Relationships.* Westport, CT: Quorum Books.

Hunt, Shelby D. (1976), "The Nature and Scope of Marketing," *Journal of Marketing,* 40 (July), 17–28.

Kahneman, Daniel, Paul Slovic, and Amos Tversky (1982), *Judgment Under Uncertainty Heuristics and Biases.* Cambridge: Cambridge University Press.

Kotler, Philip (1972), "A Generic Concept of Marketing," *Journal of Marketing,* 36 (April), 46–54.

___ and Gary Armstrong (1994), *Principles of Marketing,* 6th ed. Englewood Cliffs, NJ: Prentice Hall.

___ and Sidney J. Levy (1969), "Broadening the Concept of Marketing," *Journal of Marketing,* 33 (January), 10–15.

___ and Eduardo L. Roberto (1989), *Social Marketing Strategies for Changing Public Behavior.* New York: The Free Press.

___ and Gerald Zaltman (1971), "Social Marketing: An Approach to Planned Social Change," *Journal of Marketing,* 35 (July), 3–12.

Lindblom, Charles E. (1977), *Politics and Markets.* New York: Basic Books, Inc.

Lloyd, W.F. (1833), *Two Lectures on the Checks to Population.* Oxford.

MacInnis, Deborah J., Christine Moorman, and Bernard J. Jaworski (1991), "Enhancing and Measuring Consumers' Motivation, Opportunity, and Ability to Process Brand Information From Ads," *Journal of Marketing,* 55 (October), 32–53.

Mansbridge, Jane J. (1990), *Beyond Self Interest.* Chicago: The University of Chicago Press.

Marks, Amy Seidel (1997), "Private Sector Collaboration in Social Marketing Health Research: Examples from South Africa," presented at Innovations in Social Marketing, (May), Boston.

Matarazzo, J.D. (1984), "Behavioral Health: A 1990 Challenge for the Health Sciences Professions," in *Behavioral Health: A Handbook of Health Enhancement and Disease Prevention,* J.D. Matarazzo, S.M. Weiss, J.A. Hord, and N.E. Miller, eds. New York: John Wiley & Sons, 3–40.

Messick, M. and K. Brewer (1983), "Solving Social Dilemmas: A Review," in *Review of Personality and Social Psychology,* L. Wheeler and P. Shaver, eds. Beverly Hills, CA: Sage Publications.

Mill, John Stuart (1859), *On Liberty and Other Essays,* reprinted 1991. Oxford: Oxford University Press.

Olson, M. (1965), *The Logic of Collective Action.* Cambridge, MA: Harvard University Press.

Ouchi, William G. (1980), "Markets, Bureaucracies, and Clans," *Administrative Science Quarterly,* 25 (March), 129–41.

Park, C. Whan and Banwari Mittal (1985), "A Theory of Involvement in Consumer Behavior: Problems and Issues," in *Research in Consumer Behavior,* Vol. 1, Jagdish N. Sheth, ed. Greenwich, CT: JAI Press, 201–31.

Rangan, V. Kasturi, Sohel Karim, and Sheryl K. Sandberg (1996), "Do Better at Doing Good," *Harvard Business Review,* 74 (May/June), 42–54.

Rasmuson, M., R. Seidel, W.A. Smith, and E.M. Booth (1988), *Communication for Child Survival,* 7.

Rogers, E.M. (1962), *Diffusion of Innovations.* New York: The Free Press.

Rothschild, Michael L. (1979), "Marketing Education in Nonbusiness Situations or Why It's So Hard to Sell Brotherhood Like Soap," *Journal of Marketing,* 43 (Spring), 11–20.

Saur, Meghan (1998), "A Marketing View of Binge Drinking on College Campuses," senior honors thesis, University of Wisconsin.

Schelling, Thomas C. (1978), *Micromotives and Macrobehavior.* New York: W.W. Norton & Company.

Shapiro, Benson P. (1973), "Marketing for Nonprofit Organizations," *Harvard Business Review,* 51 (September/October), 123–32.

Sheth, Jagdish N., David M. Gardner, and Dennis E. Garrett (1988), *Marketing Theory: Evolution and Evaluation.* New York: John Wiley & Sons.

Skinner, B.F. (1935), "The Generic Nature of the Concepts of Stimulus and Response," *Journal of General Psychology,* 12, 40–65.

Smith, Adam (1776), *An Inquiry Into The Nature and Causes of the Wealth of Nations,* reprinted 1937. New York: Random House.

Smith, William (1993), "The Future of Social Marketing," presentation to the Marketing Conference on Creating Successful Partnerships, Carleton University, Ottawa, Canada.

___ (1996), "Marketing and Public Health Applying Tested Techniques to Promote Public Health Activities," paper presented to Promoting Public Health in an Era of Change; Agency for Health Care Policy and Research; User Liaison Program, Towson, MD.

Sober, Elliot, and David Sloan Wilson (1998), *Unto Others: The Evolution and Psychology of Unselfish Behavior.* Cambridge, MA: Harvard University Press.

Taylor, Michael and Sara Singleton (1993), "The Communal Resource: Transaction Costs and the Solution of Collective Action Problems," *Politics & Society,* 21 (June), 195–214.

Tellis, Gerard J. (1988), "The Price Elasticity of Selective Demand: A Meta-Analysis of Econometric Models of Sales," *Journal of Marketing Research,* 25 (November), 331–41.

UC Berkeley Wellness Letter (1997), "What's Really Killing Us," (August), 7.

Walsh, Diana Chapman, Rima E. Rudd, Barbara A. Moeykens, and Thomas W. Moloney (1993), "Social Marketing for Public Health," *Health Affairs,* (Summer), 104–19.

Weibe, G.D. (1951), "Merchandising Commodities and Citizenship on Television," *Public Opinion Quarterly,* 15 (Winter), 679–91.

Wiener, Joshua Lyle and Tabitha A. Doescher (1991), "A Framework for Promotion of Cooperation," *Journal of Marketing,* 55 (April), 38–47.

Wright, Robert (1994), *The Moral Animal.* New York: Pantheon Books.

Young, H. Peyton (1996), "The Economics of Convention," *Journal of Economic Perspectives,* 10 (Spring), 105–22.

Improving Vaccination Coverage in Urban Areas Through a Health Communication Campaign: The 1990 Philippine Experience

S. Zimicki,[1] R.C. Hornik,[1] C.C. Verzosa,[2] J.R. Hernandez,[3] E. de Guzman,[4] M. Dayrit,[5] A. Fausto,[6] M.B. Lee,[1] and M. Abad[6]

From March to September 1990 the Philippine Department of Health, with the assistance of the HEALTHCOM Project, carried out a national mass-media communication campaign to support routine vaccination services. The essential elements of the campaign strategy were as follows: focusing on measles as a way to get mothers to bring their children to the health centre; emphasizing logistic knowledge in the mass-media messages, in particular popularizing a single day of the week as "vaccination day" and giving clear information about the age for measles vaccination; and focusing on urban areas, which had lower vaccination rates than rural areas.

Evaluation of the effects of the campaign indicates an increase in vaccination coverage and a substantial increase in the timeliness of vaccination that can be attributed to improvement in carers' knowledge about vaccination. Furthermore, most of the observed increase in knowledge was related to exposure to the mass-media campaign. There was no evidence of any programmatic change that could account for the increase in vaccination or evidence that increased health education efforts at health centres could account for the change in knowledge.

These results indicate that when countries meet certain conditions—a high level of access to the media, sufficient expertise and funds available to develop and produce high-quality radio and television advertisements, and a routine system that is able to serve the increased demand—a mass communication campaign can significantly improve vaccination coverage.

Susan Zimicki, Robert C. Hornik, Cecelia C. Verzosa, José R. Hernandez, Eleanora de Guzman, Manolet Dayrit, Adora Fausto, and Mary Bessie Lee (1994), "Improving Vaccination Coverage in Urban Areas Through a Health Communications Campaign: The 1990 Philippines Experience," *Bulletin of the World Health Organization,* 72(3), 409–422.

[1]Center for International, Health, and Development Communication, Annenberg School for Communication, University of Pennsylvania, 3620 Walnut St., Philadelphia, PA 19104–6220, USA. Requests for reprints should be sent to S. Zimicki at this address.
[2]Academy for Educational Development, Washington. DC, USA.
[3]Child Survival Project, Department of Health, Manila, Philippines, Formerly: HEALTHCOM Project, Philippines.
[4]HEALTHCOM Project, Dakar, Senegal. Formerly: HEALTHCOM Project, Philippines.
[5]Public Information and Health Education Service, Department of Health, Manila, Philippines.
[6]TRENDS, Inc., Quezon City, Philippines.

Introduction

Since the institution of the WHO Expanded Programme on Immunization (EPI) in 1974, levels of vaccination coverage have increased considerably worldwide. Among the factors identified as important in achieving and maintaining high coverage are the following: an adequate supply of vaccine (*1, 2*); accessibility of vaccination sites and convenient hours for vaccination (*3–5*); short waiting times (*2, 6, 7*); and low rates of missed opportunities for vaccination (*2,5, 8–10*).

However, even when vaccines are readily available and service delivery is good, coverage rates may still be low, owing to problems arising from knowledge, attitudes and perceptions about vaccination (*5, 6, 11, 12*). These can include more general knowledge and attitudes about the utility of vaccination, such as a less scientific, more fatalistic notion of disease and a generally lower use of preventive services (*11*), lack of knowledge about what diseases vaccination prevents (*5, 11, 12*), or a belief that EPI diseases are not serious (*12*), as well as lack of "logistic knowledge" about the time and place vaccination is available (*3*) or about the appropriate age or interval at which to bring the child for vaccination (*5, 6,10, 12*).

One response to identification of these deficiencies is to provide the necessary information through the mass media. However, provision of information is usually only one of many components of programme improvement (and frequently is barely mentioned in descriptions of mass campaigns—see, e.g., 7, *14–16*); thus it has been difficult to evaluate its effect. The question is important, since the mass media are not an inevitable element of immunization programmes. Continued use of the mass media does require evidence that such use contributes to the success of programmes.

The 1990 national communications campaign to support the Philippine immunization programme provided an opportunity to assess the effectiveness of using the mass media. The immunization programme was managed by the Philippine Department of Health's Maternal and Child Health Services in collaboration with the Public Information Health Education Service, with technical assistance from the Communication for Child Survival project (HEALTHCOM) in developing, implementing, and monitoring the communication elements of the programme.

Because the campaign focused on urban areas, physical access to health facilities was not an issue. Moreover, the Philippines generally has good levels of health service provision, which did not change greatly during the campaign. Thus it provided an opportunity to examine the effect of dissemination of information about vaccination through the mass media, which could be analysed independently of other major changes in health services. The analysis demonstrates that improvement in coverage can be linked to an increase in knowledge about vaccination which in turn was related to exposure to the communication elements of the campaign.

Materials and Methods

THE COMMUNICATION CAMPAIGN

The vaccination communication campaign in the Philippines was carried out in two major phases: a pilot phase in Manila in 1988, which led to a nationwide campaign in 1990. The present article focuses on the nationwide campaign, which used the programme strategies piloted in the successful measles immunization communication campaign in Manila.[a] Three essential elements of the strategy were: focusing on measles as a way to get mothers to bring their children to the health centre; emphasizing logistic knowledge in the mass media messages, in particular popularizing a single day of the week as "vaccination day", and giving clear information about the age for measles vaccination; and focusing on urban areas, which had lower vaccination rates than rural areas.

Measles vaccination was selected for promotion because measles was the commonest childhood communicable disease recognized by mothers and because it was the third largest killer of infants and children in the country. Also, since measles vaccination is the final one in the series, its promotion could draw children who had not received earlier vaccinations, particularly diphtheria–pertussis–tetanus (DPT) and oral poliomyelitis vaccine (OPV), and ensure they received these as well. The selection of a single day of the week as vaccination day meant that mothers knew a time when they could be sure that vaccinations would be given at any health centre. After consultations with the regional immunization officers, Wednesday was selected as the vaccination day.

Because of the large number of cities to be covered by the campaign, a number of pre-campaign activities with city and health personnel had to be conducted in different parts of the country. In July and August 1989, area planning conferences were held with regional immunization officers, provincial health officers, city health officers, municipal health officers, and city/municipal EPI coordinators to give them an overview of the campaign and their roles in the activities and to address their concerns. In September 1989, meetings were held with the mayors of the campaign cities (who control the city health centres) to obtain their support and cooperation in campaign activities.

The orientation of clinic personnel to the campaign began in February 1990. There were three master "sales conferences", one-day meetings with regional health staff, who were informed about the campaign and encouraged to convene similar meetings in their own areas. These meetings were held to reinforce Department of Health policies about vaccinations, to prepare clinics for the increased demand and the focus on the Wednesday vaccination day, and to stimulate the involvement of the clinic personnel in the campaign.

---

[a]Details about the Manila campaign can be found in: **Verzosa C et al.** *Managing a communication program on immunization.* Manila, Academy for Educational Development, December 1989.

The mass-media element of the campaign was carried out between 16 March and 22 September 1990. Four television and four radio advertisements were broadcast, and advertisements were printed in newspapers reminding people that Wednesdays were free vaccination days at the health centres. Other promotional materials included posters, bunting, and welcome streamers for health centres to display, as well as stickers for *jeepneys* (shared taxi rides) and tricycles, and T-shirts for health centre staff.

The communication materials focused on the danger of measles and its complications, and recommended that children aged 9–12 months be taken to the health centre for vaccination. The materials emphasized that the vaccinations were free and that they would be available on Wednesdays at health centres. The campaign slogan, included in all communication materials, was "*Iligtas si baby sa tigdas*" ("Protect your baby from measles").

EVALUATION

The evaluation presented here is based on data obtained from two sources: two surveys of the carers of children aged <2 years in Manila, Luzon, Mindanao and Visayas; and a pre–post study of 60 health centres in the same geographical areas.

Surveys

The first survey was carried out in July and August 1989, before the campaign; and the second, in August 1990, 5 months after the start of the media campaign. Using a structured questionnaire in the relevant local language, interviewers obtained information about the family's socioeconomic status, the child's vaccination status, use of the health care system, the experience the last time the child was taken to be vaccinated, knowledge about vaccination, exposure to the mass media, and specific recall of any advertisements about vaccination. The same questionnaire was used for both surveys.

A woman was eligible to be a respondent if she was the mother or permanent carer of a child aged less than 2 years. The sample of women interviewed was obtained using a multistage cluster sampling strategy, with a cluster size of 10 (sampling stages are summarized in Table 1). Weighted analyses were used to adjust for geographical representation and to standardize the 1990 sample to the distribution of the 1989 sample for socioeconomic factors, since differences were noted in some characteristics of the respondents interviewed in the two surveys (Table 2). Unless noted otherwise, all estimates reported in this article are weighted, and cluster effects were taken into consideration in calculating statistics for testing significance (*17, 18*), except for regression analyses. Furthermore, all coverage estimates reported here are based on carers' reports as well as vaccination cards. As reported previously in the Sudan (*13*), examination of the Philippine data indicated that coverage can be substantially underestimated if card evidence alone is used; cards are often lost and vaccinations may not be recorded. The magnitude of underestimation that would occur if undocumented vaccinations were discounted is much larger than the overestimation inherent in accepting them as valid (see Annex).

TABLE 1

Summary of the Sampling Procedures Used in the Study

Stage

1		Allocation of interviews to:
	A. Manila (400 interviews)	B. Cities outside Manila (800 interviews)
2	—	Probability proportionate to size sample of:
		3 cities in Luzon
		4 cities in Visayas
		3 cities in Mindanao
3	Round 1: Random sample of voting districts with substantially D and E populations[a]	
	Round 2: Next (previously unselected) voting district on geographically ordered list	
4	Random selection of cluster start	
5	Interviews with 10 mothers/carers of children <2 years living in adjacent or nearest houses in a randomly determined direction from the cluster start	

[a]"D" and "E" are the lowest categories of the five-category "ABCDE" scale used by market researchers. Approximately 90% of the urban population in the Philippines belongs to categories "D" and "E".

TABLE 2

Differences Between the Respondents Interviewed in 1989 and 1990 (Weighted to Account for Area Representation Only)

Characteristic	1989 Survey	1990 Survey
% born in a small city	6.9 (1 200)[a]	17.7 (1 198)
% who speak English with children	19.9 (1 200)	6.0 (1 200)
% with electricity	90.3 (1 200)	94.8 (1 200)
% with a radio	71.5 (1 200)	77.8 (1 200)
% whose last child was born at home	37.3 (1 200)	30.9 (1 200)
Average income category (1–10)	4.5 (1 116)	5.5 (1 153)
Average length of schooling of respondent (years)	9.6 (1 199)	10.1 (1 198)

[a]Figures in parentheses are the number of respondents.

It is important to note that the absolute level of coverage reported here cannot be compared directly with estimates based on other procedures. The sample of mothers surveyed was restricted to relatively less well-off people, those who were considered to be in the "D" and "E" categories of the five-category "ABCDE" scale used by market researchers. Thus it might differ from other estimates, for example, those based on distributed vaccines, on card-verified data only, or with different samples; rural as well as urban people, other social classes as well as "D" and "E", or with other provinces included. This evaluation seeks to establish the effects of the campaign and the process through which it occurred. In view of the cost constraints that limited the sample, it cannot be said to represent the absolute level of vaccination in the Philippines.

Health Centre Study

A simultaneous health centre study provided parallel evidence about what was happening at the facilities that were to meet the demand stimulated by the communication campaign. This study included three components: structured interviews with the staff of 60 health centres; observations of 10 children who attended the health centre on a day when vaccinations were given in a subset of 20 centres; and exit interviews with the adults accompanying the observed children as they left these 20 health centres. All the health centres were visited from August to October 1989 and from July to September 1990.

The structured interviews with health centre staff covered general information about the particular clinic and its customary practices with regard to vaccination, supplies, and record-keeping. Observations centred on the interaction between the health centre clients and the staff providing vaccinations; and the interview with the client outside the health centre, which took less than 5 minutes, included questions about clinic accessibility, waiting time, knowledge about vaccination, and examination of the child's card to determine missed opportunities that day.

Most of the 60 health centres included in the study were selected because the majority of carers in an individual cluster (60 of the 120 clusters in the first survey) had named the centre concerned, either as the one they attended, if they used the public health system, or as the nearest health centre to where they lived, if they did not use the public health system. For a few clusters, either no health centre was named by a majority of individuals or the one that was named was unavailable for the study; in these eases another nearby health centre was substituted.

Results

EFFECT OF THE CAMPAIGN

Between the surveys conducted in 1989 and 1990 the proportion of fully vaccinated children aged 12–23 months increased from 54% to 65%, and the average number of vaccinations for all children less than 2 years of age increased from 4.32 to 5.10 (Table 3). Although vaccination levels in the Philippines had been increasing even before the campaign began, the rate of increase was too gradual to explain the extent of the observed change.[b]

The most striking change was the improvement in the proportion of children finishing "on time", estimated as the proportion of children between 9 months of age and their first birthday who had received all eight vaccinations. This apparently greater increase in timely vaccination than in overall coverage is an artifact of the timing of the evaluation. A comparison of the age-specific proportions of fully vaccinated children in 1989 and 1990 (Figure 1)

---

[b]The secular trend was estimated from the time plot of measles vaccination by 12 months of age among 12–23-month-old children determined in 51 city and provincial level EPI surveys undertaken by the Philippine Department of Health with assistance from the Resources for Child Health (REACH) project between February 1988 and March 1990.

TABLE 3

Improvement in Vaccination Coverage Between the 1989 and 1990 Surveys, According to Various Measures

Measure	1989 Survey (%)	1990 Survey (%)	Rate Difference
12–23 month coverage (proportion of children aged 12–23 months who had all 8 vaccinations)	53.6 *446*[a]	64.5 *461*	10.9 (2.8–19.0)[b]
Starting on time (proportion of children <4 months of age who had at least one vaccination)	43.3 *255*	55.6 *196*	12.3 (1.5–23.1)
Finished on time (proportion of children aged 9–11 months who had all 8 vaccinations)	32.2 *184*	56.2 *193*	24.0 (12.2–35.8)
Appropriate early vaccinations (proportion of children aged 2–8 months with at least 4 vaccinations)	47.7 *441*	56.2 *442*	8.5 (0–17.1)
Mean number of vaccinations	4.32 *1 200*	5.10 *1 195*	0.8 (0.4–1.1)

[a]Figures in italics are the denominators.
[b]Figures in parentheses are the 95% confidence limits of the rate difference based on the *t*-test statistic corrected for the design effect associated with the cluster sample procedures (ref. *17, 18*).

FIGURE 1

Age-Specific Proportions of Children Who Were Fully Vaccinated (All Eight Vaccinations) at the Time of the Surveys Completed in 1989 (before the Mass-Media Campaign) and in August 1990 (5 Months after the Start of the Campaign)

The 95% confidence limits (bars) are corrected for the design effect associated with the cluster sampling procedures (ref. *17, 18*).

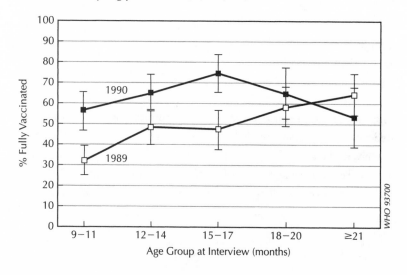

indicates that improvement occurred for children who were less than 1 year of age at the start of the campaign (i.e., <18 months of age at the time of the follow-up survey); children who were older at the start of the campaign showed no improvement. Had the "after" measure been delayed until the children who were 12 months old at the time of the 1990 survey reached their second birthday, the apparent increase in 12–23-month coverage would have been larger.

MECHANISM OF THE EFFECT

There is substantial evidence that the programme increased knowledge about vaccination among the carers of young children. There were large increases in knowledge about vaccination between 1989 and 1990, and the increases, which were associated with the improvement in vaccination practice, were also related to exposure to the mass-media campaign. There is no evidence of any changes in other programme factors that could account for the increase in vaccination coverage, e.g., increased vaccine supplies, increased outreach efforts, or reorganization of clinic services to reduce waiting times. Moreover, the findings on the interaction between health workers and those coming for vaccination suggest that greater health education efforts at the health centres cannot account for the change in knowledge.

Knowledge about Vaccinations

The surveys conducted in 1989 and 1990 included measurements of 22 items of knowledge about vaccination: eight measurements specifically about measles vaccination and 14 measurements concerning other vaccinations and vaccination in general. People knew more about measles vaccination after the campaign than before. For every question there was a statistically significant improvement between 1989 and 1990 (Table 4). When the baseline correct knowledge was over 80%, the improvements were small, but when the baseline knowledge was lower, the improvements were often more than twenty percentage points.

Knowledge about other vaccinations also improved between the two surveys, although not so sharply (Table 5). The increase in the average proportion of correct answers to these questions (4.8%) was only about a third of that for the eight questions about measles (15.2%). Such an overall comparison of the changes in knowledge about measles and about the other vaccinations can only be tentative, since not all the questions were identical. However, comparison of similar questions[c] shows that in every case a greater improvement occurred with respect to knowledge about measles vaccination than about other vaccinations. Moreover, the lack of change in knowledge about other vaccinations (questions 7, 8, 9 in Table 5), particularly about the number of doses of OPV necessary, suggests that the experience of actually obtaining the vaccinations is not the chief means of acquiring knowledge about them. The greater change in knowledge

---

[c]Question 2 in Table 4 with questions 1–3 in Table 5; question 3 in Table 4 with questions 4–6 in Table 5; and question 7 in Table 4 with question 13 in Table 5.

TABLE 4

Changes in Knowledge about Measles Vaccination among Respondents between the 1989 and 1990 Surveys

Measles Knowledge Question	% Correct Answers:		Rate Difference (%)
	1989 (n = 1 200)	1990 (n = 1 195)	
1. *Open ended:* "Some children get measles and others do not. Is there any way to protect a child from getting measles?" *If says yes:* "What can one do to protect a child from getting measles?" (*Mentions vaccination*)	53.2	73.2	20.0 (14.9–25.3)[a]
2. "Here is a list of diseases: please tell me against which of these diseases a child can be protected by vaccination?" (*Mentions measles*)	87.8	94.5	6.8 (4.0–9.4)
3. "When (child's name) has all the vaccinations he/she needs will he/she still be likely to become sick from measles?" (*Says no*)	48.0	65.4	17.4 (11.5–23.2)
4. "Would you say that measles is a serious or not so serious disease?" (*Says it is serious*)	81.1	86.6	5.5 (1.6–9.3)
5. "Would you say that measles can lead to complications or not?" (*Says it can lead to complications*)	81.0	95.9	14.9 (11.6–18.2)
6. "Mothers should never take measles for granted" (*Agrees*)	80.7	91.2	10.5 (6.0–15.0)
7. "As far as you know, at what age should a child get vaccination for measles?" (*Gives answer between 38–52 weeks*)	45.1	66.1	21.0 (15.7–26.5)
8. "The best age for a child to get measles vaccination is 3–5 months old" (*Disagrees*)	32.6	57.9	25.3 (19.3–31.4)
Average % correct	63.7	78.9	15.2

[a]See footnote *b*, Table 3.

about measles suggests the importance of the communication efforts, in view of the emphasis placed on that antigen during the mass-media campaign.

Vaccination Coverage and Knowledge

A series of regression analyses using survey year and knowledge variables to predict the number of vaccinations indicated that a subset of four of these 22 knowledge items was particularly important in explaining the influence of the campaign on vaccination practice. These four items were chosen because they were the only ones that had independent effects on the relation between survey year and vaccination performance. They included three questions about measles (questions 2, 7 and 8 in Table 4) and one about all vaccinations (question 13 in Table 5); three out of the four were about the timing of vaccinations.

Changes in Knowledge about Other Vaccinations among Respondents between the 1989 and 1990 Surveys

	% Correct Answers:		
Vaccination Knowledge Question	**1989** ($n = 1\,200$)	**1990** ($n = 1\,195$)	**Rate Difference** (%)
1. "Here is a list of diseases: please tell me against which of these diseases a child can be protected by vaccination?": Whooping cough (*Mentions*)	63.7	69.4	5.7 (0.7–10.7)[a]
2. Tuberculosis (*Mentions*)	77.0	81.9	4.9 (0.8–9.2)
3. Poliomyelitis (*Mentions*)	90.3	91.6	1.3 (−1.9 to 4.4)
4. "When (child's name) has all the vaccinations he/she needs will he/she still be likely to become sick from: Whooping cough?" (*Says no*)	39.4	48.1	8.7 (2.7–14.7)
5. ". . . tuberculosis?" (*Says no*)	61.0	70.9	9.9 (4.4–15.4)
6. ". . . poliomyelitis?" (*Says no*)	64.2	74.3	10.1 (4.8–15.3)
7. "There is no vaccination to protect a newborn baby from tetanus" (*Disagrees*)	66.2	62.5	−3.7 (−9.0 to 1.6)
8. "For a child to be fully protected against poliomyelitis, only one dose of vaccine is necessary" (*Disagrees*)	62.9	61.4	−1.5 (−7.5 to 4.5)
9. "BCG vaccination protects children from getting whooping cough" (*Disagrees*)	18.4	18.7	0.3 (−4.7 to 5.2)
10. "Poliomyelitis vaccination is given by drops in the mouth" (*Agrees*)	80.8	85.8	5.0 (1.1–9.0)
11. "Even if a child has a cold and a low fever a child should still be given vaccination" (*Agrees*)	18.2	25.1	6.9 (1.8–12.0)
12. "As far as you known, by what age should a child begin getting vaccination?" (*Answer is 4 weeks or less*)	50.7	58.8	8.1 (3.0–13.7)
13. "As far as you know, by what age should a child have all the vaccinations he/she needs" (*Answer is 38–52 weeks*)	65.0	78.1	13.1 (8.8–17.5)
14. "It's best for a child to finish getting all vaccinations by his first birthday" (*Agrees*)	91.9	90.6	−1.3 (−3.8 to 1.2)
Average % correct	60.7	65.5	4.8

[a]See footnote *b*, Table 3.

Evidence that the campaign worked by increasing knowledge can be seen clearly from Figure 2, which shows for both surveys the relationship between practice and a knowledge score (range, 0–4), obtained by summing responses to the four critical knowledge items, with respondents receiving one point for each correct answer. Strikingly, the plots are almost

Mean Number of Vaccinations for All Children Aged 0–23 Months, by Vaccination Knowledge Scores, in 1989 and 1990

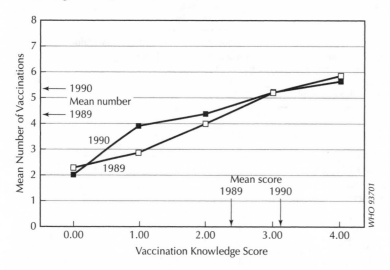

Effect of Respondents' Knowledge on the 1989–1990 Vaccination Differences[a]

	Absolute Difference	% Explained	Significance of Difference
1989–1990 difference in vaccination coverage	0.77	—	P < 0.0001
Amount of that difference accounted for by four knowledge items	0.54	70	
Remaining difference not explained by knowledge	0.23	30	NS[b]

[a]This analysis summarizes the results of a multiple regression analysis. These are the unstandardized coefficients for a variable representing the time a survey was completed, estimated with and without the knowledge items in the equation. Expressed alternatively, the simple bivariate correlation between survey year and vaccination level is 0.122 (P < 0.0001); and the partial correlation, controlling for the knowledge variables is 0.04, a non-significant coefficient (P = 0.07).
[b]NS = not significant.

identical, indicating that the relationship between knowledge and practice was about the same for both 1989 and 1990. However, respondents scored higher in 1990 for knowledge, averaging 2.97 correct responses, compared with 1989, when the average score was 2.3, a difference of 0.67 (95% confidence interval (CI): 0.55–0.78).

In 1989, before the campaign, surveyed children had an average of 4.32 vaccinations; in 1990 they had 5.10, an increase of almost 20%. If this difference was largely due to the effects of the campaign on knowledge, controlling for knowledge should essentially remove the effect. The results of a series of multiple regression analyses (summarized in Table 6) demonstrate the expected pattern. The original gap in vaccination levels between the

1989 and 1990 samples is essentially explained by knowledge differences between them. Once knowledge was controlled for, no significant difference in vaccination practice between the two years remained.

Knowledge and Campaign Exposure

There is good evidence that the changes in knowledge were related to exposure to the mass-media campaign. The public communication campaign was readily recalled by the survey respondents (Table 7), including a particularly high proportion who could complete the campaign slogan "*Iligtas si baby sa tigdas*". The low number of correct responses given to the same questions in the 1989 survey indicates that the 1990 answers were not random correct guesses. Some of the 1989 respondents gave replies suggesting they had been exposed to mass-media information about measles. Most of these respondents were in Manila and had been exposed to the roughly similar pilot campaign mounted in 1988. This permitted them to recall the catch phrase of the campaign and know that the advertisements emphasized that vaccines were available without cost. However, the 1988 campaign featured Friday as the "vaccination day", which explains why virtually no one answered that question correctly in 1989.

A second type of supporting evidence for the effects of the mass media on knowledge was the response to the general question "Can you tell me where/from whom you learned about vaccination? Anyone else/any other place?" The broad tendency was for responses to this question to focus on health system components: clinic staff or private physicians. This did not change between 1989 and 1990. However, there was a striking increase in the number of times the mass media were mentioned in the two surveys. In 1989 about 11% and in 1990 about 35% of the respondents mentioned radio or television among their sources of such knowledge (difference = 24%; 95% CI: 19–30%).

TABLE 7

Exposure of Respondents to the Mass-Media Campaign

	1989 Survey ($n = 1\,200$)	1990 Survey ($n = 1\,195$)	Rate Difference (%)
Heard or saw an advertisement (%)	31.1	83.9	52.9 (48.2–57.6)[a]
Could complete last word of campaign rhyme (%)	12.6	72.0	59.3 (54.9–63.7)
Of those who recalled the advertisement:	($n = 372$)	($n = 1\,003$)	
Agreed that it said that vaccinations were free (%)	68.2	93.7	25.5 (18.6–32.4)
Mentioned that it said that Wednesday was vaccination day (%)	6.5	74.0	67.5 (62.6–72.4)
Average score on four-point campaign recall scale (all respondents)	0.71	3.03	2.32 (2.19–2.46)

[a]See footnote *b*, Table 3.

While this is not evidence about the source of any specific knowledge, it does indicate that, in general, people viewed the mass media as a much more significant source for information about vaccination than they had before the campaign.

The third type of evidence is the most direct. A measure of recall of campaign messages was constructed from respondent's replies to the items listed in Table 7. A carer could receive from 0 to 4 points depending on how many of the items were answered in a way consistent with exposure to the media campaign ($\alpha = 0.85$). Comparison of this recall score with the level of knowledge both before and after the campaign shows the importance of the exposure in achieving greater knowledge about vaccination (Figure 3). The exposure measure was unrelated to knowledge in 1989, as expected, but was strongly related to knowledge in 1990.

The most convincing evidence that exposure to the mass-media campaign had an important influence on knowledge is obtained from an analysis of the difference in the level of knowledge before and after the campaign (Table 8). The difference between the knowledge scores of respondents in 1989 (2.3) and 1990 (2.97) is 0.67, of which almost two-thirds is accounted for by the effects of the campaign exposure variables. Once they were controlled for, the remaining gap was 0.24, less than one-third of the original. The remaining difference was not explained by any of the other variables that were measured, including area of the country, carers' education level or wealth, recency of visiting the health centre, or number of vaccinations the child had received. Overall, while exposure does not account for all of the gain in knowledge, it had a substantial influence.

FIGURE 3

Mean Knowledge Scores in 1989 and 1990, by Level of Recall of the Mass-Media Campaign. Each point displayed represents at least 50 respondents.

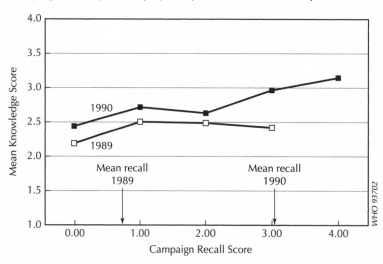

TABLE 8

Effect of Campaign Exposure on 1989–1990 Knowledge Differences ($n = 2\,395$)

	Absolute Difference	% Explained	Significance of Difference
1989–1990 difference in vaccination knowledge	0.67		$P < 0.01$
Amount of that difference accounted for by four campaign recall items	0.43	64	
Remaining difference not explained by campaign recall items	0.24	36	$P < 0.01$

Improvements in Other Programme Factors

The increase in the average level and timeliness of vaccination cannot be explained by improvements in other programme components. Available evidence indicates that most programme factors were relatively stable.

MISSED OPPORTUNITIES

One of the most important aspects of health worker practice that affects vaccination coverage is the level of missed opportunities—whether children receive fewer than all the vaccinations for which they are eligible at the time of each contact with the health system. Information from both the health centre study and the surveys indicates that a decrease in missed opportunities did not contribute to campaign results. During each of the 20 health centre visits, the cards of 10 children were examined to determine whether they had received all the vaccinations for which they were eligible that day. Considering all four antigens (with little difference among them), approximately 16% of the children were not given all the appropriate vaccines in 1989. In 1990 there was a small but not statistically significant increase in the proportion of such children to 21%.

While the presence of observers at the health centres may have decreased the likelihood of missed opportunities, the results were corroborated by analysis of the vaccination data recorded during the surveys. From these data a lower limit estimate of missed opportunities can be calculated, since no information was recorded about visits to health centres when no vaccinations were received. Children did not receive all appropriate vaccinations at 24.6% of sessions during the campaign, a rate not statistically different from that during sessions in 1988 and 1989 (22.4%).

VACCINE SUPPLY

Vaccination coverage can be inhibited by a shortage of vaccine and vaccination supplies, and hence planning for the campaign included provision for an increase in supplies. Interviews with providers during the health centre study indicated that needles, syringes, and measles vaccine were all in shorter supply in 1990 than in 1989, both on the day of the interviews and over the previous 3 months. Other vaccines were all adequately supplied. Vaccination cards were in short supply in both years, with only a slight tendency for supplies to be worse in 1990 than in 1989. These shortages suggest that demand for vaccination was greater than anticipated. However, evidence from the carer's surveys suggests that supplies very nearly met the increased demand. In the 1989 survey, 2% of carers who visited the clinics in the previous year claimed to have been turned away at least once because of shortages; that proportion was only slightly, although not significantly, greater in 1990 (4%). Overall, these data suggest that the improvement in vaccination coverage occurred despite any shortfall in vaccination supplies.

Accessibility

Few people (about 1%) claimed to have visited health centres to find them closed in either year. Waiting times for vaccination at clinics averaged about 1 hour, and they seem to have declined only slightly, by about 8 minutes (95% CI: 2.5–13.5), according to the carers' surveys.

Increases in Knowledge and Health Centre Practice

One possible explanation for the observed improvements in knowledge is that carers learned about vaccination during visits to health centres. However, evidence that health clinic personnel changed their way of interacting with their clients is less convincing than that for the mass-media exposure effects. Data for this conclusion come from two sources: the carer surveys and the exit interviews in the health centre study. In both cases there was little change in the reported character of the interaction or in the level of accurate knowledge that carers took away from their health centre visit.

The interviews with carers in their homes indicated very little change in what happened at health centres. About 36% of respondents in both years said that someone at the clinic knew them by name, and about 74% said that someone had told them about the side-effects of vaccination at the last visit. There was a small increase in the proportion who reported being told against which diseases the vaccine protected (51.9% in 1989 and 59.0% in 1990; difference: 7.1%; 95% CI: 0.6–13.4), and no change in the proportion who said that someone had reminded them about vaccination over the previous 3 months (14.4% in 1989; 18.1% in 1990; difference: 3.7%; 95% CI: −0.8 to 8.4). Differences in these factors do not explain the observed improvements in vaccination levels.

The carers interviewed as they left the health centres reported roughly similar experiences in 1989 and 1990. The time they spent with the clinic personnel was about 10 minutes in both years, and almost all (85% in 1989 and 89% in 1990) were told when to bring the child back or that the child had received all the vaccinations needed. In both years 38% said that someone had told them about possible side-effects of vaccination, and in both years about the same proportion could tell the interviewer accurately what vaccinations their child had received (63% in 1989; 72% in 1990: difference not significant). One exception to this pattern of little change was a sharply increased proportion of exit interviewees saying that "someone explained about vaccination": 18.4% in 1989, but 75.5% in 1990. However, this result is difficult to interpret, since no parallel change was observed in responses to more specific questions, whether of exit interviewees or of carers.

If an essentially unobserved change in health centre practice affected knowledge, then we could expect that better knowledge would be associated with frequency of contact with the health centre. However, in 1990 the average knowledge scores of carers who reported 0, 1–3 and $\geq$4 visits to the health centre over the past year were almost exactly identical (on average, 2.97, 2.97, and 2.92 resp.). In summary, there is little evidence that changes in the way vaccination sessions were conducted at the clinics were responsible for the increase in knowledge among the carers that would account for most of the increased vaccination levels.

Discussion

The evidence suggests that the mass-media information campaign was largely responsible for the improvement in vaccination coverage. Health centre practice was essentially the same during the campaign as previously. The rate of missed opportunities for vaccinating children was slightly worse, as were vaccine supply shortages, and only small changes in the interaction of health workers with vaccination clients was noted. In contrast, changes in knowledge about measles vaccination, in particular about the appropriate age for vaccination, were substantial.

There were three essential elements in the campaign strategy: the concentration on urban areas; the focus on measles, and the emphasis on knowledge of the details of the time, place, and age. The decision to focus on urban areas was prompted by their lower vaccination rates. While the urban areas are at an undoubted disadvantage because of higher rates of disease transmission, this is somewhat offset by easier access to services. In contrast to rural areas, the physical access of the urban population to health facilities and of health centre staff to supply sites is not a constraint; moreover, dissemination of information is likely to be greater.

In this programme, the focus on measles and logistical knowledge—the age for vaccination and the times and places vaccinations would be available—translated directly into the messages disseminated in the television and radio advertisements and mentioned on posters. The designation of a particular day for vaccination could help keep costs down, since this reduces wastage and improves efficiency (19). The change in knowledge about the appropriate age for vaccination relates directly to the major effect of the campaign on the timeliness of vaccination. This effect can be important as the Philippines moves into a later stage of measles control (20), since a one-dose vaccination strategy for young children may be more effective than a two-dose strategy that achieves the same coverage (21).

The effect of the campaign was not limited to measles vaccination. This "spillover" is most probably due to a heightening of awareness about vaccination generally, rather than the concurrent administration of other needed vaccinations when children came for measles vaccine. Improvements in vaccination levels increased well before the children reached 8.5 months of age, when they become eligible for measles vaccination (see Table 3). If the spillover was only the result of other vaccinations given when children came for measles vaccine, the improvement in coverage would have been restricted to children eligible for measles vaccination.

It is important to point out that the Philippine campaign differed from classical mass campaigns (7, 22) in a number of important respects. Most importantly, it was a communications campaign in support of routine vaccination services. There was a long planning period, so that vaccine supplies were reasonably adequate for the demand created; health service staff were alerted through the "sales conferences" and their local meetings; the campaign was centralized, in that there was a unique policy and universal provision of vaccination on Wednesdays, usually in addition to other days selected by local staff. The quality of services provided did not appear to suffer; there was no increase in waiting times or decrease in the proportion of clients told when to come back, a situation that contrasts markedly with that reported for some mass campaigns (7).

A number of factors contributed to the success of the campaign. First, the urban sample was drawn from a population with good access to the mass media. More than 60% claimed to own televisions and 73% claimed to own radios, while more than 50% owned both. In the 1990 survey, most of those who did not own such equipment claimed to be listeners and watchers, with only 2% describing themselves as neither watchers nor listeners. The intensive mass-media-based promotion campaign therefore clearly found the channels to reach its audience. Second, the high level of public access to the mass media was reflected in the expertise available to the Department of Health to develop and produce high-quality radio and television spots. Finally, and most importantly, the campaign supported a routine system that was ready to serve the increased demand that it generated.

Even with the successful media campaign, on-time vaccination coverage did not exceed 65% and the 18-month coverage was just below 80%. If measles is to be controlled and transmission interrupted in urban areas, vaccination coverage of 95% or more may be needed (J. Clements, personal communication, 1992). Achieving a high level of control will depend on using all available tools and strategies, of which mass-media-based information campaigns should certainly be one.

Acknowledgements

HEALTHCOM is a 14-year programme providing technical assistance to developing countries to promote and refine the use of communication and social marketing methods to influence health practices as an element of an effective child survival strategy. It was sponsored by the Office of Health, Bureau for Research and Development of the United States Agency for International Development, and was administered by the Academy for Educational Development (contract # DPE-5984-Z-00-9018-00). Subcontractor Porter/Novelli provided assistance with the social marketing strategies; and the Center for International, Health, and Development Communication (CIHDC), Annenberg School for Communication, University of Pennsylvania, was responsible for evaluating the impact of HEALTHCOM activities.

The surveys reported in this article were carried out by TRENDS, Inc., and the health centre studies by Kabalikat ng Pamilyang Pilipino, with technical advice from CIHDC. We thank the Department of Health, specifically Mr. M. Taguiwalo and Ms M. Bernaje, as well as the EPI staff; the staff of TRENDS; Dr M.T. Bagasao, Ms M. Pabalan and the staff of Kabalikat ng Pamilyang Pilipino; as well as the HEALTHCOM staff.

Helpful comments on previous drafts were provided by Dr J. Clements, Dr A. Andreason, Mr M. Favin, Dr S. McCombie, and Dr S. Watkins. We are grateful to Mr D. Boyd and to REACH for providing information about the results of EPI surveys carried out from 1988 to early 1990.

References

1. Subramanyam K. Vaccine distribution: an operations research study. *Reviews of infectious diseases,* 1989, 11 (suppl. 3): S623–S628.
2. Cutts FT et al. The use of evaluation to improve the Expanded Programme on Immunization in Mozambique. *Bulletin of the World Health Organization,* 1990, 68: 199–208.
3. Belcher DW et al. A mass immunization campaign in rural Ghana: factors affecting participation. *Public health reports,* 1978, 93: 170–176.
4. Friede AM et al. An epidemiological assessment of immunization program participation in the Philippines. *International journal of epidemiology,* 1985, 14: 135–141.
5. Cutts FT et al. Evaluation of factors influencing vaccine uptake in Mozambique. *International journal of epidemiology,* 1989, 18: 427–433.
6. Eng E et al. The acceptability of childhood immunization to Togolese mothers: a sociobehavioral perspective. *Health education quarterly,* 1991 (Spring), 97–110.
7. Unger J-P. Can intensive campaigns dynamize front line health services? The evaluation of an immunization campaign in Thies health district, Senegal. *Social science and medicine,* 1991, 32: 249–259.
8. Steinhoff MC et al. Evaluation of the opportunities for and contraindications to immunization in a tropical paediatric clinic. *Bulletin of the World Health Organization,* 1985, 63: 915–918.
9. Loevinsohn BP. Missed opportunities for immunization during visits for curative care: practical reasons for their occurrence. *American journal of tropical medicine and hygiene,* 1989, 41: 255–258.

10. Cutts FT et al. Application of multiple methods to study the immunization programme in an urban area of Guinea. *Bulletin of the World Health Organization*, 1990, 68: 769–776.

11. Hanlon P et al. Factors influencing vaccination compliance in peri-urban Gambian children. *Journal of tropical medicine and hygiene*, 1988, 91: 29–33.

12. Streatfield M, Singarimbun M. Social factors affecting use of immunization in Indonesia. *Social science and medicine*, 1988, 27: 1237–1245.

13. Gareaballah E-T, Loevinsohn BP. The accuracy of mothers' reports about their children's vaccination status. *Bulletin of the World Health Organization*, 1989, 67: 669–674.

14. Risi JB Jr. The control of poliomyelitis in Brazil. *Reviews of infectious diseases*, 1984, 6 (suppl. 2): S400–S403.

15. Balraj V, John TJ. Evaluation of a poliomyelitis immunization campaign in Madras city. *Bulletin of the World Health Organization*, 1986, 64: 861–865.

16. Cutts FT. Strategies to improve immunization services in urban Africa. *Bulletin of the World Health Organization*, 1991, 69: 407–414.

17. Kish L. Selection of the sample. In: Festinger L, Katz D, eds. *Research methods in the behavioral sciences.* New York, Holt, Rinehart & Winston, 1953.

18. Frerichs RR. Simple analytic procedures for rapid microcomputer assisted cluster surveys in developing countries. *Public health reports*, 1989, 104: 24–35.

19. Phonboon K et al. The Thai expanded programme on immunization: role of immunization sessions and their cost-effectiveness. *Bulletin of the World Health Organization*, 1989, 67: 181–188.

20. Cutts FT et al. Principles of measles control. *Bulletin of the World Health Organization*, 1991, 69: 1–8.

21. Mclean AR, Anderson RM. Measles in developing countries. Part II. The predicted impact of mass vaccination. *Epidemiology and infection*, 1988, 100: 419–442.

22. Robinson DA. Polio vaccination—a review of strategies. *Transactions of the Royal Society of Tropical Medicine and Hygiene*, 1982, 76: 575–581.

ANNEX

Validity of reported vaccinations with no card evidence

Information about their children's vaccination status was obtained by asking carers for their child's vaccination card. If no card was available, or if a specific vaccination was not recorded, the carer was asked whether the child had received that vaccination, and on what date.

In 1989, prior to the campaign, undocumented vaccinations reported by carers accounted for 15–31% (median, 17.5%) of the coverage levels of different vaccinations among children aged less than 1 year, and, as expected, higher proportions (33–40%; median, 35%) among older children, who were less likely to have cards (Table A1). It is clear that excluding undocumented reports would decrease the estimated coverage to levels that are probably too low. Moreover, some verification of these reports is available from BCG scar ascertainment: in 1989 scars

Total Coverage Rates for Specific Antigens and the Proportion of Coverage Based on Undocumented Carers' Reports

Vaccine[a]	Age (months)	1989 Survey		1990 Survery	
		Coverage Rate	% Undocumented	Coverage Rate	% Undocumented
Age-Appropriate Coverage in the First Year of Life:					
BCG	0–11	64.0	25	76.5	27
DPT1	2–11	70.0	18	78.6	21
OPV1		69.7	19	79.1	22
DPT2	3–11	56.9	16	69.2	21
OPV2		55.8	16	67.3	20
DPT3	4–11	45.1	17	57.0	23
OPV3		43.9	15	55.7	23
Measles	9–11	35.1	31	61.1	43
Coverage among 12–23-Month-Olds:					
BCG		84.9	40	89.4	39
DPT1		84.0	37	87.1	37
OPV1		83.8	37	85.6	38
DPT2		76.1	35	83.4	38
OPV2		75.2	35	82.8	38
DPT3		66.3	33	74.2	38
OPV3		66.2	34	73.2	37
Measles		61.2	33	71.7	42

[a]DPT = diphtheria–pertussis–tetanus; OPV = oral poliomyelitis vaccine.

were observed in 88.6% of children with card evidence of vaccination and in 82.0% of those without such evidence, suggesting that most of the reports were valid. In view of the high proportion of undocumented vaccinations, if many carers were claiming vaccinations that their children had not actually received, the difference in scar ascertainment would be greater and other distortions of basic patterns would be evident. This was generally not the case; for example, coverage levels decreased for successive vaccinations, as expected.

The proportion of undocumented vaccinations was fairly constant for the different vaccinations, except for BCG and measles. Higher proportions of undocumented BCG vaccinations were apparent for both 0–11- and 12–23-month-old children. This is not surprising, since BCG vaccine is frequently given at the place where a child is born, and may not always be recorded on the vaccination card, which is obtained at a health centre.

For measles, the proportion of undocumented reports was higher than for other vaccinations among children aged less than 1 year but not among those aged

12–23 months. This could have arisen because of the practice of some physicians of giving two doses of measles vaccine—one soon after the child reached 6 months of age, and the second after the first birthday (M.T. Bagaso, personal communication, 1992). When this is done the usual practice is not to record the first dose on the vaccination card given to the mother, which has space for only one entry for measles. Thus, young children might have had a vaccination that was not recorded; in contrast, older children would probably have received the second of the two-dose series, which was recorded.

In 1990, the proportions of reported vaccinations that were undocumented increased slightly, the proportion undocumented being consistent for all vaccinations except measles. For measles, although the possibility of some overreporting stimulated by the campaign could not be ruled out, we judged that the likelihood of underestimating coverage by discounting claimed vaccinations was probably greater than that of overestimating coverage by accepting them. However, to reduce the impact of any overreporting of measles on the analysis of the effect of the campaign, the total number of vaccinations was used as the outcome measure for the analyses we have presented here.

THE INCREDIBLE SHRINKING DUYERS

Peter Perl

Overeating and under-exercising have become a way of life. That made the Duyer family all too typical—until they decided to launch a full-scale attack on fat.

The cross-examinations make [Emma Duyer] itchy, if not angry. As if teen-parent relations aren't trouble enough, obesity inevitably raises the stakes. As early as age 10, Emma was taken for help to a nutritionist, but "she was like stone. She wouldn't say a word," [Kathy] recalls. "She just didn't want to hear it." As an elementary school kid, Emma was teased about being fat, but her parents had to learn about it from a teacher because Emma never told them. Asked about teasing now, Emma says it just doesn't happen anymore. "People know if they make fun of me," she says with a hint of playful bravado, "it'll be the last thing they ever do."

There are the photos of Emma and [Sarah] on family vacations to Maine, Assateague and Chincoteague, with Emma always looking twice the size of her little sister. The family joke is that Emma was born hungry; at birth, she had a distinct scar on her hand, and the doctor said she'd apparently been chewing on it in the womb. In the succession of family pictures, Emma expands, but Sarah stays slender. The big sister marvels at the genetic anomaly. "She's weird," Emma deadpans about Sarah. "I think she was switched at birth with the real daughter."

Something is missing: Emma. She has lost less than 10 pounds, and she hasn't been to Weight Watchers in two weeks because snow postponements forced extra play rehearsals on Saturday mornings. And Kathy suspects that nearly two weeks' worth of school cancellations also led Emma to a lot of extra snacking, so she is especially skittish about facing a weigh-in. Kathy pushes Emma to reschedule, offering to take her on a Sunday, but the conversation doesn't go well, ending with Emma exclaiming, "Why do you always try to make me feel guilty?"

From the tired scowl on her round face, it is evident that there are a million places that 15-year-old Emma Duyer would rather be at 9:30 on this Saturday morning. She could be snuggled back in bed, sleeping in her family's Germantown townhouse. Or hanging

Perl, Peter (2003), "The Incredible Shrinking Duyers," *The Washington Post Magazine,* March 30, pp. 6 ff.

with her friends. Or rehearsing her singing role in the chorus for the school musical, "Annie." Or she could be curling up in the family room to surf the various Internet fan sites of her all-time favorite TV show, the spy thriller "Alias," featuring a sleek, sexy CIA female operative.

But no. Instead, Emma reluctantly takes her spot in a long line of mostly apprehensive and substantially overweight people, including her mother, Kathy, and her father, George, who are queuing up for their weekly weigh-in at the Clopper's Mill Village Center in a jampacked storefront office of Weight Watchers. The three Duyers share a genetic tendency toward the same big, bulky body type. They are also linked by bad habits: too many years of unhealthy eating, too many late-night pizzas, too many all-you-can-eat french fry binges, too much of everything—except exercise.

The inevitable result of all that has brought them here, to this unforgiving black rectangular scale. One by one, they kick off their sneakers and peel off their jackets, then step up with a mixture of hope and dread. Emma wants to lose weight, but she's finding it a struggle. Her parents are more focused: They want to slim down and get healthier, but they also want to save their daughter from what they fear will be an unhappy future.

For nearly three months, Emma has been grudgingly accompanying them here because the Duyers have acknowledged that, for them, obesity has become a family affair. For years, Kathy, 48, a lawyer, and George, 51, who sells custom shower enclosures, have struggled unsuccessfully with their weight. The last decade, however, has been disastrous. It began when Emma was a toddler and the Duyers (pronounced Dwyers) risked all they owned for George to open his own business. After years of turmoil, he went bankrupt. Kathy, all that while, was forced to soldier on at a law firm job she hated.

Stressed out and discouraged, the Duyers developed a pattern of what they now call "emotional eating." Frequent and "supersize" portions of fast food, Italian restaurant pasta-and-bread binges, Chinese food deliveries, cookies, chips, cakes. "I self-medicate by eating," Kathy explains. The weight kept piling on, and on, until George, at 5-foot-11, reached 272 pounds, and Kathy, at 5-foot-6, passed 260.

And the bad habits were contagious, says George. "We also had to watch our daughter eating and getting very overweight." Emma, a stout, broad-shouldered 5-8, is in the 98th percentile for weight in her age and height group. Kathy was also fat in early adolescence and remembers vividly the sting of being called "Kathy Cow-Pile."

"I would so much like to save Emma from feeling the pain," she says.

But if Emma is feeling the hurt, she doesn't show it easily. She doesn't really want to be interviewed for this story, but agrees after her parents prod her. She curls up on a basement couch, hunched over and hugging a big pillow, giving brief, clipped answers between very long silences. On being big: "It's just who I am," she says matter-of-factly.

"It's who I am right now, but it's not who I want to be ... It's just hard picturing myself not being overweight, because I have always been that way."

Besides, Emma is a funny, quirky kid who says she doesn't care all that much what people think of her. Otherwise, she would not have gone to school on Valentine's Day wearing an illustrated sign taped to the back of her shapeless raincoat that said "Down With Cupid!" Nor would she have decided recently to wear a plastic silver tiara to school for several days. "People looked at me like I was insane," she says, smiling impishly. "But they think I'm insane anyway." In fact, she's an honors student at Seneca Valley High School with a grade point average above 4.0, a talented painter, a fine singer, a Girl Scout and a member of a tight circle of girlfriends.

It's just that she's also fat—although at this January weigh-in she learns she has lost weight. The digital readout behind the front desk (discreetly placed away from prying eyes) allows a Weight Watchers staffer to quietly report to Emma that she has lost a grand total of two-tenths of a pound in the last week. Emma frowns. It's been a long, hard week for her, trying to carefully record everything she eats on a Weight Watchers hand-held calculator, dutifully lugging low-fat lunches to school, and attempting to curb her after-school snack attacks. All this for a few lousy ounces. "It's not very much." She sighs. "But it's better than gaining."

Everyone at Weight Watchers preaches that it takes a long time to lose weight. So Kathy, who lost a full two pounds this week, asks Emma afterward whether she has the patience and discipline to stick with the program over the long, long haul. Emma furrows her brow a moment before answering in a distinctively teenage tone that sounds equally like a declaration and an unresolved question: "Yeah."

What happened to the Duyers is in many ways what happened to America. As a nation, our modern lifestyle has made us fat. We have the most bountiful food supply, the most powerful food-marketing machine and the most advanced labor-saving technology in human history. We are, as a people, consuming more and ever-larger portions of high-calorie restaurant meals and high-fat "convenience" foods, while also becoming increasingly sedentary. As a result, Americans in the last two decades have become virtually the fattest people on earth, exceeded only by some South Pacific islanders.

"I have the cure for obesity," says Richard Atkinson, co-founder of the American Obesity Association and head of the new MedStar weight-control clinic at Washington Hospital Center. "Let's get all of the women out of the workforce, back cooking nutritious meals at home, and get all the men back in the fields behind the mules, working hard. And let's rip up all the roads and have everyone walk everywhere. We were not a fat nation then. But unfortunately, we can't go backwards."

Since the 1980s, all measures of the bloating of America have spiked upward, with the Centers for Disease Control and Prevention declaring in 1999 that obesity had become "epidemic." The CDC's most recent estimates are that more than 60 percent of American adults are overweight, while almost one out of three is obese. In those same two decades, according to the CDC, the proportion of overweight children between ages 6 and 19 has tripled, to nearly one of every three kids. Overweight and obesity are determined by a mathematical formula known as body mass index, which measures weight relative to height. For example, a 5–6 person weighing 160 or more would be labeled overweight; while the same person weighing 186 or more would be considered obese.

The loudest governmental alarm was sounded in December 2001 by Surgeon General David Satcher, who estimated that 300,000 deaths per year are associated with overweight and obesity, and projected the annual public health cost at about $117 billion because of the life-threatening complications of diabetes, hypertension, heart disease, cancer, kidney failure and many other ailments.

Researchers say that an individual's genes can create a tendency to be slender or overweight, but that even greater determinants are personal choices, learned habits and the elusive quality called willpower.

"You can't blame obese people, but you can't totally excuse them, either," says James O. Hill, a leading obesity researcher at the University of Colorado. Though exercising willpower is important, it is ultimately futile for most people, Hill says, given America's toxic nutritional environment—awash in high-fructose corn syrup, palm oil and other high-fat or high-calorie additives, in everything from soda to cereal. "This environment is so difficult, it's hard to make good choices even if you have good willpower," says Hill.

And the cost of failure is high. Obese Americans—despite the dramatic increase in their ranks—still face discrimination and prejudice in a culture that regards slender as sexy and fat as loathsome. Studies have shown fat high schoolers are more often rejected at prestigious colleges, fat college students are more often turned down by elite medical schools, and fat adults are more likely to lose out in salaries, promotions and social life. "Obesity," says Atkinson, "is the last bastion of socially acceptable bigotry."

Some obesity experts believe that appetite-suppressing drugs will ultimately be the answer. But the small number of drugs approved by the Food and Drug Administration have shown limited effectiveness and, often, serious side effects. So the search for the magic bullet continues.

At any given time, half of the American population is said to be dieting. Weight Watchers is only the most familiar of thousands of approaches, ranging from the drastic— surgery that slices away much of the digestive system—to the almost Zenlike, the decision to focus on well-being, and ignore the numbers on the scale.

But by any method, virtually all diets are doomed. Long-term studies suggest that regardless of which weight-loss program they follow, fewer than one of every 20 dieters achieves lasting success.

"How many points is this?" Emma asks her mother, gesturing with a square of corn bread at the dinner table, where the Duyers are finishing the "white chicken chili" that Kathy whipped up after work, with white beans, chopped chicken breasts, broth and flour to thicken it, and onions, green chilies and spices to give it some kick.

Kathy takes out her Weight Watchers point-counter, a cardboard slide rule that she uses to calculate how the calories, fat and fiber content of foods translate into points. Each of the Duyers is allotted 30 to 35 points per day, depending on age and weight. Kathy keeps portion sizes moderate: a cup of chili for Emma and her sister, Sarah, who is 13 and slender, and a slightly larger bowl for the adults. Based on the nutritional labels, Kathy calculates with a pleased smile that the whole dinner, including low-fat corn bread and cut-up fresh fruit for dessert, totals only about 7 or 8 points.

Emma punches the dinner data into her blue calculator and announces that she's only had about 20 points for the whole day. Her parents are a bit skeptical. "What'd you eat today?" Kathy asks. Emma reports that she microwaved a Lean Pockets breakfast biscuit and brought an Uncle Ben's Noodle Bowl to school for lunch, totaling about a dozen points.

"You didn't eat anything else?" George asks, his doubts fed by family history; the Duyers had found that Emma's passion for snacking led her to squirrel away junk food in the mysterious jumble of her bedroom. She'd declared herself a healthy-food vegetarian a few years back, after she and Sarah became smitten with a brown-eyed cow they met at a county fair. But Emma quickly gave up vegetarianism when she acknowledged she hated almost all vegetables.

"I had an orange for a snack," Emma says.

"That's all?" George's eyebrows arch.

The cross-examinations make Emma itchy, if not angry. As if teen-parent relations aren't trouble enough, obesity inevitably raises the stakes. As early as age 10, Emma was taken for help to a nutritionist, but "she was like stone. She wouldn't say a word," Kathy recalls. "She just didn't want to hear it." As an elementary school kid, Emma was teased about being fat, but her parents had to learn about it from a teacher because Emma never told them. Asked about teasing now, Emma says it just doesn't happen anymore. "People know if they make fun of me," she says with a hint of playful bravado, "it'll be the last thing they ever do."

Emma, who hides herself in loose clothes like her father's old raincoat, is equally unrevealing to her parents about her emotions. Yet there are times when Kathy knows her daughter is hiding her pain, as when they were unable two years ago to find suitable clothes anywhere to fit Emma, forcing them to order by catalogue. "Her self-esteem took a little hit."

The point system has been a dominant topic of dinner-table conversation since Kathy coaxed the family to rejoin Weight Watchers last October, but everyone approaches it differently. Kathy, a consistently upbeat woman whose plump face is framed by short, dark hair, has been sticking to the program with an almost religious intensity. Virtually every single piece of food to pass her lips is carefully recorded in her 6-by-9-inch binder, where she tracks her points in a custom that Weight Watchers calls "journaling." (Weight Watchers' catchy phrase for this ritual: "If you bite it, write it.")

This day, Kathy had her usual breakfast, a creation she calls "Egg McMom." She makes it with a lite English muffin that's low in fat and high in fiber, a scrambled Egg Beater and a Morning Star Farms vegetable protein patty that tastes to her almost like sausage. With coffee and skim milk, breakfast was only 4 points. Her Lean Cuisine lunches that she microwaves at the office are only 5 to 7 points, with midafternoon snacks of fruit and low-fat crackers adding only a point or two. She says she's getting enough to eat to fight off hunger, and her vigilance even allows her an occasional treat of a few low-cal cookies or Hershey Kisses. Kathy, who has never been big on exercise, has also begun taking brisk half-hour lunchtime walks.

In three months, Kathy has lost 20 pounds toward her ultimate goal of losing 100. Emma has lost almost 10 pounds, while deflecting her mother's efforts to get her to commit to a specific weight goal, and George has lost 15, despite his adamant refusal to keep a journal or set a goal, regardless of Kathy's urging. George is a balding, friendly bear of a man who jokes that he grew a beard because he was tired of looking at his "two or three chins." Today, George reports, he had his customary breakfast—cinnamon raisin bagel without cream cheese, washed down by a Diet Coke. His work puts him on the road a lot, and so for lunch he hit Boston Market for a turkey carver with mashed sweet potatoes and lemonade. He has no idea about his point total, but says he's trying hard to conquer his main enemy, midafternoon snacking. Recently, he's been falling victim to Hershey Kisses, but today it was just a small pack of Oreos.

Kathy is trying to persuade George to use a journal to keep a more precise count. "It really works if you follow the program," she says. "If you don't follow the program, it doesn't work."

"That's not true," George shoots back. "It works for me—and I don't follow it." George says later that he knows from his past failures at Weight Watchers and other programs that he simply can't stand to keep count of food. "It becomes all-consuming. I felt guilty because I wasn't following the point system. I'm trying to develop a lifestyle where I would not have to think about it so much . . . To this day, I don't like being told to lose weight," he says, glancing at Kathy. "I have to decide to do it for myself."

"Uh-oh," says Kathy, laughing ominously.

But George says he is determined to stick with the program because he knows that it forces him to face a moment of truth every Saturday morning: "What works for me," he says, "is the weigh-in."

On a quiet winter evening, George and Kathy are sitting at the dining room table, reminiscing over family photos. There's a chunky Kathy as a fifth-grader at Hungerford

Elementary in Rockville. There's George as a husky teenager on the Eastern Shore, playing in a rock-and-roll band.

There's Kathy looking relatively slender at her 1983 graduation from the Catholic University School of Law. But two pregnancies and more than 100 pounds later, the more recent photos look like a different woman. George regards himself in Kathy's graduation picture.

"I had size 38 pants then," he says, confessing that in recent years he's been up to 52, and lately he's been squeezing into size 48s because he doesn't want to have to go to the Big & Tall shops, even though his pants sometimes hurt his belly.

There are the photos of Emma and Sarah on family vacations to Maine, Assateague and Chincoteague, with Emma always looking twice the size of her little sister. The family joke is that Emma was born hungry; at birth, she had a distinct scar on her hand, and the doctor said she'd apparently been chewing on it in the womb. In the succession of family pictures, Emma expands, but Sarah stays slender. The big sister marvels at the genetic anomaly. "She's weird," Emma deadpans about Sarah. "I think she was switched at birth with the real daughter."

Sarah's thin face breaks into a bashful smile when she is asked about being the only skinny Duyer. "It's kinda weird sometimes," says Sarah, an eighth-grade honors student. Two years ago, she accompanied the family to their previous attempt at Weight Watchers. "I'd cheer when they lost," she says, "and try to make them feel better if they gained." Sarah eats no red meat, tries to limit junk food, and, occasionally, fears gaining weight. "I kinda worry," she says, "but it's not a big worry."

Looking at family photographs makes Kathy distressed. "Emma was always big. She never had a waist. I feel pretty guilty about it. I'm her mom, and I fed her," she says. "I made the worst of my genetic background. My sister is not fat. I made bad choices. My sister didn't eat bags and bags and bags of cookies, and didn't spend 15 years in a job she hated." Her career was stunted, Kathy says, partly because obesity made her put limits on herself. She never tried to become a big-time litigator, because she wanted a family life but also because she believed a fat female lawyer wouldn't be taken seriously within the firm and wouldn't present well to juries.

This discussion dredges up, for George, the crushing stress he felt over the years his shower-enclosure business was failing and the everlasting stream of doughnuts, sausage-egg biscuits, hot dogs, burgers and fries he consumed in those years. He finally sold the business—and then suffered a heart attack in September 1997. He'd worried for years because heart disease runs in his family, yet he says the heart attack did not cause him to make any major changes, except for taking cholesterol and blood-pressure medicines. "I can't explain why it did not act as the proverbial wake-up call," he says. "I had worried so much about it and worried about it, and it was not nearly as bad as the elephant on my chest that I expected."

Later, Kathy is thumbing through old records that she has kept as a bitter reminder of her eight failed attempts at Weight Watchers. She explains why she believes that this time will be different. "I've reached the point in my life where life is basically under control. I have a good job, a good salary, and I pretty much have my act together," she says. "I'm also now at an age where I think about how long I am going to live, and I want to see my kids grow up and be happy and have families, and be successful, and that's why I want to be a healthy weight." She blinks a tear from her eyes.

George says he, too, wants to shed the burden of obesity. He hates the shortness of breath, pain in his joints, and excruciating gastric attacks. Kathy is quick to add mention of his heart condition. But George says that's not his primary motivation: "I can't say I'm blase about it, but it's not like it has been a big eye-opener."

"You didn't make any lifestyle changes after the first heart attack," Kathy says, her voice rising sharply, "and you had two more."

George refuses to rise to the bait. He calmly points out that the other two attacks last year were relatively minor. He steadfastly resists what he calls "panic" dieting and says he wants to go slow. Then he concedes, "I'm far too overweight, and I don't feel good, and I don't like feeling bad when I walk up stairs, or walk any length of time."

"Hell-o, George!" Kathy replies, her jaw tightening.

"I wouldn't be at Weight Watchers if I didn't want to be there," he says.

"So why are you doing it?"

"I want to lose weight, and it's easier doing it as a team . . ."

"And because I told you you were gonna die!" she exclaims.

George shakes his head, ignoring the outburst. "I want to be able to go into Kohl's and shop off the rack," he says coolly.

"If I were you," she says, "my main motivation is that I have had three heart attacks and I want to be there to see my kids grow up." She turns to their visitor. "George started Weight Watchers in October because I said I didn't want to raise our kids by myself."

George is still not rattled. "That is not why I started," he says, evenly. "I have to start on my own, for my own reasons."

There are some people, much heavier than the Duyers, for whom diets always fail, people who have nearly abandoned all hope. More than 200 of them cram into a basement auditorium on a Wednesday night at Holy Cross Hospital in Silver Spring. Some of them must walk with canes or walkers. Several can move only with wheelchairs. A huge woman carries oxygen; a gigantic man slumps over a table because he is having trouble breathing.

"I celebrate two birthdays," Doris Wray says into the microphone, "my own, and May 17th, 2002." That was when she had gastric bypass surgery. "I was 5-2, 375 pounds. And now I am a little, trim 213. I was on my way to die—and since my surgery, now I can breathe! I have no more diabetes medicine. I can walk! I am tremendously happy. I work at a school and I can play with the children now."

In the first nine months after the radical and irreversible procedure, Wray has lost up to 15 pounds a month. Three-quarters of her stomach is gone and all but three of some 20 feet of her intestine have been bypassed, making it nearly impossible for her body to absorb fat. It is potentially dangerous; roughly 1 in 200 patients die from the surgery, while post-op infections and complications have been estimated at upwards of 15 percent.

Despite the danger, it is an increasingly popular operation—more than 63,000 performed last year, according to the American Society for Bariatric Surgery, nearly triple the number just five years earlier—because there is such a large and desperate population of the severely or "morbidly" obese. The crowd at Holy Cross has gathered for an unadvertised but increasingly crowded biweekly support-group meeting of more than 50 patients who have had surgery, and more than 100 who are considering it.

Doris Wray grew up in Nashville in a close-knit, spiritual family who were heavy consumers of deep-fried Southern cooking. "I plumped up like a Ball Park frank," she says, laughing. She attended an all-girls parochial school, and her father did not allow her to date through high school. "I was eating to replace a lot of unfulfilled desires," she says. "If I'd gone out more, I would not have used food to satisfy some unrequited feelings."

After graduating from Howard University and getting her master's, Wray remained obese until serious dieting with a doctor's help in her mid-twenties shrank her to about 125 pounds. She bought a sporty car, began an active social life and had a good job teaching in the Montgomery County school system.

But then she became pregnant with twins, out of wedlock, and went into a downward emotional spiral. She felt ashamed around her family, and eventually became alienated from her sons' father. As a single mother, she says, "my needs had become secondary, and then my needs were tertiary, and then my needs were unmet altogether. To deal with that, I would eat. I would eat away the pain—I went from 150 to 165, 175 to 185, 199, 210, 230, and the next thing I knew I was 265. I mean, that weight was just whipping around me so fast, I just couldn't stop it."

Diabetes, high blood pressure, heart problems, sleep apnea, pneumonia, arthritis, shortness of breath, swollen limbs, circulation problems—Wray had all these and more. Her ankles swelled up too big for her shoes; her legs were so swollen, they oozed fluid. She could barely fit in her car, and she tired so easily she would have to pull over and rest during her 15-minute commute. She stopped going to movies because she couldn't squeeze into the seats. She feared leaving her car in parking lots, because she sometimes would get pinned in and need to ask strangers for help.

The hurt and stigma of such morbid obesity are intense. In the 1990s, University of Florida psychiatrists surveyed 47 successful gastric bypass patients who were no longer obese years later, asking them to choose whether they would rather suffer from another handicap—or be forced to return to morbid obesity. By overwhelming margins, they said they would rather be blind, deaf, dyslexic, or suffer heart disease, severe acne or an amputation, rather than become obese again. As one patient put it, "When you're blind, people want to help you. No one wants to help you when you're fat."

A cheerful and buoyant person with her friends, Wray says she often felt horrible when she encountered the unmistakable contempt that she would see in the eyes of strangers. "You can see their disgust, and you don't want to be in their presence, so you walk away and you feel bad," she says, "and what do you do? You eat!"

Since her surgery, Wray must take numerous vitamins and eat only small portions of meats, cheeses, eggs and vegetables, virtually swearing off bread, pasta, cakes and most sweets with refined white sugar. When she drank a glass of sweetened lemonade last year, she suffered violent vomiting and felt like she was having a heart attack, a phenomenon called "dumping" that is a major fear among bypass patients. Like all dieters, she is encouraged to drink lots of water and always eat slowly, reminding herself with a silent mantra: Chewyourfoodchewyourfoodchewyourfood. Her stomach, the size of a small piece of fruit, can hold only five or six forkfuls at a time. Sometimes she'll forget to eat, noticing hunger only when she feels lightheaded. But when she does eat, she says, she's actually savoring the taste of food "rather than inhaling it."

The surgery is not a panacea, and Wray, whose weight dipped to 206 by early March, knows that some patients suffer health problems and actually manage to regain weight. She still has to struggle, she says, to avoid emotional eating. Despite a post-surgery infection, a hernia and the need for abdominal surgery to remove excess skin, she says she has no regrets. "Look what I can do!!" she exclaims like an excited kid, and, beaming, she crosses her legs in her chair. "I have not been able to cross my legs in over 10 years! Do you know how good that feels? Better than any cupcake!"

Another Saturday, another weigh-in for the Duyers, another Weight Watchers support meeting that has the aura of an energetic, benevolent cult. "It's kind of entertaining," says George. "It's like being in a sorority." In this 95 percent female gathering, George is usually one of only three or four men who get to hear middle-aged women trade recipes, food-shopping tips and personal anxieties—about their bodies, their clothes, their husbands and boyfriends. They routinely have a "sharing" time for exchanging positive and negative experiences (for which they receive little silver stars for participating) followed by a "successes" segment in which people are heartily applauded for each milestone they pass.

George is not a guy who's looking to impress the ladies; he is wearing his customary outfit that he calls "my grubbies," which include a worn striped polo shirt that tents over his belly and a pair of old gray sweat pants that have worn so thin they have holes in the thighs.

Margaret Bell, a relentlessly cheery leader, is explaining to any newcomers how she joined Weight Watchers in 1994, lost 30 pounds, and kept it off. It was the best thing she ever did, she says, so she joined the company's professional staff.

Emma immediately finds the proceedings tedious, and she rests her head on her father's shoulder. She's got a ballpoint pen and is writing on the skin of her bare left arm. "EVERYTHING YOU KNOW IS WRONG," she inscribes on the upper arm. Then, on her forearm, she writes, "THE END IS NEAR." Kathy spots it and whispers, "Now you're scaring me."

"It's just about 'Friends,' the TV show," Emma explains. "The end is near." Kathy rolls her eyes.

And so it goes week after week through the winter. Emma's weight seems the most volatile: She is delighted in early January to learn she lost 3.4 pounds over the holidays. But after she misses a few meetings because of play rehearsals at a time when she is also stressed by finals and SATs, she is silently devastated because she's gained back 4.8 pounds. Then, on the week of her 16th birthday, January 30th, she's afraid of going to Weight Watchers because there was chocolate birthday cake, and not one but two dinner outings to celebrate. Yet that week, she loses a full pound, prompting Margaret to enthusiastically ooh and aah over Emma's achievement. Several times, Margaret invites Emma to share her thoughts about her successes with the group. Each time, Emma, her eyes downcast, quietly demurs.

George is making slow but steady progress. Kathy has apologized for questioning his commitment and harping on his heart attacks as they looked over the family photos; George says he understands. He loses 1.6 pounds over the holidays, and then in mid-January he stirs himself out of his favorite stuffed chair to make his first serious attempt at exercise in more than a year. He walks for 20 minutes on the old treadmill in the basement, covering less than a mile, but he finds it too boring and his back is hurting. Then George gets more serious about eating only healthy snacks, bringing oranges, yogurt and pretzel sticks to work, in pursuit of the noble goal of having an "Oreo-free week." He loses eight-tenths of a pound. By early February, he takes four walks in one week, the most exercise he's had in years; but the bad news is that it makes him hungry, and he gains two-tenths of a pound that week.

Kathy, however, is the star of the class. She is consistently losing at least two pounds a week. "Ohmygosh!! Down three pounds! Whoa!" Margaret exclaims at the January 18 meeting, where Kathy is applauded for reaching the plateau of a 10 percent loss in body weight—26 pounds. Margaret asks her to share, and Kathy is eager: She talks about how huge her ultimate goal of losing 100 pounds seems, but how determined she is to achieve it. She's been a size 24, and says she is sick of having to shop at "plus-size" departments or "fat ladies'" stores. "This week, I wore a suit I bought in August that I couldn't wear anymore, and I was able to put it on because I'd gone down a full size!" she says. The other women applaud, and, as is their hallowed custom, ooh and aah. By the end of January, Kathy is down to a size 20, hellbent on reaching 14.

After most every meeting, the Duyers file out of the storefront, walk past the fragrant Chinese restaurant next door, and go two doors further to have lunch at Subway. The fast-food chain now has more U.S. outlets than McDonald's and touts its healthy offerings through the now-legendary Jared Fogle, a TV-promotion phenomenon who lost 235 pounds through diet and exercise, while developing a taste for Subway sandwiches—without mayo or cheese. The Duyers always choose the smaller, six-inch turkey or ham subs, with lettuce, tomato and veggies (except for Emma), with no fatty dressings, small bags of Baked Lay's chips, and Diet Cokes, all for only 7 points. Besides the healthy options, Subway also offers special discounts to Weight Watchers members.

"Yeah," says George, "on Saturdays at Subway, they're just looking out the window, waiting for the fatties to start piling in."

Not everybody relies on weekly weigh-ins. In Southeast Washington, pediatrician Gloria WilderBrathwaite tells her patients to forget about the scale.

Inside a big, blue 38-foot medical van, parked curbside at a low-income housing complex, WilderBrathwaite is showing Marcel Mathis, age 12, a large laminated sheet with brightly colored drawings of portions of meat, eggs and potatoes. Each serving is roughly the size of a person's palm.

"Portions. Portions. Portions. That's what it's all about," says Doctor Gloria, as everyone calls the Children's Hospital physician in charge of its mobile health-care program. "You're not eating anything bigger than your hand, are you Marcel? For rice, or meat, or potatoes?"

"Yes, ma'am," says Marcel, as his mother, Yolanda Mathis, nods approvingly.

"And your vegetables? How much can you eat?"

"As much as I want."

His mother, a single parent of three who receives public assistance, interjects to explain that without a car, she usually can't shop at regular supermarkets. At neighborhood markets, most fresh, healthy foods are too scarce or expensive. WilderBrathwaite says later she hears this from the families of virtually all her 3,000 uninsured or Medicaid patients. "Just as we have more liquor stores in areas of poverty, we also have more really poor grocery stores, corner stores and carryouts," she says. "A lot of the kids I see are eating three meals a day from the carryout."

Marcel is headed toward obesity. His mother weighs 245, his older sister is even heavier, and he confesses he's worried about hitting 200. But Doctor Gloria tells him and his mother not to worry about numbers. Instead, the doctor urges them to focus on changing their eating habits, while making sure that Marcel gets lots of exercise by playing outside. But Yolanda Mathis says she usually won't allow that. In a gang-related shooting at their apartment complex last year, a bullet smashed through their window and lodged in a wall not far from Marcel's room.

Gloria WilderBrathwaite is all too familiar with the entire scenario faced by the Mathis family. She grew up in poverty herself in Brooklyn's tough Bedford-Stuyvesant neighborhood, the daughter of a single mother with three kids who eventually worked her way off welfare. She, too, was raised on a diet of cheap, fattening foods. Like the Mathises, WilderBrathwaite also grew up obese—and she remains so. She confesses to being "around size 22," but she says she stopped weighing herself long ago and doesn't want to estimate her weight for this story because it could undermine confidence in the medical advice she gives her patients, more than 40 percent of whom are obese. "Overweight and obesity are problems that have been in the inner city for a long time," she says. "I think the rest of the country is just kinda catching up."

From her earliest years, Gloria Wilder was fat but fit, an athletic, healthy girl who didn't let her size slow her down. Throughout her life—graduating from Howard University with honors, Georgetown University Medical School and George Washington University's master's program in public health, while also marrying her high school sweetheart and bearing four healthy, normal-weight children—WilderBrathwaite, 38, has steadfastly refused to diet.

"I come from a long line of really big women. I was destined to be big," she says in an interview over dinner with her family in their spacious home in Dumfries. Teased as a kid, she says, "I tried to diet when I was about 10 or 12. It didn't work, and I was miserable, crying. I could have kept dieting, but I don't like stress, I don't like worry . . . I decided that life is too important to be unhappy. If something superficial like size is making you unhappy, get over it."

"Over the years, I've had friends say, 'You'd be pretty, if you could just lose weight.' Well, I'm pretty now," she says, and is no longer friends with people who think that way. At 16, she fell in love with a handsome, slender Brooklyn high school track star, Carlos Brathwaite, who is now a muscular, 6-foot, 250-pound Fairfax County police officer.

"Her smile just swept me away. Her personality just overwhelms everything else. You don't even see her as a person of size," says Carlos WilderBrathwaite. He blushes, though, when she reminds him that he was initially "too embarrassed to acknowledge you had a fat girlfriend."

"I got over that fast," he says, smiling.

Two heaping ceramic bowls of fruit in the kitchen are the main snack foods of their children—Travis, 16, Kai, 10, Trent, 6, and Kyle, 19 months—who must ask permission for any cookies or chips, which are rarities in the home. The kids all love fruits and vegetables, and eat balanced diets, as do their parents—although Carlos, not Gloria, was recently diagnosed with diabetes and must cut down on his portion sizes, particularly sweets and pasta. Mom or Dad cooks dinner at home every night, except about once every two weeks, they'll get pizza or Chinese food.

Last month, WilderBrathwaite spoke on obesity to a medical conference in Washington, opening her talk by saying, "A lot of you may be surprised to hear an obese doctor talk about obesity." Summarizing her philosophy, she says, "I truly believe in the bell curve of life: There have to be some people who are supermodels in the world, and there are also gonna be some people on the other extreme. But that doesn't mean the other extreme can't be fit and healthy." She herself has normal blood pressure, low cholesterol and blood sugar, and other healthy readings. "As long as my vital signs are good, I'm happy," she says. "I don't keep track of my weight. I go by the fact I have worn the same clothes, same size, for like 10 years, so I don't worry about the numbers."

"Would I prefer if I had lived my life at like 150 pounds? Well, yeah, definitely," she says. "But we have to start swapping the way we see things. We have to get away from the blame game and all the shame, all the worry, and get focused on health.

"The big thing is, 'Are you able to do what you wanna do at your weight? Are you able to walk up a flight of steps and not be winded? Are you able to walk five blocks in any direction, even if it's uphill?' Those are my personal guides to know whether I'm staying where I want to be." She says she gets two 30-minute sessions of aerobic exercise a week, and should do more, but she is too busy.

Such advice is heresy to many obesity experts, who say the so-called "fit and fat" population such as WilderBrathwaite is very small and that most obese people should focus on achieving at least a 5 to 10 percent weight loss. But WilderBrathwaite doesn't buy it. "A lot of folks struggling with weight problems are also struggling with depression and low self-esteem," she says, and trying to diet usually makes them unhappier—and fatter. "They may not feel very good at the weights they are at, and they feel almost like they are gonna hide themselves from the rest of society, and a good way to do that is to become morbidly obese."

At 6:30 A.M. on a Friday in February, George Duyer is doing a highly uncharacteristic thing: He is sweating profusely, his face and bald head glistening. He is about to finish 25 minutes on the treadmill at a fancy new gym called Healthtrax Wellness and Fitness. "This is my fifth time this week!" he huffs while keeping up a 3.5 mph pace. When he stops, the electronic calorie counter reads 216. "I've lost a sandwich!" He smiles.

George, who only a few weeks earlier had described himself as "pretty sedentary . . . actually just plain lazy," had for years routinely started his workdays with a 45-minute hot bath. Now, he not only finishes off the treadmill, but also then hits the Lifecycle for 15 minutes more. Over the years, George tried but dropped out of other health clubs. Too many young studs in muscle shirts, too many babes in leotards. It made him feel old, ungainly, unwelcome. This place, in a 30-foot atrium with skylights, giant TV screens and a no-Spandex dress code, is more his speed, he says. "It's also easier here because you have more distractions. You watch TV, you listen to four different channels of music, and you watch the schlub in front of you." He's even invested in a fresh pair of gray sweat pants.

While George is in the shower, after burning off a total of 302 calories, Kathy comes striding purposefully in the front door, carrying her gym bag. George and Kathy arrive separately, in his-and-hers Dodge minivans, because she stays home until 7:30 to get the girls off to school. It was Kathy's brainchild to join the newly opened club, two miles from their home, because she has fully absorbed both parts of Weight Watchers' simple wisdom: Eat Less, Move More. She believes the $150-a-month membership is a crucial investment for the whole family's health, so she even has Sarah and Emma, with their busy schedules, coming to swim or exercise about twice a week.

George and Kathy reap immediate benefits in their first week at the gym, losing 3.6 and 2.8 pounds, respectively. Kathy had an all-time personal best of exercising 12 times in a week, including her five lunch-hour walks and two nights at the gym with the girls. Emma, who declared her two exercise sessions "not too bad," unfortunately gains four-tenths of a pound. Kathy, though, is elated at the prospect that her long-sedentary family actually might be changing. "The other night, we were all there, four of us standing in a row on treadmills," she recalls, chuckling. "It was like aliens came and took away our family and replaced the Duyers."

Kathy has just been diagnosed with hypertension, but she is optimistic her eating and exercise regimen can change that—and that she can become that statistical rarity, a permanent weight-loser. "I think I can be the 1-in-20 because I've had so many learning experiences over the last 30 years and I'm just not gonna have another one," she says, breathing heavily on the treadmill. "This is it for me! I'm not doing this again. I want to get stronger and healthier, in forward motion, and I am not going back!"

George, too, is enthusiastic about the budding changes, feeling more energy and vitality, despite the sore back, ankles and legs from increased activity. But after his exercise session, he betrays his doubts. "I know it's new now. When it becomes routine, it'll be harder. We'll see if I keep it up," he says. "That's the acid test."

By early March, Kathy and George Duyer are feeling pretty great. She has lost 37.2 pounds, her greatest weight loss ever. Of course she's lost impressive amounts before, but each time she returned to Weight Watchers heavier than before. This time, she is convinced, is her last. George also marvels at their life change. He's lost 24.4 pounds, his best in memory, and he has agreed with his doctor to set a target weight goal of 200 pounds, which is now less than 45 pounds away.

"Sloth and gluttony used to be our favorite sins," Kathy says with a laugh over lunch at Subway after another triumphant weigh-in, following another week of healthy eating and regular exercise. Last night, Friday night, instead of the customary pizza for the kids and Chinese for the parents, they ate baked chicken and then went to work out at the gym. "Can you believe it?" George asks. At this morning's weigh-in, she's down 2.4, and he's lost 3.4. "Nyah, nyah. I lost more," he teases as they step off the scale.

After five months, they both have begun to see actual changes: thinner faces, more energy, looser-fitting clothes. Both of them know their goals remain many months, if not years, away—and the odds are that they will not reach them. Yet both believe they have learned healthy new habits that will not change.

But something is missing: Emma. She has lost less than 10 pounds, and she hasn't been to Weight Watchers in two weeks because snow postponements forced extra play rehearsals on Saturday mornings. And Kathy suspects that nearly two weeks' worth of school cancellations also led Emma to a lot of extra snacking, so she is especially skittish about facing a weigh-in. Kathy pushes Emma to reschedule, offering to take her on a Sunday, but the conversation doesn't go well, ending with Emma exclaiming, "Why do you always try to make me feel guilty?"

"Emma would really like to lose some weight," Kathy says. "But if I was not being a nudge, I don't think she'd be doing it."

Obesity experts wonder how America, as a nation, is going to nudge itself, particularly future generations, into reversing the current alarming trend. "If we don't change something, I think the entire society will become obese," says Hill of the University of Colorado. "It is not too far-fetched to say we will all give up and become obese, except for a few lucky, genetically gifted people."

Some advocates believe our society should launch a tobacco-style public health campaign to save coming generations from all the ailments associated with overweight. A first wave of lawsuits has targeted fast-food companies for allegedly misleading consumers about the dangers of their products; and some activists want to tax junk foods and use the money to promote healthy eating. George L. Blackburn, chairman of nutrition medicine at Harvard Medical School, said recently that the government must move on the problem more forcefully, "or we are going to have the first generation of children who are not going to live as long as their parents."

Kathy is passionate enough to keep pushing her daughter, but ultimately savvy enough to realize that nagging Emma really doesn't work. But it's hard not to. She remembers the age when wearing cool clothes and looking like the other kids seem so important, and when girls start to get serious about boys, and she desperately doesn't want her daughter to be left behind.

At this Saturday's weigh-in, Kathy is again a star of the class, being applauded for passing her 35-pound milestone. She is asked to share her motivation for success, and her eyes fill with tears as she says, "I made a decision to stop looking at my past failures, and just look forward."

Back in the minivan, Kathy says she realizes she can't fully control whether Emma sticks with the program or drops out. So Kathy makes another decision. "I guess maybe Emma has to decide when it's her time to really do something," she says. "Maybe I just gotta let it ride, and maybe I just have to let her go for now."

IN CHINA, CIGARETTES ARE A KIND OF MIRACLE DRUG

Geoffrey York

Guiyang, China—Here's some exciting medical news from the Chinese government: Smoking is great for your health.

Cigarettes, according to China's tobacco authorities, are an excellent way to prevent ulcers.

They also reduce the risk of Parkinson's disease, relieve schizophrenia, boost your brain cells, speed up your thinking, improve your reactions and increase your working efficiency.

And all those warnings about lung cancer? Nonsense.

You're more likely to get cancer from cooking smoke than from your cigarette habit.

Welcome to the bizarre parallel universe of China's state-owned tobacco monopoly, the world's most successful cigarette-marketing agency.

With annual sales of 1.8 trillion cigarettes, the Chinese monopoly is responsible for almost one-third of all cigarettes smoked on the planet today.

If you believe the official website of the tobacco monopoly, cigarettes are a kind of miracle drug: solving your health problems, helping your lifestyle, strengthening the equality of women, and even eliminating loneliness and depression.

"Smoking removes your troubles and worries," says a 37-year-old female magazine editor, quoted approvingly on the website. "Holding a cigarette is like having a walking stick in your hand, giving you support.

"Quitting smoking would bring you misery, shortening your life."

Such statements are widely believed in China.

Two-thirds of Chinese men are smokers, and surveys show that as many as 90 per cent believe their habit has little effect on their health, or is good for them.

Even in China's medical community, 60 per cent of male doctors are smokers. Few are aware of the studies forecasting that cigarettes will soon be responsible for one-third of all premature deaths among Chinese men.

Little wonder that Western tobacco companies are hungrily circling the Chinese market, lobbying eagerly for entry into this lucrative market of 360 million smokers, the biggest market in the world.

York, Geoffrey, (2005). "In China, Cigarettes are a kind of miracle drug." *Globe and Mail.*

So far, 99 per cent of the market is controlled by the Chinese monopoly, but Western tobacco companies are convinced they will soon crack it, especially now that China is a member of the World Trade Organization and is obliged to reduce its tariffs on foreign cigarettes.

For the anti-smoking movement, China is the ultimate challenge. Nonetheless, this week, a group of Canadian experts arrived in southwestern China in a bid to convince Chinese smokers that cigarettes might not be quite as beneficial as they believe.

They distributed anti-smoking posters, visited cancer patients, showed the graphic warnings on Canadian cigarette packs, and lectured on how the anti-smoking campaign has reduced Canada's lung-cancer rate. But they admitted that they face an uphill struggle in a country where the tobacco industry provides 60 million jobs and 10 per cent of national tax revenue.

"The magnitude of the problem is overwhelming," said Jean Couture, a Quebec surgeon who has been travelling to China since 1990 to work on cancer-education programs.

"In China today, the economy comes first and everything else is secondary, including health care," Dr. Couture said. "You wonder if anyone in the government is conscious of how great the smoking problem is. There's no public education program. The Chinese anti-smoking association is very weak and has almost no money. Within 20 years, China could have the majority of all smoking deaths in the world."

Chinese doctors have called Dr. Couture a "second Norman Bethune"—a reference to the Canadian surgeon who became a Chinese hero after dying while giving care to Chinese Communist soldiers in 1939. The Quebec doctor, who has helped create an 80-bed cancer unit at a hospital in northeastern China, is now leading an anti-smoking campaign in four Chinese provinces.

When the Canadians arrived this week in Guizhou province in southwestern China, they were worried about the power of the local tobacco industry. The province is filled with tobacco farms and cigarette factories. As they distributed posters at a hospital in one of Guizhou's biggest cities yesterday, the Canadians saw a number of people smoking in the hospital. A hospital shop was openly selling cigarettes.

"The tobacco industry is so huge and the anti-tobacco movement is so weak," said Mark Rowswell, a Canadian television personality and Chinese celebrity (under the name Da Shan), who helps promote the anti-smoking campaign. "What we're doing is just a drop in the ocean."

While smoking rates have fallen sharply in Canada in the past two decades, the rate in China is still rising.

"Ten years ago, when we first came to China, it was unheard of for young women to smoke," said Nicole Magnan, executive director of the Quebec division of the Canadian Cancer Society, who was in the Canadian delegation this week. "Now there are more and more of them."

While China has proclaimed that the 2008 Beijing Olympics will be a smoke-free Olympics, it has done little to discourage smoking. The number of Chinese smokers is growing by three million a year, despite an estimated 1.3 million tobacco-related deaths annually.

Chinese cigarettes are cheap—as little as 30 cents a pack—and the health warnings are hidden in small print on the sides of the packages. Though cigarette advertising is technically illegal, tobacco companies are allowed to promote their corporate names. When sprinter Liu Xiang won a gold medal for China at the Athens Olympics last summer, he promptly went out and filmed a television commercial for China's biggest cigarette company.

Children can easily buy cigarettes at Chinese shops, despite an official ban on sales to those under the age of 18. "Shop owners never refuse to sell us cigarettes," said one 16-year-old boy who was smoking as he played pool near a Guizhou school this week.

"They only care about money."

Che Chuangao, a construction worker, started smoking when he was 20. "More than 90 per cent of my friends smoked, so I couldn't be different," he said. "And it's helpful for my work. Offering a cigarette is a social greeting, whenever you meet a friend or a stranger. I know that smoking isn't good. Once I stopped smoking for a month or two. But my friends persuaded me to smoke again."

While their task is daunting, the Canadians are scoring some small successes. After listening to a speech by the Canadians this week, 27-year-old medical student Li Dongbo said he was inspired to work on anti-smoking projects.

The student's uncle, who had smoked for 30 years, died of lung cancer in February. To spare his feelings, his family had never told him the truth about his illness.

"I was shocked," Mr. Li said. "The government should be doing more. We need promotion campaigns to tell people about it."

College Binge Drinking:
Administrators Struggle with Student Alcohol Consumption

Sept. 26—It's been rated the top party school in the nation. Welcome to a typical party night on campus at the University of Colorado. Alcohol abuse has long been one of the most serious problems facing America's colleges—national studies show about four out of every 10 students qualify as binge drinkers. So what are schools doing to stop it? "Dateline" spent part of the past school year at the University of Colorado, where leaders are determined to reform the campus culture of drinking. How are they doing? NBC's Josh Mankiewicz has a sobering look.

It's a hot August night. A new school year is starting. At the University of Colorado in Boulder, there's a party in progress, and the guest of honor is in a plastic cup. It turns out the drug of choice at many college campuses isn't cocaine or even marijuana. It's alcohol.

This party could be happening nearly any night at Boulder, an academic community of 22,000 undergrads in the foothills of the Rocky Mountains. Known there as "C.U.," it's a school with a reputation for scholarship, skiing and alcohol-fueled extra-curricular activities.

Tonight's party at C.U. is no different. Almost everyone drinks. Some drink too much. Often the police come to shut down these gatherings and the students run away because many of these student drinkers are under the legal age of 21. They buy alcohol with a fake ID or they have someone else do it for them. Meet Nick Hanson, a junior, a marketing major. Nick is in training.

Nick: "It's taken a long time to get my body in shape to where I can handle that much drinking."

How much? Nick says 15 to 20 drinks a night, often several times a week.

Nick: "We have 12 beers before we even leave to go out."

We're not talking about just drinking here, we're talking about binge drinking. Technically, that's when a woman downs four drinks in an evening or a man consumes five

College Binge Drinking: Administrators Struggle with Student Alcohol Consumption, *Dateline NBC*, October 26, 2003. (transcript as appears on http://msnbc.msn.com/id/3088196/)

drinks. And one national survey found that 40 percent of America's college students routinely drink that much or more, and that every year that kind of drinking accounts for 70,000 cases of sexual assault and 1,400 deaths from things like alcohol poisoning, falls and car accidents. It is an issue that America's college presidents say is a matter of life and death. But it's an issue that America's college students see differently. At Boulder, for example, we found a lot of binge drinkers. And for them, four or five drinks is just a first course.

At the beginning of the 2002 school year, "Dateline" came to Boulder, invited by both school administrators and by students themselves. We weren't undercover, we told students we were doing a story on the party scene here. And we spent several weeks watching campus life, videotaping students who offered to let us see what they do after class. It was at the local party scene that we met Nick and his pal Keiven Cosgriff.

Nick: "Study hard play, that's all we have to do."
Keiven: "Study hard, play hard."

Study hard, play hard. Keiven tells us that's his mantra. We were not in a position to know how hard he studies, but his dedication to hard drinking is undeniable. Keiven's 20, a political science and sociology major who says he's on his way to law school. He shows off his tattoo.

Josh Mankiewicz: "How hammered were you that night?"
Keiven: "I was significantly intoxicated. Definitely."
Mankiewicz: "And that would be how many drinks? Five? Ten?"
Keiven: "No, it was definitely more than five. I'd say in the 10 to 15 range."

Like Nick, Keiven admits he wasn't born with his current tolerance for alcohol—that only comes with practice.

Keiven: "The social scene that I'm interested in revolves around it."
Mankiewicz: "Revolves around drinking that much."
Keiven: "Drinking that much. See it's all about your perspective. Like to you that's a lot but to me that's the norm when people go out."

And it's not just the boys. Lily is a senior, just turning 21. At Boulder, and many other campuses, that means a birthday ritual of consuming 21 drinks. Lily's girlfriends help her keep track by marking her arm with every drink. Eight drinks, and Lily is just getting started. As the alcohol continues to flow, the first thing to go is that clever marking system. By the middle of the night Lily has lost track of how much she's had to drink.

Lily: "So I had, oh, I had at least three shots and two beers at that bar, so that's five more. Here, I've had at least two shots. I've had at least 20."

Twenty drinks, and to us, Lily doesn't even seem that drunk. She tells us that's because she can drink like a guy.

Lily: "I have a lot of guy friends and I drink with them a lot and guys have a tendency to be able to handle their alcohol a lot better, so I just have grown accustomed to drinking a lot more. I'm proud of it. I don't know why I am, but I am."

Proud to be able to keep up with the boys. But there are some in Boulder who could never keep up with Lily, like the school's chancellor, Richard Bynny.

Bynny: "I think that if you or I had four or five drinks in a row in a bar, we would be pretty dysfunctional."
Mankiewicz: "Deeply asleep in my case."
Bynny: [laughs] "Yeah, that's right."

Seven years ago when Bynny took this job, he found himself dealing with a university in an alcohol induced crisis. Drunken students rioted after a football game. They rioted after student parties were shut down. One time they rioted after a crackdown on underage drinking. Bynny resolved to change that.

Bynny: "Our job is to work with them, and try and figure out, you know, how can we get across to them the importance of finding other venues for having fun."

So in what amounted to a sort of large-scale intervention, the university tried to change its own culture, with dry events like casino night, mandatory sessions for freshmen on the fallout of too much drinking, and a program called "three strikes, you're out."

Get caught once with alcohol or drugs and you go to a substance-abuse class; twice and the school calls your parents; three times and you can be suspended. That's happened to only 84 students since the program started in 2000.

C.U. is one of the first universities to make a serious effort to deal with student drinking, and that's one of the reasons "Dateline" came here. The chancellor says his innovations are working. Some students aren't as sure.

Keiven: "You know, they tell you in orientation that three strikes you're out and all that nonsense. I just didn't take them seriously."

Consider the effectiveness of one program: a ban on alcohol sales at C.U. football games. We went along with hard-drinking Nick and Keiven to the first big game of the school year, C.U. vs. Colorado State. The kickoff was set for 11 A.M. But the party in the stadium parking lot kicked off a lot earlier.

Nick: "It was an 11:00 game, so we were up at 7:30. We got at the stadium at like 8:00."
Mankiewicz: "OK, 8:00 A.M. Have you had a beer at that point?"
Nick: "Yeah."

Mankiewicz: "Three hours to go 'till game time."

Nick: "Uh-huh."

Mankiewicz: "How many drinks do you have?"

Nick: "I think I had a lot."

Mankiewicz: "Five? Ten?"

Nick: "Ten plus. I don't, I'm not totally sure."

What is sure is that even with police on the scene, for some of these underage drinkers that alcohol ban has become meaningless.

Mankiewicz: "I just get the feeling that the students kind of confound you at every turn. I mean you make the stadium dry, well they drink in the parking lot. And they get up early and start drinking before the game, because they're going to make sure that they get that daily dose of alcohol."

Bynny: "Yup."

Mankiewicz: "Whether you like it or not."

Bynny: "I believe that that's right. As you know, people who are devious can find ways around most rules. Doesn't mean you shouldn't set standards for a community."

Keiven: "They're trying to keep student drunkenness to a minimum, that's they're objective."

Nick: "That's a lie. That's not going to happen."

Keiven: "That's their goal, but the students have a philosophy of saying, you know, f★★★ the administration."

And if what you're about to say is that parents ought to exercise more control, remember Lily's 21st birthday? Well, her mother was there, helping Lily celebrate.

Mom: "Oh that's, yeah, see now this is what my husband and I have been arguing about. He says it's terribly bad form, but she's 21 years old and it's like a rite of passage and not only will she have a few drinks, she'll probably get drunk. And she might even get sick. And, you know, it's just something you go through."

Remember that mantra of 'study hard, play hard'? Surveys make clear that the more you party the less you study. But on the other side of that equation is the simple fact that in college, in that awkward nether-world between childhood and adulthood, alcohol is the lubricant that makes a lot of social interaction possible.

Keiven: "Hey, zoom in on the sober driver. Sober driver. Yeah."

Students say they know not to drink and then get behind the wheel. But that's where the alcohol lesson ends.

Mankiewicz: "You guys have clearly gotten the message that drinking and driving is a bad idea. That it can have serious legal and health impact on you. But you don't seem to have gotten any sort of similar message about binge drinking. That's still sort of done and accepted."

Keiven: "Yeah well, yeah, you can—like all the eggheads in academia they tell you, you know, 'If you hit the sauce that hard it's not good for you,' you know, probably physically and emotionally. But for whatever reason, my generation, at least the people that I socialize with, thousands and thousands of undergraduates, don't feel that it's an issue and aren't concerned about it. This is a social scene. This is like what people do, they go out and have a good time."

Mankiewicz: "So what might seem abnormal to me is actually normal behavior around here?"

Keiven: "It really is. Like, I don't know, it's frightening for especially someone your age, and maybe possibly your background, to relate to, but this is what's going on these days."

But if Keiven is defiant, his best friend is less so. Remember when we met him, Nick Hanson was in training. When we came back at the end of the semester, we found a different Nick.

Nick: "I kind of scared myself, so I started to slow down then. Realized that I gotta, sort of get my ass in shape I guess."

Mankiewicz: "You know, I apologize for sounding like somebody's Dad here."

Nick: "Yeah."

Mankiewicz: "But you're too young to have a drinking problem like that."

Nick: "Definitely."

He doesn't believe he's an alcoholic, which might be why he hasn't quit completely. But for now Nick says he's drinking a lot less.

Mankiewicz: "So you're not getting buzzed anymore?"

Nick: "No."

Mankiewicz: "You miss that?"

Nick: "No."

Nick even went to a football game—sober.

Mankiewicz: "How was it?"

Nick: "It was good. It was the same thing. I mean, you kind of got pissed at all the drunk people but . . ."

It took awhile, but one student seems to have learned a valuable lesson. Every September though, a new freshman class will arrive, 5,000 more students who will make their own choices about how much is too much.

EXPLORING MACROMARKETING: TAKING A BROADENED VIEW OF OUR WORLD

Macromarketing

Clifford J. Shultz, II

Introduction

Marketers and marketing institutions increasingly are under pressure to address society's problems, conflicting interests, and the reciprocal effects of marketing on society and society on marketing. In other words, the world is (re)turning to macromarketing.

> *"The purpose of macromarketing . . . is to save the world." (Fisk 2001)*

Macromarketing literally deals with big/important issues, beyond comparatively simple exchanges between buyers and sellers, or even relationships between companies and customers. In a more interconnected world of markets, marketers, and their stakeholders, macromarketing is an important mechanism to study both opportunities and shortcomings of marketing, and both its intended positive effects and unintended deleterious effects. This suggests macromarketing includes an optimistic perspective; that it seeks functional mechanisms to enhance marketing processes, to the benefit of the largest number of stakeholders, the world over.

Definition

The definition of macromarketing can vary depending upon one's source, but essentially, macromarketing is differentiated by its focus on aggregations and systems, and the way marketing processes within them affect and are affected by those systems and the society in which they function. For example, Bartels and Jenkins (1977) suggested:

"(M)acromarketing" should connote an aspect of marketing which is "larger" than what is otherwise considered. . . . It has meant the marketing process in its entirety, and the *aggregate* mechanism of institutions performing it. It has meant systems and *groups* of micro institutions, such as channels, conglomerates, industries, and associations, in contrast to their individual component units . . . the social context of micromarketing, its role in the national economy, and its application to the marketing of noneconomic goods. It has also meant the *uncontrollable environment* of micro firms (p. 17).

SHULTZ, CLIFF: Macromarketing

Clifford J. Shultz, II is Professor and Marley Foundation Chair in the Morrison School of Management and Agribusiness at Arizona State University.

Similarly, Hunt (1981) suggested

> . . . macromarketing is a multidimensional construct, (which) refers to the study of (1) marketing systems, (2) the impact and consequence of marketing systems on society, and (3) the impact and consequence of society on marketing systems (p. 8; see also Hunt, 1977).

Fisk (1981) added that (macro)marketing should be viewed as social process, as (1) a life-support system provisioning technology, with concerns about (2) quality and quantity of life-goals served by marketing, (3) a technology for mobilizing and allocating resources and (4) is concerned about the consequences of marketing—the spillover effects of marketing—for those who may not seek or be aware of the intended or unintended activities of marketers (pp. 3, 4, 5) (see also Dixon, 1979; Shawver and Nickels, 1979).

The Domain of Macromarketing

The macromarketing domain is illuminated in the context of perspectives and historical development, and then six key topics.

PERSPECTIVES AND HISTORICAL DEVELOPMENT

The ideas and interests central to macromarketing have been with us for Millennia. *History of the Peloponnesian War* (Thucydides, 1972 [431~424 B.C.]), the *Magna Carta* (Danziger and Gillingham, 2004), and *The Travels* (Marco Polo, 1958 [circa late 13th Century]) provide just three examples of works in which trade, markets, marketing and concerns for societal welfare were themes. Macromarketers regularly delve into such literature, because they find it intrinsically interesting, but also because they believe there are important lessons germane to modern marketing scholarship and practice.

Macromarketing *practice* moreover is perhaps as old as society itself. Societies emerged for the welfare of the group; the need for specialization and then exchanges of items produced by specialists surely was evident early-on. Greater specialization and support for it begat trade. Eventually markets—which linked many systems in any given society, from production to consumption—were an efficient mechanism to sustain a society, which, fundamentally is a series of institutions and systems agreed upon by the members of the group. One would reasonably presume the first markets—imagine the ancient agora in Athens or a bazaar in the Fertile Crescent of Mesopotamia—must have necessitated systemic organization and coordination, bringing people together in ways to facilitate exchanges and, on balance, improving society (see also Lane, 1991; and McMillan, 2002, p. 4, who hints the oldest discovered artifact of written language may be a marketing transaction, scratched in baked clay, circa 3000 B.C.).

Within the modern marketing literature, macromarketing *orientations* were evident early in the 20th century. Sheth and Gardner (1982) suggest "the first school of marketing thought (was) *macromarketing*," a focus on problems and potential of marketing activities from a more societal perspective, rather than from the firm's perspective (p. 53).[1] More explicit glimpses of academic macromarketing were evident in textbooks written by Breyer (1934), and Vaile, Grether and Cox (1952). Their macro orientation became a cornerstone at the Wharton School of the University of Pennsylvania and was further developed by Alderson (1957).

A more prescribed macromarketing *concept* seems to have emerged between the late 1950s and mid 1960s (e.g., Holloway and Hancock, 1964; Grether and Holloway, 1967; Slater, 1968). Fisk's (1967) text on *Marketing Systems* presented a detailed macrosystems perspective, including chapters on Evolution of Marketing Systems (historical analysis), Characteristics of Marketing Systems (Micro and Macro system characteristics), Resource Allocation by Competition and the Expanding Role of Government (aggregate system constraints), and Social Performance of Marketing and Comparative Marketing (Fisk, 2004).

Macromarketing therefore is integral to society and its welfare. Despite this assertion and complexities and dangers that have accelerated in the last half century, marketing scholars ironically have become more atomistic, potentially distancing themselves from important societal contributions. This trend has raised some concerns in the academy,[2] which in turn may portend a shift back to a macromarketing focus by marketing scholars. Some substantiation of this assertion is provided by the recent inclusion of "stakeholders" in the latest definition of marketing proffered by the AMA.

In summary, marketing began because it added value to societies, and markets and the systems of which they were part emerged and thrived, because, though not flawless, they were superior to most (all?) other social institutions as a provisioning mechanism. They are among the oldest institutions that affect and are affected by society; they are among the first institutions restored in the wake of societal destruction (e.g., Shultz et al., 2005). Macromarketing addresses these complex and multi-faceted relationships by examining marketing and society, marketing systems, marketing history, marketing phenomena in the aggregate, and marketing's effects on quality of life.

MACROMARKETING TODAY

Today, macromarketing continues to morph, to draw new and diverse followers, and thus it defies neat boundaries, descriptors, and limitations. With its growth and maturation

---

[1]See also Bartels (1965); Alderson and Cox (1948); Wilkie and Moore (1999; 2003); contributions by Ely (1903), Shaw (1916) and Schumpeter (1934), for example, also come to mind (cf. Jones and Moniesen, 1990).

[2]A special session at the 2003 AMA Summer Educators' Conference, for example, assembled many leading marketing scholars who lamented the increasingly micro and concomitantly inconsequential focus of marketing scholarship.

have come new directions in the forms of sub-disciplines, as described in the following sections.[3]

Historical Analysis

History broadens and deepens understanding, and contributes to a sense of continuity and tradition. Marketing history is a vast data bank, spanning cultures, events, people, places, companies/organizations, and of course time; its exploration can be a major contribution to the marketing discipline. It puts current events and ideas into perspective; insights from it can assist contemporary marketing and marketers. The origins, growth, and development of both marketing history (as scholarly and professional activities), and marketing thought (as an intellectual pursuit) are of particular interest, and are considered a mainstream area for further study in macromarketing.

Competition and Markets

Understanding how markets work is at the core of macromarketing. The past century has shown how open markets with freely competing firms, operating within an appropriate institutional framework, can enhance our material standard of living, but as we look to the future, a number of challenges need to be addressed regarding our understanding of markets and competition. Many macromarketers therefore currently are studying several compelling issues. "Conceptualization and measurement of markets" is one important area that needs to evolve along with technology and other change. Consider the Internet, for example, and relevant questions it raises about marketplace change. Related to this, government-as-participant in markets is a key issue (e.g., as in the current transition of state-owned enterprises and privatization in many countries). Other timely topics include conflicts of interests; market homogeneity vs. diversity; value creation and good will; heterogeneous jurisdictions (e.g., EU, AFTA, NAFTA and WTO); the changing nature of firms and their role in society; resource-based views of competition; and of course markets and democracy.

Global Policy and the Environment

Globalization renders macromarketing issues increasingly critical for the survival of the world as we know it. What we do as marketers today will affect others for centuries to come; the consequences of our actions will affect our environment. As globalization

---

[3]This section of the chapter is organized vis-à-vis the editorial sections of the *Journal of Macromarketing*. The following text is gleaned largely from the ideas shared by current and former section editors, which are posted on the *Journal's* website: http://agb.east.asu.edu/jmm/from_the_editor.htm). Therefore, Stan Hollander, Brian Jones, Terry Witkowski, Andreas Falkenberg, Bill Kilbourne, Andrea Prothero, Pierre McDonagh, O.C. Ferrell, Gary Bamossy and Joe Sirgy are acknowledged for their contributions.

increases, so too will the environmental problems that accompany it. If we limit our domain of marketing concerns only to firm management the results may be catastrophic. The boundaries of inquiry therefore must be expanded. These can range from specific environmental problems and their solutions to the conceptualization of alternative paradigms within which sustainable marketing practices can be developed. Some topics of particular interest here include measurement; compatibility of contemporary marketing practices; role and consequences of anthropocentrism; materialism, including resource allocation problems, wealth distribution, waste disposal, etc.; implications of neoclassical economic models and political liberalism on the environment, perhaps including different conceptions of freedom, democracy, and property rights and how prevailing political institutions affect the environment and the conduct of marketing; new technologies and technological risks; individual value systems and their relationship to environmental perceptions and behavior; balancing economic growth and environmental quality. Environmental problems transcend specific cultures, political models, academic disciplines, geography, and time, and, accordingly, the preference is for similarly transcendent studies and solutions.

Marketing Ethics and Distributive Justice

Ethical conduct and concern for distributive justice are indispensable to the macromarketing ethos. Marketing practices and public policy need to be explored to determine the extent to which they are ethical, and to determine their impact on marketing stakeholders. Opportunities for exploration abound for theoretical work as well as empirical studies (more on ethics is available in Section IX of this book).

Marketing and Development

Economic development studies were a pillar of early macromarketing work. New challenges have created new opportunities for scholarship and practice, as the world has globalized. Studies designed to provide insights on arcane and evolving systems, social performance, host performance, elements of the marketing mix, market reforms, models, macroeconomic policy, unemployment, inflation, technology transfer, trade and investment, and business cycles still are needed. Such analyses might include comparative studies within and across political boundaries, best practices or policy recommendations, and ultimately solutions to humanity's most pressing development challenges represented by an array of human welfare indicators. Moreover, some measures, such as gross domestic product per capita, income per capita, or even the more recent purchasing power parity, though insightful, may not indicate the developmental progress for vulnerable populations within a society. Infants, women, the elderly, the sick, and ethnic minorities come to mind as examples of groups potentially at risk. Conditions and tendencies among families, communities, and the aforementioned vulnerable populations, in addition to national, regional and global trends, should be examined and measured.

Quality of Life

Quality of Life (QOL) marketing is becoming increasingly important because of the growing complexities and interdependencies of the marketing institution with other societal institutions. With the increasing role of marketing ethics on marketing thought and practice, marketers are likely to demand concepts, models, and measures that would enable them to enhance the QOL of consumers with little or no adverse effects to other organizational stakeholders. This is an important and awesome challenge for marketing scholars. Marketers need to accept this challenge by conducting studies that address the many and complicated issues facing contemporary marketing. Particularly pressing QOL studies in marketing would focus on the marketing of products, services, or programs specifically designed to enhance the QOL of consumer groups (e.g., elderly), families/ households in general or specific types of families/households (e.g., single-parent households), communities in general or specific types of communities (e.g., rural communities), and wide geographic regions/countries or specific types of regions/countries (e.g., developing countries).

Readers will see that any current marketing issue of interest likely will be relevant to more than one of these topical areas. Secondly, enthusiasm for many of these subdisciplines in turn has spun off new scholarly groups and conferences (e.g., International Society of Marketing and Development, International Society for Quality of Life Studies, Conference on Historical Analysis & Research in Marketing, etc.) that cross traditional boundaries and embrace disciplines beyond marketing, including other social sciences, as well as the arts, biological sciences, and even the physical sciences. Thus interest in macromarketing ideas continues to grow throughout the academy, ultimately driven by a fascination with the interplay between marketing and society.

Delving Deeper into Macromarketing: Selected Readings

For someone interested in learning more about this field, the *Journal of Macromarketing* is a good place to begin. The table below includes some of the *Journal*'s articles (listed chronologically) that have had the most impact. Reviewing these titles, moreover, can provide additional insights into the depth and breadth of macromarketing.

The readings for this section synthesize important movements in the discipline, from its early years, through its evolution, and into its future.

TABLE 1

Representative Articles with Substantial Impact on Macromarketing[*]

"Marketing Processes in Developing Latin American Societies" (Slater, 1968)

"Macromarketing" (Bartels and Jenkins, 1977)

"Macromarketing as a Multidimensional Concept" (Hunt, 1981)

"The Visions of Charles C. Slater: Social Consequences of Marketing" (Nason and White, 1981)

"The Political Economy of Marketing Systems: Reviving the Institutional Approach" (Arndt, 1981)

"Public Regulation of Marketing Activity: Part I: Institutional Typologies of Marketing Failure" (Harris and Carman, 1983)

"Frameworks for Analyzing Marketing Ethics" (Laczniak, 1983)

"Technological Antecedents of the Modern Marketing Mix" (Funkhouser, 1984)

"Marketing and Economic Development: Review, Synthesis and Evaluation" (Wood and Vitell, 1986)

"A General Theory of Marketing Ethics" (Hunt and Vitell, 1986)

"Measures of Structural Changes in Macromarketing Systems" (Layton, 1989)

"Retailing in Classical Athens: Gleanings from Contemporary Literature and Art" (Dixon, 1995)

"The First Dialogue on Macromarketing" (Shaw, 1995)

"Marketing and the Wealth of Firms" (Falkenberg, 1996)

"Sustainable Consumption and the Quality of Life: A Macromarketing Challenge to the Dominant Social Paradigm" (Kilbourne, McDonagh and Prothero, 1997)

"Improving Life Quality for the Destitute: Contributions from Multiple-Method Fieldwork in War-Ravaged Transition Economies" (Shultz, 1997)

"Organizational Transformations in Transitional Economies" (Carmen and Dominguez, 2001)

"Macromarketing and International Trade: Comparative Advantage versus Cosmopolitan Considerations" (Ellis and Pecotich, 2002)

"Developing a Subjective Measure of Consumer Well-being" (Lee, Sirgy, Larsen and Wright, 2002)

"Globalization and Technological Achievement: Implications for Macromarketing and the Digital Divide" (Hill and Dhanda, 2004)

---

[*]Thanks are given to Roger Dickinson, Shelby Hunt, Bob Nason, Bill Redmond, Stan Shapiro, and Joe Sirgy for sharing thoughts on articles to be included.

LAYING THE FOUNDATION FOR THE FIELD

Fisk's (1981) article initiated macromarketing as a formal scholarly discipline. Building on his body of publications in the 1960s and 1970s, Fisk's articulation of the history, nature, and scope of macromarketing institutionalized macromarketing and the *Journal of Macromarketing* as a scholarly discipline, and a prime scholarly outlet, respectively. Fisk furthermore offered a research agenda and encouraged marketing scholars to direct their research efforts toward eclectic endeavors that would serve the interests of broad communities with vested interests in marketing. Note that many of the ideas introduced remain compelling.

MARKETING SYSTEMS

The second important article is provided by Meade and Nason (1991), who made a valuable contribution by suggesting that macromarketing should develop as a unified theoretical construct, and by encouraging redirection toward systems conceptualization and research. This was an important evolutionary step in the discipline. The authors noted that macromarketing largely had been a patchwork of content topics, with no unifying philosophy and no unifying principles. To overcome these shortcomings,[4] they made a case for systems theory as a framework for the macromarketing domain and a structure for meaningful empirical research.

In a recent exchange, Nason (2004) revisited the rationale for the systems approach, and maintained the underlying logic remains sound, because (1) macromarketing is compatible with the global nature of systems science, (2) it is appropriate to use explanatory ideals from systems theory as analytical concepts in macromarketing, (3) the "balance of forces" concept from physical systems is useful, (4) open systems are structurally unstable and will exhaust either input or output potentials, and therefore (5) macromarketing deals with closed systems and needs to be framed in those terms. Moreover, Meade and Nason made the important point that macromarketing should not simply focus on systems failures, but rather should enable analysis of components, with a broader objective to recombine those components in appropriate ways. They provide an interesting case—disposable diapers—to illustrate their points. Nason, upon reflection, would extend the article by focusing on investigation of positive externalities as well as negative; looking at micromarketing as a subsystem with open links in all sorts of directions to show how myopic, and in some cases dangerous, it is without a systems perspective; expanding the system beyond marketing, for example, to consider financial measures to test *satisficing* or optimization, to look at cost systems, to focus on policy issues germane to the entire societal system in which markets and marketing exist.

SOCIAL TRAPS AND THE TRAGEDY OF THE COMMONS

The third article, by Shultz and Holbrook (1999), also looks at marketing systemically, but further develops temporal dimensions and trade-offs that people and firms must make within the marketing system. The authors argue marketing ultimately must be addressed as a contributor or solution to the commons dilemma and other forms of social

---

[4]Some macromarketers comparatively, over the years, have referred to this lack of structure or unifying theme as a strength, rather than a weakness of macromarketing.

traps—the tendency for people and organizations to engage in activities that benefit them in the short run, but eventually harm them and others in the long run. By re-examining Hardin's (1968) classic article through marketing lenses, they in some ways bring the discussion full circle (Fisk also cited Hardin in his 1981 *JMM* article), as they attempt to synthesize the massive amount of literature from several disciplines on this most insidious and pervasive societal problem. They argue that marketing can and indeed must provide solutions to the commons dilemma. They conclude their synthesis with testable propositions and an illustration.

Shultz and Holbrook recognize the growing marketing and business paradigm sweeping the globe, and contend this reality must be factored into the solution process. In other words, they understand managerial perspectives, suggest these perspectives must be addressed if commonly shared resources are to be managed prudently, and reach out to business practitioners. Rather than simply encourage marketers to be more thoughtful in their management of commonly shared resources (to date, not an especially effective strategy), they encourage marketers and their stakeholders to negotiate win-win outcomes for stakeholders of the commons. An important component toward that end is an appreciation for the social cocktail that exists in the form of corporate profit motives, consumer choice and wise management of the commons; indeed, they suggest that finding ways to balance divergent stakeholder interests must be factored into negotiated agreements, otherwise more powerful stakeholders (typically, corporations) will be inclined to eschew negotiations, reducing the probability for sustainable win-win outcomes. Management of a tract of California's redwood forest is given as a possible model. Important elements of that model include stakeholder inclusion, imaginative thinking, effective monitoring and measurement, and consideration for systems beyond those that affect and are affected by the redwood forests.

GLOBALIZATION, TECHNOLOGY, AND ADVANCEMENT

Hill and Dhanda (2004) bring our attention squarely to the phenomenon of globalization, implications for vulnerable groups, and the necessity for accurate measures, systemic action and cooperation to improve life quality and societal outcomes generally. They focus on the "digital divide"—the striking disparities within and among countries—and the imperative to close this divide if we are to alleviate interdependent socioeconomic problems and injustices, the world over. The contribution is noteworthy because the authors creatively examine extant data provided by the United Nations and other international organizations, with particular attention to an interesting subset of measures salient to marketing and consumption: equitability in distribution of consumption opportunities, gender-related development, carbon dioxide emissions, and technological achievement.

In summary, these articles capture the essence, evolution and primary foci of macromarketing:

- big issues in relation to the interplay of marketing and society;
- appreciation for the complex interaction of numerous forces—past, present and future—that affect society and are manifest in marketing systems;
- solutions that will result in sustainable quality of life for the largest number of stakeholders in various marketing systems, from local to global.

Policy in Progress: Illustrative Action Issues

The seemingly relentless progression of globalization is a convoluted series of interactive policies and actions that, by definition, affect all of us (e.g., Stiglitz, 2002). It clearly is a colossal process potentially leading to a huge, benevolent, interconnected marketing system that offers prosperity to its participants. But it also affects and is affected by humanity's biggest problems, and if not managed properly, globalization will lead to environmental degradation, war, pandemics, dehumanizing exploitation, and myriad other tragedies. It raises important macromarketing questions about how best to engage others in an evolving global system; whether win-win outcomes for the largest number of stakeholders are possible and whether the sirens' song of short-term gain from innumerable social traps can be resisted to the long-term benefit of all (e.g., *Journal of Macromarketing,* 2005).

VIETNAM AS PART OF THE GLOBAL MARKETING SYSTEM

A look at a particular country—its history, ongoing transition, and current engagement with other countries and external organizations—might help to make more concrete some of these abstract ideas. Vietnam, for example, embodies both the peril and promise of globalization. It has been ravaged by centuries of colonial exploitation and war. The years 1945–1975 were especially harsh, dominated by protracted wars with France and then the United States. The Vietnam War (or American War, as the Vietnamese refer to it) devastated infrastructure and institutions, tore apart societies in both countries, and killed more than 58,000 Americans and more than 2 million Vietnamese. Administering any country in the wake of such destruction would have been difficult; Vietnamese leaders compounded problems by embarking on a series of devastating Marxist-Leninist policies and still more war with neighboring Cambodia and China that rendered Vietnam one of the 10 poorest countries in the world. The collapse of the Soviet Union, its largest benefactor, and the geo-political shift toward market economies forced Vietnam's own transition to a more market-oriented economy (e.g., Karnow, 1997; Shultz et al., 1994).

Today, Vietnam is undergoing a socioeconomic renaissance. Marketing institutions are entrenched; Vietnamese enjoy more personal freedoms, and have access to more and better goods and services. A majority of its 80 million people, however, remain quite poor. Approximately 35 percent live below the poverty line and income per capita hovers around $400 per year. The economy is primarily agrarian and 1.5 million workers are added annually to an already crowded labor force (Shultz et al., 2006). The government recently has invoked many new policies to expedite socioeconomic development and Vietnam's more seamless integration into the global economy, including initiatives intended to enable membership in the WTO by 2005 (Xuan, 2005). Vietnam, in short, is an enigmatic political, economic, natural, social, and marketing system that is moving forward, but still needs help. It will remain dependent upon foreign assistance well into the future, if it is to reach its development goals by 2020 (Central Intelligence Agency, 2005).

Nike in Vietnam

Foreign direct investment (FDI) has been a key component of Vietnam's rebirth. Vietnam has welcomed its former adversaries to invest in and to help rebuild the country, and the United States now is one of Vietnam's largest trading partners (VOV News, 2005). Nike is among the largest investors. The factories with which it has contracts employ approximately 50,000 people, yet Nike has been criticized for its engagement in Vietnam (Vietnam Labour Watch, 2004). An article published by Greenhouse (1997) in *The New York Times,* "Nike Shoe Plant in Vietnam Is Called Unsafe for Workers," is generally regarded as the bellwether for allegations of unfair and unsafe practices in the factories in which Nike shoes are made, and thus it is included as a reading for this chapter.

Nike responded to the charges with changes. For example, a 2001 press release introduced readers to Nike's webcam and virtual tours of its Vietnamese factories, as well as its increasingly transparent policies and practices, from production, to marketing, to consumption. Nike furthermore has cooperated with organizations such as the Fair Labor Association (FLA) to monitor and measure compliance with generally accepted practices for factory management and employee relations in Vietnam and other developing economies, and to enable investors, marketers and consumers to make responsible buying decisions (Fair Labor Association, 2005a). Table 2 discloses the FLA Workplace Code of Conduct, with which Nike strives to comply.[5]

Macromarketing Solutions to Nike's Systemic Challenges

The preceding text and readings offer glimpses into Nike's efforts to improve working conditions and to be a responsible player in a growing global supply chain. They more

---

[5]Some readers may have interest to see detailed policies and lengthy reports, by Nike and the FLA, which can be found via links to "responsibility" at www.nikebiz.com.

TABLE 2

Fair Labor Association Workplace Code of Conduct[*]

Forced Labor. There shall not be any use of forced labor, whether in the form of prison labor, indentured labor, bonded labor or otherwise.

Child Labor. No person shall be employed at an age younger than 15 (or 14 where the law of the country of manufacture allows) or younger than the age for completing compulsory education in the country of manufacture where such age is higher than 15.

Harassment or Abuse. Every employee shall be treated with respect and dignity. No employee shall be subject to any physical, sexual, psychological or verbal harassment or abuse.

Nondiscrimination. No person shall be subject to any discrimination in employment, including hiring, salary, benefits, advancement, discipline, termination or retirement, on the basis of gender, race, religion, age, disability, sexual orientation, nationality, political opinion, or social or ethnic origin.

Health and Safety. Employers shall provide a safe and healthy working environment to prevent accidents and injury to health arising out of, linked with, or occurring in the course of work or as a result of the operation of employer facilities.

Freedom of Association and Collective Bargaining. Employers shall recognize and respect the right of employees to freedom of association and collective bargaining.

Wages and Benefits. Employers recognize that wages are essential to meeting employees' basic needs. Employers shall pay employees, as a floor, at least the minimum wage required by local law or the prevailing industry wage, whichever is higher, and shall provide legally mandated benefits.

Hours of Work. Except in extraordinary business circumstances, employees shall (i) not be required to work more than the lesser of (a) 48 hours per week and 12 hours overtime or (b) the limits on regular and overtime hours allowed by the law of the country of manufacture or, where the laws of such country do not limit the hours of work, the regular work week in such country plus 12 hours overtime and (ii) be entitled to at least one day off in every seven day period.

Overtime Compensation. In addition to their compensation for regular hours of work, employees shall be compensated for overtime hours at such premium rate as is legally required in the country of manufacture or, in those countries where such laws do not exist, at a rate at least equal to their regular hourly compensation rate.

Any Company that determines to adopt the Workplace Code of Conduct shall, in addition to complying with all applicable laws of the country of manufacture, comply with and support the Workplace Code of Conduct in accordance with . . . Principles of Monitoring . . . and shall apply the higher standard in cases of differences or conflicts. Any Company that determines to adopt the Workplace Code of Conduct also shall require its licensees and contractors and, in the case of a retailer, its suppliers to comply with applicable local laws and with this Code in accordance with the Principles of Monitoring and to apply the higher standard in cases of differences or conflicts.

[*]The Code is posted on the FLA website in Arabic, Bahasa Indonesia, Brazilian Portuguese, English, French, German, Greek, Hindi, Italian, Japanese, Khmer, Korean, Bahasa Malaysia, Mandarin, Portuguese Singhalese, Spanish, Tamil, Tagalog, Thai, Turkish, and Vietnamese.

broadly reveal thorny, interdependent, and evolving forces facing many marketing firms, consumer groups, and policy makers in an age of accelerating globalization. They hint at dilemmas that confront governments, companies, workers, families, communities, and consumers in a dynamic marketing system.

Nike had problems in Vietnam during the late 1990s because some of its associates did not understand a number of factors in that system, which resulted in labor difficulties, strained relations with the government, and a public relations nightmare that degraded its global brand image. A macromarketing reorientation, however indicates Nike largely has rectified policies and practices, to the benefit of many stakeholders. Nike is now among the largest employers in Vietnam and has among the most favorable working conditions. It is involved in the welfare of its employees through several assistance programs, including education support, micro-loans for entrepreneurial ventures, and programs to support women. It has refurbished local infrastructure and commenced a recycling program, which may prove to be a model for Vietnam. Unexpected consequences include new start-up enterprises (creating still more jobs and lifting still more people out of poverty), reductions in domestic violence, larger numbers of Vietnamese completing secondary education, and technology-and-skills-transfer that makes Nike employees more desirable in the labor market, which drives up these employees' wages.[6]

It would be easy to raise a cynical eye about some of these findings, but many observers believe the Vietnamese people are markedly better off from Nike's constructive engagement in their country. Sales of shoes made in Vietnam suggest Nike and its customers also are better off. In sum, managerial practices with an eye toward optimizing welfare throughout the marketing system can enable the firm to do well financially as it makes broad contributions to society. Furthermore, one can reasonably conclude that Nike has won considerably more hearts and minds in Vietnam, over the last five years, than did most other American organizations that operated there during the 1960s and early 1970s. Net effects of a macromarketing orientation or constructive engagement in Vietnam to date include corporate success, global customer satisfaction, remarkable improvements in quality of life for most Vietnamese (e.g., Nguyen, Shultz and Westbrook, 2005; United Nations, 2002; 2004), and a new era of peaceful, mutually beneficial United States-Vietnam relations.

FROM VIETNAM TO IRAQ

While Vietnam and Nike provide some tangible examples of policy in progress and relevant action issues, some readers might wonder if Iraq is a *more* compelling example of a marketing system in shambles, embodying several social traps that scream out for immediate resolution. The global forces that have come to a boil in Iraq may prove to be a macromarketing crucible. Trends to date, however, suggest that little thought has been given to important macromarketing considerations. This seems tragically ironic, given that the remnants of the aforementioned Mesopotamia—perhaps the birthplace of markets, and a marketing system so important to the advancement of civilization—are found in present-day Iraq. Similarly to reflections on Vietnam, we can only speculate

---

[6] Based on the author's interviews from 2001–2005 of several strata of Nike management, Nike factory workers—predominantly from factories in Cu Chi and Dong Nai—participants in the micro-loan program and their families, various Vietnamese government authorities at national and local levels, and representatives from the Vietnam Women's Worker Union.

what Iraq might look like today, if former and current policy makers and business persons had possessed a better understanding of and appreciation for history, competition and markets, marketing and development, environmentalism and prudent resource management, and distributive justice.[7]

Regardless of one's position concerning Iraq, *solutions* require greater understanding of historical and cultural forces, coupled with far-reaching systemic analysis beyond Iraqi borders, and ultimately a willingness to invoke polices and practices that will result in some short-term costs, but also better long-term benefits for individuals in a particular marketing system as well as the larger global community. Indeed, this perspective is now gaining currency among some corporate leaders, politicians, and pundits. Thomas Friedman (2005a, b, c), for example, now champions "The Geo-Green Alternative," essentially arguing that many of our most daunting challenges—the Iraq/Iran/Mid East saga, war, global warming, the rise of China, energy alternatives, environmentally friendly technology and product development, job creation, terrorism, political repression and religious intolerance, human rights, failed states, nuclear proliferation, and gasoline taxes and prices, etc.—all are interconnected and thus necessitate a sound integrative policy, to ensure the best long-term outcomes for societies, markets and individual consumers. They demand, in a word, macromarketing. Three final readings, a stream of Friedman's commentaries published in *The New York Times,* are included to draw attention to action issues discernible in Iraq, with repercussions for all of us.

Conclusion

One need not look far in today's world to find macromarketing action issues or "hot topics" that command attention and resolution. Recapping specific topics and adding to the list, we are faced with difficult dilemmas in the forms of environmentalism; the illicit trafficking of weapons, people, narcotics, and nuclear materials; cartels (e.g., energy suppliers); religious and cultural intolerance; intellectual property rights (protected and stolen); economic transition and/or development; public health crises (poverty, malnutrition, contaminated water, homelessness, malaria, HIV/AIDS and other pandemics); genetic engineering; societal inequities, angst and anomie; historical lessons (learned and not learned, and costs associated with ignoring them); poor/despotic governance; and, most unfortunately, societies that disintegrate into war. Many of these issues interact; that is, they are parts of broader systems and failures of those systems, increasingly of global proportions. They are tangible examples of primary foci for macromarketing

---

[7] Both Vietnam and Iraq are extraordinarily complex societies, with diverse and high context cultures that have emerged from more than 5000 years of history; space constraints preclude detailed discussion, but readers should be sensitive to the relationship between historical/cultural ignorance, and policy and marketing failures. Secondly, we could similarly speculate about many other communities, countries and regions.

research and practice. If the purpose of macromarketing is indeed to save the world, a macromarketing orientation toward their resolution may be our best hope for the most optimal outcomes for the greatest number of people, over time.

Questions for Discussion

Possible questions for discussion are asked below. The first two queries are more specific to the illustrative action issues; they are followed by more general questions regarding macromarketing.

- What are the dilemmas, or costs and benefits, of a global marketing system that encourages foreign direct investment and outsourcing?
- Is a company responsible for the conduct and welfare of the other members of its global supply chain; at what point are people no longer stakeholders of a company's actions?
- How can macromarketing tools and perspectives help to improve the welfare of particularly vulnerable groups (e.g., children, women, families, refugees, disenfranchised communities, laborers, ethnic groups, and even countries) suffering from the world's most pressing crises?
- Is it appropriate for marketers or governments to engage repressive countries to sell products that benefit consumers in those countries or other countries?
- Are any marketing systems or countries so dysfunctional that military intervention by another country is justifiable? (If the answer is "yes," then what, precisely, might be justifiable reasons for that intervention and at what financial, moral and human costs? Would you volunteer to participate in the intervention or encourage loved ones to participate?)
- How could one construct a model of a marketing system to determine impediments to desirable societal outcomes; what would be included in the model; what might be measured?
- How does one reconcile that it is unlikely all stakeholders will receive optimal outcomes from any marketing endeavor or policy (and what is "optimal")?
- What insights might be derived from history, a better understanding of competition and markets, measures of QOL, and other key topics previously discussed to help reshape or to sustain a marketing system, and to improve societal welfare?
- How can we persuade policy makers and corporate leaders to engage in seemingly costly large-scale socially responsible conduct, when their competitors do not engage in similar, desirable conduct?
- How does one manage a career—business or academic—when the short-term measures of success in one's field may be counter to the long-term welfare of the stakeholders of ones actions?

References

Alderson, Wroe. 1957. *Marketing Behavior and Executive Action,* Homewood, IL: Irwin.

Alderson, Wroe and Reavis Cox. 1948. "Towards a Theory of Marketing", *Journal of Marketing,* 12 (Oct): 137–151.

Arndt, Johan. 1981. "The Political Economy of Marketing Systems: Reviving the Institutional Approach," *Journal of Macromarketing,* 1 (2): 36–47.

Bartels, Robert. 1965. "Development of Marketing Thought: A Brief History," in *Science in Marketing.* George Schwartz, (ed.) New York: John Wiley.

Bartels, Robert and Roger L. Jenkins. 1977. "Macromarketing," *Journal of Marketing,* 41 (4): 17–20.

Breyer, Ralph. 1934. *The Marketing Institution.* New York: McGraw Hill.

Carman, James and Luis Dominguez. 2001. "Organizational Transformations in Transitional Economies," *Journal of Macromarketing,* 21 (2): 164–180.

Central Intelligence Agency. 2005. *The World Factbook* (online edition, accessed March 10), https://www.cia.gov/cia/publications/factbook/index.html

Danziger, Danny and John Gillingham. 2004. *1215: The Year of the Magna Carta.* New York: Touchstone.

Dixon, Donald. 1995. "Retailing in Classical Athens: Gleanings from Contemporary Literature and Art," *Journal of Macromarketing,* 15 (1): 74–85.

Dixon, Donald. 1979. "The Origins of Macromarketing Thought," in *Macromarketing: New Steps on the Learning Curve.* George Fisk and Robert Nason, (eds.) Boulder, CO: University of Colorado Business Research Division.

Ellis, Paul and A. Pecotich. 2002. "Macromarketing and International Trade: Comparative Advantage versus Cosmopolitan Considerations," *Journal of Macromarketing,* 22 (1): 32–56.

Ely, R. T. 1903. E. D. Jones to Ely, March 18 unpublished correspondences, Ely Papers, Madison: State Historical Society of Wisconsin in Jones, Brian and David D. Monieson (1990), "Early Development of the Philosophy of Marketing Thought," *Journal of Marketing,* 54 (Jan): 102–113.

Fair Labor Association. 2005a. "Welcome," (www.fairlabor.org), accessed March 9, July 7.

Fair Labor Association. 2005b. "Workplace Code of Conduct," (http://www.fairlabor.org/all/code/index.html), accessed March 9, July 7.

Falkenberg, Andreas W. 1996. "Marketing and the Wealth of Firms," *Journal of Macromarketing,* 16 (1): 4–24.

Fisk, George. 1981. "An Invitation to Participate in Affairs of the Journal of Macromarketing," *Journal of Macromarketing,* 1 (1): 3.

Fisk, George. 1967. *Marketing Systems: An Introductory Analysis.* New York: Harper and Row.

Fisk, George. 2001. "Reflections of George Fisk" (from plenary session presentation at the 2001 Macromarketing Conference), *Journal of Macromarketing,* 21 (2): 121–122.

Fisk, George. 2004. Correspondences with Fisk, Stan Shapiro and author, October 24.

Fitzgerald, Frances. 1972. *Fire in the Lake: The Vietnamese and Americans in Vietnam,* New York: Vintage Books.

Friedman, Thomas. 2005a. "The Geo-Green Alternative," *The New York Times,* January 30, Section 4, p. 17.

Friedman, Thomas. 2005b. "No Mullah Left Behind," *The New York Times,* February 13, Section 4, p. 15.

Friedman, Thomas. 2005c. "Geo-Greening by Example," *The New York Times,* March 27, Section 4, p. 11.

Funkhouser, G. Ray. 1984. "Technological Antecedents of the Modern Marketing Mix," *Journal of Macromarketing,* 4 (1): 17–28.

Greenhouse, Steven. 1997. "Nike Shoe Plant in Vietnam Is Called Unsafe for Workers," *The New York Times,* November 8 (accessed via http://www.mindfully.org/WTO/Nike-Vietnam-Unsafe.htm, December 3, 2004).

Grether, E.T. and Robert Holloway. 1967. "Impact of Government upon the Marketing System," *Journal of Marketing,* 31 (April): 1–5.

Hardin, Garrett. 1968. "The Tragedy of the Commons," *Science,* 162, 1243–1248.

Harris, Robert G. and James M. Carman. 1983. "Public Regulation of Marketing Activity: Part I: Institutional Typologies of Marketing Failure," *Journal of Macromarketing,* 3 (1): 49–58.

Hill, Ronald Paul and Kanwalroop Kathy Dhanda. 2004. "Globalization and Technological Achievement: Implications for Macromarketing and the Digital Divide," *Journal of Macromarketing,* 24 (2): 147–155.

Holloway, Robert J. and Robert S. Hancock. 1964. *The Environment of Marketing Behavior,* New York: Wiley.

Hunt, Shelby. 1981. "Macromarketing as a Multidimensional Concept," *Journal of Macromarketing,* 1 (1): 7–8.

Hunt, Shelby. 1977. "The Three Dicohotomies Model of Marketing: An Elaboration of Issues," in *Macro-Marketing: Distributive Processes from a Societal Perspective,* edited by Charles Slater, Boulder: Business Research Division, University of Colorado, 52–56.

Hunt, Shelby and Scott Vitell. 1986. "A General Theory of Marketing Ethics," *Journal of Macromarketing,* 6 (1): 5–16.

Jones, Brian and David D. Monieson. 1990. "Early Development of the Philosophy of Marketing Thought," *Journal of Marketing,* 54 (Jan): 102–113.

Journal of Macromarketing (1981a), 1 (1): 3–78.

Journal of Macromarketing (1981b), 1 (2): 3–80.

Journal of Macromarketing (2005), Special Issue on Globalization, 24 (2).

Karnow, Stanley. 1997. *Vietnam: A History,* New York: Penguin.

Kilbourne, William, Pierre McDonagh and Andrea Prothero. 1997. "Sustainable Consumption and the Quality of Life: A Macromarketing Challenge to the Dominant Social Paradigm," *Journal of Macromarketing,* 17 (Spring): 4–24.

Laczniak, Eugene. 1983. "Frameworks for Analyzing Marketing Ethics," *Journal of Macromarketing,* 3 (1): 7–18.

Lane, Robert. 1991. *The Market Experience,* Cambridge: Cambridge University Press.

Layton, Roger A. 1989. "Measures of Structural Changes in Macromarketing Systems," *Journal of Macromarketing,* 9 (1): 5–15.

Lee, Dong-Jin, M. Joseph Sirgy, Val Larsen and Newell Wright. 2002. "Developing a Subjective Measure of Consumer Well-being," *Journal of Macromarketing,* 22 (2): 158–169.

McMillan, John. 2002. *Reinventing the Bazaar: The Natural History of Markets,* New York: Norton.

Meade, William and Robert Nason. 1991. "Toward a Unified Theory of Macromarketing: A Systems Theoretic Approach," *Journal of Macromarketing,* 11 (1): 72–82.

Monieson, David D. 1988. "Intellectualization in Macromarketing: A World Disenchanted," *Journal of Macromarketing,* 8 (2) 4–10.

Nason, Robert. 2004. Comments on Meade and Nason 1991, by Bob Nason (e-mail correspondence, September 24).

Nason, Robert W. and Phillip D. White. 1981. "The Visions of Charles C. Slater: Social Consequences of Marketing," *Journal of Macromarketing,* 1 (2): 4–18.

Nguyen Dình Tho, C. Shultz and D. Westbrook. 2005. "Sustaining Advances in the Subjective Quality of Life: Vietnam's *Doi Moi,*" working paper, Georgetown University.

Osgood, Charles. 1962. *An Alternative to War or Surrender,* Urbana: University of Illinois Press.

Polo, Marco. 1958. *The Travels.* Ronald Latham (trans.), New York: Penguin.

Schumpeter, Joseph. 1934. *The Theory of Economic Development: An Inquiry into Profits, Capital, Credit, Interest, and the Business Cycle,* Cambridge: Harvard University Press.

Shaw, Arch Wilkinson. 1916. *An Approach to Business Problems.* Cambridge: Harvard University Press.

Shaw, Eric H. 1995, "The First Dialogue on Marketing," *Journal of Macromarketing,* 15 (1): 7–20.

Shawver, Donald and William Nickels. 1979. "A Rationalization for Macromarketing Concepts and Measures," in *Macromarketing: New Steps on the Learning Curve.* George Fisk and Robert Nason (eds.) Boulder, CO: University of Colorado Business Research Division.

Sheth, Jadgish and David Gardner. 1982. "History of Marketing Thought: An Update," in *Marketing Theory: Philosophy of Science Perspectives.* Ronald Bush and Shelby Hunt (eds.) Chicago: AMA, 52–58.

Shultz, C. 1997. "Improving Life Quality for the Destitute: Contributions from Multiple-Method Fieldwork in War-Ravaged Transition Economies," *Journal of Macromarketing,* 17 (1): 56–67.

Shultz, C., T. Burkink, B. Grbac, and N. Renko. 2005. "When Policies and Marketing Systems Explode: An Assessment of Food Marketing in the War-Ravaged Balkans and Implications for Recovery, Sustainable Peace, and Prosperity," *Journal of Public Policy & Marketing,* 24 (1): 24–37.

Shultz, C., D. Dapice, A. Pecotich, and Doan H. D. 2006. "Vietnam: Expanding Market Socialism and Implications for Marketing, Consumption and Socio-economic Development," in *Handbook of Markets and Economies: East Asia, Southeast Asia, Australia, New Zealand,* A. Pecotich & C. Shultz (eds.) New York: M.E. Sharpe, 656–688.

Shultz, C. and M. Holbrook. 1999. "Marketing and the Tragedy of the Commons: A Synthesis, Commentary, and Analysis for Action," *Journal of Public Policy & Marketing,* 18 (2): 218–22.

Shultz, C., Pecotich, A., & Le, K. 1994. "Changes in Marketing Activity and Consumption in the Socialist Republic of Vietnam," *Research in Consumer Behavior,* Vol. 7, 225–257.

Slater, Charles C. 1968. "Marketing Processes in Developing Latin American Societies," *Journal of Marketing,* 32 (July).

Stiglitz, Joseph. 2002. *Globalization and Its Discontents,* New York: W.W. Norton & Co.

Thucydides. 1954 (431~424 B.C.). *History of the Peloponnesian War.* Rex Warner (trans.) 1954, New York: Penguin.

United Nations. 2002. *Vietnam Household Living Standards Survey 2002,* General Statistical Office, Hanoi, sponsored by UNDP Hanoi.

United Nations. 2004. Raw data from Vietnam Household Living Standards Survey, sponsored by UNDP Hanoi.

Vaile, R., E. Grether and R. Cox. 1952. *Marketing in the American Economy,* New York: Ronald Press Co.

Vietnam Labour Watch. 2004. "Reports" (accessed in March 2005) (http://www.saigon.com:8081/~nike/report.html) and "Update" (http://www.saigon.com:8081/~nike/report.html).

VOV News. 2005. "AmCham Pins High Hopes on Vietnam-US Blossoming Business," July 15, accessed July 14, via (accessed in March 2005) http://www.vov.org.vn/2005_06_15/english/kinhte1.htm.

Wilkie, William and Elizabeth Moore. 1999. "Marketing's Contributions to Society," *Journal of Marketing,* 63 (Special Issue): 198–218.

Wilkie, William and Elizabeth Moore. 2003. "Scholarly Research in Marketing: Exploring the '4 Eras' of Thought Development," *Journal of Public Policy and Marketing*, 22 (2): 116–146.

Wood, Van and Scott Vitell. 1986. "Marketing and Economics Development: Review, Synthesis and Evaluation," *Journal of Macromarketing*, 6 (1): 28–48.

World Bank. 2004. *World Development Indicators 2004*. Washington: World Bank.

Xuan Danh. 2005. "Vietnam continues WTO talks with U.S., Japan," *Thanh Nien News*, March 9, accessed via (accessed in March 2005) http://www.vietnamembassy-usa.org/news/newsitem.php3?datestamp=20050310105129, March 13.

An Invitation to Participate in Affairs of the Journal of Macromarketing

George Fisk

This invitation explains our goal and illustrates specific objectives of macromarketing study. It identifies current priorities in macromarketing thought and explains why we believe the *Journal of Macromarketing* can serve the professional scholar and public and managerial social policy formulating communities concerned with marketing.

We the undersigned announce publication of the *Journal of Macromarketing*. People concerned with the effects of marketing on society and with the effects of social programs on marketing practice are invited to submit manuscripts and to subscribe to the *Journal*. We also welcome their participation in the annual macromarketing seminars and international scholarly colloquia and symposia that will be associated with publication.

We are initiating the *Journal of Macromarketing* because we believe that marketing technology has important social consequences largely ignored or rationalized in the professional marketing literature. Many groups and individuals, ranging from parents of children exposed to TV advertising to residents of third world nations are affected by marketing practice. In turn, they react and attempt to influence the behavior of marketing organizations.

People largely ignorant of marketing as a social process make decisions on a wide range of public and social policies on issues too broad to be resolved within the prevailing modes of marketing thought. Marketing literature continues to treat societal issues, either as narrow technical problems, or as philosophical questions not amenable to rational problem solving. Because many of us have been directly involved with the formulation of management, social or public policy, we recognize the need for a communication medium that will enable us to present the results of our scholarship and experience for peer review and improvement.

Goal and Objectives

Our primary goal is to provide a forum in which people can debate and clarify the role of marketing in society. To accomplish this we hope to identify social issues on which improvements in knowledge can lead to improvements in the way resources are managed

GEORGE FISK is a Professor of Marketing at Syracuse University.

George Fisk (1981), "An Invitation to Participate in Affairs of the Journal of Macromarketing," *Journal of Macromarketing,* 1 (1), 3–6.

in private and public organizations to serve society's interest. The word macromarketing implies that we care about the consequences of large marketing systems on large social issues. Examples of these issues include environmental deterioration and renewal, economic development of national economies, the influence of marketing on the quality of life, and marketing efficiency in mobilizing and allocating resources. In short, we seek knowledge to improve marketing strategies and policies that affect social welfare.

The market mechanism is only one of many instruments for raising standards of living, promoting economic stability, providing sources of income, and improving the "quality of life." However, it is more attractive in terms of cost/benefit for many groups in society than is the proposed alternative for mobilizing and allocating resources by "mutual coercion mutually agreed upon" (Hardin 1968, p. 1243). Of course, exchange for mutual benefit does not automatically produce socially and politically more desirable consequences than coercion. But we hold that an informed citizenry will know and express its own long-run interests in exchange transactions better than any doctrinaire professional elite can dictate by administrative fiat.

We regard any consideration of marketing behavior that affects a larger community or society as macromarketing (Shawver and Nickels 1979; Dixon 1979). Although we will refine and qualify this statement later on, we begin by examining four topics to initiate discussion about improving knowledge of marketing as a social process:

1. Marketing as a life supply support provisioning technology.
2. The "quality" and "quantity" of life goals served by marketing.
3. Marketing as a technology for mobilizing and allocating economic resources.
4. Societal consequences of marketing in learning societies.

To use Shelby Hunt's terms, macromarketing is both "positive" and "normative," "profit" and "nonprofit," but excludes the micromarketing phenomena of decision making to produce an intended result for an individual household, business, or public organization. Our focus is squarely on what Tucker's award winning article terms "the well being of society" (1974, p. 35).

1. Marketing as a life support/supply provisioning technology (Fisk 1974, Arndt 1978). Social benefits and costs of supply-demand equalization practices can be assessed on an industry by industry basis as well as for a total national economy in both the short and the long run. Studies on such questions as "Does Distribution Cost Too Much?" could be reported in the *Journal of Macromarketing,* emphasizing interindustry analyses of benefit and cost effects of collecting, sorting, and dispersing. Marketing effectiveness and efficiency in serving social purposes needs more conceptual clarification and study. We welcome manuscripts on market adjustments of supply demand at the industry and economy levels of aggregation.

2. *The "quality" and "quantity" of life goals served by marketing.* In recent years, a grow-ing number of people have challenged the idea that more gross national product means more gross national happiness. Rising crime, disease, and social disintegration rates have refocuscd attention on "quality" goals such as environmental improvement at the expense of rising levels of living, the traditional end of economic effort in industrialized nations. Articles dealing with the role of marketing in economic development and quality of life and levels of living are planned for the *Journal of Macromarketing.*

Given freedom of choice, people often select short run and individual consumption goals over long run and societal or public goals. Even well-informed consumers cannot make well-informed choices among technologically complicated alternatives. At present little is known about "quality of life" tradeoffs required by consumer choices favoring rising "quantity of life," for example rising energy consumption in the face of shrinking fossil fuel resources. Both consumers and marketers appear to be pursuing conflicting "quantity" and "quality" of life goals simultaneously. While major taxonomic and measurement studies of "quantity" versus "quality of life" are urgently needed, market-ing writers seem preoccupied with consumer preferences, or with technical micro-managerial questions. The *Journal of Macromarketing* will provide a vehicle for studies of aggregate consumption of goods including societal consequences and societal sanction systems for shaping consumer freedom of choice.

3. *Marketing as a technology for mobilizing and allocating economic resources.* The risk bear-ing and venture functions are elements of the same process that distributes resources among competing uses. Despite recurrent business cycles, marketing literature continues to focus on micromarketing questions pertaining to efficient order shipment, routing, and order handling size, rather than the societal business cycle consequences of inven-tory imbalances. Unemployment, spiraling prices, and inflation—"stagflation"—frighten people in the world's money and labor markets, but occasions scant notice in marketing literature. Marketing is an element of risk management technology, but within the mar-keting and behavioral science disciplines it is widely regarded as something less. Cycli-cal inventory accumulations and inflation are societal phenomena that reflect imbalances of supply with demand. A societal task of marketing is to bring supply and demand into balance in commodity markets. But since commodity markets are inextricably related to money and labor markets, we must know more about the impact of economic system interrelations on marketing practice and vice versa. We cannot adequately understand marketing behavior until we understand it in relation to the larger economic system of which it is a part.

Other questions on resource mobilization and allocation are worthy of study. How do the Japanese mobilize and allocate resources? How do multinational corporations intro-duce marketing into centrally planned societies and lesser developed nations? International marketing systems responsible for innovative competition and venture management deserve increasing attention. The building of economic infrastructures by developing entrepreneurial marketing skill warrants study. While the American Challenge, "Le Defi Americain," has receded from Europe, the Korean challenge is appearing around the world with important marketing lessons for developing nations. Comparative studies of these phenomena are welcome. The list could be much expanded, but the point remains the same: it is useful to positive science and normative policy formulation to study societal impacts of marketing in order to understand, predict and prescribe policy for mobilizing and allocating resources effectively. The *Journal of Macromarketing* will provide a medium for discussion of these issues.

4. Societal consequences of marketing in learning societies. Labor was the resource first mobilized to build early societies, and capital has been the resource used to build modern industrial states. However, accumulation and distribution of knowledge is the critical resource that learning societies will require in the future. We already know that market behavior provides rapid feedback on the effects of social policies. Although political leaders may ignore lessons taught by market feedback, these lessons are repeated with sufficient frequency to provide excellent opportunities for scholars to conduct test-retest studies. These add to knowledge about macrobehavior of people forced to choose among managerial profit and public (nonprofit) alternatives under shortage, glut, inflation, and so on. In addition, public and private statistical agencies measure and report market behavior periodically. Much of the longitudinal macromarketing data collected over time can be statistically adjusted for comparative study. *The Journal of Macromarketing* will offer a vehicle to interested persons for reports of innovation adoption, comparative studies of societal adaption to market sanctions, and other forms of social learning.

The growing interest in the diffusion of innovation, in technology assessment, in benefit cost analysis and in futures analysis, augmented by computer simulation capabilities, provides opportunities to study macromarketing behavior with respect to the diffusion of new knowledge. In learning societies, the availability of formal education institutions, research institutes, and mass media, including professional media like the *Journal of Macromarketing,* can greatly facilitate rapid dissemination of knowledge.

We need to know more about the consequences of marketing including its spillover benefits and costs. An important result of persuasion and communication is initiation of societal behavior change. But how can the persuader know which changes are desirable? Present knowledge of desirable spillover benefits compared to undesirable spillover costs is still too rudimentary for use in normative marketing studies. Every public policy decision and most private new venture decisions yield "spillovers" onto people who may neither seek nor desire them. The *Journal of Macromarketing* encourages contributors to prepare manuscripts on societal benefits and costs of marketing both in the short and long run.

How to Tell if Your Research Belongs in the Journal of Macromarketing

Four approaches now in use for identifying macromarketing can help prospective contributors and subscribers determine if their interests coincide with ours. We describe here the behavioral, historical, societal impact, and taxonomic criteria by which scholars can determine whether a paper belongs in the *Journal of Macromarketing.* To judge whether some behavior is or is not macromarketing, it is helpful to use the following criteria.

1. Behavioral. A famous early definition of operations research defined it as what operations researchers do. Macromarketing is likewise what macromarketers do. More specifically, macromarketing is concerned with specification of social tasks or purposes served by marketing. Macromarketing also includes:

- management of societal programs undertaken to secure results required by social tasks served by marketing.
- management of the reward and penalty market, i.e., social and legal sanction systems that motivate people to attain socially desirable outcomes.
- organized behavior patterns of cooperation and conflict between actors engaged in marketing.
- consequences of marketing, i.e., the social externalities of marketing that fall on people who seek neither the benefits nor costs that impact on them.
- networks of organizations in marketing channels adding marketing services to goods.
- infrastructure comprising the environment within which marketing organizations can survive.
- the "metatheoretical" questions of scientific methods appropriate to the study of marketing phenomena.

Like the rest of the criteria to follow, the list of macromarketing topics above is subject to qualification and amendment.

2. Historical. Early articles on macromarketing focused on the supply-demand balancing aspects of marketing under the heading of institutional and commodity approaches to marketing. Interferences with the market such as monopoly and product differentiation to control prices also figured prominently in economic literature on the decline of competition. Thus, the earliest studies of marketing as a formal discipline were concerned with raising the share of the consumers' food expenditures returned to farmers by improving marketing efficiency. L. H. D. Weld, Fred Clark, and the U.S. Joint Commission of Agricultural Inquiry in 1922 were all concerned with rationalizing channels of distribution to balance supply and demand more effectively to reduce market gluts and shortages while at the same time improving the organization and performance of marketing activities.

Among the most widely read of all marketing books up to 1939 was the study conducted by Paul Stewart, J. Frederick Dewhurst, and their associates, "Does Distribution

Cost Too Much?" sponsored by the Twentieth Century Fund. A sequel, *Distribution in a High Level Economy,* by Reavis Cox and associates appeared in 1965. Earlier, Stuart Chase and his associates had written *Your Money's Worth* and *One Hundred Million Guinea Pigs* leading to the organization of Consumers Research and Consumers Union. They represented another vein of macromarketing thought reflecting the views of perhaps the largest public impacted by marketing—the consumer!

Since World War II, political leaders seeking economic development and employment of their countries' resources have provided the motivation for macromarketing literature dealing with competitive market behavior, economic development, and international technology transfer. The work on marketing and economic development by Charles Slater and his students is reported in the proceedings of the 1976, 1977, and 1978 Macromarketing Seminars. Galbraith and Holton's *Marketing Efficiency in Puerto Rico* was an early work in this area, and J. J. Servan Schreiber's *The American Challenge* focused on the impact of U.S. marketing and organizational strategies on European nations.

Most recently, books such as Henion and Kinnear's *The Conserver Society* and Fisk's *Marketing and the Ecological Crisis* have directed attention to the environmental quality impacts of marketing. Normative prescriptive programs with national policy implications have also been proposed by Stanley Shapiro. These relate to considerations of marketing and the quality of life, another dimension of macromarketing gaining in significance to overall social welfare.

3. Societal impacts. Much of the current emphasis on macromarketing stems from public concern with unwanted societal consequences of marketing behavior. The environmental impacts of throwaway packages and products, the social behavior of children who have seen TV commercials for high sugar cereals, the "future shock" resulting from the planned diffusion of innovations by social marketing programs, and the economic and ecological consequences of shopping center construction on local retail stores and wetlands, have impacts that should be analyzed. Macromarketing studies are important to the people who are affected. Changes in marketing behavior affecting prevailing consumer's life styles, health, and peace of mind can be more intelligently guided if the benefits desired can be compared with the costs of resources that must be committed and societal costs that must be imposed to achieve the benefits sought.

4. Taxonomy. If macromarketing simply looks at marketing from a societal standpoint, why is it needed at all? Why not simply focus on marketing and public policy? The answer is that macromarketing deals with managerial issues, with scientific-positive questions, and with normative value questions from a higher level of aggregation than the tactical or even strategic perspective of a single firm concerned only with direct impacts on customers, competitors, and stockholders (Bartels and Jenkins 1977). Macromarketing relates to both nonprofit and profit seeking organizations. It is both a social process and a management technology; and it is concerned with normative questions as well as the descriptive, explanatory, and predictive issues posed in positive studies. Thus macromarketing is so broad in scope that it provides a large umbrella under which a highly diverse group of scholars can discover threads of common interest.

References

Arndt, Johan (1978), "How Broad Should the Marketing Concept Be?" *Journal of Marketing,* 42 (January), 101–103.

Bartels, Robert, and Roger L. Jenkins (1977), "Macromarketing," *Journal of Marketing,* 41 (October), 17–20.

Dixon, Donald F. (1979), "The Origins of Macromarketing Thought," in *Macromarketing: New Steps on the Learning Curve,* George Fisk and Robert W. Nason, eds., Boulder: University of Colorado Business Research Division.

Fisk, George (1974), *Marketing and the Ecological Crisis,* New York: Harper and Row. (See Chapter 4, "Marketing as a Provisioning Technology.")

Hardin, Garrett (1968), "The Tragedy of the Commons," *Science,* 162 (13 December), 1243.

Shawver, Donald L., and William G. Nickels (1979), "A Rationalization for Macromarketing Concepts and Definitions," in *Macromarketing: New Steps on the Learning Curve,* George Fisk and Robert W. Nason, eds., Boulder: University of Colorado Business Research Division.

Tucker, W. T. (1974), "Future Directions in Marketing Theory," *Journal of Marketing,* 38 (April), 30–35.

Toward a Unified Theory of Macromarketing: A Systems Theoretic Approach

William K. Meade II and Robert W. Nason

This article explores the analytic nature and domain of macromarketing from a systems theoretic perspective. Macromarketing is developed as the study of the complex coordination and control processes underpinning growth, evolution, and design of exchange systems. This approach provides a rich conceptual framework in which to unify the traditional themes of macromarketing and, potentially, to accelerate empirical research.

> Every science studies systems of some kind, whether natural (physical, chemical, biological, or social) or artificial (technical). Moreover, most sciences study nothing but systems. Thus, biology studies biosystems, sociology sociosystems, and technology technosystems.... Until recently every species of system was studied separately. About four decades ago a number of specialists joined efforts to launch various cross-disciplinary ventures, such as operations research and cybernetics. Their success suggested to some workers that a unified approach to problems in various fields was possible. They pointed out that (a) there are some concepts and structural principles that seem to hold for systems of many kinds, and (b) there are some modeling strategies—in particular the state space approach—that seem to work everywhere (Bunge 1979, p. 1).

Interdependence is an intuitively obvious and an analytically elusive concept. Intuitively obvious because people seem to have an innate sensitivity to competition and other modes of interdependence. This intuition has spawned a collection of intertwined economic concepts ranging from competition (Moorthy 1985) to cooperation (Telser 1985). Interdependence and how to capture value from it are near the marrow of marketing. The concept is ubiquitous in economics and in micromarketing and macromarketing, having been used to explain marketing functions (Shaw 1916), how markets work (McInnes 1964; Houston and Gassenheimer 1987), the economic mechanisms relating economic quantities to one another (Schumpeter 1954), the mixture of competitive and cooperative behavior occurring in markets (Alderson 1957; Easton 1988), and how the economy works (Dixon 1991). In these explanations the concept of

WILLIAM K. MEADE II is an Assistant Professor of Marketing in the School of Business Administration at the University of Missouri-St. Louis in St. Louis, Missouri. ROBERT W. NASON is the Department Chair of Marketing and Transportation at Michigan State University in East Lansing, Michigan.

William K. Meade, II and Robert W. Nason (1991) "Toward a Unified Theory of Macromarketing: A Systems Theoretic Approach," *Journal of Macromarketing*, 11 (1), 72–82.

interdependence is linked to the division of labor, separation of functions, competition, cooperation, economic complexity, and exchange.

Interdependence is analytically elusive, however, because it has proven to be an extraordinarily difficult concept to express mathematically in a generalizable way. Many representations have been developed, including input-output analysis (Leontief 1966), network analysis (Thorelli 1986), and game theory (Moorthy 1985), each largely incommensurable with the others. The development of a new representation is often heralded as a scientific revolution capable of changing the nature of a discipline. The ensuing competition of theories, however, allows new representations to express only the problems they represent best (Box 1984, p. 1). The result of this competition is an expanding toolkit of analytical representations of interdependence.

The toolkit expands in two ways: by covering new problems by more finely subdividing the treatment of problems already covered. The enthusiasms in a discipline can for a time attract researchers to one approach or the other in order to overwhelm measurement difficulties (Kuhn 1961, p. 196), but eventually analytical balance returns. For a discipline to be empirically productive, however, it is essential for there to be logical order in the analytical toolkit. Order is not a product of the sequence in which representations happen to develop; rather, it is the product of an organizing principle capable of arranging existing and newly emerging tools. As Reavis Cox warned, order ensures that worthy techniques are not "buried under an avalanche of literature authored by those developing new approaches."[1] (1964, p. 10). Just any organizing principle will not do. What is needed is one that brings the latent themes of the discipline to the surface. Orthodoxy can come back in fresh thinking.

This article explores the analytic nature and the domain of macromarketing from a systems science perspective. In terms of analytic nature, a unifying theme runs through the topics and analyses which are called macromarketing on an *ad hoc* basis. Whether the focus is on the social consequences of promoting infant formula in developing countries, deceptive practices, economic development, or polity,[2] understanding how exchange systems are coordinated and controlled seems to be a covert theme of macromarketing. From a systems perspective, macromarketing focuses on three logical phenomena: (1) causes of "poor" performance in exchange systems, (2) how economic interests, culture, and institutions both structure and control exchange systems and their evolution, and (3) how intervention could improve performance by changing system structure or control.

In terms of a discipline's domain, compelling content descriptions are based on analytical concepts, not common sense. Analytical concepts (such as scarcity, cost, and

---

[1] In Cox's words, "this may happen not because the new approaches are really better but rather because they attract attention of ambitious students, and by their nature lend themselves to endless proliferation" (1964, p. 10).

[2] "Polity refers to the power-and-control system of an organization of society" (Arndt 1981, p. 40).

opportunity) serve two functions. First, they point specifically to empirical phenomena. Second, they provide a rich set of expectations as to how the phenomena operate. These expectations, once confirmed by experience and experiment, become acceptable explanations. Along these lines, Becker (1976, p. 5) states that what most distinguishes economics from other social sciences is not its domain, but the fact that it approaches empirical phenomena looking for maximizing behavior. Competition was the original phenomenon to which maximizing points, but as understanding of the analytical categories of economics deepened, the domain expanded until economists came to believe these categories "are truly universal in applicability" (Hirshleifer 1985, p. 53). The domain of economics has broadened to include racial discrimination, the family, and crime, as Becker and others have searched for the limits to the applicability of economics' analytical categories (Stigler 1988, pp. 196–99). Optimization and the intertwined concepts of demand, price, and competition are analytical concepts that provide economists with expectations to test. For example, optimization makes economists expect profit maximization by firms, utility maximization by consumers, and maximization of total economic output by governments (Nicholson 1989, p. 27).

In order to develop insight into its domain, macromarketing needs to discover explanatory categories which fit its analytical nature. Some of these concepts can be supplied by systems science. For example, from a systems perspective there are three macromarketing content areas. The first is suboptimization (for example, externalities with effects that are well understood,[3] or with effects yet to be understood[4]). The second deals with the functioning of exchange system components,[5] as well as with the interplay of social, technical, and cultural subsystems of exchange systems. The third involves understanding interventions that alter exchange systems structure (domestic content laws) or control marketing flows (prohibition of advertising to children).

The systems science approach to macromarketing is consistent with previous definitions of the field, but the focus on analytical concepts tightly couples theory to practice. In contrast, approaches to macromarketing that only define content areas leave researchers without guidance as to how to begin empirical investigation or how to interpret and integrate empirical findings. Tightly coupling theory to practice is desirable because it provides unhampered feedback to guide theory development (Box 1976, p. 791; Box 1984, p. 5).

Macro-marketing refers to the study of (1) marketing systems, (2) the impact and consequence of marketing systems on society, and (3) the impact and consequence of society on marketing systems.

---

[3]For example, in the case of the developing country infant formula problem, dying babies were a significant effect of the marketing of infant formula. Babies dying as a result of product use is a relatively clear signal that something is wrong.

[4]For example, Nason (1989) categorizes these as "unforseen effects," citing Thalidomide, asbestos, auto safety defects, Three Mile Island, and Union Carbide's 1984 Bhopal disaster as examples.

[5]Hollander's (1971) "Consumer Purchasing Surrogate" is an example of an exchange system component, that is, an intermediary in a channel making a profit from market information and access.

Criterion (1) is a level of aggregation criterion which allows the inclusion of topics like comparative marketing, the institutional structure of marketing and power relationships in channels of distribution. Criterion (2) is a generalized "interests of society" criterion which brings in items like "social responsibilities" and the role of marketing in economic development. Criterion (3) recognizes that society impacts on marketing and would include topics like the legal aspects of marketing and the consequences on marketing of different political and social value systems (Hunt 1977, p. 56).

This content-only definition of macromarketing is clear, concise, and accurate. In the 15 years since it was published, however, there has been an almost complete lack of empirical research in macromarketing (Zinkhan et al. 1990). Content specifications are necessary to, but not sufficient for, expressing the work a discipline sets for itself.

> Any science must have two parts: it must have a philosophy and it must have content. The content refers to the various phenomena to be studied and explained by the particular science.... The philosophy of a science refers to the rules by which one can test statements concerning the phenomena under study (Halbert 1964, p. 29).

What Halbert calls "testing statements" are the key to understanding macromarketing definitional and empirical research enigmas. In other words, macromarketing is not making progress because it is missing a philosophy of justification.

What is a philosophy of justification? In a formalized science, it would be a symbolic system. Empirical claims would be tested against theorems developed from this symbolic system by its rules of inference (Hofstadter 1980, p. 35). At the other extreme, informal disciplines like macromarketing have philosophical rules of explanation which are verbal. These verbal arguments are more or less "accepted" by people in the discipline. Accepted explanations are what Toulmin calls "Ideals of Natural Order."

> So far as the prognosticator is concerned, the course of Nature need consist only of "one damn thing after another." He himself is not going to be caught napping, for he has discovered a way of telling what is going to happen next; but this is not to say that he understands what is happening. The scientist is in a very different position. He begins with the conviction that things are not just happening ... but rather that some fixed set of laws or patterns or mechanisms accounts for Nature's following the course it does, and that his understanding of these should guide his expectations (1961, p. 44–45).

Laws, patterns, and mechanisms guide a scientist's expectations not only because they allow prediction but also because they fit a phenomenon into a pattern of temporal (diachronic) and structural (synchronic) events (Holland et al. 1986, p. 329). Explanatory ideals provide compelling content descriptions because they are patterns that simultaneously point to and explain phenomena as cases of fundamentally intelligible types (Toulmin 1961, p. 81).

Macromarketing has relied on explanations and ontological concepts borrowed from neighboring disciplines. Consequently, macromarketing has not developed distinctive explanatory concepts to deal with the phenomena of exchange. Ontology is the study of order and structure of reality in a broad sense (Leary 1985, p. 1). The ontology of a research tradition defines the kinds of entities that exist within the discipline and the basic conceptual building blocks of theories (Anderson 1982, p. 67). Assembling macromarketing's paradigm by borrowing from abutting disciplines has resulted in a "patchwork" of content topics.

Systems theory can provide the explanatory philosophy missing from macromarketing. First, it offers a means of empirically operationalizing the complex constructs of macromarketing. Second, systems theory provides a set of explanatory ideals capable of unifying the "patchwork" of themes in macromarketing. Third, in the context of exchange systems, the explanatory ideals of systems theory point to core macromarketing phenomena that have not been clearly articulated to date. In short, systems theory can deepen macromarketing theory and encourage empirical research in two important ways. (1) It can make available ontological concepts such as "system," "component," and "flow rate," which have proven useful for empirical as well as theoretical research in many kinds of systems. (2) It can make available a systematic set of auxiliary explanatory ideals, such as "balanced flow," "feedback," and "stability," which point to and isolate the central phenomena of macromarketing.

Philosophical Background

Explanatory ideals are nothing more than ideas of how nature works (Toulmin 1961, p. 44). If I hold a large book four feet above the floor and then drop it, what will happen? The book will fall and make a sound upon impact. Expectations of how nature behaves in various situations are generated by explanatory ideals. When empirical experiences matches the expectations provided by explanatory ideals, we are not surprised. If the book made no sound upon impact, or if it did not fall when released (assuming away qualifying conditions, such as dropping the book while in Earth orbit), we would be genuinely surprised. Expectations are actually predictions, and prediction errors (unexpected outcomes) are what scientists investigate as "phenomena" (Toulmin 1961, p. 44). The success or failure of predictions is effectively a feedback signal guiding the development of knowledge (Holland et al. 1986, p. 9; Box 1976, p. 791). So, explanatory ideals are critically important to scientific progress because they point to phenomena and frame possible discoveries.

An example of explanatory ideals isolating the "phenomena" of a discipline's paradigm is given by dynamics. The explanatory ideals of motion and force evolved in three stages, marked by the contributions of Aristotle, Galileo, and Newton. Each successive "ideal of natural motion" isolated the phenomena of dynamics more precisely, converting the assumptions implicit within the "old" explanatory ideal into an explicit phenomenon of the "new" explanatory ideal.

Aristotle conceptualized natural motion in terms of how a cart behaves with and without a horse pulling it. If a cart moved, Aristotle inferred a force. His "ideal of natural motion" was rest, because when force no longer was applied to a cart, it came to a halt.

A second explanatory ideal of motion was developed by Galileo, who imagined how a ship on a calm sea would behave if all friction were removed. A ship initially at rest would remain at rest. A ship moving without resistance would circumnavigate the earth forever. Whereas Aristotle implicitly included friction in his explanatory ideal, Galileo explicitly recognized friction as a force. Galileo argued that constant circular motion and rest were both self-explanatory. These two self-explanatory states of motion, rest and constant circular motion, point to the phenomena of the world that need explanation for Galileo, namely, changes in motion.

Newton further refined Galileo's conception of motion. Newton's first law, that "a body in motion with no forces acting on it will continue to move in a straight line and at a constant velocity" (Berg 1989, p. 1), provides a criterion for determining in what respects a body's motion calls for explanation. Newton explicitly recognized the force of gravity, which was implicit in Galileo's conception of motion, and made it an explicit force. The two self-explanatory states of motion for Newton, rest and travel along a straight line at a uniform speed, point precisely to phenomena requiring explanation: disturbances from rest, disturbances from travel along a straight line, or disturbances from a constant speed.

Borrowing and Disciplinary Foundations

A discipline can study only a limited part of the world. Macromarketers, by "borrowing" the detailed ontological and explanatory concepts of nearby disciplines, to some extent have transplanted the content of those disciplines to macromarketing. Much of this borrowing is legitimate, but these subsets of phenomena are more central to the "lending" discipline than to macromarketing. Borrowed phenomena are likely to fall at the periphery of macromarketing. Borrowings from microeconomics, marketing management, and other disciplines have created within macromarketing a patchwork of peripheral phenomena without a unifying principle.

An example is the infant formula problem in developing countries. Treating it as an externality—whether as an international marketing "environmental difference," as done by Daniels and Radebaugh (1986, p. 328), or as an abstract "external diseconomy," as Stigler (1987, p. 328) suggests—does not bring macromarketing phenomena to light. What makes the problem a distinctively marketing phenomenon is that coordination and/or control of the exchange system could have minimized or eliminated it. What makes the problem a distinctively macromarketing phenomenon is the question of whether a sufficient power and control system (polity) existed to control (internalize) the externality.

The infant formula problem arose when a developed country product was transferred to another environment. The product could not meet the technical, physical, or price requirements of developing country exchange systems. The companies involved did not redesign the product to meet those requirements, babies died, and people around the world chose to boycott Nestlé. Four central macromarketing phenomena are involved in the controversy. The first is the failure of "developed country" technology and management to respond effectively to externalities as they emerged. The second is how the technical and economic systems were controlled at market, national, and international levels of organization. The third is how the structure and/or control of the technical and economic systems could have been improved to detect, respond to, and eliminate the externality. The fourth is how stakeholders around the world were able to organize boycotts against Nestlé brands (Daniels and Radebaugh 1986, p. 642), that is, coordinated nonpurchase behavior to reverse the assumed beneficial effects of branding to exert influence over Nestlé.

Disciplines usually are founded on the need for new principles of explanation (Gould 1987, p. 69). If an existing discipline could supply all the necessary explanations of macromarketing phenomena (externalities, for example), then there would be no need for a discipline of macromarketing. If those phenomena are not explained by economics or another adjacent discipline, and if the unexplained phenomena require new principles of explanation, then a potential exists for a unique intellectual space and disciplinary foundation. Macromarketing's content fragmentation (or patchwork) indicates that the operational foundations of macromarketing have yet to be discovered.

To summarize:

A lack of empirical work in macromarketing indicates that something is hindering the advance of macromarketing research.

Lack of a content definition is not what is hindering macromarketing, since Hunt's (1977) content definition has been accepted for 15 years.

Macromarketing is lacking the philosophy element of Halbert's (1964) two parts of science (content and philosophy).

Because macromarketing is still an informal science, Halbert's "philosophy" and Toulmin's (1961) explanatory ideals are interchangeable.

Explanatory ideals fill two functions: They point to the content (phenomena) of a discipline, and they provide acceptable explanations.

Borrowing the detailed concepts of neighboring disciplines has supplied macromarketing with a patchwork of peripheral content but not explanatory ideals.

Disciplines are founded on unmet needs for explanation.

Based on these premises, we argue that lack of explanatory ideals pointing to the content of macromarketing is hindering the advance of empirical research and the development of macromarketing's disciplinary foundations.

Content and Concepts

> Logic is useful for all sciences, and one cannot have a science without it.... In our borrowings from the methodological disciplines, we should not look for concepts that are directly relevant to marketing as a content area, but rather those which are relevant to the development of any science.... Marketing theory has borrowed extensively from the content area of the business disciplines, and the concept and technique area of economic theory.... It is apparent that we shall have to look increasingly to the methodological sciences to provide concepts and structure in marketing theory (Halbert 1964, p. 30).

Systems concepts can augment macromarketing in a way that specialized concepts from neighboring disciplines cannot. Because systems theory is concerned with explaining the behavior emerging from the structural characteristics of systems, global as opposed to local laws are investigated (Bunge 1979, p. 2). Transposing macromarketing into a localized systems theory is plausible, while transposing macromarketing into a globalized microeconomics is not. Furthermore, there is a logical compatibility, or isomorphism, between the global nature of systems science and macromarketing. This correspondence underlies both macromarketing's analytic nature and the systems theme running through the macromarketing literature. Given this isomorphism, we propose that it is appropriate to use explanatory ideals from systems theory as analytical concepts in macromarketing.

In order for explanatory ideals from systems theory to provide macromarketing with both content and philosophy of justification elements (Halbert 1964), and if the resulting concepts are to advance empirical and foundations research in macromarketing, three tests must be met. The explanatory ideals must (1) isolate some phenomena of macromarketing, (2) allow multiple macromarketing themes to be contrasted in a unified conceptual framework, and (3) tie some macromarketing hypotheses which are "intuitively" appealing but otherwise not theoretically integrated into a theoretical framework.

Externalities as Systems

In this section we develop a macromarketing example, an "externality," in terms of systems theory. The objective is to investigate the capacity of an analytical concept from systems theory, "balance of forces," to contribute both content expectations and philosophy of justification (explanatory ideals) to macromarketing. The example chosen is disposable diapers. We first indicate the theoretical application of systems theory to this example and then point out the implications for empirical research.

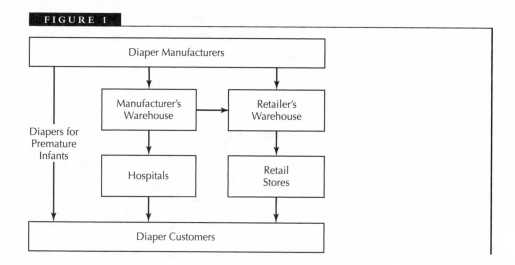

DISPOSABLE DIAPERS

Many purchasers of disposable diapers feel guilty about "what plastic does to the environment," although they often cannot cite specific negative effects. Despite this guilt, the convenience of disposability prevents the use of substitutes. Disposables currently have an 85% share of the diaper market (*Consumer Reports* 1991a, p. 551). Figure 1 presents a conventional marketing channel diagram of how selected diaper products move from production to consumption. This diagram abstracts from certain details: The number of warehouses is greater than the number of manufacturers, there are suppliers upstream from manufacturers, there are waste management suppliers downstream from diaper consumers, and so forth. The channel diagram points to the content of managerial marketing, that is, coordinating intermediaries' interconnections and interactions.

Figure 2 represents a first cut at isolating the logical structure of the disposable diaper market in the United States as a system. The "diaper manufacturers" block represents the collection and transformation of materials and energy involved in producing disposable diapers. The "diaper retailers" block represents stores where disposable diapers are sold to customers. The "diaper customers" block represents the point at which disposable diapers are used. Finally, the "landfill" block represents the final resting place of disposable diapers.

Systems theory relies on several assumptions, explanatory ideals, and ontological concepts which are auxiliary to an economic or macromarketing analysis. The "balance of forces" concept is an explanatory ideal applied by systems scientists to physical systems. To be in balance, a system first must be closed, that is, it conserves all mass and energy by recycling it though the system. In contrast, an open system (that receives or stores mass in a single component) depends on ubiquity of inputs and/or storage capacity for the outputs. Because an open system eventually will exhaust input or output potentials,

FIGURE 2

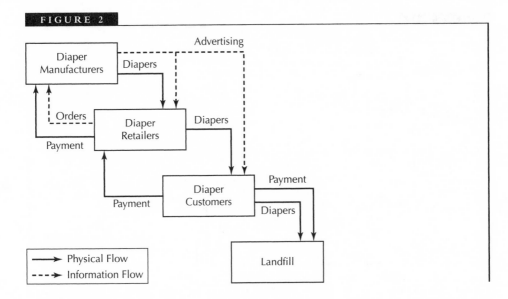

it is structurally unstable. A balanced closed system can be stable in an intuitively self-explanatory way to a systems scientist; if designed appropriately, it can run forever as long as energy is available to maintain circulation. As an explanatory ideal, the balanced system concept points to the open loop in Figure 2, between the landfill and the diaper manufacturer, as a phenomenon which needs explaining. It is not intuitively obvious how Figure 2 is a viable, let alone a good, system design.

Because the landfill perpetually takes in materials, and the diaper manufacturer continually produces diapers (without system-generated inputs), the disposable diaper exchange system is unbalanced; the system eventually will be starved of input materials and/or space in the landfill. Systems scientists call a component which "receives only" an "infinite sink"; a component which "sends only" is termed an "infinite source." Either can exist in reality. From a systems theory perspective, infinite sinks are tantamount to dumping some kind of material and/or energy into the environment, and infinite sources effectively exhaust some stock of resources.

To close the diaper system and make it stable in the long run, processing would have to occur at the landfill stage to break down organic compounds and, eventually, produce resources from which to make diapers (see Figure 3). In reality, the decomposition in the landfill liberates chemicals and energy. These leech into the environment, where chemicals accumulate and become part of the natural environment, and energy is dissipated. From a systems perspective, energy will quickly escape into the environment, as will the unreduced chemicals, but more slowly.

There is a general misconception that being biodegradable is the same as being beneficial to the environment. It is not. . . . If biodegradable products end up in landfills, they will

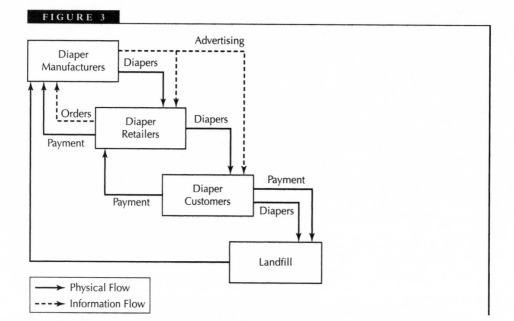

FIGURE 3

break down and form leachate and methane gas, the two major problems with all current landfills. Nonbiodegradable materials, such as plastics, are, therefore, far more desirable in landfills (Executive Director of the New York State Legislative Commission on Water Resource Needs of Long Island, in Proctor & Gamble 1989, p. 3).

Systems theory sees disposable diapers (and other consumer products requiring infinite sinks) as making the exchange system an "open loop." An obvious solution (using the balanced forces explanatory ideal) to the resulting externalities is to "close the loop." In this respect a systems approach is similar to economics, which deals with an externality by "internalizing" external costs (Allen 1988, p. 381).

When information about a system is incomplete, systems analysis can take place, whereas economic analysis is paralyzed by lack of data upon which to base economic assumptions. For example, without knowing the state of competition, market prices, or efficiency of markets, a systems analysis could reasonably hypothesize as follows: (1) landfills take up land in direct proportion to materials content; (2) real estate costs in general are based on population density; (3) as population grows, and as time passes (landfills will take up more real estate over time), landfills will cost more. From these hypotheses a conclusion can be drawn: The equilibrium price of landfills will rise and fall with population level and will rise with time. Furthermore, unless something occurs that reduces population, the artifacts put in landfills today will not be charged their actual long-run marginal costs.

At this point we can tie the more global systems analysis into a local (that is, microeconomic) theory. When economic activities impose external costs, they are likely to be overproduced (Allen 1988, p. 380). At today's prices, landfills are being overproduced.

From a systems perspective, landfills are not an externality waiting to happen, they are an existing externality waiting to be recognized. Whereas an economist would rely on the microeconomic explanatory ideal of general equilibrium to conclude that today's garbage is not tomorrow's externality, the systems scientist first would look to the explanatory ideal of system balance to evaluate structural stability. After recognizing a sink (the landfill), the systems analyst would evaluate the controls on the system. If a sink exists but controls prevent flows from entering it, the viability of the system is not threatened. The mechanisms controlling the rate of diaper flow into landfills are complex, but for present purposes the cost per diaper of storage in the landfills can be seen as the binding control mechanism. Once it has been identified, the systems analyst looks for bias in costs of storing materials in landfills. To determine bias, the physical cost structure of the system environment is reviewed. Assuming that population will continue to increase, the finding that present costs are biased below long-run landfill costs is clear. The system scientist can interpret the diaper externality as a defect either in system structure or controls.

Does the "balanced forces" concept satisfy the three tests noted earlier? First, does the balanced flow explanatory ideal "isolate some central phenomenon of macromarketing"? We believe that this concept identifies phenomena central to macromarketing at two levels, theoretical and operational. At a theoretical level, the unbalanced exchange system components are identified. Note that the diaper manufacturer is one of these. Where does s/he get materials? At an operational level, the diaper landfill demands explanation.

Second, does the balanced forces concept "allow multiple macromarketing themes to be contrasted in a unified conceptual framework"? The systems framework in Figure 2 allows the issue of suboptimization to be analyzed. This framework could accommodate other macromarketing analyses as well. The effects on the diaper exchange system of society imposing a tax, for instance, could be analyzed by incorporating the tax as a feedback source.

Third, does the balanced forces ideal "tie some macromarketing hypothesis that is intuitively appealing but otherwise not theoretically integrated into a theoretical framework"? The analysis of higher future costs appeals to the intuition of many macromarketers. These costs are not otherwise integrated into macromarketing theory, so the balanced forces ideal allows this concept to be attached to a macromarketing model and to be theoretically integrated.

The systems explanatory ideal of balanced forces does, indeed, satisfy the three criteria. Through balanced forces, feedback, and other explanatory ontological concepts, systems theory has the potential to provide macromarketing with the ability to characterize the central phenomena of the discipline, integrate the central phenomena with existing macromarketing content, and accelerate empirical work.

EMPIRICAL RESEARCH

From a systems perspective, empirical research on the diaper externality would be straightforward. First, state the primary hypothesis (H1) about the system. Second, explicitly state the primary assumptions (A1 and A2) about the system in Figure 2. Third, test the assumptions to determine whether they support the hypothesis.

H1: Use of landfills at current market prices is creating an externality.

IF

A1: Landfills do not reduce garbage (used diapers) into harmless compounds

AND IF

A2: Landfills become more expensive: (a) over time and (b) from high population densities

THEN

H1 is supported.

Checking A1 would require chemical analysis of dirty diapers in landfill conditions. Checking A2 could be accomplished by time series analysis of landfill costs, cross-sectional analysis of the effect of population on landfill costs, and/or pooled time series cross-sectional analysis of time and population effects on landfill costs. Once we ascertain whether today's landfill prices for storing diapers are systematically low, we can falsify or support the hypothesis that "today's consumption causes tomorrow's externality."

Another operationalization might be to compare disposable diapers with substitutes (diaper service or washable diapers) in terms of technical functioning and social consequences. Each substitute imposes a dual technical and economic cost structure. Washable diapers over their life cycle impose greater energy, pesticide, and water costs. Disposable diapers impose greater pollution from wood being turned into pulp and oil being turned into plastic (*Consumer Reports* 1991b, p. 555).

> Consumers won't make a big contribution to the health of the environment by choosing one type of diaper over another. They may, however, make a small contribution to the well-being of their region. If you live in an area where the solid-waste problem has become acute, ... consider using cloth diapers. If water is at a premium in your town ... disposables might be the better choice *(Consumer Reports* 1991b, p. 556).

What Is Macromarketing?

Is macromarketing the study of poorly performing exchange systems, that is, externalities? Externalities in particular and suboptimization in general are gateways to understanding the interplay of society and marketing. Externalities are limiting cases of such interplay, however, because they focus on the failure modes of exchange systems. Externalities have served well in allowing macromarketers to begin staking out a unique intellectual space, that is, the socially pathological aspects of marketing rooted in nonmarket facets of exchange systems. Systems theory can deepen this kind of analysis. For example, failures in the infant formula problem can be partitioned into three subsystems. (1) In the technical subsystem, the problem of bacterial contamination can be addressed by product design. (2) In the economic subsystem, the price of formula relative to a market segment's ability to pay can be addressed. (3) In the power and control subsystem, the issue of internalizing the externalities caused by multinational corporations can be addressed. It is now time to widen the intellectual space of macromarketing beyond social pathology to the study of exchange system regulation in general. The main thrust of systems theory goes beyond explaining failures. Systems theory is about building a hard analytical understanding of systems to allow the components of a problem to be recombined in apt—even fortuitous—ways.

Just as systems science seeks to understand system failures by understanding successful system designs, macromarketing can understand externalities in terms of successful exchange system functioning. Beyond removal of systematic inequities, macromarketing is about component functioning and the interplay of subsystems, which underpin the design and evolution of exchange systems. Exchange, which emerges in a system of technical, social, and cultural subsystems, provides society with the degrees of freedom to produce in abundance. The progressive mechanization and separation of functions inevitable to evolving systems (Bertalanffy 1968, p. 44), and that drive competition and the division of labor in exchange systems in particular (Durkheim 1893/1984, p. 208), create and intensify the need for exchange system coordination and control (regulation). Macromarketing is the study of the statics (structure) and dynamics (evolution) of the resulting socioeconomic regulation mechanisms.

Systems science can be viewed as the common sense or orthodoxy of macromarketing. We argue for an uncommonly hard interpretation of systems science, however, to tap analytical concepts outside common sense that we think are capable of unifying the latent themes of macromarketing. Applying harder systems concepts to the study of how socioeconomic regulation emerges from technological and/or socioeconomic interdependence is one approach to setting in order the toolkit and topics of macromarketing.

References

Alderson, Wroe (1957). *Marketing Behavior and Executive Action.* Homewood: Richard D. Irwin.

Allen, Bruce T. (1988). *Managerial Economics.* New York: Harper and Row.

Anderson, Paul F. (1982). "Marketing Strategic Planning, and the Theory of the Firm." *Journal of Marketing,* 46 (Spring 1982): 15–26. Quoted in Jagdish N. Sheth and Dennis E. Garrett, *Marketing Management: A Comprehensive Reader* (Cincinnati: South-Western Publishing), pp. 58–80.

Arndt, Johan (1981). "The Political Economy of Marketing Systems: Reviving the Institutional Approach." *Journal of Macromarketing,* 1 (2): 36–47.

Becker, Gary S. (1976). *The Economic Approach to Human Behavior.* Chicago: University of Chicago Press.

Berg, Glen V. (1989). *Elements of Structural Dynamics.* Englewood Cliffs, NJ: Prentice-Hall.

Bertalanffy, Ludwig von (1968), *General System Theory: Foundations, Development, Applications,* rev. ed. New York: George Braziller.

Box, George E. P. (1984). "The Importance of Practice in the Development of Statistics." *Technometrics,* 26 (February): 1–8.

___ (1976). "Science and Statistics." *Journal of the American Statistical Association,* 71 (December): 791–98.

Bunge, Mario (1979). *Treatise on Basic Philosophy: Volume 4, Ontology II: A world of Systems.* Boston: D. Reidel Publishing Co.

Consumer Reports (1991a). "Diaper Decisions: Which are Best for the Baby?" 56 (August): 551–54.

___ (1991b). "Diaper Decisions: Which are Best for the Environment?" 56 (August): 555–56.

Cox, Reavis (1964). "Introduction." In *Theory in Marketing,* second series, edited by Reavis Cox, Wroe Alderson, and Stanley J. Shapiro. Homewood, IL.: Richard D. Irwin, pp. 1–14.

Daniels, John D., and Lee H. Radebaugh (1986). *International Business: Environments and Operations,* 4th ed. Reading Mass: Addison-Wesley.

Dixon, Donald F. (1991). "Marketing Structure and the Theory of Economic Interdependence: Early Analytical Developments." *Journal of Macromarketing,* 11 (Fall): 5–18.

Durkheim, Emile (1893/1984). *The Division of Labor in Society,* Translated by W. D. Halls. New York: The Free Press.

Easton, G. (1988). "Competition and Marketing Strategy." *European Journal of Marketing,* 22 (2): 31–49.

Gould, Stephen Jay (1987). *An Urchin in the Storm: Essays about Books and Ideas.* New York: W. W. Norton & Co.

Halbert, Michael H. (1964). "The Requirements for Theory in Marketing." In *Theory in Marketing,* second series, edited by Reavis Cox, Wroe Alderson, and Stanley J. Shapiro. Homewood, IL: Richard D. Irwin, pp. 17–36.

Hirshleifer, Jack (1985). "The Expanding Domain of Economics." *American Economic Review,* 75 (December): 53–68.

Hofstadter, Douglas R. (1980). *Godel, Escher, Bach: An Eternal Golden Braid.* New York: Vintage Books.

Holland, John H., Keith J. Holyoak, Richard E. Nisbett, and Paul Thagard (1986). *Induction: Processes of Inference.* Cambridge, MA: MIT Press.

Hollander, Stanley C. (1971). "She Shops For You or With You." In *New Essays in Marketing Theory,* edited by George Fisk. Boston: Allyn and Bacon, Inc.

Houstin, Franklin S., and Jule B. Gassenheimer (1987). "Marketing and Exchange." *Journal of Marketing,* 51 (October): 3–18.

Hunt, Shelby D. (1977). "The Three Dichotomies Model of Marketing: An Elaboration of Issues." In *Macro-Marketing: Distributive Processes from a Societal Perspective,* edited by Charles C. Slater. Boulder: Business Research Division, University of Colorado, pp. 52–56.

Kuhn, Thomas S. (1961). "The Function of Measurement in Modern Physical Science." *Isis,* 52, 161–93 in Thomas S. Kuhn (1977) *The Essential Tension: Selected Studies in Scientific Tradition and Change.* Chicago: University of Chicago Press, pp. 178–224.

Leary, Rolfe A. (1985). *Interaction Theory in Forest Ecology and Management.* Boston: Martinus Nijhoff/DR W. Junk Publishers.

Leontief, W. W. (1966). *Essays in Economics: Theories and Theorizing.* New York: Oxford University Press.

McInnes, William (1964). "A Conceptual Approach to Marketing." In *Theory in Marketing,* second series, edited by Reavis Cox, Wroe Alderson, and Stanley J. Shapiro. Homewood, IL: Richard D. Irwin, pp. 51–67.

Moorthy, Sridhar (1985). "Using Game Theory to Model Competition." *Journal of Marketing Research,* 22 (August): 262–82.

Nason, Robert W. (1989). "The Social Consequences of Marketing: Macromarketing and Public Policy." *Journal of Public Policy & Marketing* 8: 242–51.

Nicholson, Walter (1989). *Microeconomic Theory: Basic Principles and Extension.* 4th ed. Chicago: Dryden Press.

Proctor & Gamble (1989). *Questions and Answers About Solid Waste.* Cincinnati: The Proctor & Gamble Co.

Schumpeter, Joseph A. (1954). *History of Economic Analysis.* New York: Oxford University Press.

Shaw, Arch Wilkinson (1916). *An Approach to Business Problems.* Cambridge: Harvard University Press.

Stigler, George J. (1987). *The Theory of Price,* 4th ed. New York: Macmillan Publishing.

___ (1988). *Memoirs of an Unregulated Economist.* New York: Basic Books, Inc.

Telser, Lester G. (1985). "Cooperation and Competition." *Journal of Law and Economics,* 28 (May): 271–95.

Thorelli, Hans B. (1986). "Networks: Between Markets and Hierarchies." *Strategic Management Journal,* 7 (January/February): 37–51.

Toulmin, Stephen (1961). *Foresight and Understanding: An Enquiry into the Aims of Science.* New York: Harper Torch Books.

Zinkhan, George M., Marilyn Y. Jones, Sarah Gardial, and Keith K. Cox (1990). "Methods of Knowledge Development in Marketing and Macromarketing." *Journal of Macromarketing,* 10 (Fall): 3–17.

MARKETING AND THE TRAGEDY OF THE COMMONS: A SYNTHESIS, COMMENTARY, AND ANALYSIS FOR ACTION

Clifford J. Shultz II and Morris B. Holbrook

The authors contend that solutions to the most pressing environmental challenges will result from understanding and solving social traps such as the commons dilemma. They propose a synthesis for analysis and action to suggest that marketing's stakeholders can cooperate to contribute solutions and ultimately develop programs that help ameliorate the tragedy of the commons.

Environmentalism will be one of the greatest challenges in the twenty-first century. The effect of marketing activities on environment preservation therefore matters increasingly to many marketers, consumers, and marketing policy scholars (e.g., Ellen, Wiener, and Cobb-Walgren 1991; Granzin and Olsen 1991; Milne, Iyer, and Gooding-Williams 1996; Pickett, Kangun, and Grove 1993; Pieters et al. 1998; Pilling, Crosby, and Ellen 1991; Schwepker and Cornwell 1991). Marketing enterprises have discovered that ecological issues often can provide a source of competitive advantage (e.g., Gifford 1997). Thus, businesses now focus on the problem of sustainable growth or development (e.g., Elkington 1994; Hart 1997; Ruckelshaus 1989), whereas marketers aspire to ecological (e.g., Fisk 1974), environmental (e.g., Polonsky and Mintu-Wimsatt 1995), green (e.g., Ottman 1993; Wasik 1996), or, more recently, enviropreneurial (e.g., Hartman and Stafford 1998; Menon and Menon 1997; Varadarajan 1992) marketing. But, when we consider the plethora of strategies, products, and advertising campaigns that purport to be "green," we cannot help but wonder how many of these truly work toward environmental protection (cf. Beder 1997; Gray-Lee, Scammon, and Mayer 1994; Kangun, Carlson, and Grove 1991; Kilbourne 1995). Even when well-intentioned, these ecologically oriented green efforts and activities may be misguided. Worse, they sometimes may represent cynical marketing tactics such as "greenwashing"—deceptive claims to cover up assaults on the environment—that would benefit from modification or termination (cf. Stauber and Rampton 1995, p. 125).

CLIFFORD J. SHULTZ II is Professor and Marley Chair, Morrison School of Agribusiness and Resource Management, Arizona State University. MORRIS B. HOLBROOK is the Dillard Professor of Marketing, Graduate School of Business, Columbia University. The authors thank Albert Bartlett, Morton Deutsch, A. Fuat Firat, George Fisk, Garrett Hardin, Geoffrey Heal, Robert Nason, Giulio Pontecorvo, Debra Scammon, Ronald Schram, and four anonymous *JPP&M* reviewers for their helpful comments on the formative stages and various drafts of this article. Debra Scammon served as editor for this article.

Clifford Shultz and Morris Holbrook (1999), "Marketing and the Tragedy of the Commons: A Synthesis, Commentary, and Analysis for Action," *Journal of Public Policy & Marketing*, 18 (2), 218–229.

In short, "it's not easy bein' green" (e.g., Judge 1997); marketers and consumers face the challenge of determining which activities are truly green enough to serve the long-term best interests of the environment and its inhabitants. But resolving these problems requires fresh thinking (cf. Daly 1996; Hart 1997; Kilbourne, McDonagh, and Prothero 1997; Nill and Shultz 1997; Shabecoff 1993; Thompson 1987). Toward this end, one important set of issues concerns the extent to which business activities, marketing plans, and consumer products are *commons-friendly,* that is, the extent to which they work toward sustaining commonly shared natural resources.

More than 30 years ago, in "The Tragedy of the Commons," Garrett Hardin (1968) argued that the world's most compelling problem was selfish exploitation of the planet's scarce resources. Hardin's arguments inspired a generation of social scientists to examine various forms of commons dilemmas. Although the empirical findings from many of these studies were enlightening, they did not succeed in halting—much less reversing—the assault on our common resources, which continues at an accelerating pace. We submit that, in the interest of human survival, marketers must take a more proactive role in the management of shared resources by involving multiple stakeholders in their decision making and seeking competitive advantages through legitimate green marketing, that is, through commons-friendly marketing. Accordingly, in this article, we examine the commons dilemma as a topic of interest to marketing strategists, policymakers or analysts, and consumers. Specifically, we discuss the logic behind the commons dilemma, we review relevant perspectives from other disciplines, we propose a synthesis for analysis and action, and we propose potential roles for marketing in the resolution of such conflicts. In this, we hope to inspire further research and encourage professional efforts toward the creation of marketing solutions to the commons dilemma.

The Commons Dilemma, Revisited

In general, the "commons dilemma" refers to a phenomenon in which the members of a social group face choices in which selfish, individualistic, or uncooperative decisions, though seeming more rational by virtue of short-term benefits to separate players, produce undesirable long-term consequences for the group as a whole. The problem has baffled humanity for centuries (cf. Aristotle [340~ BC] 1976; Lloyd 1833); obvious current examples include the overconsumption of water in arid climates, the unwise harvesting of trees to meet the demands of lumber and paper markets, or the noise- and pollution-causing use of cars. Here and elsewhere, individuals in most societies achieve short-term gains from consuming as much, polluting as extensively, and having as many children as possible; but societies, over time, suffer as a result (Dawes 1976). Furthermore and ironically, many of these problems have arisen because of economic progress, that is, because the checks that prevailed until the last 200 years or so have been destroyed by the bittersweet fruits of modern technology in general and by gains in industrial production or medical care in particular (Dawes 1980). In this context, an individualistic pursuit imperils not only our common base of resources, but also our very existence (Hardin 1968). Notice that this intractable commons dilemma reflects the combination of circumstances that Rangan, Karim, and Sandberg (1996, p. 51) deem most "disadvantageous" and most likely to make the finding of marketing-based solutions "difficult." Thus, though plenty of adjacent social issues also merit consideration, we confine our attention to this most problematic facet of social marketing.

A Synthesis of Social Science and Marketing Implications

Building on the literature in the social sciences and marketing, let us propose a synthesis for analysis of commons-related problems as a guide to action encouraging their resolution. We first review the background of attention to the commons problem in the social sciences and marketing. We next provide a synthesis of commons-related issues and indicate a set of themes to suggest one or more marketing-oriented strategies for resolution. Each issue and strategy then receives more detailed discussion in developing our understanding of the various themes in the synthesis.

BACKGROUND IN THE SOCIAL SCIENCES: EXTERNALITIES AND SOCIAL TRAPS

Economists have shown a keen interest in common property and resource management (cf. Coase 1960; Galbraith 1973; Olson 1965; Sagoff 1988). Their work has assessed the commons dilemma as involving externalities in the economic relations between people or time periods (e.g., Dasgupta 1982), often with the conclusion that common resources are managed best through variances in prices (to reflect the "true" costs of product usage) and/or by regulatory controls (such as taxation and/or usage laws). Meanwhile, behavioral scientists (cf. Dawes 1980; Edney 1980; Messick and Brewer 1983) view the commons dilemma as a social trap, that is, as an arrangement of rewards and punishments in which behavior that rewards an individual in the short-run implies long-run punishment for that and at least one other individual (Cross and Guyer 1980; Platt 1973).

Note that Cross and Guyer (1980) and Messick and Brewer (1983) make distinctions among various types of social dilemmas. For example, in addition to social traps, there exist social fences and individual traps. In social fences, short-term aversive consequences deter people from performing an act that would produce long-term positive benefits to themselves and others. In individual traps, a single person pursues immediate gain, but with long-term deleterious effects only for that person. The distinguishing characteristic of social dilemmas, including the commons dilemma, is immediate individual incentive to engage in behavior that eventually will be harmful to that person and also to others (the larger group or society) who rely on the shared commons; thus, both group (collective) and temporal (long-term) components are part-and-parcel constituents of the commons dilemma (Messick and Brewer 1983). In the context of the tragedy of the commons per se, Dawes (1980) suggests that N participants must decide between D (defecting) and C (cooperating), where D(m) is the payoff to a defector when m individuals cooperate; C(m) is the payoff to a cooperator when m individuals cooperate; and a social dilemma implies that (1) D(m) > C(m + 1) and (2) C(N) > D(0). In summary, the "tragedy" is that (1) the relevant incentives work toward the lower-payoff selfishness, yet (2) all individuals in society or interdependent groups receive a lower payoff when acting selfishly than when cooperating.

Given the ubiquitous positive and negative components in each individual's socially relevant decisions, particular interest attaches to the factors that potentially induce subjects to decide in favor of cooperative choices amid powerful incentives to choose selfish or "defecting" alternatives. The challenge confronting marketers is to devise and reconcile strategies for managing elements of the marketing mix so as to influence behavior in ways that help resolve various commons dilemmas that have a deleterious effect on the environment and the various stakeholders that share it (cf. Andreasen 1995, p. 141).

BACKGROUND IN MARKETING

Although marketing scholars have examined environmental issues since the early 1970s (e.g., Anderson and Cunningham 1972; Fisk 1973; Kassarjian 1971), the marketing literature makes few explicit references to the commons dilemma. Partial exceptions include work by Nason (1989), Pieters (1991), Wiener and Doescher (1991, 1994), Wiener (1993), Berger and Kanetkar (1995), Rangan, Karim, and Sandberg (1996), and Pieters and colleagues (1998). Nason (1989) suggests commons implications for social marketing as the summation of transactions that results in effects on all. Pieters (1991) notes commons-related problems when discussing a waste-separation program; Pieters and colleagues (1998, p. 215) contend that environmentally friendly consumer behavior is a "large-scale social dilemma." Wiener and Doescher (1991, 1994) extend a stream of research on prosocial behavior and "selling brotherhood" (cf. Bloom and Novelli 1981; Ritchie and McDougall 1985) to posit communication and cooperation as potential strategies for solving social dilemmas. Rangan, Karim, and Sandberg (1996) address what we call commons problems as their fourth type of social cause and suggest approaches more drastic than those recommended elsewhere. Thus, these studies open what has remained a rather small crack in the shutters through which marketers have begun to view the commons dilemma.

More generally, the broader themes of socially conscious, conservation-oriented, and green marketing have received considerable attention, as have some of the underlying factors that might determine environmental behavior for individuals and families (e.g., Taylor and Todd 1995, pp. 192–93) and for companies (e.g., Drumwright 1994).

TABLE 1

Synthesis of Commons Resolutions and Implications for Marketing Engagement

Remedy	Implications for Marketing Engagement
Regulation	Examples: cost/benefit incentives through privatization, taxes, fees, or prices
Organization	Examples: partnerships, alliances
Social responsibility	Example: inculcation of altruistic values
Communication	Examples: small-scale group discussion, large-scale educational campaigns; multistakeholder dialogue, negotiated outcomes, and feedback through verification measures over time

The proposition that marketing scholars and practitioners should actively pursue solutions to environmental problems in general and to the commons dilemma in particular seems especially compelling when marketing and consumer cultures are castigated so frequently for encouraging reckless resource depletion (cf. Anderson and Challagalla 1994; Kilbourne, McDonagh, and Prothero 1997).

Reflecting such beliefs, the responsible or prosocial use of marketing strategy is a logical extension of the economics and psychology literature on shared resources and social traps explored here. Indeed, prosocial marketing appears well suited to provide solutions to some aspects of the commons dilemma (cf. Andreasen 1995; Nason and White 1981). In this connection, we believe that solutions may emerge in at least four ways, as represented by the proposed synthesis to which we now turn.

A SYNTHESIS OF COMMONS RESOLUTIONS AND IMPLICATIONS FOR MARKETING ENGAGEMENT

The elements of our proposed synthesis of commons resolutions and implications for marketing engagement appear in Table 1. These derive from a review and distillation of the relevant literature. We believe they are fundamental to an analysis of factors related to commons-based issues and guides to potential marketing-oriented action. In a sense, they might be considered new thoughts and strategies for an old problem. Some solutions depend on changes at the individual level, whereas others arise from coordinated, organized, or structural changes at the group, transgroup, or collective level. Furthermore, some resolutions focus on how actions affect individual or joint selfish interests in the short run, and others on how they influence collective considerations based on social welfare in the long run. Thus, Table 1 includes four key components: regulation, organization, social responsibility, and communication. Note that these distillates should be viewed as partially overlapping themes rather than as distinct, mutually exclusive categories. We review each theme, with attention to its development in the social sciences and its prescriptive implications for marketing.

Regulation

Some solutions to commons-related dilemmas alter the pattern of self-oriented incentives that characterize social situations (Hardin and Baden 1977). Such micro-level, self-oriented resolutions often hinge on regulatory measure(s) imposed on users of the commons by an authority figure interested in reducing depletion or misdirection of scarce resources. This idea, an essential foundation for governmental intervention, is an old one (cf. Hobbes 1651; Locke [1699] 1967). Similarly, Hardin (1968, p. 1243) suggests abandoning laissez-faire mentality and implementing "mutually coercive devices" to invoke cooperative choices by means of taxes and laws typically associated with regulation. This solution presupposes the establishment of some superordinate authority to address the commons dilemma but thereby raises a second age-old quandary: Who will govern those who govern the commons?

Experimental results suggest that subjects prefer to elect leaders to manage resources when they believe that others harvest excessively (Messick et al. 1983). However, this tendency appears to be stronger for (say) Dutch subjects (Samuelson et al. 1986) than for Americans (Messick et al. 1983), which suggests that cultures differ on the issue of when leadership intervention is desirable and thus helps explain the diversity of political systems found throughout the world.

Behavioral scientists have examined the effects of changing payoff contingencies. Not surprisingly, changing incentives to reward (punish) defection decreases (increases) cooperative behavior (e.g., Komorita, Sweeney, and Kravitz 1980). Also, subjects exercise self-restraint when such restraint helps increase the overall size or quality of the resource pool (e.g., Jorgenson and Papciak 1981).

Another solution to certain types of collective social dilemmas involves the conversion of community-owned resources into privately owned resources, the logic being that private-property owners will have vested interests in preserving their personal property (Dasgupta 1982). Experimental research suggests that when resources are held privately, they are harvested nearly optimally if harvest management is publicly visible (e.g., Messick and McClelland 1983). This finding hints that information sharing or communication is integral to resource management (a theme we develop subsequently) and suggests that privatization alone should not be considered a panacea for the commons dilemma.

In contrast to privatization, taxation schemes or fee schedules show some promise as ways to resolve commons dilemmas. For example, taxes have helped control toxic waste (cf. Tietenberg 1985). Also, usage fees can help discourage abuse of the commons by assigning costs when they are incurred (cf. Cairncross 1995).

With respect to specific marketing-based resolution strategies, traditional manipulations of the marketing mix, in concert with prudent regulation, may abet commons preservation. It would be advantageous to study the effects of the marketing mix on defecting or cooperative consumer behavior. Many aspects of product development, distribution, and pricing vitally affect the commons for better or worse. These areas of impact open opportunities for the resolution of some commons dilemmas through the design of regulatory strategies that affect such areas as product design, packaging, and pricing decisions.

The differential pricing of electricity during peak versus off-peak hours would be an obvious example. Price is a particularly salient variable to many consumers when they are making what they believe to be environmentally friendly purchase decisions (e.g., Antil 1984). But the overarching message of the price-related literature indicates that, though many consumers generally are willing to pay more for green products, they are not willing to pay much more (cf. Berger and Kanetkar 1995), perhaps due to the disbelief among many consumers that green products add any real value to self or environment. To overcome this disbelief, education on the demand side must prepare the way for acceptance of commons-sensitive offerings created on the supply side (cf. Simmons and Widmar 1990).

Organization

By "organization," we mean group cooperation or group formation and incentives to create social structures or change interpersonal boundaries for the benefit of the commons. Such structural changes traditionally have been the domain of politicians, economists, and political scientists. Structural changes work through mechanisms that are likely to affect self-oriented incentives throughout the group. For example, one such structural determinant involves group size.

From one perspective, reducing group size often can work toward resolving the commons dilemma. Anecdotal evidence, lay observations, and experimental findings all suggest that incentives toward cooperation or self-constraint tend to increase as group size decreases (Komorita and Lapworth 1982). The reasons for this phenomenon are unclear and seem to be varied. Perhaps payoffs change as group size increases (Bonacich et al. 1976); perhaps individuals cooperate only when others do but perceive large groups as harboring noncooperators; or perhaps individuals in larger groups believe that their defecting decisions are less visible or have less impact on group welfare (Messick 1973).

Whatever the reason for the inverse relationship between cooperation and group size, a solution to ecological problems through population reduction does not appear imminently feasible. The population pressures on our global commons are enormous and increasing rapidly, despite various birth-control technologies and intervention policies (cf. Bartlett 1994; Keyfitz 1994).

More feasible strategies may involve approaches that actually increase group size but with an emphasis on the collective pursuit of self-interest. This strategy might be viewed as a change in the way firms and groups organize, the way in which they structure, cooperate, and form boundaries and alliances (cf. Cairncross 1992; Milne, Iyer, and Gooding-Williams 1996). For example, Merck & Co. cooperated with the government of Costa Rica, whereby that country received US$1 million and a percentage of profits by setting aside one-quarter of its rain forest as a reserve area to be used for the prudent and responsible development of biodiversity samples (Chichilnisky 1992). Environmentalists also have teamed with retailers and furniture manufacturers to form buyers' groups that demand better forest-management practices, including independent verification of those practices (Ipsen 1997). Most recently, environmentalists, state and federal governments, and the Pacific Lumber Company collaborated to preserve 10,000 acres of redwood forest (Christensen 1999). Some environmentalists might argue that optimal commons-preserving scenarios in each of these cases would have prohibited any access or exploitation of forests. We take the position that negotiation, compromise, and, ideally, win–win outcomes for multiple stakeholders are expedient; similarly, we believe that, in most cases, incremental rather than extreme measures of protection are less likely to alienate corporate stakeholders and consequently more likely to lead to the longer-term desirable outcome of better protecting the commons, which is the goal advocated by environmentalists.

Although many of these organizational efforts may begin altruistically, none will be sustained or perhaps even considered desirable without a self-interested favorable impact on the corporate bottom line. Thus, such efforts have entered a critical period in which greater numbers of managers will need to recognize that the bottom line must "factor in" preservation of the commons as a precondition for the firm's long-run survival and, therefore, as an ingredient in long-term profitability (e.g., Gifford 1997). To state the case bluntly, net present value suffers when discounted cash flows lack long-term potential. In this spirit, the emergence of the Environmental Defense Fund and subsequent cooperative efforts between corporations and environmentalists hint at possible win–win scenarios between the profit motive and responsible commons management.

Social Responsibility

Although we believe large-scale corporate involvement in resolutions to commons dilemmas may require profit incentives, some people may choose to respond cooperatively because of other-oriented concerns that altruistically place the collective welfare above self-interest (cf. Schwartz 1977). Thus, Edney (1980) suggests that the crux of the commons dilemma is not so much an issue of selfish gain through rationality of choice as it is a conflict of human values (cf. Granzin and Olsen 1991; Vining and Ebreo 1990). Saemann (1992, p. 190) frames the issue similarly and urges consumers to embrace the realities of social interdependence, namely, *Gemeinschaftsgefühl,* or a sense of social interest, community feeling, and humanistic identification that fosters "oneness in interdependence" rather than "egocentric independence" from humanity. Thompson (1995) has argued for the need to address contextual factors that should influence appropriate and responsible decision making when confronted with dilemmas. From these perspectives, we might conclude that education can teach members of the commons about the nature of social dilemmas and the need for social responsibility in individual actions. When experimental treatment groups have been coached on the long-term consequences of their actions or instructed on the moral obligation of selflessness, significant increases in cooperative behavior have occurred (e.g., Stern 1976). Furthermore, people tend to be more socially responsible in their decision making when they recognize the importance of the collective welfare and receive feedback on the impact of their choices (Sweeney 1973).

Brewer (1981) has suggested that cooperative solutions to collective social dilemmas may be facilitated by exploring the constructive incentives that arise from social identity. The sense of membership in a common group probably enhances the individual's willingness to exercise personal restraint in the interest of collective welfare (Messick and Brewer 1983). Conformity pressures seem to be higher in more cohesive groups, and members of an "in-group" tend to perceive other members more favorably, particularly in terms of trustworthiness, honesty, and cooperativeness, while perceiving themselves as part of some common fate (Rabbie and Horwitz 1969).

But, despite the potentially powerful effects of social responsibility on individual decision making, in the context of environmental marketing issues, these effects may be unpredictable and are affected by many factors and forces (e.g., Ölander and Thøgersen 1995). For example, loyalties to groups and their social norms may shift (Messick and Brewer 1983); altruism with regard to commons-friendly behavior may be situation-specific (e.g., Hopper and Nielsen 1991) or simply secondary to internalized personal norms (Thøgersen 1995). At bottom, as discussed previously, attempts to solve social dilemmas may require institutional or structural changes that support such efforts at the group level.

In drawing on potential marketing-related resolutions, such change could not occur without technological progress (discussed subsequently) and profit incentives working together. But more fundamentally, it cannot occur unless consumers care increasingly, because of revisions in their consumption-related needs and wants, and unless people believe that their commons-friendly behavior will have an impact (cf. Berger and Corbin 1992; Kinnear, Taylor, and Ahmed 1974). To the benefit of the commons and ultimately the human condition, there now exist segments of consumers that refuse to buy furniture made from rain-forest wood, cosmetics tested on animals, or food served in styrene containers (e.g., Schwepker and Cornwell 1991; Wescott 1992). For some customer segments, offering commons-friendly products or emphasizing this theme in a marketing communication strategy has become a potential source of competitive advantage or a viably unique selling proposition (cf. Gross 1990), as was the case with the forest-preservation campaign by the World Wildlife Fund.

But, as indicated previously, applications of green orientations to consumption, marketing, and protection of the commonly shared environment raise a host of issues awaiting resolution. Since the formal organization of green political movements in the Netherlands and Germany during the mid-1970s, the term "green" has acquired so many meanings as to relinquish any claims to clarity (cf. Eckersley 1992). This confusion—coupled with cynical abuses by some marketers and ensuing consumer skepticism—has sparked efforts by governments and the private sector to establish generally accepted standards for green claims (cf. Gray-Lee, Scammon, and Mayer 1994). The Federal Trade Commission (FTC) (Code of Federal Regulations 1994, p. 111) moved to curtail abuses of "environmental marketing claims." These FTC guidelines address the prominence and clarity of qualifications and disclosures; distinctions between product benefits and packaging; and the veracity of environmental marketing claims regarding, for example, general environmental benefits, degradability, compostability, recyclability, waste reduction, refillability, and ozone friendliness. Simon (1992) argues persuasively that no product should be considered green unless it meets the following criteria: reduced raw material content, high recycled content (e.g., aluminum cans); nonpolluting manufacture with nontoxic materials (e.g., chlorofluorocarbons, deinking solvents); no unnecessary animal testing (e.g., cosmetics); no unfavorable impact on protected species (e.g., dolphin-safe tuna); low energy consumption during production, use, and disposal (e.g., efficient light bulbs); minimal packaging (e.g., fast foods); reuse/refill of packages when possible (e.g., beverage or detergent containers); long, useful life with updating capacity (e.g., office machines); postconsumption collection/disassembly systems (e.g., automobiles); and remanufacturing capability (e.g., closed- or partial-loop reuse as in composting or non-toxic incineration) (cf. Samli 1998).

More succinctly, Ottman (1993, p. 49) defines green products as "typically durable, non-toxic, made from recycled materials and minimally packaged" but, perhaps more important, also asserts that green is "a relative term describing those products with less impact on the environment than alternatives." Ottman further states that regional conditions, technological changes, attitude shifts, and regulatory changes all determine what consumers deem green products and behavior. This relativistic orientation raises an important question: Is a product that assaults the environment green simply because it replaces a product that was an even more egregious threat?

Such difficulties in determining green-ness are underscored by three examples. First, sales of Mobil's Hefty garbage bags soared when first introduced because consumers believed that they decomposed over time; when it later turned out that they only partially decomposed and thus potentially did more harm than good, sales plummeted. Second and more symptomatically, McDonald's decided to eliminate styrene packaging because customers disapproved of this material, even though styrene is actually more recyclable than the paper that replaced it (Kleiner 1991). Third and even more insidiously, the consumption of products generally accepted as green may help the environment less than easily available greener alternatives, such as when paper towels made of recycled paper replace the option of using a sponge (Ottman 1993, p. 54).

In short, truly green marketing decisions must address a broad and complex variety of externalities and interactive systems that are associated with relevant assaults on the commonly shared environment (cf. Meade and Nason 1991; Mundt 1993; Sinclair-Desgagné and Gabel 1997). That is, the effect of altruism and commons-friendly behavior is as much a function of systemic interdependence as of social interdependence. Consider the simple act of choosing whether to drink a cup of coffee from a styrene, paper, or porcelain cup. Conventional green reasoning might recommend the porcelain cup. However, consumers also should consider the amount of energy used by dishwashers and the pollution caused by detergents. Quite possibly, if frequently washed, the porcelain cup may consume more energy, pollute more water, and generally damage the environment more extensively than would either styrene or paper (*The Economist* 1992). Similarly, a pressing concern is the proclivity to focus on what we would call micro-green activities instead of on macro-green or systemically commons-friendly activities. Revisiting McDonald's as an illustration, the production of beef protein (a staple of the McDonald's menu) is intrinsically more damaging to the commonly shared resources of soil and fresh water than is the production of soy protein. To draw attention only to styrene versus paper, rather than beef versus soy protein, may placate many or most green-conscious consumers but not make significant contributions toward preserving the commons (cf. Stauber and Rampton 1995). Thus, it is incorrect to claim that any organization is unilaterally green, for all its actions, with respect to all commonly shared resources, all the time. In other words, we submit that we could find the "greenest" company on Earth, but that, upon scrutiny, we would find nongreen or commons-unfriendly activity in that company. Therefore green-ness or commons friendliness is indeed a relative term and must be measured on several continua and with regard to each commons on which it has a direct or indirect bearing.

Communication

Communication within a group increases the probability that individuals will sacrifice their self-interest in favor of other-oriented resource conservation at the collective level (e.g., Hackett, Schlager, and Walker 1994). When groups have the opportunity to discuss a dilemma in advance, individuals in those groups make significantly fewer defecting choices than individuals who have engaged in no prior discussion (Dawes, McTavish, and Shaklee 1977). However, using a resource dilemma design that provided actual feedback about the behavior of others, Messick and colleagues (1983) find that such feedback can have potentially conflicting effects on individual choices. Learning that other group members are restraining their harvest introduces normative pressures to conform by behaving cooperatively; however, it also may relieve some pressure toward cooperation if one person's choice appears less essential to the collective welfare. Furthermore, when given information that other group members are making selfish, defecting choices, individuals tend to conform in favor of their self-interest. Thus, subjects given false feedback that other group members were overusing the resource pool tended to increase their own harvests across trials, whereas subjects given false feedback that others were underusing the pool tended to maintain moderate harvests across trials. Along similar lines, Dawes, McTavish, and Shaklee (1977) find a positive correlation between individuals' perceptions of how many group members would cooperate and their own degrees of cooperation. Subjects who predicted that a larger (smaller) number of the other group members would cooperate tended to cooperate more (less) themselves. In addition, subjects who communicated about the dilemma predicted more cooperation than did subjects in groups that did not communicate.

Through implicit reciprocity, a decision to make a cooperative choice often rests on the trust that others also will make cooperative decisions. Even if people are aware of the value of cooperative decisions, they are unlikely to make them if others fail to reciprocate (cf. Bingham 1996). In the commons, unilateral exercise of personal restraint in the interest of collective welfare appears futile unless one member trusts that others will behave similarly. In short, no one wants to play the sucker by cooperating while others selfishly profit at the group's expense (cf. Wiener and Doescher 1991).

Research on the relationship between trust and cooperation in social dilemmas assumes that personal trust is a function of communication through interpersonal interactions that reveal or disclose the motives and intentions of others (e.g., Kelley and Stahelski 1970). However, the commons situation may require individuals to make decisions without explicit knowledge of others. In such circumstances, choosing cooperatively requires "depersonalized trust," that is, trust formed in the absence of prior interaction with interdependent others (Brewer 1981). Such depersonalized trust thrives best in relatively homogeneous social groups or in cultures whose members share common values, attitudes, and goals.

Depersonalized trust also can be enhanced by confidence that those who fail to cooperate will be sanctioned in some fashion. In such cases, we differentiate sanctions that are agreed on and administered by the group from sanctions administered by relatively external, regulatory bodies such as governments. More specifically, when groups are empowered to punish defectors, cooperative choices significantly increase (Caldwell 1976). Furthermore, group norms can serve a similar function by providing a set of expectations while implying that violations of these norms will be punished. Thus,

Bonacich (1976) finds that communication among group members tends to focus on the normative requirement of cooperative choices and on expressions of how angry the group would be toward a defector. In these conditions, even in the face of high monetary incentives to defect, the rate of cooperative responding exceeded 90%.

The effects just noted appear to be reinforced when decisions are personally identifiable, that is, traceable. Individuals who must reveal their choice under the eye of public scrutiny increase their rate of cooperative behavior (Jorgenson and Papciak 1981). This tendency apparently holds for corporations as well. Some companies exposed as polluters have found the adverse public relations too costly to bear and have begun to refrain from commons-hostile activities (Thomas 1992; Upah and Wokutch 1985).

All this suggests a potentially positive role for communication among group members in fostering cooperation toward resolving commons dilemmas. However, as Messick and Brewer (1983) point out, the practical applications of these findings are limited because, in real-world dilemmas, the direct communication among group members found in experimental settings is not always possible. Most social dilemmas, particularly the commons dilemma, involve large collectivities that extend far too widely to permit the sort of contacts that facilitate cooperation in laboratory experiments. In such conditions, relatively large and often diffuse groups may find little or no opportunity to communicate to negotiate solutions. However, Nill and Shultz (1997) contend that the issue is not so much opportunity as will; even among large, disparate, and culturally diverse groups with seemingly adversarial interests, when all stakeholders enter a dialogue to resolve the likes of commons dilemmas, multiwin and more commons-friendly marketing activities are more probable.

That said, verification of agreements and ensuing marketing activities that emanate from communicative interactions among all stakeholders become integral to the process. It is not enough simply that all agree to cooperate and preserve. Instead, a step-series of agreed-on, incremental, and measurable results at specific periods, while the process is moving toward the final, ideal outcome, must be verified. This multistep verification schema has proven to be particularly important to ameliorate some of the most intractable crises and conflicts of the past 50 years (cf. Deutsch 1973, 1985; Osgood 1962, 1966; Pruitt and Rubin 1986). We believe it is also important to any large-scale commons-friendly marketing activity, especially when stakeholders occupy adversarial positions.

Contrary to some scholars who believe there is no technical solution to largest-scale commons dilemmas (e.g., Hardin 1968; Postman 1993; Wade 1974; Winner 1986), we believe that technology will play a significant role—not because of potential breakthroughs to replace air, water, soil, or other commonly shared resources, but rather because technological advances will facilitate dissemination of information, enhancement of communication, education of all stakeholders, and verification (cf. Christensen 1999; Saemann 1992). Hardin (1968, p. 1245) notes that "one does not know whether a man killing an elephant or setting fire to grassland is harming others until one knows the total system in which his act appears." Thus, communication will enable each of us to understand the systemic repercussions of defecting behavior. And, as the advent of the information superhighway has made clear, technology eventually will enable communication networks to reach us all. In essence, as we move into the Age of Global Information, the disconnected and disparate world collectives that Messick and Brewer (1983) argue would preclude effective communication, thereby blocking dilemma resolution, will eventually grow less disparate and more connected. Hardin (1998) recently has shifted his position on the role of technology and the extent to which it may abet commons preservation. Similarly to us, Hardin now believes that technological advancements may facilitate information dissemination and group cooperation, as well as the development of more commons-friendly products and marketing processes.

Consider, for example, the potential role(s) of computer networks and simulations, television networks, satellite photos of the rain forest, and other telecommunication technologies. Each informs and thereby empowers consumer-interest groups that, in turn, can use communication networks to advocate commons-friendly agendas, monitor program compliance, publicize conspicuous abuses, pressure regulators, and motivate marketers. Consumer empowerment and its attendant perceptions of consumer effectiveness are vital to progress in addressing commons-related environment issues (cf. Kinnear, Taylor, and Ahmed 1974). Much of the previously cited psychology literature clearly indicates that focused efforts and increased self-efficacy enhance commons-friendly activities (Kaufman and Kerr 1993), and recent field studies concur (Bromley 1992). Studies on consumers per se indicate similar conclusions (Ellen, Wiener, and Cobb-Walgren 1991).

Although Hardin (1968, p. 1244) states that progress is impossible until we "explicitly exorcise the spirit of Adam Smith," we may have entered an era in which Smith's invisible hand will play a role in the form of communication technology guided by marketing acumen. Therefore, the commons preservation message slowly is permeating the marketplace. Despite Hardin's (1968, p. 1245) argument that "the morality of an act cannot be determined by a photograph," photographs—and their evolutionary analogs in the form of digital reproductions, computer images, video screens, and so forth— become an important link in the communications network when their interpretation, contextualization, and dissemination facilitate change.

Consequently, marketing communications that inform consumers about the value of commons conservation and the pitfalls of commons degradation seem a potential catalyst for prosocial consumption and movement toward resolution of the commons dilemma (cf. Lord 1994). Such strategic applications of marketing communication have been referred to as "attacking the barriers to cooperation" (Wiener and Doescher 1991). Communicating the value of commons-friendly (cooperative) consumption and the costs of commons-unfriendly (defecting) consumption is also more likely to inspire design and production of commons-friendly products and render them less price sensitive. Again, this assertion is a reasonable extension of previously cited experimental findings (e.g., Bonacich 1976).

As a final example, we return to the case of cooperation among various stakeholders with common interests in redwood forests (Christensen 1999). This cooperative agreement, the habitat conservation plan, embodies much of our synthesis and may prove an instructive model for a type of new thinking that we encouraged in our introductory remarks. Briefly, multiple stakeholders, some with adversarial perspectives and contentious positions, enter a constructive dialogue. This communicative process leads to an alliance of sorts and a negotiated agreement with specific and measurable outcomes over time. The need for a systemic plan for action and commons management effectively is communicated and recognized by consumers, activists, regulators, marketers, and other stakeholders in ways designed to influence usage and consumption decisions that, at this juncture, would appear to be commons friendly, at least with regard to this particular commons of focus (10,000 acres of redwood forest).

In Figure 1, we delineate the essence of the extant agreement: (1) presence of redwood commons, (2) stakeholders in that commons, and (3) a negotiated agreement on how to manage it. We also suggest more expansive elements for integrative commons management. Our expansion includes a monitoring or verification program to alert stakeholders to the unfolding processes that result from the agreement. More specifically,

FIGURE 1

Stakeholder Negotiation and Compliance Model for Commons Management

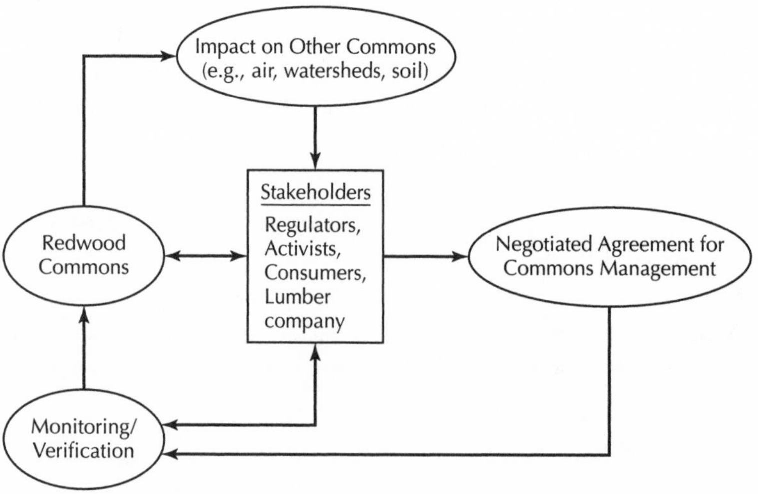

the engaged stakeholders, as well as external policy analysts, will and should monitor the prescribed activities to determine whether those activities abet redwood commons preservation, consistent with the incremental measures and agreed on time lines, to the satisfaction of the vested parties to the negotiated conservation plan. Moreover, the model requires a broader, integrative systemic approach that will determine the extent to which the agreement affects other commons beyond the specific acreage directly included, such as air, watersheds, soil, or fisheries that may be affected by harvesting, downstream production, distribution, and product usage or consumption. Finally, note that in the stakeholder negotiation and compliance model for commons management, the participating parties must literally look "outside the box" (i.e., the centrally located set of principal stakeholders) to resolve their commons dilemma.

Discussion and Directions for Further Research

Irrespective of the transnational cooperative efforts to address commons-related issues (e.g., the 1992 United Nations Conference on Environment and Development and the ongoing "Rio Process" [Jordan and Voisey 1998]), protracted environmental degradation resulting from commons dilemmas indicates that fresh thinking truly is warranted. With the increasing global influence of the marketing concept, responsible and responsive activity by marketers and effective application of marketing tools may provide one avenue of assistance in the search for resolutions to difficulties stemming from the tragedy of the commons. Toward that end, we have proposed the synthesis of commons resolutions and implications for marketing engagement (Table 1) and the stakeholder negotiation and compliance model for commons management (Figure 1). We hope that both the synthesis and the model will inspire further research. In that spirit, we propose the following topics for empirical investigation:

1. Consumers' commons-related choice processes and factors that influence those processes, including factors that enhance consumer motivations to engage in green consumption and willingness to endure such short-term costs as higher product prices or inconvenient purchase venues;
2. The source, nature, and persuasiveness of attempts at social influence leading in the direction of altruistic values;
3. The marketing communications mix (e.g., advertising, promotions. selling, public relations, sponsorship, labeling) appropriate for encouraging changes in commons-related attitudes and behavior (e.g., purchases, selfish exploitation); and
4. Perhaps most important, systemic factors and integrative forces relevant to administering the interactive effects of marketing activity, governing bodies, regulatory guidelines, enforcement programs, consumption, and their interrelated impacts on the

commons and its multiple stakeholders, in short, a systemic approach that should be integral to the analysis and solution for some of the most fractious global macrochallenges (e.g., integrative management of multiple commons).

More specifically, we believe that the following propositions are particularly compelling, lend themselves to empirical testing, and therefore should be of interest to marketing policy scholars:

P_1: Communication targeted at increasing the likelihood of commons-friendly behavior tends especially to succeed when that communication reaches all stakeholders, includes information about others, invokes a sense of trust in others, and enunciates measurable steps toward mutually agreed-on outcomes.

P_2: Communicating the value of commons-friendly behavior and the costs of commons-unfriendly behavior will tend to inspire not only commons-friendly consumption, but also the production of commons-friendly products and services and to render such offerings both less price sensitive and less cost sensitive.

P_3: Marketing activities aimed at enhancing social responsibility, altruism, and selflessness will further the prudent management of common resources.

P_4: Systemic commons-management strategies mutually agreed on by all stakeholders of that commons (regulators, activists, consumers, producers, and so forth) will yield more effective commons-friendly management and more successful environmental protection programs.

P_5: Mutually agreed-on strategies that more fully include specific, measurable outcomes and address downstream commons, as well as the commons of immediate interest, will yield more optimal management and protection programs for a longer period of time, to the benefit of a larger number of stakeholders.

By empirically investigating these and related propositions, researchers with special interests in marketing communications, ethics and social responsibility, organizational design and strategic alliances, consumer decision making, management by objectives, and so forth can enjoy opportunities, not to mention challenges, to leverage their expertise.

In conclusion, responsible and responsive prosocial activity by marketers and effective application of marketing tools to public policy may provide an avenue of assistance in the search for resolutions to difficulties stemming from environmental social traps. Because marketers typically pursue activities that predict, transact, and assess commercial exchange (cf. Bagozzi 1975), they may be positioned uniquely to ameliorate the tragedy of the commons, in so far as commercial exchanges and the product usage or consumption resulting therefrom ultimately abet or assault the commons. Further research as well as both vision and vigilance are needed to overcome the tragic consequences potentially stemming from the inertia of short-sighted and self-interested marketers. By working with consumers, regulators, interest groups, and researchers—particularly in the areas of communications and consumer decision making, product development, green advocacy, program design, and systems management—marketers might contribute to solutions in an area in which, too often, they have been vilified for encouraging social waste, wreaking ecological destruction, and contributing to the tragedy of the commons.

References

Anderson, W. Thomas and Goutam N. Challagalla (1994), "The Negative Legacy of Consumption," *International Journal of Research in Marketing,* 11 (2), 165–76.

___ and William H. Cunningham (1972), "The Socially Conscious Consumer," *Journal of Marketing,* 36 (July), 23–31.

Andreasen, Alan R. (1995), *Marketing Social Change.* San Francisco, CA: Jossey-Bass.

Antil, John (1984), "Socially Responsible Consumers: Profile and Implications for Public Policy," *Journal of Macromarketing,* 4 (Fall). 18–38.

Aristotle (1976), *The Politics of Aristotle,* Books I-V. New York: Arno Press.

Bagozzi, Richard (1975), "Marketing as Exchange," *Journal of Marketing,* 39 (4), 32–39.

Bartlett, Albert (1994), "Reflections on Sustainability, Population Growth, and the Environment— Revisited," *Population & Environment,* 16 (September), 5–35.

Beder, S. (1997), *Global Spin: The Corporate Assault on Environmentalism.* White River Junction, VT: Chelsea Green.

Berger, Ida and R.M. Corbin (1992), "Perceived Consumer Effectiveness and Faith in Others as Moderators of Environmentally Responsible Behaviors," *Journal of Public Policy & Marketing,* 11 (2), 79–89.

___ and Vinay Kanetkar (1995), "Increasing Environmental Sensitivity Via Workplace Experiences," *Journal of Public Policy & Marketing,* 14 (Fall), 205–15.

Bingham, Roger (1996), "Toward a Science of Morality," *Skeptic,* 4 (2), 48–61.

Bloom, Paul and William Novelli (1981), "Problems and Challenges in Social Marketing," *Journal of Marketing,* 45 (Spring), 79–88.

Bonacich, Phillip (1976), "Secrecy and Solidarity," *Sociometry,* 39 (September), 200–208.

___, Gerald H. Shure, James P. Kahan, and Robert J. Meeker (1976), "Cooperation and Group Size in the N-Person Prisoner's Dilemma," *Journal of Conflict Resolution,* 20 (December), 687–706.

Brewer, Marilynn B. (1981), "Ethnocentrism and Its Role in Interpersonal Trust" in *Scientific Inquiry and the Social Sciences,* M. Brewer and B. Collins, eds. San Francisco, CA: Jossey-Bass, 345–60.

Bromley, Daniel W. (1992), *Making the Commons Work.* San Francisco, CA: ICS Press.

Cairncross, Frances (1992), "UNCED, Environmentalism and Beyond," *Columbia Journal of World Business,* 27 (Fall/Winter), 12–17.

___ (1995), *Costing the Earth: The Challenge for Governments, the Opportunity for Business.* Boston, MA: Harvard Business School Press.

Caldwell, Michael D. (1976), "Communication and Sex Effects in a Five Person Prisoner's Dilemma Game," *Journal of Personality and Social Psychology,* 33 (March), 273–80.

Chichilnisky, Graciela (1992), "Market Innovation and the Global Environment," *Columbia Journal of World Business,* 27 (Fall/Winter), 36–41.

Christensen, Jon (1999), "Seeing a Forest to Save the Trees," *New York Times,* (March 7), C2.

Coase, Ronald H. (1960), "The Problem of Social Costs," *Journal of Law and Economics,* 3 (October), 1–44.

Code of Federal Regulations (1994), *Federal Trade Commission Commercial Practices,* 16, Chapter 1, Part 260. Washington, DC: Office of the Federal Register National Archives and Records Administration, 111–18.

Cross, John G. and Melvin J. Guyer (1980), *Social Traps.* Ann Arbor, MI: University of Michigan Press.

Daly, Herman (1996), *Enough Already! Beyond Growth: The Economics of Sustainable Development.* Boston, MA: Beacon Press.

Dasgupta, Partha (1982), *The Control of Resources.* Oxford: Blackwell.

Dawes, Robyn M. (1976), "Formal Models of Dilemmas in Social Decision Making," in *Human Judgment Journal and Decision Processes,* M. Kaplan and S. Schwarts, eds. New York: Academic Press, 88–107.

___ (1980), "Social Dilemmas," *Annual Review of Psychology,* 31, 169–93.

___, Jeanne McTavish, and Harriet Shaklee (1977), "Behavior, Communication, and Assumptions About Other People's Behavior in a Commons Dilemma Situation," *Journal of Personality and Social Psychology,* 35 (January), 1–11.

Deutsch, Morton (1973), *The Resolution of Conflict: Constructive and Destructive Processes.* New Haven, CT: Yale University Press.

___ (1985), *Distributive Justice.* New Haven, CT: Yale University Press.

Drumwright, M. (1994), "Socially Responsible Organizational Buying: Environmental Concern as a Noneconomic Buying Criterion," *Journal of Marketing,* 58 (July), 1–19.

Eckersley, Robin (1992), *Environmentalism and Political Theory.* Albany, NY: State University of New York Press.

The Economist (1992), (August 1), 54.

Edney, Julian J. (1980), "The Commons Problem: Alternative Perspectives," *American Psychologist,* 35 (February), 131–50.

Elkington, John (1994), "Towards the Sustainable Corporation: Win-Win-Win Business Strategies for Sustainable Development," *California Management Review,* 36 (Winter). 90–100.

Ellen, Pam Scholder, Joshua Lyle Wiener, and Cathy Cobb-Walgren (1991), "The Role of Perceived Consumer Effectiveness in Motivating Environmentally Conscious Behaviors," *Journal of Public Policy & Marketing,* 10 (Fall), 102–17.

Fisk, George (1973), "Criteria for a Theory of Responsible Consumption," *Journal of Marketing,* 37 (April), 24–31.

___ (1974), *Marketing and the Ecological Crisis.* New York: Harper and Row.

Galbraith, John K. (1973), *Economics and the Public Purpose.* Boston, MA: Houghton Mifflin.

Gifford, D. (1997), "The Value of Going Green," *Harvard Business Review,* 75 (September/October), 11–12.

Granzin, K.L. and J.E. Olsen (1991), "Characterizing Participants in Activities Protecting the Environment: A Focus on Donating, Recycling and Conservation Behaviors," *Journal of Public Policy & Marketing,* 10 (2), 1–27.

Gray-Lee, Jason W., Debra L. Scammon, and Robert N. Mayer (1994), "Review of Legal Standards for Environmental Marketing Claims," *Journal of Public Policy & Marketing,* 13 (Spring), 155–59.

Gross, Frank B. (1990), "The Weaning of the Green: Environmentalism Comes of Age in the 1990s," *Business Horizons,* 33 (September-October), 40–46.

Hackett, S., E. Schlager, and J. Walker (1994), "The Role of Communication in Resolving Commons Dilemmas: Experimental Evidence with Heterogeneous Appropriations," *Journal of Environmental Economics and Management,* 27 (September), 99–127.

Hardin, Garrett (1968), "The Tragedy of the Commons," *Science,* 162, 1243–48.

___ (1998), telephone interview, (May 27), Santa Barbara, CA.

___ and John Baden (1977), *Managing the Commons.* San Francisco, CA: W.H. Freeman.

Hart, Stuart L. (1997), "Beyond Greening: Strategies for a Sustainable World," *Harvard Business Review,* 75 (January/February), 66–76.

Hartman, Cathy L. and Edwin R. Stafford (1998), "Crafting Enviropreneurial Value Chain Strategies Through Green Alliances," *Business Horizons,* 41 (March-April), 67–72.

Hobbes, Thomas (1651), *Leviathan.* London: Dent.

Hopper, J. and J. Nielsen (1991), "Recycling as Altruistic Behavior: Normative and Behavioral Strategies to Expand Participation in a Community Recycling Program," *Environment and Behavior,* 23 (2), 195–220.

Ipsen, Erik (1997), "Selling the Doorjamb and Seeing the Forest," *International Herald Tribune,* (April 5–6), 9.

Jordan, Andrew and Heather Voisey (1998), "The 'Rio Process': The Politics and Substantive Outcomes of 'Earth Summit II'," *Global Environmental Change,* 8 (1), 93–97.

Jorgenson, Dale and Anthony S. Papciak (1981), "The Effects of Communication, Resource Feedback, and Identifiability on Behavior in a Simulated Commons," *Journal of Experimental Psychology,* 17 (July), 373–85.

Judge, P. (1997), "It's Not Easy Bein' Green," *BusinessWeek,* (November 24), 180–81.

Kangun, Norman, Les Carlson, and Stephen Grove (1991), "Environmental Advertising Claims: A Preliminary Investigation," *Journal of Public Policy & Marketing,* 10 (Fall), 47–58.

Kassarjian, Harold (1971), "Incorporating Ecology into Marketing Strategy: The Case of Air Pollution," *Journal of Marketing,* 35 (July), 61-65.

Kaufman, Cynthia M. and Norbert L. Kerr (1993), "Small Wins: Perceptual Focus, Efficacy, and Cooperation in a Stage-Conjunctive Social Dilemma," *Journal of Applied Social Psychology,* 23 (January), 3–20.

Kelley, Harold H. and Anthony J. Stahelski (1970), "Social Interaction Basis of Cooperators' and Competitors' Beliefs About Others," *Journal of Personality and Social Psychology,* 16 (October), 66–91.

Keyfitz, Nathan (1994), "The Scientific Debate: Is Population Growth a Problem?" *Harvard International Review,* 16 (Fall), 10–11, 74.

Kilbourne, William (1995), "Green Advertising: Salvation or Oxymoron," *Journal of Advertising,* 17 (2), 7–19.

___, Pierre McDonagh, and Andrea Prothero (1997), "Sustainable Consumption and the Quality of Life: A Macromarketing Challenge to the Dominant Social Paradigm," *Journal of Macromarketing,* 17 (Spring), 4–24.

Kinnear, Thomas C., James R. Taylor, and Sadrudin A. Ahmed (1974), "Ecologically Concerned Consumers: Who Are They?" *Journal of Marketing,* 38 (April), 20–24.

Kleiner, Art (1991), "What Does It Mean to Be Green?" *Harvard Business Review,* 69 (July/August), 38–47.

Komorita, Samuel S. and C. William Lapworth (1982), "Cooperative Choice Among Individuals Versus Groups in an N-Person Dilemma Situation," *Journal of Personality and Social Psychology,* 42 (March), 487–96.

___, James Sweeney, and David A. Kravitz (1980), "Cooperative Choice in the N-Person Dilemma Situation," *Journal of Personality and Social Psychology*, 38 (March), 504–16.

Lloyd, William F. (1833), *Two Lectures on the Checks to Population.* Oxford: Oxford University Press.

Locke, John ([1699] 1967), *Two Treatises of Government.* London: Cambridge University Press.

Lord, K.R. (1994), "Motivating Recycling Behavior: A Quasi-experimental Investigation of Message and Source Strategies," *Psychology and Marketing*, 11 (4), 341–58.

Meade, William K. and Robert W. Nason (1991), "Toward a Unified Theory of Macromarketing: A Systems Theoretic Approach," *Journal of Macromarketing*, 11 (Fall), 72–82.

Menon, A. and A. Menon (1997), "Enviropreneurial Marketing Strategy: The Emergence of Corporate Environmentalism as Marketing Strategy," *Journal of Marketing*, 61 (January), 51–67.

Messick, David M. (1973), "To Join or Not to Join: An Approach to the Unionization Decision," *Organizational Behavior and Human Performance*, 10 (August), 145–56.

___ and Marilynn B. Brewer (1983), "Solving Social Dilemmas," in *Review of Personality and Social Psychology*, L. Wheeler and P. Shaver, eds. Beverly Hills, CA: Sage, 11–44.

___ and Carol L. McClelland (1983), "Social Traps and 36 Temporal Traps," *Personality and Social Psychology Bulletin*, 9 (March), 105–10.

___, Henk Wilke, Marilynn B. Brewer, Roderick M. Kramer, Patricia E. Zemke, and Layton Lui (1983), "Individual Adaptations and Structural Change as Solutions to Social Dilemmas," *Journal of Personality and Social Psychology*, 44 (February), 294–309.

Milne, George R., Easwar S. Iyer, and Sara Gooding-Williams (1996), "Environmental Organization Alliance Relationships Within and Across Nonprofit, Business, and Government Sectors," *Journal of Public Policy & Marketing*, 15 (Fall), 203–15.

Mundt, JoNel (1993), "Externalities: Uncalculated Outcomes of Exchange," *Journal of Macromarketing*, 13 (Fall), 46–53.

Nason, Robert W. (1989), "The Social Consequences of Marketing: Macromarketing and Public Policy," *Journal of Public Policy & Marketing*, 8, 242–51.

___ and Phillip D. White (1981), "The Visions of Charles C. Slater: Social Consequences of Marketing," *Journal of Macromarketing*, 1 (Fall), 4–18.

Nill, A. and C. Shultz (1997), "Cross Cultural Marketing Ethics and the Emergence of Dialogic Idealism as a Decision Making Model," *Journal of Macromarketing*, 17 (Fall), 4–19.

Ölander, Folke and John Thøgersen (1995), "Understanding of Consumer Behaviour as a Prerequisite for Environmental Protection," *Journal of Consumer Policy*, 18 (4), 345–85.

Olson, Mancur (1965), *The Logic of Collective Action.* Cambridge, MA: Harvard University Press.

Osgood, Charles (1962), *An Alternative to War or Surrender.* Urbana, IL: University of Illinois Press.

___ (1966), *Perspectives in Foreign Policy.* Palo Alto, CA: Pacific Books.

Ottman, Jacquelyn (1993), *Green Marketing.* Lincolnwood, IL: NTC Business Books.

Pickett, Gregory M., Norman Kangun, and Stephen Grove (1993), "Is There a General Conserving Consumer? A Public Policy Concern," *Journal of Public Policy & Marketing*, 12 (2), 234–43.

Pieters, Rik G.M. (1991), "Changing Garbage Disposal Patterns of Consumers: Motivation, Ability, and Performance," *Journal of Public Policy & Marketing*, 10 (Fall), 59–76.

___, Tammo Bijmolt, Fred van Raaij, and Mark de Kruijk (1998), "Consumers' Attributions of Proenvironmental Behavior, Motivation, and Ability to Self and Others," *Journal of Public Policy & Marketing*, 17 (2), 215–25.

Pilling, Bruce K., Lawrence A. Crosby, and Pam Scholder Ellen (1991), "Using Benefit Segmentation to Influence Environmental Legislation: A Bottle Bill Application," *Journal of Public Policy & Marketing*, 10 (2), 28–46.

Platt, J. (1973), "Social Traps," *American Psychologist,* 28 (August), 641–51.

Polonsky, Michael J. and Alma T. Mintu-Wimsatt (1995), *Environmental Marketing.* New York: Haworth Press.

Postman, N. (1993), *Technopoly: The Surrender of Culture to Technology.* New York: Vintage.

Pruitt, Dean G. and Jeffrey Z. Rubin (1986), *Social Conflict.* New York: Random House.

Rabbie, Jacob M. and Murray Horwitz (1969), "Arousal of In-Group-Out-Group Bias by a Chance Win or Lose," *Journal of Personality and Social Psychology,* 13 (3), 269–77.

Rangan, V. Kasturi, Sohel Karim, and Sheryl K. Sandberg (1996), "Do Better at Doing Good," *Harvard Business Review,* 74 (May/June), 42–54.

Ritchie, J. Brent and Gordon McDougall (1985), "Designing and Marketing Energy Conservation Policies and Programs: Implications From a Decade of Research," *Journal of Public Policy & Marketing,* 4, 14–32.

Ruckelshaus, William D. (1989), "Toward a Sustainable World," *Scientific American,* 261 (September), 166–70, 172, 174–75.

Saemann, Ralph (1992), "The Environment and the Need for New Technology, Empowerment and Ethical Values," *Columbia Journal of World Business,* 27 (Fall-Winter), 186–93.

Sagoff, M. (1988), *The Economy of Earth.* Cambridge: Cambridge University Press.

Samli, A. Coskun (1998), "A Method for Assessing the Environmental Friendliness of Products," *Journal of Macromarketing,* 18 (1), 34–40.

Samuelson, C., D. Messick, H. Wilke, and C. Rutte (1986), "Individual Restraint and Structural Change as Solutions to Social Dilemmas," in *Psychology of Decision and Conflict: Experimental Social Dilemmas,* Vol. 3, H. Wilke, D. Messick, and C. Rutte, eds. New York: Verlag, Peter, Lang, 29–51.

Schwartz, S. (1977), "Normative Influence on Altruism," in *Advances in Experimental Social Psychology,* Vol. 10, L. Berkowitz, ed. New York: Academic Press, 221–79.

Schwepker, Charles and T. Bettina Cornwell (1991), "An Examination of Ecologically Concerned Consumers and Their Intention to Purchase Ecologically Packaged Products," *Journal of Public Policy & Marketing,* 10 (Fall), 77–101.

Shabecoff, Philip (1993), *A Fierce Green Fire: The American Environmental Movement.* New York: Hill and Wang.

Simmons, D. and R. Widmar (1990), "Motivations and Barriers to Recycling: Toward a Strategy for Public Education," *Journal of Environmental Education,* 22 (1), 13–18.

Simon, Francoise (1992), "Marketing Green Products in the Triad," *Columbia Journal of World Business,* 27 (Fall/Winter), 268–85.

Sinclair-Desgagné, Bernard and H. Landis Gabel (1997), "Environmental Auditing in Management Systems and Public Policy," *Journal of Environmental Economics and Management,* 33 (3), 331–46.

Stauber, John C. and Sheldon Rampton (1995), *Toxic Sludge Is Good for You.* Monroe, ME: Common Courage Press.

Stern, Paul C. (1976), "Effects of Incentives and Education on Resource Conservation Decisions in a Simulated Commons Dilemma," *Journal of Personality and Social Psychology,* 34 (December), 1285–92.

Sweeney, John W. (1973), "An Experimental Investigation of the Free-Rider Problem," *Social Science Research,* 2 (September), 277–92.

Taylor, Shirley and Peter Todd (1995), "Understanding Household Garbage Reduction Behavior: A Test of an Integrated Model," *Journal of Public Policy & Marketing,* 14 (2), 192–204.

Thøgersen, J. (1995), "Recycling as Moral Behavior," in *Sustainable Consumption,* E. Stø, ed. Oslo, Norway: SIFO, 375–405.

Thomas, M.L. (1992), "The Business Community and the Environment: An Important Partnership," *Business Horizons,* 35 (March–April), 21–24.

Thompson, Craig J. (1995), "A Contextualist Proposal for the Conceptualization and Study of Marketing Ethics," *Journal of Public Policy & Marketing,* 14 (2), 177–91.

Thompson, William Irwin (1987), *GAIA: A Way of Knowing.* Great Barrington, MA: Lindisfame Press.

Tietenberg, Thomas (1985), *Emissions Trading: An Exercise in Reforming Pollution Policy.* Washington, DC: Johns Hopkins Press.

Upah, Gregory D. and Richard E. Wokutch (1985), "Assessing Social Impacts of New Products: An Attempt to Operationalize the Macromarketing Concept," *Journal of Public Policy & Marketing,* 4, 166–78.

Varadarajan, P. Rajan (1992), "Marketing's Contribution to Strategy: The View from a Different Looking Glass," *Journal of the Academy of Marketing Science,* 20 (Fall), 323–43.

Vining, Joanne and Angela Ebreo (1990), "What Makes a Recycler: A Comparison of Recyclers and Nonrecyclers," *Environment and Behavior,* 22 (January), 55–73.

Wade, N. (1974), "Green Revolution: A Just Technology, Often Unjust in Use," *Science,* 186, 1094–96.

Wasik, John F. (1996), *Green Marketing and Management.* Cambridge, MA: Blackwell Publishers.

Wescott, William F. (1992), "Environmental Technology Cooperation: A Quid Pro Quo for Transnational Corporations and Developing Countries," *Columbia Journal of World Business,* 27 (Fall/Winter), 144–53.

Wiener, Joshua L. (1993), "What Makes People Sacrifice Their Freedom for the Good of Their Community," *Journal of Public Policy & Marketing,* 12 (2), 244–51.

___ and Tabitha Doescher (1991), "A Framework for Promoting Cooperation," *Journal of Marketing,* 55 (April), 38–47.

___ and ___ (1994), "Cooperation and Expectations of Cooperation," *Journal of Public Policy & Marketing,* 13 (2), 259–70.

Winner, L. (1986), *The Whale and the Reactor: A Search for Limits in an Age of High Technology.* Chicago: University of Chicago Press.

GLOBALIZATION AND TECHNOLOGICAL ACHIEVEMENT: IMPLICATIONS FOR MACROMARKETING AND THE DIGITAL DIVIDE

Ronald Paul Hill and Kanwalroop Kathy Dhanda

This article examines the impact of globalization and technological achievement on the lives of vulnerable groups in society as well as the larger environment so that the marketing community may better understand the macrolevel implications of the digital divide. Using data collected by a variety of international organizations and in cooperation with the United Nations Development Programme, this research explores the creation, diffusion, and use of technology within the context of economic inequities, gender discrimination, and carbon dioxide pollution across nations. The article opens with a brief introduction to the technology revolution and the digital divide along with a theoretical discussion of the research objectives. Data descriptions are presented in the next section, and the findings show comparisons across technology achievement categories. The article closes with suggestions for abridging the digital divide and research implications for macromarketing.

The sweeping technological changes of the late twentieth century have affected consumers worldwide. Spawned by the convergence of the computer and telecommunications industries, the development of the World Wide Web, and the globalization of markets and consumer culture, the network age has dramatically increased the diffusion of knowledge across national and geographic boundaries (Hill and Dhanda 2002; Hussein 1999; Rust and Oliver 1994). As a result, citizens of even the least developed nations have access to information that was unavailable to the richest individuals in the wealthiest countries as recently

RONALD PAUL HILL is the Founding Dean and Bank of America Professor of Corporate Social Responsibility at University of South Florida St. Petersburg. He received his Ph.D. from the University of Maryland College Park, and his research concentrates on low-income consumers, corporate social responsibility, and public policy issues in marketing. KANWALROOP KATHY DHANDA is an associate professor in the Department of Management at the College of Commerce, DePaul University. She received her Ph.D. from the University of Massachusetts–Amherst, and her research focuses on environmental management, gender rights, and global public policy issues.

The authors wish to thank Sanford Grossbart, Clifford Shultz, and the anonymous reviewers for their helpful and supportive suggestions for this article. They also thank Dr. Pamplin for his financial generosity, which helped sponsor this project.

Hill, Ronald Paul and Kanwalroop Kathy Dhanda (2004), "Globalization and Technological Achievement: Implications for Macromarketing and the Digital Divide," *Journal of Macromarketing,* 24 (2), 147–155.

Globalization can be reshaped, and when it is, when it is properly, fairly run, with all countries having a voice in policies affecting them, there is a possibility that it will help create a new global economy in which growth is not only more sustainable and less volatile but the fruits of this growth are more equitably shared

—Joseph Stiglitz
(2002, 22)

as a century ago (Stiglitz 2002). Thus, the purpose of this article is to examine the impact of technology creation, dissemination, and use on a number of social and economic variables including consumption inequities, gender discrimination, and carbon dioxide pollution.

The development and expansion of the World Wide Web, often referred to in common parlance as the Internet, was exponential during the 1990s because of these trends (United Nations Development Programme [UNDP] 2001). From approximately 20 million users in 1995 to more than 400 million users by late 2000, the United Nations now predicts that 1 billion people globally will be online by 2005. In addition, there were just 200 available Web sites on the Internet in 1993, but this figure grew dramatically to more than 20 million sites by late 2000. Global expenditures by governments and industry on information and communications technology associated with the Web were expected to progress from $2.2 trillion in 1999 to $3 trillion by the end of 2003.

Such explosive growth notwithstanding, much of this technology has yet to reach ordinary consumers in less developed nations (Bucy 2000; Metzl 1996). Haythornthwaite (2001, 365) revealed, "It is important to examine how the increasing presence and importance of the Internet in the everyday lives of those with access separates [*sic*] others from the ongoing social, economic, and commercial activity the Internet supports and creates." For example, in a global community where fewer than half of all people have used a telephone, the ability to access the Web is a remote possibility for many (Hammond 2001). The UNDP reported that just 7 percent of the world's population is online (Norris 2000). These consumers typically reside within developed Western nations, which contain 97 percent of Internet hosts, 92 percent of computer hardware and software buyers, and 86 percent of all Internet connections (also see Godlee, Horton, and Smith 2000).

These differences are encapsulated in the term *digital divide,* a concept that captures the vast disparities in accessibility of information and communications technology within and among nation states. For example, high-income Organization for Economic Cooperation and Development (OECD) countries comprise only 14 percent of the world's population, yet they contain almost 80 percent of all Internet users (UNDP 2001). Among the remainder, nearly 900 million consumers are illiterate, close to 3 billion people live on less than $2 a day, and most women face multiple forms of discrimination (Hill, Peterson, and Dhanda 2001). Scholars believe that the digital divide that separates the "knowledge rich" from the "knowledge poor" continues to grow (Hussein 1999), condemning entire regions of the world to even greater poverty and inequity (Hanshaw 2000; Persaud 2001). In the end, globalization and technological advancement may be exacerbating the gap between the haves and the have-nots within and among countries (Hunter and Yates 2002).

Research Directions

Given these dire circumstances, a call for more research investigating the impact of information and communications technology on human development is warranted (see Wade 2002). This complex relationship, however, has yet to be clarified in the broader social science and human rights literatures. The UNDP (2001) has described the relationship as reciprocal, with technology advancing quality of life in terms of health, education, and consumption opportunities, and improved quality of life increasing access to and innovation of technology goods and services.

Macromarketing scholars have a long history of work on quality of life (QOL), and they have contributed significantly to this debate (see Sirgy 2001 for an excellent comprehensive review). One particularly relevant study, conducted by Peterson and Malhotra (1997), used factor analysis to determine the underlying dimensions of the QOL construct. Their findings reveal a three-dimensional model, which the authors termed benefits, costs, and sustainability. In addition, they found that measures of infrastructure, including the level of information and communications technology, are excellent "proxies" for the consumption (benefits and costs) portion of QOL. Consistently, this investigation uses technological achievement as an indicator of QOL across nations.

What is clear, as described previously, is that vast differences in technological achievement exist worldwide, resulting in tremendous inequities. James (2002a, 71) reported that

> recent evidence indicates that globalization based on technical advances in information technology is creating a dualistic situation in the world economy, whereby the benefits tend to accrue to a narrow group of relatively affluent countries, while the majority lags behind.

His rationale is that technological innovations typically are designed with the needs of developed countries in mind, almost to the exclusion of less developed nations. Regardless of the origin, most scholars believe that "the move toward an increasingly digital society has had economic and social impacts that threaten to exacerbate existing inequalities" (Servon and Nelson 2001, 280). Improving macromarketers' understanding of the impact of globalization and technological achievement on such inequities is the basis of this study.

One issue that has received some attention within the macromarketing field is global poverty. For example, using information reported by the United Nations, Hill and Adrangi (1999) estimated that approximately one-half of the world's population lives under conditions of ill health, low literacy, and a lack of financial resources. Although potential causes are multifaceted, authors such as Cawkell (2001, 56) posited, "Material poverty and information poverty go hand-in-hand." Wade (2002) concurred and believed that the digital divide may be exacerbating economic differences both within and between countries. Others, referred to in the literature as *cyber-optimists,* have taken a more hopeful perspective, hypothesizing that information technology benefits citizens through improved educational opportunities that lead to greater economic development (see Barrett and Greene 2001; Garson 2001). Consistently, Norris (2001) put forward an Internet engagement model that suggests Internet technology is intimately tied to material success. Thus, *research proposition 1* is that technological advancement by a nation will reduce income disparities among its citizens.

A second area of concern involves consumption inequities that result from gender discrimination (Hill and Dhanda 1999). The UN acknowledged that, although significant improvement has occurred during the previous decades, inequalities still exist between men and women in every nation of the world (UNDP 1998). These disparities cross several domains of basic human progress, including life expectancy, educational attainment, and income (Hill, Peterson, and Dhanda 2001). Mazrui and Mazrui (2001) advanced a possible link between technological achievement and gender development, contending that information technology provides significant economic and political opportunities for women, including those living in traditionally Muslim nations. Access to adequate health care, which has been a vexing problem for women worldwide, also has been enhanced through Internet access (Sorensen 2001). Thus, *Research Proposition 2* is that technological achievement by a nation will improve human development opportunities for female citizens.

The third and final proposition is influenced by the findings of Peterson and Malhotra (1997), who demonstrated the multidimensional nature of the QOL construct. Their findings showed that the consumption aspects (benefits and costs) were separate from the sustainability factor, which includes the long-term integrity of the environment. In support of this result, Ger (1997, 112) opined, "Consumption and production patterns of affluent countries are responsible for most transboundary problems, such as ozone layer depletion, ocean pollution, and chemicalization of the habitat." The latest *Human Development Report* from the United Nations (UNDP 2003) provides supporting evidence that the countries that are most technologically advanced, including in information and communications technologies, are the primary culprits of environmental degradation. Thus, consistent with the extrapolation in proposition two above, *Research Proposition 3* is that technological achievement by a nation will increase the amount of environmental damage from its citizens.

Technological Achievement and Quality of Life

DATA DESCRIPTION AND ANALYSES

The UN assesses QOL worldwide through the activities of the UNDP. Founded nearly forty years ago, this unit has offices around the globe that conduct and assimilate hundreds of individual data-collection projects (Hill and Adrangi 1999; Hill, Peterson, and Dhanda 2001). Major sources of standardized data include the International Monetary Fund, the World Bank, the World Health Organization, and a wide variety of UN-supported agencies such as the United Nations Educational, Scientific, and Cultural Organization (UNESCO).

These efforts culminate in its annual publication of the *Human Development Report,* which has updated the status of the international community of nations for the past thirteen years. The focal topic of a recent volume is "Making Technologies Work for Human Development," and it is the source of all data in this research. For the first time, the UNDP (2001, 46) presented its technological achievement index (TAI), "which aims to capture how well a country is creating and diffusing technology and building a human skill base." This index is a composite of several indicators involving the creation of technology, the diffusion of recent innovations, the diffusion of older innovations, and human skills. Although it has yet to meet all of the valid criticisms of QOL scholars such as Sirgy (2001), it is consistent with the infrastructure model described by Peterson and Malhotra (1997).

Creation of technology is determined by two indicators, patents granted per capita and receipts of royalty and license fees from abroad per capita, and the sources of these data are the World Intellectual Property Organization (WIPO 2001) and the World Bank (2001b) respectively. Diffusion of recent innovations is measured by Internet hosts per capita and high- and medium-technology exports as a share of all exports, using data from the International Telecommunication Union (ITU 2001a) to estimate Internet dispersion and data from Lall (2001) and the UN (2001a) to calculate export share. Diffusion of old innovations is composed of the logarithm of telephone lines per capita and the logarithm of electricity consumption per capita; the data source for the former is the ITU (2001b) and for the latter is the World Bank (2001b). Finally, human skills are measured by mean years of schooling within a nation along with gross enrollment at the tertiary level in science, mathematics, and engineering. These data were abstracted from Barro and Lee (2000) for the mean years of schooling and from UNESCO (1998, 1999, 2001a) for tertiary-level training. The range of the combined indicators is from 0 to 1, with higher numbers suggesting greater technological achievement.

The measurement of income insecurity and disparity has received considerable attention by the United Nations, consistent with their interest in eradicating poverty by the early twenty-first century (see UNDP 1997 for more details). Unfortunately, their Human Poverty Index (HPI), which was designed to expose the dimensions of impoverishment worldwide, varies between developed and developing countries, making comparisons difficult. Therefore, this investigation uses the Gini Index for Research Proposition 1, which measures the equitability in the distribution of consumption opportunities among citizens within a nation (UNDP 2001). Values close to 0 suggest nearly equitable consumption potentialities, and values close to 100 suggest vast disparities between higher and lower socioeconomic groups within a society. The original source of these data is the World Bank (2001b).

The UN measures human development through an index composed of longevity (life expectancy), knowledge dissemination (adult literacy and school enrollments), and standard of living (GDP per capita; see Hill and Dhanda 1999). The Gender-Related Development Index (GDI) adjusts this construct to reflect disparities between men and women across all three variables, providing an appropriate indicant for Research Proposition 2. GDI values close to 1 intimate near equality in development between genders, whereas numbers close to 0 imply significantly lower development possibilities for women. Data on longevity were provided by the UN (2001b), data on adult literacy and schooling by UNESCO (2001a, 2001b), and on per capita GDP by the World Bank (2001a).

Although there are several possible causes of environmental destruction, one of the leading culprits is carbon dioxide (CO_2), which is a byproduct of consumption for a wide variety of personal and industrial uses. The burning of fossil fuels has nearly quintupled since 1950, and emissions of carbon dioxide annually have quadrupled as a result (UNDP 1998). Dhanda (1999, 258) asserted, "Not surprisingly, the world's dominant consumers are concentrated in the industrialized west, where high levels of consumption are matched with serious environmental damage." Thus, the measure used for research proposition 3 is CO_2 emissions per capita within a nation, and the source of these data is the Carbon Dioxide Information Analysis Center (CDIAC; 2000).

The research propositions were tested using ANOVA, which was used to examine differences in three dependent variables across the four technology achievement categories described below. The first step was to determine whether changes in these variables are in the predicted directions, with the expectation that the GDI and CO_2 emissions would increase and the Gini Index would decrease as TAI values rise from one category to the next. The second step used the F test to determine whether these differences are statistically significant. Results from the analyses are provided in the following subsection.

FINDINGS

An examination of the TAI among nations shows great disparities in the ability of countries to participate in the network age. Values range from a high of .744 in Finland to a low of .066 in Mozambique, and the mean TAI across the seventy-two nations for which reliable data existed is .374. The average TAI is .556 among the relatively wealthy OECD countries for which information is available. In contrast, the developing countries of the world have a mean TAI of .272, and within the few least developed states among this group, the index drops to .075. (Table 1 provides a complete listing of countries by TAI values, along with data for the three other variables.)

Further examination of the developing world reveals differences across geographic boundaries. For example, East Asia and the Pacific have the greatest technological

TABLE 1

Listing of Countries by TAI Values

Country	TAI	TAI Category	GDI	Gini Index	CO_2 Per Capita
Finland	.744	Leaders	.923	25.6	10.9
United States	.733	Leaders	.932	40.8	20.1
Sweden	.703	Leaders	.931	25.0	5.4
Japan	.698	Leaders	.921	24.9	9.2
Republic of Korea	.666	Leaders	.868	31.6	9.4
Netherlands	.630	Leaders	.926	32.6	10.4
United Kingdom	.606	Leaders	.920	36.1	8.9
Canada	.589	Leaders	.934	31.5	16.2
Australia	.587	Leaders	.935	35.2	17.3
Singapore	.585	Leaders	.871	NA	23.4
Germany	.583	Leaders	.916	30.0	10.2
Norway	.579	Leaders	.937	25.8	NA
Ireland	.566	Leaders	.908	35.9	10.0
Belgium	.553	Leaders	.928	25.0	10.2
New Zealand	.548	Leaders	.910	NA	8.3
Austria	.544	Leaders	.915	23.1	7.5
France	.535	Leaders	.922	32.7	5.8
Israel	.514	Leaders	.888	35.5	9.7
Spain	.481	Potential leaders	.901	32.5	6.2
Italy	.471	Potential leaders	.903	27.3	7.1
Czech Republic	.465	Potential leaders	.842	25.4	11.9
Hungary	.464	Potential leaders	.826	24.4	5.7
Slovenia	.458	Potential leaders	.871	28.4	7.5
Hong Kong (SAR)	.455	Potential leaders	.877	NA	3.5
Slovakia	.447	Potential leaders	.829	19.5	6.9
Greece	.437	Potential leaders	.874	32.7	7.6
Portugal	.419	Potential leaders	.870	35.6	5.0
Bulgaria	.411	Potential leaders	.770	26.4	5.9
Poland	.407	Potential leaders	.826	31.6	9.0
Malaysia	.396	Potential leaders	.768	49.2	6.2
Croatia	.391	Potential leaders	.799	29.0	4.2
Mexico	.389	Potential leaders	.782	51.9	3.9
Cyprus	.386	Potential leaders	.872	NA	7.1
Argentina	.381	Potential leaders	.833	NA	3.9
Romania	.371	Potential leaders	.769	28.2	4.8
Costa Rica	.358	Potential leaders	.813	45.9	1.3
Chile	.357	Potential leaders	.817	57.5	4.0
Uruguay	.343	Dynamic Adopters	.825	42.3	1.6
South Africa	.340	Dynamic Adopters	.695	59.3	8.2
Thailand	.337	Dynamic Adopters	.755	41.4	3.5
Trinidad/Tobago	.328	Dynamic Adopters	.789	40.3	17.2
Panama	.321	Dynamic Adopters	.782	48.5	2.8
Brazil	.311	Dynamic Adopters	.743	59.1	1.8
Philippines	.300	Dynamic Adopters	.746	46.2	1.0
China	.299	Dynamic Adopters	.715	40.3	2.7
Bolivia	.277	Dynamic Adopters	.640	58.9	1.4
Columbia	.274	Dynamic Adopters	.760	57.1	1.7
Peru	.271	Dynamic Adopters	.724	46.2	1.2

(Continued)

█ TABLE 1 █

Continued

Country	TAI	TAI Category	GDI	Gini Index	CO_2 Per Capita
Jamaica	.261	Dynamic Adopters	.736	36.4	4.3
Iran	.260	Dynamic Adopters	.696	NA	4.5
Tunisia	.255	Dynamic Adopters	.700	41.7	1.8
Paraguay	.254	Dynamic Adopters	.725	57.7	.7
Ecuador	.253	Dynamic Adopters	.711	43.7	1.7
El Salvador	.253	Dynamic Adopters	.694	50.8	.9
Dominican Republic	.244	Dynamic Adopters	.712	47.4	1.6
Syrian Republic	.240	Dynamic Adopters	.677	NA	3.2
Egypt	.236	Dynamic Adopters	.620	28.9	1.7
Algeria	.221	Dynamic Adopters	.673	35.3	3.2
Zimbabwe	.220	Dynamic Adopters	.548	56.8	1.6
Indonesia	.211	Dynamic Adopters	.671	31.7	1.2
Honduras	.208	Dynamic Adopters	.623	59.0	.7
Sri Lanka	.203	Dynamic Adopters	.732	34.4	.4
India	.201	Dynamic Adopters	.553	37.8	1.1
Nicaragua	.185	Marginalized	.628	60.3	.7
Pakistan	.167	Marginalized	.466	31.2	.7
Senegal	.158	Marginalized	.412	41.3	.4
Ghana	.139	Marginalized	.538	39.6	.2
Kenya	.129	Marginalized	.512	44.5	.2
Nepal	.081	Marginalized	.461	36.7	.1
Tanzania	.080	Marginalized	.432	38.2	.1
Sudan	.071	Marginalized	.413	NA	.1
Mozambique	.066	Marginalized	.309	39.6	.1

achievement with a mean TAI of .354. Latin America and the Caribbean are next with an average TAI of .292, and the Arab states follow as the TAI drops to .238. South Asia, one of the least developed regions of the globe, has a mean TAI of only .182. Finally, data reports from Sub-Saharan Africa provide an average TAI of .150, the lowest mean value among geographic regions.

For the purpose of comparison, the UNDP (2001) divided countries of the world into four technology creation, diffusion, and use categories: *leaders* (TAI values of .50 and above), *potential leaders* (TAI values of .35 to .49), *dynamic adopters* (TAI values from .20 to .34), and *marginalized nations* (TAI values below .20). Eighteen countries are categorized as *leaders* in technology achievement with an average TAI of .609; they are located primarily in North America, Western Europe, Scandinavia, and parts of Asia, and also include Australia. Nineteen countries are in the *potential leaders* category with a mean TAI of .418, and they are found principally in Eastern Europe with substantial representation in Latin America and the Caribbean. Twenty-six countries are considered *dynamic adopters* with

ANOVA Statistics

	GDI		Gini		CO$_2$	
Leader	.916	(.021)	30.707	(5.275)	11.347	(4.961)
Potential leaders	.834	(0.044)	34.094	(11.035)	5.879	(2.34)
Dynamic adopters	0.702	(0.066)	45.883	(9.602)	2.758	(3.369)
Marginalized	0.463	(0.090)	41.425	(8.533)	0.289	(0.252)
F statistic	150.30*		10.91*		29.39*	

Note: Each number represents the mean and the numbers in parentheses are standard deviations.
*$p < .01$.

an average TAI of .266, and this category is dominated by nations in Latin America and the Caribbean as well as some East Asia and Pacific and Arab countries. Finally, nine nations are deemed *marginalized* with a mean TAI of .119, and they are from Sub-Saharan Africa and South Asia.

The Gini Index values largely support research proposition 1, demonstrating critical differences in the appropriate direction across technology achievement categories. The correlation coefficient for the TAI/Gini combination is −.484, consistent with lower numbers revealing less disparity across socioeconomic groups. For example, technology leaders boast a mean Gini statistic of 30.707. In contrast, potential leaders have an average Gini of 34.094, and dynamic adopters have an average of 45.883. Surprisingly, marginalized nations show a slight improvement with a mean Gini of 41.425. This result may be due to the small sample size of the cell (as noted by a reviewer), or it may be an artifact of the "low" high range of economic opportunities in these least developed nations. Regardless, ANOVA results confirm these differences as statistically significant ($F = 10.91$, $p < .01$). Table 2 provides additional information.

The GDI values and the correlation coefficient for the TAI/GDI (.894) are consistent with research proposition 2. Technology leaders have the highest GDI of .916, followed by potential leaders at .834, dynamic adopters at .702, and marginalized nations at .463. These differences are statistically significant (ANOVA with $F = 150.30, p < .01$). In addition, the results for research proposition 3, using carbon dioxide pollution as a proxy for environmental damage, demonstrate that technological achievement is matched with increasing levels of ecological degradation. The correlation coefficient of the TAI and per capita emissions is .796, and CO$_2$ values move from a high of 11.347 for technology leaders to 5.879 for potential leaders, 2.758 for dynamic adopters, and a low of only .289 for marginalized nations. These ANOVA results also are statistically significant ($F = 29.39, p < .01$).

Discussion and Implications

SUMMARY OF FINDINGS

Using data collected by the United Nations, its affiliates, and other international organizations, this article explores technology creation, diffusion, and use among nations through the Technology Achievement Index advanced by the UNDP. The findings reveal great differences between developed and developing countries, with the least developed nations facing acute deficits in technological advancement. These differences expose a north-south divide in capability, with Scandinavia, Western Europe, and North America as technology leaders, and South Asia and Sub-Saharan Africa as technology laggards. Most of the rest of the world—Latin America and the Caribbean, East Asia and the Pacific, and the Arab states—reside somewhere in between. The exceptions to this rule are Japan, the Republic of Korea, and Australia.

In large part, the research propositions of this investigation are supported. For example, inequalities of consumption opportunities in a society are reduced with increased technological achievement, suggesting that the digital divide may exacerbate the plight of the impoverished in nations without the capacity to create or disseminate basic and/or advanced technology. In addition, equity in human development capabilities between men and women improves with technological achievement, which may be the result of educational and employment options that transcend traditional gender roles and boundaries. Finally, technological achievement within a society as a quality of life proxy is associated with greater environmental pollution and its concomitant ecological devastation. These findings reveal that globalization and technological achievement are a mixed bag that has positive economic and social benefits along with serious environmental consequences.

ABRIDGING THE DIGITAL DIVIDE

Our results suggest that the creation and diffusion of technology associated with the Internet contribute to the advancement of vulnerable consumers within developed countries. Such nations possess the necessary infrastructure in telephony and electricity that allows for the widespread dissemination of increasingly affordable Internet connections. Nevertheless, the least developed nations globally have few of these assets. Telephony and electricity in their countries typically are lacking, and the cost of service and the necessary computer hardware and software are beyond the reach of most consumers. For example, the UNDP (2001) reported that access charges are approximately 1 percent of the monthly income of U.S. citizens, but represent 614 percent of the monthly income in Madagascar, 278 percent in Nepal, and 191 percent in Bangladesh. As a consequence, the Internet only is widely available to the wealthiest consumers in much of the developing world.

Dholakia and Kshetri (2002) aptly noted that bridging the digital divide is dependent on identifying and meeting the needs of "digitally-excluded" consumers, and designing appropriate and affordable goods and services that are consonant with their requirements. Of course, one essential prerequisite is improvement in basic telephony service, especially in rural areas of developing countries (see James 2002a). One possible solution that has been advanced calls for the use of mobile phone networks to bypass the need for a traditional telecommunications infrastructure. Described as Mobile E-Development Models (MED), these flexible networks allow consumers and small business operators to access information and opportunities previously unavailable within their communities (Dholakia and Kshetri 2003).

In addition, the cost of the necessary computer technology is a fundamental road-block to resolving this global dilemma. Wade (2002, 451–52) presented the situation in ominous terms:

> In several ways, developing country users are being tied more tightly into hardware and software escalation with ramifications difficult to anticipate. . . . The effect of this techno-logical arms race is to keep widening the digital divide between the prosperous democracies and the rest of the world.

Once again, Dholakia and Kshetri (2002) posited that the solution lies in the creation of systems that are simple in design, adequate for the intended uses, affordable to the target market, and easily implemented and used.

A possible source of technology that may help meet these demands is the discarded personal computers from the developed world, which are of growing concern to environmentalists as scarce landfill space increasingly is filled with their remains. James (2002b) reported that at least 20 million PCs become obsolete annually in the United States alone, with only a small number currently recycled. The private firm New Deal, Inc., has stepped in to take advantage of this opportunity by renovating old 486 and early Pentium machines and selling them for approximately $100 each (James 2001a). They infuse these computers with "sustainable software" that includes word processing, spreadsheet, database, and Internet access applications (James 2001b).

Another possible source of technology is nongovernmental organizations such as the World Computer Exchange, which operates as a clearinghouse for donated secondhand personal computers from organizations in developed nations. Their explicit charter is to reduce the digital divide by shipping technological products to partner institutions in the developing world that install, maintain, and connect these machines to the Internet (James 2002b). Ten separate shipments of 3,800 PCs were transported to 500 schools that educate more than 200,000 students around the globe. The use of open-source software based on the Linux protocol may help keep the overall cost of these systems reasonable throughout their lifetimes.

Successes of such ventures notwithstanding, the ability of most consumers in developing counties to own telephones and computers and to have Internet services is severely constrained. As an alternative, James (2002a, 4) recommended, "In the poorer regions of the world reality demands a much more modest target, namely, to provide members of the community with reasonable *access* to (as opposed to individual ownership of) these technologies." One option may be the so-called Simputer, which is priced at less than $200 and contains a slot for smart cards that may be purchased for as little as $1. Impoverished consumers are able to rent these machines within their communities for about 20 cents an hour and have the ability to use its functions and storage capabilities. An additional benefit is that these PCs are designed for local conditions, and services can be delivered in a variety of languages as well as formats for nonliterate users (James 2001a).

Governments also have a role to play in closing the digital divide. For example, Dholakia and Kshetri (2002) suggested that policy makers accelerate technology diffusion and adoption through need identification of the underserved, development of appropriate network architectures to meet these needs, and tax incentives/reduced tariffs on information and communication technology goods and services. In addition, governmental entities may join together with multinational organizations such as the United Nations or World Bank to form what Yunus (2001, 25) called an "International Center for Information Technology to Eliminate Global Poverty." Such an agency's primary responsibility would be to collect, summarize, and distribute information on the varieties of low-cost technology currently available (see James 2002a for more details).

MACROMARKETING RESEARCH IMPLICATIONS

One troublesome finding, the environmental results of QOL defined in technology infrastructure terms, and issues of causality provide impetus for additional study. For instance, the implications of a decrease in the Gini Index by the lowest technology achievement countries are unclear. As noted earlier, this discrepancy may be due to the relatively "low-high" among the least developed nations, leading to smaller absolute differences across socioeconomic groups. One reviewer, however, suggested an alternative explanation based on the macrolevel of this analysis, contending that some countries with lower TAI values have pockets of significant achievement that are masked by these national aggregates. Thus, a possible future investigation might examine the impact of wide variations in the creation and dissemination of technology products within rather than among nation states on this set or a similar set of variables.

Inferences from the results on environmental degradation are particularly vexing, especially in light of the recent conflict over the Kyoto Protocol (UNDP 2001). Under this accord, developed nations tentatively decided to reduce their carbon dioxide emissions by more than 5 percent on or before 2012. Although no targets were established for developing or less developed nations, postindustrial countries could meet their goals by supporting emission-reduction programs in less affluent nations. For example, the United States could reach its target reduction of CO_2 more cheaply by helping producers in developing countries make factories less polluting than by making their facilities less polluting. Such trading would result in the transfer of advanced technologies that are estimated to exceed \$100 billion. Of course, this exchange of wealth depends on the ratification of the Kyoto agreement by the most affluent countries—including the United States, which has failed to do so at this point in time.

Issues of causality and rival explanations for these findings present a third avenue for additional investigation by macromarketers. Although the research propositions are grounded in multidisciplinary studies that triangulate around the rationales provided, the cross-sectional and selective nature of the data make the findings less compelling. Consider the results involving gender development. Is it possible that advancing the educational status of women leads to greater diffusion of information and communication technologies throughout a society? In addition, is it possible that gender development and technological achievement covary and are influenced by overall advancement of a society as measured by more comprehensive QOL measures? Exploration of such issues will become possible as the number of countries reporting the TAI increases and longitudinal data become available.

Macromarketing scholars interested in QOL issues may contribute to this debate through additional study and the development of technology measures. The current UN index clearly captures the influence of important indicators that are associated with the ability of a nation to exploit the benefits of an information-based economy. Which aspect of the TAI, however, drives the environmental damage revealed in this investigation? Is this relationship potentially causal, or do intervening variables such as economic success and its impact on per capita purchasing power play a role? In addition, macromarketers may consider advancing alternative technology achievement constructs that tap into the creation and dissemination of environmentally friendly technologies, which enhance QOL while avoiding or reducing damage to the ecology. Policy makers interested in global legislation could use such measures to bolster their positions and persuade reluctant national representatives.

On a larger level, it may be an appropriate time for macromarketing scholars to reconsider the QOL construct that is so closely tied to the field. The seminal work of Joe Sirgy at Virginia Tech has advanced thinking in this area for several decades, with intermittent contributions from a number of other scholars (Sirgy 2001). The beginning of the twenty-first century, however, with its postmodern hue in the developed world and the intimate tie of technology to work, leisure, and entertainment, represents a significant shift in how we define ourselves. The prototypical consumer in the industrialized West is in contact with information and communications technology at virtually every waking moment through pagers, cell phones, laptops, desktops, cable television, and more. Imagine their lives if these devices disappeared even for twenty-four hours. Now imagine living without the hope of ever having them. It may be time to recognize that the quality of consumers' lives is significantly influenced by access to a host of technology goods and services, representing a fundamental change in how we conceptualize QOL.

References

Barrett, K., and R. Greene. 2001. *Powering up: How public managers can take control of information technology.* Washington, DC: CQ Press.

Barro, R. J., and J. W. Lee. 2000. International data on educational attainment: Updates and implications. NBER working paper no. 7911. Cambridge, MA: National Bureau of Economic Research.

Bucy, E. 2000. Social access to the Internet. *Harvard International Journal of Press/Politics* 5 (Winter): 50–61.

Carbon Dioxide Information Analysis Center (CDIAC). 2000. *Trends: A compendium of data on global change.* December. http://cdiac.esd.ornl.gov/trends/trends.htm.

Cawkell, T. 2001. Sociotechnology: The digital divide. *Journal of Information Science* 27 (1): 55–60.

Dholakia, N., and N. Kshetri. 2002. Electronic architectures for bridging the global digital divide: A comparative assessment of e-business systems designed to reach the global poor. In *Architectural issues of Web-enabled electronic business,* edited by N. Shi and V. K. Murthy. Hershey, PA: Idea Group.

———. 2003. Mobil commerce as a solution to the global digital divide: Selected cases of e-development. In *The digital challenge: Information technology in the development context,* edited by S. Madon and S. Krishna. Aldershot, UK: Ashgate.

Garson, G. D. 2001. *Social dimensions of information technology: Issues for the new millennium.* Hershey, PA: Idea Group.

Ger, G. 1997. Human development and humane consumption: Well-being beyond the good life. *Journal of Public Policy and Marketing* 16 (1): 110–25.

Godlee, F., R. Horton, and R. Smith. 2000. Global information flow. *Lancet* 356 (9236): 1129–30.

Hammond, A. S. 2001. Digitally empowered development. *Foreign Affairs* 80 (March-April): 96–106.

Hanshaw, M. 2000. Venture philanthropist. *Harvard Business Review* 78 (July-August): 26.

Haythornthwaite, C. 2001. The Internet in everyday life. *American Behavioral Scientist* 45 (November): 363–82.

Hill, R. P., and B. Adrangi. 1999. Global poverty and the United Nations. *Journal of Public Policy and Marketing* 18 (Fall): 135–46.

Hill, R. P., and K. K. Dhanda. 1999. Gender inequity and quality of life: A macromarketing perspective. *Journal of Macromarketing* 19 (December): 140–52.

———. 2002. Advertising, technology, and the digital divide: A global perspective. *Advances in International Marketing: New Directions in International Advertising Research* 12: 175–93.

Hill, R. P., R. M. Peterson, and K. K. Dhanda. 2001. Global consumption and distributive justice: A Rawlsian perspective. *Human Rights Quarterly* 23 (February): 171–87.

Hunter, J. D., and J. Yates. 2002. In the vanguard of globalization: The world of American globalizers. In *Many globalizations: Cultural diversity on the contemporary world,* edited by P. L. Berger and S. P. Huntington, 323–57. New York: Oxford University Press.

Hussein, N. A. 1999. Keys to the global village. *New Perspectives Quarterly* 16 (Fall): 53–55.

International Telecommunication Union (ITU). 2001a. *World Internet reports: Telephony*. Geneva: International Telecommunication Union.

____. 2001b. *World Telecommunication indicators: Database*. Geneva: International Telecommunication Union.

James, J. 2001a. Bridging the digital divide with low-cost information technologies. *Journal of Information Technologies* 27 (4): 211–17.

____. 2001b. Low-cost computing and related ways of overcoming the global digital divide. *Journal of Information Science* 27 (6): 385–92.

____. 2002a. *Technology, globalization and poverty*. Cheltenham, UK: Edward Elgar.

____. 2002b. The human development report 2001 and information technology for developing countries: An evaluation. *International Journal of Technology Management* 23 (6): 643–52.

Lall, S. 2001. Harnessing technology for human development. Background paper, United Nations.

Mazrui, A., and A. Mazrui. 2001. The digital revolution and the new reformation: Doctrine and gender in Islam. *Harvard International Review* 23 (1): 52–55.

Metzl, J. F. 1996. Information technology and human rights. *Human Rights Quarterly* 18 (4): 705–46.

Norris, P. 2000. Information poverty and the wired world. *Harvard International Journal of Press / Politics* 5 (Summer): 1–6.

____. 2001. *Digital divide: Civic engagement, information poverty, and the Internet worldwide*. Cambridge, UK: Cambridge University Press.

Persaud, A. 2001. The knowledge gap. *Foreign Affairs* 80 (March–April): 107–17.

Peterson, M., and N. K. Malhotra. 1997. Comparative marketing measures of societal quality of life: Substantive dimensions in 186 countries. *Journal of Macromarketing* 17 (Spring): 25–38.

Rust, R. T., and R. W. Oliver. 1994. The death of advertising. *Journal of Advertising* 23 (December): 71–77.

Servon, L. J., and M. K. Nelson. 2001. Community technology centers: Narrowing the digital divide in low-income, urban communities. *Journal of Urban Affairs* 23 (3–4): 279–90.

Sirgy, M. J. 2001. *Handbook of quality-of-life research: An ethical marketing perspective*. Boston: Kluwer.

Sorensen, A. A. 2001. Promoting public health through electronic media: A challenge for schools of public health. *American Journal of Public Health* 91 (8): 1183–85.

Stiglitz, J. E. 2002. *Globalization and its discontents*. New York: W. W. Norton.

United Nations. 2001a. Correspondence on technology exports, statistics division. January. New York: United Nations.

____. 2001b. *World population prospects 1950–2050: The 2000 revision: Comprehensive tables*. New York: United Nations, Department of Economic and Social Affairs, Population Division.

United Nations Development Programme (UNDP). 1997. *Human development report 1997*. New York: Oxford University Press.

____. 1998. *Human development report 1998*. New York: Oxford University Press.

____. 2001. *Human development report 2001: Making new technologies work for human development*. New York: Oxford University Press.

____. 2003. *Human development report 2003: Millennium development goals—A compact among nations to end poverty*. New York: Oxford University Press.

United Nations Educational, Scientific, and Cultural Organization (UNESCO). 1998. *Statistical yearbook 1998*. Paris: UNESCO.

____. 1999. *Statistical yearbook 1999*. Paris: UNESCO.

___. 2001a. *Correspondence on gross enrollment ratios*. March. Paris: UNESCO.

___. 2001b. *Correspondence on net enrollment ratios*. March. Paris: UNESCO.

Wade, R. H. 2002. Bridging the digital divide: New route to development or new form of dependency? *Global governance* 8: 443–66.

World Intellectual Property Organization (WIPO). 2001. Basic facts about the patent cooperation treaty. April (accessed on original publication date) http://www.wipo.int/pct/en/basic_facts/basic_facts.htm.

World Bank. 2001a. *Correspondence on income poverty*. February. Washington, DC: World Bank.

___. 2001b. *World development indicators 2001*. CD-ROM. Washington, DC: World Bank.

Yunus, M. 2001. Microcredit and IT for the poor. *New Perspectives* 18 (Winter): 25–26.

Nike Shoe Plant in Vietnam Is Called Unsafe for Workers

Steven Greenhouse

Undermining Nike's boast that it maintains model working conditions at its factories throughout the world, a prominent accounting firm has found many unsafe conditions at one of the shoe manufacturer's plants in Vietnam.

In an inspection report that was prepared in January for the company's internal use only, Ernst & Young wrote that workers at the factory near Ho Chi Minh City were exposed to carcinogens that exceeded local legal standards by 177 times in parts of the plant and that 77 percent of the employees suffered from respiratory problems. The report also said that employees at the site, which is owned and operated by a Korean subcontractor, were forced to work 65 hours a week, far more than Vietnamese law allows, for $10 a week.

The inspection report offers an unusually detailed look into conditions at one of Nike's plants at a time when the world's largest athletic shoe company is facing criticism from human rights and labor groups that it treats workers poorly even as it lavishes millions of dollars on star athletes to endorse its products.

Though other American manufacturers also have problems in overseas plants, Nike has become a lightning rod in the debate because it is seen as able to do more since it earned about $800 million last year on sales of $9.2 billion.

Critics of Nike's working conditions, who had been given a copy of the internal report by a disgruntled employee, made it available to The New York Times and several other reporters, prompting the company to call a news conference Friday to address the allegations.

"We believe that we look after the interests of our workers," said Vada Manager, a Nike spokesman. "There's a growing body of documentation that indicates that Nike workers earn superior wages and manufacture product under superior conditions."

He and other Nike officials said the company had carried out "an action plan" to improve working conditions since the report was issued last January, 17 months after the factory opened. The company said it had slashed overtime, improved safety and ventilation and reduced the use of toxic chemicals.

Greenhouse, Steven (1997), "Nike Shoe Plant in Vietnam I Called Unsafe for Workers," *The New York Times,* November 8 (accessed via http://www.mindfully.org/WTO/Nike-Vietnam-Unsafe.htm, December 3, 2004).

The company also asserted that the report showed that its internal monitoring system had performed exactly as it should have.

"This shows our system of monitoring works," Manager said. "We have uncovered these issues clearly before anyone else, and we have moved fairly expeditiously to correct them."

While Nike has often been attacked over low pay and long hours, the Ernst & Young report pushed hard on a relatively new front for Nike's critics: air quality in its factories. Ernst & Young found that toluene, a carcinogen, was in the air at different sites in the factory studied, six to 177 times the amount allowed by Vietnamese regulations, which itself is about four times as strict as American toluene standards. Extended exposure to the carcinogen toluene is known to cause damage to the liver, kidneys and central nervous system.

The fact that such conditions existed in one of Nike's newer plants and were given a withering assessment by Nike's own consultants made for yet another embarrassing episode in a continuing saga.

Only five months ago, the company had taken out full page newspaper ads excerpting Andrew Young, the civil rights advocate and former United Nations representative, who had inspected 15 Nike factories last spring at Nike's behest. After completing his two-week tour covering three countries, he informed Nike it was doing a "good job" in treating its workers, though he allowed it "should do better." Young was widely criticized by human rights groups and labor groups for not taking his own translators and for doing slipshod inspections, an assertion he repeatedly denied.

Like many American apparel makers, Nike uses many subcontractors in Asia, with some 150 factories employing more than 450,000 workers. And like many, that tricky relationship is often offered as a reason why it is hard to impose American-style business practices on factories in that part of the world.

The Tae Kwang Vina factory, which was inspected by Ernst & Young, is one of Nike's larger plants. It has 9,200 workers and makes 400,000 pairs of athletic shoes each month at Bien Hoa City, some 25 miles northeast of Ho Chi Minh City, formerly Saigon. The Ernst & Young report painted a dismal picture of thousands of young women, most under age 25, laboring 10 1/2 hours a day, six days a week, in excessive heat and noise and in foul air, for slightly more than $10 a week. The report also found that workers with skin or breathing problems had not been transferred to departments free of chemicals and that more than half the workers who dealt with dangerous chemicals did not wear protective masks or gloves.

In plain, unemotional language, the report detailed problem after problem. "Dust in mixing room exceeded the standard 11 times," the report said. And, it added, "There's a high rate of labor accidents caused by carelessness of employees." Later, the report pointed to two other problems: "workers' inadequate understanding of the harmful effect of chemicals" and "increasing number of employees" with health problems conti- nue to work with chemicals.

The report also stated that "more than half of employees" in several departments who use chemicals "do not wear protective equipment (mask and gloves)—even in highly hazardous places where the concentration of chemical dust, fumes exceeded the standard frequently."

The Transnational Resource and Action Center, a nonprofit group based in San Francisco that often criticizes conditions at American factories overseas, made the report available. The center obtained the report from Dara O'Rourke, an environmental con- sultant for the United Nations Industrial Development Organization whose job involves inspecting factories in Vietnam and who was given a copy of the report by a disgruntled Nike employee.

O'Rourke, who is also a research associate at the Transnational Center, said he was making the report public because he wanted to pressure Nike to treat its workers better and because he was convinced that Ernst & Young's inspection report let Nike off easy. O'Rourke said wages at the plant were the lowest of any of the 50 factories he visited in Vietnam, and that working conditions were well below average.

Tien Nguyen, Nike's labor practices manager in Vietnam, said at a news conference Friday that as soon as Ernst & Young made its confidential report 10 months ago, the company took numerous steps to improve working conditions.

Nguyen said the number of hours worked a week had been reduced to 45, from 65. He said that many more fans had been installed, but he acknowledged that the company had done no measurements to determine whether chemical levels were now low enough to meet legal standards.

With the improvements, "it's markedly better than shoe factories in the United States," said Dusty Kidd, Nike's director of labor relations. "The shoe factories in Vietnam are among the most modern in the world. The factories there are excellent factories, but there are a lot of things they could get better."

But O'Rourke, who has visited the Nike factory three times as part of his United Nations duties, said that when he visited Vietnam last month, several workers said the plant was hardly better than in January. He said many workers still failed to wear pro- tective equipment, that pay remained low and that managers still yelled at or otherwise harassed workers.

Young, who made his visits in June, did not inspect this particular plant. And his report, which pronounced the plants to be "clean, organized, adequately ventilated and well lit" had few findings in common with the Ernst & Young report.

Was he aware of the Ernst & Young study prior to the trip? Doug Gatlin, who toured the Nike factories with Young, said they were. "We didn't see or read all of the reports they did prior to our going," said Gatlin, who nonetheless defended the job they did.

"Nike always said they were asking for the facts," said Gatlin, who was working for Young's consulting firm, Goodworks International.

Young could not be reached for comment because he was traveling.

As far as the Ernst & Young report went in shedding light on Nike's practices, some found fault with it, too. O'Rourke, for instance, criticized its conclusion that most employees were happy with the wages and working conditions. O'Rourke said the workers whom Ernst & Young interviewed were scared to speak candidly. O'Rourke said his interviews found much discontent.

O'Rourke said the Ernst & Young report had so many inadequacies that it showed the benefits of using noncommercial monitors, like human rights groups, to inspect factories.

THE GEO-GREEN ALTERNATIVE

Thomas L. Friedman

Davos, Switzerland

One of the most striking things I've found in Europe these past two weeks is the absolute conviction that the Bush team is just itching to invade Iran to prevent it from developing nuclear weapons. Pssssssst. Come over here. A little closer. Now listen: Don't tell the Iranians this, but the Bush team isn't going to be invading anybody. We don't have enough troops to finish the job in Iraq. Our military budget is completely maxed out. We couldn't invade Grenada today. If Iran is to forgo developing nuclear weapons, it will only be because the Europeans' diplomatic approach manages to persuade Tehran to do so.

For two years the Europeans have been telling the Bush administration that its use of force to prevent states from developing nuclear weapons has been a failure in Iraq and that the Europeans have a better way—multilateral diplomacy using carrots and sticks. Well, Europe, as we say in American baseball, "You're up."

"I think this is an absolute test case for Europe's ability to lay out its own idea for a joint agenda with the United States to deal with a problem like Iran," said the Oxford historian Timothy Garton Ash, author of "Free World: America, Europe and the Surprising Future of the West." "O.K., we think bombing Iran is a bad idea. What is a good idea?" For the Europeans to be successful, though, Mr. Ash said, they can't just be offering carrots. They have to credibly convey to Iran that they will wield their own stick. They have to credibly convey that they will refer Iran to the U.N. Security Council for real sanctions, if it is unwilling to strike a deal involving nuclear inspections in return for normalized economic relations with the West.

"Very often there is the notion that Europe is the soft cop and the U.S. is the hard cop," Mr. Ash said. "Here it must be the other way around. Europe has to talk as credibly about using economic sanctions as some in Washington have talked about using military force."

The U.S. has to help. The carrot the Iranians want for abandoning their nuclear program is not just unfettered trade with the West, but some kind of assurances that if they give up their nuclear research programs, the U.S. will agree to some kind of

---

Friedman, Thomas (2005a), "The Geo-Green Alternative," *The New York Times,* January 30, Section 4, p. 17.

nonaggression accord. The Bush team has been reluctant to do this, because it wants regime change in Iran. (This is a mistake; we need to concentrate for now on changing the behavior of the Iranian regime and strengthening the reformers, and letting them handle the regime change.)

If multilateral diplomacy is to work to defuse the brewing Iran nuclear crisis, "the Europeans have to offer a more credible stick and the Americans need to offer a more credible carrot," Mr. Ash said. But the Europeans are not good at credibly threatening force.

That's why this is a serious moment. If Britain, France and Germany, which are spearheading Europe's negotiations with Iran, fail, and if the U.S. use of force in Iraq (even if it succeeds) proves way too messy, expensive and dangerous to be repeated anytime soon, where are we? Is there any other way the West can promote real reform in the Arab-Muslim world?

Yes, there is an alternative to the Euro-wimps and the neocons, and it is the "geo-greens." I am a geo-green. The geo-greens believe that, going forward, if we put all our focus on reducing the price of oil—by conservation, by developing renewable and alternative energies and by expanding nuclear power—we will force more reform than by any other strategy. You give me $18-a-barrel oil and I will give you political and economic reform from Algeria to Iran. All these regimes have huge population bubbles and too few jobs. They make up the gap with oil revenues. Shrink the oil revenue and they will have to open up their economies and their schools and liberate their women so that their people can compete. It is that simple.

By refusing to rein in U.S. energy consumption, the Bush team is not only depriving itself of the most effective lever for promoting internally driven reform in the Middle East, it is also depriving itself of any military option. As Richard Haass, president of the Council on Foreign Relations, points out, given today's tight oil market and current U.S. consumption patterns, any kind of U.S. strike on Iran, one of the world's major oil producers, would send the price of oil through the roof, causing real problems for our economy. "Our own energy policy has tied our hands," Mr. Haass said.

The Bush team's laudable desire to promote sustained reform in the Middle East will never succeed unless it moves from neocon to geo-green.

No Mullah Left Behind

Thomas L. Friedman

The Wall Street Journal ran a very, very alarming article from Iran on its front page last Tuesday. The article explained how the mullahs in Tehran—who are now swimming in cash thanks to soaring oil prices—rather than begging foreign investors to come into Iran, are now shunning some of them. The article related how a Turkish mobile-phone operator, which had signed a deal with the Iranian government to launch Iran's first privately owned cellphone network, had the contract frozen by the mullahs in the Iranian Parliament because they were worried it might help the Turks and their foreign partners spy on Iran.

The Journal quoted Ali Ansari, an Iran specialist at the University of St. Andrews in Scotland, as saying that for 10 years analysts had been writing about Iran's need for economic reform. "In actual fact, the scenario is worse now," Ansari said. "They have all this money with the high oil price, and they don't need to do anything about reforming the economy."

Indeed, The Journal added, the conservative mullahs are feeling even more emboldened to argue that with high oil prices, Iran doesn't need Western investment capital and should feel "free to pursue its nuclear power program without interference."

This is a perfect example of George W. Bush's energy policy at work, and the Bush energy policy is: "No Mullah Left Behind."

By adamantly refusing to do anything to improve energy conservation in America, or to phase in a $1-a-gallon gasoline tax on American drivers, or to demand increased mileage from Detroit's automakers, or to develop a crash program for renewable sources of energy, the Bush team is—as others have noted—financing both sides of the war on terrorism. We are financing the U.S. armed forces with our tax dollars, and, through our profligate use of energy, we are generating huge windfall profits for Saudi Arabia, Iran and Sudan, where the cash is used to insulate the regimes from any pressure to open up their economies, liberate their women or modernize their schools, and where it ends up instead financing madrassas, mosques and militants fundamentally opposed to the progressive, pluralistic agenda America is trying to promote. Now how smart is that?

The neocon strategy may have been necessary to trigger reform in Iraq and the wider Arab world, but it will not be sufficient unless it is followed up by what I call a

Friedman, Thomas (2005b), "No Mullah Left Behind," *The New York Times,* February 13, Section 4, p. 15.

"geo-green" strategy. As a geo-green, I believe that combining environmentalism and geopolitics is the most moral and realistic strategy the United States could pursue today. Imagine if Bush used his bully pulpit and political capital to focus the nation on sharply lowering energy consumption and embracing a gasoline tax.

What would that buy? It would buy reform in some of the worst regimes in the world, from Tehran to Moscow. It would reduce the chances that the United States and China are going to have a global struggle over oil—which is where we are heading. It would help us to strengthen the dollar and reduce the current account deficit by importing less crude. It would reduce climate change more than anything in Kyoto. It would significantly improve America's standing in the world by making us good global citizens. It would shrink the budget deficit. It would reduce our dependence on the Saudis so we could tell them the truth. (Addicts never tell the truth to their pushers.) And it would pull China away from its drift into supporting some of the worst governments in the world, like Sudan's, because it needs their oil.

Most important, making energy independence our generation's moon shot could help inspire more young people to go into science and engineering, which we desperately need.

Sadly, the Bush team won't even consider this. It prefers cruise missiles to cruise controls. We need a grass-roots movement. Where are college kids these days? I would like to see every campus in America demand that its board of trustees disinvest from every U.S. auto company until they improve their mileage standards. Every college town needs to declare itself a "Hummer-free zone." You want to drive a gas-guzzling Humvee? Go to Iraq, not our campus.

And an idea from my wife, Ann: free parking anywhere in America for anyone driving a hybrid car.

But no, Bush has a better project: borrowing another trillion dollars, which will make us that much more dependent on countries like China and Saudi Arabia that hold our debt—so that you might, if you do everything right and live long enough, get a few more bucks out of your Social Security account.

The president's priorities are totally nuts.

GEO-GREENING BY EXAMPLE

Thomas L. Friedman

How will future historians explain it? How will they possibly explain why President George W. Bush decided to ignore the energy crisis staring us in the face and chose instead to spend all his electoral capital on a futile effort to undo the New Deal, by partially privatizing Social Security? We are, quite simply, witnessing one of the greatest examples of misplaced priorities in the history of the U.S. presidency.

"Ah, Friedman, but you overstate the case." No, I understate it. Look at the opportunities our country is missing—and the risks we are assuming—by having a president and vice president who refuse to lift a finger to put together a "geo-green" strategy that would marry geopolitics, energy policy and environmentalism.

By doing nothing to lower U.S. oil consumption, we are financing both sides in the war on terrorism and strengthening the worst governments in the world. That is, we are financing the U.S. military with our tax dollars and we are financing the jihadists—and the Saudi, Sudanese and Iranian mosques and charities that support them—through our gasoline purchases. The oil boom is also entrenching the autocrats in Russia and Venezuela, which is becoming Castro's Cuba with oil. By doing nothing to reduce U.S. oil consumption we are also setting up a global competition with China for energy resources, including right on our doorstep in Canada and Venezuela. Don't kid yourself: China's foreign policy today is very simple—holding on to Taiwan and looking for oil.

Finally, by doing nothing to reduce U.S. oil consumption we are only hastening the climate change crisis, and the Bush officials who scoff at the science around this should hang their heads in shame. And it is only going to get worse the longer we do nothing. Wired magazine did an excellent piece in its April issue about hybrid cars, which get 40 to 50 miles to the gallon with very low emissions. One paragraph jumped out at me: "Right now, there are about 800 million cars in active use. By 2050, as cars become ubiquitous in China and India, it'll be 3.25 billion. That increase represents an almost unimaginable threat to our environment. Quadruple the cars means quadruple the carbon dioxide emissions—unless cleaner, less gas-hungry vehicles become the norm."

All the elements of what I like to call a geo-green strategy are known:

We need a gasoline tax that would keep pump prices fixed at $4 a gallon, even if crude oil prices go down. At $4 a gallon (premium gasoline averages about $6 a gallon

Friedman, Thomas (2005c), "Geo-Greening by Example," *The New York Times,* March 27, Section 4, p. 11.

in Europe), we could change the car-buying habits of a large segment of the U.S. public, which would make it profitable for the car companies to convert more of their fleets to hybrid or ethanol engines, which over time could sharply reduce our oil consumption.

We need to start building nuclear power plants again. The new nuclear technology is safer and cleaner than ever. "The risks of climate change by continuing to rely on hydrocarbons are much greater than the risks of nuclear power," said Peter Schwartz, chairman of Global Business Network, a leading energy and strategy consulting firm. "Climate change is real and it poses a civilizational threat that [could] transform the carrying capacity of the entire planet."

And we need some kind of carbon tax that would move more industries from coal to wind, hydro and solar power, or other, cleaner fuels. The revenue from these taxes would go to pay down the deficit and the reduction in oil imports would help to strengthen the dollar and defuse competition for energy with China.

It's smart geopolitics. It's smart fiscal policy. It is smart climate policy. Most of all—it's smart politics! Even evangelicals are speaking out about our need to protect God's green earth. "The Republican Party is much greener than George Bush or Dick Cheney," remarked Mr. Schwartz. "There is now a near convergence of support on the environmental issue. Look at how popular [Arnold] Schwarzenegger, a green Republican, is becoming because of what he has done on the environment in California."

Imagine if George Bush declared that he was getting rid of his limousine for an armor-plated Ford Escape hybrid, adopting a geo-green strategy and building an alliance of neocons, evangelicals and greens to sustain it. His popularity at home—and abroad—would soar. The country is dying to be led on this. Instead, he prefers to squander his personal energy trying to take apart the New Deal and throwing red meat to right-to-life fanatics. What a waste of a presidency. How will future historians explain it?

EXPLORING PROSPECTS FOR BETTER DECISIONS: MARKETING ETHICS

Nature and Scope of Marketing Ethics

O.C. Ferrell

Introduction

Marketing ethics is viewed as important because of marketing's interface with many diverse stakeholders. Marketing is a key functional area in the business organization that provides a visible interface with not only customers, but other stakeholders such as the media, investors, regulatory agencies, channel members, trade associations, as well as others. It is important when addressing marketing ethics to recognize that it should be examined from an individual, organizational, and societal perspective. Examining marketing ethics from a narrow issue perspective does not provide foundational background that provides a complete understanding of the domain of marketing ethics. The purpose of this chapter is to define, examine the nature and scope, identify issues, provide a decision-making framework, and trace the historical development of marketing ethics from a practice and academic perspective.

Definition of Marketing Ethics

Ethics has been termed the study and philosophy of human conduct, with an emphasis on the determination of right and wrong. For marketers, ethics in the workplace refers to rules (standards, principles) governing the conduct of organizational members and the consequences of marketing decisions (Ferrell, 2005). Therefore, ethical marketing from a normative perspective approach is defined as "practices that emphasize transparent, trustworthy, and responsible personal and organizational marketing policies and actions that exhibit integrity as well as fairness to consumers and other stakeholders (Murphy, Laczniak, Bowie and Klein, 2005). Marketing ethics focuses on principles and standards that define acceptable marketing conduct, as determined by various stakeholders and the organization responsible for marketing activities. While many of the basic principles have been codified as laws and regulations to require marketers to conform to society's expectations of conduct, marketing ethics goes beyond legal and regulatory issues.

FERRELL, O.C.,: Marketing Ethics

O.C. Ferrell is Professor of Marketing and Creative Enterprise Scholar in the Robert O. Anderson School and Graduate School of Management at the University of New Mexico.

Ethical marketing practices and principles are core building blocks in establishing trust, which help build long-term marketing relationships. In addition, the boundary-spanning nature of marketing (i.e. sales, advertising, and distribution) presents many of the ethical issues faced in business today. .

Both marketing practitioners and marketing professors approach ethics from different perspectives. For example, one perspective is that ethics is about being a moral individual and that personal values and moral philosophies are the key to ethical decisions in marketing. Virtues such as honesty, fairness, responsibility, and citizenship are assumed to be values that can guide complex marketing decisions in the context of an organization. On the other hand, approaching ethics from an organizational perspective assumes that establishing organizational values, codes, and training is necessary to provide consistent and shared approaches to making ethical decisions (Ferrell and Ferrell, 2005).

The Domain of Marketing Ethics

SUBSTANTIVE DOMAIN

The relationship between a customer and an organization exists because of mutual expectations built on trust, good faith, and fair dealing in their interaction. In fact, there is an implied covenant of good faith and fair dealing, and performance cannot simply be a matter of the firm's own discretion (Ferrell, 2004). Not only is this an ethical requirement but it has been legally enforced in some states. The implied covenant of good faith and fair dealing is to enforce the contract or transaction in a manner consistent with the parties' reasonable expectations (1998 WL 1991608 Mich. App.) Courts may impose "implied duties of good faith" in marketing exchanges (Gundlach and Murphy, 1993). This obligation of good faith appears to be an institutional or legal approach to enforcing ethical conduct in marketing.

Marketing ethics not only requires an attempt to make ethical decisions, but also to avoid the unintended consequences of marketing activities. This requires consideration of key stakeholders and their relevant interests (Fry and Polonsky, 2004). Market orientation has been found as the key variable in the successful implementation of marketing strategies (Homburg, Krohmer, and Workman, 2004). But a successful marketing strategy has not always been associated with meeting the needs and demands of all stakeholders (Miller and Lewis, 1991). While Wal-Mart customers get low prices, Wal-Mart has many critics, including "organized labor, feminists, human rights activists, environmentalists, local businesses, and anti-sprawl activists . . . resulting in a growing negative consumer perception of Wal-Mart's corporate citizenship" (Hemphill, 2005). Unfortunately, most approaches to market orientation select to elevate the interests of one stakeholder—the customer—over those of others (Ferrell, 2004). Now that Wal-Mart has focused mainly on customers and profits, a new direction should include all stake-holders that have an interest in the firm's operations and conduct. There is evolving concern that organizations must focus on not just their customers, but also the important communities and groups that hold the firm accountable for its actions. A new emerging logic of marketing is that it exists to provide both social and economic processes, including a network of relationships to provide skills and knowledge to all stakeholders (Vargo and Lusch, 2004).

This logic is captured in the new definition of marketing developed by the American Marketing Association (2004) which states that, "marketing is an organizational function and a set of processes for creating, communicating, and delivering value to customers and for managing customer relationships in ways that benefit the organization and its stakeholders". This definition emphasizes the importance of delivering value and the responsibility of marketers to be able to create meaningful relationships that provide benefits to all relevant stakeholders. This is the first definition of marketing to include concern for stakeholders beyond the organization and customers.

One difference between an ordinary decision and an ethical one is that accepted rules may not apply and the decision-maker must weigh values in a situation that he or she may not have faced before. Another difference is the amount of emphasis placed on a person's values when making an ethical decision. An ethical dilemma evolves when the choice between alternative actions with moral content is unclear. Whether a specific behavior is right or wrong, ethical or unethical, is often determined by the concerned stakeholders and an individual's personal ethics. Consequently, values, judgments, and complex situations all play a critical role in ethical decision making.

Stakeholders designate the individuals, groups and communities that can directly or indirectly affect, or be affected by, a firm's activities (Freeman, 1984). Marketing stakeholders can be viewed as both internal and external. Internal stakeholders include various departments, the board of directors, employees, and other interested internal parties. External stakeholders include competitors, advertising agencies, suppliers, regulators and others such as special interest groups (Miller and Lewis, 1991). The various relationships should be identified and interests understood. The complexity surrounding a determination of the effects of marketing transactions on all relevant stakeholders requires the identification of stakeholders in the exchange process (Fry and Polonsky, 2004). The re-conceptualization of the marketing concept based on a long-term, multiple stakeholder approach has also been suggested as a prescriptive model for organizational responsibility in marketing (Kimery and Rinehart, 1998). Based on these developments, there is a need for marketing to develop more of a stakeholder orientation rather than a narrow customer orientation. Stakeholder orientation in marketing goes beyond markets, competitors, and channel members to understanding and addressing all stakeholder demands. As a result, organizations are now under pressure to demonstrate initiatives that take a balanced perspective on stakeholder interests (Maignan, Ferrell, and Ferrell, 2005).

HISTORICAL DEVELOPMENT OF MARKETING ETHICS

The historical background for marketing ethics is derived from early concerns during the turn of the 20th century concerning antitrust and consumer protection, especially adulterated food products. From the beginning of advertising, there have always been concerns about misrepresentations and purposeful deception of consumers. Frank Chapman Sharp started teaching a course in business ethics at the University of Wisconsin in 1913 and Sharp and Fox (1937) published a textbook on business ethics. The book was based on the concept of "fair service" and the authors stated "it will be possible to reduce our study of fair service to the principles of fair salesmanship" (Sharp and Fox, 1937). The book could have been titled 'Marketing Ethics' and had chapters on commercial coercion, let the buyer beware, the limits of persuasion, fair pricing, and the ethics of bargaining. Within the academic history of marketing, one of the first articles that appeared in the *Journal of Marketing* was an article by Charles F. Phillips (1939) entitled, "Some Theoretical Considerations Regarding Fair Trade Laws." In this article, ethics was not directly addressed, but the impact of resale price maintenance on competition, especially channel members and customers, was addressed. The concern was that customers were not receiving information about prices and might assume that the quality of coffee offered by all stores was identical. Most academic publishing in the 1950s focused on issues such as fair trade, antitrust, advertising and pricing.

During the 1960s American society turned to causes. An anti-business attitude developed as many critics attacked the vested interests that controlled the economic and political sides of society—the so-called military-industrial complex. The 1960s saw the decay of inner cities and the growth of ecological problems, such as pollution and the disposal of toxic and nuclear wastes. This period also witnessed the rise of consumerism—activities undertaken by independent individuals, groups, and organizations to protect their rights as consumers. In 1962 President John F. Kennedy delivered a "Special Message on Protecting the Consumer Interest," in which he outlined four basic consumer rights: the right to safety, the right to be informed, the right to choose, and the right to be heard. These came to be known as the Consumers' Bill of Rights (Ferrell, Fraedrich, and Ferrell, 2005).

During this period of time, Robert Bartels (1967) contributed the first comprehensive model for ethics in marketing. This first academic conceptualization of the variables that influence marketing ethics decision making tried to determine the logical basis for marketers to determine what is right or wrong. It presented a schematic plan for analyzing the variables inherent in the ethics of decision making; and provided a framework for social and personal ethics in marketing decisions. The model did a good job in delineating variables that influence ethical decision making, including participants, cultural influencers, role expectations, and the complexity of ethical decision making. During this same period of time, Richard Farmer (1967) published an article, "Would You Want Your Daughter to Marry a Marketing Man?" that maintained that much of marketing is unethical and irrelevant. This article was received so well that in 1977, Farmer published an article entitled, "Would You Want Your Son to Marry a Marketing Lady?" and in 1987 published another article entitled, "Would You Want Your Granddaughter to Marry a Taiwanese Marketing Man?" The titles of these articles indicate that possibly marketing ethics was not considered a serious academic research area. The 1967 Bartels article provided a foundation for empirical research that followed in the 1970s.

In the 1970s significant research was conducted to describe the beliefs of managers about marketing ethics. Carroll (1975) found that young managers would go along with their supervisors to show loyalty in dealing with matters related to judgments on morality. A follow-up study by Bowman (1976) supported these findings. Ferrell and Weaver (1978) provided insights into organizational relationships that influence marketing mangers' ethical beliefs and behavior. The findings indicated that respondents perceived that the ethical standards of their peers and top management were lower than their own standards. Empirical research in the 1970s set the stage for frameworks that describe ethical decision making within the context of a marketing organization.

The Ferrell and Gresham (1985) "A Contingency Framework for Understanding Ethical Decision Making in Marketing" emphasized the interaction of the individual and organization, including organization culture, co-workers, and opportunity to explain how ethical decisions are made. Most of the propositions in this model have been tested to provide a grounded understanding of ethical decision making. Hunt and Vitell (1986) "A General Theory of Marketing Ethics" is widely accepted and also provides an empirically grounded model to illustrate how ethical decision making occurs in an organization. Research followed in both marketing and management literature that helped test the Ferrell and Gresham and Hunt and Vitell models (Hunt and Vitell, 2005).

In the 1980s, business academics and practitioners acknowledged business ethics as an important field of study. Industry developments, such as the Defense Industry Initiative on Business Ethics and Conduct, established a method for discussing best practices and working tactics to link organizational practice and policy to successful ethical compliance. In the 1990s, the government also provided support and rewards for ethics programs through the Federal Sentencing Guidelines for Organizations, approved by Congress in 1991. The Guidelines broke new ground by codifying into law incentives to reward organizations for taking action to prevent misconduct. A special task force provided a report for updating and refining the guidelines in 2003 (United States Sentencing Commission, 2003). In 2005, a federal amendment to the Federal Sentencing Guidelines added oversight of ethics and compliance programs to the responsibilities of board of director positions. The amendment places more responsibility on board members to monitor and audit ethics programs, including marketing ethics.

While the regulatory system was developing incentives for ethical conduct in organizations, Hunt, Wood and Chonko (1989) conducted research demonstrating a strong link between corporate ethical values and organizational commitment in marketing. Their corporate ethical values scale is widely used in organizational ethics research. Gundlach and Murphy (1993) build a normative framework for relational marketing exchanges based on the ethical exchange dimensions of trust, equality, responsibility, and commitment. They develop foundational understanding of the interrelationship of ethics and law in marketing exchange. This is a significant contribution because some observers take the perspective that the legal and ethical dimensions of exchange are independent. They conclude that ethical marketing exchanges require a managerial emphasis on ethical corporate culture, ethics training programs, and on ethical audits.

Dunfee, Smith and Ross (1999) suggest the need for a normative framework for marketing ethics. Integrative Social Contract Theory (ISCT) links the decision-making process, multiple communities, hypernorms, and ethical judgments based on the dominant legitimate norms. This framework can be used for resolving ethical issues that arise among different communities and is significant because marketers frequently engage in boundary-spanning relationships and cross-cultural activities. This normative framework is significant to marketing because it emphasizes the exchange relationship between the firm and its stakeholders, including the right to exist and even prosper in society. This theory can be used to bridge normative and descriptive research in marketing ethics (Dunfee, Smith and Ross, 1999).

As the 21st century arrived, ethics in the world of business became a major issue with scandals associated with Enron, WorldCom, Tyco, Qwest, Sunbeam, and Arthur Andersen. While most of these scandals were associated with accounting fraud, in many cases companies such as Sunbeam, using inventory sales shifting strategies (buy and hold), relied on salespersons to help implement the fraud. These activities resulted in the passage of the Sarbanes-Oxley Act in 2002, which is the most far-reaching change in organization control, corporate governance, and government oversight since the Securities and Exchange Act of 1934. During this time (2000–2006) the *Journal of Marketing* published no articles with the word ethics in the title, but articles did appear dealing with ethical issues (Klein, Smith and John, 2004). There is still a need to continue both theory development and empirical testing of theories of ethical decision making in marketing.

Key Issues in Marketing Ethics[1]

By its very nature, marketing ethics is controversial, and there is no universally accepted approach for resolving questions. Ethical issues address a problem, situation, or opportunity that requires an individual, group, or organization to choose among several actions that must be evaluated as right or wrong (Ferrell, Fraedrich, and Ferrell, 2005). The organization and stakeholders define marketing ethical issues that must be identified and resolved to build trust and effective relationships with stakeholders. Because marketing ethics sometimes deals with subjective moral choices, this requires decisions about the moral standards to apply and the definition of ethics issues (Murphy, Laczniak, Bowie and Klein, 2005). However, many groups in society, including government, are defining ethical and legal issues and proactive approaches to deal with these issues. For example, millions of blogs or personal web logs exist on the Internet without any formal code of ethics or regulation. Many firms, such as Audi, have their own blogs with many stakeholders requesting the formation of an ethics committee to create unified standards. Organizations are being asked to prevent and control misconduct by implementing ethical compliance programs. Ethics brings many rewards to organizations that nurture it, but managing ethics requires activity and attention on several levels—complying with the law, setting ethical standards, and dealing with the complex decisions related to trade-offs between the bottom line and ethical conduct. For example, the Securities and Exchange Commission is looking into retailers such as Saks, Inc. and other major department stores investigating collections or "charge backs" to manufacturers. Manufacturers often guarantee a certain profit margin or compensate retailers for items that did not sell well. Saks may have improperly collected over $21 million from its vendors (D'Innocenzio, 2005).

High ethical standards require both organizations and individuals to conform to sound moral principles. Fair Trade has emerged to link ethically minded consumers with marketers concerned with disadvantaged producers in developing nations. Starbucks works to treat coffee farmers fairly in their business relationships by paying premium prices, long-term contracts, affordable credit, direct purchasing, and investing in social projects in coffee communities (http://www.starbucks.com/aboutus/StarbucksAndFairTrade. pdf; accessed July 5, 2005). However, general special factors must be considered when applying ethics to marketing. First, to survive, marketers must contribute to profits or other organizational objectives. Second, marketers must balance their desire for success against the needs and desires of society. Maintaining this balance often requires compromises or tradeoffs. To address these unique aspects, society has developed rules—both legal and implicit—to guide marketers in their efforts to reach their objectives in ways that do not harm individuals or society as a whole.

---

[1]Some of the material in this section has been adapted from LeClair, Ferrell, and Fraedrich (1998), with the permission of O'Collins Corporation.

External stakeholders interests, concerns, or dilemmas help trigger ethical issue intensity. For example, the National Do-Not Call Registry has tremendous impact on telemarketers' business practices. Organizational culture (internal stakeholders) and individual moral philosophies and values influence the recognition of ethical issues and marketing ethics decisions. New Belguim Brewing Company, the third largest craft beer brewer in the United States, uses only wind energy and co-generation as well as a vigorous recycling initiative. In addition, the company practices open-book management. The decisions or outcomes are evaluated by both internal and external stakeholders.

Marketing ethics relates to issues such as honesty and fairness, conflicts of interest, discrimination, privacy, and fraud. Government regulatory agencies and self-regulatory groups such as the Better Business Bureau have developed formal mechanisms to deal with ethical issues related to marketing. The Federal Trade Commission (FTC) enforces consumer protection laws. Within this agency, the Bureau of Consumer Protection works to protect consumers against unfair, deceptive, or fraudulent practices. In addition to the FTC, other federal agencies such as the Food and Drug Administration, the Consumer Product Safety Commission, and the Federal Communications Commission try to assist consumers in addressing deceptive, fraudulent, or damaging conduct. At the state level, consumer protection statutes exist, and deceptive trade practices laws exist in most states. In New Jersey, the Attorney General's office has filed a lawsuit against Blockbuster, Inc. for not properly disclosing terms associated with its "No More Late Fees" policy. Overdue rentals are automatically converted to sales on the eighth day after the due date. The New Jersey Consumer Fraud Act could result in Blockbuster paying civil penalties of up to $10,000 for each violation (Merritt, 2005). These regulatory agencies help define many of the issues that should be an ethical concern for marketers. Examples of issues include marketing communications that are false and misleading, material misrepresentations in external and internal communications, and the use of telecommunications to deceive customers. Antitrust, deception in pricing, product liability, and marketing channel relationships all encompass ethical decisions.

A FRAMEWORK FOR UNDERSTANDING ETHICAL DECISION MAKING IN MARKETING

Ethical decision making in marketing parallels ethical decision making across all organizational domains. There is much overlap between marketing ethics and business ethics because the basic frameworks that describe ethical decision making in an organization include decisions that encompass marketing. In other words, within the context of an organization, there is an ethical component to business decisions, regardless of whether it is marketing or some other functional area component. External stakeholder interests, concerns or dilemmas help trigger ethical issue intensity. For example, PETA has encouraged KFC and other fast-food restaurants to make the ethical treatment of animals a priority. Organizational culture (internal stakeholders) and individual moral philosophies and values influence the recognition of ethical issues and marketing ethics decisions. The decisions or outcomes are evaluated by both internal and external stakeholders. While it is impossible to describe precisely how or why an individual or a work group may make a specific decision, we can generalize about average or typical behavior patterns within organizations.

First, as previously discussed, marketing can identify the importance of stakeholders, stakeholder issues, and gather information to respond to significant individuals, groups, and communities. Next, in the decision-making process, marketers should identify the importance or relevance of a perceived issue—i.e., the intensity of the issue (Jones, 1991). The fast food industry is being pressured by government agencies, consumers, and special interest groups to offer healthier menu options, particularly for children. The intensity of a particular issue is likely to vary over time and among individuals and is influenced by the organizational culture, values and norms; the special characteristics of the situation; and the personal pressures weighing on the decision. McDonald's restaurants were the targets of negative publicity associated with the release of the movie *Super Size Me*. In response, the company introduced more salads and healthful portions and alternatives. Individual factors are obviously important in the evaluation and resolution of ethical issues, and familiarity with principal, theoretical frameworks from the field of moral philosophy is helpful in determining ethical decision making in marketing (Murphy, Laczniak, Bowie, and Klein, 2005). Personal moral development and philosophy, organizational culture, and coworkers determine why different people perceive issues with varying intensity (Robin, Reidenbach, and Forrest, 1996).

The ethical climate of an organization is a significant element of organizational culture. Whereas a firm's overall culture establishes ideals that guide a wide range of behaviors for members of the organization, its ethical climate focuses specifically on issues of right and wrong. The ethical climate is the organization's character or conscience. Codes of conduct and ethics policies, top management's actions on ethical issues, the values and moral development and philosophies of coworkers, and the opportunity for misconduct all contribute to an organization's ethical climate. In fact, the ethical climate actually determines whether or not certain dilemmas are perceived as having an ethical intensity level that requires a decision.

Opportunity usually relates to employees' immediate job context—where they work, with whom they work, and the nature of the work. The specific work situation includes the motivational "carrots and sticks" that superiors can use to influence employee behavior. Pay raises, bonuses, and public recognition are carrots, or positive reinforcement, whereas reprimands, pay penalties, demotions, and even firings act as sticks, the negative reinforcement. For example, a salesperson who is publicly recognized and given a large bonus for making a valuable sale that he or she obtained through unethical tactics will probably be motivated to use unethical sales tactics in the future, even if such behavior goes against one's personal value system. Research has shown that there is a general tendency to discipline top sales performers more leniently than poor sales performers for engaging in identical forms of unethical selling behavior (Bellizzi and Hasty, 2003). Neither a company policy stating that the behavior in question was unacceptable nor a repeated pattern of unethical behavior offsets the general tendency to favor the top sales performers. A superior sales record appears to induce more lenient forms of discipline despite managerial actions that are specifically instituted to produce more equal forms of discipline. Based on their research, Bellizzi and Hasty concluded that an opportunity exists for top sales performers to be more unethical than poor sales performers.

In 2004, the American Marketing Association approved a new code of ethics entitled, "Ethical Norms and Values for Marketers" (see Appendix). The AMA code provides values which are assumptions about appropriate behavior, as well as norms that provide suggested behaviors. The AMA recognizes the diversity of marketing, and encourages members to access codes of ethics that address specific functional areas such as marketing research, direct selling, direct marketing, and advertising.

Delving Deeper into Marketing Ethics: Selected Readings

The following three academic articles have been selected to provide more in-depth understanding of marketing ethics. These articles provide a foundational framework for understanding marketing ethics.

Two conceptual articles provide both a normative and descriptive understanding of the dimensions of ethical decision making in a marketing organization. The first of these, by Ferrell and Gresham, provides a basic descriptive model of ethical decision making in a marketing organization. This was the first framework that attempted to integrate the various elements of ethical decision making in marketing. The second article, by Gundlach and Murphy, provides a perspective of relational exchange built on ethical and legal foundations. This article is significant in that it examines the interrelationship of contract law and ethics for building and sustaining marketing exchanges. Managerial and research implications provide directions for research and practice to improve marketing ethics.

The third article describes an empirical study that provides a positive association between corporate ethical values and organizational commitment. This article, by Hunt, Wood and Chonko, is significant in that it develops a measure of corporate ethical values and associates these values with organizational commitment in marketing. The strong link between commitment and other organizational benefits provides evidence that ethics is not just a personal or societal issue, but a key organizational issue as well.

These three articles are excellent examples of progress in increasing knowledge within the domain of marketing ethics.

Policy in Progress: Illustrative Action Issues

CONTROVERSY AT WAL-MART

Even though Wal-Mart is the world's largest corporation and employs 1.6 million, as described in the article by Serwer (2005), *Wal-Mart: Bruised in Bentonville,* its success has not come without controversy. The company has focused on serving customers, in Sam Walton's vision, assuming that the rest would fall into place. Unfortunately, today, many stakeholders are involved in disputes, lawsuits, and boycotts related to its business practices. Issues of concern relate to urban sprawl and damage to area small businesses, fairness in treatment and compensation of employees, discrimination, supplier treatment and compensation, executives' and board member's improper use of company resources, and even alledged attempts to fight unions improperly. To combat its problems, the company is using public relations, legal teams, its financial resources, and is even considering adopting a more balanced approach to managing its stakeholder interests.

QUESTIONS

1. Because Wal-Mart became successful by saving consumers billions of dollars, how has its legacy for success been affected by the interests and actions of other stakeholders?
2. What does Wal-Mart need to do today to improve upon its reputation?
3. In the long run, how will concerns about Wal-Mart's ethical conduct influence its success?

CHILDHOOD OBESITY AND FOOD MARKETING

There is a growing controversy about how food and beverages should be marketed to children. As the article by McKay (2005), *Study Tries to Link Obesity in Children with Food Marketing,* describes advertising aimed at pre-schoolers using cartoon characters to promote cereals and snacks are coming under fire. There is a belief that the marketing activities of food companies are contributing to epidemic levels of childhood obesity. Research is being conducted in an attempt to link obesity in children with food marketing. Some companies such as General Mills are responding by using whole grains in its cereals and some companies are attempting to eliminate transfats from their food products.

QUESTIONS

1. Who should be responsible for children's food choices: parents, food marketers or the government?
2. What are the ethical and social responsibilities of food marketers when targeting their products to children?
3. What is the role of the government and special interest groups in impacting childrens' food choices?

COUNTERFEIT GOODS

As described in the article *Fakes!* by Balfour et al (2005), the world market for counterfeit goods continues to grow, fueled by developing countries that are attempting to advance their economic development. Many counterfeit products are almost impossible to distinguish from the real product. In some cases, authorized manufacturers of licensed products are making supplemental inventories to market on their own. There is a concern that channel members, transportation companies, and even retailers are aware of the problem and do nothing about it as long as they can capitalize on the trend. The manufacturer of Louis Vuitton leather goods spent more than $16 million over the last year investigating and attempting to stop the counterfeiting of its products.

QUESTIONS

1. What are the ethical ramifications of counterfeit products?
2. How can manufacturers deal with this problem in a global marketplace?
3. How do you feel as a consumer about having the opportunity to purchase an exclusive name brand product at a fraction of its retail price?

Conclusions

Much progress has been made in advancing theory and research in marketing ethics. In addition, the practice of marketing has been elevated to higher levels of ethics from professional codes of conduct provided by the American Marketing Association, Direct Selling Association, Direct Marketing Association, Marketing Research Association, American Federation of Advertising and the National Advertising Division of the Council of Better Business Bureaus. In addition, most corporations have developed comprehensive codes of conduct that address specific ethical risk areas in marketing practice. Recent regulatory changes that require boards of directors to be responsible for oversight on all ethics issues within an organization elevate the importance of marketing ethics. It is clear that marketing ethics is part of organizational responsibility and individuals cannot make independent decisions about appropriate conduct. There is recognition through academic research and regulatory initiatives that corporate culture plays a key role in improving marketing ethics.

STATE OF THE FIELD AND FUTURE DIRECTIONS

The latest description of the Hunt and Vitell (2005) theory of marketing ethics and their discussions of empirical tests of the theory provides an excellent framework for understanding the "why" questions about marketing ethics. The model shows why peoples' ethical judgments differ in an organizational context. This theory, as well as Ferrell and Gresham (1985), provide directions for future empirical descriptive research in marketing ethics. While many researchers and managers believe that personal ethics determines organizational ethics, these frameworks and empirical research question this assumption. The role of corporate culture along with internal control of opportunity to engage in misconduct remains a key determinant of marketing ethics.

The development of stakeholder theory and the importance of stakeholder orientation provide a new direction for integrating ethics into marketing decisions (Maignan, Ferrell and Ferrell, 2004). This perspective focuses on understanding and responding to important stakeholder groups that hold marketing accountable for its actions. This approach assumes that stakeholders are knowledgeable on key ethics issues and that the organization can respond in a manner that maintains marketing relationships.

Stakeholder orientation has the potential to redefine the strategic concept of market orientation by including the interests of all stakeholders in marketing decisions. Marketing can be viewed more as a network of relationships providing skills and knowledge to all stakeholders (Vargo and Lusch, 2004). From this perspective marketing ethics would be an important part of the strategic planning process (Greenley, Hooley, Broderick, and Rudd, 2004).

The role of normative theory (Dunfee, Smith and Ross, 1999) and cognitive moral development (Goolsby and Hunt, 1992) continues to be a part of the pluralistic approach used to discover and evaluate marketing ethics. Both descriptive and normative researchers agree that marketers do develop guidelines and rules for ethical conduct based on accepted norms and moral philosophies. Integrative Social Contract Theory (ISCT) (Dunfee, Smith and Ross, 1999), based on norms as the foundation of rules within communities, provides a direction for future research. Stakeholder theory can be linked with ISCT to examine multiple conflicting norms and discovery of norms that should have priority in marketing decisions.

Insights

For most organizations, trade associations define minimum acceptable ethical behavior and the regulatory system provides the foundation for acceptable conduct in society. While acceptable ethical behavior is derived from the professional, cultural, industry, and organizational environments, individual behavior may differ based on ethical judgments (Hunt and Vitell, 2005). Marketing ethics remains a complex area to understand and offers the opportunity for research on many different dimensions that have been discussed in this section. Marketing will be under pressure from organizational efforts to institutionalize formal ethics programs in order to satisfy stakeholder demands. Both normative and descriptive understanding will be required to improve marketing ethics. There are many opportunities to contribute to the advancement of knowledge in this important area of marketing.

Questions for Discussion

1. Define the nature and scope of marketing ethics from both a descriptive and normative perspective.
2. What can be found in examining the history of marketing ethics that could be used in understanding marketing ethics today?
3. How does the contingency framework for understanding ethics in a marketing organization assist in designing an effective program to maintain and improve ethics in marketing?
4. What is the interrelationship between contract law and ethics in building and sustaining marketing exchanges?
5. Discuss the relationship between corporate ethical values and organizational performance in marketing.

References

1998 WL 1991608 Mich. App.

American Marketing Association. "What Are The Definitions of Marketing and Marketing Research?," available at http://www.marketingpower.com/content4620.php, accessed December 8, 2004.

Balfour, Frederik, Carol Matlack, Amy Barrett, Kerry Capell, Dexter Roberts, Jonathan Wheatley, William C. Symonds, Paul Magnusson, and Diane Brady. 2005. "Fakes!" Business Week, February 7, www.businessweek.com/@@AENS@YYQ4mWr6QUA/magazine/content/05_06/ (accessed July 5, 2005).

Bartels, R. 1967. "A Model for Ethics in Marketing," *Journal of Marketing,* Vol. 31, 20–26.

Bellizzi, J.A. and R.W. Hasty. 2003. "Supervising Unethical Sales Force Behavior: How Strong Is the Tendency to Treat Top Sales Performers Leniently?" *Journal of Business Ethics,* Vol. 43, 337–351.

Bowman, James S. 1976. "Managerial Ethics in Business and Government," *Business Horizons,* October, 50.

Carroll, Archie B. 1975. "Managerial Ethics: A Post-Watergate View," *Business Horizons,* April, 79.

D'Innocenzio, Anne. 2005. "Apparel Suppliers, Retailers Spar over Finances," *Coloradoan,* April 24, E3.

Dunfee, T.W., N.C. Smith, and W.T. Ross Jr. 1999. "Social Contracts and Marketing Ethics," *Journal of Marketing,* 63 (3): 14–33.

Farmer, R.N. 1967. "Would You Want Your Daughter to Marry a Marketing Man?" *Journal of Marketing,* Vol. 31, 1–3.

Farmer, R.N. 1977. "Would You Want Your Son to Marry a Marketing Lady?" *Journal of Marketing,* Vol. 41, 15–18.

Farmer, R.N. 1987. "Would You Want Your Granddaughter to Marry a Taiwanese Marketing Man?" *Journal of Marketing,* Vol. 51, 111–116.

Ferrell, O.C. 2004. "Business Ethics and Customer Stakeholders," *Academy of Management Executive,* Vol. 18, No. 2, 126–129.

Ferrell, O.C. 2005. "A Framework for Understanding Organizational Ethics," in *Business Ethics: New Challenges for Business Schools and Corporate Leaders*. R.A. Peterson and O.C. Ferrell, (eds.) Armonk, New York: M.E. Sharpe, 3–17.

Ferrell, O.C. and L. Ferrell. 2005. "Ethics and Marketing Education." *Marketing Education Review*, forthcoming.

Ferrell, O.C., J. Fraedrich, and L. Ferrell. 2005. *Business Ethics: Ethical Decision Making and Cases*. Boston: Houghton Mifflin.

Ferrell, O.C. and L.G. Gresham. 1985. "A Contingency Framework for Understanding Ethical Decision Making in Marketing." *Journal of Marketing*, 49 (3).

Ferrell, O.C. and K. Mark Weaver. 1978. "Ethical Beliefs of Marketing Managers," *Journal of Marketing*, 42 (3): 69–73.

Freeman, R.E. 1984. *Strategic Management: A Stakeholder Approach*. Boston: Pitman.

Fry, M. and M.J. Polonsky. 2004. "Examining the Unintended Consequences of Marketing," *Journal of Business Research*, Vol. 57, 1303–1306.

Goolsby, J.R., and S.D. Hunt. 1992. "Cognitive Moral Development and Marketing." *Journal of Marketing* 56 (1): 55–70.

Greenley, G.E., G.J. Hooley, A.J. Broderick, and J.M. Rudd. 2004. "Strategic Planning Differences Among Different Multiple Stakeholder Orientation Profiles." *Journal of Strategic Marketing*, Vol. 12, 163–182.

Gundlach, G.T., and P.E. Murphy. 1993. "Ethical and Legal Foundations of Relational Marketing Exchanges." *Journal of Marketing*, 57 (4): 35–47.

Hemphill, T.A. 2005. "Rejuvenating Wal-Mart's Reputation." *Business Horizons*, Vol. 48, 11–21.

Homburg, C., H. Krohmer, and J.P. Workman. 2004. "A Strategy Implementation Perspective of Market Orientation," *Journal of Business Research*, Vol. 57, 1331–1340.

Hunt, Shelby D. and Scott Vitell. 2005. "Personal Moral Codes and the Hunt-Vitell Theory of Ethics," in *Business Ethics: New Challenges for Business Schools and Corporate Leaders*, Robert A. Peterson and O.C. Ferrell (eds.) Armonk, New York: M.E. Sharpe, 18–37.

Hunt, S.D., V.R. Wood, and L.B. Chonko. 1989. "Corporate Ethical Values and Organizational Commitment in Marketing." *Journal of Marketing*, 53 (3).

Hunt, S. D. and S. Vitell. 1986. "A General Theory of Marketing Ethics." *Journal of Macromarketing* 6 (Spring): 5–15.

Jones, T.M. 1991. "Ethical Decision Making by Individuals in Organizations: An Issue-Contingent Model," *Academy of Management Review*, Vol. 16, 366–395.

Kimery, K.M. and S.M. Rinehart. 1998. "Markets and Constituencies: An Alternative View of the Marketing Concept." *Journal of Business Research*, Vol. 43, 117–124.

Klein, J.G., N.C. and John A. Smith. 2004. "Why We Boycott: Consumer Motivations for Boycott Participation." *Journal of Marketing*, 68 (3): 92–110.

LeClair, D.T., O.C. Ferrell, and J.P. Fraedrich. 1998. *Integrity Management: A Guide to Managing Legal and Ethical Issues in the Workplace*. Tampa, Florida: University of Tampa Press.

Maignan, I., O.C. Ferrell, and L. Ferrell. 2005. "A Stakeholder Model for Implementing Social Responsibility in Marketing." *European Journal of Marketing*, forthcoming.

Maignan, I., O.C. Ferrell, and L. Ferrell. 2004. "Corporate Social Responsibility and Marketing: An Integrative Framework." *Journal of the Academy of Marketing Science*, 32 (1): 3–19.

McKay, Betsy. 2005. "Study Tries to Link Obesity in Children with Food Marketing," *The Wall Street Journal*, (January 27): B1.

Merritt, Athena D. 2005. "N.J. AG Sues Blockbuster Over Ads." *Philadelphia Business Journal,* February 18, 42.

Miller, R.L. and W.F. Lewis. 1991. "A Stakeholder Approach to Marketing Management Using the Value Exchange Models," *European Journal of Marketing,* Vol. 25, No. 8, 55–68.

Murphy, P.E., G.R. Laczniak, N.E. Bowie, and T.A. Klein. 2005. *Ethical Marketing,* Upper Saddle River, N.J: Pearson Prentice-Hall.

Phillips, C.F. 1939. "Some Theoretical Considerations Regarding Fair Trade Laws." *Journal of Marketing,* Vol. 3, 242–250.

Robin, D.P., R.E. Reidenbach, and P.J. Forrest. 1996. "The Perceived Importance of an Ethical Issue as an Influence on the Ethical Decision-Marking of Ad Managers." *Journal of Business Research,* Vol. 35, 17–29.

Serwer, Andy. 2005. "Wal-Mart: Bruised in Bentonville," *Fortune,* http://money.cnn.com/magazines/fortune/fortune_archive/2005/04/18/8257005/index.htm (accessed July 5, 2005).

Sharp, F.C. and P.G. Fox. 1937. *Business Ethics,* New York: D. Appleton-Century Company.

United States Sentencing Commission (2003), "Report of the Ad Hoc Advisory Group on the Organizational Sentencing Guidelines," www.ussc.gov/corp/advgrprpt/advgrprpt.htm.

Vargo, S.L. and R.F. Lusch. 2004. "Evolving to a New Dominant Logic for Marketing." *Journal of Marketing,* Vol. 68 (January 2004): 1–17.

Appendix
Ethical Norms and Values for Marketers

http://www.marketingpower.com/content435.php

Preamble

The American Marketing Association commits itself to promoting the highest standard of professional ethical norms and values for its members. Norms are established standards of conduct that are expected and maintained by society and/or professional organizations. Values represent the collective conception of what people find desirable, important, and morally proper. Values serve as the criteria for evaluating the actions of others. Marketing practitioners must recognize that they not only serve their enterprises but also act as stewards of society in creating, facilitating, and executing the efficient and effective transactions that are part of the greater economy. In this role, marketers should embrace the highest ethical norms of practicing professionals and the ethical values implied by their responsibility toward stakeholders (e.g., customers, employees, investors, channel members, regulators and the host community).

General Norms

1. Marketers must do no harm. This means doing work for which they are appropriately trained or experienced so that they can actively add value to their organizations and customers. It also means adhering to all applicable laws and regulations and embodying high ethical standards in the choices they make.
2. Marketers must foster trust in the marketing system. This means that products are appropriate for their intended and promoted uses. It requires that marketing communications about goods and services are not intentionally deceptive or misleading. It suggests building relationships

that provide for the equitable adjustment and/or redress of customer grievances. It implies striving for good faith and fair dealing so as to contribute toward the efficacy of the exchange process.

3. Marketers must embrace, communicate, and practice the fundamental ethical values that will improve consumer confidence in the integrity of the marketing exchange system. These basic values are intentionally aspirational and include honesty, responsibility, fairness, respect, openness and citizenship.

Ethical Values

Honesty—to be truthful and forthright in our dealings with customers and stakeholders.

- We will tell the truth in all situations and at all times.
- We will offer products of value that do what we claim in our communications.
- We will stand behind our products if they fail to deliver their claimed benefits.
- We will honor our explicit and implicit commitments and promises.

Responsibility—to accept the consequences of our marketing decisions and strategies.

- We will make strenuous efforts to serve the needs of our customers.
- We will avoid using coercion with all stakeholders.
- We will acknowledge the social obligations to stakeholders that come with increased marketing and economic power.
- We will recognize our special commitments to economically vulnerable segments of the market such as children, the elderly and others who may be substantially disadvantaged.

Fairness—to try to balance justly the needs of the buyer with the interests of the seller.

- We will represent our products in a clear way in selling, advertising, and other forms of communication; this includes the avoidance of false, misleading, and deceptive promotion.
- We will reject manipulations and sales tactics that harm customer trust.
- We will not engage in price fixing, predatory pricing, price gouging, or "bait-and-switch" tactics.
- We will not knowingly participate in material conflicts of interest.

Respect—to acknowledge the basic human dignity of all stakeholders.

- We will value individual differences even as we avoid stereotyping customers or depicting demographic groups (e.g., gender, race, sexual orientation) in a negative or dehumanizing way in our promotions.
- We will listen to the needs of our customers and make all reasonable efforts to monitor and improve their satisfaction on an ongoing basis.
- We will make a special effort to understand suppliers, intermediaries, and distributors from other cultures.
- We will appropriately acknowledge the contributions of others, such as consultants, employees and coworkers, to our marketing endeavors.

Openness—to create transparency in our marketing operations.

- We will strive to communicate clearly with all our constituencies.
- We will accept constructive criticism from our customers and other stakeholders.

- We will explain significant product or service risks, component substitutions or other foreseeable eventualities that could affect customers or their perception of the purchase decision.
- We will fully disclose list prices and terms of financing as well as available price deals and adjustments.

Citizenship—to fulfill the economic, legal, philanthropic and societal responsibilities that serve stakeholders in a strategic manner.

- We will strive to protect the natural environment in the execution of marketing campaigns.
- We will give back to the community through volunteerism and charitable donations.
- We will work to contribute to the overall betterment of marketing and its reputation.
- We will encourage supply chain members to ensure that trade is fair for all participants, including producers in developing countries.

Implementation

Finally, we recognize that every industry sector and marketing subdiscipline (e.g., marketing research, e-commerce, direct selling, direct marketing, advertising) has its own specific ethical issues that require policies and commentary. An array of such codes can be accessed through links on the AMA Web site. We encourage all such groups to develop and/or refine their industry and discipline-specific codes of ethics to supplement these general norms and values.

A Contingency Framework for Understanding Ethical Decision Making in Marketing

O.C. Ferrell and Larry G. Gresham

This article addresses a significant gap in the theoretical literature on marketing ethics. This gap results from the lack of an integrated framework which clarifies and synthesizes the multiple variables that explain how marketers make ethical/unethical decisions. A contingency framework is recommended as a starting point for the development of a theory of ethical/unethical actions in organizational environments. This model demonstrates how previous research can be integrated to reveal that ethical/unethical decisions are moderated by individual factors, significant others within the organizational setting, and opportunity for action.

Most people agree that a set of moral principles or values should govern the actions of marketing decision makers, and most marketers would agree that their decisions should be made in accordance with accepted principles of right and wrong. However, consensus regarding what constitutes proper ethical behavior in marketing decision situations diminishes as the level of analysis proceeds from the general to the specific (Laczniak 1983a). For example, most people would agree that stealing by employees is wrong. But this consensus will likely lessen, as the value of what is stolen moves from embezzling company funds, to "padding" an expense account, to pilfering a sheet of poster board from company supplies for a child's homework project. In fact, a Gallup poll found that 74% of the business executives surveyed had pilfered homework supplies for their children and 78% had used company telephones for personal long-distance calls (Ricklefs 1983a).

Because of the lack of agreement concerning ethical standards, it is difficult to find incidents of deviant behavior which marketers would agree are unethical. For example, in the Gallup poll cited above, 31% had ethical reservations in accepting an expensive dinner from a supplier, but most of the respondents indicated that bribes, bid rigging, and price collusion had become more common in recent years (Ricklefs 1983a, 1983b). Dishonesty is reportedly perverting the results of market tests (Hodock 1984).

O.C. FERRELL is Associate Professor, and LARRY G. GRESHAM is Assistant Professor, Department of Marketing, Texas A&M University. The authors wish to thank Patrick E. Murphy, Gene R. Laczniak, Mary Zey-Ferrell, Charles S. Madden, Steven Skinner, Terry Childers, and two anonymous reviewers for their helpful suggestions and constructive comments.

Ferrell, O.C. and Gresham, Larry G. (1985), "A Contingency Framework for Understanding Ethical Decision Making in Marketing," *Journal of Marketing,* 49(3) 87–96.

Obviously, there is a wide-ranging definition of what is considered to be ethical behavior among marketing practitioners.

Absence of a clear consensus about what is ethical conduct for marketing managers may lead to deleterious results for a business. Due to faulty test marketing results, potentially successful products may be scrapped and unwise market introductions may be made. In either case, both the consumer and the "cheated" firm are losers. Productivity and other measures of efficiency may be low because employees maximize their own welfare rather than placing company goals as priorities.

Absence of a clear consensus about ethical conduct among marketers has resulted in much confusion among academicians who study marketing ethics. These academicians have resorted to analyzing various lists of activities to determine if marketing practitioners feel specific behaviors are ethical or unethical. This research seems unenlightened by evidence that ethical standards are constantly changing and that they vary from one situation/organization to another. Individuals have different perceptions of ethical situations and use different ethical frameworks to make decisions. Thus, no attempt is made here to judge what is ethical or unethical (the content of the behavior). Our concern is with the *determinants* of decision-making behavior which is ultimately defined as ethical/unethical by participants and observers. Rather than advocate a particular moral doctrine, we examine contexts and variables that determine ethical decisions in the managerial process.

This article intends to fill a significant gap in the theoretical literature related to marketing ethics. The conceptual framework developed and discussed focuses on a multistage contingency model of the variables that impact on ethical decisions in an organizational environment. The article's specific objectives are (1) to review empirical research and logical evidence useful in creating a contingency framework to explain ethical decisions of marketers, (2) to defend the contingency framework with existing empirical research and logical evidence, and (3) to suggest additional research to test portions of the contingency framework.

Definitions and Approach

We assume that the operating exigencies of the firm bring the marketer into contact with situations that must be judged as ethical or unethical (right or wrong). Such situations may include placing marketers in positions to use deceptive advertising, fix prices, rig bids, falsify market research data, or withhold product test data. The opportunity variable is especially salient since the marketer performs a boundary spanning role for the organization. That is, the marketer links the task environment to the organization by defining consumer needs and satisfaction. As Osborn and Hunt (1974) note, those parts of the organization most exposed to the environment will be under more pressure to deviate. Therefore, many of the ethical questions developing in any firm are related to marketing decisions. The model described is equally applicable to other functional areas of the organization, such as accounting, management, etc. However, the opportunity to deviate from ethical behavior may be less prevalent in nonmarketing areas, due to a lower frequency of boundary spanning contacts.

The proposed framework for examining ethical/unethical decision making is multidimensional, process oriented, and contingent in nature. The variables in the model can be categorized into individual and organizational contingencies. The individual variables consist of personal background and socialization characteristics, such as educational and business experiences. The organizational characteristics consist of the effects of organizations external to the employing organization (customers, other firms) and intraorganizational influences (e.g., peers and supervisors). These variables are interdependent as well as ultimately affecting, either directly or indirectly, the dependent variable—ethical/unethical marketing behavior.

The general framework is a contingency approach to individual decision making, which suggests that we can observe wide variations in ethical decision making, but this variation is not random. Theoretical and practical contributions are achieved through identifying important contingency variables that distinguish between contexts in which decisions are made. This simply means that the decision making of marketers is dependent on contingencies external to the decision-making process. These contingency factors may be found within the individual, in the organizational context, or external to both the individual and the organization (i.e., in the interorganizational environment).

The contingency framework presented in Figure 1 demonstrates that multifaceted factors affect the likelihood of ethical actions by individual decision makers. Individual factors (including knowledge, values, attitude, and intentions) are posited as interacting with organizational factors (including significant others and opportunity factors) to influence individuals involved in an ethical/unethical decision-making dilemma. The societal/environmental criteria used to define an ethical issue are treated as exogenous variables in this theoretical framework and are, therefore, beyond the scope of this analysis.

Constructs in the Contingency Framework

INDIVIDUAL FACTORS

It is impossible to develop a framework of ethical decision making without evaluating normative ethical standards derived from moral philosophy. Based on the emphasis of normative approaches in the literature, it is assumed that marketers develop guidelines and rules for ethical behavior based on moral philosophy. Various philosophies related to utilitarianism, rights, and justice explain how individuals create ethical standards.

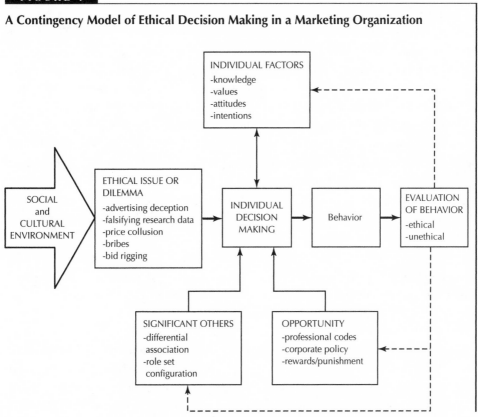

FIGURE 1

A Contingency Model of Ethical Decision Making in a Marketing Organization

The oldest approach to ethics is based on the study of moral philosophy. It is assumed that, knowingly or unknowingly, individuals may use a set of philosophical assumptions as a basis for making ethical decisions. This assumption about the influence of cultural and group norms/values on individual decision-making processes is soundly based in marketing literature (cf. Engel and Blackwell 1982, Fishbein and Ajzen 1975).

Philosophy divides assumptions about ethics into two basic types—teleological and deontological (Beauchamp and Bowie 1979). These two approaches differ radically in terms of judging ethical behavior. Teleological philosophies deal with the moral worth of behavior determined totally by the consequences of the behavior. One's choice should be based on what would be best for all affected social units. For many marketing decision makers, ethical action is tied into the business and their ability to meet company performance objectives (Sherwin 1983). The assumption is that the economic success of a firm's marketing activities should benefit employees, management, stockholders, consumers, and society. Utilitarianism is a teleological philosophy that attempts to establish morality not in the motives or intentions of marketers' decisions but in the consequences of such decisions (Velasquez 1982).

Utilitarianism. The act is ethical only if the sum total of utilities produced by the act is greater than the sum total of utilities produced by any other act. That is when the greatest possible balance of value for all persons is affected by the act. Under utilitarianism, it is unethical to select an act that leads to an inefficient use of resources. Also, it is unethical to engage in an act which leads to personal gain at the expense of society in general. Implicit in the utilitarian principle is the concept of utility and the measurement and comparison of value. For example, it may cost the public more through higher prices to redesign an automobile than to pay damages to a few people who are injured from a safety defect in the automobile.

Deontological philosophies stress the methods or intentions involved in a particular behavior. This focus on intentions is consistent with marketing theories of consumer choice (cf. Engel and Blackwell 1982, Howard 1977), which specify behavioral intentions as a cognitive precedent of choice behavior. Results of action are the focus of deontological philosophies. Standards to defend personal ethics are often developed from the types of deontological philosophies described in the following summaries (Velasquez 1982).

Rights principle. This principle specifies minimum levels of satisfaction and standards, independent of outcomes. Moral rights are often perceived as universal, but moral rights are not synonymous with legal rights. The rights principle is based on Kant's categorical imperative which basically incorporates two criteria for judging an action. First, every act should be based on a reason(s) that everyone could act on, at least in principle (universality). The second criterion is that action must be based on reasons the actor would be willing to have all others use, even as a basis of how they treat the actor (reversibility). For example, consumers claim that they have a "right to know" about probable defects in an automobile that relate to safety.

Justice principle. This principle is designed to protect the interests of all involved. The three categories are distributive, retributive, and compensatory. Basically, distributive justice holds that equals should be treated equally and unequals should be treated unequally. Retributive justice deals with blaming and punishing persons for doing wrong. The person must have committed the act out of free choice and with knowledge of the consequences. The punishment must be consistent with or proportional to the wrongdoing. Compensatory justice is concerned with compensation for the wronged individual. The compensation should restore the injured party to his/her original position. Corporate hierarchies and executive prerogatives are examples of distributive justice in practice. Antitrust legislation allowing criminal prosecution of corporate officials is based on the notion of retributive justice. Class action suits embody compensatory principles.

It is important to note that all of these philosophies produce standards to judge the act itself, the actor's intentions, or the consequences of the act. Also, these philosophies are based on assumptions about how one should approach ethical problems. Standards developed from utilitarianism, justice principles, and rights principles are used to socialize the individual to act ethically and may be learned with no awareness that the standards are being used. The precise impact of these philosophies on ethical behavior is unknown, but there is widespread acceptance in the marketing literature that such culturally derived standards impact on the decision-making process.

Ethical decision making may be influenced by the Individual Factors identified in Figure 1. Beliefs may serve as inputs affecting attitude formation/change and intentions to resolve problems. Also, evaluation or intention to act (or even think about an ethical dilemma) may be influenced by cognitive factors that result from the individual's socialization processes. It is at this stage that cultural differences would influence perceptions of problems. For example, variations in ethical standards are illustrated by what Mexicans call la mordida—*the bite.* The use of payoffs and bribes are commonplace to business and government officials and are often considered tips for performing required functions. U.S. firms often find it difficult to compete in foreign environments that do not use American moral philosophies of decision making.

ORGANIZATIONAL FACTORS

The preceding discussion explored philosophies that have an impact on individuals' knowledge, values, attitudes, and intentions toward ethical issues. In this section, recognition is given to the fact that ethics is not only a matter of normative evaluation, but is also a series of perceptions of how to act in terms of daily issues. From a positive perspective, success is determined by managers' everyday performances in achieving company goals. According to Cavanaugh (1976, p. 100), "Pressure for results, as narrowly measured in money terms, has increased." Laczniak (1983a) suggests that this pressure to perform is particularly acute at levels below top management because "areas of responsibility of middle managers are often treated as profit centers for purposes of evaluation. Consequently, anything that takes away from profit—including ethical behavior—is perceived by lower level management as an impediment to organizational advancement and recognition" (p. 27). Thus, internal organizational pressures seem to be a major predictor of ethical/unethical behavior.

SIGNIFICANT OTHERS

Figure 1 posits Significant Others as a contingency variable in individual decision making. Individuals do not learn values, attitudes, and norms from society or organizations but from others who are members of disparate social groups, each bearing distinct norms, values, and attitudes. Aspects of differential association theory and role-set theory provide theoretical rationales for including organizational factors in the decision framework. These theories, and empirical tests of their relevance to the ethical decision-making process, are discussed in the following sections.

Differential association theory. Differential association theory (Sutherland and Cressey 1970) assumes that ethical/unethical behavior is learned in the process of interacting with persons who are part of intimate personal groups or role sets. Whether or not the learning process results in unethical behavior is contingent upon the ratio of contacts with unethical patterns to contacts with ethical patterns. Cloward and Ohlin (1960) are responsible for incorporating an opportunity variable (discussed in a later section) in the differential association model of deviant behavior. Thus, as posited in our model, it is expected that association with others who are perceived to be participating in unethical behavior, combined with the opportunity to be involved in such behavior oneself, are major predictors of unethical behavior.

In the Zey-Ferrell, Weaver, and Ferrell (1979) study of marketing managers, differential association with peers and opportunity were found to be better predictors of ethical/unethical behavior than the respondent's own ethical belief system. This finding contradicts DeFleur and Quinncy's (1966) reformulation of Sutherland's differential association model, which specifies internalization of group norms as a necessary second step in the development of deviant behavior. The Zey-Ferrell, Weaver, and Ferrell (1979) conclusion that an individual may act in compliance with group pressure without internalizing group norms is, however, congruent with the value/behavior inconsistency noted by Newstrom and Ruch (1975) in their survey of marketing practitioners.

Empirical support for the impact of superiors on the ethics of their subordinates is provided by a variety of studies of business ethics spanning the last two decades. For example, more than 75% of the manager/respondents ($n = 1200$) to Baumhart's (1961) ethics survey reported experiencing conflict between personal standards and what was expected of them as managers. In Brenner and Molander's (1977) replication of the Baumhart research, 57% of those responding ($n = 1227$) indicated similar role conflict situations. Carroll (1975) found that young managers in business indicated they would go along with their superiors to demonstrate loyalty in matters related to judgment of morality. Almost 60% of the respondents ($n = 236$) agreed that young managers in the business world would have done just what junior members of Nixon's re-election committee had done. In Bowman's (1976) follow-up, an even higher percentage (70%) of public officials expressed this same opinion.

Central to the application of differential association theory to the model of ethical/unethical marketing behavior is the identification of referent others in the decision process. This perspective is provided via a consideration of the decision maker's (focal person's) role-set configuration.

Role-set theory. A role set refers to the complement of role relationships which focal persons have by virtue of their social status in an organization (Merton 1957). A role-set configuration is defined as the mixture of characteristics of referent others who form the role set, and may include their location and authority, as well as their perceived beliefs and behaviors. Previous evidence (Merton 1957, Miles 1977) suggests that role-set characteristics provide clues for predicting behaviors of a focal person.

One important dimension of role-set configuration appears to be the organizational distance between the referent other and the focal person. Organizational distance in this context is defined as the number of distinct intra- and interorganizational boundaries that separate the focal person and the referent other. Persons in the same department as the focal person tend to be least differentiated. They are hired and socialized within the same immediate organizational context and share the focal person's functional specialization and knowledge base. People in different departments within the same organization are more similar than people separated by organizational boundaries. Those in other organizations have different socialization and reinforcement under systems which pursue separate and sometimes varying objectives with different personnel selection criteria. Boundaries within and between departments serve to reduce the focal person's knowledge of referent others' attitudes and behaviors. Further, referent others outside the focal person's own organization are likely to differ from the focal person in orientation, goals, interests, and modus operandi. Thus, one would expect that the greater the distance between the focal person and the referent other, the less likely their influence on the focal person's ethical/unethical behavior.

In the only reported direct test of the distance hypothesis, Zey-Ferrell and Ferrell (1982) compared responses from ad agency account executives with those from their corporate clients. The expectation that neither of those groups would be perceived by the other as influencing their own behavior (due to the interorganizational distance involved) was confirmed. Further support for the distance proposition came from the ad agency respondent type. Peer group, the referent other closest to the focal person, was the strongest predictor of ethical/unethical behavior. But, for the corporate respondent, top management, rather than peer group, was the most influential. The latter finding does not support the distance hypothesis but is consistent with predictions deriving from the relative authority dimension of the role configuration.

The relative authority dimension is a measure of the amount of legitimate authority referent others have, relative to the focal person, on issues requiring contact between them. Kahn et al. (1964) view powerful referent others in a role set as those capable of restricting the range of behavior available to the focal person. They posit the status and powers of referent others as directly related to the amount of pressure they can exert on the focal person to conform to their role expectations. Thus a role set configured with referent others who are superior in authority relative to the focal person would be in a position to exert strong role pressures for compliance to their expectations. Applying this logic to business settings, one would anticipate that top management, as referent others with greater authority, would have more influence than peer groups on the focal person's ethical/unethical behavior.

The Baumhart (1961) and Brenner and Molander (1977) surveys support this relative authority proposition—*behavior of superiors* was perceived by respondents in both studies as the number one factor influencing ethical/unethical decisions. Similar results are also reported in a study by Newstrom and Ruch (1975). Hunt, Chonko, and Wilcox (1984) found the actions of top management to be the single best predictor of perceived ethical problems of marketing researchers. Ferrell and Weaver (1978) suggest that top management must assume at least part of the responsibility for the ethical conduct of marketers within their organization. In addition, the general conclusion that the ethical tone for an organization is set by upper management is common to most attempted syntheses of ethics research (cf. Dubinsky, Berkowitz, and Rudelius 1980; Laczniak 1983a; Murphy and Laczniak 1981).

Responses from the Zey-Ferrell and Ferrell (1982) ad agency executive sample do not support the authority proposition—this group was influenced by peers, rather than top management. The authors speculate that this unexpected outcome may have been attributable to the high frequency of contact among ad agency account executives and their relatively infrequent associations with superiors. Such an explanation is congruent with differential association theory and appears to indicate that frequency of contact with referent others is a more powerful predictor (than relative authority) of ethical/unethical behavior. Corporate client responses from the same survey also support a differential association explanation of the results obtained—top management, rather than peers, was perceived as the relevant referent other. In a corporation, the advertising director does not have a number of individuals at the same level with whom to interact. Thus, the frequency of interaction with upper management levels is usually higher for advertisers in corporations because the advertising director does not have anyone else performing the same job tasks.

OPPORTUNITY

Figure 1 depicts opportunity as having a major impact on the process of unethical/ethical decision making. Opportunity results from a favorable set of conditions to limit barriers or provide rewards. Certainly the absence of punishment provides an opportunity for unethical behavior without regard for consequences.

Rewards are external to the degree that they bring social approval, status, and esteem. Feelings of goodness and worth, internally felt through the performance of altruistic activities, for example, constitute internal rewards. External rewards refer to what an individual in the social environment expects to receive from others in terms of values externally generated and provided on an exchange basis. It is important to note that deontological frameworks for marketing ethics focus more on internal rewards, while teleological frameworks emphasize external rewards.

Cloward and Ohlin (1960) are responsible for incorporating an opportunity variable in the differential association model of ethical/unethical behavior. Zey-Ferrell and Ferrell (1982) empirically confirm that the opportunity of the focal person to become involved in ethical/unethical behavior will influence reported behavior. In this study, opportunity for unethical behavior was found to be a better predictor of behavior than personal or peer beliefs. Therefore, we can conclude that professional codes of ethics and corporate policy are moderating variables in controlling opportunity.

Weaver and Ferrell (1977) suggest that codes of ethics or corporate policy on ethics must be established to change individual beliefs about ethics. Their research indicates that beliefs are more ethical where these standards exist. Also, it was found that the enforcement of corporate policy on ethical behavior is necessary to change the ethical behavior of respondents. Their research discovered a poor correlation between ethical beliefs and ethical behavior. Opportunity was a better predictor of ethical behavior than individual beliefs. This research supports the need to understand and control opportunity as a key determinant (as indicated in Figure 1) in a multistage contingency model of ethical behavior.

A Contingency Framework for Ethical Decisions

A contingency framework for investigating behavioral outcomes of ethical/unethical decisions across situations is shown in Figure 1. The basic elements of the framework are: (a) the individual's cognitive structure—knowledge, values, beliefs, attitudes, and intentions; (b) significant others in the organizational setting; and (c) opportunity for action.

Figure 1 specifies that the behavioral outcome of an ethical dilemma is related to the first order interaction between the nature of the ethical situation and characteristics associated with the individual and the organizational environment. Potential higher order interactions are anticipated in the basic postulate. At this stage of development, there is no claim that this is an all-inclusive framework; rather, it is the initial step toward constructing such a framework.

Propositions from the Contingency Framework

Each of the constructs associated with the framework were discussed in the preceding sections. Some propositions incorporating the previously defined constructs are presented in the section that follows. These propositions are stated so that testable hypotheses can be derived to direct future research efforts. The elements and propositions discussed were selected on the basis of the past research and logical evidence used to construct the contingency framework in Figure 1. They are presented as a representative subset of potential propositions that can be derived from the paradigm.

PROPOSITIONS CONCERNING THE INDIVIDUAL FACTORS

Proposition 1: The more individuals are aware of moral philosophies for ethical decision making, the more influence these philosophies will have on their ethical decision.

   a. Individuals will be influenced by moral philosophies learned through socialization, i.e., family, social groups, formal education.
   b. Within the educational system, courses, training programs, and seminars related to ethics will influence ethical beliefs and behavior.
   c. The cultural backgrounds of individuals will influence ethical/unethical behavior.

PROPOSITIONS CONCERNING ORGANIZATIONAL FACTORS

Proposition 2: Significant others located in role sets with less distance between them and the focal individual are more likely to influence the ethical behavior of the focal person.

   a. Top management will have greater influence on the individual than peers, due to power and demands for compliance.
   b. Where top management has little interaction with the focal person and peer contact is frequent, peers will have a greater influence on ethical behavior.

Proposition 3: In general, differential association (learning from intimate groups or role sets) predicts ethical/unethical behavior.

   a. Internalization of group norms is not necessary to develop ethical/unethical behavior through differential association.
   b. Unethical behavior is influenced by the ratio of contacts with unethical patterns to contacts with ethical patterns.

PROPOSITIONS CONCERNING THE OPPORTUNITY VARIABLE

Proposition 4: The opportunity for the individual to become involved in unethical behavior will influence reported ethical/unethical behavior.

   a. Professional codes of ethics will influence ethical/unethical behavior. Ethics related corporate policy will influence ethical/unethical behavior.
   b. Corporate policy and codes of ethics that are enforced will produce the highest level of compliance to established ethical standards.
   c. The greater the rewards for unethical behavior, the more likely unethical behavior will be practiced.
   d. The less punishment for unethical behavior, the greater the probability that unethical behavior will be practiced.

Developing and Testing Contingency Propositions

The research program for developing and testing contingency hypotheses outlined by Weitz (1981) provides valuable guidance for future studies of marketing ethics. This program, recommended for tests of his contingency framework of effectiveness in sales interactions, is adaptable to examinations of ethical phenomena. The three stages of the research program are hypotheses generation, hypotheses testing in a laboratory environment, and hypotheses testing in a field setting.

HYPOTHESES GENERATION

The primary objectives of this step in the research program are to (1) add specificity to the propositions presented in the preceding section, i.e., move from "bridge laws" (Hunt 1983, p. 195) to research hypotheses; (2) identify additional propositions from the theoretical framework; and (3) develop a richer taxonomy of moderator variables within the Individual Factors, Significant Others, and Opportunity subsets.

Past studies of business ethics (cf. Darden and Trawick 1980; Dubinsky, Berkowitz, and Rudelius 1980), with their foci on identifying perceptions of ethical/unethical situations, provide a useful starting point for achieving the first objective of adding specificity to propositions. The theoretical framework of ethical decision making developed in this article requires identification of a variety of ethical issues to make the hypotheses derived from the specified relationships empirically testable. In addition, the practical and theoretical value of the proposed contingency framework can only be determined by testing its explanatory power *across* a variety of ethical situations.

Theories in use methodologies (Zaltman, LeMasters, and Heffring 1982) might be useful in generating additional theoretical propositions and developing a richer taxonomy of moderator variables, as well as in identifying a wide range of ethical dilemmas. Such methodologies involve observing and questioning marketing decision makers. Examples of how these techniques might be employed in ethics research include studies of verbal protocols recorded during the decision-making process, interviews with marketing practitioners concerning their behavior in specific decision situations, and investigations of the characteristics marketers use to classify ethical/unethical situations. Levy and Dubinsky (1983) have developed a methodology for studying retail sales ethics that applies the protocol technique. Their approach starts by generating situations that might be ethically troublesome to the retailer's sales personnel. This is first addressed by meeting with 8 to 12 retail sales personnel from different departments with a moderator to generate, individually and silently, ethical problems they confront on their jobs, and to record these on a sheet of paper.

EXPERIMENTAL TESTING

Regardless of the procedure used to develop contingency hypotheses from the theoretical framework, the next step in the ethics research program is to test these hypotheses in a laboratory environment, using an experimental design. The advantages of laboratory experiments to researchers attempting to assess causal relationships between variables are widely recognized (cf. Cook and Campbell 1976) as including control of exogenous variables and elimination of potential alternative explanations for the results obtained. However, the difficulties involved in testing hypotheses concerning marketing ethics in lab settings is evidenced by the absence in the marketing/business literature of reports of such experiments. The subjective nature of self-report operationalizations of constructs from the ethical decision-making framework and the problem of achieving experimental realism (Carlsmith, Ellsworth, and Aronson 1976, p. 83) in laboratory tests of ethical issues represent major threats to the internal validity of these studies.

However, the management literature on collective bargaining contains numerous examples of laboratory studies of negotiation techniques (cf. DeNisi and Dworkin 1981, Johnson and Tullar 1972, Notz and Stark 1978), which are very similar to the type of experiment needed in ethics research, i.e., unobtrusive, experimenter-controlled predictor variables and clearly defined behavioral outcomes. Such studies illustrate how complex cognitive phenomena (e.g., attitudes) can be operationalized, manipulated, and measured while minimizing threats to internal validity.

Applying similar techniques to studies of marketing ethics might involve, for example, manipulating the "opportunity" to engage in unethical behavior through the presence/absence of specific experimenter instructions regarding the rules of the game, or varying the impact of significant others through the use of a confederate in experimental groups. Laboratory experiments represent quick and effective ways for testing behavioral propositions. In addition, the primary value of such studies to a research program for marketing ethics may well lie in the purification of existing measures of the constructs under consideration, as well as the development of new and more valid and reliable operationalizations.

FIELD TESTING

The survey procedures used in earlier tests of some of the relationships posited in the theoretical framework of ethical decision making (Zey-Ferrell, Weaver, and Ferrell 1979) represent efficient and practical methods of examining these linkages. However, the correlational nature of the results obtained in these studies prohibits causal inference. In addition, the validity of the self-report measures used in these studies is open to question.

Future research programs on marketing ethics should address the latter problem in the laboratory testing phase. Lab studies focusing on the purification of existing measures of the constructs of interest and the identification of new and different measurement methods (e.g., physiological measures) may well result in the valid and reliable instruments needed for the field testing portion of the research program.

The ethical problems inherent in experimental manipulation of ethical issues/problems in field settings make solutions to the former problem much more difficult to overcome. Some of the hypotheses derived from the propositions presented earlier (e.g., those concerning the effects of corporate policy and training programs/seminars) are more amenable to field testing than others. For example, multi-unit corporations might institute training programs/seminars related to ethics at some locations and not at others. Before and after indices of ethical/unethical behavior (e.g., employee theft, customer complaints) could then be compared for the treatment and control units. Cook and Campbell (1976) indicate that "quasi-experimental" designs of this sort are acceptable surrogates for "true experiments" in field settings where random assignment of subjects to treatment control conditions is frequently impossible or impractical.

Nevertheless, the ethical issues and practical problems associated with random assignment of subjects to treatment conditions and unobtrusive assessment (or inducement) of ethical/unethical behavior present major obstacles to the implementation of experimental designs in field settings.

Conclusion

Research and theoretical development in marketing ethics have not been based on multidimensional models that are contingent in nature. Most articles in the field of marketing ethics focus on moral philosophies, researchers provide descriptive statistics about ethical beliefs, and correlational linkages of selected variables. This article attempts to integrate the key determinants of ethical/unethical behavior in a multistage contingency model. The framework is based on the assumption that the behavioral outcome of an ethical dilemma is related to first order interaction between the nature of the ethical situation and characteristics associated with the individual (cognitive factor), significant others, and opportunity. The framework provides a model for understanding the significance of previous theoretical work and empirical research and provides direction for future studies.

The contingency framework is process oriented, with events in a sequence causally associated or interrelated. The contingency variables represent situtional variables to the marketing decision maker. The complexity and precision of the framework developed in this paper should increase as research is conducted that permits more scientific conclusions about the nature of ethical decision making in marketing. Our framework is a start toward developing a comprehensive framework of ethical decision making. We have attempted to construct a simple and direct representation of variables based on the current state of research and theory development.

Propositions concerning individual factors and propositions concerning the organizational factors of significant others and opportunity were developed to be used in a research program for testing contingency hypotheses. Based on a research program for testing contingency hypotheses outlined by Weitz (1981), we suggest hypotheses generation, hypothesis testing in a laboratory environment, and hypothesis testing in a field setting. Both retail store management and field sales management provide excellent opportunities for testing the contingency framework in Figure 1. For example, Dubinsky (1985) has developed a methodology for studying the ethical problems of field salespeople as an approach for designing company policies. Dubinsky's methodology could be tested using the contingency framework of ethical decision making, hypotheses generation, laboratory testing, and field testing.

To develop new directions in research and theory construction, new propositions are needed to test the contingency framework. More research to develop a taxonomy of ethical standards (Velasquez 1982) and attempts to incorporate these standards into marketing (Fritzche 1985) are needed to understand more about individual factors related to beliefs, values, attitudes, or intentions. Attempts to develop logical decision rules for individual decision making (Laczniak 1983b) also contribute to understanding individual factors. Chonko and Burnett (1983) provide an example of descriptive research classifying individual beliefs about sales situations that are a source of role conflict. Their research may assist in developing additional propositions, especially as it relates to pinpointing new ethical issues. In addition, marketers should be able to draw from a rich source of research on organizational behavior to develop and test propositions related to significant others and opportunity.

The importance of ethical decision making in marketing is becoming more evident. Laczniak and Murphy (1985) suggest organizational and strategic mechanisms for improving marketing ethics, including codes of marketing ethics, marketing ethics committees, and ethics education modules for marketing managers. To improve specific recommendations for marketing ethics, more needs to be learned about the process of ethical decision making. We suggest an integrated approach to understanding marketing ethics with improved propositions that test the contingency model presented in this article. By taking a multidimensional view of ethical decision making, a new level of rigor in research should be achieved.

References

Baumhart, Raymond C. (1961), "How Ethical Are Businessmen?", *Harvard Business Review,* 39 (July–August), 6–19, 156–176.

Beauchamp, Tom L. and Norma E. Bowie, eds. (1979), *Ethical Theory and Business,* Englewood Cliffs, NJ: Prentice-Hall.

Bowman, James S. (1976), "Managerial Ethics in Business and Government," *Business Horizons,* 19 (October), 48–54.

Brenner, Steven N. and Earl A. Molander (1977), "Is the Ethics of Business Changing?," *Harvard Business Review,* 55 (January–February), 57–70.

Carlsmith, J. Merrill, Phoebe C. Ellsworth, and Eliot Aronson (1976), *Methods of Research in Social Psychology,* Reading, MA: Addison-Wesley.

Carroll, Archie B. (1975), "Managerial Ethics: A Post-Watergate View," *Business Horizons,* 18 (April), 75–80.

Cavanaugh, G. F. (1976), *American Business Values in Transition,* Englewood Cliffs, NJ: Prentice-Hall.

Chonko, Lawrence B. and John J. Burnett (1983), "Measuring the Importance of Ethical Situations as a Source of Role Conflict: A Survey of Salespeople, Sales Managers, and Sales Support Personnel," *Journal of Personal Selling and Sales Management* (May), 41–47.

Cloward, R. A. and L. E. Ohlin (1960), *Delinquency and Opportunity,* Glencoe, IL: Free Press.

Cook, Thomas D. and Donald T. Campbell (1976), "The Design and Conduct of Quasi-Experiments and True Experiments in Field Settings," in *Handbook of Industrial and Organizational Psychology,* M. D. Dunnette, ed., Chicago: Rand McNally.

Darden, William R. and Fred D. Trawick (1980), "Marketers' Perceptions of Ethical Standards in the Marketing Profession: Educators and Practitioners," *Review of Business and Economic Review,* 6 (Fall), 1–17.

DeFleur, M. L. and R. Quinncy (1966), "A Reformulation of Sutherland's Differential Association Theory and Strategy for Empirical Verification," *Journal of Research in Crime and Delinquency,* 3 (no. 1), 1–22.

DeNisi, Angelo S. and James B. Dworkin (1981), "Final-Offer Arbitration and the Naive Negotiator," *Industrial and Labor Relations Review,* 35 (October), 78–87.

Dubinsky, Alan J. (1985), "Ethical Policies for Sales Force Management," in *Marketing Ethics Guidelines for Managers,* Gene R. Laczniak and Patrick E. Murphy, eds., Lexington, MA: Heath.

___, Eric N. Berkowitz, and William Rudelius (1980), "Ethical Problems of Field Sales Personnel," *MSU Business Topics,* 28 (Summer), 11–16.

Engel, James F. and Roger D. Blackwell (1982), *Consumer Behavior,* 4th ed., New York: Dryden.

Ferrell, O. C. and K. Mark Weaver (1978), "Ethical Beliefs of Marketing Managers," *Journal of Marketing,* 42 (July), 69–73.

Fishbein, Martin and Icek Ajzen (1975), *Belief, Attitude, Intention and Behavior,* Reading, MA: Addison-Wesley.

Fritzche, David J. (1985), "Ethical Issues in Multinational Marketing," in *Marketing Ethics Guidelines for Managers,* Gene R. Laczniak and Patrick E. Murphy, eds., Lexington, MA: Heath.

Hodock, Calvin L. (1984), "Intellectual Dishonesty Is Perverting the Results from Various Market Tests," *Marketing News,* 18 (no. 2), 1.

Howard, John A. (1977), *Consumer Behavior: Application of Theory,* New York: McGraw-Hill.

Hunt, Shelby D. (1983), *Marketing Theory: The Philosophy of Marketing Science,* Homewood, IL: Irwin.

___, Lawrence B. Chonko, and James B. Wilcox (1984), "Ethical Problems of Marketing Researchers," *Journal of Marketing Research,* 21 (August), 304–324.

Johnson, Donald F. and William Tullar (1972), "Style of Third Party Intervention, Face Saving, and Bargaining Behavior," *Journal of Experimental Social Psychology,* 8 (March), 312–320.

Kahn, R. L., D. M. Wolfe, R. P. Quinn, J. D. Snoek, and R. A. Rosenthal (1964), *Organizational Stress: Studies in Role Conflict and Ambiguity,* New York: Wiley.

Laczniak, Gene R. (1983a), "Business Ethics: A Manager's Primer," *Business,* 33 (January–March), 23–29.

___ (1983b), "Framework for Analyzing Marketing Ethics," *Journal of Macromarketing,* 5 (Spring), 7–17.

___ and Patrick E. Murphy (1985), "Implementing Marketing Ethics," in *Marketing Ethics Guidelines for Managers,* Gene R. Laczniak and Patrick E. Murphy, eds., Lexington, MA: Heath.

Levy, Michael and Alan J. Dubinsky (1983), "Identifying and Addressing Retail Salespeople's Ethical Problems: A Method and Application," *Journal of Retailing,* 59 (no. 1), 46–66.

Merton, R.K. (1957), "The Role Set," *British Journal of Sociology,* 8 (June), 106–120.

Miles, R.H. (1977), "Role-Set Configuration as a Predictor of Role Conflict and Ambiguity in Complex Organizations," *Sociometry,* 40 (no. 1), 21–34.

Murphy, Patrick E. and Gene R. Laczniak (1981), "Marketing Ethics: A Review with Implications," in *Review of Marketing,* Ben M. Enis and Kenneth J. Roering, eds., Chicago: American Marketing, 251–266.

Newstrom, John W. and William A. Ruch (1975), "The Ethics of Management and the Management of Ethics," *MSU Business Topics,* 23 (Winter), 29–37.

Notz, William W. and Frederick A. Starke (1978), "Final Offer versus Conventional Arbitration as Means of Conflict Management," *Administrative Science Quarterly,* 23 (June), 189–203.

Osborn, Richard N. and James C. Hunt (1974), "Environment and Organizational Effectiveness," *Administrative Science Quarterly,* 19 (June), 231–246.

Ricklefs, Roger (1983a), "Executives and General Public Say Ethical Behavior Is Declining in U.S.," *Wall Street Journal* (October 31), 25.

___ (1983b), "Public Gives Executives Low Marks for Honesty and Ethical Standards," *Wall Street Journal* (November 2), 29.

Sherwin, Douglas S. (1983), "The Ethical Roots of the Business System," *Harvard Business Review,* 61 (November–December), 183–192.

Sutherland, E. and D. R. Cressey (1970), *Principles of Criminology,* 8th ed., Chicago: Lippincott.

Velasquez, Manuel (1982), *Business Ethics,* Englewood Cliffs, NJ: Prentice-Hall.

Weaver, K. Mark and O.C. Ferrell (1977), "The Impact of Corporate Policy on Reported Ethical Beliefs and Behavior of Marketing Practitioners," in *Contemporary Marketing Thought,* Barnett Greenberg and Danny N. Bellenger, eds., Chicago: American Marketing.

Weitz, Barton A. (1981), "Effectiveness in Sales Interactions: A Contingency Framework," *Journal of Marketing,* 45 (Winter), 85–103.

Zaltman, Gerald, Karen LeMasters, and Michael Heffring (1982), *Theory Construction in Marketing,* New York: Wiley.

Zey-Ferrell, Mary and O. C. Ferrell (1982), "Role-Set Configuration and Opportunity as Predictors of Unethical Behavior in Organizations," *Human Relations,* 35 (no. 7), 587–604.

___, K. Mark Weaver, and O. C. Ferrell (1979). "Predicting Unethical Behavior among Marketing Practitioners," *Human Relations,* 32 (no. 7), 557–569.

Ethical and Legal Foundations of Relational Marketing Exchanges

Gregory T. Gundlach and Patrick E. Murphy

Previous study of exchange by marketing scholars has emphasized events and conditions leading to and the outcomes of exchange interaction. However, limited attention has been directed toward the role of ethics and law in exchange. The emerging perspective of relational exchange suggests the importance of these foundations. The authors examine the interrelationship of contract law and ethics for building and sustaining marketing exchanges. They explore dimensions of ethical exchange and offer managerial and research implications.

A recent theme in marketing distinguishes short-term, discrete exchange transactions from exchange involving long-term repetitive interaction with a relational emphasis (i.e., open-ended supplier contracts, franchisor-franchisee arrangements, strategic partnering, and joint ventures). Relational exchanges can facilitate heightened customer satisfaction, lower costs through transaction routinization, and raise barriers to competitive market entry. Examples of this trend are common today:

- Motorola plans to cut substantially the number of outside law firms it retains. In an attempt to obtain higher quality legal services at a lower cost, the company intends to establish and build relationships with only a few primary legal service providers (Pollock 1991).
- Toyota, a leader in production efficiency, is teaming with small American suppliers in an effort to enhance these firms' productivity. Rather than taking their business elsewhere, Toyota is cultivating relationships with the suppliers and teaching them their production know-how. Toyota's commitment to these firms has led to design advances and quality improvements (White 1991).
- American Express is changing from a focus on product marketing to relationship marketing. The firm plans on emphasizing consumer needs to increase loyalty and usage for its green, gold, and platinum cards. Adopting a relationship management model, according to Phillip Riese, AmEx executive vice president, "is the way the customer battle will be won in the 1990s" (McCormack 1992).

GREGORY T. GUNDLACH is Assistant Professor and PATRICK E. MURPHY is Professor, Department of Marketing, College of Business Administration, University of Notre Dame. The authors extend their appreciation to Bob Dwyer, Jule Gassenheimer, Pat Kaufmann, Gene Laczniak, Donald Robin, Joshua Wiener, members of the Department of Marketing at the University of Notre Dame, three anonymous *JM* reviewers, and the editor for their helpful comments.

Gundlach, G.T., Murphy, P. E., (1993), "Ethical and Legal Foundations of Relational Marketing Exchanges," *Journal of Marketing*, 57(4), 35–47.

Beginning with Adler's (1966) conception of symbiotic marketing, scholars have explored the trend toward relational exchange in marketing (Varadarajan and Rajaratnam 1986). In early work on personal selling, Goodman (1971) emphasized the importance of sustaining relationships with customers. Arndt (1979) later noted the tendency of some exchanges to be circumscribed by long-term associations, labeling this phenomenon "domesticated markets." More recently, Dwyer, Schurr, and Oh (1987) extended this concept to include consumer transactions in which key distinctions occur across phases in the development of buyer-seller exchange relationships. In the context of service exchanges, both Lovelock (1983) and Crosby, Evans, and Cowles (1990) highlight the importance of relationship management. Internationally, the Industrial Marketing and Purchasing Group provides a rich characterization of the elements in buyer/seller interactions that foster relational bonds (Hakansson 1982).

For many business exchanges, emphasis on relational exchange has brought about greater communication, coordination, and planning between partners (Frazier, Spekman, and O'Neal 1988; Jackson 1985; Salmond and Spekman 1986; Spekman and Johnston 1986). Within consumer exchanges, marketing strategies such as those utilized by book and record clubs and frequent flyer programs illustrate the benefits of procuring long-term relationships. In the service sector, relationship-building approaches are employed by lawyers, bankers, and physicians, as well as nonprofit organizations. Together, these examples suggest the importance of exchange relationship development and its foundations.

Various legal theories, including contract law, facilitate the process of exchange development. A system of law and enforcement enables parties to plan, negotiate, and consummate their exchanges. Reliance on the law, however, can be costly in terms of both resources and time and may potentially erode buyer-seller interdependence. Empirical evidence indicates that relational exchange participants rely more often on extra-legal governance to maintain their relationships and resolve disputes (Beale and Dugdale 1975; Macaulay 1963). Non-legal alternatives are especially notable in Asian cultures. According to NEC Corporation legal chief Satoshi Nakaichi (Galen, Cunes, and Greising 1992),

> when disputes arise ... attorneys often are the last to get involved. Salesmen and front-line managers are the chief problem-solvers. In part, that's to avoid spoiling a long-term relationship.... [T]he idea is to coexist and win that money back on future deals.

The Japanese *Keiretsu* exemplifies this alternative model of exchange with its admonishment of confrontation as a solution to legal dispute resolution.

Mechanisms of extra-legal governance encompass standards of conduct, including the personal and organizational ethics that each party brings to the exchange. Both can be distinguished from group norms or standards that emanate from the relationship itself. Ethics is the branch of moral philosophy that deals with moral judgments, standards, and rules of conduct. Focus on ethics in exchange has received limited emphasis in marketing: influencing the value received (Bagozzi 1975), potency (Alderson 1957), and utility created (Houston and Gassenheimer 1987).

Our goal is to examine ethics and law as mechanisms for guiding exchange. We initially discuss the perspectives of exchange as a discrete event versus exchange involving long-term interaction. Our attention then turns to the legal and ethical foundations of exchange and the exploration of their interrelationship for governing exchange. Finally, we propose several dimensions of ethical conduct and offer implications for managers and researchers.

Exchange Events to Exchange Relationships

Various marketing scholars have characterized the operational forms of exchange as a continuum anchored by the polar archetypes of discrete and relational exchange. Incorporating work by Williamson (1985), Macneil (1978, 1980) and others (Stinchcombe 1985), Dwyer, Schurr, and Oh (1987) propose that transitions to long-term relationships evolve through five phases: (1) awareness, (2) exploration, (3) expansion, (4) commitment, and (5) dissolution. Jackson (1985) suggests a similar continuum for industrial marketers in her normative discussion of transactional versus relationship marketing. These authors distinguish various exchange elements, including their temporal nature, situational and strategic characteristics, and outcomes.

POLAR ARCHETYPES OF EXCHANGE

Table 1 summarizes these elements along a continuum. A key element regarding the polar exchange forms is the time horizon or duration of the exchange relationship. At its extreme, *transactional* exchange involves single, short-term exchange events encompassing a distinct beginning and ending. Goldberg (1976, p. 49) describes this form as a transaction in which "no duties exist between the parties prior to formation [of the exchange], and in which the duties of the parties are determined completely" up-front. Obtaining emergency medical treatment away from home or stopping at an off-brand gas station when traveling illustrate consumer exchange transactions, whereas true spot markets are examples of organizational exchange transactions.

In contrast, *relational* exchange involves transactions linked together over an extended time frame. These exchanges trace back to previous interactions and reflect an ongoing process. The close, long-term relationships established between certain vendors and their industrial customers, such as those between some automobile manufacturers and their

TABLE 1

Continuum of Exchange

Exchange Elements	Forms of Exchange[1]		
	Transactional	**Contractual**	**Relational**
Temporal Dimensions			
Time horizon	Short	Intermediate to extended	Extended
Nature of transactions	Short duration; transaction has distinct beginning and end	Longer duration; transactions linked together	Longest duration; transactions merged together
Situational/Strategic Characteristics			
Investment	Small	Moderate	Large
Switching costs	Low	Medium	High
Purpose of exchange	Narrow; economic; substance of exchange	Moderate; economic and social elements; creation of longer-term initiatives	Broad; economic and social elements; creation of longer-term initiatives
Strategic emphasis	Low	Moderate	High
Outcomes			
Complexity	Simple offer—acceptance	Increasing complexity	Complex web of operational and social interdependence
Division of benefits and burdens	Distinct, sharp division	Trade-offs and compromise	Blurring as goals converge

[1]Adapted from Dwyer, Schurr, and Oh (1987) and Jackson (1985).

suppliers (e.g., Ford Motor Company and A. O. Smith), exemplify this exchange form. Relationship banking, frequent-stay programs at hotels, and priority acceptance for alumni family members at universities are examples of relational exchanges directed toward consumers.

Within relational exchange, emphasis is placed on purposeful cooperation. Extended planning and the establishment of complex webs of operational and social interdependence occur. Turnbull and Wilson (1989) suggest "structural" and "social" bonding can create substantial barriers to competition. Similar results can happen when strong interpersonal relationships develop between many service providers/professionals and their clients.

CONTRACTUAL EXCHANGE

Table 2 depicts examples of contractual or intermediate exchange forms. The types fall on a continuum with subcategories of true contractual exchanges, which are nearest the

TABLE 2

Examples of Contractual Exchanges

Transactional Exchange	Contractual Exchange	Relational Exchange

—True Contractual Exchange—
   —Interorganizational/Interparty Systems—
      —Transorganizational/Transparty Systems—
         —Joint Ventures—

Contractual Exchange	Description	Examples	
		Business Exchange	Consumer Exchange

True Contractual Exchanges[1]

Contractual Exchange	Description	Business Exchange	Consumer Exchange
Executory bilateral contract	Simple contractual exchange involving a future act or obligation.	Simple vendor contract	Purchase of a home
Sequential contingent contract	A series of contracts linked serially and conditional on one another.	Contractor/ subcontractor relationships	Yearly lawn care services; maid or housekeeping services
Open-ended contract	A contract in which certain terms (e.g., order amount, price, terms of trade) are deliberately left open to be agreed on at a later date.	Open-ended supplier and vendor contracts	Adjustable rate financing contracts for mortgages and credit cards
Interorganizational/ Interparty Systems[2]	Interfirm/party exchange relationship involving traditional (e.g., purchasing, sales, vendors, etc.) boundary spanning linkages and coordination.	Licensing arrangements for trademarks and/or patents; traditional channel relationships; franchisor/franchisee contracts	Consumer financial planners or accountants; legal service and their providers consumer clients
Transorganizational/ Transparty Systems[2]	Interfirm/party coalition composed of a system of interpartner roles and responsibilities organized interfunctionally (e.g., research and development, marketing, production, etc.) and supported by a network of coordination, liaison, and decision-making linkages (Achrol, Scheer, and Stem 1992).	Strategic partnering for research and development, marketing, production and other functional areas	Nursing home care; military and boarding schools; child care services
Joint Ventures	Interfirm/party creation of an autonomous entity, usually organized by function, with or without equity positions by the partners in the entity.	Non-equity arrangements involving research and development, production and marketing; equity sharing arrangements; satellite organizations	Consumer buying cooperatives

[1]Adapted from Goetz and Scott (1981).
[2]Terms denote organizational and consumer exchanges.

transactional end, and joint ventures, which approach the relational archetype. Inter-organizational/interparty and transorganizational/transparty systems of exchange are positioned between these forms. Each is arranged to represent its perceived relative location along the continuum with some latitude of placement.[1] Recognition of these intermediate exchanges supplements perspectives that emphasize the largely hypothetical archetypes.

Legal Foundations of Exchange

For the development of exchange relationships, each party must possess some expectation of its partner's intentions and performance. Without assurance of future conduct, one party's provision of value for the promise of future delivered value by the other likely will not occur. For any exchange, the level of assurance may be assessed directly by contemplating the expected value to be received or indirectly by referring to some facilitating governance mechanism. According to Houston and Gassenheimer (1987, p. 9):

> Party A may believe future receipt is unlikely but the gain received today compensates for value deferred to the future . . . [or] because of past experience or legal or moral strictures, he or she [A] is willing to defer more value into the future.

Most of marketing management emphasizes strategies directed at promoting the evolution of buyer-seller exchange toward the relational archetype (Dwyer, Schurr, and Oh 1987). Indeed, the general premise underlying the marketing concept (i.e., fulfilling customer needs) promotes the development of exchange relationships and future interaction.

CONTRACT LAW AND EXCHANGE RELATIONSHIPS

Contract law applies to the legal rights of exchange parties and guides the planning and conduct of exchange. Largely composed of classic contract doctrine embodied in common law (i.e., case law), it also embraces new legislative enactments bearing on exchange relationships. The latter foundation represents "modern" legal contract and can be found across corporate, insurance, partnership, and commercial law (i.e., Uniform Commercial Code [UCC]).[2]

The classic case law of contract views exchange as composed of single, independent, and static transactions. Precise rules dictate the steps—"offer," "acceptance," and

---

[1]Dwyer, Schurr, and Oh (1987) call for the development of a framework that specifies the differing organizational exchange forms along the continuum from discrete to relational exchange. A variety of authors have discussed exchange in terms of a continuum (Achrol, Scheer, and Stern 1992; Borys and Jemison 1989; Thorelli 1986). Their discussions parallel and are consistent with the array presented in Table 2.

[2]The common law of contract refers to that found in the *Restatement of Contracts* (1932). This treatise is considered to represent traditional concepts of legal contract prevalent during the early 1900s. A more modern interpretation of contract law is found in the *Second Restatement of Contracts* (1981) and the Uniform Commercial Code (1978). These documents reflect concepts of contract law that are currently accepted.

"performance"—reflecting the perceived one-time nature of a singular transaction. Prior dealings are of little consequence in the interpretation of exchange with events not contemplated originally by the parties excluded. These elements mirror the transactional form of exchange (Table 1).

The shortcomings of classic contract law for the facilitation of relational exchange has led researchers to question its contemporary relevance. Macaulay's (1963) early examination of exchange relationships contends that reliance on legalistic strategies lessens the chance of future interaction. He concludes that business people prefer to rely on "a handshake, or common honesty and decency"—even when the transaction is risky (p. 58). Recent studies support Macaulay's findings in the automotive (Frazier and Summers 1984; Whitford 1968) and rail freight industries (Palay 1985) and within supplier exchanges involving complex goods (Beale and Dugdale 1975). The theoretical inconsistency of contract law as a basis for these exchanges has also been noted (Gilmore 1974; Macneil 1980, 1985; Williamson 1991). For one-time transactions (e.g., spot market exchanges and some real estate transactions), classic contract doctrine provides an efficient system of governance. Many long-term exchanges, however, have been likened to marriages or partnerships between buyers and sellers. In these associations, parties often avoid reference to formal contractual rights as a basis for gaining compliance and cooperation.

EXCHANGE AND MODERN CONTRACT LAW

Modern interpretations of contract law, contained within the UCC and other areas of law (e.g., corporate, partnership, etc.), illustrate the law's attempt to deal with the dynamic intercourse of intermediate- and extended-term exchanges. Several adaptations for these exchanges are identified subsequently—i.e., exchange planning and contract formation, adjustments to existing contracts, and resolution of contractual conflicts.

Exchange planning and contract formation. A legal prerequisite to contract formation is an agreement or mutual manifestation of assent (*Cessna Financial Corporation v. Mesilla Valley Flying Service* 1970). Planning for every material term prior to an exchange is difficult, however, because future events may be unknown. Often parties wish to rely on custom, prior dealings, or third parties. Under common law, indefinite contracts are void (Calamari and Perillo 1987). Modern contract law is flexible in its interpretation of assent. Under "gap filler" provisions of the UCC (1978), exchange is allowed when parties reach an agreement, but have not worked out the necessary details:

> Terms not specified by exchange partners may be agreed to and incorporated into their contract even after the contract has been formed (Section 2-204(3)).

> A contract may be concluded even though the price, place of delivery, time of performance or other particulars have not been settled (Section 2-305 through 2-311).

Adjustments to existing contract relationships. Adjustments may be required if one party fails to perform, both parties wish to amend their relationship, or unilateral action necessitates alteration of the original agreement (Macneil 1978). The "doctrine of impossibility" addresses those circumstances in which parties cannot carry out their obligations because of extreme impracticability (e.g., *Portland Section of Council of Jewish Women v. Sisters of Charity* 1983). The common law rule was "Pacta Sunt Servada"— promises must be kept even if impossible to perform (Sharp 1941). More recent interpretation of this doctrine under the UCC covers unforeseen outcomes:

> Delay or non-delivery is not considered a breach when the agreed upon carrier becomes unavailable and a substitute carrier is used (Section 2-614).

> When the contemplated form of payment is impossible, substantially equivalent means of payment is allowed (e.g., countertrade or foreign currency) (Section 2-615).

The "doctrine of mistake" is another method by which parties can amend their obligations (Foulke 1911). Increasingly, this doctrine indicates that the contract can be amended when enforcement would result in an inequitable exchange and little hardship would be imposed through recision (*Da Silva v. Musso* 1981). Some restrictions apply (e.g., unilateral mistakes); however, allowing parties to correct errors promotes fairness and continued interaction.

Resolution of contractual conflict. Under the classic common law "perfect tender rule," buyers could reject goods unless delivery conformed in every respect to the contract (Calamari and Perillo 1987). Modern contract law encourages parties to amicably resolve their differences. The UCC interpretation of this rule attempts to sustain exchange relationships in spite of conflict (White and Summers 1988):

> If a buyer rejects goods delivered in a manner not in accordance with the original agreement, the seller has the right to make a conforming delivery before the contract time expires (Section 2-508(1)).

> Where a buyer fails to perform a purchase obligation, the seller may identify the goods involved in the contract and resell them at a private or public sale (Section 2-704).

DEVELOPMENT OF MORALITY-BASED LEGAL DOCTRINES

For many contractual exchanges, changes found in modern contract law are sufficient to govern conduct and ensure proper performance. However, greater complexities of exchanges closer to the relational archetype suggest a need for guiding mechanisms beyond contract law. Legal scholars have long acknowledged the importance and role of ethical principles for complex exchange relationships (cf. Gottlieb 1983; Macaulay 1963; Macneil 1983, 1986; Shell 1991b). Ethics provide guidance for exchange behavior while affording the flexibility necessary for sustaining relational exchanges. Modern contract law specifically embraces the moral basis of exchange through a variety of doctrines:

- *Doctrine of unconscionability.* Courts can refuse to enforce contracts "so unfair that no honest person would accept" (*Earl of Chesterfield v. Janssen* 1790, at 100). Though not explicitly defined under the UCC, unconscionability is recognized to embrace tenets of fairness, equity, and good faith (Burton 1980).
- *Promissory estoppel.* Reflecting contract law's advancement of moral and ethical ideals, this principle states that a promise made between exchange parties with the expectation of furthering economic interests should be enforced without regard to the stringent formalities of traditional contract law (Shell 1988). This doctrine is "an attempt by the courts to keep (contract) remedies abreast of increased moral consciousness of honesty and fair representation in all business dealings" (*Peoples National Bank of Little Rock v. Linebarger Construction Co.* 1951, 16).
- *Fiduciary standards.* Underlying many commercial exchange relationships (i.e., franchisor-franchisee or agency-client), fiduciary standards require full disclosure and fair treatment regardless of self-interest (Kronman 1978). According to one commentator, the term *fiduciary* reflects an ideal "stricter than the morals of the marketplace" (Shell 1988).

Good faith in contract. The obligation of "good faith" provides a particularly relevant example of the law's embrace of ethical precepts. Courts may impose "implied" duties of good faith both in the negotiation (*Channel Hose Centers, Grace Retail v. Grossman* 1986) and performance (*Empire Gas Corp. v. American Bakeries Co.* 1988) of contractual exchanges. In *Jordan v. Duff and Phelps, Inc.* (1987, p. 438) the court notes:

> One term implied in every written contract and therefore, we suppose every unwritten one, is that neither party will try to take opportunistic advantage of the other.

The duty of good faith has also been extended to certain exchange relationships, (e.g., joint venture partners recognizing fiduciary obligations, *Arnott v. American Oil Co.* 1979). Under the UCC (1978), "[E]very contract or duty within this Act imposes an obligation of good faith in its performance or enforcement" (Section 1-203) and "honesty in fact and the observance of reasonable commercial standards of fair dealing in the trade" (Section 1-201).

Good faith is defined in contract as "fairness" and "fair dealing" (Hillman 1979; Holmes 1978, 1980), "decency" (Farnsworth 1963), and "common ethical sense" (Unger 1976). Reiter (1983, pp. 106–7) describes good faith as "standards of appropriate behavior relevant in the community.... [T]he 'appropriate' range will include the 'very best' behavior, but will also incorporate less virtuous conduct." The development of various doctrines within contract law that embrace ethical principles underscores the importance of ethics in providing a foundation for exchange development.

Ethical Foundations of Exchange

Ethics involves perceptions regarding right or wrong. It requires an individual to behave according to the rules of moral philosophy. In marketing, several scholars (Ferrell and Gresham 1985; Ferrell, Gresham, and Fraedrich 1989; Hunt and Vitell 1986; Robin and Reidenbach 1987; Williams and Murphy 1990) have applied ethical theories including utilitarianism, deontology, and virtue ethics to marketing decision making. Though ethics in the philosophical sense is individually oriented, these authors have adopted the perspective that decision makers operate within a marketing organization and its corporate culture. Various observers outside marketing have also examined the moral basis of exchange. Their common theme suggests that much of the law addressing exchange is drawn from and formalizes moral principles.

EQUALITY IN EXCHANGE

The evolution of exchange can be traced from the Greek and Roman traditions to modern European and American interpretations (Gordley 1981). Most of the early writing on contract law evolved from the thinking of Aristotle, who believed that exchange requires equality as a matter of commutative justice so that neither party is enriched at the other's expense. Aristotle's (Irwin 1985, Book V, 1133b17) notion of exchange, originally expressed in *Nichomachean Ethics,* was: "for there would be no association without exchange, no exchange without equality, no equality without commensurability." Though Aristotle was discussing personal exchanges in pursuit of a virtuous life, these notions seem particularly appropriate, given their implied emphasis on equality, for the development, adjustment, and resolution of conflict in marketing exchanges. Contemporary analysis of fair or just exchanges postulates that parties to a fair exchange are equal in terms of need (Cordero 1988). Participants may not be equal in wealth, intelligence, experience, or moral goodness, but if they are equally interested in obtaining something the other has, mutually advantageous exchange will occur. Furthermore, a recent essay on this topic (Koehn 1992, p. 341) argues that "the practice of exchange properly understood reveals itself to be inherently, ethically good."

THE PROMISE PRINCIPLE

Legal scholars (Atiyah 1981, Fried 1981) have undertaken an in-depth examination of ethics' relationship to law in the exchange context. They view exchange from the Kantian perspective, which interprets contract law as promise based. This "promise principle" provides the moral basis for contract law. Individuals can voluntarily impose obligations on themselves under which they can choose to join together for mutual advantage. Trust is one tool through which people can cooperate with others to actively serve one another's purposes, and promising is thought to be the best vehicle for generating trust (Harris 1983). Both contract and exchange are rooted in promise keeping (Fried 1981). Therefore, parties planning an exchange seem to rely more on promises made to each other than legal principles in forming their relationship with adjustments or conflict handled similarly.

Promises should be binding per se to better understand the underlying law of contracts (Atiyah 1981). Promissory obligations are a refutation of utilitarian philosophical thinking (greatest good for greatest number) because individuals would not break a promise to create greater happiness. The obligation to "keep a promise" is a classic example of a duty emanating from principle-based ethical theory. The promise principle rejects the classical model of contract as not reflecting contemporary law or legal values. Following this approach, marketers would be morally obligated to deliver on their promises whether or not they were legally binding.

MORALITY OF DUTY AND ASPIRATION

Fuller (1969) proposed a dichotomy of moralities, arising out of exchange. The morality of duty, characterized by "thou shalt nots," specifies minimum standards of conduct. Grounded in the Ten Commandments, it condemns people for failing to respect the basic moral rules governing individuals and societies. Under the morality of duty, penalties take precedence over rewards. Its application places a negative burden on exchange parties to follow the rules and to not do harm knowingly to one another (Drucker 1974).

The morality of aspiration is characterized by "thou shalts"—exhortations to realize one's fullest potential—and exemplifies the Greek philosophy of Aristotle and Plato (Fuller 1969). Its orientation reflects the top of human achievement, in which proper conduct and functioning at one's best exists. It represents the fullest realization of the good life. Rewards and praise, not punishment and disapproval (i.e., morality of duty), play a central role. For exchange, application of the morality of aspiration would include recognition awards for suppliers who meet planned goals, forgiving errors made by an exchange partner, and the amicable resolution of conflict.

The Interrelationship of Law and Ethics in Exchange

Figure 1 depicts a conceptualization of the relative significance of ethical and contract law principles for guiding relationships across the continuum of exchange. The horizontal axis contains our three delineated exchange forms—transactional, contractual, and relational (Table 2). The vertical axis shows the *significance* of contract law and ethics as one moves from left to right on this continuum. The arrows illustrate the increasing impact and importance of ethics and the declining significance of contract law as one moves toward relational exchange.

FIGURE 1

Interrelationship of Contract Law and Ethics Across Exchange Forms

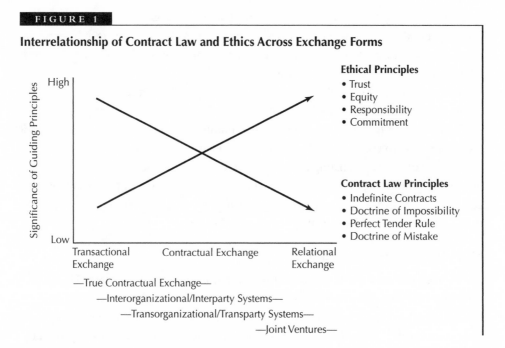

GUIDING PRINCIPLES ACROSS THE CONTINUUM OF EXCHANGE

Transactional exchange. Because this exchange involves short-term and infrequent inter-action, principles guiding it are predominantly legal. Classic contract law is supportive of these exchanges. The simultaneous transfer of goods within transactional exchanges mirrors contract law's view of exchange. Formal terms of the contract supersede less formal ones, and precise rules of construction guide the transaction. We do not imply that ethics are unimportant, but they are less significant than in other forms of ex-change (cf. Baumol and Blackman 1991). This fact stems from their simple and direct nature. Transactional exchanges are readily subsumed in contract law's "offer," "accep-tance," and "performance" criteria. If parties forthrightly discharge their duties, they have met the necessary prerequisites for completing the exchange. In fact, deviation from these steps or cultivation of the exchange beyond its transactional nature may not be desirable to the parties involved. From an ethical perspective, each party should follow Fuller's (1969) morality of duty and Drucker's (1974) responsibility to "not knowingly do harm." Though transactional exchanges can sometimes be characterized by relatively high prices because of their spot nature, the exchange is ethical if it is straightforward.

Contractual exchange. Both legal and ethical principles play a significant role in con-tractual exchange (Figure 1). Though the contract between the exchange parties spells out legal conditions, more than just a binding legal agreement is present. For reasons cited previously, many aspects of these exchanges are not reducible to contractual terms. Moreover, strict reliance on the contract itself for enforcement may impact negatively other aspects of these exchanges. Exchanges identified in Table 2 involve obligations with complex duties. In this sense, doctrines found in contemporary contract law support contractual exchange. Modern contract law is somewhat flexible in its interpretation of exchange relationships, as illustrated by its adaptations for contract planning and formation, adjustments to existing contracts, and resolution of contracts. For this form of exchange to work efficiently, however, more than just principles of modern contract law are required. Ethical precepts, such as trust, appear especially important for guiding these relationships through areas not addressed in the formal contract. Evidence of this position is found in contract law's embrace of ethical principles and morality-based doctrines cited previously (e.g., good faith, unconscionability, etc.).

Relational exchange. The significance of ethical principles for exchange conduct occurs most prominently in relational exchanges. Their long-term, complex nature requires administrative mechanisms not found in contract law. Though a contract may exist, these relationships endure for reasons beyond reliance on the law. For these exchanges to work and merit continuance, exchange parties must rely on principles that address all aspects of the exchange relationship. Such a mode must also be resilient to change and evolution of the exchange association. Contract law, even its most contemporary legacy, fails these criteria. Following ethical principles allows administration of exchange relationships in ways that depend on mutual respect and honor for one another's word. The moral foundations of exchange transcend differing circumstances, parties, and occasions. Perhaps more so than contract law, tenets of moral philosophy are known and understood. In addition, these basic principles do not change as do interpretations of contract law.

Ethical principles called for in relational exchanges closely approximate Fuller's (1969) "moralities of aspiration." That is, partners must work together to achieve their mutual goals and conduct themselves in an ethical manner. The spirit rather than the letter of the law should serve to guide the relationship. Only in this way can the benefits of these exchanges be obtained by both parties and their association endure. Literature in industrial and consumer marketing indicates that more emphasis is currently being placed on collaboration and cooperation rather than hard-nosed negotiation in buyer-seller interactions (Dion and Banting 1988; Kapron 1991; Perdue, Day, and Michaels 1986). Brought about by maturing markets, escalating costs of attracting new customers, rising global competition, and more complex exchanges, many firms are placing a premium on building strong, durable relationships with their customers. The growing use of single sourcing, companies and suppliers working closely together to achieve global competitiveness, and consumer and business marketers' embrace of relationship marketing are trends that seem to suggest an increasing emphasis on highly ethical relationships.

Focusing on these exchanges in the future mandates concern for incorporation of morally based principles by exchange partners.

Dimensions of Ethical Exchange

The limiting role of contract law suggests the importance of ethics as a foundation for exchange development. The adoption of morality-based doctrines in contract law indicates that ethical precepts are increasingly central for consummating exchanges. Trust, equity, responsibility, and commitment are required for fair and open exchanges to occur.

TRUST

The variable most universally accepted as a basis for any human interaction or exchange is trust—a faith or confidence that the other party will fulfill obligations set forth in an exchange. Trust means taking another's word as fact and reducing the likelihood that the other party will act opportunistically (Bradach and Eccles 1989). Zaltman and Moorman (1988) define trust as a three-stage process: an interpersonal or interorganizational state that reflects the extent to which the parties can predict one another's behavior; a dependence on one another when it counts; and a faith that the other will continue to act in a responsive manner despite an uncertain future (p. 17).

Trust is a salient factor in influencing interpersonal, group, and organizational dynamics (Gambetta 1988; Golembiewski and McConkie 1975). As part of a self-heightening cycle (i.e., trusting behavior begets trusting behavior), trust influences a range of relevant exchange variables: communication and feedback, problem solving, effective delegation, and the acceptance of common goals and sharing of responsibility. Mutual trust can assist parties with conflicting interests and is a prerequisite for coordination and collaboration leading to relational exchange (Pruitt 1981). Schurr and Ozanne (1985) conclude that high trust causes more favorable attitudes regarding loyalty than low trust. Trust is influenced by experience and attributions of trustworthiness (Swan and Nolan 1985; Swan, Trawick, and Silva 1985). Furthermore, personal attributes (dependable, honest/candid, competent, customer orientation, and likable/friendly) contribute to feelings of trust. The importance of bilateral trust in developing and maintaining relationships has been affirmed (Moorman, Zaltman, and Deshpande 1992; Zaltman and Moorman 1988). Trust's pervasive nature suggests its importance as an essential foundation for creating relational exchange.

EQUITY

A second critical dimension for building relational exchange is equity. The notion of equity or fairness is widely recognized as essential for mutually satisfying exchanges and is tied to the concept of distributive justice (Cook and Messick 1983; Jasso 1980;

Messick and Sentis 1979). Perceived equity is dependent on an individual's assessment of the value and relevance of participants' inputs and outcomes (Walster, Walster, and Berscheid 1973). Equity leads to forthright negotiations concerning exchange details and the development of conditions enhancing the establishment of relational exchanges. It tends to be the guiding principle when economic productivity is a goal of a cooperative venture (Deutsch 1975). Fairness dominates satisfaction judgments in exchange whereas future intentions are primarily a function of prior perceptions (Oliver and Swan 1989). Lack of equity can stimulate retaliatory acts (e.g., lawsuits and lobbying for increased regulation) by some exchange parties. A recent study of slotting allowance practices and minority matching policies indicates that perceptions of inequity can lead to reduced satisfaction and trust in exchange relationships (Smith 1990). Fair exchanges are those that transcend legal mandates. Exchange participants striving to build relationships should rely on equity as a cornerstone.

RESPONSIBILITY

Responsibility implies an obligation, which is the manifestation of individual ethical duties. It is the link between the manager, his or her position, and the organization. The essence of managing means taking responsibility for one's actions. Three types of responsibility are identified—role, causal, and capacity (Toffler 1986). Role responsibilities refer to the activities and obligations specified by one's formal role. Causal responsibility states simply that if one has caused a problem or harm, he or she has the ethical responsibility to correct it. Capacity responsibility implies that one has a responsibility to deal with a situation if one has the capability to do so.

Four managerial responsibilities—leadership, delegation, communication, and motivation—are essential for enacting ethical exchange policies (Murphy 1988). These responsibilities tie classic managerial duties to ethical policies. Furthermore, these responsibilities can be linked to the morality of duty (negative rules and sanctions) and aspiration (positive factors such as open communication, trust in delegation, and empathetic motivation) notions for the marketing manager.

COMMITMENT

For an exchange to occur, participants must be committed. Characteristics of a commitment are thought to be stability, sacrifice, and loyalty. Commitment is applicable to both interorganizational (O'Reilly and Chatman 1986) and interpersonal (Burgess and Huston 1979) exchange. Commitment should go beyond a strictly utilitarian evaluation of the situation's costs and benefits. As conflict and negotiation accompany exchange, commitment to working out differences is essential. The work of Williamson (1983), who uses "the term commitment to be reserved to describe exchange," can be directly applied to our legal and ethical perspective. In addition, his notion of "credible commitments" closely align with the ethical precepts discussed here. Unless trust, equity, and responsibility are apparent, commitment by an exchange party lacks credibility.

Commitment may also be employed to describe a phase of exchange relationship development (Dwyer, Schurr, and Oh 1987). Commitment refers to an implicit or explicit pledge of relational continuity between exchange partners. It is a function of each side's perception of the other's commitment, "pledges" made by each, and factors such as communication levels (Anderson and Weitz 1992). Commitment deepens when bilateral communication is the norm and both sides are willing to assume risk in a relationship.

Trust, equity, responsibility, and commitment are important for the development of relational marketing exchanges. Each guides the conduct of exchange between parties who desire more relational interaction or anticipate establishing an enduring relationship. One rationale for relying on these characteristics is the notion of "enlightened self-interest" advanced by Adam Smith. Self-interest refers to self-love/selfish interests or simply designating those interests with which one is most intimately concerned. Some observers believe that enlightened self-interest, perhaps more than anything else, justifies ethical exchange behavior. One researcher has argued that self-interest is not necessarily based on selfishness—"For Smith, then, a rational person is prudent, cooperative and fair, both naturally and because it is to her advantage to be so" (Werhane 1989, p. 680).[3] This perspective seems especially compatible with the characteristics noted here.

Implications for Managers and Researchers

Several implications can be drawn from our examination of the ethical and legal foundations of exchange. For marketing managers, they pertain to the increasing emphasis on relationship marketing and the promotion of ethical managerial practices. For academic researchers, implications include questions for further inquiry and avenues for future research.

Some predict that many future exchanges will be conducted in close, extended relations (Salmond and Spekman 1986). A number of organizations already are encouraging the cultivation of long-term relational exchanges. In Europe, "relationship managers" oversee exchanges with key customers (Ford 1980). In the U.S., Nestle and Baxter International encourage long-term relationships through sales force incentives to stay in the same territory (with the same customers) for longer periods (Schellhardt 1991). These examples and those offered in the introduction of this article (Motorola, Toyota, and American Express) highlight current relationship marketing efforts by firms.

---

[3]For more detail on the ethical component of Adam Smith's works and classical economics, see Dixon (1982).

In some instances, the development of relational exchanges may not provide results compatible with the mission and strategies of an organization. Spot market or transactional exchanges represent a viable and needed form of business for some commodities and goods. Moreover, the use of and strict reliance on formal contracts remains an accepted and essential practice. For these exchanges, ethical principles, though not paramount, still provide a necessary foundation for the transaction. Without moral principles to guide conduct, even the simplest of exchanges risks failure.

Beyond exchange relationships, a potential concern for relational exchange is an anticompetitive outcome. Though relational exchanges can enhance the individual efficiency of participants, anticompetitive results in terms of aggregate social costs also can occur. Relational exchange can facilitate the creation of cartels (Posner 1976) and elevate entry barriers to an anticompetitive level (Williamson 1979). Less persuasive arguments have also been advanced relative to excessive product differentiation (Comanor 1968) and the negative effect of relational exchange on industry dynamics (Goldberg 1979). Relational interaction can serve as a basis for collusion in restraint of trade, especially among rivals. Sharing of information and other proprietary property between exchange parties also can raise implications for innovations and related advances (i.e., trademark and copyright). However, recent case law and enforcement initiatives by the U.S. Department of Justice and the Federal Trade Commission suggest that concern for the anticompetitive effects of relational exchange in vertical relationships is not paramount. Consistent with policy articulated in the 1970s, neither agency has devoted substantial resources to this area. Current case law parallels this trend (Ornstein 1989; Steuer 1989).

ETHICAL MANAGERIAL PRACTICES

We offer several avenues for firms desiring to use ethical principles for guidance and marketers who wish to move toward more relational exchanges. The organization should go beyond the existence of an ethical code or public proclamations by the chief executive officer on ethics. Specific proposals include the following:

- *Creating an ethical corporate culture*—A long-term objective in building primarily relational exchanges is to create a culture that reinforces ethical behavior. Through a system of rewards and open communication, a company can foster a culture in which employees know they will be rewarded for doing the right thing. The Business Roundtable (Keogh 1988) discusses such programs at companies like Xerox, Boeing, and Hewlett-Packard. The purpose of this approach is to create a climate in which ethics is a hallmark of the firm.
- *Instituting ethics training programs*—Such programs should sensitize salespeople, purchasing personnel, and other marketing department employees to their ethical

duties. As Browning and Zabriskie (1983) point out, these programs are needed for both new and experienced personnel. The purpose of the training programs should be to place emphasis on collaborative and trustworthy relationships rather than competition and suspicion. Furthermore, Goolsby and Hunt (1992, p. 65) advocate a specific focus—"marketers who want to encourage a corporate culture embodying high ethical values may want to emphasize cognitive moral development in training programs."

- *Conducting an ethical audit*—An ethical audit is similar to the social audit suggested by Kizilbash and his coauthors (1979). A series of questions can be developed to ensure that ethical guidelines are being carried out. They can serve as a basis for evaluating a firm's ethical standing. Such an audit would be useful for a firm with high ethical standards, such as Johnson & Johnson, to use in evaluating a new supplier or dealing with a firm without an explicit credo or code of conduct (Williams and Murphy 1990). The purpose of an ethical audit is to ensure that ethically relevant questions are being asked so that truly relational exchanges can be fostered.

ACADEMIC RESEARCH DIRECTIONS

For researchers examining law and ethics in exchange, several implications are apparent. Research that investigates issues central to the propositions advanced here is needed. These fall into four areas:

- *Examination of ethics across exchange types*—Several questions need further study, for example, what role do ethical considerations play in advancing relationships from transactional toward relational exchanges? How do individual ethical considerations differ from group-generated norms such as solidarity and reciprocity (Nooteboom 1992)? How do these differing mechanisms of governance work together within exchange relationships? Are there differences in the level of ethical values present across differing exchange forms? What specific ethical values are important in establishing trust, commitment, and solidarity of association in exchange relationships? Research examining these issues should consider the use of longitudinal analysis and ideally be conducted across several different types of organizational and consumer exchanges in order to track the changing nature and impact of these values.

- *Operationalization of ethical dimensions*—Measures are available in the literature to operationalize the dimensions of ethical exchange proposed as central to moving toward the relational form. For example, Swan and others have developed a scale to measure trust (Swan, Trawick, and Silva 1985; Swan et al. 1988; Moorman, Zaltman, and Deshpande 1992); Anderson and Weitz (1992) have undertaken a similar process for commitment; and the work of Oliver and Swan (1989) in equity contains viable operationalizations. The next step is to refine these measures and utilize them together. The area of responsibility needs measurement development. Specifically, role, causal, and capacity responsibilities must be clearly defined.

- *Analysis of functional areas*—Functional areas in marketing, such as advertising and personal selling, could benefit from similar ethical and legal analysis as provided here. For example, ethical implications surrounding deception in advertising and bad faith in negotiations could be fruitfully explored. Interestingly, a review of the case law that addresses bargaining and negotiation indicates the law has become infused with ethical standards and norms of conduct (Shell 1991a, 1991b). In this respect, legal scholars have suggested "a new standard of business ethics" has resulted in the shift of legal doctrines related to nondisclosure in recent years (Keeton et al. 1984). Research that focuses on the interplay of ethics and law prior to an exchange or development of a relationship was not explored here and is a needed area of inquiry.

- *Investigation of international exchange*—Cross-cultural studies investigating the preceding issues are also required. What ethical values are associated with exchange development in other societies, such as those in Japan and Eastern Europe? Which ethical dimensions (e.g., trust, equity, responsibility, commitment) are most important in different cultures? Can researchers use similar instruments and scales to study global legal and ethical questions?

Answers to these questions can prove invaluable in understanding and enhancing exchange associations. Research by Hunt, Wood, and Chonko (1989) suggests that corporate ethical values are important for establishing intrafirm commitment by marketers. Companies that promote high ethical values also appear to increase the commitment of their marketing employees. These findings can also apply for exchange relationships. Reinforcing ethical behavior is important for improving performance and achieving success in the marketplace.

Conclusion

Several conclusions can be drawn from this article. First, an understanding of the legal and ethical foundations underlying exchange is essential to the development of exchange relationships. Second, analyses of both foundations of exchange highlight the growing significance of ethical principles as one moves across the exchange continuum. Third, implications for marketers interested in moving toward more relational exchanges are that greater emphasis should be placed on implementing ethical considerations into their firms' decision making. Building trust, establishing equity, developing responsibility, and solidifying commitment appear to be important exchange dimensions. Finally, future academic researchers might study ethical versus legal considerations, operationalization of relevant variables, analysis of functional marketing issues, and cross-cultural exchange.

References

Achrol, Ravi, Lisa K. Scheer, and Louis W. Stern (1992), "Designing Successful Transorganizational Marketing Alliances," Marketing Science Institute, Manuscript #92–101.

Adler, Lee (1966), "Symbiotic Marketing," *Harvard Business Review,* 44 (November–December), 59–71.

Alderson, Wroe (1957), *Marketing Behavior and Executive Action.* Homewood, IL: Richard D. Irwin, Inc.

Anderson, Erin and Barton Weitz (1992), "The Use of Pledges to Build and Sustain Commitment in Distribution Channels," *Journal of Marketing Research,* 29 (February), 18–34.

Arndt, Johan (1979), "Toward a Concept of Domesticated Markets," *Journal of Marketing,* 43 (Fall), 69–75.

Arnott v. American Oil Company (1979), 609 F. 2d 873.

Atiyah, P.S. (1981), *Promises, Morals, and Law.* Oxford: Clarendon Press.

Bagozzi, Richard P. (1975), "Marketing as Exchange," *Journal of Marketing,* 39 (October), 32–39.

Baumol, William J. and Sue Anne Batey Blackman (1991), *Perfect Markets and Easy Virtue.* Cambridge, MA: Blackwell Publications.

Beale, Hugh and Tony Dugdale (1975), "Contracts Between Businessmen: Planning and the Use of Contractual Remedies," *British Journal of Law and Society,* 2, 45–60.

Borys, Bryan and David B. Jemison (1989), "Hybrid Arrangements as Strategic Alliances: Theoretical Issues in Organizational Combinations," *Academy of Management Review,* 14 (2), 239–49.

Bradach, Jeffrey L. and Robert G. Eccles (1989), "Price, Authority, and Trust: From Ideal Types to Plural Forms," *Annual Review of Sociology,* 15, 97–118.

Browning, John and Noel B. Zabriskie (1983), "How Ethical Are Industrial Buyers," *Industrial Marketing Management,* 12 (October), 219–24.

Burgess, Robert L. and Ted L. Huston (1979), eds., *Social Exchange in Developing Relationships.* New York: Academic Press.

Burton, Steven J. (1980), "Breach of Contract and the Company Law Duty of Good Faith," *Harvard Law Review,* 94, 369–404.

Calamari, John D. and Joseph M. Perillo (1987), *Contracts.* St. Paul, MN: West Publishing.

Cessna Financial Corporations v. Mesilla Valley Flying Services (1969), 462 P. 2d 144, cert. denied 397 U.S. 1076, (1970).

Channel Hose Centers, Grace Retail v. Grossman (1986), 795, F. 2d 291.

Comanor, William S. (1968), "Vertical and Territorial Restrictions: White Motors and its Aftermath," *Harvard Law Review,* 81, 1419–38.

Cook, Karen S. and David M. Messick (1983), "Psychological and Sociological Perspectives on Distributive Justice: Convergent, Divergent, and Parallel Lines," in *Equity Theory: Psychological and Sociological Perspectives,* David M. Messick and Karen S. Cook, eds. New York: Praeger Publishers, 1–12.

Cordero, Ronald A. (1988), "Aristotle and Fair Deals," *Journal of Business Ethics,* 7 (September), 681–90.

Crosby, Lawrence A., Kenneth R. Evans and Deborah Cowles (1990), "Relationship Quality in Services Selling; An Interpersonal Influence Perspective," *Journal of Marketing,* 54 (July), 68–81.

Da Silva v. Musso (1981), 428 N.E. 2d 382.

Deutsch, Morton (1975), "Equity, Equality, and Need: What Determines Which Value Will Be Used as the Basis of Distributive Justice?" *Journal of Social Issues,* 31 (3), 137–49.

Dion, Paul A. and Peter M. Banting (1988), "Industrial Supplier-Buyer Negotiations," *Industrial Marketing Management,* 17 (February), 43–47.

Dixon, D.F. (1982), "The Ethical Component of Marketing: An Eighteenth-Century View," *Journal of Macromarketing,* 2 (Spring), 38–46.

Drucker, Peter (1974), *Management: Tasks, Responsibilities and Practice.* New York: Harper & Row.

Dwyer, F. Robert, Paul H. Schurr, and Sejo Oh (1987), "Developing Buyer-Seller Relationships," *Journal of Marketing,* 51 (April), 11–27.

Earl of Chesterfield v. Janssen (1790), 28 English Reports 82.

Empire Gas Corporation v. American Bakeries Company (1988), 840 F. 2d 1333.

Farnsworth, E. Allan (1963), "Good Faith Performance and Commercial Reasonableness Under the Uniform Commercial Code," *University of Chicago Law Review,* 30, 666–79.

Ferrell, O.C. and Larry Gresham (1985), "A Contingency Framework for Understanding Ethical Decision Making in Marketing," *Journal of Marketing,* 49 (Summer), 87–96.

___, ___, and John Fraedrich (1989), "A Synthesis of Ethical Decision Models for Marketing," *Journal of Macromarketing,* 9 (Fall), 55–64.

Ford, David (1980), "The Development of Buyer-Seller Relationships in Industrial Markets," *European Journal of Marketing,* 19 (5/6), 339–53.

Foulke, Ronald R. (1911), "Mistake in Formation and Performance of Contract," *Columbia Law Review,* 11, 197–230.

Frazier, Gary L., Robert E. Spekman, and Charles R. O'Neal (1988), "Just-In-Time Exchange Relationships in Industrial Markets," *Journal of Marketing,* 52 (October), 52–67.

___ and John O. Summers (1984), "Interfirm Influence Strategies and Their Application Within Distribution Channels," *Journal of Marketing,* 48 (Summer), 43–55.

Fried, Charles (1981), *Contract as Promise: A Theory of Contractual Obligation.* Cambridge, MA: Harvard University Press.

Fuller, Lon L. (1969), *The Morality of Law,* revised edition. New Haven, CT: Yale University Press.

Galen, Michele, Alice Cunes, and David Greising (1992), "Guilty! Too Many Lawyers and Too Much Litigation: Here's a Better Way," *Business Week* (April 13), 60–66.

Gambetta, D. (1988), "Can We Trust Trust?" in *Trust: Making and Breaking Cooperative Relations,* D. Gambetta, ed. New York: Blackwell Publications.

Gilmore, Grant (1974), *The Death of Contract.* Columbus, OH: Ohio State University Press.

Goetz, Charles J. and Robert E. Scott (1981), "Principles of Relational Contracts," *Virginia Law Review,* 67 (6), 1089–150.

Goldberg, Victor P. (1976), "Toward an Expanded Economic Theory of Contract," *Journal of Economic Issues,* 10 (March), 45–61.

___ (1979), "The Law and Economics of Vertical Restrictions: A Relational Perspective," *Texas Law Review,* 58, 19–129.

Golembiewski, Robert T. and Mark McConkie (1975), "The Centrality of Interpersonal Trust in Group Processes," in *Theories of Group Processes,* Cary L. Cooper, ed. London: John Wiley & Sons, 131–85.

Goodman, Charles Schaffer (1971), *Management of the Personal Selling Function.* New York: Holt, Rinehart, & Winston.

Goolsby, Jerry R. and Shelby D. Hunt (1992), "Cognitive Moral Development and Marketing," *Journal of Marketing,* 56 (January), 55–68.

Gordley, James (1981), "Equality in Exchange," *California Law Review,* 69 (December), 1587–656.

Gottlieb, Gidon (1983), "Relationalism: Legal Theory for a Relational Society," *The University of Chicago Law Review,* 50, 567–612.

Hakansson, H., ed. (1982), *International Marketing and Purchasing of Industrial Goods: An Interaction Approach.* Ann Arbor, MI: Books on Demand.

Harris, Donald (1983), "A Review Article Based on Contract as Promise," *International Review of Law and Economics,* 3, 69–77.

Hillman, Robert A. (1979), "Policing Contract Modifications Under the Uniform Commercial Code: Good Faith and the Doctrine of Economic Duress," *Iowa Law Review,* 64, 849–902.

Holmes, Eric M. (1980), "Is There Life After Gilmore's Death of Contract?—Inductions From A Study of Commercial Good Faith in First Party Insurance Contracts," *Cornell Law Review,* 65, 330–89.

___ (1978), "A Contextual Study of Commercial Good Faith: Good-Faith Disclosure in Contract Formation," *University of Pittsburgh Law Review,* 39, 381–452.

Houston, Franklin S. and Jule B. Gassenheimer (1987), "Marketing and Exchange," *Journal of Marketing,* 41 (October), 3–18.

Hunt, Shelby D. and S. Vitell (1986), "A General Theory of Marketing Ethics," *Journal of Macromarketing,* 6 (Spring), 5–16.

___,Van R. Wood, and Lawrence B. Chonko (1989), "Corporate Ethical Values and Organizational Commitment in Marketing," *Journal of Marketing,* 53 (July), 79–90.

Irwin, Terence, transl. (1985), Aristotle's *Nicomachean Ethics.* Indianapolis: Hackett.

Jackson, Barbara B. (1985), *Winning and Keeping Industrial Customers: The Dynamics of Customer Relationships.* New York: The Free Press.

Jasso, Guilermina (1980), "A New Theory of Distributive Justice," *American Sociological Review,* 45 (February), 3–32.

Jordan v. Duff and Phelps, Inc. (1987), 815 F. 2d 429.

Kapron, Jill Reynaud (1991), "Encouraging Cooperative Behavior in Channels of Distributions: A Social Motives Perspective," in *Enhancing Knowledge Development in Marketing,* Mary C. Gilly et al., eds. Chicago: American Marketing Association, 260–68.

Keeton, W.P., D.B. Dubbs, R.E. Keeton, and D.G. Owen (1984), *Prosser and Keeton on the Law of Torts.* St. Paul, MN: West.

Keogh, James, ed., (1988), *Corporate Ethics: A Prime Business Asset.* New York: Business Roundtable.

Kizilbash, A.H., William O. Hancock, Carlton A. Maile, and Peter Gillett (1979), "Social Auditing for Marketing Managers," *Industrial Marketing Management,* 8 (February), 1–6.

Koehn, Daryl (1992), "Toward an Ethic of Exchange," *Business Ethics Quarterly,* 2 (July), 341–55.

Kronman (1978), "Mistake, Disclosure, Information and the Law of Contracts," *Journal of Legal Studies,* 7 (1), 1–34.

Lovelock, Christopher H. (1983), "Classifying Services to Gain Strategic Marketing Insights," *Journal of Marketing,* 47 (Summer), 9–20.

Macaulay, Stewart (1963), "Non-Contractual Relations in Business: A Preliminary Study," *American Sociological Review,* 28, 55–69.

Macneil, Ian R. (1986), "Exchange Revisited: Individual Utility and Social Solidarity," *Ethics,* 96, 567–593.

___ (1985), "Relational Contract: What We Do and Do Not Know," *Wisconsin Law Review,* 483–525.

___ (1983), "Values in Contract: Internal and External," *Northwestern University Law Review,* 78, 340–418.

___ (1980), *The New Social Contract: An Inquiry into Modern Contractual Relations.* New Haven, CT: Yale University Press.

___ (1978), "Contracts: Adjustment of Long-Term Economic Relations Under Classical, Neoclassical, and Relational Contract Law," *Northwestern Law Review,* 72, 854–905.

McCormack, Kevin (1992), "AMEX Builds Its Relationships," *Adweek* (June 8), 10.

Messick, David M. and Keith P. Sends (1979), "Fairness and Preference," *Journal of Experimental Social Psychology,* 15 (July), 418–34.

Moorman, Christine, Gerald Zaltman, and Rohit Deshpande (1992), "Relationships Between Providers and Users of Market Research: The Dynamics of Trust Within and Between Organizations," *Journal of Marketing Research,* 29 (August), 314–28.

Murphy, Patrick E. (1988), "Implementing Business Ethics," *Journal of Business Ethics,* 7 (December) 907–15.

Nooteboom, Bart (1992), "Marketing, Reciprocity and Ethics," *Journal of Business Ethics* 1 (April), 110–116.

Oliver, Richard L. and John E. Swan (1989), "Consumer Perceptions of Interpersonal Equity and Satisfaction in Transactions: A Field Survey Approach," *Journal of Marketing,* 53 (April), 21–35.

O'Reilly, Charles and Jennifer Chatman (1986), "Organizational Commitment and Psychological Attachment: The Effects of Compliance, Identification, and Internationalization on Prosocial Behavior," *Journal of Applied Psychology,* 72 (3), 492–9.

Ornstein, Stanley I. (1989), "Exclusive Dealing of Antitrust," *The Antitrust Bulletin,* (Spring) 65–98.

Palay, Thomas M. (1985), "Avoiding Regulatory Constraints: Contracting Safeguards and the Role of Informal Agreements," *Journal of Law, Economics and Organization,* 1 (1), 155–175.

Peoples National Bank of Little Rock v. Linebarger Construction Co. (1951), 240 S.W. 2d 12.

Perdue, B.C., R.L. Day, and R.E. Michaels (1986), "Negotiation Styles of Industrial Buyers," *Industrial Marketing Management,* 15 (August), 171–6.

Pollock, Ellen Joan (1991), "Corporations Scale Back Use of Outside Counsel," *Wall Street Journal* (October 15), B1.

Portland Section of Council of Jewish Women v. Sisters of Charity (1983), 513 P. 2d 1183.

Posner, Richard A. (1976), *Antitrust Law: An Economic Perspective.* Chicago: University of Chicago Press.

Pruitt, Dean G. (1981), *Negotiation Behavior.* New York: Academic Press.

Reiter, B. J. (1983), "Good Faith in Contracts," *Valparaiso University Law Review,* 17, 705–34.

Restatement of Contracts, Second (1981), American Law Institute.

Restatements of Contracts (1932), American Law Institute.

Robin, D.P. and E.E. Reidenbach (1987), "Social Responsibility, Ethics, and Marketing Strategy: Closing the Gap Between Concept and Application," *Journal of Marketing,* 51 (January), 44–58.

Salmond, Deborah and Robert Spekman (1986), "Collaboration as a Mode of Managing Long-Term Buyer-Seller Relationships," in *Proceedings of the 1986 AMA Educators' Conference,* Terence A. Shimp and George John, eds. Chicago: American Marketing Association, 162–6.

Schellhardt, Timothy D. (1991), "Moving Up May Not Mean Moving Around as Much," *Wall Street Journal* (October 4) B1.

Schurr, Paul H. and Julie L. Ozanne (1985), "Influences on Exchange Processes: Buyers' Preconceptions of a Seller's Trustworthiness and Bargaining Toughness," *Journal of Consumer Research,* 11 (March), 939–53.

Sharp, Malcolm P. (1941), "Pacta Sunt Servada," *Columbia Law Review,* 41, 783–98.

Shell, G. Richard (1991a), Opportunism and Trust in the Negotiation of Commercial Contracts: Toward a New Cause of Action," *Vanderbilt Law Review,* 44 (2), 221–82.

___ (1991b), "When Is It Legal to Lie in Negotiations," *Sloan Management Review,* 90 (Spring), 93–101.

___ (1988), "Substituting Ethical Standards for Common Law Rules in Commercial Cases: An Emerging Statutory Trend," *Northwestern University Law Review* 82, 1198–254.

Smith, Kelly L. (1990), "An Equity Theory Approach to Examining the Effects of Unethical Practices in Marketing Channels," in *Proceedings of the 1990 AMA Summer Educators Conference,* William Bearden and A. Parasuraman, eds. Chicago: American Marketing Association, 380–385.

Spekman, Robert and Wesley Johnston (1986), "Relationship Management: Managing the Selling and Buying Interface," *Journal of Business Research,* 14 (December), 519–33.

Steuer, Richard M. (1989), "Clarity and Confusion in Vertical Restraints," *Antitrust Law Journal,* 58, 421–32.

Stinchcombe, A.L. (1985), "Contracts as Hierarchical Documents,'' in *Organizational Theory and Project Management,* A.L. Stinchcombe and C.A. Heiner, eds. London: Oxford University Press, 121–70.

Swan, John E. and Johannah Jones Nolan (1985), "Gaining Customer Trust: A Conceptual Guide for the Salesperson," *Journal of Personal Selling & Sales Management,* 5 (November), 39–48.

___, I.F. Trawick, David R. Rink, and Jenny J. Roberts (1988), "Measuring Dimensions of Purchaser Trust of Industrial Salespeople," *Journal of Personal Selling & Sales Management,* 8 (May), 1–9.

___, ___, and David W. Silva (1985), "How Industrial Salespeople Gain Customer Trust," *Industrial Marketing Management,* 14 (August), 203–11.

Thomas, Gloria P. and Gary F. Soldow (1988), "A Rules-Based Approach to Competitive Interaction," *Journal of Marketing,* 52 (April), 63–74.

Toffler, Barbara L. (1986), *Tough Choices: Managers Talk Ethics.* New York: John Wiley & Sons.

Turnbull, Peter W. and David T. Wilson (1989), "Developing and Protecting Profitable Customer Relationships," *Industrial Marketing Management,* 18, 233–8.

Unger, Roberto Mangabeira (1976), *Law in Modern Society: Toward a Criticism.* New York: The Free Press.

Uniform Commercial Code (1978), American Law Institute and the National Conference of Commissioners on Uniform State Laws.

Varadarajan, Rajan P. and Daniel Rajaratnam (1986), "Symbiotic Marketing Revisited," *Journal of Marketing,* 50 (January), 7–17.

Walster, Elaine G., William Walster, and Ellen Berscheid (1973), "New Directions in Equity Research," *Journal of Personality and Social Psychology,* 25 (2), 151–76.

Werhane, Patricia H. (1989), "The Role of Self-Interest in Adam Smith's Wealth of Nations," *Journal of Philosophy,* 86 (11), 669–80.

White, John and Richard Summers (1988), *Uniform Commercial Code,* 3rd ed. St. Paul, MN: West Publishing.

White, Joseph B. (1991), "Japanese Auto Makers Help U.S. Suppliers Become More Efficient," *Wall Street Journal* (September 9), A1.

Whitford, William C. (1968), "Law and the Consumer Transaction: A Case Study of the Automobile Warranty," *Wisconsin Law Review,* 1006–98.

Williams, Oliver F. and Patrick E. Murphy (1990), "The Ethics Virtue: A Moral Theory for Marketing," *Journal of Macromarketing,* 10 (Spring), 19–29.

Williamson, Oliver E. (1991), "Comparative Economic Organization: The Analysis of Discrete Structural Alternatives," *Administrative Science Quarterly,* 36, 269–96.

___ (1985), *The Economic Institutions of Capitalism.* New York: The Free Press.

___ (1983), "Credible Commitments: Using Hostages to Support Exchange," *The American Economic Review,* 73 (4), 519–40.

___ (1979), *Markets and Hierarchies: Analysis and Antitrust Implications.* New York: The Free Press.

Zaltman, Gerald and Christine Moorman (1988), "The Importance of Personal Trust in the Use of Research," *Journal of Advertising Research,* 28 (October/November), 16–23.

CORPORATE ETHICAL VALUES
AND ORGANIZATIONAL COMMITMENT
IN MARKETING

Shelby D. Hunt, Van R. Wood, and Lawrence B. Chonko

The authors explore corporate ethical values and organizational commitment in marketing. They (1) discuss corporate ethical values as a component of corporate culture, (2) review the literature on organizational commitment, (3) hypothesize a positive relationship between corporate ethical values and organizational commitment, and (4) empirically test the relationship with data from more than 1200 professional marketers, representing subsamples of marketing managers, marketing researchers, and advertising agency managers. The study results provide strong evidence of a positive association between corporate ethical values and organizational commitment. Given previous research demonstrating a strong link between commitment and specific organizational benefits, corporate ethics may be not only an important *societal* issue, but a key *organizational* issue as well.

Corporate[1] values have long been referred to as *the* central dimension of an organization's culture and have been recognized as powerful influences differentiating one firm from another (Alchian and Demsetz 1972; Chamberlin 1933). Recent work suggests that the unique values shared by organizational members may explain the superior and sustained performance of some corporations (Barney 1986; Bonoma 1984; Deal and Kennedy 1982; Leontiades 1983). To paraphrase Schein (1985), corporate values, as a major dimension of corporate culture, define the standards that guide the external adaptation and internal integration of organizations. Corporate values influence organizations' product and service quality, advertising content, pricing policies, treatment of employees, and relationships with customers, suppliers, communities, and the environment. Our discussion pertains to the ethical dimensions of corporate values. Our central issue is the extent to which corporate ethical values are associated with the loyalty or commitment of marketers to their respective organizations. Though there is no universally accepted definition, corporate ethical values are considered to be a composite of the individual

---

[1]We use the term "corporate" (e.g., "corporate values" and "corporate ethical values") in the generic and not the legal sense. "Corporate" is likened to "company," "firm," or "organization."

SHELBY D. HUNT is the Paul Whitfield Horn Professor of Marketing and VAN R. WOOD is Associate Professor of Marketing, Texas Tech University. LAWRENCE B. CHONKO is the Holloway Professor of Marketing, Baylor University.

Hung, Shelby D., Van R. Wood, and Lawrence B. Chonko (1989), "Corporate Ethical Values and Organizational Commitment in Marketing," *Journal of Marketing*, 53 (3), 79–90.

ethical values of managers and both the formal and informal policies on ethics of the organization.

Like corporate ethical values, the subject of employee organizational commitment has been much discussed because of its strong association with many valuable organization outcomes, including employee satisfaction (Hunt, Chonko, and Wood 1985), performance (Morris and Sherman 1981), absenteeism (Hammer, Landau, and Stern 1981; Steers 1977), employee turnover (Abelson 1983), and organizational adaptability (Angle and Perry 1981). In general, low levels of commitment are thought to be dysfunctional to both the organization and the individual (Randall 1987).

Alarmingly, organizational commitment is declining. Recent empirical indicants of this decline include (1) a Harris poll of middle managers in which 65% said salaried employees are less loyal to their companies than they were 10 years ago (Nussbaum 1986) and (2) research findings by Yankelovich, Skelly, and White that managerial commitment (the bond between employees and their companies) dropped markedly during the 1980s (Kiechel 1985). Further, executive mobility between firms is at unprecedented levels (Mowday, Porter, and Steers 1982; Randall 1987).

Though marketing managers, like other managers, want committed employees, interest in the formal construct of organizational commitment in marketing is relatively recent (see Hunt, Chonko, and Wood 1985; Still 1983). However, the marketing literature has long addressed issues related to ethical values: ethical theory, marketing research ethics, ethical values and consumers, and ethical problems in marketing management (for a review of these and related issues, see Murphy and Laczniak 1981). Past works indicate that ethical values play an important role in many marketing settings. However, no study has investigated ethical values as a motivating force related to marketers' organizational commitment.

One could hypothesize that there is no relationship between ethical values and commitment in marketing. After all, marketers' ethics often have been described as questionable at best and abusive at worst (Baumhart 1961; Murphy and Laczniak 1981). Likewise, marketers (in contrast to other employees) have been theorized to be less committed to their organizations (Still 1983). If these characteristics are inherent in marketers, little association would be expected between marketers' corporate ethical values and organizational commitment. Recently, however, several empirical studies in marketing have indicated that top managers must take an active role in promoting ethical values if such values are to have positive effects (Chonko and Hunt 1985; Hunt, Chonko, and Wilcox 1984). These studies found that the actions of top managers can reduce the perceived ethical problems of their employees. Similarly, one might hypothesize that when top managers create a corporate culture that emphasizes high ethical values, marketers' commitment to the organization will increase.

Is the organizational commitment of marketers associated with corporate ethical values? Should corporations desiring highly committed marketing employees take an active role in promoting ethical values in their organizations? We report the results of empirical research designed to explore these questions. The managerial significance of these questions lies in the fact that a strong link has long been recognized between organizational commitment and such desirable outcomes as high performance and low absenteeism. More specifically, we (1) discuss the subject of corporate ethical values as a component of corporate culture, (2) briefly review the literature on organizational commitment (see Hunt, Chonko, and Wood 1985 for a more extensive review), (3) hypothesize a positive relationship between corporate ethical values and organizational commitment, and (4) empirically test the relationship using data from more than 1200 professional marketers (499 marketing managers, 417 marketing researchers, and 330 advertising agency managers).

Background

CORPORATE CULTURE AND ETHICAL VALUES

Corporate culture is a multifaceted construct. For example, in describing corporate culture, Goffman (1959, 1967) focused on the *observed behavioral regularities* in people's interactions, Homans (1950) wrote of the *norms* that evolve in working groups, Ouchi (1981) stressed the *philosophy* that influences organizational policy, and Van Maanen (1976) emphasized the *rules* for getting along in an organization. More recently, corporate culture has been defined as the assumptions, beliefs, goals, knowledge and *values* that are shared by organizational members (Deal and Kennedy 1982; Sathe 1984; Schein 1985; Schwartz and Davis 1981). Though values, according to this view, are but one dimension of corporate culture, they have been theorized to be highly influential in directing the actions of individuals in society in general and organizations in particular (Rokeach 1968, 1973; Yankelovich 1971, 1981). For *society,* values help define the "core" of people—what they love, hate, or are just indifferent to. They help explain why people make sacrifices and what they are willing to give up to attain goals. Values encompass a larger view of what people are, can be, and will become (Mitchell 1971). For an *organization,* values serve to convey a sense of identity to its members, enhance the stability of its social system, direct managers' attention to important issues, guide subsequent decisions by managers, and (most important for our research) *facilitate commitment to something larger than self* (Deal and Kennedy 1982; Smircich 1983).

Organizations may have many values that are distinctly marketing in character—for example, values that guide product and service quality, advertising content, selection of distribution channels, and treatment of customers. However, underpinning all of these specific values are corporate *ethical* values. These values help establish and maintain the standards that delineate the "right" things to do and the things "worth doing" (Jansen and Von Glinow 1985). In turn, such ethical standards can influence individuals' choices and lead to actions that are desirable to organizations (Conner and Becker 1975). More specifically, when the ethical standards/values of an organization are widely shared among its members, organizational success will be enhanced (Badovick and Beatty 1987; Brown 1976; England 1967; Keeley 1983; Koch and Fox 1978). As Peters and Waterman (1982) point out in their study of excellent companies, virtually all the superior performance firms have at the core a well-defined set of shared values, particularly ethical values.

Over the last several decades, marketing has increasingly considered exchange to be its central concept, a trend that culminated in 1985 with the AMA's new definition of marketing. Insight into the influence of shared values on desirable organizational outcomes can be gained by examining the exchange relationship between individuals and their organizations. As in all *exchange relationships,* two sides are involved, each with something of value, freedom to agree or disagree, and the ability to communicate what is being offered. On one side are individuals, who come to organizations with certain needs and desires. Within the organization they expect to find a work environment in which they can use their abilities to satisfy many of these needs. On the other side, organizations hire individuals to accomplish the tasks necessary for the survival, growth, and prosperity of the organization. In essence, organizations satisfy individuals' needs and, in return, individuals work hard to accomplish organizational goals (Steers 1977). When organizations provide an environment or "culture" conducive to such exchanges (e.g., when they are dependable, broadminded, or ethical), the likelihood of receiving desirable responses from employees (e.g., high productivity and loyalty) is theorized to increase (Hrebiniak and Alutto 1972; March and Simon 1958). Though top managers must recognize that this exchange relationship is important in both the recruitment and retention (or commitment) of employees, our study focuses on the latter.

ORGANIZATIONAL COMMITMENT

Scholarly works on organizational commitment are numerous (see Randall 1987). Though recent reviews reveal more than 30 different forms of work commitment, they also show that each form can be relatively stable over time (Morrow 1983). Similarly, though definitions of organizational commitment abound, a common theme in most of them is that committed individuals tend to identify with the objectives and goals of their organizations and want to remain with their organizations (Buchanan 1974; Hrebiniak and Alutto 1972). Thus, organizational commitment has been described as a "psychological bond" to the organization that influences individuals to act in ways consistent with the interests of the organization (Mowday and McDade 1979; Porter, Mowday, and Boulin 1974).

As noted previously, commitment has been associated with many desirable organizational outcomes, including satisfaction, performance, reduced turnover, and flexibility. Most researchers acknowledge its value on both theoretical and empirical grounds and most managers prefer loyal and devoted employees on practical grounds. The *important issue* from both research and managerial viewpoints is: How can organizations instill and maintain a high level of commitment in their members? In other words, before managers can hope to influence commitment in an informed way, the antecedents of commitment must be identified (Morris and Sherman 1981; Randall 1987).

Previous research has shown certain personal characteristics (including age, income, and education) and certain job characteristics (including variety, autonomy, identity, and feedback) to be robust predictors of many organizational behaviors. For example, in the organization literature, age and income have been found to be related positively to commitment (Brief and Aldag 1980; Steers 1977) whereas education has been related negatively (Brief and Aldag 1980; Morris and Sherman 1981). Further, Herzberg (1966), Hackman and Lawler (1971), and Becherer, Morgan, and Richard (1982) found positive relationships between satisfaction and certain intrinsic job characteristics as measured by the Job Classification Index (JCI) (see Sims, Szilagyi, and Keller 1976). Similarly, in the marketing literature, positive relationships have been found between organizational commitment and age, income, variety, autonomy, and feedback (Hunt, Chonko, and Wood 1985). What has not been investigated *empirically* in *any* literature is the association between corporate ethical values and commitment.

Research Issue and Hypotheses

The preceding discussion, in conjunction with the established relationship between organizational commitment and desirable organizational outcomes, warrants the examination of the following research issue.

RI: Controlling for the effects of specific personal characteristics and intrinsic job characteristics, what is the nature of the relationship (if any) between shared ethical values and organizational commitment in marketing?

To investigate this issue, we hypothesize the following linkages.

H_1: Organizational commitment in marketing is a positive function of age and income and a negative function of education.

H_2: Organizational commitment in marketing is a positive function of the job characteristics (variety, autonomy, identity, and feedback).

H_3: Organizational commitment in marketing is a positive function of shared ethical values.

On the basis of past research findings, we use the independent variables examined in H_1 and H_2 as controls so that the direction and strength of the relationship postulated in H_3 can be examined. Taken together, these hypotheses represent both a partial replication (H_1 and H_2) and an extension (H_3) of our previous work (Hunt, Chonko, and Wood 1985).

Method

DATA

The data reported here came from two self-administered questionnaires mailed to (1) professional marketing managers and researchers and (2) professional advertising agency managers. The two questionnaires were identical in the constructs investigated, though other distinct issues[2] (not reported here) also were examined.

Responses from marketing managers and researchers were obtained by drawing a systematic sample of one of every four practitioners in the American Marketing Association (AMA). In total, 4282 practitioners were sent questionnaires and 1076 usable responses were returned, a response rate of 25.1%. From the total usable responses, those of 916 individuals who identified themselves as sales, product, or marketing managers (n = 499) or as marketing researchers (n = 417) were retained for the study. Advertising agency employees (because they were too few to analyze) and consultants were excluded from the analysis (for more specific details about this sample, see Hunt, Chonko, and Wood 1985).

To broaden the scope and increase the generalizability of the study, a second self-administered questionnaire was mailed to 3064 advertising agency executives whose names and addresses were secured from a commercial source. A total of 330 usable questionnaires were returned, an effective response rate of 17%.[3]

We first merge and analyze responses from the marketing managers, marketing researchers, and advertising agency managers into one combined sample. We then treat each professional marketing group as a subsample or segment of the larger sample and present analysis results for each group. The overall response rate for the combined sample is 20.4%, based on an initial effective universe of 6114 marketers and n = 1246 respondents.

The characteristics of all respondents, along with the breakdown of marketing managers, researchers, and advertising agency managers, are reported in Table 1. The majority of our combined sample and subsamples are married, male, more than 30 years of age, and earning $30,000 or more a year. In education, the vast majority of each subsample has at least a bachelor's degree. Likewise, within each subsample, a large variance is seen in respondents' job titles, business experience, and number of firms worked for, though the advertising managers tend to have worked for considerably more firms during their careers than marketing managers or researchers. The majority of marketing managers and researchers work for larger firms (500 employees or more), and the majority of advertisers work for smaller firms (less than 100 employees).

---

[2]These issues included Machiavellianism and social responsibility in marketing.

[3]If we assume an attrition rate on the mailing list of 35% (Vitell 1986), the effective universe is 1992. The procedure suggested by Armstrong and Overton (1977) revealed no response bias problems.

TABLE 1

Characteristics of Sample (in percentage)

	Marketing Managers (n = 499)	Marketing Researchers (n = 417)	Advertising Agency Managers (n = 330)	Combined Sample (n = 1246)
Job Title				
Entry positions[a]	12	6	7	9
District manager[b]	9	29	4	14
Division manager[c]	21	12	21	18
Corporate manager[d]	29	33	18	27
Vice president	20	13	14	16
President, owner	9	7	37	16
Size of Firm Worked for (number of employees)				
<100	19	20	88	38
100–499	22	18	9	17
500–999	12	11	1	9
1000+	48	51	2	37
Education Level of Sample				
No college degree	4	4	13	6
Bachelor's degree	34	34	64	42
Graduate degree	62	62	22	52
Income ($)				
<30,000	21	37	23	27
30,000–49,999	44	40	25	38
50,000+	35	22	51	36
Total Business Experience (number of years)				
1–5	9	20	5	12
6–10	22	23	12	20
11–15	22	19	20	20
16–20	17	11	14	15
20 or more	30	26	49	33
Number of Firms Worked for (during career)				
1	14	16	5	12
2	21	26	11	20
3	24	21	23	23
4	20	14	20	18
5+	21	23	42	27
Age (years)				
20–29	13	24	11	16
30–39	44	38	30	38
40–49	24	19	27	24
50+	19	17	32	22

(Continued)

TABLE 1				

Characteristics of Sample (in percentage) (*Continued*)

	Marketing Managers (n = 499)	Marketing Researchers (n = 417)	Advertising Agency Managers (n = 330)	Combined Sample (n = 1246)
Sex				
Male	78	61	73	71
Female	22	39	26	29
Marital Status				
Married	74	67	78	73
Single	26	33	22	27

[a]Includes junior analysts, media schedulers, creative assistants, and salespeople.
[b]Includes associate analysts and assistant directors.
[c]Includes analysts and directors.
[d]Includes specialized vice presidents.

Though our overall sample size is very large for social science research and our sample's characteristics compare favorably with those of other samples of marketing professionals, readers are cautioned (given the inevitably small response rate) to view the study results as exploratory and as only a useful "first step" toward verifying the relationships examined. As with all cross-sectional studies, one must be cautious not to overgeneralize results.

MEASURES

Some of the measures used (i.e., age, education, income) are self-explanatory and are listed in Table 1, but measures such as corporate ethical values, organizational commitment, and job characteristics require some elaboration.

Corporate ethical values. Because of their time, place, and issue specificity, ethical values have been described as one of the "most difficult" concepts to measure and study in organizations (Payne 1980). Many broad generalizations in the area are based solely on theory or speculation. Most previous efforts to measure corporate ethical values have been highly qualitative (Deal and Kennedy 1982). Quantitative efforts to develop scales in this general area have tended to center on either broad-based concepts such as organizational culture (Kilman and Saxton 1983) or issues such as value priorities (Marshall 1985). Because of the changing nature of what constitutes ethical issues in organizations, researchers frequently have been encouraged to measure the broad principles underlying ethical values rather than the domain-specific ethical issues *per se* (Trevino 1986). On the basis of these considerations, our measure of corporate ethical values attempts to capture the broader principles of the degree to which organizations take an interest in ethical issues and act in an ethical manner, rather than product, service, or industry-specific issues.

Another consideration that guided our measurement is the need to incorporate "reward systems" into the study of corporate ethical values (Jansen and Von Glinow 1985). Reward systems often are posited to shape and maintain behaviors. More specifically, if the observance of ethical standards is not rewarded explicitly by the organization, ethical ambivalence in the organization (at the very least) is likely to result (Kerr 1975). Therefore, our measure also attempts to capture the extent to which ethical behavior is *rewarded* in the organization.

The measure of corporate ethical values (Table 2) was developed to capture three broad-based perceptions: (1) the extent to which employees perceive that managers are *acting* ethically in their organization (see item 1), (2) the extent to which employees perceive that managers are *concerned* about the issues of ethics in their organization (see item 3), and (3) the extent to which employees perceive that ethical (unethical) behavior is *rewarded (punished)* in their organization (see items 2, 4, and 5). Table 2 shows the factor analysis of the corporate ethical values scale developed by using the total sample and a 7-point Likert format (1 = strongly disagree and 7 = strongly agree).

The exploratory factor analysis (principal components) shows a unidimensional structure. Likewise, results indicate a reasonably high reliability (coefficient alpha = .78). Therefore, the scale appears reasonable for the study's purpose.

Organizational commitment. Commitment of marketing managers, researchers, and advertising agency managers to their organizations was measured on our previous

---

TABLE 2

Principal Components Solution: Corporate Ethical Values[a]

	F_1	h^2
1. Managers in my company often engage in behaviors that I consider to be unethical.[b]	.54	.30
2. In order to succeed in my company, it is often necessary to compromise one's ethics.[b]	.55	.31
3. Top management in my company has let it be known in no uncertain terms that unethical behaviors will not be tolerated.	.60	.35
4. If a manager in my company is discovered to have engaged in unethical behavior that results primarily in *personal gain* (rather than corporate gain), he or she will be promptly reprimanded.	.70	.49
5. If a manager in my company is discovered to have engaged in unethical behavior that results primarily in *corporate gain* (rather than personal gain), he or she will be promptly reprimanded.	.84	.71

% variance = 43%
Eigenvalue = 2.14
Coefficient alpha = .78

[a]1 = strongly disagree and 7= strongly agree.
[b]Reverse scored.

4-item scale (Hunt, Chonko, and Wood 1985), which also has a 7-point Likert format:

1. I would be willing to change companies if the new job offered a 25% pay increase.
2. I would be willing to change companies if the new job offered more creative freedom.
3. I would be willing to change companies if the new job offered more status.
4. I would be willing to change companies if the new job was with people who were more friendly.

The scale is drawn from previous definitions and research in this area (Alutto, Hrebiniak, and Alonzo 1973; Becker 1960; Buchanan 1974) and captures the strength of intentions to remain with and psychological bonds to the organization. As before (Hunt, Chonko, and Wood 1985), our factor analysis indicated a unidimensional structure and a high degree of reliability (coefficient alpha = .87).

Job characteristics. Both theory and empirical research have demonstrated that certain intrinsic job characteristics can enrich organizational work and influence employee commitment (Alutto 1969; Hertzberg 1966; Hunt, Chonko, and Wood 1985; Steers 1977). Basically, when organizations fail to provide individuals with challenging and meaningful work, commitment decreases. We measured job characteristics by using the Job Classification Index (JCI; see Sims, Szilagyi, and Keller 1976). The JCI analyzes four dimensions of job characteristics (variety, autonomy, identity, and feedback) and has been widely accepted as a valid and reliable measure (Griffin et al. 1980; Pierce and Dunham 1976).

Results

The data were analyzed in the same way as in our previous study (Hunt, Chonko, and Wood 1985). First, univariate comparisons (Table 3) were made between marketing managers, researchers, and advertising agency managers for the principal constructs; second, recursive equations (Table 4) were estimated for the total sample and each subsample to test H_1, H_2, and H_3.

Table 3 compares marketing managers, researchers, and advertising agency managers on corporate ethical values, organizational commitment, and the four job characteristics (JCI). On perceived levels of corporate ethical values, the three professional marketing groups are significantly different (Sheffé test). Advertising managers perceived their companies to have the highest ethical values ($\bar{x} = 5.88$), followed by marketing managers ($\bar{x} = 5.33$) and researchers ($\bar{x} = 5.08$), indicating that marketers' perceptions of corporate ethical values seem to be related to the specific area of marketing in which they work. Similarly, the commitment level of the advertising agency managers is significantly higher than that of either the marketing managers or the researchers ($\bar{x} = 4.79$ vs. 4.18 and 4.16, respectively). As a tentative explanation, note that our subsample of advertising

TABLE 3

ANOVA: Corporate Ethical Values, Commitment, and the Job Characteristics Inventory[a]

Variables	Marketing Managers (n = 499)		Marketing Researchers (n = 417)		Advertising Agency Managers (n = 330)		Combined Sample (n = 1246)		Coefficient Alpha
	x̄	S.D.	x̄	S.D.	x̄	S.D.	x̄	S.D.	
Corporate ethical values	5.33[b]	1.12	5.08[b]	1.17	5.88[b]	1.22	5.40	1.18	.78
Commitment	4.16[b]	1.43	4.18[b]	1.44	4.79[b]	1.77	4.37	1.59	.87
Autonomy	6.03[c]	0.95	5.96[c]	1.06	6.17[c]	0.90	6.04	.97	.76
Variety	5.71[b]	1.10	5.52[b]	1.10	5.84[b]	1.08	5.68	1.10	.77
Feedback	4.77[b]	1.47	4.73[b]	1.54	5.36[b]	1.29	4.92	1.46	.90
Identity	5.64	1.09	5.72	1.08	5.91	1.05	5.70	1.08	.81

Corporate ethical values: All three groups differ.
Commitment: Advertising agency managers differ from marketing managers and marketing researchers.
Autonomy: No two groups differ.
Variety: Marketing researchers differ from marketing managers and advertising agency managers.
Feedback: Advertising agency managers differ from marketing managers and marketing researchers.
Identity: No two groups differ.

[a]Results of Scheffé test (level of significance = .01). Mean scores of corporate ethical values, commitment, and JCI scales on 7-point scales (high scores mean higher perceived levels of each variable).
[b]Significant at .01 level (F-test).
[c]Significant at .05 level (F-test).

agency managers has a higher percentage of presidents/owners than the other two sub-samples and hence they may naturally be more committed to their organizations. In any case, the differences in self-reported commitment levels, though statistically significant, probably lack *substantive* significance because the difference at the extreme is less than two thirds of a scale point on our 7-point Likert scale.

Though the four job characteristics (JCI) are not central constructs in this study (other than as control variables), Table 3 also reports their rating results. Overall, perceptions of the amount of autonomy, variety, feedback, and identity in their jobs are very similar for marketing managers, researchers, and advertising agency managers. The mean scores indicate that all three groups perceived more autonomy than the other three job characteristics in their work. *Statistically,* researchers perceived less variety than the other groups, whereas advertising managers perceived more feedback. *Substantively,* however, given the relatively small magnitude of these differences, the three groups' perceptions of the four job characteristics appear to differ little.

Table 4 reports the results of the recursive equation analyses; estimates are presented in five separate equations (l_A through l_E), first for the total marketing sample and then for each subsample. As we reported previously (Hunt, Chonko, and Wood 1985), the

TABLE 4

The Corporate Ethical Values–Commitment Relationship

Dependent Variable	Age	Education	Income	Feedback[a]	Identity[a]	Autonomy[a]	Variety[a]	Corp. Ethical Values[b]	Constant	R^2	F (Model)
1. Combined Sample (n = 1246)											
Commitment[c]											
1_A	.09[d]	-.28[d]							13.9	.15	61.91[d]
1_B			.71[d]						23.7	.21	76.12[d]
1_C				.19[d]	-.03	.42[d]	.31[d]	.44[d]	4.3	.17	241.54[d]
1_D	.07[d]	-.26[d]	.47[d]	.15[d]	-.02	.38[d]	.24[d]		21.7	.27	64.66[d]
1_E	.06[d]	-.25[d]	.37[d]	.11[d]	-.03	.31[d]	.20[d]	.23[d]	14.9	.32	66.72[d]
2. Advertising Agency Managers (n = 330)											
Commitment											
1_A	.09[d]	-.20[e]							13.78	.18	22.72[d]
1_B			.79[d]						28.3	.28	29.24[d]
1_C				.23[d]	-.05	.56[d]	.50[d]	.58[d]	2.1	.21	82.51[d]
1_D	.05	-.25[d]	.53[d]	.20[d]	-.01	.50[d]	.39[d]		25.6	.35	24.30[d]
1_E	.04	-.21[e]	.42[d]	.17[e]	-.04	.33[e]	.36[d]	.29[d]	16.0	.40	24.93[d]
3. Marketing Managers (n = 499)											
Commitment											
1_A	.03	-.08							13.8	.03	4.64[d]
1_B			.38[d]						21.2	.17	23.71[d]
1_C				.09[e]	-.02	.60[d]	.14[e]	.31[d]	7.1	.10	49.15[d]
1_D	.01	-.07	.18	.08	-.02	.58[d]	.13		20.7	.17	14.20[d]
1_E	.01	-.11	.13	.06	-.02	.52[d]	.10	.17[d]	16.4	.20	14.19[d]
4. Marketing Researchers (n = 417)											
Commitment											
1_A	.11[d]	-.37[d]							14.1	.17	26.93[d]
1_B			.72[d]						21.5	.18	20.46[d]
1_C				.14[d]	-.02	.26[e]	.30[d]	.37[d]	5.7	.14	62.11[d]
1_D	.11[d]	-.28[e]	.47[d]	.11[e]	-.06	.24[e]	.23[d]		18.6	.27	20.73[d]
1_E	.10[d]	-.29[d]	.37[d]	.09[e]	-.08	.21[e]	.19[d]	.21[d]	13.2	.31	21.52[d]

[a]Measured by mean score on JCI scale.
[b]Mean score on corporate ethical values scale.
[c]Measured by mean score on commitment scale.
[d]Significant at .01 level.
[e]Significant at .05 level.

personal characteristics of age, education, and income, along with certain job characteristics, are related to marketers' organizational commitment. Therefore, these characteristics were included as control variables so that the relative association of corporate ethical values and organizational commitment could be explored. Equations 1_A and 1_B of analyses 1 through 4 (Table 4) are the test results for the control variables.

In general, the results are very uniform. For the combined sample, all control variables, with the exception (as expected) of identity, are related significantly to commitment and all the signs are consistent in directionality with our hypotheses. These results conform with, and thus partially replicate, those of a larger sample we examined (Hunt, Chonko, and Wood 1985). When the combined sample is subdivided by type of marketing profession, the directionality of all signs remains stable though the magnitudes of the coefficients for age and education for marketing managers are not significant. Note also that the variance in commitment explained by job characteristics is reasonably high, especially in the case of advertising agency managers ($R^2 = .28$).

Equations 1_C, 1_D, and 1_E (analyses 1 through 4) are the results for the third hypothesis and our central research issue. We see in 1_C that corporate ethical values are related significantly ($p < .01$) to commitment for advertising agency managers, marketing managers, and marketing researchers with the explained variance being .21, .10, and .14, respectively. These initial results (in conjunction with the combined sample results, $p < .01, R^2 = .17$) provide evidence that corporate ethical values, taken alone, may be a strong predictor of commitment. If personal and job characteristics are used as control variables, will the ethical values–commitment linkage hold? Equations 1_D and 1_E, when examined together, reveal the incremental influence of ethical values (in conjunction with the control variables) on organizational commitment. Note the incremental change in R^2 from equation 1_D to 1_E. Observe also that in each case, when all variables are entered into the equation (1_E), the relationship between corporate ethical values and organizational commitment remains highly significant ($p < .01$). Further, in the case of marketing managers, corporate ethical values and autonomy are the *only* variables that remain significant predictors of commitment. Also of interest is the fact that the amount of explained variance in commitment increases in each case when all variables are entered into the equations. This increase is particularly striking for advertising agency managers and marketing researchers ($R^2 = .40$ and .31, respectively). In all subsamples, however, corporate ethical values remain a significant and substantive predictor of organizational commitment.

Finally, observing the results for the combined sample of marketers, we conclude that in general, with the single exception of "identity," a strong relationship is present between the marketers' organizational commitment levels and all the hypothesized variables. More important, and of more salience for our discussion, is the consistency in the findings that corporate ethical values are significant and substantive predictors of organizational commitment in marketing. Not only does this relationship hold across three distinct professional marketing groups taken separately, but also, as revealed in Table 4 (analysis 1), when all three subsamples are combined.

Discussion

Is organizational commitment in marketing associated with corporate ethical values? Should managers who want committed employees take an active role in promoting ethical values in their organizations? The results of our broad-based research appear tentatively to give an affirmative response to these questions. Our findings indicate that though there may be contextual differences among marketing areas (i.e., advertising agency managers, marketing managers, and marketing researchers do "anatomically" different jobs; see Porter, Lawler, and Hackman 1975), the direct impact of such *area* differences on the corporate ethical values–commitment relationship is small. The magnitude of the relationship varies among the areas of marketing, but the directionality and significance of the relationship stay the same. Likewise, when the corporate ethical values–organizational commitment association is analyzed in combination with specific control variables (i.e., personal and job characteristics), the results appear even firmer.

One must be aware, however, that organizational commitment may blind some employees to the ethical problems in their firms (i.e., "I am committed, therefore no ethical problems are present in my organization"). At issue here is: Under what circumstances can a person engage in "perceptual distortion" about the commitment–corporate ethical values relationship? Numerous studies clearly indicate that perception is determined, in part, by the motivation and need-value system of the observer (Bruner and Goodman 1947; Bruner and Postman 1951; Edwards 1941; Jenkins 1957). In general, research has shown that perceptual distortion is higher when the relevant object or construct is highly valued. Perceptual distortion decreases when the object or construct is considered unimportant or trivial. Similar logic applies to commitment if we consider the spectrum of objects to which one can be committed. For example, a person can be committed to a church, a spouse (possibly "love is blind"), children, family, country, an organization, and so on. In theory, the more one absolutely values the object of his or her commitment, the more likely it is that the attributes of that object will be perceptually distorted. Where does the organization stand on this spectrum of objects? We would be remiss to classify the organization as unimportant or trivial. Nevertheless, the position that the absolute commitment level of most employees to their organizations (especially in today's times) would be so high as to make them blind (high perceptual distortion) to the presence of ethical problems in their organizations seems theoretically less reasonable than the alternative—namely, that employees who perceive correctly that their organizations have high ethical standards will be more committed.

With this argument in mind, we ask to what extent our findings can be generalized to the universe of professional marketers. Though the usual caveats about inferring causality from cross-sectional data certainly apply, data were collected and analyses performed across three distinct professional groups within marketing. Further, the nature of the samples analyzed and the consistency of the empirical findings give some credence to generalizing our findings to marketing in general.

An underlying premise of our work is that ethical values are a managerial issue and not "just" a societal issue. Obviously, society has an interest in marketing managers maintaining high ethical standards. Not so obviously, our research shows that high ethical values may be a key organizational construct as well. Indeed, though causality cannot be shown with certainty, our study *suggests* that the most fruitful way to influence marketers' commitment to their organizations may be through emphasizing our major construct of interest—corporate ethical values.

Though our ability to compare our results with those of previous studies is hampered by the lack of empirical research in this area (this is the only study to date that has examined corporate ethical values and organizational commitment across a spectrum of vocational areas), our results do indicate that organizational commitment is influenced strongly by perceptions of corporate ethical values. Equally important, our results may lend insight into an ongoing controversy about the role of managers in forming corporate values and subsequently influencing organizational outcomes.

On one side of the controversy are persons who argue that, though values are a powerful force in explaining the behavior of individuals and groups within organizations, they are unperceived, unspoken, and taken for granted. To this side, values are the "common sense" of the firm and therefore require no articulation (Barney 1986; Berger and Luckman 1967; Polanyi 1958). On the other side of the controversy are persons who argue that increased "formalization" of ethical values in organizations (i.e., increasing the extent to which employees are aware of written rules, explicitly stated norms, and set values) is the key to influencing employee behavior. These writers argue that formalization facilitates job and role clarity (Ferrell and Weaver 1978; Kaikati and Label 1980; Morris and Steers 1980). Essentially this group believes that top managers' articulation and action are required if values are to influence behavior. Our results lend support to this group, because the more marketers perceive their companies as showing concern for ethics, acting ethically, and rewarding ethical behavior, the more positive is the resulting influence on marketers' commitment to their organizations.

Implications and Conclusions

A foremost implication of our study for marketing managers is that a distinct style of leadership may be *required* if having committed marketing employees is *desired*. Given the consistent association between corporate ethical values and commitment, managers wanting to instill and maintain a high level of loyalty in their employees may have to be *more* than just task directors of their organizations. Rather, they may have to think of themselves as the standard bearers, mood setters, and moral leaders of their organizations. More specifically, these leaders must show concern for, act upon, and reward ethical behavior. In essence, top managers should define, refine, evaluate, communicate, and thus *institutionalize* the ethical principles underlying their policies, practices, and goals. They should decide what will be considered right, what will be considered wrong, and what things are worth doing from an ethical perspective in their organizations. In marketing, these decisions involve product and service quality, advertising content, pricing policies, relationships with customers, suppliers, and all other *exchange relationships* that affect organizational success.

Top managers in marketing might also consider developing commitment and corporate ethical values indexes. Periodically employees might be asked to respond *anonymously* to a series of questions designed to measure their perceptions of ethical values in the organization and their levels of commitment. Such indexes could be used to monitor changes in employees' perceptions over time and could provide early warning signals of potential *future* problems (e.g., losing valuable employees) or opportunities (e.g., raising levels of commitment).

Several research implications are also apparent. First, though our findings demonstrate that the corporate ethical values–commitment relationship is consistent across three marketing areas, replications with such groups as sales and retailing would be desirable. Our study could be used as a "norm" score for comparison. Second, our findings have implications for longitudinal studies. Research that tracks the changing nature and impact of ethical values in organizations over time is needed. Ethical values are said to be situational and time specific. How do those values change over time and place? What specific actions by managers cause such changes? Which specific ethical values have the most staying power and impact over time?

Finally, cross-cultural studies investigating the relationships we examined would be useful. Are corporate ethical values associated with commitment in other societies, such as those in Europe and Japan? Which specific ethical values dominate in different cultures and what are their implications for U.S. marketers? The answers to these and other questions could prove to be invaluable in the continuous quest for a sustained competitive advantage in the international arena.

The search for efficiency, productivity, and success constitutes a core dimension of the discipline of management in general and marketing management in particular. Our research indicates that corporate ethical values (given their relationship to commitment and commitment's long-established relationship to improved performance) may be a key ingredient for success. Companies that promote high ethical values in their organizations may find themselves richer in loyal talent than ones that ignore or abjure such values.

Research conducted for the American Management Association in the mid-1980s (as reported by Kiechel 1985, p. 207) led to the conclusion that:

> ... while corporate loyalty has declined considerably, [employees] still wish for a bond [with their organization]. They want to belong to something they can believe in. ...

A sense of high corporate ethical values appears to be one of those "things" they can believe in.

References

Abelson, Michael A. (1983), "The Impact of Goal Change on Permanent Perceptions and Behaviors of Employees," *Journal of Management,* 9 (Spring-Summer), 65–79.

Alchian, A. and H. Demsetz (1972), "Production, Information Costs and Economic Organization," *American Economic Review,* 62, 777–95.

Alutto, J. A. (1969), "Men, Motivation, and Productivity," *Administrative Management Society Bulletin,* 1 (August), 1–8.

___, L. G. Hrebiniak, and R. C. Alonzo (1973), "On Operationalizing the Concept of Commitment," *Social Forces,* 51 (4), 448–54.

Angle, Harold L. and James L. Perry (1981). "An Empirical Assessment of Organizational Commitment and Organizational Effectiveness," *Administrative Science Quarterly,* 20 (March), 1–14.

Armstrong, J. Scott and Terry S. Overton (1977), "Estimating Nonresponse Bias in Mail Surveys," *Journal of Marketing Research,* 14 (August), 396–402.

Badovick, Gordon J. and Sharon E. Beatty (1987), "Shared Organizational Values: Measurement and Impact Upon Strategic Marketing Implication," *Journal of the Academy of Marketing Science,* 1 (Spring), 19–26.

Barney, Jay B. (1986), "Organizational Culture: Can It Be a Source of Sustained Competitive Advantage?" *Academy of Management Review,* 11 (3), 656–65.

Baumhart, R. C. (1961), "How Ethical Are Businessmen," *Harvard Business Review,* 39 (6–9), 156–7.

Becherer, Richard C., Fred W. Morgan, and Lawrence M. Richard (1982), "The Job Characteristics of Industrial Salespersons: Relationship to Motivation and Satisfaction." *Journal of Marketing,* 46 (Fall), 125–35.

Becker, H. S. (1960), "Notes on the Concept of Commitment," *American Journal of Sociology,* 6 (1), 32–40.

Berger, P. L. and T. Luckman (1967), *The Social Construction of Reality.* Garden City, NY: Anchor.

Bonoma, Thomas V. (1984). "Making Your Marketing Strategy Work," *Harvard Business Review,* 62 (March–April), 69–76.

Brief, Arthur P. and Ramon J. Aldag (1980). "Antecedents of Organizational Commitment Among Hospital Nurses," *Sociology of Work and Occupation,* 7 (2), 210–21.

Brown, Martha (1976), "Values—A Necessary But Neglected Ingredient of Motivation on the Job," *Academy of Management Review,* 1 (October), 1523.

Bruner, J. and C. Goodman (1947), "Values and Needs as Organizing Factors in Perception," *Journal of Abnormal and Social Psychology,* 42 (1), 33–44.

___ and L. Postman (1951), "An Approach to Social Perception," in *Current Trends in Social Psychology,* Wayne Dennis, ed. Pittsburgh: University of Pittsburgh Press.

Buchanan, Bruce (1974), "Building Organizational Commitment: The Socialization of Managers in Work Organizations," *Administrative Science Quarterly,* 19 (4), 533–46.

Chamberlin, E. H. (1933), *The Theory of Monopolistic Competition.* Cambridge, MA: Harvard University Press.

Chonko, Lawrence B. and Shelby D. Hunt (1985), "Ethics and Marketing Management: An Empirical Examination," *Journal of Business Research,* 13 (August), 339–59.

Conner, Patrick E. and Boris W. Becker (1975), "Values and the Organization—Suggestions for Research," *Academy of Management Journal,* 18 (3), 550–61.

Deal, Terrence E. and Allan A. Kennedy (1982), *Corporate Cultures.* Reading, MA: Addison-Wesley Publishing Company.

Edwards, A. L. (1941), "Political Frame of Reference as a Factor Influencing Recognition," *Journal of Abnormal and Social Psychology,* 36 (1), 34–50.

England, George (1967), "Personal Value Systems of American Managers," *Academy of Management Journal,* 10 (1), 53–68.

Ferrell, O. C. and K. Mark Weaver (1978), "Ethical Beliefs of Marketing Managers," *Journal of Marketing,* 42 (July), 69–73.

Goffman, E. (1959), *The Presentation of Self in Everyday Life.* New York: Doubleday.

___ (1967), *Interactional Ritual.* Hawthorne, NY: Al-dine Publishing Company.

Griffin, R. W., Gregory Moorhead, Bruce Johnson, and Lawrence B. Chonko (1980), "The Empirical Dimensionality of the Job Characteristic Inventory," *Academy of Management Journal,* 23 (2), 772–7.

Hackman, J. R. and E. F. Lawler (1971), "Employee Reactions to Job Characteristics," *Journal of Applied Psychology,* 55 (2), 259–86.

Hammer, T., J. Landau, and R. Stern (1981). "Absenteeism When Workers Have a Voice: The Case of Employee Ownership," *Journal of Applied Psychology,* 66 (5), 561–73.

Herzberg, Fredrick (1966), *Work and the Nature of Man.* New York: World Publishing.

Homans, G. (1950), *The Human Group.* New York: Harcourt Brace Jovanovich.

Hrebiniak, Lawrence and Joseph A. Alutto (1972), "Personal and Role Related Factors in the Development of Organizational Commitment." *Administrative Science Quarterly,* 17 (3), 555–72.

Hunt, Shelby D., Lawrence B. Chonko, and James B. Wilcox (1984), "Ethical Problems of Marketing Researchers," *Journal of Marketing Research,* 21 (August), 304–24.

___, ___, and Van R. Wood (1985), "Organizational Commitment and Marketing." *Journal of Marketing,* 49 (Winter), 112–26.

Jansen, Erik and Mary Ane Von Glinow (1985), "Ethical Ambience and Organizational Reward Systems," *Academy of Management Review,* 10 (4), 814–22.

Jenkins, Noel (1957), "Affective Processes in Perception," *Psychological Bulletin,* 54 (2), 100–27.

Kaikati, Jack and Wayne A. Label (1980). "American Bribery Legislation: An Obstacle to International Marketing," *Journal of Marketing,* 44 (Fall), 38–43.

Keeley, Michael (1983), "Values in Organizational Theory and Management Education," *Academy of Management Review,* 8 (3), 376–86.

Kerr, S. (1975), "On the Folly of Rewarding A While Hoping for B," *Academy of Management Journal,* 18 (4), 769–83.

Kiechel, Walter (1985), "Resurrecting Corporate Loyalty," *Fortune* (December 9), 209–11.

Kilman, R. and M. J. Saxton (1983), *Kilman-Saxton Culture Gap Survey.* Pittsburgh: Organizational Design Consultants.

Koch, James L. and Colin L. Fox (1978), "The Industrial Relations Setting, Organizational Forces and the Form and Content of Worker Participation," *Academy of Management Review,* 3 (3), 572–83.

Leontiades, Milton (1983), "The Importance of Integrating Marketing Planning with Corporate Planning," *Journal of Business Research,* 11 (4), 457–73.

March, James G. and Herbert A. Simon (1958), *Organizations.* New York: John Wiley & Sons, Inc.

Marshall, Claudia E. (1985), "Can We Be 'Consumer Oriented' in a Changing Financial Service World," in *Services Marketing in a Changing Environment,* Thomas M. Black et al., eds. Chicago: American Marketing Association.

Mitchell, Arnold (1971), "Changing Values," *International Advertiser,* 12 (March), 5–9.

Morris, James and J. Daniel Sherman (1981), "Generalizability of Organizational Commitment Model," *Academy of Management Journal,* 24 (3), 512–26.

___ and Richard M. Steers (1980), "Structural Influence on Organizational Commitment," *Journal of Vocational Business,* 17 (1), 50–7.

Morrow, Paula C. (1983), "Concept Redundancy in Organizational Research: The Case of Work Commitment," *Academy of Management Review,* 8 (3), 486–500.

Mowday, Richard T. and Thomas W. McDade (1979), "Linking Behavior and Attitudinal Commitment: A Longitudinal Analysis of Job Choice and Job Attitudes," *Academy of Management Proceedings,* 84–8.

___, L. W. Porter, and R. M. Steers (1982), *Organizational Linkages.* New York: Academic Press, Inc.

Murphy, Patrick E. and Gene Laczniak (1981), "Marketing Ethics: A Review with Implications for Managers, Educators and Researchers," in *Review of Marketing 1981,* Ben M. Enis and Kenneth J. Roering, eds. Chicago: American Marketing Association, 251–66.

Nussbaum, Bruce (1986), "The End of Corporate Loyalty?" *Business Week* (August 4), 42–9.

Ouchi, W. G. (1981), *Theory Z.* Reading, MA: Addison-Wesley Publishing Company.

Payne, Stephene L. (1980), "Organizational Ethics and Antecedents to Social Control Processes," *Academy of Management Review,* 5 (3), 409–14.

Peters, T. J. and R. H. Waterman (1982), *In Search of Excellence.* New York: Harper & Row Publishers, Inc.

Pierce, J. L. and R. B. Dunham (1976), "Task Design: A Literature Review," *Academy of Management Review,* 1 (3), 83–97.

Polanyi, M. (1958), *Personal Knowledge.* Chicago: University of Chicago Press.

Porter, L. W., E. E. Lawler, and J. R. Hackman (1975), *Behavior in Organizations.* New York: McGraw-Hill Book Company.

___, Richard T. Mowday, and P. V. Boulin (1974), "Organizational Commitment, Job Satisfaction and Turnover Among Psychiatric Technicians," *Journal of Applied Psychology,* 59 (5), 603–9.

Randall, Donna M. (1987), "Commitment and the Organization: The Organization Man Revisited," *Academy of Management Review,* 12 (3), 460–71.

Rokeach, M. J. (1968), *Beliefs, Attitudes and Values.* San Francisco: Jossey-Bass Inc., Publishers.

___ (1973), *The Nature of Human Values.* New York: The Free Press.

Sathe, Vijay (1984), "Implications of Corporate Culture: A Manager's Guide to Action," *Organizational Dynamics,* 12 (Autumn), 4–23.

Schein, Edgar H. (1985), *Organizational Cultures and Leadership,* San Francisco: Jossey-Bass Inc., Publishers.

Schwartz, Howard and Stanley Davis (1981), "Matching Corporate Culture and Business Strategy," *Organizational Dynamics,* 10 (Summer), 30–48.

Sims, H. P., A. D. Szilagyi, and R. I. Keller (1976), "The Measurement of Job Characteristics," *Academy of Management Journal,* 21 (3), 123–8.

Smircich, Linda (1983), "Concepts of Culture and Organizational Analysis," *Administrative Science Quarterly,* 28 (September), 339–58.

Steers, Richard M. (1977), "Antecedents and Outcomes of Organizational Commitment," *Administrative Science Quarterly,* 22 (1), 46–56.

Still, Leonie V. (1983), "Part-Time Versus Full-Time Salespeople: Individual Attributes, Organizational Commitment, and Work Attitudes," *Journal of Retailing,* 59 (Summer), 55–79.

Trevino, Linda K. (1986), "Ethical Decision Making in Organizations: A Person-Situation Interaction Model," *Academy of Management Review,* 11 (3), 601–17.

Van Maanen, J. (1976), "Breaking In: Socialization to Work," in *Handbook of Work, Organization and Society,* R. Dubin, ed. Chicago: Rand McNally, Inc.

Vitell, Scott (1986), *Marketing Ethics: Conceptual and Empirical Foundations of a Positive Theory of Decision Making in Marketing Situations Having Ethical Content,* unpublished Ph.D. dissertation, Texas Tech University.

Yankelovich, Daniel (1981), *New Rules.* New York: Random House, Inc.

____ (1971), "What New Life Styles Mean to Market Planners," *Marketing Communication,* 299 (June), 38–45.

BRUISED IN BENTONVILLE

Andy Serwer

By some financial measures, the No. 1 company in the FORTUNE 500 had a pretty good year in '04. Wal-Mart yet again defied the laws of large numbers, with sales climbing 10% to an astonishing $288 billion. Profits rose 13%, to more than $10 billion, in spite of a soft Christmas season. (For more on how it drives its business, see following story.)

And yet Wal-Mart is embattled as it has never been before. Sex-discrimination litigation, wage and pay disputes, fights with unions, and other workplace problems have left the company at loggerheads with plaintiffs lawyers, federal investigators, and even the chattering classes. From Chicago to New Orleans to California to New York (never mind Quebec and Mexico), news that Wal-Mart is coming to town is now often greeted with protests. Every week, it seems, a new untoward story comes to light: a multimillion-dollar settlement with immigration authorities over illegal workers; the resignation of a top company officer after allegations of financial improprieties; lawsuits delaying construction of dozens of Supercenters in California, a market critical to the company's growth. With characteristic zeal and efficiency, Wal-Mart has marched itself straight into a management and public relations quagmire.

As with most things at Wal-Mart, the problem goes back at least in part to Sam Walton, the visionary founder and leader of the company until he died in 1992. Sam disdained the press, publicists, and government relations, regarding them as wasteful distractions. Focus on serving the customers, Sam said, and everything else will take care of itself. Even after the company grew large enough to draw criticism as a destroyer of small-town America, Wal-Mart's buyers and merchandisers were moneymakers and heroes, and its lawyers and personnel execs were cost centers and zeros.

But now Wal-Mart is the biggest company in the world—inevitably a global symbol of business power—and it can't get away with such corporate isolationism anymore. It has other constituencies that need to be taken care of—millions of employees and local citizens, for example. Yet Sam's successors too often have followed the letter of his rules, not the spirit. He might have been an obsessive merchandiser, but Sam never would have put stonewalling the outside world above growing the company. "I think if Sam were

ANDY SERWER, Fortune New York: Apr 18, 2005. Vol. 151, Iss. 8, p. 84–89 (4 pp.)
Copyright Time Incorporated Apr 18, 2005

Andy Serwer (2005) "Wal-Mart: Bruised in Bentonville," *Fortune*, April 18, Vol. 151, Iss. 8, p. 84–89 (4 pp.)

alive today he wouldn't be jumping for joy over all the external communications we have to do," says Jay Alien, Wal-Mart's senior vice president of corporate affairs. "But he would see the need for it now."

Until recently the company was unable even to admit that its world had changed, that it must address these problems. It is starting to do so now, but it has dug itself such a hole that so far it has not had much success. Wal-Mart has hired legions of publicists, lobbyists, and lawyers, and its senior execulives have taken to giving tub-thumping speeches in defense of its actions. But the company's stock price is stuck where it was six years ago.

Defining Wal-Mart's problems isn't easy. Some have occurred because the company, now with 1.6 million employees worldwide, is just so big. Like other giant institutions (the military and post office come to mind), it is bound to have bad apples. Some problems stem from an ingrained attitude that the bottom line supersedes all. Some are the result of actions by antagonists such as unions. Still others seem to be the product of simple tone-deafness.

It is difficult, too, to assess the impact these problems have had on Wal-Mart's business. True, the company built or expanded 242 Supercenters in the U.S. last year—each producing an estimated $79.5 million in revenues on average, according to Morgan Stanley—and plans to build 240 to 250 more this year. But it has also had to scrap or delay plans to build stores in California, Illinois, and New York. Each unbuilt store is a marginal hit to revenues. And whenever there is a unionizing action or local friction over a new store, the company sends out lawyers, PR people, and anti-union teams—a marginal increase in costs. The flat stock price is attributable in part to what Deutsche Bank analyst Bill Dreher calls "headline risk." The overhang of a potential multibillion-dollar settlement from a gender-discrimination class-action lawsuit couldn't be helping matters much either.

To combat its problems, Wal-Mart has employed a variety of tactics, including carrots, sticks, money, lawyers, and jawboning. That's appropriate, given that it faces all manner of difficulties, but its actions can appear muddled and uncoordinated too.

Facing a raft of cases alleging workplace malfeasance, for instance, Wal-Mart is litigating some and settling others. On its website the company acknowledges that it is the subject of "more than 40 pending wage-and-hour cases seeking class certification status." Those are generally complaints in which employees claim managers tolerated or required off-the-clock work; the company is fighting the claims. On the other hand, the company recently paid a record $11 million settlement to U.S. Immigration and Customs Enforcement, settling a four-year-old federal investigation into the hiring of hundreds of illegal immigrants to clean floors at 60 stores around the country. The biggie, though, is the class-action gender-discrimination lawsuit certified last year, which could encompass the claims of 1.6 million women who have worked at Wal-Mart since

1998. The lawsuit alleges that women are underpaid and underpromoted relative to their male peers. It is the largest civil rights class ever certified and could potentially cost the company billions. For the time being, Bentonville is fighting this one tooth and nail.

As for employee misconduct, Wal-Mart CEO Lee Scott says he's now taking a hard line. "The world has changed, and so you have to react more dramatically and more aggressively, in a less forgiving, harsher way," he said in a recent interview. That seems to apply to the highest levels of the company. On March 25 board member Tom Coughlin, the onetime head of Wal-Mart's stores division, stepped down as a director. According to an SEC filing, Coughlin resigned because of a disagreement with the company over an investigation into alleged unauthorized use of corporate gift cards and reimbursements valued between $100,000 and $500,000.

When it comes to unions, Wal-Mart's stance is implacable. And this fight may provide the clearest example yet of how the company's adherence to the old ways of doing business is hurting it in the present.

In the mid-1990s, Wal-Mart's growth slowed, and CEO David Glass and chairman Rob Wallon saw the need to move beyond selling dry goods to middle America. They decided to bet on the Supercenter concept of huge stores as large as 200,000 square feet that include a full supermarket. They would plop down these Supercenters everywhere, in Texas, Florida, and New York. And they began eyeing California, too, where the company had a small presence. The plan was a smash hit. Within a matter of years, Wal-Mart became a giant in the supermarket business, and the company's stock took off again. Supermarkets like Kroger, Albertsons, Safeway, and Winn-Dixie (now in bankruptcy) came under tremendous pressure, and so did the union representing many of the workers in those stores, United Food and Commercial Workers.

In 2002, Wal-Mart announced it would build up to 40 Supercenters in California. To compete, California grocery-store managements began looking to pare costs. The following year Safeway presented to its workers a contract that slashed medical benefits and wages. Safeway workers went out on strike. Soon thereafter the two other major chains in Southern California—Kroger, which owns Ralphs supermarkets, and Albertsons— locked out UFCW members at their stores. What followed was a bitter strike/lockout that left more than 60,000 grocery workers out of work until February 2004. In the end it was a draw—benefits were cut, but not as severely as management had wanted.

Today Wal-Mart has only three Supercenters in California (another three are under construction), compared with, for instance, more than 200 in Texas and more than 100 in Florida. Why so few? In part it's because lawsuits funded by local businesses and UFCW chapters are holding back construction. The lawsuits take advantage of California's tough Environmental Quality Act, which requires studies not only of wildlife and air quality but also of potential economic decay caused by store closings.

Wal-Mart officials say the suits will slow but not stop them. "The horse-and-buggy industry wasn't permitted to crush the car," argues Scott. "The candle lobby wasn't allowed to stop electric lights. Ultimately that's what this debate is all about."

There is a softer side to Wal-Mart's battle plan, though. For the first time the company is publicizing the millions of dollars it contributes to local community organizations. It is running a national TV image-advertising campaign. It has started a website, walmartfacts.com, to rebut its critics. It has engaged another PR firm, Hill & Knowlton, and it has hired dozens of communications specialists and dropped them into regional offices, state capitals, and Washington, D.C.

And not a minute too soon. Lots of big companies develop image problems, and a few even become part of a broad cultural debate (think McDonald's and nutrition policy). But Wal-Mart at this point seems to have moved into a league of its own. After a long critique of the company was published in the New York Review of Books, of all places, Scott responded with an open letter to the publication's readers. The University of California at Santa Barbara hosted a conference last April titled "Wal-Mart: A Template for 21st-Century Capitalism?" As you might imagine, the discussion was in no way Wal-Mart friendly. The conference's organizer, Nelson Lichtenstein, proposed this central thesis: Throughout U.S. history there has usually been one dominant company that essentially sets a benchmark living wage for the American worker. "Today that company is Wal-Mart, but its pay is so low, it can't be considered a living wage," Lichtenstein says.

On this point, Wal-Mart management says, there is a tradeoff. The more than a million Americans working at Wal-Mart are paid wages that might be higher, but if they were, Wal-Mart's goods would cost more, to the detriment of the 296 million of us who can shop at Wal-Mart. There is something coldly reductionist, though, about Wal-Mart's paying its workers so little that the only store where they can afford to shop is Wal-Mart. It brings to mind an old Bob & Ray routine, a fictitious interview with one Hudley Pierce, CEO of the Great Lakes Paper Clip Co. When asked how his employees can possibly live on a wage of 14 cents a week, Pierce responds, "We don't pry into the personal lives of our employees. But as I understand it, our people live in caves on the edge of town, and they forage for food." Wal-Mart argues that retailing has always been a low-wage sector, and that the company has actually raised the standard in this business.

Away from university campuses and journals of opinion, though, can Wal-Mart find a way to stem the tide of criticism? "I look at it this way," says Jay Allen. "Thirty percent of the country don't care one way or the other about Wal-Mart. Thirty percent love us. Thirty per cent have sincere questions about us. And 10% hate us. We need to focus on the 30% that have sincere questions about us and work to answer their questions."

Wal-Mart is learning, but in some cases it's still bungling. Last year it raised public ire in Inglewood, Calif., when it attempted to circumvent local laws and essentially construct a Supercenter in the dead of night. Locals got wind of the project, organized, and voted it down. Plans for a store there have been scrapped. "What we did in Inglewood was wrong," says Allen. "We have to learn from those mistakes."

But is it doing so? In Dunkirk, Md., a local ordinance was passed recently limiting the size of a store to 75,000 square feet to keep out big-box retailers. Wal-Mart has proposed building a 74,998-square-foot store there—and then erecting a 22,689-square-foot garden center right next door. That's following the letter of the law, but isn't it violating the spirit?

"We are going to find a way to serve customers," Allen says.

THE CHILDREN'S MENU: DO ADS MAKE KIDS FAT?

Betsy McKay

DO SPONGEBOB SquarePants Cereal and Scooby-Doo Fruit Snacks Make Kids Fat?

Amid a growing battle over how food and beverages are marketed to children, the question is surprisingly tough to answer. While it might seem obvious that bombarding kids with sales pitches for cartoon-character cereal and snacks contributes to the obesity epidemic among U.S. children, scientists say the hard evidence is thin.

In one of the few studies so far, Stanford University researchers in 2001 found that watching food ads on TV can influence preschoolers' food choices. The study showed that preschoolers who were shown videos with food commercials were more likely to ask for those foods than preschoolers who watched videos without ads.

Trying to fill the void of solid science on marketing and childhood obesity, the Centers for Disease Control and Prevention is sponsoring a major study of the effects of food marketing on the diets and health of children. The agency wants to lay a scientific foundation for the possible tightening of government oversight of food marketing if proof of a link is found. The CDC also hopes the research will teach the agency itself how to harness the power of marketing to convince kids to pester their parents for carrots and celery sticks instead.

The study, now under way, is being conducted by the Institute of Medicine, a branch of the National Academy of Sciences that advises the government on scientific and health issues. A second study led by the CDC is examining how to get kids more interested in healthy foods. The federal government last undertook a comprehensive study on food marketing to children in 1978, when public concern that television ads were leading to childhood dental cavities and other problems prompted the Federal Trade Commission to consider regulation. The agency abandoned the effort in 1981 after its staff and Congress ruled against restrictions.

"For the government to write guidelines or institute more-formal policy, we have to be very clear about what the science says or doesn't say," says Casey Hannan, policy director for CDC's division of nutrition and physical activity. The panel also will try to determine the biggest gaps in research connecting obesity to marketing.

Many nutrition and food-policy experts say enough indirect evidence already exists linking advertising and childhood obesity to justify restrictions. "I've got five inches of papers that document the effect of food marketing on kids," says Marion Nestle, professor of nutrition at New York University and an outspoken critic of food-industry marketing practices.

In a 2003 report on diet, nutrition, and preventing chronic diseases, the World Health Organization concluded that the evidence of a link between junk-food marketing and childhood obesity was strong enough to warrant action, and subsequently said governments should discourage ads that promote unhealthy eating to children. The European Union threatened last week to impose restrictions on advertising to children if the industry doesn't make its own moves.

But even the CDC's study may not go far enough to prove beyond any doubt that clever food marketers are making kids fat. "There's not going to be a smoking gun," says Susan Linn, a psychologist at Judge Baker Children's Center in Boston and author of "Consuming Kids: The Hostile Takeover of Childhood." "Why is the burden on the underfunded public health community to prove this? Where is the evidence it isn't having an effect?"

Recent moves by the food industry make government action even more urgent, say nutrition and child-health advocates. A new lobbying group formed recently by food companies and advertising agencies plans to fight restrictions by touting self-policing efforts and research supporting its right to advertise to children.

A lack of regulation means that companies are setting their own rules about what they market. Kraft Foods Inc. said it won't advertise regular Kool-Aid to kids between six years old and 11 years old, but will continue to market its sugar-free version to them. In a small symbol on its box, General Mills Inc. touts Cocoa Puffs cereal as a good source of whole grain, although a one cup serving has only one gram of dietary fiber.

In a report last year, the American Psychological Association recommended restrictions on ads aimed at children under eight years old, concluding that they are prone to accept advertising as truthful and unbiased. An IOM report on childhood obesity published last September concluded that food marketing can affect children's food choices, urging the food and beverage industries to develop and "strictly adhere" to marketing and advertising guidelines that would minimize the risk of obesity.

The CDC's effort to sift through the evidence was prompted by Sen. Tom Harkin (D-Iowa), who won Congressional approval for $1 million in funding for the two studies. Food and beverage companies spend an estimated $10 billion to $12 billion a year pitching products to children and adolescents, the IOM says. A proliferation of new media has expanded their reach beyond television and print advertising to the Internet, videogames and cell phones. The typical child now sees about 40,000 TV ads a year, according to a report on the role of media in childhood obesity by the Henry J. Kaiser Family Foundation, a nonprofit foundation focusing on health-care issues.

"There isn't a place where children go in their day where they're not encouraged to eat," says Margo Wootan, director of nutrition policy for the Center for Science in the Public Interest, a nonprofit advocacy group that is urging restrictions on marketing to children under 18 years old.

The committee sponsored by the Atlanta-based CDC includes nutritionists and psychologists who have documented negative consequences of food marketing, as well as scientists who have served as consultants to food companies and a former FTC official. The panel expects to deliver its report to the CDC by early September.

FAKES!

Frederik Balfour, Carol Matlack, Amy Barrett, Kerry Capell, Dexter Roberts, Jonathan Wheatley, William C. Symonds, Paul Magnusson, and Diane Brady

The global counterfeit business is out of control, targeting everything from computer chips to life-saving medicines. It's so bad that even China may need to crack down. A year and a half ago, Pfizer Inc. got a disturbing call on its customer hotline. A woman who had been taking its cholesterol-lowering drug Lipitor complained that a new bottle of tablets tasted bitter. She sent the suspicious pills to the company, which tested them at a lab in Groton, Conn. The white oblong tablets looked just like the real thing—and even contained some of the active ingredient in Lipitor. But Pfizer soon determined that they were counterfeits. Over the next two months, distributors yanked some 16.5 million tablets from warehouses and pharmacy shelves nationwide.

An isolated case? Hardly. Last October, Brazilian police got a tip-off about a hoard of bogus Hewlett-Packard Co. inkjet cartridges and seized more than $1 million worth of goods. Chinese police last year conducted raids confiscating everything from counterfeit Buick windshields to phony Viagra. In Guam, the Secret Service in July uncovered a network selling bogus North Korean-made pharmaceuticals, cigarettes, and $100 bills. In June, French customs seized more than 11,000 fake parts for Nokia Corp. cell phones—batteries, covers, and more. In January, U.S. Commerce Secretary Donald Evans blasted the Chinese on a visit to Beijing, demanding they step up efforts to police intellectual-property violations. Evans singled out the case of a General Motors Corp. subsidiary that is suing Chinese carmaker Chery Automotive for ripping off the design of its Chevrolet Spark minicar. The uncanny resemblance between the two cars, said Evans, "defies innocent explanation."

Critical Mass

Kiwi shoe polish, Callaway Golf clubs, Intel computer chips, Bosch power drills, BP oil. Pick any product from any well-known brand, and chances are there's a counterfeit version of it out there. Of course, as anyone who has combed the back alleys of Hong Kong, Rio, or Moscow knows, fakes have been around for decades. Only the

Frederik Balfour, Carol Matlack, Amy Barrett, Kerry Capell, Dexter Roberts, Jonathan Wheatley, William C. Symonds, Paul Magnusson, and Diane Brady (2005) "Fakes!" *Business Week,* February 7.

greenest rube would actually believe that the $20 Rolex watch on Silom Road in Bangkok or the $30 Louis Vuitton bag on New York's Canal Street is genuine.

But counterfeiting has grown up—and that's scaring the multinationals. "We've seen a massive increase in the last five years, and there is a risk it will spiral out of control," says Anthony Simon, marketing chief of Unilever Bestfoods. "It's no longer a cottage industry." The World Customs Organization estimates counterfeiting accounts for 5% to 7% of global merchandise trade, equivalent to lost sales of as much as $512 billion last year—though experts say this is only a guess. Seizures of fakes by U.S. customs jumped by 46% last year as counterfeiters boosted exports to Western markets. Unilever Group says knockoffs of its shampoos, soaps, and teas are growing by 30% annually. The World Health Organization says up to 10% of medicines worldwide are counterfeited—a deadly hazard that could be costing the pharmaceutical industry $46 billion a year. Bogus car parts add up to $12 billion worldwide. "Counterfeiting has gone from a local nuisance to a global threat," says Hanns Glatz, DaimlerChrysler's point man on intellectual property.

The scale of the threat is prompting new efforts by multinationals to stop, or at least curb, the spread of counterfeits. Companies are deploying detectives around the globe in greater force than ever, pressuring governments from Beijing to Brasilia to crack down, and trying everything from electronic tagging to redesigned products to aggressive pricing in order to thwart the counterfeiters. Even some Chinese companies, stung by fakes themselves, are getting into the act. "Once Chinese companies start to sue other Chinese companies, the situation will become more balanced," says Stephen Vickers, chief executive of International Risk, a Hong Kong–based brand-protection consultant.

China is key to any solution. Since the country is an economic gorilla, its counterfeiting is turning into quite the beast as well—accounting for nearly two-thirds of all the fake and pirated goods worldwide. Daimler's Glatz figures phony Daimler parts—from fenders to engine blocks—have grabbed 30% of the market in China, Taiwan, and Korea. And Chinese counterfeiters make millions of motorcycles a year, with knockoffs of Honda's workhorse CG125—selling for about $300, or less than half the cost of a real Honda—especially popular. It's tales like this that prompt some trade hawks in the U.S. to call for a World Trade Organization action against China related to counterfeits and intellectual-property rights violations in general. Such pressure is beginning to have some effect. "The Chinese government is starting to take things more seriously because of the unprecedented uniform shouting coming from the U.S., Europe, and Japan," says Joseph Simone, a lawyer specializing in IPR issues at Baker & McKenzie in Hong Kong.

Yet slowing down the counterfeiters in China and elsewhere will take heroic efforts. That's because counterfeiting thrives on the whole process of globalization itself. Globalization, after all, is the spread of capital and knowhow to new markets, which in turn contribute low-cost labor to create the ideal export machine, manufacturing first the cheap stuff, then moving up the value chain. That's the story of Southeast Asia. It's the story of China. Now it's the story of fakes. Counterfeiting packs all the punch of skilled labor, smart distribution, and product savvy without getting bogged down in costly details such as research and brand-building.

The result is a kind of global industry that is starting to rival the multinationals in speed, reach, and sophistication. Factories in China can copy a new model of golf club in less than a week, says Stu Herrington, who oversees brand protection for Callaway Golf Co. "The Chinese are extremely ingenious, inventive, and scientifically oriented, and they are becoming the world's manufacturer," he says. The company has found counterfeiters with three-dimensional design software and experience cranking out legitimate clubs for other brands, so "back-engineering a golf club is a piece of cake" for them, he says. And counterfeiters are skilled at duplicating holograms, "smart" chips, and other security devices intended to distinguish fakes from the genuine article. "We've had sophisticated technology that took years to develop knocked off in a matter of months," says Unilever marketing boss Simon.

The ambition of the counterfeiters just keeps growing. In China, recent raids have turned up everything from fake Sony PlayStation game controllers to Cisco Systems router interface cards. "If you can make it, they can fake it," says David Fernyhough, director of brand protection at investigation firm Hill & Associates Ltd. in Hong Kong. Don't believe him? Shanghai Mitsubishi Elevator Co. discovered a counterfeit elevator after a building owner asked the company for a maintenance contract. "It didn't look like our product," says Wang Chung Heng, a lawyer for Shanghai Mitsubishi. "And it stopped between floors."

Many fakes, though, are getting so good that even company execs say it takes a forensic scientist to distinguish them from the real McCoy. Armed with digital technology, counterfeiters can churn out perfect packaging—a key to duping unwitting distributors and retail customers. GM has come across fake air filters, brake pads, and batteries. "We had to cut them apart or do chemical analysis to tell" they weren't real, says Alexander Theil, director of investigations at General Motors Asia Pacific. The parts might last half as long as the real thing, but that's not apparent until long after the sale.

The counterfeiters even ape the multinationals by diversifying their sourcing and manufacturing across borders. Last August, Philippine police raided a cigarette factory in Pampanga, two hours outside of Manila. What they found was a global operation in miniature. The factory was producing fake Davidoffs and Mild Sevens for export to Taiwan. The $6 million plant boasted a state-of-the-art German cigarette-rolling machine capable of producing some 3 billion fake smokes, worth $600 million, annually. The top-quality packaging came from a printer in Malaysia. The machinery itself was manned by 23 Chinese brought in by a Singapore-based syndicate, says Josef Gueta, director of Business Profiles Inc., a Manila firm that tracks counterfeit rings for multinationals. "They have shipping, warehousing, and the knowledge and network to move things around easily," he says.

As such counterfeiters get more entrenched and more global, they will be increasingly hard to eradicate. Financing comes from a variety of sources, including Middle East middlemen, local entrepreneurs, and organized crime. Sometimes the counterfeiters are fly-by-night operations, but just as often they're legitimate companies that have a dark side. In fact, many are licensed producers of brand-name goods that simply run an extra, unauthorized shift and sell out the back door. Or they are former licensees who have kept the molds and designs that allow them to go into business for themselves. Shoemaker New Balance Athletic Shoe Inc. is suing a former contract manufacturer in Guangdong province for selling unauthorized New Balance sneakers that have turned up as far away as Australia and Europe. In the Philippines, semiconductor distributor Sardido Industries says it has been burned by counterfeiters that have sold it microprocessors rejected by inspectors from the likes of Intel and Advanced Micro Devices. These are doctored with logos and serial numbers to look like genuine parts and sold off cheaply as returns or production overruns. Other counterfeiters are generic manufacturers who moonlight as makers of fakes. Yamaha Corp. has licensed five plants in China to make its motorcycles, but almost 50 factories have actually produced bikes branded as Yamaha.

It's easy to find the counterfeiters, too. The Ziyuangang market in the sprawling city of Guangzhou, two hours north of Hong Kong, looks pretty much like any recently built Chinese shopping mall. But venture inside, and you'll find row upon row of shops offering bogus Gucci, Versace, Dunhill, Longines, and more. Each shop has just a few dozen samples but offers vast catalogs of goods that can be made and delivered in less than a week. At one outlet, a clerk offers counterfeit Louis Vuitton bags in various sizes. "Even fakes have many grades of quality, and these fakes are really, really good," she boasts. Exports? She's happy to arrange shipping to the country of your choice.

Once those goods leave China, they can sneak into the legitimate supply chain just about anywhere. Sometimes, phony components get used in authentic products. Last year, for example, Kyocera Corp., had to recall a million cell-phone batteries that turned out to be counterfeit, costing the company at least $5 million. Unscrupulous wholesalers will fob off fakes on small auto-repair shops, office-supply stores, or independent pharmacies by saying they have bargain-priced—but not suspiciously cheap—oil filters, printer cartridges, or bottles of shampoo that another retailer returned, or which are close to their sell-by date. Some traders mix phonies in with authentic goods. "It's easy to slide a stack of fake Levis under the real ones," says one investigator based in Shanghai. "Most inspectors and buyers can't tell the difference."

Counterfeiters can also disguise their wares before they reach their final destination. Some ship unmarked counterfeit parts in several consignments to be assembled and labeled at their destination. And last May, Shanghai customs officials were inspecting a Dubai-bound shipment of 67 100cc motorcycles labeled with the brand name Honling. But when they peeled back stickers on the machines' crank cases, they found "Yamaha" engraved on the casting. "They are very sneaky and cunning, and that's very frustrating," laments Masayuki Hosokawa, chief representative of Yamaha Motor Co. in Beijing.

Strategic Defense

They are also making big bucks. Counterfeiting has become as profitable as trading illegal narcotics, and is a lot less risky. In most countries, convicted offenders get off with a slap on the wrist and a fine of a few thousand dollars. Counterfeiters, after all, don't have to cover research and development, marketing, and advertising costs, and most of the expense goes into making goods look convincing, not performing well. Fake Marlboros that cost just pennies a pack to make in China could end up selling for $7.50 in Manhattan. Phony New Balance shoes can be stitched together for about $8 a pair and retail for as much as $80 in Australia, while real ones cost between $11 and $24 to make, and sell for up to $120. Gross margins for knockoff printer cartridges are north of 60%. Counterfeiters "use low-paid employees and cut corners on safety," says Richard K. Willard, general counsel for Gillette Co., which turns up hundreds of thousands of imitation Duracell batteries every week. "If they can push them off as a high-quality product, there is a big margin for them."

While the counterfeiters are piling up profits, the multinationals are spending ever more on stopping them. Luxury house LVMH Möet Hennessy Louis Vuitton spent more than $16 million last year on investigations, busts, and legal fees. GM has seven full-time staffers sleuthing the globe, and Pfizer has five people working in Asia alone. Last September, Nokia started making batteries with holographic images and 20-digit identification codes that can be authenticated online. Cigarette maker JT International has boosted its anti-counterfeiting budget from $200,000 to $15 million in the past six years, spending the money on a network of investigators, lawyers, and informants in factories suspected of making fakes.

Pfizer will soon introduce radio-frequency ID tags on all Viagra sold in the U.S., which will enable it to track drugs all the way from the laboratory to the medicine cabinet. Other companies simply try to make life as difficult as possible for manufacturers and distributors by raiding factories and warehouses or by slightly altering the look of products, making it tough for counterfeiters to keep up with the changes. JT International—which sells Camels and Winstons outside the U.S.—sometimes digs through dumpsters at suspect factories looking for counterfeit packaging. Callaway patrols the

Web looking for suspiciously cheap clubs bearing its brand—though as soon as it shuts one dealer down, another is sure to pop up. "Getting rid of the problem altogether is too much to ask," says Callaway's Herrington. "We just try to do our best and give the counterfeiters a really bad day."

One tactic is to outwit the counterfeiters in the marketplace. Anheuser-Busch Cos., for instance, was plagued by knockoff Budweiser in China. A big problem was that counterfeiters were refilling old Bud bottles, so the company started using expensive imported foil on the bottles that was very hard to find in China. The company also added a temperature-sensitive label that turned red when cold. The result: "We've been able to keep [counterfeiting] at a pretty low level," says Stephen J. Burrows, chief executive and president of Anheuser-Busch International. Yamaha, meanwhile, overhauled the way it manufactures and designs motorcycles to lower costs. Now it charges $725 for its cheapest bikes in China, down from about $1,800. To stay competitive, counterfeiters have since lowered their prices from around $1,000 to roughly half that.

The biggest challenge is getting cooperation from China. For years, Chinese authorities turned a blind eye to the problem, largely because most of the harm was inflicted on foreign brand owners and most counterfeiting was seen as a victimless offense. The only time China got tough on counterfeiters was when there was a clear danger to Chinese. Last year, for example, 15 infants died from phony milk powder. The ringleader was sentenced to eight years in prison. But when the victim is a company not an individual, the courts are far less severe. Last June, a Guangdong businessman was found guilty of producing fake windshields under 15 different brand names, including General Motors, DaimlerChrysler, and Mitsubishi Motors. He was fined just $97,000 and given a suspended sentence. It's unclear just how much he made selling fakes, but GM gumshoe Theil says "there is no way the fine is commensurate with the profits he made."

But more Chinese corporate interests have seen profits hit because of counterfeiting—which may lead to a tougher response from Beijing. Li-Ning Co., China's No. 1 home-grown athletic footwear and apparel company, has gotten the ultimate compliment from counterfeiters: They're faking its shoes. So today, Li-Ning has three full-time employees who track counterfeiters. The state tobacco monopoly is conducting joint raids with big international tobacco companies, since counterfeiters have started cranking out Double Happiness, Chunghwa, and other Chinese smokes. The crackdown, investigators believe, has forced some cigarette counterfeiters to decamp to Vietnam and Burma. And the government is finally realizing that piracy—which accounts for 92% of all software used in the mainland—isn't just setting back the likes of Microsoft Corp. "Piracy is a big problem for the development of the local software industry," says Victor Zhang, senior representative for China of the Business Software Alliance, an industry group. Some fear that Western companies may cut research spending in China if the mainland doesn't crack down.

Now, China is toughening its legal sanctions. In December, Beijing lowered the threshold for criminal prosecution of counterfeiters. Prior to the changes, an individual needed to have $12,000 worth of goods on hand before police could prosecute. It was easy to skirt that rule by spreading the wares around. Today, that threshold stands at $6,000 for counterfeiters caught with one brand and $3,600 for those with two or more. And in late January, Beijing began the trial of two Americans who are accused of selling $840,000 in knockoff CDs and DVDs made in China over the Internet. The two could face up to 15 years in jail if convicted.

One big problem: Too many scammers have ties to local officials, who see counterfeit operations as a major source of employment and pillars of the local economy. "Two or three of our raids have failed because of local protection," says Joseph Tsang, chairman of Marksman Consultants Ltd., a Hong Kong-based company that has helped conduct raids on behalf of Titleist and Nike Golf. Take the example of a raid last August in Fujian province. The police found a dirt-covered hatch hiding a stairway that led into a pitch-black cave. Inside was a rolling machine, cigarette paper, and a die for stamping Marlboros and Double Happiness packaging. But the counterfeiters themselves had cleared out and taken the smokes with them. "They knew we were coming," sighs a Hong Kong-based investigator who participated in the raid.

Embattled Beijing

Beijing says it's doing what it can. The government has raised intellectual-property issues to the highest levels: Trade czar and Vice-Premier Wu Yi, for instance, has held regular meetings with the Quality Brands Protection Committee since 2003. "China customs is taking the fight seriously," says Meng Yang, director general for the Policy & Legal Affairs Dept. of the General Administration of Chinese Customs. The agency in November held a conference in Shanghai with brand owners and customs officers from around the world to map out strategies. But delegates acknowledged their biggest challenge is finding the funds to fight counterfeiting, as most governments are more concerned with preventing the smuggling of drugs and arms.

Could the U.S. apply stronger pressure to get China to crack down? "The answer is for the Administration to bring a WTO case against the Chinese," says one leader of the intellectual-property bar in Washington. The challenge is to secure evidence from U.S. companies, which desperately want relief but don't want to anger Beijing. More calls for a WTO action may come soon, after the U.S. Trade Representative's office finishes a review of IPR in China in March.

Hard as it is, there's every reason to try to keep up the fight to stop counterfeiting. One is safety. Novartis says counterfeiters have used yellow highway paint to get the right color match for fake painkillers. And in some African countries, counterfeit or illegal medicines account for as much as 40% of the drugs on the market. "You even have antibiotics without the ingredients," says Daniel L. Vasella, chairman of Novartis. Pfizer says police and regulators in Asia uncovered more than 1.5 million counterfeit doses of its hypertension drug Norvasc in 2003. "You are seeing counterfeiters exploit a loose supply chain and moving from lifestyle drugs to life-saving drugs," says Pfizer's vice-president for global security, John Theriault. "That should make people nervous."

The other reason to mount an offensive against the counterfeits is, obviously, the hit to corporate profits—and the likelihood developed markets will one day be seriously contaminated. It's already happening. In June, 2003, Tommy Hilfiger Corp. successfully sued Goody's Family Clothing Inc. for $11 million for carrying fake shirts. The incidence of fake prescription drugs in the U.S., though small, is rising sharply. The U.S. Food & Drug Administration began 58 investigations of counterfeit drugs in its fiscal 2004, up from 22 in 2003.

More alarming, say police, is counterfeiting's connection to the underworld. "Organized crime thrives on counterfeiting," says Ronald K. Noble, Secretary General of Interpol. So does terrorism. Noble says profits from pirated CDs sold in Central America have funded Hezbollah in the Middle East. One cigarette executive estimates North Korea earns $100 million per year in fees from pirates producing there. That kind of activity proves that buying fakes "isn't innocent, and it's not a game," says Bernard Arnault, chairman of luxury goods maker LVMH.

The counterfeiting scourge, meanwhile, continues to spread. Pakistan and Russia are huge producers of fake pharmaceuticals, while in Italy an estimated 10% of all designer clothing is fake, much of it produced domestically. Gangs in Paraguay funnel phony cosmetics, designer jeans, and toys from China to the rest of South America. Bulgarians are masters at bootlegging U.S. liquor brands. This is one fight that will take years to win.

Expertise

Current and former employees of licensed manufacturers of branded goods can disassemble products and reengineer them. Licensed factories may add another shift to crank out counterfeits, using cheaper materials. Sophisticated packaging equipment is acquired to give the appearance of authenticity. In the case of memory chips, discards from real chip plants are smuggled to counterfeiters, who then etch brand names such as Intel into them.

Distribution

The most important step. Authorized licensees who decide to counterfeit can tap legitimate channels to enter retail outfits, auto shops, and more. Some counterfeiters mix real items with fake ones. Containers loaded with fakes are deliberately shipped through so many ports that it becomes impossible to determine their origin.

INDEX

About TEXERE

Texere, a progressive and authoritative voice in business publishing, brings to the global business community the expertise and insights of leading thinkers. Our books educate, enlighten, and entertain, and provide an intersection where our authors and our readers share cutting edge ideas, practices, and innovative solutions. Texere seeks to cultivate, enhance, and disseminate information that illuminates the global business landscape.

www.thomson.com/learning/texere

About the Typeface

This book was set in 10.5 Bembo. Bembo was cut by Francesco Griffo for the Venetian printer Aldus Manutius in 1495 for the publication of *De Aetna* by Cardinal Pietro Bembo. Stanley Morison supervised a revival of the Bembo design for the Monotype Corporation in 1929. The Bembo is a readable and classical typeface known for its well-proportioned letterforms, functional serifs, and lack of peculiarities.

Library of Congress Cataloging-in-Publication Data

Explorations of marketing in society/Gregory T. Gundlach, Lauren G. Block, William L. Wilkie [editors].
      p. cm.
  Assembles academic contributions that have already been published in journals, coupled with invited commentaries.
  Includes bibliographical references and index.
  ISBN-13: 978-0-324-30430-5 (alk. paper)
  ISBN-10: 0-324-30430-7 (alk. paper)
  1. Marketing—Social aspects. 2. Consumer behavior. 3. Social marketing.
  4. Marketing—Moral and ethical aspects. 5. Public interest. I. Gundlach, Gregory T. (Gregory Thomas) II. Block, Lauren G. III. Wilkie, William L.
  HF5414.E96 2007
  306.3'4—dc22

      2006101636